Library and Book Trade Almanac™

Almanac™

formerly **The Bowker Annual**

2012 | 57th Edition

Library and Book Trade Almanac ™

formerly **The Bowker Annual**

2012 | 57th Edition

Editor Dave Bogart
Consultant Betty J. Turock

 **Information Today, Inc.**

Published by Information Today, Inc.
Copyright © 2012 Information Today, Inc.
All rights reserved

International Standard Book Number 978-1-57387-439-7
International Standard Serial Number 2150-5446
Library of Congress Catalog Card Number 55-12434

Information Today, Inc.
143 Old Marlton Pike
Medford, NJ   08055-8750
Phone: 800-300-9868 (customer service)
              800-409-4929 (editorial queries)
Fax: 609-654-4309
E-mail (orders): custserv@infotoday.com
Web Site: http://www.infotoday.com

Printed and bound in the United States of America

Contents

Part 1
Reports from the Field

Part 2
Legislation, Funding, and Grants

Part 3
Library/Information Science Education, Placement, and Salaries

Part 4
Research and Statistics

Book Trade Research and Statistics

Part 5
Reference Information

Bibliographies

Ready Reference

Distinguished Books

Part 6
Directory of Organizations

Preface

Welcome to this 57th edition of the *Library and Book Trade Almanac,* which presents a valuable and useful compilation of information of broad interest to the library and publishing worlds.

As change accelerates, driven by advances in technology, librarians and publishers are daily faced with new challenges. Add to the mix a continuing economic recession that shows only slight signs of improvement, and the picture becomes increasingly complex.

This edition examines the current concerns of the information industry from many points of view.

First come the Special Reports:

- Alan S. Inouye takes an in-depth look at the future of libraries as the digital revolution progresses.
- Robert Bocher and Bonnie Tijerina detail the burgeoning e-book phenomenon, with a particular emphasis on its effects on libraries.
- Kristin Fontichiaro examines the concept of digital literacy and its growing importance across society and the information world.
- Karen E. Downing, Mark Winston, and Alexandra Rivera discuss the evolution of library leadership in light of the rapid and accelerating changes in modern organizations.
- Nancy Kranich studies how all types of libraries are taking advantage of new opportunities to extend their reach further into the realm of civic engagement in an effort to foster the development of a civil society.

Part 1 continues with reports on the activities of federal libraries, federal agencies, and national and international library and publishing organizations.

Recent and current legislation and regulations affecting libraries are detailed in Part 2, as are the activities of two major funding and grant-making agencies, the National Endowment for the Humanities and the Institute of Museum and Library Services.

Part 3 offers professional information for librarians, ranging from advice on finding job opportunities to a listing of the year's major library scholarship and award winners.

Part 4 presents a varied abundance of research and statistics—tables of library acquisition expenditures, book and periodicals prices, detailed data on publishing, and reports on noteworthy research. Among Part 4 features are Jim Milliot's survey of the year in publishing, an assessment by Robert Molyneux of the "consortial effect" that occurs when public libraries join in a resource-sharing consortium, and Albert Greco's analysis of the U.S. import/export trade in books, with a particular emphasis on the effect of the e-book boom.

Reference information makes up Part 5, from lists of major literary prize winners, bestsellers, and recommended books to guidance on how to obtain an ISBN, SAN, or ISSN.

Part 6 is our directory of library and publishing organizations at the state, national, and international levels, followed by a calendar of major upcoming information industry events.

The *Library and Book Trade Almanac* represents the dedicated work of many people, and we are grateful to all those who assembled reports, contributed articles, supplied statistics, and responded to our requests for information. Particular thanks are due Consultant Editor Betty J. Turock, whose guidance and assistance with our "Special Reports" section was invaluable; to Contributing Editor Catherine Barr; and to Christine McNaull, who turns it all into a book and whose diligence and skill make everyone else's job easier.

We believe you will find this 57th *Library and Book Trade Almanac* a valuable resource to which you will turn often, and, as always, we welcome your comments and suggestions for future editions.

Dave Bogart
Editor

Part 1
Reports from the Field

Special Reports

The Future of Libraries

Alan S. Inouye

Director, Office for Information Technology Policy, American Library Association

In the two decades since the creation of the World Wide Web, there has been a revolution in how Americans access, manage, and create information. This digital revolution is not a secret, as the latest technological developments and trends are continually chronicled by the media. Terms emerging from this revolution—Google, Kindle, Facebook, Twitter, e-book, laptop, smartphone, Amazon, Android, Netflix, iPhone, iPad, and more—have become common in household conversation, and the revolution shows no signs of slowing.

As the quintessential information institution, libraries have been swept up in the digital revolution. Library professionals recognized early on the need to incorporate new technologies and services to provide improved services for users. However, they also saw that the revolution would engender in libraries a more profound transformation extending beyond adoption of the latest technologies to a fundamental reevaluation of the library's place in the information ecosystem and society. Of course, the adoption of new technologies does have value, but the value is often narrow, limited, and inherently incremental and transitory as technologies evolve. In particular, from a national or public policy perspective, this kind of short-sighted framing overlooks the larger phenomenon taking place within the library world.

ALA's Perspective on the Digital Revolution

There has never been a press release or grand announcement of the revolution in libraries. Rather, librarians and other participants in the information ecosystem have come to perceive and understand this revolution at different times.

At the American Library Association (ALA), the recognition that a fundamental shift in libraries was taking place occurred in the latter part of the last decade. ALA took an important action in 2008 by creating the Program on America's Libraries for the 21st Century (AL21C) within the Office for Information Technol-

Alan Inouye began his career in the computer industry in Silicon Valley, then returned to school full-time to earn his Ph.D. in library and information studies at the University of California, Berkeley. In addition, he holds degrees in mathematics, social sciences and education, management and finance, systems engineering, and information systems. He joined the American Library Association in 2007 as director of its Office for Information Technology Policy (OITP) and also serves as director of its Program on America's Libraries for the 21st Century (AL21C).

Program on America's Libraries for the 21st Century

Overview

The fundamental changes that underlie the ways in which much information is now created, modified, disseminated, and accessed offer both opportunities and challenges for libraries and access to information. ALA's Program on America's Libraries for the 21st Century (AL21C) focuses on monitoring and evaluating trends in technology and society to assist the library community in shaping its future to the maximum benefit of the nation.

In which roles may libraries be most useful in serving the nation? Physical library spaces continue to have value for communities, although their roles are evolving. The explosion in online information enables users to access many nonlibrary information sources readily, but the online environment also affords tremendous opportunity for libraries both to serve existing clients in new ways and to reach out to new clients. How should the library and information science community's core principles of equal access, intellectual freedom, and objective stewardship of information be represented in the future online environment?

Major Areas of Focus

The AL21C Program has six major areas of focus:

- Monitor technological and societal trends that are relevant to libraries and public access to information, and encourage and contribute to discussion of these trends in forums inside and outside of ALA
- Identify relevant data sources for these trends, and strive to improve the usefulness and visibility of these data
- Advocate for appropriate policies and practices based on those trends that have identifiable, direct implications for the library and information science community
- Identify scenarios, models, and specific directions in technology and society that hold the most promise for advancing the interests of the library and information science community
- Engage the library and information science community in the development of appropriate visions, strategies, positions, and messages
- Assist the library and information science community in taking a greater leadership role in shaping its future in the digital world

Work Process of the AL21C Program

The work of the program is conducted by a number of individuals with deep knowledge of academic, school, public, and other kinds of libraries, as well as expertise in a wide array of relevant disciplines and professions beyond the library community. ALA members participate through the AL21C Subcommittee, which provides guidance and feedback on the various program activities.[i] A significant portion of the research, writing, review, editing, and publication work is completed by OITP staff,[ii] an OITP fellow,[iii] an OITP research associate,[iv] and a number of consultants.[v]

In addition to the core team described above, the program consults with subject matter experts and experienced practitioners from the various ALA units; the library community at large; and entities outside of the library community in academia, industry, government, and the nonprofit sector. The program's work is funded by ALA and private foundations.

---

i. Further information about the AL21C Subcommittee is available at http://www.ala. org/ala/mgrps/committees/ala/ala-al21c.cfm.

ii. See http://www.ala.org/ala/aboutala/offices/oitp/people/staff/index.cfm.

iii. See http://www.ala.org/ala/aboutala/offices/oitp/people/oitpfellows/index.cfm.

iv. See http://www.districtdispatch.org/2011/11/oitp-appoints-its-first-research-associate/.

v. See http://www.ala.org/offices/oitp/people/consultants.

ogy Policy (OITP). This program explores all aspects of the future of American libraries and develops recommendations for the library community and its stakeholders.[1]

While some are pessimistic about the future of libraries, ALA, like many in the community, envisions future library services that incorporate new philosophies, new technologies, and new physical and virtual spaces to meet the needs of all users more effectively than ever before. This perspective entails rethinking the very core of what defines a library—the sense of place, of service, and of community that has characterized the modern library for the last century. The AL21C Program took this optimistic lens as the point of departure for its work on the future of libraries.

The core of the program's work since its founding is summarized in three policy briefs. *Checking Out the Future,* released in February 2010,[2] surveys the literature relating to the future of libraries. Published in June 2010, *There's an App for That!* focuses on the rise of mobile technology and the implications for libraries.[3] Finally, *Confronting the Future,* released in June 2011,[4] lays out visions and strategies for public libraries to consider as they address the opportunities and challenges arising from the digital revolution. Much of the content that follows represents a synthesis of these policy briefs, although it is supplemented with more recent developments as appropriate, such as the AL21C Program's recent focus on digital content, especially e-books.

Beyond the World of Libraries

In-depth description or analysis of the radical changes that have occurred in the information ecosystem over the past few decades is far beyond the scope of this article. Nonetheless, some understanding of the larger forces at work is essential to understanding how and why libraries have found themselves in the midst of a revolution.[5] Two trends—technological innovation and the upheaval experienced by creators, intermediaries, and users—provide the primary foundation for the discussion that follows. Two additional trends—a tightening financial environment and shifting user demographics—provide important context.

Technological Innovation

By invoking the digital revolution, this article already has identified one key trend: the extraordinary advances that have occurred in digital media and technology. Already, most newly published material is being made available first in digital form. Moreover, the conversion of existing analog materials to digital form continues apace.

Storage, communication, computation, and display technologies are expected to continue increasing in quality and capability. Storage will become faster, more compact, and less expensive and will be available in ever-increasing capacities to accommodate the growing data needs of users.[6] Widespread access to broadband via wired and wireless devices and the availability of multicore processors capable of trillions of operations per second will be realized. Advances will also continue in display technologies, with ever-improving resolution, color range, and compactness, available in very small or very large form factors.[7]

Also expected to continue is the trend toward the devolvement of software and technology services from the user's experience. For example, cloud computing services are transferring more and more of the direct management of technology to intermediary organizations. Widgets, applications, and services increasingly substitute for traditional software packages that users previously needed to purchase, configure, and maintain. And these widgets, applications, and services are becoming ever more sophisticated, exploiting technological advances in text, graphics, audio, video, gaming, and social interactivity. Google's "Chromebooks," for example, rely almost exclusively on widgets and applications, and they keep much of a user's data stored in the cloud rather than locally on the computer's hard drive.[8] Meanwhile, in the mobile technology space, almost all new functionality is already represented by applications (or "apps") that users purchase or download to their smartphones or devices. This is a trend that is likely to continue for some time.[9]

Upheaval for Creators, Intermediaries, and Users

Continued rapid change in the information ecosystem can be expected for content creators, intermediaries, and users alike. For example, new forms of social and other media, coupled with the ease of distribution made possible by the Internet, are changing what we think of as content creation. Meanwhile, bricks-and-mortar stores for music, videos, and books have declined drastically in number, replaced by online stores and services of varying types. In some instances, the replacement service comes in the form of a more sophisticated version of the old-fashioned mail-order service (that is, online ordering with physical delivery); in others, new services provide for direct and instantaneous digital access.

Indeed, the role of every kind of intermediary—book publisher, newspaper and magazine publisher, search engine company, social media company, and many others (and yes, libraries, too)—is being critically challenged. Which entities could (or should) provide what services for which audiences at what prices? The answers are all up for grabs.

Commensurate with this institutional upheaval is a fundamental change in user expectations. In the past, users expected information to be provided in controlled, professionally managed institutions, whether by the mass media, bookstores, libraries, or otherwise. In general, users did not expect their needs to be fulfilled immediately. Today, users expect to access information from a much larger set of sources of varying quality on a real-time basis, and increasingly from wherever they happen to be at the moment.

Tightening Financial Environment and Shifting User Demographics

The global economic crisis of recent years has had significant ramifications for libraries. All parts of the library community have experienced considerable financial stress. Essentially, all funders of libraries have seen significant decreases in available funding, and the outlook for the next several years is flat and uncertain at best. Governments at all levels, but especially many state and local governments, have seen a general decline in their budget trajectories since at least 2007.[10] Philanthropy from private foundations and corporations also has decreased.[11] Meanwhile, the demand for funding in the library world has increased in the face of the severe recession.

The demographic makeup of the nation also is undergoing transformation, and libraries today are challenged to meet the needs of new and shifting users. In the next few decades, for example, the population is expected to increase by more than 100 million, to more than 400 million. The Hispanic population is growing faster than expected and over the last decade has accounted for more than half of the nation's growth, with the group's increase driven by births and immigration.[12] The U.S. Census Bureau is projecting that the non-Hispanic white population of the United States will drop to 46.3 percent by 2050.

The baby boomers are fueling considerable growth in the over-65 population. A recent survey by the Pew Research Center shows that by 2030, "when all Baby Boomers will have turned 65, fully 18% of the nation's population will be at least that age."[13] This demographic shift will have wide-ranging implications for libraries, as evidence suggests that traditional library services for seniors will not satisfy the interests or needs of baby boomers, a group that already accounts for 32 percent of traffic on the Internet on any given day.[14]

The Digital Revolution and Its Implications for Libraries

Three key developments of the digital revolution have major implications for the future of libraries: born-digital materials, digitization of analog materials, and the diffusion of mobile technology. These developments are changing the very nature of library services and spaces.

Born-Digital Materials

Library access to born-digital materials has been an issue for several decades. The focus was initially on databases and then on electronic journal subscriptions. Difficult, sometimes heated, discussions took place among libraries, consortia, and publishers over usage terms and, especially, journal pricing. In the past decade or so, however, most information of primary concern to libraries has been born digital. Journals, newspapers, magazines, newsletters, and other periodicals are published online, and often in formats enhanced beyond what is available in print. E-books have become a mass market phenomenon. And physical photo albums have become Flickr sites or Facebook albums.

While born-digital materials offer many potential advantages for libraries and society at large, they also pose formidable challenges. Licensing, which has replaced copyright as the legal regime for obtaining access to much born-digital content, is at the core of a number of these challenges. Under copyright law, libraries have rights that have enabled their core functions. In particular, the "first sale" doctrine enables library lending. Licensing, on the other hand, entails no inherent lending right, as all privileges are subject to contract negotiation. In 2012 the problematic nature of licensing and lending is most apparent in the e-book market, in which some major publishers impose significant restrictions on what materials libraries may lend, while others (including at least two of the largest publishers) permit no library lending at all.[15]

Library licensing challenges extend beyond lending. The purchase of materials under the first sale doctrine also enables archiving, and other provisions of the copyright law enable preservation by libraries. Moreover, copyright law facilitates the means of making materials accessible to those with disabilities. In the licensing regime, however, all of these functions must be negotiated with each licensor.[16]

Libraries face still other challenges beyond licensing. For example, they may be required to provide born-digital materials only via an infrastructure managed by a vendor. Library access to e-books, for instance, often is made possible through an intermediary for-profit service provider. Thus, information about a borrower's identity, as well as details on reader behavior (for example, which pages or passages of a work a reader accesses) is now—at least in principle if not in reality—accessible to parties outside the library. Patron privacy, previously managed exclusively and carefully within the walls of the library, now is subject to negotiation with and supervision of vendors and other intermediaries.

Digitization of Analog Materials

Digitization projects are under way in many organizations, including libraries. In recent years the most visible, and arguably most important, of these is Google Books. The vision of this project is ambitious: to digitize millions of books and make them available online. While some of these works are in the public domain, others remain protected by copyright—and that is the crux of the controversy and lawsuit in which the project is embroiled. In October 2008 a proposed settlement between Google and authors and publishers addressed the concerns of some parties, but this settlement ultimately was rejected by U.S. District Court Judge Denny Chin.[17] As of early 2012 the parties were preparing for trial, but many observers believe a final resolution will not be reached any time soon.[18]

Despite the present controversy, digitization projects have been taking place for decades. Perhaps the first major such effort was Project Gutenberg, begun in 1971 with the goal of making public domain literary works available electronically for free.[19] In the 1990s JSTOR was founded to make scholarly articles broadly accessible,[20] the Library of Congress embarked on its National Digital Library Program,[21] and the Internet Archive began to archive the Web.[22] More recently, the Hathi Trust has been working to ensure that the cultural record is preserved and accessible far into the future, with about 10 million volumes available.[23] The newest major project is the Digital Public Library of America (DPLA), which began in 2010. Its focus is on developing a prototype of the DPLA system with specially digitized materials.[24]

In the last two years, one OITP priority has been the digitization of collections of materials with unique local value, such as documentation of an important historical community figure or event. Such collections often are not the focus of the larger national efforts, but they nevertheless have significant value. Indeed, materials of more local value that are not digitized and made available online become essentially invisible. Given that smaller public libraries and other institutions in many communities lack the infrastructure to undertake the digitization of these materials, more support and collective efforts are needed in this area at the regional, state, and national levels.[25]

It is painfully clear to those working on these digitization projects that two major policy issues remain as challenges: funding and copyright. Digitization that is carried out for long-term archival purposes with proper metadata requires specific equipment, expertise, and infrastructure. While some funding is available for such undertakings, it is far less than the need. At the same time, the copyright issues surrounding digitization remain difficult, and the resolution of these issues is ongoing with no end in sight. For these reasons, it is understandable that most digitization efforts to date have focused on out-of-copyright materials. But is this limitation necessarily in the best interests of users or society?

Diffusion of Mobile Technology

The proliferation of mobile technology being seen today has significant implications for libraries.[26] One consequence is the increasing demand for wireless access while users are in libraries. This growing demand is a major component of libraries' increasing need for broadband connectivity.[27]

Library services also are directly affected; indeed, libraries can better serve their users by embracing the growing capabilities of mobile technology. Libraries expand their existing services by offering mobile access to their Web sites and online public access catalogs; by supplying mobile reference services; and by providing mobile access to e-books, journals, video, audiobooks, and other multimedia content. These new capabilities also have the potential to increase access to text and media for the reading impaired and other persons with disabilities.

However, some of the issues generated by the growing mobile environment are new to the library community. Many of the aspects that make mobile devices powerful—such as pervasive connectivity, location awareness, and close integration with social networks and online profiles—call for careful scrutiny. Mobile devices and services deliver or interact with digital content that is more easily tracked and associated with individual users than other forms of information. For example, it is much easier to determine who is using a given smartphone to access the Internet (likely its registered owner or account holder) than it is to determine who is using an Internet-connected public terminal at any given time. Furthermore, the relationships between librarians and their users are changing as patrons access content and services online with mobile devices. The continued evolution from primarily physical, in-person interaction with patrons and content to increasingly virtual, digital, and mobile interaction creates unique challenges for libraries.[28]

A particular concern is privacy, which becomes more vulnerable in the context of mobile technology. The use of mobile devices typically involves wireless communications. Therefore, privacy depends in part on the security of the communications medium, which may vary greatly with the particular network in use, as well as security measures deployed on the device and at the service provider. Mobile devices also typically involve cloud-based services, so that privacy depends on the security measures employed by those services as well—both the technology of the cloud and the specific applications being used.

One issue that is decidedly not new and is exacerbated by mobile technology is licensing of digital content. In many respects, this issue is not tied to mobile technology specifically, as the general issue is access to digital content. But the brevity and limitations of communications and display via mobile technology imply greater needs for slicing and dicing information and therefore additional complexities and demands for licensing regimes.

Library Services and Spaces, Physical and Virtual

It is all too easy to become caught up in the innovations in information technology and services that the digital revolution is bringing. For the library community, however, the ultimate question must be how services for clients can be improved even as the venue for those services is becoming more complex, expanding far beyond the traditional bricks-and-mortar library building. While library services continue to occur in such buildings, they also are provided through all manner of technological applications, in kiosks[29] (a technological extension of bookmobiles), and in classrooms as librarians increasingly collaborate with teachers. In 2009 OITP established a mechanism for recognizing libraries that display best practices in offering services via cutting-edge technology.[30]

At the same time, we suspect that while mobile computing, online materials, and other new technologies and applications will continue to alter library services dramatically, a critical need will remain for many of the physical resources and characteristics present in today's libraries. Yet greater flexibility in physical spaces will be necessary as physical collections shrink in space and more information becomes accessible online. Like many segments of the economy, libraries may well evolve to services less focused on products (such as print books) and more focused on experiences in which patrons engage while visiting.[31] These experiences are likely to evolve from centering primarily on information access to entailing user participation and the creation of information—resulting in more collaborative activities.[32]

In its work on the future of libraries, OITP reconsiders some of the foundations of libraries, such as the act of reading itself or processing information. For example, a growing body of literature addresses the way new generations—"digital natives"—create, access, and absorb information.[33] The retirement of the baby boomer generation, just now getting under way, also will generate new demands for library services and spaces.

How to Take Action: The Manager's View

Clearly, many important trends and developments are affecting the future of libraries. In this context, one might ask what an individual practitioner can do. Accordingly, one area of focus for the AL21C Program has been how a library manager can think about the future in a systematic way, without having to comprehend every major trend taking place in technology and in society. The goal has been to produce a synthesis of our thinking that is future oriented, but also is directly useful for practitioners.

The initial plan for the *Confronting the Future* policy brief was to undertake this synthesis for all library types. However, it became clear that such an undertaking would require far more resources than were available at the time, given the significant differences across library types. Thus, we focused this policy brief on public libraries, being mindful of how this work could be applied to school, academic, and other types of libraries.

The Unique Advantages of Public Libraries

While the context of public (and all) libraries is changing in a profound way, the library community retains some fundamentally unique strengths and advantages. *Confronting the Future*[34] summarizes these as the six Ps (people, place, price, principles, pride, and package).

Unique Strengths and Advantages of Libraries: The Six Ps

- **People**—Librarians provide unbiased services and advice based on expertise and professional norms.
- **Place**—Libraries are physical spaces conducive to individual or group contemplative work.
- **Price**—Library services are generally provided at no charge to the user, and access is available regardless of the individual ability to pay.
- **Principles**—Library services are provided under the rubric of intellectual freedom, privacy, and trust.
- **Pride**—An excellent library is an indicator of a community with quality public services and high quality of life.
- **Package**—Libraries provide successful integration of information services across disparate functions.

A Model for Revisiting a Library's Mission and Strategy

In general, libraries have substantial strategic autonomy in the way they meet their community's needs within a general policy framework. To address the challenges outlined in this article, library managers must make strategic choices within four distinct dimensions, each consisting of a continuum of additional choices that lie between two extremes. Collectively, these choices create a vision for the library and how it understands and serves its users.

One dimension focuses on the primary clients for a library's services. Some libraries may emphasize work by individuals by providing appropriate study carrels and one-on-one reference services. Other libraries will give greater priority to support for group work and projects, community events, local archives, and shared spaces.

Another dimension addresses the nature of the information managed by the library. Some libraries will emphasize their traditional role of managing a collection of information that is relevant to their community—meaning information largely published by others. Others will offer relatively greater support for the production of information by, for example, providing video or audio production facilities.

The extent of a library's ownership of the media its patrons access is the focus of a third dimension. At one extreme, a library will serve only as a portal to information owned and hosted by other organizations. At the other extreme, a library will own and manage all of the information available to its patrons.

The final dimension is the extent to which a library exists primarily as a physical or a virtual entity. Of course, a purely physical library likely no longer exists. But some libraries may emphasize their physicality more than others.

Strategic Decision Making

In determining where their library fits in this model, library managers must begin by assessing and possibly re-evaluating the library's mission and goals to ensure that it is meeting the needs of its users. Then still at this macro level, library managers must carefully consider the most relevant external trends and forces and develop a set of assumptions to articulate an explicit view of the world that forms the library's context.

Following this external analysis, the next step is to assess the library's strengths relative to its competitors. These strengths include its operational capabilities and strategic assets in addition to the broader advantages outlined earlier as the Six Ps. This assessment, coupled with the external analysis, should yield a number of strategic imperatives—or actions—that a library should undertake. Library managers then should ask which vision from the above model best accords with these strategic imperatives. Implementation of the vision follows, and the cycle then begins again, as the external world and users' needs will continue to evolve.[35]

Directions for ALA in 2012 and Beyond

The challenge in thinking about and working on the future of libraries is the abundance of worthwhile topics that could and should be pursued. The topics given greatest priority will naturally evolve as circumstances change. In 2012 two of the topics that ALA is pursuing with significant emphasis are digital content and libraries, and contemplation.

Digital Content and Libraries

Certainly one of the major areas of focus for ALA will be digital content, particularly e-books. While digital content has been on the library agenda for several decades, e-books have achieved critical mass in the last year or two and have evolved from a niche product to something more mainstream. It is now generally accepted that e-books will largely replace print books for new releases by the end of the decade. OITP will be increasing its focus on digital content, but so will all of ALA through the newly created Digital Content and Libraries Initiative. Activities associated with digital content will be coordinated across the entities within ALA, and strategy and advocacy will be developed and coordinated through this initiative. In late 2011 ALA created a Digital Content and Libraries Working Group to provide advice from across the association.[36]

The phenomenon of e-books, and digital content more generally, extends beyond technology and services. The digital revolution challenges the profession itself. Librarianship, at least in the 20th century, was built on the cornerstone of professional control. Librarians were the decision-makers. While they exercised this role with the best of intentions, librarians had considerable latitude in determining how best to serve their patrons, armed with a robust body of knowledge and professional norms. However, the digital revolution fundamentally changed this position of control.

Control of collections now is shared with publishers and other information service intermediaries. Likewise, access to information was determined primarily by librarians but is now a shared responsibility with external parties. Licensing agreements and service provider infrastructure (e-book lending systems, for instance) fundamentally alter the practice of librarianship. Archiving, preservation, and privacy also were mainly under the control of librarians but now are subject to negotiation in licensing and service provision agreements—in the best case when agreements are even negotiated.

Thus, the digital revolution means a revolution in the library culture and profession. Professional knowledge and control are increasingly morphing into collaboration, cooperation, and negotiation.[37]

Contemplation

The foundation for the development of knowledge and for global economic competitiveness has always been thoughtful pursuits—or, more precisely, contemplation. Historically, libraries have been central to promoting contemplation through book lending and the provision of spaces and the right environment for thoughtful work, story hours, or places to plan careers and search for jobs. But contemplation in society is in jeopardy.

Such technologies and services as smartphones, instant messaging, search engines, and social media sites, to name a few, encourage short-term, brief communication exchanges. These developments have many benefits, of course, but they also come with considerable cost to society.[38] In particular, we are becoming increasingly a nation of information gatherers rather than information processors.

Libraries and librarians can play a useful role in promoting and restoring contemplation. Meanwhile, many others—from software developers, educators, and information service providers to social scientists, foundation officials, and policymakers—can orient their work to better support contemplation[39] and the benefits it provides.

A Final Word

Perhaps the greatest challenge for the library community in the past few years has been accepting fully that we are not facing fundamentally a digital revolution, but a full library revolution. Book publishers, newspapers, online information service providers, bookstores, higher education institutions, and myriad other entities are struggling to determine how they can survive and even prosper. Libraries, like all other information institutions, need to define a new role that best benefits their users in this new and evolving information ecosystem.

The word "struggling" above was selected carefully. Meeting this challenge will continue to be a struggle. But libraries—and particularly public libraries—contribute to society in ways that differ from those of most other stakeholders. As more online information is provided by entities driven by the profit motive, libraries seek only to satisfy the needs of their communities, regardless of users' ability to pay. The library mission of ensuring equitable access to information for all and advocating for national policies in the public interest is more important now than ever. To achieve this mission, we will have to become more visible activists, hardened negotiators, effective marketers, and successful innovators than ever before.

Acknowledgments

Many people have contributed to OITP's body of work since the 2008 inception of the Program on America's Libraries for the 21st Century (AL21C). I deeply appreciate the contributions of those who served on the AL21C Subcommittee, OITP fellows, OITP Google policy fellows, our OITP research associate, and OITP staff and consultants. I would also like to acknowledge those who provided reviews of drafts and general guidance, both individuals within the library community and those beyond. I am grateful to the John D. and Catherine T. MacArthur Foundation, the Bill and Melinda Gates Foundation, and the American Library Association for their financial support of this work. I appreciate as well the guidance and support of Betty Turock, the substantive and editorial assistance of David Padgham, and the editing of Rona Briere in the preparation of this article.

Notes

1. Further information about this program is available at http://www.ala.org/ala/aboutala/offices/oitp/programs/al21c/index.cfm.

2. Jennifer C. Hendrix. *Checking Out the Future: Perspectives from the Library Community on Information Technology and 21st-Century Libraries.* Policy Brief No. 2. Office for Information Technology Policy, American Library Association. February 2010.

3. Timothy Vollmer. *There's an App for That! Libraries and Mobile Technology: An Introduction to Public Policy Considerations.* Policy Brief No. 3. Office for Information Technology Policy, American Library Association. June 2010.

4. Roger E. Levien. *Confronting the Future: Strategic Visions for the 21st Century Public Library.* Policy Brief No. 4. Office for Information Technology Policy, American Library Association. June 2011.

5. The section was adapted from Levien, op. cit., pp. 10-12.

6. Indeed, IBM recently made an announcement about a breakthrough in computer memory that might have far-reaching implications. See Alex Knapp. "IBM Shrinks Computer Memory Into Only Twelve Atoms." *Forbes,* January 17, 2012. http://www.forbes.com/sites/alexknapp/2012/01/17/ibm-shrinks-computer-memory-into-only-twelve-atoms.

7. For further information on several of these trends, see Kevin Bullis. "The Year in Materials." *Technology Review,* December 29, 2011. http://www.technologyreview.com/energy/39397.

8. For a description of how Google's Chromebooks work, see https://www.google.com/intl/en/chromebook/#features.

9. See http://www.pwc.com/us/en/industry/entertainment-media/publications/assets/consumer-research-series-smartphones.pdf.

10. For more information on these trends, see Elizabeth McNichol, Phil Oliff, and Nicholas Johnson. "States Continue to Feel Recession's Impact." Center on Budget and Policy Priorities, updated January 9, 2012. http://www.cbpp.org/cms/index.cfm?fa=view&id=711.

11. For example, research by the Foundation Center found that foundation support declined in 2009 for most major funding areas; see http://foundationcenter.org/media/news/20111013.html.

12. See Sudeep Reddy. "Latinos Fuel Growth in Decade." *Wall Street Journal,* March 25, 2011. http://online.wsj.com/article/SB10001424052748704604704576220603247344790.html.

13. See D'Vera Cohn and Paul Taylor. "Baby Boomers Approach Age 65—Glumly." Pew Research Center Publications, December 20, 2010. http://pewresearch.org/pubs/1834/baby-boomers-old-age-downbeat-pessimism.

14. See http://www.slideshare.net/PewInternet/baby-boomers-in-the-digital-age-3476910.

15. See, for example, Randall Stross. "Publishers vs. Libraries: An E-Book Tug of War." *New York Times,* December 24, 2011. http://www.nytimes.com/2011/12/25/business/for-libraries-and-publishers-an-e-book-tug-of-war.html.

16. See Carrie Russell. "Threats to Digital Lending." *American Libraries,* January 12, 2012. http://americanlibrariesmagazine.org/features/01122012/threats-digital-lending.

17. See http://www.nysd.uscourts.gov/cases/show.php?db=special&id=115.

18. Further information about the lawsuit can be found at http://wo.ala.org/gbs.

19. See http://www.gutenberg.org/cache/epub/27045/pg27045.html.

20. See http://about.jstor.org/sites/default/files/jstor-factsheet-20110610.pdf.

21. See http://memory.loc.gov/ammem/dli2/html/lcndlp.html.

22. The Internet Archive is at http://www.archive.org.

23. See http://www.hathitrust.org and http://www.hathitrust.org/documents/christenson-lrts-201104.pdf.

24. See http://dp.la.

25. See Gwen Glazer. *Digitizing Hidden Collections in Public Libraries.* OITP Perspectives No. 1. June 2011. http://www.ala.org/ala/aboutala/offices/oitp/publications/oitpperspectives/oitp_perspectives_ju.pdf.

26. Much of this section was adapted from or inspired by *There's an App for That!,* op. cit.

27. For public libraries, see John Windhausen, Jr. and Marijke Visser. *Fiber to the Library: How Public Libraries Can Benefit from Using Fiber Optics for their Broadband Internet Connection. Policy Brief No. 1.* Office for Information Technology Policy, American Library Association. September 2009.

28. These issues are explored in much greater detail in *There's an App for That!* op. cit.

29. See, for example, Will Reisman. "BART to Unveil Book-lending Machine at Millbrae Station." *San Francisco Examiner,* May 4, 2011. http://www.sfexaminer.com/topics/library-go-go.

30. http://www.ala.org/offices/oitp/cuttingedge.

31. Discussed in more detail in *Checking Out the Future,* op. cit.

32. See work by R. David Lankes on libraries as conversation, such as in *The Atlas of New Librarianship.* MIT Press and the Association of College and Research Libraries. 2011.

33. The John D. and Catherine T. MacArthur Foundation has been at the forefront of this line of thinking through its Digital Media and Learning Initiative. See http://www.macfound.org/ site/c.lkLXJ8MQKrH/b.946881/k.B85/Domestic_Grantmaking_Digital_Media_Learning. htm.

34. Levien, op. cit.

35. This strategic decision-making process is discussed in greater depth in a fall 2011 webinar by Roger Levien, which can be viewed at http://www.districtdispatch.org/2011/10/ confronting-the-future-of-public-libraries-webinar-video. Generally, this section on strategic planning comes from *Confronting the Future,* op. cit., although the presentation here is necessarily much condensed. Readers are referred to the full policy brief for elaboration.

36. See http://connect.ala.org/node/159669 for further information about the working group.

37. For further discussion of this change in control, see Alan S. Inouye. "The Revolution Isn't Just Digital." *American Libraries.* January/February 2012. http://americanlibrariesmagazine. org/features/01112012/revolution-isn-t-just-digital.

38. See, for example, Nicholas Carr. *The Shallows.* New York: W. W. Norton. 2010; and William Powers. *Hamlet's BlackBerry: A Practical Guide for Building a Good Life in the Digital Age.* HarperCollins. 2010.

39. See the article by Jessie L. Mannisto in the *OITP Perspectives* series forthcoming in spring 2012, http://www.ala.org/oitp.

E-Books and Their Impact on Libraries

Robert Bocher

Bonnie Tijerina

It is difficult to engage librarians and library supporters in discussions about the future of libraries without the topic of e-books being quickly brought into the conversation.[1] While there is no defined moment when e-books suddenly took center stage in the psyche of the library community, a rapid series of technology and market developments have moved e-books to the front-and-center place they now occupy. These recent developments include a new generation of ever more powerful—but also ever more affordable—e-book readers.[2] Extensive marketing is driving the sale of millions of e-book readers, and e-books themselves are assuming an ever greater percentage of book sales. For example, in May 2011 Amazon announced that over the previous six weeks its customers purchased more e-books for its Kindle e-reader than all print books, both hardcover and paperback.[3] The Association of American Publishers (AAP) also reported that from February 2010 to February 2011 e-book sales increased by more than 200 percent.[4]

> Librarians are increasingly concerned about how e-books will affect their audience and many believe a tipping point is not far off. Libraries need to anticipate this shift and become part of the e-book story.—Chief Officers of State Library Agencies. *COSLA: eBook Feasibility Study for Public Libraries.* June 2010.

Along with the increase in the sale of e-books, there has been a parallel rise in the number of libraries offering e-books to their patrons. In 2006 just 38.3 percent of the nation's public libraries offered e-books, but in 2010 this increased to 67.2 percent.[5] However, whether a library offers e-books is highly dependent on the size of the community the library serves. For urban libraries, 82.8 percent offer e-books, but this figure falls to 48.3 percent for libraries serving smaller and rural communities.[6] The soaring interest in e-books is evident in the dramatic increase in use over the past year. For example, Wisconsin's public libraries saw an annual rise of more than 700 percent in e-book circulation from 2010 to 2011.[7] Higher use is documented not just in hard data but anecdotally. It was also witnessed by public library staff nationwide in the first weeks after the 2011 holiday shopping season as thousands of patrons, some new customers, walked through the library door with their new e-readers in hand wanting to know how to access e-books.

The recent emergence of e-books has surprised some in the library community, especially those who thought that the quintessential service of public libraries—the circulation of print books—was immune to change. Yet the dramatic growth in the popularity of e-books is challenging the assumption that lending print books will remain as important in the future as it was in the past. E-books are not a passing fancy and the library community ignores their increasing influence at its own peril. The community must step forward, embrace this change, and take actions

Robert Bocher is a technology consultant at the Wisconsin State Library and Fellow, American Library Association (ALA) Office for Information Technology Policy (OITP). Bonnie Tijerina is assistant director of collections services at Claremont Colleges, chairs the OITP Advisory Committee, and is a member of ALA's Digital Content and Libraries Working Group.

to ensure that library patrons are afforded access to e-books as they are afforded access to printed books.

In this article the authors will review the e-book landscape and its impact on library services. Several of the areas covered are:

- Setting the background for the recent emergence of e-books by placing them in the context of the long-term trends in technology and the digitization of print resources
- Providing an overview of key issues that libraries and staff confront in delivering e-books to their patrons
- Highlighting several initiatives or programs that individual libraries, library consortia, or states are undertaking to address the demand for e-books
- Reviewing recent e-book related actions and activities of the American Library Association (ALA) as it articulates a message and advocates for libraries on this critical subject

The Past Is Prologue

With the emergence of e-books, libraries and publishers are witnessing one of the last bastions of the print world change dramatically, that is, providing access to popular fiction and nonfiction trade titles. But this transition to a digital format has been happening in other areas of the collection for several decades. For example, many libraries in the early 1990s procured reference databases on CD-ROM and currently more than 99 percent of public libraries[8] and many other libraries have Web access to periodical and reference databases. As a result, libraries have reduced their subscriptions to print periodicals and print reference resources.[9] E-books—while not as visible as access to digitized periodical and reference resources—have been available for many years, too, from a variety of sources and in various formats. In this regard, the increase in popularity and visibility of e-books over the past several years is part of a much longer continuum. Several major projects or programs highlight this continuum.

- *Project Gutenberg*—One of the earliest attempts to undertake large-scale digitization of texts was Project Gutenberg.[10] The brainchild of the late Michael Hart, Project Gutenberg was founded in 1971, long predating the PC revolution or the Internet. The Declaration of Independence was the first digitized text available, entered by Hart himself. Since its inception the project has digitized more than 36,000 books that can be downloaded and viewed on a variety of devices from PCs and smart phones to e-book readers. Most books in the project's archive are in the public domain. For many years the titles were available only in plain ASCII text, but many are now also available in HTML and EPUB formats.
- *Google Book Project*—Started in 2004, the Google Book Project[11] does not have the longevity of Project Gutenberg. Nevertheless, it has very much caught the attention of the library, publishing, and author communities. Unlike Project Gutenberg, which is relatively low-key and relies on volunteers, the Google project receives considerable publicity and it draws on

the deep financial pockets of Google, Inc. About 20 libraries are participating, most from the academic community. The project is scanning titles both in the public domain (over 1 million thus far) and those still under copyright protection. It is these latter titles that are the cause of considerable controversy, and the result is several lawsuits filed by the Authors Guild, the Association of American Publishers, and others. One key legal issue is whether Google's actions in undertaking unauthorized scanning of copyright-protected books and making available small segments of them (which Google terms "snippets") constitutes "fair use" under U.S. copyright law.[12] These legal issues provide a graphic example of one of the complex issues[13] libraries, publishers, and authors confront in trying to make more e-books available through libraries.[14]

- *Internet Archive*—The not-for-profit Internet Archive was founded in 1996. It now has scanned more than 2 million books and makes another 1 million available from other libraries.[15] More than 100 people are involved in digitizing books in scanning centers at 27 libraries and more than 1,000 books are scanned each day. The Chief Officers of State Library Agencies (COSLA) voted unanimously in October 2011 to enter into a memorandum of understanding with the Internet Archive to help make more e-books available in public libraries. Jim Scheppke, then Oregon state librarian, stated, "COSLA and Internet Archive share the vision that every public library in the U.S. should provide e-books, at no charge, to their communities." The Internet Archive's Open Library initiative allows an individual to check out an e-book. If the title is still under copyright, only one patron at a time can have access, and the print title will not circulate while the digitized version is checked out.

- *American Memory Project*—The Library of Congress's American Memory Project[16] is one of the oldest and largest digitization efforts undertaken by a specific library. Started as a pilot project in 1990, it has digitized more than 9 million books, posters, photographs, maps, and phonograph records. Many of these are rare or unique items from the library's collections, and some are items contributed by other cooperating institutions. Digitized titles are available in a wide variety of formats (such as MP3, TIFF, pdf) depending on the type of item.

E-book readers also have a relatively long history, with the first ones coming to market almost 15 years ago. One of the first was the RocketBook. Introduced by NuvoMedia in 1998, it weighed 22 ounces, had just 4MB memory (holding about ten digitized books), and retailed for $500. It was widely panned for its poor display[17] and was discontinued after five years. But all these limitations are not surprising—the first generation of many electronic devices suffered the same fate because they were too large, too limited, and too "clunky."[18] No one viewed the RocketBook as a threat to the publishing industry's reliance on the sale of printed books. And they were right. But within a few years, the technology evolved and the new generation of e-book readers has addressed many of the RocketBook's flaws. Most now weigh less than 14 ounces, the screen display technology on some models is nearly the same as looking at a page in a book, and costs have decreased dramatically, with some readers now under $100. Parallel to this, the new generation of e-readers has been introduced in an environment in which a large segment of the public already has daily interaction with other handheld or portable devices, such as smartphones, laptops, or tablets.

Some Current Issues

There likely is not a librarian working in a public service position who does not encounter, on a daily basis, patrons with e-readers in hand asking how they can get e-books from the library onto their device. Unfortunately, such a simple question often does not engender a simple answer. The bewildering environment of e-reader devices, file format incompatibilities,[19] and convoluted download processes continue to be a frustrating issue for library staff and patrons as well. Added to this mix are a growing number of patrons who do not want to purchase another physical device but would rather read e-books on their netbook, tablet, or even the small screen on their smartphone. This diversity of technology places considerable stress on library staff, who are often overwhelmed by questions that may be highly technical, or are related to licensing or use restrictions that patrons, and often staff, find difficult to understand. As John Stoneberg, director of the L. E. Philips Public Library in Eau Claire, Wisconsin, stated, "We simply do not have the staff resources to offer help or support for every e-book device or tablet that patrons bring into the library. Assistance with e-book downloading is one issue, but often even more daunting are the follow-up technical questions about specific devices. These are often difficult or impossible for staff in small and medium-sized public libraries to address."

As referenced earlier in this article, many Web sites provide access to e-books in the public domain. However, when accessing titles still under copyright—which includes most popular fiction and nonfiction—many libraries work with companies that act as intermediaries between the library and the publisher. In other words, few libraries work directly with major publishers to get access to e-books. This arrangement is similar to the acquisition of print titles, where libraries often order titles through book jobbers or intermediaries, not directly from publishers. To some extent, such companies as Barnes & Noble and Amazon serve as intermediaries to address the needs of the consumer market. One of the largest e-book intermediary service companies is OverDrive,[20] which offers libraries access to more than 500,000 e-books and audiobooks from more than 500 publishers. EBSCO Publishing, through its EBSCOhost program, also offers an e-book service, and in mid-2011 3M entered the market. In acting as intermediaries or aggregators, these companies address both the needs and demands of the publishers and the needs and demands of the library community. To no one's surprise, the needs and demands of these two constituencies are not always the same. While performing a valuable service for publishers and libraries, these companies have also been the subject of pointed criticism from the library community. Some of this criticism relates to technical issues, from elaborate e-book download processes[21] to concerns about licensing and contract issues. The last issue has become particularly important because of questions many libraries have about the actual ownership of e-books.[22]

One of the most contentious issues in the library community is exactly what having access to an e-book means. Are e-books owned in the same manner as print books? The traditional lending of print books and other materials is protected under U.S. copyright law by the "first sale" doctrine, which has its antecedents in a Supreme Court case from more than a century ago.[23] In brief, first sale allows libraries to purchase printed materials and then lend them to patrons with virtually no restrictions. It also allows private citizens to purchase books and resell them at whatever price the market will bear.[24] Many in the library community would like to see libraries, and by extension their patrons, have the same rights to an e-book that are accorded to print books. But in many instances e-books are *licensed to* the library, not *owned by* the library. This is a fundamental difference, because what can and cannot be done with an e-book is not subject to protections under the first sale doctrine but is subject to the terms and conditions specified by license. For example, when accessing e-books on the Simon & Schuster Web site, users will encounter restrictive language using such terms as "revocable," "non-assignable," and "non-transferable."[25] While the licensing of e-books has become a heated issue, licensing has been used by software companies for years and was recently upheld in a court case[26] that could have a significant impact on the e-book rights of libraries and private citizens. Libraries have experience with licensing content because this is a common provision of periodical and reference databases. With few exceptions, companies license the content of these databases—and if a library decides not to renew a contract, access to thousands of magazines and newspapers will cease. A fundamental difference with many periodical database licenses is that they usually allow an unlimited number of patrons to simultaneously view any of the content an unlimited number of times. Licensing of e-books is much more restrictive and seldom allows for simultaneous use of a specific title unless the library pays for this use by licensing multiple copies. Licensing is also used to control who among a library's patrons can have access to an e-book. For example, publisher-imposed restrictions mean that some libraries can allow access to e-books only by residents within the specific boundaries of a community, even if the library serves non-community residents on an equal basis.[27]

In addition to using licensing to control access, the publishing industry often places other technical restrictions on the use of e-books with the intention of preventing the illegal downloading of titles. Publishers are very aware of what has happened to the music industry over the past 15 years with easy access to file-sharing sites offering free downloads of music protected by copyright, and they are anxious to avoid this fate. As a result, most publishers or e-book aggregators use digital rights management (DRM) to retain as much control as possible over who can access/download the digitized content and what can be done with it once it is downloaded onto an e-reading device.[28] DRM can be used in a manner that

> Loaning licensed ebooks is like playing with another kid's ball on the playground. The kid may suddenly claim you're not playing fair and will take her ball and go home, leaving you empty-handed.
> —Chris Harris

> The delicate balance set by copyright between owners and users via the "First Use" doctrine is derailed in the e-book world where licensing nearly always prevails. It will be difficult get libraries back to the copyright-driven model.—Mary Minow

makes it difficult or impossible to transfer an e-book downloaded to one's PC to an e-reader or tablet, and it can make it difficult or impossible to print or copy/paste text. This tool is often used to enforce e-book due dates, rendering a title inaccessible when it passes its date. Licensing and DRM are closely related in that DRM helps to enforce the restrictive language found in most e-book license agreements. As ALA has stated, "DRM, if not carefully balanced, limits the ability of libraries and schools to serve the information needs of their users and their communities . . ."[29]

In addition to restrictive licensing provisions and DRM, publishers often use a variety of other methods and strategies to control e-book use. In March 2011 HarperCollins came under criticism from the library community when it announced that an e-book expired, and thus would have to be repurchased, after it had circulated 26 times. This figure is based on a two-week loan period over one year. And in November 2011 one of the nation's largest publishers, Penguin Group USA, suspended access by libraries to new titles in e-book format citing "security concerns." [30] This action was related to a dispute with Amazon, and libraries were caught in the middle. Several days later Penguin partly reversed itself, saying titles that libraries already had would be restored until the end of the year. And in an extreme example of control, several of the nation's largest publishers have taken the ultimate head-in-the-sand position and simply refuse to make any of their e-books available to libraries. In a hopeful sign, in late January 2012 several key representatives from ALA, including ALA President Molly Raphael and Executive Director Keith Fiels held meetings with high-level management from several major publishing houses including Simon & Schuster, Macmillan, and Penguin.[31] Other publishers have since agreed to meet with the ALA team. Perhaps the dialog will lead to a win-win situation, suiting both libraries and publishers.

As libraries lease or license content rather than own it, they lose their role as stewards of that information going forward. Some publishers allow libraries to own and house digital copies of content, but the majority keep the leased materials on their servers or with a third party. This eliminates libraries' traditional role in preserving their materials and safeguarding them for future use. Librarians are left wondering what will happen in five, ten, or thirty years to the books they are now paying for, and how the original published work is safe from changes, edits, and deletions after it is published. One of the major publishers of popular books, Random House, states that it has the right to "Replace, edit, or modify the contents" of its e-books.[32] This allows Random House to change a book that has already been published. The shift away from stewardship of information may be a loss for libraries and their patrons today and in the future.

Another issue that perplexes and frustrates many librarians is why e-books cost so much. After all, parts of the traditional book-publishing process—printing, binding, and distribution—are removed from the economic equation. Yet some of the costs incurred in the print model still hold for the e-book model, including editing, advertising, author royalties, and the costs incurred to make the book conform to various file formats for viewing on an e-reader. It is ironic that while the cost of e-readers has decreased substantially, the cost of e-books has increased substantially, especially for popular authors and bestsellers. One does not have to be a believer in conspiracy theories to think that the relatively high cost of e-books in relation to print versions may be the result of a deliberate, collective decision by several large publishers. This claim that some major publishers are illegally colluding to keep e-book costs high is the subject of a class action lawsuit filed in August 2011.[33] The suit claims that when the industry saw inexpensive e-books, offered initially by Amazon for $9.99, threatening their longstanding print-based business model, they "coordinated their activities to fight back in an effort to restrain trade and retard innovation." Among other assertions, the suit says that the publishing industry is "hidebound" and has been "lacking innovation for decades." While not part of this suit the library community obviously has a vested interest in the outcome of any legal action impacting the availability, use, and cost of e-books. Several related suits have been filed since August 2011.[34] In addition, both the U.S. Justice Department and the European Commission have investigations open on e-book pricing.[35]

The issues outlined demonstrate that the publishing industry itself is having difficulties developing a simple and fair way to ensure library access to e-books. Of course what may be viewed as simple and fair to publishers may not be viewed the same way by librarians.[36]

Meanwhile, the frustration in the library community continues to grow. Many librarians feel they are being buffeted by the winds of technological change and economic forces over which they have little or no control but which will have a profound impact on the services they deliver.

Concerns about privacy and confidentiality are also being raised relating to the circulation of e-books to patrons.[37] All 50 U.S. states have opinions from their attorneys general[38] that protect the personal information collected when a patron checks out a book, and confidentiality has been part of the ALA Code of Ethics for many years.[39] But a library patron's checking out of e-books has raised questions related to who retains and has access to the critical privacy data that links the patron to the e-book. This has become more of an issue with the long-awaited September 2011 announcement by OverDrive that it had reached an agreement with Amazon to allow Kindle users access to the libraries e-book content provided via OverDrive. To complete the transaction, Kindle users are taken to the Amazon site, which is outside the legal protections provided by states' library privacy laws. Now many patrons have likely entered personally identifiable information on a company's Web site. But since it is the library that is offering the goods in the form of e-books, some libraries believe they should at least place a warning on their Web site to make patrons aware of the sites to which their information is going and the implications of it going there.[40]

In 2011 California enacted two laws intended to help protect the privacy of patrons checking out e-books. The laws prohibit companies such as Amazon from disclosing to any other party what e-books a patron, or any Amazon customer, has read without the patron's consent or a court order.[41] Privacy will likely become an even more important issue as more of a reader's e-books are stored not on their e-reader but on a non-library-controlled server somewhere else, for instance in the cloud. However, even titles stored on one's e-reader can vanish, as happened in 2009 when Amazon remotely removed illegal copies of George Orwell's *1984*

> We have a professional responsibility to inform patrons that their library use data may now be outside the control and protection of the library.—Sarah Houghton, San Rafael, California, Public Library.

from more than 2,000 customers' Kindles.[42] This remote take-back feature is possible because Kindles, like many e-readers, can access the Web via wireless connectivity, meaning that Amazon can access customers' Kindles.

For years the publishing industry has complained that by providing books free of charge, libraries reduce publishers' sales.[43] Whether this complaint had any validity or not, in an interesting turn libraries now may be viewed as marketing tools to increase sales because the agreement between OverDrive and Amazon allows Amazon to encourage patrons to purchase the e-book. Some question whether libraries want to be viewed as a marketing arm for any commercial firm or product, especially when they have no ability to opt out unless they decline to offer the service. It should be noted that some libraries have provided links to Amazon or other commercial sites in their online catalogs that predate the more recent e-book linkages.

While the issues relating to digitized content have grown in complexity, so has the management of such content. In the print world, when a print book was needed, it was ordered, cataloged, processed, shelved. In the digital world, licenses are negotiated, business terms determined, access set up and checked, and URLs added to the catalog and other access points. After the initial setup, ongoing management is required. All of this complicates the workflows and processes that are in place in libraries. The more complex management of electronic content has required libraries to re-envision workflows, staffing needs, and continuing professional development.

For many years public libraries have relied heavily on circulation statistics to help engender community support, especially for budget increases. An integrated library system (ILS) has facilitated more-accurate collection of circulation and acquisition data. As e-book circulation increases and purchasing models change, libraries need to be able to extract data and reports from systems that can accommodate libraries' new needs.

Librarians need new tools to assist in managing more-complex materials. Tools meant to support library processes in the print world are often unable to handle the new complexities. Managing license terms, renewal dates, usage, and link-checking often associated with various electronic resources requires tools that can hold this information and make it easy for library staff to pull reports and know what they have acquired. New tools exist in managing e-content. The market is constantly changing in this area. In addition, many librarians and information providers are working closely on standards and best practices to improve efficiencies.[44]

The exploding area of self-publishing is something public libraries are only beginning to address. While some think of self-published books as vanity publishing, an ever-growing number of these books are valuable and of high quality. On a given week, a few self-published books are among the top ten bestsellers, showing the interest in these books on the part of many readers. While the number of traditionally published books remains flat, the increase in self-published, or non-traditionally published books is increasing exponentially every year.[45]

COSLA's e-book study, *COSLA: eBook Feasibility Study for Public Libraries,* published in June 2010, suggests that libraries support self-publishing by celebrating high-quality self-published books and representing some of these materials in the catalog and other discovery tools. They also suggest that libraries facilitate self-publishing through workshops or by hosting digital publishing platforms, already prevalent in academic libraries. The recent news that Apple has thrown its hat into the self-publishing e-book and e-textbook market with iBooks 2 adds to the growing need for librarians to think about their role in getting authors to readers in the self-publishing arena.[46]

Examples from the Field

Many libraries or library consortia have taken the initiative to make the availability of e-books and e-content a key part of their service model.

Douglas County Libraries

Like many public libraries that provide e-books, the Douglas County (Colorado) Libraries contract with OverDrive as a key source of e-books. The library also has an excellent reference section to help patrons in the process of downloading e-books to their portable readers, with an extensive list of what devices are and are not compatible with the e-books provided by OverDrive. What makes the library different from many others is that it has mounted its own servers to deliver content, including an Adobe Content Server (ACS) for DRM-protected e-books and other content. In addition, the library has signed agreements with the Colorado Independent Publishers Association to facilitate easier access to e-books. Library Director Jaime LaRue believes that too many libraries focus on content from the big multinational publishing houses while ignoring valuable content much closer to home. The library must be a leader in working with local and regional authors and publishers.

> Our intent is to place the library at the center of the e-book revolution, not at its periphery—James LaRue, director, Douglas County Libraries

Wisconsin Public Library Consortium

Most of Wisconsin's public library access to e-books is made available via the Wisconsin Public Library Consortium (WPLC). Founded in 2001, WPLC has a contract with OverDrive for e-books and audiobooks. A fall 2010 ALA survey showed that only 5.5 percent of Wisconsin libraries did not offer e-books—the second-lowest percentage among all the states surveyed—and now all 385 public libraries in the state offer e-books. In May 2011 the Wisconsin state library agency sponsored a one-day E-book Summit[47] attended by representatives of all types of libraries throughout the state. Wisconsin has the highest per capita interlibrary loan in the United States, and one of the key issues of the summit was how to retain a robust and cooperative interloan environment as more titles become available in electronic format. Two key recommendations from the summit dealt with the need to be more assertive in combining the purchasing power of libraries, and the need to establish a statewide e-book buying pool. Moving forward with these key recommendations, WPLC members committed to raise a $1 million e-content acquisitions pool. The state library used $300,000 in Library Services and Technology Act (LSTA) funds as an incentive to help the state's public library community reach the $1 million goal. The funding effort, coordinated by the state's regional library systems, reached its goal by mid-September 2011. About 70 percent of the funding has been allocated to OverDrive for e-books and audiobooks. The remaining funds are held in reserve pending review of other options. This funding initiative will increase the number of titles available by about 50 percent. But a strong consensus coming out of the summit was that, from a long-term perspective, local libraries must start (or continue) to allocate more of their acquisitions budgets toward the purchase of e-content.

Sacramento Public Library

Through grant support from the California State Library and the Institute of Museum and Library Services, the Sacramento Public Library is diving into local self-publishing through the I Street Press: A Community Writing and Publishing Center.[48] Starting in early 2012, participants from the community can take classes to improve writing skills and learn about self-publishing and print-on-demand (POD) services. The library purchased an Espresso Book Machine, a device that prints and binds books ranging from 40 to more than 800 pages in length, to allow authors to print their self-published book as well as more than 3 million other books available to them. I Street Press engages the community in understanding the growing self-publishing environment and gives them the tools to publish their own works. Sacramento Public Library Outreach and Community Services Supervisor Manya Shorr sees this as filling a void created by the closure of the University of California, Davis extension program in creative writing. She sees this as a way to support the community and celebrate the written word at a time when libraries have a foot in both the digital and print worlds.[49]

Genesee Valley Educational Partnership

When Christopher Harris, coordinator of the school library system of New York's Genesee Valley Educational Partnership, tells school librarians not to buy e-books for their libraries, it is only because be believes the benefits of consortia purchasing are so much more powerful. "We need to be buying e-books for our school libraries so that we can continue to engage in resource sharing, provide more equitable levels of access, and create a common knowledge pool for learning. The challenge then is finding a model for purchasing that works within a consortium." At the partnership, they are using technology and crowd-sourcing to select and purchase regional resources. Using a model similar to the crowd-funding site Kickstarter. com, the libraries commit to spending a percentage of their materials budgets for regional electronic purchases. That money is pledged toward the purchase of a book at the level that it would cost a single library to acquire it. When enough libraries commit to a book to reach the level of a consortium purchase price, they buy the book for the regional library. Harris explains that ". . . this means each library is only ever paying out what they would have paid to buy the book on their own. If more libraries pledge to buy a book than needed to match the consortium price, then each pledging library pays less. Our system also has a reserve fund that we can use to help push worthy books over the edge to trigger a purchase."

ALA Actions and Activities

While much work is being done at the local level, ALA—a 60,000-member organization—is using its power to research the myriad issues associated with e-books, to work with publishers to make them more aware of library issues, and to establish policy agendas in this area. In 2010 ALA Council passed "A Resolution to Ensure Equitable Access to All Formats of Electronic Content Through Libraries."[50] The resolution referenced ALA's policy statement "Principles for the Networked World" and called for the formation of a presidential task force.

As a result of that resolution, the Presidential Task Force on Equitable Access to Electronic Content (EQUACC) was created with the charge of evaluating the current environment and making recommendations for what ALA should do to support members on this issue. This group was given an extensive set of responsibilities. Specifically, EQUACC was directed not only to describe challenges but also bring forth solutions on migrating from print to electronic access spanning various areas of stewardship from preservation to distribution. This task force was to bring forth suggestions on how ALA and libraries might work collaboratively with regard to distribution infrastructures, as well, and outline digital content access possibilities. This charter is expected to provide specific new ALA policy recommendations and changes, where needed. EQUACC was also charged with working with the already-existing Office of Information Technology Policy's E-Book Task Force whose focus was to support the needs of membership through programming and publications around these issues, such as "Frequently Asked E-book Questions from Public Librarians."[51]

As a result of the task force's work, EQUACC made multiple recommendations. First, resources were requested to complete an environmental scan of all data and reports in order to support and educate ALA members. An economic analysis of e-content licensing models, current and emerging, was also supported. EQUACC strongly urged that the issues pertaining to accessibility for people with disabilities be addressed with specific recommendations.[52]

The Digital Content in Libraries Working Group emerged out of this report. Made up of about 20 ALA members representing various divisions and interest groups, the working group will advise the association regarding libraries and digital content and where that overlaps with ALA's commitment to equitable access to digital content. The group will help members better understand the issues surrounding digital content and will suggest strategies for working with key stakeholders such as publishers, government officials, and interest groups.[53]

In addition to this new working group, ALA is committing staff resources and leadership to this issue. As stated earlier in this report, current ALA President Molly Rapheal and President-Elect Maureen Sullivan are addressing these matters. They held meetings with several of the "big six" publishers in late 2012, accompanied by ALA Executive Director Keith Fiels and OITP Director Alan Inouye.[54] The combined efforts of the association, its members, and leadership have positioned ALA to negotiate a well-reasoned future for both the nation's libraries and publishers.

Conclusion

How the e-book revolution will play out and its ultimate impact on library services is still an open question. There are those who think libraries, especially public libraries, will become a hollow shell of themselves. There are various apocalyptic interpretations of this scenario, one of them viewing small storefront libraries staffed by surly clerks whose only job is to check out e-book readers to patrons who can't afford their own.[55] But an optimistic alternative is also widely voiced; there are those who believe libraries will assert their mission and be viable players as e-books steadily erode the sale and use of legacy print stock.

To reiterate, e-books are not a passing fad and the library community must step forward—as some are definitely doing—and continue to embrace this change, to the ultimate benefit of all library patrons. As Douglas County Libraries' Jaime LaRue aptly stated, "We need to place the library at the center of the e-book revolution, not on its periphery."

Notes

1. Readers seeking basic background information on e-books should see the report "Frequently Asked E-book Questions from Public Librarians" from the American Library Association's E-book Task Force. June 2011. Accessed January 29, 2012, http://www.ala.org/ala/aboutala/offices/oitp/e-book_faq.pdf.

2. "Popularity of Books in Digital Platforms Continues to Grow . . . " Last modified April 14, 2011. Accessed January 29, 2012, http://www.publishers.org/press/30.

3. *New York Times.* "E-Books Outsell Print Books at Amazon." Last modified May 19, 2011. Accessed January 29, 2012, http://www.nytimes.com/2011/05/20/technology/20amazon.html?_r=1. And "Amazon.com Now Selling More Kindle Books Than Print Books." Accessed January 29, 2012, http://phx.corporate-ir.net/phoenix.zhtml?c=176060&p=irol-news Article&ID=1565581&highlight.

4. Association of American Publishers. "E-Books Rank as #1 Format Among All Trade Categories for the Month." Last modified April 14, 2011. Accessed January 29, 2012, http://www.publishers.org/press/30.

5. *American Libraries* Digital Supplement. "2010–2011 Public Library Technology Landscape." P.7. Accessed January 29, 2012, http://www.ala.org/research/sites/ala.org.research/files/content/initiatives/plftas/2010_2011/plftas11-techlandscape.pdf. American Library Association Research Series. "Libraries Connect Communities, 2006–2007." Figure 27. Accessed January 29, 2012, http://www.ala.org/research/sites/ala.org.research/files/content/initiatives/plftas/previousstudies/0607/finalreport.pdf.

6. American Library Association Research Series. "2010–2011 Public Library Funding and Technology Access Survey: Survey Findings and Results." Figures 35 and 37. Accessed January 29, 2012, http://www.ala.org/research/sites/ala.org.research/files/content/initiatives/plftas/2010_2011/techsvcs1011.pdf.

7. Data from the Wisconsin Public Library Consortium. In 2010 a total of 30,099 e-books circulated. This figure increased to 231,644 in 2011.

8. "2010–2011 Public Library Funding and Technology Access Survey: Survey Findings and Results." Figure 34. Accessed January 29, 2012, http://www.ala.org/research/sites/ala.org.research/files/content/initiatives/plftas/2010_2011/techsvcs1011.pdf.

9. This transition is happening well beyond the library world too as exemplified by the steady decline in print newspaper subscriptions as more people rely on online news resources.

10. Project Gutenberg. Accessed January 29, 2012, http://www.gutenberg.org.

11. Google Books Library Project. Accessed January 29, 2012, http://www.google.com/googlebooks/library.html.

12. Jonathan Band. "A Guide for the Perplexed Part IV: The Rejection of the Google Books Settlement." Accessed January 29, 2012, http://www.districtdispatch.org/wp-content/uploads/2011/04/GuideIV-FINALV3.pdf.

13. To show the bewildering nature of this lawsuit, see the flow chart developed by Jonathan Band for the Library Copyright Alliance. Accessed January 29, 2012, http://www.arl.org/bm~doc/gbs-march-madness-diagram-final.pdf.

14. As of January 29, 2012, this case was still before the courts. To track its progress, see the ALA blog at http://wo.ala.org/gbs/articles-blog-posts-links. Accessed January 29, 2012.

15. The Internet Archive Book Drive. Accessed January 29, 2012, http://openlibrary.org/bookdrive.

16. The Library of Congress American Memory Project. Accessed January 29, 2012, http://memory.loc.gov/ammem/index.html.

17. Matt Ellis. "A Rocket Misfires." Accessed January 29, 2012, http://www.wordpillediting.com/wordpillblog/2011/11/a-rocket-misfires. The SoftBook reader, also introduced in 1998, weighed almost 3lbs.

18. The author recalls seeing a demonstration of a fax machine, ca. 1979. It was the size of a washing machine and took 5 minutes to print one page on waxy paper. He thought at the time, "This will never fly."

19. This is very similar to the early 1980s in what was then termed "microcomputers," when there were many different hardware manufacturers, operating systems (DOS, Apple, CP/M), floppy disk formats, and so forth.

20. OverDrive. Accessed January 29, 2012, http://overdrive.com.

21. For a somewhat humorous look at download issues from a frustrated patron, see "Why DRM Doesn't Work." Accessed January 29, 2012, http://bradcolbow.com/archive/view/the_brads_why_drm_doesnt_work/?p=205.

22. One of the most contentious issues in this regard is the dispute between the Kansas State Library and OverDrive on the issue of who owns the e-books. The state library claims that based on its contract (now expired) with OverDrive that it has purchased, not licensed, its e-book content. Interview with Joanne Budler, Kansas State Librarian, in *American Libraries Newsmaker.* January 3, 2012. Accessed February 27, 2012, http://americanlibrariesmagazine.org/columns/newsmaker/joanne-budler.

23. 210 U.S. 339 *Bobbs-Merrill Co.* v. *Isidor Straus, et al.* (1908). First sale is codified Section 109(a) of the Copyright Act of 1976.

24. There have been several recent court cases impacting the first sale doctrine. See http://www.publishersweekly.com/pw/by-topic/digital/copyright/article/48587-second-circuit-copyright-ruling-could-affect-libraries-and-jobs.html. Accessed January 29, 2012.

25. Simon & Schuster. "Terms of Service." Accessed January 29, 2012, http://www.simonandschuster.com/about/terms_of_use.

26. *Vernor* v *AutoDesk.* U.S. Ninth Circuit Court of Appeals. No. 09-35969. Accessed January 29, 2012, http://www.ca9.uscourts.gov/datastore/opinions/2010/09/10/09-35969.pdf.

27. Sarah Houghton (Librarian in Black) Blog entry, December 9, 2011. Accessed February 27, 2012, http://overdriveblogs.com/library/2011/12/12/ensuring-access-to-the-largest-ebook-catalog-for-libraries.

28. Random House, Inc. "Terms of Sale." The terms say that any reseller of its e-books will "Utilize digital rights management, encryption and security technology approved by RH to

secure the eBooks from Misappropriation." Accessed January 29, 2012, http://www.randomhouse.biz/booksellers/pdfs/eBooksLibraryTOS1210.pdf.

29. American Library Association. "Digital Rights Management (DRM) and Libraries." Accessed January 29, 2012, http://www.ala.org/ala/issuesadvocacy/copyright/digitalrights/index.cfm.

30. Penguin Group USA to No Longer Allow Library Lending of New Ebook Titles. Accessed January 31, 2012, http://www.thedigitalshift.com/2011/11/ebooks/penguin-group-usa-to-no-longer-allow-library-lending-of-new-ebook-titles.

31. Statement by Molly Raphael at the ALA Office for Information Technology Policy Advisory Committee meeting, January 19, 2012.

32. Random House, Inc. Terms of Sale. Accessed January 31, 2012, http://www.randomhouse.biz/booksellers/pdfs/eBooksLibraryTOS1210.pdf.

33. "The Lawsuit Against Apple and Big Publishers: What's In It." Accessed January 29, 2012, http://paidcontent.org/article/419-class-action-suit-against-apple-and-big-publishers-whats-in-it. Text of the actual suit is at http://www.hbsslaw.com/file.php?id=761&key=ecdb5cfd51c029dd03eab73f6ccdd096. Accessed January 29, 2012. The suit challenges the "agency model" used by the major publishers to sell e-books.

34. "Price-Fixing Case Against Apple, Major Book Publishers Mushrooms." Accessed January 29, 2012, http://paidcontent.org/article/419-price-fixing-case-against-apple-major-book-publishers-mushrooms.

35. "US Joins EU in Investigating Ebook Price Fixing Claims." Accessed January 29, 2012, http://www.techradar.com/news/portable-devices/portable-media/us-joins-eu-in-investigating-ebook-price-fixing-claims-1046474.

36. While not directly library related, it is of interest that when Amazon announced its e-book lending program in November 2011, none of the major publishers participated. The publishers argue that Amazon's terms are too onerous. See, "Amazon Launches Lending Library Without the Big Six." Accessed January 29, 2012, http://www.publishersweekly.com/pw/by-topic/digital/content-and-e-books/article/49374-amazon-launches-lending-library-without-the-big-six.html.

37. "2010: E-Book Buyer's Guide to E-Book Privacy." Accessed January 29, 2012, https://www.eff.org/deeplinks/2010/12/2010-e-book-buyers-guide-e-book-privacy.

38. American Library Association. "State Privacy Laws Regarding Library Records." Accessed January 29, 2012, http://www.ala.org/ala/aboutala/offices/oif/ifgroups/stateifcchairs/stateifcinaction/stateprivacy.cfm.

39. American Library Association. "Code of Ethics of the American Library Association." Accessed January 29, 2012, http://www.ala.org/ala/issuesadvocacy/proethics/codeofethics/codeethics.cfm.

40. The Wisconsin Public Library Consortium Web site warns patrons that they will be leaving the site and going to a third party site (Amazon) that "does not have the same policies used by the library for your session privacy or use of your user information."

41. Grayson Barber. "Reader Privacy and E-Books in California." Commented in "LibraryLaw Blog." Accessed January 29, 2012, http://blog.librarylaw.com/librarylaw/2011/10/reader-privacy-and-e-books-in-california-by-grayson-barber.html.

42. New York Times. "Amazon Erases Orwell Books from Kindle." Accessed January 29, 2012, http://www.nytimes.com/2009/07/18/technology/companies/18amazon.html. Orwell's book "1984" is still under copyright protection.

43. "Survey Says Library Users Are Your Best Customers." This 2011 survey not only questions this assumption, but perhaps debunked it. Accessed January 29, 2012, http://www.publishersweekly.com/pw/by-topic/industry-news/publishing-and-marketing/article/49316-survey-says-library-users-are-your-best-customers.html.

44. An alphabetical listing of all NISO standards and recommended practices is available at http://www.niso.org/apps/group_public/projects.php. Accessed January 31, 2012.

45. Based on Bowker's 2010 report at http://www.bowker.com/index.php/press-releases/ 616-bowker-reports-traditional-us-book-production-flat-in-2009.

46. Apple Unveils iBooks 2 and iBooks Author, New E-Book Creation Software. Accessed January 31, 2012, http://www.digitalbookworld.com/2012/apple-unveils-ibooks-2-and-ibooks-author-new-e-book-creation-software.

47. State E-Book Summit—May 4, 2011. Accessed January 29, 2012, http://dpi.wi.gov/pld/ ebooksummit.html.

48. More information on the Community Writing and Publishing Center is available at http:// www.saclibrary.org/?pageId=1599. Accessed January 31, 2012.

49. From the article "Sacramento Public Library: Self-Publishing Made Possible Through Espresso Book Machine." Accessed January 31, 2012, http://www.sacramentopress.com/ headline/59057/Sacramento_Public_Library_Selfpublishing_made_possible_through_ Espresso_Book_Machine.

50. Accessed January 31, 2012, http://www.equacc.ala.org/wp-content/uploads/2011/03/ cd_44rev_equitable_a.pdf.

51. OITP E-Book Task Force Releases an FAQ on E-Books. Accessed January 31, 2012, http:// www.districtdispatch.org/2011/06/oitp-e-book-task-force-has-releases-an-faq-on-e-books-ala11.

52. Report of the Presidential Task Force on Equitable Access to Electronic Content (EQUACC). Accessed January 31, 2012, http://www.equacc.ala.org/wp-content/uploads/2011/07/ EQUACC-Council-report-final.pdf.

53. Digital Content and Libraries Working Group. Accessed January 31, 2012, http://connect.ala. org/node/159669.

54. ALA Midwinter 2012: ALA to Meet with Top Executives of Macmillan, Simon & Schuster, and Penguin on Ebook Lending. Accessed January 31, 2012, http://lj.libraryjournal. com/2012/01/publishing/ala-to-meet-with-top-executives-of-macmillan-simon-schuster-and-penguin-on-ebook-lending.

55. "2010-2011 Public Library Technology Landscape." Accessed January 29, 2012, http://www. ala.org/research/sites/ala.org.research/files/content/initiatives/plftas/2010_2011/plftas11-techlandscape.pdf. This survey documented (p. 32) that just 28.7 percent of libraries lend e-readers or netbooks. A more apocalyptic view of how e-books will affect libraries is epitomized by Eli Neiburger's "Libraries Are Screwed" presentation at the Library Journal/School Library Journal Online Summit in September 2010. Accessed January 29, 2012, http://www. youtube.com/watch?v=KqAwj5ssU2c.

A Holistic Look at Digital Literacy

Kristin Fontichiaro

What is digital literacy? Often, it depends on one's point of view. Elementary school librarians see the first mouse clicks and the earliest, often misspelled, Web searches. To them, digital literacy starts with teaching students the fundamentals of computer use. High school librarians may spy students attempting to cut-and-paste or bypass the filter to get to Facebook. In those moments, digital literacy manifests itself as an issue of citizenship online. A public librarian helps a patron videoconference with a family member overseas and glimpses digital literacy as the ability to communicate globally. A young adult librarian checks out a digital video camera to a group of adolescent filmmakers and sees digital literacy as content creation. An academic librarian creates a pathfinder to help academics see the range of digital journalism resources available at the library; in this case, digital literacy appears to be knowledge of available resources. A law librarian is gathering the most relevant cases for a team of attorneys, and digital literacy is comprehension and understanding.

All of them are right—and yet not completely right. While each event gives us one perspective into digital literacy, it is only by uniting our collective observations and experiences that we can see, understand, and take action to promote a digitally literate culture. This report undertakes a holistic review of digital literacy and suggests avenues for future commitment of resources and staff time. The digital stakes are high for our culture, and libraries are an essential piece of the solution.

Common Roots

In the hurried, ever-changing world in which we live, libraries remain steadfast symbols of the possibility for individual and societal growth. Today's libraries and librarians are repositories for communal resources, community centers, safe study spaces, performance halls, storytelling circles, discovery zones, multimedia environments, business incubators, and solitary spaces for quiet contemplation. And yes, they are centers for learning.

The idea of a library as a learning hub may seem like a 21st century idea. However, libraries as educational institutions can be traced back to Melvil Dewey himself. In 1917 Dewey reiterated his words from the first issue of *American Libraries,* stating:

> The time *was* when a library was very like a museum, and a librarian was a mouser in musty books, and visitors looked with curious eyes at ancient tomes and manuscripts. The time *is* when a library is a school, and the librarian is in the highest sense a teacher . . . (p. 45)

To be engaged in teaching and learning is to return to some of the library profession's classical foundations.

Kristin Fontichiaro is a clinical assistant professor at the University of Michigan School of Information, where she coordinates the school library media program and teaches courses in library and information science.

Bibliographic Instruction and Information Literacy

Libraries have a long tradition of helping patrons of all ages navigate through their information worlds. For many decades in the mid- to late 20th century, these efforts were focused on the term *bibliographic instruction*. Librarians helped their patrons find their way from the sometimes dizzying drawers of the card catalog to the book on the shelf, from the table of contents and index to the words on the page, from the first draft of the essay to the final references page.

In 1974 the term bibliographic instruction began to give way gradually to Zurkowski's term *information literacy*. Grassian and Kaplowitz (2009) credit Zurkowski (1974). They summarized his definition this way:

> An information literate individual is anyone who has learned to use a wide range of information sources in order to solve problems at work and in his or her daily life.

It is important to notice that Zurkowski intended information literacy to encompass both work and home lives. For several years between Zurkowski's definition and the digital era, information literacy was erroneously attributed primarily to academic tasks, not personal or consumer ones.

A similar definition was found in the classic American Library Association (ALA) definition of information literacy. More than 20 years ago, the final report of ALA's Presidential Committee on Information Literacy defined it as

> . . . a survival skill in the Information Age. Instead of drowning in the abundance of information that floods their lives, information-literate people know how to find, evaluate, and use information effectively to solve a particular problem or make a decision—whether the information they select comes from a computer, a book, a government agency, a film, or any number of other possible resources. (ACRL 1989)

Sixteen years later UNESCO released a single-page document formally titled "Beacons of the Information Society: The Alexandria Proclamation of Information Literacy and Lifelong Learning," frequently referred to as the Alexandria Declaration of 2005. It made information literacy a worldwide endeavor. Like the earlier ALA definition, the Alexandria Declaration focuses on both work and personal life, with an additional emphasis on development, inclusion, cultural context, and human rights:

> [I]nformation literacy and lifelong learning are the beacons of the Information Society, illuminating the courses to development, prosperity and freedom.

> Information Literacy lies at the core of lifelong learning. It empowers people in all walks of life to seek, evaluate, use and create information effectively to achieve their personal, social, occupational and educational goals. It is a basic human right in a digital world and promotes social inclusion of all nations . . .

> Information literacy

> - comprises the competencies to recognize information needs and to locate, evaluate, apply and create information within cultural and social contexts;
> - is crucial to the competitive advantage of individuals, enterprises . . . regions and nations;

- provides the key to effective access, use and creation of content to support economic development, education, health and human services, and all other aspects of contemporary societies . . . and
- extends beyond current technologies to encompass learning, critical thinking and interpretative skills across professional boundaries and empowers individuals and communities. (p. 1)

As in the 1989 ALA statement, technology is referenced. It is interesting to note that UNESCO redefined its terminology in 2011, bundling information literacy with media literacy—the ability to understand, critique, and evaluate the messages of mass media—under the term *media and information literacy* (MIL), and articulated digital literacy as one subset of MIL.

Digital Literacy

To the chagrin of many information literacy aficionados, the term *information literacy* and adoption of its tenets rarely took place outside library settings. Today, the coin of the realm is *digital literacy,* and adoption of the term helps librarians connect their practice with that of educational technology practitioners, politicians, community organizations, and federal initiatives. The California ICT (Information and Communications Technologies) Digital Literacy Leadership Council has defined digital literacy as

> . . . a lifelong learning process of capacity building for using digital technology, communications tools, and/or networks in creating, accessing, analyzing, managing, integrating, evaluating, and communicating information in order to function in a knowledge-based economy and society. (2010, p. 3)

As in previous definitions, there is an understanding that digital literacy skills are essential not only in school, but in life.

The federal government's foray into digital literacy, announced by U.S. Secretary of Commerce Gary Locke in May 2011, is an initiative created through the department's National Telecommunications and Information Administration to expand economic and educational opportunities in the United States that complement a strengthened national broadband infrastructure and augment Recovery Act investments. DigitalLiteracy.gov, in which ALA and nine federal agencies are partners, highlights school, library, and community efforts to develop the technical and operational skills of digital literacy. This emphasis is reflected in DigitalLiteracy.gov's fact sheet, which states:

> High-speed Internet access and online skills are not only necessary for seeking, applying for, and getting today's jobs, but also to take care of the growing educational, civil, and health care advances spurred by broadband. For example, an increasing amount of activities, such as taking college classes, monitoring chronic medical conditions, renewing your driver's license, tracking your child's school assignments, are now commonly conducted online. (National Telecommunications and Information Administration, n.d.)

Many of DigitalLiteracy.gov's projects focus on learning how to use computer equipment and software and not on the evaluation of resources, reading comprehension, or critical thinking. However, the resources provided to the site by the

American Association of School Librarians and other divisions of ALA make the connection between cognition and tools.

In November 2011 ALA Literacy Officer Dale Lipschultz introduced this definition at a conference of the U.S. Council on Adult Literacy. It succinctly encapsulates the ideas presented above:

> Digital literacy is the ability to use information and communication technologies to find, evaluate, create, and communicate information; it requires both technical and cognitive skills.

The recognition that digital literacy requires a combination of both technical or operational skills and cognitive or mental-processing skills is at the core of our understanding of the power of digital literacy and, similarly, of the perils should these skills not be developed.

Transliteracy and Metaliteracy

While the term *digital literacy* has the strongest foothold in larger conversations beyond libraries, other terms are emerging. The first is *transliteracy*. Thomas et al. (2007) define transliteracy as:

> . . . the ability to read, write and interact across a range of platforms, tools and media from signing and orality through handwriting, print, TV, radio and film, to digital social networks . . . The word "transliteracy" is derived from the verb "to transliterate," meaning to write or print a letter or word using the closest corresponding letters of a different alphabet or language . . . [T]ransliteracy extends the act of transliteration and applies it to the increasingly wide range of communication platforms and tools at our disposal . . . the concept of transliteracy calls for a change of perspective away from the battles over print versus digital, and a move instead towards a unifying ecology not just of media, but of all literacies relevant to reading, writing, interaction and culture, both past and present. It is, we hope, an opportunity to cross some very obstructive divides.

Transliteracy is a 21st century renaming and clustering of skills earlier reflected as multiple literacies or multimedia literacies. As Thomas notes, transliteracy includes the notion of digital literacy, but it is a broader term that recognizes non-digital genres as well. For example, Brian Selznick's Caldecott Medal-winning chapter book *The Invention of Hugo Cabret* is told in alternating forms. At times, the plot is moved forward solely through a series of pencil drawings. At others, the story is told through text. The ability to synthesize the meaning of the written text with that of the illustrations, resulting in a holistic understanding, requires transliteracy skills. However, as a non-digital product, the book does not require digital literacy skills. On the other hand, a product such as the app iDrakula, authored by Bekka Black (2010), weaves a modern version of Bram Stoker's *Dracula* through texts, e-mails, Web screenshots, recipes, photographs, and audio. The skills needed to fully experience iDrakula could be called, interchangeably, transliterate or digitally literate ones.

Coming full circle, Mackey and Jacobson (2011) argue that information literacy itself is a 21st century *metaliteracy* that encompasses all forms of literacy. They write:

[T]here are many challenges to the standard information literacy definition based on the emergence of new social technologies. While new literacy movements have similar foundation elements to information literacy, specifically related to critical reading and critical thinking, as well as proficiencies in finding, synthesizing, and creating information, differences are often emphasized based on the specificity of technology or media formats. As each new form of literacy is introduced, the shared literacy goals related to critical thinking and information skills are often overlooked, creating an unnecessary divide between information literacy and other literacy types. The information literacy literature has also contributed to this separation in an effort to clarify important distinctions between information and computer skills, or between traditional bibliographic instruction and new media literacy. Metaliteracy reinforces stronger connections between information literacy and other literacy frameworks. This approach looks at the foundation principles that unite information and technology, rather than focusing on differences based on discrete skills, distinct technologies, or media formats . . . Information literacy is the metaliteracy for a digital age because it provides the higher order thinking required to engage with multiple document types through various media formats in collaborative environments . . . Metaliteracy provides an integrated and all-inclusive core for engaging with individuals and ideas in digital information environments. (p. 70)

Here, for the first time, the emerging social technologies are made part of the digital literacy discussion.

This 35-year journey of naming schemes points out one of the fundamental tensions in librarianship: we disagree on how we define and use particular terms, and those differences are heightened depending on the type of library in which a librarian works. For this reason and because vocabulary is insufficient to reduce the silos, a deeper dive into *digital literacy* definitions and practices is in order to clarify nomenclature within the library field and beyond in the larger community.

Deepening Our Understanding of Digital Literacy

As this report's introduction pointed out, librarians can stumble when they assume that each experience is like their own. When instead they pool their experiences with others working in different environments, a fuller picture emerges. As an example, the University of Michigan School of Information places a high value on practical engagement, internship, and practicum experiences. Certainly, these experiences allow students to make active connections between theory and practice. But these experiences are also brought back into the classroom and inform the face-to-face classroom experience. As in many programs of library and information science today, students are rarely separated by library type; instead, there is a commingling of school, public, academic, and special librarians of all kinds. The students' individual practicum experiences help faculty, staff, and students recognize the nuances of practice, which continually refines and updates syllabi and discussion content. As the 21st century marches on, instead of types of libraries being silos, separated and distinct from one another, they are converging in terms of user-centered experiences, challenges, and digital literacy, which helps all of us see better the complete picture.

Students' experiences examining digital literacy practices in a variety of settings have demonstrated the value of unpacking definitions, sharing observations and strategies across library types, and seeking points of commonality in pre-professional practice. In deconstructing the definition into its many potential components, libraries and librarians can discover new avenues and paths to support their academic and neighborhood communities. By unpacking digital literacy, examining each category in detail and pointing to existing practices for the development of skills and operations, librarians of all specialties can find guidance for practice.

Technology Operations and Concepts

The International Society for Technology in Education (ISTE), in its National Educational Technology Standards for Students (2007), uses the term "technology operations and concepts" to define the "how to do it" technology skills: the ability to point, click, highlight, double-space, print, format, and surf. We might think of it as technological "how to do it." Long the focus of digital instruction in all kinds of libraries, the foundation of digital literacy is knowing how hardware, operating systems, and basic software packages work. As sites such as DigitalLiteracy. gov show, the ability to use a mouse, print a document, or fill out an online form remain important basic skills, especially in communities where desk-based work is not predominant. Early technology integration efforts in K–12 schools often focused their curriculum efforts around the development of skills like these. Having the how-to is a starting point, but it is not sufficient. Similarly, stocking libraries with computers and software and making them available to patrons supports access, but, again, this is only a starting point. Examples of library-based work in this area abound. A quick visit to a local public library's Web site or to a K–12 school demonstrate an ongoing commitment to teaching fundamental skills.

To strengthen patron literacy in this area, libraries and librarians can

- Continue existing practice leading orientation or "how-to" classes using common business software (such as Microsoft products)
- Expand instruction in free or open-source productivity tools (such as Google Docs or OpenOffice)
- Include orientation for popular tablets, e-readers, cell phones, cameras, and smartphones
- Partner with local businesses to bring these tools and resources to the library as free technology "petting zoos" so patrons can try a range of tools before making a purchase
- Use beginning orientation sessions as the bottom rung of a scaffold of increasingly complex and advanced skills (such as "Advanced Microsoft Word Features")
- Take advantage of free and low-cost screencasting, videocasting, or other tutorial tools to create or link to software guides so that patrons can access on-demand instruction from home
- Keep a current collection of illustrated tutorials and manuals in the print collection while keeping some past-generation tutorials for those working with older equipment

Communication, Collaboration, and Community

A digitally literate citizen is one who is also able to partner social skills with digital tools to communicate, collaborate, and build community effectively with others. Unlike past generations—who relied on face-to-face interaction, phone calls, or the postal service to communicate—today's generation is used to instantaneous interaction in multiple media, including e-mail, Twitter, Facebook, instant messages, texts, voice mail, and more. Our grandparents may have swapped ideas while leaning over their porch railings, but the world of today is vastly different. There is a difference between knowing how to navigate one's address book and make a call in Skype and knowing how to comport oneself during the call. There is a contrast between knowing which toolbar command to click on to open a new e-mail window and the ability to craft a thoughtful, polite message. The how-to is a start, but the art of online communication requires "soft skills" or "people skills" as well.

Consider how a library might model, offer one-on-one support, or lead courses in communication skills such as creating

- A multimedia, Web-based employment portfolio or résumé to organize, highlight, and share achievements
- Effective structures for business e-mail—when to "reply all," when to send a blind copy to a third party, appropriate opening and closing statements, signatures, and so forth—as well as business English vocabulary and language
- Facebook and Twitter etiquette and settings
- Collaborative tools such as wikis, Google Docs, Google Hangouts, Skype, or Webspiration

While it is relatively easy to teach patrons to click and drag, developing interpersonal ("soft") skills requires deft interaction and well-developed communication savvy. Helping patrons develop collaboration skills is difficult, but not impossible, for public or academic librarians who may have limited access to their patrons. One option is to partner with local business facilitators, life coaches, psychologists, or psychiatrists who specialize in interpersonal relations. These community experts can share their communication expertise and help librarians develop finesses in "soft skills" workshops.

In developing collaborative skills, school librarians may be the best positioned to work with students and their teachers over extended periods of time, from weeks to years. Learning to collaborate is an active, ongoing learning activity that is integrated into the American Association of School Librarians' *Standards for the 21st-Century Learner* (2007).

Reflect on how a librarian might partner with others to help students and patrons to develop these skills and strategies:

- The art of active listening
- Strategies for taking turns and ensuring that all voices are heard and none overshadow another
- Brainstorming protocols and civil participation in dialogs

- Collaborative tools such as mind-mapping tools (such as Webspiration. com), online whiteboards (such as Dabbleboard.com), productivity tools (such as Google Docs), Webinar software (such as WebEx.com, Adobe Connect, Elluminate.com, Google Hangouts, and Skype)

Development of these communication skills requires both online and face-to-face practice. As an example, school librarians in Ann Arbor, Michigan, are creating plans to bring these "soft skills" into their library practice as they consider how to adopt the Common Core State standards, which include speaking and listening skills at all grade levels. Similarly, school librarian Buffy Hamilton of Creekview High School in Georgia partners with classroom teachers to engage students in "fishbowl" conversations that involve students deeply in face-to-face conversations even as they practice resource exchanges using online tools like Symbaloo. com, Delicious.com, and Diigo.com.

Creating community involves developing and sharing online norms for civility, including agreements about etiquette, privacy, personal safety, cyberbullying, and an understanding of the line between copyright protections and creative mashups that feed the creation of new works. ISTE (2007) refers to this as digital citizenship, which can carry an unpleasant connotation from the days of classroom rules and school behavior codes. Instead, when discussing these skills, consider the term *community,* which recalls positive emotions and experiences. When we think of the online world as our digital neighborhood and its participants as our digital neighbors, our online experiences are less anonymous. As a result, our level of civility rises. Of all the aspects of digital literacy, this area is likely the category where there is the largest gap of understanding between librarians and patrons. Who hasn't heard a patron or student say, "If it's on the Internet, it's free," or "I can use that image because I got it on Google"? Many are uncertain about the nuances or impacts—positive and negative—of Google's 2012 revised privacy policies, Facebook's automatic Timeline creation, or the impact of hacked credit card numbers from popular shopping sites.

Even citation, the warhorse of our past as bibliographic instructors, is a variation of community, a Golden Rule. When we credit the work of others, we are extending them the courtesy of a thank-you, joining what Paul Courant calls a "community of authors" (Cunningham, 2011), and pointing our readers, viewers, or consumers toward additional helpful resources. Two keys help reach patrons on these thorny issues. First, for live events and educational sessions, marketing is key. Upbeat language wins out over negative, nagging, or disapproving wording. A session titled "What you need to know about copyright" is less likely to attract attendees than "How much of the Web can you use before you have to ask permission?" or "Are mashups legal?" or "Will I get in trouble if I watch a stolen video?" Second, there are issues about which a student may not wish to speak with a librarian. Here online resources like FAQs will go a long way toward preserving patron privacy. Similarly, librarians can realize that some topics may be uncomfortable for adults to raise in face-to-face librarian interactions. For example, parents anxious about cyberbullying may seek online resources first. For a sampling of discreet, online resources about cyberbullying, see New York Public Library's http://www.nypl.org/blog/2011/07/21/cyberbullying-safety or Denver Public Library's http://denverlibrary.org/content/what-you-need-know-about-cyberbullying.

School libraries like that at Rochester (Michigan) High School can spearhead digital citizenship modules that are compatible with Moodle, a software package for producing Internet-based courses and Web sites. School and public libraries can host parent sessions about cyberbullying and adolescents' safe use of social networking, recognizing the balance between their children's desire for full-time communication with the potential concerns or hazards that exist in "Web life."

Finally, academic libraries are leading the way in having conversations about Creative Commons, licensing, remixing, and traditional copyright. As an example, the University of Michigan's library system will offer sessions on citation and copyright, while its Copyright Office (http://www.lib.umich.edu/copyright), housed under the library's auspices, provides campus advice on an as-needed basis.

Some additional topics to consider discussing in creating community:

- What does Google know about me? What is the impact of its 2012 privacy policy on my online interactions? On the search results I see?
- What should I share online on Facebook? How do I set my privacy settings? How does Timeline work?
- How do I stay out of trouble when I use online resources?
- Is it really free if it's on the Internet?
- How do I block cyberbullying?
- What are Creative Commons and Open Access? How do they help me as a user of content? What are the advantages and disadvantages to me as a creator?
- How do I give credit? Why do I have to cite, anyway?
- What's cool to say publicly online? What's OK to say on my blog? What kinds of discussions and writing will bring me more followers and friends online? What practices are turn-offs?

Ambient Knowledge, Search, and Credibility

A pre-service teacher in my information literacy class surveyed her high school German class about how and where they search for information. They told her something she predicted: that they use Wikipedia for research. When she probed for the reason, however, their response surprised her. While librarians might predict that they selected Wikipedia because it shows up in the top three search results for most search engine queries, because it is seen as having content to answer any kind of query, or because its format is predictable, none of these were articulated as their rationale.

Instead, these college-bound students at a nationally ranked high school revealed that the reason they use Wikipedia is that—despite the millions of sites available online and via subscription—it is the only place they saw as a "go-to" site for answers. If someone could help them find other places to search, the teacher found out, they'd be happy to learn about them. This response directly contradicts our popular thinking about resource abundance and, perhaps, even some scholarly research on the topic. But it reveals something potentially powerful about how people construct their sense of the information landscape. What if people are loyal users of Wikipedia and Google's top three results because they have limited or no ambient understanding of some reliable anchor sites for their most common information needs?

Certainly, databases would remain key resources for those engaged in scholarly work, but what might someone's go-to site be for stock updates? Or biographical information? Or objective health information? Consumer price comparisons? Mortgage rates? Just as the Great Books program of the past century helped to canonize some titles as being core to human enlightenment (albeit a non-multicultural one), librarians might think about how they could practice their collection development and weeding skills to help their patrons have a core set of reliable resources.

We are so often eager to show how helpful we can be that we inundate our users with numerous available resources. Perhaps we should curate that list down to a "Top Ten List of Web Sites That Can Help You Live Long and Prosper." Maybe our patrons' search skills are predictable because they have no other way of narrowing down an endless list of choices.

Of course, not every query can be answered with one of ten Web sites, so search strategies remain important. Librarians have mastered the shortcuts and tips so that they find buffalo mozzarella, not the Buffalo Bills or Buffalo Bill or buffalo nickels, and when we share those strategies and search language with our patrons, we can help them get to better information faster. If we see librarianship, at least in part, as removing the barriers between patrons and information, then we recognize that our patrons are going to use the easiest means possible to get to a useful result. Let's teach strategies in Google, Bing, Duck Duck Go, and other search engines they use. Let's help them narrow the morass of results. Let's share how to skim results to quickly find links worth clicking. These strategies take seconds, but save minutes in search time. Finally, once patrons reach a site, they need skills in evaluating what they find there for accuracy, currency, relevance, reading level, comprehensiveness, and more. Librarians can support patrons' skill development in these areas by

- Designing tightly curated lists of reliable Web sites that answer most consumer queries, instead of inundating patrons with lengthy pathfinders
- Teaching search strategies for the open Web, not just library-acquired databases
- Guiding patrons in developing skills in Web site evaluation and credibility

Comprehension and Understanding

The Web was primarily designed for a general audience with middle school reading abilities and comprehension skills, similar to the reading level of the average newspaper. However, many Web viewers are children, English-language learners, or people struggling with literacy issues. Digital literacy is inextricably intertwined with traditional reading comprehension skills, with new twists. For example, skimming, rather than close reading, is far more common onscreen than with a paper document or book. This fundamentally shifts how patrons read and find meaning. In addition, many adults learned to read primarily fiction in K–12 education and lack skimming and scanning strategies for informational text, where one tends to read less in a linear format and more in search of particular information. As a result, literacy support remains key. Here are some strategies to help develop patron skills in this area:

- Partner with existing literacy organizations to include digital reading as part of the definition of adult literacy.
- Teach digital reading skills, such as skimming and scanning; identifying section headers and specially formatted text; interpreting charts, graphs, tables, and infographics; and scrolling the length of the document to get a basic main idea before reading in depth.
- Strengthen instructional support for reading informational text.
- Align library collections and programming to support K–12 students and teachers as they adopt the Common Core State Standards, which dramatically increases the amount of informational text being written in school.
- Build skills in looking for bias, point of view, and subjectivity in online content and communication.
- Build awareness of how spammers work and develop skills for how to recognize fraudulent, phishing, or scamming contacts.

Algorithmic Thinking

Many well-intentioned digital literacy efforts focus on how patrons can interface with existing software products and online systems. While these skills are valuable, they do not help patrons understand how the Web works, how to do logic-oriented planning, or how to make simple fixes when HTML coding on a Web template fails to work as anticipated.

Digital humanist Cathy Davidson refers to this as the "fourth R," for algorithm (building on reading, 'riting, and 'rithmatic), saying:

> [L]ike the other literacies, algorithmic thinking is foundational. Wikipedia defines "algorithm" as "a set of rules that precisely defines a sequence of operations." It is a step-by-step approach to calculation. You use algorithms to program a computer or for Webcraft . . . It provides an alternative to fact-based mastery and proposes, instead, iterative, process-oriented, constructive, innovative thinking. In the most general sense, algorithms can be child's play: a five-year-old customizing his Pokemon characters and game is already engaged in algorithmic thinking . . . They develop both design and problem-solving skills, alone or within a world-wide community . . . What is marvelous about algorithmic thinking and Webmaking is that you can actually see abstract thinking transformed into your own customized multimedia stories on the Web, offered to a community, and therefore contributing to the Web. Algorithmic thinking is less about learning code than learning to code. Code is never finished, it is always in process, something you build on and, in many situations that you build together with others. Answers aren't simply right guesses among pre-determined choices, but puzzles to be worked over, improved, and adapted for the next situation, the next iteration. You look at examples, you try your own, you run the program, and you see if it works. If it doesn't, you see where you started to go wrong, return to that place, and try something else. The better you become, the more possibilities open for you. (2012)

Davidson's view of the multidimensional learning opportunities with coding range from logic development to the value of iterative design to engagement with other coders and open Web sharing. Informally called the year of coding, it is hoped that 2012 is the year when not only formal programmers but also amateur experimenters will deepen their engagement with creation at the core level. As Manjoo writes, "There's no better way to learn how computers work than to start programming" (2012). Projects like Codeyear.com, sponsored by Codecademy. com, are bringing programming lessons to the general public free of charge in 2012.

Librarians can help by

- Offering programming courses for students, as the Darien (Connecticut) Library does
- Starting a CodeYear or similar programming club for multiple age groups
- Hosting "hackathons" or other marathon coding sessions in which products and sites are created in a very short time frame
- Hosting outside coding groups (ideally during non-peak or extra hours, so as not to use up all of the library's bandwidth)
- Partnering aspiring programmers with not-for-profit and community organizations in need of Web support
- Downloading Scratch (http://scratch.mit.edu), a free building blocks programming module created by the Lifelong Kindergarten Group of the MIT Media Lab to enable beginning programmers of all ages to gain a conceptual framework for programming, or Hackasaurus.org, which allows users to customize Web pages (Davidson 2012)
- Providing appealing workspaces where aspiring programmers can feel comfortable settling in, making noise, playing music, and eating

Self-Expression, Innovative Thinking, and Problem-Solving

Sometimes any user-generated content that looks colorful or animated online is considered creative even if the majority of the creativity was exercised by the tool's programmers and the user merely uploaded a few photographs. The terms self-expression and innovative thinking more clearly delineate the difference between plugging a few resources into someone else's multimedia tool and creating something that reflects one's own view of the world and innovative solutions for it. Clearly, the Web of 2012 has abundant options for people to share in multimedia formats. But it's more than harnessing existing creativity tools; it's the ability to use technology's tools and resources to create innovative ideas. Work force examples include designing or redesigning workflow or manufacturing processes, considering ways to cut costs while maintaining jobs, or knowing where to install roof vents.

School applications might include the ability to engage with Web-based simulations to explore a problem and consider solutions, the use of technology tools to create original multimedia works to express understandings, or using one's understanding of the Depression of the 1930s to consider solutions for today's economic recession.

In today's world of overabundant information, there is no need for citizens to re-create and recall factual information when there is so much of this content online. Rather than merely reciting facts found online, digitally literate citizens are able to move from ideas to action. This journey requires synthesis, deep thinking, and the ability to sort out information in order to make a useful decision. Front-line managers might review data about cashier speed or rates of error to identify areas that need improvement. Students might investigate alternative energies before identifying types that can be employed in their community. Public library patrons might access several medical Web sites and databases to come up with a personal plan for living with cancer.

Moving from recall or retelling to synthesis and action is very difficult for most people; this area can be developed strongly in K–12 settings, where there is more regular interaction between librarian, teacher, and student. Librarians can support this effort by

- Modeling synthesis
- Serving as a meeting point for creative artists, both amateur and professional
- Helping creators find online means of publication
- Engaging in virtual or physical exhibitions, as well as digital publishing, to promote the work of their communities
- Leading workshops about how to synthesize information for schoolwork rather than just reporting back a list of facts

Going Mobile

The pathway to digital literacy is a long and rocky road with many twists and turns. To fully embrace a holistic vision of digital literacy will require openness to innovation and working toward implementing the vision across library types. For decades, libraries have provided front-line digital access to its patrons, almost exclusively via desktop terminals inside the physical library. In the past few years, however, desktop access has shrunk as a primary method of Web access for patrons. Mobile devices are dominating the landscape. It's time for libraries to catch up and increase their education about and services for mobile users. Many library OPAC systems already convert into mobile-friendly format for cell phones, but there is more work to do in this arena as we shift from the tools librarians use in the workplace to those that our patrons use on-the-go in their daily lives.

We have to go mobile in a society where 2011 statistics from the Pew Internet and American Life Project show that 85 percent of adults (those over age 18) own a mobile phone. That figure jumps to 92 percent of users ages 35 to 46 and 95 percent of those ages 18 to 34. While smartphones offer the most sophisticated kinds of information interactions, even today's regular cell phones offer the options of sharing photos, shooting video, texting, and voice calls. Libraries must work with vendors to create content that is mobile-friendly, expand texting-based reference services, deepen patrons' ability to use cell phones more effectively, and discuss safety concerns relating to mobile use and the resultant need for attentiveness.

Action Steps

The challenge is large for libraries, even as time, resources, and staff are limited. How do we work together to meet these goals and make digital literacy progress in our communities? Let's next examine several strategies for success.

Partnering Across Library and Organization Types

Certainly, the easiest way to strengthen library-based digital literacy initiatives is to engage in ongoing, substantive planning and implementation between types of libraries. An academic library may be able to host a school field trip, providing an opportunity to demonstrate that knowledge of resources and search skills are important high school skills to develop (Mulder, 2011). Public and school librarians might partner to create a cyberbullying or Internet safety presentation for parents or children, delivering a single, balanced message that focuses on proactive behavior instead of hyperbolic fears. Inviting a local sister library to co-plan professional development events and cross-train two libraries at once can start the formulation of an active collaborative agenda.

Librarians might also partner with other organizations. For example, many public libraries now have business centers to support start-up entrepreneurs. (See Baltimore's Enoch Pratt Library Business Center at http://www.prattlibrary.org/locations/businesscenter/index.aspx.) These libraries can build partnerships with local accounting agencies, angel investors, municipal licensing agencies, and more to help the library become one-stop shopping for a potential business owner. Many small businesses may be unaware of the subscription resources, such as Bloomberg Terminal's financial news service (Darien Library, 2012), that could positively influence their bottom line.

Staff Training and Evaluation

In the rapidly changing technology arena, ongoing staff development is a necessity for all library personnel to retain competence in digital literacy. At a time when there is a widespread belief that communities no longer need libraries because we have the Internet, those on the front line must walk the walk. If a circulation desk clerk cannot delete a hold, if the information desk sends a patron elsewhere for help connecting their laptop to the wireless network, or if numerous computer terminals are marked "out of order," the fundamental rules of marketing have been broken. Patrons and students must see our digital literacy to believe it.

Online tutorials, replicable programs like the Public Library of Charlotte and Mecklenburg County's 23 Things program (http://plcmcl2-things.blogspot.com), and self-paced training tools like Atomiclearning.com put learning at the fingertips of all employees. Similarly, library staff needs to know what digital resources are available to patrons. Recently, a database vendor visited a public library and asked what kind of feedback the librarian had received about a competitor's database, which the vendor had seen on the library's Web site. The librarian said that she didn't know. In fact, she asserted that the library didn't subscribe. When a database vendor has to show librarians what is on their own institution's Web site, their credibility is marred. Librarianship is about connecting people to resources.

A systemic, ongoing plan for in-house professional development is essential to keeping digital literacy skills fresh. Professional development is more than demonstrations of new tools. Librarians are professionals who need time to discuss such professional issues as the impact of licensing versus ownership, filtering versus open access, streaming versus the acquisition of physical items. These discussions are not intended to convince staff members to adopt every new tool or trend. A thoughtful discussion about rolling out tablet computers for checkout in the children's room should be just that: a discussion—not a mandate. Librarians are right to debate cost, impact, appropriateness, physical development of the child, and what pediatricians recommend in terms of screen time. Libraries facing the future engage their staff in these conversations so that any staff member can provide exemplary service. The 21st century is a time of flattened hierarchies. Great librarians know that knowledge is power, and shared knowledge exponentially increases collective power.

Finally, if libraries are committed to digital literacy, professional development experiences must be followed by staff evaluations that require evidence of digital fluency. While some librarians may, in their homes, prefer not to have technology gadgets, broadband, or smartphones, they do not have the option to opt out of technological engagement on the job. Libraries have not been "all about books" since the days before vinyl records, and communities cannot afford librarians who will only engage with a single slice of the collection. Digital isn't always best, but it must be among the options.

Partnering at State and Federal Levels

Many digital initiatives are created at the state or federal level. For example, individual states adopted the Common Core State Standards and later joined one of two consortia to develop assessments that will be delivered online. This puts many school libraries, which double as building-level tech centers, in an uncomfortable position as they scramble to find enough working technology equipment to accommodate both testing and ongoing learning activities. Librarians have a role in conversations about these decisions, but they cannot occur if they stand outside decision making circles.

Similarly, the ALA Office of Information Technology Policy (http://ala.org/oitp) develops relationships with federal organizations and thought leaders to include librarians as partners in digital literacy initiatives while asserting ALA's traditions of intellectual freedom and lifelong learning. A January 31, 2012, presentation by the chairman of the Federal Communications Commission (FCC) indicated the impact of this work. In the press release accompanying the speech by FCC Chairman Julius Genachowski, it was stated that "A Further Notice of Proposed Rulemaking seeks comment on using savings from other Universal Service Fund reforms to increase digital literacy training at libraries and schools, a key step in increasing broadband adoption" (FCC 2012, p. 2).

Coming to Grips with the Idea of 'Satisficing'

Nobel Prize-winning economist Herbert Simon coined the term "satisficing" to denote our natural inclination to do what is good enough (Herbert Simon, 2009):

[P]eople, in many different situations, seek something that is "good enough," something that is satisfactory. Humans, for example, when in shopping mode, aspire to something that they find acceptable, although that may not necessarily be optimal. They look through things in sequence and when they come across an item that meets their aspiration level they go for it.

Certainly, "satisficing" applies to many people's approach to school, work, or home-based research. Since the Internet began to flourish, many librarians have wrung their hands when their patrons, faculty, or students, are satisfied with the top three search engine results, with Wikipedia as a single source, or with unverified facts spread by e-mail chain letters. Librarians need to find a way to make peace with this concept lest they fall prey to information arrogance, in which we see ourselves as superior to those we support.

Supporting Digital Literacy in K–12 Schools

If librarians are truly committed to developing a digitally literate, information literate, transliterate, or metaliterate society, we must devote maximum resources to K–12 classrooms and libraries. Programs of library education are a future school librarian's first introduction to 21st century librarianship. Often, library classes are by default designed around an academic, or public library model. This kind of marginalization cuts off the tree of librarianship at its roots. The only place where patrons are required to have regular interaction with librarians is at the K–12 level. The profession must commit to supporting foundational digital skill development in the childhood years. For that, school library students must be well supported within the master's degree curriculum. School library instruction cannot be marginalized. Aspiring school librarians need deep, rigorous, ongoing instruction and conversations about instructional practice in digital and information literacies. They need to develop fluency in policies such as the Children's Internet Protection Act, which sets out strict legal guidelines for what must be filtered. They need strong mentors in the field, as well as visiting university field instructors who help them convert theory into effective practice. They need to be regularly challenged so that they can develop their leadership skills and have the confidence to assert a multidimensional view of the digital and information skills that children and adolescents need. This increased effort should not benefit school librarians alone. As technological change envelops libraries faster and faster, more and more librarians need these skills.

Let's not hide behind inaccurate jargon like "digital native" (describing children born in an era of ubiquitous computer access) and "digital immigrants" (describing those who grew up before or as the digital era was developing), as Prensky (2001) advocated. The latter may have served us well in early days of digital life. However, let us not confuse digital speed or digital fearlessness with the complex, iterative, and long-term development of digital fluency (Fontichiaro 2011). Whether we host K–12 students in our academic libraries, enter classrooms as guest teachers, partner with school librarians to lower the teacher-to-student ratio when difficult skills are being developed, or lobby elected officials to support congressional initiatives such as the SKILLS Act, we must realize that the best approach to digital literacy is to support skill development proactively over time and not allow students to flounder until they find their way to public or academic libraries.

Libraries are a brand. Just as we recognize the Golden Arches as a symbol of McDonald's or the winged red horse as a sign for Mobil gas, the blue-and-white symbol of a seated figure holding a book is our logo. Brand loyalty begins early. Many of us still use the same brand of toothpaste, soap, or laundry detergent that our parents used during our childhood. If we consider libraries a brand, then it is in our professional interest to develop brand loyalty from the earliest ages. While all children have the option to attend public libraries, it is in K–12 schools that library engagement is required of students. All library types are served when students have regular interactions with capable, intelligent, and nimble K–12 school librarians. We must advocate sending skilled librarians into schools and lobby local school boards to see the importance of regular, ongoing instruction by certified school librarians. We must build sound digital habits when students are young and most malleable. The recession has brought hard times to school libraries, as it has to all libraries. The digitally literate community demands that we educate, hire, and retain leader librarians who can transform libraries into centers of learning that make digital literacy skills available to all within their borders.

Conclusion

Librarians believe in the joy of tumbling into a great story, the democratic ideal of shared resources, the life-changing potential of access, and the power of supplying information to solve problems. The digital future forces us to rethink how we can remain not only viable, but also influential in our communities and how we can use our skills and expertise to support everyone's digital development. Let's pool our perspectives, see the complete picture, and get to work.

References

"Algorithm." 2012. Wikipedia. Feb. 1. Retrieved February 1, 2012, from http://en.wikipedia.org/wiki/Algorithm.

ACRL (Association of College and Research Libraries). 1989. *Presidential Committee on Information Literacy: Final Report. 1989.* Retrieved January 8, 2012, from http://www.ala.org/acrl/publications/whitepapers/presidential.

American Association of School Librarians (AASL). 2007. *Standards for the 21st-Century Learner.* Retrieved January 28, 2012, from http://www.ala.org/aasl/standards.

Black, Bekka. 2010. iDrakula. Smartphone app. Retrieved January 28, 2012, from http://itunes.apple.com/us/app/idrakula/id387791516?mt=8.

California ICT Digital Literacy Leadership Council. 2010. "Digital Literacy Pathways in California: ICT Leadership Council Action Plan Report." Retrieved January 31, 2012, from http://www.cio.ca.gov/Government/Publications/pdf/Digital%20LiteracyMaster_Final_July_2010.pdf.

Cunningham, Kelly. 2011. "Courant Says Copyright Lawsuit Involving Digitized Books Is 'Misguided and Unnecessary'." Sept. 19. Retrieved February 1, 2012, from http://ur.umich.edu/1112/Sep19_11/2616-courant-says-copyright.

Darien Library. 2012. "Bloomberg Terminal." Feb. 13. Retrieved February 17, 2012, from http://www.darienlibrary.org/node/1705.

Davidson, Cathy. 2012. "Why We Need a 4th R: Reading, wRiting, aRithmetic, algoRithms." Retrieved January 31, 2012, from http://dmlcentral.net/blog/cathy-davidson/why-we-need-4th-r-reading-writing-arithmetic-algorithms.

Dewey, Melvil. 1917. "A New Profession." In "What the A.L.A. Was Intended to Be and to Do." *Wisconsin Library Bulletin,* Feb., 41–50. Retrieved January 31, 2012, from http://books.google.com/books?id=AmnpAAAAMAAJ&dq =what%20the%20a.l.a.

Federal Communications Commission (FCC). 2012. "FCC Reforms, Modernizes Lifeline to Keep Low-Income Americans Connected to Jobs, Family, 911 Services" (Press Release). Jan. 31. Retrieved January 31, 2012, from http://transition.fcc.gov/Daily_Releases/Daily_Business/2012/db0131/DOC-312210A1.pdf.

Fontichiaro, Kristin. 2011. "The Legend of the Digital Native." *UMSI Monthly.* Dec. 9. Retrieved February 17, 2012, from http://monthly.si.umich.edu/2011/12/09/the-legend-of-the-digital-native.

Grassian, Esther S., and Joan R. Kaplowitz. 2009. *Information Literacy Instruction: Theory and Practice.* Neal-Schuman.

"Herbert Simon." 2009. The *Economist.* March 20. Retrieved January 31, 2012, from http://www.economist.com/node/13350892.

ISTE (International Society for Technology in Education). 2007. "National Educational Technology Standards for Students." Retrieved February 23, 2012, from http://www.iste.org/Libraries/PDFs/NETS-S_Standards.sflb.ashx.

Mackey, Thomas, and Trudi E. Jacobson. 2011. "Reframing Information Literacy as a Metaliteracy." *College & Research Libraries* 72:1 (December 2011) pp. 62–78.

Manjoo, Farhad. 2012. "You Need to Learn How to Program: Make a Free Weekly Coding Lesson Your New Year's Resolution." *Slate.* January 4. Retrieved January 31, 2012, from http://www.slate.com/articles/technology/technology/2012/01/learn_to_program_make_a_free_weekly_coding_lesson_your_new_year_s_resolution_.html.

Mulder, Natalie. 2011. "The Importance of Academic Library K–12 Outreach." In *Information Literacy in the Wild* (e-book). Ed. by Kristin Fontichiaro. Retrieved February 17, 2012, from http://www.smashwords.com/books/view/115254.

National Telecommunications and Information Administration, http://www.commerce.gov. n.d. DigitalLiteracy.gov. Retrieved January 31, 2012, from http://digitaliteracy.gov.

National Telecommunications and Information Administration, U.S. Department of Commerce. 2011. "Digital Literacy Initiative: Fact Sheet." Retrieved January 31, 2012, from http://www.digitalliteracy.gov/sites/digitalliteracy.gov/files/Digital_Literacy_Fact_Sheet_051311.pdf.

Pew Internet and American Life Project. 2011. "A Closer Look at Generations and Cell Phone Ownership." February 3. Retrieved February 1, 2012, from http://pewinternet.org/Infographics/2011/Generations-and-cell-phones.aspx.

Prensky, Marc. 2001. "Digital Natives, Digital Immigrants." *On the Horizon.* MCB University Press, 9(5), September. Retrieved February 1, 2012, from http://www.marcprensky.com/writing/Prensky%20-%20Digital%20Natives,%20Digital%20Immigrants%20-%20Part1.pdf.

Thomas, Sue, Chris Joseph, Jess Laccetti, Bruce Mason, Simon Mills, Simon Perril, and Kate Pullinger. 2007. "Transliteracy: Crossing Divides." *First Monday* [Online], 12:12 December 3, 2007. Retrieved January 28, 2012, from http://firstmonday.org/htbin/cgiwrap/bin/ojs/index.php/fm/article/view/2060/1908.

UNESCO. 2005. "Beacons of the Information Society: The Alexandria Proclamation on Information Literacy and Lifelong Learning." Retrieved January 31, 2012, from http://bit.ly/AgO3dw.

UNESCO. 2011. "Media and Information Literacy Curriculum for Teachers." Retrieved January 31, 2012, from http://unesdoc.unesco.org/images/0019/001929/192971e.pdf.

U.S. Council on Adult Literacy. 2011. Digital Literacy: Skills, Tools, and Opportunities to Reshape Adult Literacy, Learning, and Instruction. November 3. Retrieved January 26, 2012, from http://connect.ala.org/files/67893/dig_lit_presentation_final_pdf_20843.pdf.

Zurkowski, Paul G. 1974. "The Information Service Environment: Relationships and Priorities." National Commission on Libraries and Information Science. In Grassian, Esther S., and Joan R. Kaplowitz, *Information Literacy Instruction: Theory and Practice.* 2009. Neal-Schuman.

Library Leadership 2.0:
Leading from Throughout the Organization

Karen E. Downing

Mark Winston

Alexandra Rivera

Why Leadership Now?

Since so many articles, books, and Web sites are devoted to the topic of leadership, why are we endeavoring to add to the literature at this time? After reading hundreds of works on the topic, two main reasons emerge:

- While there is an abundance of attention to the study and practice of management, there is not much new on library leadership.
- With the rapid, revolutionary changes in today's organizations, the demand for a fresh look at leadership is critical if we are to develop leaders for the emerging library environment.

The way we work in libraries today, it is not unusual to serve as a member of team-based or project-based groups to accomplish organizational goals. With the ongoing integration of changing technologies and a distributed mode of work, a wider variety of expertise is spread throughout the typical library. Gone are the days when leadership was practiced by a few; the norm now is for the same person to act in a leadership capacity in one group and as a follower in others. This model of distributed or shared leadership makes timely an in-depth look at leadership needs within the profession, and a fresh conceptualization of leadership within libraries.

This report presents a brief look at the evolution of leadership thought, ideas about leadership in various settings, and the authors' thoughts about the application of recent leadership research. We discuss issues of demographic changes within the profession and within the communities we serve, and the impact of rapid technological changes and other forces on the type and content of our work.

What Is Leadership?

Always it seems, the concept of leadership eludes us or turns up in another form to taunt us again with its slipperiness and complexity (Bennis 1959, p. 260).

Karen E. Downing is university learning communities liaison and foundation and grants librarian, University of Michigan. Mark Winston is assistant chancellor, Rutgers University–Newark, and director of its John Cotton Dana Library. Alexandra Rivera is student enrichment and community outreach librarian, University of Michigan.

Despite the length of time researchers and scholars have studied and written about leadership, no consensus exists on one commonly accepted definition. As Ford (2005) writes, "Despite attempts to trace the development in leadership thought, a clear definition of the concept continues to evade us" (p. 237). In fact, 20 years earlier, Bennis and Nanus (1985) acknowledged virtually the same thing.

> Decades of academic analysis have given us more than 350 definitions of leadership . . . thousands of empirical investigations of leaders have been conducted . . . but no clear and unequivocal understanding exists as to what distinguishes leaders from non-leaders . . . [and] effective leaders from ineffective leaders" (Bennis and Nanus 1985, p. 4).

Some scholars define leadership as a set of characteristics possessed by a person (the leader), that distinguishes the leader from his/her followers (Walter and Bruch 2009). Others define leadership through a set of behavior-based competencies practiced by the leader (Hall 2004; Kouzes and Posner 2007; Kouzes and Posner 2011; Pellegrini and Scandura 2008; Riggs 2001; Winston and Quinn 2005; Winston and Dunkley 2002). Still others define leadership not as being attached to one or more persons per se, but as a process of social influence that occurs *between* people, any one of whom may switch between being in the leader role and the follower role in any given context that requires a particular expertise and leader (Chemers 1997; Lubans 2010; Parolini, Patterson and Winston 2008). In other words, leaders are those who effectively and ethically practice social influence in order to affect positive change, even if they lack authority (or administrative power). As Kouzes and Posner (2007) write, "Leadership opportunities are everywhere" (p. 8) and "leadership is ultimately about creating a way for people to contribute to making something extraordinary happen" (p. 3).

Ultimately, the authors of this report draw upon the extensive scholarship of leadership as being about the management of meaning and narrative within a given context (library department, organization, community, or campus) to influence an outcome or set of outcomes, while empowering others to do the same. In her book *Organizational Storytelling for Librarians,* Marek (2011) describes the uses of storytelling (or "leadership narrative") for leadership purposes. Drawing on the work of Denning (2005 and 2007), Marek inserts the idea of library organizations as "communities," whereby a shared narrative about the past, present, and future of that organizational community "ties us together—in good ways—and gives us a sense of belonging to a larger group or purpose" (p. 46). It is through narrative and shared meaning, which any leader must usher, that our library communities can make those extraordinary things happen.

Later in this report we will discuss in depth our vision of what we call "Library Leadership 2.0,"—a process of influence and framing preferred futures that is a shared responsibility among those throughout the library organization.

Differences Between Leadership and Management

Scholars have shown increasing interest in the study of leadership, resulting in a growing body of theory and scholarly discussion, including increasing professional discussion in the library and information science (LIS) field (Kreitz 2009; Riggs 2001; Winston 2001a). While there has been expanded discussion of leadership in the LIS literature in recent years, debate about the theoretical underpinnings of the successful leadership of organizations is not new. The growing research and societal interest is not unrelated to issues of accountability and ethical leadership, and to the enhanced scrutiny of leaders and evaluation of leadership performance. In addition, in library and information services, there has been enhanced focus on leadership development, as will be discussed in greater detail.

Conceptually, leadership is not easily defined and is often equated with management, which is a narrower concept and often position-specific (Winston 2001a). In the ongoing efforts to define leadership in the literature, a common element among hundreds of definitions is that of equating leadership with influence. Conceptually, "Leadership occurs any time a person attempts to influence the behavior of an individual or group, regardless of the reason" (Hersey and Blanchard 1992, p. 5).

In considering the distinction between management and leadership, leadership is the broader concept; "Management is a kind of leadership in which the achievement of organizational goals is paramount" (Hersey and Blanchard 1992, p. 5). While leadership can and should focus on achieving organizational success, leadership also relates to exerting influence (over the attitudes, thinking, and behavior) on others, in pursuit of goals that may or may not be consistent with organizational goals.

Leadership is also broader than management in that management is position-specific, reflecting the responsibilities and authority associated with certain positions within an organizational hierarchy. Leadership, or the ability to exert influence, can and should exist at all levels within organizations—senior and middle management, supervisors, front-line staff, and everyone else. Research on the concept of "power" indicates that the capacity to direct or influence the behavior of others is not limited to those in managerial roles (Kanter 1981). One specific type of power, or "authority," is tied to one's position within a given organization—often, but not only, managerial. Power can also be associated with expertise or the admiration of others, for example, and therefore is not position-specific.

Why Leadership Is Important to Libraries and Librarianship

Leadership influences a library's effectiveness, institutional role, and adaptability (Weiner 2003, p. 5).

We would be hard pressed to find another type of organization and/or profession that has experienced the amount of change that libraries and librarianship have over the last several decades. The discipline of library science has morphed into library and information science, which incorporates people from many related fields. Burgeoning technological advances have had impact on every aspect of librarianship and libraries. The depth and breadth of scholarship has increased, and the pace and output of publishing has expanded, as have complications associated with scholarly communication. The need for technologists within librarianship has enlarged, user expectations have changed with regard to preferences for accessing collections and library staff and services, and libraries face competition from various sources, such as Google and e-book providers. At the same time, demands for accountability increase as economic stresses strain communities, campuses, and every other type of setting in which libraries are found (Hernon 2010). These economic stresses have increased the need for new organizational structures, planned abandonment of legacy services, cuts in library staff, and finding new ways to deliver much-needed services and collections (Evangeliste and Furlong 2011; Carpenter 2012).

We also know that much more upheaval is on the way. The demographics of library users, along with the pool of potential users (or non-users), are rapidly changing, while the demographics within librarianship are not (Adkins and Hussey 2005; Alire 2001; Davis and Hall 2007; de la Peña McCook 2000; Winston 2001). Globalization trends, in the form of immigration, global collaboration/exchange, and the interconnectedness of global markets and economies, all point to the increasing need to incorporate diversity leadership in the profession and the workplace (al Ansari and al Khadher 2011; Ford 2005). And, of course, ongoing technological advances will make more and more information available, and open unlimited possibilities for librarians to deliver service in new and exciting ways.

In their seminal works, Kouzes and Posner (2007 and 2011) attribute the growing interest in and need for modern leadership to many mega-trends, including the power shift that distributed computing and global connectedness has brought to organizations and societies. In a distributed (or now "cloud") world, we have both the access and the ability to empower people throughout the world and between and within our organizations. Recent examples of these co-occurring phenomena can be found in the power of Twitter and other social networking tools to enlist political and social engagement in such phenomena as the Arab Spring and the Occupy movement. New access to more information and the ability to win support and to coalesce around ideas from anywhere within society and within organizations demand a new way to think about leadership. With this individual power and global connectedness come flattened organizational structures and distinct power shifts. As Kouzes and Posner (2007) observe, "Power has gone to the people" (p. xviii), and thus the previous need to be managed by others is now more a need to be self-led. With the rapid pace of change, and change coming from every direction, "sensemaking," as Bolman and Gallos (2011) write, "is the difficult art at the heart of . . . leadership" (p. 17).

Donald Riggs's prescient thoughts a decade ago on the importance of library leadership are echoed in today's world. He writes, "Libraries will continue to undergo rapid change in the years ahead. People who work in libraries will have to learn how to lead change and to live positively with ambiguity" (Riggs 2001). Ambiguity is not something librarians traditionally have suffered well. Research on the predominant personality "types" in the profession indicates a high representation of individuals who prefer order, organization, and clarity. (Agada 1998; Hendrickson and Giesecke 1994; Scherdin 1995). Anyone who has viewed the YouTube video *So You Want to Be an [Academic] Librarian* knows there is an inkling of truth that our profession attracts people who like to organize, manage, and control the information landscape. It is what we do.

Winston (2005), stressing the importance of leadership within the library profession, noted the "need for effective, informed, forward-thinking, innovative, and ethical leadership." Among the many factors driving this need for more focus on leadership, Winston writes,

In general, a range of professional challenges necessitates effective and informed leadership in organizations: increased accountability and enhanced scrutiny of leaders and organizations of all types (required by funding agencies and other stakeholders), limited financial resources, enhanced competition, changing organizational structures, including greater use of teams, the proliferation of communication and information technology in the design and provision of products and services, including information services, as well as greater opportunities for ethical abuses and the overall importance of effective decision making to ensure organizational performance and success. There is also the leadership issue associated with recruiting the most well prepared graduates who have a choice among potential employers. All of these challenges have led to greater research and practical interest in the study and application of effective leadership strategies (p. 234).

Change is here and more is coming—there is no question about that, and the pace of new development is increasing (al Ansari and al Khadher 2011; Garman and Johnson 2006). The question is, as Hernon (2010) writes, "what will we [libraries and librarianship] become?" As Riggs stated, "Without strong, dynamic, and visionary leadership, libraries are certain to drift backward into the future" (Riggs 2001, p. 5).

Leadership within libraries and within the profession of library and information services is of critical importance in order to successfully position libraries as the centers of information delivery, cultural exchange, and innovation in our schools, universities, government, communities, hospitals, and corporations. It is through enlightened leadership—via vision, influence, and shared narrative—that we can harness unrelenting change to navigate libraries in ways that are true to our professional values.

Conceptions of Leadership in the Literature

Leadership has been studied, written about, and characterized in many ways. Historically, the vast majority of library, business, and education literature characterizes leadership as being attached to a single person or a few people at the apex of a hierarchical organizational structure (al Ansari and al Khadher 2011; Pellegrini and Scandura 2008; Popper, Mayseless, and Castelnovo 2000; Riggs 2001; Walter and Bruch 2009).

Early concepts of leadership concentrated on the idea that leaders were born, not made. Concepts such as the "great man," "paternalistic leadership," and "charismatic leadership" were all based on the idea that certain individuals were imbued with an innate set of traits that allowed them to lead others to do their bidding by sheer force of personality and ultimate authority (Ford 2005). Conceptually, these theories were based on the study of successful leaders, as identified by their ability to get others to support their vision. These leadership theories gave way to ideas of "servant leadership," "transformational leadership," and "stewardship" in the 1980s and 1990s (Block 1993; Greenleaf and Spears 1998; Parolini, Patterson, and Winston 2008). These latter conceptualizations suggested that leaders could be made and that individuals could be taught leadership skills and competencies, yet they still concentrated on defining leadership based on power and authority at the apex of the organization.

Following the servant leadership trends, scholars more recently have envisioned leadership as a set of teachable competencies that allow those who are poised for leadership to develop the knowledge and abilities to lead effectively (Hall 2004; Kouzes and Posner 1997; Kouzes and Posner 2007; McWilliams 2007; Winston and Dunkley 2002). While there is not universal agreement on which competencies are necessary to lead others, Kouzes and Posner (1990, 1997, 2007) determined via research conducted over a decade that the four most admired characteristics of leaders are honesty, forward vision, competence, and the ability to inspire others to action (Mason and Wetherbee 2004).

Recently, such concepts as "ethical leadership," "shared leadership," "followership," "self-leadership," "open leadership," and "sustainable leadership" also share ideas of learned competencies, but they shift the focus of leadership from one administrator/leader to processes of influence and the democratization of organizations, whereby leaders are found at every level of the organizational structure, and there is less of a distinction between leaders and followers (Ford 2005; Lambert 2011; Lubans 2010; Stewart, Courtright, and Manz 2011; Yun, Cox, and Sims 2006).

Leadership and Diversity

Without addressing context, our theories of leadership remain incomplete, making it more difficult to offer practical guidelines to address the leadership demands of changing organizations in contemporary society (Ospina and Foldy 2009).

The study of diversity in the leadership literature has been concerned with the characteristics of leaders, followers, and situational context, which all contribute to leadership processes and outcomes (Hsieh 2010). Much of the original diversity leadership literature was written in the 1970s and concentrated on black/white stylistic differences and followers' racial preferences regarding their leaders.

A growing body of 21st century literature includes intersections of leadership and feminism, globalism, and race-ethnicity, and points to the growing concern among researchers for incorporating diversity more regularly into all leadership literature (Ford 2005; Hsieh 2010; Ospina and Foldy 2009). Ospina and Foldy (2009) examined leadership through context, power, and collective lenses to understand race-ethnicity in the leadership literature. Ford (2005) and Turock (2001) have examined leadership through the lens of feminism.

Current diversity and leadership literature stresses the importance of societal and institutional context and issues of power inequities in the understanding of leadership, including historical inequalities among groups of people (al Ansari and al Khadher 2011; Ospina and Foldy 2009). As demographics continue to change, as a nation we continue to experience the "fundamental fault line" of race-ethnicity (Marable 1996), and the legacy of gender inequality, even in a primarily female-oriented profession. Diversity and leadership must be inextricably linked as we strategize about the next generation of leadership in our profession.

The need for more diversity leadership literature is twofold: first there is simply not enough of it, and second, what exists has been faulted for examining cultural contexts only from the perspective of the "dominant cultural value orientations" (Hsieh 2010, p. 107). Therefore, the contextualization of diversity "probably [reflects] biases due to ignoring the variation within countries" (Graen 2006,

p. 96, cited in Hsieh 2010, p. 107). As has been considered in the literature on diversity and leadership, "cultural values have been proven to have a profound effect on leadership concepts, values behaviors, and leadership styles" (Hsieh 2010, p. 99). And therefore, "What is expected of leadership, what leaders may or may not do, and the status and influence bestowed upon them vary considerably as a result of the cultural forces in the countries or regions in which the leaders function" (Hsieh 2010, p. 100). As a profession, we need a firmer grasp of the ways cultural influences and traditions impact our leadership and followership roles.

The idea of the importance of narrative and meaning-making to leadership, presented earlier in this report, is also linked to diversity. As Ford (2005) suggests, "cultural understanding of leadership requires an understanding of local meaning . . . leadership can be defined as 'about influencing the construction of reality—the ideas, beliefs and interpretations of what and how things can and should be done'" (Alvesson 2002, cited by Ford 2005, p. 242). In her research on the relationship between social identity and role performance in libraries, Downing (2009) found that race/ethnicity, gender, and age all significantly affected the ways in which librarians enact their work, including leadership roles.

And finally, much more insight is needed into the ways globalization affects leadership in library settings and in the profession as a whole. As Hsieh writes, "with the trend of globalization, leaders have more chances to live and work with those coming from very diverse cultural origins including differences in language, norms and lifestyles" (Hsieh 2010, p. 99).

As a profession, we need a firmer grasp of the many ways in which cultural influences and traditions may impact, enhance, and/or limit our leadership practices and needs.

Leadership 2.0: Leadership Is All of Us!

When thinking of leadership . . . include yourself, no matter what your position or job title in the library. Building leadership skills is something everyone should consider, because leadership comes from all across the organization (Marek 2011, p. 7).

Leadership is never a person; it is a process between leaders and followers (Lubans 2010, p. 12).

Over the last decade, leadership scholarship in the business and education realms has changed considerably (and our library leadership literature needs to catch up). The concept that leadership rests only with library deans, directors, or department heads (Riggs 2001; Weiner 2003) is changing out of necessity—no longer can one or a few people in a library organization lead the masses through turbulent times. Because of the proliferation of distributed technology and increasingly segmented expertise and knowledge bases operating within libraries and library contexts, no one person or small group of people can know everything that needs to be known to make sound decisions and envision the strongest futures for libraries. Some of that expertise resides in each and every library worker, and successful organizations will figure out how to foster and grow the multitude of leadership qualities in all of their employees.

No longer is leadership considered the exclusive realm of top administrators; rather, it is now seen as something that each individual within the organization must develop in order for positive organizational futures. Recent literature has also emphasized that leadership does not reside within only one person or set of people but rather it is a *process* that occurs between people (Ford 2005; Lubans 2010; Marek 2011). In this conceptualization, it is the interplay between leaders and followers that is important. With these changes in emphases come new competencies that leaders and followers must master or incorporate into their increasingly collaborative work.

In addition to including everyone in the leadership model, the line in the sand between those who are leaders and those who are followers is largely erased, as any one person may be a leader in one context (project or work group) and a follower in another. Leadership 2.0 emphasizes that we will all need to possess leadership skills, but we will all need to be followers as well. On a given day, on any given set of projects, the same person may need to fluidly move between leadership and followership roles, and thus the competencies of each must be distributed among all our library workers.

At first blush, it may seem a radical and somewhat contradictory notion to distribute leadership among all people in the library, but already the profession is straining for the next generation of library administrators (this is dealt with later under the heading "Retirements and Succession Planning"). What better way to increase the pipeline of dynamic administrators than to open the teaching of leadership to all of the library's members? Furthermore, in today's rapidly changing information environment, the idea that any one person or small group of people can know and act on cues from the environment is hardly sustainable.

In sum, Ford (2005) envisioned a new type of leadership, with which we agree. She writes:

> Instead of focusing on styles and contingencies of leadership and the heroic qualities of leaders . . . leadership is the work of many people in an organization. The focus thus shifts from leaders to followers, in terms of giving voice to all people in an organization, to harness the collective intelligence of the workforce as part of a process of building new relationships within, across and outside the organization (p. 240).

Figure 1 illustrates the components and concepts of Library Leadership 2.0. It is an amalgamation of the concepts of self-leadership, open leadership, and ethical leadership prevalent in the leadership literature and applied to the library context.

Unlike traditional library leadership, which has leaders primarily at the apex of the organization, Leadership 2.0 necessitates developing and locating leadership throughout the entire organization. Each staff member has the potential and is encouraged to develop leadership skills and competencies to enable effective team-based work processes. In Leadership 2.0, complexity and ambiguity are the norm, and therefore the traditional taking command and seeking control of situations and people is not well-suited to the new information environment. Complexity, flexibility, and ambiguity are acknowledged and even encouraged as opposed to being considered environmental faults that need to be fixed or overcome. Leaders throughout the organization are able to employ organizational narratives that effectively persuade teams and stakeholders to take a course of action, or secure resources for particular purposes. And finally, rather than focusing primarily on a select set of current leaders, Leadership 2.0 recognizes the pressing need to continuously develop new leadership in order to sustain the organization at all levels, and the profession of librarianship.

Figure 1 / Library Leadership 2.0 versus Traditional Leadership

Library Leadership 2.0	Traditional Library Leadership
• Distributed throughout the organization	• Concentrated in top or middle-level administrators
• Uses complexity and persuasion as part of context	• Uses persuasion as an extension of the leader
• Harnesses the talents and deep knowledge of the collective	• Uses "command and control"
• Is open to criticism and change	• Leaders and followers are separate people
• Synthesizes information and trends	• Does not actively seek feedback from followers
• Effectively employs organizational/ professional narrative	• Focuses on current leaders
• The same people are leaders and followers at different times or on different projects	• Emphasizes leadership as residing in people rather than process
• Sustains itself through active development of new leadership	
• Is viewed as a process between people	

What Is Happening Now

The need to stop and take stock of where we are as a profession with regard to leadership, leadership needs, and leadership development is an essential step before taking any course of action. The next several sections of the report discuss pressing issues with regard to leadership, including retirements, succession planning, and neglected areas that need attention.

Retirements and Succession Planning

Many predictions have been associated with the fact that librarians are older than the average for professions in the United States (Kyrillidou and Young 2008) and the potential impact of that fact on the profession. For example, "between 2010–2020, 45% of librarians will reach the retirement age of 65 years old" (Chu 2009, n.p.). Or, "58 percent of professional librarians will reach the age of 65 between 2005 and 2019" (American Library Association [ALA] 2011). Other researchers have estimated that "40% of librarians are set to retire by 2014" (Sheardown and Woroniak 2007, pp. 64–65). As Jason Martin (2009) and others have noted, "With the recent economic downturn it is unclear if that number, 40%, will hold true. But the economy will eventually take a turn for the better, and, when that happens, retirement will once again become an option for many Boomer librarians" (p. 652).

There are those who suggest that ongoing fiscal restraint may lead to the loss of many positions as librarians retire. As Steams (2009) has suggested, it is not clear that "large numbers of upcoming retirements are bound to create multiple job opportunities." Positions could be eliminated as individuals retire (p. 44). However, it is likely that with retirements, remaining and redefined positions, and "a shortage of younger, mid-career librarians and a shortage of new recruits into the profession" (Nixon 2008, p. 249), the profession is likely to experience libraries "with more open positions . . . than we can fill" (p. 249). While this overall shortage is a concern for the profession, there is likely to be "a shortage of librarians who are willing and able to take on leadership positions" (Martin 2009, p. 652). This loss of experienced librarians, including experienced managers, and the aversion of many to leadership positions, highlight the increased need to focus on succession planning and the expansion of leadership development. Blakesley (2011) pointed out that "The concept of succession planning emerged in the business literature in the late 1960s" (p. 1); however, the discussion of succession planning in libraries is a relatively recent phenomenon and is largely tied to the anticipated retirements.

Recent library and information science publications on the topic of succession planning have included a 2009 theme issue of the *Journal of Library Administration* that focused on leadership development programs in the profession, such as the Association of Research Libraries' (ARL's) Research Libraries Leadership Fellows Program, and *Succession Planning in the Library: Developing Leaders, Managing Change* (2010) by Paula Singer and Gail Griffith, which focuses mostly on the public library context. In relation to published research, Blakesley (2011) has indicated that "Most studies of succession planning in the U.S. have focused on public libraries" (p. 2).

Conceptually, succession planning might be considered to be central to or a major component of the strategic planning in organizations. In this regard, it is necessary for the organization to define its context, goals, needs—including its leadership needs—and the potential staffing changes, such as retirements, that are anticipated. Succession planning helps to define the leadership needs of the organization and to explore, with some specificity, how to develop current staff, recruitment needs, and factors to consider in the recruitment of new staff, in order to prepare for anticipated leadership gaps. The well-defined succession plan, as a part of overall organizational planning, should provide the opportunity to focus resources and organizational efforts on ensuring that organizations are conscious about anticipating and preparing to meet leadership needs.

Leadership Needs in Specific Realms

Placing the discussion of leadership within more specific professional contexts helps to narrow the vast breadth and complexity of leadership as a topic. The following sections highlight particular leadership needs within library organizations, across the profession, and within library associations, as examples of more specific library-related contexts.

Within Organizations

This section considers leadership needs within individual organizations, focusing to a large extent on common elements across types of library organizations. Conceptually, many broad principles of leadership apply across types of library organizations. While the organizational missions will vary, as will the user populations—from children to graduate students to adults, for example—the overall goals of supporting fulfillment of the larger parent organization (for example, the university, school, or local government) and the goals of libraries in fostering access to information are similar. In addition, the principles associated with organizational behavior and leadership, while developed and defined in the context of corporate entities to a large extent (as much of the empirical research has involved private sector organizations), the general principles are applicable more broadly; the common elements of human resources, financial resources (and limitations), products and services, and the client base (and potential client base) exist among all types of organizations.

In the organizational context, one key issue, as noted, is that of fostering leadership, including the shared building of and appreciation for the organizational vision by those at all levels in the organizational hierarchy. As leadership has often been equated to management, the need for organizational vision has often been seen as the exclusive work of managers and administrators. This limited view ignores the fact that much of organizational decision making is done by those who are not in clearly defined managerial roles. Similarly, those in non-managerial roles have much of the responsibility for interaction with library users. In the case of both decision making and user interaction, an understanding of organizational mission and goals as well as input into direction and vision is critical to organizational success. In addition, the expertise, experience, and guidance of those who are closer to the "front lines" can provide a much more informed perspective in evaluating organizational circumstances than would be the case with managers, who are often removed from users and who could not (and should not) make all of the organizational decisions themselves. To encourage not only consistency in decisions made throughout the organization but also high-quality decisions, encouraging a sense that all of those employed have the opportunity for input and influence is likely to foster greater buy-in and a realization that the parts of the organization are interconnected, with individuals having a shared stake in organizational success. Thus, fostering leadership at all levels requires the commitment of those in management to provide necessary information throughout the organization that fosters shared vision; to provide all staff with opportunities for professional development; and to provide support for others in their decision making and interactions with users.

The needs of organizations will vary by type and even among organizations of the same type. Public libraries, for example, will define their user populations based on the local community, with such issues as "local standards" providing some framework or limitations for defining how success is measured. Among academic libraries, the research university mission will vary somewhat from that of the community college library. However the organizational mission is defined, the role of leadership is one of exerting influence to fulfill that mission.

Leadership in the Library Profession

Beyond leading specific libraries into a preferred future, the library profession as a whole is in need of leaders and leadership awareness in order to guide the profession into the future. Profession-based leadership is concerned with both the overarching mega-issues that face the profession and with the micro-issues that cut across all types of information settings and have societal impacts. This necessarily includes advocacy leadership, collaboration with other related professions and entities, working with publishers, and making the case to the general public, government, and other stakeholders that libraries are an essential part of a free society.

Providing leadership for the profession includes defining the national library agenda by providing guidance about profession-wide topics such as diversity, and advocating for federal, state, municipal, and campus funding support for all types of libraries. It also includes participating in efforts to influence aspects of public policy, such as those relating to scholarly communication; copyright; issues of access to information, such as making digital collections publicly available (open access); fighting against censorship; and adopting technologies to provide more-effective and more-efficient provision of information.

Examples of these types of profession-wide leaders can be found in *Library Journal*'s annual "Movers and Shakers" issue, which recognizes leadership within the profession at every level of professional career. Leaders can range from front-line librarians to senior administrators—the title of the celebrated individuals does not matter; their leadership contribution to the profession is what qualifies them to be included. The profession needs more champions willing to take on important societal issues that are larger than any one library organization—which leads to the next section, on library association responses to leadership needs.

Library Associations

Library associations, like libraries and the profession, have originated programs that address the need for leadership within their member volunteers. Several are laudable efforts that have arisen from concern about the lack of leaders in the pipeline, and the acknowledgement that it is not always easy for those who aspire to leadership to navigate large, complex associations. Leadership development programs share the basic premise that leaders are not born, but are developed, mentored, and encouraged. This narrative, as well as Table 1, builds on and updates the work originated by Mason and Wetherbee (2004), characterizing the different types of leadership development programs currently available. All of the major efforts have a selective admissions process, and all—with the exception of ALA's Emerging Leaders Program—have residential leadership institutes that vary in length.

Current major efforts include those of ARL and the International Federation of Library Associations and Institutions (IFLA). ALA has a series of five programs, including the Emerging Leaders Program, Committee Internships, Legislative Day, the Spectrum Scholarship Program, and the ACRL/Harvard Leadership Institute.

ALA Programs

Emerging Leaders

ALA's Emerging Leaders Program develops a yearly cohort of approximately 100 leaders from across the nation for the profession as well as for the association. The program emphasizes the development of problem-solving skills through group work and peer networking. First offered in 1997, it now holds one-day events at both its Midwinter Meeting and Annual Conference. The program emphasizes the practice of leadership within ALA at an early point in a career, in the hope of creating association leadership succession planning. It provides mentors and coaches, and recognizes that leadership needs to occur at all levels throughout the association as well as throughout libraries.

Committee Internships

ALA Committee Internships are another association leadership pathway. Interns learn about roles and issues of concern to ALA-wide or division committees with the intent of interns going on to become active committee and association leaders.

Library Legislative Day

National Library Legislative Day is sponsored by ALA's Washington Office in collaboration with state library association chapters. This day, along with the planning activities leading up to it, provides librarians at all levels the opportunity to advocate for libraries in the halls of Congress. ALA provides training and tips for speaking with Congress members and their staff about specific issues impacting all libraries.

Spectrum Scholarship Program

Developed in 1996 and first offered in 1997, the Spectrum Scholarship Program has, as part of its design, a three-day leadership institute during the association's Annual Conference. Each year, Spectrum Scholars are recruited through a competitive selection process. The scholars each receive $5,000 for tuition or other education expenses plus $1,500 for the institute. The program is intended to increase the diversity of the profession and provide training for future leadership in libraries, the profession, and its associations. The program also includes mentors and coaching. More than 750 scholarships have been awarded from the program's inception through 2012.

ACRL/Harvard Leadership Institute

The Association of College and Research Libraries (ACRL)/Harvard Leadership Institute, begun in 1997, is directed to academic library directors and associate directors. The emphasis of the five-day program is on planning and strategizing to prepare transformational leaders. It is the only ALA-affiliated program that does not provide mentoring and coaching.

ARL Programs

The Association of Research Libraries (ARL) offers a series of four programs, the first three of which promote and develop leaders from under-represented populations. All provide mentors and coaches for participants while introducing major issues in library leadership. Included in these efforts are the Career Enhancement Program (CEP), the Initiative to Recruit a Diverse Workforce (IRDW), the Leadership and Career Development Program (LCDP), and the Research Library Leadership Fellows Program (RLLF).

Career Enhancement Program

CEP, begun in 2009, prepares its fellows for careers as leaders of research libraries. Emphasis is placed on developing global perspectives for higher education and the skills to meet the challenges of changing demographics. Once every two years, participants receive a 6- to 12-week paid for-credit internship at an ARL institution and a two-day leadership institute. A total of 53 individuals have been chosen for this fellowship program to date.

Initiative to Recruit a Diverse Workforce

IRDW has an emphasis on research library leadership. Those accepted into the program receive a $10,000 stipend over two years and $2,500 for professional development, a paid membership in ARL, and a two-day leadership institute. There have been 108 ARL Diversity Fellows so far.

Leadership and Career Development Program

LCDP, begun in 1997, targets mid-career librarians with more than five years of service in academic libraries to foster diversity in upper administrative positions for academic libraries. It is an 18-month program with two four-day leadership institutes, a research project, and a poster session where the research is presented. The program also offers opportunities to create networks and advanced leadership skills. To date 111 librarians have completed.

Research Library Leadership Fellows

RLLF, which began in 2004, is open to all library staff who have the desire and the potential to become senior-level leaders in large research libraries. The program lasts 18 months, with three strategic issues institutes, multiple site visit opportunities of which one is required, and attendance at ARL membership meetings. RLLF has had 64 participating fellows.

IFLA New Professionals

IFLA's New Professionals Special Interest Group began from a grassroots movement started by new professionals interested in association leadership. Its purview is to develop opportunities for aspiring leaders and succession planning within IFLA.

Table 1 presents a composite of other leadership development programs. The table illustrates the larger national leadership programs sponsored by professional associations and particular institutions. All of these programs have a selective admissions process and all have residential leadership institutes that vary in length.

Leadership Development for the Profession

The ability to learn is important in leadership training. At the most basic level, the ability to learn leadership skills is a complex mix of motivation, personal orientation, and skills (Mason and Wetherbee 2004, p. 195).

Leadership competencies are acquired in many different ways—on the job, through life experience, through mentoring, and through training programs designed to develop leadership skills. Leadership development programs are based on the premise that certain leadership competencies can be developed rather than inherently residing in a select few. Such programs are critically needed to prepare library leaders in response to a rapidly changing environment.

Table 1 / Current Library Leadership Development Programs

Program	First Offered	Target Audience	Primary Emphasis	Length
EDUCAUSE Institute Leadership Program	1998	A new CIO or an experienced senior-level leader aspiring to CIO/executive-level leadership	Critical success skills for executive leaders and keys to understanding institution-wide IT strategy	Week-long program
Frye Leadership Institute (cosponsored by EDUCAUSE and CLIR)	1999	A CIO, librarian, information technology professional, or administrator with at least seven years' experience	To learn how to create a collaborative community that takes leadership on critical issues to develop a platform for collective action	Intensive, week-long residential seminar, coupled with online project meetings
National Library of Medicine/AAHSL Leadership Fellows Program	2002	Minimum of five years experience as department head or higher in an academic health sciences library and interested in a directorship	Preparing emerging leaders for the position of library director in academic health sciences libraries	One year with multiple elements including three leadership institutes and a two-week site visit
University of California Senior Fellows Program	1982	Senior-level library administrators	Multi-modal learning opportunities in strategic thinking, management models, and the development of practical and theoretical solutions to issues in higher education and libraries	Three-week program with an advance assignment and follow-up project
University of Minnesota Leadership Training Institute for Librarians of Color	1999	Early-career minority librarians with one to three years' experience	Leadership, management, and decision making as well as self-knowledge and complex organizational behavior	Eight days with advance reading assignment
University of Wisconsin Archives Leadership Institute	2008	Mid-level archives professionals or senior staff who aspire to leadership roles	Prepares participants to influence policy and affect change on behalf of the profession and the public served now and in the future	Seven days
Institute for Academic Library Leadership, Peabody College, Vanderbilt University	2006	College and university library deans and heads and those who aspire to library leadership roles	Prepares participants to consider the library in context of the university mission and to serve as campus leaders, central to decision making	Four days
Snowbird Leadership Institute (no longer in existence)	1990	Early-career librarians	Training to utilize creativity, encourage risk-taking, develop self-knowledge, and development and use of change strategies as a path to leadership	Five days

The 1990s and 2000s saw the introduction and growth of a number of leadership development programs in the profession, as well as changes in the types of programs being offered and the ultimate demise of some programs. The programs came into being in response to perceived needs in the profession and the opportunity to address those needs through means other than LIS or other degree programs.

As leadership theories have evolved, so too have the programs designed to develop leadership skills. Formerly targeted at administrators and managers and to prepare individuals to take on such positions, today's leadership development programs are more inclusive in the populations they serve: non-librarian professionals; new librarians; librarians of color; and early, mid-career, and senior librarians. The article "Learning to Lead: An Analysis of Current Training Programs for Library Leadership" (Mason and Wetherbee 2004) identified and analyzed more than 30 leadership development programs.

The longest-standing leadership development program is the Senior Fellows Program offered by the University of California, Los Angeles. Developed in 1982, this program is for senior-level academic librarians and "offers a unique combination of management perspectives, strategic thinking, and practical and theoretical approaches to the issues confronting academic institutions and their libraries" (UCLA Senior Fellows Program 2011). It was one of a handful of leadership development programs offered before the mid-1990s, after which time there was a sudden and large increase in such programs. Many of the programs identified in "Learning to Lead" (Mason and Wetherbee 2004) still exist, some have been suspended, and many more have since been added. These programs, almost without exception, are in the United States. They each have a niche, serving different populations, including those at different stages in their career or in different types of libraries. The programs are delivered via different modes, though most of them are residential, with participants spending multiple days, often a week or longer, in a shared environment. Some programs serve a national audience, and there are more than a dozen that have a statewide or regional focus. Some shared elements that have been noted as beneficial by the participants include mentoring/coaching components and sharing a cohort experience (Neely and Winston 1999; Neely 2009).

A common thread found throughout the curricula and assessment of all of these leadership development programs is that leadership development is not a one-time activity. Rather, leadership development is a negotiated process that utilizes learned and inherent competencies that are practiced in all activities in which a "leader" is engaged (McCall, Lombardo, and Morrison 1988; Kouzes and Posner 2011). Libraries and library-related organizations should explicitly and continually develop leadership skills through staff development efforts and provide leadership opportunities to all of their library workers. One unique leadership development program is being piloted by the Library of Congress Center for Learning and Development. It is offered solely to "high potential employees from diverse backgrounds who are interested in broadening their knowledge and developing the skills that are the foundation of effective leadership" (Library of Congress 2011). This 15-month competency-based training program is designed to meet the succession planning goals outlined in the library's fiscal years 2011–2016 strategic plan. It serves as a model for individual organizations that should be concerned with leadership development—not just for succession planning, but for fostering excellence throughout their work force. Workplace experience has been cited as one of the most valuable means of developing leadership expertise (McCall, Lombardo, and Morrison 1988). However, an executive study found that:

> No amount of experience could possibly prepare an executive for all the expected requirements much less the unexpected challenges of these jobs . . . as a group they seemed ready to grab or create opportunities for growth, wise enough not to believe that there's nothing more to learn, and courageous enough to look inside themselves and grapple with their frailties. (McCall, Lombardo, and Morrison 1988, p. 122).

Individuals should take responsibility for acquiring and practicing leadership skills in all aspects of their lives, and current leaders should recognize and make opportunities for new leaders to develop their budding skills.

Likewise, Kouzes and Posner (2011), who have been conducting research and writing about leadership development for several decades, write that "leadership begins with an inner journey . . . the quest for leadership, therefore, is first an inner quest to discover who you are and what you care about, and it's through this process of self-examination that you find the awareness needed to lead" (p. 22).

Assessing Leadership Development Programs

Measures exist that indicate the success of library leadership development programs, including the extent to which those who have completed the programs have taken on senior leadership roles in libraries (Lynch 1994; Neely and Winston 1999). However, there are some limitations associated with the leadership development program model, whether the program content focuses on skills development, self-awareness, or discussions of leadership as a concept, or if the program is structured around the use of experiential learning, or some combination of these elements and others.

Even with the increasing number of programs over time and the expansion and broadening of existing programs, it is typically the case that a small percentage of librarians have the opportunity to participate. In addition, while the level of awareness of leadership development opportunities may be limited, the potential for exclusivity is increased because of the expense of participating in such programs and the fact that not all library organizations provide for release time, travel expenses, and stipends for this type of professional development (this is particularly so because program participants may be seen as preparing for future roles at other institutions). Generally speaking, few school librarians or those in small academic or public libraries may be able to participate in such programs. It is likely the case that the limited participation possible in the national programs was part of the basis for the establishment of state and regional programs. While there have been changes in the demographic composition of the senior management of libraries over time, the research suggests that far fewer minorities and women participate in such programs than might be suggested by their representation in the profession overall (Winston and Neely 2001).

Another design limitation relates to the identification of program content and delivery methods, which will be of relevance and usefulness for program participants and their current and future employing organizations. Some programs have supplemented classroom time with ongoing mentoring activities in order to expand learning beyond the formal curriculum. In addition, some leadership development programs have been criticized for providing more in terms of management training than leadership development.

Finally, it is often difficult to measure the success of leadership development programs. Progression to more senior leadership roles is a measure of success, but this one yardstick may be contrary to the premise of a broad definition of leadership, which involves leadership opportunities at all levels of an organization. Similarly, the research suggests that individuals have identified other ways in which they have expanded their leadership participation beyond movement into senior management after participation in leadership development programs. In addition, it is certainly difficult to state definitively that individuals who progress to senior management have done so as a direct or indirect consequence of participation in leadership development (Winston and Neely 2001). Much more research is needed, both qualitative and quantitative explorations into the outcomes of these important programs, as our profession relies on them for our next generation of leaders.

Conclusion

The intersection of rapid changes in society (demographics, adaptation of technology, economic strains, and increased calls for accountability, among others) all conspire to make leadership a pressing topic for discussion. While leadership is a broad, complex, and evolving topic, understanding the importance of leadership in the library profession and throughout our library organizations is essential to the continued health of the profession.

As Ford (2005) writes, "Understanding leadership calls not only for the consideration of social processes and cultural context" (p. 247), but also calls for rejection of models of leadership that concentrate power and influence in one or a few people within an organization (patriarchal/charismatic leadership), a practice that "perpetuates a model that is exclusionary" (p. 247), and robs the profession of powerful voices of potential leaders found throughout our libraries and at all points of their career ladders.

This broad overview of leadership in libraries and the library profession points to the need for more deliberate and concerted efforts to develop and encourage stronger leadership participation at all levels of an organization. This would include continuing education, professional development, job mentoring, opportunities for those at all levels who show interest in taking the lead on projects, programs, committees, and so forth, and being deliberate about feedback and coaching new leaders. This means nothing short of empowering library workers at all levels of library organizations to develop leadership competencies.

While LIS programs have changed dramatically over time, the lack of curricular emphasis on professional and societal leadership has remained constant. In 2001, Riggs challenged LIS degree programs to move beyond teaching administration and management to teaching emerging librarians about leadership. LIS programs often rightly bristle when library practitioners chide them for not teaching specific job skills. However, leadership preparation goes far beyond skills training—it is a professional value and philosophy with a body of theory and published research (mostly from other professions and contexts, unfortunately) to support its inclusion in the curriculum.

Many scholars and researchers have called for librarians to advance and update their own leadership skills, and for advanced library leaders to actively influence the development of leadership throughout the profession (al Ansari and al Khadher 2011; Carpenter 2012; Riggs 2001; Winston 2006; Winston 2008).

There is a great and pressing need to study leaders at all levels of library organizations and at all points along the career ladder. Too much of the library leadership literature concentrates on deans and directors, and, as newer leadership models stress, the rapid pace of change dictates the need for leadership throughout the organization and the profession.

Bibliography

Adkins, Denice, and Isabel Espinal. 2004. "The Diversity Mandate." *Library Journal* 129: 52–54.

Adkins, Denice, and Lisa K. Hussey. 2005. "Unintentional Recruiting for Diversity." *Public Libraries* 44: 229–233.

Agada, John. 1998. "Profiling Librarians with the Myers-Briggs Type Indicator: Studies in Self Selection and Type Stability." *Education for Information* 16: 57–68.

al Ansari, Hussain, and Othman al Khadher. 2011. "Developing a Leadership Competency Model for Library Information Professionals in Kuwait." *Libri* 61: 239–246.

Alire, Camila. 2001. "Diversity and Leadership: The Color of Leadership." *Journal of Library Administration* 32: 95–109.

Alvesson, Mats. 2002. *Understanding Organizational Culture.* Sage.

American Library Association. 2011. "Library Leadership Training Resources." Accessed December 23, 2011. http://www.ala.org.proxy.lib.umich.edu/offices/ hrdr/abouthrdr/hrdrliaisoncomm/otld/leadershiptraining.

Armstrong, Ann, and Ashraf S. Nouman. 2010. "Leadership Competencies in a Diverse Culture." In *Leadership in Nonprofit Organizations: A Reference Handbook,* ed. by Kathryn A. Agard. 267–274. Sage.

Association of Academic Health Sciences Libraries. 2009. "NLM/AAHSL Leadership Fellows Program." Accessed December 23, 2011. http://www.aahsl. org/mc/page/leadershipfellows.

Association of Research Libraries. 2011. "Research Library Leadership Fellows." Accessed December 23, 2011. http://www.arl.org.proxy.lib.umich.edu/ leadership/rllf.

Association of Research Libraries. 2011. "Career Enhancement Program." Accessed December 23, 2011. http://www.arl.org.proxy.lib.umich.edu/diversity/ cep/index.shtml.

Association of Research Libraries. 2011. "Initiative to Recruit a Diverse Workforce." Accessed December 23, 2011. http://www.arl.org/diversity/init/index. shtml.

Association of Research Libraries. 2011. "Leadership and Career Development Fellows." Accessed December 25, 2001. http://www.arl.org.proxy.lib.umich.edu/diversity/lcdp.

Bedard, Martha. 2009. "Introduction to Our Commitment to Building Leaders: Programs for Leadership in Academic and Special Libraries." *Journal of Library Administration* 49: 777.

Bennis, Warren G. 1959. "Leadership Theory and Administrative Behavior: The Problem of Authority." *Administrative Science Quarterly* 4: 259–301.

Bennis, Warren G., and Burt Nanus. 1985. *Leaders: The Strategies for Taking Charge*. Harper & Row.

Blakesley, Elizabeth. 2011. "Planning for the Future: Sources to Explore about Succession Planning." *Library Leadership & Management* 25 (2): 1–4.

Block, Peter. 1993. *Stewardship*. Berrett-Koehler.

Bolman, Lee G., and Joan V. Gallos. 2011. *Reframing Academic Leadership*. Jossey Bass.

Brown, Michael E., and Linda K. Trevino. 2006. "Ethical leadership: A Review and Future Directions." *Leadership Quarterly* 17: 595–616.

Carpenter, Maria Taesil Hudson. 2012. "Cheerleader, Opportunity Seeker, and Master Strategist: ARL Directors as Entrepreneurial Leaders." *College & Research Libraries* 73: 11–32.

Chemers, Martin M. 1997. *An Integrative Theory of Leadership*. Lawrence Erlbaum Associates.

Chu, Melanie. 2009. "Ageism in Academic Librarianship." *E-JASL: The Electronic Journal of Academic and Special Librarianship.* 10: n.p.

Davis, Denise M., and Tracie D. Hall. 2007. *Diversity Counts*. American Library Association.

Denning, Stephen. 2005. *The Leader's Guide to Storytelling*. Jossey Bass.

Denning, Stephen. 2007. *The Secret Language of Leadership: How Leaders Inspire Action Through Narrative*. John Wiley.

de la Peña McCook, Kathleen. 2000. "Ethnic Diversity in Information and Library Science." *Library Trends* 49: 1–214.

Downing, Karen. 2009. "The Relationship Between Social Identity and Role Performance. Dissertation." University of Michigan. Accessed December 23, 2011. http://deepblue.lib.umich.edu/handle/2027.42/62396.

EDUCAUSE. 2012. "EDUCAUSE Institute Management and Leadership Programs." Accessed February 13, 2012. http://www.educause.edu/institute.

Evangeliste, Mary, and Katherine Furlong. 2011. "When Interdependence Becomes Codependence: Knowing When and How to Let Go of Legacy Services." Paper presented at the conference of the Association of College and Research Libraries, Philadelphia, March 30–April 2. Accessed January 17, 2012. http://66.158.92.95/ala/mgrps/divs/acrl/events/national/2011/papers/when_interdependence.pdf.

Ford, Jackie. 2005. "Examining Leadership Through Critical Feminist Readings." *Journal of Health Organization and Management* 19: 236–251.

Frye Institute. 2011. "The Frye Leadership Institute—What Is the Program?" Accessed December 23, 2011. http://www.fryeinstitute.org/program.asp.

Gardner, Howard. Feb. 2006. "The Synthesizing Leader." *Harvard Business Review* 84: 36–37.

Gardner, William L., Kevin B. Lowe, Todd W. Moss, Kevin T. Mahoney, and Claudia C. Cogliser. 2010. "Scholarly Leadership of the Study of Leadership: A Review of the *Leadership Quarterly*'s Second Decade, 2000–2009." *Leadership Quarterly* 21: 922–958.

Garman, Andrew N., and, Matthew P. Johnson. 2006. "Leadership Competencies: An Introduction." *Journal of Healthcare Management* 51: 13–17.

Graen, George B. 2006. "In the Eye of the Beholder: Cross-Cultural Lesson in Leadership from Project GLOBE: A Response Viewed from the Third Culture Bonding (TCB) Model of Cross-Cultural Leadership." *Academy of Management Perspectives* 45: 95–101.

Greenleaf, Robert K., and Larry C. Spears. 1998. *The Power of Servant-Leadership: Essays.* Berrett-Koehler.

Hall, Lee. 2004. "A Palette of Desired Leadership Competencies: Painting the Picture for Successful Regionalization." *Healthcare Management Forum* 17: 18–22.

Harvard Graduate School of Education. 2011. "Leadership Institute for Academic Librarians." Accessed December 23, 2011. http://www.gse.harvard.edu.proxy.lib.umich.edu/ppe/programs/higher-education/portfolio/leadership-academic-librarians.html.

Hendrickson, Kent, and Joan Giesecke. 1994. "Myers-Briggs Type Indicator Profile and the Organization." *Faculty Publications, UNL Libraries.* Paper 89. 8: 218–222. http://digitalcommons.unl.edu/libraryscience/89.

Hernon, Peter, ed. 2010. *Shaping the Future: Advancing the Understanding of Leadership.* Libraries Unlimited.

Hersey, Paul, and Ken. H. Blanchard. 1992. *Management of Organizational Behavior: Utilizing Human Resources.* 2nd ed. Prentice Hall.

Hsieh, Su-Chin. 2010. "Literature Review on Global Leadership Competency." *Journal of Human Resources and Adult Learning* 6: 99–109.

International Federation of Library Associations and Institutions. 2010. "About New Professionals Special Interest Group." Accessed December 23, 2011. http://www.ifla.org/en/about-new-professionals.

Joyce, Mary Ellen, and William C. Adams. 2010. "Leadership Competencies." In *Political and Civic Leadership,* ed. by Richard A. Couto, 874–886. Sage. http://www.sage-ereference.com.proxy.lib.umich.edu/view/civicleadership/n98.xml.

Kanter, Rosabeth Moss. 1981. "Power, Leadership, and Participatory Management." *Theory into Practice* 20: 219–224.

Klein, Robert R. 2009. "A Review of Becoming a Resonant Leader (McKee, Boyatzis, and Johnston): Contextualizing the Place of Emotional Intelligence Skills with Respect to Team Leadership and Group Dynamics." *Organization Management Journal* 6: 58–63.

Kouzes, James, M., and Barry Z. Posner. 2011. "Leadership Begins with an Inner Journey." *Leader to Leader* 60: 22–27.

———. 1990. *The Leadership Challenge.* Jossey-Bass.

———. 2007. *The Leadership Challenge.* 4th ed. Jossey-Bass.

———. 1997. *The Leadership Practices Inventory.* Jossey-Bass.

Kreitz, P. A. 2009. "Leadership and Emotional Intelligence: A Study of University Library Directors and Their Senior Management Teams." *College & Research Libraries* 70: 531–554.

Kyrillidou, Martha, and Mark Young. 2008. *2006–2007 ARL Statistics.* Accessed December 3, 2011. http://www.arl.org/bm~doc/arlstat08.pdf.

Lambert, Steven. 2011. "Sustainable Leadership and the Implication for the General Further Education College Sector." *Journal of Further and Higher Education* 35: 131–148.

Library of Congress. 2011. "Center for Learning and Development: Leadership Development Program." Accessed December 23, 2011. http://www.loc.gov/extranet/cld/ldp/index.html.

Lubans, John. 2010. *Leading from the Middle, and Other Contrarian Essays on Library Leadership.* Libraries Unlimited.

Lynch, Beverly P. 1994. "Taking on the Issues in a Changing Environment: The Senior Fellows Program" [at the UCLA Graduate School of Library and Information Science]. *Journal of Library Administration* 20 (2): 5–15.

McCall, Morgan W., Michael M. Lombardo, and Ann M. Morrison. 1988. *The Lessons of Experience: How Successful Executives Develop on the Job.* Lexington.

McWilliams, Margaret A. 2007. "A Leadership Competency Model: Guiding NAON Processes." *Orthopaedic Nursing* 26: 211–213.

Marable, Manning. 1996. *Speaking Truth to Power: Essays on Race, Resistance and Radicalism.* West View.

Marek, Kate. 2011. *Organizational Storytelling for Librarians: Using Stories for Effective Leadership.* American Library Association.

Martin, Jason. 2009. "The Art of Librarianship: Thoughts on Leadership Skills for the Next Generation of Academic Library Leaders." *College & Research Libraries News* 70: 652–654.

Mason, Florence M., and Louella V. Wetherbee. 2004. "Learning to Lead: An Analysis of Current Training Programs for Library Leadership." *Library Trends* 53: 187–217.

Merrill, Alex N., and Elizabeth Blakesley Lindsay. 2009. "Growing Your Own: Building an Internal Leadership Training Program." *Library Leadership and Management* 23: 85-87.

Neely, Theresa. 2009. "Assessing Diversity Initiatives: The ARL Leadership and Career Development Program." *Journal of Library Administration* 49: 811–835.

Neely, Theresa, and Mark Winston. 1999. "Snowbird Leadership Institute: Leadership Development in the Profession." *College & Research Libraries* 60: 412–425.

Nixon, Judith M. 2008. "Growing Your Own Leaders: Succession Planning in Libraries." *Journal of Business & Finance Librarianship* 13: 249–260.

Olson, Christi A., and Paula M. Singer. 2004. *Winning with Library Leadership: Enhancing Services through Connection, Contribution, and Collaboration.* American Library Association.

Ospina, Sonia, and Erica Foldy. 2009. "A Critical Review of Race and Ethnicity in the Leadership Literature: Surfacing Context, Power and the Collective Dimensions of Leadership." *Leadership Quarterly* 20: 876–896.

Parolini, Jeanine, Kathleen Patterson, and Bruce Winston. 2008. "Distinguishing Between Transformational and Servant Leadership." *Leadership & Organization Development Journal* 30: 274–291.

Pellegrini, Ekin K., and Terri A. Scandura. 2008. "Paternalistic Leadership: A Review and Agenda for Future Research." *Journal of Management* 34: 566–593.

Popper, Micha, Ofra Mayseless, and Omri Castelnovo. 2000. "Transformational Leadership and Attachment." *Leadership Quarterly* 11(2): 267–289.

Riggs, Donald E. 2001. "The Crisis and Opportunities in Library Leadership." *Journal of Library Administration* 32: 5–17.

Roberts, Sue, and Jennifer Rowley. 2008. *Leadership: The Challenge for the Information Profession.* Facet.

Scherdin, Mary Jane, ed. 1994. *Discovering Librarians: Profiles of a Profession.* Association of College and Research Libraries, American Library Association.

Scherdin, Mary Jane, and Anne Beaubien. 1995. "Shattering Our Stereotype: Librarians' New Image." *Library Journal* 120: 35–38.

Sheardown, Jana, and Monique Woroniak. 2007. " 'Mind the Gap': Future Librarians Preparing to Take on Leadership Roles." *Feliciter* 53: 64–65.

Singer, Paula, and Gail Griffith. 2010. *Succession Planning in the Library: Developing Leaders, Managing Change.* ALA Editions.

Steams, Robert. 2009. "Back to the Future." *American Libraries* 40: 44.

Stewart, Greg L., Stephen H. Courtright, and Charles C. Manz. 2011. "Self-Leadership: A Multilevel Review." *Journal of Management* 37: 185–222.

Turock, Betty. 2001. "Women and Leadership." *Journal of Library Administration* 32: 115–137.

UCLA Senior Fellows Program. 2011. Accessed January 17, 2012. http://is.gseis.ucla.edu/events/seniorfellows/index.htm.

Vanderbilt Peabody College. 2010. Academic Library Leadership. Accessed December 23, 2011. http://www.peabody.vanderbilt.edu/peabody_professional_institutes/upcoming_institutes/academic_library_leadership.xml.

Walter, Frank, and Heike Bruch. 2009. "An Affective Events Model of Charismatic Leadership Behavior: A Review, Theoretical Integration, and Research Agenda." *Journal of Management* 35: 1428–1452.

Webster, Duane E., and DeEtta Jones Young. 2009. "Our Collective Wisdom: Succession Planning and the ARL Research Library Leadership Fellows Program." *Journal of Library Administration* 49: 781.

Weiner, Sharon Gray. 2003. "Leadership of Academic Libraries: A Literature Review." *Education Libraries* 26: 5–18.

Wikipedia. 2012. "Leadership." Accessed January 5, 2012. http://en.wikipedia. org/wiki/Leadership#cite_note-0.

Winston, M. D. 2001. "The Importance of Leadership Diversity: The Relationship Between Diversity and Organizational Success in the Academic Environment." *College & Research Libraries* 62: 517–526.

——— (2001a). Introduction (Theme issue on Leadership). *Journal of Library Administration* 32: 1–3.

——— (2001b). "Recruitment Theory: Identification of Those Who are Likely to be Successful as Leaders." *Journal of Library Administration* 32: 19–35.

———. 2005. "Library Leadership in Times of Crisis and Change." *New Library World* 106: 395–415.

———. 2006. "Ethical Leadership: Professional Challenges and the Role of LIS Education." *New Library World* 106: 234–243.

———. 2008. *Opportunity for Leadership: Full and Informed Participation*. Libraries Unlimited.

———, and Lisa Dunkley. 2002. "Leadership Competencies for Academic Librarians: The Importance of Development and Fund-Raising." *College & Research Libraries* 63: 171–182.

———, and Teresa Y. Neely. 2001. "Leadership Development and Public Libraries" [survey of participants in the Snowbird Leadership Institute]. *Public Library Quarterly* 19: 15–32.

———, and Susan Quinn. 2005. "Library Leadership in Times of Crisis and Change." *New Library World* 106: 395–415.

Yun, Seokhwa, Jonathan Cox, and Henry P. Sims, Jr. 2006. "The Forgotten Follower: A Contingency Model of Leadership and Follower Self-Leadership." *Journal of Managerial Psychology* 21: 374–388.

Libraries and Civic Engagement

Nancy Kranich

For the first two-thirds of the 20th century a powerful tide bore Americans into ever deeper engagement in the life of their communities, but a few decades ago—silently, without warning—that tide reversed and we were overtaken by a treacherous rip current. Without at first noticing, we have been pulled apart from one another and from our communities over the last third of the century. (Putnam 2000, p. 27)

Americans are more disconnected from each other and from the institutions of civic life than ever before. Over the last 40 years, many citizens stopped voting, curtailed their work with political parties and service organizations, and attended fewer community meetings and political events. They have even diminished their pleasurable get-togethers, with fewer people entertaining friends at home. Americans are also less public spirited, giving fewer dollars to charities. Without a sustained, broad-based social movement to restore civic life and participation in our democracy, we will not reclaim our nation's civic culture.

Librarians share concerns about the erosion of civic engagement[1] and participation in our communities. With a burgeoning movement to engage citizens, libraries—school, public, and academic—are taking advantage of new opportunities to extend their reach further into the realm of civic activities. Libraries have long recognized their role in promoting access to a diversity of ideas, serving as depositories for government, community, and other useful information. But many are also expanding that civic role by facilitating the exchange and sharing of those ideas. Why? Because libraries uphold and strengthen some of the most fundamental democratic ideals of our society; they not only make information freely available to all, but also foster the development of a civil society. They also provide comfortable, inviting, neutral, safe civic spaces conducive to democratic discourse—spaces where citizens can work together to solve public problems. As Ray Oldenburg (1989) describes in *The Great Good Place,* libraries are places essential to the political processes of democracy; places that reinforce the notion of association. Many use their public spaces to host programs that offer people a chance to learn together, frame issues of common concern, deliberate about choices for solving problems, deepen understanding about others' opinions, and connect citizens across the spectrum of thought.

Nationwide, libraries are undertaking new approaches to engage communities and assist them in meeting today's most pressing civic challenges. Their efforts are rekindling civic engagement, connecting citizens, boosting citizen participation, and encouraging increased involvement in community problem solving and decision making. These new services increase social capital—the glue that holds people together and enables them to build bridges to others (Putnam 2000, pp.

Nancy Kranich lectures at the Rutgers University School of Communication and Information and works on special projects at Rutgers University Libraries. Her theme as president of the American Library Association in 2000–2001 was Libraries and Democracy. She founded and chairs both the ALA Libraries Foster Civic Engagement Membership Initiative Group and the ALA Center for Civic Life. She is a former member of the National Issues Forum Institute Board.

22–24). They also help libraries garner greater community support and position libraries as even more essential community-based institutions.

The State of Civic Engagement

In the words of Robert Putnam (2000), Americans are "bowling alone." They simply have too few opportunities that expose them to people with different views and engage them in authentic dialogue about pressing problems, as documented by Diana Mutz (2006). And dialogue about possibilities declines as people flee the public square. At forums in 2006 titled "Democracy's Challenge: Reclaiming the Public's Role," participants reflected on Putnam's and Mutz's findings, lamenting that there was something dreadfully off track in the nation. They expressed feelings of alienation from politics and community affairs and powerlessness to do much about them. They also said they had become consumers in democracy, rather than citizen proprietors—bystanders rather than active members with a sense of ownership in their democracy. Others saw themselves as local but not national participants, like citizens of city-states rather than of a national democracy. Forum participants expressed concern about the loss of public space where citizens meet informally to discuss community problems and political issues. In short, they saw the average citizen as unrepresented and voiceless.

At the same time, forum participants recognized that the nation faces a variety of economic, moral, and political issues—among them improving schools, expanding job opportunities, combating crime, reducing poverty, and determining America's role in the world. These require engagement in democratic discourse in order to understand the issues, determine options for action, and choose among competing policy alternatives. But too often, participants felt, these civic responsibilities are abrogated to politicians and professionals, making citizens passive spectators in the political process. Nevertheless, participants also felt that increased public engagement could rejuvenate hope and public-mindedness. They concluded that they had a significant role to play, recognizing that democracy's challenge is "our" problem and not "their" problem (Doble 2006).

Reinvigorating Citizen Participation

To Vaclav Havel (1997), "Civil Society . . . means a society that makes room for the richest possible self-structuring and the richest possible participation in public life." After the collapse of the Soviet Union, civil society began to blossom in Havel's Czech Republic and other parts of Eastern Europe. At the same time in America, the associations and activities that had created the glue that strengthened civil society—notably described by Alexis de Tocqueville in *Democracy in America* in 1835—and that ensured a structure and climate for active citizen participation were declining. Widespread acknowledgement of the crisis prompted social scientists to propose new models to invigorate a weakened democracy and to encourage more active citizen involvement with governance.

Among the early voices was that of Benjamin Barber, who prescribes "strong democracy" as a remedy to incivility and apathy, where "active citizens govern themselves in the only form that is genuinely and completely democratic" (1984,

p. 148). Barber claims that "community grows out of participation and at the same time makes participation possible," and that "strong democracy is the politics of amateurs, where every [person] is compelled to encounter every other [person] without the intermediary of expertise" (1984, p. 152). From his perspective, "citizens are neighbors bound together neither by blood nor by contract but by their common concerns and common participation in the search for common solutions to common conflicts" (1984, p. 219). In a later work, Barber calls for "a place for us in civil society, a place really for us, for what we share and who, in sharing, we become. That place must be democratic: both public and free" (1998, p. 38).

David Mathews applies practical techniques to this active citizenship model, engaging lay citizens in deliberation about issues of common concern. As president of the Kettering Foundation, he has developed a national network for civic forums that teaches citizens to frame issues, make choices, find common ground, and act in their community's best interest (1999; Mathews and McAfee 2001). James Fishkin has also helped pioneer this framework for citizen deliberation (1995; 1997; 2009), joined by Daniel Yankelovich and his colleagues at the public opinion research and public engagement organization Public Agenda (1991; 1999; Yankelovich and Friedman 2010). Harry Boyte (1989; 2004; Boyte and Evans 1986; Boyte and Kari 1996), another political scientist instrumental in developing theories of active citizenship, has advanced new models for reinvigorating communities through the creation of free spaces or commons for public discourse and deliberation. These civil society theorists were joined by a rash of other scholars in the last two decades (Verba, Scholzman, and Brady 1995; Elkin and Soltan 1999; Skocpol 1999; Putnam 2000; Fong 2004; Gutmann 2004; Dzur 2008)—scholars who are strong proponents of citizen participation in public life. Echoing these theorists is a cadre of librarians advocating a broader new "civic librarianship" where libraries strengthen democracy by building and renewing communities, and by engaging citizens in public work (Molz and Dain 1999; McCook 2000; McCabe 2001; Kranich 2001; Schull 2004).

Stages of Public Engagement

A question Americans have debated since the early days of the republic is: What role should the public play in a participatory democracy? The answer lies in the "stage" of involvement they wish to have with their government. Citizens in the "Information Stage" (OECD 2001) of involvement maintain only a one-way relationship in which government compiles and delivers information to them. These informed citizens—referred to by Michael Schudson (1998; 2003) as "monitorial" citizens—only pay attention when things go wrong. While Schudson believes citizens need to know what their government is doing, he also expects them to "know what they need to do with what they know" (p. 311). Barber (1984) considers this informed citizen model of governance as "thin democracy" dominated by representative institutions with relatively passive citizens.

In the "Consultation Stage" (OECD 2001), citizens interact in a two-way relationship with government in which their voices are heard through public opinion surveys and commentary about proposed policies. During this stage, citizens express their preferences—a stage that Barber (2003) refers to as "plebiscitary democracy."

In the third stage of involvement, "Active Participation" (OECD 2001), citizens engage directly in the decision making and policy making process by proposing policy options and shaping policy dialogue. Barber (1984) calls this "strong democracy," where citizens "regard discourse, debate, and deliberation as essential conditions for reaching common ground and arbitrating differences among people in a large, multicultural society" (Barber 2003, p. 37). As a remedy to incivility and apathy, Barber contends that this stage enables active citizens to "govern themselves in 'the only form that is genuinely and completely democratic'" (1984, p. 148). A more active, participatory citizenry depends upon an information environment that Leah Lievrouw describes as shifting from "informing" to "involving" (1994, p. 350). And, according to Paul Jaeger and Gary Burnett, it also depends on a policy environment that relies on "Libraries, as established guardians of diverse perspectives of information . . . to protect and preserve information access *and exchange* [italics mine] in this new policy environment . . . facilitating and fueling deliberative democracy" (2005, p. 464).

Educating Citizens for Democracy

Since the days of John Locke, political philosophers have stressed the importance of civic education to the success of democracy. John Dewey (1910; 1916) recognized the value of small groups deliberating to make choices in problematic situations. In the 1920s and 1930s a public forum movement emerged that educated voters through discussions embodying democratic principles and practices (Keith 2007). Like Dewey, Eduard Lindeman (1935) articulated the need to educate adults about their civic responsibilities through discussion groups, an approach later affirmed by Norman Nie, Jane Junn, and Kenneth Stehlik-Barry (1996). Jurgen Habermas contends that citizens pursue "the rationally motivating force of achieving understanding" (Habermas 1992a, p. 80) to seek agreement through a democratic process that depends on hearing all relevant voices, based on everyone having knowledge of different perspectives and deferring to others with better arguments (Habermas 1992b). Learning to act democratically, then, requires citizens not only to learn and apply deliberative decision making processes but also to navigate through the contradictions and tensions of democracy.

Little is understood about the informal civic learning required for citizens to participate effectively in the processes of democracy (Schugurensky 2006). But evidence suggests that when citizens participate in deliberation and decision making, they learn how to take responsible social and political action, particularly at the local level. Carole Pateman observes that "Participation develops and fosters the very qualities necessary for it; the more individuals participate the better able they become to do so" (1970, pp. 42–43). This shift from what Daniel Schugurensky calls "passivity to the feeling of agency" (2006, p. 172) helps individuals become public, and not just private, citizens, while they develop a political culture that eliminates exclusive control by political elites. Hence, public participation in political discussions builds citizens' capacity for self-governance and political efficacy, enabling them to go beyond spectators to become actors, to move from occasional voters to participants in the deliberative act of making choices together.

Concerns about declining civic engagement have prompted educators to consider how best to prepare more-active citizens. Many schools are renewing their civic mission and helping "young people acquire and learn to use the skills, knowledge, and attitudes that will prepare them to be competent and responsible citizens throughout their lives" (Gibson and Levine 2003, p. 4). Colleges and universities have also reaffirmed their once vital tradition of civic education (Boyte 2000, p. 46). Many have incorporated public engagement into their overall institutional mission, following the leadership of higher education organizations such as the Association of American Colleges and Universities, American Association of State Colleges and Universities, and Campus Compact. Adult learners also need opportunities to learn civic skills and responsibilities. As John Gastil asserts, "Adult lives are already immersed in rich community contexts, which are replete with (often missed) opportunities for public action" (2004, p. 309). The need to impart the skills to participate in a strong democracy provides ideal opportunities for libraries in schools, on campus, and in towns not only to inform, but also to educate and engage today's and tomorrow's citizens in a safe, neutral environment.

History of Libraries and Civic Engagement

Benjamin Franklin founded the first public lending library in America in the 1730s. His idea of sharing information resources departed from much of the rest of the civilized world, where libraries were often the property of the ruling classes and religious institutions. Public tax-supported libraries were organized in the mid-19th century as supplements to the public schools as well as "civilizing agents and objects of civic pride in a raw new country" (Molz and Dain 1999, p. 3). Later in the century, public libraries continued "the educational process where the schools left off and by conducting a people's university, a wholesome capable citizenry would be fully schooled in the conduct of a democratic life" (Ditzion 1947, p. 74). By the 1920s libraries became recognized as informal education centers where all could gain access to ideas needed for self governance (Learned 1924).

Following World War II librarians joined civic groups, politicians, and educators to rejuvenate the democratic spirit in the country. The New York Public Library sponsored a series of discussions about the meaning of the American democratic tradition. These programs, according to Ruth Rutzen, chair of the American Library Association's (ALA's) Adult Education Board, offered libraries ideal opportunities to assume a leadership role in their communities, proclaiming, "Let us all make our libraries active community centers for the spread of reliable information on all sides of this vital issue and for the encouragement of free discussion and action" (Preer 2008, p. 3). In 1952 ALA, in conjunction with its 75th anniversary, sought to increase political support for libraries by launching the American Heritage Project, which enabled citizens to consider the issues of the day through discussions at their local libraries (Preer 1993). In the words of Jean Preer, "the group setting [in libraries] offered an experience of democracy as well as a consideration of it" (Preer 2001, p. 151). Just as important, libraries defined themselves as agencies that promoted not only access to but also engagement with a diversity of ideas.

Paralleling the decline of civic participation in America in the late 20th century was the suspension of democratic discussion groups in local libraries. Following the social upheaval of the 1960s, public libraries shifted away from the democratic process of group life toward broadening information access for a greater number of individuals. Ronald McCabe suggests that public libraries adopted a more utilitarian purpose where "usefulness is a function of effective planning that ensures responsiveness to the information needs of individuals" (McCabe 2001, p. 37). That diminished focus on community engagement is reflected in a 2006 report by Public Agenda that found libraries were among the most trusted public institutions, but needed to "look carefully at opportunities to strengthen their role in addressing serious problems in their own communities" (p. 13).

Engaging Citizens Through Libraries

After a hiatus of several decades, libraries around the country are undertaking a vast array of engaging programs that bring citizens together to share interests, concerns, and decision making. The challenge for libraries in the digital age is to extend their reach well beyond educating and informing into a realm where they increase social capital, rekindle civil society, and expand public participation in democracy. Nancy Kranich (2005/6) has documented civic initiatives under way in school, academic, public, and special libraries over the last decade and has found it useful to group them into the following seven distinct categories:

1 *The Library as Civic Space.* Libraries offer safe, neutral spaces where citizens can turn to solve personal and community problems. Over the past two decades, communities, schools, colleges, and universities have refurbished or built exciting new spaces for their libraries—spaces that also serve as public gathering spots that anchor neighborhoods, downtowns, schools, and campuses. A good example is the Salt Lake City Public Library, which built a dramatic new facility designed by Moshe Safdie—an award-winning facility considered the community gathering place where "citizens practice democracy" (Berry 2006, p. 32).

2 *The Library as Enabler of Civic Literacy.* Children and adults alike must learn a broad range of 21st century literacy skills if they are to become smart seekers, recipients, and creators of content, as well as effective citizens. School libraries, academic libraries, and, increasingly, public libraries—long committed to enabling information literacy—can extend their offerings into the realm of civic literacy[2] (Milner 2002; Partnership for 21st Century Skills n.d.) so that their constituents can gain critical thinking skills along with a sense of civic agency[3] (Boyte 2007, 2009). Different approaches to civic literacy all encompass active engagement with the civic life of communities, helping civic actors to apply skills for participation in civil discourse. An example of a civic literacy initiative used by an academic library is the application of James Fishkin's (2010) deliberative polling technique at Kansas State University Libraries. Donna Schenck-Hamlin (et al. 2010) used the technique to measure whether students think more complexly and revise their opinions after a deliberative dialogue about the death penalty.

3 *Library as Public Forum and Conversation Catalyst.* Many school, public, and academic libraries host public programs that facilitate the type of discourse that offers citizens a chance to frame issues of common concern,

deliberate about choices for solving problems, create deeper understanding about others' opinions, connect citizens across the spectrum of thought, and recommend appropriate action that reflects legitimate guidance from the whole community. Libraries that sponsor deliberative forums see benefits in connecting them more closely and deeply to their communities. These forums and community conversations often follow the formats developed by such organizations as the Kettering Foundation's National Issues Forums Institute, Study Circles (now called Everyday Democracy), Choices, Conversation Cafes, the Harwood Institute for Public Innovation, and others. Libraries are among those offering deliberative public forums in State College, Pennsylvania; Johnson County, Kansas; and Des Moines, Iowa. Topics range from democracy and immigration to energy and health care and involve citizens holding different perspectives in learning and participatory democracy. Librarians in Virginia Beach, Virginia, helped citizens collect and assess community concerns about redevelopment, learn about civic action, participate in democratic discourse, and develop civic leadership skills (Caywood 2010). In Des Plaines, Illinois, librarians joined forces with community partners by framing and deliberating the question "What does it take to meet the needs of Des Plaines residents?" These community conversations resulted in greater awareness of local services and new collaborative approaches for taking action (Griffin 2006). In Youngstown, Ohio, community conversations helped the public library gain more knowledge of citizen's aspirations and apply it as agents for change, thereby strengthening community ties as well as public perceptions about the library that resulted in a successful tax levy referendum that increased the library's budget in November 2010.

4   *The Library as Civic Information Center.* Using both electronic and print technologies, libraries now deliver numerous local databases and Web sites about vital services within their communities. Joan Durrance (2004) and her colleagues at the University of Michigan School of Information have identified and evaluated successful civic library projects in communities throughout the country that help immigrants and minorities, teach youth to participate in community problem solving, and pull together essential information and communication resources that might otherwise be difficult to identify or locate. Beyond access, libraries are also facilitating e-government services (Bertot et al. 2006; Jaeger 2005; Horrigan 2004). A good example is Florida's Pasco County library system, which helps people transact government business, search for jobs, and file online forms for food stamps, Medicaid, unemployment compensation, and more through its extensive e-government program.

5   *The Library as Community-Wide Reading Club.* For many years, school, public, and academic libraries have hosted community-wide "one-book" reading initiatives. The idea was launched by the Seattle Public Library, but Chicago advanced it considerably, promoting reading by "giving a 'public voice' to what is usually considered a private activity . . . to discover or build unity in a diverse city" (Putnam and Feldstein 2003, p. 53). The Kentucky State Library linked with Kentucky Educational Television to launch a highly successful statewide reading effort with outreach and

engagement activities involving a mix of 130 partners (Pennsylvania State University Public Broadcasting 2002). Other libraries offer shared reading experiences through the Civically Engaged Reader program (Project on Civic Reflection, n.d.), a diverse collection of provocative short articles designed to inspire contemplation about the central questions of civic life. With a grant from the Fetzer Institute, the ALA Public Programs Office is training librarians to use this reflection technique as part of its "Building Common Ground: Discussions of Community, Civility and Compassion" project (ALA Public Programs Office n.d.).

6 *The Library as Partner in Public Service.* Pennsylvania State University (2002) launched Partners in Public Service (PIPS) in 1999 to demonstrate how collaborative projects between public broadcasting stations, libraries, museums, and educational institutions could enhance services to participating communities. With support from the Corporation for Public Broadcasting and the Institute of Museum and Library Services (IMLS), PIPS produced a useful guide with case studies on how to undertake these institutional partnerships to help communities revitalize by utilizing digital technologies and fulfilling unmet needs. Considered a vision for a "community as a learning campus," IMLS built upon the PIPS idea by funding numerous collaborative civic projects around the country that bring libraries, museums, and public media together. An example is a collaboration between the Princeton (New Jersey) Public Library, AllPrinceton.com, and Princeton Community Television that "applies the power of digital media to the civic, cultural, and commercial life of Princeton" (AllPrinceton. com, n.d.).

7 *The Library as Service Learning Center.* Service learning combines meaningful public service with curriculum or program-based learning. Schools, colleges, and universities use service learning to strengthen academic skills, foster civic responsibility, and develop leadership abilities. Today, many require students to participate in service learning in order to graduate. An example of a school library involved with service learning is at the Urban School in San Francisco, which works with faculty and students to facilitate their co-curricular community-based research and engagement projects (Urban School n.d.). Even though one-third of college students now participate in service learning activities (Campus Compact, 2010), Lynn Westney (2006) found academic library contributions to service learning sparse. A number of MLIS programs do incorporate service learning into their curriculum. These include the University of Texas School of Information project to create a National Virtual Museum of the American Indian and a University of Wisconsin–Madison Jail Library Group student project to provide reading materials for incarcerated adults (Roy 2009; Riddle 2003). Another, based at the University of Illinois Graduate School of Library and Information Science program in Community Informatics, involves students interested in the experiences of underserved groups in Professor Ann Bishop's class onsite at Paseo Boricua Community Library Project in Chicago (Bishop, Bruce, and Jeong 2009).

Opportunities to Partner and Participate

Public Libraries

Public librarians aspire to realign their civic mission, embed their services in their communities, convene community conversations, and build partnerships that deliver impact and results (Hill 2009; IMLS 2009; Lankes et al. 2007; Putnam and Feldstein 2003; Urban Libraries Council 2005). Kranich (2010a) has written and spoken extensively about the importance of public librarians engaging community members in democratic discourse and community renewal. Likewise, in 2011, the Urban Libraries Council issued a leadership brief on community civic engagement, calling on public libraries "to shape and lead discussions, decisions, and strategies that encourage active and purposeful civic engagement." The brief recommends that librarians identify new roles that move them "from supporting players to valued leaders in today's civic engagement space . . . [that will] broaden their impact as the go-to resource for building a culture of enlightened, engaged, and empowered citizens" (Urban Libraries Council 2011).

Numerous national and community-based organizations look to public libraries as partners in civic activities. Such dialogue and deliberation organizations as the National Issues Forums Institute and Everyday Democracy provide resources and training for deliberative forums that are conducted in many libraries around the country. AmericaSpeaks is another national group that has involved libraries in national conversations, including the 2010 Our Budget/Our Economy (OBOE) dialogue hosted in 19 locations around the country, including the Johnson County (Kansas) Library. Teams from Grand Forks, North Dakota, and Columbia, South Carolina, both included representatives from their public libraries. Locally, libraries are partnering with community groups related to particular issues under discussion. For example, in Johnson County and Kansas City, the libraries worked with United Community Services, Kansas City Consensus, and the Kansas Small Business Development Center for a dialogue about the economy. Johnson County has also partnered with the Ewing Marion Kauffman Foundation, University of Kansas School of Public Administration, Kansas City Public Television (KCPT), St. Luke's Health System, the Center for Practical Bioethics, community nonprofits, Mid America Regional Council, and the League of Women Voters Johnson County. In Des Moines, the public library collaborated with Pioneer Hi-Bred and the Iowa Council for International Understanding on international dialogue issues. In State College, Pennsylvania, the Schlow Regional Library worked with the school district's community education department, the Centre Daily Times, and the local community foundation to sponsor its dialogue series, in conjunction with such groups as the United Way, the League of Women Voters, and various Penn State units. Finally, in Virginia Beach, the public library has teamed up with the mayor's office, the League of Women Voters, the Hampton Roads Center for Civic Engagement, and others to spur community redevelopment and subsequent initiatives.

Academic Libraries

In colleges and universities, academic librarians are promoting deeper engagement by embedding services in the teaching, learning, and research processes, as well as becoming more involved with their communities (ACRL 2007; ARL 2009; Lougee 2002; Westney 2006; Williams 2009). Kranich (2004) and her colleagues (Kranich, Reid, and Willingham 2004) have encouraged academic libraries to "play a critical role in kindling civic spirit by providing not only information, but also expanded opportunities for dialogue and deliberation as a practice ground for democracy" (Kranich 2010b).

Recognizing that a robust democracy and the public welfare depend on an engaged and informed citizenry, colleges and universities endeavor to strengthen both the study and practice of deliberative democracy in a diverse and interdependent world. In 1946 President Harry Truman created a Commission on Higher Education for Democracy, which published a report the following year (U.S. President's Commission on Higher Education for Democracy 1947). The commission considered the principal goal for American higher education "a fuller realization of democracy in every phase of living" (p. 8). It also called for the integration of democratic principles into the active life of the American people, noting that such an integration "is not to be achieved merely by studying or discussing democracy . . . [but democracy] must be lived to be thoroughly understood. It must become an established attitude and activity, not just a body of remote and abstract doctrine—a way for men to live and work harmoniously together, not just words in a textbook or a series of slogans" (p. 14). The report also stated that "The democratic way of life can endure only as private careers and social obligations are made to mesh, as personal ambition is reconciled with public responsibility" (p. 10). Finally, the commission concluded that college graduates of the day may have acquired career-oriented competencies, but they "fall short of that human wholeness and civic conscience which the cooperative activities of citizenship require" (p. 48).

Decades later, in 1999, the presidents of American colleges and universities challenged higher education to re-examine its public purposes and its commitments to the democratic ideal (Campus Compact 1999) and programs have sprung up on campuses around the country to motivate young people toward lifelong participation in civic life. The following year, academic leaders proclaimed:

> We believe that our institutions serve not only as agents of this democracy, but also as its architects—providing bridges between the aims and aspirations of individuals and the public work of the larger world. To that end, we commit our institutions to wide-ranging examinations of our civic and democratic purposes through curricula and extracurricular activities, socially engaged scholarship, civic partnerships, and community-based learning and research (Kellogg Commission 2000, p. 24).

Nationally, college and university libraries can participate in efforts to stimulate deliberative democracy by working with organizations committed to revitalizing democracy, such as the Association of American Colleges and Universities, the American Association of State Colleges and Universities (AASCU) American Democracy Project, the American Association of University Professors, Campus Compact, and the Democracy Imperative. On many campuses, public engagement is now a critical part of the overall institutional mission—with faculty incorporating civic content into their curricula and encouraging students to participate in socially responsible extracurricular activities. According to Nancy Thomas of the Democracy Imperative, "Practicing the arts of democracy can be infused across disciplines, and it can be built into nearly all structures on campus, such as student clubs and activities, athletic programs, cultural and intellectual events, residential life, and volunteer opportunities. There are no venues on campus that could not be practice grounds for democracy" (Thomas 2007, p. 7). Civic engagement initiatives on campus offer a perfect opportunity for libraries to fulfill their traditional roles of promoting civic literacy and ensuring an informed and engaged citizenry. They can also deepen understanding of the relationship between liberal education and civic responsibility, helping students to look beyond the classroom to the world's major questions and encouraging them to apply their analytical skills and ethical judgment to significant problems around them.

Beyond their local campuses, a number of academic libraries are collaborating with public libraries and other organizations to advance regional or statewide civic initiatives. For example, as participants in the American Democracy Project at Illinois State University, librarians are working with other libraries in the area to sponsor deliberative forums. Likewise, at the University of Georgia Russell Library, archivists convene deliberative forums in collaboration with the Carter Presidential Library and public libraries throughout the state, while Kansas State University librarians who are affiliated with the Kansas State University Institute for Civic Discourse and Democracy are training librarians throughout the state to host forums about the future of broadband in their communities.

School Libraries

In schools, librarians seek to collaborate closely with teachers and engage more directly with students by integrating their resources and services into the curriculum (Darrow 2009; Loertscher 2008; Loertscher, Koechlin, and Zwaan 2008). As she has done with academic librarians, Kranich (2006) has called upon school librarians to join forces with organizations such as the Campaign for the Civic Mission of Schools to provide substantial opportunities for young people to participate in civic activities and learn skills for democratic deliberation. Beyond redesigning facilities, collaborating with teachers, and developing resources, school librarians can enhance civic participation by teaching students sophisticated information literacy skills to live, learn, and work in the digital age as well as to carry out the day-to-day activities of citizens in a developed democratic society.

Ever since the days of John Dewey, educators have recognized the vital role of education in teaching civic understanding and active citizenship (Burstyn 1996; Gutmann 1987; Westbrook 1991). When librarians facilitate the development of critical thinking, creativity, and problem solving, students develop the necessary skills to exercise the rights and responsibilities of citizenship. States Jerilyn Fay Kelle, ". . . if we don't afford students the opportunity within their schools to live in and be active members of a democratic community, they will not become active participatory citizens in the wider society" (1996, p. 63).

Like colleges, universities, and local communities, schools are undertaking major initiatives to teach students the skills for active citizenship. In the early 1990s the Center for Civic Education (CCE) (1991; 1994) laid out a framework along with standards for teaching civics in schools, stating, "The aim of civic education is . . . not just any kind of participation by any kind of citizen; it is the participation of informed and responsible citizens, skilled in the arts of effective action and deliberation" (CCE 1991, summary). Shortly thereafter, a number of leading education organizations, including the Education Commission of the

States, the American Federation of Teachers, and the National Council for the Social Studies (NCSS), joined the call for enhanced civics study, launching the National Alliance for Civic Education.

NCSS has declared that "a primary goal of public education is to prepare students to be engaged and effective citizens. It has defined an effective citizen as one who has the knowledge, skills, and attitudes required to assume the 'office of citizen' in our democratic republic." It then went on to commit the organization to "revitalizing citizenship education in our schools and to empowering all students with a positive vision of their role as citizens in a democracy" (NCSS 2001). A few years later, the education community reached a consensus on the need for national action sparked by publication of a report, *The Civic Mission of Schools* (Gibson and Levine 2003; Levine 2006). The report recommends that schools help "young people acquire and learn to use the skills, knowledge, and attitudes that will prepare them to be competent and responsible citizens throughout their lives" (Gibson and Levine 2003, p. 4), and encourages communities and local institutions to collaborate to provide civic learning opportunities. Subsequently, more than 40 organizations joined forces to launch the Campaign for the Civic Mission of Schools (n.d.) while numerous advocacy organizations have begun their own civic engagement initiatives for youth.

The most recent gauge of progress is reflected by *The Nation's Report Card: Civics 2010* (National Assessment of Educational Progress 2011), which measured only limited progress in the mastery of civic skills over the last decade. Although civic education falls outside the focus of No Child Left Behind and is threatened in an era of strong standards and accountability measures, Donovan Walling (2007) predicts that a comeback is in sight with hopeful signs from a rebound in youth volunteerism and increasing political engagement. Thanks to the efforts of the campaign and organizations like the Center for Information and Research on Civic Learning and Engagement (CIRCLE), many states have ramped up their civics requirements for schools, providing substantial opportunities for young people to participate in civic activities and learn skills for democratic deliberation. School librarians are ideally positioned to bolster these fledgling initiatives, following the example of a school librarian and social studies teacher (Eastman and McGrath 2006) who collaborated to promote civics and media literacy by engaging high school students in a voluntary, out-of-school course called Primary Research Through the History of Beverly, Massachusetts.

Library Education

If librarians are to embrace their role in engaging citizens, they need both formal and informal training that offers conceptual and practical approaches. Diantha Schull (2004), in her study of "The Civic Library," found little formal training at the master's and doctoral levels or in professional development. Neither did she uncover much of a pedagogical base for school librarians about democratic values or civic roles. She laments that "Graduate programs offer courses on community information networks, digital communities, community information systems, and outreach to local communities, but almost nothing that offers the background required for new professionals to actualize the civic value of their library" (Schull 2004, p. 60). Nevertheless, a number of library educators are leading impressive (although scattered) efforts to teach civic librarianship. Noteworthy is Ann Bishop, who leads the University of Illinois Graduate School of Library and Information Science program in Community Informatics, a program that is mentoring students eager for a career that gives them the opportunity to contribute to their communities (Bishop, Bruce, and Jeong 2009). At the University of Michigan, Durrance and her colleagues (2004) started the Libraries and Community-Engagement Initiative to study information needs and use in communities, community informatics, and community-focused library services. Kathleen de la Peña McCook's (2000) research and teaching at the University of South Florida have focused on libraries as community builders. And, finally, Loriene Roy at the University of Texas has spearheaded new models for service learning in LIS education (Roy, Jensen, and Meyers 2009).

National Library Organizations

Much evidence indicates that librarians across the nation are working together to enhance their role in developing the civic capacity of citizens in an effort to revitalize communities and strengthen democracy. A number of ALA presidents have spearheaded these efforts, beginning with Sara Long, who focused on libraries building community in 1999. She was followed by Kranich, whose initiative on libraries and democracy has seeded subsequent civic initiatives. Leslie Burger in 2006 led an effort titled "Libraries Transform Communities" that helped inform Molly Raphael's 2011 initiative "Empowering Voices," which encourages community engagement.

Beyond its leaders, ALA has worked for more than a decade to foster public deliberation through library forums using materials produced by the National Issues Forums Institute and others. The association has hosted moderator training sessions and other programs relating to community building and engagement. In 2004 several ALA members formed a Membership Initiative Group—Libraries Foster Civic Engagement (ALA Libraries Foster Civic Engagement n.d.)—to provide an official presence within ALA and to create a learning community. In 2010 ALA launched the ALA Center for Civic Life (CCL) (ALA Center for Civic Life n.d.) in conjunction with the Kettering Foundation in order to play a more visible role in promoting community engagement and fostering public deliberation through libraries. The center is building the capacity of libraries and librarians to help citizens get more engaged in the civic life of their communities. It is documenting the growing involvement of libraries with deliberation and the challenges and opportunities they face in conducting a nationwide program that supports local public institutions such as libraries. Members of the center's advisory committee worked with the ALA Intellectual Freedom Round Table to frame and design an issue map for deliberative forums titled "Who Do I Trust to Protect My Privacy?" as part of the Office for Intellectual Freedom's Privacy Revolution initiative launched in spring 2010 (ALA Office for Intellectual Freedom n.d.). CCL is also forming national partnerships with organizations such as AmericaSpeaks and AASCU, as well as helping local libraries identify and link with partners pursuing similar civic goals.

Many librarians are also taking part in the annual September Project—which is designed "to break the silence following September 11 [2001], and to invite all people into libraries for conversations about patriotism, democracy, and citizenship" (The September Project n.d.). In April 2011 librarians, journalists, and civic-minded citizens attended a workshop titled "Beyond Books: News, Literacy, Democracy for America's Libraries" where they explored what is possible for communities and democracies. Participants ended their conversations by issuing a consensus statement that commits them to: "work together to create informed, engaged communities and advance 21st century democracy . . . Journalists and librarians are well positioned to join with the public to strengthen community networks that engage and empower people. Together, we can fill a deficit in the information ecology of 21st century communities" (Beyond Books 2011).

Related developments in the library community include a study supported by ALA's Office for Information Technology Policy (OITP) and authored by then OITP fellow David Lankes titled "Participatory Networks: The Library as Conversation" (2007). More recently, Lankes (2011) extended that study by calling on all libraries to shift conceptually from focusing on the collection of artifacts to the facilitation of knowledge creation through conversation in a safe environment. David Carr (2011) has made similar recommendations based on his work with IMLS, encouraging both librarians and museum curators to move beyond the documentation of the past to reinventing their institutions as places for the expression of American voices—for open conversations as the public mode of learning in museums and libraries. Finally, IMLS (2011) has focused its 2012–2016 strategic plan on the civic role of libraries, with a mission statement that calls on IMLS to "inspire libraries and museums to advance innovation, learning, and cultural and civic engagement by providing leadership through research, policy development and grant-making."

Conclusion

Leaders across the library profession recognize the need to engage, embed, and integrate libraries into the life of their communities, schools, and universities if they are to remain relevant and appreciated in the digital age. No single approach can work for every library. A plethora of relevant efforts provide role models and stories that can create a new professional narrative that resonates with colleagues and community members alike. But without a critical mass of public, academic, school, and special libraries seizing opportunities to engage their communities in authentic, meaningful ways, libraries will not emerge as widely acknowledged institutions that foster strong democracy. Libraries need to realign their programs and services strategically to reflect the civic attitudes and concerns of their specific communities and increase their impact. In the words of Chrystie Hill, "If we stay focused on our users, stakeholders, and their needs, and continually design to them, we'll be better positioned to stay engaged with our communities no matter what's taking place around us" (2009, p. 53).

Efforts abound that encourage more active citizenship. They offer libraries ideal opportunities to engage with their communities and to join forces with the many organizations and institutions already committed to strengthening participation in democracy. All types of libraries can forge civic partnerships with other organizations and individuals that extend their reach and help them achieve their mission. These partnerships can also establish new constituencies that widen and deepen public support, broaden and diversify sources of funding, and strengthen public involvement with local affairs.

Repositioning libraries as informal civic learning agents fits the theory and practice of community inquiry conceived a century ago by John Dewey (1916). Dewey believed that people need the opportunity to share ideas through multiple media in order to understand and solve everyday problems together. To this formulation, libraries bring their role as trusted boundary spanners. Whether face-to-face or virtual, libraries build learning communities that bring people with mutual interests together to exchange information and learn about and solve problems of common concern. Civic librarians need to become more aware of their assets as public conveners and more intentional in developing programs, services, and spaces that promote public engagement, infused and embedded into the mainstream of everyday practice and professional training. Through the facilitation of community conversations, libraries can deepen their involvement with their constituents, serving not only as agents but as architects of the civic life of their communities.

Librarian of Congress Archibald Macleish (1940, p. 388) once avowed that "Librarians must become active not passive agents of the democratic process." With renewed interest in promoting civic literacy and deliberative democracy around the country, libraries are poised to grasp this cause, build civic space, and reclaim their traditional role. If they are to fulfill their civic mission in the digital age, libraries must find active ways to engage community members in democratic discourse and community renewal. Working closely with a rich and diverse array of partners, libraries of all types can rekindle civic engagement, promote greater citizen participation, and increase community problem solving and decision making. For, as Putnam has stated, "Citizenship is not a spectator sport" (2000, p. 342).

References

AllPrinceton.com. n.d. AllPrinceton.com Web site. Retrieved December 31, 2011, from http://allprinceton.com/content/about-us.

American Library Association (ALA) Center for Civic Life. n.d. Center for Civic Life Blog. American Library Association. Retrieved December 31, 2011, from http://discuss.ala.org/civicengagement.

American Library Association (ALA) Libraries Foster Civic Engagement Membership Initiative Group. n.d. Libraries Fostering Civic Engagement ALA Connect Site. American Library Association. Retrieved December 31, 2011, from http://connect.ala.org/node/64933.

American Library Association (ALA) Office for Intellectual Freedom. n.d. "Who Should I Trust to Protect My Privacy?" *Moderator and Public Forum Guides.* American Library Association. Retrieved December 31, 2011, from http://www.privacyrevolution.org/index.php/resources/for_libraries/civic_engagement.

American Library Association (ALA) Public Programs Office. n.d. "Building Common Ground: Discussions of Community, Civility and Compassion." American Library Association. Retrieved December 31, 2011, from http://ppo.ala.org/commonground.

American Psychological Association. n.d. "Definition of Civic Engagement." American Psychological Association. Retrieved December 30, 2011, from http://www.apa.org/education/undergrad/civic-engagement.aspx.

Association of College and Research Libraries (ACRL). 2007. *Establishing a Research Agenda for Scholarly Communication: A Call for Community Engagement.* American Library Association. Retrieved December 30, 2011, from http://www.acrl.ala.org/scresearchagenda/index.php?title=Main_Page.

Association of Research Libraries (ARL). 2009. *Public Engagement.* ARL, SPEC Kit 312.

Barber, Benjamin. 1984. *Strong Democracy.* University of California Press.

Barber, Benjamin. 1998. *A Place for Us: How to Make Society Civil and Strong.* Hill and Wang.

Barber, Benjamin. 2003. "Which Technology and Which Democracy?" in *Democracy and New Media,* ed. by Henry Jenkins and David Thorburn, 33–47. MIT Press.

Berry, John. 2006. "Where Democracy Happens." *Library Journal* 131 (11) June 15: pp. 32–35.

Bertot, John, Paul Jaeger, Lesley Langa, and Charles McClure. 2006. "Public Access Computing and Internet Access in Public Libraries: The Role of Public Libraries in E-Government and Emergency Situations." *First Monday* 11 (9) September. Retrieved December 31, 2011, from http://firstmonday.org/htbin/cgiwrap/bin/ojs/index.php/fm/article/view/1392/1310.

Beyond Books: News, Literacy, and Democracy for America's Libraries. 2011. "A Consensus Statement on Libraries, Journalism and Participatory Democracy." Retrieved December 31, 2011, from http://www.mediagiraffe.org/wiki/index.php/Biblionews-work-statement.

Bishop, Ann, Bertram Bruce, and Sunny Jeong. 2009. "Beyond Service Learning: Toward Community Schools and Reflective Community Learners." In *Service Learning: Linking Library Education and Practice,* ed. by Loriene Roy, Kelly Jensen, and Alex Hershey Meyers. American Library Association: pp. 16–31.

Boyte, Harry. 1989. *Commonwealth: A Return to Citizen Politics.* Free Press.

Boyte, Harry. 2000. "The Struggle Against Positivism." *Academe* 86 (4). Retrieved December 28, 2011, from http://www.aaup.org/AAUP/pubsres/academe/2000/JA/Feat/Boyt.htm.

Boyte, Harry. 2004. *Everyday Politics: Reconnecting Citizens and the Public Life.* University of Pennsylvania Press.

Boyte, Harry. 2007. "Building Civic Agency: The Public-Work Approach." *Open Democracy.* November 21. Retrieved December 31, 2011, from http://www.opendemocracy.net/article/building_civic_agency_the_public_work_approach.

Boyte, Harry. 2009. *Civic Agency and the Cult of the Expert.* Kettering Foundation. Retrieved December 31, 2011, from www.csc.vsc.edu/cai/sources/agency_and_experts.pdf.

Boyte, Harry, and Sara Evans. 1986. *Free Spaces: The Sources of Democratic Change in America.* Harper and Row.

Boyte, Harry, and Nancy Kari. 1996. *Building America: The Democratic Promise of Public Work.* Temple University Press.

Burstyn, Joan, ed. 1996. *Educating Tomorrow's Valuable Citizen.* State University of New York Press.

Campaign for the Civic Mission of Schools. n.d. "Welcome to the Campaign for the Civic Mission of Schools." Retrieved December 31, 2011, from http://www.civicmissionofschools.org.

Campus Compact. 1999. *President's Declaration on Civic Responsibility of Higher Education.* Retrieved December 31, 2011, from http://www.compact.org/resources-for-presidents/presidents-declaration-on-the-civic-responsibility-of-higher-education/about-the-declaration.

Campus Compact. 2010. *Campus Compact Annual Membership Survey, 2010.* Campus Compact. Retrieved December 31, 2011, from http://www.compact.org/about/statistics.

Carr, David. 2011. *Open Conversations: Public Learning in Libraries and Museums.* Libraries Unlimited.

Caywood, Carolyn. 2010. "Civic Engagement at the Virginia Beach Public Library." Telephone interview with Nancy Kranich, March 5.

Center for Civic Education (CCE). 1991. *Civitas: A Framework for Civic Education.* CCE. Retrieved December 31, 2011, from http://www.civiced.org/index.php?page=civitas_executive_summary.

Center for Civic Education (CCE). 1994. *National Standards for Civics and Government.* CCE.

Darrow, Rob. 2009. "School Libraries Are Essential." *Knowledge Quest* 37 (5), May/June: pp. 78–83.

Dewey, John. 1910. *How We Think.* D. C. Heath and Co.

Dewey, John. 1916. *Democracy and Education: An Introduction to the Philosophy of Education.* Macmillan.

Ditzion, Sidney. 1947. *Arsenals of a Democratic Culture: A Social History of the American Public Library Movement in New England and the Middle States from 1850–1900.* American Library Association.

Doble Research Associates. 2006. *Public Thinking About Democracy's Challenge: Reclaiming the Public's Role.* Kettering Foundation.

Durrance, Joan, Karen E. Fisher, and Marian Bouch Hinton. 2004. *How Libraries and Librarians Help: A Guide to Identifying User-Centered Outcomes.* American Library Association.

Dzur, Albert. 2008. *Democratic Professionalism: Citizen Participation and the Reconstruction of Professional Ethics, Identity, and Practice.* Pennsylvania State University Press.

Eastman, W. Dean, and Kevin McGrath. 2006. "Encouraging Civic Virtues: A Collaborative Model Developed by a Teacher-Librarian and a Classroom Teacher." *Knowledge Quest* 34 (4), March/April: pp. 28–31.

Elkin, Stanley, and Karol Soltan, eds. 1999. *Citizen Competence and Democratic Institutions.* Pennsylvania State University Press.

Fishkin, James. 1995. *The Voice of the People: Public Opinion and Democracy.* Yale University Press.

Fishkin, James. 1997. *Democracy and Deliberation: New Directions for Democratic Reform.* Yale University Press.

Fishkin, James. 2009. *When the People Speak: Deliberative Democracy and Public Consultation.* Oxford University Press.

Fishkin, James. 2010. *Deliberative Polling: Toward a Better-Informed Democracy.* Center for Deliberative Democracy, Stanford University. Retrieved December 31, 2011, from http://cdd.stanford.edu/polls/docs/summary.

Fong, Archon. 2004. *Empowered Participation: Reinventing Urban Democracy.* Princeton University Press.

Gastil, John. 2004. "Adult Civic Education Through the National Issues Forums: Developing Democratic Habits and Dispositions Through Public Deliberation." *Adult Education Quarterly* 54 (4) August: pp. 308–328.

Gibson, Cynthia, and Peter Levine. 2003. *The Civic Mission of Schools.* Carnegie Corporation of New York. Retrieved December 28, 2011, from http://civic missionofschools.org/cmos/site/campaign/cms_report.html.

Griffin, Joanne. 2006. "Building Community Through Creative Conversations: Report on Public Forums—Meeting the Needs of Des Plaines Residents— What Does It Take?" Des Plaines Public Library, May.

Gutmann, Amy. 1987. *Democratic Education.* Princeton University Press.

Gutmann, Amy. 2004. *Why Deliberative Democracy?* Princeton University Press.

Habermas, Jurgen. 1992a. *Autonomy and Solidarity: Interviews with Jurgen Habermas.* Rev. ed. Verso.

Habermas, Jurgen. 1992b. *Postmetaphysical Thinking: Philosophical Essays.* MIT Press.

Havel, Vaclav. 1997. "State of the Republic" presidential address to the Parliament and Senate of the Czech Republic, December 9.

Hill, Chrystie. 2009. *Inside, Outside, and Online: Building Your Library Community.* American Library Association.

Horrigan, John. 2004. *How Americans Get in Touch with Government.* Pew Internet and American Life Project. Retrieved December 31, 2011, from http://www.pewinternet.org/Reports/2004/How-Americans-Get-in-Touch-With-Government.aspx.

Institute of Museum and Library Services (IMLS). 2009. *Museums, Libraries, and 21st Century Skills.* IMLS. Retrieved December 30, 2011, from http://www.imls.gov/about/museums_libraries_and_21st_century_skills.aspx.

Institute of Museum and Library Services (IMLS). 2011. *Creating a Nation of Learners: Strategic Plan 2012–2016.* IMLS. Retrieved December 30, 2011, from http://www.imls.gov/about/strategic_plan.aspx.

Jaeger, Paul. 2005. "Deliberative Democracy and the Conceptual Foundations of Electronic Government." *Government Information Quarterly* 22 (4): pp. 702–719.

Jaeger, Paul, and Gary Burnett. 2005. "Information Access and Exchange Among Small Worlds in a Democratic Society: The Role of Policy in Shaping Information Behavior in the Post-9/11 United States," *Library Quarterly* 75 (4) (October): pp. 464–495.

Keith, William. 2007. *Democracy as Discussion: Civic Education and the American Forum Movement.* Lexington.

Kelle, Jerilyn Fay. 1996. "To Illuminate or Indoctrinate: Education for Participatory Democracy." In *Educating Tomorrow's Valuable Citizen,* ed. by Joan Burstyn. State University of New York Press: pp. 61–77.

Kellogg Commission on the Future of State and Land Grant Universities. 2000. *Renewing the Covenant: Learning, Discovery, and Engagement in a New Age and Different World.* National Association of State Universities and Land-Grant Colleges. Retrieved December 31, 2011, from www.aplu.org/NetCommunity/Document.Doc?id=186.

Kranich, Nancy. 2001. *Libraries and Democracy: Cornerstones of Liberty.* American Library Association.

Kranich, Nancy. 2004. "Promoting Civic Engagement Through the Campus Library." *Friends of Libraries USA (FOLUSA) Newsletter* 27 (5), October: pp. 9, 11. Retrieved December 30, 2011, from http://www.nifi.org/news/news_detail.aspx?itemID=3856&catID=2871

Kranich, Nancy. 2005/6. "Civic Partnerships: The Role of Libraries in Promoting Civic Engagement," in "Creative Collaborations: Libraries Within Their Institutions and Beyond," Special issue of *Resource Sharing and Information Networks* 18 (1 and 2): pp. 89–103. Retrieved December 30, 2011, from http://www.nifi.org/news/news_detail.aspx?itemID=3856&catID=2871.

Kranich, Nancy. 2006. "The Civic Mission of School Libraries," *Knowledge Quest* 34 (4) March/April: pp. 10–17.

Kranich, Nancy. 2010a. "Promoting Adult Learning Through Civil Discourse in the Public Library," In *Adult Education in Cultural Institutions: Libraries, Museums, Parks, and Zoos,* ed. by Marilyn Parrish and Edward Taylor, in series *New Directions for Adult and Continuing Education* 127 (Fall): pp. 15–24.

Kranich, Nancy. 2010b. "Academic Libraries as Hubs for Deliberative Democracy," *Journal of Public Deliberation* special issue on Higher Education and Deliberative Democracy. 6 (1) Article 4, Retrieved December 30, 2011, from http://services.bepress.com/jpd/vol6/iss1/art4.

Kranich, Nancy, Michele Reid, and Taylor Willingham. 2004. "Civic Engagement and Academic Libraries," *College and Research Libraries News* 65 (4), July/August: pp. 380–383, 388, 393.

Lankes, R. David. 2011. *The Atlas of New Librarianship.* MIT Press.

Lankes, R. David, Joanne Silverstein, Scott Nicholson, and Todd Marshall. 2007. "Participatory Networks: The Library as Conversation. *Information Research* 12 (4), October. Retrieved December 30, 2011, from http://InformationR.net/ir/12-4/colis05.html.

Learned, William. 1924. *The American Public Library and the Diffusion of Knowledge.* Harcourt, Brace.

Levine, Peter. 2006. "The Civic Mission of Schools: Chief Findings and Next Steps." *Knowledge Quest* 34 (4), March/April: pp. 18–21.

Lievrouw, Leah. 1994. "Information Resources and Democracy: Understanding the Paradox." *Journal of the American Society for Information Science* 45 (6): pp. 350–357.

Lindeman, Eduard. 1935. "The Place of Discussion in the Learning Process." Reprinted in S. D. Brookfield. *Learning Democracy: Eduard Lindeman on Adult Education and Social Change.* Croom Helm, 1987.

Loertscher, David. 2008. "Flip This Library: School Libraries Need a Revolution." *School Library Journal* November 1. Retrieved December 30, 2011, from http://www.schoollibraryjournal.com/article/CA6610496.html.

Loertscher, David, Carol Koechlin, and Sandi Zwaan. 2008. *The New Learning Commons Where Learners Win: Reinventing School Libraries and Computer Labs.* Hi Willow Research and Publishing.

Lougee, Wendy. 2002. *Diffuse Libraries: Emergent Roles for the Research Library in the Digital Age.* Council on Library and Information Resources. http://www.clir.org/pubs/reports/pub108/contents.html.

McCabe, Ronald. 2001. *Civic Librarianship: Renewing the Social Mission of the Public Library.* Scarecrow.

McCook, Kathleen de la Peña. 2000. *A Place at the Table: Participating in Community Building.* American Library Association.

Macleish, Archibald. 1940. "The Librarian and the Democratic Process." *ALA Bulletin* 34, June: pp. 385–388; 421–422.

Mathews, David. 1999. *Politics for People,* 2nd ed. University of Illinois Press.

Mathews, David, and Noelle McAfee. 2001. *Making Choices Together: The Power of Public Deliberation.* Charles F. Kettering Foundation.

Milner, Henry. 2002. *Civic Literacy: How Informed Citizens Make Democracy Work.* University Press of New England.

Molz, Redmond Kathleen, and Phyllis Dain. 1999. *Civic Space/Cyberspace: The American Public Library in the Digital Age.* MIT Press.

Mutz, Diana. 2006. *Hearing the Other Side: Deliberative Versus Participatory Democracy.* Cambridge University Press.

National Assessment of Educational Progress (NAEP). 2011. *The Nation's Report Card: Civics 2010.* National Center for Education Statistics. Retrieved December 31, 2011, from http://nces.ed.gov/nationsreportcard/pubs/main2010/2011466.asp.

National Council for the Social Studies (NCSS), 2001. *Creating Effective Citizens Position Statement.* NCSS. Retrieved December 31, 2011, from http://www.socialstudies.org/positions/effectivecitizens.

Nie, Norman, Jane Junn, and Kenneth Stehlik-Barry. 1996. *Education and Democratic Citizenship in America.* University of Chicago Press.

Oldenburg, Ray. 1989. *The Great Good Place.* Paragon.

Organisation for Economic Cooperation and Development (OECD). 2001. Citizens as Partners: Information, Consultation and Public Participation in Policy-making. OECD. Retrieved December 30, 2011, from http://www.oecd.org/

LongAbstract/0,3425,en_2649_34129_2672752_119669_1_1_37405,00. html.

Partnership for 21st Century Skills. n.d. "Civic Literacy." Partnership for 21st Century Skills. Retrieved December 31, 2011, from http://www.p21.org/ overview/skills-framework/258.

Pateman, Carole. 1970. *Participation and Democratic Theory.* Cambridge University Press.

Pennsylvania State University Public Broadcasting. 2002. *Digital Alliances— Partnerships in Public Service: Models for Collaboration,* Benton Foundation. Retrieved December 31, 2011, from http://www.benton.org/publibrary/ partners/pips.pdf.

Preer, Jean. 1993. "The American Heritage Project: Librarians and the Democratic Tradition in the Early Cold War," *Libraries and Culture* 28 (2) Spring: pp. 166–188.

Preer, Jean. 2001. "Exploring the American Idea at the New York Public Library." *American Studies* 42 (3) Fall: pp. 135–154.

Preer, Jean. 2008. "Promoting Citizenship: How Librarians Helped Get Out the Vote in the 1952 Election," *Libraries and the Cultural Record* 43 (1) Spring: pp. 1–28.

Project on Civic Reflection. n.d. *The Civically Engaged Reader,* Project on Civic Reflection. Retrieved December 31, 2011, from http://civicreflection.org.

Public Agenda. 2006. *Long Overdue: A Fresh Look at Public and Leadership Attitudes About Libraries in the 21st Century.* Public Agenda. Retrieved December 30, 2011, from http://www.publicagenda.org/reports/long-overdue.

Putnam, Robert. 2000. *Bowling Alone: The Collapse and Revival of American Community.* Simon & Schuster.

Putnam, Robert, and Lewis M. Feldstein. 2003. "Branch Libraries: The Heartbeat of the Community," in *Better Together: Restoring the American Community.*: Simon & Schuster: pp. 34–54.

Riddle, John. 2003. "Where's the Library in Service Learning? Models for Engaged Library Instruction." *Journal of Academic Librarianship* 29, March: pp. 71–81.

Roy, Loriene, Kelly Jensen, and Alex Hershey Meyers, eds. 2009. *Service Learning: Linking Library Education and Practice.* American Library Association.

Schenck-Hamlin, Donna, Bill Schenck-Hamlin, Timothy Steffensmeier, and Phillip Marzluf. 2010. "Employing Deliberative Polling in a University Classroom: Results of a Pilot Test." *Institute for Civic Discourse and Democracy Working Paper.* Kansas State University.

Schudson, Michael. 1998. *The Good Citizen: A History of American Civic Life.* Free Press.

Schudson, Michael. 2003. "Click Here for Democracy: A History and Critique of an Information-Based Model of Citizenship," in *Democracy and New Media,* ed. by Henry Jenkins and David Thorburn. MIT Press: pp. 49–59.

Schugurensky, Daniel. 2006. "This Is Our School for Citizenship: Informal Learning in Local Democracy," in Svi Bekerman, Nicholas Burbeules, and Diana

Silberman-Keller (eds.) *Learning in Places: The Informal Education Reader*: p. 249. Peter Lang.

Schull, Diantha. 2004. "The Civic Library: A Model for 21st Century Participation." *Advances in Librarianship* 28: pp. 55–82.

The September Project: Connecting the World One Library at a Time. n.d. Web Site. Retrieved December 31, 2011, from http://theseptemberproject.org/join.

Skocpol, Theda. 1999. *Civic Engagement in American Democracy*. Brookings Institution.

Thomas, Nancy. 2007. "Why It Is Imperative to Strengthen American Democracy Through Study, Dialogue, and Change in Higher Education," Catalyst Paper 1, The Democracy Imperative. Retrieved December 31, 2011, from http://www.unh.edu/democracy/catalyst-papers.html.

Tocqueville, Alexis de, 1835. *Democracy in America.*

U.S. President's Commission on Higher Education for Democracy. 1947. *Higher Education for Democracy*. Government Printing Office.

Urban Libraries Council. 2005. *The Engaged Library: Chicago Stories of Community Building*. Urban Libraries Council. Retrieved December 30, 2011, from http://urbanlibraries.org/displaycommon.cfm?an=1&subarticlenbr=553.

Urban Libraries Council. 2011. "Library Priority: Community Civic Engagement, Leadership Brief." Urban Libraries Council. Retrieved December 30, 2011, from http://urbanlibraries.org/displaycommon.cfm?an=1&subarticlenbr=553

Urban School. n.d. "About Us." San Francisco: The Urban School. Retrieved December 31, 2011, from http://www.urbanschool.org/page.cfm?p=2.

Verba, Sidney, Kay Scholzman, and Henry Brady. 1995. *Voice and Equality: Civic Voluntarism in American Politics*. Harvard University Press.

Walling, Donovan. 2007. "The Return of Civic Education," *Phi Delta Kappan* 89 (04), December: pp. 285–289.

Westbrook, Robert B. 1991. *John Dewey and American Democracy*. Cornell University Press.

Westney, Lynn. 2006. "Conspicuous by Their Absence: Academic Librarians in the Engaged University," *Reference & User Services Quarterly* 45 (3), Spring: pp. 200–203.

Williams, Karen. 2009. "A Framework for Articulating New Library Roles." *Research Library Issues: A Bimonthly Report from ARL, CNI, and SPARC*, no. 265. August: pp. 3–8. Retrieved December 30, 2011, from http://www.arl.org/resources/pubs/rli/archive/rli265.shtml.

Yankelovich, Daniel. 1991. *Coming to Public Judgment: Making Democracy Work in a Complex World*. Syracuse University Press.

Yankelovich, Daniel. 1999. *The Magic of Dialogue*. Simon & Schuster.

Yankelovich, Daniel, and Will Friedman, eds. 2010. *Toward Wiser Public Judgment*. Vanderbilt University Press.

Notes

1. The term civic engagement takes many forms, but for this paper, a definition from the American Psychological Association will pertain: "Individual and collective actions designed to identify and address issues of public concern." (APA n.d.).

2. Henry Milner defines civic literacy as "the knowledge and ability of citizens to make sense of their world and to act as competent citizens" (2002, p. 3). The Partnership for 21st Century Skills (n.d.) considers civic literacy: (1) Participating effectively in civic life through knowing how to stay informed and understanding governmental processes; (2) Exercising the rights and obligations of citizenship at local, state, national and global levels; and (3) Understanding the local and global implications of civic decisions.

3. Harry Boyte (2007, 2009) uses the term "civic agency" to mean: "the capacity of human communities and groups to act cooperatively and collectively on common problems across their differences of view."

Federal Agency and
Federal Library Reports

Library of Congress

10 First St. S.E., Washington, DC 20540
202-707-5000
World Wide Web http://www.loc.gov

James H. Billington
Librarian of Congress

Founded in 1800, the Library of Congress is the nation's oldest federal cultural institution and the largest library in the world, with more than 151 million items in various languages, disciplines, and formats. As the world's largest repository of knowledge and creativity, the library's mission is to support the Congress in fulfilling its constitutional duties and to further the progress of knowledge and creativity for the benefit of the American people.

The library's collections are housed in its three buildings on Capitol Hill, and in special climate-controlled facilities for books at Fort Meade, Maryland, and for audiovisual materials at the Packard Campus in Culpeper, Virginia. The library also provides global access to its resources through its award-winning Web site, http://www.loc.gov.

Legislative Support to Congress

Serving Congress is the library's highest priority, particularly in the area of legislative support. The library provides legislative support to Congress through the Congressional Research Service (CRS), the Law Library, and the U.S. Copyright Office.

During the past year CRS delivered to Congress an array of products focused on the key public-policy issues deemed likely to be on the legislative agenda. CRS supported Congress with policy analyses as it considered increasingly complex domestic legislative issues such as national security, economic stimulus and job creation, employment and training, unemployment compensation, food safety, transportation, and judicial nominations. In the area of foreign affairs, CRS supported congressional debate on U.S. relations with China, continuing unrest in the Middle East, military operations in Iraq, Afghanistan, and Libya, and foreign assistance programs.

Report compiled by Audrey Fischer, Public Affairs Specialist, Library of Congress.

CRS worked with others in the library to provide for the next generation of the Legislative Information System (LIS), which was developed by the library more than a decade ago for use by Congress and congressional staff members. CRS developed a Web-based Text Analysis Program (TAP) to identify similarities in congressional bills. A complement to LIS, TAP provides rankings of bills according to individual searches within a specific Congress (dating back to the 103rd Congress). CRS also launched a new feature on its Web site that makes it easier for Congress to place requests online, track policy issues, receive notifications of new products, and register for CRS events.

The Law Library provided Congress with comprehensive international, comparative, and foreign law research based on the most current information available from the world's largest law library, comprising 2.8 million volumes. During the year Law Library staff prepared 373 legal research reports, special studies, and memoranda in response to congressional inquiries. Foreign law specialists provided foreign and comparative law reports relating to U.S. legislative issues including banking, citizenship, cybersecurity, government procurement, immigration, marriage, mining, nuclear power, taxation, and terrorism.

The *Global Legal Monitor*, a continually updated online publication that covers legal news and developments worldwide, remained a popular page on the Law Library's Web site. At year's end the publication had more than 16,000 subscribers. In its first year the Law Library's blog, "In Custodia Legis," had 15,000 subscribers.

The Global Legal Information Network (GLIN) provided Congress and other participating parliamentary bodies with more than 200,000 laws, judicial decisions, and related legal materials contributed by 38 member nations and international organizations. In 2011 more than 13,000 legal materials were added to the GLIN database. Legal information analysts at the Law Library added more than 1,800 laws to the database for 16 nations outside the network.

During the year the Law Library completed an eight-year business plan for the One World Law Library (OWLL), which will be accessible at http://www.law. gov. The site will serve as a repository for global legal and legislative information and use emerging technologies for search-and-retrieval of content contained in divergent information sources.

The U.S. Copyright Office provided policy advice and technical assistance to Congress on important copyright laws and related issues. On March 14, 2011, acting Register of Copyrights Maria Pallante testified before the House Judiciary Subcommittee on Intellectual Property, Competition, and the Internet. The hearing's subject was "Promoting Investment and Protecting Commerce Online: Legitimate Sites v. Parasites." Pallante discussed the need to protect legitimate commerce from rogue Web sites that sell pirated copies of copyrighted works such as books, feature films, television programs, and music.

Pallante, who assumed the position of Copyright Register on June 1, testified that day before the House Judiciary Subcommittee at its hearing on illegal streaming of television, motion pictures, and other copyrighted works. The hearing also explored the current impediments to effective prosecution of those who infringe on the right to publicly perform such works by willfully streaming them worldwide. She testified in support of a legislative proposal that would elevate the penalties for the latter, recognizing that as streaming has become a viable business model for legitimate content distribution, it has also become a mechanism for large-scale infringement.

Security

The security of the library's staff, visitors, facilities, and collections is of paramount importance. The focus of the Office of Security and Emergency Preparedness in 2011 was placed on enhancing the emergency-preparedness program, improving security at the library's Capitol Hill buildings and outlying facilities, and strengthening its personnel-security programs.

Work continued to develop a Continuity of Operations (COOP) management site from which key library personnel can operate in the event Capitol Hill facilities are compromised. Emergency planners, logistics staff, and information-technology teams finalized the installation of enhanced voice and data systems, secure storage for sensitive equipment, and outfitting of senior management workstations.

The library continued to improve its electronic and physical security controls to safeguard its priceless collections and assets in all library buildings on Capitol Hill. Important security projects were completed at the library's off-site facilities, including Modules 3 and 4 at Fort Meade.

The Information Technology Security (ITS) program ensures that the library's mission-critical systems are reliable and secure and that the technology infrastructure that supports these systems is uncompromised. The library's technology infrastructure includes four data centers, more than 650 servers, 250 enterprise systems and applications, and wide-area, metropolitan-area, and local-area networks that consist of 350 network devices. The data centers house more than 3.8 terabytes of disk storage and over 6.5 petabytes of tape storage. ITS also supports more than 8,400 voice connections, 11,000 data network connections, and 5,300 workstations.

Strategic Planning

The library made significant progress during the year in implementing its Strategic Plan for fiscal years 2011 through 2016 and the related planning and budgeting framework. The plan describes the library's goals and strategies for serving Congress and the American people and demonstrates the organization's commitment to the Government Performance and Results Act. The framework integrates planning and budgeting processes, adds rigor to the library's planning and budgeting activities, and enhances the organization's ability to measure progress toward achieving the plan's outcomes and goals.

In April 2011 the library published the fiscal 2011 Library of Congress Annual Plan. Annual objectives define the first set of incremental steps toward achieving the intended results of the Strategic Plan. Detailed performance targets, standards, and milestones for each of these annual objectives improve the library's ability to establish clear lines of accountability for meeting the goals of the Strategic Plan as well as tracking and measuring progress toward achieving results.

Budget

On April 15, 2011, President Barack Obama signed the fiscal 2011 spending agreement [P.L. 112-10], which enacted a full-year continuing resolution and budgetary realignment for the Library of Congress. The act provided an appropriation for the library of $671.5 million, including authority to spend up to $42.9 million in offsetting receipts.

Development

During fiscal 2011 the library's fund-raising activities brought in a total of $11.3 million, representing 706 gifts from 571 donors. Those gifts, including $235,650 received through planned gifts, were made to 63 library initiatives. The library forged partnerships with 292 first-time donors. New donors gave $3.1 million, representing 27 percent of the gifts received during the year.

Private gifts supported a variety of new and continuing initiatives throughout the library, including exhibitions, acquisitions, symposia, and other scholarly programs. Donors committed $2.7 million to create a Residential Scholars Center to provide convenient, affordable accommodations for students, teachers, and researchers.

Gifts from the James Madison Council—the library's private sector advisory group—in fiscal 2011 totaled more than $4.6 million, bringing the council's total support since 1990 to more than $203 million. Gifts from the council supported the "Gateway to Knowledge" traveling exhibition, the World Digital Library, the National Book Festival, and the Junior Fellows Summer Intern Program.

Target Corp., the *Washington Post,* Wells Fargo & Co., and a host of contributors gave nearly $1.2 million to support the 2011 National Book Festival. David M. Rubenstein added $1.3 million for the year, of which $300,000 was given specifically to allow the event to become a two-day festival. (In 2010 he announced the award of $5 million over five years to support this event.)

Educational Outreach

The library's Educational Outreach Office makes its online resources useful and accessible to teachers and students through the Teachers Page (http://www.loc.gov/teachers) and through its Teaching with Primary Sources (TPS) program. During the year, TPS provided professional development to more than 19,000 teachers throughout the country. The TPS Educational Consortium grew to 28 educational institutions delivering professional development to educators in 17 states. Through the TPS Regional Program, 152 organizations delivered TPS programming to teachers in 36 states and the District of Columbia. Held at the library, the TPS Summer Teacher Institute taught 150 educators from 31 states how best to use the library's digitized primary sources in the classroom. In 2011 the program was expanded from four to five days. The Educational Outreach Office collaborated with PBS Teacherline in launching a 45-hour online course titled "Teaching with Primary Sources from the Library of Congress." Nearly 200 teachers across the country have completed the course. More than 100 educators from 13 states attended teacher institutes focused on the primary resources on display in "The Last Full Measure," the library's Civil War exhibition.

The Teachers Page—the library's home for teacher resources—was augmented with primary sources and teaching guides about the New Deal; the Harlem Renaissance; maps from the World Digital Library; political cartoons in U.S. history; children's lives at the turn of the 20th century; Washington, Jefferson, and Lincoln; and U.S. symbols.

Literacy Promotion

The Library of Congress promotes reading and literacy through the Center for the Book, the National Book Festival, collaborative public-service advertising campaigns, the appointment of a National Ambassador for Young People's Literature, and through its popular literacy-promotion Web site, http://www.Read.gov.

With its network of affiliates in all 50 states and more than 80 organizational partners, the Center for the Book led the library's reading-promotion efforts. During the year the center reprised its national signature projects, Letters about Literature and River of Words, which inspire young people to write about how books have changed their lives. The center also provided oversight for the Read.gov Web site. Read.gov is supported by an advertising campaign directed by the library's Public Affairs Office in cooperation with the private, nonprofit Advertising Council. Since its launch in September 2009, the site has featured multimedia resources designed specifically for children, teens, parents, and educators. A highlight of the Read.gov site is the exclusive serial story, "The Exquisite Corpse Adventure," a project of the Center for the Book and the National Children's Book and Literacy Alliance (NCBLA). The online story grew to include 27 episodes by 16 different authors and five illustrators. The work was published in its entirety by Candlewick Press in August 2011.

In collaboration with the Children's Book Council (CBC) and the CBC Foundation, and with support from publishers, the center sponsors the National Ambassador for Young People's Literature. Children's author Katherine Paterson held the post throughout 2011—the second year of her two-year appointment that began in January 2010. [For more on the center's activities, see the following article, "Center for the Book"—*Ed.*]

To reach out to children and teens, the library opened a Young Readers Center in its Thomas Jefferson Building in October 2009. Visitors can choose to read a book from an up-to-date collection of noncirculating titles, they can browse the Web's child-friendly sites, or they can attend programs especially designed for young readers. In its second fiscal year in operation, the Young Readers Center attracted more than 29,000 visitors. The collection was enhanced with the donation of juvenile-interest books by Diane Roback, children's book editor at *Publishers Weekly*.

On March 2, 2011, the library played host to the National Education Association's 14th Annual Read Across America Day. First Lady Michelle Obama and U.S. Secretary of Education Arne Duncan were among guests at the event, which marked the 107th anniversary of the birth of author Theodor Seuss Geisel (Dr. Seuss). The first lady, Duncan, and National Education Association President Dennis Van Roekel joined Librarian of Congress James H. Billington in the library's Great Hall for the event, designed to highlight the importance of reading. Local schoolchildren were greeted by costumed characters the Cat and the Hat and Things 1 and 2, and treated to storytelling by actress Jessica Alba, "Top Chef" Padma Lakshmi, and Green Bay Packers receiver Donald Driver.

Collections

During 2011 the size of the library's collections grew to 151.7 million items, an increase of 4.6 million from the previous year. This figure included more than 34.5 million cataloged books and other print materials, 66.5 million manuscripts, 16.6 million microforms, 5.4 million maps, 6.5 million pieces of sheet music, 15.4 million visual materials (photographs, posters, moving images, prints, and drawings), 3.4 million audio materials, and more than 1 million items in miscellaneous formats.

Important Acquisitions

The library receives millions of items each year from copyright deposits, federal agencies, and purchases, exchanges, and gifts.

In 2011 the Copyright Office forwarded to the library more than 700,000 copies of works with a net value estimated at $31 million. About half were received from publishers under the mandatory-deposit provisions of the copyright law. The library also received the first 300 electronic serial issues obtained through the eDeposit program that provides for the receipt of electronic serials demanded under copyright law.

Significant acquisitions made possible by the Madison Council included correspondence and other materials documenting the life of American composer and conductor Leonard Bernstein and Agostino Tofanelli's *View of Rome,* a four-volume set of books, completed in 1833, for the library's Rare Book and Special Collections Division. Madison Council member David M. Rubenstein purchased and gave the library stewardship of Abel Buell's rare and historically significant map, "A New and Correct Map of the United States of North America Layd [sic] Down from the Latest Observations and Best Authorities Agreeable to the Peace of 1783." Published shortly after the Treaty of Paris ended the Revolutionary War, it is the first map of the new American nation and the first to depict the Stars and Stripes.

The library also acquired many significant items and collections by gift or purchase, including the following:

- Ten American silent films from Gosfilmofond, the state film archive of Russia, of which no known copies existed in the United States
- Two volumes of an extraordinarily rare 1478 edition of the *Casus breves* of Johannes de Turnhout (c. 1446–1492), the first example of case law in legal history
- A gift of 200,000 master disc and tape recordings from the Universal Music Group, the library's first significant acquisition of commercial master recordings
- A total of 130,569 items from the Ira and Leonore Gershwin Trust in San Francisco, which tripled the library's preeminent Gershwin Collection

- A collection of 10,000 set designs, sketches, and drawings from the estate of theatrical designer Oliver Smith
- Scripts, correspondence, photographs, and other items from the estate of actor and singer John Raitt, including papers from the original Broadway productions of "Carousel" and "The Pajama Game"
- Courtroom drawings by Marilyn Church, including thousands of color sketches depicting notable trials of the late 20th century
- The John Miley Sports Broadcast Collection of thousands of rare radio sports broadcasts captured prior to 1972
- The *Difesa di Galileo Galilei* (Venice: J. Baglioni, 1607), Galileo's second book and his first work on astronomy

Cataloging

The library cataloged 524,812 new works in 2011. Production of full- and standard-level original cataloging totaled 225,314 bibliographic records. The library and other member institutions of the international Program for Cooperative Cataloging created 339,104 name and series authority records, and 11,444 subject authorities. The library served as secretariat for the program and created 110,637 of the name and series authority records and 8,624 of the subject authorities. Dewey Decimal Classification numbers were assigned to 86,712 titles as a service to other libraries throughout the world that use that system to organize their collections.

Bibliographic Control and Standards

The Library of Congress, along with the National Library of Medicine and the National Agricultural Library, coordinated the testing of the new cataloging standard Resource Description and Access (RDA). Approximately 26 institutions conducted RDA tests between July 1 and December 31, 2010. A coordinating committee led by the library's director for acquisitions and bibliographic access analyzed the test results and questionnaire responses and submitted its report on May 9 to the senior management of the three U.S. national libraries. The decision to implement RDA jointly, no earlier than January 2013, was announced on June 13, 2011. The intervening period will allow time to fulfill a list of recommendations based on test findings.

Reference Services

In addition to serving Congress, the library provides reference services to the public in its reading rooms and through its Web site. During the year, library staff handled more than 508,000 reference requests received in person, over the telephone, and through written and electronic correspondence. The library's digital reference staff also responded to more than 16,000 questions posed by patrons using the Ask a Librarian feature on the library's Web site. Nearly 1.1 million items were circulated for use within the library.

In its second year of operation, a total of 34,879 new on-site patrons were registered in the automated Reader Registration System, bringing the total to more than 105,000 since its inception in April 2009.

Work continued on an upgrade to the Automated Call Slip system. The system allows patrons in the library's reading rooms to request library materials from the general collections through the library's online public access catalog, instead of using paper call slips. The upgraded system will be implemented early in the next fiscal year.

During the year the library added 384 new encoded archival description (EAD) finding aids to its redesigned search system at http://www.loc.gov/finding aids. The system offers 1,480 finding aids to more than 43.2 million archival items in the library's Manuscript, Music, American Folklife Center, Prints and Photographs, and Motion Picture, Broadcasting, and Recorded Sound divisions, and other Library of Congress research centers.

Online Resources

Through the National Digital Library program and digitization efforts of several of its divisions, the library has been adding high-quality digital content to its award-winning Web site, http://www.loc.gov. Consistently recognized as one of the top federal sites, the Web site recorded 73.4 million visits and 512 million page-views in 2011.

The library's Web site gives users access to the institution's vast resources, including its online catalog, selected collections in various formats, copyright and legislative information, webcasts and podcasts of library events, and exhibitions. Special presentations are dedicated to the achievements of African Americans, Asians, Hispanics, Jews, women, and veterans.

As a portal to the library's 31.4 million online primary source files, the Wise Guide (http://www.loc.gov/wiseguide) continued to introduce new and returning users to the library's Web site. The site is updated monthly with a series of articles containing links to the library's online resources.

Also accessible on the Web site is the public legislative information system known as THOMAS (http://thomas.loc.gov), which tracks federal legislation. THOMAS received 10.3 million visits during the year. The Law Library implemented numerous improvements to THOMAS, making it significantly easier to find and access legislative action.

By subscribing to the library's RSS feeds and e-mail update service, users can stay up-to-date about areas of the library's site that interest them. To sign up for either service, visit http:/www.loc.gov/rss.

The library continued to promote its activities by producing podcasts and making them accessible on its Web site at http://www.loc.gov/podcasts. The podcasts include interviews conducted with authors participating in the National Book Festival. Webcasts of selected lectures, readings, conferences, and symposia held at the library were also added to the site at http://www.loc.gov/webcasts.

Web 2.0

To develop new communication channels and new relationships, to reach new audiences, and to experiment with and explore new technologies, the Library of

Congress continued to participate in media-sharing and social networking sites such as YouTube, iTunes U, Facebook, Twitter, and Flickr. Videos added to the library's YouTube channel included the 2011 National Book Festival, selected concerts, and a series on "Hidden Treasures of the Library of Congress." New educational content on Library's iTunes U site includes the 2011 National Book Festival, collections from the Veterans History Project and Civil War sheet music. In addition to its main Facebook site, the library supports Facebook pages for the Law Library, American Folklife Center, and the National Digital Information Infrastructure and Preservation Program. The library's Twitter presence includes feeds for the World Digital Library, the digital preservation program, THOMAS, the Congressional Research Service, Copyright issues and maps. A live Twitterfall could be viewed by attendees of the 2011 National Book Festival.

The library's main blog—among the first federal blogs at the time of its launch on April 24, 2007—has since been joined by blogs generated by the library's Music Division, Science and Technology Division, and Law Library at http://blogs. loc.gov. In fiscal 2011 new blogs were introduced by the National Digital Preservation Program, the Prints and Photographs Division, and the Education Outreach office. The library also added more than 3,500 images to its Flickr site at http:// www.flickr.com/photos/library_of_congress. The library's blog site contains links to all library Web 2.0 sites.

Global Access

The Library of Congress acquires global resources through cooperative agreements and exchanges with other nations, through its overseas offices, and through the World Digital Library initiative. The overseas offices collect and catalog materials from 86 countries in some 150 languages and 25 scripts, from Africa, Asia, Latin America, and the Middle East. These items are accessible in the library's area studies reading rooms. Selected items have been digitized—many through cooperative digitizing projects—and are accessible on the library's Web site.

Overseas Offices

The library's six overseas offices (in Rio de Janeiro, Cairo, New Delhi, Jakarta, Nairobi, and Islamabad) acquired, cataloged, and preserved materials from parts of the world where the book and information industries are not well developed. These offices brought in and distributed 291,805 items to the library and, on a cost-recovery basis, provided 385,132 items to other U.S. libraries.

During 2011 the library commissioned the Council of American Overseas Research Centers (CAORC) to test a new model for acquiring materials from difficult-to-access regions of the world. CAORC, with its network, tested the acquisition model in the 11 francophone countries of sub-Saharan West Africa. In its first year of operation, the project yielded 1,355 titles for cataloging, including many titles that were published in regional areas of West Africa.

World Digital Library

Launched in April 2009, the World Digital Library (WDL) Web site (http://www. wdl.org) makes available significant primary materials in various formats from cultures around the world. Its collections are available on the Internet free of charge and in multilingual format. Since its inception, there have been nearly 18 million visits to the site, comprising 116 million page views. Of the seven WDL interface languages (Arabic, Chinese, English, French, Portuguese, Russian, and Spanish), Spanish was the most heavily used, followed by English.

During 2011 work focused on recruiting additional partners and adding content. At year's end 135 partners from 72 countries were participating in the project. The first meeting of the WDL Executive Council took place at UNESCO in January 2011. The council endorsed a long-term plan developed by the Library of Congress that includes targets for collections to be added and cites the need to recruit partners in countries and regions of the world that currently are underrepresented in WDL. Efforts are being made to build a global audience of users through outreach efforts to teachers, students, and researchers.

Noteworthy content added to the WDL site during the year from partner institutions included translations of Arabic scientific works printed in Venice in the late 1400s (from the Central Library, Qatar Foundation); Korean manuscripts from the 15th to the early 19th century (National Library of Korea); 18th- and 19th-century Persian manuscripts (University of Kashmir, India); Matteo Ricci's 1602 map of the world in Chinese (James Bell Ford Library, University of Minnesota); and classic works of western science (Smithsonian Institution). Also added were outstanding items from the international collections of the Library of Congress, including rare Chinese books, late-19th-century photochromes, Japanese prints, and the Prokudin-Gorskii collection of early color photographs of the Russian Empire.

A key objective of the WDL project is to build digital library capabilities in the developing world. In support of this objective, the Library of Congress provided technical assistance and training to a number of library partners around the world. In exchange, the library received high-quality digital images of books, manuscripts, and other materials for inclusion on the WDL Web site.

Preservation

Preserving its unparalleled collections—from cuneiform tablets to born-digital items—is one of the library's major activities in support of its vision to further human understanding and wisdom. During the year nearly 10.7 million items from the library's collections were bound, repaired, mass-deacidified, microfilmed or otherwise reformatted. The Preservation Directorate surveyed the preservation needs of nearly 548,000 items from the library's general and special collections, including books, photographs, maps, audiovisual materials, and other formats. Of these, nearly 292,000 items were housed in protective containers.

The library announced Twitter's donation of its digital archive of public tweets on April 14, 2010. In December 2010 Twitter identified the company Gnip as its agent for the transfer of tweets to the library. From January to June 2011, the library and Gnip tested the packaging and transfer of files. In September the library's Twitter accessioning application went into production. At the end of the fiscal year, more than 24 billion public tweets had been transferred to the library's custodial care.

Books

The library transferred 354,154 items to its climate-controlled off-site storage facility at Fort Meade, during the year, bringing the total there to more than 3.9 million collection items. Fiscal 2011 additions to the facility included 235,569 books and 118,585 special-format materials such as more than 81,000 reels of microfilm masters.

The library continued to sustain the book digitization program, which was initially created with a grant of $2 million from the Alfred P. Sloan Foundation to address at-risk "brittle books" in the library's public domain general collection. The scanning facilities are shared by the library with other federal libraries through a FedLink master contract. The scanned materials are accessible for reading online or for download on the Internet Archive's Web site. In fiscal 2011, some 28,000 volumes in the public domain general collections were scanned, comprising 5 million pages. This brought the total to 116,000 volumes comprising 21.8 million pages since the project's inception.

The library joined other research library partners as a member of the HathiTrust, a digital repository for the books scanned by American libraries. The library submitted more than 67,000 digitized volumes to this shared online collection. All of these works were pre-1923 American imprints, and thus in the public domain and freely available on the Internet. The library has participated in the establishment of governance and planning for the trust as it has grown in size and significance in the research community. At year's end, the HathiTrust comprised more than 9 million digital volumes.

Newspapers

The Library of Congress, in partnership with the National Endowment for the Humanities, is participating with the National Digital Newspaper Program in a project to digitize and provide free and public access to American newspapers that are in the public domain. During 2011 the number of state projects contributing digitized content grew to 28, and 200 new newspaper titles were added to the project. At year's end the Web site comprised 4.3 million pages. Since March 2007 the library has been making this material accessible on the Chronicling America Web site, a free, national searchable database of historic American newspaper pages published between 1860 and 1922. A redesign of the site was launched in May. The site hosted more than 2.4 million visits and provided 23 million page views during the year.

Photographs

More than 1.2 million of the library's nearly 14 million photographs have been digitized and are accessible on the library's Prints and Photographs Online Catalog at http://www.loc.gov/pictures. Cataloging records exist for approximately 95 percent of the division's holdings. During the year the library added more than 3,500 new photos to its Flickr account, including new sets of images on subjects such as the Civil War and World War I. Through this media-sharing site, the public is assisting the library in identifying people, places, and scenes depicted in these images.

Maps

The library reached a milestone during the year with the digitization of its 30,000th map. Working amid giant scanners, the staff of the library's Geography and Map Division digitized and placed online the record-breaking item—the Berks County, Pennsylvania, land ownership atlas from 1862, one of the earliest known county land-ownership atlases produced in the United States.

The library's online maps include some of the world's great cartographic treasures, such as the 1507 Waldseemüller World Map—the first map to show the word "America"—and, most recently, Abel Buell's "A New and Correct Map of the United States of North America Layd Down from the Latest Observations and Best Authorities Agreeable to the Peace of 1783." During the year the Preservation Directorate began working to design a protective anoxic display case for the rare map. The case will be tailored to reduce damage to the map by prolonged exposure to light.

Audiovisual Collections

Opened in July 2007, the library's Packard Campus for Audio Visual Conservation in Culpeper, Virginia, consolidated the library's sound, film, and video collections—the world's largest and most comprehensive—previously housed in library buildings in four states and the District of Columbia.

Philanthropist David Woodley Packard and the Packard Humanities Institute donated the state-of-the-art facility, the largest-ever private gift to the legislative branch of the U.S. government. The $155 million facility was financed jointly by the gift from Packard and appropriations from Congress totaling $82.1 million.

The Packard Campus comprises a collections building, where 5.7 million items (1.2 million moving images, nearly 3 million sound recordings, and 1.5 million related items, such as manuscripts, posters, and screenplays) are housed under ideal conditions; a conservation building, where the collections are acquired, managed, and preserved; and a separate facility with 124 vaults where combustible nitrate films can be stored safely. Researchers in the library's related reading rooms on Capitol Hill will be able to access derivative copies of the digital files through high-speed fiber-optic connections from Culpeper.

During fiscal 2011 the Packard Campus Film Laboratory processed 1,360 original reels of nitrate film—more than double the amount processed the previous year. Each reel of original nitrate film was inspected, cleaned, and hand-repaired prior to transfer to safety-preservation copies. More than 33,000 recorded sound and moving image collections were digitally preserved.

Films

It is estimated that half of the films produced before 1950 and 80 percent to 90 percent of those made before 1920 have disappeared forever. The Library of Congress is working with many organizations to prevent such losses and to preserve motion pictures through the National Film Registry. Under the terms of the National Film Preservation Act of 1992, the Librarian of Congress—with advice from the National Film Preservation Board—began selecting 25 films annually for the National Film Registry, to be preserved for all time. The films are chosen based on whether they are "culturally, historically, or aesthetically significant." The library works to ensure that registry films are preserved by its staff or through collaboration with other archives, motion-picture studios, and independent filmmakers.

A new documentary, *These Amazing Shadows,* tells the story of the library's National Film Registry, an effort to preserve the nation's film heritage. With sequences shot in the Jefferson Building and at the library's Packard Campus for Audio Visual Conservation, the documentary features interviews with members of the library staff and clips from nearly 200 classic films on the registry. The film, which debuted at the Sundance Film Festival in January 2011, won press attention, as did the library's December 28, 2011, announcement of the following additions to the National Film Registry, which brought the total of films on the list to 575:

Allures (1961)
Bambi (1942)
The Big Heat (1953)
A Computer Animated Hand (1972)
Crisis: Behind a Presidential Commitment (1963)
The Cry of the Children (1912)
A Cure for Pokeritis (1912)
El Mariachi (1992)
Faces (1968)
Fake Fruit Factory (1986)
Forrest Gump (1994)
Growing Up Female (1971)
Hester Street (1975)
I, an Actress (1977)
The Iron Horse (1924)
The Kid (1921)
The Lost Weekend (1945)
The Negro Soldier (1944)
Nicholas Brothers Family Home Movies (1930s–1940s)
Norma Rae (1979)
Porgy and Bess (1959)
The Silence of the Lambs (1991)
Stand and Deliver (1988)
Twentieth Century (1934)
War of the Worlds (1953)

Sound Recordings

Sound preservation got a boost in 2011 with the launch of the library's National Jukebox at a May 10 news conference featuring a performance by Grammy-winning pianist, singer, and actor Harry Connick, Jr. The interactive Web site (http://www.loc.gov/jukebox) allows users to play thousands of historic sound recordings—many of them unavailable to the public for more than a century. More than 1 million visits to the site were recorded within its first two days. Developed by the library, with assets provided by Sony Music Entertainment, the National Jukebox offers free online access to more than 10,000 out-of-print music and spoken-word recordings produced in the United States between the years 1901 and 1925.

The agreement for the National Jukebox grants the Library of Congress usage rights to Sony Music's entire pre-1925 catalog—comprising thousands of recordings produced by Columbia Records, OKeh, and Victor Talking Machine Co., among others, and represents the largest collection of such historical recordings ever made publicly available for study and appreciation online. Visitors to the National Jukebox can listen to available recordings on a streaming-only basis, as well as view thousands of label images, record-catalog illustrations, and artist and performer biographies. In addition, users can access interactive features, listening to playlists developed by library staff and creating and sharing their own playlists.

The National Recording Preservation Act of 2000 tasks the Librarian of Congress with annually choosing recordings that are "culturally, historically or aesthetically significant." In April 2011 the following 25 sound recordings were added to the National Recording Registry, bringing the total to 325:

Phonautograms recorded by Édouard-Léon Scott de Martinville (c. 1853–1861)

"Take Me Out to the Ballgame," Edward Meeker, accompanied by the Edison Orchestra (1908)

Cylinder recordings of Ishi (1911–1914)

"Dark Was the Night, Cold Was the Ground," Blind Willie Johnson (1927)

"It's the Girl," Boswell Sisters with the Dorsey Brothers Orchestra (1931)

"Mal Hombre," Lydia Mendoza (1934)

"Tumbling Tumbleweeds," Sons of the Pioneers (1934)

"Talking Union," Almanac Singers (1941)

"Jazz at the Philharmonic" (July 2, 1944)

"Pope Marcellus Mass" (Palestrina), Roger Wagner Chorale (1951)

"The Eagle Stirreth Her Nest," Rev. C. L. Franklin (1953)

"Tipitina," Professor Longhair (1953)

"At Sunset," Mort Sahl (1955)

Interviews with Jazz Musicians for the Voice of America, Willis Conover (1956)

"Music from 'Peter Gunn,'" Henry Mancini (1959)

United Sacred Harp Musical Convention in Fyffe, Alabama, field recordings by Alan Lomax and Shirley Collins (1959)

"Blind Joe Death," John Fahey (1959, 1964, 1967)

"Stand by Your Man," Tammy Wynette (1968)

"Trout Mask Replica," Captain Beefheart and His Magic Band (1969)

"Songs of the Humpback Whale," (1970)

"Let's Stay Together," Al Green (1971)

"Black Angels (Thirteen Images from the Dark Land)," George Crumb, CRI Recordings (1972)

"Aja," Steely Dan (1977)

"3 Feet High and Rising," De La Soul (1989)

GOPAC Strategy and Instructional Tapes (1986–1994)

Oral History

The library's American Folklife Center continued its mandate to "preserve and present American folklife" through a number of outreach and oral history programs such as the Veterans History Project and StoryCorps.

Established by Congress in 2000, the Veterans History Project (VHP) is a major program of the center. For more than a decade, this oral history program has preserved the memories of those who served in the nation's armed services and others who shared America's wartime experience in the 20th and early 21st centuries.

In 2011 the project collected more than 5,000 personal recollections from across the nation, bringing the total to more than 78,000. In May 2011 the project reached a milestone by digitizing its 10,000th collection, making these recorded interviews, photographs, letters, and other historical documents fully accessible on the Internet. The milestone collection was from World War II Coast Guard veteran George A. Travers. Special presentations added to the site during the year honored military aviators and military chaplains. Selected content from the VHP Web site is also accessible on iTunes U.

StoryCorps, launched in 2003 by MacArthur Fellow Dave Isay and his award-winning documentary company, Sound Portraits Productions, is one of the nation's largest oral narrative projects. Isay was inspired by the Works Progress Administration's (WPA's) Federal Writers' Project of the 1930s, which recorded oral history interviews with everyday Americans across the country. In fiscal 2011 more than 7,400 audio files of interviews were added to the StoryCorps collection, bringing the total to more than 40,000 housed in the American Folklife Center. In addition to weekly broadcasts on National Public Radio's "Morning Edition," selected StoryCorps stories are available as downloadable podcasts.

In its first year of operation, the Historias mobile booth gathered contemporary personal narrative recordings of Latinos and Latinas in 20 cities in the United States and Puerto Rico. The recorded oral narratives of Latino Americans will be housed in the American Folklife Center.

The Civil Rights History Project Act of 2009 (P.L. 111-19) requires the Library of Congress and the Smithsonian Institution's National Museum of African American History and Culture (NMAAHC) to establish a joint five-year oral-history project to collect and make publicly accessible documentation relevant to the personal histories of participants in the civil rights movement. A cooperative agreement between the library and the Smithsonian, signed in July 2009, specified that the American Folklife Center would conduct a survey of libraries, archives, museums and other institutions to determine the extent of existing documentary recordings of the civil rights movement. The Smithsonian will record interviews with individuals about their experiences in the movement. The interviews and memorabilia will be made accessible to researchers at the library, NMAAHC, and online through the project Web site.

On August 26 the library announced the completion of phase one of the project—the launch of the Civil Rights History Project Web site (http://www.loc.gov/folklife/civilrights). The Web portal presents the results of a nationwide survey of oral history interviews. Developed by Library of Congress catalogers and Web designers, the database and search tool will enable researchers to locate hundreds of collections in repositories around the country.

Digital Preservation and Management

The library's National Digital Information Infrastructure and Preservation Program (NDIIPP) is a unique strategic initiative mandated by Congress in 2000 to collect and preserve at-risk digital content of cultural and historical importance. Under the auspices of the library's Office of Strategic Initiatives, NDIIPP has grown to a decentralized network of 200 partners with expertise in handling digital content. These partners are seeking to preserve a wide range of born-digital records, including public and commercial content, and are working collaboratively to establish standards for digital preservation. The project also includes Web capture to address the problem of the limited lifespan of the average online site as well as plans to manage the influx of born-digital collections.

The NDIIPP partners met in July to present project results, share expertise, and conduct working group meetings of the National Digital Stewardship Alliance, which was established in 2010. At the end of the fiscal year, 96 organizations were members of the alliance. Alliance members are working to build a national digital collection, develop and adopt digital preservation standards, share tools and services, support innovation of practice and research, and promote national outreach for digital preservation.

Work accomplished in 2011 included the following:

State Records

Most states lack the resources to ensure the preservation of the information they produce in digital form only, such as legislative records, court-case files, and executive-agency records. As a result, much state government digital information—including content useful to policymakers—is at risk. In 2011 the four projects making up the NDIIPP Preserving State Government Information initiative worked with institutions in 35 states, adding valuable digital information to the network. The projects represent a geographically and thematically diverse body of important state government digital information.

Standards

The Federal Agency Digitization Guidelines Working Group, under NDIIPP, is a collaborative effort by 18 federal agencies to define common guidelines, methods, and practices to digitize historical content in a standard manner. Two main working groups—still images and audiovisual—continued their work of developing guidelines and tools that can be broadly applied.

The Still Image group evaluated file formats (such as JPEG 2000) for archival and other benefits. The group also focused on the area of color accuracy for production scanning projects. The Audiovisual Working group continued developing of a Material Exchange Format (MXF) standard, suitable for the creation and management of files for video and other moving-image content. Drafts were distributed for comment in October 2010 and August 2011. The audiovisual group also continued to develop a specification for Broadcast WAVE file (BWF) metadata, a file header for audio files, which is used by the European Broadcast Union.

Web Archiving

In fiscal 2011 the library's Web Archiving team in the Office of Strategic Initiatives provided project management and technical support for a growing number of Web archive collections for Library Services and the Law Library, and continued to develop tools and strengthen the infrastructure at the library for the long-term storage and preservation of Web archive content. The Web Archiving Team managed 22 Web archive collections, which included more than 6,300 nominated Web sites. At year's end the library's Web archives comprised more than 5 billion Web documents or 250 terabytes of data.

The team worked with Library Services to archive sites about the Civil War's sesquicentennial. It partnered with other organizations to archive sites relating to the 2011 earthquake in Japan, and the "Arab Spring" and "Jasmine Revolution" events in North Africa and the Middle East. The team also worked with the library's overseas offices to build Web archives for the 2010 elections in Brazil, Burma/Myanmar, and Sri Lanka; the 2011 elections in Laos, Thailand, and Vietnam; the Maoist Movement in India; Pakistan Nationalism; and the beginnings of Timor Leste (East Timor) as an independent country.

The team also provided support to the Law Library as it archived U.S. Senate, House, and committee Web sites that will be made available through the public legislation information system known as THOMAS.

U.S. Copyright Office

The U.S. Copyright Office in the Library of Congress administers the U.S. copyright law, under which authors of creative works register claims to protect their intellectual property. Congress enacted the first copyright law in May 1790; in 1870 it centralized the national copyright function in the Library of Congress. The collections of the library have been created largely through the copyright deposit system.

During the fiscal year the Copyright Office registered 670,044 copyright claims, eliminating a backlog of outstanding claims that developed during the transition to electronic processing, which began in 2007. By the close of the fiscal year, electronic submissions accounted for more than 80 percent of all incoming claims.

In its effort to maintain a mint record of American creativity, the Copyright Office continued its large-scale effort to digitize some 70 million pre-1978 copyright records and make the records available online. In fiscal 2011 the office digitized 10 million assignment-card records, bringing the total scanned to 12.5 million. The office also digitized 318 volumes of the Catalog of Copyright Entries (representing an additional 10 million claim records).

The Copyright Royalty Judges (CRJ) administer the provisions of Chapter 8 of Title 17 of the Copyright Act, which relates to setting royalty rates and terms as well as determining the distribution of royalties for certain copyright statutory licenses. In 2011 CRJ facilitated the collection of more than $326 million in copyright royalties and directed distribution of more than $144 million to copyright owners.

National Library Service for the Blind and Physically Handicapped

Established in 1931 when President Herbert Hoover signed the Pratt-Smoot Act, the National Library Service for the Blind and Physically Handicapped (NLS) marked the 80th anniversary of its braille and talking-book services in March 2011. NLS used the occasion to increase awareness of its digital talking-book program through a direct mail marketing campaign in collaboration with its network of regional libraries. NLS also marketed its services to more than 250,000 institutions serving people with visual and physical disabilities, including veterans, seniors, and students.

During the year, NLS circulated more than 25 million copies of braille and recorded books and magazines to some 800,000 readers through a network of 103 cooperating libraries. NLS also provides a free service known as the 102 Talking-Book Club to more than 3,700 patrons who are 100 years of age or older.

Through its digital talking-book program, NLS distributes digital players and audiobooks on flash-memory cartridges in specially designed mailing containers to libraries nationwide. Approximately 310,000 users are enjoying digital talking-book players and books. Patrons can select among 8,500 titles on cartridges and approximately 25,000 titles on the Braille and Audio Reading Download (BARD) Web site. Responsibility for administering BARD, which has 40,415 registered users, was turned over to the network of cooperating libraries this year. Web portals were customized with respective library logos, making service provision seamless to patrons.

John W. Kluge Center

The John W. Kluge Center was established in 2000 with a gift of $60 million from the late John W. Kluge, Metromedia president and founding chairman of the James Madison Council (the library's private sector advisory group). Located within the library's Office of Scholarly Programs, the center's goal is to bring the world's best thinkers to the Library of Congress, where they can use the institution's resources and can interact with policymakers in Washington.

During the fiscal year the Kluge Center continued to attract outstanding senior scholars and postdoctoral fellows. The center conducted eight fellowship competitions internally and participated in eight fellowship competitions managed primarily by external partners. The spring saw a record number of senior scholars-in-residence—seven for the mid-March to mid-April period. Working under the auspices of the center, a total of 104 individuals produced or contributed to the production of scholarly works that drew from the library's collections, databases, and staff resources.

For more information about the center, visit http://www.loc.gov/kluge.

Publications

Each year the library publishes books, calendars, and other printed products featuring its vast holdings. All told, 200 library publications currently are in print and can be ordered in bookstores nationwide and from the Library Shop.

Among the titles published in 2011 were several issued in conjunction with the sesquicentennial of the Civil War (*The Library of Congress Illustrated Timeline of the Civil War* and *Long Remembered: Lincoln and His Five Versions of the Gettysburg Address*) and three new titles in the Fields of Vision series that feature the photographs of Carl Mydans, Gordon Parks, and Arthur Rothstein. Rounding out the list of new publications was a facsimile of *The Washington Haggadah,* a reproduction of the rare 15th-century tome held by the library's Hebraic Division, and *Photographic Memory,* a book celebrating photography and the photograph album.

Exhibitions

A new major exhibition, "The Last Full Measure," showcased rare Civil War photographs from the Liljenquist family collection, which were donated to the Library of Congress to mark the war's sesquicentennial. Nearly 400 ambrotype and tintype photographs of both Union and Confederate soldiers were featured.

Displays in the Performing Arts Reading Room foyer featured material from the Federal Theater Project (1935–1939) and marked the 60th anniversary of the iconic television show "I Love Lucy." The Geography and Map Division mounted the third in a series of Landsat map displays titled "Earth as Art."

During the year the library opened three graphic arts galleries in the Thomas Jefferson Building to showcase its visual arts collections. The Herblock Gallery celebrates the work of editorial cartoonist Herbert L. Block—better known as "Herblock"—who donated his body of work to the library. The Swann Gallery presents caricatures, political cartoons, comics, animation art, graphic novels, and illustrations. A third gallery showcases the graphic arts collections in the Prints and Photographs Division on a rotational basis, beginning with "Timely and Timeless: New Comic Art Acquisitions."

Throughout the year the traveling exhibition "Gateway to Knowledge" brought facsimiles of many of the library's top treasures to small towns across the nation. Mounted in a specially fitted truck, the exhibition traveled to 90 small towns in 34 states and drew about 85,000 people. After a year on the road, "Gateway to Knowledge" made its final stop at the 2011 National Book Festival in Washington, D.C.

The library's exhibitions can be viewed online at http://www.loc.gov/exhibits.

Special Events

During fiscal 2011 the library presented hundreds of public events such as poetry and literary programs, concerts, lectures, and symposia, many of which were broadcast live or archived on the library's Web site at http://www.loc.gov/webcasts. For a list of upcoming events, visit http://www.loc.gov/loc/events. For concert information, go to www.loc.gov/concerts.

Literary Events

An estimated 200,000 book-lovers gathered on the National Mall in Washington, D.C., for the first two-day National Book Festival on September 25 and 26. The festival was organized by the Library of Congress, with President Obama and First Lady Michelle Obama serving as honorary chairpersons. The festival has drawn an estimated 1.2 million people since its inception in 2001.

The 2011 National Book Festival featured presentations by more than 100 of the nation's bestselling authors, illustrators, and poets in pavilions devoted to various genres: works for children, for teens, history and biography, fiction and mystery, contemporary life, and poetry and prose. Three new pavilions—The Cutting Edge, Graphic Novels, and State Poets Laureate—gave festival-goers the opportunity to learn about authors and genres not previously represented. Also new to the festival was the Family Storytelling Stage, sponsored by the Target store chain, which featured presentations by more than 20 authors and musicians whose books and performances were geared to young readers.

The festival attracted numerous well-known authors, including Toni Morrison, Julianne Moore, Dave Eggers, David McCullough, Tomie dePaola, Terry McMillan, Katherine Paterson, Garrison Keillor, Jim Lehrer, and Hoda Kotb. In the Children's pavilion, National Ambassador for Young People's Literature Katherine Paterson rolled out the newly published book version of "The Exquisite Corpse Adventure"—a year-long, serialized story written by various children's authors and illustrated by notable artists. The story originated online at http://www.Read. gov.

Robert Casper, programs director for the Poetry Society of America, was named the head of the Poetry and Literature Center in the Office of Scholarly Programs at the Library of Congress in March 2011. During the year the center sponsored a number of programs featuring new and renowned poets reading from their works. W. S. Merwin served as the 17th Poet Laureate Consultant in Poetry for the 2010–2011 literary season. During a 60-year writing career, Merwin has received many major literary awards, including his second Pulitzer Prize in 2009 for *The Shadow of Sirius*. He gave the final reading of his term on May 4, 2011. On October 17, Philip Levine began his tenure as the 18th Poet Laureate Consultant in Poetry for 2011–2012.

The library's African and Middle Eastern Division marked the centennial of the publication of *The Book of Khalid* with a symposium on Arab American author Ameen Rihani on March 29.

In September a two-day symposium, "Literatura de Cordel: Continuity and Change in Brazilian Popular Literature," was sponsored by the American Folklife Center in collaboration with the Poetry and Literature Center, the Hispanic Division, the Embassy of Brazil, and the library's office in Rio de Janeiro.

Concerts

Since 1925 the library's Coolidge Auditorium has provided a venue for world-class performers and world premieres of commissioned works. Sponsored by its Music Division, the library's annual concert series reflects the diversity of music in America and features many genres: classical, jazz, musical theater, dance, pop, and rock.

The library saluted the American composer and the American songbook as the centerpiece of its 85th concert season (2010–2011), offering 36 concerts, two film series, and lectures by notable scholars. The focus was on new American music at the intersection of many genres: classical music, jazz, country, folk, and pop.

All concerts were presented free of charge in the library's 500-seat Coolidge Auditorium.

The noontime folklife concert series "Homegrown: The Music of America" featured diverse musical traditions. Presented by the American Folklife Center and the Music Division in cooperation with the Kennedy Center Millennium Stage, the 11-concert series presented a range of musical genres including Chicano music from California, bluegrass from Indiana, blues from Mississippi, fiddle music from Connecticut, and Chinese Zheng music from Florida.

Symposia and Lectures

Various library divisions sponsored programs and lectures on a wide range of topics during the year. These programs provided an opportunity to share ideas, celebrate diversity, and showcase the library's collections. Examples of these programs include the following:

- The library's Interpretive Programs Office presented nine public programs relating to "The Last Full Measure," the Civil War exhibition. These included talks by donor Tom Liljenquist and Adam Goodheart, author of *1861: The Civil War Awakening.*
- The American Folklife Center's Benjamin A. Botkin Lecture Series presented nine programs highlighting the best of current research and practice in folklore, folklife, and related fields.
- The Asian Division commemorated the 25th anniversary of the 1986 People Power Revolution in the Philippines that toppled Ferdinand Marcos's 20-year regime with a program held on February 23.
- In honor of former Supreme Court Chief Justices Edward Douglass White (1845–1921) and Oliver Wendell Holmes, Jr. (1841–1935), on March 8 the Law Library presented excerpts from "Father Chief Justice," a play by Louisiana State University law professor Paul R. Baier about the court's ninth chief justice.
- The library's Center for Architecture, Design, and Engineering organized the program "Marvels of Roadside and Main Street America: The Itinerant Eye of John Margolies" to discuss the work of that photographer and historian.
- The Preservation Directorate organized "Preservation Roadmaps for the 21st Century: Assessing Options for Large Collections," a symposium held March 15.
- The Kluge Center sponsored more than 40 public programs during the year, including lectures, symposia, book talks, and a concert. On April 26, the Kluge Center sponsored a panel discussion on "Dignity of the Human Person" moderated by Cardinal Theodore McCarrick.
- The Geography and Map Division sponsored a symposium in May titled "Re-Imagining the U.S. Civil War: Reconnaissance, Surveying and Cartography."
- Art historian and archaeologist David Stuart, expert on Mayan hieroglyphs, delivered the fifth Jay I. Kislak Lecture, in September, "Deciphering the Art of the Ancient Maya and the Year 2012."

Film Screenings

The library's Packard Campus Theater in Culpeper, Virginia, continued its popular film screenings that showcase the film, television, radio, and recorded sound collections of the Library of Congress. The Art-Deco-style theater is one of only five venues in the country equipped to show original classic film prints on nitrate film stock as they would have been screened in theaters before 1950. The theater also features a custom-made organ that provides live music accompaniment for silent movies. During the year the theater offered 131 public screenings, attended by more than 13,000 people, of more than 245 titles held by the library.

Honors and Awards

Gershwin Prize for Popular Song

On September 28, the library announced that Grammy- and Academy-Award-winning songwriters Burt Bacharach and Hal David would each receive the library's Gershwin Prize for Popular Song at an all-star tribute in Washington, D.C. This is the fourth time the honor has been awarded, and the first time to a songwriting team. The prize commemorates brothers George and Ira Gershwin; an extensive manuscript collection of the songwriting team resides in the library. The prize is awarded to musicians whose lifetime contributions in the field of popular song exemplify the standard of excellence associated with the Gershwins. The first Gershwin Prize was awarded in May 2007 to Paul Simon, the second to Stevie Wonder in February 2009, and the third to Paul McCartney in June 2010.

Creative Achievement Award

Nobel Prize and Pulitzer Prize-winner Toni Morrison was presented with the National Book Festival Creative Achievement Award at the 2011 National Book Festival.

Additional Sources of Information

Library of Congress telephone numbers for public information:

Main switchboard (with menu)	202-707-5000
Reading room hours and locations	202-707-6400
General reference	202-707-3399
	TTY 202-707-4210
Visitor information	202-707-8000
	TTY 202-707-6200
Exhibition hours	202-707-4604
Copyright information	202-707-3000
Copyright hotline (to order forms)	202-707-9100
Library of Congress Shop (credit card orders)	888-682-3557

Center for the Book

Library of Congress, Washington, DC 20540
World Wide Web http://www.loc.gov/cfbook

John Y. Cole
Director

Congress established the Center for the Book in the Library of Congress by statute (Public Law 95-129) in 1977. The center's purpose was to use the resources and prestige of the Library of Congress to stimulate public interest in books and reading. Through the years, the center's mission has expanded to include literacy and library promotion and encouraging the historical study of books, reading, libraries, and print culture. A network of affiliated state centers was inaugurated in 1984, and in 1987 the center started to develop a partnership program that included both nonprofit organizations and interested government agencies.

The Center for the Book is an early example of a successful public-private partnership. The Library of Congress supports its five staff positions; all of its activities must be supported by private contributions.

Highlights of 2011

During 2011 the Center for the Book

- Completed its second year of administering the Library of Congress Young Readers Center in the Jefferson Building, the first space in the institution's history devoted to the reading interests of people under the age of 16.
- Played a major role in the organization and program development of the 2011 National Book Festival, which attracted an estimated 200,000 people to the National Mall on September 24 and 25.
- Organized and hosted "Making Appalachian Spring," a public program and book talk on October 7 that celebrated the Library of Congress's 1944 commissioning and presentation of Aaron Copland's ballet "Appalachian Spring."
- Hosted an awards ceremony October 21 for the National Collegiate Book Collecting Contest, working in partnership with the library's Rare Book and Special Collections Division, the Antiquarian Booksellers Association of America, and the Fellowship of American Bibliophilic Societies.
- Presented 20 public book talks and signings in its "Books & Beyond" author series at the library.
- Cosponsored poetry presentations by Library of Congress Witter Bynner fellows in Providence and Seattle with the Rhode Island and Washington state centers for the book.
- Cosponsored, with the library and the University of Texas Press in Austin, publication of *The Library of Congress and the Center for the Book: Historical Essays in Honor of John Y. Cole.*

Young Readers Center

Opened in 2009, the Young Readers Center is increasingly seen by families as a major reason for visiting the Library of Congress, making available current and classic books for browsing and reading aloud and media and Internet resources. The center is open to readers 16 and younger provided they are accompanied by an adult. During 2011 it attracted more than 30,000 visitors, more than twice as many as the previous year. Programs included author appearances; events cosponsored with such Center for the Book reading-promotion partners as Reading Is Fundamental, Inc., a weekly story hour for children; and participation in the annual Kids Euro Festival (an annual festival organized by the nations of the European Union) in the fall.

National Ambassador

Award-winning children's author Katherine Paterson completed her second and final year as National Ambassador for Young People's Literature, a program developed with the Children's Book Council to promote the importance of young people's literature nationwide. Her many national appearances included the launching of Children's Book Week in New York in May, appearances at the National Book Festival in September, and two programs at the Louisiana Book Festival on October 29. She also served as part of the panel that voted to recommend to Librarian of Congress James H. Billington that he choose noted author Walter Dean Myers to serve as her successor in 2012–2013.

Letters About Literature

The six national winners of the 2010–2011 Letters About Literature reading and writing contest were announced in April, along with the national honors and the state winners. To enter, a young (grades 4 through 12) reader writes a personal letter to an author, living or dead, from any genre—fiction or nonfiction, contemporary or classic—explaining how that author's work changed the student's way of thinking about the world or himself or herself. For the second straight year, more than 70,000 letters were submitted. The contest is cosponsored by the Center for the Book, its state centers, and the Target store chain, which donated gift cards to all winners, $10,000 to a library designated by each of the six national winners, and $1,000 to a library designated by each of the 12 national honorable mention winners.

River of Words

Since its inception in 1995 under the leadership of Robert Hass, U.S. Poet Laureate 1995–1997, the Center for the Book has cosponsored the River of Words, an annual environmental poetry and art competition for students ages 5 to 19. The contest was on hiatus during 2011 as a new funding sponsor was sought. In May the center and River of Words cosponsored a concert in Washington, D.C., featuring River of Words poems set to music by young musicians under the mentorship of composer Libby Larsen. A new home for River of Words was announced in the fall: the St. Mary's College Center for Environmental Literacy in Moraga, California.

Online Resources

A new multimedia Web site overseen by the Center for the Book, www.read.gov, was launched in September 2009. The Center for the Book's Web site, www.loc. gov/cfbook, is part of this overall site. Read.gov comprises four subsites tailored to kids, teens, adults, and educators and parents. A new National Ambassador for Young People's Literature subsite was added in 2010. Read.gov is one of the few sites on www.loc.gov that offers contemporary programming related to reading and to current books and authors. This occurs primarily through the webcasts of the Books & Beyond authors series and its complementary Facebook page. More than 180 Books & Beyond webcasts are currently available. The major upgrade of the site in 2011 was the addition of many more digitized public domain books, most of them for young people. The books are presented in a page-turning format that simulates the experience of reading a physical book.

The Center for the Book Web site, www.loc.gov/cfbook, includes links to more than 200 organizations, including national reading-promotion partners and affiliated state centers, that share the center's interest in promoting books and reading and encouraging the study of books, libraries, and print culture.

Exquisite Corpse Adventure

The Exquisite Corpse Adventure, a cooperative online project that began in 2009, concluded with the publication of a book by Candlewick Press in 2011. The project centered on a serialized story written exclusively for the Center for the Book's Read.gov Web site by 20 notable authors and illustrators for young people. The National Children's Book and Literacy Alliance was the cosponsor. The imaginative tale, a continuing challenge to its creators, ran biweekly for 27 online episodes, gaining an enthusiastic national and international audience. The online version ended in September 2010 in conjunction with a "performance" of episode 27 at the 2010 National Book Festival by several of the authors and illustrators, orchestrated and written by Katherine Paterson, the author of episode 27. The publication by Candlewick of The Exquisite Corpse Adventure was celebrated at the 2011 National Book Festival during a presentation by project organizers and several of the participating authors and illustrators.

National Book Festival

As it has done since 2001, the Center for the Book took the lead in organizing the 2011 National Book Festival. The expansion to a two-day schedule, the weekend of September 24 and 25, meant an increase to 112 participating authors, illustrators, and poets from 71 the previous year. Presentations ran for 45 minutes (they were previously 30 minutes), and many writers who would otherwise have been unavailable on Saturday, September 24, were able to take part on the second day.

The festival's theme was "Celebrate the Joys of Reading Aloud," and it drew record crowds: approximately 100,000 each day. In addition to the author pavilions (Children, Teens, Contemporary Life, Poetry and Prose, Fiction and Mystery, and History and Biography), on Sunday three mini-pavilions offered presentations in genres not previously represented: Graphic Novels, The Cutting Edge (Urban Fiction), and State Poets Laureate.

Featured writers included Nobel Laureate Toni Morrison, who received the festival's Creative Achievement Award; 2011 Pulitzer Prize-winners Jennifer Egan, Eric Foner, and Siddhartha Mukherjee; NPR personality Garrison Keillor; former Poet Laureate and Pulitzer-winner Rita Dove; historian David McCullough; and National Ambassador for Young People's Literature Katherine Paterson.

The most popular attraction at the festival, the Pavilion of the States, was organized by the Center for the Book and staffed by representatives from affiliated state centers for the book, state libraries, state humanities councils, and affiliates from various U.S. territories. They provided handouts and information about their states' writers, libraries, book festivals, book awards, and reading-promotion activities. In addition, several festival authors and illustrators made scheduled visits to their state's table to greet fans and sign autographs.

An especially popular Pavilion of the State feature among young readers and their families was "Discover Great Places Through Reading," a free map of the United States that visitors presented at each table for an appropriate state sticker or stamp. The map included "52 Great Reads About Great Places," a reading list of books for young people recommended by each state or territory.

Reading-Promotion Networks

The center's partnership program, which includes more than 80 national nonprofit and governmental organizations, strengthens and supports its reading and literacy projects nationwide. The annual partners idea exchange meeting was held at the Library of Congress on March 17, 2011. The principal topic at the meeting was the planned forthcoming launch of the Read It LOUD! project. Speakers included Wally Amos, chair of the Read It LOUD! Foundation (RILF); Carlos Collazo, founder and CEO of MARSYS, an international information technology company based in San Francisco and the principal RILF corporate sponsor; and the Librarian of Congress.

The state affiliates of the Center for the Book must renew their partnerships with the national center every three years. The purpose of the network is to link reading-promotion resources and ideas from the Library of Congress to related projects and interests at the state and local level. The annual idea exchange meeting is an important way for representatives from the state centers to learn how their peers around the country promote reading, literacy, and libraries. Book awards, literary maps, databases about state authors, book festivals, and participation in Letters About Literature and River of Words are prominent state center for the book projects.

At the 2011 state center idea exchange on May 9–10, coordinators from 36 state affiliates discussed current and potential projects as well as topics such as fund raising and board development.

National Agricultural Library

U.S. Department of Agriculture, Abraham Lincoln Bldg.,
10301 Baltimore Ave., Beltsville, MD 20705-2351
E-mail agref@nal.usda.gov
World Wide Web http://www.nal.usda.gov

Mary Ann Leonard

Special Assistant to the Director

The U.S. Department of Agriculture's National Agricultural Library (NAL) is one of the world's largest and most accessible agricultural research libraries, offering service directly to the public via its Web site, http://www.nal.usda.gov.

The library was instituted in 1862 at the same time as the U.S. Department of Agriculture (USDA). It became a national library in 1962 when Congress established it as the primary agricultural information resource of the United States (7 USCS § 3125a). Congress assigned to the library the responsibilities to:

- Acquire, preserve, and manage information resources relating to agriculture and allied sciences
- Organize agricultural information products and services and provide them within the United States and internationally
- Plan, coordinate, and evaluate information and library needs relating to agricultural research and education
- Cooperate with and coordinate efforts toward development of a comprehensive agricultural library and information network
- Coordinate the development of specialized subject information services among the agricultural and library information communities

NAL is located in Beltsville, Maryland, near Washington, D.C., on the grounds of USDA's Henry A. Wallace Beltsville Agricultural Research Center. Its 15-story Abraham Lincoln Building is named in honor of the president who created the Department of Agriculture and signed several of the major U.S. laws affecting agriculture.

The library employs about 100 librarians, information specialists, computer specialists, administrators, and clerical personnel, supplemented by about 50 volunteers, contract staff, and cooperators from NAL partnering organizations.

NAL's reputation as one of the world's foremost agricultural libraries is supported and burnished by its expert staff, ongoing leadership in delivering information services, expanding collaborations with other U.S. and international agricultural research and information organizations, and its extensive collection of agricultural information, searchable through AGRICOLA (AGRICultural On-Line Access), the library's bibliographic database.

The Collection

The NAL collection dates to the congressionally approved 1839 purchase of books for the Agricultural Division of the Patent Office, predating the 1862 establishment of USDA itself. Today NAL provides access to billions of pages of agricultural information—an immense collection of scientific books, journals, audiovisuals, reports, theses, artifacts, and images—and to a widening array of digital media, as well as databases and other information resources germane to the broad reach of agriculture-related sciences.

The library's collection contains nearly 3.6 million items, dating from the 16th century to the present, including the most complete repository of USDA publications and the world's most extensive set of materials on the history of U.S. agriculture. NAL also acquires annually approximately 13,100 serial titles in agriculture and related sciences, including nearly 5,500 digital journals. More than 3,000 of these digital journals are purchased with permanent data storage rights.

Building the Collection

NAL has primary responsibility for collecting and retaining publications of USDA and its agencies, and it is the only U.S. national library with a legislated mandate to collect in the following disciplines: plant and animal health, welfare, and production; agricultural economics, products, and education; aquaculture; forestry; rural sociology and rural life; family and consumer science; and food science, safety, and nutrition. In addition to collecting as comprehensively as possible in these core subject areas, NAL collects extensively in many related subjects, such as biology, bioinformatics, biochemistry, chemistry, entomology, environmental science, genetics, invasive species, meteorology, natural resources, physics, soil science, sustainability, water quality, and zoology.

In general, NAL's acquisition program and collection development policy are based upon its responsibility to provide service to the staff of the Department of Agriculture, U.S. land-grant universities, and the general public in all subjects pertaining to agriculture. The NAL Collection Development Policy (http://www.nal.usda.gov/about/policy/coll_dev_toc.shtml) outlines the scope of subjects collected and the degree of coverage for each subject. NAL collection policies also reflect and differentiate the collecting responsibilities of the National Library of Medicine and the Library of Congress. Together, these three national libraries have developed cooperative collection development policy statements for the subject areas of biotechnology, human nutrition and food, and veterinary sciences.

Rare and Special Collections

The NAL Rare and Special Collections program emphasizes access to and preservation of rare and unique materials documenting the history of agriculture and related sciences. Items in the library's special collections include rare books, manuscripts, nursery and seed trade catalogs, posters, objects, photographs, and other rare materials documenting agricultural subjects. Materials date from the 1500s to the late 1900s and include many international sources. Detailed information about these special collections is available on the NAL Web site at http://www.nal.usda.gov/speccoll.

Special collections of note include the following:

- The U.S. Department of Agriculture History Collection (http://www.nal. usda.gov/speccoll/collect/history.html), assembled over 80 years by USDA historians, includes letters, memoranda, reports, and papers of USDA officials, as well as photographs, oral histories, and clippings covering the activities of the department from its founding through the early 1990s.
- The U.S. Department of Agriculture Pomological Watercolor Collection includes more than 7,000 detailed, botanically accurate watercolor illustrations of fruit and nut varieties developed by growers or introduced by USDA plant explorers. Created between 1880 and the 1940s, the watercolors served as official documentation of the work of the Office of the Pomologist and were used to create chromolithographs in publications distributed widely by the department. Although created for scientific accuracy, the works are artistic treasures in their own right. The full collection has been digitized and is now available online at http://usdawatercolors. nal.usda.gov.
- The Henry G. Gilbert Nursery and Seed Trade Catalog Collection (http:// www.nal.usda.gov/speccoll/collectionsguide/nurserycatalogs.shtml), begun in 1904 by USDA economic botanist Percy L. Ricker, has grown to comprise more than 200,000 American and foreign catalogs. The earliest items date from the late 1700s, but the collection is strongest from the 1890s to the present. Researchers commonly use the collection to document the introduction of plants to the United States, study economic trends, and illustrate early developments in American landscape design.
- The Rare Book Collection (http://www.nal.usda.gov/speccoll/collections guide/rarebooks.shtml) highlights agriculture's printed historical record. It covers a wide variety of subjects but is particularly strong in botany, natural history, zoology, and entomology. International in scope, the collection documents early agricultural practices in Britain and Europe, as well as the Americas. Of particular note are the more than 300 books by or about Carl Linnaeus, the "father of taxonomy," including a rare first edition of his 1735 work *Systema Naturae*.
- Manuscript collections, now numbering more than 400, document the story of American agriculture and its influence on the world. The collections guide is at http://www.nal.usda.gov/speccoll/collectionsguide/mssindex1. shtml.

NAL continues to digitize these and other unique materials to share them broadly via its Web site and has published detailed indexes to the content of many manuscript collections to improve discovery. AGRICOLA, NAL's catalog, includes bibliographic entries for special collection items, manuscripts, and rare books. The library provides in-house research and reference services for its special collections and offers fee-based duplication services.

Preservation

NAL is committed to the preservation of its print and nonprint collections. It continues to monitor and improve the environmental quality of its stacks to extend the longevity of all materials in the collection. The library has instituted a long-term strategy to ensure the growing body of agricultural information is systematically identified, preserved, and archived.

NAL's digital conversion program has resulted in a growing digital collection of USDA publications and many non-USDA historical materials not restricted by copyright. These materials are now part of the expanding NAL Digital Collections.

NAL Digital Collections

NAL has undertaken several projects to digitize, store, and provide online access to nearly 1 million pages of historic print documents and images, primarily from USDA. In an effort to unify all digital content, the library launched a new interface for the NAL Digital Collections (http://naldc.nal.usda.gov) accompanied by new policies for collecting, storing, and making publicly available federally funded research outcomes published by USDA scientists and researchers. Long-range plans include collecting, maintaining, and providing access to a broad range of agricultural information in a wide variety of digital formats. The end result will be a perpetual, reliable, publicly accessible collection of digital documents, datasets, images, and other items relating to agriculture.

AGRICOLA

AGRICOLA catalogs and indexes NAL collections and delivers worldwide access to agricultural information through its searchable Web interface (http://agricola. nal.usda.gov). Alternatively, users can access AGRICOLA on a fee basis through several commercial vendors, or they can subscribe to the complete AGRICOLA file, also on a fee basis, from the National Technical Information Service within the U.S. Department of Commerce.

The AGRICOLA database covers materials in all formats, including printed works from the 16th century onward. The records describe publications and resources encompassing all aspects of agriculture and allied disciplines. More than 390,000 AGRICOLA records contain links to networked Web resources. AGRICOLA comprises the following two components:

- NAL Public Access Catalog, containing more than 1 million citations to books, audiovisual materials, serial titles, and other materials in the NAL collection. (The catalog also contains some bibliographic records for items cataloged by other libraries but not held in the NAL collection.)
- NAL Article Citation Database, consisting of 3.4 million citations to serial articles, book chapters, reports, and reprints.

Information Management and Information Technology

Over the past quarter century, NAL has applied increasingly sophisticated information technology to support the ever more complex and demanding information needs of researchers, practitioners, policymakers, and the general public. Technological developments spearheaded by the library date back to the 1940s and 1950s, when NAL Director Ralph Shaw invented "electronic machines" such as the photo charger, rapid selector, and photo clerk. Over the years NAL has made numerous technological improvements, from automating collections information to delivering full-text and image collections digitally on the Internet.

NAL has fully implemented the Voyager integrated library management system from Ex Libris, Ltd. The system supports ordering, receiving, and invoice processing for purchases; creating and maintaining indexing and cataloging records for AGRICOLA; circulating print holdings; and providing a Web-based online catalog for public searching and browsing of the collection. In addition, the system is fully integrated with an automated interlibrary loan and document delivery system by Relais International that streamlines services and provides desktop delivery of needed materials.

English-Spanish Agricultural Thesaurus and Glossary

NAL is known for its expertise in developing and using a thesaurus, or controlled vocabulary, a critical component of effective digital information systems. The NAL Agricultural Thesaurus (NALT) (http://agclass.nal.usda.gov/agt.shtml) is a hierarchical vocabulary of agricultural and biological terms, organized according to 17 subject categories. It comprises primarily biological nomenclature, with additional terminology supporting the physical and social sciences.

In January 2012 NAL released the 11th edition of NALT, which has grown to approximately 87,000 terms. This edition now includes updated terminology associated with life cycle assessment, sustainable agriculture, antibiotics, soil, viruses, angiosperm, and ferns. In addition, collaboration with the Inter-American Institute for Cooperation on Agriculture and other partners resulted in the significant addition of Latin American plant species.

In 2011 NALT became available as Linked Open Data. Linked Open Data translates information into a form both readable and understandable by computers, a shift that makes it possible to provide integrated access to data, virtually eliminating data silos. NAL can now connect its vocabulary to other linked data vocabularies, which, in turn, will connect the NALT to the larger semantic web. Such interconnections will help programmers create meaningful relationships that will make it easier to locate related content.

Associated with the NALT, the NAL Glossary provides definitions of agricultural terms. The 2012 edition contains 3,302 definitions ranging across agriculture and its many ancillary subjects, an increase of 332 definitions (in both Spanish and English) over last year. Most definitions are composed by NALT staff. (Suggestions for new terms or definitions can be sent by e-mail to agref@ars.usda.gov.)

NAL publishes Spanish-language versions of the thesaurus and glossary, which carry the names *Tesauro Agrícola* and *Glosario,* respectively. Both are updated concurrently with the annual release of the English-language version. The 2012 edition of the Spanish-language version of NALT contains more than 75,000 terms.

The thesaurus and glossary are primarily used for indexing and for improving the retrieval of agricultural information, but they can also be used by students from fifth grade up, teachers, writers, and others who are seeking precise definitions of words from the agricultural sciences. Users can download all four publications—English and Spanish thesaurus and glossary—in both machine-readable (MARC 21, RDF-SKOS, and XML) and human-readable (doc, pdf) formats at http://ag-class.nal.usda.gov/download.shtml.

Library Services

NAL serves the agricultural information needs of customers through a combination of Web-based and traditional library services, including reference, document delivery, and information center services. The NAL Web site offers access to a wide variety of full-text resources, as well as online access to reference and document delivery services. In 2011 the library delivered more than 95 million direct customer service transactions throughout the world via its Web site and other Internet-based services.

The main reading room in the library's Beltsville facility features a walk-up service desk, access to an array of digital information resources (including full-text scientific journals), current periodicals, and an on-site request service for materials from NAL's collection. NAL also operates a walk-in reference and digital services center at USDA headquarters in downtown Washington, D.C. Services at both facilities are available 8:30 to 4:30 Monday through Friday, except federal holidays.

NAL's reference services are accessible online using the Ask a Question form on the NAL Web pages; by use of e-mail addressed to agref@ars.usda.gov; by telephone at 301-504-5755; or by mail to Reference Research Services, National Agricultural Library ARS/USDA, 10301 Baltimore Avenue, Beltsville, MD 20705. Requesters receive assistance from Reference Research Services staff in all areas and aspects of agriculture, but staff particularly answer questions, provide research guidance, and make presentations on topics not addressed by the seven subject-focused information centers of the library.

NAL's seven information centers are reliable sources of comprehensive, science-based information on key aspects of U.S. agriculture, providing timely, accurate, and in-depth coverage of their specialized subject areas. Their expert staff offer extensive Web-based information resources and advanced reference services. Each NAL information center has its own Web site and is a partner in the Agriculture Network Information Center (AgNIC) Alliance (see heading AgNIC later in this report).

- The Alternative Farming Systems Information Center (AFSIC) (http://afsic.nal.usda.gov) specializes in identifying and accessing information relating to farming methods that maintain the health and productivity of the entire farming enterprise, including the world's natural resources. This focus includes sustainable and alternative agricultural systems, crops, and livestock.
- The Animal Welfare Information Center (AWIC) (http://awic.nal.usda.gov) provides scientific information and referrals to help ensure the proper care and treatment of animals used in biomedical research, testing, teaching, and exhibitions, and by animal dealers. Among its varied outreach

activities, the center conducts workshops for researchers on meeting the information requirements of the Animal Welfare Act.

- The Food and Nutrition Information Center (FNIC) (http://fnic.nal.usda. gov) provides credible, accurate, and practical resources for nutrition and health professionals, educators, government personnel, and consumers. FNIC maintains a staff of registered dietitians who can answer questions on food and human nutrition.
- The Food Safety Research Information Office (FSRIO) (http://fsrio.nal. usda.gov) delivers information on publicly funded—and, to the extent possible, privately funded—food safety research initiatives. Its Research Projects Database, with more than 7,000 projects cited, provides ready access to the largest searchable collection of food safety research being conducted within U.S. and international governmental agencies.
- The National Invasive Species Information Center (NISIC) (http://www. invasivespeciesinfo.gov) delivers accessible, accurate, referenced, up-to-date, and comprehensive information on invasive species drawn from federal, state, local, and international sources.
- The Rural Information Center (RIC) (http://ric.nal.usda.gov) assists local officials, organizations, businesses, and rural residents working to maintain the vitality of rural areas. It collects and disseminates information on such diverse topics as community economic development, small business development, health care, finance, housing, environment, quality of life, community leadership, and education.
- The Water Quality Information Center (WQIC) (http://wqic.nal.usda.gov) collects, organizes, and communicates scientific findings, educational methodologies, and public policy issues relating to water resources and agriculture.

In addition to these information centers, NAL manages the popular Nutrition. gov Web site (http://www.nutrition.gov) in collaboration with other USDA agencies and the Department of Health and Human Services. This site provides vetted, science-based nutrition information for the general consumer and highlights the latest in nutrition news and tools from across federal government agencies. The site is an important tool for disseminating the work of multiple federal agencies in a national obesity prevention effort. A team of registered dietitians at NAL's Food and Nutrition Information Center maintains Nutrition.gov and answers questions on food and nutrition issues.

Web-Based Products and Services

In 2011 the NAL Web sites, which encompass nearly all the content and services described here, collectively received an average of 7.5 million page views per month from people seeking agricultural information.

NAL has had growing success using Twitter to disseminate information about agriculture to a broad audience. Through 2011, the eight NAL Twitter feeds—a general NAL account and seven subject-specific streams—have together acquired more than 59,000 followers.

DigiTop

DigiTop, USDA's Digital Desktop Library, delivers the full text of thousands of journals and hundreds of newspapers worldwide, provides 18 agriculturally significant citation databases, supplies a range of digital reference resources, and offers focused, personalized services. DigiTop is available around the clock to the entire USDA work force worldwide—more than 100,000 people. NAL staff provides help desk and reference services, continuous user education, and training for DigiTop users. During fiscal year 2011 more than 1,330,000 articles were downloaded through DigiTop.

Document Delivery Services

NAL's document delivery operation responds to thousands of requests each year from USDA employees and from libraries and organizations around the world. NAL uses the Relais Enterprise document request and delivery system. With Relais fully integrated with the Voyager library system, with DigiTop, and with other Open-URL and ISO ILL compliant systems, NAL customers can request materials or check on the status of their requests via the Web, and the needed materials can be easily delivered electronically. Document requests can also be submitted via OCLC (NAL's symbol is AGL) and DOCLINE (NAL's libid is MDUNAL). Visit http://www.nal.usda.gov/services/request.shtml for details.

Networks of Cooperation

The NAL collection and information resources are supplemented by networks of cooperation with other institutions, including arrangements with agricultural libraries at U.S. land-grant universities, other U.S. national libraries, agricultural libraries in other countries, and libraries of the United Nations and other international organizations.

AgNIC

The library serves as secretariat for the Agriculture Network Information Center (AgNIC) Alliance, a voluntary, collaborative partnership that hosts a distributed network of discipline-specific agricultural information Web sites at http://www. agnic.org. AgNIC provides access to high-quality agricultural information selected by its 63 partner members, which include land-grant universities, NAL, and other institutions globally. Together they offer 71 subject-specific sites and reference services, with additional sites and resources regularly added.

During 2011 AgNIC partners continued to build full-text content through a variety of projects. One project, metadata harvesting, uses the Open Archives Initiative protocols to harvest metadata for full-text resources from targeted institutional repositories and collections. Once the metadata is harvested, AgNIC delivers it through a single point of access with the bibliographic citations linked to another service to help users find items in nearby libraries. Over the last year AgNIC partners reviewed more than 400 other institutional repositories to identify additional agricultural content to be harvested. The AgNIC system now links to more than 5 million full-text and bibliographic items.

AGLINET

Through the Agricultural Libraries Network (AGLINET), NAL serves as the U.S. node of an international agricultural information system that brings together agricultural libraries with strong regional or country coverage and other specialized collections. NAL functions as a gateway to U.S. agricultural libraries and resources, fulfilling requests for information via reciprocal agreements with several other libraries, information centers, and consortia. As an AGLINET member, NAL agrees to provide low-cost interlibrary loan and photocopy service to other AGLINET libraries. Most materials requested through AGLINET are delivered digitally, although reproductions via fiche or photocopy are used when appropriate. AGLINET is administered by the Food and Agriculture Organization of the United Nations.

National Library of Medicine

8600 Rockville Pike, Bethesda, MD 20894
301-496-6308, 888-346-3656, fax 301-496-4450
E-mail publicinfo@nlm.nih.gov
World Wide Web http://www.nlm.nih.gov

Kathleen Cravedi
Director, Office of Communications and Public Liaison

Melanie Modlin
Deputy Director, Office of Communications and Public Liaison

Founded in 1836, the National Library of Medicine (NLM), a component of the National Institutes of Health (NIH), celebrated 175 years of public service and information innovation in 2011.

The world's largest biomedical library, NLM

- Produces authoritative electronic information sources such as PubMed, MedlinePlus, and GenBank that are searched billions of times by millions of people each year
- Coordinates a 6,000-member National Network of Libraries of Medicine that promotes and provides access to health information in communities across the United States
- Supports and conducts research, development, and training in biomedical informatics and health information technology
- Houses and shares with the world a collection of more than 17 million books, journals, artworks, audiovisuals, and other materials in more than 150 languages

NLM remains focused on the goals of its 2006–2016 long-range plan, including key activities in support of interoperable electronic health records, more-effective disaster and emergency response, and development of a robust knowledge base for personalized health care.

Through its advanced information systems, informatics research and training, and extensive partnerships, NLM plays a pivotal role in catalyzing and supporting the translation of basic science into new treatments, improved practice, useful decision support for health professionals and patients, and effective disaster and emergency preparedness and response.

NLM's information systems disseminate an enormous range of information, including genetic, genomic, chemical, toxicology, and clinical trials data; images; published and unpublished research results; decision support resources; standards for scientific and health data and publications; informatics tools for system developers; and high-quality health information for the public.

Scientists, health professionals, and members of the public search or download much of this information directly from an NLM Web site, find it via an Internet search engine, or use an externally developed app that provides value-added access to NLM data. Commercial and nonprofit system developers regularly use the applications programming interfaces (APIs) that NLM provides to promote innovation and facilitate use of its information in products and services produced by others.

As the use of electronic health records expands, new opportunities are emerging to link patient data to NLM's large and rapidly expanding stores of electronic scientific data, research results, and high-quality health information in ways that can increase understanding of disease onset and progression, identify new therapeutic avenues, and speed the translation of such discoveries into improved health and health care.

Developments in 2011

During 2011 NLM continued to expand and refine its current information services, focusing on improved access to these services in underserved communities and support for research, development, and education that will help to take advantage of new opportunities to advance biomedical research, health care, and public health. The following are some of the major themes and activities that characterized the year.

Biomedical and Health Information Services

At the core of NLM are the world's largest, continually expanding collection of biomedical literature and a broad array of authoritative databases for health professionals, scientists, the public, and the librarians and information specialists who serve them.

During 2011 the library again saw significant increases in the information available in its existing databases, such as PubMed/MEDLINE, its flagship database of references and abstracts for medical journal articles, which grew by more than 725,000 indexed citations; PubMed Central, which now provides public access to more than 2.3 million research articles, including those produced by NIH-funded researchers; and ClinicalTrials.gov, the world's largest clinical trials database, which now also includes summary results data for many trials. NLM also expects to release new information sources in 2012, including an expanded one-stop shop for systematic reviews of clinical effectiveness, a new Genetic Testing Registry, and a database of clinical significant human genetic variants.

NLM continued to deploy or develop specialized information services designed to assist those responding to natural or man-made disasters and emergencies, as it has done in the past for the Gulf oil spill, earthquakes in Haiti and Chile, and floods in Pakistan. In 2011 the Radiation Emergency Medical Management (REMM) tool—previously developed by NLM in cooperation with the Health and Human Services (HHS) assistant secretary for preparedness and response and other HHS agencies—was used in Japan following the March earthquake, tsunami, and nuclear reactor disaster. A new Chemical Emergency Medical Management (CHEMM) tool is now available to help physicians and other health professionals deal with patients exposed to toxic chemicals.

NLM continued to tap the power of social media to reach new audiences. NLM's 13 Twitter feeds—including @medlineplus and the Spanish-language version @medlineplusesp—are companions to its popular consumer health Web site, six Facebook pages, and new YouTube channel. All are a testament to the library's wide range of content and its diverse audiences. NLM also produces a range of mobile applications and mobile-friendly versions of its premier Web services.

Increasing Public Awareness and Access

NLM has active outreach programs to make biomedical researchers, health professionals, librarians, patients, and the public aware of NLM's diverse information services and improve public access to reliable health information. The library will continue to work through the National Network of Libraries of Medicine and through other formal partnerships, including Partners in Information Access for the Public Health Workforce and the Environmental Health Information Outreach Partnership with Historically Black Colleges and Universities, tribal colleges, and other minority-serving institutions.

MedlinePlus is the library's main portal for consumer health information. Available in English and Spanish, with selected materials in nearly 50 other languages, it includes information from NIH and other trusted sources on more than 900 diseases and conditions, and is updated daily. There are directories; a medical encyclopedia and medical dictionary; easy-to-understand tutorials on common conditions, medical tests, and treatments; extensive information on prescription and over-the-counter drugs; health information from the media; and links to thousands of clinical trials.

NLM fosters informal partnerships, such as the Information Rx program to promote MedlinePlus usage by encouraging physicians to write "information prescriptions" for their patients. Recognizing the critical importance of reducing health disparities, NLM uses exhibitions, the media, and new technologies in its efforts to reach underserved populations.

In 2011 NLM opened a major new exhibition, "Native Voices: Native Peoples' Concepts of Health and Illness," as part of its outreach to populations with serious health disparities and in response to congressional interest in documenting traditional Native Hawaiian healing practices. NLM also continues to expand its successful traveling exhibitions program. Examples include the well-received "Harry Potter's World: Renaissance Science, Magic, and Medicine," and "Life and Limb: The Toll of the Civil War."

With assistance from other NIH components and outside partners, NLM continues to increase the distribution of its popular *NIH MedlinePlus* magazine. The free quarterly, which is available online in Spanish and English, is distributed to doctors' offices, health science libraries, Congress, the media, federally supported community health centers, select hospital emergency and waiting rooms, and other locations where the public receives health services. Each issue may be read by more than 5 million people.

In 2011 NLM experimented with the use of contests to promote awareness and innovative use of its authoritative databases. Users were invited to celebrate NLM's 175th anniversary by submitting videos expressing their appreciation of its programs and services, with the winners posted on the NLM YouTube channel. "Show Off Your Apps," NLM's first software-development challenge, elicited 42 entries that made use of dozens of NLM data sources. HHS Secretary Kathleen Sebelius, HHS Chief Technology Officer Todd Park, and U.S. Chief Technology Officer Aneesh Chopra helped to congratulate the winners. Based on the success of this first foray, more NLM challenges are likely to follow.

Promoting Scientific Discovery, Speeding Translation of Research into Practice

For more than 40 years, NLM has conducted and funded research and research training in biomedical informatics—the application of computer and information sciences to health care and biomedical research. Since the National Center for Biotechnology Information (NCBI) was established by law at NLM in 1988, the library has also promoted scientific discovery by organizing and providing rapid access for scientists to the massive amounts of genetic sequence data, now resulting from new sequencing technologies that allow complete genomes to be sequenced in days, rather than years.

NLM also has supported much of the fundamental work on clinical information systems and plays a key role in funding and developing standard terminologies for electronic health records. The increasing availability of standardized electronic health records already enables direct links from patient data to related medical knowledge, as illustrated by expanding use of NLM's MedlinePlus Connect feature, which returns authoritative information relating to specific problems, medications, and test results in an electronic patient record.

NLM has also been a leader in biomedical natural language understanding research by developing, funding, and sharing innovative algorithms, resources, and tools, including the Unified Medical Language System resources. This research has been applied successfully to indexing, information retrieval, question-answering, and literature-based discovery at NLM and by many external researchers, including those working on IBM's Watson project. The IBM computer's success in playing "Jeopardy!" has highlighted the value of rapid parallel computing of large stores of text and simultaneous execution of multiple hypotheses as an aid to question-answering.

NLM and its grantees continue to bring many threads together—genomic data, standardized electronic health records, natural language understanding applied to clinical text and published knowledge, low-cost parallel processing—to make reliable information available when and where it is needed.

Administration

NLM Director Donald A. B. Lindberg, M.D., is guided in matters of policy by a Board of Regents consisting of 10 appointed and 11 ex officio members.

Table 1 / Selected NLM Statistics*

Library Operations	Volume
Collection (book and non-book)	18,790,404
Items cataloged	21,268
Serial titles received	19,793
Articles indexed for MEDLINE	724,831
Circulation requests processed	401,699
For interlibrary loan	244,701
For on-site users	102,054
MEDLINE/PubMed Searches	1,834,317,403
Budget authority	$391,514,000
Staff	804

*For the year ending September 30, 2011.

United States Government Printing Office

732 North Capitol St. N.W., Washington, DC 20401
World Wide Web http://www.gpo.gov

Gary Somerset
Media and Public Relations Manager
202-512-1957, e-mail gsomerset@gpo.gov

The U.S. Government Printing Office (GPO) was created when President James Buchanan signed Joint Resolution 25 on June 23, 1860. GPO opened its doors for business nine months later on March 4, 1861, the same day Abraham Lincoln took the oath of office to become the 16th President of the United States. On that day, GPO began operation in buildings purchased by Congress, at the same address it occupies today. In March 2011 GPO marked its 150th anniversary.

Under Title 44 of the United States Code, GPO is responsible for the production and distribution of information products for all three branches of the federal government. These include the official publications of Congress, federal agencies, and the courts. Today, GPO provides products in print and a variety of digital forms, all of which are born digital. In addition, GPO produces passports for the Department of State and secure credentials for many government agencies. As the federal government's primary resource for gathering, producing, cataloging, providing access to, and preserving published information in all forms, GPO has disseminated millions of publications to the public.

GPO's Superintendent of Documents and its Library Services and Content Management (LSCM) organizations administer the Federal Depository Library Program (FDLP). Included in FDLP is the provision of free online access to government publications via GPO's Federal Digital System (FDsys). GPO also prepares a catalog of government publications published during the preceding month, with information on where they are obtainable and the price. Today the *Catalog of U.S. Government Publications* (*CGP*) is a primary finding tool for federal publications. It includes descriptive records for historical and current publications and direct links those that are available for sale on the GPO Bookstore Web site.

FDLP has roots back to 1813 when Congress first authorized legislation to ensure the provision of certain congressional documents to selected universities, historical societies, and state libraries. At that time, the secretary of state was responsible for distributing publications. In 1857 the secretary of the interior assumed oversight of printing and the designation of depositories. In the Printing Act of 1895, the governance of the depository program was transferred to the Office of the Superintendent of Documents at GPO. Fast forward to 1993, when Public Law 103-40, the Government Printing Office Electronic Information Access Enhancement Act, amended GPO's duties to not only provide the public access to printed publications but Internet-accessible publications as well. Almost 200 years after the start of FDLP, the program continues to serve a vital need of the public through the partnership with federal depository libraries located in almost every congressional district.

LSCM is responsible for current and future access to published U.S. government information. Operations are divided into four main categories: FDLP, cataloging and indexing, distribution of government publications to the International Exchange Service, and distribution of certain government publications to members of Congress and other government agencies, as mandated by law. IES operates under the direction of the Library of Congress; GPO distributes tangible government publications to foreign governments that agree to send to the United States similar publications of their governments.

In addition to the administration of FDLP, GPO is charged with cataloging and indexing all publications issued by the federal government that are not confidential in character.

Finally, LSCM also administers the dissemination of certain tangible publications as specified by public law. Under Title 44, U.S.C., GPO is required to provide copies of publications to certain federal agencies and others at the direction of Congress. Additionally, on behalf of the Department of State, LSCM distributes copies of publications to foreign legions. This is known as the By-Law program.

The GPO of today is obviously a much different agency in the digital age than it was 150 years ago, but its mission has always remained the same. FDLP and GPO's information dissemination programs are examples of its longstanding commitment to permanent public access to U.S. government information.

Acting Public Printer Named

Davita Vance-Cooks became acting public printer in January 2012 and is the first woman to serve as GPO's chief executive officer. Vance-Cooks has 30 years of business executive experience in both the private and government sectors. During her time at GPO, she has held a succession of senior management positions including chief of staff, managing director of GPO's Customer Services and Procurement business unit, and managing director of publication and information sales. Prior to GPO, Vance-Cooks held private sector management positions such as senior vice president of operations for NYLCare MidAtlantic Health Plan where, among other duties, she was responsible for a digital print work center for production of variable data printing products. In addition, she also served as director of customer service and claims, director of membership and billing, and director of market research and product development for Blue Cross Blue Shield Plans.

New Superintendent of Documents

Mary Alice Baish was appointed to the position of assistant public printer, superintendent of documents, in January of 2011. Throughout Baish's career she has worked with all sectors of the library community, has testified before congressional committees on behalf of GPO, and has been a leading voice in developing electronic systems to disseminate government information.

As assistant public printer, she focuses her efforts on FDLP, in cooperation with Congress and GPO's library partners. She also oversees policy and strategy for LSCM.

150th Anniversary History Exhibit

GPO is marking 150 years of service to the nation with a major exhibit. The exhibit uses images and examples of GPO's output to describe "What We Do" (the nature and variety of GPO's work for Congress, the White House, federal agencies, and the courts), "Who We Are" (focusing on the GPO staff), and "How We Do It" (describing the interaction of technology and skill through which GPO makes information available).

Among other features are copies of the memorable work produced by GPO throughout its history.

The exhibit is open from 8 A.M. to 4 P.M. Monday through Friday at 732 North Capital St. N.W. A companion volume to the exhibit is available at GPO's bookstore or online at http://bookstore.gpo.gov/collections/gpo-keeping-america-informed-jsp.

Collaboration/Partners in Progress

Digital Partnerships with Federal Depository Libraries

GPO has been developing digital partnerships with federal depository libraries and other federal agencies to increase access to electronic federal information since 1997. With an increasing amount of federal information available electronically, partnerships ensure permanent public access to electronic content and provide services to assist depositories in providing access to electronic material and in managing their depository collections. These partnerships also allow GPO to take advantage of the expertise of federal depository librarians and the services they have developed in the depository collections.

Partnership Updates

During fiscal year (FY) 2011, GPO

- Signed a partnership with the University of Iowa Libraries for permanent public access to the libraries' collection of digitized federal posters that date from before World War II through the 1990s
- Signed a partnership with the U.S. Department of Labor and the National Technical Information Service for permanent public access to Davis Bacon Act wage determinations on the Wage Determinations Online (WDOL) Web site
- Renewed a partnership with the University of Illinois at Chicago for the Government Information Online Ask a Librarian service, under which the participating depository libraries provide e-mail and chat reference service for questions about government information
- Continued to process bibliographic records for the U.S. Forest Service that are submitted by the University of Montana; as of the end of FY 2011 there were 50 such records available

PACER Access and Education Program

Public Access to Court Electronic Records (PACER) is an online service of the United States Judiciary that provides case and docket information from federal appellate, district, and bankruptcy courts. At the direction of Congress, the judiciary funds PACER through user fees. In September 2010 the Judicial Conference approved the establishment of a program involving GPO, the American Association of Law Libraries (AALL), and the Administrative Office of the United States Courts (AOUSC) that "would provide training and education to the public about PACER service, and would exempt from billing the first $50 of quarterly usage by a library participating in the program." GPO, through FDLP, is working in collaboration with AALL and AOUSC to implement the PACER Access and Education Program. This program will fulfill the conference's vision of an education program that will result in greater public awareness of and access to PACER.

The program builds on training activities already undertaken by libraries. Librarians from participating libraries will conduct training sessions and develop and share training materials.

The Law Library of Congress and the San Bernardino (California) County Law Library created some training materials and tested processes and procedures. A program Web site was launched, and training materials were made available through GPO's FDLP Desktop (FDLP Desktop is detailed later in this report). FY 2012 will bring more federal depository libraries into the program, which ultimately will be open to all federal depository libraries, public libraries, and public law libraries in the United States. More information about the PACER Access and Education Program is available on FDLP Desktop.

Participation and Collaboration

During the year LSCM staff participated and collaborated with a number of outside groups relevant to the FDLP community, including AALL; the Legal Information Preservation Alliance; the Cartographers Users Advisory Council; Commerce Energy NASA Defense Information (CENDI) and CENDI Policy Working Group; the CENDI Digitization Specification Working Group; the End of Term Harvest of Government Web Sites Group; Ex Libris Users of North America; Federal Agencies Digitization Guidelines Initiative, Audio-Visual Working Group; Federal Agencies Digitization Guidelines Initiative, Still Image Digitization Working Group; Federal Library and Information Center Committee, Preservation Working Group; Federal Library and Information Network, Federal Library Shared Collection; Imaging Science and Technology Archiving; International Internet Preservation Consortium; the National Digital Strategy Advisory Board; the National Federation of Advanced Information Services; the National Information Standards Organization; the North American Serials Interest Group; and the Science.gov Alliance.

LSCM also hosted two groups of international visitors through the Department of State's International Visitor Leadership Program. The areas of focus were the role and function of the libraries in FDLP and partnerships and best practices for technology and information literacy in public, school, and academic libraries.

LSCM also collaborated with various professional library programs in FY 2011, including the Careers in Federal Libraries Panel at the University of North Carolina, the Careers in Federal Information Panel at the University of Washington, the Federal Librarians Networking Symposium, and San José State University to offer a virtual internship through LSCM.

FY 2011 LSCM Events

Federal Depository Library Conference

The 2010 Depository Library Council Meeting and Federal Depository Library Conference was held in Arlington, Virginia, October 18–20, 2010. More than 300 attendees participated in more than 40 Depository Library Council meetings and educational sessions.

Depository Library Council Meeting

The 2011 spring Depository Library Council Meeting was held April 4–6, 2011, in San Antonio. The three-day event showcased 18 Depository Library Council sessions and education programs for more than 150 attendees.

Interagency Depository Seminar

The Interagency Depository Seminar was held at GPO headquarters in Washington, D.C., August 1–5. The event provided a blend of depository library management information and training on federal agency information products and services. Tours of the U.S. Senate Library, the Library of Congress, and GPO were also given to the nearly 40 attendees.

Key GPO Tools

Federal Digital System

GPO's Federal Digital System (FDsys) is a one-stop site for online access to authentic published information. This system automates the collection and dissemination of electronic information for all three branches of the federal government. Information is submitted directly into FDsys, permanently available in electronic format, authenticated and versioned, and publicly accessible for searching and downloading. FDsys is a content management system; it securely controls digital content throughout its life cycle to ensure content integrity and authenticity. It is a preservation repository that follows archival system standards to ensure long-term preservation and access of digital content.

Catalog of Government Publications (CGP)

GPO is charged with cataloging and indexing all publications issued by the federal government that are not confidential in character. This task serves libraries and the public nationwide and enables people to locate desired government publications in all formats. The main public interface for the access of cataloging records is the *Catalog of U.S. Government Publications (CGP)*, accessible at http://catalog.gpo.gov.

GPO's goal is to expand *CGP* to a more comprehensive online index of public documents, both historic and current, to increase the visibility and use of government information products. Electronic information dissemination and access have greatly expanded the number of publications that require cataloging and indexing.

FDLP Desktop

FDLP Desktop (http://www.fdlp.gov) serves as a centralized resource for FDLP. Desktop users can stay up to date with innovations and the progress of the program, and federal depository libraries can utilize its various tools to enhance public services.

FDLP Desktop is created and maintained by GPO staff and serves as the main informational hub for FDLP. An easy-to-use navigation system, including RSS feeds and links to social bookmarks, it provides multiple ways to stay in touch with the latest developments in FDLP.

FDLP Community

The FDLP Community Web site (http://community.fdlp.gov) is designed to give members of the federal library community an opportunity to connect, collaborate, and learn from each other in a secure environment. All members of the federal depository library community can create an account, then share knowledge, experiences, and resources through such means as writing blogs, posting to a forum, collaborating in groups, uploading documents, or submitting Web links. While GPO maintains informational pages and at times will generate forum topics, most of the content on FDLP Community is generated by its members. As participation increases, the resources become more helpful and relevant.

Enhancement/Progression/Innovation

FDsys Accomplishments

FY 2011 saw numerous accomplishments regarding GPO's Federal Digital System (FDsys). As of December 2010 FDsys became GPO's official system of record for online government information. This transformation was accompanied by a new logo; FDsys tagline, America's Authentic Government Information; and a redesigned, more user-friendly interface.

GPO focused efforts toward increasing the amount of content managed and preserved within FDsys, which includes at-risk born-digital content.

In February 2011, at the direction of the Joint Committee on Printing, GPO announced a collaborative initiative with the Library of Congress to digitize some of the nation's most important legal and legislative documents. Drawing on the strengths of both agencies, volumes 65–94 of the *United States Statutes at Large* became the first digitized collection to be released on FDsys the following month. The collection spans the period from 1951 through 1980 (the 82nd through 96th Congresses). In June GPO released volumes covering 1981 through 2001 (the 97th through 107th Congresses).

The Library of Congress scanned the documents in this collection, and GPO digitally signed them to ensure authentication of the material. Both the library and GPO maintain the archival collection and share the content for their individual uses.

In June 2011, in collaboration with the National Oceanic and Atmospheric Administration (NOAA) Coastal Services Center, GPO began providing digital access to the Coastal Zone Information Collection, which contains more than 5,000 coastal-related documents. The collection provides nearly 30 years of data and information crucial to the understanding of U.S. coastal management and NOAA's mission to sustain healthy coasts. NOAA sought GPO's preservation repository services on FDsys after planning to discontinue public access to the collection. The collection on FDsys features documents from 1951 through 1999.

Another FDsys partnership in FY 2011 was with the Administrative Office of the United States Courts (AOUSC). With an interest in increasing public access to court opinions, the Judicial Conference approved a recommendation of its Court Administration and Case Management Committee for a pilot project to make lower federal court opinions available through FDsys.

The United States Courts Opinions collection in FDsys (public beta launched in early FY 2012) contains opinions from the federal appellate, district, and bankruptcy courts. The pilot moved from the development phase to the test phase in September 2011. Initial testing was with three courts: the United States Court of Appeals for the Eighth Circuit, United States District Court District of Rhode Island, and United States Bankruptcy Court for the Southern District of Florida. The number of courts participating in the pilot will rapidly expand to 12 and, after further testing, to more than 30. The content of this collection dates back to April 2004, although searchable electronic holdings for some courts may be incomplete for this earlier time period.

The opinions are electronically transferred to GPO from the AOUSC's Case Management/Electronic Case Filing system. With the secure transfer of files, the chain of custody is maintained, allowing GPO to authenticate the files. Users are afforded the same advanced fielded search options and faceted navigation features as in other FDsys collections, as well as some features that are unique to this collection.

Having legal opinions accessible through FDsys provides the ability to search for opinions from one court, from select courts, or from all available courts, along with the ability to search for opinions in conjunction with other FDsys content. In addition to being a new collection for FDsys, the lower federal court opinions represent new content for FDLP.

GPO also focused during the fiscal year on increasing the ways content within FDsys can be used and reused.

- In March 2011 the Public Papers of the Presidents collection was updated to be able to accept XML data. The XML data is also available through Data.gov.
- In May the *Journal of the House of Representatives* from 2000 to 2006 was added to FDsys.
- In June, beginning with the 112th Congress, the Constitutional Authority Statements (CASs) printed in the *Congressional Record* were made available in FDsys as individual documents. This enables users to perform a search on and then link directly to the individual document CAS in HTML and pdf formats.
- Also in June, at the request of the Library of Congress, predictable links were added to Congressional Calendar documents.

• In August Excel spreadsheets were added to the Economic Indicators collection, and the *U.S. Government Manual* collection was updated to be able to accept XML data.

Authentication Initiative

GPO's authentication policies and technologies are developed around a "user-centric" approach to content authentication, where GPO provides a suite of tools to help users make determinations about the authenticity of a particular piece of content. As the field of content authenticity develops, technology changes, and user requirements are identified, GPO's policies and technologies will continue to evolve.

In April 2011 GPO demonstrated its leadership in this area by partnering with the Library of Congress in creating the Content Authentication Working Group to bring agencies together to define common guidelines, methods, and best practices to authenticate digital content. Among the tasks of this working group are to create a glossary so that all have a common understanding of some basic vocabulary regarding such terms as "authentic," "integrity," "verification," "chain of custody," and "trust."

The working group is expected to devise common authentication guidelines and best practices that will enhance the exchange of research results and developments, encourage collaborative authentication practices for projects among federal agencies and institutions, and provide the public with an enhanced level of trust in the authenticity of federal information products.

Additionally, in June 2011 GPO released two papers, "Authenticity of Electronic Federal Government Publications" and "Overview of GPO's Authentication Program," to further explain GPO's content authentication goals. More information about the initiative can be found on GPO's Web site.

FDLP and FDsys Promotion

In early FY 2011 GPO contracted with North American Precis Syndicate (NAPS) on an FDsys campaign. NAPS staff worked with GPO to disseminate informational articles about FDsys to 10,000 print and online publications nationwide, as well as a radio spot to about 400 FM stations.

In June LSCM launched a suite of five informational brochures: *Easy as FDL: Federal Depository Libraries; FDsys: GPO's Federal Digital System; Research Federal Rulemaking in FDsys; Search the Catalog of U.S. Government Publications*; and *Tracking Federal Legislation in FDsys*.

GPO made these brochures available free of charge by mail and as downloadable high-resolution pdf versions.

As of November 2011 GPO Access made the switch over to FDsys, marking the start of an archive-only state for GPO Access; new content will only be uploaded to FDsys. During this phase, GPO Access will remain publicly accessible as a reference archive. Federal depository libraries were asked to assist in promoting or using FDsys and to discontinue promoting or using GPO Access in FY 2011. The following GPO Access flyers were also noted as being outdated: *Authenticated Federal Government Documents, Explore Federal Rules and Regulations Using*

GPO Access, Research Each Step in the Lawmaking Process Using GPO Access, and *U.S. Government Bookstore.*

Digitization Projects Registry

The Registry of U.S. Government Publication Digitization Projects contains records for projects that include digitized copies of publications originating with the U.S. government. It serves as a locator tool for publicly accessible collections of digitized U.S. government publications; increases awareness of U.S. government publication digitization projects that are planned, in progress, or completed; fosters collaboration for digitization projects; and provides models for future digitization projects.

During FY 2011 the Registry of U.S. Government Publication Digitization Projects was examined as part of a content and technological refresh. As a result, the site was renamed the Digitization Projects Registry and relaunched in May 2011. The relaunch also introduced a new interface design and enhanced functionality. Examples of enhancements include the ability to showcase projects through a rotating slideshow, a dynamic bar graph that illustrates the various statuses of digitization projects on the site, and a listing of contributing institutions.

Cataloging Record Distribution Project

In October 2009 GPO announced the launch of a one-year pilot project to address the need for the distribution of cataloging records, produced by GPO, to libraries in FDLP. The pilot project (the Cataloging Record Distribution Project or CDRP) tested the MARC21 record distribution workflows from GPO's Integrated Library System (ILS), matching with library profile information and finally disseminating bibliographic records to pilot libraries for inclusion in their local online public access catalogs. GPO contracted with MARCIVE, Inc. to use MARCIVE's existing MARC record distribution infrastructure to deliver cataloging records to 48 participating depository libraries.

Based on the success of the pilot, GPO implemented a one-year expansion of the cataloging record distribution process, successfully delivering records to 75 participating libraries from September 25, 2010, to September 24, 2011. Participating libraries received 12 months' worth of records, beginning with records produced in October 2010.

In March 2011 GPO administered a survey of participating libraries that generated generally positive feedback. Highlighted benefits for CRDP participants include customizable output profiles, automatic updates to project selection profiles, an easy process of retrieving records, and hands-on customer service provided by MARCIVE staff. Ultimately, CRDP allows libraries to cut down on staff cataloging time and helps them provide greater access to federal government information.

A continuation of this service began on October 1, 2011, and is slated to end on September 31, 2012. More than 70 libraries are participating in the project. GPO is taking lessons learned to assess long-term solutions for bibliographic record distribution. For more information on the project, visit the FDLP Desktop CRDP page.

Integrated Library System

FY 2011 saw numerous enhancements to the Integrated Library System (ILS). Among them:

- Aleph software: A minor service pack was applied for the implementation of fields for the new cataloging standard Resource Description and Access (RDA).
- Historic Shelflist records: GPO continued to make Historic Shelflist records publicly viewable; more than 100,000 were unsuppressed in FY 2011.
- New Electronic Titles: In FY 2011 GPO added the new fields "OCLC number," "GPO System Number," and "New GPO Cataloged Date" to the .csv format of the New Electronic Titles static monthly reports.

Also in FY 2011 MetaLib, a service of *CGP*, saw a key enhancement. Meta-Lib is a federated search tool that is used to retrieve reports, articles, and citations by simultaneously searching across multiple databases. FDsys was configured, as a MetaLib target, to enable the simultaneous searching of FDsys and *CGP* through a predefined search set, "GPO Resources," in MetaLib. FDsys can also now be searched by itself in MetaLib, and it is one of the resources included in all of the 14 subject-specific, pre-defined search sets, except "Catalogs." The subject-specific search sets are General Resources, Business and Economy, Education, History, Reference, GPO Resources, Environment, Politics and Law, Science and Technology, Agriculture, Defense and Military, Health and Safety, Recreation, Travel and Transportation, and Catalogs.

Document Discovery

Publications that may be in scope of FDLP but are not yet cataloged and disseminated through FDLP have traditionally been known as "fugitive documents" or "lost docs." In recent years GPO revitalized the program that aims to identify these publications and bring them into FDLP, now known as the Document Discovery Program. Document Discovery progress in FY 2011 included the following:

- FDLP librarians are submitting more document discovery requests through askGPO, enabling GPO to more easily track the progress of such requests. These requests receive priority routing and monitoring. AskGPO questions about Document Discovery are being handled expeditiously.
- A flyer was designed for outreach visits and presentations to federal agencies. In addition, a new agency Web page and form on GPO's Web site were created to guide agency staff and encourage them to cooperate with GPO. These tools were designed to help LSCM make informed decisions about federal publications regarding the content, its various formats, and its appropriateness for GPO programs. FDLP librarians who have agency contacts were also asked to help LSCM by directing their agency contacts to GPO's Document Discovery federal agency Web page.

Pre-1976 Shelflist Conversion Project

GPO's shelflist contains bibliographic information on publications dating from the 1870s to the shelflist's closure in 1992. The more than 1 million cards are arranged in Superintendent of Documents (SuDoc) classification order and are still used by GPO staff to verify the creation of new SuDoc numbers.

While not a complete inventory of all publications distributed through FDLP, the shelflist contains information on publications in all formats (monographs, serials, maps, integrating resources, and microfiche) as well as publications distributed directly to depositories by the publishing agency. The cards were also used by GPO staff to record information about how to obtain copies of a title, information discovered about publication history, and contact information for staff at the publishing agencies.

Two projects are currently under way to make the information included in the shelflist more accessible to both GPO staff and the depository community.

Shelflist Transcription

Until recently, the bibliographic information on the cards created before GPO joined OCLC in July 1976 was not available in *CGP*. Since January 2010 a team of contract staff from the LAC Group has been at work transcribing the cards into MARC21 records using the GPO ILS. GPO does not have the publications in hand to consult, so the bibliographic information is being transcribed as it is found on the cards. In FY 2011 progress continued with the transcription. As of the end of the fiscal year, there were 108,360 shelflist records available through *CGP*.

Shelflist Digitization

As part of its records management requirement, GPO has been planning for the eventual transfer of the tangible shelflist to the National Archives and Records Administration for long-term preservation and archiving. The cards date back to the 19th century, and despite meticulous care over the years their condition is beginning to deteriorate. The goal of the digitization project, which should be complete in 2012, is to ensure that a high-quality image of all shelflist cards remains accessible to GPO staff. GPO contracted out the scanning and digitization of the cards, and the contract was awarded in January 2011. By the end of FY 2011 approximately two-thirds of the drawers had been digitized.

GPO Access Transition

On December 20, 2010, FDsys was released as GPO's official system of record for online government information, and on that date the countdown to the shutdown of GPO Access began. With more than 15 years of service, GPO Access is a well-respected and heavily accessed resource for users throughout the world. In order to ensure continuity of access from GPO Access to FDsys, a plan was developed to provide a seamless transition to FDsys for federal depository libraries, Congress, federal agencies, and the general public. The plan divided the shutdown into three phases: the system-of-record phase, the archive phase, and the shutdown phase.

The system-of-record phase began with the announcement that FDsys was officially GPO's system of record, and it continued through October 2011. This phase focused on introducing GPO Access users to FDsys while GPO Access and

FDsys were maintained in tandem. Users were notified of the official release of FDsys and given a link to the site through the implementation of a pop-up banner on strategic GPO Access Web pages.

In early November 2011 the GPO Access pop-up banner was modified to announce the implementation of the archive phase of GPO Access. Starting on November 5, FDsys became GPO's only site for both current and historical information from all three branches of the federal government. GPO Access is accessible as a reference archive.

As part of the final preparations for the shutdown of GPO Access, GPO is in the process of creating one-to-one redirects from GPO Access content to the FDsys equivalent. This will ensure that bookmarks, Web links, URLs in print publications, and other GPO Access references point to valid Web resources. Once this has been completed, phase three will be implemented, and GPO Access will be taken offline. A date has not yet been established for the final shutdown of GPO Access, but it is slated for FY 2012.

FDsys Training Initiative

Part of LSCM's efforts to educate the public on the use of FDsys is the creation of a formal FDsys training plan. In summer 2011 LSCM staff began the design of a plan with two major components: developing a comprehensive FDsys curriculum and curriculum tools, and planning for the implementation of the curriculum and tools in live, virtual, and recorded video environments.

For the curriculum team, LSCM assembled staff who had previous experience giving GPO Access and FDsys training, staff who have worked extensively in the development of FDsys, and staff with backgrounds in education. In August 2011 the curriculum was completed. It includes detailed scripts for recorded video modules, step-by-step talking points and instructions for educators, presentation material for each session, and a user manual to bring it all together. The curriculum includes the following: introduction, background, basic searching, advanced searching, browsing government publications, retrieving by citation, tracking legislation (including seven sub-parts), tracking regulations (including four sub-parts), help, and "tips and tricks" (including 15 sub-parts and counting).

LSCM posted questions about online training tools and learning software applications on the FDLP Community site. Comments were received about how content is created and delivered, favorite features, and other online training informational resources. The information LSCM gained from the federal depository library community was used to develop a document that identifies requirements for a system to be used for depository library training and to manage training materials and activities.

Through this training initiative, LSCM will increase awareness of FDsys, help users navigate its content effectively, and enhance access to federal government information.

Online Learning

In August 2011 Online Programming for All Libraries (OPAL) became unavailable for GPO's use. Since that time, and in conjunction with LSCM's FDsys training initiative, LSCM staff has been working toward replacing OPAL with a dynamic resource to assist the depository community in sharing their expertise and to receive training from GPO. FY 2011 saw many sessions of Chat with GPO, including "Going Mostly Electronic—Part I: The Basics," "Going Mostly Electronic—Part II: Options and Opportunities," "Going Mostly Electronic—Part III: Chat with GPO," "Modeling a Sustainable FDLP for the 21st Century," "WEBTech Notes," "FDsys: Advanced Search Techniques and Tips," "Searching the Catalog of U.S. Government Publications," and "Digitization Projects Registry: A Tool for Discovery, Collaboration, and Preservation."

All past Chat with GPO sessions, along with all other past OPAL sessions, remain available in the OPAL archive. In addition to past Chat with GPO sessions, there are sessions given by FDLP community members and GPO staff covering topics from Preservation to Maps and GIS.

FDLP Connection

In August 2011 LSCM launched *FDLP Connection,* an online newsletter that highlights the goals, achievements, activities, and stories of the FDLP community. Designed to instruct, inspire, and educate, this monthly Web-based newsletter features

- Columns from the Superintendent of Documents and the Depository Library Council
- Information on the organizations and staff within GPO that work behind the scenes to produce, protect, preserve, and distribute documents of the American democracy
- Insights from GPO staff, depository librarians, federal agencies, and other FDLP community members
- Spotlights on depositories and partnerships that are making a difference in providing free public access to and long-term preservation of federal government information
- Updates on GPO projects relating to FDLP
- Tips about FDLP and how to promote services to local communities

Each monthly edition has a different theme. FY 2011 issues of *FDLP Connection* featured articles by Tim Byrne, senior outreach librarian, Office of Scientific and Technical Information, U.S. Department of Energy; Robert Lopresti, government information librarian, Western Washington University; Bev Godwin, director of the Federal Citizen Information Center, GSA Office of Citizen Services and Innovative Technologies; Marianne Mason, federal information librarian, University of Iowa Libraries; and Daniel Rooker, technical services librarian and depository library coordinator, Downey City (California) Library.

Harvesting Initiative

GPO has undertaken an initiative to modernize GPO's Web harvesting program. In light of the fact that 97 percent of all government information is born digital and disseminated over the Web, a robust harvesting program is essential to GPO's mission. In FY 2011 a task force was developed to tackle this issue. As a result, GPO entered into a one-year contract with Internet Archive's "Archive-It" Web harvesting service to harvest and host Web-based federal agency publications within the scope of FDLP. LSCM staff will manage the process of site selection, acquisition, and cataloging, while outsourcing the actual harvesting and content hosting to Internet Archive. In the future, the Web content collection will be made accessible through an upcoming search feature on FDsys.

Web Enhancements

As part of its technology refresh strategy, FDLP Desktop, FDLP Community site, and Ben's Guide are all scheduled for an aesthetic redesign and a content management system version upgrade in FY 2012. During FY 2011 extensive research and planning was conducted based on Web standards, technologies, and trends. Lessons learned from the research and planning will be applied to the redesign of these Web services. The redesign of the FDLP Community site is on hold in order to focus attention on FDLP Desktop and Ben's Guide.

Work is continuing in FY 2012 with testing and refinement of both FDLP Desktop and Ben's Guide. Next steps include content development, content migration, site testing, and bug corrections, which will lead to the relaunch of these services.

Depository Library Spotlight

Each month GPO Depository Library Spotlight highlights a different federal depository library and describes the featured library and the unique services it offers. The feature appears on gpo.gov and in the *FDLP Connection* newsletter. Libraries included in FY 2011 were Snell Library at Northwestern University, Boston; Calvin T. Ryan Library at the University of Nebraska, Kearney; Contra Costa County Library, Pleasant Hill, California; Six State Virtual Conference; Trinity College Library, Hartford, Connecticut; Murphy Library at the University of Wisconsin, La Crosse; Roberts-LaForge Library at Delta State University, Cleveland, Mississippi; Alaska State Court Law Library, Anchorage; Library of Virginia, Richmond; Middletown (New York) Thrall Library; Raymond H. Fogler Library at the University of Maine, Orono; and Gordon B. Olson Library at Minot (North Dakota) State University.

Metrics

Notable LSCM metrics for FY 2011:

• New titles acquired (online and tangible)	22,225
• Searches of the *Catalog of U.S. Government Publications*	24,110,479
• Total titles cataloged	21,907
• Total PURLs created	13,376
• Total titles distributed	10,206
• Total copies distributed	1,648,615
• Number of federal depository libraries	1,209

Performance Measures/Quality Assurance

Legal Requirements and Program Regulations

In June 2011 GPO released *Legal Requirements and Program Regulations of the Federal Depository Library Program,* which provides member libraries with a single resource for current obligations of libraries in the FDLP system.

The document is divided into three parts: an Authority Statement prefaces the document and explains the basis for the content; Legal Requirements provides a concise summary of the legal requirements found in Title 44 U.S.C. 1901–1916 (2010); FDLP Program Regulations lists the Superintendent of Documents' current FDLP regulations governing FDLP member libraries. This publication supersedes the *FDLP Handbook* (2008) and the *Federal Depository Library Requirements* (2009).

Public Access Assessment

A Public Access Assessment (PAA) is a review by GPO staff of an individual library's federal depository operations and services. GPO has the responsibility, pursuant to 44 U.S.C. 19, to ensure that the resources it distributes to federal depository libraries are made accessible to the general public and that participating libraries comply with the requirements and regulations of FDLP.

The review is intended to be supportive of each individual depository library and involves sharing of best practices and recognition of notable achievements that will help each library continue to enhance its operations and services. The PAA is organized according to the same categories found in *Legal Requirements and Program Regulations of the Federal Depository Library Program.*

2011 Biennial Survey

The Biennial Survey provides GPO with important information concerning the conditions of both individual depository libraries and FDLP as a whole. This data is used to administer the program and to assist in the assessments of the conditions and services of depository libraries. Completion of the survey is required of all libraries participating in FDLP.

On the very last day of FY 2011, the 2011 Biennial Survey was released and ready for completion by federal depository coordinators. The 2011 survey was prepared with a focus on keeping it simple, relevant, and easy to use. Multi-part questions were eliminated, and the number of questions was kept low by asking only for information that GPO intended to use.

The survey tool, developed by GPO staff members, was created so that federal depository coordinators could print, save, and e-mail the survey as necessary. The tool was tested by a pilot group whose input was included in the final version.

The 2011 survey consisted of 31 questions and spanned seven pages.

Library User Survey

In its efforts to address the value of FDLP membership and to determine baseline outcomes-based performance measures, GPO, working with Outsell, Inc. and the Depository Library Council, developed a survey for depository library users. The survey ran from October 10, 2010, through March 4, 2011, and drew more than

3,300 responses from users of nearly 550 depository libraries, yielding a confidence level of about 95 percent. Submissions were well distributed, both geographically and across different library types.

The survey report, "FDLP Users Speak: The Value and Performance of Libraries Participating in the Federal Depository Library Program," conveys the overall results and compares results by library segment and by selective and regional designations.

Survey respondents were asked about the purposes for which they were accessing materials from federal depository libraries. A series of questions followed that related outcomes in light of their objectives when using the information they retrieved.

GPO learned that most depository library patrons sought government information for academic research (65 percent), educational (40 percent), or personal (33 percent) purposes. Other uses for depository resources ranged from lobbying and legal needs to charity work and civic participation to business and scientific needs.

In the opinion of respondents, the overall quality of depository library resources and services and of other important performance indicators is positive. Of the respondents, 85 percent were "somewhat" or "extremely" satisfied with the overall quality of resources and services, and 84 percent were "somewhat" or "extremely" satisfied with levels of service provided by library staff.

Individual depository reports contain charts that compare the library's results with the aggregated results for its state or territory, library sector, and for all libraries. Any comments made by users were included.

Quality Control for Classification and Cataloging

LSCM continued in FY 2011 to refine its quality control processes for classification and cataloging. By means of various searches that LSCM's Library Technical Services Support unit runs on a monthly or biweekly basis, staff members check cataloging records for issues with the item, class numbers, and the PURL. Staff members run a monthly check of records for authorities and make corrections as appropriate. Supervisors pull records at random on a quarterly basis and check them carefully for errors. Internal processes and forms have been developed for increasing communication among staff and peer quality checking. Additionally, GPO staff members continue to review and implement quality control measures identified by GPO's Cataloging Quality Control Team.

Serials Management Plan

GPO has embarked upon a serials management strategy to create a streamlined serials processing workflow to provide better intellectual control of federal government serials in all formats and to provide improved electronic tools for locating and accessing serial publications in *CGP*.

The goals of this project are to migrate serials processing from the legacy ACSIS system to GPO's ILS; enhance access to serial information at the piece or issue level and make this information available through *CGP*; and increase information about historic and current serial titles for the FDLP and Cataloging and Indexing programs. This two- to three-year project (with more than 28,000 active serial titles in *CGP*) is driven by the development of new workflows and procedures. It replaces information previously available in the printed *Monthly Catalog of U.S. Government Publications Serials Supplement.*

During FY 2011 work was completed on numerous serials projects. Serials from GPO's historic shelflist were added to *CGP*; serial policy and desk instructions were created, including prediction patterns, serials check-in instructions, and an item-level description; a total of 78,870 serials that were distributed to libraries were checked in to ILS; and a rework of GPO's internal workflow to process new serials was begun.

LSCM sponsored two virtual practicum students in FY 2011. Working in conjunction with a supporting librarian at a depository library with a large collection, students assisted in projects aimed at the goal of identifying fugitive documents not in *CGP.*

RDA Compliance Project

Since early spring 2011 all staff members in LSCM's Library Technical Information Services have been making preparations for the implementation of Resource Description and Access (RDA). The cataloging team has been training in RDA via reading, webinars, tests, and training records since February 2011. The ILS interface was updated to reflect labels for the new RDA MARC fields (336, 337, and 338). Several RDA records were created in ILS and were made available for the public to view. A GPO Cataloging Policy on RDA capitalization rules was prepared and released on the FDLP Desktop.

In FY 2011 GPO continued to monitor the discussion of the Joint Steering Committee for the Development of RDA. RDA is based on Functional Requirements for Bibliographic Records (FRBR) and was released in 2010. It has undergone testing at the Library of Congress, the National Library of Medicine, the National Agricultural Library, and at RDA National Test Partner Libraries. In July 2011 the test partner libraries concluded that they will delay implementation of RDA until January 2013, pending some improvements the steering committee and partner libraries need to make to the RDA documentation and toolkit.

The FDLP RDA announcement with major policy documentation appended can be found on FDLP Desktop.

Selling Government Information

GPO's Sales Program currently offers for sale approximately 2,500 individual government titles on a broad array of subjects. These are sold principally via the Internet, e-mail, telephone, fax, mail, and through the GPO main bookstore. The program operates on a cost-recovery basis. Publications for sale include books, e-books, forms, posters, pamphlets, and CD-ROMs. Subscription services for both dated periodicals and basic-and-supplement services (involving an initial volume and supplemental issues) also are offered.

GPO's U.S. Government Online Bookstore (http://bookstore.gpo.gov) is the prime source of information on its sales inventory. The bookstore includes a searchable database of all in-print publications. It also includes a broad spectrum of special publication collections featuring new and popular titles and key product lines. GPO uses Pay.gov, a secure government-wide financial management transaction portal available around the clock to provide timely and efficient processing of online orders. Free shipping is included. The online bookstore also gives customers the options of expedited shipping, new and improved shopping cart and order confirmation e-mails, and expanded ordering options for international customers.

Express service, which includes priority handling and expedited delivery, is available for orders placed by telephone for domestic delivery. Orders placed before noon Eastern Time for in-stock publications and single-copy subscriptions will be delivered within two working days. For more information, call the GPO Contact Center toll-free at 866-512-1800 (or 202-512-1800 within the Washington, D.C., area). The Contact Center is open from 8 A.M. to 5:30 P.M. Eastern time.

GPO also offers publications for sale through the main bookstore, which is located at 710 North Capitol St. N.W., in Washington, D.C., which has recently undergone a major renovation. Hours of operation are 8 A.M. to 4 P.M. Eastern time. The bookstore is available by telephone at 202-512-0132 or by e-mail at mainbks@gpo.gov.

Consumer-oriented publications also are either sold or distributed at no charge through the Federal Citizen Information Center in Pueblo, Colorado, which GPO operates on behalf of the General Services Administration.

Interested parties can register to receive e-mail updates free of charge when new publications become available for sale through GPO's New Titles by Topic e-mail alert service, which can be accessed at http://bookstore.gpo.gov/alertservice. jsp.

Standing order service is available to ensure automatic receipt of many of GPO's most popular recurring and series publications. Standing order customers receive each new edition automatically as soon as it is published. This service can be set up using a MasterCard, American Express, or Discover credit card, or through a Superintendent of Documents deposit account. For more information on how to set up a standing order for recurring or series publications, e-mail contactcenter@gpo.gov or call 866-512-1800 (toll free) or 202-512-1800 within the Washington, D.C., area.

The GPO sales program has begun using print-on-demand technology to increase the long-term availability of publications. The program also has brought its bibliographic practices more in line with those of the commercial publishing sector by utilizing ONIX (Online Information Exchange), the publishing industry's standard electronic format for sharing product data with wholesale and retail booksellers, other publishers, library buyers, and anyone else involved in the sale of books. ONIX enables GPO to have government publications listed, promoted, and sold by commercial book dealers worldwide. In 2010 GPO began Government Book Talk (http://govbooktalk.gpo.gov), a blog that reviews government publications past and present. In its first year and a half, the new blog received more than 210,000 page views and added more than 1,760 subscribers.

National Technical Information Service

U.S. Department of Commerce, Alexandria, VA 22312
800-553-NTIS (6847) or 703-605-6000
World Wide Web http://www.ntis.gov

Wayne Strickland
Manager, Office of Product and Program Management

The National Technical Information Service (NTIS) is the nation's largest and most comprehensive source of government-funded scientific, technical, engineering, and business information produced or sponsored by U.S. and international government sources. NTIS is a federal agency within the U.S. Department of Commerce.

Since 1945 the NTIS mission has been to operate a central U.S. government access point for scientific and technical information useful to American industry and government. NTIS maintains a permanent archive of this declassified information for researchers, businesses, and the public to access quickly and easily. Release of the information is intended to promote U.S. economic growth and development and to increase U.S. competitiveness in the world market.

The NTIS collection of more than 2 million titles contains products available in various formats. Such information includes reports describing research conducted or sponsored by federal agencies and their contractors; statistical and business information; multimedia training programs; databases developed by federal agencies; and technical reports prepared by research organizations worldwide. NTIS maintains a permanent repository of its information products.

More than 200 U.S. government agencies contribute to the NTIS collection, including the National Aeronautics and Space Administration; the Environmental Protection Agency; the departments of Agriculture, Commerce, Defense, Energy, Health and Human Services, Homeland Security, Interior, Labor, Treasury, Veterans Affairs, Housing and Urban Development, Education, and Transportation; and numerous other agencies. International contributors include Canada, Japan, Britain, and several European countries.

NTIS on the Web

NTIS offers Web-based access to information on government scientific and technical research products. Visitors to http://www.ntis.gov can search the entire collection dating back to 1964 free of charge. NTIS provides many of the technical reports for purchase on CD, paper copies, or downloaded pdf files. RSS feeds of recently catalogued materials are available in 39 major subject categories at http://www.ntis.gov/rss/RSSNTISCategoryList.aspx.

NTIS Database

The NTIS Database offers unparalleled bibliographic coverage of U.S. government and worldwide government-sponsored research information products acquired by NTIS since 1964. Its contents represent hundreds of billions of research dollars and cover a range of important topics including agriculture, biotechnology, business, communication, energy, engineering, the environment, health and safety, medicine, research and development, science, space, technology, and transportation.

The NTIS Database can be leased directly from NTIS and can also be accessed through several commercial services. For an updated list of organizations offering NTIS Database products, see http://www.ntis.gov/products/commercial. aspx.

To lease the NTIS Database directly from NTIS, contact the NTIS Office of Product Management at 703-605-6515. For more information, see http://www. ntis.gov/products/ntisdb.aspx.

NTIS National Technical Reports Library

The National Technical Reports Library (NTRL) enhances accessibility to the NTIS technical reports collection. Subscription rates are based on institutional FTE levels. NTRL operates on a system interface that allows users to do queries on the large NTIS bibliographic database. The intent is to broadly expand and improve access to more than 2.5 million bibliographic records (pre-1960 to the present) and 600,000 full-text documents in pdf format that are directly linked to that bibliographic database. For more information, visit http://www.ntis.gov/products/ntrl.aspx.

Other Databases Available from NTIS

NTIS offers several valuable research-oriented database products. To find out more about accessing the databases, visit http://www.ntis.gov/products/data.aspx.

AGRICOLA

As one of the most comprehensive sources of U.S. agricultural and life sciences information, the AGRICOLA (Agricultural Online Access) Database contains bibliographic records for documents acquired by the U.S. Department of Agriculture's National Agricultural Library. To access an updated list of organizations offering AGRICOLA Database products, see http://www.ntis.gov/products/agricola.aspx.

AGRIS

The International Information System for the Agricultural Science and Technology (AGRIS) Database is a cooperative system for collecting and disseminating information on the world's agricultural literature. More than 100 national and multinational centers take part in the system. References to citations for U.S. publications given coverage in the AGRICOLA Database are not included in AGRIS. To access an updated list of organizations offering AGRIS Database products, see http://www.ntis.gov/products/agris.aspx.

Energy Science and Technology

The Energy Science and Technology Database (EDB) is a multidisciplinary file containing worldwide references to basic and applied scientific and technical research literature. The information is collected for use by government managers, researchers at the national laboratories, and other research efforts sponsored by the U.S. Department of Energy, and the results of this research are transferred to the public. To access an updated list of organizations offering EDB products, see http://www.ntis.gov/products/engsci.aspx.

FEDRIP

The Federal Research in Progress Database (FEDRIP) provides access to information about ongoing federally funded projects in such fields as the physical sciences, engineering, and life sciences. To access an updated list of organizations offering FEDRIP Database products, see http://www.ntis.gov/products/fedrip.aspx.

Online Subscriptions

NTIS offers quick, convenient online access, on a subscription basis, to the following resources:

World News Connection

World News Connection (WNC) is an NTIS online news service accessible only via the World Wide Web. WNC makes available English-language translations of time-sensitive news and information from thousands of non-U.S. media. Particularly effective in its coverage of local media, WNC provides the power to identify what is happening in a specific country or region. The information is obtained from speeches, television and radio broadcasts, newspaper articles, periodicals, and books. The subject matter focuses on socioeconomic, political, scientific, technical, and environmental issues and events.

The information in WNC is provided to NTIS by the Open Source Center (OSC), a U.S. government agency. For more than 60 years, analysts from OSC's domestic and overseas bureaus have monitored timely and pertinent open source material, including gray literature. Uniquely, WNC allows subscribers to take advantage of the intelligence-gathering experience of OSC. WNC is updated every government business day. New information is added hourly.

Access to WNC is available through Dialog Corporation. To use the service, complete the WNC form at http://www.dialog.com/contacts/forms/wnc.shtml.

U.S. Export Administration Regulations

U.S. Export Administration Regulations (EAR) provides the latest rules controlling the export of U.S. dual-use commodities, technology, and software. Step by step, EAR explains when an export license is necessary and when it is not, how to obtain an export license, policy changes as they are issued, new restrictions on exports to certain countries and of certain types of items, and where to obtain further help.

This information is available through NTIS in looseleaf form, on CD-ROM, and online. An e-mail update notification service is also available. For more information, see http://www.ntis.gov/products/export-regs.aspx.

Special Subscription Services

NTIS Alerts

More than 1,000 new titles are added to the NTIS collection every week. NTIS prepares a list of search criteria that is run against all new studies and research and development reports in 16 subject areas. An NTIS Alert provides a twice-monthly information briefing service covering a wide range of technology topics.

For more information, call the NTIS Subscriptions Department at 703-605-6060 or see http://www.ntis.gov/products/alerts.aspx.

NTIS Selected Research Service

NTIS Selected Research Service (SRS) is a tailored information service that delivers complete electronic copies of government publications based on your needs, automatically, within a few weeks of announcement by NTIS. SRS includes the full bibliographic information in XML format. Customers choose between Standard SRS (selecting one or more of the 320 existing subject areas) or Custom SRS, which creates a new subject area to meet their particular needs. Custom SRS requires a one-time fee to cover the cost of strategy development and computer programming to set up a profile. Except for this fee, the cost of Custom SRS is the same as the Standard SRS. Through this ongoing subscription service, customers download copies of new reports pertaining to their field(s) of interest, as NTIS obtains the reports.

This service is also available in CD-ROM format as Science and Technology on CD, which delivers the documents digitized and stored in pdf format.

For more information on SRS, see http://www.ntis.gov/products/SRS.aspx. To place an order, call 800-363-2068 or 703-605-6060. For more information on Science and Technology on CD, see http://www.ntis.gov/products/STonCD.aspx.

Federal Science Repository Service

Collections of scientific and technical documents, images, videos and other content represent the mission and work of an agency or other institution. To help preserve these collections, NTIS formed a joint venture with Information International Associates, Inc. of Oak Ridge, Tennessee, to develop for federal agencies a searchable, digital Federal Science Repository Service (FSRS). Now available, FSRS provides a supporting infrastructure, long-term storage, security, interface design, and content management and operational expertise. An agency can utilize this entire service or select components, resulting in the design of an agency-specific repository that serves as a distinct gateway to its content.

NTIS Customer Service

NTIS's automated systems keep it at the forefront when it comes to customer service. Shopping online at NTIS is safe and secure; its secure socket layer (SSL) software is among the best available.

Electronic document storage is fully integrated with NTIS's order-taking process, allowing it to provide rapid reproduction for the most recent additions to the NTIS document collection. Most orders for shipment are filled and delivered anywhere in the United States in five to seven business days. Rush service is available for an additional fee.

Key NTIS Contacts for Ordering

Order by Phone

Sales Desk   800-553-6847 or 703-605-6000
8:30 A.M.–5:00 P.M. Eastern time, Monday–Friday

Subscriptions   800-363-2068 or 703-605-6060
8:30 A.M.–5:00 P.M. Eastern time, Monday–Friday

TDD (hearing impaired only)   703-487-4639
8:30 A.M.–5:00 P.M. Eastern time, Monday–Friday

Order by Fax

24 hours a day, seven days a week   703-605-6900

To verify receipt of fax, call 703-605-6090, 7:00 A.M.–5:00 P.M. Eastern time, Monday–Friday

Order by Mail

National Technical Information Service
5301 Shawnee Rd.
Alexandria, VA 22312

RUSH Service (available for an additional fee)   800-553-6847 or 703-605-6000
Note: If requesting RUSH Service, please do not mail your order.

Order Online

Direct and secure online ordering   http://www.ntis.gov

National Archives and Records Administration

700 Pennsylvania Ave. N.W., Washington, DC 20408-0001

8601 Adelphi Rd., College Park, MD 20740
301-837-2000
World Wide Web http://www.archives.gov

The National Archives and Records Administration (NARA), an independent federal agency, is the nation's record keeper. NARA safeguards and preserves the records of the federal government, so that the people can discover, use, and learn from this documentary heritage. NARA ensures continuing access to the essential documentation of the rights of American citizens and the actions of their government.

NARA is singular among the world's archives as a unified federal institution that accessions and preserves materials from all three branches of government. It carries out its mission through a national network of archives and records services facilities stretching from Washington, D.C., to the West Coast, including presidential libraries documenting administrations back to Herbert Hoover. NARA assists federal agencies in documenting their activities, administering records management programs, scheduling records, and retiring non-current records to federal records centers. The agency also administers the National Historical Publications and Records Commission, a grants program for archives across the nation, the papers of key figures in American history, and state and local government records. It publishes the laws, regulations, presidential documents, and other official notices of the federal government through the *Federal Register*. In cooperation with other federal agencies, it administers the National Declassification Center, providing a systematic, collaborative approach to the referral process, essential to the proper declassification and release of information. It also administers the Information Security Oversight Office, which oversees the government's security classification program, and the Office of Government Information Services, responsible for the review of agencies' Freedom of Information Act (FOIA) administration practices and compliance with FOIA.

NARA constituents include the federal government, educators and their students at all levels, the public, family historians, the media, the archival community, and a broad spectrum of professional associations and researchers in such fields as history, political science, law, library and information services, and genealogy.

The size and breadth of NARA's holdings are enormous. Together, NARA's facilities hold approximately 4.5 million cubic feet (equivalent to more than 11 billion pieces of paper) of original textual and non-textual materials from the executive, legislative, and judicial branches of the federal government. Its multimedia collections include more than 120,000 motion picture films; more than 8 million maps, charts, and architectural drawings; about 250,000 sound and video recordings; more than 27 million aerial photographs; more than 14 million still pictures and posters; and about 165 terabytes of electronic records.

Records and Access

Electronic Records Archives

The critical Electronic Records Archives (ERA) system captures electronic records and information, regardless of format, saves them permanently, and provides access to them. In 2010 NARA deployed the Congressional Records Instance, providing for management and access to congressional assets. It met another major milestone in late 2011 with the release of a prototype of Online Public Access (OPA), the portal for public access to and information about NARA's holdings. Early public feedback has been positive. NARA also drafted a Preservation Framework, defining the principles for long-term preservation and access to permanent electronic records in ERA.

NARA works to continue moving data from its legacy systems into ERA, as well as ingesting new electronic records from federal agencies. Electronic records from the presidential libraries bring the total volume in ERA to more than 145 terabytes, an information content equivalent to more than 60 billion textual pages of records. ERA development was completed at the end of fiscal year (FY) 2011, and ERA moved to an operations and maintenance phase at the beginning of FY 2012. NARA's focus shifted to advancing user adoption in anticipation of ERA becoming mandatory by the end of 2012 for federal agency use in scheduling and transferring permanent electronic records to NARA. NARA's goal of transferring 10 terabytes per quarter from agencies was quickly dwarfed in late 2011 when it accepted 488 terabytes of 2010 census records into a secured part of the system. For more information about ERA, visit http://www.archives.gov/era.

NARA's Applied Research serves as its premier center for advanced and applied research capabilities in the fields of computer science, engineering, and archival science. Applied Research conducts research on new technologies, both to be aware of new types of electronic records it will need to preserve, and to evaluate new technologies that might be incorporated into the ERA system or other systems to increase their value. The center will also help NARA managers and employees acquire the new knowledge and skills they need to function effectively in e-government. For more information about Applied Research, visit: http://www.archives.gov/applied-research/index.html.

National Declassification Center

In an executive order signed in December 2009, President Barack Obama directed an overhaul of the way documents created by the federal government are classified and declassified. This initiative is aimed at promoting transparency and accountability of government. The president also directed the creation of the National Declassification Center (NDC), now located within NARA.

NDC is leading the streamlining of the declassification process throughout the federal government. In particular, it is accelerating the processing of historically valuable classified records in which more than one federal agency has an interest. It oversees the development of common declassification processes among agencies, and it is prioritizing declassification based on public interest and the likelihood of declassification. For more information about NDC, visit http://www.archives.gov/declassification.

Online Research Catalog

Today anyone connected to the Internet can search descriptions of nearly 80 percent of NARA's nationwide holdings and view digital copies of some of its most popular documents through its Online Public Access portal prototype. Because of the volume of NARA holdings, it will take several more years to fully populate the catalog. At present, the catalog contains more than 5 million descriptions of archival holdings, representing approximately 80 percent of NARA's total. Included in the catalog are nearly 160,000 digital copies of high-interest documents, representing many of the holdings highlighted in the Public Vaults, NARA's permanent interactive exhibition. The catalog is available on the Internet at http://www.archives.gov/research.

Office of Government Information

Congress refers to the Office of Government Information (OGIS) as "the federal FOIA ombudsman." In short, this means OGIS serves as a bridge between requesters and agencies, particularly in situations where clear, direct communication has been lacking.

OGIS was created within the NARA when the OPEN Government Act of 2007 amended the Freedom of Information Act (5 U.S.C. 552). OGIS's key responsibilities include the following:

- *Review compliance and policy.* OGIS reviews policies and procedures of administrative agencies under FOIA, reviews compliance with FOIA by agencies, and recommends policy changes to Congress and the president to improve the administration of FOIA.
- *Mediate disputes.* OGIS offers mediation services to resolve disputes between persons making FOIA requests and agencies (as a nonexclusive alternative to litigation). It may issue advisory opinions if mediation has not resolved the dispute.
- *Serve as ombudsman.* OGIS solicits and receives comments and questions from federal agencies and the public regarding the administration of FOIA to improve FOIA processes and facilitate communication between agencies and FOIA requesters.

In addition to these responsibilities, OGIS also provides dispute resolution training for the FOIA staff of federal agencies, and works closely with key FOIA stakeholders such as the requester community and open government advocates. For more information, visit http://www.archives.gov/ogis.

Internet

NARA's Web site, http://www.archives.gov, redesigned in late 2010, provides the most widely available means of electronic access to information about and services available from NARA. Feedback from visitors to the Web site, as well as visitors to the National Archives Building in Washington, D.C., led to portals designed to support the particular needs of researchers, veterans and their families, educators and students, and the general public, as well as easily found information for records managers, journalists, information security specialists, members of Congress, and federal employees. The site includes directions on how to contact NARA and do research at its facilities; descriptions of holdings in an online catalog at http://www.archives.gov/research/search; direct access to certain archival electronic records at http://www.archives.gov/aad; digital copies of selected archival documents; a form for customer questions, reference requests, comments, and complaints; electronic versions of *Federal Register* publications; online exhibits; classroom resources for students and teachers; and online tools, such as the Web-based interactive inquiry program at http://www.archives.gov/veterans/military-service-records that allows veterans and the next-of-kin of deceased veterans to complete and print, for mail-in submission, requests for their service records. At http://www.archives.gov/presidential-libraries visitors can link to individual presidential library Web sites to explore the history of the nation through its chief executives.

Copies of military pension records from the American Revolution through World War I, census pages, land files, court records, and microfilm publications can be ordered online, as can books, apparel, and accessories. Researchers can also submit reference questions about various research topics online.

Visitors to NARA's Web site can interact with NARA staff through a wide variety of social media including Facebook, Twitter, blogs, Flickr, and YouTube, and can obtain Really Simple Syndication (RSS) feeds for the "Document for Today" feature, NARA news, and press releases.

In cooperation with several federal agencies, NARA also has established a Web portal, http://www.regulations.gov, providing access to federal rules and instructions for submitting comments on federal regulatory actions.

Digitization Projects

NARA is working to digitize its traditional holdings to benefit their preservation and to provide greater access to the public. Although its online catalog gives users the ability to identify many archival holdings (except for the relatively small amount of material digitized and made available via catalog), it does not provide online access to the holdings themselves. Most of NARA's holdings currently are available only from the archival facility in which they are stored. Through a series of digitization projects, NARA is working to vastly increase online public access to more of its holdings. In 2008 it created a strategy to deal with digitization efforts, which includes working with partners in the private sector. Currently, more than 1,300 catalog descriptions link to millions of digital copies on partners' Web sites and many thousands more will be made available in the future; for instance, the 1940 census was scheduled to be available in 2012. More information about NARA's digitization partnerships is available at http://www.archives.gov/digitization/index.html.

Social Media

As the use of social media grows, so does its use at the National Archives. NARA has embraced social media as an important tool for open government. NARA's main goals are to increase awareness about archival holdings and programs and to enrich NARA's relationship with the public through conversations about its services and holdings. Social media projects are also a way for NARA to learn more about its researchers and the general public and what they seek from the National Archives.

NARA shares historical videos from its holdings and videos of recent public events through YouTube, and photographs and documents from its collections through Flickr Commons. NARA can also be found on Facebook and regularly "tweets" about news and events.

The AOTUS (Archivist of the United States) and NARAtions blogs have sparked many conversations about ideas NARA is exploring to do its work better. NARA also plans to use a blog to share information and collect feedback from the public on updating its Open Government plan and activities. NARA uses IdeaScale, an idea generation and social voting tool, as a way to get input from the general public, stakeholders, and staff.

For more information about NARA's Web 2.0 projects, visit http://www.archives.gov/social-media.

National Archives Experience

The National Archives Experience, a set of interconnected resources made possible by a public-private partnership between NARA and the Foundation for the National Archives, provides a variety of ways of exploring the power and importance of America's records.

The Rotunda for the Charters of Freedom at the National Archives Building in Washington, D.C., is the cornerstone of the National Archives Experience. On display are the Declaration of Independence, the Constitution, and the Bill of Rights, known collectively as the Charters of Freedom. The Public Vaults is a 9,000-square-foot permanent exhibition that conveys the feeling of going beyond the walls of the Rotunda and into the stacks and vaults of the working Archives. Dozens of individual exhibits, many of them interactive, reveal the breadth and variety of NARA's holdings. Complementing the Public Vaults, the O'Brien Gallery hosts a changing array of topical exhibits based on National Archives records. The 290-seat McGowan Theater is a state-of-the-art showplace for NARA's extensive audiovisual holdings and serves as a forum for lectures and discussion. It also is home to the Charles Guggenheim Center for the Documentary Film at the National Archives. Inside the Boeing Learning Center, the ReSource Room is an access point for teachers and parents to explore documents found in the exhibits and to use NARA's records as teaching tools. The center's "Constitution-in-Action" Learning Lab, is designed to provide an intense field trip adventure for middle and high school students.

Recently launched DocsTeach is an education Web site designed to provide instruction to teachers in the best practices of teaching with primary sources. Using documents in NARA's holdings as teachable resources, DocsTeach strongly supports its goal to promote civic literacy. This tool gives all teachers access to primary sources, instruction in best practices, and opportunities to interact with teachers across the nation. When developing the site, NARA established an online community that served as a virtual meeting place for its education team and colleagues from schools, institutions, and organizations to collaborate and share innovative ideas and best practices for this online Web resource. For more information, visit http://www.docsteach.org.

A set of Web pages now makes the entire National Archives Experience available to people who may not be able to travel to Washington. An illustrated history of the Charters of Freedom can be found, as well as information on educational programs, special events, and exhibits currently at the National Archives. Those traveling to Washington can make online reservations at http://www.recreation.gov. For more information, see The National Archives Experience at http://www.archives.gov/national-archives-experience.

National Archives Building Research Center

At the Robert M. Warner Research Center, researchers can consult with staff experts on records in the National Archives building and can submit requests to examine original documents. The center houses approximately 275,000 rolls of microfilmed records, documenting military service prior to the First World War, immigration into the United States, the federal census, Congress, federal courts in the District of Columbia, the Bureau of Indian Affairs, and the Freedmen's Bureau. The center also contains an ever-expanding system of reference reports.

Archives Library Information Center

The Archives Library Information Center (ALIC) provides access to information on American history and government, archival administration, information management, and government documents. ALIC is physically located in the National Archives at College Park, Maryland. Customers also can visit ALIC on the Internet at http://www.archives.gov/research/alic, where they will find "Reference at Your Desk" Internet links, staff-compiled bibliographies and publications, an online library catalog, and other resources. ALIC can be reached by phone at 301-837-3415.

Government Documents

U.S. government publications are generally available to researchers at many of the 1,250 congressionally designated federal depository libraries throughout the United States. A record set of these publications also is part of NARA's archival holdings. Publications of the U.S. government (Record Group 287) is a collection of selected publications of government agencies, arranged by the SuDoc classification system devised by the Office of the Superintendent of Documents, Government Printing Office (GPO). The core of the collection is a library established in 1895 by GPO's Public Documents Division. By 1972, when NARA acquired the library, it included official publications dating from the early years of the federal government and selected publications produced for and by federal government agencies. Since 1972 the 25,000-cubic-foot collection has been augmented periodically with accessions of U.S. government publications selected by the Office of the Superintendent of Documents as a byproduct of its cataloging activity. As with the federal depository library collections, the holdings in NARA's Record Group 287 comprise only a portion of all U.S. government publications.

NARA Publications

NARA publishes guides and indexes to various portions of its archival holdings; catalogs of microfilmed records; informational leaflets and brochures; general interest books about NARA and its holdings that will appeal to anyone with an interest in U.S. history; more-specialized publications that will be useful to scholars, archivists, records managers, historians, researchers, and educators; facsimiles of certain documents; and *Prologue*, a scholarly journal published quarterly. Some publications are also available on NARA's Web site, at http://www.archives.gov/publications/online.html. Many are available from NARA's Customer Service Center in College Park, by phoning toll-free 800-234-8861 or 866-272-6272 (in the Washington, D.C., area 301-837-2000) or faxing 301-837-0483. The NARA Web site's publications homepage, http://www.archives.gov/publications, provides detailed information about available publications and ordering.

Federal Register

The *Federal Register* is the daily gazette of the U.S. government, containing presidential documents, proposed and final federal regulations, and public notices of federal agencies. It is published by the Office of the Federal Register and printed and distributed by GPO. The two agencies collaborate in the same way to produce the annual revisions of the *Code of Federal Regulations* (*CFR*). Free access to the full text of the electronic version of the *Federal Register* and *CFR*, and to an unofficial, daily-updated electronic *CFR* (the *e-CFR*), is available at http://www.federalregister.gov. Federal Register documents scheduled for future publication are available for public inspection at the Office of the Federal Register (800 North Capitol St. N.W., Washington, D.C.) or online at the electronic Public Inspection Desk (http://www.federalregister.gov). Access to rules published in the *Federal Register* and open for public comment, and a portal for submitting comments is provided through the multiagency Web site http://www.regulations.gov.

Access to the full texts of other Federal Register publications, including the *Compilation of Presidential Documents, Public Papers of the President,* slip laws, *U.S. Statutes at Large,* and the *United States Government Manual* is available via http://www.federalregister.gov. Printed editions of these publications also are maintained at all federal depository libraries. The Public Law Electronic Notification Service (PENS) is a free subscription e-mail service available for notification of recently enacted public laws. The *Federal Register* Table of Contents Service is a free e-mail service available for delivery of the daily table of contents from the *Federal Register* with direct links to documents.

The Office of the Federal Register also publishes information about its ministerial responsibilities associated with the operation of the Electoral College and ratification of constitutional amendments, and provides access to related records. Publication information concerning laws, regulations, and presidential documents and services is available from the Office of the Federal Register (202-741-6000). Information, as well as additional finding aids for Federal Register publications, the Electoral College, and constitutional amendments, is also available through the Internet at http://www.archives.gov/federal-register.

Publications can be ordered by contacting GPO at http://bookstore.gpo.gov, and toll-free at 866-512-1800. To submit orders by fax or by mail, see http://bookstore.gpo.gov/help/index.jsp.

Customer Service

Few records repositories serve as many customers as NARA. In FY 2011 there were nearly 130,000 researcher visits to NARA facilities nationwide, including archives, presidential libraries, and federal records centers. At the same time, more than 1.5 million customers requested information in writing. NARA also served the executive agencies of the federal government, the courts, and Congress by providing records storage, reference service, training, advice, and guidance on many issues relating to records management. Federal records centers replied to more than 8.2 million requests for information and records, including more than 1.4 million requests for information regarding military and civilian service records provided by the National Personnel Records Center in St. Louis, Missouri. NARA also provided informative public programs at its various facilities for nearly 13,000 people. More than 1 million visited the National Archives Experience in Washington, D.C., and exhibits in the presidential library museums were visited by more than 2 million.

NARA knows it must understand who its customers are and what they need to ensure that people can discover, use, and learn from their documentary heritage in the National Archives. Customers are surveyed regularly to help NARA align its standards of performance with their expectations. By repeating surveys at frequent, systematic intervals, changes in NARA's performance are measured and appropriate management actions are taken to ensure that service levels reflect an appropriate balance between customer needs and NARA resources. NARA also maintains an Internet form (http://www.archives.gov/contact/inquire-form.html) to facilitate continuous feedback from customers about what is most important to them and what NARA might do better to meet their needs.

Grants

The National Historical Publications and Records Commission (NHPRC) is the grant-making affiliate of NARA's national grants program. The Archivist of the United States chairs the commission and makes grants on its recommendation. The commission's 14 other members represent the president (two appointees), the U.S. Supreme Court, the U.S. Senate and House of Representatives, the Departments of State and Defense, the Librarian of Congress, the American Association for State and Local History, the American Historical Association, the Association for Documentary Editing, the National Association of Government Archives and Records Administrators, the Organization of American Historians, and the Society of American Archivists.

The commission fulfills a statutory mission to ensure understanding of the nation's past by promoting the preservation and use of essential historical documents. It supports the creation and publication of documentary editions and research in the management and preservation of authentic electronic records, and it works in partnership with a national network of state archives and state historical records advisory boards to develop a national archival infrastructure. NHPRC grants help state and local governments, and archives, universities, historical societies, professional organizations, and other nonprofit organizations to establish or strengthen archival programs, improve training and techniques, preserve and process records collections, and provide access to them through finding aids, digitization of collections, and documentary editions of the papers of significant historical figures and movements in American history. For more information about the commission, visit http://www.archives.gov/nhprc.

Information Security Oversight Office

The Information Security Oversight Office (ISOO) is responsible to the president for policy and oversight of the government-wide security classification system and the National Industrial Security Program. ISOO is a component of NARA and receives policy and program guidance from the National Security Council. ISOO oversees the security classification programs (classification, safeguarding, and declassification) in both government and industry. It is also responsible for carrying out NARA's authorities and responsibilities as the Executive Agent for Controlled Unclassified Information. ISOO contributes materially to the effective implementation of the government-wide security classification program and has a direct impact on the performance of thousands of government employees and contract personnel who work with classified national security information. For more information on ISOO, visit http://www.archives.gov/isoo.

Administration

NARA employs approximately 3,500 people, of whom nearly 2,600 are full-time permanent staff members.

Federal Library and Information Center Committee

101 Independence Ave. S.E., Washington, DC 20540-4935
202-707-4800, fax 202-707-4818, e-mail flicc@loc.gov

Blane K. Dessy
Executive Director

Highlights of the Year

During fiscal year (FY) 2011 the Federal Library and Information Center Committee (FLICC) continued its mission to achieve better utilization of federal library and information resources; to provide a cost-effective and efficient administrative mechanism for delivering necessary services and materials to federal libraries and information centers; and to serve as a forum for discussion of federal library and information policies, programs, and procedures.

The FLICC membership focused its quarterly meetings on a variety of broad federal information topics, including a grant by the Council on Library and Information Resources to the Library of Congress to catalog African map sets; the U.S. Government Printing Office Federal Digital System (FDsys); the Resource Description and Access (RDA) cataloging code; the Library of Congress Collection Assessment project; and the Federal Inventory of Legal Materials for the Law Library of Congress's One World Library.

FLICC working groups completed an ambitious agenda during the fiscal year. Notably, the Membership and Governance Working Group prepared revisions to the FLICC bylaws and presented them to the membership and to the Library of Congress. The revised bylaws were scheduled to be formally approved during 2012.

The Human Resources Working Group launched its revision of the FLICC Competencies for Federal Librarians and held its annual networking fair for those interested in working in the federal library system. The Education Working Group presented a variety of seminars, workshops, and institutes on preservation issues, vendor portfolio management, strategic planning, Great Escapes library tours, and a three-day technicians institute.

FLICC also established a working group for federal librarians new to federal service. The NewFeds Working Group will support the development and advancement of early-career professionals with fewer than five years of federal service.

In conjunction with the working groups, FLICC offered 38 seminars, workshops, brokered conferences, and lunchtime discussions to more than 1,600 members of the federal library and information center community.

FLICC's cooperative network, FEDLINK, continued to enhance its fiscal operations while providing its members with $80.9 million in transfer-pay services, $6.7 million in direct-pay services, and an estimated $48.8 million in Direct Express services.

FLICC's budgeting efforts projected costs and revenue for FY 2010, looking at both private sector and historic costs based on vendor and Government Accountability Office (GAO) predictions. After examining FEDLINK program growth and savings realized through program management and program reserves,

FLICC/FEDLINK's governing bodies recommended that fees remain the same in FY 2012.

FEDLINK also began exploring strategic sourcing of federal information products and services with the Office of Management and Budget (OMB) and the General Services Administration (GSA). After detailed data and trend analysis, FEDLINK staff is identifying a number of core service areas that would offer other federal agencies an opportunity to streamline their information-resource purchasing. Using a similar model, FEDLINK also sponsored several planning meetings with a variety of federal agencies to explore the possibilities of a shared collection management plan. The group created a charter to identify common goals and responsibilities for a multi-agency dark storage operation for print materials.

FEDLINK gave federal agencies cost-effective access to automated information retrieval services for online research, cataloging, and resource sharing. FEDLINK members procured print serials, electronic journals, books and other publications, document delivery, and digitization and preservation services via Library of Congress/FEDLINK contracts with more than 120 vendors. The program obtained further discounts through consortia and enterprise-wide licenses for journals, aggregated information retrieval services, and electronic books. New in FY 2011 were a vendor that provides Web-based online foreign-language courseware, two additional book jobbers, and seven additional database vendors. FEDLINK established a contract with Information International Associates to support CENDI, an interagency working group of senior scientific and technical information managers from 14 federal agencies. FEDLINK also awarded 23 contracts to support preservation, conservation, and digitization services.

Accomplishments by Trends

FEDLINK performs a regular environmental scan of the information community to gain an overview of the external factors that may influence the organization. Identifying these factors allows for such strategic actions as adding services, adjusting budgets, and training staff.

The scan includes a review of materials from a variety of organizations and materials produced by the federal government, among them documents on reforming information technology within the government, information on transparency in government, and samples of resources making use of new technologies.

After analysis, the environmental scan identified seven major trends that define future efforts for federal libraries. FEDLINK focused on five of these goals:

Trend 1: Demonstrate returns on investment. FEDLINK worked with a variety of governmental and private sector colleagues to identify new ways to quantify its successes. In FY 2011 FEDLINK developed a workshop on managing the library's portfolio of vendors and supported the Outsell annual benchmarking survey; created a directory of federal libraries that contains basic benchmarking information on the federal library community; re-examined its cost-savings calculations; worked on designing strategic sourcing efforts with OMB and GSA to maximize savings and work efficiencies for federal agencies; and commissioned a study on the federal information marketplace and trends in government information purchasing.

Trend 2: Establish mission-critical programs. New program and budget paradigms within the federal information community influenced a number of FEDLINK's approaches to its performance markers and strategic planning. During the fiscal year FEDLINK prepared its five-year business plan revision and opted to use a "balanced scorecard" approach to improve program management in fiscal years 2012–2016; introduced new services including 60 contracts and agreements covering preservation, conservation, digitization, cataloging, Web content development, information retrieval, monograph acquisitions, online language learning, CENDI, and Science.gov support; developed a new program to support federal shared print repositories; and streamlined its organizational bylaws to reduce administrative overhead activities to focus on mission-critical programs.

Trend 3: Integrate mobile devices, apps, and dashboards into workflows. FEDLINK promoted demonstrations and provided information on vendor developments in support of mobile devices and apps. With a focus on the development of better access to and management of government data, FEDLINK cosponsored a number of educational programs and CENDI activities to discuss this new direction in serving information to varied users.

Trend 4: Expand roles as analyst, educator, and consultant. Efforts to evaluate and assist users with the continued rapid proliferation of information will grow exponentially. Librarians will need to integrate evaluation tools with the newest software and devices and expand instruction in digital literacy and online searching techniques. The release of a revised FLICC Competencies for Federal Librarians served as a centerpiece for developing FEDLINK's education programming. Outreach efforts for FY 2012, reaching a record number of participants both in person and virtually, combine the use of online learning systems, continued efforts on mentoring, and the creation of the working group NewFeds. The working group is concerned in part with building a sense of community among new FLICC members, advocating for new professionals, promoting careers in federal libraries, and developing partnerships with other FLICC working groups and library professional associations.

Trend 5: Cultivate use of the Semantic Web, cloud computing and Web 3.0. Library use of social collaboration and interactive responsibility will combine with Web 3.0 technologies to create a Semantic Web that includes human intelligence combined with data management where content and technology are now one. With increasingly cloud-based sources and tools, librarians will serve as a bridge to share information and support projects that cross agency lines. FEDLINK responded to this trend by identifying related initiatives for federal libraries in the FY 2012–2016 business plan.

Trend 6: Customize and personalize information to meet the needs of users. As this trend is critical to all facets of the FLICC/FEDLINK program, multiple efforts identified it as central to ongoing work. FEDLINK encouraged vendors to provide better support of end-user access to electronic information and data sets; continued work on implementation of the Customer Account Management System to support user needs directly; and continued work on implementation of its SYMIN II financial management system to improve management of customer accounts.

Trend 7: Collaborate via knowledge transfer and information sharing. In combination with the trends above, libraries will need to discover forthcoming agency efforts and package their services to serve the project mission. Librarians will need to merge information from various groups and identify information available from external sources. FEDLINK responded by identifying related initiatives for federal libraries in its latest performance in the 2012–2016 business plan.

Working Group Highlights

Awards

To honor the innovative ways in which federal libraries, librarians, and library technicians fulfill the information demands of government, business, research, scholarly communities, and the public, the FLICC Awards Working Group recognized the following libraries and staff:

Federal Library/Information Center of the Year (large library/information center category)—The Environmental Protection Agency (EPA) National Library Network was recognized for its leadership role in creating a collaborative community and responding to patron needs. EPA libraries worked together to digitize 7,500 agency publications during FY 2010, adding to the growing inventory of more than 45,000 digital documents available to the public at no cost. EPA libraries also implemented an internal live-chat reference service and began using webinar technology to bring locally developed library classes to an agency-wide audience. Serving as a point of contact for public inquiries, EPA libraries collectively addressed nearly 9,000 public reference questions and lent more than 8,000 documents, saving taxpayers an estimated $266,000.

Small Library/Information Center (staff of ten or fewer)—Medical Library, U.S. Army Medical Research Institute of Infectious Diseases, Fort Detrick, Maryland, was recognized for providing an array of educational and informational opportunities to increase its value to other agencies at Fort Detrick and to the Department of Homeland Security's National Biodefense and Countermeasures Center. In addition to designing an innovative combination of support and outreach efforts, the library digitized and preserved laboratory notebooks and developed a collection of published research papers from junior scientists. By providing searchable electronic access to these digitized resources and by maintaining its broader collection of e-resource, database, document, and traditional materials, the library served more than 850 institute employees and sister-agency staff members throughout the command.

Federal Librarian of the Year—Eleanor G. Frierson, deputy director of the National Agricultural Library (NAL) in Beltsville, Maryland, was recognized for her leadership as deputy director of NAL and her service as co-chair of the Science.gov Alliance. Frierson has nurtured partnerships across government and has advocated for federal libraries and the value of open access to information. Internationally, she chairs the International Federation of Library Associations and Institutions (IFLA) Government Information and Official Publications Section and serves as the U.S. representative to the WorldwideScience.org Alliance.

Federal Library Technician of the Year—Laura (Layne) Bosserman, a library technician with the U.S. Department of Justice in Washington, D.C., was recognized for her initiative, flexibility, and persistence in meeting the goals of the departmental libraries. Her work with the Washington offices and three field offices helped update their resource collections and saved the agency more than $100,000.

Budget and Finance

The FLICC Budget and Finance Working Group developed the FY 2012 FEDLINK budget and fee structure in the spring quarter. The group reviewed survey results from FEDLINK members and used the results to verify assumptions for the budget. The final budget held membership fees steady. The FEDLINK Advisory Council and FLICC Executive Board approved the budget in May, followed by the FLICC membership in July. Library of Congress officials approved the budget in September 2011.

Education

During the fiscal year the Education Working Group, in partnership with other FLICC working groups, sponsored 38 seminars, workshops, brokered conferences, and lunchtime discussions for members of the federal library and information center community. These programs featured such topics as preservation and digitization; resource, description, and access (RDA) testing; vendor portfolio management; and collection development and access. A two-day institute for federal library technicians focused on developing competencies.

The working group sponsored a series of orientations to libraries and information centers to provide an opportunity for federal librarians to become acquainted with a variety of institutions and collections in the Washington, D.C., area.

Human Resources

The Human Resources Working Group revised and published the FLICC Competencies for Federal Librarians in April. With the Federal Research Division, it produced the report *The Positive Education Requirements for Federal Librarians.* The working group's Federal Librarians Networking Symposium attracted registrants and vendors from nearly 25 agencies. The program also featured a series of well-attended sessions on résumé writing, federal applications, interviews, and the selection process.

Libraries and Emerging Technologies

The Libraries and Emerging Technologies working group focused its discussions on a variety of topics ranging from cybersecurity problems and solutions to making content readily available to people working at remote locations. The group also heard case studies and presentations by experts on topics including usability testing in libraries, the National Digital Stewardship Alliance, and the use of geospatial technology. They also cooperated with Information Today, Inc., to coordinate a government stream at the Computers in Libraries conference.

NewFeds

The newly established NewFeds working group ended FY 2011 with more than 36 members. Group leadership also spent most of the first year making presentations on federal career opportunities at a variety of workshops, symposia, and conferences. The group also coordinated a virtual event on sharing highlights from library professional associations and cosponsored a Web meeting with the FLICC Human Resources Working Group to provide a facilitated discussion about the future of the "federal librarian" position.

Nominating

The Nominating Working Group oversaw the election process for FLICC rotating members, FLICC Executive Board members, the FEDLINK Advisory Council, and a FEDLINK delegate to the OCLC Members Council. Nominees represented a variety of federal agencies.

Preservation

During FY 2011 the Preservation Working Group cosponsored, with CENDI and the Federal Agency Digitization Guidelines Initiative, a successful series of webinars on topics relating to digitization. The series, "Issues and Answers in Digitization," touched on copyright issues, best practices for converting audiovisual materials, and making digital and multimedia assets compliant with Section 508 requirements. The group also presented a program on the U.S. Government Printing Office Federal Digital System (FDSys), offering a behind-the-scenes view of the system. Later in the year the group presented a program on contracting for emergency response services. In July the Working Group and the Northeast Document Conservation Center cosponsored the biennial FLICC Preservation Institute, a week-long course on the fundamentals of library and archives preservation, taught by staff of the Library of Congress. Working group members assisted FEDLINK staff by serving as subject matter experts during the source-selection phase of a solicitation that resulted in 23 basic ordering agreements for procuring preservation services for the federal community.

Executive Director's Office

FLICC Executive Director Blane K. Dessy was keynote speaker at the International Gray Literature Conference in Prague and hosted visitors from China interested in emulating FLICC/FEDLINK concepts. Dessy also served on the Library of Congress Human Resources Working Group, spoke at the International Association of Intelligence Analysis at Johns Hopkins University, and served on the Catholic University of America School of Library Sciences Intelligence Analysis Advisory Committee.

Publications and Education Office

In FY 2011 FLICC continued its publication program as a digital communication provider and used the FEDLIB listserv to electronically distribute critical advocacy and program information to more than 3,000 subscribers.

FLICC revised mission-critical materials and developed targeted resources to support the FEDLINK program, including revisions to the FLICC bylaws and three FEDLINK Information Alerts. It also produced the minutes of the four FY 2010 Quarterly Meetings and six FLICC Executive Board meetings, and all FLICC education program promotional and support materials. In addition, it produced announcements to promote FLICC education programs and other materials for FEDLINK membership meetings, the brown-bag lunch discussion series, and education institutes.

Staff members continued to convert all publications, announcements, alerts, member materials, meeting minutes, and working group resources into HTML and pdf formats. New resources for the fiscal year included a federal library affiliate's page, photographic coverage of FLICC programs, research papers, and the revised Competencies for Federal Librarians. Staff members maintained many Web links throughout the FLICC/FEDLINK Web site, worked on quality assurance efforts with the Library of Congress's Library Services branch and the Office of Strategic Initiatives, and enhanced and expanded the site. Staff also participated in the Federal Consortium on Second Life as part of ongoing efforts to influence federal agency use of Web 2.0 emerging technologies.

FLICC increased its distance-learning offerings by using Web conferencing software for a number of its free events, and routinely incorporated electronic versions of PowerPoint and other presentation materials to enhance access to the resources available at educational programs. Staff used Web conferencing services to offer live and interactive attendance to quarterly membership and other meetings to participants at remote locations.

With its working groups, FLICC offered a total of 38 seminars, workshops, brokered conferences, and lunchtime discussions to members of the federal library and information center community. Institutes and workshops on emerging technologies, collections management, preservation, and digitization drew more than 1,600 attendees.

FLICC demonstrated its ongoing commitment to library technicians' continuing education by hosting its Institute for Federal Library Technicians and its annual teleconference series "Soaring to . . . Excellence," produced by the College of DuPage. Federal and academic librarians also joined FLICC professionals to discuss various areas of librarianship, including virtual reference, preservation, and disaster preparedness, Web writing and content management, and federal appropriations law. The ongoing FLICC Great Escapes series returned, with library tours at the U.S. State Department, the National Institute of Standards and Technology (NIST), the Library of Congress Culpepper, Virginia, facility and the U.S. Agency for International Development (USAID) Knowledge Services Center in Washington, D.C. FLICC also provided organizational, promotional and logistical support for FEDLINK meetings and events including a variety of career development meetings and 33 vendor presentations.

Staff members also continued to support the variety of initiatives and projects of all FLICC governing bodies including meetings, listservs, projects, graphic design initiatives, surveys, and the development of a variety of multimedia resource materials.

FEDLINK

FEDLINK (the Federal Library and Information Network) continued to give federal agencies cost-effective access to an array of automated information retrieval services for online research, cataloging, information management, and resource sharing. FEDLINK members also procured print and electronic journals, print and electronic books, sound recordings, audiovisual materials, document delivery, technical processing services, digitization, digital archiving, and preservation and conservation services via Library of Congress/FEDLINK contracts with more than 130 vendors. The program obtained further discounts for customers through consortia and enterprise-wide licenses for journals, aggregated information retrieval services, and books.

FEDLINK issued requests for proposals (RFPs) for preservation and digitization services, completing agreements with 23 companies. It held open seasons to establish new agreements with five book jobbers and one new online language learning system, and established seven new agreements with information retrieval vendors. FEDLINK also issued an RFP and awarded a contract for a Web development project for the Department of Defense, and issued requests for quotes for nearly 200 libraries' serials subscription services, 11 online language learning systems, four preservation and digitization projects, and two libraries' cataloging services. FEDLINK assisted 15 agencies in procuring services for digitization and digital archiving from the Internet Archive. It established a contract to support the interagency group CENDI, whose members represent 97 percent of the federal research and development budget, and an interagency agreement with Department of Energy to support Science.gov. It also established an agreement with National Archives and Records Administration to support a new print repository for federal libraries.

The fall FEDLINK membership meeting featured an overview of the Library of Congress Veterans History Project and the National Digital Stewardship Alliance. The spring membership meeting featured MaryBeth Dowdell of the Naval Research Laboratory, chair of the FLICC Budget and Finance Working Group, who presented the proposed budget for FY 2011. There were also updates on FLICC working groups and activities, including proposed changes to the bylaws.

In support of outreach, FLICC/FEDLINK staff continued to support Web conferencing via the Elluminate application. FEDLINK staff highlighted services at national conferences including those of American Library Association (ALA), the Military Librarians Workshop, and the Special Libraries Association, and regional events including the Government Accountability Office Expo. Staff also assisted the ALA Federal and Armed Forces Librarians Round Table in tracking activities affecting federal libraries. During ALA's Annual Conference in Washington, D.C., FLICC cosponsored a successful session on careers in federal libraries. Staff also participated in other national conferences, workshops, and meetings including Computers in Libraries, Internet Librarian, FOSE, and the Sixth International Digital Curation Conference.

FEDLINK negotiated discounted rates for several national conferences with Information Today, Inc., for Computers in Libraries 2011, WebSearch University, and the Internet Librarian conference, for a total savings to the government of nearly $80,000.

FEDLINK Fiscal Operations

FEDLINK continued to enhance its fiscal operations while providing its members with $80.9 million in transfer-pay services, $6.7 million in direct-pay services, and an estimated $48.8 million in Direct Express services, saving federal agencies more than $19.1 million in vendor volume discounts and approximately $17.1 million more in cost avoidance.

Accounts Receivable and Member Services

FEDLINK processed registrations from federal libraries, information centers, and other federal offices for 387 signed interagency agreements (IAGs) and 1,878 IAG amendments for agencies that added, adjusted, or ended service funding. These IAGs and IAG amendments represented 6,611 individual service requests to begin, move, convert, or cancel service from FEDLINK vendors. FEDLINK executed service requests by generating 6,156 delivery orders.

Transfer-Pay Accounts Payable Services

Staff processed 47,650 vendor invoices and earned $19,255 in discounts in excess of interest payment penalties levied for the late payment of invoices to FEDLINK vendors. FEDLINK continued to maintain open accounts for three prior years to pay publications service invoices for members using books and serials services.

Direct Express Services

The FEDLINK Direct Express Program now includes 73 vendors offering database retrieval services. The program is set up to provide customers procurement and payment options similar to GSA, in which the vendors pay a quarterly service fee to FEDLINK based on customer billings for usage.

Financial Management, Reporting, and Control

FEDLINK successfully passed the Library of Congress Financial Audit of FY 2010 transactions and completed vulnerability assessments of program financial risks for Library Services. As a follow-up requirement, staff members completed detail control reviews of program financial operations. Support for these audits includes financial systems briefings, documented review and analysis of the financial system, testing and verification of account balances in the central and subsidiary financial systems, financial statement preparation support, security briefings and reviews, and research and documented responses to follow-up audit questions and findings.

FEDLINK continued to provide central accounting for customer agency account balances to meet Treasury Department reporting requirements. FEDLINK also completed all aspects of its revolving fund status reporting, including preparation, review, and forecasts of revenue and expenses for each quarter.

National Center for Education Statistics Library Statistics Program

U.S. Department of Education, Institute of Education Sciences
Elementary/Secondary and Libraries Studies Division
1990 K St. N.W., Washington, DC 20006

Tai A. Phan
Program Director

In an effort to collect and disseminate more complete statistical information about libraries, the National Center for Education Statistics (NCES) initiated a formal library statistics program in 1989 that included surveys on academic libraries, school library media centers, public libraries, and state libraries.* At the end of December 2006, the Public Libraries Survey and the State Library Agencies Survey were officially transferred to the Institute of Museum and Library Services (IMLS). The Academic Libraries Survey and the School Library Media Centers Survey continue to be administered and funded by NCES, under the leadership of Tai A. Phan, program director, Library Statistics Program. [For detailed information on the surveys now being handled by IMLS, see "Institute of Museum and Library Services Library Programs" in Part 2 and "Highlights of IMLS Surveys" in Part 4—*Ed.*]

The library surveys conducted by NCES are designed to provide comprehensive nationwide data on the status of libraries. Federal, state, and local officials, professional associations, and local practitioners use these surveys for planning, evaluating, and making policy. These data are also available to researchers and educators.

The Library Statistics Program's Web site, http://nces.ed.gov/surveys/libraries, provides links to data search tools, data files, survey definitions, and survey designs for each survey. The two library surveys are described below.

Academic Libraries

The Academic Libraries Survey (ALS) provides descriptive statistics from more than 3,600 academic libraries in the 50 states, the District of Columbia, and the outlying areas of the United States. NCES surveyed academic libraries on a three-year cycle between 1966 and 1988. From 1988 to 1998, the ALS was a component of the Integrated Postsecondary Education Data System (IPEDS), and was on a two-year cycle. Since fiscal year 2000, the survey has no longer been a component of IPEDS, but remains on a two-year cycle. IPEDS and ALS data can still be linked by the identification codes of the postsecondary education institutions. In aggregate, these data provide an overview of the status of academic libraries nationally and by state. The survey collects data on libraries in the entire universe of degree-granting postsecondary institutions, using a Web-based data collection system.

*The authorization for the National Center for Education Statistics (NCES) to collect library statistics is included in the Education Sciences Reform Act of 2002 (PL 107-279), under Title I, Part C.

The ALS has an established working group composed of representatives of the academic library community. Its mission is to improve data quality and the timeliness of data collection, processing, and release. NCES also works cooperatively with the American Library Association (ALA), the Association of Research Libraries, the Association of College and Research Libraries, and academic libraries.

The survey collects data on the number of academic libraries, operating expenditures, full-time-equivalent library staff, number of service outlets, collection size, circulation, interlibrary loans, number of public service hours, gate count, information services to individuals, library visits, consortia services, number of presentations, attendance at presentations, electronic services, information literacy, and virtual reference. Academic libraries are also asked whether they provide reference services by e-mail or the Internet, have technology for patrons with disabilities, and whether documents are digitized by library staff.

An NCES First Look report "Academic Libraries, 2010" (NCES 2012-365) was released on the NCES Web site in December 2011, as were the final data file and documentation for the 2010 ALS public use data file (NCES 2011-367). NCES has developed a Web-based peer analysis tool for the ALS called "Compare Academic Libraries." This tool currently uses the ALS 2010 data.

Additional information on academic library statistics can be obtained from Tai A. Phan, Elementary/Secondary and Libraries Studies Division, telephone 202-502-7431, e-mail tai.phan@ed.gov.

School Library Media Centers

National surveys of school library media centers in elementary and secondary schools in the United States were conducted in 1958, 1962, 1974, 1978, and 1986, 1993–1994, 1999–2000, and 2003–2004. The 2007–2008 data was available in summer 2009.

NCES, with the assistance of the U.S. Bureau of the Census, conducts the School Library Media Centers Survey as part of the Schools and Staffing Survey (SASS). SASS is the nation's largest sample survey of teachers, schools, and principals in K–12 public and private schools. Data from the school library media center questionnaire provide a national picture of public school library staffing, collections, expenditures, technology, and services. Results from the 2007–2008 survey can be found in *Public and Bureau of Indian Education Elementary and Secondary School Library Media Centers in the United States: 2007–08 Schools and Staffing Survey* (NCES 2009-322).

NCES also published a historical report about school libraries entitled *Fifty Years of Supporting Children's Learning: A History of Public School Libraries and Federal Legislation from 1953–2000*. Drawn from more than 50 sources, this report presents descriptive data about public school libraries since 1953. Along with key characteristics of school libraries, the report also presents national and regional standards, and federal legislation affecting school library media centers. Data from sample surveys are presented at the national, regional, and school levels, and by state.

NCES has included some library-oriented questions relevant to the library usage and skills of the parent and the teacher instruments of the new Early Childhood Longitudinal Study (ECLS). For additional information, visit http://nces.

ed.gov/ecls. Library items also appear in National Household Education Survey (NHES) instruments. For more information about that survey, visit http://nces. ed.gov/nhes.

NCES also included a questionnaire about high school library media centers in the Education Longitudinal Study of 2002 (ELS: 2002). This survey collected data from tenth graders about their schools, their school library media centers, their communities, and their home life. The report, *School Library Media Centers: Selected Results from the Education Longitudinal Study of 2002 (ELS: 2002)* (NCES 2005-302), is available on the NCES Web site. For more information about this survey, visit http://nces.ed.gov/surveys/els2002.

Additional information on school library media center statistics may be obtained from Tai A. Phan, National Center for Education Statistics, telephone 202-502-7431, e-mail tai.phan@ed.gov.

How to Obtain Printed and Electronic Products

Reports are currently published in the First Look format. First Look reports consist of a short collection of tables presenting state and national totals, a survey description, and data highlights. NCES also publishes separate, more in-depth studies analyzing these data.

Internet Access

Many NCES publications (including out-of-print publications) and edited raw data files from the library surveys are available for viewing or downloading at no charge through the Electronic Catalog on the NCES Web site at http://nces.ed.gov/ pubsearch.

Ordering Printed Products

Many NCES publications are also available in printed format. To order one free copy of recent NCES reports, contact the Education Publications Center (ED Pubs) at: http://www.edpubs.org, by e-mail at edpubs@edpubs.ed.gov, by toll-free telephone at 877-4-ED-PUBS (1-877-433-7827) or TTY/TDD 877-576-7734, by fax at 703-605-6794, or by mail at ED Pubs, P.O. Box 22207, Alexandria, VA 22304.

Many publications are available through the Educational Resources Information Clearinghouse (ERIC) system. For more information on services and products, visit the EDRS Web site at http://www.eric.ed.gov.

Out-of-print publications and data files may be available through the NCES Electronic Catalog on the NCES Web site at http://nces.ed.gov/pubsearch or through one of the 1,250 federal depository libraries throughout the United States (see http://catalog.gpo.gov/fdlpdir/FDLPdir.jsp). Use the NCES publication number included in the citations for publications and data files to quickly locate items in the NCES Electronic Catalog. Use the GPO number to locate items in a federal depository library.

Defense Technical Information Center

Fort Belvoir, VA 22060-6218
World Wide Web http://www.dtic.mil

Sandy Schwalb
Public Affairs Officer

The Defense Technical Information Center was formed in 1945 to collect and catalog scientific and technical documents from World War II. In the 21st century DTIC continues to serve as a vital link in the transfer of information within the defense community.

The center offers engineers, researchers, scientists, information professionals, and those in laboratories, universities, and the acquisitions field access to more than 2 million publications.

DTIC's mission is "to provide essential, technical, research, development, testing and evaluation information rapidly, accurately and reliably to support our customers' needs." The center is a Department of Defense (DoD) "field activity" and is in the Office of the Under Secretary of Defense for Acquisition, Technology, and Logistics and reports to the assistant secretary of defense, research and engineering.

The year 2011 was one of transition for the center. In late 2010 Christopher Thomas, DTIC's chief technology officer, was named its acting administrator.

Reaching Customers

DTIC offers its suite of services to a diverse population of the defense community. Because of the nature of the information it handles, individuals must be eligible to register with DTIC. By registering with DTIC, one can take advantage of value-added services, for instance having research performed by trained information professionals, and having access to limited (not publicly available) information. More information about who is eligible to register with DTIC can be found at http://www.dtic.mil/dtic/registration.

In addition to individuals in DoD and federal sectors, DTIC's registered customers can also be found in academia, the intelligence community, foreign governments (there are negotiated agreements with Australia, Canada, France, Germany, the Netherlands, the Republic of Korea, and the United Kingdom) as well as military school students and the American public at large.

DTIC's registered users include acquisition instructors, active duty military personnel, congressional staff, DoD contractors, faculty and students at military schools, historians, information professionals/librarians, logistics management specialists, business owners, security managers, and software engineers and developers.

Suite of Services

To gain access to the organization's suite of services—DoDTechipedia, Aristotle, and DTIC Online Access Controlled—individuals must be registered with DTIC.

DoDTechipedia

DTIC designed DoDTechipedia, a wiki used by the defense community. A secure online system, it facilitates the sharing of knowledge throughout that community. A collaborative tool, DoDTechipedia ensures greater transparency and communication among DoD scientists, engineers, and program managers. It helps members of the DoD community collaborate, identify solutions for technology challenges, and ensure taxpayer dollars are spent efficiently. Among its numerous features are a live forum, a "sandbox" for users to practice posting and editing content, and interest-area pages for DoD personnel and DoD contractors to work together on challenges and solutions.

Aristotle

Launched in August 2010, Aristotle is a secure, Web-based professional networking tool designed for federal government and DoD employees and contractors in the science and technology community. Aristotle connects federal and DoD customers and provides the capability to search for people, projects, and topics.

DTIC Online Access Controlled

DTIC Online Access Controlled is a secure site that offers a gateway to DoD "unclassified, controlled" (not public) science, technology, research, and engineering information. Users can get congressional budget information, DoD science and technology planning documents, the Biomedical Research Database, more than 2 million technical reports, research summaries of work in progress, and numerous other resources, all free of charge.

Web Hosting Expertise

DTIC hosts more than 100 Web sites sponsored by components of the Office of the Secretary of Defense, military service headquarters organizations, and several defense agencies, including the Joint Chiefs of Staff and Defense Prisoner of War/ Mission Personnel Office. As a leader in information storage and retrieval, DTIC has been able to advise DoD components concerning policy, law, best practices, and security strategies that relate to the transmission and use of all types of information. This is an effective support program for senior-level planners and other users of information resources. The shared infrastructure allows many organizations to obtain technologies and resources that no single organization could afford on its own.

As the nation geared up for the 2012 presidential election, DTIC staff continued its work on the Federal Voter's Assistance Program (FVAP) Web site, http:// www.fvap.gov. A high-profile site, it is heavily used by active duty members of the Armed Forces, Merchant Marine, Public Health Service, National Oceanic and Atmospheric Administration, and their family members, in addition to U.S. citizens living in other countries for work, school, or other reasons. DTIC staff has the site and its applications up and running to ensure that all U.S. citizens, wherever they are living around the world, can cast their votes during the 2012 presidential election cycle.

Security of Information

A priority of DTIC in handling information is to safeguard national security, export control, and intellectual property rights. While there is much publicly accessible material in the DTIC collection, some information is restricted by security classifications. The DoD's scientific and technical information is always categorized (or "marked") by the office that originates the document. This marking determines how, and to whom, the information can be disseminated.

Resources

DTIC's holdings include technical reports on completed research; research summaries of planned, ongoing, and completed work; independent research and development summaries; defense technology transfer agreements; DoD planning documents; DoD directives and instructions; conference proceedings; security classification guides; command histories; and special collections that date back to World War II. DoD-funded researchers are required to search DTIC's collections to ensure that they do not "reinvent the wheel" and undertake unnecessary or redundant research.

Information Sources

DTIC information is derived from many sources, including DoD organizations (civilian and military) and DoD contractors; U.S. government organizations and their contractors; non-profit organizations working on DoD scientific, research, and engineering activities; academia; and foreign governments. DTIC accepts information in print, nonprint (CDs and DVDs), and electronically over the Web. DTIC gets information from the defense community, for the defense community, about defense and beyond. Having a full range of science and technology and research and development information within the DTIC collection ensures that technological innovations are linked to defense development and acquisition efforts. New research projects can begin with the highest level of information available. This avoids duplication of effort, maximizing the use of DoD project dollars.

Information Analysis Centers

The Information Analysis Centers (IACs) are research and analysis organizations established by DoD and managed by DTIC to help researchers, engineers, scientists, and program managers use existing scientific and technical information. IACs identify, analyze, and use scientific and technical information in specific technology areas and develop information and analysis products for the defense science and engineering communities. Staffed by experienced technical area scientists, engineers, and information specialists, they help users locate and analyze scientific and technical information in specific subject areas.

Many of the products and services produced by the IACs are free and include announcements of reports relevant to the particular IAC's field of interest, authoritative bibliographic search reports, latest scientific and engineering information on specific technical subjects, consultation with or referral to world-recognized technical experts, and status of current technologies. For more information, visit http://iac.dtic.mil.

As of December 2011, the DTIC-managed IACs were: AMMTIAC: Advanced Materials, Manufacturing and Testing Information IAC; CBRNIAC: Chemical, Biological, Radiological, Nuclear Defense IAC; CPIAC: Chemical Propulsion IAC; DACS: Data and Analysis Center for Software; IATAC: Information Assurance Technology Analysis Center; MSIAC: Modeling and Simulation IAC; RIAC: Reliability IAC; SENSIAC: Sensors IAC; SURVIAC: Survivability IAC; and WSTIAC: Weapons Systems Technology IAC.

Annual Conference

DTIC hosted its first-ever annual conference as both an on-site and virtual event. It took place April 4–5 at DTIC headquarters in Fort Belvoir, Virginia, and while a limited number of individuals were able to participate in the conference on-site, the meeting was viewed over a secure DoD network (Defense Connect Online). The conference theme was "DTIC: Your Authoritative Source of Defense Information for the Front Line and Homeland." There were speakers from DoD, representing the laboratory program and the office of the assistant secretary of defense for research and engineering. Conference attendees represented DoD, other federal agencies, and their contractors and potential contractors (representing small businesses and academia).

DTIC's 2012 Conference, "Connecting Lab Research with the Warfighter," was held March 26–30, once again as an on-site and virtual event.

Training Opportunities

"DTIC Boot Camp: S&T Resources for Labs," offers hands-on training, including sessions about DTIC Online Access Controlled, DoDTechipedia, and Aristotle, as well as instruction on how to submit documents. This one-day interactive workshop is held monthly to enable customers to learn how to maximize DTIC's suite of services to meet their information needs. The boot camp model has proven to be effective, and demand for training increased during 2011. DTIC users have requested additional training sessions at Fort Belvoir and at their own locations.

Another facet of DTIC's free training is the "DoDTechipedia 101" webinars, which provide online information about the DoD wiki. DTIC has also produced online tutorials to help individuals learn how to use the wiki's key features.

DoD Scientific and Technical Information (STINFO) training can help attendees gain a better understanding of this program. The training, which can be held at DTIC or off-site, provides instruction on the management and conduct of an organizational STINFO program, and enables more direct information exchange among those who oversee this program Training information can be found at http://www.dtic.mil/dtic/customer/training/training.html.

Note: DTIC is a registered service mark of the Defense Technical Information Center.

National Library of Education

Knowledge Utilization Division
National Center for Education Evaluation and Regional Assistance
Institute of Education Sciences, U.S. Department of Education
400 Maryland Ave. S.W., Washington, DC 20202
World Wide Web http://ies.ed.gov/ncee/projects/nat_ed_library.asp

Ruth Curran Neild

Acting Director, National Library of Education
202-208-1200, e-mail ruth.neild@ed.gov

The U.S. Department of Education's National Library of Education (NLE), which marked 17 years of service in 2011, is the primary resource center for education information in the federal government, serving the research needs of the education community through the Education Resources Information Center, better known as ERIC, and the Education Department Research Library/Reference Center (RL/RC). These programs are the center for the collection, preservation, discovery, and retrieval of education information, especially information produced by and for the U.S. Department of Education. The program resides in the department's Institute of Education Sciences and reports to the Commissioner for Education Evaluation and Regional Assistance through the Knowledge Utilization Division.

Created by Public Law 103-227, the Educational Research, Development, Dissemination, and Improvement Act of 1994, and reauthorized under Public Law 107-279, the Education Sciences Reform Act of 2002, NLE is directed to perform four primary functions:

- Collect and archive information, including products and publications developed through, or supported by, the Institute of Education Sciences; and other relevant and useful education-related research, statistics, and evaluation materials and other information, projects, and publications that are consistent with scientifically valid research or the priorities and mission of the institute, and developed by the department, other federal agencies, or entities

- Provide a central location within the federal government for information about education

- Provide comprehensive reference services on matters relating to education to employees of the Department of Education and its contractors and grantees, other federal employees, and members of the public

- Promote greater cooperation and resource sharing among providers and repositories of education information in the United States

NLE's programs—ERIC and RL/RC—share these functions by complementing and supporting one another and by eliminating duplication of effort. ERIC collects and archives information and provides a central location within the federal government for information about education, while RL/RC offers comprehensive reference services. Both address promoting cooperation and resource sharing, although in different ways. To carry out these responsibilities, the NLE director, who is required by the legislation to be qualified in library science, is assisted by six federal staff, including the ERIC director, as well as ERIC and NLE contractors.

ERIC, established in 1966, pre-existed NLE, but became part of the library upon its creation in 1994. ERIC is responsible for providing a comprehensive, easy-to-use, searchable, Internet-based bibliographic and full-text database of education research and information for educators, researchers, and the general public. Its digital library is centered around a collection of more than 1.3 million bibliographic records of education resources, including journal articles, books, research syntheses, conference papers, technical reports, policy papers, and other education-related materials, and more than 330,000 full-text documents. In 2010 ERIC users conducted more than 125 million searches through the ERIC Web site (http://www.eric.ed.gov) and through commercial and noncommercial sites. Because ERIC serves as the major public program and outreach arm of NLE, it is covered separately. [See the following article, "Education Resources Information Center"—*Ed.*] This article, providing only a brief overview of NLE, is devoted to the activities of RL/RC.

Research Library/Reference Center

RL/RC has as its prime responsibility providing information services to agency staff and contractors, the general public, other government agencies, and other libraries. Located in the agency's headquarters building in Washington, D.C., it houses current and historical collections and archives of information on education issues, research, statistics, and policy; there is a special emphasis on agency publications and contractor reports, as well as current and historical federal education legislation. RL/RC makes a special effort to support Institute of Education Sciences programs by collecting journals indexed in the ERIC database, and through research supporting the What Works Clearinghouse and the Regional Educational Laboratories. Because of space considerations and increasing customer demand, RL/RC is moving toward a predominately electronic collection; to date, about 98 percent of current journal subscriptions are received in electronic format, and about two-thirds of all monographs added to the collection in 2010 were electronic—about 2,100 new electronic titles as opposed to 320 paper titles.

In addition to providing more electronic books and journals, RL/RC provides agency staff with desktop access to a comprehensive collection of digital information resources covering the subjects of education, psychology, sociology, public policy, and law. To promote its information services, manage customer requests, and grow its own internal information bank, RL/RC employs virtual reference technology to provide reference services to department staff and contractors and to support the activities of the IES Regional Educational Laboratories Virtual Reference Desk Program. RL/RC continues to deliver the great majority of its products and services in digital formats, with usage increasing year by year. Promoting and improving services remains a primary consideration in achieving RL/RC objectives.

With a staff of 12—three full-time federal staff and nine contract librarians—RL/RC has two units: Collection Management (formerly Technical Services and Serials Management) and Public Services (formerly Reference and Document Delivery). Staffing and organizational structure are kept flexible to support changing needs and to allow for fast, competent response to customer requests, institutional initiatives, and advances in technology. The RL/RC primary customer base includes about 5,000 department staff nationwide; department contractors performing research; education organizations and media; and academic, special, and government libraries. All services are supported by NLE's budget for RL/RC, which in fiscal year 2011 was $2 million.

Use of the Library

RL/RC receives about 18,500 requests a year. Document delivery and interlibrary loan continue to show the greatest growth, with requests for reference assistance remaining constant. While most information requests come from the general public, most staff time (more than 70 percent) is devoted to responding to the information needs of department staff and contractors as their requests tend to be complex, often requiring services that extend over several weeks or months. This group generated nearly 7,000 requests, or about 37 percent of the total, in 2010. It also accessed more electronic journal articles and conducted more database searches than in the previous year, showing an increase in usage of 6.1 percent. With most access taking place on the RL/RC portal, usage of the "Ask a Librarian" feature nearly doubled over the previous year.

The general public also generated nearly 7,000 requests—about 38 percent of the total number—down slightly from the previous year; most were for reference assistance. Of these, around 12 percent were referrals generated by the department's EDPubs service, the 800-USA-LEARN service, Regional Education Laboratories Virtual Reference Desk, and ERIC Help Desk. The characteristics of public users remain almost the same as in previous years. More than 71 percent of the general public contacting RL/RC in 2010 consisted of K–12 educators, students in institutions of higher education, or researchers; 26 percent were parents; and about 2.5 percent were unknown. The majority of these customers continued to access RL/RC by telephone (55 percent) and e-mail (43.2 percent); less than 1.8 percent visited the facility.

Academic, government, and special libraries make up RL/RC's third-largest user group; together they generated slightly more than 4,700 requests (25 percent of total requests), which was somewhat higher than the previous year. Most requests continued to be for interlibrary loan services. While in the past the most frequently requested items were historical documents of all types (such as policy, research, and contractor reports, including those on ERIC microfiche) and other publications released prior to 1985, in 2010 more than 50 percent of all requests were for more recently published documents (since 1990), with libraries in institutions of higher education initiating the largest number of requests. Nearly 80 percent of RL/RC's library customers are institutions of higher education, followed by special libraries, including law libraries (15 percent) and government libraries (5 percent). Public and school libraries represent less than 1 percent. Outreach to academic libraries includes interlibrary loan and a gift books program that has become increasingly popular in recent years with more than 200 libraries participating in 2010.

Collections

RL/RC's collection focus has remained the same since its creation: education issues, with an emphasis on research and policy; and related topics, including law, public policy, economics, urban affairs, sociology, history, philosophy, psychology, cognitive development, and library and information science. In 2010 RL/RC added about 2,100 new electronic titles and 320 paper titles to its monograph collection. This represents a significant change in collection development, as in the previous year RL/RC added about 2,650 print monographs and 404 electronic publications, excluding agency publications. The number of paid journal subscriptions increased to 418, up from 322 in 2009. With 98 percent of current subscriptions being desktop-accessible, staff demand for journals has increased, which explains why RL/RC added 96 new titles during the year.

RL/RC has maintained special collections of historical documents associated with its parent agency, having a complete collection of ERIC microfiche; research reports supporting the work of the What Works Clearinghouse and special panels; and publications of or relating to the department's predecessor agencies, including the National Institute of Education and the U.S. Office of Education in the Department of Health, Education, and Welfare. These collections include reports, studies, manuals, statistical publications, speeches, and policy papers. With the digitization of the ERIC microfiche collection of about 340,000 documents, RL/RC now has electronic access to the full text of all ERIC microfiche indexed between 1966 and 1992. In contrast, the ERIC Web site at http://www.ed.eric.gov provides public access only to those documents for which copyright clearance was obtained—the full text of nearly 192,000 documents or almost 55 percent of the collection. All digitized documents from the ERIC microfiche collection are available through interlibrary loan upon request. RL/RC also serves as a federal depository library under the Government Printing Office program.

Services

RL/RC provides reference and other information services, including legislative reference and statistical information services, to department staff and contractors, to the education community at large, and to the general public, as well as providing document delivery services to department staff and contractors and interlibrary loan services to other libraries and government agencies. Services to agency staff and contractors continue to grow, resulting in additional being focused on serving this community. Through its involvement in the Regional Education Laboratories Virtual Reference Desk, the library provides resources and reference services to researchers and end users alike.

On another front, RL/RC has seen an increased interest in news feeds by various offices and individuals within the agency, especially by those with responsibility for communications. In addition, RL/RC tracks research on specific topics for agency and contractor staff and publishes, at least weekly, an electronic newsletter on education research of general interest to agency staff.

Of the nearly 7,000 inquiries from the general public received in 2010, most pertained to the same issues that were of interest in the previous year: agency programs, student achievement and assessment, charter schools, teacher quality and preparation, early childhood education, and national statistics. Requests for information on No Child Left Behind dropped from the previous year; however, new to this list is the reauthorization of the Elementary and Secondary Education Act (ESEA). Other topics of public interest included agency policy and budget; federal funding to states and local school districts; current education issues in the news, such as Common Core State Standards, local school funding, technology in the schools, community colleges, after-school and summer programming, school choice, and failing schools; teacher certification requirements; school safety; and bullying and cyberbullying.

Agency staff conducted more than 30,000 searches of RL/RC's databases. Results of these searches coupled with department staff and contractor requests for specific titles generated requests for more than 7,000 journal articles and other documents. Although more full-text journal articles are available to agency staff online, the number of requests for journal articles and other documents continues to grow steadily, up from the 6,800 requests in 2009 and the 6,000 requests in 2008. The library filled about 65 percent of requests from its own collections, with the remaining 35 percent filled from other sources—about 8 percent were borrowed from other libraries, 19 percent came from document delivery services, and 8 percent were purchased from vendors and sponsoring organizations. Increasingly, RL/RC has been able to fill more staff and contractor requests from its own collections; this was especially true during 2010 because of the addition of 96 new journal titles. Also, with the increased acquisition of e-books, RL/RC is able to provide access to new publications more quickly than in previous years.

The U.S. Department of Education Research Library/Reference Center can be contacted by e-mail at library@ed.gov. The library's reference desk is available by telephone at 800-424-1616 (toll free), 202-205-5015, 202-205-5019, or 202-205-7561 (TTY); and by fax at 202-401-0547. Located in the department's headquarters building at 400 Maryland Ave. S.W., it is open from 9 A.M. to 5 P.M. weekdays, except federal holidays.

Education Resources Information Center

National Library of Education
National Center for Education Evaluation and Regional Assistance
Institute of Education Sciences, U.S. Department of Education
400 Maryland Ave. S.W., Washington, DC 20202
World Wide Web http://www.eric.ed.gov

Ashley Branca

Acting Director, ERIC Program
202-208-2321, e-mail ashley.branca@ed.gov

The Education Resources Information Center (ERIC) is the world's largest education library, featuring an electronic collection of more than 1.3 million bibliographic records from 1966 to the present along with about 332,000 full-text documents. The U.S. Department of Education's Institute of Education Sciences (IES) administers ERIC as part of the National Library of Education.

Background

For decades ERIC has served the information needs of schools, institutions of higher education, educators, parents, administrators, policymakers, researchers, and public and private entities through a variety of library services and formats, first in paper copy, then in microfiche, and today exclusively in electronic format. ERIC provides service directly to the public via its Web site, http://www.eric. ed.gov.

With a 45-year history of public service, ERIC is one of the oldest programs in the U.S. Department of Education. As the world's largest education resource, it is distinguished by two hallmarks: free dissemination of bibliographic records, and the collection of gray literature such as research conference papers and government contractor reports.

The authorizing legislation for ERIC is part of the Education Sciences Reform Act of 2002, Public Law 107-279. This legislation envisioned ERIC subject areas or topics (previously covered by the ERIC Clearinghouses) as part of the totality of enhanced information dissemination to be conducted by the Institute of Education Sciences. In addition, information dissemination includes material on closing the achievement gap and educational practices that improve academic achievement and promote learning. The Department of Education awarded a single contract for the operation of ERIC to Computer Sciences Corporation (CSC) in 2009.

ERIC Mission

The ERIC mission is to provide a comprehensive, easy-to-use, searchable, Internet-based bibliographic and full-text database of education research and information for educators, researchers, and the general public. Terms defining the ERIC mission are explained as follows:

- *Comprehensive,* consisting of journal articles and non-journal materials, including materials not published by commercial publishers, that are directly related to education
- *Easy-to-use and searchable,* allowing database users to find the information they need quickly and efficiently
- *Electronic,* making ERIC operations accessible to the maximum extent feasible and linking to publishers and commercial sources of journal articles
- *Bibliographic and full-text,* with bibliographic records conveying the information that users need in a simple and straightforward manner, and whenever possible including full-text journal articles and non-journal materials free of charge

Following this mission, the overarching goal of ERIC is to increase the availability and quality of research and information for ERIC users.

Activities that fulfill the ERIC mission are broadly categorized as collection development, content authorizations and agreements, acquisitions and processing, database and Web site operations, and communications. These five functions continue to evolve and improve as suggestions and guidance are received from a variety of sources including public comments and the ERIC Steering Committee, Content Experts, and Library Committee.

Selection Standards

The broad selection standard provides that all materials added to the ERIC database are directly related to the field of education. The majority of the journals indexed in ERIC are peer-reviewed, and the peer-reviewed status is indicated for all journals indexed from 2004 forward, when this data began to be documented by the ERIC system. The collection scope includes early childhood education through higher education, vocational education, and special education; it includes teacher education, education administration, assessment and evaluation, counseling, information technology, and the academic areas of reading, mathematics, science, environmental education, languages, and social studies. In addition, the collection also includes resources addressing one of the three objectives identified in Section 172 of the Education Sciences Reform Act: closing the achievement gap, encouraging educational practices that improve academic achievement, and conducting education research.

Within that standard, there are three sets of specific criteria providing guidance for document selection. The quality criteria consist of five basic factors: completeness, integrity, objectivity, substantive merit, and utility/importance. Selection is further determined by sponsorship criteria, and preference for inclusion in ERIC is given to those resources with identified sponsorship (for example, professional societies and government agencies). Detailed editorial criteria also provide factors for consideration, especially with regard to journals considered for comprehensive indexing.

All submissions considered for selection must be in digital format and accompanied by author permission for dissemination. For individual document submissions, authors (copyright holders) register through the ERIC Web site feature

"My ERIC"; follow the steps to enter bibliographic information, abstract, and document file; and submit the electronic document release form authorizing ERIC to disseminate the materials. Journal publishers, associations, and other entities with multiple documents also submit electronic content following guidance and instructions consistent with provider agreements from ERIC. Once publishers have signed an ERIC agreement, files can be submitted by e-mail or disk or by upload to ERIC's ftp site.

ERIC Collection

In addition to being the largest education library, ERIC is one of the few collections to index non-journal materials as well as journal literature. The largest share of the collection consists of citations to journal articles (874,100 records), and a smaller portion consists of non-journal materials (499,500 records). The non-journal materials are frequently called gray literature, materials that are not easy to find and are not produced by commercial publishers. In ERIC, the gray literature consists of research syntheses, dissertations, conference proceedings, and such selected papers as keynote speeches, technical reports, policy papers, literature reviews, bibliographies, congressional hearings and reports, reports on federal and state standards, testing and regulations, U.S. Department of Education contractor reports (such as the What Works Clearinghouse and the National Center for Education Statistics), and working papers for established research and policy organizations.

To support consistency and reliability in content coverage, most education journals are indexed comprehensively so that all articles in each issue are included. ERIC currently indexes a total of 1,143 journals; 1,046 journals comprehensively and 97 selectively. Articles from selectively covered journals are acquired by ERIC subject specialists, who identify individual documents for the ERIC database according to the ERIC selection policy.

The complete list of journals indexed in ERIC, including the years of coverage and the number of articles indexed, is a tool on the ERIC Web site enabling users to identify more easily specific journal literature. There is also a non-journal source list of more than 800 organizations producing education-related materials providing content to ERIC. Another convenience for users that is designed to streamline the process of obtaining full text is the "Find in a Library" feature, which leverages the Open URL Gateway and WorldCat to provide a link from ERIC records to electronic and print resources available in libraries. For all journals currently indexed in ERIC, there are links to publishers' Web sites if users choose to purchase full-text articles.

To facilitate electronic access to more archived materials, ERIC launched a microfiche digitization project in 2006; this project was concluded in 2009. The project scope was to digitize and archive microfiche full-text documents containing an estimated 43 million pages and to provide copyright due diligence by seeking permission from the copyright holders to make the electronic version available to users.

Approximately 340,000 full-text documents, indexed 1966–1992, were converted from microfiche to digital image files, and more than 65 percent of these documents were added to the ERIC digital library. The ERIC Web site provides various lists for librarians to manage microfiche collections in their institutions based on what is now available in pdf format on the ERIC Web site.

In 2010 ERIC established a partnership with ProQuest to begin indexing education-related doctoral dissertations from 700 academic institutions worldwide. More than 1,700 recent records from the ProQuest Dissertations and Thesis Database have been added to the ERIC collection. As the project expands, records will reach back to 1997, the year digital copies of dissertations were first acquired.

ERIC Web Site

Recent enhancements to ERIC focus on increased access for special audiences and new search features. For example, the home page provides links with information for publishers and authors, librarians, and licensors of the ERIC database. Searchers can mark records for placement in a temporary workspace called "My Clipboard." This feature permits users to print, e-mail, or export records, or save them to a "My ERIC" account. Additional Web site improvements include search-term highlighting so that users see where and how frequently their search terms occur in the results set; a metadata field indicating peer-reviewed articles for records acquired 2004 to the present; and quicker loading of search results. Search facets are a new feature, allowing users to narrow searches by author, descriptor, date, audience, source, education level, and publication type, with each category offering the most frequently occurring names or terms in the results set.

Refinements to ERIC's technical architecture continue to improve system functionality and user satisfaction. Usability tests with participant groups including librarians, researchers, and students provide input on issues such as online submission, the "Help" section, and an extensive range of search operations. With all database enhancements, the development process contributes to increasing accessibility, efficiency, and quality.

Automated systems for acquisition and processing help to reduce the total time required to produce a database record, and most records are processed in less than 30 days. New content is added to the ERIC database every day, and ERIC publishes approximately 4,000 new records to the ERIC digital library each month. Commercial vendors receive updates to the database monthly.

RSS feeds enable users to keep up to date with new content from several sources. For example, users can receive regular updates from specific U.S. Department of Education programs: the Regional Educational Laboratories, the What Works Clearinghouse, and the National Assessment of Educational Progress (NAEP). Moreover, any ERIC search can become an RSS feed, or users can click to one of several education topics including community colleges, financial aid for college, and teacher effectiveness.

Tutorials provide added support for users searching the ERIC collection, helping searchers take advantage of Web site features. Tutorials include author search using full name, citation management, field code search, refining a search, and many more titles found under the ERIC "Help" section.

While the ERIC database has traditionally used narrative abstracts to describe full-text documents, database contributors now have the option of writing structured abstracts for their research papers and conference presentations. Structured abstracts present important details about research studies and their outcomes under predefined headings or elements such as research design types and study sample.

The Web site also provides links to find ERIC on Facebook and Twitter. This feature provides frequent news updates, links, and downloadable materials, with the goal of broadening ERIC outreach.

ERIC Access

There were more than 125 million searches of the ERIC digital library in 2010. In addition to the government-sponsored Web site at http://www.eric.ed.gov, ERIC is carried by search engines, including Google and Google Scholar, MSN, and Yahoo!, and by commercial database providers, including EBSCO, OCLC, OVID, ProQuest, SilverPlatter, and Dialog. ERIC is also available through statewide networks in Ohio, Texas, Kentucky, and North Carolina.

The ERIC digital library can be reached by toll-free telephone in the United States, Canada, and Puerto Rico at 800-LET-ERIC (800-538-3742), Monday through Friday, 8 A.M. to 8 P.M. eastern time. Questions can also be transmitted via the message box on the "Contact Us" page on the ERIC Web site.

National Association and Organization Reports

American Library Association

50 E. Huron St., Chicago, IL 60611
800-545-2433
World Wide Web http://www.ala.org

Molly Raphael
President

The American Library Association—the world's oldest, largest, and most influential library association—was founded in 1876 in Philadelphia and later chartered in the Commonwealth of Massachusetts. ALA has nearly 60,000 members, including librarians, library trustees, and other interested people from every U.S. state and many nations. The association serves public, state, school, and academic libraries, as well as special libraries for people working in government, commerce and industry, the arts, and the armed services or in hospitals, prisons, and other institutions.

ALA's mission is "to provide leadership for the development, promotion, and improvement of library and information services and the profession of librarianship in order to enhance learning and ensure access to information for all."

ALA is governed by an elected council, which is its policy making body, and an executive board, which acts for the council in the administration of established policies and programs. In this context, the executive board is the body that manages the affairs of the association, delegating management of its day-to-day operation to the executive director. ALA also has 37 standing committees, designated as committees of the association or of the council. ALA operations are directed by the executive director and implemented by staff through a structure of programmatic offices and support units.

ALA is home to 11 membership divisions, each focused on a type of library or library function. They are the American Association of School Librarians (AASL); the Association for Library Collections and Technical Services (ALCTS); the Association for Library Service to Children (ALSC); the Association of College and Research Libraries (ACRL); the Association of Library Trustees, Advocates, Friends, and Foundations (ALTAFF); the Association of Specialized and Cooperative Library Agencies (ASCLA); the Library and Information Technology Association (LITA); the Library Leadership and Management Association (LLAMA); the Public Library Association (PLA); the Reference and User Services Association (RUSA); and the Young Adult Library Services Association (YALSA).

ALA also hosts 18 round tables for members who share interests that lie outside the scope of any of the divisions. A network of affiliates, chapters, and other organizations enables the association to reach a broad audience.

Key action areas include diversity, equitable access to information and library services, education and lifelong learning, intellectual freedom, advocacy for libraries and the profession, literacy, and organizational excellence.

ALA offices address the broad interests and topics of concern to ALA members; they track issues and provide information, services, and products for members and the general public. Current ALA offices are the Chapter Relations Office, the Development Office, the Governance Office, the International Relations Office (IRO), the Office for Accreditation (OA), the Office for Diversity (OFD), the Office of Government Relations (OGR), the Office for Human Resource Development and Recruitment (HRDR), the Office for Information Technology Policy (OITP), the Office for Intellectual Freedom (OIF), the Office for Library Advocacy (OLA), the Office for Literacy and Outreach Services (OLOS), the Office for Research and Statistics (ORS), the Public Information Office (PIO), the Public Programs Office (PPO), and the Washington Office.

ALA's headquarters is in Chicago; OGR and OITP are housed at the association's Washington Office. ALA also has an editorial office for *Choice,* a review journal for academic libraries, in Middletown, Connecticut.

ALA is a 501(c)(3) charitable and educational organization.

Focus on Advocacy and Diversity

In her presidential year, 2011–2012 ALA President Molly Raphael, former director of libraries at Multnomah County (Oregon) Library and the District of Columbia Public Library, focused initiatives on two ALA priority areas: advocacy and diversity.

Raphael's "Why Libraries Matter: Empowering Community Voices" initiative concentrated on how librarians can engage their communities to speak out more effectively for libraries of all types—not just during times of crisis, but at all times. "Libraries are so essential for learning and for life," she said. "ALA is the only organization that speaks for all types of libraries, and we can all benefit from working together to serve our communities. Libraries will not just survive but will thrive when those who use and value libraries join with those who work in libraries to sustain the critical roles of libraries in our society."

Raphael's diversity initiative built on efforts to significantly increase funding for the Spectrum Scholarship program, ALA's national diversity and recruitment effort designed to address the under-representation of minority librarians in the profession; it also promoted inclusiveness in library leadership development efforts to help ensure that the library leaders of today and tomorrow are as diverse as the communities they serve. Strategies included linking diversity efforts to ALA leadership-development programs; pursuing diversity, inclusiveness, and leadership development by building on one another's work through collaborative efforts across many ALA constituencies and units; and including the populations libraries serve in formulating and implementing plans.

Raphael also pledged to continue to vigorously defend intellectual freedom, the right to privacy, and open access to information. "We must continue to be vigilant and watchful," she said, "for those who wish to restrict access to information remain unrelenting in their quest. People across this country and, indeed, around the world have witnessed the impact of the ALA's leadership in protecting intellectual freedom, privacy, and open access to information. We must continue to build coalitions with those individuals and institutions, both in the United States and globally, that believe in the fundamental right and value of the free flow of ideas and an individual's right to privacy."

Highlights of the Year

Survey: Libraries Are Tech Centers—And Havens During Disasters

A 2011 survey found that U.S. public libraries continue to expand as technology centers for communities, providing essential resources for job-seekers and support for critical e-government services. In addition, as the demand for e-books increases, libraries are a prime source for free downloads. However, budget cuts have forced libraries nationwide to reduce operating hours and access to services at a time when their resources are most needed.

The 2011 Public Library Funding and Technology Access Study reported that virtually all public libraries—99 percent—provided public access to computers and the Internet. More than 87 percent of libraries provided technology training, and more than two-thirds (67 percent) offered access to e-books, up 12 percent from two years earlier.

Conducted by ALA and the Information Policy and Access Center at the University of Maryland, the survey builds on the largest study of Internet connectivity in public libraries, which began in 1994. The study, funded by the Bill and Melinda Gates Foundation and ALA, functions as an annual "state of the library" report on the technology resources brokered by libraries and the funding that enables free public access to these resources.

In addition to regular services and resources, libraries often play a key role in helping communities recover after a major disaster. Libraries were "life-savers" in the aftermath of Hurricane Katrina, said Melinda Gates, co-chair of the Gates Foundation, as she greeted ALA Annual Conference attendees via video during the June 2011 conference's opening general session in New Orleans. "They have also been community anchors during the long rebuilding process," Gates said. "Through the hard work of many library leaders and community members, libraries have returned, and they're even stronger than they were before."

ALA's Office of Government Relations worked with Sen. Jack Reed (D-R.I.) to help secure a change to Federal Emergency Management Agency (FEMA) policy that will allow libraries to be eligible for temporary relocation during major disasters and emergencies under the FEMA Public Assistance Program. Prior to the policy change, libraries were specifically excluded from the list of eligible public facilities.

"This is a commonsense change that I have been calling for since Hurricane Katrina," Reed said. "It will help libraries in need relocate so they can keep serving the public in the wake of a flood or other emergency. Libraries are vital information hubs, and in the aftermath of a disaster libraries take on an even greater community role, providing free and easy access to technology and essential information."

ALA continued its efforts to help libraries around the world affected by major disasters. Immediately following the earthquake and tsunami in Japan on March 11, 2011, ALA set up a fund to take in donations on behalf of the Japan Library Association to help rebuild affected libraries in northeastern Japan. ALA also continued its fund-raising efforts for libraries hit by the 2010 earthquake in Haiti, reaching a milestone of $50,000.

AASL announced that total grants awarded through Beyond Words: The Dollar General School Library Relief Fund had passed $1 million. Beyond Words provides funding to public schools affected by disasters to help rebuild and expand library programs; grants can be used to defray the cost of replacing or supplementing books, media, and/or equipment in the school library. A collaboration of AASL, ALA, and the National Education Association, the program is funded by the Dollar General Literacy Foundation.

New Web Site for Advocates Features Library Quotes

In January 2011 ALTAFF and ilovelibraries.org launched Library Quotes, a resource supporting libraries, reading, books, and literacy. This collection of quotes by authors, celebrities, politicians, historic figures, activists, philanthropists, and others helps library advocates make the case for libraries in their communities. Library Quotes was an initiative of 2010–2011 ALA President Roberta Stevens, ALTAFF, and OLA.

Spectrum Initiative Nears $1 Million Goal

As of October 2011 more than $950,000 of a $1 million goal had been raised through the Spectrum Presidential Initiative for the Spectrum Scholarship Program. The initiative, begun in 2009, aims to support the immediate need of additional scholarships, offer two $25,000 doctoral scholarships, increase the scholarship endowment, and develop special programs for recruitment and career development.

Choose Privacy Week

OIF celebrated its second Choose Privacy Week, an initiative that invites library users into a national conversation about privacy rights in a digital age. The 2011 events included Data Privacy Day, along with a webinar, "Hot Topics in Privacy," with national experts on library privacy. New sponsors included the Society of American Archivists. OIF and the Open Society Foundation also sponsored a Privacy and Youth Conference in Chicago March 24–25, 2011, inviting 25 scholars, librarians, journalists, privacy activists, and government officials to discuss the work they are doing to engage and educate young people in privacy protection.

Banned Books Week Virtual Readout

The 30th annual Banned Books Week (BBW)—held September 24 through October 1 with the theme "Free Your Mind: Read a Banned Book"—included for the first time a "virtual readout" on its redesigned Web site, http://www.bannedbooks week.org. The OIF event doubled its media coverage from the previous year, with 2,300 TV, radio, and newspaper media placements; drew millions of friends and fans on Facebook; and saw 800 videos posted on BBW's YouTube channel.

YALSA Marks Teen Read Week

More than 3,500 libraries joined in Teen Read Week, October 16–22, 2011, with the theme "Picture It @ your library." The week-long initiative by YALSA encouraged teens to read graphic novels and other illustrated materials, seek out creative books, or imagine the world through literature. More than 9,000 teens voted in the 2011 Teens' Top Ten, with *Clockwork Angel* by Cassandra Clare chosen as the most popular young adult book from the previous year. The 2012 theme will be "It Came from the Library."

Library Copyright Alliance Weighs In

ALA, ACRL, and the Association of Research Libraries continued during 2011 to partner in the Library Copyright Alliance (LCA). Over the course of the year, LCA issued comments on pending legislation and a number of court cases, joined briefs, and released papers and guides on a wide range of copyright and fair use issues, including the Google Book Search settlement and the lending rights of libraries.

In response to the March 2011 rejection of the proposed Google Book Search Settlement, LCA issued a statement saying that copyright law continues to present significant barriers to libraries interested in mass digitization initiatives because of "orphan works" issues. The group also released *A Guide for the Perplexed Part IV: The Rejection of the Google Books Settlement,* an analysis of the latest developments in the Google Books case and its potential effect on libraries. This guide is the latest in a series prepared by LCA legal counsel Jonathan Band to help inform the library community about this landmark legal dispute.

In the wake of the settlement rejection, several interested parties began discussing with renewed vigor the issues of orphan works, mass digitization, and even modernization of Section 108 of the U.S. Copyright Act. As part of this initiative, LCA released a statement describing the key features that copyright reform proposals should include in order to constitute significant improvement over current law for libraries and their users.

In April 2011 ACRL sent letters to the National Institutes of Health (NIH), U.S. Department of Health and Human Services (HHS), and the White House Office of Science and Technology Policy (OSTP) in support of public access to federally funded research. The letters, sent to commemorate the third anniversary of the NIH Public Access Policy on April 7, asked NIH to shorten the current embargo, and asked HHS and OSTP to expand public access policies to other federal agencies.

Money Smart Week @ your library

ALA became the first national partner of the Federal Reserve Bank of Chicago's Money Smart Week initiative to promote personal financial literacy. Libraries in 30 states participated in Money Smart Week @ your library, held April 2–9, 2011, partnering with community groups, financial institutions, government agencies, educational organizations, and other financial experts to help consumers learn to manage their personal finances more effectively.

USAPatriot Act Watch Continues

In May 2011 Congress approved reauthorization of three key sections of the USA-Patriot Act, without any changes, until June 1, 2015. OGR has actively worked with ALA colleagues throughout the association for USAPatriot Act reform since the law was introduced in 2001 and will continue to monitor activity and work to address ongoing problems.

Library Legislative Day

National Library Legislative Day, held May 9–10, 2011, drew 361 people from 47 states, plus another 5,000 who participated in Virtual Library Legislative Day. A first day of briefings was followed by a reception with members of Congress and their staff; participants met with other federal officials the next day. Library advocates who couldn't make it to Capitol Hill for the event were able to be a part of the effort by calling or e-mailing their elected officials; Virtual Library Legislative Day was led by ALTAFF, ALA's Washington Office, CRO, and OLA. The 2011 effort saw four times as many messages sent as the previous year.

Gates Foundation Funds Technology Access Benchmarks

OITP and PLA joined with other library and government leaders to develop a series of public access technology benchmarks for public libraries. With $2.8 million in funding from the Bill and Melinda Gates Foundation and with the Urban Libraries Council as the project lead and facilitator, the coalition will develop guidelines that define high-quality technology services at libraries. After an initial test of benchmarks in California, Oklahoma, and Texas, the prototypes were refined and launched for broad use in spring 2012.

PLA Offers 'Turning the Page 2.0'

PLA renewed its partnership with the Gates Foundation for Turning the Page 2.0, the next generation of its popular Turning the Page: Building Your Library Community program. The free training program addresses the same core issues of advocacy, communications, and relationship building, this time in a convenient blended-learning format. In a six-week facilitated online course to be offered six times in 2011–2012, library staff and supporters learn how to create and tell their library's story, deliver effective presentations, develop a compelling case for support, and build and sustain partnerships along the way. Participants choose an advocacy goal for their library and are guided through the creation of an advocacy work plan.

AASL Launches Interactive Planning Tool

AASL joined with Britannica Digital Learning to copublish an online, interactive planning module to help with school library program development and implementation. "A Planning Guide for Empowering Learners" is a program evaluation, planning, implementation, and advocacy tool to ensure that school library program planners go beyond the basics to provide goals, priorities, criteria, and general principles for establishing effective library programs. The guide includes a revised "School Library Program Rubric," a tool that allows school librarians to assess their programs using 16 sets of criteria.

2011 Emerging Leaders

ALA's Emerging Leaders program began its fifth year with a day-long session at the 2011 Midwinter Meeting. Eighty-three individuals were selected through a competitive process for the program, which enables librarians and library staff from across the United States to participate in project-planning work groups, to network with peers, to gain an inside look into ALA structure, and to have an opportunity to serve the profession in a leadership capacity early in their careers.

Participants received two days of orientation and education with Maureen Sullivan, an organizational development consultant whose practice focuses on leadership development for the profession, and Peter Bromberg, assistant director of the Princeton (New Jersey) Public Library.

Following the opening session, the program continued in an online learning and networking environment for six months, culminating in a poster session at the 2011 Annual Conference in New Orleans that showcased the results of their project planning work. Nearly half the participants received sponsorships from ALA divisions, offices, roundtables, state chapters, affiliate groups, and other organizations.

Helping Libraries Address Privatization

PLA President Audra Caplan, along with Carolyn Anthony, Christine Hage, and Kathleen Hage, joined the ALA Committee on Library Advocacy's Task Force on Privatization to create "Keeping Public Libraries Public: A Checklist for Communities Considering Privatization of Public Libraries." This publication revised and improved a previous PLA resource, "Outsourcing: A Public Library Checklist." The new publication is designed to help librarians, trustees, friends, and other library supporters address the issue of privatization and prepare for any discussions about it that might arise in their communities.

Campaign for the World's Libraries

During 2011 the Library Association of Barbados and the Library Association of the Republic of China (Taiwan) became the newest members of the Campaign for the World's Libraries. Developed by ALA and the International Federation of Library Associations and Institutions (IFLA), the campaign showcases the vital roles played by public, school, academic, and special libraries worldwide. Nearly 40 countries have joined the campaign and had its @ your library logo translated into their country's language. The @ your library logo is currently available in 32 languages and in the colors of each partner country's flag.

Programs and Partners

Campaign Partnerships

The Campaign for America's Libraries continued to work with partners to generate public awareness about the value of libraries and librarians, to reach new audiences, and to amplify pro-library messages.

Season five of the Step Up to the Plate @ your library program, developed by ALA and the National Baseball Hall of Fame and Museum, concluded with a grand-prize drawing at the Hall of Fame in Cooperstown, New York. Hall of Famer Andre Dawson chose Josh Smith, 13, of Haverhill, Massachusetts, as the winner. The program encouraged fans of all ages to use the print and electronic resources at their library to answer a series of baseball trivia questions developed by library staff and the Hall of Fame. The start of season six of the program coincided with Major League Baseball opening day in March.

Launched at the ALA Annual Conference in New Orleans, Connect with your kids @ your library positions the library as the place for quality family time. Campaign partner Lifetime Networks provided a grant to support the development of two television public service announcements featuring families visiting the library, and donated air time for them.

The 75 public libraries participating in the American Dream Starts @ your library program, funded by the Dollar General Literacy Foundation, continued to develop literacy services for adult English-language learners and their families. The participating libraries expanded their print and digital collections, adding new technologies, increasing outreach and bookmobile services, building effective community partnerships, and engaging the media to promote library resources. Over the year, the 75 American Dream libraries partnered with nearly 400 local organizations, agencies, and businesses; 95 percent used a portion of their funding to improve their English-as-a-second-language and bilingual collections; and five libraries hosted naturalization ceremonies for hundreds of new Americans.

Smart Investing @ your library

In February 2011 the Smart Investing @ your library program gave $1.4 million in grants to 20 recipients to help them provide patrons with effective, unbiased financial education resources. Jointly administered by RUSA and the Financial Industry Regulatory Authority (FINRA) Investor Education Foundation, the program also offered the webinar "Taking a Blended Approach to PR in a Web 2.0 World" and enhanced its online presence with a redesigned Web site offering downloadable tools, multimedia materials to publicize programs, survey instruments, and staff training templates, as well as a new YouTube channel featuring videos developed by grantees.

In its first four years, Smart investing @ your library awarded $4.69 million in grants and grew a network of dozens of grantees representing more than 600 library facilities that together serve almost 23 million people.

LibrariUS Initiative Shares Library Stories

PLA and OLA partnered with Public Insight Network at American Public Media to promote a new initiative, LibrariUS. A journalism project undertaken in collaboration with libraries, LibrariUS uses an interactive Web site to explore the information, social, and civic needs of communities through the lens of local libraries. A simple widget installed on a library's Web site links patrons to the LibrariUS Web site, enabling them to share why they're visiting the library or using the library's Internet site. Responses are displayed on a dynamic map, updated in real time, and contact information is also requested for possible media follow-up.

PPO by the Numbers

PPO was awarded more than $2.2 million in funding in fiscal year 2011 to bring cultural programming grant opportunities and resources to libraries, and school, public, academic, and special libraries nationwide benefited from PPO initiatives; more than 600 libraries and community centers received grant awards totaling $592,300. Recipients included 320 public, 155 academic, 25 special, and 57 school libraries, along with more than 50 community centers.

Building Common Ground

PPO announced in June 2011 that it had received funding from the Fetzer Institute to support "Building Common Ground: Discussions of Community, Civility, and Compassion," a multiformat discussion program for public audiences. By bringing adult audiences together in the library for programs and events that include reading, viewing, reflection, discussion, and civic engagement initiatives, the program is supporting public libraries as they strive to enhance the quality of life and learning in their communities. Following a competitive application, conversations are being convened in 30 public libraries in 2012.

Talking About the Civil War

"Let's Talk About It: Making Sense of the American Civil War" follows the popular Let's Talk About It model, which engages participants in discussion of a set of common texts selected by a nationally known scholar for their relevance to a larger, overarching theme. PPO and the National Endowment for the Humanities (NEH) announced that 65 public, academic, and community college libraries would host reading and discussion program grants under the program. The selected libraries received a cash grant to support program expenses and support materials, including 30 copies of three titles, promotional materials, and training for the local project director.

On the Road with PPO

In 2011 PPO toured eight ongoing traveling exhibitions to 82 public, academic, and special libraries, reaching an estimated audience of nearly 100,000 library patrons: "Benjamin Franklin: In Search of a Better World," "Forever Free: Abraham Lincoln's Journey to Emancipation," "Harry Potter's World: Renaissance Science, Magic, and Medicine," "John Adams Unbound," "Lewis and Clark and the Indian Country," "Lincoln: The Constitution and the Civil War," "Pride and Passion: The African American Baseball Experience," and "Visions of the Universe: Four Centuries of Discovery."

Teen Tech Week Promotes Nonprint Resources

The fourth annual Teen Tech Week, held March 6–12 with the theme "Mix & Mash @ your library," drew registration from more than 1,700 libraries. Teen Tech

Week encourages teens to explore the nonprint resources available at their libraries, including DVDs, databases, audiobooks, and electronic games. It also urges teens to learn how to safely and properly navigate these new technologies. Promotional partners included ALA Graphics, Figment.com, the Margaret Edwards Trust, and Tutor.com; DoSomething.org and the Federal Trade Commission are nonprofit supporters.

Conferences and Workshops

2011 Annual Conference

Five years after ALA held the first major convention in New Orleans following Hurricane Katrina, more than 20,000 librarians, library supporters, and exhibitors returned to the city for the 2011 ALA Annual Conference June 23–28.

As with the 2006 Annual Conference, librarians ushered in the event by stepping up to provide community service. More than 220 volunteers gathered for "Libraries Build Communities," a program that involved visiting 15 sites, including public and school libraries. The group shelved books, reorganized and updated collections, and entered data, among other activities. "Libraries Build Communities" was launched by ALA's CRO in the wake of Katrina and has since become an Annual Conference tradition.

"When ALA came to New Orleans in 2006, there was an unimaginable amount of work that needed to be done throughout the city," said Michael Dowling, director of CRO. "In a few short days, ALA was able to make a difference and illustrate that libraries do in fact build communities."

Disaster preparedness was the focus of the conference's ALA Washington Office Briefing. "It's not a matter of if a disaster will happen; it's simply a matter of when," said panelist Katherine Zeringue of the Federal Emergency Management Agency (FEMA) Environmental Liaison Office. Everyone, she said, including libraries, needs to be prepared to work with response teams.

Roberta Stevens's President's Program featured Sue Gardner, executive director of the Wikimedia Foundation, which operates Wikipedia. Gardner noted that Wikipedia staff "are lovers of the institutions of knowledge," and definitely of libraries. The wiki is not opposed to traditional media, she said, adding that "we want you as Wikipedians." Gardner posited that Wikipedia has turned people into "more aware, more critical consumers of information." Saying she was well aware that "we're not perfect," she emphasized that "the people in this room are the people who can make it better, and we want you to do that with us."

Opening General Session speaker Dan Savage, author of the syndicated column "Savage Love" and editorial director of Seattle's weekly newspaper *The Stranger,* spoke about the growth of the "It Gets Better Project," which addresses lesbian, gay, bisexual, and transgender youth—children who experience rough times and even bullying to the point of pushing them to suicide.

A standing ovation greeted Daniel Ellsburg, whom Richard M. Nixon called the "most dangerous man in America" after Ellsburg's release of "The Pentagon Papers" in 1971. Ellsburg told the audience at the "War and Secrecy" program that he regretted not releasing the documents earlier because it would have made a difference by exposing lies that had been used to justify the Vietnam War.

PPO hosted six programs addressing issues in cultural and community programming and also presented readings from 26 authors and poets on the LIVE! @ your library Reading Stage on the exhibits floor. More than 500 conference-goers took a break to enjoy live readings from many award-winning and up-and-coming authors and poets, including Mark Doty, Daniel Handler, Tayari Jones, R. Zamora Lindmark, and Nalini Singh.

The RUSA President's Program, "Marketing Reference on a Dime," featured a panel presentation of successful initiatives for marketing library reference services. Other topics included applying user experience to library public services, the business of social media and how librarians can help business owners leverage their social capital, and virtual reference.

The PLA President's Program and awards presentation recognized award winners and hosted as keynote speakers writer-producer David Simon and mystery author Laura Lippman. PLA also cosponsored "Consultants Giving Back," an opportunity for attendees to meet one-on-one in complimentary half-hour sessions with nationally recognized library consultants.

The 14th Annual Diversity and Outreach Fair, with more than 300 attendees, showcased 28 participants highlighting diverse services, including library-based family literacy programs and library services to underserved or under-represented communities. The event, organized by OLOS and sponsored by DEMCO, celebrates extraordinary examples of diversity in America's libraries and demonstrates possibilities for other libraries in search of "diversity-in-action" ideas.

For the fifth year, OLOS and the Subcommittee on Bookmobiles presented the Parade of Bookmobiles, bringing bookmobiles from across the country onto the exhibit floor. The parade provides an opportunity to showcase libraries' ability to reach rural and other communities where access to conventional library facilities is a challenge.

The Jean E. Coleman Library Outreach Lecture was presented by Robert Wedgeworth, a member of the National Museum and Library Services Board, former ALA executive director, and president of ProLiteracy. Wedgeworth's lecture, "The Future of Literacy in Libraries: Our Challenges, Our Opportunities," explored why library literacy programs have not been more successful and how they might become more accountable, developing and replicating innovative strategies and demonstrating the impact of library literacy services to influence stakeholders and decision-makers.

ALSC and REFORMA, the National Association to Promote Library and Information Services to Latinos and the Spanish-Speaking, held a coming-of-age ceremony gala for the Pura Belpré Award in honor of the award's 15th anniversary. The *Quinceañera Celebración* featured the 2011 medal and honor Belpré authors and illustrators.

ALSC's annual Charlemae Rollins President's Program focused on the theme "How Libraries Can Best Serve Special Needs Patrons, Especially Those with Autism Spectrum Disorders (ASD)" and featured keynote speaker Ricki Robinson, a leader in developing multidisciplinary treatment plans for children with ASD. Joining Robinson in a panel discussion were authors Cynthia Lord and Francisco X. Stork, as well as librarian Patricia Twarogowski, who has been recognized for her effective programming for special-needs children.

2012 Midwinter Meeting

A total of 6,236 attendees and 3,693 exhibitors participated in the 2012 January 20–24 Midwinter Meeting in Dallas.

Key topics included support for school libraries and library budgets, and attendees were encouraged to support AASL President Carl Harvey's petition to ensure that every child in America has access to an effective school library program by providing dedicated funding as part of the reauthorization of the Elementary and Secondary Education Act (ESEA).

The program "Empowering Voices: Transforming Libraries" emphasized the transformational role librarians play in their communities. ALA President's Program speaker Rich Harwood of the Harwood Institute of Public Innovation envisioned a transformative role in society. "We need you to listen to our political debate and see what's going on in so many of our communities," he said, "to see the isolation and fragmentation of people, to see the need for us to illuminate the knowledge that we need to make choices in our democracy."

At the LITA Top Technological Trends program, panelist Stephen Abram of Cengage Learning discussed how such trends as direct downloads of digital music and books are changing the ways librarians serve their communities.

Some 1,400 attended the annual Youth Media Awards program recognizing the best in children's and young adult literature, and another 18,900 watched the announcements via webcast. The 2012 John Newbery Medal for most distinguished contribution to children's literature went to *Dead End in Norvelt* by Jack Gantos; *A Ball for Daisy,* illustrated and written by Chris Raschka, earned the 2012 Caldecott Medal for the most distinguished American picture book for children; and John Corey Whaley's *Where Things Come Back* won the Michael L. Printz Award for excellence in literature for young adults.

Ashley Bryan—the storyteller, artist, author, poet, and musician who in 1962 became the first African American to both write and illustrate a children's book— was recognized with the Coretta Scott King Virginia Hamilton Award for Lifetime Achievement. The Coretta Scott King Book Award for authors went to Kadir Nelson, author and illustrator of *Heart and Soul: The Story of America and African Americans,* and the award for illustrators was won by Shane W. Evans, illustrator and author of *Underground: Finding the Light to Freedom.*

At "A Library Occupies Occupy Wall Street," librarians Betsy Fagin, Mandy Henk, and Zachary Loeb shared their experiences in building the Occupy Wall Street People's Library. The library—which held a collection of more than 5,000 items and provided free access to books, magazines, newspapers, and other materials—was seized by police November 15 during a planned raid to evict Occupy Wall Street protesters from Zuccotti Park.

Susan Cain, author of Quiet: The Power of Introverts in a World That Can't Stop Talking, opened the Auditorium Speakers Series, where she touted the contributions of such introverts as Charles Darwin, Theodor Seuss Geisel (Dr. Seuss), and Warren Buffett. The series also included bestselling author John Green, whose most recent book is *The Fault in Our Stars.*

Jamal Joseph, activist and author of *Panther Baby: A Life of Rebellion and Reinvention,* delivered the keynote speech at the 13th Annual Arthur Curley Memorial Lecture. Joseph's personal odyssey led him from the streets of Harlem to

Rikers Island and Leavenworth prison, and then to Columbia University, where he currently serves as chair of the School of the Arts film division.

The keynote speaker at the Martin Luther King, Jr. Sunrise Celebration was Lewis Baldwin, professor of religious studies at Vanderbilt University and author of *"Thou, Dear God": Prayers That Open Hearts and Spirits,* the first published collection of King's prayers.

Other meeting highlights included a three-hour interactive "Unconference" session, which addressed such topics as the current job market for librarians, the challenges faced by library administrations, and online privacy, and featured a Wrap Up/Rev Up Closing Session by pop musician and children's recording artist Lisa Loeb.

PLA Virtual Spring Symposium

More than 675 online attendees took part in PLA's first Virtual Spring Symposium March 30, 2011. The interactive event featured eight programs highlighting topics in technology, youth services, administration/leadership, and adult services. Special programs included a lunchtime interview with author Diane Ackerman (*A Natural History of the Senses, The Zookeeper's Wife*) led by *Booklist* editor Donna Seaman, and a lively closing session, "The Sustainable Library," with George Needham and Joan Frye Williams.

ACRL Conference Draws Record Registration

More than 5,300 library staff, exhibitors, speakers, and guests from around the world met March 30–April 2 in Philadelphia and online for the ACRL 2011 conference, which had the highest combined registrant participation ever, with 3,532 in-person and virtual attendees from all 50 states and 24 other countries. The conference offered more than 300 programs that explored the interdependency that exists in academic and library communities and the changing nature and role of academic and research librarians.

A new conference feature was the IdeaPower Unconference, a forum for the exploration of ideas to transform academic libraries. About 20 presenters volunteered to share, in a six-minute presentation, an idea with the power to transform academic libraries.

Publishing

ALA Editions

ALA Editions and ALA TechSource produced and disseminated a record number of books (46), serial publications, and online learning opportunities (27) during 2011. Formats ranged from traditional print books to print/online periodicals including *Library Technology Reports* and *Smart Libraries Newsletter,* from combined print/e-book bundles to multipart online workshops, and from articles in *American Libraries* magazine to partnerships with other publishers. Products included content reorganized to meet the different needs expressed by readers and learners, such as *Children's Programming Monthly,* a pdf subscription magazine filled with ready-to-use programs, ideas for storytimes, and planning resources.

ALA Graphics

Among the top celebrity READ and character posters of the year were Harry Potter movie stars (Daniel Radcliffe, Rupert Grint, and Emma Watson) and the cast of the Fox television series *Glee,* each launching with social media marketing campaigns. Popular children's characters featured on posters included Judy Moody, Phineas and Ferb, Five Little Monkeys, Bad Kitty, and Scaredy Squirrel. For tweens and teens, the selection included mini posters for Dork Diaries and Wimpy Kid, exclusive art by John Rocco for the Lost Hero Poster, as well as Witch and Wizard products based on the manga adaptation of James Patterson's popular series.

RDA Toolkit and Training

The first official subscribers to the RDA (Resource Description and Access) Toolkit came on board in late 2010 after an initial 90-day open-access period. Under the direction of the three U.S. national libraries—the Library of Congress, the National Agricultural Library, and the National Library of Medicine—a select group of libraries then tested RDA. Based on analysis of the testing results, the three national libraries recommended implementation of RDA with certain conditions after January 2013. ALA Digital Reference worked to help catalogers and other users prepare for implementation.

Training in RDA and related matters was offered from a number of sources, including introductory webinars archived on the RDA Toolkit site. Special outreach to LIS instructors and students continues to help them integrate RDA into their teaching/learning. Translation and distribution agreements were initiated, with German, French, and Spanish leading the way. ALA Digital Reference Publisher Troy Linker attended the Frankfurt Book Fair to work with international colleagues in both publishing and the library fields.

ALA JobLIST

ALA JobLIST, the association's library jobs site and a top source for both job seekers and employers, continues to embrace new opportunities. With JobLIST content syndicated through numerous avenues—including RSS, Twitter, Facebook, LinkedIn, Indeed.com, SimplyHired.com, search engine optimization, and e-newsletters—the number of impressions shows continuous growth. Despite a reduced number of jobs available because of the national economic crisis, this joint project of ACRL, *American Libraries,* and HRDR listed more than 1,400 open positions during 2011 and showed a significant increase in online advertising revenue.

American Libraries

American Libraries, ALA's flagship publication, offered more content in more channels than ever before by the end of the fiscal year, with an increasingly robust suite of electronic products to complement the print magazine. Offerings now include six print issues of *American Libraries* plus five digital supplements during the year; americanlibrariesmagazine.org, which averages more than 85,000 visitors a month; *American Libraries Direct,* the award-winning weekly e-newsletter; video archives at AL Focus, with coverage of conferences and events, interviews, and profiles; occasional webinars in partnership with ALA offices covering such major trends as new technologies and privacy; and a growing family of blogs, including "Inside Scoop" and "Ask the ALA Librarian."

An online readership survey in April 2011 received responses from more than 3,700 readers, with some clear patterns emerging. More than half of the respondents gave print *American Libraries* high marks for relevance, reliability, variety, and depth. More than 75 percent said that print *American Libraries* and e-newsletter *American Libraries Direct* (which maintains a weekly click-through rate of at least 33 percent per issue) are regarded as essential professional reading. Requests for additional coverage included more articles on academic libraries, school librarianship, youth services, cataloging, and international librarianship, as well as more about the needs of job seekers, those new to the profession, and retired librarians.

Publishing a digital version of "The State of America's Libraries" in April was the magazine's first joint initiative with PIO. In one month, nearly 8,000 visited the report. In another collaborative outreach, *American Libraries* printed a limited-edition international supplement promoting the benefits of ALA membership to the attendees of the IFLA conference in San Juan, Puerto Rico.

Booklist Publications

Booklist Publications introduced several new electronic publications in 2011 and further developed its sponsored webinar program while still publishing 22 print issues of *Booklist* and four print *Book Links* supplements.

The webinar program grew to 26 free webinars during the fiscal year, moderated by *Booklist* editors and guests and including presentations from numerous publishing experts. More than 50,000 people registered and either attended in person or accessed the recordings after the event. The webinars covered a broad range of topics including reluctant readers, graphic novels, resources on bullying, multimedia in the library, high-demand mysteries, fresh voices for teen readers, authority in reference, book groups, crafts and gardening, and math and science.

Booklist Online Video Review, Bookmakers, and *Corner Shelf* joined the lineup of Booklist Online e-newsletters, which also include *REaD Alert, Booklist Online Exclusives,* and *Booklist's Quick Tips for Schools and Libraries.* The January 2011 issue of the e-newsletter *Booklist Online Exclusives* was the debut of a new business model: the single-sponsor newsletter, with Amazon Publishing signing on to sponsor the monthly issues throughout the year.

At the end of fiscal 2011, *Booklist Online* rolled out a new look and added features. Updates included links to related editor-selected recommended reading, book awards, and feature articles being placed alongside reviews for easiest access; Facebook, Twitter, and Google buttons, as well as a general Share widget, for easy sharing of favorite content; new icons for awards and e-book editions; "Great Reads" recommended by *Booklist* editors; and user-created subject heading searches on the main review page.

Leadership

Molly Raphael, former director of libraries at Multnomah County (Oregon) Library and the District of Columbia Public Library, was inaugurated as ALA president at the 2011 Annual Conference in New Orleans.

Raphael retired from the Oregon library in 2009 after serving in urban public libraries for 40 years. She had been recruited in 2003 to lead the library, where she increased diversity in library employment, collections, and programming and was awarded the Arthur Flemming Civil Rights Award. Under her leadership, the library achieved consistently high national rankings among urban public libraries and the highest gross circulation of any library in the United States, surpassing libraries serving much larger populations. The library—a nationally recognized leader in developing early literacy services and programs to reach out to underserved, culturally diverse communities—received the National Medal for Museum and Library Service, awarded by the Institute of Museum and Library Services, in 2009.

Raphael's previous 33 years at the District of Columbia Public Library began as a youth librarian and culminated in her appointment as director in 1997. During her tenure there, she led efforts to create an adult literacy program, developed services for at-risk children and families, and managed the implementation of new technologies that changed the way libraries deliver services. She also co-developed the first public library service in the United States serving the deaf community.

Maureen Sullivan, an organization development consultant from Baltimore, was named ALA president-elect in the 2011 election. Sullivan serves as president-elect for the 2011–2012 term and is to be inaugurated as president at the 2012 Annual Conference in Anaheim.

Three new ALA Executive Board members were elected by the ALA Council in a vote taken at the 2011 ALA Midwinter Meeting in San Diego: Dora Ho, young adult librarian at the Los Angeles Public Library; Michael Porter, president of Library Renewal in Seattle; and Sylvia Norton, a state-level coordinator for school libraries in Maine. They will each serve three-year terms beginning in July 2011 and concluding in June 2014.

Grants and Contributions

IMLS Grant Extends Doctoral Studies Program

The Institute of Museum and Library Services' Laura Bush 21st-Century Librarian Program awarded the Office for Diversity and Spectrum Scholarship Program a grant of $886,499 to extend the Spectrum Doctoral Fellowship Program, Building Change. The effort will continue ALA's work to recruit doctoral candidates from ethnically diverse backgrounds and to work with participating academic programs to support their education. Selected Spectrum doctoral fellows will receive full tuition and stipends for two years beginning in fall 2013, support for participation in professional conferences where they can share their research, and participation in two Spectrum doctoral fellows institutes to prepare for their doctoral studies and dissertation work. More than 20 LIS doctoral programs have agreed to participate in the project, each pledging to provide full tuition and stipends for the candidates after the first two years.

Grants Support Understanding of Louisa May Alcott

Thirty libraries received $2,500 grants to support five reading, viewing, and discussion programs featuring the documentary *Louisa May Alcott: The Woman Behind Little Women* and the companion biography of the same name. The library outreach program for the documentary is a collaboration among NEH, PPO, and Nancy Porter and Harriet Reisen for Filmmakers Collaborative. The film, biography, and library programs will introduce or reintroduce audiences to Alcott by presenting a story full of insights, discoveries about the author, and an understanding of American culture during her lifetime.

YALSA and ALSC Win Literacy Foundation Funding

YALSA and ALSC received funding to support Everyone Reads @ the library, a new youth literacy program, through a grant from Dollar General Literacy Foundation. Each division received $70,000 to support its efforts. YALSA used its money to create materials to help librarians serve Spanish-speaking teens, develop an iPhone application, and offer mini-grants for Teen Read Week and summer reading. The grant also supported distributing sets of the 2011 Teens' Top Ten nominees to needy libraries.

Major Awards and Honors

Honorary Membership

ALA bestowed its highest honor, honorary membership, on librarian and author Yohannes Gebregeorgis, founder of Ethiopia Reads, at the 2011 Annual Conference. Nonprofit Ethiopia Reads establishes children's libraries in Ethiopia and publishes bilingual and trilingual children's books, providing the children an opportunity to discover the love of reading and increasing literacy in an entire nation.

Madison Award

Patrice McDermott was the recipient of the 2011 James Madison Award. McDermott, director of OpenTheGovernment.org, received the award during the 13th annual National Freedom of Information Day Conference celebration. McDermott previously served as deputy director of OGR, where she led the office's work on government information and privacy policy and e-government policy issues, and as assistant director of OIF.

American Booksellers Association

200 White Plains Rd., Tarrytown, NY 10591
914-591-2665
World Wide Web http://www.BookWeb.org

The American Booksellers Association (ABA) and its more than 1,900 independent bookstore locations had a busy and fruitful year in 2011. Despite a challenging first quarter, the overall year was quite strong. In the fourth quarter holiday season, independent stores showed continued resilience, with reported online and in-store sales well up from the same period a year earlier.

ABA member in-store book sales as tracked by Nielsen Bookscan for Thanksgiving week—which included Black Friday and culminated in Small Business Saturday—increased 15.5 percent over the same week in 2010. Online sales through ABA-member Web sites during that week increased 60 percent over the previous year, and these strong sales continued through the end of the year.

In addition, a national survey gathering data from 1,768 independent businesses across 49 states—conducted by the Institute for Local Self-Reliance in partnership with several business organizations, including ABA—further demonstrated these sales increases, and showed how the "shop local" movement continues to grow in strength.

The survey found that independent businesses experienced strong sales growth over the holidays and appeared to be benefiting from increased public interest in supporting locally owned retail stores, banks, restaurants, and other enterprises.

These were among the key findings:

- Independent businesses in communities with an active "buy local" campaign operated by a local business organization reported revenue growth of 7.2 percent in 2011, compared with 2.6 percent for those in areas without such an initiative. ("Buy local" campaigns run by Independent Business Alliances and Local First groups are now under way in about 150 cities.)
- Independent retailers, which composed about half the survey respondents, reported stronger holiday sales than the industry average. While overall holiday sales were up 4.1 percent in 2011, the independent retailers surveyed said their holiday sales increased 6.7 percent on average.
- More than three-quarters of the businesses surveyed said that public awareness of the benefits of supporting locally owned businesses had increased in the last year.
- Looking specifically at retail respondents, the survey found that those in areas with an active "buy local" campaign reported holiday sales growth of 8.5 percent in 2011, compared with 5.2 percent for retailers in areas without such an initiative.

Continued Membership Growth

Forty-one ABA member bookstores opened in 2011, including seven branches of existing businesses and eight that sell primarily used books. Two of the new indie booksellers—Avid Bookshop in Athens, Georgia, and Hello Hello Books in Rockland, Maine—opened after waging successful campaigns to obtain financial support from their local communities, showcasing growing community support for locally owned businesses and bricks-and-mortar stores. The openings included two new stores for Maple Street Book Shop in New Orleans as well as the return of independent bookselling to Nashville, where bestselling author Ann Patchett and co-owner Karen Hayes opened Parnassus Books.

The model for independent bookstore success continues to include an engaging, curated inventory; strong community ties; a full events calendar; and complementary gift items—all focused on the goal of providing a rewarding customer experience.

Nationally, new ABA member stores have multiplied in the last two years. The association's more than 1,900 storefront member locations represent an increase of 15.5 percent since January 2010. Since 2005 more than 614 stores have opened and joined ABA, 74 since January 2010.

Association and Governance Activity

In March 2011 ABA bookstore members approved a bylaws amendment that moved ABA from a nine-person board of directors to a ten-person board by making the position of board president a separate and distinct position involving a single two-year term.

Said outgoing ABA President Michael Tucker of the California bookstore group Books, Inc., "Creating a two-year term for future presidents will prove to be a great benefit for ABA's governance and for achieving the association's ends policies [which express the board's long-term goals] by enhancing the diversity of the board's deliberations and by helping to ensure the frequent infusion of new energy and ideas while maintaining the responsiveness and collegiality of a small group."

Following the bylaws vote, the association announced the results of balloting by bookstore members. Elected to serve three-year terms as directors beginning May 2011 were: John Evans, a co-owner of Diesel bookstores in California; Matt Norcross, co-owner of McLean & Eakin Booksellers in Petoskey, Michigan; and Ken White, manager of the General Books Department at San Francisco State University Bookstore.

Under the amended bylaws, the membership elected Becky Anderson, co-owner of Anderson's Bookshops in Naperville, Illinois, to serve a two-year term as ABA president, and Steve Bercu, co-owner of BookPeople in Austin, to serve a two-year term as vice president. The association's vice president/secretary is elected for a single term of two years, which, unlike the office of president, is subject to, and not in addition to, the six-year limit on terms of service established for directors.

Following Anderson's election to the presidency, the board appointed Valerie Koehler of Blue Willow Bookshop in Houston to fill the resulting vacancy. Koehler will serve a one-year term and will be eligible to stand for election to a full three-year term during the next election cycle.

Call for Innovation

Speaking at ABA's Annual Meeting May 24, 2011, during its major trade show, BookExpo America (BEA), CEO Oren Teicher noted that "These are not normal times in the book business. We are living through a period of unprecedented change and staggering challenges."

Teicher emphasized that in order for booksellers and publishers to ensure that "we will create a business environment where everyone grows and prospers," ABA and its members need to chart a creative new course. "We need to come up with new and innovative ways in which we do business together," he said. "It can no longer be 'business as usual.'" The first step, he said, would be "for publishers and booksellers, together, to take out a clean sheet of paper and ask themselves: If we were to design a business model that would give all stakeholders in our industry the best possible opportunity for success, what would it look like?"

Teicher noted that long-term solutions would build on the core strengths of bookselling while adapting to and implementing new technology. A key reality of retailing, he said, was that "bricks-and-mortar bookstores—and not just indies, but all bricks-and-mortar bookstores—remain the essential showroom in ensuring the sales of a broad spectrum of titles."

Regarding online sales and other new forms of marketing, Teicher said, "We at ABA are leaving no stone unturned in helping empower our member stores to make it as easy as possible for customers to buy digital content" from indie booksellers. Teicher reported that ABA now has more than 300 bookstores able to sell Google eBooks.

He noted, however, that "ABA in no way believes that print books are going away. We remain convinced that the lion's share of books sold in our member stores for the foreseeable future will be sold in traditional book format."

Regarding new business models, Teicher said, "It is time for our industry to acknowledge that new challenges require new business practices." Noting that independent booksellers "understand that publishers are facing significant financial pressures and constraints, too," Teicher said ABA has held a number of meetings with publishers about "the direction of the industry and steps booksellers and publishers might take to improve their collective future."

Book Awards

BookExpo America (BEA) was also the site of the presentation of the 2011 Indies Choice Book Awards and the E. B. White Read-Aloud Awards, as chosen by the owners and staff at member stores.

The winners of the 2011 Indies Choice Book Awards were: (adult fiction) *Room* by Emma Donoghue (Little, Brown); (adult nonfiction) *Unbroken* by Laura Hillenbrand (Random); (adult debut) *Matterhorn* by Karl Marlantes (Atlantic Monthly Press and El León Literary Arts); and (young adult) *Revolution* by Jennifer Donnelly (Delacorte).

The E. B. White Read-Aloud Awards—formerly offered by the Association of Booksellers for Children, which merged with ABA in 2010—recognize books that reflect the playful, well-paced language, engaging themes, and universal appeal of White's well-known works. They replace the Indies Choice Book Awards in the categories of "middle reader" and "new picture book."

The 2011 E. B. White winners were: (middle reader) *The Strange Case of Origami Yoda* by Tom Angleberger (Amulet); and (picture book) *Children Make Terrible Pets* by Peter Brown (Little, Brown).

ABA members chose Laurie Halse Anderson as the year's "most engaging author." Halse Anderson was recognized for her involvement and responsiveness during in-store appearances and for having a strong sense of the importance of indie booksellers to their local communities.

And, in a very tight race, ABA inducted four all-time favorites into the Indies Choice Book Awards Picture Book Hall of Fame: *Corduroy* by Don Freeman (Viking), *Mike Mulligan and His Steam Shovel* by Virginia Lee Burton (Houghton Mifflin Harcourt), *The Snowy Day* by Ezra Jack Keats (Viking), and *The Very Hungry Caterpillar* by Eric Carle (Philomel).

ABA Personnel Changes

In August ABA announced that Len Vlahos, the association's chief operating officer and a longtime staff member, had been selected as the executive director of the Book Industry Study Group, Inc. (BISG), effective September 12.

In November Joy Dallanegra-Sanger joined the association as senior program officer, a newly created senior executive position. Dallanegra-Sanger's experience includes 15 years in publishing and 13 years in book retailing. Most recently, she was senior vice president and director of marketing for Macmillan Children's Publishing Group, and earlier held senior positions at Random House, including vice president and director of field sales for Random House Children's Books and vice president and associate publisher, trade paperbacks, for Doubleday/Broadway Publishing Group. In addition, she held a number of positions at Waldenbooks with responsibilities that included merchandising, marketing, and buying.

Shannon O'Connor joined the ABA staff in the newly created position of ABC Children's Group Manager. She will be ABA's point person for children's booksellers and, working closely with other staff, will oversee the management of the ABC Group's programs, including children's bookseller educational offerings at both the Winter Institute and BookExpo America, the ABC silent auction, the author tea and speed dating events at BEA in conjunction with the Children's Book Council, the annual *ABC Best Books for Children Catalog,* and other projects.

Also during 2011, ABA CEO Teicher was elected vice president of the International Booksellers Federation (IBF). Teicher, who will continue to serve on the IBF Council, was installed as vice president at the October meeting of IBF in conjunction with the Frankfurt Book Fair. In his new role, Teicher said, he would continue to work with the council "to re-energize IBF as a vehicle for bookseller associations from around the world to learn from each other, as increasingly the challenges faced by booksellers in one country are similar to the issues being faced everywhere."

Member Education

More than 500 new and experienced booksellers took part in the 2012 ABA Winter Institute in New Orleans, the association's seventh such annual educational event. The three-day program January 18–20 gave participants practical ideas for improving their businesses and networking opportunities with colleagues from across the country. The institute's programming covered an array of topics, including new business models, e-books, events, the children's book market, buying and spending for success, and new partnerships between booksellers and authors. Its lead sponsor is the Ingram Content Group.

The 2013 Winter Institute is scheduled for Kansas City February 22–25.

In August 2011 ABA held its first one-day mini-institute, the IndieCommerce Institute (ICI). The event, attended by about 70 booksellers, was sponsored by the Ingram Content Group and designed to accommodate three tracks of booksellers—introductory, experienced, and a master class. The feedback received from attendees is providing ABA with both a sense of the event's success and information to plan for future programming.

ABA also continues its full range of educational programming for bookstore members at BEA. At the 2011 conference, more than a thousand independent booksellers representing approximately 400 ABA member stores participated. The program spotlighted children's bookselling, with educational sessions and panels on such topics as "turning mind share into market share" in the children's market, creating events for children, and reaching the young adult audience.

The schedule also featured programming for general booksellers, including beginner and advanced e-books sessions, panels on strategic thinking, effective marketing, a review of the latest ABACUS data, and a session on how to increase nonfiction sales.

Preceding the opening of BEA, the association offered a free, full-day "Introduction to Retail Bookselling" seminar. The workshop was facilitated by Donna Paz Kaufman and Mark Kaufman of the bookstore training group Paz & Associates. The free workshop was open to ABA provisional members and employees of ABA regular member stores.

ABA also continued to offer free education seminars and panels in conjunction with the nine regional trade shows organized by the industry's regional booksellers' associations, and a series of ABA forums for members, also organized in conjunction with the regional trade associations.

IndieCommerce

ABA continued in 2011 to introduce enhancements and new features to IndieCommerce, its e-commerce business solution for member stores, and the bookstore user base for IndieCommerce continued to grow.

At year's end approximately 360 member stores subscribed to IndieCommerce, and in September ABA announced that it would lower the monthly price from $225 to $175, beginning October 1. Earlier in the year the association said it would be able to lower the fee if it reached its goal of 300 subscribers by October. ABA member stores looking to take advantage of IndieCommerce's customizable platform and growing e-book sales helped ABA exceed that goal by mid-September.

IndieCommerce Web sites experienced an 84 percent jump in sales in 2011, with e-book sales increasing from 0.7 percent in 2010 to 5.2 percent in 2011. Of note was the fact that there was a nearly 300 percent increase in the number of stores that had more than $10,000 in gross sales on their sites.

Creative bookseller marketing efforts that employed a number of different publisher e-book promotions continued to publicize the availability of Google eBooks on store sites. A prime example of this was a promotion in partnership with ABA from Unbridled Books that highlighted 25 Unbridled eBooks for 25 cents. The titles, all Google eBooks, were to be available for 25 cents via IndieCommerce Web sites for three days, June 9–11. The 25 Unbridled titles for 25 cents include 16 Indie Next List selections, including three No. 1 picks, *The Singer's Gun* by Emily St. John Mandel, *The Pirate's Daughter* by Margaret Cezair-Thompson, and *The Green Age of Asher Witherow* by M. Allen Cunningham.

To meet the demand of consumers for a mobile retail solution for reading and purchasing e-books, in 2011 ABA launched a device-based reading application, the IndieBound Reader, developed by Bluefire Productions, an independent software company in Seattle. The app is available for devices using the Android operating system and iOS devices.

"With the release of IndieBound Reader, independent bookstores are taking another major step forward as players on the digital stage," said ABA Technology Director Matt Supko. "A year after the launch of Google eBooks, indies have become a vital and fast-growing part of the e-book market. . . . The IndieBound Reader app gives independent bookstores a home on the most popular mobile devices, making it easier than ever for customers to shop local when they shop digital."

In addition, a number of improvements to the IndieCommerce product were introduced, including storage of customer credit card numbers for easy repeat use, bulk upload of non-book items, search for non-book items, and browse by category (using BISAC codes) for books and Google eBooks.

In another area of bookstore adoption of technology, in 2011 ABA and On Demand Books (ODB), the maker of the Espresso Book Machine (EBM), entered into a joint marketing agreement under which ABA will market EBM to member bookstores and help permission publisher titles to the EBM sales channel.

"The Espresso Book Machine provides a unique opportunity to help our members differentiate themselves from their competitors," said then-ABA COO Len Vlahos. "By offering retail-level on-demand printing, indie bookstores can explore new custom publishing business models and more quickly and efficiently meet consumer demand for books. This new relationship between ABA and ODB helps lower the barrier to entry for our members to participate."

Advocacy

ABA continued its robust advocacy efforts on behalf of member bookstores during 2011. Of prime importance was the continued campaign for sales tax equity, and ABA worked closely with booksellers nationwide to help them make their views known to elected officials regarding the importance of equitable enforcement of sales tax legislation on the state level and, on the federal level, the passage of "e-fairness" legislation. ABA staff offered booksellers help in meeting with legislators and state officials, providing background information and support materials, and working with a growing number of allied trade associations and organizations.

In November ABA led an advocacy day in Washington, D.C., in support of a federal solution to the issue of sales tax equity. Participating with ABA and indie booksellers in 31 meetings with key legislators and senior staff in the Senate and House of Representatives were retail members and association staff from the American Specialty Toy Retailing Association, the National Bicycle Dealers Association, the National Association of College Stores, and the National Retail Hobby Stores Association. ABA also worked with the Retail Industry Leaders Association and the Alliance for Main Street Fairness in organizing the advocacy day.

The meetings followed the introduction of bipartisan sales tax fairness legislation in the House and the expected introduction of new legislation in the Senate.

In addition, ABA continued to work closely with the Small Business Administration (SBA) to help booksellers access SBA resources, including SBA-backed small business loans. One result was nine educational sessions in 2011 at the fall regional trade shows organized by ABA in conjunction with SBA, focusing on sources of capital and on small business professional development resources, and a similar session at the Winter Institute where SBA also participated in a number of one-on-one meetings with booksellers.

Association of Research Libraries

21 Dupont Circle N.W., Washington, DC 20036
202-296-2296, e-mail arlhq@arl.org
World Wide Web http://www.arl.org

Lee Anne George
Publications Program Officer

The Association of Research Libraries (ARL) is a nonprofit organization of 126 research libraries in the United States and Canada. Its mission is to influence the changing environment of scholarly communication and the public policies that affect research libraries and the diverse communities they serve. ARL pursues this mission by advancing the goals of its member research libraries, providing leadership in public and information policy to the scholarly and higher education communities, fostering the exchange of ideas and expertise, facilitating the emergence of new roles for research libraries, and shaping a future environment that leverages its interests with those of allied organizations.

ARL and its member libraries addressed a number of strategic issues in 2011. Key areas included copyright and fair use, orphan works, digitization of collections, licensing of online content, and implementation of e-science programs. The association's diversity and leadership initiatives continue to expand the capacity of libraries to reflect society's diversity in staffing, collections, leadership, and programs. Ongoing and new assessment activities support research libraries' ability to effectively measure their performance. Following are highlights of the association's programs and activities.

Influencing Public Policies

A primary goal of ARL's Influencing Public Policies program is to influence legislative and executive branch action that is favorable to the research library and higher education communities. To achieve this goal, the program helps association members keep abreast of rapidly changing issues, players, regulations, and community priorities. The program analyzes, responds to, and seeks to influence public initiatives on information, intellectual property, and telecommunications policies among others. In addition, the program promotes funding for numerous agencies and national institutions and advances ARL members' interests on these issues.

The Influencing Public Policies program monitors Canadian information policies, such as copyright and intellectual property and access to government information, through the Canadian Association of Research Libraries (CARL). More information about this ARL strategic direction is available at http://www.arl.org/pp.

Copyright and Intellectual Property

In March 2011 the Library Copyright Alliance (LCA)—made up of ARL, the American Library Association (ALA), and the Association of College and Research

Libraries (ACRL)—participated in a U.S. Department of Commerce "listening session" on the proposed treaty on Traditional Cultural Expression and provided analysis of the draft treaty. The analysis is available at http://www.librarycopyright alliance.org/bm~doc/lca_tcecomments21march11-2.pdf.

On May 16, 2011, LCA released a statement describing the key features that copyright reform proposals should include in order to constitute significant improvement over current law for libraries and their users. The statement is available at http://www.arl.org/bm~doc/lca_copyrightreformstatement_16may11.pdf.

In June ARL participated in a series of roundtable discussions at the U.S. Copyright Office regarding the risks and possible benefits of bestowing federal protection on sound recordings made prior to February 15, 1972. The discussions were part of the Copyright Office's preparation of a report on the subject commissioned by Congress as part of the PRO-IP Act. ARL's and ALA's Reply Comments are available at http://www.arl.org/bm~doc/arl-ala_ soundrecordingcomments_13apr11.pdf. ARL's post on its Policy Notes blog is at http://policynotes.arl.org/post/4587677896/arl-and-ala-on-federal-copyright-for-pre-1972-sound.

Also in June, ARL joined the Electronic Frontier Foundation (EFF) in a letter regarding the U.S. Senate Judiciary Committee endorsing the PROTECT IP Act (S. 968). The letter warned that the PROTECT IP Act might hamper free expression and undermine Internet security. The letter is available at https://www.eff.org/files/filenode/coica_files/pub_interest_pipa_ltr.pdf.

In September ARL developed and released the Orphan Works Resource Packet, a compilation that provides general information on legal and policy issues concerning orphan works and the University of Michigan's Orphan Works Project, an FAQ, and a legal memorandum by Jonathan Band of policyband-width that describes the legal issues associated with making orphan works digitally available. The packet is available at http://www.arl.org/bm~doc/resource_ orphanworks_13sept11.pdf.

In October U.S. Rep. Lamar Smith (R-Texas and chair of the Committee on the Judiciary) introduced the Stop Online Piracy Act (SOPA), a bill that could raise significant new risks of liability for research libraries. ARL wrote multiple letters to representatives in response to the bill and to its companion bill in the Senate, the Protect IP Act. For additional information, see http://www.arl.org/pp/ppcopyright/index.shtml.

Court Cases and Related Activities

Costco v. Omega

On December 13, 2010, the Supreme Court decided *Costco* v. *Omega* in a manner that eliminated none of the uncertainty caused by the lower court's ruling in that case. Jonathan Band, legal counsel to LCA, released a memorandum on the impact http://www.arl.org/bm~doc/lcacostco013111.pdf and LCA filed an amicus (friend-of-the-court) brief, available at http://www.librarycopyrightalliance.org/bm~doc/lca-costco-amicus.pdf.

The following month Verizon filed a notice of appeal in the U.S. Court of Appeals for the D.C. Circuit challenging the Federal Communication Commission's authority to regulate broadband Internet access service. For more information, the issue brief is available at http://www.arl.org/bm~doc/issue-brief-nn-rules implications-012411.pdf and the amicus brief filed by LCA is at http://www.arl.org/bm~doc/fccvs_att_amicus.pdf.

Google Books Settlement

There were many updates to the Google Books settlement in 2011, including Judge Denny Chin's rejection of the proposed settlement on March 22, 2011; his April 14 decision to give the parties in the Google Books litigation until June 1 to prepare for a status conference, and his decision to set another extension for September 15—at which time, having seen no movement on the settlement, he set a "generous" trial schedule to begin July 2012. ARL commented on each step of the suit via the ARL Policy Notes blog http://policynotes.arl.org. Additionally, in April, Band released *A Guide for the Perplexed Part IV: The Rejection of the Google Books Settlement,* the latest in his series on the evolving Google Books settlement saga. The guide is available at http://www.arl.org/bm~doc/guideiv-final-1.pdf.

In response to the complex nature of the Google Books settlement, ARL, with the Washington College of Law, organized and conducted a two-day workshop on next steps following a Google Books settlement decision, with a focus on best practices. In addition, LCA updated Band's "March Madness: Paths Forward for the Google Books Settlement." The diagram is available at http://www.arl.org/bm~doc/gbs-march-madness-diagram-final.pdf.

In May ARL commented via the ARL Policy Notes blog on *Cambridge University Press et al.* v. *Patton et al.,* the legal dispute over Georgia State University's e-reserves and course management systems (http://policynotes.arl.org/tagged/gsu), which began in May 2011 and ended in June. Additional analysis of the ruling is available on the ARL Policy Notes blog at http://policynotes.arl.org/post/6395517300/publishers-lose-another-claim-as-gsu-trial-comes-to-a-close.

In June ARL participated in an amicus brief in *Lawrence Golan* v. *Eric H. Holder, Jr., et al.* before the U.S. Court of Appeals, Tenth Circuit, concerning works remaining in the public domain, as well as in *Timothy S. Vernor* v. *Autodesk, Inc.,* before the U.S. Court of Appeals for the Ninth Circuit, concerning the first sale doctrine. Both amicus briefs can be found at http://www.librarycopyright alliance.org.

International Copyright Activities

In May 2011 the ARL Board of Directors affirmed that it is the right of North American research libraries to participate in international interlibrary loan (ILL) and document delivery (DD) activities. Over the previous year questions had been raised concerning the current ILL practices of some U.S. research libraries. The focus of concern was on the delivery of resources from U.S. libraries to non-U.S. libraries. U.S. copyright law supports the ability of domestic libraries to participate in ILL arrangements and to send copies of copyrighted works to foreign libraries provided the libraries meet the requirements of the law. The *ARL Task Force Report on International Interlibrary Loan and Document Delivery Practices* is available at http://publications.arl.org/1acgvq.pdf.

In November LCA submitted comments to the Library of Congress in response to its Notice of Inquiry regarding section 1201 of the Copyright Act. LCA asked that the previous exemptions to the prohibition of circumvention of copyright protection systems for access control technologies be renewed. The comments are available at http://www.librarycopyrightalliance.org/bm~doc/lca_1201comments_29nov11.pdf.

LCA participated in discussions at the World Intellectual Property Organization (WIPO) on issues relating to access to copyrighted works by the print disabled, traditional cultural expression, and discussions concerning a possible library-related treaty. ARL and ALA actively engaged members of the U.S. delegation. LCA commented and provided an analysis on the Proposed WIPO Cultural Expressions Treaty. The comments are available at http://www.arl.org/bm~doc/lca_wipo_tce_072110.pdf.

Fair Use and Related Initiatives

In January 2011 ARL released *Fair Use Challenges in Academic and Research Libraries,* a report that summarizes research into the current application of fair use and other copyright exemptions to meet the missions of U.S. academic and research libraries. In dozens of interviews with research and academic librarians, the researchers learned how copyright law comes into play as interviewees perform core library functions. The research was conducted in partnership with the Center for Social Media and the Program on Information Justice and Intellectual Property at American University. The report is part of a three-stage project funded by the Andrew W. Mellon Foundation with the ultimate goal of developing and promoting a code of best practices in fair use for research and academic libraries. The full report is available at http://www.arl.org/bm~doc/arl_csm_fairusereport.pdf.

Public Access Policies

Open Access and Public Access Policies

In April 2011, to build upon the success of the three-year-old Public Access Policy of the National Institutes of Health, ARL and its affiliate SPARC (the Scholarly Publishing and Academic Resources Coalition) wrote to key U.S. policymakers requesting that they expand the policy's scope and shorten its embargo period. The letters are available at http://www.arl.org/sparc/advocacy/nih/11-0407.shtml.

The following month the Senate passed the Faster FOIA Act of 2011 (S. 627), which was introduced by Sen. Patrick Leahy (Chair, Senate Judiciary Committee and D-Vt.). ARL wrote in support of the act with OpenTheGovernment.org.

With SPARC, the Max Planck Institute, and the Howard Hughes Medical Institute, ARL organized the Berlin 9 conference (http://www.arl.org/sparc/media/11-0324.shtml), an international conference that focused on the impact of open access. A significant number of ARL libraries sponsored the conference.

Open Government

In January 2011 ARL joined with more than 30 organizations and well over 100 individuals in thanking the National Archives and Records Administration for its leadership in investigating the Central Intelligence Agency's destruction of federal records showing the torture of detainees at CIA "black sites." The full letter is available at http://www.openthegovernment.org/otg/CIA-Accountability-Groups. pdf. Throughout the year ARL participated in OpenTheGovernment letters and participated in meetings concerning the Freedom of Information Act (FOIA), preservation of government records with a particular focus on digital records, whistleblower legislation, and Executive Branch open and transparent initiatives.

Federal Depository Library Program

In April 2011 the University of Minnesota Libraries proposed to establish a multi-state regional Federal Depository Library (FDL) for the states of Minnesota, South Dakota, and Michigan. This proposal came in response to an announcement by the Library of Michigan that it was dropping its designation as a regional FDL for the state. In addition, the Association of Southeastern Research Libraries (ASERL) initiated a collaborative Centers of Excellence project for academic and research libraries in the Southeast. ARL collaborated with the University of Minnesota, the State Library of Michigan, and other FDLs on changes to the Federal Depository Library Program (FDLP). ARL compiled communication from the U.S. Government Printing Office (GPO) and the libraries on this subject. For more information, see http://www.arl.org/pp/access/fdlp/fdlp-dev/index.shtml. In October the ARL Board of Directors issued an "ARL Statement on Recent USGPO Decisions Concerning the FDLP" that was endorsed by a large number of academic and research libraries and consortia throughout the country. The statement is available at http://www.arl.org/bm~doc/fdlp_arlstatement_12oct11.pdf.

Privacy and Civil Liberties Issues

In January 2011 ARL joined the Electronic Frontier Foundation and others in the not-for-profit sector in an open letter to U.S. government officials calling on them to respect freedom of expression. The letter focused on the public debate over controversial disclosures by WikiLeaks. The signatories of the letter urged caution "against any legislation that could weaken the principles of free expression vital to a democratic society or hamper online freedoms." The full letter is available at http://www.openthegovernment.org/otg/wikileaks_open_letter_final.pdf.

In February ARL and ALA sent a letter to Sen. Leahy, chair of the Senate Committee on the Judiciary, supporting S. 193, the USAPatriot Act Sunset Extension Act of 2011. The full letter is available at http://www.arl.org/bm~doc/lt_leahy patriot020211.pdf. In May the House of Representatives and the Senate voted to renew three expiring provisions of the USAPatriot Act for four more years. Due to expire were the "lone wolf" provision, the roaming wiretaps provision, and the "library provision" (Section 215). ARL wrote a post on the ARL Policy Notes blog http://policynotes.arl.org.

ARL, along with others in the public and private sectors, issued a "Statement of Concern about Expansion of CALEA." The purpose of the statement was to influence the Obama administration on extending the mandates of the Communications Assistance for Law Enforcement Act (CALEA), and to help policymakers assess whatever CALEA proposals there are. The statement is available at http://cdt.org/files/CALEA_II_Joint_Statement_with_sigs.pdf.

In March ARL participated in Sunshine Week, a national initiative to promote dialogue about the importance of the public's right to know what its government is doing, and why. Sunshine Week coincides with National Freedom of Information (FOI) Day and James Madison's birthday on March 16. As in years past, OpenTheGovernment, of which ARL is a member, recruited host sites across the country where people could watch the webcast and then discuss local open government issues.

In April ARL filed comments with the Federal Trade Commission (FTC) and suggested that it require strong protection for reader privacy in the Google Books service. In its comments to FTC, ARL noted the privacy concerns libraries and other organizations had raised about the proposed Google Books settlement. While the settlement was rejected by the court, many of the privacy concerns raised in that context remain relevant to the existing Google Books service. The comments to FTC are available at http://www.arl.org/bm~doc/gbs-privacycomments_26apr11.pdf.

ARL, ALA, and several other library groups joined the Electronic Frontier Foundation (EFF) in an April amicus brief that asked a federal appeals court to apply well-established rules that protect online service providers from being sued for copyright infringement by their users. Viacom and other rights holders have sued Google (parent company of YouTube) over infringing videos uploaded by users to YouTube, arguing for a very cramped reading of the "safe harbor" provisions in the Digital Millennium Copyright Act. The trial court rejected these interpretations.

ARL is a member of the Digital Due Process Coalition, which focuses on updating current law to ensure strong privacy protections for communications and associated data, and in 2011 issued a Joint Statement on Principles. For more information, see http://www.digitaldueprocess.org.

Net Neutrality

ARL, ALA, and EDUCAUSE held meetings with congressional staff in both the House of Representatives and the Senate, and sent letters in support of network neutrality and broadband deployment. ARL, as a member of the Open Internet Coalition (OIC), filed numerous comments on telecommunications issues and participated in meetings with relevant congressional and administration staff. For additional information, see http://www.arl.org/pp/telecom/index.shtml.

Federal Agency Funding

As a member of the Science Coalition, ARL supported increased funding for the National Science Foundation (NSF) and joined in coalition testimony. ARL also participated in an American Association for the Advancement of Science letter in support of funding NSF's Directorate for Social and Behavioral and Economic Science. In addition, ARL participated in many letters and meetings on international program funding at the Department of Education as a member of the Coalition for International Education. For example, ARL filed testimony in support of Title VI funding with House of Representatives and Senate Appropriations Committees and opposed cuts to the programs.

ARL filed a statement before the Senate Judiciary Committee in support of Development, Relief, and Education for Alien Minors (DREAM) Act legislation. The ARL statement is available at http://www.arl.org/bm~doc/ltdream_27june11.pdf.

Reshaping Scholarly Communication

ARL's Reshaping Scholarly Communication program works to develop effective, extensible, sustainable, and economically viable models of scholarly communication that provide barrier-free access to quality information in support of the mission of research institutions. The program encourages the creation and implementation of new models for scholarly exchange that build on the widespread adoption of digital technologies, advocates for improved terms and conditions under which content is made available, and establishes alliances and develops relationships that promote open collaboration among stakeholders in the scholarly communication system. Additional information about this ARL strategic direction is available at http://www.arl.org/sc.

ARL Endorses Berlin Declaration on Open Access

In November ARL joined more than 300 organizations and institutions to endorse the Berlin Declaration on Open Access to Knowledge in the Sciences and Humanities. In a letter to Peter Gruss, president of the Max Planck Society, Winston Tabb, ARL president and Sheridan Dean of University Libraries and Museums at Johns Hopkins University, wrote, "The Association of Research Libraries has been a longtime and consistent supporter of Open Access and has worked hard to advance its principles internationally. During the October 2011 meeting of the Board of Directors a decision was taken to become a signatory to the Berlin Declaration." Thirty-two additional research institutions, associations, and foundations in the United States, Canada, and Mexico also signed the Berlin Declaration before the Berlin 9 Open Access Conference in November. For more information, see http://www.arl.org/news/pr/Berlin-1nov11.shtml.

ARL Registers as ORCID Participant

The ARL Board supported a recommendation from the ARL Reshaping Scholarly Communication Steering Committee that the association register to participate in the ORCID initiative. ORCID (Open Researcher and Contributor ID) is a nonprofit organization dedicated to solving the problem of name ambiguity in scholarly research. The organization brings together universities, funding organizations, societies, publishers, libraries, and corporations from around the world with the goal of establishing a registry that can be adopted and embraced as the de facto standard by the whole community. For information about ORCID, visit http://orcid.org.

ARL, LYRASIS in Licensing Agreement

In November ARL and the library consortium LYRASIS signed an agreement designating LYRASIS as an agent to negotiate licenses for online content on behalf of interested ARL member libraries. This was the culmination of an effort that began in 2010 to identify a strategy for ARL to influence the marketplace regarding licensing rights, technical specifications, and business terms to meet the needs of research libraries. For more information, see http://www.arl.org/news/pr/LYRASIS-29nov11.shtml.

Publishing Support for Small Print-Based Publishers

In March 2011 ARL released the report *Publishing Support for Small Print-Based Publishers: Options for ARL Libraries.* The report summarizes a project funded by ARL to investigate how research libraries might provide support to print-only publishers in order to ensure long-term digital access to their content. The final report was prepared for ARL by project consultants October Ivins and Judy Luther. A PDF of the report is available at http://www.arl.org/bm~doc/pub-support_7mar11.pdf.

Transforming Research Libraries

The transformation of research libraries mirrors, to a large degree, the ongoing evolution of research institutions and the practices of research and scholarship. ARL's Transforming Research Libraries (TRL) strategic direction focuses on articulating, promoting, and facilitating new and expanding roles for ARL libraries that support, enable, and enrich the transformations affecting research and research-intensive education. Additional information about this ARL strategic direction is available at http://www.arl.org/rtl.

2030 Scenarios Project

As a follow-up to the release of the ARL 2030 Scenarios in 2010, ARL offered "Planning with the ARL 2030 Scenarios," a two-and-a-half day workshop at the Georgia Institute of Technology in Atlanta. This experiential learning event used real library cases to take participants through a process of assessing an organization's needs and mapping out a custom plan for effectively incorporating the ARL 2030 Scenarios in the case organizations. Each participant worked through a diagnostic process to define the needs of his or her organization, mastered the concept of a strategic agenda, and learned techniques for implementing scenario planning activities. This was an active learning event, minimizing lecture and presentation and maximizing interaction and activity. For more information about the ARL 2030 Scenarios, see http://www.arl.org/rtl/plan/scenarios/index.shtml.

Library Collections Task Force

In January 2011 ARL launched the 21st Century Research Library Collections Task Force that was charged to "articulate an action plan on 21st century research library collections and some of the emerging functions related to content managed by research libraries in a digital age." The nine members of the task force and Visiting Program Officer Christine Avery (Pennsylvania State University) consulted broadly on a range of related initiatives and with leadership groups within ARL and beyond. In their work, which considered content broadly, the task force developed a new vision of research library collections content and strategies for advancing joint initiatives among member libraries.

E-Science Institute

ARL and CLIR/DLF jointly developed an E-Science Institute to support member libraries seeking to build or enhance their capacity to advance e-science. The institute consists of four modules, beginning with a "baseline" module to establish common understanding of the issues and concluding with an in-person workshop event. The set of designed experiences will take small teams of individuals chosen by participating research libraries through a process that strengthens and advances their e-science support role. The development and delivery of the 2011 institute was funded by sponsoring libraries that are members of ARL and the Council on Library and Information Resources/Digital Library Federation (CLIR/DLF). Information on the institute, including a list of sponsors and supporters is available at http://www.arl.org/rtl/eresearch/escien/escieninstitute.

The first of the three ARL/DLF E-Science Institute capstone events took place in Atlanta November 30–December 2. The second and third capstone events were held in early 2012. Teams from 22 ARL institutions convened to network with one another and with institute faculty. Building on months of on-campus interviews, data gathering, and analysis, the teams collaborated to create strategic agendas for implementing e-science programs and services at their institutions.

Digital Curation for Preservation

In March 2011 ARL released the first report in the New Roles for New Times series, *Digital Curation for Preservation,* authored by Tyler Walters (Virginia Tech University) and Katherine Skinner (Educopia Institute). The report explores a "promising set of new roles that libraries are currently carving out in the digital arena," describing emerging strategies for libraries and librarians and highlighting collaborative approaches through a series of case studies of key programs and projects. The report also provides helpful definitions and offers recommendations for libraries considering how best to make or expand their investments in digital curation. A PDF of the report is available for download at http://www.arl.org/bm~doc/nrnt_digital_curation17mar11.pdf.

In April ARL hosted a webcast to complement the report. Report co-authors discussed the new roles and services being developed in the arena of digital curation for preservation. Also featured were four members of a reactor panel who explored and expanded on key findings and recommendations in the report. View the archive of the webcast on ARL's YouTube channel at http://www.youtube.com/watch?v=mrys17cfg-c. The co-authors and webcast panelists wrote responses to questions asked during the webcast, providing a deeper understanding of digital curation issues.

NSF Data Sharing Policy Guide

The ARL publication *Guide for Research Libraries: The NSF Data Sharing Policy* by Patricia Hswe and Ann Elisabeth Holt (Pennsylvania State University) was updated several times to incorporate new resources that are emerging to support the National Science Foundation policy. Many of the linked items are broadly relevant to data sharing activities beyond the specific requirements of NSF. The guide is available at http://www.arl.org/rtl/eresearch/escien/nsf/index.shtml.

Sustainability of Digitized Special Collections

In November 2010 ARL and Ithaka S+R partnered in a two-year study, funded by the Institute of Library and Museum Services (IMLS), of how libraries, archives, and museums are sustaining digitized special collections. Together they are developing a survey that will be sent to all ARL members and to cultural institutions that have received National Leadership Grants to create or enhance digitized special collections. In November 2001 Ithaka S+R and ARL led the webcast "Sustainability of Digitized Special Collections: A Participant's Guide" for ARL libraries. The second presentation of the webcast, targeted toward additional institutions that have received IMLS National Leadership Grants to create or enhance digitized special collections, was held in late November. To view the webcast archives and additional information about the project, visit http://www.ithaka.org/ithaka-s-r/research/sustainability-of-digitized-special-collections.

Diversity, Professional Workforce, and Leadership Development

ARL works closely with member libraries, graduate library and information science programs, and other libraries and library associations to promote awareness of career opportunities in research libraries and support the success of library professionals from racial and ethnic groups currently under-represented in the profession. ARL's Diversity Programs support member libraries as they strive to reflect society's diversity in their staffing, collections, leadership, and programs. Central to the diversity agenda are programs that facilitate the recruitment, preparation, and advancement of librarians into leadership positions in research libraries. The themes and curricula of these programs introduce participants to major trends affecting research libraries and the communities they serve: the changing nature of scholarly communication, the influence of information and other public policies, and new and expanding library roles in support of research and scholarship.

Leadership Symposium

More than 50 MLIS students attended the seventh annual ARL Leadership Symposium held in San Diego January 8–9, 2011. Program participants included ARL Career Enhancement Program (CEP) Fellows, ARL Diversity Scholars, and other MLIS students and new professionals from around the country. The symposium curriculum included presentations by ARL staff on the major strategic areas of the association, as well as on developing job-search skills, and on the evolving professional roles in ARL libraries. The event was underwritten by IMLS, Preservation Technologies, EBSCO, and ARL member libraries. More information about the annual Leadership Symposium can be found at http://www.arl.org/diversity/leadinst. An eighth symposium was held in Boston January 21–22, 2012.

Initiative to Recruit a Diverse Workforce

The ARL Initiative to Recruit a Diverse Workforce (IRDW) reflects the commitment of ARL members to create a diverse academic and research library community that will better meet the challenges of changing demographics in higher education and the emphasis on global perspectives in the academy. The IRDW offers numerous financial benefits, leadership development provided through the annual ARL Leadership Symposium, a formal mentor program, career placement assistance, and a research library visit hosted by the Purdue University Libraries. The program is funded by IMLS and by contributions from 52 ARL member libraries.

The research library visit introduces the ARL Diversity Scholars to the advanced operations of a research library, with the goals of raising the students' awareness of issues facing such libraries and increasing their interest in working in these organizations. For the seventh consecutive year, Purdue University Libraries hosted participants in the 2010–2012 IRDW for a two-day visit in April that included sessions on e-science, digital initiatives, information literacy, information technology and learning environments, liaison librarianship, promotion and tenure, and scholarly communications. Small-group sessions were held on topics of special interest, including administration, archives and special collections, liaison librarianship in various disciplines, and marketing. The group also met with Purdue Provost Tim Sands and Vice Provost for Diversity Christine Taylor. New on the agenda for this year was a research poster session, which gave participants an opportunity to talk one-on-one with library faculty and staff about their research on a wide variety of topics.

In July the ARL Committee on Diversity and Leadership selected 13 MLIS students to participate in the 2011–2013 IRDW. For more information, including a list of the 2011–2013 ARL Diversity Scholars, see http://www.arl.org/news/pr/IRDWjuly11.shtml.

Leadership and Career Development

Since 2007 ARL has offered the Leadership and Career Development Program (LCDP), an 18-month fellowship experience designed to help prepare mid-career librarians from under-represented racial and ethnic groups to take on increasingly demanding leadership roles in research libraries. For more information about the LCDP, visit http://www.arl.org/diversity/lcdp.

The 2011–2012 class met in March 2011 in Washington, D.C., for a five-day leadership institute with curricula focused on public policy issues and research methodologies. The event included site visits hosted by the Georgetown University Library and the National Archives and Records Administration.

In June ARL hosted its first Leadership and Career Development Program Forum at the ALA Annual Conference in New Orleans. The program featured a panel presentation by three former LCDP participants, plus a "research showcase" where program alumni shared information about their research projects and other significant contributions to the profession. The formal presentation was followed by a networking event. The program was coordinated by several LCDP alumni and generously underwritten by current and former LCDP sponsoring directors.

Career Enhancement Program

In summer 2011, 19 Fellows in ARL's Career Enhancement Program (CEP) interned at eight CEP host institutions across the United States. Each fellow spent 6 to 12 weeks at his or her host institution, working closely with a mentoring librarian and supervisor. The paid internship is the final component of the CEP fellowship, which gives MLIS students from under-represented racial and ethnic groups an opportunity to pursue careers in research libraries. For more information on the program, including lists of fellows and host institutions, visit http://www.arl.org/diversity/cep.

Library Leadership Fellows

The Research Library Leadership Fellows (RLLF) executive leadership development program seeks to meet increasing demands for succession planning for research libraries by preparing the next generation of deans and directors. The fourth offering of the RLLF Program is designed and sponsored by seven ARL member libraries: University of British Columbia Library, University of Illinois at Chicago Library, University of Colorado at Boulder Libraries, Dartmouth College Library, University of Miami Libraries, University of North Carolina at Chapel Hill Libraries, and Northwestern University Library. The 2011–2012 RLLF applicant pool was highly competitive. The selection committee, composed of the ARL directors sponsoring the program, chose 25 fellows representing a broad array of backgrounds and experiences from multiple ARL institutions. An overview of the RLLF program, as well as a complete list of the fellows, is available at http://www.arl.org/leadership/rllf.

The University of North Carolina at Chapel Hill hosted the fellows for their first Strategic Issues Institute in April 2011. The institute theme was "Better Together: Research Libraries in a Multi-University Environment" and the program design emphasized the benefits of collaborations among nearby Duke University, North Carolina State University, and North Carolina Central University.

In July OCLC hosted the fellows at its Dublin, Ohio, campus. Meeting participants explored the future of print collections and their relationship to the growing investment in digital resources, funding for higher education and the need to secure major cost savings, and transitions in the leadership of organizations important to research libraries.

In September the fellows visited with Donald Waters, senior program officer for scholarly communication at the Andrew W. Mellon Foundation and had a conversation on leadership with James G. Neal, vice president for information services and university librarian at Columbia University.

The University of British Columbia (UBC) Library and its director, Ingrid Parent, hosted the fellows for their second Strategic Issues Institute in October. Highlights of the institute included a presentation on the topic of leadership by John Furlong, CEO of the Vancouver 2010 Olympic and Paralympic Games; a discussion with the library's administrative team on the challenges of strategic change; and a guided tour of the UBC Museum of Anthropology.

Diversity and Inclusion Initiative

In November ARL began accepting applications for the ARL/Music Library Association (MLA) Diversity and Inclusion Initiative (DII). This scholarship program, funded by a grant from IMLS and by ARL member libraries, offers minority candidates an opportunity to pursue an MLIS degree while gaining hands-on experience in a large academic music library. The total award package for the ARL/MLA DII is in excess of $20,000 and includes a tuition stipend in support of MLIS education; a paid internship in a partner music/performing arts library for up to one year; financial assistance for relocation; paid student membership in MLA and ALA for one year; and support for attendance at an MLA Annual Meeting. MLA will develop and host a career development workshop that will address strategies for job searching, skills development, résumé writing, interviewing skills, and other topics relating to job placement. More information can be found at http://www.arl.org/diversity/arl-mla-dii.

Statistics and Assessment

The ARL Statistics and Assessment program focuses on describing and measuring the performance of research libraries and their contributions to research, scholarship, and teaching. ARL serves a leadership role in the development, testing, and application of academic library performance measures, statistics, and management tools.

The program provides analysis and reports of quantitative and qualitative indicators of library collections, personnel, and services by using a variety of evidence-gathering mechanisms and tools. The program hosts the StatsQUAL (Statistics and Service Quality) suite of services that focus on developing new approaches for describing and evaluating library service effectiveness, value and return on investment, digital library services, the impact of networked electronic services, diversity, leadership, and organizational climate, among others. StatsQUAL tools include LibQUAL+, ClimateQUAL, MINES for Libraries, and ARL Statistics. Research and development efforts have featured projects including efforts to articulate the dimensions of digital library service quality and tools focusing on demonstrating the value of the library. More information is available at http://www.arl.org/stats and http://www.statsqual.org.

LibQUAL+ and LibQUAL+ Lite

In 2011 a total of 160 institutions registered for the LibQUAL+ survey and library users completed more than 185,500 survey forms. The optional LibQUAL+ Lite protocol had higher response rates and shortened response times than the longer version of the survey. In September the LibQUAL+ team began offering User Subgroup Custom Analysis notebooks. This new analysis can be performed for each of three different user groups: undergraduate, graduate, and faculty. For example, an Undergraduate User Subgroup Custom Analysis notebook will drill down into the undergraduate data and provide analysis for first-year, second-year, third-year, fourth-year, fifth-year and above, and non-degree students.

LibQUAL+ Triads Pilot

In fall 2011 libraries were invited to join the LibQUAL+ Triads pilot project, the third protocol option within the LibQUAL+ suite, joining the original long version and LibQUAL+ Lite. LibQUAL+ Triads defines clear priorities for survey items that score close to one another so libraries can act on those priorities that are most important to users; eases respondent burden, as this version takes less time to complete than the long form; and provides valid data by computing intra-individual score reliability coefficients to help screen out untrustworthy responses.

An annual membership subscription provides access to the full LibQUAL+ Data Repository and Analytics tools. For details, see http://www.libqual.org/about/about_lq/fee_schedule.

ClimateQUAL

The centerpiece of the ClimateQUAL: Organizational Climate and Diversity Assessment project is an online survey of staff perceptions of an organization's commitment to the principles of diversity, organizational policies and procedures, and staff attitudes. The survey addresses such issues as diversity, teamwork, learning, fairness, current managerial practices, and staff attitudes and beliefs. ARL offers the protocol in partnership with the University of Maryland Industrial/Organizational Psychology Program.

The ClimateQUAL learning community—which is composed of those libraries that have implemented or are interested in implementing the internal staffing survey—convened in New Orleans in June to discuss best practices and actions to follow up on the data collected through the survey. A session on ClimateQUAL that highlighted how the University of Connecticut, Northwestern University, and Wayne State University had followed up on their survey implementations was held during the May 2011 ARL Membership Meeting.

Integrating library assessment into the university-wide environment is key to understanding how libraries can benefit researchers, faculty, and students. As libraries are presenting their successful experiences with ARL assessment tools at the campus level, university colleges and departments are becoming interested in ARL's R&D services. In 2011 ARL began working closely with the College of Geosciences at Texas A&M University to launch a pilot that would bring ClimateQUAL to the college-level experience.

Organizational Performance Assessment

Organizational Performance Assessment for Libraries (OPAL) is a new consulting service developed and offered in 2011 to help academic libraries effectively integrate strategy, planning, and assessment within the institution so that the library is well prepared to demonstrate its value in advancing the organization. OPAL can guide the library to establish effective strategies aligned with its university mission and vision, to monitor and document progress toward plans and goals, and to provide stakeholders with a persuasive and easily understandable summary of the library's role in the academy. OPAL can focus the library on strategic decision making and on collecting, analyzing, and presenting information that demonstrates the library's impact, outcomes, and value. OPAL is the successor to, and builds upon, the Effective, Sustainable, and Practical (ESP) Assessment service. More information is available at http://www.arl.org/stats/initiatives/opal and in "Living the Future: Organizational Performance Assessment" in *Journal of Library Administration* 51, no. 7–8 (2011).

Statistics Review Task Force

In 2011 ARL formed a task force to review and implement changes in annual statistical surveys. The task force gathered feedback from the ARL survey coordinators and SPEC Liaisons, the Personnel Administrators and Staff Development Officers discussion group, the Preservation Administrators Forum, and ARL member representatives. At the October ARL Membership Meeting, the ARL Statistics and Assessment Committee discussed recommendations from four subgroups on the future revisions to the annual surveys and provided an update to members. It is expected that revised surveys will be available in summer 2012.

Publications

Annual electronic and print publications produced by the program describe salary compensation and collection, staffing, expenditures, and service trends for research libraries. The series includes the *ARL Annual Salary Survey, ARL Statistics, ARL Academic Law Library Statistics,* and *ARL Academic Health Sciences Library Statistics.* Online access to these publications from 2006 to the present is available through ARL Digital Publications (http://publications.arl.org).

ARL Profiles: Research Libraries 2010—Final Report

This report includes a thorough analysis of narrative descriptions of research libraries in the early 21st century. The profile analysis engaged qualitative methods that complement the annual quantitative ARL statistics. The contextual information provided in this report documents the importance of the public good research libraries provide in an increasingly globalized environment. For additional information, see http://www.arl.org/news/pr/ARL-Profiles21july11.shtml.

MINES for Libraries: Measuring the Impact of Networked Electronic Services and the Ontario Council of University Libraries' Scholar Portal, Final Report 2011

This study summarizes findings on 34,000 randomly captured uses of electronic resources over a 12-month period from the 21 members of the Ontario Council of University Libraries (OCUL). ARL worked collaboratively with OCUL's Scholars Portal staff to implement a second iteration of the Measuring the Impact of Networked Electronic Services (MINES for Libraries) methodology that captures data on library user demographics, the purpose of use, and the location of the user at point of use when accessing electronic resources and services. The results show the increasing value derived from the use of digital content, the emerging use of digital resources in the humanities, and the soaring use of electronic resources from off-campus locations. The data are currently used by Scholars Portal staff, as well as staff in OCUL institutions, to: determine how specific populations apply digital content to their work; identify where library use originates to tailor services accordingly; gather usage data on digital collections to justify funding and inform collection development decisions; and assess the impact of networked electronic resources and services on teaching, learning, and research. ARL implemented this methodology in collaboration with OCUL in 2004–2005 and again in 2010–2011. The latest summary report focuses on the 2010–2011 findings and provides a description of the major differences between the two implementations. The report is available at http://www.libqual.org/documents/LibQual/publications/MINES_OCUL2011.pdf.

SPEC Surveys and Kits

The SPEC survey program gathers information on current research library operating practices and policies on topics relevant to the association's strategic directions, and publishes the SPEC Kit series as guides for libraries as they face ever-changing management issues. Six SPEC Kits were published in 2011: *SPEC Kit 322 Library User Experience, SPEC Kit 323 Socializing New Hires, SPEC Kit 324 Collecting Global Resources, SPEC Kit 325 Digital Preservation, SPEC Kit 326 Digital Humanities,* and *SPEC Kit 327 Reconfiguring Service Delivery.* Links to the tables of contents and executive summaries of SPEC Kits are available at http://www.arl.org/resources/pubs/spec/complete.shtml. PDFs of complete SPEC Kits from 1977 through 2005 are available through Google Books http://books.google.com and HathiTrust http://www.hathitrust.org. Online access to complete SPEC Kits from 2006 to the present is available through ARL Digital Publications (http://publications.arl.org).

Workshops and Other Events

The Statistics and Assessment program also offers workshops on such related topics as XML development and METS. Presentations at research conferences on topics relating to the value of libraries, analytics, and library assessment also took place throughout the year. For information on upcoming events, see http://www.arl.org/stats/statsevents/index.shtml.

Communications

The communications capability engages in many activities that support ARL's strategic directions. Using electronic and print media as well as direct outreach, the communications capability disseminates information and sparks conversations about ARL and strategic issues relating to research libraries. The primary audiences are ARL member libraries as well as the broader higher education and scholarly communities, especially policy and decision makers.

This capability publishes a full range of resources to assist library and higher education communities in their efforts to improve the delivery of scholarly communication. See especially the quarterly *Research Library Issues* (http://publications.arl.org/rli) and the monthly *E-News for ARL Directors* (http://www.arl.org/news/enews) for coverage of issues of strategic importance.

News Feeds

News about ARL activities and publications is available through several public e-mail lists that reach a large audience in the library and higher education communities. To subscribe, visit http://www.arl.org/resources/emaillists.

ARL also has a presence on Twitter (http://twitter.com/ARLnews and http://twitter.com/ARLpolicy); Facebook (http://www.facebook.com/association.of.research.libraries); Google+ (http://plus.google.com/116038873630463451082); YouTube (http://www.youtube.com/arladmin); and Flickr (http://www.flickr.com/photos/arl-pix). In addition, ARL offers information via blogs on public policy issues (http://policynotes.arl.org), and on library service assessment, evaluation, and improvement (http://libraryassessment.info). For more information about these and other news feeds from ARL, see http://www.arl.org/news/feeds.

Digital Publications Web Site

In December the association launched the ARL Digital Publications Web site. The site provides convenient online access to collections of ARL popular publications from 2006 to the present: *ARL Annual Salary Survey, ARL Statistics, Research Library Issues,* and *SPEC Kits. Research Library Issues* is freely available. Access to the ARL Statistics Collection and ARL Annual Salary Survey Collection is free to ARL members as a benefit of membership; an annual subscription is available to others. Access to the SPEC Kit collection is available by annual subscription. For more information, visit http://publications.arl.org.

ARL partnered with the CLOCKSS (Controlled Lots of Copies Keep Stuff Safe) Archive to preserve these flagship digital publications in its geographically and geopolitically distributed network of redundant archive nodes, located at 12 major research libraries around the world. This action provides for content to be freely available to everyone after a "trigger event" and ensures an author's work will be maximally accessible and useful over time.

ARL makes many of its publications available electronically via the ARL Web site; some are available in excerpted form for preview before purchase and others are available in their entirety. See http://www.arl.org/resources/pubs for more information.

Governance and Membership Meetings

Spring Membership Meeting

The 158th ARL Membership Meeting convened in Montreal May 4–6, 2011, in conjunction with the Canadian Association of Research Libraries (CARL). ARL President Carol A. Mandel and CARL President Ernie Ingles welcomed members and guests. Under the theme of "Transcending National Borders," 173 ARL and CARL members, speakers, and guests took part in program sessions examining a range of issues including emerging data policies, STM journal market trends, scholarly communication partnerships, international copyright, and legal issues in building 21st century collections. Many of the speakers' presentations are available at http://www.arl.org/resources/pubs/mmproceedings/158mm-proceedings.shtml.

Fall Membership Meeting and Forum

ARL President Carol A. Mandel convened the 159th ARL Membership Meeting October 12–13 in Washington, D.C. Under the theme of "Expanding Capacity and

Partnerships in the Digital World," 114 ARL member library representatives participated in sessions about digital research collections and orphan works. R. Michael Tanner of the Association of Public and Land-grant Universities presented the luncheon keynote speech. Audio and slide presentations of speakers are available at http://www.arl.org/resources/pubs/mmproceedings/159mm-proceedings.shtml.

At the ARL business meeting on October 13, member library representatives ratified the ARL Board of Directors' election of Wendy Pradt Lougee (Minnesota) as ARL vice president/president-elect and elected three new board members: Joan Giesecke (Nebraska–Lincoln), Judith Russell (Florida), and Jay Schafer (Massachusetts Amherst). Committee chairs provided progress reports and members received outlines of current activities and projects in five ARL program areas: Public Policies; Scholarly Communication; Transforming Research Libraries; Diversity and Leadership; and Statistics and Assessment. At the conclusion of the business meeting, Mandel presented the gavel to Winston Tabb (Johns Hopkins), who began his term as ARL president.

The ARL-CNI Fall Forum, "21st-Century Collections and the Urgency of Collaborative Action," was held October 13–14 in Washington. Speakers' slides and audio recordings of sessions are available at http://www.arl.org/resources/pubs/fallforumproceedings/forum11.shtml.

SPARC—The Scholarly Publishing and Academic Resources Coalition

Heather Joseph

Executive Director

21 Dupont Circle, Suite 800, Washington, DC 20036
202-296-2296, fax 202-872-0884, e-mail sparc@arl.org
World Wide Web http://www.arl.org/sparc

Background and Mission

SPARC (the Scholarly Publishing and Academic Resources Coalition) is a global organization that promotes expanded sharing of scholarship in the networked digital environment. It believes that faster and wider sharing of outputs of the research process increases the impact of research, fuels the advancement of knowledge, and increases the return on research investments.

Established in 1997, SPARC was launched by the Association of Research Libraries to act on library concern that the promise of the Internet to improve scholarly communication was inhibited by pricing and access barriers in the journals marketplace. SPARC has been an innovative leader in the rapidly expanding international movement to make scholarly communication more responsive to the needs of researchers, students, the academic enterprise, funders, and the public.

SPARC is a catalyst for action. Its pragmatic agenda focuses on collaborating with other stakeholders to stimulate the emergence of new scholarly communication norms, practices, and policies that leverage the networked digital environment to support research, expand the dissemination of research findings, and reduce financial pressures on libraries.

As support for and conversations about "open access" have emerged at ever higher levels, SPARC has had increasing opportunities to participate and contribute to policy-making in multiple arenas. The growth of SPARC's influence parallels that of the open access movement, which is expanding in scale and becoming more global. Open access is now a factor in the valuation of companies and a considerable force that is gaining power.

Today SPARC is supported by a membership of more than 220 academic and research libraries and works in cooperation with affiliates in Europe and Japan. Together, SPARC and its affiliates in Europe and Japan represent more than 800 libraries worldwide.

Strategy

SPARC's strategy focuses on reducing barriers to the access, sharing, and use of scholarship. SPARC's highest priority is advancing the understanding and implementation of policies and practices that ensure open access to scholarly research outputs. While much of SPARC's focus to date has been on journal literature, its evolving strategy reflects an increasing interest in open access to research outputs and digital data of all kinds, in all subject areas. SPARC's role in stimulating change centers on three key program areas:

- Educating stakeholders about the problems facing scholarly communication and the opportunities for them to play a role in achieving positive change
- Advocating policy changes that advance scholarly communication and that explicitly recognize that dissemination of scholarship is an essential, inseparable component of the research process
- Incubating demonstrations of new publishing and sustainability models that benefit scholarship and academe

Priorities

SPARC actions were designed to advance acceptance and long-term sustainability of a more-open system of scholarship, with a primary focus on advancing open access models for both publishing and archiving the results of scholarly research. In particular, as interest in public access to the results of federally funded research has continued to accelerate, SPARC has worked to deploy a focused and disciplined advocacy strategy.

SPARC's program activity recognizes that cultural, economic, and technical differences exist in various disciplines and that, in some areas, the interests of scholarship may best be served in the near term by equitable fee-based publishing solutions. Its programs aim at building a broader understanding of opportunities for change in all fields, and place an emphasis on identifying areas of common advantage to all stakeholders in the scholarly communications community—particularly scholarly and scientific researchers, universities and colleges, and university presses and society publishers.

Key areas of focus in 2011 included expanding adoption of public access policies throughout the U.S. federal government, expanding SPARC's role in supporting the "open data" and "open educational resources" movements, and the international expansion of SPARC.

Activities and Outcomes for 2011

Advocacy and Policy Front

During 2011 SPARC continued policy advocacy with the Open Access Working Group (OAWG), an alliance of leading organizations that support open access, and served as the organizational focal point for the Alliance for Taxpayer Access (ATA).

SPARC served as the leading coordinator for the 2011 open access movement's response to the White House Office of Science and Technology Policy's request for information on public access policies.

As legislative and policy proposals affecting open access were explored in Washington, D.C., SPARC continued to play an active role. In 2010 the Federal Research Public Access Act (FRPAA) was introduced in the Senate (it had been introduced in the House in 2009). SPARC worked to prepare for expected reintroduction of the legislation in 2012. FRPAA would require that 11 U.S. government agencies with annual extramural research expenditures of more than $100 million make manuscripts of journal articles stemming from that research publicly available via the Internet. The manuscripts would be maintained and preserved in a digital archive maintained by the agency or in another suitable repository that permits free public access, interoperability, and long-term preservation. Each manuscript would be freely available to users without charge within six months after its publication in a peer-reviewed journal.

During the year SPARC deepened its ties with the "open science" and "open educational resource" (OER) communities. It participated in an advocacy coalition for OER. SPARC also endorsed the work of Michael Nielsen to raise awareness of open science globally, expanding interest beyond scholars to gain mainstream support.

SPARC was the primary organizer for the Berlin 9 Open Access conference held in Maryland in November 2011. It was the first time the group convened in North America and brought together policymakers from the Obama administration, university presidents and provosts, and the library community. The meeting advanced the agenda of open access with a focus on impact over ideology.

Plans called for establishing a U.S. counterpart of the Berlin open access meeting; the first was set for March 2012 in Kansas City, and the series is intended to continue biennially in North America.

In 2011 SPARC partnered with the Health Resources Alliance to begin to put together a set of resources for disease-specific foundations to develop guides for open access policies for research funders. They were expected to be released in 2012, with the support of numerous funders.

SPARC continued to support campus-based policy action in conjunction with the panel of experts first convened in 2009 to help develop a set of resources that support data-driven, community-engaging, and successful open access policy development. More than 100 institutions have taken advantage of the project to initiate policy discussions to date.

SPARC also established a home for the newly formed Coalition of Open Access Policy Institutions (COAPI). It provided space and resources to host the group, which plans to meet regularly to share best practices concerning the implementation of campus open access policies.

In response to media requests for information on public access issues, SPARC provided materials to reporters and expert sources for interviews. Its staff has also authored articles for various publications. For examples of SPARC in the press, see http://www.arl.org/sparc/media/inthenews/index.html.

SPARC participated in a new Open Educational Resources advocacy coalition to leverage messaging and membership in support of Open Access and OER policies. In addition, work continued in 2011 with the Committee for Economic Development (CED), a Washington-based think tank whose board of trustees includes several dozen university and college presidents as well as leaders in private industry. In conjunction with the Kauffman Foundation, CED developed a paper to be released in 2012 exploring the impact on scientific discovery and economic development of the National Institutes of Health (NIH) public access policy. (Under that policy, investigators funded by NIH agree to submit their final, peer-reviewed manuscripts to the National Library of Medicine's PubMed Central to be made publicly available no later than 12 months after the official date of publication.)

During 2011 SPARC worked in collaboration with Confederation of Open Access Repositories (COAR), an association of repository initiatives launched in October 2009 that unites 59 institutions in 23 countries in Europe, Latin America, Asia, and North America.

SPARC continued to actively partner in the open access space promoting the adoption of policies and practices with PLoS, Open Access Scholarly Publishing Association, bePress, ePrints, and Dura Space.

International Expansion

Because change in scholarly communication is needed on a global scale, SPARC continued to amplify its impact by working with partners worldwide. SPARC worked to restructure its international presence and move from a series of stand-alone organizations each with its own name to globalize the SPARC brand and create a global network. The structural reorganization was completed in December with new leadership. Alma Swan has been named director of European advocacy and Lars Bjørnshauge will serve as director of European library relations.

Campus Education

SPARC sponsored International Open Access Week in October 2011, in partnership with several organizations in the United States and internationally, to spread the word about and highlight the research community's commitment to open access.

Participation expanded greatly in 2011 with thousands of students and scholars observing the week on campuses in more than 130 countries. The 2012 Open Access Week is scheduled for October 22–28.

On college and university campuses, SPARC continued to encourage and aid libraries' grassroots advocacy efforts to support open access with presentations, consulting, and new or enhanced resources. In 2011 SPARC provided webcasts to libraries every other month and conducted briefing calls with open access experts. Its staff met directly with faculty members, department heads, deans, and campus administrators on SPARC member campuses (at the request of SPARC member organizations) to provide one-on-one information and advice on campus open access advocacy and other scholarly communication issues. Author rights management continues to be a core element in SPARC's effort to engage faculty and advance more open practices for sharing research.

During the year SPARC continued support of Peter Suber's monthly *SPARC Open Access Newsletter* and "Open Access News" blog. SPARC offered programs to connect directors with thought leaders in scholarly communication.

The popular SPARC Innovator Series continued in 2011, highlighting the efforts of key individuals and institutions in successfully promoting positive change in scholarly communications. Profiled in 2011 were Ventura Perez, a faculty member of the University of Massachusetts Amherst's College of Social and Behavioral Sciences, and *PLoS One,* an interactive open access journal for the communication of peer-reviewed scientific and medical research.

SPARC-ACRL Forum

A major component of SPARC's community outreach occurs at meetings of the American Library Association (ALA) when SPARC works with ALA's Association of College and Research Libraries (ACRL) and its scholarly communication committee to bring current issues to the attention of the community.

In January 2011 the SPARC-ACRL forum, "Marketplace: Open Access and the Changing State of Scholarly Publishing," was held in San Diego. It painted a picture of the rapidly changing, and maturing, open access publishing sphere, illustrated the growing range of options and approaches that are emerging, and offered help to the library community to make sense of what it all means.

In June 2011 a second SPARC-ACRL forum was held in New Orleans.

Student Campaign

SPARC continues to expand its partnership with student groups and to educate the next generation of academics on issues relating to scholarly communication. The student Right to Research Coalition is now an established body representing organizations with more than 7 million students. In 2011 SPARC expanded the coalition to include 12 European and international student organizations. The first European Union Right to Research Coalition student leadership summit was held in Berlin in spring 2011, bringing together representatives of a dozen European student organizations.

Also in 2011, SPARC hosted the third annual "Student Leadership Summit" in Washington, D.C., which brought together active leaders from campuses. Students talked about strategies and ways to deepen engagement in the coalition.

To help students articulate the characteristics they value about the open Web and electronic communication using new media and technology, SPARC hosted the 5th annual SPARKY Awards contest. It was cosponsored by Campus Movie-Fest, Open Video Alliance, New Media Consortium, the Center for Social Media, Students for Free Culture, the Association of Research Libraries, ACRL, Penn Libraries at the University of Pennsylvania, and the organization Student PIRGs (Public Interest Research Groups).

Publisher Partnership Programs

SPARC supports and promotes useful examples of open access or other innovative publishing initiatives, and participates in programs that highlight areas of common concern to libraries and not-for-profit publisher communities and where collaborative action can be beneficial.

SPARC continued to assist arXiv, BioOne, Project Euclid, and others in evolving sound and sustainable business practices needed to become leading platforms for digital dissemination of independent journals.

Business Consulting Services

SPARC provides ongoing consulting support to the library and publishing communities. Subsidized advisory services were made available to more than a dozen organizations and alternative publishing ventures in 2011.

SPARC developed a free online Open Access Journal Publishing Resource Index with information and documents to support the launch and operation of open access journals. Materials in the index will help libraries, presses, and other academic units on campuses as they strive to make the work of their researchers more widely available.

Governance

SPARC is guided by a steering committee. Members of the 2012 committee are David Carlson (chair), Southern Illinois University at Carbondale; Jun Adachi, Japanese National Institute of Informatics (for SPARC Japan); Maggie Farrell, University of Wyoming; Lorraine Harricombe, University of Kansas; Rick Luce, Emory University; Lee Van Orsdel, Grand Valley State University; Rosann Bazirjian, University of North Carolina at Greensboro; Gerald Beasley, Concordia University; Richard Clement, Utah State University; Brian Schottlaender, University of California, San Diego; Kevin Smith, Duke University; and Martha Whitehead, Queen's University.

Council on Library and Information Resources

1752 N St. N.W., Suite 800, Washington, DC 20036
202-939-4754, fax 202-939-4765
World Wide Web http://www.clir.org

Kathlin Smith
Director of Communications

The Council on Library and Information Resources (CLIR) is an independent, nonprofit organization that forges strategies to enhance research, teaching, and learning environments in collaboration with libraries, cultural institutions, and communities of higher learning. Its staff of 11 is led by its president, Charles Henry.

CLIR is supported by fees from sponsoring institutions, grants from public and private foundations, contracts with federal agencies, and donations from individuals. CLIR's board of directors establishes policy, oversees the investment of funds, sets goals, and approves strategies for their achievement. In 2011 the board appointed new members Leslie Weir, university librarian at the University of Ottawa, and Herman Pabbruwe, chief executive officer of Brill. A full listing of board members is available at http://www.clir.org/about/governance.html.

G. Sayeed Choudhury and Elliott Shore continued their affiliations with CLIR as senior presidential fellows in 2011. Choudhury is associate dean for library digital programs and Hodson Director of the Digital Research and Curation Center at the Sheridan Libraries, Johns Hopkins University. Shore is chief information officer and Constance A. Jones Director of Libraries and professor of history at Bryn Mawr College.

Activities

While continuing its ongoing work in leadership, preservation, and scholarly communication, CLIR is increasingly focused on identifying models of collaboration that could redefine the concept of the research library and produce more cost-effective services and programs to improve support of research and teaching. Such collaboration might include building campus cyberinfrastructures, developing connections between institutional repositories, collectively negotiating with commercial and external entities in large-scale digitization, cooperative cataloging, participating in academic and research computing roles on campus, and creating print repository and "insurance" models, among others. The following is an overview of CLIR's 2011 activities.

Cyberinfrastructure

Study and Workshop on Linked Data

In March 2011 the Andrew W. Mellon Foundation awarded grants to CLIR and to Stanford University to commission a survey and conduct a workshop, respectively, on linked data. The aims of the survey and workshop were to better understand the current landscape for linked data work and to develop specifications, requirements, and a basic technical design for a multinational, multi-institutional prototype demonstrating the viability and efficacy of a linked data environment for improving discovery and navigation.

The survey, which was commissioned as background for the workshop, reviews and analyzes existing projects and programs that use semantic Web, linked data, and Resource Description Framework (RDF) Triples Technologies—elements critical to a linked data environment that will enable improved discovery and navigation across multiple information genres and formats.

The workshop was held June 27–July 1, 2011, at Stanford University. Discussion focused on outlining a national agenda for developing linked data environments, reducing redundancy of effort, and creating a more sophisticated context in which practitioners and planners can develop future projects.

The survey and a report from the workshop were published in October and are available at http://www.clir.org/pubs/abstract/pub152abst.html.

Building Data Curation Skills

In April 2011 the Alfred P. Sloan Foundation awarded CLIR funds for research on how to build capacity for data curation in varying disciplines. Most graduate programs in the sciences, social sciences, and humanities are not designed to cultivate the data management skills of their students, or even to help them understand why such skills are important to their fields of study. Nonetheless, in every discipline, at least some professionals must master the complex demands relating to the creation, access, reuse, and preservation of digital research data that have traditionally been the purview of the library and information technology professions and of schools of library, information, and computer science.

The data curation project, managed by CLIR's Digital Library Federation (DLF) program, consists of three interrelated activities that are scheduled for completion by summer 2013. The first activity is an environmental scan of professional development needs and of education and training opportunities for digital curation in the academy; it was scheduled to be issued early in 2012. The second, to be issued later in the year, is an anthropological study of five sites where digital curation activities are under way. The third is a report that analyzes the results of the two research efforts and includes a proposal, informed by the findings, for amending the curriculum for CLIR's Postdoctoral Fellowship in Academic Libraries program.

Assessment of 'Digging into Data' Challenge

In January 2010 CLIR entered a cooperative agreement with the National Endowment for the Humanities (NEH) Office of Digital Humanities to provide a strategic assessment of the Digging into Data (DID) Challenge, a grant competition that had been jointly sponsored by NEH, the United Kingdom's Joint Information Systems Committee (JISC), the U.S. National Science Foundation, and Canada's Social Sciences and Humanities Research Council. The goals of the DID Challenge are to encourage international, multidisciplinary collaborations that explore the application of computational techniques to large corpora and to begin to understand the kinds of research that are possible when advanced search algorithms are applied to these corpora. The program's sponsors announced the first eight awards in December 2009. Encouraged by the success of the inaugural challenge, the cooperating agencies have joined with four additional sponsors to fund a second cycle for the program. The second round of grant recipients was announced in January 2012.

The CLIR/NEH cooperative assessment addresses how well the DID Challenge met its objectives and identifies the next steps agencies and researchers might take to best support continued development in this area. In early 2011 CLIR staff visited all eight project teams funded in the program's first cycle. In June 2011 the teams delivered public reports on their findings in Washington, D.C., and eight expert respondents delivered assessments of these reports. CLIR held focus group meetings with project principal investigators and expert respondents before and after this meeting.

CLIR will issue its final reports on the project in 2012. The first report will discuss implications of the findings for the future of computationally intensive scholarship in the humanities, and for the roles of academic institutions and public and private funding agencies in fostering this research. The second will be a technical summary that addresses the administrative history of the program and gives an account of the study methodology, summary of findings, next steps, and recommendations.

Infrastructure for Humanities Scholarship

With funding from the Institute of Museum and Library Services (IMLS), CLIR continued its work with Tufts University on a planning process to identify what is needed to advance an infrastructure to support humanities scholarship, with a particular focus on the classics. In October 2010 CLIR hosted a meeting of classics scholars to discuss a literature review of existing digital projects in the classics and to outline goals and objectives for a strategic plan that describes the technical requirements for a classics infrastructure.

The literature review, written by Alison Babeu of Tufts University's Perseus Project, was circulated broadly for comment. A final version, issued in August 2011, is available at http://www.clir.org/pubs/abstract/pub150abst.html. Work on the strategic plan continues under the leadership of Gregory Crane, editor-in-chief of Perseus Digital Library. A final version of the plan is anticipated in 2012.

ARL/DLF E-Science Institute

Early in 2011 CLIR's DLF program joined with the Association for Research Libraries (ARL) to create the ARL/DLF E-Science Institute, which formally launched July 1, 2011. The institute seeks to give participants a basis for developing a sound strategic approach to exploring and supporting e-science within their organizations. It comprises a set of designed learning experiences that take small teams of individuals through a process that strengthens their e-science support role. Specific member institutions of ARL and CLIR/DLF are funding design of the institute's training program.

The first of three capstone events for the E-Science Institute took place December 1–2, 2011. The second and third events took place in January 2012, in Phoenix and Dallas.

DLF Forum

CLIR's DLF program hosts an annual forum, a working meeting where the DLF community, and those interested in joining, come together to collaborate on common challenges. It provides an opportunity for practitioners to share experiences and practices. The 2011 forum was held October 31–November 1 in Baltimore.

New Models

DPLA Prototype

The Digital Public Library of America (DPLA) is envisioned as a large-scale digital library that will "make the cultural and scientific heritage of humanity available, free of charge, to all." Planning for the DPLA began in late 2010. The Berkman Center for Internet and Society at Harvard University serves as the secretariat. The DPLA is currently organized by six workstreams that are defined and coordinated through a steering committee. The workstreams include audience and participation; financial/business models; governance; legal issues; technical aspects; and content and scope. Rachel Frick, director of the DLF program, is co-chair of the content and scope workstream.

In May 2011 the steering committee announced a "Beta Sprint" to solicit models, prototypes, tools, and interfaces that demonstrate how the DPLA might index and provide access to a wide range of broadly distributed content. CLIR's DLF program and the Center for Informatics Research in Science and Scholarship (CIRSS) at the Graduate School of Library and Information Science at the University of Illinois submitted a prototype to the Beta Sprint, which was among those chosen for presentation at the October 2011 DPLA Plenary Meeting. The DLF/CIRSS project prototype leverages the IMLS Digital Collections and Content (IMLS DCC) resource and DLF Aquifer content as a core collection for the DPLA. The IMLS DCC, launched in 2003, is an aggregation of digital collections from libraries, museums, and archives, supported by IMLS and developed collaboratively by CIRSS and the University of Illinois Library.

As part of the project to develop the prototype, CLIR commissioned a comparative report that reviews the research on and practical efforts to aggregate large-scale collections. The report sheds light on how and why such projects succeed or fail. The report also identifies potential content providers for the DPLA and will estimate the time, effort, and other costs required to ingest these resources into the resulting prototype.

Postdoctoral Fellowship in Academic Libraries

CLIR Postdoctoral Library Fellows work on projects that forge, renovate, and strengthen connections between academic library collections and their users. The program offers scholars who have recently earned Ph.D.'s a chance to work in academic libraries on projects relating to their disciplines that benefit both the scholar and the library. The fellows have the opportunity to develop research models, collaborate with information specialists, and explore new career opportunities. Participating libraries benefit from the expertise of accomplished scholars who can invigorate approaches to collection use and teaching, contribute field-specific knowledge, and provide insight into the future of scholarship. In 2011, its eighth year, the program had its largest cohort of fellows ever, with 16 current and continuing fellows. To date, 55 fellows have participated in the program.

The Next Scholar

Cataloging Hidden Special Collections and Archives

CLIR's Cataloging Hidden Special Collections and Archives Program supports cataloging projects that expose unknown or underutilized cultural materials to communities of scholars, students, and other users who need them for their work. The program, funded by the Andrew W. Mellon Foundation, completed its fourth review cycle in 2011. The review panel selected 19 projects to receive a total of $4 million in awards.

Since the program's inception, 66 projects, representing a wide range of institutions across the United States, have been funded. The projects have already made accessible to scholars impressively large volumes of cultural materials in diverse formats.

Work continues on a multiyear study to describe successful strategies for engaging users with collections. The study, titled "Observations on Scholarly Engagement with Hidden Special Collections and Archives," is being undertaken by a team of former participants in CLIR's Postdoctoral Fellowship in Academic Libraries Program. Results of the study, to date, are available on the Hidden Collections program Web site (http://www.clir.org/hiddencollections/engagement/SEdocuments.html).

This year the study team will focus on three subject areas that are well represented among funded projects: civil rights, natural history, and literature. Rather than reporting their findings to CLIR, the team will focus on describing the impact of hidden collections cataloging and related programming for the communities of scholars and students who work with these collections. The teams plan to host a webinar, curate an online exhibit, and submit articles for publication in relevant scholarly and professional journals.

Mellon Fellowships for Dissertation Research

The Mellon Dissertation Fellowship program helps junior scholars in the humanities and related social science fields gain skill and creativity in developing knowledge from original sources; enables dissertation writers to do research wherever relevant sources may be, rather than just where financial support is available; encourages more extensive and innovative uses of original sources in libraries, archives, museums, historical societies, and related repositories in the United States and abroad; and provides insight from the viewpoint of doctoral candidates into how scholarly resources can be most effectively developed for access in the future.

The program marked its eleventh year in 2011. It has supported 127 graduate students who have carried out their dissertation research in a variety of public and private libraries and archives.

A research study is under way on the Mellon Fellowship Program's first ten years. Surveys and interviews are being conducted to better understand the fellows' experiences in the program; their introduction to and integration into teaching and research following the fellowship; and methodologies in their field—what has changed, and what has remained constant.

Preservation

Preservation Symposia

In 2010–2011 CLIR partnered with the Library of Congress in presenting three of its Future Directions symposia. The first, "Understanding the Physical Environment," in fall 2010, reviewed 25 years of research by the Image Permanence Institute that have produced resources and recommendations now widely used to preserve a broad range of media. The second symposium, "Assessing Options for Large Collections," was held in March 2011. Senior preservation administrators, scientists, digital collection experts, and conservators described options for managing large collections in the context of environmentally controlled remote storage, mass-deacidification treatments, and digitization. The third, held in October 2011, focused on the road ahead, as cultural agencies work together to devise strategies for providing broad and long-term access to the mixed collection formats of the 21st century.

CLIR/Library of Congress Fellowship

In spring 2011 CLIR established the CLIR/Library of Congress Fellowship, which supports original-source dissertation research in the humanities or related social sciences in the Preservation Research and Testing Division of the library's Preservation Directorate. The fellowship is offered as part of the Mellon Fellowships for Dissertation Research in Original Sources. Amy Brady of the University of Massachusetts Amherst was awarded the fellowship for 2011 for research on where and how the proletarian avant-garde contributed to the shaping of the Federal Theatre Project.

The Emerging Library

Workshops on Participatory Design in Academic Libraries

In 2011 CLIR launched a new workshop series, based on its successful workshops on faculty research behavior and undergraduate research practices begun in 2007, and at the time this report was prepared more than people had participated. Led by Nancy Fried Foster, director of anthropological research at the University of Rochester's River Campus Libraries, the new workshops provide attendees with an overview of the participatory design process and strategies for including faculty members, graduate students, undergraduates, and library staff in the design process. The workshops feature extensive interaction among participants and between participants and research subjects.

CIOs Group

CLIR's Chief Information Officers (CIOs) Group is composed of 33 directors of organizations that have merged their library and technology units on liberal arts college campuses. The group met twice in 2011 to discuss common concerns and to exchange ideas about possible solutions for organizational and policy problems unique to their campus environments. They explored such topics as open access; how the recession has affected organizational structure, technology, business strategies, and attitudes; cloud computing; portals versus Web 2.0; strategies for measuring the use and effectiveness of services; and ideas for prioritizing services. Throughout the year members exchange ideas and solutions through a listserv.

Leadership

Leadership Through New Communities of Knowledge

Launched in July 2009 as a partnership between CLIR and the Council of Independent Colleges (CIC), this program offers professional development opportunities for library staff at small-to-midsize private colleges and universities. Since the program's inception, CLIR has sent participants from CIC schools to numerous workshops on data curation, work restructuring, archival practice, undergraduate research behavior, and information fluency.

Supported with funds from IMLS, the program has offered numerous workshops on topics including work restructuring in the library, archival principles for nonarchivists, and undergraduate research behavior. CLIR cosponsored with CIC workshops on information fluency in history and literature. Scholarships were offered to the University of North Carolina's Digital Curation Institute in January 2011.

The program also held a symposium on the future of the liberal arts college library October 10–11, 2011, at Alverno College in Milwaukee.

Frye Leadership Institute

The Frye Leadership Institute, created to prepare and develop the next generation of leaders in libraries, information services, and higher education, welcomed its first class of students in 1999. Institutes were held annually thereafter until 2009.

In 2010 the institute took a one-year hiatus to develop and articulate a new program that addresses higher education's leadership needs in an era of unprecedented change. It resumed with a new curriculum June 5–10, 2011, in Atlanta. The new program engages individuals who are already leaders in their profession and seek to further develop their skills, particularly in the area of advocacy. The institute addresses challenges in higher education through a variety of topics, empowering librarians and information technologists to start conversations and take action on issues that are important not only to their own institutions but also to the entire higher education community.

The Frye Leadership Institute is cosponsored by CLIR, EDUCAUSE, and Emory University.

Academic Library Advisory Committee

The Academic Library Advisory Committee (ALAC) meets once a year in person, and conducts two or three teleconference calls annually. It represents research libraries that are not members of ARL, and many small liberal arts institutions that sponsor CLIR. The last few years have been focused on leadership in libraries: confronting the crisis of many vacancies, difficult searches, and a shrinking pool of interested candidates at the director level at college and university libraries. More recently ALAC continues to discuss and review literature on this crisis, and has also begun to work more concertedly with CLIR on macrosolutions as an aspect of new leadership and the potential transformational impact these large-scale projects may have on the way libraries (and higher education) are conceptualized.

Awards

Peterson Fellowship

In 2011, in partnership with the National Institute for Technology in Liberal Education (NITLE), CLIR established a fellowship in honor of Richard Allen Peterson. Peterson, who died in early 2011, was an active promoter of collaboration in the area of information technology services and digital libraries. He last served as chief technology officer at Washington and Lee University.

The fellowship will be awarded annually to an early-career information technology professional or librarian who has reached beyond traditional boundaries to resolve a significant challenge facing digital libraries. The fellowship supports participation in the annual NITLE Symposium and in CLIR's DLF Forum.

The 2011 fellowship was granted to Meghan Frazer, digital resource librarian at Kenyon College.

Rovelstad Scholarship in International Librarianship

Timothy Thompson, a dual-degree master's student in library science and Latin American and Caribbean studies at Indiana University, was awarded the 2011 Rovelstad Scholarship in International Librarianship. Thompson is studying advanced Portuguese at the University of Brasilia and undertaking fieldwork for his master's thesis. He is conducting a survey and meta-analysis of major digital library projects being developed in Brazil and their social impact on community development.

Instituted in 2002, the Rovelstad Scholarship encourages library students who have an interest in international library work by enabling them to attend the World Library and Information Congress, the annual meeting of the International Federation of Library Associations and Institutions (IFLA).

Zipf Fellowship

Kathleen Fear, a Ph.D. candidate in the School of Information at the University of Michigan, was selected to receive the A. R. Zipf Fellowship in Information Management for 2011. Her research focuses on how scientific data can best be preserved, managed, and accessed.

The Zipf Fellowship is awarded annually to a graduate student in a field of information management or systems who best exemplifies the ideals of Al Zipf, the information science pioneer for whom the award is named.

Publications

Linked Data for Libraries, Museums, and Archives: Survey and Workshop Report. October 2011. Available at http://www.clir.org/pubs/abstract/pub152abst. html. The survey and workshop report address the practical aspects of understanding and applying linked data practices and technologies to the metadata and content of libraries, museums, and archives.

Rome Wasn't Digitized in a Day: Building a Cyberinfrastructure for Digital Classicists by Alison Babeu. August 2011. Available at http://www.clir.org/pubs/abstract/pub150abst.html. The author provides a summative and recent overview of the use of digital technologies in classical studies, focusing on classical Greece, Rome, and the ancient Middle and Near East, and generally on the period up to about 600 AD. The report explores what projects exist and how they are used, examines the infrastructure that currently exists to support digital classics as a discipline, and investigates larger humanities cyberinfrastructure projects and existing tools or services that might be repurposed for the digital classics.

Ruminations Series

In February 2011 CLIR launched a new publication series, Ruminations. The series features short research papers and essays that bring new perspectives to issues relevant to planning for and managing organizational and institutional change in the evolving digital environment for scholarship and teaching. Two papers have been issued:

Supporting Humanities Doctoral Student Success: A Collaborative Project Between Cornell University Library and Columbia University Libraries by Gabriela Castro Gessner, Damon E. Jaggars, Jennifer Rutner, and Kornelia Tancheva. October 2011. Available at http://www.clir.org/pubs/ruminations/02cornellcolumbia/report.html.

Bibliographic Indeterminacy and the Scale of Problems and Opportunities of "Rights" in Digital Collection Building by John P. Wilkin. February 2011. Available at http://www.clir.org/pubs/ruminations/01wilkin/wilkin.html.

Association for Library and Information Science Education

ALISE Headquarters, 65 E. Wacker Place, Suite 1900, Chicago, IL 60601-7246
312-795-0996, fax 312-419-8950, e-mail contact@alise.org
World Wide Web http://www.alise.org

Lynne C. Howarth
President 2011–2012

The Association for Library and Information Science Education (ALISE) is an independent, nonprofit professional association. Its mission is to promote excellence in research, teaching, and service for library and information science (LIS) education through leadership, collaboration, advocacy, and dissemination of research. ALISE was founded in 1915 as the Association of American Library Schools (AALS). In 1983 it changed its name to its present form to reflect more accurately the mission, goals, and membership of the association.

In June 2011, following extensive member feedback and final approval by its board of directors, ALISE adopted its planning framework, "Expanding Our Horizons: Strategic Directions, 2011–2014." The association's vision states that

> By 2014, ALISE will be known as the international leader in Library and Information Science education with strong links to schools and faculty around the world. We will also engage with other organizations and scholars in cognate disciplines. ALISE will showcase innovative research, including the scholarship of teaching and learning, promote greater diversity and inclusion as a hallmark of membership, and build and communicate its strength through greater visibility and voice.

Strategic Directions

The planning document commits to four key strategic directions for the 2011–2014 timeframe:

Areas for Strategic Development

- Strategic Direction 1: Consolidating and expanding the membership base by positioning the association as an organization of members
- Strategic Direction 2: Enhancing collaboration and extending ALISE membership to scholars in cognate disciplines and affiliated organizations, nationally and internationally

Core Strategic Areas (ongoing)

- Strategic Direction 3: Focusing on the scholarship of teaching and learning and the promotion of outstanding research
- Strategic Direction 4: Providing sound fiscal management, fostering administrative best practice, and advancing effective communication strategies for ALISE and its members

Membership

Membership categories are personal and institutional. Personal members can include anyone who has an interest in the objectives of the association, with categories including full-time (faculty member, administrator, librarian, researcher, or other interested individual); part-time/adjunct (retired or part-time faculty member); and doctoral student. Institutional members include schools with programs accredited by the American Library Association (ALA) and other U.S. and Canadian schools that offer a graduate degree in library and information science or a cognate field. International affiliate institutional membership is open to any school outside the United States or Canada that offers a program to educate persons for the practice of librarianship or other information work at the professional level as defined or accepted by the country in which the school is located.

Structure and Governance

Operational groups within ALISE include the board of directors; committees; the council of deans, directors, and program chairs; school representatives; and special interest groups. Since 2006 the Medical Library Association has provided management services for ALISE, with Kathleen Combs serving as ALISE executive director.

The board of directors is made up of seven elected officers serving three-year terms. Officers for 2011–2012 were Lynne Howarth (University of Toronto), president; Melissa Gross (Florida State University), vice president/president-elect; Lorna Peterson (University at Buffalo, State University of New York), past president; Jean Preer (Indiana University), secretary/treasurer; Ann Carlson Weeks (University of Maryland), director for membership services; Louise Spiteri (Dalhousie University), director for external relations; and Andrew Wertheimer (University of Hawaii at Manoa), director for special interest groups. At the end of the January 2012 ALISE Annual Conference, Peterson, Preer, and Wertheimer concluded their terms of service on the board and newly elected officers joined the board: Eileen G. Abels (Drexel University), vice president/president-elect; Steven L. MacCaul (University of Alabama), secretary/treasurer; and R. David Lankes (Syracuse University), director for special interest groups.

The board establishes policy, sets goals and strategic directions, and provides oversight for the management of ALISE. Face-to-face meetings are held in January in conjunction with the Annual Conference and in April to focus on strategic planning. For the remainder of the year, business is conducted through teleconferences and e-mail.

Committees have important roles in carrying out the work of the association. Since fall 2008, an open call for volunteers to serve on committees has been used to ensure broader participation in committee service, with members for the coming year appointed by the vice president/president-elect. Principal areas of activity include awards, budget and finance, conference program planning, governance, membership, nominations, publications, research competitions, and tellers (see http://www.alise.org/mc/page.do?sitePageId=86452 for a full list). Each committee is given an ongoing term of reference to guide its work as well as the specific charges for the year. Task forces can be charged to carry out tasks outside the scope of the existing standing committees. For example, a Diversity Statement Task Force was established in January 2011 and chaired by Clara M. Chu (University of North Carolina–Greensboro). The task force presented a two-hour session, "Extending ALISE's Reach: Expanding Our Diversity Horizon" at the 2012 Annual Conference. Speakers Sarah Park (St. Catherine University) and André Brock (University of Iowa) set the stage for small-group discussions on preliminary work toward developing an ALISE diversity statement. With additional consultation and feedback, a draft will be completed over the coming year and put forward to the board and ALISE membership for approval.

The ALISE Council of Deans, Directors, and Program Chairs consists of the chief executive officers of each ALISE institutional member school. The group convenes at the Annual Conference and can discuss issues via e-mail in the interim. Susan Roman (Dominican University), Mary Stansbury (University of Denver), and Deborah Grealy (St. Catherine University) shared chair duties for 2011–2012.

Within each institutional member school, a school representative is named to serve as a direct link between the membership and the ALISE Board of Directors. These individuals communicate to the faculty of their school about ALISE and the organization's events and initiatives, providing input on membership issues to the ALISE board.

Special interest groups (SIGs) enable members with shared interests to communicate and collaborate, with a particular emphasis on programs at the Annual Conference. New SIGs are established as new areas of interest emerge. The 18 current SIGs, grouped in three broad themes, are:

- *Roles and Responsibilities Cluster*: Assistant/Associate Deans and Directors; Doctoral Students; New Faculty; and Part-time and Adjunct Faculty
- *Teaching and Learning Cluster*: Curriculum; Distance Education; and Teaching Methods
- *Topics and Courses Cluster*: Archival/Preservation Education; Gender Issues; Historical Perspectives; Information Ethics; Information Policy; International Library Education; Multicultural, Ethnic and Humanistic Concerns; Research; School Library Media; Technical Services Education; and Youth Services

Notable activities for the SIGs at the 2012 conference included a cross-disciplinary session, "Cultural Heritage Preservation: Identifying Concepts, Communities, and Constructs," presented by the Archival/Preservation Education SIG; "Telling Our Stories: Extending Our Reach," a Youth Services SIG interactive discussion on the role of storytelling in LIS youth services education; and a luncheon hosted by San José State University for the Part-time and Adjunct Faculty SIG.

Publications

The ALISE publications program has four components:

- The *Journal of Education for Library and Information Science* (*JELIS*) is a peer-reviewed quarterly journal edited by Kathleen Burnett and Michelle Kazmer of Florida State University. Under their leadership, *JELIS* has published a number of research articles, brief communications and discussions of research in progress, and the ALISE 2011 Best Conference Papers. The journal will continue to showcase outstanding contributed papers presented at each ALISE Annual Conference. The editors continue management and updating of the companion Web site, http://jelis.org. The goal is to raise the visibility of the journal and to create an interactive Web site that engages the ALISE membership and others interested in LIS education in scholarly conversation. Examples in advancing that goal are announcements such as the posting of the 2011 ALISE Best Conference Paper award winners. Articles developed from these papers appeared in Volume 52, no. 4, published in October 2011.

- The *ALISE Directory of LIS Programs and Faculty in the United States and Canada* is published annually. It is now made available to members only in electronic form through the ALISE Web site. Listings of faculty for each school include indications of teaching and research areas, using codes from the LIS Research Areas Classification Scheme that ALISE maintains.

- The *ALISE Library and Information Science Education Statistical Report* publishes data collected in cooperation with ALA's Committee on Accreditation. It is an annual compilation of statistical data on curriculum, faculty, students, income and expenditures, and continuing professional education. Danny Wallace (University of Alabama), since his appointment as ALISE statistical data manager in 2008, has worked to bring publication of the annual volumes up to date. Currently members can gain access to the 2005, 2006, 2009, and 2010 reports. In October 2011 Wallace and his team rolled out a database application for collecting online, in real time, survey data that had previously been recorded on spreadsheets, or before that, recorded manually on printed forms. The system has been designed not only to support customized reports of summative and trend data as output but also for managing all aspects of the annual statistical data gathering process and retrospective inclusion of data for all years since 1980.

- The ALISE Web site keeps members informed with posting of updates on association activities and issues of the *ALISE News*, published three times a year. Information compiled from each Annual Conference and made available on the Web site includes abstracts of papers and posters presented and the president's report.

During summer 2011 ALISE launched a Facebook page; individual members used Twitter to tweet updates to the 2012 conference in Dallas. ALISE continues to explore options for effective communication with its members using a variety of social media and other platforms.

Annual Conference

The ALISE Annual Conference is held each year immediately before the ALA Midwinter Meeting. The 2012 conference in Dallas January 17–20 drew 471 attendees to explore the theme "Extending Our Reach: Expanding Horizons, Creating Opportunity." The program co-chairs, Toni Carbo (Drexel University) and Andrew Dillon (University of Texas–Austin), assembled a rich array of program sessions, including a keynote address by Archivist of the United States David S. Ferriero. His presentation, "Expanding Horizons: Including Your Customers" (available on the ALISE 2012 Conference Web site at http://www.alise.org/assets/documents/conf_2012/alise_2012_ferreiro_presentation_12_01_18.pdf), sparked a lively discussion, setting the stage for sessions that crossed disciplinary, geographic, cultural, institutional, and career boundaries.

Two poster sessions—Works-in-Progress and the Doctoral Student Research Poster Session—offered opportunities to engage with a wide range of research. The Birds of a Feather brown-bag lunch fostered discussions of teaching in various content areas. Concurrent sessions included presentations of award-winning and juried (peer-reviewed) papers, panel and interactive roundtable discussions, a presidential program on indigenous knowledge, and SIG-sponsored programs.

The first day of the conference was devoted to continuing professional development, with a workshop on pedagogical practices in online LIS education sponsored by the Web-based Information Science Education (WISE) consortium, and the ALISE Academy sponsored by the H. W. Wilson Foundation. The ALISE Academy initiative, in its fourth year, is a continuing education opportunity designed to provide support and inspiration to members at all stages of their careers. For the 2012 conference, the academy, co-convened by Connie Van Fleet (University of Oklahoma) and Melissa Gross (Florida State University), focused on leadership development needs in three critical areas: teaching leadership, leadership for professionals, and leadership as a career choice. Asking the question "How can I develop new leaders?" Peter Hernon (Simmons College) conducted "Leading from the Classroom: Teaching Leadership" for those with a goal of empowering leadership in students. For faculty interested in leadership, but not in administrative positions, John Bertot (University of Maryland) offered "Leading from Where You Are: Modeling Leadership." Co-facilitators Elizabeth Aversa (University of Alabama) and Cecelia Brown (University of Oklahoma) facilitated the workshop "Leading from Administration: Choosing Leadership" for faculty considering administration, and administrators committed to developing new leaders.

The Annual Conference has an active placement service, facilitating support for job candidates through résumé and portfolio reviews and scheduled interviews. Representatives of several institutional member schools conducted interviews for a greater number of open positions than have been available over the past two to three years. New to the ALISE conference for 2012 was access to résumés of those seeking part-time and adjunct faculty positions. These were made available in binders on-site, and via a recently launched adjunct faculty portal that complements a Web portal designed for individual and institutional members targeting full-time faculty appointments.

Grants and Awards

ALISE seeks to stimulate research and recognize accomplishments through its grants and awards programs. Research competitions include the ALISE Research Grant Competition, the ALISE/Bohdan S. Wynar Research Paper Competition, the ALISE/Dialog Methodology Paper Competition, the ALISE/Eugene Garfield Doctoral Dissertation Competition, the ALISE/Linworth Youth Services Paper Award, and the OCLC/ALISE Library and Information Science Research Grant Competition. Support for conference participation is provided by the University of Washington Information School Youth Services Graduate Student Travel Award and the Doctoral Student to ALISE Award. Awards recognizing outstanding accomplishments include the ALISE/Norman Horrocks Leadership Award (for early-career leadership), the ALISE/Pratt-Severn Faculty Innovation Award, the ALISE Service Award, the ALISE Award for Teaching Excellence, and the ALISE Award for Professional Contribution. Winners are recognized at an awards reception at the Annual Conference. [For a list of award winners, see "Library Scholarship and Award Recipients, 2011" in Part 3—Ed.]

Collaboration with Other Organizations

ALISE seeks to collaborate with other organizations on activities of mutual interest. ALISE is represented on the ALA Committee on Education (COE) by Director for External Relations Louise Spiteri, who has also been actively engaged, on behalf of ALISE, with the ALA COE Diversity Working Group. Several ALISE institutional members collaborate on staffing an ALISE booth anchoring the LIS Education Pavilion area of the exhibit hall at the ALA Annual Conference each summer.

During 2011 ALISE past president for 2011–2012 Lorna Peterson registered the association in, and agreed to serve as a member of, the Coalition on the Academic Workforce. The coalition listserv will keep ALISE members apprised of developments relating to the academic workplace and work force.

In June 2011 ALISE responded to an invitation to participate in the National Digital Stewardship Alliance (NDSA), a program initiated by the Library of Congress through its National Digital Information Infrastructure and Preservation Program (NDIIPP). NDSA and its outreach committee are interested in making connections with the many communities of practice in library and information science, and particularly LIS students, ". . . because they are our next generation of leaders and could have a lasting impact on digital preservation issues" (NDSA communication, 6/3/2011). ALISE membership on NDSA will allow for input on such initiatives as a "Digital Preservation in a Box" product that will be shared with students and faculty in terms of development, curriculum integration, student projects, and so forth.

ALISE is seeking to build more international connections. For the fourth year, Executive Director Kathleen Combs organized a dinner for ALISE members attending the 2011 IFLA World Library and Information Congress in San Juan, Puerto Rico, in August. In addition, a number of ALISE members attending the IFLA conference helped to staff the ALISE table. Situated immediately inside the entrance to the exhibits hall, the ALISE presence attracted steady traffic and interest in membership activities. ALISE continues to seek opportunities to partner with the IFLA Sections on Education and Training (SET) and Library Theory and Research (LTR), and has initiated discussions on a possible joint session on Innovations in LIS Education to be offered at the IFLA 2013 conference in Singapore. The ALISE board is also exploring mechanisms for encouraging and supporting association members who wish to seek election to an IFLA Standing Committee. ALISE will be represented at the IFLA Conference in Helsinki in August 2012.

Conclusion

As ALISE looks ahead to celebrating its 100th anniversary in 2015, its board of directors has appointed a committee, chaired by Elizabeth Aversa (University of Alabama), to launch a Centennial Campaign to raise significant funding for the ALISE endowment. Concurrently, a centennial celebration committee, chaired by Michele Cloonan (Simmons College), is planning activities and events to showcase the association and the accomplishments of its members over the past century. The ALISE archives, housed at the University of Illinois, will be an invaluable resource in this endeavor, as the ALISE board and management services staff continue to ensure that records documenting the work of the association are readily accessible and maintained well into the future. Through its programs, the work of its personal and institutional members, and its focus on outreach to cognate disciplines, and to international affiliates, ALISE is uniquely positioned to provide leadership for library and information science research and education in the 21st century.

International Reports

International Federation of Library Associations and Institutions

P.O. Box 95312, 2509 CH The Hague, Netherlands
Tel. 31-70-314-0884, fax 31-70-383-4827, e-mail ifla@ifla.org
World Wide Web http://www.ifla.org

Beacher Wiggins
Director for Acquisitions and Bibliographic Access, Library of Congress
American Library Association Representative to the Standing Committee on Government
Libraries, 2011–2013

The International Federation of Library Associations and Institutions (IFLA) is the preeminent international organization representing librarians, other information professionals, and library users. Like many other nonprofit and international organizations, in 2011 IFLA was challenged by worldwide economic constraints, political upheaval, and natural disasters. Nevertheless, IFLA promoted high standards of provision and delivery of library and information services; encouraged widespread understanding of the value of good library and information services; and represented the interests of its members throughout the world. Throughout the year, IFLA promoted an understanding of libraries as cultural heritage resources that are the patrimony of every nation.

World Library and Information Congress

The World Library and Information Congress/77th IFLA General Conference and Council (WLIC) attracted 2,418 registered participants from 116 countries to San Juan, Puerto Rico, August 13–18, 2011. The number of registered participants was 25 percent lower than the 3,236 at the 2010 WLIC in Gothenburg, Sweden, and nearly one-third lower than the 3,568 who registered at the WLIC in Milan, Italy, in 2009. The decreases reflected the continuing weakness of the global economy, the aging of the library profession, financial constraints on many libraries, and the arrival of Hurricane Irene over Puerto Rico during the conference week. The 2011 conference theme, "Libraries Beyond Libraries: Integration, Innovation, and Information for All," struck an upbeat note, focusing on technological and political progress that makes libraries more central than ever to the community life of nearly every nation.

    The keynote speaker at the opening session of the Congress was Fernando Picó, a Jesuit priest and professor at the University of Puerto Rico, whose address in Spanish was on "The Afterlife of Texts: When Paradise Is an Internet Site." Mayra Santos-Febres, an author and professor of literature at the University of Puerto Rico; documentary filmmaker Luis Molina-Casanova, who teaches at San Juan's University of the Sacred Heart; and Trevor C. Clarke, assistant director general for culture and creative industries, World Intellectual Property Organization (WIPO), were the other speakers for each day's plenary session of the Congress.

Fourteen satellite meetings—in Barbados, Cuba, Guatemala, Guyana, Jamaica, Mexico, the United States (Atlanta, Georgia), the U.S. Virgin Islands, and Puerto Rico—permitted intensive focus on special topics. The Guatemala satellite meeting on "Cooperation Among Multiple Types of Libraries and Affiliated Information Services of Archives and Museums" pointed out the growing convergence of libraries with other cultural heritage institutions. Two satellite meetings highlighted interest in sustainability: "Francophones, Libraries, and Sustainable Development" in Guyana, cosponsored by the IFLA Preservation and Conservation Section and Association Internationale Francophone des Bibliothécaires et Documentalistes; and in Cuba, "Social Science Libraries: A Bridge to Knowledge for Sustainable Development," sponsored by the IFLA Social Science Libraries Section. The IFLA Cataloguing Section sponsored a satellite meeting at the National Library of Puerto Rico on the new cataloging instructions, "RDA: Resource Description and Access." Three meetings on "Collections in Islands" (Museum of Art of Puerto Rico), "Art Bibliography and Information in Latin America and the Caribbean" (Mexico City), and "Building Cross-Cultural Capacities in Library and Information Science: African and Caribbean Reflections" (Barbados) reflected the Caribbean setting for the 2011 Congress, while other satellite meetings focused on health and school librarianship, information literacy, technology, and specialized collection development.

The next World Library and Information Congresses will take place in Helsinki, Finland (2012) and Singapore (2013). Under the current IFLA WLIC conference planning guidelines, the conference cities are selected three years in advance, and at each WLIC the IFLA Governing Board announces the specific location of the conference that will take place two years later. The 2014 conference will take place in a European city, to be followed by conferences in Africa (2015), North America (2016), Europe (2017), Latin America or the Caribbean region (2018), and again in Europe (2019). The IFLA Governing Board is committed to continuously improving both the conference experience for participants and the financial security of the organization. The WLIC in Puerto Rico enjoyed sponsorship by OCLC, Inc., Infor, De Gruyter Saur, Gale Cengage Learning, SirsiDynix, and Elsevier, in addition to subsidies by local civic and tourism bodies. Although the WLIC exhibitor fees and registration are higher than for most conferences in the library community, the conference does not make money for IFLA, and the custom of convening all registered participants in opening and closing ceremonies limits the number of cities that can host the conference to those with conference halls seating at least 3,000 people. Furthermore, member organizations have reported that the scheduling requirements make it difficult to send representatives to both the general conference and the numerous specialized satellite meetings. The current seven-year planning cycle and conference model were adopted after a consultation in early 2010 that Pleiade Management and Consultancy of Amsterdam conducted for IFLA among four major stakeholder groups: delegates and members who were represented at recent conferences; IFLA Section Standing Committees, special interest groups, and core activities; former national conference committee members; and conference sponsors and exhibitors. In the resulting model, each IFLA conference is organized around three to five tracks or themes. In San Juan, the five tracks were: open access and digital resources; policy, strategy, and advocacy; users driving access and services; tools and techniques; and ideas, innovation, and anticipating the new. Through its governing board, IFLA retains overall ownership of each conference, and the governing board, IFLA headquarters, and the conference national committee (the local organizing committee) are responsible for each conference overall. Program content is guided by the IFLA Professional Committee. Actual conference planning and services are contracted to a "provider of conference organization," or event management company; in San Juan the contractor was CongrexUK. A more extensive review of conference governance, the host city selection process, the planning cycle, and financial management is planned for 2015–2016, after the site of the 2018 conference is announced and all of IFLA's regions have hosted at least one conference.

Conference of Directors of National Libraries

The Conference of Directors of National Libraries (CDNL) is an independent association that meets in conjunction with IFLA's WLIC to promote cooperation on matters of common interest to national libraries around the world. At the 2011 meeting, CDNL discussed the recovery of national libraries from natural disasters, digitization projects, electronic legal deposit, copyright, and the role of literacy and reading programs in national libraries. In 2011 the chair of CDNL was John Tsebe, national librarian and chief executive officer of the National Library of South Africa, which hosted the CDNL Secretariat.

Response to War and Natural Disaster

Since 1996 IFLA has been a founding member of the International Committee of the Blue Shield (ICBS) to protect cultural property in the event of natural and human disasters. Its current partners in ICBS are the International Council on Archives, the International Council on Monuments and Sites, the International Council of Museums, and the Co-ordinating Council of Audiovisual Archives Associations. In 2011 ICBS and numerous IFLA sections responded with direct aid and consultations after the devastating earthquakes in Chile (February 2010), New Zealand (September 2010; February and June, 2011), and Japan (March 2011) as well as after the Tunisian and Egyptian revolutions in January and February in which many libraries were damaged. ICBS also continued its concern for the preservation of cultural heritage in the ongoing aftermath of earlier wars and disasters. The IFLA North American regional center for preservation and conservation, hosted at the Library of Congress, continued to develop a network of colleague institutions to provide a safety net for library collections during emergencies. In March 2011 IFLA and the Prince Claus Fund of the Netherlands, with additional funding from the City of Geneva, Switzerland, established an Ark or treatment center for damaged documents and collections in Port-au-Prince, Haiti, in order to support cultural reconstruction in that country after the massive earthquake there in January 2010.

Bibliographic Control

The federation has worked steadily over the decades to improve bibliographic control, through practical workshops, support of the International Standard Bibliographic Description, and research that seeks to establish basic principles of bibliographic control and to identify areas where cataloging practice in different cultures can be harmonized to make library catalogs less expensive to produce and easier for patrons to use. In July 2011 De Gruyter Saur published a new edition of the consolidated *International Standard Bibliographic Description* (ISBD), edited by the Standing Committee of IFLA's Cataloguing Section. The 2011 edition features corrections and additions arising from experience with using the preliminary consolidated edition issued in 2007. The Cataloguing Section is now working with the Joint Steering Committee for the Development of RDA and the international ISSN Network to harmonize the ISBD; RDA: Resource Description and Access; and the ISSN (International Standard Serial Number), a widely used unique identifier. Also within the Cataloguing Section, the ISBD/XML Study Group, charged in 2008 to develop an XML/RDF schema for the ISBD, extended this project for a third year. An XML/RDF schema will move the ISBD into the Semantic Web environment and ensure the interoperability of the ISBD with other schemas such as MARCXML.

In December 2011 IFLA announced that it would close its core activity ICADS. In 2009 IFLA had reshaped its core activity ICABS, the IFLA-CDNL Alliance for Bibliographic Standards, into ICADS, the IFLA-CDNL Alliance for Digital Strategies, with CDNL and seven national libraries as founding members. Awareness of digital activities has increased tremendously in recent years, and a special national libraries group to highlight digital strategies is no longer necessary.

The separate IFLA UNIMARC Core Activity (UCA) maintains, develops, documents, and promotes the four UNIMARC formats for bibliographic, authority, classification, and holdings data. Since 2003, when it succeeded IFLA's former Universal Bibliographic Control and International MARC program, UCA has been hosted by the National Library of Portugal. Under UCA, the Permanent UNIMARC Committee maintains the formats and also advises ICADS on matters relating to UNIMARC. The Permanent UNIMARC Committee is currently chaired by Alan Hopkinson of Middlesex University in London.

The IFLA Governing Board in December 2011 established a Committee on Standards that could make recommendations for standards in cataloging, classification, indexing, and related areas in the digital realm as well as in other areas of librarianship.

Copyright Issues

The IFLA Committee on Copyright and Other Legal Matters (CLM) works to ensure a proper balance between the claims of intellectual property rights holders and the needs of library users worldwide. In 2009 CLM developed a list of 12 basic "Core Exceptions to Copyright" law that are essential if libraries throughout the world are to fulfill their mission of providing open access to information and knowledge for all people. In 2010 CLM encouraged WIPO to recognize the core exceptions, striving for a global copyright strategy based on libraries' real-life needs. In November 2010 the WIPO Standing Committee on Copyright and Related Rights adopted a work plan for 2011–2012 that placed the core exceptions and their possible adoption in treaty form on the agenda for formal discussion by WIPO member states in 2011. The efforts of CLM bore fruit as the WIPO Standing Committee considered copyright exceptions for print-disabled people during its meeting in Geneva, Switzerland, June 14–25, 2011. At this meeting a draft treaty proposal on Copyright Exceptions and Limitations for Libraries and Archives was introduced. The WIPO Standing Committee's next regular meeting, November 21–December 2, 2011, devoted three days to discussions of the proposal and ended with agreement for discussion in 2012 of a draft compilation of copyright exceptions of interest to libraries, to include preservation, right of reproduction and supply of copies, legal deposit, library lending, parallel importation, cross-border uses, orphan works, retracted and withdrawn works, liability of libraries and archives, technological measures of protection, contracts, and the right to translate works.

FAIFE

One of IFLA's core activities is Freedom of Access to Information and Freedom of Expression, or FAIFE, which is defined in Article 19 of the United Nations Universal Declaration of Human Rights as a basic human right.

FAIFE has been a leader within IFLA in adopting social media such as Facebook and YouTube and began publishing a new online newsletter in 2010. FAIFE has a presence at the annual Internet Governance Forum, which in 2011 took place in Nairobi, Kenya, in September. In 2011 FAIFE paid particular attention to the important role of social media in the Tunisian and Egyptian revolutions. Through its "FAIFE Spotlight," it also opposed restrictions on access to information in Hungary, Turkey, and Venezuela.

Grants and Awards

The federation continues to work with corporate partners and national libraries to maintain programs and opportunities that would otherwise not be possible, especially for librarians and libraries in developing countries. The Jay Jordan IFLA/ OCLC Early Career Development Fellowships provide four weeks of intensive experience, based in OCLC headquarters in Dublin, Ohio, for library and information science professionals from countries with developing economies who are in the early stages of their careers. The fellows for 2011 were from Botswana, China, Malawi, the Philippines, and Serbia. As announced at the Puerto Rico conference, the fellows for 2012 will be from Bangladesh, Ghana, Kenya, Nigeria, and Pakistan. The American Theological Library Association is the third sponsor of the program, and one of the fellows must be a theological librarian. Since its inception in 2001, the program has supported 60 librarians from 33 developing countries.

The Frederic Thorpe Awards, established in 2003, are administered by the IFLA Libraries Serving Persons with Print Disabilities Section and the Ulverscroft Foundation of Leicester, England, which Thorpe founded to support visually impaired people. The Ulverscroft Foundation renewed the program as the Ulverscroft/IFLA Best Practice Awards (Frederic Thorpe Awards) in 2006, 2007, 2008, 2010, and 2011, with no award in 2009. In 2011 the Ulverscroft/IFLA Best Practice Awards were presented to Marianne Kraack of the Royal New Zealand Foundation for the Blind; Jelena Lesaja of the Croatian Library for the Blind; Kristina Janc of the National and University Library, Slovenia; and Megan Gilks of RNIB (Royal National Institute of Blind People), U.K., and Marieke Belt of the Loket aangepast-lezen (Center for Adapted Reading), the Netherlands, who will visit each others' institutions.

The Bill and Melinda Gates Foundation Access to Learning Award in 2011 was presented at the Puerto Rico conference to the Arid Lands Information Network that administers 12 information centers in Kenya, Uganda, and Tanzania. This annual award presents up to $1 million to libraries, library agencies, or comparable organizations outside the United States that have been innovative in providing free public access to information.

Numerous awards and grants encourage travel to the annual IFLA conferences. For the 2010 conference in Gothenburg, De Gruyter Saur provided grants for travelers from the Pacific Region; the Swedish Library Association and the IFLA Foundation made €60,000 available to support participation from developing countries; and Axiell Library Group provided €16,000 for travel grants. The IFLA Academic and Research Libraries Section instituted an annual essay contest, awarding conference registration for three contestants from Africa, Latin America, and the Asia/Pacific region. The Section on Education and Training sponsors a Student Paper Award for library science students. The IFLA International Marketing Award includes a stipend and travel to the conference. In 2002, 2003, and 2004 IFLA and 3M Library Systems cosponsored the marketing awards. After a hiatus in 2005, IFLA cosponsored the awards with SirsiDynix in 2006 and 2007. The Emerald Group has sponsored the award since 2008. The Council on Library and Information Resources (CLIR) sponsors the Rovelstad Scholarship that brings one international library science student to WLIC each year. The Dr. Shawky Salem Conference Grant supports conference attendance from an Arab country. While many national library professional associations subsidize travel to the IFLA conference, the Comité Français IFLA supports travelers from any francophone country. The newest travel award is the Aspire Award, established to support travel to conferences of IFLA and of CILIP, the Chartered Institute of Library and Information Professionals (Britain). The Aspire Award honors the memory of Bob McKee (1950–2010), chief executive of CILIP. For 2011 and 2012, the Aspire Award supports travel to WLIC by librarians from Ukraine.

The Guust van Wesemael Literacy Prize was awarded biennially to a school or public library in a country with a developing economy from 1993 to 2009.

The IFLA Honorary Fellowships, the IFLA Medal, and the IFLA Scroll of Appreciation recognize service to IFLA by individuals.

Membership and Finances

IFLA has more than 1,500 members in 150 countries. Initially established at a conference in Edinburgh, Scotland, in 1927, it has been registered in the Netherlands since 1971 and has headquarters facilities at the Koninklijke Bibliotheek (Royal Library) in The Hague. Although IFLA did not hold a General Conference outside Europe and North America until 1980, there has since been steadily increasing participation from Asia, Africa, South America, and Australia. The federation now maintains regional offices for Africa (in Pretoria, South Africa); Asia and Oceania (in Singapore); and Latin America and the Caribbean (moved from Rio de Janeiro to Mexico City in 2011). The organization has seven official working languages—Arabic, Chinese, English, French, German, Russian, and Spanish. It offers a range of membership categories: international library associations, national library associations, other associations (generally regional or special library associations), institutions, institutional sub-units, one-person libraries, school libraries, association affiliates, personal affiliates, student affiliates, new graduate members, and non-salaried personal members. Association and institution members have voting rights in the IFLA General Council and IFLA elections and may nominate candidates for IFLA offices. Institutional sub-units, one-person libraries, and school libraries have limited voting rights for section elections; affiliates and personal members do not have voting rights, but may submit nominations for any IFLA office and individuals may run for office themselves. Except for affiliates, membership fees are keyed to the UNESCO Scale of Assessment and the United Nations List of Least Developed Countries, to encourage participation regardless of economic circumstances. The IFLA Core Activity Fund is supported by national libraries worldwide.

UNESCO has given IFLA formal associate relations status, the highest level of relationship accorded to non-governmental organizations by UNESCO. In addition, IFLA has observer status with the United Nations, WIPO, the International Organization for Standardization, and the World Trade Organization, and associate status with the International Council of Scientific Unions. The federation continues joint activities with the World Summit on the Information Society, including its Forum in Geneva, Switzerland, in May 2011, where IFLA introduced its Statement on Open Access of all people to scientific research, particularly on the Internet.

More than two dozen corporations in the information industry have formed working relationships with IFLA as Corporate Partners, providing financial and in-kind support. Gold Corporate Partners that contributed more than €3,500 to IFLA in 2011 were Australian Science; OCLC, Inc.; SirsiDynix; and publishers De Gruyter Saur, Elsevier, Emerald, InTech, nbd/biblion, Sabinet, and Sage.

The IFLA Foundation (Stichting IFLA) was established in 2007. The foundation accepts private donations and also is funded by other IFLA income. It gives funding priority to proposals and projects that promise to have a long-term impact in developing and strengthening IFLA; are clearly related to at least one of the foundation's three pillars; and are not likely to be funded by other bodies.

IFLA's Three Pillars: Society, Members, and Profession

The operational model for IFLA is based on the three pillars of society, membership, and professional matters. All of the federation's core functions relate to three strategic factors: the societal contexts in which libraries and information services operate; the membership of the federation; and the library profession.

Although the three pillars and the infrastructure of IFLA are interdependent, they can be roughly analyzed as follows: The Society Pillar focuses on the role and impact of libraries and information services in society. Activities supported by the Society Pillar include FAIFE, CLM, Blue Shield, IFLA's presence at the World Summit on the Information Society, and the advocacy office at IFLA headquarters—all activities that preserve memory, feed development, enable education and research, and support international understanding and community well-being. The Profession Pillar focuses on IFLA's role as the global voice for libraries and information services. The Members Pillar includes IFLA's member services, conferences, and publications.

The federation's operational infrastructure—consisting of IFLA Headquarters, the IFLANET Web site, and the IFLA governance structure—support and receive strategic direction from the three pillars. The three pillars enable IFLA to promote its four core values: freedom of access to information and expression, as stated in Article 19 of the Universal Declaration of Human Rights; the belief that such access must be universal and equitable to support human well-being; delivery of high-quality library and information services in support of that access; and the commitment to enabling all members of IFLA to participate without regard to citizenship, disability, ethnic origin, gender, geographical location, political philosophy, race, or religion.

In 2010 the IFLA Governing Board adopted a new Strategic Plan for the years 2010–2015. The plan, grounded in the four core values, sets forth four strategic directions: empowering libraries to enable their user communities to have equitable access to information; building the strategic capacity of IFLA and that of its members; transforming the profile and standing of the library profession; and representing the interests of IFLA's members and their users throughout the world. The governing board determines priority activities every two years under the strategic plan. Priority activities for 2010–2011 included support for FAIFE, CLM, Action for Development through Libraries (ALP), advocacy, and the Preservation and Conservation core activity (PAC).

Personnel, Structure, and Governance

The secretary general of IFLA is Jennefer Nicholson, former executive director of the Australian Library and Information Association. Sjoerd M. J. Koopman retired as IFLA's professional programs director on August 1, 2011. Joanne Yeomans joined IFLA headquarters as professional support officer in September. Wiebke Dalhoff joined headquarters as the new policy officer in August. The editor of the quarterly *IFLA Journal* is J. Stephen Parker. In 2008 IFLA hired Stuart Hamilton as its first director for policy and advocacy, also a headquarters position. IFLA has expanded its staffing for communications under Ingeborg Verheul, director for communications and services, with communications officers Susan Schaepman and Louis Takács and webmaster Simon Lemstra. The IFLA conference officer is Josche Ouwerkerk.

After IFLA's biennial elections in spring 2011, new officers and board members took office at the close of the Puerto Rico conference. The new president of IFLA is Ingrid Parent, university librarian, University of British Columbia, Vancouver. She succeeded Ellen R. Tise of the University of Stellenbosch, South Africa, at the close of the San Juan conference. Parent's presidential theme is "Libraries—A Force for Change," reflecting the values of inclusion, transformation, innovation, and convergence.

The new president-elect of IFLA is Sinikka Sipilä, president of the Finnish Library Association. The new treasurer is Donna Scheeder of the Congressional Research Service, Library of Congress.

Under the revised 2008 IFLA Statutes, the 19 members of the IFLA Governing Board (plus the secretary general, ex officio) are responsible for the federation's general policies, management and finance. Additionally, the board represents the federation in legal and other formal proceedings. The board comprises the president, president-elect, treasurer, nine directly elected members, the chair of the IFLA Professional Committee, the chairs of each IFLA division, and the chair of the standing committee of the Management of Library Associations Section, currently Gerald Leitner, secretary general of the Austrian Library Association. Current members, in addition to Parent, Sipilä, Scheeder, Nicholson, and Leitner, are Kent Skov Andreasen (Denmark), Frédéric Blin (France), Ingrid Bon (Netherlands), Genevieve Clavel-Merrin (Switzerland), Barbara Lison (Germany), Inga Lundén (Sweden) Christine Mackenzie (Australia), Buhle Mbambo-Thata (South Africa), and Paul Whitney (Canada), plus the chairs of the professional committee and divisions, named below.

The Governing Board delegates responsibility for overseeing the direction of IFLA between board meetings, within the policies established by the board, to the IFLA Executive Committee, which includes the president, president-elect, treasurer, chair of the professional committee, two members of the Governing Board (elected every two years by members of the board from among its elected members), and IFLA's secretary general, ex officio. The current elected Governing Board members of the executive committee are Mbambo-Thata and Whitney.

The IFLA Professional Committee monitors the planning and programming of professional activities carried out by IFLA's two types of bodies: professional groups—five divisions, 48 sections, and discussion groups—and core activities (formerly called core programs). The Professional Committee is composed of one elected officer from each division, plus a chair elected by the outgoing committee; the president, the president-elect, and the professional support officer, who serves as secretary; the chairs of the CLM and FAIFE committees, and two elected members of the governing board, currently Skov Andreasen and Clavel-Merrin. Ann Okerson, special advisor on electronic strategies, Center for Research Libraries (New Haven, Connecticut), chairs the committee.

The five divisions of IFLA and their representatives on the professional committee are: Library Types (Lynne M. Rudasill, USA); Library Collections (formerly Ann Okerson, USA; now vacant with Okerson's assumption of the chairmanship); Library Services (Tone Eli Moseid, Norway); Support of the Profession (Anna Maria Tammaro, Italy); and Regions (Filiberto Felipe Martínez-Arellano,

Mexico). The new chair of the IFLA Copyright and Legal Matters Committee is Victoria Owen (Canada). The chair of the IFLA Freedom of Access to Information and Freedom of Expression Committee is Kai Ekholm (Finland). A total of 43 sections focus on topical interests, such as statistics and evaluation, library theory and research, and management and marketing, or on particular types of libraries or parts of the world.

The five core activities are Action for Development Through Libraries (ALP, formerly Advancement of Librarianship); Preservation and Conservation (PAC); IFLA UNIMARC Core Activity, which maintains and develops the Universal MARC Format, UNIMARC; Free Access to Information and Freedom of Expression (FAIFE); and Copyright and Other Legal Matters (CLM). The IFLA-CDNL Alliance for Digital Strategies (ICADS) core activity ceased at the end of 2011 as its work has been absorbed by numerous IFLA sections. Two other longstanding IFLA projects are the IFLA World Wide Web site IFLA.org and the IFLA Voucher Scheme, which replaced the IFLA Office for International Lending. The Voucher Scheme enables libraries to pay for international interlibrary loan requests using vouchers purchased from IFLA rather than actual currency or credit accounts. By eliminating bank charges and invoices for each transaction, the voucher scheme reduces the administrative costs of international library loans and allows libraries to plan budgets with less regard to short-term fluctuations in the value of different national currencies. The voucher scheme has also encouraged participating libraries to voluntarily standardize their charges for loans at the rate of one voucher for up to fifteen pages.

To ensure an arena within IFLA for discussion of new social, professional, or cultural issues, the Professional Committee approves the formation of special interest groups for a limited time period. There currently are discussion groups for Access to Information Network/Africa (ATINA); Agricultural Libraries; E-Learning; E-Metrics; Environmental Sustainability and Libraries; Indigenous Matters; Library and Information Science Education in Developing Countries; Library History; National Information and Library Policy; National Organizations and International Relations; New Professionals; RFID; Semantic Web; and Women, Information, and Libraries.

Canadian Library Association

1150 Morrison Drive, Suite 400., Ottawa, ON K2H 8S9
613-232-9625, fax 613-563-9895, e-mail info@cla.ca
World Wide Web http://www.cla.ca

Kelly Moore
Executive Director

The Canadian Library Association/Association Canadienne des Bibliothèques (CLA) is Canada's major national professional association for the library and information community. It is predominantly English-language, with selected activities also in French. It recently drafted a new mission: "CLA is the national public voice for Canada's library communities. We champion library values and the value of libraries. We influence public policy impacting libraries. We inspire and support learning. We collaborate to strengthen the library community."

Founded in 1946, CLA is a federally incorporated not-for-profit organization. It is governed by a six-person executive council, which is advised by appointed advisory and standing committees and as-needed task forces.

Membership includes both individuals (librarians, library staff, other information professionals, and library board trustees) and institutions (mainly libraries, but also suppliers to the library and information community).

There are CLA student chapters at six English-language library and information science post-graduate programs in Canada, and there is a student chapter at one library technician program.

To facilitate sharing of information in specific areas of interest, CLA currently has 21 "networks" focusing on topics as diverse as accessible collections and services, evidence-based library and information practice, human resources, library history, government library and information management professionals, and voices for school libraries. New networks are forming regularly.

Governance

In May 2011 the role of CLA president was assumed by Karen Adams, director of libraries, University of Manitoba. She succeeded Keith Walker, director of library services, Medicine Hat College Library, who had served as president since June 2010.

Others serving as officers for 2012 are Vice President/President-Elect Pilar Martinez, Treasurer Mary-Jo Romaniuk, and Executive Director Kelly Moore.

Major Activities

Following a major strategic planning exercise initiated in 2010, CLA entered a period of change. At the organization's 2011 Annual General Meeting, CLA members voted on a resolution to adopt major changes to the governance and professional structures of the association. The resolution was approved unanimously. Major implications included the introduction of networks to address issues identified by and for members, a reduction in size of the executive council, the establishment of a number of advisory and standing committees, and the dissolution of the five former type-of-library divisions.

CLA continues to lead a variety of national advocacy initiatives and to offer professional development opportunities. Major activities have focused on these two elements, with federal advocacy taking a predominant role.

Advocacy and Public Awareness

Canada Post has maintained the Library Book Rate for 2012 with only a slight increase in costs, the first increase since 2005. CLA continues to support MP Merv Tweed (Brandon-Souris) on his private member's bill (C-321) to create legislation supporting the rate. The bill has the support of the government and all opposition parties, but still awaited action at the time this report was prepared.

During 2011 CLA met with members of parliament and officials and staff in federal government ministries to raise awareness of key issues. National and international developments in the area of copyright and related rights were a major focus. CLA produced an analysis—"Protecting the Public Interest in the Digital World Revisited for Bill C-11: The views of the Canadian Library Association/ Association canadienne des bibliothèques on Bill C-11, 'An Act to Amend the Copyright Act' "—of the government's latest proposed copyright legislation, and suggested technical amendments to the bill. With other library organizations, CLA has been present at meetings of the World Intellectual Property Organization's Standing Committee on Copyright and Related Rights and engaged in efforts to promote a draft treaty on limitations and exceptions for libraries and archives.

CLA continues to track intellectual freedom issues in Canada through its annual survey of challenges to library materials and policies. The survey, now conducted in both English and French, captures details of challenges from libraries of all types across the country.

The association also spearheads Canadian Library Month/Le Mois Canadien des Bibliothèques, partnering with provincial, regional, and territorial library associations and governments. Under the theme "Your Library: A Place Unbound/ Votre Bibliothèque: Un Peu, Beaucoup, à l'Infini," this bilingual collection of events helped raise awareness during 2011 of all types of libraries—public, academic, school, and special—and their roles for Canadians of all ages.

Professional Development

CLA's major contribution to continuing professional development continues to be its annual National Conference. The 2011 CLA National Conference and Trade Show was held in Halifax May 25–28.

International Activities

CLA has maintained strong contact with the international library community, mainly through its involvement with the International Federation of Library Associations and Institutions (IFLA). CLA President Karen Adams and Executive Director Kelly Moore attended the 2011 IFLA Congress in San Juan, Puerto Rico, along with a large Canadian delegation. The Canadian library community supports Ingrid Parent, university librarian at the University of British Columbia, as Canada's first president of IFLA. She assumed presidency of the federation in August 2011 for a two-year term.

Communications

As information professionals, Canadian librarians depend on timely and attractive publications and resources from their professional association, and those outside the community look to the association as a significant source of information.

CLA's bimonthly publication, *Feliciter,* published since 1956, explores core themes in the library community, among them the future of print, challenges faced by small libraries, and open access. A second publication, *CLA Digest,* is a biweekly e-newsletter for members, with links to more in-depth news.

Awards and Honors

CLA recognized individuals from the library and information community with awards and honors in 2011.

CLA's most significant award is for Outstanding Service to Librarianship. It is presented only in years when there is a candidate deemed worthy to receive it. In 2011 CLA presented the award to Stephen Abram of Gale Cengage Learning.

The CLA Award for the Advancement of Intellectual Freedom was presented to A. Alan Borovoy. Since 1988 the award has recognized outstanding contributions to intellectual freedom of individuals and groups, both in and outside the library community.

The CLA/Ken Haycock Award—established in honor of educator, administrator, advocate, and former CLA President Ken Haycock—honors an individual for demonstrating exceptional success in enhancing public recognition and appreciation of librarianship. The 2011 recipient was Allan Wilson, chief librarian, Prince George (British Columbia) Public Library.

The CLA/Information Today Award for Innovative Technology went to the Red Deer (Alberta) Public Library. The award recognizes innovative use of technology to foster community awareness and engagement in the political process.

The CLA/3M Canada Award for Achievement in Technical Services was presented to the Wilfred Laurier University Library for the project "Voyager-Banner Financials Interface Project."

The 28th annual student article contest was won by Richard Anderson for "Information Visualization in Children's Picture Books."

Conclusion

CLA is constantly adapting to meet the needs of its members and the broader library community in Canada. The association achieved tangible success with government on some key files, and efforts continued to advance issues such as copyright and the library book rate. Promoting public awareness of the role and importance of libraries and literacy remains a key CLA function.

Special Libraries Association

331 South Patrick St., Alexandria, VA 22314
703-647-4900, fax 703-647-4901
E-mail membership@sla.org
World Wide Web http://www.sla.org

Janice R. Lachance
Chief Executive Officer

Headquartered in Alexandria, Virginia, the Special Libraries Association (SLA) is a global organization for information professionals and their strategic partners. SLA represents thousands of information experts and knowledge managers in 85 countries who collect, analyze, evaluate, package, and disseminate information to facilitate strategic decision making. SLA members are known for finding innovative ways to contribute to the overall goals of their organizations, regardless of industry.

SLA's 9,000-plus members work in various settings including Fortune 500 companies, not-for-profit organizations, consulting firms, government agencies, technical and academic institutions, museums, law firms, and medical facilities. SLA promotes and strengthens its members through learning, advocacy, and networking initiatives.

History and Membership

SLA was founded in 1909 by John Cotton Dana and a group of librarians who believed that libraries serving business, government, social agencies, and the academic community were very different from other libraries. Dana recognized a need for unity within the special librarian profession, and his initial goal was to provide numerous and continuous opportunities to achieve that unity. The association still identifies with this initial goal more than a century later. The founders believed that these libraries operated using a different philosophy and more-diverse resources than the typical public or school library.

These "special"—or, more aptly, "specialized"—libraries at first were distinguished by being subject collections with a specialized clientele, but gradually it was recognized that their chief characteristic was that they existed to serve the organization of which they were a part. Their purpose was not education per se, but the delivery of practical, focused, and decision-ready information to the executives and other clients within their organizations. Specialist librarians, commonly referred to today as "information professionals," are unique in their relationship with their users and customers, and are proactive partners in information and knowledge management.

SLA members are focused on early adoption of technology tools, and are increasingly assuming nontraditional roles to benefit their organizations through information service. SLA defines information professionals as people who strategically and expertly use information to advance their organizations.

Information professionals contribute to a diverse variety of industries, but their expertise can be classified into a few broad categories.

Corporate information professionals synthesize and analyze information to help executives make sound business decisions that contribute to short- and long-term growth. This information includes market research, competitive intelligence, product research and due diligence, and financial portfolio analyses.

Government information professionals organize and deliver information for congressional, parliamentary, judicial, and executive leaders to enable policy decisions at the local, state, and federal levels.

Academic librarians organize, digitize, and deliver research information so that faculty can effectively relay knowledge to students, and students can follow the right methods of gathering information for research projects and dissertations.

Legal librarians contribute case research, package that research in ways that are accepted in civil and criminal courts, and conduct patent research for publishing firms and other organizations that are responsible for and use intellectual property and protected materials.

Medical librarians conduct research to support hospitals, medical practices, and pharmaceutical companies pursuing patents, issuing papers and reports to their communities, and serving their constituents through medicine and medical equipment and facilities.

SLA empowers its members by focusing on three crucial areas: learning, networking, and advocacy. These underpinnings prompted the organization's founders to form a cooperative association, and they are still the fundamental benefits SLA provides information professionals today.

Core Values

The association's core values are:

- Leadership—Strengthening members' roles as information leaders in their organizations and communities
- Service—Responding to clients' needs by adding qualitative and quantitative value to their information services
- Innovation and continuous learning—Embracing innovative solutions for the enhancement of services and intellectual advancement within the profession
- Results and accountability—Delivering measurable results in the information economy and members' organizations; the association and its members are expected to operate with the highest level of ethics and honesty
- Collaboration and partnering—Providing opportunities and a consistent platform, both online and in person, to meet, communicate, collaborate, and partner within the information industry and the business community

Chapters, Divisions, and Caucuses

SLA chapter membership provides a network of information professionals in geographic communities or regions, while SLA division membership links information professionals within topical areas of expertise. SLA membership includes membership in one chapter and one division. For a small fee, members can join additional chapters, divisions, and caucuses.

SLA is organized into 55 regional chapters in the United States, Canada, Europe, Asia, and the Middle East; 27 divisions representing a variety of industries; and 10 special-interest caucuses.

SLA's regional chapters elect officers, issue bulletins or e-newsletters, hold three to nine program meetings a year, hold niche conferences, and manage blogs. Members may affiliate with the chapter nearest their own mailing address (either business or residence).

SLA divisions represent the fields to which SLA members contribute their expertise and information services. Each division elects officers, publishes a newsletter, manages a Web site, and holds meetings both in person and virtually to discuss current trends and connect with corporate partners. They also conduct sessions, panels, and, in some cases, continuing education courses during the association's Annual Conference. The association added an Academic Division in 2008 and a Taxonomy Division in 2009.

A caucus is an informal network of members gathered to discuss a specific topic or discipline, not necessarily relating to their individual day-to-day work. Examples of SLA caucuses include the Futurist Caucus (using science fiction films and stories to find parallels to where the profession is headed in the digital age), the User-Experience Caucus (the association's newest caucus, examining how users interact with libraries and information centers, and how this interaction can be made more efficient and valuable), and the Baseball Caucus (discussing everything from current events in the baseball community to methods of organizing and analyzing baseball statistics).

Governance

SLA is governed by a board of directors elected by the membership. The board and the association both operate on a calendar year, with newly elected officers, as well as chapter and division leaders, taking office in January. SLA's president in 2012 is Brent Mai, head librarian of Concordia University in Portland, Oregon. Its president-elect is Deb Hunt, principal of Information Edge, a research firm she started. Janice R. Lachance is the association's chief executive officer. [Additional officers are listed in SLA's directory entry in Part 6 of this volume—*Ed.*].

Programs and Services

Click University

SLA's Click University (Click U), launched in 2005, is an online learning community focusing on continuing professional education for information professionals. Click U is primarily designed to give SLA members state-of-the-art learning opportunities in partnership with industry thought leaders. Courses on new software, new technology, management, communications, copyright laws and issues, leadership, and research uses of social media enhance the skills acquired through traditional library and information science education. Click U and its programs are available to SLA members and nonmembers. The majority of the webinars offered through Click U are offered free of charge as SLA membership benefits, and are available to members only. The offerings that carry an additional fee are noted as "Click U Premium," including Click U at Annual Conference and Click U Certificate Programs, which members can use to improve their résumés and skill sets. Click U regularly adds programs and courses on topics ranging from public speaking to copyright law.

Click U Certificate Programs (Premium)

Click U provides certificate programs for information professionals who want to augment their information skills in such fields as knowledge management and copyright management. Thirteen Certificate in Copyright Management (CCM) and Certificate in Knowledge Management (CKM) programs are being offered in 2012, including two full-day courses at SLA's 2012 Annual Conference in Chicago July 15–18.

Continuing Education at Conference

The association offers in-person training and continuing education at its Annual Conference. Workshops (half day) or learning forums (full day) at the conference are designed to inspire participants to make an impact in their organizations. These courses give professionals tools they can use to make improvements in their organizations or bolster their personal toolkits and résumés. A total of 17 courses will be offered in 2012.

Future Ready Toolkit

A new resource and member benefit, the Future Ready Toolkit, was completed in late 2011 and is designed to give information professionals new and enhanced career skills. The toolkit builds upon SLA's Alignment Research project completed in 2009. Examples of tools include "Five Ways to Use Social Media in Your Job Search;" "Planning, Writing, and Presenting a Budget;" "Marketing and Branding;" and "Building a Network to Engage and Partner with Stakeholders." The toolkit can be found on SLA's Web site, and is a members-only benefit.

Advocacy

SLA serves the profession by advocating publicly on the value of the information profession. Its activities range from communicating with executives and hiring professionals on the important role information professionals play in the workplace to sharing the membership's views and opinions with government officials.

Public Policy Program

Government bodies and related international organizations play a critical role in establishing the legal and social framework within which SLA members conduct information services. Because of the importance of governments and international organizations to its membership, SLA maintains an active public policy program. SLA staff and the association's Public Policy Advisory Council monitor and proactively work to shape legislation and regulatory proposals that affect the association's membership.

SLA supports government policies that

- Strike a fair and equitable balance among the rights and interests of all parties in the creation, distribution, and use of information and other intellectual property
- Strengthen the library and information management operations of government agencies
- Promote access to government public information through the application of modern technologies and sound information management practices
- Encourage the development and application of new information and communications technologies to improve library services, information services, and information management
- Protect individual intellectual freedom and the confidentiality of library records, safeguard freedom of expression, and oppose government censorship
- Foster international exchange of information

With regard to the actions of government bodies and related international organizations in the policy areas listed above, the association will

- Monitor executive, legislative, and judicial actions and initiatives at the national and international level, and to the extent practical at various local levels
- Educate key decision-makers on the concerns of SLA's members, and highlight the importance of these concerns
- Provide timely updates to the membership on critical issues and actions
- Encourage and empower members to influence public action and legislation by expressing their opinions
- Develop cooperative relationships with like-minded organizations to expand SLA's visibility and impact

In 2012 SLA will oppose the Research Works Act, and will support the Lubuto Library Project, amendments to the Presidential Records Act, OpenTheGovernment.org, and any initiative to improve the transparency of public institutions and the availability of their records and research.

Employment and Career Services

SLA's online Career Center includes a variety of services to meet the career needs of members, including career coaching, articles and resources such as podcasts, and career disruption assistance mentoring. It includes a job board where employers publicize library job opportunities to a targeted audience of professionals with master's degrees in library and information science. SLA members and nonmembers have access to the listings on the job board, but only members are able to utilize resources such as career coaching articles.

SLA Career Connections is the in-person educational component of SLA's career services and takes place at the Annual Conference. At the 2012 conference, speakers will address how résumés can be leveraged as marketing tools, how to make the most of difficult situations at work and in the job market, and how to elevate a career role to a leadership position. Speakers will be information professionals who also carry deep experience of career coaching and career-focused presentations.

SLA invites universities specializing in library and information science education to partner with it in providing student members with information on the job market, job search strategies, and relevant job opportunities.

Information Center

The SLA Information Center provides referral services and resources to members to assist them in their day-to-day tasks and management decisions, and in their roles as SLA leaders.

Professional and Student Networks

SLA's student groups are affiliated with accredited graduate schools of library and information science around the world. Student members enjoy all the benefits of SLA membership at a lower cost. They become part of a network of peers, gain professional advice, and make industry contacts well in advance of officially starting their careers as information professionals.

Publications, Blogs, and Newsletters

Information Outlook

SLA's magazine *Information Outlook* provides news, features, and evaluation of trends in information management. Articles are written by information industry thought leaders, SLA's senior editor and chief executive officer, and SLA members who have professional writing experience. Columns include "10 Questions," a member-spotlight that provides a platform for individual members to share on-the-job accomplishments and discuss their experience with SLA.

SLA Connections

The e-newsletter *SLA Connections* covers breaking information industry news and SLA's ongoing events and stories. The e-newsletter includes content from SLA's blogs.

Future Ready 365 Blog

Cindy Romaine, 2011 SLA president, started a blog aimed at "a daily blog post throughout the year of 2011 discussing how we are an adaptable, resilient, 'Future Ready' force of information professionals." The blog received more than 5 million hits within a year.

Unit-Blogs, Industry-Outreach Blogs, Division Newsletters

Aside from the blogs created on the association level, many chapters and divisions of SLA actively write their own blogs to keep their members and the rest of the association community informed on their recent activities. Many divisions (such as the Science and Technology Division) publish a monthly bulletin or newsletter featuring industry news as it relates to new technologies.

Social Media and Web 2.0

SLA has a presence on various social media networking sites, including Twitter, LinkedIn, and Facebook. These give members an opportunity to build community among themselves when physical meetings aren't possible. They also provide a way to share SLA information and are a route for customer service inquiries directed to SLA staff. Aside from social networks, SLA started a podcast, "My SLA," which is an avenue for member-to-member discussions. The podcast is available at http://my.sla.org.

SLA Awards and Honors

The SLA awards and honors program was created in 1948 to honor exceptional individuals, achievements, and contributions to the association and the information profession. The program's purpose is to bring attention to the important work of special librarians and information professionals within the corporate and academic setting.

SLA's highest honor is named after founder John Cotton Dana, and is granted to recognize a lifetime of professional achievement and contribution to the association. For a full list of past and current award recipients, visit the "Awards and Honors" page on SLA's Web site, http://www.sla.org. [The major SLA awards are included in "Library Scholarship and Award Recipients, 2011" in Part 3—*Ed.*]

Fund Raising

Launched in January 2012, SLA's Loyalty Club will help the association provide international networking opportunities at SLA Annual Conferences, deliver Click University webinars free of charge to members, and publish salary surveys, all of which carry costs that are not covered by annual membership dues. As donations increase, they will support other existing programs and services or fund the development and delivery of new ones. For more information, click the "Donate" button within the "Inside SLA" tab of http://www.sla.org.

Research

SLA funds surveys and projects, endowment fund grants, and research studies relating to all aspects of information management.

Grants

SLA offers grants on a rolling basis for research projects for the advancement of library sciences, the support of programs developed by SLA chapters, divisions, or committees, and the support of the association's expanding international agenda. Additionally, grants, scholarships, and stipends are offered separately by many of SLA's chapters and divisions. The program has been temporarily suspended, but the association plans to re-launch it in the coming year.

Events and Conferences

SLA's Annual Conference and INFO-EXPO brings together thousands of information professionals and provides a forum for discussion on issues shaping the information industry. The conference offers more than 400 events, programs, panel discussions, and seminars, and includes an exhibit hall with more than 200 participating companies.

The 2012 Annual Conference and INFO-EXPO will be held in Chicago beginning July 15. The scheduled keynote speaker is Guy Kawasaki, author, former chief technology evangelist for Apple, and founder of the online "digital magazine rack" Alltop. The theme of the conference is "Future Now: Operation Agility," which will build upon the previous theme of "Future Ready: Building Community" to arm attendees with skills and ideas for remaining integral components of the evolving global economy. Sessions and panels are planned to address the current need for enhanced search skills, adoption of new technologies and tools, connecting with new service and solution providers, and strengthening relationships with existing providers.

Part 2
Legislation, Funding, and Grants

Legislation

Legislation and Regulations Affecting Libraries in 2011

Emily Sheketoff
Executive Director, Washington Office, American Library Association

Jacob Roberts
Communications Specialist, Washington Office, American Library Association

Federal Funding

On December 23, 2011, President Barack Obama signed a $915 billion budget bill for fiscal year (FY) 2012. The bill, which passed the House 296–121 on December 16 and cleared the Senate the following day 67–32, provides year-long funding for departments including Defense, Energy, Homeland Security, Interior, Labor/Health and Human Services/Education, State, financial services, and the legislative branch. An FY 2012 budget bill was passed a month earlier for the departments of Agriculture, Commerce, Justice, and Transportation, in addition to other operations. The more recent bill covered many library programs, including money for school libraries, the Library Services and Technology Act (LSTA), and the U.S. Government Printing Office (GPO).

There was good news for literacy programs, with funding reinstated after a year's lapse. Congress had zeroed out funding for FY 2011 for the program Improving Literacy Through School Libraries. Run by the Department of Education, the program was designed to improve student literacy skills and academic achievement by providing schools with up-to-date library materials, and to ensure that school library media centers were staffed by state-certified school library media specialists. In developing the 2012 budget, both the Senate and House recognized that they cut the primary source of federal funding to school libraries, and the new budget appropriated $28.6 million for literacy. A minimum of half the appropriation must go to school libraries serving low-income communities while the rest will go to national not-for-profit organizations active in childhood literacy efforts, with the aim of making books available to children in low-income communities.

The budget appropriation for the Institute of Museum and Library Services (IMLS) included $185 million for Library Services and Technology Act (LSTA) funding. This is a 2 percent cut from the FY 2011 amount of $189 million. Under LSTA, the Grants to States program was funded at $156.6 million, Native American Library Services at $3.8 million, National Leadership Grants for Libraries at $11.9 million, and the Laura Bush 21st Century Librarian program at $12.5 million.

GPO was funded at $126.2 million, including Congressional Printing and Binding at $90.7 million and the Superintendent of Documents at $35 million.

President Obama made his FY 2013 budget request to Congress in February 2012.

Elementary and Secondary Education Act

The Elementary and Secondary Education Act (ESEA), which includes what was previously known as No Child Left Behind (NCLB), was scheduled to be reauthorized but Congress had not yet acted at the time this report was prepared. However, both the Senate and House held hearings and meetings throughout 2010 and 2011 on what should be included in a reauthorized ESEA bill. During this time, the American Library Association's (ALA's) Office of Government Relations (OGR) met with key legislators and staff to ensure that school libraries were adequately included in the considerations.

In a bipartisan effort in July 2011, Sen. Jack Reed (D-R.I.) and Sen. Thad Cochran (R-Miss.) introduced the Strengthening Kids' Interest in Learning and Libraries (SKILLS) Act (S. 1328), which would amend ESEA to include school libraries and help improve student academic achievement by ensuring that more students have access to effective school library programs. This bill received co-sponsorship from Sens. John Kerry (D-Mass.), Patty Murray (D-Wash.), John Rockefeller (D-W.V.), Tim Johnson (D-S.D.), and Sheldon Whitehouse (D-R.I.).

On October 20, 2011, the Senate Health, Education, Labor, and Pensions Committee voted on an ESEA reauthorization bill. In committee Senators Whitehouse and Murray introduced a measure that would amend ESEA to include the SKILLS Act and require the inclusion of effective school library programs in school improvement programs. However, Sen. Whitehouse was forced to withdraw this amendment before a committee vote because of a lack of support from other committee members. Whitehouse stated in committee that he hoped to work on this amendment and reintroduce it should ESEA reauthorization be brought to the Senate floor.

Consumer Product Safety Improvement Act

After three years of dispute, resolution was reached on the Consumer Product Safety Improvement Act (CPSIA) issue late in 2011. The legislation, introduced in 2008, sought to decrease the levels of lead and phthalates in products intended for children under the age of 12, with enforcement in the hands of the Consumer Product Safety Commission (CPSC) (http://www.cpsc.gov). Under the CPSC General Counsel's interpretation of the measure, children's books were to be subject to the same testing standards as toys. Given the high cost of testing, this was not a feasible option for libraries, and OGR, with other concerned parties, spent much time seeking changes to the proposal.

Late in the year a bill was introduced and quickly passed into law (becoming Public Law 112-28) to provide CPSC with greater authority and discretion in enforcing the consumer product safety laws. The law resulted in clarifying libraries' responsibilities for CPSIA requirements in two ways: first, it requires manufacturers of books to ensure that their processes are safe and fall within the limits of the law, and second, it excludes ordinary books and paper-based printed materials from third-party testing requirements.

The bill specifies that "each limit set forth . . . shall apply only to a children's product . . . that is manufactured after the effective date of such respective limit," requiring book manufacturers to ensure that their processes are safe and fall within the limits of the law. Later, it states that "the third party testing requirements established . . . shall not apply to ordinary books or ordinary paper-based printed materials," then defines both "ordinary books" and "ordinary paper-based printed materials."

The revised bill quickly passed the House (421–2) then was passed by the Senate, without amendment, by unanimous consent.

Copyright Legislation

Over the course of the year three antipiracy copyright-related bills were introduced in the Senate and the House. The bills shared a common characteristic, in that they took aim at any Web site beyond U.S. borders that was found to be distributing copyright-infringing products. Two of the three bills went further, however, incentivizing Internet companies to cut off access to infringing Web sites. This was felt to have a potential chilling effect on first amendment free speech rights and intellectual freedom, and threatened to weaken cybersecurity and privacy as well. OGR engaged ALA members in significant grassroots advocacy and worked to significantly slow the progress of the legislation. Work on the bills or similar measures was likely to continue in 2012.

ALA applauded Internet providers' efforts to protest two congressional bills, PIPA (S. 968, the Preventing Real Online Threats to Economic Creativity and Theft of Intellectual Property Act of 2011) and SOPA (H.R. 3261, the Stop Online Piracy Act). By either going dark or otherwise masking their Web sites, Wikipedia, Reddit, Craigslist, Google, Tumblr, and many others demonstrated the potential impact of these bills. The day-long darkening or blocking of Web sites highlighted fears that the bills would probably impose outright denial of access to information.

A third bill, the OPEN (Online Protection and Enforcement of Digital Trade) Act, introduced December 17 by Sens. Ron Wyden (D-Ore.), Jerry Moran (R-Kan.), and Maria Cantwell (D-Wash.), was seen by many as a more acceptable alternative to the other two bills, but ALA believes it needs considerable further study.

ALA has taken a stance in opposition to all three bills and has a "PIPA, SOPA and OPEN Act Quick Reference Guide" (http://www.districtdispatch.org/2012/01/pipa-sopa-and-open-act-quick-reference-guide). In addition, ALA opposes any legislation that would incentivize and likely increase surveillance of online activity, as promoted by these bills.

In another area of concern, Rep. Darrell Issa (R-Calif.) introduced the Research Works Act (H.R. 3699) in mid-December. This bill, cosponsored by Rep. Carolyn Maloney (D-N.Y.), would effectively turn back the clock on the National Institutes of Health (NIH) Public Access policy, put into place in 2008, which requires that the public have access to the published results of NIH-funded research.

The bill was referred to the U.S. House Committee on Oversight and Government Reform, of which Rep. Issa is chairman.

The Federal Research Public Access Act (FRPAA) (H.R. 5037), introduced in the 111th Congress, was modeled on the NIH Public Access policy. ALA strongly supported FRPAA as it aimed to ensure free, timely, online access to the published results of federally funded research by 11 U.S. federal agencies and departments. The bill, which had bipartisan support, mirrored a Senate version of FRPAA (S. 1373); a brief history of these bills is available at http://www.ala.org/ala/issues advocacy/access/accesstoinformation/publiclyfundedresearch/s1373.cfm.

ALA has been an ardent supporter of increasing access to information of all types, including federally funded research. It strongly opposes the Research Works Act and will keep it under close examination.

International Copyright

ALA's Office for Information Technology Policy (OITP) in Washington, with the Library Copyright Alliance (LCA), coordinates U.S. library advocacy at the Standing Committee on Copyright and Related Rights (SCCR) of the World Intellectual Property Organization (WIPO). LCA consists of three major library associations: ALA, the Association of College and Research Libraries (a division of ALA), and the Association of Research Libraries. LCA's current primary interests at WIPO are library copyright exceptions and limitations, a proposed treaty for an exception for people with print disabilities, and a proposed treaty on the protection of "traditional cultural expressions" or TCEs (also called "expressions of folklore," these include music, art, designs, names, signs and symbols, performances, architectural forms, and so forth).

A treaty or legal instrument for copyright exceptions would mandate that all WIPO member countries endorse and potentially implement exceptions for libraries and archives regarding TCEs, such as preservation, reproduction and supply, library lending, and liability limits. Under U.S. Copyright Law, these exceptions already exist, but some other countries don't have them. LCA has worked closely with the U.S. delegation to WIPO to advance library exceptions, and a U.S. statement on the importance of library exceptions and limitations was introduced to SCCR.

LCA continues to oppose a treaty or other legal instrument that would give copyright protection to TCEs. The alliance recognizes the issues facing indigenous communities in the United States that want to restrict access to TCEs, particularly sacred objects or ceremonies, but instead of a treaty it supports collaboration with indigenous communities to identify shared interests to address both TCE protection and access to information. These collaborations already take place in U.S. libraries and archives. LCA believes a TCE treaty would threaten the public domain, freedom of inquiry, research, scholarship and critique, preservation, and the ability to create derivative works. This is a highly contentious issue at the WIPO Intergovernmental Committee on the Protection of Traditional Cultural Expressions, Traditional Knowledge, and Genetic Resources (IGC), and is thought likely to continue for many more years.

Also at WIPO, a treaty on an exception for people with print disabilities has been on the agenda for four years. LCA supports a treaty that would allow that accessible copies of works be created for the print-disabled without authorization (similar to the U.S. Chafee Amendment §121). In addition, a treaty would allow the cross-border sharing of accessible content. English-speaking nations could borrow accessible content from the United States to meet the needs of the print-disabled. The international publishing community is strongly opposed to this proposal, but there were signs that some type of instrument would be successfully created.

Net Neutrality

As a supporter of Internet neutrality, ALA worked through OGR during 2011 to defeat anti-net-neutrality legislation in the Senate. The Federal Communications Commission (FCC) had codified and put into place an order to help ensure net neutrality principles during the year, but proposed Senate legislation would have stripped FCC of the ability to enforce the order. Grassroots advocacy by ALA members, coupled with targeted lobbying by OGR, helped defeat the bill in a close partisan vote. Defeat of the bill sent a message to Congress that libraries and the public they serve care deeply about a nondiscriminatory Internet and depend on it to provide unfettered access to all types of information.

National Library Legislative Day

On May 9–10, 2011, ALA hosted its annual National Library Legislative Day. On the first day, the Washington Office hosted a series of briefings at the Liaison Hotel in Washington, D.C., and later held a reception honoring Rep. Raul Grijalva (D-Ariz.) for his support of libraries. Also attending the reception was Sen. John Boozman (R-Ariz.) and more than 100 congressional staffers from a variety of House and Senate offices.

The following day, participants met with their elected officials. A total of 361 people from 47 states participated. More than 5,000 more participated in Virtual Library Legislative Day, in which librarians and their supporters were urged to contact the federal representatives via the Internet.

Emerging Advocacy Techniques

OGR continues to use Capwiz—an online program that supports the sending of advocacy messages—to send legislative action alerts to a list of more than 80,000 library supporters. Additionally, in November OGR organized a "Twitter blast" in which more than 1,000 "tweets" were sent to members of Congress on the same day asking them to support the inclusion of school libraries in the Elementary and Secondary Education Act (ESEA). OGR will continue to look for ways to utilize social media platforms for library advocacy.

Libraries for the 21st Century

The Program on America's Libraries for the 21st Century (AL21C) continued its work to identify and disseminate examples of outstanding applications of technology in library services, and to publish reports that discuss key topics of interest and their future implications for the profession.

The AL21C selected programs at Creekview High School in Canton, Georgia; Orange County Library System in Orlando, Florida; North Carolina State University Libraries in Raleigh; and OhioLINK in Columbus as winners of its second annual contest. Leaders from these libraries spoke at the 2011 ALA Annual Conference in New Orleans, and reprised the panel in the ALA Virtual Conference. Their presentations and case studies about their work are archived online at http://www.ala.org/cuttingedge.

A 2011 policy brief authored by ALA OITP fellow Roger Levien, "Confronting the Future: Strategic Visions for the 21st Century Public Library," also captured attention at the conference, where it was presented both live and via webinar. In the brief, Levien outlined challenges facing today's libraries, highlighted roles and functions of libraries, laid out alternate visions for public libraries of the future, and suggested a process for strategic decision making. He proposed that libraries must make strategic choices in four dimensions, each consisting of a continuum of choices between two extremes: a totally physical versus totally virtual library; an individual focus versus community focus; a collection library versus creation library; and portal versus archive. The report and webinar are archived at http://www.ala.org/oitp.

OITP also launched a publications series called OITP Perspectives in 2011. The purpose of the new series is to provide an outlet for topics that are more specialized than those covered by policy briefs. The series also provides a needed outlet for OITP to make a more rapid response to current issues. The first publication in the series was authored by Gwen Glazer, 2010 Google Policy Fellow at ALA. Titled "Digitizing Hidden Collections in Public Libraries," the paper offers an overview of digitization challenges facing small and medium-sized libraries, presents options for large-scale digitization projects, and suggests ways to share newly created digital collections. Two panels, one focused on digitization and one on discoverability, also were created to continue the conversation.

Benchmarks for Public Libraries

A national coalition was formed in 2011 to design and pilot a series of public access technology benchmarks for public libraries, with $2.8 million in funding from the Bill and Melinda Gates Foundation. The Edge Initiative (http://www.libraryedge.org)—an effort driven by a coalition of leading library and government organizations, including OITP and the Public Library Association—is developing the Edge benchmarks, a framework of goals and indicators intended to help libraries evaluate and continually improve their public technology services for communities.

The Edge benchmarks will be supported by training and a toolkit of customizable materials that will help library staff demonstrate the quality of their technology services to the communities they serve and convince decision-makers to continually reinvest in public technology access in libraries. The benchmarks and toolkit will be designed to be responsive to the library needs.

With the Urban Libraries Council as the project lead and facilitator, the coalition includes the state libraries of California, Oklahoma, and Texas; the library consortium Lyrasis; OCLC's WebJunction, an online community dedicated to the emerging technology and training needs of librarians; researchers at the University of Maryland and University of Washington; the International City/County Management Association; TechSoup Global; and the Gates Foundation.

Benchmark development will include three phases. To begin, the coalition will draft prototype benchmarks and collect feedback from the library field and local government leaders to ensure the benchmarks are meaningful and useful. Next, the group will test an initial set of benchmarks in communities in California, Oklahoma, and Texas. Finally, the prototype benchmarks will be refined with feedback from the pilot communities and the library field. It is anticipated the Edge benchmarks will be launched in the second half of 2012.

Digital Content and Libraries

During 2011 the continuing proliferation of e-books stimulated increasing demand for them in libraries. However, libraries only have limited access to e-books because of restrictions placed by publishers on how they are lent. Several ALA units were addressing the e-books issue, and digital content more generally. ALA leadership determined that an association-wide body was needed to develop the association's strategy and policy and coordinate work across ALA units. Consequently, the Digital Content and Libraries Initiative was created, with the Digital Content and Libraries Working Group as the principal entity to provide advice to the association on a variety of digital content issues.

ALA 2011–2012 President Molly Raphael appointed the members of the working group in October 2011. Sari Feldman, executive director of the Cuyahoga County Public Library, and Robert Wolven, associate university librarian at Columbia University, were named co-chairs. An ALA Connect site, e-mail list, and background materials were assembled and the group's first conference call was in November. Subgroups were formed to address business models/licensing, library produced/digitized content, accessibility, privacy, communications to the library community, and communications beyond the library community.

Digital Literacy

After the release of the National Broadband Plan (NBP) in 2010, federal agencies focused on issues that were identified as barriers to broadband adoption in the home. Of particular interest to libraries is a study showing that 23 percent of people who do not subscribe to broadband stated that it was lack of skills, lack of relevancy, and fear of going online that prevented them from doing so. Together, these issues have been combined under the umbrella of digital literacy by the Federal Communications Commission (FCC) and the National Telecommunications and Information Administration (NTIA), two government agencies tasked with carrying out recommendations made in the NBP.

Libraries of all types have always had programs that build information literacy skills for students and patrons. As technologies have changed and influenced how people search for, find, and use information, libraries have adapted their programs to ensure their users have the requisite skills—both technical and cognitive—to be able to take advantage of the resources and opportunities afforded by the digitization of information and the Internet. As national attention on these issues increased, OITP began working closely with FCC and NTIA staff to make sure that libraries were front and center in the conversations.

In response to one of the recommendations made in the NBP, NTIA, in partnership with nine other federal agencies, created a digital literacy portal (Digitalliteracy.gov) to collect resources for librarians, educators, and other professionals who provide digital literacy training. OITP staff reviewed the portal functionality and collected library resources for inclusion in the portal prior to its launch in May 2011. Since that time, materials from school, public, and academic libraries, as well as state library initiatives, continue to be added to the portal. Emphasis on job creation, work force development, and economic growth make the portal a strong resource for those librarians working with populations looking for a job or in need of upgrading their skills to 21st century requirements.

In fall 2011 FCC Chairman Julius Genachowski announced a series of digital literacy initiatives including a public-private partnership, Connect to Compete (http://connect2compete.org), which will provide eligible low-income families with less-expensive computers and Internet connections, as well as skills training. Genachowski also announced a plan to create a digital literacy corps that would provide training in schools and libraries across the country. Both projects are in the planning stages and are being further developed in 2012.

One outgrowth of OITP's work with FCC and NTIA was to establish a digital literacy task force consisting of ALA members from school, public, and academic libraries. The task force is charged with identifying best practices among libraries, where there might be gaps in practice, and where there are opportunities for libraries to excel in digital literacy work. The work of the task force will highlight the multiple roles libraries play in supporting a digitally literate society. For more information, visit http://www.districtdispatch.org/2011/05/oitp-digital-literacy-task-force-is-up-and-running).

Funding Programs and Grant-Making Agencies

National Endowment for the Humanities

1100 Pennsylvania Ave. N.W., Washington, DC 20506
202-606-8400, 800-634-1121
TDD (hearing impaired) 202-606-8282 or 866-372-2930 (toll free)
E-mail info@neh.gov, World Wide Web http://neh.gov

The National Endowment for the Humanities (NEH) is an independent federal agency created in 1965. It is one of the largest funders of humanities programs in the United States.

Because democracy demands wisdom, NEH promotes excellence in the humanities and conveys the lessons of history to all Americans, seeking to develop educated and thoughtful citizens. It accomplishes this mission by providing grants for high-quality humanities projects in six funding areas: education, preservation and access, public programs, research, challenge grants, and digital humanities.

Grants from NEH enrich classroom learning, create and preserve knowledge, and bring ideas to life through public television, radio, new technologies, museum exhibitions, and programs in libraries and other community places. Recipients typically are cultural institutions, such as museums, archives, libraries, colleges and universities, and public television and radio stations, as well as individual scholars. The grants

- Strengthen teaching and learning in the humanities in schools and colleges
- Preserve and provide access to cultural and educational resources
- Provide opportunities for lifelong learning
- Facilitate research and original scholarship
- Strengthen the institutional base of the humanities

Over the past 47 years, NEH has reached millions of Americans with projects and programs that preserve and study the nation's culture and history while providing a foundation for the future.

The endowment's mission is to enrich cultural life by promoting the study of the humanities. According to the National Foundation on the Arts and the Humanities Act, "The term 'humanities' includes, but is not limited to, the study of the following: language, both modern and classical; linguistics; literature; history; jurisprudence; philosophy; archaeology; comparative religion; ethics; the history, criticism, and theory of the arts; those aspects of social sciences which have humanistic content and employ humanistic methods; and the study and application of the humanities to the human environment with particular attention to reflecting our diverse heritage, traditions, and history and to the relevance of the humanities to the current conditions of national life."

The act, adopted by Congress in 1965, provided for the establishment of the National Foundation on the Arts and the Humanities in order to promote progress and scholarship in the humanities and the arts in the United States. The act included the following findings:

- The arts and the humanities belong to all the people of the United States.
- The encouragement and support of national progress and scholarship in the humanities and the arts, while primarily matters for private and local initiative, are also appropriate matters of concern to the federal government.
- An advanced civilization must not limit its efforts to science and technology alone, but must give full value and support to the other great branches of scholarly and cultural activity in order to achieve a better understanding of the past, a better analysis of the present, and a better view of the future.
- Democracy demands wisdom and vision in its citizens. It must therefore foster and support a form of education, and access to the arts and the humanities, designed to make people of all backgrounds and locations masters of technology and not its unthinking servants.
- It is necessary and appropriate for the federal government to complement, assist, and add to programs for the advancement of the humanities and the arts by local, state, regional, and private agencies and their organizations. In doing so, the government must be sensitive to the nature of public sponsorship. Public funding of the arts and humanities is subject to the conditions that traditionally govern the use of public money. Such funding should contribute to public support and confidence in the use of taxpayer funds. Public funds provided by the federal government ultimately must serve public purposes the Congress defines.
- The arts and the humanities reflect the high place accorded by the American people to the nation's rich culture and history and to the fostering of mutual respect for the diverse beliefs and values of all persons and groups.

What NEH Grants Accomplish

Since its founding, NEH has awarded more than 67,700 competitive grants.

Interpretive Exhibitions

Interpretive exhibitions provide opportunities for lifelong learning in the humanities for millions of Americans. Since 1967 NEH has awarded more than $268 million in grants for interpretive exhibitions, catalogs, and public programs, which are among the most highly visible activities supported by the endowment. During 2011 NEH support financed 30 exhibitions; reading, viewing, and discussion programs; Web-based programs; and other public education programs at venues across the country.

Renewing Teaching

Over NEH's history, nearly 96,000 high school and college teachers have deepened their knowledge of the humanities through intensive summer study supported by the endowment; tens of thousands of students benefit from these better-educated teachers every year.

Reading and Discussion Programs

Since 1982 NEH has supported reading and discussion programs in the nation's libraries, bringing people together to discuss works of literature and history. Scholars in the humanities provide thematic direction for the discussion programs. Using selected texts and themes such as "Work," "Family," "Diversity," and "Not for Children Only," these programs have attracted more than 2 million Americans to read and talk about what they've read.

Chronicling America

NEH's National Digital Newspaper Program is supporting projects to convert microfilm of historically important U.S. newspapers into fully searchable digital files. Developed in partnership with the Library of Congress, this long-term project ultimately will make more than 30 million pages of newspapers accessible online. For more on this project, visit http://chroniclingamerica.loc.gov.

Stimulating Private Support

More than $1.685 billion in humanities support has been generated by NEH's Challenge Grants program, which requires most grant recipients to raise $3 in nonfederal funds for every dollar they receive.

Presidential Papers

Ten presidential papers projects, from Washington to Eisenhower, have received support from NEH. Matching grants for the ten projects have leveraged $7.65 million in nonfederal contributions.

New Scholarship

NEH grants enable scholars to do in-depth study. Jack Rakove explored the making of the Constitution in his *Original Meanings* and James McPherson chronicled the Civil War in his *Battle Cry of Freedom*. Projects supported by NEH grants have earned 18 Pulitzer Prizes and 20 Bancroft Prizes.

History on Screen

Since 1967 NEH has awarded more than $291 million to support the production of films for broad public distribution, including the Emmy Award-winning series *The Civil War,* the Oscar-nominated films *Brooklyn Bridge, The Restless Conscience,* and *Freedom on My Mind,* and film biographies of John and Abigail Adams, Eugene O'Neill, and Ernest Hemingway. Twenty million Americans have watched Ken Burns' critically acclaimed *The War* (2007), which chronicles the United States in World War II. More than 8 million people saw the April 2010 debut of

The Buddha, a documentary made for PBS by filmmaker David Grubin, and it has been streamed into nearly 550 classrooms across the country.

American Voices

NEH support for scholarly editions makes the writings of prominent and influential Americans accessible. Ten presidents are included, along with such key figures as Martin Luther King, Jr., George C. Marshall, and Eleanor Roosevelt. Papers of prominent writers—among them Emily Dickinson, Walt Whitman, Mark Twain, and Robert Frost—are also available.

Library of America

Millions of books have been sold as part of the Library of America series, a collection of the riches of the nation's literature. Begun with NEH seed money, the more than 170 published volumes include the works of such figures as Henry Adams, Edith Wharton, William James, Eudora Welty, and W. E. B. Du Bois.

The Library of America also received a $150,000 grant for the publication of *American Poetry: The Seventeenth and Eighteenth Centuries* (two volumes) and an expanded volume of selected works by Captain John Smith—a key figure in the establishment of the first permanent English settlement in North America, at Jamestown, Virginia—and other early exploration narratives.

Technical Innovation

NEH support for the digital humanities is fueling innovation and new tools for research in the humanities. Modern 3D technology allows students to walk the sands of ancient Egypt alongside Ramses II in Digital Karnak (http://dlib.etc.ucla.edu/projects/karnak) or visit the 1964–1965 New York World's Fair (http://mcl.ucf.edu/nywf). Spectral imaging is being used to create an online critical edition of explorer David Livingstone's previously unreadable field diary.

Science and the Humanities

The scientific past is being preserved with NEH-supported editions of the letters of Charles Darwin, the works of Albert Einstein, and the 14-volume papers of Thomas Edison. Additionally, NEH and the National Science Foundation have joined forces in Documenting Endangered Languages (DEL), a multiyear effort to preserve records of key languages that are in danger of becoming extinct.

EDSITEment

EDSITEment (http://www.edsitement.neh.gov) assembles the best humanities resources on the Web, drawing more than 400,000 visitors each month. Incorporating these Internet resources, particularly primary documents, from more than 350 peer-reviewed Web sites, EDSITEment features more than 500 online lesson plans in all areas of the humanities. Teachers use EDSITEment's resources to enhance lessons and to engage students through interactive technology tools that hone critical-thinking skills.

Federal-State Partnership

The Office of Federal-State Partnership links NEH with the nationwide network of 56 humanities councils, which are located in each state, the District of Columbia, Puerto Rico, the U.S. Virgin Islands, the Northern Mariana Islands, American Samoa, and Guam. Each council funds humanities programs in its own jurisdiction.

Directory of State Humanities Councils

Alabama

Alabama Humanities Foundation
1100 Ireland Way, Suite 101
Birmingham, AL 35205-7001
205-558-3980, fax 205-558-3981
http://www.ahf.net

Alaska

Alaska Humanities Forum
161 E. First Ave., Door 15
Anchorage, AK 99501
907-272-5341, fax 907-272-3979
http://www.akhf.org

Arizona

Arizona Humanities Council
Ellis-Shackelford House
1242 N. Central Ave.
Phoenix, AZ 85004-1887
602-257-0335, fax 602-257-0392
http://www.azhumanities.org

Arkansas

Arkansas Humanities Council
407 President Clinton Ave., Suite 201
Little Rock, AR 72201
501-320-5761, fax 501-537-4550
http://www.arkhums.org

California

Cal Humanities
312 Sutter St., Suite 601
San Francisco, CA 94108
415-391-1474, fax 415-391-1312
http://www.calhum.org

Colorado

Colorado Humanities
1490 Lafayette St., Suite 101
Denver, CO 80218
303-894-7951, fax 303-864-9361
http://www.coloradohumanities.org

Connecticut

Connecticut Humanities Council
37 Broad St.
Middletown, CT 06457
860-685-2260, fax 860-685-7597
http://www.ctculture.org

Delaware

Delaware Humanities Forum
100 W. Tenth St., Suite 1009
Wilmington, DE 19801
302-657-0650, fax 302-657-0655
http://www.dhf.org

District of Columbia

Humanities Council of Washington, D.C.
925 U St. N.W.
Washington, DC 20001
202-387-8393, fax 202-387-8149
http://wdchumanities.org

Florida

Florida Humanities Council
599 Second St. S.
St. Petersburg, FL 33701-5005
727-873-2000, fax 727-873-2014
http://www.flahum.org

Georgia

Georgia Humanities Council
50 Hurt Plaza S.E., Suite 595
Atlanta, GA 30303-2915
404-523-6220, fax 404-523-5702
http://www.georgiahumanities.org

Hawaii

Hawai'i Council for the Humanities
First Hawaiian Bank Bldg.
3599 Waialae Ave., Room 25
Honolulu, HI 96816
808-732-5402, fax 808-732-5432
http://www.hihumanities.org

Idaho

Idaho Humanities Council
217 W. State St.
Boise, ID 83702
208-345-5346, fax 208-345-5347
http://www.idahohumanities.org

Illinois

Illinois Humanities Council
17 N. State St., No. 1400
Chicago, IL 60602-3296
312-422-5580, fax 312-422-5588
http://www.prairie.org

Indiana

Indiana Humanities
1500 N. Delaware St.
Indianapolis, IN 46202
317-638-1500, fax 317-634-9503
http://www.indianahumanities.org

Iowa

Humanities Iowa
100 LIB RM 4039
Iowa City, IA 52242-5000
319-335-4153, fax 319-335-4154
http://www.humanitiesiowa.org

Kansas

Kansas Humanities Council
112 S.W. Sixth Ave., Suite 210
Topeka, KS 66603
785-357-0359, fax 785-357-1723
http://www.kansashumanities.org

Kentucky

Kentucky Humanities Council
206 E. Maxwell St.
Lexington, KY 40508

859-257-5932, fax 859-257-5933
http://www.kyhumanities.org

Louisiana

Louisiana Endowment for the Humanities
938 Lafayette St., Suite 300
New Orleans, LA 70113-1782
504-523-4352, fax 504-529-2358
http://www.leh.org

Maine

Maine Humanities Council
674 Brighton Ave.
Portland, ME 04102-1012
207-773-5051, fax 207-773-2416
http://www.mainehumanities.org

Maryland

Maryland Humanities Council
108 W. Centre St.
Baltimore, MD 21201-4565
410-685-0095, fax 410-685-0795
http://www.mdhc.org

Massachusetts

Mass Humanities
66 Bridge St.
Northampton, MA 01060
413-584-8440, fax 413-584-8454
http://www.masshumanities.org

Michigan

Michigan Humanities Council
119 Pere Marquette Drive, Suite 3B
Lansing, MI 48912-1270
517-372-7770, fax 517-372-0027
http://michiganhumanities.org

Minnesota

Minnesota Humanities Center
987 E. Ivy Ave.
St. Paul, MN 55106-2046
651-774-0105, fax 651-774-0205
http://www.minnesotahumanities.org

Mississippi

Mississippi Humanities Council

3825 Ridgewood Rd., Room 311
Jackson, MS 39211
601-432-6752, fax 601-432-6750
http://www.mshumanities.org

Missouri

Missouri Humanities Council
543 Hanley Industrial Court, Suite 201
St. Louis, MO 63144-1905
314-781-9660, fax 314-781-9681
http://www.mohumanities.org

Montana

Humanities Montana
311 Brantly
Missoula, MT 59812-7848
406-243-6022, fax 406-243-4836
http://www.humanitiesmontana.org

Nebraska

Nebraska Humanities Council
215 Centennial Mall South, Suite 330
Lincoln, NE 68508
402-474-2131, fax 402-474-4852
http://www.nebraskahumanities.org/

Nevada

Nevada Humanities
1034 N. Sierra St.
Reno, NV 89507
775-784-6587, fax 775-784-6527
http://www.nevadahumanities.org

New Hampshire

New Hampshire Humanities Council
117 Pleasant St.
Concord, NH 03301-3852
603-224-4071, fax 603-224-4072
http://www.nhhc.org

New Jersey

New Jersey Council for the Humanities
28 W. State St., 6th floor
Trenton, NJ 08608
609-695-4838, fax 609-695-4929
http://www.njch.org

New Mexico

New Mexico Humanities Council
MSC06 3570
1 University of New Mexico
Albuquerque, NM 87131-0001
505-277-3705, fax 505-277-6056
http://www.nmhum.org

New York

New York Council for the Humanities
150 Broadway, Suite 1700
New York, NY 10038
212-233-1131, fax 212-233-4607
http://www.nyhumanities.org

North Carolina

North Carolina Humanities Council
122 North Elm St.
Greensboro, NC 27401
336-334-5325, fax 336-334-5052
http://www.nchumanities.org

North Dakota

North Dakota Humanities Council
418 E. Broadway, Suite 8
P.O. Box 2191
Bismarck, ND 58502
701-255-3360, fax 701-223-8724
http://www.nd-humanities.org

Ohio

Ohio Humanities Council
471 E. Broad St., Suite 1620
Columbus, OH 43215-3857
614-461-7802, fax 614-461-4651
http://www.ohiohumanities.org

Oklahoma

Oklahoma Humanities Council
Festival Plaza
428 W. California, Suite 270
Oklahoma City, OK 73102
405-235-0280, fax 405-235-0289
http://www.okhumanitiescouncil.org

Oregon

Oregon Council for the Humanities
813 S.W. Alder St., Suite 702

Portland, OR 97205
503-241-0543, fax 503-241-0024
http://www.oregonhum.org

Pennsylvania

Pennsylvania Humanities Council
325 Chestnut St., Suite 715
Philadelphia, PA 19106-2607
215-925-1005, fax 215-925-3054
http://www.pahumanities.org

Rhode Island

Rhode Island Council for the Humanities
131 Washington St., Suite 210
Providence, RI 02903
401-273-2250, fax 401-454-4872
http://www.rihumanities.org

South Carolina

Humanities Council of South Carolina
P.O. Box 5287
Columbia, SC 29250
803-771-2477, fax 803-771-2487
http://www.schumanities.org

South Dakota

South Dakota Humanities Council
1215 Trail Ridge Rd., Suite A
Brookings, SD 57006
605-688-6113, fax 605-688-4531
http://sdhumanities.org

Tennessee

Humanities Tennessee
306 Gay St., Suite 306
Nashville, TN 37201
615-770-0006, fax 615-770-0007
http://www.humanitiestennessee.org

Texas

Humanities Texas
1410 Rio Grande St.
Austin, TX 78701
512-440-1991, fax 512-440-0115
http://www.humanitiestexas.org

Utah

Utah Humanities Council

202 W. 300 North
Salt Lake City, UT 84103
801-359-9670, fax 801-531-7869
http://www.utahhumanities.org

Vermont

Vermont Humanities Council
11 Loomis St.
Montpelier, VT 05602
802-262-2626, fax 802-262-2620
http://www.vermonthumanities.org

Virginia

Virginia Foundation for the Humanities and
    Public Policy
145 Ednam Drive
Charlottesville, VA 22903-4629
434-924-3296, fax 434-296-4714
http://www.virginiafoundation.org

Washington

Humanities Washington
1204 Minor Ave.
Seattle, WA 98101-2825
206-682-1770, fax 206-682-4158
http://www.humanities.org

West Virginia

West Virginia Humanities Council
1310 Kanawha Blvd. East
Charleston, WV 25301
304-346-8500, fax 304-346-8504
http://www.wvhumanities.org

Wisconsin

Wisconsin Humanities Council
222 S. Bedford St., Suite F
Madison, WI 53703-3688
608-262-0706, fax 608-263-7970
http://www.wisconsinhumanities.org

Wyoming

Wyoming Humanities Council
1315 E. Lewis St.
Laramie, WY 82072-3459
307-721-9243, fax 307-742-4914
http://www.uwyo.edu/humanities

American Samoa

Amerika Samoa Humanities Council
P.O. Box 5800
Pago Pago, AS 96799
684-633-4870, fax 684-633-4873
http://amerikasamoahumanitiescouncil.org

Guam

Guam Humanities Council
222 Chalan Santo Papa
Reflection Center, Suite 106
Hagatna, Guam 96910
671-472-4460, fax 671-472-4465
http://www.guamhumanitiescouncil.org

Northern Marianas Islands

Northern Marianas Humanities Council

P.O. Box 506437
Saipan, MP 96950
670-235-4785, fax 670-235-4786
http://www.nmihumanities.org

Puerto Rico

Fundación Puertorriqueña de las Humanidades
Box 9023920
San Juan, PR 00902-3920
787-721-2087, fax 787-721-2684
http://www.fphpr.org

Virgin Islands

Virgin Islands Humanities Council
1826 Kongens Gade
St. Thomas, VI 00802-6746
340-776-4044, fax 340-774-3972
http://www.vihumanities.org

NEH Overview

Bridging Cultures

Bridging Cultures is a special endowment-wide initiative that highlights the role of the humanities in enhancing understanding and respect for diverse cultures and subcultures within America's borders and around the globe.

The initiative encourages projects that explore the ways in which cultures have influenced society. With the aim of revitalizing intellectual and civic life through the humanities, NEH welcomes projects that expand both scholarly and public discussion of diverse countries, peoples, and cultural and intellectual traditions worldwide.

Contact: 202-606-8337, e-mail bridgingcultures@neh.gov.

Division of Education Programs

Through grants to educational institutions and professional development programs for scholars and teachers, this division is designed to support study of the humanities at all levels of education.

Grants support the development of curriculum and materials, faculty study programs among educational institutions, and conferences and networks of institutions.

Contact: 202-606-8500, e-mail education@neh.gov.

Seminars and Institutes

Grants support summer seminars and institutes in the humanities for college and school teachers. These faculty development activities are conducted at colleges and universities in the United States and abroad. Those wishing to participate in seminars should submit their seminar applications to the seminar director.

Contact: 202-606-8471, e-mail sem-inst@neh.gov.

Landmarks of American History and Culture

Grants for Landmarks workshops provide support to school teachers and community college faculty. These professional development workshops are conducted at or near sites important to American history and culture (such as presidential residences or libraries, colonial era settlements, major battlefields, historic districts, and sites associated with major writers or artists) to address central themes and issues in American history, government, literature, art history, and related subjects in the humanities.

Contact: 202-606-8463, e-mail landmarks@neh.gov.

Division of Preservation and Access

Grants are made for projects that will create, preserve, and increase the availability of resources important for research, education, and public programming in the humanities.

Support may be sought to preserve the intellectual content and aid bibliographic control of collections; to compile bibliographies, descriptive catalogs, and guides to cultural holdings; and to create dictionaries, encyclopedias, databases, and electronic archives. Applications also may be submitted for education and training projects dealing with issues of preservation or access; for research and development leading to improved preservation and access standards, practices, and tools; and for projects to digitize historic U.S. newspapers and to document endangered languages. Grants are also made to help smaller cultural repositories preserve and care for their humanities collections. Proposals may combine preservation and access activities within a single project.

Contact: 202-606-8570, e-mail preservation@neh.gov.

Division of Public Programs

Public humanities programs promote lifelong learning in American and world history, literature, comparative religion, philosophy, and other fields of the humanities. They offer new insights into familiar subjects and invite conversation about important humanities ideas and questions.

The Division of Public Programs supports a wide range of public humanities programs that reach large and diverse public audiences through a variety of program formats, including interpretive exhibitions, radio and television broadcasts, lectures, symposia, interpretive multimedia projects, printed materials, and reading and discussion programs.

Grants support the development and production of television, radio, and digital media programs; the planning and implementation of museum exhibitions, the interpretation of historic sites, the production of related publications, multimedia components, and educational programs; and the planning and implementation of reading and discussion programs, lectures, symposia, and interpretive exhibitions of books, manuscripts, and other library resources.

Contact: 202-606-8269, e-mail publicpgms@neh.gov.

Division of Research Programs

Through fellowships to individual scholars and grants to support complex, frequently collaborative research, the Division of Research Programs contributes to the creation of knowledge in the humanities.

Fellowships and Stipends

Grants provide support for scholars to undertake full-time independent research and writing in the humanities. Grants are available for a maximum of one year and a minimum of two months of summer study.

Contact: 202-606-8200, e-mail (fellowships) fellowships@neh.gov, (summer stipends) stipends@neh.gov.

Research

Grants provide up to three years of support for collaborative research in the preparation of publication of editions, translations, and other important works in the humanities, and in the conduct of large or complex interpretive studies, including archaeology projects and humanities studies of science and technology. Grants also support research opportunities offered through independent research centers and international research organizations.

Contact: 202-606-8200, e-mail research@neh.gov.

Office of Challenge Grants

Nonprofit institutions interested in developing new sources of long-term support for educational, scholarly, preservation, and public programs in the humanities may be assisted in these efforts by an NEH Challenge Grant. Grantees are required to raise $3 in nonfederal donations for every federal dollar offered. Both federal and nonfederal funds may be used to establish or increase institutional endowments and therefore guarantee long-term support for a variety of humanities needs. Funds also may be used for limited direct capital expenditures where such needs are compelling and clearly related to improvements in the humanities.

Contact: 202-606-8309, e-mail challenge@neh.gov.

Office of Digital Humanities

The Office of Digital Humanities encourages and supports projects that utilize or study the impact of digital technology on research, education, preservation, and public programming in the humanities. Launched as an initiative in 2006, Digital Humanities was made permanent as an office within NEH in 2008.

NEH is interested in fostering the growth of digital humanities and lending support to a wide variety of projects, including those that deploy digital technologies and methods to enhance understanding of a topic or issue; those that study the impact of digital technology on the humanities; and those that digitize important materials, thereby increasing the public's ability to search and access humanities information.

The office coordinates the endowment's efforts in the area of digital scholarship. Currently, NEH has numerous programs throughout the agency that are actively funding digital scholarship, including Humanities Collections and Resources, Institutes for Advanced Topics in the Digital Humanities, Digital Humanities Challenge Grants, Digital Humanities Start-Up Grants, and many others. NEH is also actively working with other funding partners in the United States and abroad in order to better coordinate spending on digital infrastructure for the humanities. *Contact:* 202-606-8401, e-mail odh@neh.gov.

A full list of NEH grants programs and deadlines is available on the endowment's Web site, http://www.neh.gov.

Institute of Museum and Library Services
Office of Library Services

1800 M St. N.W., Ninth Floor, Washington, DC 20036-5802
202-653-4657, fax 202-653-4625
World Wide Web http://www.imls.gov

Susan H. Hildreth
Director

Mary L. Chute
Deputy Director for Libraries

Mission

The mission of the Institute of Museum and Library Services (IMLS) is to inspire libraries and museums to advance innovation, lifelong learning, and cultural and civic engagement. It provides leadership through research, policy development, and grantmaking.

Strategic Goals

- IMLS places the learner at the center and supports engaging experiences in libraries and museums that prepare people to be full participants in their local communities and the global society.
- IMLS promotes museums and libraries as strong community anchors that enhance civic engagement, cultural opportunities, and economic vitality.
- IMLS supports exemplary stewardship of museum and library collections and promotes the use of technology to facilitate discovery of knowledge and cultural heritage.
- IMLS advises the president and Congress on plans, policies, and activities to sustain and increase public access to information and ideas.
- IMLS achieves excellence in public management and performs as a model organization through strategic alignment of IMLS resources and prioritization of programmatic activities, maximizing value for the public.

There are 123,000 libraries and 17,500 museums in the United States. IMLS supports the full range of libraries, including public, academic, research, special, and tribal, and the full range of museums including art, history, science and technology, children's museums, historical societies, tribal museums, planetariums, botanic gardens, and zoos. Nearly 170 million people in the United States over the age of 14 (69 percent of the population) are library users, and every year 148 million over the age of 18 visit a museum.

Overview

Libraries and museums help create vibrant, energized learning communities. Our achievement as individuals and our success as a democratic society depend on learning continually, adapting to change readily, and evaluating information critically.

As stewards of cultural heritage, information, and ideas, libraries and museums traditionally have played a vital role in helping people experience, explore, discover, and make sense of the world. Through building technological infrastructure and strengthening community relationships, libraries and museums can offer the public unprecedented access and expertise in transforming information overload into knowledge.

The role of IMLS is to provide leadership and funding for the nation's museums and libraries, resources these institutions need to fulfill their mission of becoming centers of learning crucial to achieving personal fulfillment, a productive work force, and an engaged citizenry.

Under the Library Services and Technology Act (LSTA), these are among IMLS's responsibilities:

- To promote improvements in library services in all types of libraries to better serve the people of the United States
- To facilitate access to resources and in all types of libraries for the purpose of cultivating an educated and informed citizenry
- To encourage resource sharing among all types of libraries for the purpose of achieving economical and efficient delivery of library services to the public

In fiscal year (FY) 2011, Congress appropriated $200,856,000 for the programs and administrative support authorized by LSTA. The Office of Library Services within IMLS, under the policy direction of the IMLS director and deputy director, administers LSTA programs. The office comprises the Division of State Programs, which administers the Grants to States program, and the Division of Discretionary Programs, which administers the National Leadership Grants for Libraries program, the Laura Bush 21st Century Librarian program, the Native American Library Services program, and the Native Hawaiian Library Services program. IMLS also presents annual awards to libraries through the National Medal for Museum and Library Service program. Additionally, IMLS is one of the sponsoring organizations supporting the National Arts and Humanities Youth Program Awards (formerly the Coming Up Taller awards; in conjunction with the President's Committee on the Arts and the Humanities, the National Endowment for the Arts, and the National Endowment for the Humanities).

Library Statistics

The president's budget request for FY 2011 included funds for IMLS to continue administering the Public Libraries Survey and the State Library Agencies Survey, effective October 1, 2008. FY 2009 marked the first year that IMLS administered these surveys over a full collection cycle, from survey planning to collection and dissemination. Responding to concerns from the professional community, IMLS has reduced the time it takes to release survey results by six months. In addition to producing annual reports reporting the survey data, IMLS introduced new, shorter research products to highlight report findings. These new reports leverage the survey data to address a wide range of public policy priorities, including education, employment, community and economic development, and telecommunications policy.

In the Library Statistics section of the IMLS Web site (http://www.imls.gov/research), visitors can link to data search tools, the latest available data for each survey, other publications, data files, and survey definitions.

Public Libraries Survey

Descriptive statistics for more than 9,000 public libraries are collected and disseminated annually through this voluntary census. The Public Libraries Survey is conducted through the Public Library Statistics Cooperative (PLSC, formerly the Federal-State Cooperative System [FSCS]). In FY 2012 IMLS will complete the 24th collection of this data.

The Public Libraries Survey collects identifying information about public libraries and each of their service outlets, including street address, city, county, zip code, telephone number, library Web address, and library mailing address. The survey collects data about staffing; type of legal basis; type of geographic boundary; type of administrative structure; type of interlibrary relationship; type and number of public service outlets; operating revenue and expenditures; capital revenue and expenditures; size of collection (including number of electronic books and databases); current serial subscriptions (including electronic); and such service measures as number of reference transactions, interlibrary loans, circulation, public service hours, library visits, circulation of children's materials, number of children's programs, children's program attendance, total number of library programs, total attendance at library programs, number of Internet terminals used by the general public, and number of users of electronic resources per year.

This survey also collects several data items about outlets, including the location of an outlet relative to a metropolitan area, number of books-by-mail-only outlets, number of bookmobiles by bookmobile outlet, and square footage of the outlet.

The 50 states and the District of Columbia have participated in data collection from the survey's inception in 1989. In 1993 Guam, the Commonwealth of the Northern Mariana Islands, Puerto Rico, and the U.S. Virgin Islands joined in the survey. The first release of Public Libraries Survey data occurred with the release of the updated Compare Public Libraries Tool on the Library Statistics section of the IMLS Web site (http://www.imls.gov/research). The data used in this Web tool are final, but do not include imputations for missing data (imputation is a statistical means for providing an estimate for each missing data item).

Final imputed data files that contain FY 2009 data on more than 9,000 responding libraries and identifying information about their outlets were made available in August 2011 in the Library Statistics section of the IMLS Web site. The FY 2009 data were aggregated to state and national levels in a report, *Public Libraries in the United States: Fiscal Year 2009,* and released in June 2010 on the IMLS Web site. The Compare Public Libraries Tool and the Find Public Libraries

Tool were updated with FY 2009 data. FY 2010 data are expected to be available on these tools in 2012.

An important new feature of the public library data tools is the availability of locale codes for all administrative entities and outlets. These locale codes allow users to quickly identify which library outlets and administrative entities are located in cities, suburbs, towns, or rural areas. The new locale codes are based on an address's proximity to an urbanized area (a densely settled core with densely settled surrounding areas). The locale code system classifies territory into four major types: city, suburban, town, and rural. Each type has three subcategories. For city and suburb, these gradations are based on population size—large, midsize, and small. Towns and rural areas are further distinguished by their distance from an urbanized area. They can be characterized as fringe, distant, or remote. The coding methodology was developed by the U.S. Census Bureau as a way to identify the location of public schools in the National Center for Education Statistics' Common Core of Data. As of FY 2008, each library outlet and administrative entity survey has one of the 12 locale codes assigned to it.

Locale codes provide a new way to analyze library services. By incorporating objective measures of rurality and urbanicity into the data files, researchers and practitioners can benchmark services in a fundamentally different way by basing comparisons on community attributes as well as the attributes of the libraries themselves. Once communities of interest have been selected, comparisons can be made to any data available in the Public Library Survey whether they are financial, operational, or related to service output.

State Library Agencies Survey

The State Library Agencies Survey collects and disseminates information about the state library agencies in the 50 states and the District of Columbia. A state library agency (StLA) is the official unit of state government charged with statewide library development and the administration of federal funds under LSTA. StLAs' administrative and developmental responsibilities affect the operation of thousands of public, academic, school, and special libraries in the nation. StLAs provide important reference and information services to state government and sometimes also provide service to the general public. StLAs often administer state library and special operations such as state archives and libraries for the blind and physically handicapped and the state Center for the Book.

The State Library Agencies Survey began in 1994, and was administered by the National Center for Education Statistics (NCES) until 2007. The FY 2009 State Library Agencies Survey collected data on the following areas: direct library services; adult literacy and family literacy; library development services; resources assigned to such allied operations as archive and records management; organizational and governance structure within which the agency operates; electronic networking; staffing; collections; and expenditures. The FY 2010 survey was the 16th in the StLA series. The data are edited electronically, and before FY 1999, missing data were not imputed. Beginning with FY 1999 data, however, national totals included imputations for missing data. Another change is that beginning with FY 1999 data, the StLA became a Web-based data collection system. The most recent data available are for FY 2010. The survey database and report were released in December 2011.

National Medal for Museum and Library Service

The National Medal for Museum and Library Service honors outstanding institutions that make significant and exceptional contributions to their communities. Selected institutions demonstrate extraordinary and innovative approaches to public service, exceeding the expected levels of community outreach and core programs generally associated with its services. The medal consists of a prize of $10,000 to each recipient and there is an awards ceremony in Washington, D.C. The 2011 ceremony was held December 5, with journalist and author Cokie Roberts presenting the keynote address.

The winners of the 2011 National Medal for Museum and Library Service were Alachua County Library District, Gainesville, Florida; Brooklyn (New York) Museum; Columbus (Ohio) Metropolitan Library; EdVenture Children's Museum, Columbia, South Carolina; Erie (Pennsylvania) Art Museum; Hill Museum and Manuscript Library, Collegeville, Minnesota; Lewis Ginter Botanical Garden, Richmond, Virginia; Madison (Wisconsin) Children's Museum; San Jose (California) Public Library; and Weippe (Idaho) Public Library and Discovery Center.

State-Administered Programs

In FY 2011 approximately 85 percent of the annual federal appropriation under LSTA was distributed, through the Grants to States program, to the State Library Administrative Agencies (SLAAs) according to a population-based formula. The formula consists of a minimum amount set by law plus a supplemental amount based on population. The 2010 reauthorization requires that base allotments of $680,000 go to the states and $60,000 go to the Pacific Territories.

For FY 2011 the Grants to States program total appropriation was $160,032,000 (Table 1). State agencies can use the appropriation for statewide initiatives and services. They may also distribute the funds through competitive subgrants or cooperative agreements to public, academic, research, school, or special libraries. For-profit and federal libraries are not eligible applicants. LSTA state grant funds have been used to meet the special needs of children, parents, teenagers, the unemployed, senior citizens, and the business community, as well as adult learners. Many libraries have partnered with community organizations to provide a variety of services and programs, including access to electronic databases, computer instruction, homework centers, summer reading programs, digitization of special collections, access to e-books and adaptive technology, bookmobile service, and development of outreach programs to the underserved. The act limits the amount of funds available for administration at the state level to 4 percent and requires a 34 percent match from nonfederal state or local funds.

Grants to the Pacific Territories and the Freely Associated States (FAS) are funded under a Special Rule, 20 USCA 9131(b)(3), that authorizes a small competitive grants program in the Pacific region and the U.S. Virgin Islands. There are seven eligible entities: Guam, American Samoa, Commonwealth of Northern Mariana Islands, Federated States of Micronesia, Republic of the Marshall Islands, Republic of Palau, and U.S. Virgin Islands. The funds for this grant program are taken from the allotment amounts for the FAS (Micronesia, the Marshall Islands, and Palau). The territories (Guam, Samoa, the Northern Marianas, and the Virgin

Islands) receive allotments through the Grants to States program and, in addition, may apply for funds under the competitive program. In FY 2011 $389,806 was available for the seven entities. This amount included a set-aside of up to 5 percent for Pacific Resources for Education and Learning (PREL), based in Hawaii, to facilitate the grants review process. Therefore, the total amount awarded in FY 2011 was $376,942.

The LSTA-funded programs and services delivered by each SLAA support the purposes and priorities set forth in legislation. The individual SLAAs set goals and objectives for their state regarding the expenditure of Grants to States funds within the statutorily required five-year plan on file with IMLS. These goals and objectives are determined through a planning process that includes statewide needs assessments.

On a rotating basis, IMLS Grants to State program staff members conduct site visits to SLAAs to provide technical support and to monitor the states' success in administering the LSTA program. In 2011 program officers visited 13 SLAAs in Arkansas, California, Connecticut, the District of Columbia, Illinois, Iowa, Massachusetts, Nevada, New Hampshire, Pennsylvania, Puerto Rico, Utah, and Wyoming. Each site visit includes the critical review of the administration of the LSTA program at the SLAA as well as trips into the field to visit libraries that are recipients of subgrants or beneficiaries of statewide LSTA projects.

Table 1 / Library Services and Technology Act, State Allotments, FY 2011 (P.L. 112-10)
Total Distributed to States: $160,032,000[1]

State	Federal Funds from IMLS (66%)[2]	State Matching Funds (34%)	Total Federal and State Funds
Alabama	$2,567,650	$1,322,729	$3,890,379
Alaska	960,008	494,550	1,454,558
Arizona	3,324,148	1,712,440	5,036,588
Arkansas	1,838,337	947,022	2,785,359
California	15,497,372	7,983,495	23,480,867
Colorado	2,694,346	1,387,996	4,082,342
Connecticut	2,090,429	1,076,888	3,167,317
Delaware	1,034,832	533,095	1,567,927
Florida	8,111,592	4,178,699	12,290,291
Georgia	4,620,382	2,380,197	7,000,579
Hawaii	1,199,217	617,778	1,816,995
Idaho	1,299,688	669,536	1,969,224
Illinois	5,766,746	2,970,748	8,737,494
Indiana	3,254,929	1,676,782	4,931,711
Iowa	1,885,804	971,475	2,857,279
Kansas	1,809,993	932,421	2,742,414
Kentucky	2,409,463	1,241,239	3,650,702
Louisiana	2,480,805	1,277,990	3,758,795
Maine	1,208,487	622,554	1,831,041
Maryland	2,964,835	1,527,339	4,492,174
Massachusetts	3,323,269	1,711,987	5,035,256
Michigan	4,676,712	2,409,215	7,085,927

Minnesota	2,791,145	1,437,863	4,229,008
Mississippi	1,863,411	959,939	2,823,350
Missouri	3,080,330	1,586,837	4,667,167
Montana	1,070,859	551,655	1,622,514
Nebraska	1,400,237	721,334	2,121,571
Nevada	1,632,613	841,043	2,473,656
New Hampshire	1,211,002	623,850	1,834,852
New Jersey	4,170,801	2,148,594	6,319,395
New Mexico	1,485,647	765,333	2,250,980
New York	8,513,873	4,385,935	12,899,808
North Carolina	4,160,471	2,143,273	6,303,744
North Dakota	939,310	483,887	1,423,197
Ohio	5,307,272	2,734,049	8,041,321
Oklahoma	2,158,082	1,111,739	3,269,821
Oregon	2,213,648	1,140,364	3,354,012
Pennsylvania	5,633,066	2,901,882	8,534,948
Rhode Island	1,102,216	567,808	1,670,024
South Carolina	2,508,533	1,292,275	3,800,808
South Dakota	1,005,672	518,073	1,523,745
Tennessee	3,204,074	1,650,584	4,854,658
Texas	10,614,851	5,468,257	16,083,108
Utah	1,796,291	925,362	2,721,653
Vermont	929,254	478,707	1,407,961
Virginia	3,763,502	1,938,774	5,702,276
Washington	3,351,575	1,726,569	5,078,144
West Virginia	1,409,521	726,117	2,135,638
Wisconsin	2,946,913	1,518,107	4,465,020
Wyoming	898,190	462,704	1,360,894
District of Columbia	920,394	474,142	1,394,536
Puerto Rico	2,270,426	1,169,613	3,440,039
American Samoa	86,309	44,462	130,771
Northern Marianas	80,639	41,541	122,180
Guam	131,530	67,758	199,288
Virgin Islands	104,027	53,590	157,617
Pacific Territories[3]	257,272	132,534	389,806
Total[4]	$160,032,000	$82,440,727	$242,472,727

1 Maintenance of effort (MOE) reductions that resulted from MOE shortfalls reported on the FY 2008 Financial Status Report (reported and reviewed in FY 2010) have been applied to the FY 2011 allotment distribution. Those funds deducted from the states that did not meet their MOE requirement have been distributed proportionately across the states that did meet their FY 2008 MOE requirements.

2 IMLS federal funds are calculated using the current minimum base set into law (P.L. 108-81) and population figures from the U.S. Census Bureau.
Population data comes from the Census Bureau. Data used in the state allotment table are the most current published population estimates available on the first day of the fiscal year. Therefore, the population data used in the FY 2011 table is what was available on the Census Bureau Web site (http://www.census.gov/popest/states/index.html) on October 1, 2010. Population data for American Samoa, Commonwealth of Northern Mariana Islands, Guam, Virgin Islands, Republic of the Marshall Islands, Federated States of Micronesia, and Republic of Palau can be accessed at http://www.census.gov/cgi-bin/ipc/idbrank.pl. This table reflects what was available on October 1, 2010.

3 Aggregate allotments (including administrative costs) for Republic of Palau, Republic of the Marshall Islands, and Federated States of Micronesia are awarded on a competitive basis to eligible applicants, and are administered by Pacific Resources for Education and Learning (PREL).

4 Because of rounding to whole dollar amounts in the state allotments, some totals may be slightly adjusted to reflect actual total amounts.

Discretionary Grants Programs

IMLS began administering the discretionary grants programs of LSTA in 1998. In FY 2011 a total of $29,003,321 was allocated for discretionary programs. Individual discretionary grant programs awarded funds as follows: National Leadership Grants, $14,461,217; Laura Bush 21st Century Librarian Program, $11,227,761; Native American Library Services, $3,545,078; and Native Hawaiian Library Services, $565,700. (Several awards were made from non-FY 2011 funds, accounting for an additional distribution of $796,435 more than the FY 2011 allocation.)

National Leadership Grants for Libraries

The National Leadership Grants for Libraries program provides funding for research and innovative model programs to enhance the quality of library services nationwide. National Leadership Grants are competitive and intended to produce results useful for the broader library community.

During 2011 IMLS awarded 48 National Leadership Grants totaling $14,461,217 (Table 2). The program received a total of 210 applications requesting more than $80 million. Projects were funded in four categories: advancing digital resources, demonstration, research, and library-museum collaboration. In addition, IMLS offered Collaborative Planning Grants in all categories of the National Leadership Grants program. Collaborative Planning Grants were offered at two levels: Level 1 planning grants of up to $50,000 enable project teams from libraries, museums, or other partner organizations to work together on the planning of a single collaborative project in any of the National Leadership Grants categories; Level 2 planning grants of up to $100,000 support workshops, symposia, or other convenings of experts to discuss issues of national importance to libraries, archives, and/or museums, with the goal of producing a white paper that encourages multiple National Leadership Grant proposals addressing issues raised in the report. Partnerships with museums are not required for any projects except those in the library-museum collaboration category.

Advancing Digital Resources (maximum award $1 million)

Advancing Digital Resources grants support the creation, use, preservation, and presentation of significant digital resources as well as the development of tools to manage digital assets, incorporating new technologies or new technology practice. IMLS supported projects that

- Developed and disseminated new tools to facilitate management, preservation, sharing, and use of digital resources
- Increased community access to institutional resources through innovative use of existing technology-based tools
- Increased community access to institutional resources by improving practice in use, dissemination, and support of existing technology-based tools
- Developed or advanced participation in museum and/or library communities using social technologies in new ways

- Developed new approaches or tools for digital curation

Demonstration (maximum award $1 million)

Demonstration projects use available knowledge to address key needs and challenges facing libraries and museums, and transform that knowledge into formal practice. Funded projects

- Demonstrated and/or tested new practices in library and/or museum operations
- Demonstrated how libraries and/or museums serve their communities by fostering public value and implementing systemic changes in the field
- Established and/or tested standards and tools for innovative learning
- Demonstrated and/or tested an expansion of preservation or conservation practices

Research (maximum award $1 million)

Research grants support projects that have the potential to improve library and museum practice, resource use, programs, and services. Both basic and applied research projects are encouraged. Funded projects

- Evaluated the impact of library or museum services
- Investigated how learning takes place in libraries and museums, and how use of library and/or museum resources enhance learning
- Investigated how to improve the quality, effectiveness, or efficiency of library or museum management programs or services
- Investigated ways to enhance the archiving, preservation, management, discovery, and use of digital assets and resources
- Investigated or conducted research to add new knowledge or make improvements in the conservation and preservation of collections

Library-Museum Collaboration (maximum award $1 million)

This category helps to create new opportunities for libraries and museums to engage with each other, and with other organizations as appropriate, to support the educational, economic, and social needs of their communities. A partnership of at least one eligible library entity and one eligible museum entity is required. Additional partners are encouraged where appropriate. Both research and implementation projects are eligible. Grant funds supported innovative collaborative projects, whether they were new partnerships or were building on an existing collaboration. Funded projects

- Addressed community civic and educational needs
- Increased the organizations' capacity to serve as effective venues and resources for learning
- Used technology in innovative ways to serve audiences more effectively

Table 2 / National Leadership Grants for Libraries, FY 2011

Advancing Digital Resources

Brown University, Office of Research Administration　　　　　　　　$249,509

The libraries of Brown University and Wheaton College will collaborate to offer a new shared repository and a suite of publishing and preservation services for humanities scholars who wish to create electronic texts using Text Encoding Initiative (TEI) guidelines. The centralized TEI Archiving, Publication, and Access Service (TAPAS) responds to a need, particularly at small liberal arts colleges, for solutions that do not require extensive technical resources or large-scale funding.

Cornell University, Office of Sponsored Programs　　　　　　　　$249,495

To help academic libraries better serve scholars who are producing digital research data, the libraries of Cornell University and Washington University in St. Louis will conduct user needs analysis for selected scholars at both universities who wish to create and share research datasets with other scholars.

Northern Illinois University　　　　　　　　$575,000

The Northern Illinois University Libraries and partner libraries at Chicago State University, Illinois State University, Illinois Wesleyan University, and Western Illinois University will simultaneously test multiple collaborative digital preservation solutions and evaluate the suitability of each option for small and medium-sized college and university libraries.

Regents of the University of Michigan　　　　　　　　$948,122

University of Michigan Libraries, with partners at other universities, will continue work that has already investigated and recorded reliable determinations of the copyright status of more than 117,000 U.S. titles published from 1923 to 1963. The library and its partners will also begin making reliable copyright status determinations for foreign-published titles. Project partners include the college and university libraries of Baylor; Columbia; Dartmouth; Duke; Indiana; Johns Hopkins; Northwestern; Pennsylvania State; Princeton; California, Irvine; California, Los Angeles; California, San Francisco; Illinois at Urbana-Champaign; Maryland; and Minnesota.

Trustees of Indiana University　　　　　　　　$947,963

The Indiana University Digital Library Program, in partnership with Northwestern University Libraries, will develop an open-source software system to help academic libraries and archives manage digital audio and video collections and provide enhanced access to these collections.

University of Kentucky Research Foundation　　　　　　　　$195,853

University of Kentucky Libraries has created an Oral History Metadata Synchronizer (OHMS) tool that allows users to more easily search for specific terms within recorded interviews, and to know exactly at what times in the interview these terms occur. Working with the MATRIX Center at Michigan State, and with partner libraries at Baylor, Oklahoma State, and Cleveland State, the project team will further develop the OHMS into an open-source software tool that will be more compatible and interoperable with a variety of digital library and content management systems.

University of North Texas　　　　　　　　$268,458

To promote best practices and to increase the capacity of academic libraries to reliably preserve electronic theses and dissertations (ETDs), University of North Texas Libraries—together with the Networked Digital Library of Theses and Dissertations, the Educopia Institute/MetaArchive Cooperative, and the libraries of Virginia Tech, Rice, Boston College, Indiana State, Pennsylvania State, and the University of Arizona—will develop and share a toolkit of guidelines, educational materials, and software tools for lifecycle data management and preservation of ETDs.

Table 2 / National Leadership Grants for Libraries, FY 2011 *(cont.)*

Washington State University $484,772

Researchers at Washington State University will partner with Smallbean, Inc.; University of California, Berkeley; Association of Tribal Archives, Libraries, and Museums; CivicActions, Inc.; National Anthropological Archives; and the National Museum of the American Indian to deploy, evaluate, and refine a software tool, to be named Mukurtu, designed to accommodate tribal organizations' particular needs. The tool will subsequently be made available freely as open-source software.

Research

Drexel University $378,014

The Drexel University College of Information Science and Technology will investigate how teenagers use social networking Web technologies to find information, and identify key issues and preferences libraries should consider as they try to construct new reference and information services for teens online.

Drexel University $413,378

Drexel University's College of Information Science and Technology will lead a study, in cooperation the University at Buffalo, Getty Research Institute, ARTstor, and Indianapolis Museum of Art, to investigate and evaluate ways of improving library and museum searching and social tagging by presenting users with thesauri, taxonomies, and other structured vocabularies as a method of discovery for relevant content.

Health Sciences Libraries Consortium $434,231

The consortium will partner with the Pennsylvania School Librarians Association and the Education Law Center of Pennsylvania to identify and measure current gaps in Pennsylvania school libraries that may deter school systems statewide from effectively teaching needed 21st century skills to students. The project will also provide data and projections on the investments that would be needed to close identified gaps and achieve higher levels of student achievement.

Johns Hopkins University $600,000

The Johns Hopkins University Library System and its partners from Tufts University and the University of Illinois at Urbana-Champaign will develop collaborative virtual workspace, including collections and services, designed to support a new "collaborative lab culture" to explore and demonstrate ways that libraries can support new modes of collaboration in research and learning.

Kent State University $219,386

The project will explore strategies and develop prototype tools to support libraries and museums in efforts to find standards and practices that support greater interoperability of the descriptive and administrative information surrounding online resources.

Portland State University $999,493

The university, in collaboration with its partners, will conduct extensive mining and analysis of data for more than 23,000 adult users of the IMLS-funded Learner Web, a learning support system for adults. This research will provide information about the learning processes of various hard-to-serve populations and how libraries can better tailor tutoring opportunities to meet diverse needs. Partners include the state libraries of California, Louisiana, Minnesota, New York, and Texas.

Rutgers University $250,000

The university's School of Communication and Information will work with OCLC to investigate new models that permit more collaborative and sustainable delivery of virtual reference services, including models that rely on more extensive collaboration between librarians and subject experts.

Table 2 / National Leadership Grants for Libraries, FY 2011 *(cont.)*

Syracuse University $190,687

This study will evaluate the relationship between free voluntary reading in public library summer reading programs for youth and the development of information literacy skills.

University of Washington $635,000

Building on a 2009 research planning grant from IMLS, researchers from the university's Information School and partners (including the Early Learning Public Library Partnership, the Foundation for Early Learning, and the State Library of Washington) will investigate and test new ways to measure the effectiveness of early literacy programs in public libraries.

Demonstration

Board of Trustees, University of Illinois at Urbana-Champaign $239,528

Librarians and staff from the university library will demonstrate a nontraditional approach to library services by working with students and taking a "bottom up" collaborative design approach for mobile applications that support academic library users.

Purdue University $249,391

Purdue University Libraries will partner with the libraries of Stanford University, University of Minnesota, and University of Oregon to develop a training program in data information literacy for graduate students who will become the next generation of scientists.

Southeastern New York Library Resources Council $429,392

The council will lead a unique partnership of libraries, museums, community organizations, audio producers, broadcasters, and oral history digitization and content management consultants to digitize oral histories selected from repositories in the region. The effort will include producing a series of radio broadcasts from excerpts; creating linked and dynamic Web sites that showcase the collections, and creating innovative mobile applications.

University of Oregon $249,904

Building on previous work in other institutions and consortia, University of Oregon Libraries will build, evaluate, and demonstrate a new tool for searching across large numbers of collection descriptions from 36 different archives, and will link to other regional and national efforts. Partner institutions in this effort are the Orbis Cascade Alliance, Lewis and Clark College, Oregon State University, Pacific University, Seattle Municipal Archives, Western Washington University, Washington State University, and the University of Montana.

University of Utah $439,142

Working with OCLC, the Digital Library Federation, and Mountain West Digital Library, the University of Utah Libraries will test and evaluate a strategy for making library digital collections significantly more visible in common Web search engines.

Westchester Library System $450,000

Westchester Library System, in partnership with Lifetime Arts, Inc., and the American Library Association's Public Programs Office, will demonstrate a new model for public libraries to deliver and sustain meaningful instructional arts programs for an aging population.

Planning

American Antiquarian Society $49,639

The society, in partnership with the American Social History Project at the City University of New York Graduate Center, will conduct a collaborative planning project designed to lay the foundation for a long-term project called Contextualizing the Visual Archive for

Table 2 / National Leadership Grants for Libraries, FY 2011 *(cont.)*

Teaching. The goal is an online, open-source resource that will allow visual images from any library or museum collection to be linked to collection records and other materials.

American Library Association $33,968

The association will conduct a four-month planning grant as the beginning of a multiyear collaboration making StoryCorps services accessible to public libraries. StoryCorps is a nonprofit organization whose mission is to record, preserve, and share the stories of Americans from all backgrounds.

American Library Association $99,985

Two national summits will be convened to recommend strategies that help academic libraries better demonstrate their value, and better explain how their services align with the institutional goals of colleges and universities. The events will serve as the basis for a white paper that summarizes findings and establishes recommendations for future action.

California State University, Long Beach Foundation $49,960

The university and Pacific Directions will develop a strategy to collect and conserve documentation relating to genocide during the Pol Pot regime in Cambodia.

Orange County (Florida) Library System $50,000

The library system will work with community partners to prototype and evaluate the feasibility of creating, as a library service, an accessible online database of obituaries, and in so doing help build a meaningful history of the residents of the community.

Regents of the University of Michigan $49,957

This collaborative planning project will help shape an anticipated large-scale research project focusing on enhancement of health information infrastructures for marginalized urban communities.

University of Minnesota Libraries $99,500

The university libraries and the Penumbra Theatre will conduct a one-year collaborative planning project to assess interest in and barriers to archival preservation of a theater's full range of activities. The project will convene a national forum of artistic directors, board chairs, and administrative or marketing staff from regional and local theaters of varying sizes to identify factors that would assist theaters in archival preparation and planning.

University of North Carolina at Chapel Hill $99,074

The university's School of Information and Library Science, in partnership with the School of Library and Information Science at North Carolina Central University, will host a summit titled "Building a Bridge to Literacy for African-American Male Youth: A Call to Action for the Library Community."

University of Utah $49,943

The university library and its partners Orbis Cascade Alliance, the University of New Mexico, and Utah Academic Library Consortium will explore ways to improve the usability of software and systems designed to search groups of encoded descriptions of archival collections.

University of Virginia $66,187

The Miller Center of Public Affairs at the university will conduct initial planning and early-stage development of "Connecting Presidential Collections," a digital resource that will provide open access to archival collections on, about, or relating to all presidents of the United States.

Table 2 / National Leadership Grants for Libraries, FY 2011 *(cont.)*

University of Washington, Office of Sponsored Programs $49,623

The University of Washington, Kent State University, the University of North Carolina, JES and Company, and Talis, Inc., will plan for the development of an integrated online learning platform to teach library and museum staff the principles and process of creating metadata for the modern Web environment, with particular focus on designing for an open linked data environment.

University of Washington $50,000

The university's Project Information Literacy is conducting a planning project to help shape a future investigation into the ways college graduates use information literacy training they received during college during their first year after graduation as they seek employment, join the work force, and continue in their daily lives as "early adults."

University System of Georgia $97,843

The Georgia Public Library Service will organize a planning committee from approximately 40 national leaders with expertise in library accessibility to plan the development of an open-source software system for libraries that serve users with visual or other impairments that prevent their use of traditional printed and text-based materials.

Virginia Library Association $50,000

The association, in conjunction with the nonprofit Liberty's Promise, will work to produce a strategy for engaging low-income immigrant youth in rural communities through exposure to libraries and library careers.

Laura Bush 21st Century Librarian Program (maximum award $1 million)

This program was established in 2003 as the Librarians for the 21st Century program; the name was changed in 2006 in accordance with the provisions of IMLS's congressional appropriation. The program provides competitive funding to support projects to recruit and educate the next generation of librarians and library leaders, build institutional capacity in graduate schools of library and information science and develop faculty who will help in this endeavor, conduct needed research on the demographics and needs of the profession, and support programs of continuing education and training in library and information science for librarians and library staff.

In FY 2011 IMLS awarded 24 grants under the program, totaling $11,227,761 (see Table 3; additional awards were made from non-FY 2011 funds). A total of 114 applications requesting $55,826,525 were received.

The 2011 priorities for funding were

Doctoral Programs

- To develop faculty to educate the next generation of library professionals. In particular, to increase the number of students enrolled in doctoral programs that will prepare faculty to teach master's students who will work in school, public, and academic libraries.

- To develop the next generation of library leaders. In particular, to increase the number of students enrolled in doctoral programs that will prepare them to assume positions as library managers and administrators.

Master's Programs

- To educate the next generation of librarians; in particular, to increase the number of students enrolled in nationally accredited graduate library programs preparing for careers of service in libraries.

Research

- *Early Career Development Program*—To support the early career development of new faculty members who are likely to become leaders in library and information science by supporting innovative research by untenured, tenure-track faculty.
- *Research*—To provide the library community with information needed to support successful recruitment and education of the next generation of librarians; in particular, through funded research, to establish baseline data on professional demographics and job availability, and to evaluate current programs in library education for their capacity to meet the identified needs; and to conduct research and establish ongoing research capacity in the field of library and information science, particularly the evaluation of library and information services, assessment of the value and use of public libraries and their services by the public, and assessment of the public value and use of the Internet.

Preprofessional Programs

- To recruit future librarians. In particular, to attract promising junior high school, high school, or college students to consider careers in librarianship through statewide or regional pilot projects employing recruitment strategies that are cost-effective and measurable; and to introduce high school or college students to potential careers in library and information science.

Programs to Build Institutional Capacity

- To develop or enhance curricula within graduate schools of library and information science. In particular, to develop or enhance courses or programs of study for library and archives professionals in the creation, management, preservation, presentation, and use of digital assets; to broaden curricula by incorporating perspectives from other disciplines and fields of scholarship; to develop or enhance programs of study that address knowledge, skills, abilities, and issues of common interest to libraries, museums, archives, and data repositories; and to develop projects or programs in data curation as training programs for graduate students in library and information science.

Continuing Education

- To increase professional development and library and archive staff knowledge, skills, and abilities through programs of continuing formal education, informal education, and training.

Table 3 / Laura Bush 21st Century Librarian Program, FY 2011

Doctoral Programs

American Library Association $886,499

The association's Spectrum Doctoral Fellowship Program: Building Change will provide tuition and stipends for at least seven ethnically diverse students pursuing a Ph.D. in library and information science. Currently, only 15 percent of doctoral degrees awarded by library school programs are to ethnic minorities.

Syracuse University $741,936

Syracuse will recruit six doctoral students and provide them with an education, stressing research in issues relating to e-science librarianship or data curation. Syracuse will also disseminate its curricular materials to other library and information science programs, helping them produce future faculty with this specialization.

University of California, Los Angeles $609,344

The university and its partners, the University of Michigan and the University of Oklahoma, will provide scholarship support to doctoral students and untenured junior faculty to participate in week-long Archival Education and Research Institutes where they will train as archival professionals and scholars. The institutes stress the skills, knowledge base, and abilities to address current and emergent needs associated with rapid technological change, new forms of archiving and archival documentation, and cultural and societal diversity.

University of Tennessee $546,472

The SciData project at the university's School of Information Sciences will advance the field of digital scientific data curation by training a core group of eight master's graduates with a thorough understanding of digital data curation and scientific publishing. It will build a model for scientific data curation that other programs may adopt, and will continue previous recruiting relationships with minority-rich schools to attract more racially and ethnically diverse students to the field.

Master's Programs

Association of Research Libraries $456,807

The Association of Research Libraries/Music Library Association Diversity and Inclusion Initiative will provide financial support, a mentoring program, paid internships at partner institutions, and career placement services for a group of 15 master's degree students from traditionally under-represented racial and ethnic minority groups with educational backgrounds in music. Other partners are the music libraries at the University of Pittsburgh, University of Buffalo, University of Illinois at Urbana-Champaign, and University of North Texas.

Dance Heritage Coalition $526,072

The coalition is partnering with the Dance Division of the New York Public Library for the Performing Arts, Dance Notation Bureau, Theatre Research Institute of Ohio State University, Jacob's Pillow Dance Festival, American Dance Festival Archives, Herberger Institute School of Dance Archives of Arizona State University, and the Museum of Performance and Design Library on an innovative program to increase the number of professional librarians who specialize in dance and promote the visibility of and access to historically and culturally valuable material on dance.

University of Central Missouri $843,613

The Preparing PRAXIS Certified Librarians for Practice Project at the University of Central Missouri will prepare 50 school librarians to develop and maintain up-to-date school libraries. The project will offer scholarships enabling these librarians to earn a master's degree in library science and information services.

Table 3 / Laura Bush 21st Century Librarian Program, FY 2011 *(cont.)*

Preprofessional Programs

El Paso Area Library Consortium $500,000

The consortium, representing 193 public, school, university, and other libraries, and its partners—People Skills, Inc., Dona Ana Community College at New Mexico State University, and Ysleta del Sur Pueblo—will continue a successful librarian recruitment program in the Trans-Pecos border region of Texas and expand into southern New Mexico, offering two programs.

Northern Kentucky University $860,677

Northern Kentucky University will partner with the West Virginia Library Commission and Mountwest Community and Technical College to expand its successful Bridging the Gap (Kentucky) project. Through a combination of financial assistance, a mentoring system, online colloquia, and travel stipends, 40 library workers will be assisted and encouraged to progress through online undergraduate programs in library science at Northern Kentucky University and Mountwest Community and Technical College.

Research

University of Maryland $497,006

Researchers at the university's College of Information Studies will study the demographics and skills of library administrators, who have not been the subject of extensive research since the late 1960s. This study will explore the current roles and responsibilities of district library supervision offices in the 100 largest school districts and 100 midsized school districts in the United States.

Research—Early Career Development

Rutgers University $334,641

In this early career development project, Jacek Gwizdka will develop and validate a new framework for non-intrusive, continuous monitoring and assessment of cognitive load (mental effort) experienced by users of digital libraries.

Simmons College $123,436

Katherine Wisser will study manuscript finding aids that have been constructed using one new descriptive standard, Encoded Archival Context—Corporate Bodies, Persons, and Families (EAC–CPF). As a form of controlled vocabulary for the names of creators or subjects of archival materials, EAC–CPF carries the promise of linking the holdings of archives together, making it easier for researchers to see connections in the past.

Programs to Build Institutional Capacity

University of Arizona $844,965

The university's School of Information Resources and Library Science Knowledge River Program and partners will recruit and matriculate 33 culturally competent information professionals to work in public libraries, archives, and medical libraries that serve Hispanic American and Native American communities.

University of Illinois at Urbana-Champaign $725,923

The university's Graduate School of Library and Information Science, along with five community partners (Champaign County Juvenile Detention Center, Don Moyer Boys and Girls Club, Best Interest of Children, TAP in Leadership Academy, and Urbana Neighborhood Connections Center), will recruit and educate ten master's degree fellows from under-represented groups in a dual youth services and community informatics certificate program.

University of North Carolina at Chapel Hill $897,449

The university's School of Library and Information Science and School of Government will support one doctoral student and ten dual-degree students, providing them with

Table 3 / Laura Bush 21st Century Librarian Program, FY 2011 *(cont.)*

both a master of library and information science and a master of public administration degree in a program emphasizing the curation and stewardship of digital public information.

University of North Texas $226,786

To take full advantage of the nation's investment in research, federal agencies and other funders increasingly are asking investigators to share the data generated by their endeavors. The university, in cooperation with the Council on Library and Information Resources, proposes a 24-month research project to investigate how the library and information science profession can best respond to the emerging needs of universities as they seek to manage the ever-increasing amount of data generated by their faculty, staff, and students.

University of North Texas $624,663

The College of Information and the university libraries will collaborate to build and deliver a post-master's graduate academic certificate in digital curation and data management. In addition to curriculum development, it will also craft an online environment populated with educational tools designed to foster active experimentation and discovery learning on the part of students.

Continuing Education

Heritage Preservation $407,023

Heritage Preservation will conduct a series of eight structured webinars and create an online community to help the staff of smaller libraries and archives improve care of their special collections, prepare for emergencies, and expand their public outreach.

New York Public Library $200,262

The library will implement Money Matters, a staff training initiative that will educate staff on the core concepts and related reference sources of personal finance. It will also give staff the opportunity to host presentations by experts from partnering agencies and associations and/or conduct personal finance training that their neighborhood communities need most.

Valley City State University $232,029

Valley City State University and its partner, the North Dakota Leadership and Educational Administration Development Center, will implement a continuing education delivery model to train and support 25 three-person school-based collaborative teams consisting of a school administrator, the library media specialist, and a classroom teacher. These teams will develop, implement, and disseminate projects that will integrate national content standards and skills in classrooms across North Dakota and neighboring states.

Level 1 Planning

San José State University $45,968

San José School of Library and Information Science will partner with the Association of College and Research Libraries, Public Library Association, Urban Libraries Council, and OCLC to explore a residency program model for recent MLIS graduates. "Catalysts for Emerging Technology Integration: Exploring a New Model for Library Residency Programs" is aimed at building a scalable and replicable residency program model that will help new librarians and library leaders integrate emerging technology in diverse types of libraries.

University of Alabama $24,007

The university's School of Library and Information Studies, unique among library schools in offering a self-contained book arts program, will join with the Alabama Center for the

Table 3 / Laura Bush 21st Century Librarian Program, FY 2011 *(cont.)*

Book and academic experts in a planning process to explore a dual master's degree program in library and information studies and the book arts.

University of Illinois at Urbana-Champaign $22,194

Field Strength, a project to be led by the university library in collaboration with the Graduate School of Library and Information Science, will begin to identify best practices in field experience in LIS education.

University of Tennessee $22,194

The university will partner with the University of Arizona on a planning grant to build La SCALA, a program to educate a new generation of Hispanic/Latino scholars and educators in the field of library and information science.

Native American Library Services

The Native American Library Services program provides opportunities for improved library services to an important part of the nation's community of library users. The program offers three types of support to serve the range of needs of Indian tribes and Alaska Native villages and corporations.

In FY 2011 IMLS distributed $3,545,078 in grants under the program. This included some funds recovered from previous budget years and reallocated to the 2011 awards. The program offers three types of support:

- Basic library services grants in the amount of $6,000, which support core library operations on a noncompetitive basis for all eligible Indian tribes and Alaska Native villages and corporations that apply for such support. IMLS awarded basic grants to 30 tribes in 2011.
- Basic library services grants with a supplemental education/assessment option of $1,000, totaling $7,000. IMLS awarded basic grants with the education/assessment option to 193 tribes. The purpose of the education/assessment option is to provide funding for library staff to attend continuing education courses and/or training workshops onsite or offsite, for library staff to attend or give presentations at conferences relating to library services, and/or to hire a consultant for an onsite professional library assessment.
- Enhancement grants, which support new levels of library service for activities specifically identified under LSTA. Of the 45 applications received, IMLS awarded 15 enhancement grants for a total of $2,010,695 (Table 4).

Native Hawaiian Library Services

The Native Hawaiian Library Services program provides opportunities for improved library services through grants to nonprofit organizations that primarily serve and represent Native Hawaiians, as the term "Native Hawaiian" is defined in section 7207 of the Native Hawaiian Education Act (20 U.S.C. 7517). In FY 2011 two Native Hawaiian Library Services grants were awarded: to Alu Like, Inc.'s Native Hawaiian Library for $407,578, and to Kanu o ka 'Aina Learning 'Ohana for $158,122.

Table 4 / Native American Library Services Enhancement Grants, FY 2011

Chilkat Indian Village $149,994

Chilkat Indian Village's Klukwan Community and School Library, Xux' Daaka Hídí, serves the cultural and educational needs of this small Tlingit village in Alaska. Collection development activities will help fill in gaps in the current library holdings, and a special component of the project will be the creation of 12 short local history/Tlingit culture bilingual books telling the story of recent village projects relating to traditional knowledge and subsistence activities. Tribal resources will be consolidated and organized in the library for increased public access.

Chilkoot Indian Association $135,696

The Chilkoot Indian Association, in partnership with the Haines Borough (Alaska) Public Library, will develop a Chilkat Valley Storyboard using the Microsoft Surface platform. The electronic interactive exhibit will share Tlingit place names, Tlingit language, and stories of local and natural history with the local community and visitors.

Crow Tribe of Montana $135,311

On behalf of the tribe, the Little Big Horn College Library will implement a project designed to reveal the wealth of information on the Crow people that is currently "hidden" in the college's Crow Collection. The goal is to make the entire Crow Collection accessible to patrons through in-depth cataloging that adds extensive content notes.

Jamestown S'Klallam Tribe $150,000

The tribe, in Sequim, Washington, will begin the transformation of its tribal library by establishing it as an active partner and valuable resource in program delivery. The library will generate cultural and educational tools using both the in-house collections as well as the new "House of Seven Generations" online archive.

Lac Courte Oreilles Band of Lake Superior Chippewa Indians $149,960

The Lac Courte Oreilles Ojibwa College Community Library will play an enhanced role by offering language and cultural resources and services to area schools and the community at large.

Nisqually Indian Tribe $149,604

The tribe in Olympia, Washington, will expand its children's library services beyond the walls of the newly refurbished tribal library to include the isolated reservation and allotment land communities. Weekly bookmobile services will be offered to a variety of tribal facilities, providing year-round children's services, with a tribal member serving as a youth services coordinator.

Petersburg Indian Association $149,681

The association and the Petersburg (Alaska) Public Library will jointly implement the Many Voices, One Community project with programming on topics such as preparation of traditional foods and medicines, subsistence methods, Northwest Coast art and design, and Tlingit language and history.

Pueblo of Acoma $95,149

The Pueblo of Acoma in New Mexico will develop the Acoma Historical Storytelling Project, led by the pueblo's Learning Center and Library. It will engage youth, senior citizens, and families in a book-publishing project through traditional and contemporary storytelling that will result in the production of two books on Acoma's history.

Pueblo of Santa Clara $150,000

The Pueblo of Santa Clara's Community Library in Espanola, New Mexico, will continue to develop its literacy programs for all ages, including the Every Child Ready to Read (ECRR) program, which will include training parents in ECRR techniques and adapting the program to the Santa Clara community. It also will build on the intergenerational elder-and-child activities of the Tewa Language Program and coordinate with other tribal

Table 4 / Native American Library Services Enhancement Grants, FY 2011 *(cont.)*

programs to integrate literacy development activities into programs for at-risk families, children, and youth.

Quapaw Tribe of Indians $126,590

The Quapaw Tribe will enhance its library services and collections by providing new materials, additional staff for extended hours, virtual library services, and cultural programs for Quapaw, Oklahoma, and the surrounding area. Based on a comprehensive community assessment, the library will provide virtual library services by joining a consortium of Oklahoma libraries subscribing to e-books, audiobooks, videos, and music for download.

Saginaw Chippewa Indian Tribe of Michigan $81,719

The tribe plans to transform its tribal library into a place where families play and learn together. An engaging children's area with a birch bark reading house, new books, educational toys, musical instruments, and early literacy stations will be the centerpiece for activities under a "Prime Time Family Reading Time" program.

Sealaska Corporation $149,935

The Sealaska Heritage Institute of Juneau, Alaska, on behalf of Sealaska Corporation, will increase access to its valuable "hidden collections" by focusing on 137 Tlingit-language recordings that contain Tlingit oral histories and traditional ecological knowledge.

Shingle Springs Band of Miwok Indians $133,859

In response to a community survey, the Shingle Springs (California) Band of Miwok Indians will transform their library into an inviting space for children and adults, with culturally relevant programming and a focused collection about Native American culture and the Native American experience.

Squaxin Island Tribe $103,786

The Squaxin Island Tribe of Shelton, Washington, will initiate the Squaxin Legends and Storytelling Project as a youth engagement and storytelling documentation project that will take place at the Squaxin Island Museum Library and Research Center. The project will build cultural awareness for Squaxin youth as they listen to traditional stories and learn to use technological skills to express their new knowledge.

Washoe Tribe of Nevada and California $149,411

The tribe intends to develop the full potential of its Woodfords Community Library in response to community feedback requesting more library staff, evening and weekend hours, organized family activities, and relevant materials on which to draw for increased cultural programming. New youth activities will include "read-a-thons," preschool story time with a focus on preliteracy skills, "pillows and PJs" movie nights, a creative writing club, and digital literacy classes in their new computer center.

Partnerships

Connecting to Collections

IMLS, along with the American Association for State and Local History and Heritage Preservation, is building on the six successful webinars held in fall 2010 for members of the Connecting to Collections community by offering the Connecting to Collections Online Community (http://www.connectingtocollections. org), which was launched in the early summer of 2011. All collecting institutions are eligible to belong without cost, and 876 organizations are now members of the community. This interactive resource connects staff at small museums, archives, and libraries with each other and with solid information about collections care. The site features a meeting room, featured resources, a discussion forum, a calendar, and an archive of past discussions. Topics have included "The Care of Videotapes," "Cold Storage for Photographic Materials," and "Integrated Pest Management"; the latter was the best attended of the 11 webinars offered to date. The series continued in January 2012, with one or two webinars scheduled each month through March 2013.

Campaign for Grade-Level Reading

IMLS has become a partner in the Campaign for Grade-Level Reading, a ten-year effort by funders, led by the Annie E. Casey Foundation, and nonprofit organizations nationwide to promote third grade reading proficiency and address the developmental and academic targets that children need to reach to be successful. The effort promotes policies to better coordinate alignment of early learning services and programs, improve instruction and evaluation, and tackle obstacles to achievement. Research indicates that the most important predictor of school success through high school graduation is grade-level reading by the end of the third grade. Data show, however, that two-thirds of U.S. fourth graders are not proficient readers and more than 4 out of 5 low-income students fail to meet this milestone. The campaign aims to make grade-level reading proficiency for all children by the end of the third grade a national priority and targets three challenges to reading success: the readiness gap, chronic absence, and summer learning loss. In addition to the campaign, the federal departments of Education and Health and Human Services have signaled the urgency of this issue at a federal level and have prioritized early learning objectives as part of the Promise Neighborhoods and Invest in Innovation grant programs. Last summer, these agencies launched a $500 million grant competition, the Race to the Top—Early Learning Challenge, to promote statewide early learning progress.

With an intention to provide up to $2 million of National Leadership Grant (NLG) funds over two years for library-museum collaborations in support of community efforts to further various goals, the Library-Museum Collaboration Category of the NLG program for FY 2012 and FY 2013 will focus on museums and libraries promoting early learning (learners ages 0–8 and their parents and caregivers). Libraries and museums are encouraged to partner with each other and/or with applicable community organizations to address at least one of the challenges identified by the campaign.

National Arts and Humanities Youth Program Awards

The National Arts and Humanities Youth Program (NAHYP) Awards (formerly the Coming Up Taller awards) are the nation's highest honor for out-of-school, after-school, and summer arts and humanities programs that celebrate the creativity of youth, particularly young people from underserved communities. Each year the NAHYP Awards recognize and support excellence in programs that open new pathways to learning, self-discovery, and achievement, in addition to presenting high-quality arts and humanities learning opportunities. Award recipients receive

$10,000 each, a plaque, and an opportunity to attend the annual awardees conference in Washington, D.C., where they receive capacity-building and communications support designed to strengthen their organizations.

Launched in 1998, this awards program is a signature initiative of the President's Committee on the Arts and the Humanities, in partnership with IMLS, the National Endowment for the Arts, and the National Endowment for the Humanities. Libraries and museums are encouraged to apply. For more information, see http://www.nahyp.org.

Twenty-First Century Skills, Competitive Work Force, Engaged Citizens

President Barack Obama has called for the development of 21st century skills, including problem solving, critical thinking, entrepreneurship, and creativity. Combining traditional strengths in creating powerful learning experiences with strategic investment in modern communications infrastructures, libraries and museums are well equipped to build the skills needed to succeed.

As part of its effort to engage libraries and museums, community stakeholders, and policymakers at the national, state, and local levels to meet the educational, economic, civic, and cultural needs of communities, IMLS worked with more than 100 museum and library experts as well as representatives from the private and education sectors to produce *Museums, Libraries, and 21st Century Skills*. The publication and its companion Web site (http://www.imls.gov/about/21stCSkills.shtm) provide a framework for museums and libraries to align their programs and services to deliver 21st century skills and outline possibilities for broader community partnerships and engagement.

Since its release in August 2009, the publication has been received with enthusiasm; more than 12,000 copies have been distributed. Success stories range from individual institutions to statewide initiatives that use the framework as a strategic planning tool. Especially in a time of economic stress, smart planning is needed to align programs and services where they are needed most.

IMLS is continuing a dissemination, training, and communications effort to raise awareness and encourage action. This involves grant making with a 21st century skills focus as well as outreach to federal, state, and local policymakers.

In addition, IMLS continued "Making the Learning Connection," a seven-city tour begun in FY 2010 to spotlight success stories and identify barriers to success. The tour concluded in FY 2011. "Making the Learning Connection" workshops brought together museum and library leaders with representatives from local community foundations, the United Way, AARP, the K–12 education system, and representatives of universities and colleges to foster collaboration and coordination of communitywide efforts to fulfill the community's learning needs. Workshops were held in Baltimore; Columbia, South Carolina; San Francisco; Miami; Chicago; Albuquerque; and Detroit. These workshops built on IMLS's long history of supporting collaborative activity among libraries, museums, and other community partners, with significant results. New materials relating to libraries, museums, and 21st century skills included additional case studies, practitioner videos, and a community workshop planning toolkit to be available on the IMLS Web site.

Learning Labs at Libraries and Museums

In a speech to the National Academies of Science, President Obama challenged all Americans to join the cause of elevating STEM (science, technology, engineering, and mathematics) education as a national priority. He announced a series called "Educate to Innovate" to highlight public-private partnerships to advance this goal. In accordance with the Office of Management and Budget guidance on cross-agency goals, IMLS has collaborated with the White House Office of Science and Technology Policy to highlight ongoing IMLS support for library and museum STEM programming and to leverage private support.

In partnership with the John D. and Catherine T. MacArthur Foundation, along with the Urban Libraries Council and the Association for Science and Technology Centers, IMLS will build the capacity of library and museum professionals to develop effective STEM programs by supporting a national competition to create up to 30 new learning labs in libraries and museums across the country. Recognizing that a real change in science education requires the participation of many national and community partners, the John S. and James L. Knight Foundation, the Pearson Foundation, the New York Community Trust, the Chicago Community Trust, the Mozilla Foundation, and the Grable Foundation are providing additional resources to support the design and construction of teen-focused, research-based learning labs.

Inspired by an innovative new teen space at the Chicago Public Library called YOUmedia and innovations in science and technology centers, these labs will help young people become makers and creators of content, rather than just consumers of it. In addition to the planning and development of the labs, grantees will be active participants in a "community of practice" that will encourage shared research, successful learning outcomes, and sustainable spaces that fulfill community needs and leverage community partnerships.

The first round of awardees, announced in November 2011, included 12 institutions—eight libraries and four museums in 11 states. Many of the awarded institutions are partnering with a wide range of community institutions such as libraries, museums, parks and recreation, media outlets, universities, and nonprofit community organizations. The second round of funding will be announced in 2012.

National Student Poets Program

IMLS, along with the President's Committee on the Arts and the Humanities (PCAH), and in partnership with the Alliance for Young Artists and Writers, launched a national initiative in November 2011 that will elevate and highlight the work of young poets for a national audience, leverage the resources of museums and libraries to help inspire other young people to excellence in their creative endeavors, and showcase the essential role of writing and the arts in academic and personal success. The program will honor five outstanding student poets, chosen by an expert jury, whose work exhibits a dedication to craft, promise, and excellence. The project expands educational opportunities by promoting core competencies in writing and reading, as well as creativity and innovation, and by providing forums for the poets and the public to interact, learn, and grow. The winning poets will be notified in July 2012 and officially invited to be appointed in a national awards ceremony in Washington, D.C., during the National Book Festival in late September. Throughout their terms, and especially during the month of April (National Poetry Month), the young poets will be engaged in poetry events in targeted communities coordinated by PCAH in partnership with IMLS, local libraries and museums, state arts and humanities councils, and other entities.

IMLS and the Department of Labor

Through communications, grant making, and federal partnerships, IMLS is working to support libraries in their roles as "first responders" in the economic downturn. As the nation experiences its first recession in the online age, job seekers are turning to libraries in record numbers. People are seeking library services to get assistance in looking for and applying for work, using e-government services, and developing new businesses. IMLS issued a series of podcast interviews with state library chief officers in five states who described how libraries were stepping up to meet new needs. Many libraries are working in cooperation with state work force organizations.

Recognizing that throngs of job seekers were using the library for support, on June 29, 2010, IMLS and the Employment and Training Administration (ETA) at the U.S. Department of Labor announced a partnership to encourage collaborations between the work force investment system and public libraries, collaborations aimed at improving the quality of employment and training services to job seekers and unemployed individuals. Assistant Secretary of Labor Jane Oates released a training and education notice to the entire public work force system encouraging work with public libraries.

IMLS and ETA have hosted webinars with the National Governors Association and other private partners to help public libraries and the work force system share data, best practices, and tools. In addition, IMLS has awarded two grants to WebJunction, an online learning community, and the State Library of North Carolina for Project Compass, which seeks to assess the needs of libraries and provide nationwide work force development training for librarians. In the past two years, Project Compass has supported training and assessment opportunities for every state library, and in FY 2011 it offered local training opportunities in high-need areas for nearly 2,000 librarians. The program continues in FY 2012.

IMLS plans additional work with other federal agencies particularly in the area of developing better e-government-related services, such as filing taxes, applying for citizenship, enrolling children in schools, and applying for social services—activities that increasingly take place at the public library.

International Collaboration

Salzburg Global Seminar

IMLS and the Salzburg Global Seminar partnered to host "Libraries and Museums in an Era of Participatory Culture," in Salzburg, Austria, October 19–23, 2011. Fifty-six leaders of libraries and museums, cultural and educational policymakers, cultural sector researchers, and technology experts from 31 countries gathered at the seminar to consider the multiple roles that libraries and museums will play as their communities demand more access to and participation in their institutions.

A combination of plenary sessions and working groups (the latter of which were charged with making concrete recommendations on their topic) focused on five key areas: culture and communities, learning transformed, communication and technologies, building the skills of library and museum professionals, and demonstrating public value. Vishahka Desai, president and CEO of the Asia Society, gave the keynote speech, "Connections and Collaboration Across Cultures in a Digital Age," and regular blogs were posted to both the library and museum communities throughout the conference. At the close of the conference, participants committed themselves to "one thing I will do differently as a result of the seminar," a listserv was set up, and an evaluation conducted. A major report on the seminar, to be disseminated globally, will be published in 2012.

Film Forward

Film Forward: Advancing Cultural Dialogue is an international filmmaker and film exchange program supported by IMLS since 2006, in partnership with the President's Committee on the Arts and the Humanities, the National Endowment for the Arts, and the National Endowment for the Humanities, and in cooperation with the Sundance Institute.

The goal of the program is to foster intercultural dialogue and engage domestic and global audiences around films. U.S. and international filmmakers are paired and sent to U.S. embassies around the world, and to various U.S. domestic film venues, including libraries, museums, arts organizations, and theaters. These venues screen the films and convene educational programs. The 2012 film program launched in December 2011. For more information, see http://www.sundance.org/filmforward.

Evaluation of IMLS Programs

In addition to outcome-based evaluation support for grantees, IMLS has instituted a new series of in-depth evaluations of its own programs on a rolling basis. In FY 2011 IMLS completed a comprehensive evaluation of the Museums for America grant program, the results of which are available on its Web site. A retrospective evaluation of the Laura Bush 21st Century Librarian Program was under way at the time this report was prepared. The evaluations, which span approximately 18 months, employ techniques for determining the impact of federal grant receipts on individual program participants and the institutions that receive support. Data used for these studies include application data, financial and narrative reports, post-award follow-up surveys, and qualitative case studies.

Research Sponsored and Conducted by IMLS

The IMLS Office of Planning, Research, and Evaluation (OPRE) released four major reports in FY 2011.

In February the FY 2009 StLA report, on state library agencies, was released, containing data on state library agencies in the 50 states and the District of Columbia for FY 2009. The data were collected through the State Library Agencies

(StLA) Survey, the product of a cooperative effort between the Chief Officers of State Library Agencies (COSLA), IMLS, and the U.S. Census Bureau.

The second report on public access computing was released in June. This report, *Opportunity for All: How Library Policies and Practices Impact Public Internet Access,* offers an analysis of the service in four public library systems and makes recommendations for strategies that help to sustain and improve public access service.

In July OPRE released its fourth research brief, titled *Who Is in the Queue: Public Access Computer Users.* The brief provides a demographic analysis of public access computer users and demonstrates that public libraries are providing much more than basic technology access.

In August the Museums for America (MFA) evaluation report, *Supporting Museums—Serving Communities,* was released. This report presents findings from a two-year study conducted by RMC Research Corporation, which looked at the program's efficacy in serving the museum community and the impact of the MFA program and MFA-funded projects. The analysis drew on IMLS administrative data from applications and awards, responses to an online survey administered by RMC to a subset of MFA applicants and grant recipients, interviews with representatives of 26 completed exemplary projects, and site visits to 6 of those 26 museums.

Future research from OPRE will examine library services in a variety of contexts from small towns and remote rural areas to central cities and suburbs. OPRE also will look at the intersection of library service with other public policy priorities, including education, employment, immigration, and public health.

Conferences and Activities

Grants to States Conference

The 11th Grants to States Conference was held in Baltimore March 14–16, 2011. A total of 120 participants representing the State Library Administrative Agencies in the 50 states, the District of Columbia, Puerto Rico, Guam, American Samoa, and the Northern Mariana Islands attended. The conference included presentations on LSTA priorities identified in the 2010 reauthorization of the Library Services and Technology Act; new evaluation guidance and developing better results-based management protocols; and review of grants administration reporting requirements, including the reporting of subgrants and executive compensation as mandated by the Federal Funding Accountability and Transparency Act.

WebWise

The 12th annual WebWise conference on Libraries and Museums in the Digital World was held March 9–11, 2011, in Baltimore, with the theme "Libraries, Museums, and STEM in Research, Education, and Practice." Co-sponsored by the University of Denver's Penrose Library and Library and Information Science Program, with additional support from the John D. and Catherine T. MacArthur Foundation, the conference brought together 400 participants to discuss the role of libraries and museums in improving STEM (science, technology, engineering, and mathematics) education in the United States. Three preconference sessions were offered on March 9, along with an opening reception sponsored by the MacArthur Foundation at the National Aquarium in Baltimore.

Library Statistics State Data Coordinators Conference

The fourth IMLS-sponsored Library Statistics State Data Coordinators Conference was held in Kansas City December 6–9. Fifty-five participants represented the 50 states, the District of Columbia, Puerto Rico, and Palau. The conference included training on data collection and input, review of existing data elements included in the Public Libraries Survey, workshops on data presentation and analysis, and discussion and a comprehensive review of survey data elements for the FY 2011 survey and beyond.

IMLS Web Site and Publications

The Grants to States program provides state LSTA program administrators with full-time access to a Web site that facilitates communication about program requirements and guidance.

The IMLS Web site (http://www.imls.gov) provides information on the various grant programs, the National Medal for Museum and Library Service, funded projects, application forms, and staff contacts. The Web site also highlights model projects developed by libraries and museums throughout the country and provides information about IMLS-sponsored conferences, publications, and studies. Through an electronic newsletter, *Primary Source,* IMLS provides information on grant deadlines and opportunities. Information on subscribing to the IMLS newsletter is located on the Web site.

The following recent publications are available at the Web site: *Creating a Nation of Learners: Strategic Plan 2012–2016; Proposed Framework for Digitally Inclusive Communities: Final Report; Public Libraries in the United States, Fiscal Year 2009; Opportunity for All: How Library Policies and Practices Impact Public Internet Access;* the *2011 National Medal for Museum and Library Service* brochure; and guidelines for each of the grant programs.

Part 3
Library/Information Science Education, Placement, and Salaries

Library Employment Sources on the Internet

Catherine Barr

Contributing Editor

Challenges abounded for library school graduates in 2011, with continuing cuts in budgets and staffing in almost all sectors of library and information science. The site http://www.losinglibraries.org is still monitoring closures and reductions at school libraries around the country. Positions were also being eliminated or left unfilled at public, academic, and special libraries, and new library graduates were experiencing long searches for employment. For facts, figures, and anecdotes relating to the situation in 2010, see *Library Journal*'s annual "Placements and Salaries" report for 2011: "The Long Wait" [See the following article for the full report.—*Ed.*]

The following is not a comprehensive list of the hundreds of job-related sites on the Internet of interest to librarians and information professionals. These are, however, the best starting places for a general job search in this area. Many offer additional information that will be helpful to those considering a career in librarianship, including advice on conducting a successful search, writing résumés, preparing for interviews, and negotiating salaries.

Before spending a lot of time on any Web site, users should check that the site has been updated recently and that out-of-date job listings no longer appear. Many sites do not reflect the current difficulties that jobseekers are encountering.

The Directory of Organizations in Part 6 of this volume may also prove useful.

Background Information

The Bureau of Labor Statistics of the Department of Labor provides a thorough overview of the work of a librarian, necessary qualifications, and the job and salary outlook at http://www.bls.gov/oco/ocos068.htm. Similar pages are available for archivists, curators, and museum technicians (http://www.bls.gov/oco/ocos065.htm) and for library technicians and library assistants (http://www.bls.gov/oco/ocos316.htm). Salary information can also be found at salary.com, which offers a page of library options at http://www1.salary.com/Library-Services-Salaries.html.

The American Library Association (ALA) provides a user-friendly overview of librarianship at all levels—from page and library assistant to managers and directors—at LibraryCareers.org (http://www.ala.org/ala/educationcareers/careers/librarycareerssite/home.cfm), and Info*Nation: Choose a Career in Libraries (http://www.cla.ca/infonation/welcome.htm) is an excellent Canadian site that describes the work of librarians, combining brief information on a variety of career options with statements by individual librarians about why they love their jobs. These two sites will be particularly useful for young people considering a possible career in librarianship.

San José State University's School of Library and Information Science has created a "Career Development" page (http://slisweb.sjsu.edu/resources/career_development/index.htm) that aims to "help our students, alumni, and prospective students navigate a myriad of career opportunities, learn about emerging trends in the field, and develop an effective job search strategy." It includes "Library and Information Careers: Emerging Trends and Titles," a pdf dated 2011 that provides facts and figures on the profession and clearly lays out the responsibilities of librarians in various fields and the skills required.

The October 2010 issue of *Knowledge Quest* has a feature story titled "Public Librarian" in which three public librarians describe their jobs and the aspects that they particularly enjoy. And the April 2010 issue of *College and Research Library News* includes an article—"Making the Best of the Worst of Times: Global Turmoil and Landing Your First Library Job"—that looks at job listings and how to prepare for an interview.

Also of interest to aspiring librarians is Rachel Singer Gordon's article in the September 15, 2009, *Library Journal* (http://www.libraryjournal.com/article/CA605244.html), "How to Become a Librarian—Updated." In this, she covers all the basics and recommends paths to the profession.

In response to the difficulties facing both new and mid-career librarians, ALA in 2009 created a site called Get a Job! (http://www.getajob.ala.org). Subtitled "ALA's Toolkit for Getting a Job in a Tough Economy," this provides helpful information under headings such as "Especially in a Tough Job Market." Podcasts and stories offer real-life experiences and users can ask questions and contribute comments.

Finally, How to Apply for a Library Job (http://www.liswiki.com/wiki/HOWTO:Apply_for_a_library_job) offers thoughtful advice and practical interview tips.

General Sites/Portals

American Library Association: http://www.ala.org/
Education and Careers   ala/educationcareers/index.cfm
Maintained by ALA. A useful source of information on library careers, education and professional development, scholarships, and salaries.

ALA JobLIST   http://joblist.ala.org
Sponsored by ALA and the Association of College and Research Libraries. This site incorporates the former job sites of *American Libraries* magazine and *C&RL News*. Registration is free for jobseekers, who can post their résumés and search jobs by library type, date, state, institution name, salary range, and other parameters. Employers can choose from a menu of print and electronic posting combinations.

Canadian Library Association: http://www.cla.ca/
Library Careers   AM/Template.cfm?Section=Library_Careers

The Canadian Library Association lists Canadian job openings here (select Job Search) and provides guidance on recognition of foreign credentials.

Employment Resources: http://slisweb.sjsu.edu/resources/employment.htm
Organizations and Associations
Maintained by San José State University's School of Library and Information Science. Gives links to organizations that will be of interest to students at the university, including a number of California sites. A related page, Professional Associations in the Information Sciences (http://slisweb.sjsu.edu/resources/orgs.htm), is a comprehensive listing of associations in the United States and abroad. And excellent information on conducting job searches and professional development in general can be found at http://slisgroups.sjsu.edu/alumni/jobseekers/index.html.

Library Job Postings on the Internet   http://www.libraryjobpostings.org/
Compiled by Sarah L. Johnson of Booth Library, Eastern Illinois University, co-author of *The Information Professional's Guide to Career Development Online* (Information Today, Inc., 2002); there is a link to the book's companion Web site on this site. Provides links to library employment sites in the United States and abroad, with easy access by location and by category of job.

LIScareer.com: Career Strategies for Librarians   http://www.liscareer.com
Relaunched in 2009, this helpful site is maintained by Priscilla Shontz and offers "practical career development advice for new librarians and information professionals, MLS students, and those considering a library-related career." There are no job listings, but the site offers interesting articles in the areas of career exploration, education, job searching, experience, networking, mentoring, interpersonal skills, leadership, publishing and presenting, and work/life balance. This is an excellent place to begin research on library jobs. Shontz is also coauthor with Richard A. Murray of *What Do Employers Want? A Guide for Library Science Students* (Libraries Unlimited, 2012).

I Need a Library Job   http://inalj.com/
Maintained by Naomi House, this attractive site offers daily e-mails/digest of job openings, links to international jobs pages, and interviews with recent successful job hunters.

The Riley Guide   http://www.rileyguide.com
This redesigned (and not immediately user-friendly site) allows users to explore all aspects of job hunting, from proper preparation to résumés and cover letters, researching and targeting employers, and networking, interviewing, and negotiating.

Sites by Sector
Public Libraries

Public library openings can be found at all the general sites/portals listed above.

Careers in Public Librarianship   http://www.ala.org/pla/tools/careers
The Public Library Association offers information on public librarianship, with a section on the experiences of PLA members and a webcast on finding and keeping public library jobs.

Competencies for Librarians   http://www.ala.org/ala/mgrps/
Serving Children in Public Libraries   divs/alsc/edcareeers/alsccorecomps/
A detailed listing of skills and knowledge required to be a children's librarian in a public library.

School Libraries

School library openings can be found at many of the sites listed above. Sites with interesting material for aspiring school librarians include those listed below.

AASL: http://www.ala.org/ala/mgrps/divs/aasl/aasleducation/
Recruitment to School Librarianship   recruitmentlib/aaslrecruitment.cfm
The American Association of School Librarians hosts this site, which describes the role of school librarians, salary and job outlooks, and mentoring programs; provides testimonials from working library media specialists; and offers state-by-state information on licensure, scholarships, library education, job hunting, mentoring, and recruitment efforts.

General education sites usually include school library openings. Among sites with nationwide coverage is:

Education America   http://www.educationamerica.net
Library openings can be searched by geographic location.

Special and Academic Libraries

AALL Career Center http://www.aallnet.org/main-menu/Careers/career-center
Maintained by the American Association of Law Librarians, this site, with an on-line job board, an extensive FAQ section (under the heading "Support," and useful tips for job seekers.

Careers in Law Librarianship   http://www.lawlibrarycareers.org/
This excellent site answers the question "Is a career as a law librarian right for you?" and provides broad information on the profession, educational requirements, and available financial assistance.

Association of College and Research Libraries
See ALA JobLIST above.

ALISE: Job Placement   http://www.alise.org/
The Association for Library and Information Science Education posts jobs (under the heading Job Placement) for deans, directors, and faculty, organized by position and alphabetically by school.

ASIS&T: Careers   http://www.asist.org/careers.html
The Careers page maintained by the American Society for Information Science and Technology offers access to a Jobline, profiles of selected members, and continuing education information.

Association of Research Libraries: http://www.arl.org/
Career Resources   resources/careers/index.shtml
In addition to listings of openings at ARL member institutions and at other organizations, there is information on ARL's diversity programs plus a database of research library residency and internship programs. A video, *Faces of a Profession,* highlights the roles played by academic librarians and includes interviews with current staff.

Chronicle of Higher Education   http://chronicle.com/jobs
Listings can be browsed, with geographical options, under the category "Library/information sciences" (found under "Professional fields") or searched by simple keyword such as "library." Articles and advice on job searching are also available.

EDUCAUSE Job Posting Service   http://www.educause.edu/Jobs
EDUCAUSE member organizations post positions "in the broad field of information technology in higher education."

HigherEdJobs.com   http://www.higheredjobs.com
The category "Libraries" is found under Administrative Positions.

Major Orchestra Librarians' Association   http://www.mola-inc.org
A nice site for a field that might be overlooked. The Resources section includes an introduction to the work of an orchestra librarian.

Medical Library Association: http://www.mlanet.org/career/index.html
Career Development
The Medical Library Association offers much more than job listings here, with brochures on medical librarianship, a video, career tips, and a mentor program.

Music Library Association Job Openings   http://www.musiclibraryassoc.org/
employment.aspx?id=95
Along with job postings and a résumé review service, this site features an article titled "Music Librarianship—Is It for You?" and a listing of resources for both beginning and mid-career music librarians.

SLA: Career Center   http://www.sla.org/content/jobs/index.cfm
In addition to salary information and searchable job listings that are available to all users, the Special Libraries Association provides many services for association members.

Government

Library of Congress   http://www.loc.gov/hr/employment
An extensive survey of what it's like to work at the library, the kinds of employees the library is seeking, the organizational structure, benefits, current job openings, internships, fellowships, and volunteering.

National Archives and Records Administration   http://www.archives.gov/
careers/
In addition to information on employment opportunities, internships, and volunteering, NARA provides profiles of employees and interns, describing the kinds of work they do.

Serials

NASIG Jobs   http://nasigjobs.wordpress.com
Managed by the North American Serials Interest Group. Accepts serials-related job postings.

Library Periodicals

American Libraries
See ALA JobList above.

Library Journal   http://www.libraryjournal.com
Job listings are found under the Job Zone tab. The Careers tab leads to archived articles relating to employment.

School Library Journal   http://www.schoollibraryjournal.com
Click on the Jobs tab for access to a general list of job openings (jointly maintained with *Library Journal*; you must filter by Children's/Young Adult to access school positions.

Employment Agencies/Commercial Services

A number of employment agencies and commercial services in the United States and abroad specialize in library-related jobs. Among those that keep up-to-date listings on their Web sites are:

Advanced Information Management   http://www.aimusa.com
Specializes in librarians and support staff in a variety of types of libraries across the country.

LAC Group   http://careers.lac-group.com/
An easy-to-use list of openings that can be sorted by function, location, and keyword.

Listservs and Networking Sites

Many listservs allow members to post job openings on a casual basis.

jESSE   http://web.utk.edu/~gwhitney/jesse.html
This worldwide discussion group focuses on library and information science education; LIS faculty position announcements frequently appear here.

LibGig   http://www.libgig.com
Along with news, blogs, career profiles, "who's hiring" job alerts, and résumé consultation, this professional networking site offers easily accessed job postings.

LIBJOBS   http://www.ifla.org/en/mailing-lists
LIBJOBS is a mailing list for librarians and information professionals seeking employment. It is managed by the International Federation of Library Associations and Institutions (IFLA). Subscribers to this list receive posted job opportunities by e-mail.

LIS New Professionals Network   http://lisnpn.spruz.com
A forum with news, blogs, and postings of general and specific interest (job openings, grants, and so forth).

PUBLIB   http://lists.webjunction.org/publib
Public library job openings often appear on this list.

Blogs

Career Q&A with the Library Career People   http://www.lisjobs.com/
careerqa_blog
This attractive and user-friendly blog is maintained by librarians Tiffany Allen and Susanne Markgren and is intended to "create an enlightening discussion forum of professional guidance and advice for librarians, library staff, and those thinking of entering the profession." Categories include job satisfaction, job seeking, and professional development.

Placements and Salaries 2011: The Long Wait

Stephanie L. Maatta

"It's tough out there!" echoed from Boston to Seattle and Minneapolis to Miami. For 2010 library and information science (LIS) graduates, the past year presented challenges in finding professional jobs with adequate living wages; however, it also offered unexpected opportunities and sounded positive notes despite a battered economy.

A total of 1,789 LIS graduates responded to *Library Journal*'s (*LJ*'s) annual Placements and Salaries Survey, representing a solid 37.3 percent of the approximately 4,790 graduates from the class of 2010 at 38 participating schools.

In another sign of the times, fewer LIS schools participated, and the ones that did once again reported that graduation rates were down (8.4 percent below 2009), ranging from 2 percent to almost 50 percent lower.

Average starting salaries were basically flat, improving by less than 1 percent to $42,556—which could be seen as good news, given the economy, but is nonetheless bad news for a profession that is already widely considered to be underpaid. On the upside, the gender gap narrowed significantly to a 3.7 percent difference (from 8.3 percent) between wages for women and men. And the new graduate unemployment rate went down slightly, with 6.7 percent reporting they were still unemployed compared with 7.8 percent in 2009.

On the downside, finding employment in a distressed economy was very challenging. Fewer jobs were reported in public libraries, which have been among the hardest hit, with branch closures, hiring freezes, and layoffs. The struggles to find public library placements was borne out by reports from the LIS programs, with 34 percent indicating there was less demand for talent to fill positions than previous years. Despite the downturn in public library placements, there was healthy growth in placements for children's librarians (31.6 percent more placements than in 2009) and for public librarians entering reference and information services (an improvement of 22.8 percent over 2009). The job search remained lengthy, averaging more than five months, and some graduates were still searching more than 18 months after receiving their degrees.

Survey participants once again cited too many applicants for too few entry-level positions, and employers described getting 200 or more applications for a single available spot. Several graduates pointed out that they were competing for jobs with other new graduates as well as with applicants with many years of professional experience who had lost jobs through library closures and staff reductions. On the flip side, some graduates also reported landing the perfect job through perseverance and patience—and with a whole lot of luck.

Stephanie Maatta is an assistant professor at Wayne State University School of Library Information Science, Detroit

Adapted from *Library Journal,* October 14, 2011.

Jobs, But Fewer Professional Ones

A moderate level of stability began to surface in the job market for the current graduates; for the second year running, full-time placements improved slightly, rising to 75.8 percent of the reported jobs (up from 72.9 percent in 2009 and a depressing 69.8 percent in 2008). Also, unlike in 2009, when 83.3 percent reported a job of any sort, approximately 86.5 percent of the participating graduates reported finding a job either within or outside LIS professions. Some graduates who identified terrific full-time permanent positions with benefits were counterbalanced by others who took on jobs in restaurants and retail while questing for those elusive professional jobs.

The challenge for many was finding a permanent professional position. Of the 1,547 graduates reporting a job of any type, a mere 59.2 percent described those jobs as being both permanent and professional. This was another year of decline in permanent positions, dropping from 61 percent in 2009 and a high of 75.8 percent in 2007.

Temporary placements, however, held steady in 2010 at levels equal to those in 2009 (10.1 percent of the jobs in 2010; 10.6 percent in 2009), hinting at stabilization even though other indications suggest a leaner and tighter job market. Graduates spoke of accepting temporary positions with the hope these positions would grow into permanent placements, explaining that it provided one way to get in front of those making the hiring decisions.

Nonprofessional positions in library and information agencies provided similar challenges for graduates as did the accepting of temporary positions. On a positive note, reports of nonprofessional positions dropped from 19.4 percent of the placements in 2009 to 17.5 percent in 2010, although they are still high compared to reports prior to 2008. Nonprofessional positions historically have lower pay scales, carry fewer benefits (such as health care, paid sick leave and vacation leave, and so on), and are among the first to be eliminated during periods of budget constraints.

Graduates expressed concern about these roles. "I'm worried that being in a nonprofessional job will hinder my ability to be considered for professional positions later," one graduate commented, because of accruing the "wrong experiences and no responsibilities matching my graduate degree." They also worried about being laid off or furloughed when tough budget decisions had to be made.

About 43 percent of the respondents remained with an employer while working toward a master's degree (MLIS). This has been consistent for the last several years. For some it meant ongoing employment in an economic recession despite having to continue in a support staff role. Others expected a promotion and a salary bump once the diploma was in hand, and some were still waiting. The libraries most profoundly affected by the inability to provide promotion or salary increases were academic libraries; 44.7 percent of new academic librarians remained with their current employer, but only 22.1 percent reported receiving any positive change in status or rank upon completion of their MLIS. Graduates in public libraries fared much better in this regard, with 48.8 percent remaining with the same employer, and 46.1 percent of those achieving a change in status, either to professional staff from support positions, a salary increase, or a promotion within the system.

Taking part-time positions continues to be a compromise made by LIS graduates, either by choice or by circumstance. The number of reported part-time placements rose once again, with a full quarter of the reported jobs described as part-time (compared to a low of 16.3 percent in 2007 and 22.8 percent in 2009). Of those with part-time jobs, 32.9 percent held multiple positions (two or more), slightly down from 34 percent in 2009. Part-timers worked as few as 10 to 15 hours per week to as many as 32 hours, or nearly full-time. For some, the wages were "dismal"—just above minimum wage.

Others, although far fewer, were successful in achieving above-average salaries ($45,000–$60,000) and full-time hours by combining two part-time jobs, including part-time consulting. The challenge for them was the nature of part-time jobs: few benefits (health insurance or sick/vacation leave accrual) and less stability. One positive note came from recent graduates who discussed how part-time employment presented the opportunity to explore different environments while seeking the perfect job and gaining valuable experience in different types of libraries or information agencies. This developed more flexible skills, applicable to multiple types of library and information agencies and, they believed, broadening their chances at professional employment.

Public library positions continued to feel the deepest cuts, with approximately 33 percent of the reported jobs being part-time (equivalent to 2009 levels of 32.7 percent); among those, circulation (46.7 percent) and adult services (36.9 percent) had the highest part-time rates. Even jobs within private industry—noted for high salaries and strong benefits packages—were not immune to the trend to part-time (31.6 percent of the reported placements in private industry were part-time). Surprisingly, placements in the western states had the highest levels of part-time jobs in 2010, when historically the jobs in the West have been the most lucrative opportunities. Rates of part-time placements in the Northeast fell from 37.5 percent in 2009 to 26.8 percent, and even more encouraging was the overall increase in available positions in the same region (up 22.3 percent compared to 2009).

It was not unusual for graduates to report multiple part-time jobs. Some worked as booksellers during the day and catalogers on weekends; others pulled duty at a reference desk part of the week and in archives the rest. Others worked outside LIS professions as restaurant or office workers and then moved onto shifts in public or community college libraries. Jobs as substitute teachers and substitute librarians were also common among the class of 2010.

Where the Jobs Are

Considered from a regional perspective, salaries for new graduates experienced slow to moderate growth in 2010. Average annual growth in salaries nationwide ran approximately 1 percent, with the Midwest winning the prize with a 5.7 percent improvement in starting salaries ($42,857 in 2010 compared to $40,418 in 2009); salaries in the Midwest were also just above the overall average starting wage ($42,857 compared to $42,556) for new grads. This was helped along by a 7.4 percent rise in salaries for women in the Midwest ($42,077, up from $38,965 in 2009) as well as the higher salaries commanded by graduates of such institutions as University of Michigan (who earned an average overall starting salary of $55,000).

The Midwest, as well as enjoying the best salary growth, experienced the strongest placement rate with 36.1 percent of all of the reported jobs (full-time and part-time combined, both inside and outside the profession). These gains were a surprise, given reports of how difficult the economic recession has been in the upper Midwest.

Another bit of good news came out of the Northeast. In 2009 graduates there experienced salary compression, with starting salaries nearly 4 percent below those of 2008 ($42,436 compared to $43,854). Grads in 2010 regained a portion of that loss, with averages rising 1.7 percent to $43,088.

Men experienced the best rate of growth in salaries in the Northeast, with a healthy 14 percent jump to $44,148 (up $6,183 from 2009). These strong signs were further enhanced by a reduction in the overall unemployment rate in the region from a high of 7 percent in 2009 to 5.2 percent in 2010, highlighted by the strong placement rate among graduates (33.4 percent reporting employment of some sort).

The Southeast's tradition of having the lowest salary levels remained, with average starting salaries at $40,383 (5.4 percent below the overall average). Yet 2010 graduates felt a small boost of 1.1 percent in salaries in the Southeast compared to previous years (average salary had actually dropped from $39,964 in 2008 to $39,925 in 2009). There were a few glimmers of light; some graduates finding jobs in the Southeast reported salaries at the top of the overall range—the highest reported salary was $97,000 for a federal government position. Salaries were helped along by high-paying federal jobs in Washington, D.C., as well as good results experienced by graduates of Valdosta State University in Georgia and Louisiana State University.

In the Southeast, graduates claiming minority status and men enjoyed healthy growth in salaries (the former averaged $45,652 for an increase of 5.2 percent and the latter averaged $42,477 or an 8.2 percent hike). Reported unemployment also stabilized in the Southeast, dropping from 8.5 percent in 2009 to 4.0 percent in 2010.

Jobs by Library Type, Assignment

Salary is only one way to measure the ongoing health of a profession. Placement by specific types of agency or types of job assignment also suggests areas of strength and of concern. Academic libraries, for example, saw an increase in the percentage of overall placements. In 2009 positions for academic librarians comprised 20.7 percent of the reported jobs; in 2010 academic positions made up 28.7 percent of these same jobs. While it can be seen as both a negative with no progress being made and a positive with no measurable losses, the average starting salaries for academic librarians held steady between 2009 and 2010, hovering at $40,315 (up less than 1 percent from 2009 when salaries averaged $40,065). Academic libraries in the Southwest gained the most, with a 4.8 percent increase in reported salaries (to $40,561).

On the other hand, the graduates also had a lot to say about job postings for academic libraries, citing far too few entry-level positions. They reported that although many job announcements did not include a preference or requirement for a second advanced subject degree, they were eliminated from the applicant pool because of a lack of such a degree. Another complaint: the required skills and competencies for some jobs were so specific, the new graduates believed they couldn't measure up to employer expectations.

Public libraries, as anticipated, lost jobs in 2010. Nationwide, public library systems are being forced to close branches and consolidate operations in order to maintain a minimal level of service to the community with, in some locations, severely restricted funding. As a result, public libraries are experiencing hiring freezes, early retirements, and layoffs. This meant new LIS graduates interested in public library service had fewer choices. Public library placements dropped from 24.2 percent of the jobs in 2009 to 22.7 percent in 2010. This decline was readily apparent in the Northeast, where reported positions fell from 34.2 percent in 2009 to 28.2 percent in 2010. An exception was children's librarians, who saw available positions in public libraries grow from 4.2 percent of the overall placements in 2009 to 7.3 percent in 2010.

Special libraries also experienced a drop in the availability of positions, slipping from 7.1 percent to 5.1 percent of reported placements in 2010. Salaries for special librarians followed suit, falling an average of 3.1 percent ($41,791 in 2010 compared to $43,090 in 2009). In a continuing trend, special libraries or information centers in corporations, hospitals, and similar agencies are being done away with, reducing the number of available positions. Nonetheless, some graduates who sought out special library jobs looked to archives and special collections for similarities in job functions, and these types of positions increased to 7.2 percent of jobs from 5.6 percent in 2009, explaining in part the growth in the number of jobs in academic libraries, where archives and special collections are readily found. New graduates also landed positions in academic special libraries, such as law, medical, or pharmacy school libraries.

Those who did find roles in special libraries described their jobs in terms of enjoying multiple areas of responsibility. They combined traditional reference and information services with roles in digitization and metadata, took on instructional activities, and became highly involved in digital rights management and the development of scholarly repositories.

New archivists saw small steps forward for their specialized skills. The 2010 graduates regained ground lost in 2009 to garner salaries averaging $40,044. They found jobs in universities and colleges as well as corporations, history centers, and archives. While there were no strong reports of jobs in preservation and conservation in 2010, graduates working in both archives and in special collections described day-to-day activities that uniquely focused on these functions and a growing emphasis in digital preservation. Many new archivists got started in part-time positions in 2010, with 34.2 percent reporting less than full-time work.

Jobs in reference and information services also sprang back from previous years. Reference jobs continue to be highly popular among new LIS graduates. They find themselves in academic, public, and special libraries as well as providing similar functions in archives, research foundations, and records management agencies. Placements in reference jobs grew from a low of 15.4 percent of the overall jobs in 2009 to an impressive 23.8 percent, echoing levels of the mid-2000s. This hike may be due to the restructuring of public library jobs, where adult service librarians have had their roles broadened to incorporate adult and youth services with other public services, including outreach and programming, with a the broader title of reference/information librarian. Additionally, the emphasis on instruction and information literacy in academic libraries has changed the nature of the reference role, aligning education closely with information seeking. One of the unique opportunities reported in this area was the role of residence hall librarian at a university, which involves providing assistance on-site in the residence halls while also serving as the liaison between the academic library and the residents. Regardless of the job description, however, salaries for new reference librarians eased back slightly to $40,759 (losing 2.5 percent) from a high of $41,795 in 2009.

Cataloging continues to be a subject of discussion and concern among new graduates. Cataloging salaries, while up, remained well below the overall average for recent graduates ($39,574 compared to $42,556), though they improved $2,016 (5.1 percent) from 2009 ($39,574 compared to $37,558). In 2010 the majority of the cataloging placements (54 percent) were in academic libraries. New graduates expressed dismay that cataloging jobs are frequently considered to be nonprofessional rather than professional, hence lower salaries, fewer benefits, and part-time hours. While they did not have the highest rate of part-time positions (circulation jobs have that distinction at 47.2 percent), approximately 22 percent of the reported cataloging jobs required less than full-time hours.

Jobs Beyond Libraries

Jobs in private industry continued to be lucrative for new LIS graduates, comprising 9.4 percent of all reported placements, up slightly from 2009. Salaries for these positions rose approximately 2.1 percent to $56,526 (up $1,225), though they didn't reach the 2008 average of $58,194. The University of Michigan, Drexel University, and the University of Texas at Austin continued to dominate private sector placement, both in number (with a combined 53.4 percent of jobs) and with starting salaries that averaged $60,951 (approximately 30.1 percent higher than the overall salary).

Graduates from an array of LIS programs identified their new employers as companies such as Google, Wolfram Alpha, and AT&T. They also found placements in software and Internet companies, engaging in responsibilities relating to information architecture, user interface analysis and design, and software engineering. This same group of graduates also took on jobs in hospitals and medical centers as well as with pharmaceutical companies, working with systems and as knowledge managers.

The 2010 graduates found the best private industry employment in the Northeast. The region claimed 32.6 percent of the reported private industry positions, and there graduates won the highest average starting salaries at an average of $63,046 (compared to $56,526 for all private industry positions). The Southeast also offered better earning power in private industry than in other types of jobs, with average starting salaries of $43,480 (7.1 percent higher than the average Southeast starting salary of $40,383), although these same graduates reported the lowest rates of employment in the private sector (8.4 percent). By comparison, graduates in the West felt the greatest impact from the economic recession, with both lower placements (11.6 percent of the total jobs in private industry in 2010 compared to 16.9 percent in 2009) and salaries averaging $53,000 (down $13,150 from 2009 highs of $66,150).

Women fared almost as well as men in the private sector marketplace. Unlike in 2008, when the salary gap yawned at 24.4 percent between the sexes, it tightened for 2010 grads to a mere 4.7 percent difference in women's and men's average starting salaries ($55,809 and $58,545, respectively) for private industry jobs. This suggests that women may be more aggressively pursuing jobs that require high-level business and computing skills or backgrounds in information technology and information science.

Besides private industry, the graduating class of 2010 took jobs in other "other" agencies (those falling outside of the library and information professions). On the one hand, graduates accepted positions in nonprofit agencies, hospitals, law firms, and corporations working with information technology and communications, global information policy, and business analysis and research. On the other hand, they accepted positions at lower salaries and part-time hours as retail clerks, office assistants, or coffee shop baristas in order to pay the bills.

Helped along by jobs in private industry, full-time jobs falling outside LIS were slightly better paid than 2009 (up to $49,218 from $47,790), and were well above the overall starting average ($42,556) for new grads. Across the board, jobs falling in the "other" category displayed the best salary improvement in the Northeast, which boosted 11.8 percent compared to 2009 ($49,487 vs. $43,624). Graduates claiming minority status also experienced strong success in placement rates (19 percent of all minority jobs) and average salary levels ($47,129) for other agencies.

Gender Equity Gap Evolves

In a year that brought disappointment to many graduates, both women and men found modest salary growth in a number of areas. Nationwide, the overall starting salaries for men and women grew slightly (by 0.8 percent) from the levels achieved in 2009 ($42,556 compared to $42,215), with the best overall rate in the Midwest (5.7 percent). Women enjoyed the best salary growth in the West, leaping from $48,170 in 2009 to $52,340; men had similar luck in the Northeast, with 14 percent growth, moving from $37,965 in 2009 to $44,148.

As a positive sign of stabilization in the profession, for the class of 2010 the salary disparity was much smaller; there was a 3.7 percent difference between women and men compared to 2009, when average starting salaries diverged by 8.3 percent. Unfortunately, however, this is probably because men struggled in the salary race, losing 2.4 percent of their average starting salaries ($43,845 compared to $44,945 in 2009). In 2010 men's salaries hovered 2.9 percent above the nationwide average, while women's salaries were less than 1 percent below the average at $42,205. For the men, there was a significant reversal of fortunes in both the Southwest and the West (23.1 percent and 26.3 percent reductions respectively), and in the West, men earned a whopping 17.4 percent less ($44,600 vs. $52,340) than women.

A number of factors helped bridge the salary gap. For example, women—even though they landed 40 percent of the jobs described as "information technology" (IT)—negotiated salaries averaging $60,380 that were approximately 7.4 percent higher than men who accepted equivalent positions ($55,942). This is a complete turnaround from 2009, when women made 17 percent less than men in IT jobs. Women also did exceptionally well in winning high salary levels in knowledge management ($66,875 compared to men's $40,750) and in the area of automation and systems ($47,833 compared to men's $39,800). Unlike in previous years, women graduates in 2010 were able to achieve consistently high-end salaries that were equivalent to and occasionally surpassed the higher salaries landed by their male counterparts. Men still took home the choicest salaries at $115,000 and $120,000, but women came in at levels nearly as hefty (in the mid- to high $90,000s to upward of $100,000).

Men achieved success in school library media specialist positions, historically dominated by women. Men from the 2010 class increased their salary levels in these types of positions from $43,448 to $51,649 between 2009 and 2010. During the same period and in equivalent positions, women drifted down slightly from $45,737 to $45,087. Interestingly, the grads reported that approximately 12.5 percent of school media positions were part-time, where they worked as substitute teachers or in two separate schools or school districts.

Women remained in or accepted 80 percent of the nonprofessional positions, such as circulation or technical services, at a much lower salary level than the men, averaging $30,226 compared to $34,164. This drove down salary growth for the graduating class as a whole and the women in particular; it also contributed to the frustration and dissatisfaction expressed by graduates overall. Among special librarians, women also lost a good portion of the gains they had achieved in 2009 (down from $43,858 to $41,206), with those in the Northeast feeling the greatest impact, dropping by 18.5 percent ($49,108 in 2009 to $41,427).

Minorities See Gains

Graduates claiming minority status recovered much of what was lost in 2009, but inequity persisted. Once again the pool was consistent, with approximately 11.7 percent of the respondents claiming minority status. When compared to all LIS graduates for 2010, the minority graduates enjoyed salaries that averaged 4.6 percent higher ($44,602 vs. $42,556) and saw more impressive growth between 2009 and 2010 (up $4,127, or 9.3 percent). The real bright note was the recovery of salaries regionally, surpassing the levels set in 2008 by 4.4 percent.

Minority graduates saw the strongest rates of placement in academic libraries (22.4 percent) and in other agencies (19 percent). They also experienced the highest salary growth with these two types of employers. In academic libraries, where national average salaries grew less than 1 percent ($40,315 in 2010), minority graduates received starting salaries that were 5.5 percent higher than 2009 levels ($39,712 vs. $37,529). Yet these same academic library salaries were 1.5 percent below the national average in 2010. A similar situation occurred in other agencies. Salaries for minority placements surpassed 2009 levels by 13 percent ($47,129 compared to $40,993), but were 4.4 percent less than the average starting salary of $42,918 achieved by all graduates in similar jobs.

With the exception of the Midwest, where salaries held steady ($39,609), minority placements obtained higher salaries region to region than they did in 2009. The strongest growth was in the West, where salaries grew by 15.7 percent (up to $55,121 from $46,467) even though they had the lowest level of placement at 10 percent of all jobs; this was also a serious decline from 2009 when they comprised 17.2 percent of the placements. Interestingly, these same salaries in the West sprinted past the average for all students landing in the West ($55,121 compared to $50,792), helped by placements in government agencies and private industry. Minority graduates also made a strong showing in the Northeast, with salary growth topping 8.4 percent to $50,088 ($4,184 above 2009).

However, the gender gap was seriously evident among graduates claiming minority status. Minority women earned 1.5 percent more than all of their female peers ($42,834 compared to $42,205), but these same women fell 18.6 percent below the men who self-identified as minorities ($42,834 vs. $50,781). A contributor was the salary extreme in private industry jobs: minority women earned 36.5 percent less than minority men in equivalent jobs. The disparity was also compounded by the number of minority women who took on nonprofessional positions (12.4 percent) at salary levels well below national averages ($28,383 compared to $31,244 for all graduates and compared to $30,226 for all women).

The Grads' Perspective

Many of the 2010 graduates found that wearing multiple hats was the norm. They found it much more challenging to delineate a single job assignment than in the past. Multiple part-time positions aside, they identified dual roles in their day-to-day jobs. In the area of reference and information services, for example, some of the more unique examples included taking information services to the user outside of the library, combining outreach with education, and being responsible for developing social media resources along with duties in other areas of the library.

Other roles combined reference services with acquisitions and collection development functions. While not a particularly unusual combination, the dual role clearly illustrates the changing nature of the information professional's routine. Similarly, in public libraries new graduates reported spending a portion of the day in circulation and another portion in either children's or adult programming. Children's and youth services librarians also served as liaisons with the local school district and school library media specialists, planning programs and in resource-sharing opportunities. Instruction and outreach were inseparable in some cases and not limited to academic libraries; public librarians as well as special librarians engaged in similar activities. As they described their multiple responsibilities, new grads emphasized the need to be flexible and the willingness to learn and think creatively about how to approach new challenges and, more important, to develop skills that are applicable to many roles.

Solo librarians expressed some of the greatest challenges in meeting the needs of their individual agencies. Most echoed, "I do it all!" They took on administrative responsibilities, research, information dissemination, cataloging, digitization, organization, and in some cases even swept the floor. Despite the complex dimensions of their jobs, the average starting salary for solo librarians came in at $41,043, which was 3.6 percent under the overall average. This was, however, a huge leap (8.8 percent) from 2009 (up from $37,449).

Like other positions, solo librarians found themselves in academic, public, and special libraries as well as government libraries and private industry. They

(text continues on page 356)

Table 1 / Status of 2010 Graduates*

Region	Number of Schools Reporting	Number of Graduates Responding	Permanent Professional	Temporary Professional	Non-professional	Total	Graduates Outside of Profession	Unemployed or Status Unreported
Northeast	13	631	299	65	118	482	45	104
Southeast	8	251	152	15	36	203	30	18
Midwest	10	602	343	56	85	484	58	60
Southwest	5	196	77	5	17	151	14	31
West	2	77	25	10	15	50	11	16
Total	38	1,789	916	153	270	1,391	156	242

* Table based on survey responses from schools and individual graduates. Figures will not necessarily be fully consistent with some of the other data reported. Tables do not always add up, individually or collectively, since both schools and individuals omitted data in some cases.

Table 2 / Placements and Full-Time Salaries of 2010 Graduates by Region*

Region	Number of Placements	Salaries			Low Salary		High Salary		Average Salary			Median Salary		
		Women	Men	Total	Women	Men	Women	Men	Women	Men	All	Women	Men	All
Northeast	385	260	63	323	$13,337	$17,000	$94,000	$120,000	$42,831	$44,148	$43,088	$41,000	$40,000	$40,000
Southeast	1,196	118	35	153	16,050	20,000	97,000	87,400	40,058	41,477	40,383	40,000	41,000	40,000
Midwest	416	259	80	340	10,000	13,000	100,000	115,000	42,077	45,375	42,857	40,000	43,300	40,000
Southwest	100	61	14	75	22,000	16,000	71,000	62,571	41,152	38,163	40,594	40,000	35,500	40,000
West	34	20	5	25	25,000	29,000	100,000	65,000	52,340	44,600	50,792	48,920	48,000	48,000
Combined	1,151	730	198	929	10,000	13,000	100,000	120,000	42,205	43,845	42,556	40,000	41,000	40,000

* This table represents only salaries and placements reported as full-time. Some data were reported as aggregate without breakdown by gender or region. Comparison with other tables will show different numbers of placements.

Table 3 / 2010 Total Graduates and Placements by School

Schools	Graduates			Employed		
	Women	Men	Total	Women	Men	Total
Alabama	85	28	113	25	6	31
Albany	70	35	105	27	10	37
Arizona*	47	12	59			
Buffalo*	16	6	23	16	6	23
Catholic	22	3	25	14	3	18
Clarion	111	33	144	29	4	33
Denver	43	12	55	7	6	13
Dominican	249	70	319	33	13	46
Drexel	214	101	315	56	20	76
Florida State	1	—	1	1	—	1
Illinois*	47	9	56	43	7	50
Indiana	211	62	273	54	16	70
Iowa	40	4	44	15		15
Kent State	206	65	271	55	14	69
Kentucky	56	15	71	19	6	25
Long Island	40	20	60	12	2	14
Louisiana State	46	13	59	37	9	46
Michigan**	92	66	158	79	42	121
Missouri–Columbia	81	27	108	25	10	35
N.C. Chapel Hill	95	23	118	3	3	6

North Texas	54	11	65	38	10	48
Oklahoma	43	16	59	17	8	25
Pittsburgh	127	31	158	23	6	29
Pratt	104	20	124	37	3	40
Rhode Island	57	9	66	13	3	16
Rutgers*	60	11	71	51	11	62
San Jose	350	80	430	43	10	54
Simmons**	188	45	233	164	40	204
South Carolina	129	27	156	30	8	38
St. John's University	11	—	11	9	—	9
Syracuse	76	13	89	5	1	6
Texas (Austin)**	37	15	55	35	14	52
Texas Woman's	193	13	206	27	2	29
UCLA*	59	22	81	—	—	—
Valdosta State	47	10	57	51	16	67
Washington	63	14	77	7	1	8
Wayne State	157	43	200	23	5	28
Wisconsin (Madison)*	59	10	70	56	10	67
Wisconsin (Milwaukee)	157	48	205	37	7	44
Total	3,743	1,042	4,790	1,216	332	1,555

Tables do not always add up, individually or collectively, since both schools and individuals omitted data in some cases.

* For schools that did not fill out the institutional survey, data were taken from graduate surveys, thus there is not full representation of their graduating classes.

** Some schools completed the institutional survey, but responses were not received from graduates, or schools conducted their own survey and provided reports. This table represents placements of any kind. Comparison with other tables will show different numbers of placements.

Table 4 / Placements by Average Full-Time Salary of Reporting 2010 Graduates*

	Average Salary			Median Salary		Low Salary		High Salary		Salaries		Total Placements
	Women	Men	All	Women	Men	Women	Men	Women	Men	Women	Men	
Michigan	$50,000	$65,000	$55,000	$45,750	$51,000	$10,000	$25,000	$100,000	$115,000	49	25	107
St. John's	54,625	—	54,625	46,750	—	40,000	—	85,000	—	4	—	4
Pratt	51,266	67,500	52,039	50,850	67,500	30,000	67,500	72,000	67,500	20	1	28
San Jose	53,753	40,500	50,296	50,000	39,500	25,000	20,000	100,000	65,000	17	6	31
Rutgers	47,737	50,896	48,304	49,000	52,000	24,000	39,500	65,000	62,000	32	7	51
Drexel	44,925	57,100	47,756	43,000	52,000	17,680	28,000	94,000	120,000	33	10	54
Catholic University	46,373	53,500	47,561	47,464	53,500	39,800	52,000	51,000	55,000	10	2	16
Rhode Island	44,893	50,000	45,744	42,000	50,000	33,753	45,000	65,000	55,000	10	2	12
Washington	43,250	—	43,250	44,500	—	34,000	—	50,000	—	4	—	4
Albany	46,068	33,400	43,189	44,150	34,000	21,500	17,000	90,000	47,000	17	5	25
Texas Woman's	43,179	—	43,179	45,000	—	22,000	—	71,000	—	19	—	26
Illinois	43,774	40,417	43,163	41,800	42,500	22,505	25,000	100,000	51,000	27	6	35
Alabama	42,890	42,333	42,810	32,640	35,000	17,000	34,000	97,000	58,000	18	3	26
Valdosta State	41,235	44,173	41,937	40,000	41,000	22,000	29,000	67,350	87,400	35	11	61
Wisconsin (Milwaukee)	42,073	40,827	41,783	40,440	41,000	19,000	30,000	81,000	52,000	23	7	37
Buffalo	40,141	46,390	41,480	38,555	41,000	27,000	38,170	70,000	60,000	11	3	17
Dominican	42,006	38,623	41,190	41,000	38,000	23,000	30,000	63,000	52,000	22	7	34
Wisconsin (Madison)	41,136	40,167	41,054	40,000	38,500	13,000	13,000	84,000	70,000	36	6	47

Simmons	40,281	40,586	40,341	38,500	36,000	21,000	28,000	70,000	101,872	103	25	113
Denver	39,700	39,940	39,820	42,000	36,000	28,500	24,000	49,000	61,000	5	5	12
Indiana	39,428	40,483	39,702	40,000	40,000	10,000	27,222	71,000	62,000	40	14	57
North Texas	40,721	34,929	39,667	40,000	35,000	11,000	10,000	67,000	62,571	27	6	41
South Carolina	40,348	37,840	39,646	39,950	41,000	21,000	24,881	62,000	55,000	18	7	31
Kentucky	37,958	40,250	38,613	38,750	44,500	27,800	24,000	49,000	48,000	10	4	16
Iowa	38,372	—	38,372	36,000	—	19,968	—	80,000	—	9	—	10
Long Island	38,162	—	38,162	34,000	—	27,000	—	65,000	—	5	—	7
NC Chapel Hill	33,833	40,833	37,333	31,500	38,500	22,000	34,000	48,000	50,000	3	3	6
Louisiana State	37,226	36,680	37,146	36,000	40,000	16,050	20,000	55,000	44,000	29	5	39
Syracuse	36,900	38,000	37,120	35,800	38,000	26,000	38,000	50,000	38,000	4	1	6
Pittsburgh	34,808	44,126	36,770	36,400	37,753	13,337	36,000	49,700	65,000	15	4	22
Oklahoma	36,605	33,752	35,892	35,680	33,604	23,900	28,000	48,000	39,800	12	4	20
Missouri (Columbia)	35,227	36,933	35,796	33,500	38,000	24,000	22,800	62,000	48,000	16	8	30
Clarion	37,149	30,000	35,644	36,000	30,000	24,000	26,000	52,000	34,000	15	4	25
Wayne State	36,458	32,467	35,460	36,000	30,000	24,000	23,000	47,919	44,400	9	3	19
Kent State University	33,442	39,338	34,621	31,096	40,500	17,600	25,700	75,000	55,000	32	8	44

* This table represents only placements and salaries reported as full-time. Some individuals or schools omitted some information, rendering information unusable. Comparisons with other tables will show different numbers of placements and salaries.

(continued from page 350)
noted that they were intrigued that each day is different, with new possibilities and new problems.

Numbers and statistics do not convey the complete story. The words of the graduates provide a sense of what is really happening. The graduating class of 2010 spoke of both triumphs and disappointments in reaching their postgraduation goals and expectations.

Regardless of prior professional experience in another discipline or some type of work experience within libraries or information agencies, the job search was lengthy for the 2010 graduates—even for those who ended up in temporary or part-time positions. Some spent three or four months landing a job, only to end up unemployed again after only a couple of months when the recession caught up with their employers. Respondents remarked that the job search seemed interminable after being dropped back into the job market unexpectedly. Graduates also expressed frustration with potential employers who did not take time to acknowledge the receipt of résumés; the grads found not knowing worse than outright rejection. Some decided to delay their job search until 2012 in hope that the job market would turn around or at least grow no worse. The lucky ones found employment before or upon graduation. Such coups did not, however, guarantee either permanence, stability, or a professional position.

Members of the graduating class agree that library experience was a prerequisite to landing a job. Nose to nose in competition with mature professionals for jobs, it was critical to be able to show meaningful experience in the type of agency targeted. Many, however, commented on the Catch-22 of the situation, asking how they would obtain that experience when they couldn't land a temporary placement or part-time job and were trying to enter the LIS job market without any "real" library or information science experience.

Table 5 / Average Salary Index Starting Library Positions 2000–2010

Year	Library Schools	Average Starting Salary	Dollar Increase in Average Salary	Salary Index	BLS-CPI*
2000	37	$34,871	$895	197.26	175.1
2001	40	36,818	1,947	208.09	177.1
2002	30	37,456	638	211.70	179.9
2003	43	37,975	519	214.63	184.0
2004	46	39,079	1,104	220.87	188.9
2005	37	40,115	1,036	226.73	195.3
2006	45	41,014	899	231.81	201.6
2007	43	42,361	1,347	239.42	207.3
2008	40	41,579	-782	235.00	215.3
2009	42	42,215	636	238.60	214.5
2010	38	42,556	341	240.52	218.1

U.S. Department of Labor, Bureau of Labor Statistics, Consumer Price index, All Urban Consumers (CPI-U), U.S. city average, all items, 1982–1984=100. The average beginning professional salary for that period was $17,693.

Graduates were unable to agree on whether specialization (library type, subject specialization, and so forth) hindered or helped them. For some, the very nature of specialization landed them a professional position. They were able to fill a need for the employer by having knowledge and skills in a specific area, such as children's services or social media resources. The combination of coursework and on-the-job experience (as part-time student workers, support staff, or through carefully planned practicums) gave them an edge over peers with more generalized backgrounds. One graduate suggested that "intellectual knowledge had to be coupled with experiential knowledge" in order to be successful in a tough job market. Others found the job search difficult for specific jobs and said it would have been better to focus broadly and more generally on their studies.

(text continues on page 361)

Table 6 / Salaries of Reporting Professionals by Area of Job Assignment*

Assignment	Number	Percent of Total	Low Salary	High Salary	Average Salary	Median Salary
Access Services	6	0.4	$30,000	$45,000	$39,667	$44,000
Acquisitions	11	0.8	25,000	72,000	37,356	35,500
Administration	40	3.0	26,000	52,000	39,072	38,440
Adult Services	23	1.7	25,000	53,000	39,568	41,250
Archives	97	7.2	21,450	94,000	40,044	40,000
Automation/Systems	18	1.3	29,000	62,500	45,433	44,000
Cataloging & Classification	62	4.6	22,000	65,000	39,574	39,897
Children's Services	98	7.3	16,000	57,468	35,211	35,000
Circulation	85	6.3	19,968	65,000	33,644	33,140
Collection Development	8	0.6	32,000	42,600	38,350	39,000
Database Management	20	1.5	32,000	78,500	48,125	45,000
Electronic or Digital Services	31	2.3	22,800	62,000	39,393	40,000
Government Documents	5	0.4	40,000	68,230	54,410	55,000
Information Architecture	9	0.7	36,000	81,000	60,427	62,000
Info Technology	29	2.2	32,000	120,000	55,581	52,000
Instruction	23	1.7	29,960	70,000	43,000	39,220
Interlibrary Loan/ Document Delivery	14	1.0	22,495	50,000	34,249	33,500
Knowledge Management	16	1.2	32,000	100,000	61,650	57,500
Other	102	7.6	13,337	65,000	35,768	33,703
Records Management	14	1.0	18,000	70,500	39,202	39,500
Reference/Info Services	320	23.8	16,050	97,000	40,759	40,000
School Library Media Specialist	190	14.1	10,000	101,872	45,634	45,000
Solo Librarian	53	3.9	20,000	67,500	41,043	40,000
Technical Services	11	0.8	30,000	42,000	36,800	37,000
Telecommunications	2	0.1	52,000	55,000	53,500	53,500
Usability/User Experience	6	0.4	50,000	70,000	64,330	68,660
Youth Services	40	3.0	13,000	54,369	38,176	37,396
Total	1,346		10,000	120,000	41,379	40,000

* This table represents placements of any type reported by job assignment, but only salaries reported as full-time. Some individuals omitted placement information, rendering some information unusable. Comparison with other tables will show different numbers of placements.

Table 7 / Comparison of Salaries by Type of Organization

	Salaries		Low Salary		High Salary		Average Salary			Median Salary		
Total Placements	Women	Men	Women	Men	Women	Men	Women	Men	All	Women	Men	All
Public Libraries												
All Public 251	185	40	$13,000	$20,000	$72,000	$52,000	$37,253	$36,952	$37,203	$36,500	$37,000	$36,896
Northeast 71	56	9	21,000	25,700	57,100	47,700	39,746	34,219	38,981	41,000	32,000	40,000
Southeast 50	33	10	13,000	20,000	51,000	52,000	33,942	36,786	34,603	34,000	36,750	35,000
Midwest 89	65	14	13,000	23,000	57,000	47,000	36,168	37,171	36,346	36,000	38,500	36,971
Southwest 20	16	3	22,000	32,208	49,000	51,000	35,541	41,003	36,403	36,000	39,800	3,600
West 13	10	1	29,000	48,000	72,000	48,000	42,877	48,000	43,343	36,150	48,000	36,500
Canada/International 2	—	—	—	—	—	—	—	—	—	—	—	—
School Libraries												
All School 170	131	7	10,000	16,000	90,000	101,872	45,087	51,649	45,420	44,000	48,000	44,325
Northeast 57	46	4	27,000	38,170	90,000	101,872	48,307	62,511	49,443	45,000	55,000	45,500
Southeast 29	21	—	17,000	—	67,350	—	43,347	—	43,347	42,000	—	42,000
Midwest 44	36	1	10,000	48,000	75,000	48,000	39,932	48,000	40,150	42,000	48,000	42,000
Southwest 29	23	1	31,000	16,000	71,000	16,000	46,201	16,000	44,943	45,000	16,000	44,750
West 5	2	1	50,000	47,500	54,000	47,500	52,000	47,500	50,500	52,000	47,500	50,000
Canada/International 2	2	—	38,000	—	88,000	—	63,000	—	63,000	63,000	—	63,000
College and University Libraries												
All Academic 317	196	72	16,050	17,000	68,000	87,400	40,199	40,587	40,315	40,000	40,000	40,500
Northeast 86	55	19	23,000	30,000	66,000	65,000	41,967	41,446	41,854	40,000	40,000	40,000
Southeast 79	49	20	16,050	24,000	62,000	87,400	39,619	39,200	39,497	42,000	40,000	41,000
Midwest 83	54	19	24,000	17,000	50,400	55,000	38,011	38,698	38,190	40,000	41,000	40,000
Southwest 44	25	6	26,000	30,500	55,000	58,000	39,996	42,917	40,561	40,000	43,000	40,000

West	20	12	6	26,000	31,000	68,000	65,000	45,341	40,500	43,727	41,554	36,000	36,554
Canada/International	2	—	1	—	50,000	—	50,000	—	50,000	50,000	—	50,000	50,000
Special Libraries													
All Special	56	40	10	25,500	24,000	60,000	67,500	41,206	44,191	41,791	40,000	41,940	40,000
Northeast	23	15	3	27,000	31,200	60,000	67,500	41,427	45,233	42,061	40,000	37,000	39,390
Southeast	14	11	2	32,000	30,000	120,000	45,000	42,682	37,500	43,179	41,500	37,500	43,750
Midwest	8	7	1	30,000	38,880	46,000	38,880	37,920	38,880	38,040	40,000	38,880	39,440
Southwest	5	4	1	25,500	24,000	44,000	24,000	35,150	24,000	32,920	35,550	24,000	33,600
West	5	2	2	47,000	45,760	60,000	62,571	53,500	54,166	49,666	53,500	54,166	47,000
Canada/International	1	1	—	52,500	—	52,500	—	52,500	—	52,500	52,500	—	52,500
Government Libraries													
All Government	19	15	1	30,000	55,000	97,000	55,000	56,851	55,000	56,736	52,000	55,000	53,500
Northeast	1	1	—	52,000	52,000	52,000	52,000	52,000	—	52,000	52,000	—	52,000
Southeast	12	9	1	35,000	55,000	97,000	55,000	61,678	55,000	61,010	41,600	55,000	55,000
Midwest	3	3	—	30,000	—	68,230	—	46,223	—	46,223	40,000	—	40,440
Southwest	1	—	—	—	—	—	—	—	—	—	—	—	—
West	1	1	—	62,000	—	62,000	—	62,000	—	62,000	62,000	—	62,000
Library Cooperatives and Networks													
All Co-op./Nets.	2	2	—	35,000	—	38,000	—	36,500	—	36,500	36,500	—	36,500
Northeast	2	2	—	35,000	—	38,000	—	36,500	—	36,500	36,500	—	36,500
Vendors													
All Vendors	17	10	6	25,000	38,000	70,000	70,000	46,990	51,800	48,593	43,950	50,000	45,000
Northeast	6	4	1	41,000	40,000	70,000	40,000	57,625	40,000	54,100	59,750	40,000	49,500
Southeast	4	2	2	37,000	61,000	52,000	70,000	44,500	65,500	55,000	44,500	65,500	56,500
Midwest	4	2	1	25,000	38,000	42,900	38,000	43,696	38,000	35,300	33,950	38,000	38,000
West	1	1	—	45,000	—	45,000	—	45,000	—	45,000	45,000	—	45,000
Canada/International	1	1	—	—	50,000	—	50,000	—	50,000	50,000	—	50,000	50,000

Table 7 / Comparison of Salaries by Type of Organization *(cont.)*

	Total Placements	Salaries		Low Salary		High Salary		Average Salary			Median Salary		
		Women	Men	Women	Men	Women	Men	Women	Men	All	Women	Men	All
Other Organizations													
All Other	273	126	61	$10,000	$13,000	$100,000	$120,000	$47,940	$51,857	$49,218	$42,250	$47,000	$45,000
Northeast	61	29	15	13,337	32,000	90,000	120,000	48,885	60,600	49,487	45,000	59,000	48,000
Southeast	41	31	4	17,600	34,000	90,000	55,000	42,296	43,750	42,520	40,000	43,000	40,000
Midwest	75	38	19	24,000	13,000	80,000	75,000	44,481	45,811	44,924	39,500	44,000	43,500
Southwest	30	10	10	23,900	28,000	75,000	62,000	41,927	42,090	42,008	37,000	41,500	40,500
West	39	25	12	35,000	29,000	100,000	115,000	63,486	63,583	63,524	65,000	59,000	65,000
Canada/International	8	7	1	10,000	25,000	50,000	25,000	34,375	25,000	32,500	38,750	25,000	35,000

These tables represent only full-time salaries and placements reported by type. Some individuals omitted placement information, rendering some information unusable. Comparison with other tables will show different numbers of total placements due to completeness of the data reported by individuals and schools. Totals within the table represent all reported placement data but will not necessarily correspond to regional or gender breakdown.

(continued from page 357)

Other graduates did find the right job in the right type of agency. They acknowledged that in some instances the search was long and disheartening, but noted that persistence and patience helped them through. Many treated the search for permanent placement itself as a full-time job, spending a regular eight-hour day on searching, preparing résumés and cover letters, and making contacts with potential employers.

The graduating class had many words of advice and encouragement for their future colleagues. As a group they advised, "Keep a positive and professional attitude; something will come along eventually." Many also suggested that new graduates will need to be even more willing than before to accept part-time, support staff positions in order to get in the door and prove one's worth.

One grad offered these sage words: "Look beyond libraries. It is very rough out there even if you do all of the right things. And acquire other relevant experiences."

For the 2010 graduates, volunteering, fieldwork, and internships were critical to finding a job and ultimately being successful in a position. They reiterated that in such endeavors they gained valuable experience and also found many opportunities to network with professionals. Grads also suggested maintaining good, comprehensive portfolios of work completed during practicums to illustrate skills and competencies to a potential employer.

Other recommendations made by new graduates include knowing when school districts actually begin the process of recruiting and hiring for the upcoming school year. Documentation and certification need to be up-to-date before hiring begins.

Far and away, however, the most important factor in landing a position, according to the 2010 graduates, is people. Tap into professional networks, keep in contact with friends made during the degree program, and continue to cultivate professional relationships with internship supervisors, they advised. They also cited mentors as being very influential for their contacts in the field and as references that may have more impact than a more generic letter from a one-semester instructor. Some graduates who landed jobs quickly suggested that finding a job wasn't the result of the hundreds of résumés they sent out but rather because of a single internal job announcement that was forwarded to them by a mentor, friend, or classmate.

Accredited Master's Programs in Library and Information Studies

This list of graduate programs accredited by the American Library Association is issued by the ALA Office for Accreditation. Regular updates and additional details appear on the Office for Accreditation's Web site at http://www.ala.org/ Template.cfm?Section=lisdirb&Template=/cfapps/lisdir/index.cfm. More than 150 institutions offering both accredited and nonaccredited programs in librarianship are included in the 65th edition (2012–2013) of *American Library Directory* (Information Today, Inc.).

Northeast: Conn., D.C., Md., Mass., N.J., N.Y., Pa., R.I.

Catholic University of America, School of Lib. and Info. Science, 620 Michigan Ave. N.E., Washington, DC 20064. Ingrid Hsieh-Yee, Interim dean. Tel. 202-319-5085, fax 202-219-5574, e-mail cua-slis@cua.edu, World Wide Web http://slis.cua.edu. Admissions contact: Louise Gray. Tel. 202-319-5085, e-mail grayl@cua.edu.

Clarion University of Pennsylvania, College of Educ. and Human Services, Dept. of Lib. Science, 210 Carlson Lib. Bldg., 840 Wood St., Clarion, PA 16214. Janice M. Krueger, chair. Tel. 866-272-5612, fax 814-393-2150, World Wide Web http://www.clarion.edu/lib sci. Admissions contact: Lois Dulavitch. Tel. 866-272-5612, e-mail ldulavitch@clarion. edu.

Drexel University, College of Info. Science and Technology, 3141 Chestnut St., Philadelphia, PA 19104-2875. David E. Fenske, dean. Tel. 215-895-2474, fax 215-895-2494, e-mail istinfo@drexel.edu, World Wide Web http://www.ischool.drexel.edu. Admissions contact: Matthew Lechtenburg. Tel. 215-895-1951, e-mail ml333@ischool.drexel. edu.

Long Island University, Palmer School of Lib. and Info. Science, C. W. Post Campus, 720 Northern Blvd., Brookville, NY 11548-1300. Jody K. Howard, interim dir. Tel. 516-299-4109, fax 516-299-4168, e-mail palmer @cwpost.liu.edu, World Wide Web http:// www.liu.edu/palmer. Admissions contact: Geraldine Kopczynski. Tel. 516-299-2857, e-mail gkopski@liu.edu.

Pratt Institute, School of Info. and Lib. Science, 144 W. 14 St., New York, NY 10011. Tula Giannini, dean. Tel. 212-647-7682, fax 202-367-2492, e-mail infosils@pratt.edu, World Wide Web http://www.pratt.edu/academics/ information_and_library_sciences. Admissions contact: Quinn Lai. E-mail infosils@ pratt.edu.

Queens College, City Univ. of New York, Grad. School of Lib. and Info. Studies, Rm. 254, Rosenthal Lib., 65-30 Kissena Blvd., Flushing, NY 11367-1597. James Marcum, chair/ dir. Tel. 718-997-3790, fax 718-997-3797, e-mail gc_gslis@qc.cuny.edu, World Wide Web http://www.qc.cuny.edu/academics/ degrees/dss/gslis/Pages/default.aspx. Admissions contact: Roberta Brody. E-mail roberta_ brody@qc.edu.

Rutgers University, School of Communication and Info., Dept. of Lib. and Info. Science, New Brunswick, NJ 08901-1071. Marie L. Radford, chair. Tel. 732-932-7500 ext. 8218, fax 732-932-6916, e-mail scilsmls@comminfo. rutgers.edu, World Wide Web http://www. comminfo.rutgers.edu. Admissions contact: Kay Cassell. Tel. 732-932-7500 ext. 8264.

Saint John's University, College of Liberal Arts and Sciences, Div. of Lib. and Info. Science, 8000 Utopia Pkwy., Queens, NY 11439. Jeffery E. Olson, dir. Tel. 718-990-6200, fax 718-990-2071, e-mail dlis@stjohns.edu, World Wide Web http://www.stjohns.edu/academics/ graduate/liberalarts/departments/lis/library_ science_langing_page.stj. Admissions contact: Deborah Martinez. Tel. 718-990-6209.

Simmons College, Grad. School of Lib. and Info. Science, 300 The Fenway, Boston, MA 02115. Michele Cloonan, dean. Tel. 617-521-2800, fax 617-521-3192, e-mail gslis@

simmons.edu, World Wide Web http://www. simmons.edu/gslis. Admissions contact: Sarah Petrakos. Tel. 617-521-2868.

Southern Connecticut State University, School of Educ., Communication, Dept. of Info., and Lib. Science, 501 Crescent St., New Haven, CT 06515. Chang Suk Kim, chair. Tel. 203-392-5781, fax 203-392-5780, e-mail ils@southernct.edu, World Wide Web http://www.southernct.edu/ils. Admissions contact: Kathy Muldowney.

Syracuse University, School of Info. Studies, 343 Hinds Hall, Syracuse, NY 13244. Elizabeth D. Liddy, dean. Tel. 315-443-2911, fax 315-443-6886, e-mail ischool@syr.edu, World Wide Web http://www.ischool.syr. edu. Admissions contact: R. David Lankes, dir. Tel. 315-443-2911, e-mail mslis@syr. edu.

University at Albany, State Univ. of New York, College of Computing and Info., Dept. of Info. Studies, Draper 113, 135 Western Ave., Albany, NY 12222. Philip B. Eppard, chair. Tel. 518-442-5110, fax 518-442-5367, e-mail infostudies@albany.edu, World Wide Web http://www.albany.edu/information studies/index.php. Admissions contact: Frances Reynolds. E-mail freynolds@albany. edu.

University at Buffalo, State Univ. of New York, Graduate School of Educ., Lib. and Info. Studies, 534 Baldy Hall, Box 1020, Buffalo, NY 14260. Dagobert Soergel, chair. Tel. 716-645-2412, fax 716-645-3775, e-mail ub-lis@buffalo.edu, World Wide Web http:// gse.buffalo.edu/lis. Admissions contact: Radhika Suresh. Tel. 716-645-2110, e-mail gse-info@buffalo.edu.

University of Maryland, College of Info. Studies, 4105 Hornbake Bldg., College Park, MD 20742. Jennifer Preece, dean. Tel. 301-405-2033, fax 301-314-9145, e-mail ischool admission@umd.edu, World Wide Web http://ischool.umd.edu. Admissions contact: Cassandra B. Jones. Tel. 301-405-2038, e-mail ischooladmission@ umd.edu.

University of Pittsburgh, School of Info. Sciences, 135 N. Bellefield Ave., Pittsburgh, PA 15260. Martin B. Weiss, acting chair and assoc. dean. Tel. 412-624-9420, fax 412-648-7001, e-mail lisinq@mail.sis.pitt.edu, World Wide Web http://www.ischool.pitt.

edu. Admissions contact: Debbie Day. Tel. 412-624-9420, e-mail dday@sis.pitt.edu.

University of Rhode Island, Grad. School of Lib. and Info. Studies, Rodman Hall, 94 W. Alumni Ave., Kingston, RI 02881. Gale Eaton, dir. Tel. 401-874-2878, fax 401-874-4964, e-mail gslis@etal.uri.edu, World Wide Web http://www.uri.edu/artsci/lsc.

Southeast: Ala., Fla., Ga., Ky., La., Miss., N.C., S.C., Tenn., P.R.

Florida State University, College of Communication and Info., School of Lib. and Info. Studies, 142 Collegiate Loop, P.O. Box 3062100, Tallahassee, FL 32306-2100. Corinne Jorgensen, dir. Tel. 850-644-5775, fax 850-644-9763, World Wide Web http:// slis.fsu.edu.

Louisiana State University, School of Lib. and Info. Science, 267 Coates Hall, Baton Rouge, LA 70803. Beth Paskoff, dean. Tel. 225-578-3158, fax 225-578-4581, e-mail slis@lsu.edu, World Wide Web http://slis. lsu.edu. Admissions contact: LaToya Coleman Joseph. E-mail lcjoseph@lsu.edu.

North Carolina Central University, School of Lib. and Info. Sciences, P.O. Box 19586, Durham, NC 27707. Irene Owens, dean. Tel. 919-530-6485, fax 919-530-6402, World Wide Web http://www.nccuslis.org. Admissions contact: Tysha Jacobs. Tel. 919-530-7320, e-mail tjacobs@nccu.edu.

University of Alabama, College of Communication and Info. Sciences, School of Lib. and Info. Studies, Box 870252, Tuscaloosa, AL 35487-0252. Heidi Julien, dir. Tel. 205-348-4610, fax 205-348-3746, e-mail info@slis. ua.edu, World Wide Web http://www.slis. ua.edu. Admissions contact: Beth Riggs. Tel. 205-348-1527, e-mail briggs@slis.ua.edu.

University of Kentucky, School of Lib. and Info. Science, 320 Little Lib., Lexington, KY 40506-0224. Jeffrey T. Huber, dir. Tel. 859-257-8876, fax 859-257-4205, e-mail ukslis@uky.edu, World Wide Web http:// www.uky.edu/cis/slis. Admissions contact: Will Buntin. Tel. 859-257-3317, e-mail wjbunt0@uky.edu.

University of North Carolina at Chapel Hill, School of Info. and Lib. Science, CB 3360,

100 Manning Hall, Chapel Hill, NC 27599-3360. Gary Marchionini, dean. Tel. 919-962-8366, fax 919-962-8071, e-mail info@ils.unc.edu, World Wide Web http://www.sils.unc.edu. Admissions contact: Lara Bailey.

University of North Carolina at Greensboro, School of Educ., Dept. of Lib. and Info. Studies, 446 School of Educ. Bldg., Greensboro, NC 27402-6170. Clara M. Chu, chair. Tel. 336-334-3477, fax 336-334-4120, World Wide Web http://lis.uncg.edu. Admissions contact: Touger Vang. E-mail t_vang@uncg.edu.

University of Puerto Rico, Info. Sciences and Technologies, P.O. Box 21906, San Juan, PR 00931-1906. Luisa Vigo-Cepeda, acting dir. Tel. 787-763-6199, fax 787-764-2311, e-mail egcti@uprrp.edu, World Wide Web http://egcti.upr.edu. Admissions contact: Migdalia Dávila-Perez. Tel. 787-764-0000 ext. 3530, e-mail migdalia.davila@upr.edu.

University of South Carolina, College of Mass Communications and Info. Studies, School of Lib. and Info. Science, 1501 Greene St., Columbia, SC 29208. Samantha K. Hastings, dir. Tel. 803-777-3858, fax 803-777-7938, e-mail hastings@sc.edu, World Wide Web http://www.libsci.sc.edu. Admissions contact: Tilda Reeder. Tel. 800-304-3153, e-mail tildareeder@sc.edu.

University of South Florida, College of Arts and Sciences, School of Lib. and Info. Science, 4202 E. Fowler Ave., CIS 1040, Tampa, FL 33620. James Andrews, dir. Tel. 813-974-3520, fax 813-974-6840, e-mail lisinfo@usf.edu, World Wide Web http://si.usf.edu. Admissions contact: Daniel Kahl. Tel. 813-974-8022, e-mail djkahl@usf.edu.

University of Southern Mississippi, College of Educ. and Psychology, School of Lib. and Info. Science, 118 College Drive, No. 5146, Hattiesburg, MS 39406-0001. M. J. Norton, dir. Tel. 601-266-4228, fax 601-266-5774, e-mail slis@usm.edu, World Wide Web http://www.usm.edu/slis. Admissions tel. 601-266-5137, e-mail graduatestudies@usm.edu.

University of Tennessee, College of Communication and Info., School of Info. Sciences, 451 Communication Bldg., Knoxville, TN 37996. Edwin M. Cortez, dir. Tel. 865-974-2148, fax 865-974-4967, World Wide Web http://www.sis.utk.edu. Admissions contact:

Tanya Arnold. Tel. 865-974-2858, e-mail tnarnold@utk.edu.

Valdosta State Univ., Dept. of Info. Studies, 1500 N. Patterson St., Valdosta, GA 31698-0133. Wallace Koehler, dir. Tel. 229-333-5966, fax 229-259-5055, e-mail mlis@valdosta.edu, World Wide Web http://www.valdosta.edu/mlis. Admissions contact: Sheila Peacock.

Midwest: Ill., Ind., Iowa, Kan., Mich., Mo., Ohio, Wis.

Dominican Univ., Grad. School of Lib. and Info. Science, 7900 W. Division St., River Forest, IL 60305. Susan Roman, dean. Tel. 708-524-6845, fax 708-524-6657, e-mail gslis@dom.edu, World Wide Web http://www.dom.edu/gslis. Admissions contact: Teresa Espinoza. Tel. 708-524-6848, e-mail tespinoza@dom.edu.

Emporia State University, School of Lib. and Info. Management, 1200 Commercial, Campus Box 4025, Emporia, KS 66801. Gwen Alexander, dean. Tel. 620-341-5203, fax 620-341-5233, e-mail sliminfo@emporia.edu, World Wide Web http://slim.emporia.edu. Admissions contact: Matthew Upson. Tel. 620-341-6159, e-mail sliminfo@emporia.edu.

Indiana University, School of Lib. and Info. Science, 1320 E. 10 St., LI 011, Bloomington, IN 47405-3907. Debora Shaw, dean. Tel. 812-855-2018, fax 812-855-6166, e-mail slis@indiana.edu, World Wide Web http://www.slis.indiana.edu. Admissions contact: Rhonda Spencer.

Kent State University, School of Lib. and Info. Science, P.O. Box 5190, Kent, OH 44242-0001. Don A. Wicks, interim dir. Tel. 330-672-2782, fax 330-672-7965, e-mail slis inform@kent.ed, World Wide Web http://www.kent.edu/slis. Admissions contact: Cheryl Tennant.

University of Illinois at Urbana-Champaign, Grad. School of Lib. and Info. Science, 501 E. Daniel St., Champaign, IL 61820-6211. John Unsworth, dean. Tel. 217-333-3280, fax 217-244-3302, e-mail gslis@Illinois.edu, World Wide Web http://www.lis.illinois.edu. Admissions contact: Penny Ames. Tel. 217-333-7197, e-mail pames@illinois.edu.

University of Iowa, Graduate College, School of Lib. and Info. Science, 3087 Main Lib., Iowa City, IA 52242-1420. Daniel Berkowitz, interim dir. Tel. 319-335-5707, fax 319-335-5374, e-mail slis@uiowa.edu, World Wide Web http://slis.grad.uiowa.edu. Admissions contact: Kit Austin. E-mail caroline-austin@uiowa.edu.

University of Michigan, School of Info., 4322 North Quad, 105 W. St., Ann Arbor, MI 48109-1285. Jeffrey MaKie-Mason, dean. Tel. 734-763-2285, fax 734-764-2475, e-mail si.admissions@umich.edu, World Wide Web http://www.si.umich.edu. Admissions contact: Laura Elgas.

University of Missouri, College of Educ., School of Info. Science and Learning Technologies, 303 Townsend Hall, Columbia, MO 65211. John Wedman, dir. Tel. 877-747-5868, fax 573-884-0122, e-mail sislt@missouri.edu, World Wide Web http://sislt.missouri.edu. Admissions tel. 573-882-4546.

University of Wisconsin–Madison, College of Letters and Sciences, School of Lib. and Info. Studies, 600 N. Park St., Madison, WI 53706. Christine Pawley, dir. Tel. 608-263-2900, fax 608-263-4849, e-mail uw-slis@slis.wisc.edu, World Wide Web http://www.slis.wisc.edu. Admissions contact: Tanya Cobb. Tel. 608-263-2909, e-mail studentservices@slis.wisc.edu.

University of Wisconsin–Milwaukee, School of Info. Studies, P.O. Box 413, Milwaukee, WI 53211. Dietmar Wolfram, interim dean. Tel. 414-229-4707, fax 414-229-6699, e-mail soisinfo@uwm.edu, World Wide Web http://www4.uwm.edu/sois.

Wayne State University, School of Lib. and Info. Science, 106 Kresge Lib., Detroit, MI 48202. Stephen T. Bajjaly, assoc. dean. Tel. 313-577-1825, fax 313-577-7563, e-mail asklis@wayne.edu, World Wide Web http://www.slis.wayne.edu. Admissions contact: Matthew Fredericks. Tel. 313-577-2446, e-mail mfredericks@wayne.edu.

Southwest: Ariz., Okla., Texas

Texas Woman's University, School of Lib. and Info. Studies, P.O. Box 425438, Denton, TX 76204-5438. Ling Hwey Jeng, dir. Tel. 940-898-2602, fax 940-898-2611, e-mail slis@twu.edu, World Wide Web http://www.twu.edu/slis. Admissions contact: Brenda Mallory. E-mail bmallory@mail.twu.edu.

University of Arizona, College of Social and Behavioral Sciences, School of Info. Resources and Lib. Science, 1515 E. 1 St., Tucson, AZ 85719. P. Bryan Heidorn, dir. Tel. 520-621-3565, fax 520-621-3279, e-mail sirls@email.arizona.edu, World Wide Web http://www.sirls.arizona.edu. Admissions contact: Geraldine Fragoso. Tel. 520-621-5230, e-mail gfragoso@u.arizona.edu.

University of North Texas, College of Info., Dept. of Lib. and Info. Sciences, 1155 Union Circle, No. 311068, Denton, TX 76203-5017. Suliman Hawamdeh, chair. Tel. 940-565-3690, fax 940-369-7600, e-mail ci-dean@unt.edu, World Wide Web http://www.ci.unt.edu/main. Admissions contact: John Pipes. Tel. 940-565-3562, e-mail john.pipes@unt.edu.

University of Oklahoma, School of Lib. and Info. Studies, College of Arts and Sciences, 401 W. Brooks, Norman, OK 73019-6032. Cecelia Brown, dir. Tel. 405-325-3921, fax 405-325-7648, e-mail slisinfo@ou.edu, World Wide Web http://www.ou.edu/cas/slis. Admissions contact: Maggie Ryan.

University of Texas at Austin, School of Info., Suite 5.202, 1616 Guadalupe St., Austin, TX 78701-1213. Andrew Dillon, dean. Tel. 512-471-3821, fax 512-471-3971, e-mail info@ischool.utexas.edu, World Wide Web http://www.ischool.utexas.edu. Admissions contact: Carla Criner. Tel. 512-471-5654, e-mail criner@ischool.utexas.edu.

West: Calif., Colo., Hawaii, Wash.

San José State University, School of Lib. and Info. Science, 1 Washington Sq., San José, CA 95192-0029. Sandy Hirsh, dir. Tel. 408-924-2490, fax 408-924-2476, e-mail sanjose slis@gmail.com, World Wide Web http://slisweb.sjsu.edu. Admissions contact: Linda Main. Tel. 408-924-2494, e-mail linda.main@sjsu.edu.

University of California, Los Angeles, Graduate School of Educ. and Info. Studies, Dept.

of Info. Studies, Box 951520, Los Angeles, CA 90095-1520. Gregory Leazer, chair. Tel. 310-825-8799, fax 310-206-3076, e-mail info@gseis.ucla.edu, World Wide Web http://is.gseis.ucla.edu. Admissions contact: Susan Abler. Tel. 310-825-5269, e-mail abler@gseis.ucla.edu.

University of Denver, Morgridge College of Educ., Lib. and Info. Science Program, 1999 E. Evans Ave., Denver, CO 80208-1700. Mary Stansbury, chair. Tel. 303-871-2747, fax 303-871-2709, e-mail mary.stansbury@du.edu, World Wide Web http://www.du.edu/lis. Admissions contact: Nick Heckart. E-mail nheckart@du.edu.

University of Hawaii, College of Natural Sciences, Lib. and Info. Science Program, 2550 McCarthy Mall, Honolulu, HI 96822. Andrew Wertheimer, chair. Tel. 808-956-7321, fax 808-956-5835, e-mail slis@hawaii.edu, World Wide Web http://www.hawaii.edu/lis.

University of Washington, The Info. School, 370 Mary Gates Hall, Seattle, WA 98195-2840. Harry Bruce, dean. Tel. 206-685-9937, fax 206-616-3152, e-mail ischool@uw.edu, World Wide Web http://ischool.uw.edu. Admissions contact: Admissions coordinator. Tel. 206-543-1794, e-mail mlis@ischool.uw.edu.

Canada

Dalhousie University, School of Info. Management, Kenneth C. Rowe Management Bldg., Halifax, NS B3H 3J5. Louise Spiteri, dir. Tel. 902-494-3656, fax 902-494-2451, e-mail sim@dal.ca, World Wide Web http://www.sim.management.dal.ca. Admissions contact: JoAnn Watson. E-mail mlis@dal.ca.

McGill University, School of Info. Studies, 3661 Peel St., Montreal, QC H3A 1X1. France Bouthillier, dir. Tel. 514-398-4204, fax 514-398-7193, e-mail sis@mcgill.ca, World Wide Web http://www.mcgill.ca/sis.

Admissions contact: Kathryn Hubbard, Tel. 514-398-4204 ext. 0742.

Université de Montréal, École de Bibliothéconomie et des Sciences de l'Information, C.P. 6128, Succursale Centre-Ville, Montreal, QC H3C 3J7. Clément Arsenault, dir. Tel. 514-343-6044, fax 514-343-5753, e-mail ebsiinfo@ebsi.umontreal.ca, World Wide Web http://www.ebsi.umontreal.ca. Admissions contact: Alain Tremblay. Tel. 514-343-6044, e-mail alain.tremblay.1@umontreal.ca.

University of Alberta, School of Lib. and Info. Studies, 3-20 Rutherford S., Edmonton, AB T6G 2J4. Ernie Ingles, dir. Tel. 780-492-4578, fax 780-492-2430, e-mail slis@ualberta.ca, World Wide Web http://www.slis.ualberta.ca. Admissions contact: Lauren Romaniuk. Tel. 780-492-4140, e-mail slis admissions@ualberta.ca,

University of British Columbia, School of Lib., Archival, and Info. Studies, Irving K. Barber Learning Centre, Suite 470, 1961 East Mall, Vancouver, BC V6T 1Z1. Caroline Haythornthwaite, dir. Tel. 604-822-2404, fax 604-822-6006, e-mail slais@interchange.ubc.ca, World Wide Web http://www.slais.ubc.ca. Admissions contact: Michelle Mallette. E-mail slaisad@interchange.ubc.ca.

University of Toronto, Faculty of Info., 140 George St., Toronto, ON M5S 3G6. Seamus Ross, dean. Tel. 416-978-3202, fax 416-978-5762, e-mail inquire.ischool@utoronto.ca, World Wide Web http://www.ischool.utoronto.ca. Admissions contact: Adriana Rossini. Tel. 416-978-8589, e-mail adriana.rossini@utoronto.ca.

University of Western Ontario, Grad. Programs in Lib. and Info. Science, Faculty of Info. and Media Studies, Room 240, North Campus Bldg., London, ON N6A 5B7. Thomas Carmichael, dean. Tel. 519-661-4017, fax 519-661-3506, e-mail mlisinfo@uwo.ca, World Wide Web http://fims.uwo.ca. Admissions contact: Shelley Long.

Library Scholarship Sources

For a more complete list of scholarships, fellowships, and assistantships offered for library study, see *Financial Assistance for Library and Information Studies,* published annually by the American Library Association (ALA). The document is also available on the ALA Web site at http://www.ala.org/educationcareers/sites/ ala.org.educationcareers/files/content/education/financialassistance/20102011_ FALIS_Booklet.pdf.

American Association of Law Libraries. (1) A varying number of scholarships of varying amounts for graduates of an accredited law school who are degree candidates in an ALA-accredited library school; (2) a varying number of scholarships of varying amounts for library school graduates working on a law degree and non-law graduates enrolled in an ALA-accredited library school; (3) the George A. Strait Minority Stipend for varying numbers of minority librarians working toward a library or law degree; and (4) a varying number of $200 scholarships for law librarians taking courses relating to law librarianship. For information, write to: AALL Scholarship Committee, 105 W. Adams, Suite 3300, Chicago, IL 60603.

American Library Association. (1) The Marshall Cavendish Scholarship and (2) the David H. Clift Scholarship, both of $3,000, for two students who have been admitted to ALA-accredited library schools; (3) the Tom and Roberta Drewes Scholarship of $3,000 for library support staff; (4) the Mary V. Gaver Scholarship of $3,000 for an individual specializing in youth services; (5) the Miriam L. Hornback Scholarship of $3,000 for an ALA or library support staff member; (6) the Christopher J. Hoy/ERT Scholarship of $5,000 for a student who has been admitted to an ALA-accredited library school; (7) the Tony B. Leisner Scholarship of $3,000 for a library support staff member; (8) the Peter Lyman Memorial/Sage Scholarship in New Media of $2,500 for a student admitted to an ALA-accredited library school who will specialize in new media; (9) the Cicely Phippen Marks Scholarship of $1,500 for a student admitted to an ALA-accredited program who will specialize in federal librarianship; (10) Spectrum Initiative Scholarships of $6,500 for a varying number of minority students admitted to a master's degree program at an ALA-accredited library school. For information, write to: ALA Scholarship Clearinghouse, 50 E. Huron St., Chicago, IL 60611, or see http://www.ala.org/scholarships.

ALA/Association for Library Service to Children. (1) The Bound to Stay Bound Books Scholarship of $7,000 each for four U.S. or Canadian citizens who have been admitted to an ALA-accredited master's or doctoral program, and who will work with children in a library for one year after graduation; (2) the Frederic G. Melcher Scholarship of $6,000 each for two U.S. or Canadian citizens admitted to an ALA-accredited library school who will work with children in school or public libraries for one year after graduation. For information, write to: ALA Scholarship Clearinghouse, 50 E. Huron St., Chicago, IL 60611, or see http://www.ala. org/scholarships.

ALA/Association of College and Research Libraries and Thomson Reuters. (1) The ACRL Doctoral Dissertation Fellowship of $1,500 for a student who has completed all coursework, and submitted a dissertation proposal that has been accepted, in the area of academic librarianship; (2) the Samuel Lazerow Fellowship of $1,000 for a research, travel, or writing project in acquisitions or technical services in an academic or research library; (3) the ACRL and Coutts Nijhoff International West European Specialist Study Grant of $3,000 to pay travel expenses, room, and board for a ten-day trip to Europe for an ALA member (selection is based on a proposal outlining the purpose of the trip). For information, write to: Megan Griffin, ALA/ACRL, 50 E. Huron St., Chicago, IL 60611.

ALA/Association of Specialized and Cooperative Library Agencies. Century Scholarship of up to $2,500 for a varying number of disabled U.S. or Canadian citizens admitted to an ALA-accredited library school. For information, write to: ALA Scholarship Clearinghouse, 50 E. Huron St., Chicago, IL 60611, or see http://www.ala.org/scholarships.

ALA/International Relations Committee. The Bogle Pratt International Library Travel Fund grant of $1,000 for a varying number of ALA members to attend a first international conference. For information, write to: Michael Dowling, ALA/IRC, 50 E. Huron St., Chicago, IL 60611.

ALA/Library and Information Technology Association. (1) The LITA/Christian Larew Memorial Scholarship of $3,000 for a disabled U.S. or Canadian citizen admitted to an ALA-accredited library school; (2) the LITA/OCLC Minority Scholarship in Library and Information Technology of $3,000; and (3) the LITA/LSSI Minority Scholarship of $2,500, each for a minority student admitted to an ALA-accredited program. For information, write to: ALA Scholarship Clearinghouse, 50 E. Huron St., Chicago, IL 60611, or see http://www.ala.org/scholarships.

ALA/Public Library Association. The Demco New Leaders Travel Grant Study Award of up to $1,500 for a varying number of PLA members with MLS degrees and five years or less experience. For information, write to: PLA Awards Program, ALA/PLA, 50 E. Huron St., Chicago, IL 60611.

American-Scandinavian Foundation. Fellowships and grants for 25 to 30 students, in amounts from $5,000 to $23,000, for advanced study in Denmark, Finland, Iceland, Norway, or Sweden. For information, write to: Fellowships and Grants, American-Scandinavian Foundation, 58 Park Ave., New York, NY 10026, or see http://www.amscan.org/fellowships_grants.html.

Association for Library and Information Science Education (ALISE). A varying number of research grants of up to $2,500 each for members of ALISE. For information, write to: Association for Library and Information Science Education, 65 E. Wacker Place, Suite 1900, Chicago, IL 60601.

Association of Bookmobile and Outreach Services (ABOS). (1) The Bernard Vavrek Scholarship of $1,000 for a student with a grade-point average of 3.0 or better admitted to an ALA-accredited program and interested in becoming an outreach/bookmobile librarian; (2) the John Philip Award of $300 to recognize outstanding contributions and leadership by an individual in bookmobile and outreach services; (3) the Carol Hole Conference Attendance Travel Grant of $500 for a public librarian working in outreach or bookmobile services. For information, write to President, ABOS, c/o MLNC, 3610 Barrett Office Drive, Suite 206, Ballwin, MO 63021, or visit http://www.abos-outreach.org.

Association of Jewish Libraries. The AJL Scholarship Fund offers up to two scholarships of $500 each for MLS students who plan to work as Judaica librarians. For information, write to: Shulamith Berger, AJL Scholarship Committee, Yeshiva University Library, 500 W. 185 St., New York, NY 10033.

Association of Seventh-Day Adventist Librarians. The D. Glenn Hilts Scholarship of $1,200 for a member of the Seventh-Day Adventist Church in a graduate library program. For information, write to: Lee Wisel, Association of Seventh-Day Adventist Librarians, Columbia Union College, 7600 Flower Ave., Takoma Park, MD 20912.

Beta Phi Mu. (1) The Sarah Rebecca Reed Scholarship of $2,000 for a person accepted in an ALA-accredited library program; (2) the Frank B. Sessa Scholarship of $1,500 for a Beta Phi Mu member for continuing education; (3) the Harold Lancour Scholarship of $1,750 for study in a foreign country relating to the applicant's work or schooling; (4) the Blanche E. Woolls Scholarship for School Library Media Service of $2,250 for a person accepted in an ALA-accredited library program; (5) the Eugene Garfield Doctoral Dissertation Scholarship of $3,000 for a person who has approval of a dissertation topic. For information, write to: Christie Koontz, Executive Director, Beta Phi Mu, College of Information, Florida State University, 101H Louis Shores Bldg., 142 Collegiate Loop, Tallahassee, FL 32306-2100.

Canadian Association of Law Libraries. The Diana M. Priestly Scholarship of $2,500 for a student enrolled in an approved Canadian law school or accredited Canadian library school. For information, write to: Ann Marie Melvin, Librarian, Saskatchewan Court of Appeal, 2425 Victoria Ave., Regina, SK S4P 4W6.

Canadian Federation of University Women. (1) The Alice E. Wilson Award of $6,000 for five mature students returning to graduate studies in any field, with special consideration given to those returning to study after at least three years; (2) the Margaret McWilliams Pre-Doctoral Fellowship of $13,000 for a female student who has completed at least one full year as a full-time student in doctoral-level studies; (3) the Marion Elder Grant Fellowship of $11,000 for a full-time student at any level of a doctoral program; (4) the CFUW Memorial Fellowship of $10,000 for a student who is currently enrolled in a master's program in science, mathematics, or engineering in Canada or abroad; (5) the Beverly Jackson Fellowship of $2,000 for a student over the age of 35 at the time of application who is enrolled in graduate studies at an Ontario university; (6) the 1989 Ecole Polytechnique Commemorative Award of $7,000 for graduate studies in any field; (7) the Bourse Georgette LeMoyne award of $7,000 for graduate study in any field at a Canadian university (the candidate must be studying in French); (8) the Margaret Dale Philp Biennial Award of $3,000 for studies in the humanities or social sciences; (9) the Canadian Home Economics Association Fellowship of $6,000 for a student enrolled in a postgraduate program in Canada. For information, write to: Fellowships Program Manager, Canadian Federation of University Women, 251 Bank St., Suite 305, Ottawa, ON K2P 1X3, Canada, or see http://www.cfuw.org.

Canadian Library Association. (1) The CLA Dafoe Scholarship of $5,000 and (2) the H. W. Wilson Scholarship of $2,000, each given to a Canadian citizen or landed immigrant to attend an accredited Canadian library school; (3) the Library Research and Development Grant of $1,000 for a member of the Canadian Library Association, in support of theoretical and applied research

in library and information science. For information, write to: CLA Membership Services Department, Scholarship Committee, 1150 Morrison Drive, Suite 400, Ottawa, ON K2H 8S9, Canada.

Catholic Library Association. (1) The World Book, Inc., Grant of $1,500 divided among no more than three CLA members for continuing education in children's or school librarianship; (2) the Rev. Andrew L. Bouwhuis Memorial Scholarship of $1,500 for a student accepted into a graduate program in library science. For information, write to: Scholarship Committee, Catholic Library Association, 205 W. Monroe St., Suite 314, Chicago, IL 60606-5061.

Chinese American Librarians Association. (1) The Sheila Suen Lai Scholarship and (2) the C. C. Seetoo/CALA Conference Travel Scholarship, each $500, to a Chinese descendant who has been accepted in an ALA-accredited program. For information, write to: MengXiong Liu, Clark Library, San José State University, 1 Washington Sq., San Jose, CA 95192-0028.

Church and Synagogue Library Association. The Muriel Fuller Memorial Scholarship of $200 (including texts) for a correspondence course offered by the association. For information, write to: CSLA, 2920 S.W. Dolph Court, Suite 3A, Portland, OR 97280-0357.

Council on Library and Information Resources. (1) The Rovelstad Scholarship in International Librarianship, to enable a student enrolled in an accredited LIS program to attend the IFLA Annual Conference; (2) the A. R. Zipf Fellowship in Information Management of $10,000, to a U.S. citizen enrolled in graduate school who shows exceptional promise for leadership and technical achievement. For more information, write to: A. R. Zipf Fellowship, Council on Library and Information Resources, 1752 N St. N.W., Suite 800, Washington, DC 20036.

Massachusetts Black Librarians' Network. Two scholarships of at least $500 and $1,000 for minority students entering an ALA-accredited master's program in library science with no more than 12 semester hours completed toward a degree. For information, write to: Pearl Mosley, Chair, Massachusetts Black Librarians' Network, 17 Beech Glen St., Roxbury, MA 02119.

Medical Library Association. (1) The Cunningham Memorial International Fellowship of $3,500 for each of two health sciences librarians from countries other than the United States and Canada; (2) a scholarship of $5,000 for a person entering an ALA-accredited library program, with no more than one-half of the program yet to be completed; (3) a scholarship of $5,000 for a minority student for graduate study; (4) a varying number of Research, Development, and Demonstration Project Grants of $100 to $1,000 for U.S. or Canadian citizens, preferably MLA members; (5) the MLA Doctoral Fellowship of $2,000 for doctoral work in medical librarianship or information science; (6) the Rittenhouse Award of $500 for a student enrolled in an ALA-accredited library program or a recent graduate working as a trainee in a library internship program. For information, write to: Professional Development Department, Medical Library Association, 65 E. Wacker Place, Suite 1900, Chicago, IL 60601-7298.

Mountain Plains Library Association. A varying number of grants of up to $600 for applicants who are members of the association and have been for the preceding two years. For information, write to: Judy Zelenski, Interim Executive Secretary, MPLA, 14293 W. Center Drive, Lakewood, SD 80228.

Society of American Archivists. (1) The F. Gerald Ham Scholarship of $7,500 for up to two graduate students in archival education at a U.S. university that meets the society's criteria for graduate education; (2) the Mosaic Scholarship of $5,000 for up to two U.S. or Canadian minority students enrolled in a graduate program in archival administration; (3) the Josephine Foreman Scholarship of $10,000 for a U.S. citizen or permanent resident who is a minority graduate student enrolled in a program in archival administration; (4) the Oliver Wendell Holmes Travel Award to enable foreign students involved in archival training in the United States or Canada to attend the SAA Annual Meeting; (5) the Donald Peterson Student Travel Award of up to $1,000 to enable graduate students or recent graduates to attend the meeting; and (6) the Harold T. Pinkett Minority Student Awards to enable minority students or graduate students to attend the meeting. For details, write to: Debra Noland, Society of American Archivists, 17 N. State St., Suite 1425, Chicago, IL 60607, or visit http://www2.archivists.org/recognition.

Southern Regional Education Board. A varying number of grants of varying amounts to cover in-state tuition for graduate or postgraduate study in an ALA-accredited library school for residents of various southern U.S. states (qualifying states vary year by year). For information, write to: Academic Common Market, c/o Southern Regional Education Board, 592 Tenth St. N.W., Atlanta, GA 30318-5790.

Special Libraries Association. (1) Three $6,000 scholarships for students interested in special-library work; (2) the Plenum Scholarship of $1,000 and (3) the ISI Scholarship of $1,000, each also for students interested in special-library work; (4) the Affirmative Action Scholarship of $6,000 for a minority student interested in special-library work; and (5) the Pharmaceutical Division Stipend Award of $1,200 for a student with an undergraduate degree in chemistry, life sciences, or pharmacy entering or enrolled in an ALA-accredited program. For information on the first four scholarships, write to: Scholarship Committee, Special Libraries Association, 331 S. Patrick St., Alexandria, VA 22314-3501. For information on the Pharmaceutical Division Stipend, write to: Susan E. Katz, Awards Chair, Knoll Pharmaceuticals Science Information Center, 30 N. Jefferson St., Whippany, NJ 07981.

Library Scholarship and Award Recipients, 2011

Compiled by the staff of the *Library and Book Trade Almanac*

Scholarships and awards are listed by organization.

American Association of Law Libraries (AALL)

AALL and Thomson West/George A. Strait Minority Scholarship. *Winners:* Donyele Darrough, Domonique Roberts.

AALL Distinguished Lectureship. *Winner:* Jolande E. Goldberg.

AALL Public Access to Government Information Award. *Winner:* Citizens for Responsibility and Ethics in Washington (CREW), Washington, D.C.

AALL Scholarships. *Winners:* (library degree for law school graduates) Andrea Alexander; (law librarians in continuing education courses) Donna Fisher, Katherine Solon.

AALL Spectrum Article of the Year Award. *Winner:* Steven J. Melamut for "Freeing Creativity: Understanding the Creative Commons licenses" (*AALL Spectrum*, April 2010).

AALL/Wolters Kluwer Law and Business Research Grant. *Winner:* John Cannan.

Marian Gould Gallagher Distinguished Service Award. To recognize extended and sustained service to law librarianship. *Winners:* Laura N. Gasaway, Frank G. Houdek, M. Kathleen Price.

Marcia J. Koslov Scholarship. To provide funding for members to attend seminars and conferences that provide continuing education for state, court, or county law librarians. *Winner:* Janine Liebert.

Law Library Journal Article of the Year. *Winners:* Amanda M. Runyon and Leslie A. Street for "Finding the Middle Ground in Collection Development: How Academic Law Libraries Can Shape Their Collections in Response to the Call for More Practice-Oriented Legal Education."

Law Library Publications Award. *Winners:* (nonprint division) Library of the U.S. Courts for the Seventh Circuit, Chicago, for "Bill's Bulletin"; Mendik Library, New York Law School, for "DRAGNET"; (print division) Jacob Burns Law Library, George Washington University Law School, for *A Legal Miscellanea.*

LexisNexis/John R. Johnson Memorial Scholarships. *Winners:* (library degree for law school graduates) Andrea Alexander, Michael McArthur, Jeff McGowan, Ellen Richardson; (dual library degree and law degree) Kathryn Crandall.

Minority Leadership Development Award. *Winner:* Michelle Cosby.

Robert L. Oakley Member Advocacy Award. To recognize an AALL member who has been an outstanding advocate and has contributed significantly to the AALL policy agenda at the federal, state, local, or international level. *Winner:* Joan M. Bellistri, director and law librarian, Anne Arundel County Public Law Library, Annapolis.

American Library Association (ALA)

ALA/Information Today Library of the Future Award ($1,500). For a library, consortium, group of librarians, or support organization for innovative planning for, applications of, or development of patron training programs about information technology in a library setting. *Donor:* Information Today, Inc. *Winner:* Orange County (Florida) Library System Technology and Education Center.

ALA Presidential Citations for Innovative International Library Projects. To libraries outside the United States for significant contributions to the people they serve. *Winners:* RISE Videoconferencing Network, Alberta, Canada; National Library Board of Singapore Quest Library Reading Program; E-Publication System Platform Project at the National Central Library, Taiwan; Expanding Information Access for Visually Impaired People Project, Vietnam.

Hugh C. Atkinson Memorial Award. For outstanding achievement (including risk taking) by academic librarians that has contributed significantly to improvements in library automation, management, and/or development or research. *Offered by:* ACRL, ALCTS, LLAMA, and LITA divisions. *Winner:* Carol A. Mandel.

Carroll Preston Baber Research Grant (up to $3,000). For innovative research that could lead to an improvement in library services to any specified group(s) of people. *Donor:* Eric R. Baber. *Winner:* Mary Wilkins Jordan, Simmons College, for "Public Library Stressors: Identification and Elimination."

Beta Phi Mu Award ($1,000). For distinguished service in library education. *Donor:* Beta Phi Mu International Library Science Honorary Society. *Winner:* Lesley Farmer.

Bogle-Pratt International Library Travel Fund Award ($1,000). To ALA member(s) to attend their first international conference. *Donors:* Bogle Memorial Fund and Pratt Institute School of Information and Library Science. *Winner:* Madeline Mundt.

W. Y. Boyd Literary Novel Award. *Winner:* See "Literary Prizes, 2011" in Part 5.

David H. Clift Scholarship ($3,000). To worthy U.S. or Canadian citizens enrolled in an ALA-accredited program toward an MLS degree. *Winner:* Christine Noel Malinowski.

Melvil Dewey Medal ($2,000). To an individual or group for recent creative professional achievement in library management, training, cataloging and classification, and the tools and techniques of librarianship. *Donor:* OCLC/Forest Press. *Winner:* Deanna B. Marcum.

Tom and Roberta Drewes Scholarship ($3,000). To a library support staff member pursuing a master's degree. *Donor:* Quality Books. *Winner:* Kelly Anne Durkin.

EBSCO/ALA Conference Sponsorship Award ($1,000). To enable librarians to attend the ALA Annual Conference. *Donor:* EBSCO. *Winners:* Elissia Buell, Tina Chan, Jonathan Chima, Megan Hodge, Miranda Rodriguez, Win Shih, Carrie L. Waibel.

Equality Award ($1,000). To an individual or group for an outstanding contribution that promotes equality in the library profession. *Donor:* Scarecrow Press. *Winner:* Joan R. Giesecke.

Elizabeth Futas Catalyst for Change Award ($1,000). A biennial award to recognize a librarian who invests time and talent to make positive change in the profession of librarianship. *Donor:* Elizabeth Futas Memorial Fund. *Winner:* To be awarded next in 2012.

Loleta D. Fyan Public Library Research Grant (up to $10,000). For projects in public library development. *Donor:* Fyan Estate. *Winner:* Mary Mann and Terry O'Connor, in partnership with the Lac du Flambeau Public Library in Wisconsin, for "Revitalizing Libraries in Indian Country: The Lac du Flambeau Ojibwe Research Center."

Gale Cengage Learning Financial Development Award ($2,500). To a library organization for a financial development project to secure new funding resources for a public or academic library. *Donor:* Gale Cengage Learning. *Winner:* St. Charles (Missouri) City-County Library District.

Mary V. Gaver Scholarship ($3,000). To a student pursuing an MLS degree and specializing in youth services. *Winner:* Shanna Shadoan.

Greenwood Publishing Group Award for Best Book in Library Literature ($5,000). To recognize authors of U.S. or Canadian works whose books improve library management principles and practice. *Donor:* Greenwood Publishing Group. *Winner:* Ellyssa Kroski for *The Tech Set* (Neal-Schuman).

Ken Haycock Award for Promoting Librarianship ($1,000). For significant contribution to public recognition and appreciation of librarianship through professional performance, teaching, or writing. *Winner:* Wendy Newman.

Honorary ALA Membership. To recognize outstanding contributions of lasting importance to libraries and librarianship. *Honoree:* Yohannes Gebregeorgis, founder of Ethiopia Reads.

Miriam L. Hornback Scholarship ($3,000). To an ALA or library support staff person pursuing a master's degree in library science. *Winner:* Kai Alexis Smith.

Paul Howard Award for Courage ($1,000). Awarded biennially to a librarian, library board, library group, or an individual for exhibiting unusual courage for the benefit of library programs or services. *Donor:* Paul Howard Memorial Fund. *Winner:* Not awarded in 2011.

John Ames Humphry/OCLC/Forest Press Award ($1,000). To one or more individuals for significant contributions to international librarianship. *Donor:* OCLC/Forest Press. *Winner:* Sally Tseng.

Tony B. Leisner Scholarship ($3,000). To a library support staff member pursuing a master's degree program. *Donor:* Tony B. Leisner. *Winner:* Christopher Danald Marcum.

Joseph W. Lippincott Award ($1,000). For distinguished service to the library profession. *Donor:* Joseph W. Lippincott III. *Winner:* Camila Alire.

Peter Lyman Memorial/Sage Scholarship in New Media ($2,500). To support a student seeking an MLS degree in an ALA-accredited program and pursuing a specialty in new media. *Donor:* Sage Publications. *Winner:* Fredrica Lush.

James Madison Award. To recognize efforts to promote government openness. *Winner:* Patrice McDermott, director of OpenTheGovernment.org.

Marshall Cavendish Excellence in Library Programming Award ($2,000). To recognize either a school library or public library that demonstrates excellence in library programming by providing programs that have community impact and respond to community need. *Donor:* Marshall Cavendish. *Winner:* Burnsville (Mississippi) Public Library for its model aircraft program, "ALOFT: A Learning Opportunity," and "SAFE: Stop Abductions Forever."

Marshall Cavendish Scholarship ($3,000). To a worthy U.S. or Canadian citizen to begin an MLS degree in an ALA-accredited program. *Winner:* Brenda Marie Hall.

Schneider Family Book Awards. *Winners:* See "Literary Prizes, 2011" in Part 5.

Scholastic Library Publishing National Library Week Grant ($3,000). For the best public awareness campaign in support of National Library Week. *Donor:* Scholastic Library Publishing. *Winner:* Southern State Community College Library, Hillsboro, Ohio.

Spectrum Doctoral Fellowships. To provide full tuition support and stipends to minority U.S. and Canadian LIS doctoral students. *Donor:* Institute of Museum and Library Services. *Winners:* To be awarded next in 2013.

Spectrum Initiative Scholarships ($5,000). Presented to minority students admitted to ALA-accredited library schools. *Donors:* ALA and Institute of Museum and Library Services. *Winners:* Neel Agrawal, Barbara Alvarez, Mikako Koyama Baker, Nataly Blas, Robina Button, Carla Davis-Castro, Ana Elisa de Campos Salles, LaToya Devezin, Jarrett Drake, Crystal Duran, Sabrina Dyck, Valeria Estrada, Andrea Galbo, Marissa Garcia, Jennifer Gibson, Neyda Gilman, Hannah Gomez, Lily Grant, Tonya Grant, Judith Guzman-Montes, Carlyn Hudson, Nicole Husbands, Mayu Ishida, Don Jason, Marika Jeffery, Rebecca M. King, Daniel Lee, Mirna Lessinger, Jameka B. Lewis, Margita Lidaka, Michelle Loera, Wai Yi Ma, Ebony Magnus, Michael David Miller, Casey Ann Mitchell, Linda Nguyen, Vy Nguyen, Johana Orellana Cabrera, John Parker, Ashley Payan, Beatriz Preciado, Diamond Sankey, Timothy Nalin Senapatiratne, Teresa Silva, Curtis Small, Nicole Thomas, Marisol Vasquez, Sharell Walker, Rhea Watson, Alyssa N. Willis, Dawn Wing, Aditi Worcester, Cara Young.

Sullivan Award for Public Library Administrators Supporting Services to Children. To a library supervisor/administrator who has shown exceptional understanding and support of public library services to children. *Donor:* Peggy Sullivan. *Winner:* Sol M. Hirsch, Alachua County (Florida) Library District.

H. W. Wilson Library Staff Development Grant ($3,500). To a library organization for a program to further its staff development goals and objectives. *Donor:* H. W. Wilson Company. *Winner:* University of Kansas Center for Research, University of Kansas Libraries, Lawrence, for "Enhancing Service and Engagement Through Understanding Staff Strengths: Individuals, Teams, and the Organization."

Women's National Book Association/Ann Heidbreder Eastman Grant ($500). To support library association professional development in a state in which WNBA has a chapter. *Winner:* Not awarded in 2011.

World Book/ALA Information Literacy Goal Awards ($5,000). To promote exemplary information literacy programs in public and school libraries. *Donor:* World Book. *Winners:* Award suspended in 2009.

ALA/Allied Professional Association

SirsiDynix Award for Outstanding Achievement in Promoting Salaries and Status for Library Workers. *Donor:* SirsiDynix. *Winners:* Award discontinued.

American Association of School Librarians (AASL)

AASL/ABC-CLIO Leadership Grant (up to $1,750). For planning and implementing leadership programs at state, regional, or local levels to be given to school library associations that are affiliates of AASL. *Donor:* ABC-CLIO. *Winner:* Texas Association of School Librarians (TASL).

AASL/Baker & Taylor Distinguished Service Award ($3,000). For outstanding contributions to librarianship and school library development. *Donor:* Baker & Taylor Books. *Winner:* Violet H. Harada.

AASL Collaborative School Library Award ($2,500). For expanding the role of the library in elementary and/or secondary school education. *Donor:* Highsmith, Inc. *Winners:* Lucy Kempton, Laurie Williams, and Marisa Fiorito, Deerfield (Illinois) High School, for their Medieval Narrative Project.

AASL Crystal Apple Award. To an individual, individuals, or group for a significant impact on school libraries and students. *Winner:* Dolly Parton and her literacy organization, Imagination Library.

AASL Distinguished School Administrators Award ($2,000). For expanding the role of the library in elementary and/or secondary school education. *Donor:* ProQuest. *Winner:* Donna Have, assistant superintendent of curriculum and instruction, Atlantic City (New Jersey) school district.

AASL/Frances Henne Award ($1,250). To a school library media specialist with five or fewer years in the profession to attend an AASL regional conference or ALA Annual Conference for the first time. *Donor:* ABC-CLIO. *Winner:* Shannon Hyman.

AASL Innovative Reading Grant ($2,500). To support the planning and implementation of an innovative program for children that motivates and encourages reading, especially with struggling readers. *Sponsor:* Capstone Publishers. *Winner:* Shanna Miles, Tech High School, Atlanta.

Information Technology Pathfinder Award ($1,000 to the specialist and $500 to the library). To library media specialists for innovative approaches to microcomputer applications in the school library media center. *Donor:* Follett Software Company. *Winners:* (elementary) Stephanie Rosalia; (secondary) Glovis South.

Intellectual Freedom Award ($2,000 plus $1,000 to the media center of the recipient's choice). To a school library media specialist and AASL member who has upheld the principles of intellectual freedom. *Donor:* ProQuest. *Winner:* Dee Venuto, Rancocas Valley Regional High School, Mount Holly, New Jersey.

National School Library Media Program of the Year Award ($10,000). To school districts and two single schools for excellence and innovation in outstanding library media programs. *Donor:* Follett Library Resources. *Winners:* (district) Northeast Independent School District, San Antonio; (single schools) Pine Grove Middle School, East Syracuse, New York; Henrico County (Virginia) Public Schools.

Association for Library Collections and Technical Services (ALCTS)

ALCTS/LBI George Cunha and Susan Swartzburg Preservation Award ($1,250). To recognize cooperative preservation projects and/or individuals or groups that foster collaboration for preservation goals. *Sponsor:* LBI: The Library Binding Institute. *Winner:* California Preservation Program.

ALCTS Presidential Citations for Outstanding Service. *Winners:* Kristin Martin, Mary Beth Weber.

Hugh C. Atkinson Memorial Award. *See under* American Library Association.

Ross Atkinson Lifetime Achievement Award ($3,000). To recognize the contribution of an ALCTS member and library leader who has demonstrated exceptional service to ALCTS and its areas of interest. *Donor:* EBSCO. *Winner:* Jan Merrill-Oldham.

Paul Banks and Carolyn Harris Preservation Award ($1,500). To recognize the contribution of a professional preservation specialist who has been active in the field of preservation and/or conservation for library and/or archival materials. *Donor:* Preservation Technologies. *Winner:* Roberta Pilette.

Blackwell's Scholarship Award. See Outstanding Publication Award.

Coutts Award for Innovation in Electronic Resources Management ($2,000). To recognize significant and innovative contributions to electronic collections management and development practice. *Donor:* Coutts Information Services. *Winner:* Jason Price.

First Step Award (Wiley Professional Development Grant) ($1,500). For librarians new to the serials field to attend the ALA Annual Conference. *Donor:* John Wiley & Sons. *Winner:* Not awarded in 2011.

Leadership in Library Acquisitions Award ($1,500). For significant contributions by an outstanding leader in the field of library acquisitions. *Donor:* Harrassowitz. *Winner:* Eleanor Cook.

Margaret Mann Citation (includes $2,000 award to the U.S. or Canadian library school of the winner's choice). To a cataloger or classifier for achievement in the areas of cataloging or classification. *Donor:* Online Computer Library Center (OCLC). *Winner:* Edward Swanson.

Outstanding Collaboration Citation. For outstanding collaborative problem-solving efforts in the areas of acquisition, access, management, preservation, or archiving of library materials. *Winners:* Indiana University Libraries and American Folklore Society for the Open Folklore Project.

Outstanding Publication Award (formerly the Blackwell's Scholarship Award). To honor the author(s) of the year's outstanding monograph, article, or original paper in the field of acquisitions, collection development, and related areas of resource development in libraries. *Winner:* Karen Coyle for "Understanding the Semantic Web: Bibliographic Data and Metadata," published in *Library Technology Reports* (46:1).

Esther J. Piercy Award ($1,500). To a librarian with no more than ten years' experience for contributions and leadership in the field of library collections and technical services. *Donor:* YBP Library Services. *Winner:* Marielle Veve.

Edward Swanson Memorial Best of *LRTS* Award ($250). To the author(s) of the year's best paper published in the division's official journal. *Winner:* Whitney Baker and Liz Dube for "Identifying Standard Practices in Research Library Book Conservation" (54:1).

Ulrich's Serials Librarianship Award ($1,500). For distinguished contributions to serials librarianship. *Sponsor:* ProQuest. *Winner:* Peter McCracken.

Association for Library Service to Children (ALSC)

ALSC/Book Wholesalers, Inc. BWI Summer Reading Program Grant ($3,000). To an ALSC member for implementation of an outstanding public library summer reading program for children. *Donor:* Book Wholesalers, Inc. *Winner:* West Palm Beach (Florida) Public Library.

ALSC/Booklist/YALSA Odyssey Award. To the producer of the best audiobook for children and/or young adults available in English in the United States. See "Literary Prizes, 2011" in Part 5.

ALSC/Candlewick Press "Light the Way: Library Outreach to the Underserved" Grant ($3,000). To a library conducting exemplary outreach to underserved populations. *Donor:* Candlewick Press. *Winner:* Richmond (California) Public Library.

May Hill Arbuthnot Honor Lectureship. To an author, critic, librarian, historian, or teacher of children's literature who prepares a paper considered to be a significant contribution to the field of children's literature. *Winner:* Author Lois Lowry for "Unleaving: The Staying Power of Gold."

Mildred L. Batchelder Award. *Winner:* See "Literary Prizes, 2011" in Part 5.

Louise Seaman Bechtel Fellowship ($4,000). For librarians with 12 or more years of professional-level work in children's library collections, to read and study at Baldwin Library, University of Florida. *Donor:* Bechtel Fund. *Winners:* Victoria Penny, Allison G. Kaplan.

Pura Belpré Award. *Winners:* See "Literary Prizes, 2011" in Part 5.

Bookapalooza Program Awards. To provide three libraries with a collection of materials that will help transform their collection. *Winners:* Houston Elementary School, Spartanburg, South Carolina; Meade County (Kentucky) Public Library, Brandenburg; Florence County (South Carolina) Library System.

Bound to Stay Bound Books Scholarships ($7,000). For men and women who intend to pursue an MLS or advanced degree and who plan to work in the area of library service to children. *Donor:* Bound to Stay Bound Books. *Winners:* Nancy Graves, Danielle Gregori, Rachel Ortiz, Robyn Woods.

Randolph Caldecott Medal. *Winner:* See "Literary Prizes, 2011" in Part 5.

Andrew Carnegie Medal. To the U.S. producers of the most distinguished video for children in the previous year. *Sponsor:* Carnegie Corporation of New York. *Winners:* Paul R. Gagne and Melissa Reilly Ellard of Weston Woods Studios for *The Curious Garden.*

Carnegie-Whitney Awards (up to $5,000). For the preparation of print or electronic reading lists, indexes, or other guides to library resources that promote reading or the use of library resources at any type of library. *Donors:* James Lyman Whitney and Andrew Carnegie Funds. *Winners:* Spencer Acadia for "A Resources Guide to Medical Sociology and Medical Anthropology"; Dana Braccia for "Write Local Online Toolkit for Aspiring Community Authors"; Shannon Farrell and Benjamin Rodriquez for "A Web-Enabled Videogame Collection Companion"; Michael Gallaway and Alison Miller for "Infusing Innovation in Rural Libraries: An Annotated List of WI Electronic and Print Resources"; Ellen Greenblatt for "Creating a Database of LGBTQ-related Literature for Children and Young Adults"; Nadean Meyer and Rayette Sterling for "What's My Story? American Indians of the Pacific Northwest Youth Resources."

Distinguished Service Award ($1,000). To recognize significant contributions to, and an impact on, library services to children and/ or ALSC. *Winner:* Dudley Carlson.

Theodor Seuss Geisel Award. *Winner:* See "Literary Prizes, 2011" in Part 5.

Maureen Hayes Author/Illustrator Visit Award (up to $4,000). For an honorarium and travel expenses to make possible a library talk to children by a nationally known author/il-

lustrator. *Sponsor:* Simon & Schuster Children's Publishing. *Winner:* McArthur Public Library, Biddeford, Maine, and Biddeford Intermediate School Literacy Team.

Frederic G. Melcher Scholarships ($6,000). To two students entering the field of library service to children for graduate work in an ALA-accredited program. *Winners:* Donna Hanley, Patricia Prodanich.

John Newbery Medal. *Winner:* See "Literary Prizes, 2011" in Part 5.

Penguin Young Readers Group Awards ($600). To children's librarians in school or public libraries with ten or fewer years of experience to attend the ALA Annual Conference. *Donor:* Penguin Young Readers Group. *Winners:* Patricia Carroll, Allison Hill, Mellissa Sanchez, Laura Simeon.

Robert F. Sibert Medal. *Winner:* See "Literary Prizes, 2011" in Part 5.

Laura Ingalls Wilder Medal. *Winner:* See "Literary Prizes, 2011" in Part 5.

Association of College and Research Libraries (ACRL)

ACRL Academic or Research Librarian of the Year Award ($5,000). For outstanding contributions to academic and research librarianship and library development. *Donor:* YBP Library Services. *Winner:* Janice Welburn.

ACRL Distinguished Education and Behavioral Sciences Librarian Award ($2,500). To an academic librarian who has made an outstanding contribution as an education and/or behavioral sciences librarian through accomplishments and service to the profession. *Donor:* John Wiley & Sons. *Winner:* Douglas Cook.

ACRL/DLS Haworth Press Distance Learning Librarian Conference Sponsorship Award ($1,200). To an ACRL member working in distance-learning librarianship in higher education. *Winner:* Cassandra Kvenild.

ACRL Doctoral Dissertation Fellowship ($1,500). To a doctoral student in the field of academic librarianship whose research has potential significance in the field. *Winner:* Not awarded in 2011.

ACRL/EBSCO Community College Learning Resources Leadership/Library Program Achievement Awards ($500). To recognize outstanding achievement in library programs or leadership. *Sponsor:* EBSCO Information Services. *Winners:* (leadership) Melora P. Mirza; (program achievement) Leslie Bussert.

ACRL Special Presidential Recognition Award. To recognize an individual's special career contributions to ACRL and the library profession. *Winner:* Not awarded in 2011.

ACRL/WGSS Award for Career Achievement in Women's Studies Librarianship. *Winner:* Kay Cassell.

Hugh C. Atkinson Memorial Award. See under American Library Association.

Coutts Nijhoff International West European Specialist Study Grant ($3,000). Supports research pertaining to West European studies, librarianship, or the book trade. *Sponsor:* Coutts Information Services. *Winner:* Mara Degnan Rojeski, Dickinson College, for her proposal to construct a bibliography of the pamphlets of the Deutscher Fichte Bund, a propaganda organization active in Germany from 1914 to 1941.

Miriam Dudley Instruction Librarian Award. For a contribution to the advancement of bibliographic instruction in a college or research institution. *Winner:* Not awarded in 2011.

Excellence in Academic Libraries Awards ($3,000).To recognize outstanding community college, college, and university libraries. *Donor:* Blackwell's Book Services. *Winners:* (university) Wake Forest University, Winston-Salem, North Carolina; (college) Grinnell College, Grinnell, Iowa; (community college) Santa Barbara (California) City College.

Instruction Section Innovation Award ($3,000). To librarians or project teams in recognition of a project that demonstrates creative, innovative, or unique approaches to information literacy instruction or programming. *Donor:* ProQuest. *Winners:* Kimberly Davies Hoffman and Michelle Costello, State University of New York at Geneseo, for LILAC (Library Instruction Leadership Academy), a collaborative professional development project.

Marta Lange/CQ Press Award ($1,000). To recognize an academic or law librarian for contributions to bibliography and information service in law or political science. *Donor:* CQ Press. *Winner:* Stephen E. Atkins.

Samuel Lazerow Fellowship for Research in Collections and Technical Services in Academic and Research Libraries. To foster advances in acquisitions or technical services by providing librarians a fellowship for travel or writing in those fields. *Winner:* Award discontinued.

Katharine Kyes Leab and Daniel J. Leab American Book Prices Current Exhibition Catalog Awards (citations). For the best catalogs published by American or Canadian institutions in conjunction with exhibitions of books and/or manuscripts. *Winners:* Hartman Center for Sales, Advertising, and Marketing History at Duke University; Sanford University Libraries and Bancroft Library at the University of California, Berkeley; John Carter Brown Library at Brown University; Linda Hall Library of Science, Engineering, and Technology; Sheridan Libraries at Johns Hopkins University; University of Rochester River Campus Libraries.

Oberly Award for Bibliography in the Agricultural or Natural Sciences. Awarded biennially for the best English-language bibliography in the field of agriculture or a related science in the preceding two-year period. *Winner:* William R. Shurtleff for "History of Soybeans and Soyfoods in Africa (1857–2009): Extensively Annotated Bibliography and Sourcebook."

Ilene F. Rockman Instruction Publication of the Year Award ($3,000). To recognize an outstanding publication relating to instruction in a library environment. *Sponsor:* Emerald Group Publishing. *Winner:* Megan Jane Oakleaf for "Information Literacy Instruction Assessment Cycle: A Guide for Increasing Student Learning and Improving Librarian Instructional Skills."

Association of Library Trustees, Advocates, Friends and Foundations (ALTAFF)

ALTAFF/Baker & Taylor Awards. To recognize library friends groups for outstanding efforts to support their libraries. *Donor:* Baker & Taylor. *Winners:* (public library group with assistance from paid staff) Friends of the Princeton (New Jersey) Public Library, Friends of the Salt Lake City Public Library; (public library group without assistance from paid staff) Friends of the Carpinteria (California) Library.

ALTAFF/Gale Outstanding Trustee Conference Grant Award ($850). *Donor:* Gale Cengage Learning. *Winner:* Dottie Bell.

ALTAFF Major Benefactors Citation. To individuals, families, or corporate bodies that have made major benefactions to public libraries. *Winner:* Public Service Enterprise Group Foundation for its contribution of $812,500 to fund the "Live Homework Help NJ" program.

ALTAFF Public Service Award. To a legislator who has been especially supportive of libraries. *Winner:* U.S. Rep. Raúl M. Grijalva (D-Ariz).

Trustee Citations. To recognize public library trustees for individual service to library development on the local, state, regional, or national level. *Winners:* Dave Hargett, Rose Mosley.

Association of Specialized and Cooperative Library Agencies (ASCLA)

ASCLA Cathleen Bourdon Service Award. To recognize an ASCLA personal member for outstanding service and leadership to the division. *Winner:* Elizabeth Ann Ridler.

ASCLA Century Scholarship (up to $2,500). For a library school student or students with disabilities admitted to an ALA-accredited library school. *Winner:* Not awarded in 2011.

ASCLA Exceptional Service Award. To recognize exceptional service to patients, the homebound, inmates, and to medical, nursing, and other professional staff in hospitals. *Winner:* Hennepin County (Minnesota) Library Outreach Services.

ASCLA Leadership and Professional Achievement Award. To recognize leadership and achievement in the areas of consulting, multitype library cooperation, statewide service and programs, and state library development. *Winner:* Diane Walden, correctional libraries senior consultant, Colorado State Library.

Francis Joseph Campbell Award. For a contribution of recognized importance to library service for the blind and physically handicapped. *Winner:* Jamal Mazrui, deputy di-

rector, Accessibility and Innovation Initiative, Federal Communications Commission.

KLAS/National Organization on Disability Award for Library Service to People with Disabilities ($1,000). To a library organization to recognize an innovative project to benefit people with disabilities. *Donor:* Keystone Systems. *Winner:* Queens Library Mail-A-Book Program with interactive programming for the homebound.

Black Caucus of the American Library Association (BCALA)

BCALA Trailblazer's Award. Presented once every five years in recognition of outstanding and unique contributions to librarianship. *Winner:* To be awarded next in 2015.

DEMCO/BCALA Excellence in Librarianship Award. To a librarian who has made significant contributions to promoting the status of African Americans in the library profession. *Winner:* Pamela Goodes.

Ethnic and Multicultural Information and Exchange Round Table (EMIERT)

David Cohen/EMIERT Multicultural Award ($300). To recognize articles of significant research and publication that increase understanding and promote multiculturalism in North American libraries. *Donor:* Routledge. *Winner:* Not awarded in 2011.

Gale/EMIERT Multicultural Award ($1,000). For outstanding achievement and leadership in serving the multicultural/multiethnic community. *Donor:* Gale Research. *Winner:* Not awarded in 2011.

Exhibits Round Table (ERT)

Christopher J. Hoy/ERT Scholarship ($5,000). To an individual or individuals who will work toward an MLS degree in an ALA-accredited program. *Donor:* Family of Christopher Hoy. *Winner:* Lori Kristen Neumeier.

Federal and Armed Forces Librarians Round Table (FAFLRT)

FAFLRT Achievement Award. For achievement in the promotion of library and information service and the information profession in the federal government community. *Winner:* Not awarded in 2011.

Adelaide del Frate Conference Sponsorship Award ($1,000). To encourage library school students to become familiar with federal librarianship and ultimately seek work in federal libraries; for attendance at ALA Annual Conference and activities of FAFLRT. *Winner:* Not awarded in 2011.

Distinguished Service Award (citation). To honor a FAFLRT member for outstanding and sustained contributions to the association and to federal librarianship. *Winner:* Lucille M. Rosa, Eccles Library, U.S. Naval War College.

Cicely Phippen Marks Scholarship ($1,500). To a library school student with an interest in working in a federal library. *Winner:* Rebecca Carlson.

Rising Star Award. To a FAFLRT member new to the profession in a federal or armed forces library or government information management setting. *Winner:* Aimee Babcock-Ellis, U.S. Drug Enforcement Administration Library.

Gay, Lesbian, Bisexual, and Transgendered Round Table (GLBT)

Stonewall Book Awards. *Winners:* See "Literary Prizes, 2011" in Part 5.

Government Documents Round Table (GODORT)

James Bennett Childs Award. To a librarian or other individual for distinguished lifetime contributions to documents librarianship. *Winner:* Tim Byrne, Office of Scientific and Technical Information, U.S. Department of Energy.

Bernadine Abbott Hoduski Founders Award. To recognize documents librarians who may not be known at the national level but who have made significant contributions to the field of local, state, federal, or international documents. *Winner:* Laura Harper, John Davis Williams Library, University of Mississippi.

Margaret T. Lane/Virginia F. Saunders Memorial Research Award. *Winner:* George Dehner, for "WHO Knows Best? National and International Responses to Pandemic Threats and the 'Lessons' of 1976" published in the

Journal of the History of Medicine and Allied Sciences, October 2010.

NewsBank/Readex Catharine J. Reynolds Award ($2,000). To documents librarians for travel and/or study in the field of documents librarianship or an area of study benefiting performance as documents librarians. *Donor:* NewsBank and Readex Corporation. *Winner:* Not awarded in 2011.

Proquest/GODORT/ALA Documents to the People Award. To an individual, library, organization, or noncommercial group that most effectively encourages or enhances the use of government documents in library services. *Winner:* Lou Malcomb, head of government information, Kent Cooper Services and Geosciences Library, Indiana University, Bloomington.

W. David Rozkuszka Scholarship ($3,000). To provide financial assistance to an individual who is currently working with government documents in a library while completing a master's program in library science. *Winner:* Laurie Aycock.

Intellectual Freedom Round Table (IFRT)

John Phillip Immroth Memorial Award for Intellectual Freedom ($500). For notable contribution to intellectual freedom fueled by personal courage. *Winners:* Mike Blasenstein and Mike Iacovone.

Eli M. Oboler Memorial Award. See "Literary Prizes, 2011" in Part 5.

ProQuest/SIRS State and Regional Achievement Award ($1,000). To an innovative and effective intellectual freedom project covering a state or region during the calendar year. *Donor:* ProQuest Social Issues Resource Series (SIRS). *Winner:* Award discontinued in 2011.

Library and Information Technology Association (LITA)

Hugh C. Atkinson Memorial Award. See under American Library Association.

Ex Libris Student Writing Award ($1,000 and publication in *Information Technology and Libraries*). For the best unpublished manuscript on a topic in the area of libraries and information technology written by a student or students enrolled in an ALA-accredited library and information studies graduate program. *Donor:* Ex Libris. *Winner:* Abigail McDermott for "Copyright: Regulation Out of Line with Our Digital Reality?"

LITA/Christian Larew Memorial Scholarship ($3,000). To encourage the entry of qualified persons into the library and information technology field. *Sponsor:* Informata.com. *Winner:* Fredrica Lush.

LITA/Library Hi Tech Award ($1,000). To an individual or institution for a work that shows outstanding communication for continuing education in library and information technology. *Donor:* Emerald Group Publishing. *Winner:* John Wilkin.

LITA/LSSI Minority Scholarship in Library and Information Technology ($2,500). To encourage a qualified member of a principal minority group to work toward an MLS degree in an ALA-accredited program with emphasis on library automation. *Donor:* Library Systems and Services. *Winner:* Andrea L. Galbo.

LITA/OCLC Frederick G. Kilgour Award for Research in Library and Information Technology ($2,000 and expense-paid attendance at the ALA Annual Conference). To bring attention to research relevant to the development of information technologies. *Donor:* OCLC. *Winner:* Daniel J. Cohen.

LITA/OCLC Minority Scholarship in Library and Information Technology ($3,000). To encourage a qualified member of a principal minority group to work toward an MLS degree in an ALA-accredited program with an emphasis on library automation. *Donor:* OCLC. *Winner:* Diamond Camille Sankey.

LITA/OITP Award for Cutting-Edge Technology in Library Services. To honor libraries that are serving their communities with novel and innovative methods. *Winners:* Contra Costa County, Pleasant Hill, California; New Canaan (Connecticut) High School Library; New York Public Library; Scottsdale (Arizona) Public Library.

Library History Round Table (LHRT)

Phyllis Dain Library History Dissertation Award ($500). Awarded biennially to the author of a dissertation treating the history of books, libraries, librarianship, or information science. *Winner:* Susan Reynolds for "The Establishment of the Library of the Supreme Court of Victoria, 1851–1884: Antecedents, Foundation, and Legacy."

Donald G. Davis Article Award (certificate). Awarded biennially for the best article written in English in the field of U.S. and Canadian library history. *Winner:* To be awarded next in 2012.

Eliza Atkins Gleason Book Award. Presented every third year to the author of the best book in English in the field of library history. *Winner:* To be awarded next in 2013.

Justin Winsor Prize Essay ($500). To an author of an outstanding essay embodying original historical research on a significant subject of library history. *Winner:* Cody White for "Rising from the Ashes: Lessons Learned from the Impact of Proposition 13 on Public Libraries in California."

Library Leadership and Management Association (LLAMA)

Hugh C. Atkinson Memorial Award. See under American Library Association.

Diana V. Braddom Fundraising and Financial Development Section Scholarship ($1,000). To enable attendance at the ALA Annual Conference. *Donor:* Diana V. Braddom. *Winner:* Award discontinued.

John Cotton Dana Library Public Relations Awards. To libraries or library organizations of all types for public relations programs or special projects ended during the preceding year. *Donors:* H. W. Wilson Company and H. W. Wilson Foundation. *Winners:* Loudoun County Public Library, Leesburg, Virginia; Anythink Libraries, Adams County, Colorado; University of California, Santa Cruz, Library; Edmonton (Alberta) Public Library; Worthington (Ohio) Libraries.

Library Research Round Table (LRRT)

Ingenta Research Award (up to $6,000). To sponsor research projects about acquisition, use, and preservation of digital information; the award includes $1,000 to support travel to a conference to present the results of that research. *Sponsor:* Ingenta. *Winner:* Award discontinued.

Jesse H. Shera Award for Distinguished Published Research ($500). For a research article on library and information studies published in English during the calendar year. *Winner:* M. Christina Patuelli for "Modeling Domain Ontology for Cultural Heritage," published in the *Journal of the American Society for Information Science and Technology* 62:2, February 2011.

Jesse H. Shera Award for Support of Dissertation Research ($500). To recognize and support dissertation research employing exemplary research design and methods. *Winner:* Amy VanScoy for "Exploring the Meaning of Reference Work for Librarians in Academic Research Libraries."

Map and Geospatial Information Round Table (MAGIRT)

MAGIRT Honors Award. *Winners:* Janet Dixon (in memoriam), Christine Kollen, Scott McEathron.

New Members Round Table (NMRT)

NMRT/Marshall Cavendish Award (tickets to the Newbery/Caldecott/Wilder Banquet at the ALA Annual Conference). *Winners:* Emily Frances Calkins, Catharine Potter.

Shirley Olofson Memorial Award ($1,000). To an individual to help defray costs of attending the ALA Annual Conference. *Winner:* Eamon Tewell.

Student Chapter of the Year Award. To an ALA student chapter for outstanding contributions to the association. *Winner:* Student Chapter at Indiana University.

3M Professional Development Grant. To new NMRT members to encourage professional development and participation in national ALA and NMRT activities. *Donor:* 3M. *Winners:* Natalie Traylor Clewell, Jessica Nadine Hernandez, Julie N. Kane.

Office for Diversity

Achievement in Diversity Research Honor. To an ALA member who has made significant contributions to diversity research in the profession. *Winner:* Camila Alire.

Diversity Research Grants ($2,500). To the authors of research proposals that address critical gaps in the knowledge of diversity is-

sues within library and information science. *Winners:* Clara M. Chu, Trae Middlebrooks, Leatha Miles-Edmonson, and Ashanti White for "Information Needs and Barriers of Southeast Asian Refugee Undergraduates"; Daniella Smith for "Diversity in Technology Integration Leadership"; Jian-zhong Zhou for "Achievement Gap of Asian American Professional Librarians at the Top of Career Ladders."

Office for Information Technology Policy

L. Ray Patterson Copyright Award. To recognize an individual who supports the constitutional purpose of U.S. copyright law, fair use, and the public domain. *Sponsor:* Freedom to Read Foundation. *Winner:* Peter Suber.

Office for Intellectual Freedom

Freedom to Read Foundation Gordon M. Conable Conference Scholarship. To enable a library school student or new professional to attend the ALA Annual Conference. *Winner:* Audrey Barbakoff.

Freedom to Read Foundation Roll of Honor (citation): To recognize individuals who have contributed substantially to the foundation. *Winner:* Christopher M. Finan, president, American Booksellers Foundation for Free Expression (ABFFE).

Office for Literacy and Outreach Services (OLOS)

Jean E. Coleman Library Outreach Lecture. *Sponsor:* OLOS Advisory Committee. *Winner:* Robert Wedgeworth.

Diversity Fair Awards. To outreach librarians for their institutions' diversity-in-action initiatives. *Winners:* (first place) University of Illinois Graduate School of Library and Information Science; (second place) Chinese American Librarians Association; (third place) ACRL Racial and Ethnic Diversity Committee.

Estela and Raúl Mora Award ($1,000 and plaque). For exemplary programs celebrating Día de Los Niños/Día de Los Libros. *Winners:* Santa Ana (California) Public Library, Springfield (Oregon) Public Library.

Public Awareness Committee

Scholastic Library Publishing National Library Week Grant ($3,000). To libraries or library associations of all types for a public awareness campaign in connection with National Library Week in the year the grant is awarded. *Sponsor:* Scholastic Library Publishing. *Winner:* Southern State Community College, Ohio.

Public Library Association (PLA)

Advancement of Literacy Award (plaque). To a publisher, bookseller, hardware and/or software dealer, foundation, or similar group that has made a significant contribution to the advancement of adult literacy. *Winner:* Award discontinued.

Baker & Taylor Entertainment Audio Music/Video Product Grant ($2,500 worth of audio music or video products). To help a public library to build or expand a collection of either or both formats. *Donor:* Baker & Taylor. *Winner:* Huntsville (Texas) Public Library.

Gordon M. Conable Award ($1,500). To a public library staff member, library trustee, or public library for demonstrating a commitment to intellectual freedom and the Library Bill of Rights. *Sponsor:* LSSI. *Winner:* Melanie Miller, former director, Hays (Kansas) Public Library.

Demco New Leaders Travel Grants (up to $1,500). To PLA members who have not attended a major PLA continuing-education event in the past five years. *Winners:* Anna Bates, Rebecca Clarke, Jenna Hecker,

EBSCO Excellence in Small and/or Rural Public Service Award ($1,000). Honors a library serving a population of 10,000 or less that demonstrates excellence of service to its community as exemplified by an overall service program or a special program of significant accomplishment. *Donor:* EBSCO Information Services. *Winner:* Independence (Kansas) Public Library.

Highsmith Library Innovation Award ($2,000). To recognize a public library's innovative achievement in planning and implementing a creative community service program. *Donor:* Highsmith. *Winner:* Noble County (Indiana) Public Library.

Allie Beth Martin Award ($3,000). To honor a public librarian who has demonstrated extraordinary range and depth of knowledge about books or other library materials and has distinguished ability to share that knowledge. *Donor:* Baker & Taylor. *Winner:* Angelina Benedetti, King County (Washington) Library System.

Polaris Innovation in Technology John Iliff Award ($1,000). To a library worker, librarian, or library for the use of technology and innovative thinking as a tool to improve services to public library users. *Sponsor:* Polaris. *Winner:* David Newyear, Mentor (Ohio) Public Library.

Charlie Robinson Award. To honor a public library director who, over a period of seven years, has been a risk taker, an innovator, and/or a change agent in a public library. *Donor:* Baker & Taylor. *Winner:* Not awarded in 2011.

Romance Writers of America Library Grant ($4,500). To a library to build or expand a fiction collection and/or host romance fiction programming. *Donor:* Romance Writers of America. *Winner:* Donald Dugan Library, Costa Mesa, California.

Public Programs Office

Sara Jaffarian School Library Program Award ($4,000). To honor a K–8 school library that has conducted an exemplary program or program series in the humanities. *Donors:* Sara Jaffarian and ALA Cultural Communities Fund. *Winner:* Ronda Hassig, librarian, Harmony Middle School, Overland Park, Kansas.

Reference and User Services Association (RUSA)

ABC-CLIO Online History Award ($3,000). A biennial award to recognize professional achievement in historical reference and librarianship. *Donor:* ABC-CLIO. *Winners:* Stephen Robertson, Shane White, Stephen Garton, and Graham White, University of Sydney (Australia) for "Digital Harlem: Everyday Life, 1915–1930" (http://acl.arts. usyd.edu.au/harlem).

ALA/RUSA Zora Neale Hurston Award. To recognize the efforts of RUSA members in promoting African American literature. *Sponsored by:* Harper Perennial Publishing. *Winner:* Theresa Venable, Children's Defense Fund Haley Farm's Langston Hughes Library, Clinton, Tennessee.

Virginia Boucher-OCLC Distinguished ILL Librarian Award ($2,000). To a librarian for outstanding professional achievement, leadership, and contributions to interlibrary loan and document delivery. *Winner:* Ed Rivenburgh, State University of New York, Geneseo.

BRASS Award for Outstanding Service to Minority Business Communities ($2,000). To a librarian or library to recognize creation of an innovative service to a minority business community or achievement of recognition from that community for providing outstanding service. *Winner:* Award suspended in 2011.

BRASS Emerald Research Grant Awards ($5,000). To ALA members seeking support to conduct research in business librarianship. *Donor:* Emerald Group Publishing. *Winners:* Diane K. Campbell and Ronald G. Cook, Rider University; Peter Jacso, University of Hawaii.

BRASS Gale Cengage Learning Student Travel Award ($1,000). To enable a student enrolled in an ALA-accredited master's program to attend the ALA Annual Conference. *Donor:* Gale Cengage Learning. *Winner:* Danielle Salomon.

BRASS Public Librarian Support Award ($1,000). To support attendance at the ALA Annual Conference of a public librarian who has performed outstanding business reference service. *Donor:* Morningstar. *Winner:* Suzanne J. Kaller.

Sophie Brody Medal. *Winner:* See "Literary Prizes, 2011" in Part 5.

Gale Cengage Award for Excellence in Business Librarianship ($3,000). For distinguished activities in the field of business librarianship. *Donor:* Gale Cengage Learning. *Winner:* Nicolette Warisse Sosulski, Portage (Michigan) Public Library.

Gale Cengage Award for Excellence in Reference and Adult Library Services ($3,000). To recognize a library or library system for developing an imaginative and unique library resource to meet patrons' reference needs. *Donor:* Gale Cengage Learning. *Winner:* Government and Heritage Library at the State Library of North Carolina for its Web site NCpedia.

Genealogical Publishing Company/History Section Award ($1,500). To encourage and commend professional achievement in historical reference and research librarianship. *Donor:* Genealogical Publishing Company. *Winner:* Mary K. Mannix, Frederick County (Maryland) Public Libraries.

Margaret E. Monroe Library Adult Services Award (citation). To a librarian for his or her impact on library service to adults. *Winner:* Joyce Saricks, Dominican University.

Isadore Gilbert Mudge–Gale Cengage Award ($5,000). For distinguished contributions to reference librarianship. *Donor:* Gale Cengage Learning. *Winner:* Diane Zabel, Pennsylvania State University.

Reference Service Press Award ($2,500). To the author or authors of the most outstanding article published in *RUSQ* during the preceding two volume years. *Donor:* Reference Service Press. *Winners:* Jenny S. Bossaller, Denice Adkins, and Kim Michelle Thompson for "Describing Vernacular Literacy Practices to Enhance Understanding of Community Information Needs: A Case Study with Practical Implications" (*RUSQ*, Fall 2009).

John Sessions Memorial Award (plaque). To a library or library system in recognition of work with the labor community. *Donor:* Department for Professional Employees, AFL/CIO. *Winner:* Russell Library, Middletown, Connecticut.

Louis Shores–Greenwood Publishing Group Award ($3,000). To an individual, team, or organization to recognize excellence in reviewing of books and other materials for libraries. *Donor:* Greenwood Publishing Group. *Winner:* Bill Ott, editor and publisher, *Booklist*.

STARS-Atlas Systems Mentoring Award ($1,000). To a library practitioner new to the field of interlibrary loan, resource sharing, or electronic reserves, to attend the ALA Annual Conference. *Donor:* Atlas Systems. *Winner:* Micquel Little.

Social Responsibilities Round Table (SRRT)

Jackie Eubanks Memorial Award ($500). To honor outstanding achievement in promoting the acquisition and use of alternative media in libraries. *Donor:* SRRT Alternatives in Publication Task Force. *Winner:* Not awarded in 2011.

Coretta Scott King Awards. *Winners:* See "Literary Prizes, 2011" in Part 5.

Young Adult Library Services Association (YALSA)

Alex Awards. *Winners:* See "Literary Prizes, 2011" in Part 5.

Baker & Taylor/YALSA Scholarship Grants ($1,000). To young adult librarians in public or school libraries to attend the ALA Annual Conference for the first time. *Donor:* Baker & Taylor. *Winners:* Yvonne Miller, Sarah Wethern.

BWI/YALSA Collection Development Grants ($1,000). To YALSA members who represent a public library and work directly with young adults, for collection development materials for young adults. *Donor:* Book Wholesalers, Inc. *Winners:* Melanie Feyerherm, Keri Weston.

Margaret A. Edwards Award. *Winner:* See "Literary Prizes, 2011" in Part 5.

Great Books Giveaway (books, videos, CDs, and audiocassettes valued at a total of $25,000). *Winners:* Oakhurst Middle School, Clarksdale, Mississippi; Colleton County High School, Walterboro, South Carolina; Fletcher (Oklahoma) Public School.

Frances Henne/YALSA/VOYA Research Grant ($1,000). To provide seed money to an individual, institution, or group for a project to encourage research on library service to young adults. *Donors: Voice of Youth Advocates* and Scarecrow Press. *Winner:* Shannon Crawford Barniskis.

Michael L. Printz Award. *Winner:* See "Literary Prizes, 2011" in Part 5.

YALSA/ABC-CLIO/Greenwood Publishing Group Service to Young Adults Achievement Award ($2,000). Awarded biennially to a YALSA member who has demonstrated unique and sustained devotion to young adult services. *Donor:* Greenwood. *Winner:* To be awarded next in 2012.

YALSA/MAE Award ($500 for the recipient plus $500 for his or her library). For an exemplary young adult reading or literature program. *Sponsor:* Margaret A. Edwards Trust. *Winner:* Katie George.

YALSA William C. Morris YA Debut Award. *Winner:* See "Literary Prizes, 2011" in Part 5.

YALSA/Sagebrush Award. See YALSA/MAE Award.

American Society for Information Science and Technology (ASIS&T)

ASIS&T Award of Merit. For an outstanding contribution to the field of information science. *Winner:* Gary Marchionini.

ASIS&T Best Information Science Book. *Winner:* Katy Börner for *Atlas of Science: Visualizing What We Know* (MIT).

ASIS&T History Fund Grant Award Winner ($1,000). *Winners:* Trudi Bellardo Hahn and Diane Barlow for "The Fortuitous Confluence of Helen Brownson, the National Science Foundation, and Information Science."

ASIS&T New Leaders Award. To recruit, engage, and retain new ASIS&T members and to identify potential for new leadership in the society. *Winners:* Caroline Whippey, Vivienne Houghton, Eugenia Kim, Julia Martin, Chrysta Meadowbrooke, Chaoqun Ni, Jacob Ratliff, William Senn.

ASIS&T ProQuest Doctoral Dissertation Award ($1,000 plus expense-paid attendance at ASIS&T Annual Meeting). *Winner:* Shelagh K. Genuis for "Making Sense of Evolving Health Information: Navigating Uncertainty in Everyday Life."

ASIS&T Research in Information Science Award. For a systematic program of research in a single area at a level beyond the single study, recognizing contributions in the field of information science. *Winner:* Christine Borgman.

James M. Cretsos Leadership Award. *Winner:* Not awarded in 2011.

Watson Davis Award. For outstanding continuous contributions and dedicated service to the society. *Winner:* Robert Williams.

Pratt Severn Best Student Research Paper Award. To encourage student research and writing in the field of information science. *Winner:* Brooks Breece for "Local Government Use of Web GIS in North Carolina."

Thomson Reuters Doctoral Dissertation Proposal Scholarship ($2,000). *Winner:* Amber Cushing for "Possession and Self Extension in Digital Environments: Implications for Maintaining Personal Information."

Thomson Reuters Outstanding Teacher Award ($1,500). To recognize the unique teaching contribution of an individual as a teacher of information science. *Winner:* Howard Rosenbaum, Indiana University.

John Wiley Best *JASIST* Paper Award. *Winners:* Jim Jansen and Soo-Young Rieh for "The Seventeen Theoretical Constructs of Information Searching and Information Retrieval."

Art Libraries Society of North America (ARLIS/NA)

ARLIS/NA Distinguished Service Award. To honor an individual whose exemplary service in art librarianship, visual resources curatorship, or a related field, has made an outstanding national or international contribution to art information. *Winner:* Margaret Webster.

ARLIS/NA Internship Award. To provide financial support for students preparing for a career in art librarianship or visual resource librarianship. *Winner:* Bailey Diers.

ARLIS/NA Student Conference Attendance Award. *Winner:* Diane Bockrath.

ARLIS/NA Worldwide Books Award for Electronic Resources. *Winner:* Samantha Deutch for *Archives Directory for the History of Collecting in America.*

ARLIS/NA Worldwide Books Award for Publications. *Winner:* Richard Minsky for *The Art of American Book Covers* (George Braziller).

AskART Conference Attendance Award. *Winner:* Sarah Osborne Bender.

Andrew Cahan Photography Award ($1,000). *Winner:* Matthew Carson, International Center of Photography.

Melva J. Dwyer Award. To the creators of exceptional reference or research tools relating to Canadian art and architecture. *Winner:* Gerald McMaster for *Inuit Modern: Masterworks from the Samuel and Esther Sarick Collection* (Douglas & McIntyre).

Judith A. Hoffberg Award for Student Attendance. *Winner:* Anna Simon.

Howard and Beverly Joy Karno Award. *Winner:* Nina Stephenson.

Samuel H. Kress Foundation Award for European Travel. *Winner:* Deborah Kempe.

Samuel H. Kress Foundation Summer Educational Institute Scholarships. *Winners:* Melissa A. Gill, Andrea Hagy, Jennifer Kniesch, Jessica Shaykett, Emma Wolman.

Gerd Muehsam Award. To one or more graduate students in library science programs to recognize excellence in a graduate paper or project. *Winner:* Katherine L. Kelley.

Merrill Wadsworth Smith Travel Award in Architecture Librarianship. *Winner:* Holly Hathaway.

H. W. Wilson Research Awards. *Winners:* Robert Craig Bunch, Hillary Veeder.

George Wittenborn Memorial Book Awards. See "Literary Prizes, 2011" in Part 5.

Asian/Pacific Americans Libraries Association (APALA)

APALA Scholarship ($1,000). For a student of Asian or Pacific background who is enrolled in, or has been accepted into, a master's or doctoral degree program in library and/or information science at an ALA-accredited school. *Winner:* Jina Park.

APALA Travel Award ($500). To a library professional possessing a master's-level degree in library and/or information science to attend the ALA Annual Conference. *Winner:* Cynthia Mari Orozco.

Association for Library and Information Science Education (ALISE)

ALISE Award for Teaching Excellence in the Field of Library and Information Science Education. *Winner:* Denise Agosto, Drexel University.

ALISE/Dialog Methodology Paper Competition ($500). To stimulate communication on research methodologies at ALISE annual conferences. *Sponsor:* Dialog. *Winner:* John

M. Budd, University of Missouri–Columbia, for "Phenomenological Critical Realism: A Practical Method for LIS."

ALISE/Eugene Garfield Doctoral Dissertation Award ($500). *Winners:* Cassidy Sugimoto, Indiana University–Bloomington for "Mentoring, Collaboration, and Interdisciplinary: An Evaluation of the Scholarly Development of Information and Library Science Doctoral Students"; Shari Ann Lee, St. John's University, for "Teen Space: Designed for Whom?"

ALISE/Norman Horrocks Leadership Award ($500). To recognize a new ALISE member who has demonstrated outstanding leadership qualities in professional ALISE activities. *Winner:* Lauren Mandel.

ALISE/LMC Paper Award. *Winner:* Marianne Martens, Rutgers University, for "The Librarian Lion: Constructing Children's Literature Through Connections, Capital, and Criticism (1910–1941)."

ALISE/Pratt-Severn Faculty Innovation Award ($1,000). To recognize innovation by full-time faculty members in incorporating evolving information technologies in the curricula of accredited master's degree programs in library and information studies. *Winner:* Scott Nicholson, Syracuse University.

ALISE/Bohdan S. Wynar Research Paper Competition. *Winner:* Catherine A. Johnson, University of Western Ontario, for "'I'm Like the Librarian Bartender sometimes': How Informal Interactions Between Library Staff and Patrons Help to Create Social Capital."

ALISE Professional Contribution to Library and Information Science Education Award. *Winner:* Eileen Abels, Drexel University.

ALISE Research Grant Awards (one or more grants totaling $5,000): *Winners:* Gail Dickinson and Shana Pribesh, Old Dominion University, for "The Impact of National Board Certification of Library Media Specialists on Student Academic Achievement."

ALISE/University of Washington Information School Youth Services Graduate Student Travel Award ($750). To support the costs associated with travel to and participation in the ALISE Annual Conference. *Winner:* Lucia Cedeira Serantes, University of Western Ontario.

Doctoral Students to ALISE Grant ($500). To support the attendance of one or more promising LIS doctoral students at the ALISE Annual Conference. *Winner:* Beth St. Jean, University of Michigan.

OCLC/ALISE Library and Information Science Research Grant Program. To promote independent research that helps librarians integrate new technologies into areas of traditional competence and contributes to a better understanding of the library environment. *Winners:* Christina Pattuelli, Chirag Shah, Bei Yu.

Service to ALISE Award. *Winner:* Michele Cloonan.

Association of Jewish Libraries (AJL)

AJL Scholarships ($1,000). For students enrolled in accredited library schools who plan to work as Judaica librarians. *Winners:* Meira Chefitz, Joyce "Jodi" Wortsman.

Fanny Goldstein Merit Award. To honor loyal and ongoing contributions to the association and to the profession of Jewish librarianship. *Winner:* Etta D. Gold.

Life Membership Award. To recognize outstanding leadership and professional contributions to the association and to the profession of Jewish librarianship. *Winner:* Pearl Berger.

Association of Research Libraries

ARL Diversity Scholarships (stipend of up to $10,000). To a varying number of MLS students from under-represented groups who are interested in careers in research libraries. *Sponsors:* ARL member libraries and the Institute of Museum and Library Services. *Winners (2011–2013):* Regina Carter, Amber D'Ambrosio, Carlos Duarte, Jennifer Garrett, Jennifer Gibson, Don Jason, Nabil Kashyap, Arthur Liu, Yumi Ohira, Brandon Taylor, Megan Threats, Sarah Velasquez, Kimberly Yang.

Association of Seventh-Day Adventist Librarians

D. Glenn Hilts Scholarship ($1,500) for a member of the Seventh-Day Adventist Church in a graduate library program. *Winners:* Melissa Faifer, Marianne Kordas.

Beta Phi Mu

Beta Phi Mu Award. See under American Library Association.

Eugene Garfield Doctoral Dissertation Fellowships ($3,000). *Winners:* Sofia Athenikos, Amber Cushing, Keisuke Inoue, Amy VanScoy, Hollie White, Yong Yi.

Harold Lancour Scholarship for Foreign Study ($1,500). For graduate study in a country related to the applicant's work or schooling. *Winner:* Natalia Ermolaev.

Sarah Rebecca Reed Scholarship ($2,000). For study at an ALA-accredited library school. *Winners:* Kalsang, Eric Ambler.

Frank B. Sessa Scholarship for Continuing Professional Education ($1,250). For continuing education for a Beta Phi Mu member. *Winner:* Santi Thompson.

Blanche E. Woolls Scholarship ($1,500). For a beginning student in school library media services. *Winner:* Jennifer Colby.

Bibliographical Society of America (BSA)

BSA Fellowships ($1,500–$6,000). For scholars involved in bibliographical inquiry and research in the history of the book trades and in publishing history. *Winners:* (Fredson Bowers Award, $1,500) Michael Johnson; (BSA-ASECS Fellowship for Bibliographical Studies in the 18th Century, $3,000) Jeremy Dibbell; (BSA-Mercantile Library Fellowship in North American Bibliography, $2,000) Laura Helton; (McCorison Fellowship for the History and Bibliography of Printing in Canada and the United States, $2,000) Hester Blum; (one-month fellowships, $2,000) Liangyu Fu, Abhijit Gupta, Joad Raymond; (Katharine F. Pantzer Senior Fellowship in Bibliography and the British Book Trades, $6,000) Earle Havens; (Katharine Pantzer Fellowship in the British Book Trades, $2,000) Madeleine Thompson; (Reese Fellowship for American Bibliography and the History of the Book in the Americas, $2,000) Lise Jaillant.

William L. Mitchell Prize for Research on Early British Serials ($1,000). Awarded triennially for the best single work published in the previous three years. *Winner:* To be awarded next in 2012.

St. Louis Mercantile Library Prize in American Bibliography ($2,000). Awarded triennially to encourage scholarship in the bibliography of American history and literature. *Sponsor:* St. Louis Mercantile Library, University of Missouri, St. Louis. *Winner:* Andrea Krupp for *Bookcloth in England and America, 1823–1850* (Oak Knoll).

Justin G. Schiller Prize for Bibliographical Work on Pre-20th-Century Children's Books ($2,000). A triennial award to encourage scholarship in the bibliography of historical children's books. *Winner:* To be awarded next in 2013.

Canadian Library Association (CLA)

Olga B. Bishop Award (C$200). To a library school student for the best paper on government information or publications. *Winner:* Not awarded in 2011.

Chancellor Group Conference Grant (C$500). To support attendance of newly qualified teacher-librarians at the next conference of the Canadian Association for School Libraries (CASL). *Winners:* Not awarded in 2011.

CLA Award for the Advancement of Intellectual Freedom in Canada. *Winner:* Alan Borovoy.

CLA Elizabeth Dafoe Scholarship (C$5,000). *Winner:* Hope Hutchins.

CLA/Ken Haycock Award for Promoting Librarianship (C$1,000). For significant contributions to the public recognition and appreciation of librarianship. *Winner:* Allan Wilson, chief librarian, Prince George Public Library.

CLA/Information Today Award for Innovative Technology. *Donor:* Information Today, Inc. *Winner:* Red Deer (Alberta) Public Library.

CLA Library Research and Development Grant (C$1,000). *Winner:* Not awarded in 2011.

CLA Outstanding Service to Librarianship Award. *Donor:* Bowker. *Winner:* Stephen Abram.

CLA Student Article Award. *Winner:* Richard Anderson for "Information Visualization in Children's Picture Books."

CLA/3M Canada Award for Achievement in Technical Services (C$1,000). *Winner:* Wilfrid Laurier University Library for its Voyager-Banner Financials Interface project.

CLA/H. W. Wilson Scholarship ($2,000). *Winner:* Sarah Felker.

CLA/YBP Award for Outstanding Contribution to Collection Development and Management (C$1,000). To recognize a CLA member who has made an outstanding local, national, or international contribution in the field of library collection development or management. *Sponsor:* YBP Library Services. *Winner:* Not awarded in 2011.

W. Kaye Lamb Award for Service to Seniors. Awarded biennially to recognize a library that has developed an ongoing service, program, or procedure of benefit to seniors and/or a design and organization of buildings or facilities that improve access and encourage use by seniors. *Sponsors:* Ex Libris Association and CLA. *Winner:* To be awarded next in 2012.

Canadian Association for School Libraries (CASL)

CASL Follett International Teacher Librarian of the Year Award. *Winner:* Judith Comfort.

CASL Margaret B. Scott Award of Merit. For the development of school libraries in Canada. *Winner:* Heather Daly.

CASL Angela Thacker Memorial Award. To honor teacher-librarians who have made contributions to the profession through publications, productions, or professional development activities. *Winner:* Moira Ekdahl.

Canadian Association of College and University Libraries (CACUL)

CACUL/Robert H. Blackburn Distinguished Paper Award ($200). To acknowledge nota-

ble research published by CACUL members. *Winner:* Ken Ladd for "An Examination of the Failure Rate and Content Equivalency of Electronic Surrogates and the Implications for Print Equivalent Preservation" published in *Evidence Based Library and Information Practice* (5:4).

CACUL/Miles Blackwell Award for Outstanding Academic Librarian. *Sponsor:* Baker & Taylor/YBP Library Services. *Winner:* Melody Burton, University of British Columbia, Okanagan.

CACUL Innovation Achievement Award ($1,000). *Sponsor:* OCLC. *Winner:* Canadian Research Knowledge Network (CRKN) for its License Information Module.

CTCL Award for Outstanding College Librarian. *Winner:* Linda Schneider, Library Resource Centre, Conestoga College Institute of Technology and Advanced Learning, Kitchener, Ontario.

CTCL Innovation Achievement Award. *Sponsor:* OCLC. *Winners:* Librarians of Okanagan College Library for the development and implementation of Course Integrated Library Research Instruction (CILRI) at Okanagan College, Kelowna, British Columbia.

Canadian Association of Public Libraries (CAPL)

CAPL/Brodart Outstanding Public Library Service Award. *Winner:* Eric Stackhouse, Pictou Antigonish Regional Library.

Canadian Association of Special Libraries and Information Services (CASLIS)

CASLIS Award for Special Librarianship in Canada. *Winner:* Ingrid C. Langhammer.

Canadian Library Trustees Association (CLTA)

CLTA/Stan Heath Achievement in Literacy Award. For an innovative literacy program by a public library board. *Donor:* ABC Canada. *Winners:* Edmonton Public Library Board, Winnipeg Public Library Board.

CLTA Merit Award for Distinguished Service as a Public Library Trustee. *Winner:* Andy Ackerman.

Catholic Library Association

Regina Medal. For continued, distinguished contribution to the field of children's literature. *Winner:* Patricia Polacco.

Chinese-American Librarians Association (CALA)

CALA Distinguished Service Award. To a librarian who has been a mentor, role model, and leader in the fields of library and information science. *Winner:* Rush G. Miller, University of Pittsburgh.

CALA President's Recognition Award. *Winners:* Camila Alire, Dora Ho, Priscilla Yu.

CALA Scholarship of Library and Information Science ($500). *Winner:* Jennifer Shuang.

Sheila Suen Lai Scholarship ($500). *Winner:* Pei Yu Lin.

C. C. Seetoo/CALA Conference Travel Scholarship ($500). For a student to attend the ALA Annual Conference and CALA program. *Winner:* Yanjuan Zou.

Sally C. Tseng Professional Development Grant ($1,000). *Winner:* The 2011 and 2012 grants were scheduled to be announced in June 2012.

Huang Tso-ping and Wu Yao-yu Scholarship Memorial Research Grant ($200): *Winner:* Sara Wang.

Church and Synagogue Library Association (CSLA)

CSLA Award for Outstanding Congregational Librarian. For distinguished service to the congregation and/or community through devotion to the congregational library. *Winner:* Margaret Lefever, Craig Eder Library, Saint Columba's Church, Washington, D.C.

CSLA Award for Outstanding Congregational Library. For responding in creative and innovative ways to the library's mission of reaching and serving the congregation and/ or the wider community. *Winner:* Ellen Perkins Memorial Library, Vienna (Virginia) Presbyterian Church.

CSLA Award for Outstanding Contribution to Congregational Libraries. For providing inspiration, guidance, leadership, or resources to enrich the field of church or synagogue librarianship. *Winner:* Carol Campbell, Saint Thomas Episcopal Church, Sunnyvale, California.

Helen Keating Ott Award for Outstanding Contribution to Children's Literature. *Winner:* Not awarded in 2011.

Pat Tabler Memorial Scholarship Award. *Winner:* Not awarded in 2011.

Coalition for Networked Information

Paul Evan Peters Award. Awarded biennially to recognize notable and lasting international achievements relating to high-performance networks and the creation and use of information resources and services that advance scholarship and intellectual productivity. *Sponsors:* Association of Research Libraries, Coalition for Networked Information, EDUCAUSE. *Winner:* Christine Borgman.

Paul Evan Peters Fellowship ($5,000 a year for two years). Awarded biennially to a student pursuing a graduate degree in librarianship or the information sciences. *Sponsors:* Association of Research Libraries, Coalition for Networked Information, EDUCAUSE. *Winner:* To be awarded next in 2012.

Council on Library and Information Resources (CLIR)

CLIR Postdoctoral Fellowships in Scholarly Information Resources. *Current fellows:* Jessica Aberle, Erin Aspenlieder, Peter Broadwell, Arthur "Mitch" Fraas, Korey Jackson, Spencer Keralis, Jennifer Redmond, Donald Sells, Christopher Teeter, Nicole Wagner; *Continuing current fellows* Andrew Asher, Tamar Boyadjian, Brian Croxall, John Maclachlan, Noah Shenker, Yi Shen.

Mellon Fellowship Program for Dissertation Research in the Humanities in Original Sources (stipends of up to $20,000 to support dissertation research). *Current fellows:* Matthew Amato, Nora Barakat, Amy Brady, Meaghan Brown, Rowan Dorin, Alice Goff, M. Scott Heerman, Philippa Hetherington, Philip Johnston, Eugenia Kisin, Konstanze

Kunst, Melissa Lo, Anne Phillips, Naomi Pitamber, Lena Suk, Gene Tempest.

Rick Peterson Fellowship. To an early-career information technology professional or librarian who has reached beyond traditional boundaries to resolve a significant challenge facing digital libraries. *Cosponsors:* CLIR and the National Institute for Technology in Liberal Education (NITLE). *Winner:* Meghan Frazer.

Rovelstad Scholarship in International Librarianship. To enable a student enrolled in an accredited LIS program to attend the IFLA World Library and Information Congress. *Winner:* Timothy Thompson.

A. R. Zipf Fellowship in Information Management ($10,000). To a student enrolled in graduate school who shows exceptional promise for leadership and technical achievement. *Winner:* Kathleen Fear.

Friends of the National Library of Medicine

Michael E. DeBakey Library Services Outreach Award. To recognize outstanding service and contributions to rural and underserved communities by a practicing health sciences librarian. *Winner:* Ann Duesing, Claude Moore Health Sciences Library, University of Virginia.

Bill and Melinda Gates Foundation

Access to Learning Award ($1 million). To public libraries or similar organizations outside the United States for innovative programs that provide the public free access to information technology. *Administered by:* Gates Foundation Global Libraries initiative. *Winner:* Arid Lands Information Network (ALIN) for its creation of 12 Maarifa (knowledge) Centers in remote regions of Kenya, Uganda, and Tanzania.

Institute of Museum and Library Services

National Medal for Museum and Library Service. For extraordinary civic, educational, economic, environmental, and social contributions ($10,000). *Winners:* (libraries) Alachua County Library District, Gainesville, Florida; Columbus (Ohio) Metropolitan Library; Hill Museum and Manuscript Library, Collegeville, Minnesota; San José (California) Public Library; Weippe (Idaho) Public Library and Discovery Center.

International Association of School Librarians (IASL)

Ken Haycock and Jean Lowrie Leadership Development Grants ($1,000). To enable applicants in developing nations to attend their first IASL Annual Conference. *Winners:* (Haycock award) Not awarded in 2011; (Lowrie award) Nguyen Tan Thanh Truc, Vietnam.

International Federation of Library Associations and Institutions (IFLA)

De Gruyter Saur/IFLA Research Paper Award (€1,000). For the best unpublished research paper on a topic of importance to publishing and access to information by an author or authors with no more than eight years of professional experience in library and information services. *Sponsors:* IFLA and De Gruyter Saur. *Winners:* Erin Thomas, Grace Costantino, Bianca Crowley, and Rebecca Morin for "Heeding the Call: User Feedback Management and the Digital Library."

Dr. Shawky Salem Conference Grant (up to $1,900). To enable an expert in library and information science who is a national of an Arab country to attend the IFLA Conference for the first time. *Winner:* Ibrahim F. Farah, American University of Beirut Libraries, Beirut, Lebanon.

Frederick Thorpe Organizational Award (up to £15,000). To a library organization for development of service delivery to the visually impaired. *Winners:* Not awarded in 2011.

Ulverscroft Foundation/IFLA Libraries Serving Persons with Print Disabilities Section Best Practice Awards. To assist the development of library services for print-disabled people and foster cooperation between library services serving these persons. *Winners:* (individual awards) Marianne Kraack, Royal New Zealand Foundation for the Blind; Jelena Lesaja, Croatian Library for the Blind; Kristina Janc of the National and University Library, Slovenia; and Megan Gilks of the Royal National Institute of Blind People (RNIB UK) and Marieke Belt of Loket aangepast-lezen (Center for Adapted Reading), the Netherlands.

Library Journal

Library Journal Teaching Award ($5,000). To recognize excellence in LIS education. *Offered by: Library Journal. Sponsored by:* ProQuest. *Winner:* Martin B. Wolske, Graduate School of Library and Information Science, University of Illinois at Urbana-Champaign.

Medical Library Association (MLA)

Virginia L. and William K. Beatty MLA Volunteer Service Award. To recognize a medical librarian who has demonstrated outstanding, sustained service to the Medical Library Association and the health sciences library profession. *Winner:* Kay E. Wellik.

Estelle Brodman Award for the Academic Medical Librarian of the Year. To honor significant achievement, potential for leadership, and continuing excellence at midcareer in the area of academic health sciences librarianship. *Winner:* Nancy Tannery.

Lois Ann Colaianni Award for Excellence and Achievement in Hospital Librarianship. To a member of MLA who has made significant contributions to the profession in the area of overall distinction or leadership in hospital librarianship. *Winner:* Barbara J. Henry.

Cunningham Memorial International Fellowships. Provides grants and travel expenses in the United States and Canada for one or more librarians from other countries. Includes attendance at the MLA Annual Meeting and observation and supervised work in one of more medical libraries. *Winners:* Midrar Ullah, Pakistan; Satish Munnolli, India.

Louise Darling Medal. For distinguished achievement in collection development in

the health sciences. *Winner:* Not awarded in 2011.

Janet Doe Lectureship. *Winner:* T. Scott Plutchak. *Topic:* "Breaking the Barriers of Time and Space: The Dawning of the Great Age of Librarians."

EBSCO/MLA Annual Meeting Grants (up to $1,000). To enable four health sciences librarians to attend the MLA Annual Meeting. *Winners:* Trish Chatterley, Anna Katherine Crawford, Lara Handler, and Ryan Rafferty.

Ida and George Eliot Prize. To recognize a work published in the preceding calendar year that has been judged most effective in furthering medical librarianship. *Winner:* Not awarded in 2011.

Carla J. Funk Governmental Relations Award ($500). To recognize a medical librarian who has demonstrated outstanding leadership in the area of governmental relations at the federal, state, or local level, and who has furthered the goal of providing quality information for improved health. *Winner:* J. Michael Homan.

Murray Gottlieb Prize. For the best unpublished essay on the history of medicine and allied sciences written by a health sciences librarian. *Donors:* Ralph and Jo Grimes. *Winner:* Not awarded in 2011.

T. Mark Hodges International Service Award. To honor outstanding achievement in promoting, enabling, or delivering improved health information internationally. *Winner:* Not awarded in 2011.

David A. Kronick Traveling Fellowship ($2,000). *Sponsor:* Bowden-Massey Foundation. *Winner:* Linda C. Butson.

Joseph Leiter NLM/MLA Lectureship. *Winner:* Peter J. Hotez. *Topic:* "Open Access and Control of the Neglected Tropical Diseases."

Donald A. B. Lindberg Research Fellowship ($10,000). To fund research aimed at expanding the research knowledge base, linking the information services provided by librarians to improved health care and advances in biomedical research. *Winner:* Thane Chambers for "How Health Sciences Librarians in North America Are Involved in Health Research."

Lucretia W. McClure Excellence in Education Award. To an outstanding educator in the field of health sciences librarianship and informatics. *Winner:* Gale G. Hannigan.

Majors/MLA Chapter Project of the Year Award. *Sponsor:* J. A. Majors Co. *Winner:* Medical Library Group of Southern California and Arizona.

John P. McGovern Award Lectureship. *Winner:* Clay Shirky. *Topic:* "Technology/Media: The Future, Innovation, Business Strategy, Marketing and Sales, Ethics, and Culture."

Medical Informatics Section Career Development Grant ($1,500). To support a career development activity that will contribute to advancement in the field of medical informatics. *Winner:* Melissa Resnick.

MLA Continuing Education Awards ($100–$500). *Winner:* Beth A. Lewis.

MLA Fellowships. For sustained and outstanding contributions to health sciences librarianship and to the advancement of the purposes of MLA. *Honorees:* Trenton Boyd, Karen Butter, Lynn M. Fortney.

MLA Research, Development, and Demonstration Project Grants ($100 to $1,000). To provide support for research, development, or demonstration projects that will help to promote excellence in the field of health sciences librarianship and information sciences. *Winner:* Kristine M. Alpi.

MLA Scholarship (up to $5,000). For graduate study at an ALA-accredited library school. *Winner:* Karen Gutzman.

MLA Scholarship for Minority Students (up to $5,000). For graduate study at an ALA-accredited library school. *Winner:* Phill Jo.

Marcia C. Noyes Award. For an outstanding contribution to medical librarianship. *Winner:* Carol G. Jenkin.

President's Award. To an MLA member for a notable or important contribution made during the past association year. *Winner:* Susan S. Star.

Rittenhouse Award. For the best unpublished paper on medical librarianship submitted by a student enrolled in, or having been enrolled in, a course for credit in an ALA-accredited library school or a trainee in an internship program in medical librarianship.

Donor: Rittenhouse Book Distributors. *Winner:* Mahria Lebo.

Thomson Reuters/Frank Bradway Rogers Information Advancement Award. To recognize outstanding contributions for the application of technology to the delivery of health science information, to the science of information, or to the facilitation of the delivery of health science information. *Sponsor:* Thomson Reuters. *Winner:* Lei Wan.

Music Library Association

Carol June Bradley Award. To support studies that involve the history of music libraries or special collections. *Winner:* Beverly M. Wilcox.

Vincent H. Duckles Award. For the best book-length bibliography or other research tool in music. *Winner:* Not awarded in 2011.

Dena Epstein Award for Archival and Library Research in American Music. To support research in archives or libraries internationally on any aspect of American music. *Winner:* Nancy Yunhwa Rao.

Kevin Freeman Travel Grants. To colleagues who are new to the profession to enable them to attend the association's annual meeting. *Winners:* Langston Bates, Sally Bauer, Zach Coble, Carolyn Doi, Molly O'Brien, Lindy Smith.

Walter Gerboth Award. To members of the association who are in the first five years of their professional library careers, to assist research-in-progress in music or music librarianship. *Winner:* Anna E. Kijas.

Richard S. Hill Award. For the best article on music librarianship or article of a music-bibliographic nature. *Winner:* Tim Brooks for "Copyright and Historical Sound Recordings: Recent Efforts to Change U.S. Law" in *Notes* 65:3, 464–474.

MLA Citation. Awarded in recognition of contributions to the profession over a career. *Winner:* Not awarded in 2011.

Eva Judd O'Meara Award. For the best review published in *Notes. Winner:* Kofi Agawu, for a review of *A Theory of Musical Narrative* in *Notes* 66:2, 275–277.

Donor: K. G. Saur Verlag. *Winner:* Not awarded in 2011.

National Library Service for the Blind and Physically Handicapped, Library of Congress

Library of the Year Awards ($1,000). *Winners:* (network library of the year) (co-winners) Ohio Library for the Blind and Physically Disabled, part of the Cleveland Public Library, and the State Library of Ohio Talking Book Service; (network subregional library of the year) Detroit Subregional Library for the Blind and Physically Handicapped of the Detroit Public Library.

REFORMA (National Association to Promote Library and Information Services to Latinos and the Spanish-Speaking)

REFORMA Scholarships (up to $1,500). To students who qualify for graduate study in library science and who are citizens or permanent residents of the United States. *Winners:* Lauren Campbell, Pablo Morales Henry, Melissa Nicholas, Jeri Ramos-Morton, Jimena Sagas.

Arnulfo D. Trejo Librarian of the Year Award. To recognize a librarian who has promoted and advocated services to the Spanish-speaking and Latino communities and made outstanding contributions to REFORMA. *Winner:* Juan Carlos Rodriguez, Grand Valley State University, Grand Rapids.

K. G. Saur Verlag (Munich, Germany)

Award for Best *Libri* Student Paper (€500). To recognize the most outstanding article published in *Libri* during the preceding year.

Society of American Archivists (SAA)

C. F. W. Coker Award for Description. To recognize creators of tools that enable archivists to produce more-effective finding aids. *Winner:* John F. Kennedy Presidential Library and Museum, Boston.

Colonial Dames of America Scholarship (up to $1,200). To enable new archivists to attend the Modern Archives Institute of the National Archives and Records Administration. *Winner:* Award discontinued in 2010.

Council Exemplary Service Award. *Winner:* Mary Jo Pugh.

Distinguished Service Award. To recognize an archival institution, education program, nonprofit organization, or governmental organization that has given outstanding service to its public and has made an exemplary contribution to the archives profession. *Winner:* Not awarded in 2011.

Fellows' Ernst Posner Award. For an outstanding essay dealing with a facet of archival administration, history, theory, or methodology, published in *American Archivist*. *Winner:* Paul Conway, University of Michigan, for "Modes of Seeing: Digitized Photographic Archives and the Experienced User," *American Archivist* 73:2.

Josephine Forman Scholarship. *Winner:* Nidya G. Gonzalez.

F. Gerald Ham Scholarship ($7,500). To recognize an individual's past performance in a graduate archival studies program and his or her potential in the field. *Winner:* Eric Willey.

Philip M. Hamer and Elizabeth Hamer Kegan Award. For individuals and/or institutions that have increased public awareness of a specific body of documents. *Winner:* University of Wisconsin–Milwaukee Libraries for its March On Milwaukee civil rights history project.

Oliver Wendell Holmes Travel Award. To enable overseas archivists already in the United States or Canada for training to attend the SAA annual meeting. *Winners:* Patrick Ansah, Umi Asma' Mokhtar.

J. Franklin Jameson Award. For individuals and/or organizations that promote greater public awareness of archival activities and programs. *Winner:* NBC television for the series "Who Do You Think You Are?"

Sister M. Claude Lane, O.P., Memorial Award. For a significant contribution to the field of religious archives. *Winner:* Malachy R. McCarthy, Claretian Missionaries Archives.

Waldo Gifford Leland Prize. For writing of superior excellence and usefulness in the field of archival history, theory, or practice. *Winner:* Laura A. Millar for *Archives: Principles and Practices* (Neal-Schuman).

Theodore Calvin Pease Award. For the best student paper. *Winner:* Lora Davis, University of Wisconsin–Milwaukee, for "Providing Virtual Services to All: A Mixed-Method Analysis of the Web Site Accessibility of Philadelphia Area Consortium of Special Collections Libraries (PACSCL) Member Repositories."

Donald Peterson Student Scholarship Award (up to $1,000). To enable a student or recent graduate to attend the SAA Annual Meeting. *Winner:* Brittany Turner.

Harold T. Pinkett Minority Student Award. To encourage minority students to consider careers in the archival profession, and to promote minority participation in SAA. *Winners:* Melvin J. Collier, Kelly Lau.

Preservation Publication Award. To recognize an outstanding work published in North America that advances the theory or the practice of preservation in archival institutions. *Winner:* Ross Harvey for *Digital Curation: A How-to-Do-It Manual* (Neal-Schuman); (special commendation) Matthew G. Kirschenbaum, Richard Ovenden, Gabriela Redwine, and Rachel Donahue, for *Digital Forensics and Born-Digital Content in Cultural Heritage Collections* (CLIR).

SAA Fellows. To a limited number of members for their outstanding contribution to the archival profession. *Honored:* George Bain, Kaye Lanning Minchew, Timothy Murray, Janice Ruth, Bradley Westbrook, Deborah Wythe, Julia Marks Young, Tanya Zanish-Belcher.

SAA Mosaic Scholarship ($5,000). To minority students pursuing graduate education in archival science. *Winners:* Rose Chou, Helen Kim.

SAA Spotlight Award. To recognize the contributions of individuals who work for the good of the profession and of archival collections, and whose work would not typically receive public recognition. *Winner:* Teresa Kiser.

Special Libraries Association (SLA)

Diversity Leadership Development Program Award ($1,000 stipend). *Sponsor:* EBSCO. *Winner:* Elizabeth Edwards.

Dow Jones Leadership Award ($2,000). For excellence in special librarianship. *Winner:* Peggy Garvin.

ProQuest and Dialog Member Achievement Award ($1,000). To an SLA member for raising visibility, awareness, and appreciation of the profession, SLA unit, or the association. *Winner:* Debal Kar.

SLA John Cotton Dana Award. For exceptional support and encouragement of special librarianship. *Winner:* Lynne McCay.

SLA Fellows. *Honored:* Kate Arnold, Leoma Dunn, Karen Huffman, James King, Marlene Vogelsang.

SLA Hall of Fame Award. For outstanding performance and distinguished service to SLA. *Winners:* Susan DiMattia, Doris Helfer.

SLA Research Grant (incorporating the Steven I. Goldspiel Memorial Research Grant Fund) (up to $25,000). To support outstanding research. *Winner:* Not awarded in 2011.

Rose L. Vormelker Award. *Winners:* Mary Talley, Judith Tapiero.

Other Awards of Distinction

Robert B. Downs Intellectual Freedom Award. To recognize individuals or groups who have furthered the cause of intellectual freedom, particularly as it impacts libraries and information centers and the dissemination of ideas. *Offered by:* Graduate School of

Library and Information Science, University of Illinois at Urbana-Champaign. *Winner:* Marianna Tax Choldin.

I Love My Librarian Awards ($5,000, a plaque, and a $500 travel stipend to attend the awards ceremony). To recognize librarians for service to their communities, schools, and campuses. Winners are nominated by library patrons. *Sponsors:* Carnegie Corporation of New York and the *New York Times. Winners:* (public librarians) Venetia V. Demson, Martha Ferriby, Jennifer O. Keohane, Saundra Ross-Forrest; (school librarians) Jennifer U. LaGarde, Betsy Long, Michelle Luhtala; (college, community college, and university librarians) Rhonda Allison Rios Kravitz, Rebecca Traub, Barbara K. Weaver.

RWA Librarian of the Year. To a librarian who demonstrates outstanding support of romance authors and the romance genre. *Offered by:* Romance Writers of America. *Winner:* Wendy Crutcher, Orange County (California) Public Libraries.

Women's National Book Association Award. Awarded biennially to a living American woman who derives part or all of her income from books and allied arts and who has done meritorious work in the world of books. *Offered by:* Women's National Book Association (WNBA). *Winner:* Not awarded in 2011.

Part 4
Research and Statistics

Library Research and Statistics

Research and Statistics on Libraries and Librarianship in 2011

Denise M. Davis

The predominant issues facing libraries in 2011, once again, were funding stability and e-content acquisition, specifically e-books. Although limited national library data were available at the time this article was prepared, news appearing throughout 2011 in *Library Journal, American Libraries* and the American Library Association (ALA) report *The State of America's Libraries 2011*[1] indicated that the economic climate did not improve during the year. Not only did libraries continue to struggle with flat or decreasing operating revenue resulting from the ongoing national (and international) economic slump, they also struggled to meet the rapidly increasing consumer demand for e-book content. Publishers and distributors responded in interesting ways, demonstrating their uncertainty about the e-book markets for everything from K–12 and higher education textbooks to popular mass market titles, and about how best to support library patron access.

This article will highlight available library statistics for 2011, including the National Center for Education Statistics (NCES) "First Look" publication *Academic Libraries: 2010,* the latest American Association of School Librarians (AASL) study *School Libraries Count!*, the Public Library Funding and Technology Access Study, and SPEC Kits released by the Association of Research Libraries (ARL).

Winners of research awards and grants conferred by ALA and its divisions, and by Beta Phi Mu, the American Society for Information Science and Technology, the Association for Library and Information Science Education, and the Medical Library Association also are highlighted.

Among noteworthy studies released during 2011 was the ALA Young Adult Services Association's (YALSA's) *National Research Agenda on Libraries, Teens and Young Adults 2012–2016.* The agenda targets four priorities: the impact of libraries on young adults, young adult reading and resources, information-seeking behaviors and needs of young adults, and informal and formal learning environments and young adults.

Developed from data gathered by library science educators in graduate schools of library science across the United States, the survey identified research gaps and how best to respond to those gaps. In its introduction, the report notes that "The

Denise M. Davis was director of the American Library Association's Office for Research and Statistics through late 2010. She is now deputy director of the Sacramento (California) Public Library.

research called for in this agenda will help guarantee that librarians serving young adults are able to provide the best service possible as well as advocate for funding and support in order to ensure that teens are served effectively by their libraries." Questions to be answered in each priority area are included in the report. It is available as a pdf at (http://www.ala.org/yalsa/sites/ala.org.yalsa/files/content/guidelines/research/researchagenda12-16.pdf).

Facts and Figures About Libraries

Public Libraries

The Public Library Association's Public Library Data Service (PLDS) 2011 Statistical Report[2] provides results from fiscal year (FY) 2010 public library data collected from a self-selected response pool representing very small to very large libraries in North America. All results are actual and unweighted. The results are influenced by a higher response from smaller libraries than in the previous year. For instance, circulation declined 23.7 percent from the prior fiscal year, although circulation per capita increased overall. Despite this influence, there are some interesting findings, such as average library revenue (income) falling below average expenditures for libraries serving 500,000 or more residents, meaning that the largest libraries were using savings to operate. It will be interesting to see the FY 2010 public library data that were scheduled for release in spring 2012 by the Institute of Museum and Library Services, which will show whether the national weighted data align with the PLDS sample data.

ALA sponsors an annual household survey that follows public library use. Harris Interactive conducted the 2010 and 2011 telephone surveys, and the 2011 results identified some modest changes; for example, the number of in-person visits adjusted down, with 2 percent fewer reporting monthly or more-frequent visits; however, "visits" by telephone increased.[3] In fact, for individuals reporting increased use of the library, use by telephone rose 12 percent in 2011 from 2010, for a net hike of 3 percent of all reporting increased use. Satisfaction remained largely unchanged from 2010, and more respondents reported as "somewhat" to "very" important the following services: help in starting a business (up 9 percent); access to computers, training, and support (up 7 percent); providing accurate and up-to-date financial information (up 6 percent); and providing information for school and work (up 5 percent).

These household survey findings were echoed in Patron Profiles, a new quarterly study series launched by Library Journal.[4] The first in the series analyzed results from 2,421 participants on a range of baseline information (demographics, library use patterns, and so forth) and drilled specifically into patron e-book use. The results identify characteristics of "power patrons" and occasional users to present a fairly comprehensive picture of public library use and media consumption overall. The Patron Profiles results provide greater detail on the types of library use. For instance, the ALA-Harris Interactive study indicates that 71 percent of respondents access the library by computer, and the Patron Profiles study reports that "databases accessed at home from a library website" averaged 7.4 times during a six-month period, but 16.4 times by "power patrons."[5] Together, these studies provide a wealth of information on public library use. More on the Patron Profiles study appears in the e-book section of this article.

ALA's *Libraries Connect Communities: Public Library Funding and Technology Access Study 2010–2011*[6] highlighted some trends that are closely aligned with the continued national and regional economic slump. A decline in opening hours was reported by 15.9 percent of libraries, nearly a four-fold increase from 2008 to 2009, with some states reporting more significant reductions (Ohio 49.9 percent, California 44.5 percent, and Georgia 31.5 percent.)[7] Delayed replacement or purchase of public-access computers was reported by 47 percent of libraries, and about 60 percent reported flat or decreased operating budgets. Some positive findings included wifi installation reported by 86 percent of public libraries, and e-book availability reported by 67.2 percent.

Return on Investment (ROI) research continues. A concise article was published by Joseph R. Matthews in *Library Leadership & Management*[8] outlining the benefits of ROI analysis and providing a useful summary of large and small-scale ROI studies that have been completed.

Academic Libraries

NCES released its *Academic Libraries: 2010*[9] biennial report, describing key metrics including staffing, collections, circulation, expenditures, and services. Most significant changes occurred in circulation, collections, and expenditures. Total circulation (general collections and reserve) continued to show a decline (about 2 percent from 2008), while interlibrary lending remained about the same. Collections grew in all areas except microform, audiovisual, and current serial subscriptions, where modest declines were reported. A substantial decline was reported for electronic reference sources and aggregation services, down about 51 percent from 2008. Considerable growth was reported for e-books, up about 54 percent from 2008.

Reported staffing also was down from 2008, but the number of institutions reporting decreased from 3,911 to 3,689, which may account for the variation. Overall expenditures increased fractionally from 2008 (by about $8 million), but declined in specific institutional characteristic areas. Overall reductions of more than $1 billion (about 30 percent) were reported by public institutions. Expenditures for salaries and wages increased about 16.7 percent from 2008, rising from about 42.7 percent of total expenditures to 49.8 percent. Other operating expenditures also increased slightly from 2008, up about 4 percent.

An updated ten-year trend report of NCES academic library data, *Academic Library Trends, 1998–2008,* was released by ALA in 2011 and is available through the ALA Office for Research and Statistics at http://www.ala.org/ala/research/librarystats/academic/ALS%209808%20comparison.pdf.

ALA's Association of College and Research Libraries revised its *Standards for Libraries in Higher Education* (*SLHE*), available at http://www.ala.org/ala/mgrps/divs/acrl/standards/standardslibraries.cfm. Also worth reviewing is an article by Gregory Crawford and Glenn McGuigan, "An Exploratory Quantitative Analysis of Academic Library Services," in *Library Leadership & Management* (August 2011). It compares various national academic library data sets, 1996–2008, to develop "total service indexes" to establish actual library use. The study identified three variables as the most significant—cost per service, cost per enrollment, and total service per enrollment.

ARL released new SPEC Kits in 2011, among them *Digital Preservation* (SPEC Kit 325), *Collecting Global Resources* (SPEC Kit 324), *Socializing New Hires* (SPEC Kit 323), and *Library User Experience* (SPEC Kit 322). The tables of contents and executive summaries are available on the ARL Web site at http://www.arl.org/resources/pubs/index.shtml, and each report is available for purchase.

School Libraries

AASL released a new edition of *School Libraries Count!* The fifth in a series of longitudinal analyses of U.S. public and private K–12 school libraries, the study was conducted by KRC Research and provides five-year comparisons of core metrics, with 4,887 libraries responding, and includes supplemental questions investigating digital citizenship.[10] Most notable findings in 2011 were reduced hours worked by "other" (non-librarian) staff, especially in libraries in the 95th percentile (40 hours in 2011 compared with 45 in 2010 and 56 in 2009). Most notable findings in 2011 were more individual visits per typical week (an average of 315.1 visits compared with 304 in 2010) and slightly more group visits per typical week (an average of 32.3 in 2011 from 31 in 2010).

School library budget data should be viewed with an eye to specific school responses because of the impact of average increases reported by all high schools—about 1,320 respondents or about 27 percent of total responses, with budgets up 29 percent in 2011 from 2010; and, sizeable reductions reported by all middle schools—about 929 respondents or about 19 percent of total responses, with budgets down 23.2 percent in 2011 from 2010. The impact of increases in high school budgets offsets the decreases reported by middle schools, and is sufficient to influence the overall average increase reported, about $677 in 2011 from 2010.

The Supplemental Report on Digital Citizenship[11] found that 71 percent of schools incorporate digital citizenship—knowing how to use technology appropriately—in the curriculum, while 35 percent do not; and that nearly all schools (95 percent) incorporate intellectual property (plagiarism, copyright, and so forth). The results indicate that issues such as "e-commerce, physical safety, social networking, and hardware and data protection" have not yet been incorporated into curricula. Further, school librarians reported that barriers to teaching digital citizenship include a lack of collaborative curriculum (42 percent), lack of community/parent involvement (19 percent), and technology challenges (such as filtering and lack of access to technology by students and in schools, 39 percent). Equal access to technology must be achieved (29 percent report this is the "biggest hurdle") to educate youth about digital citizenship, the report finds.

Another study released in 2011 was the *AASL Urban Schools Task Force Survey Report*,[12] which presents the results of two national surveys conducted in October–November 2010 to gather information from urban school librarians and library administrators about current work environment and needs. Data were collected from school districts with student enrollment of 40,000 or more, as were building-level data for schools in such districts. The report presents detailed findings from 798 respondents regarding grade levels served, school lunch program eligibility, hours of library operation, staffing, race/ethnicity of students, books and materials (counts and budgets), time spent doing various tasks, and so on. This is a useful data set for researchers interested in understanding more about urban libraries, data that are not available from NCES surveys about primary and secondary school library media centers.

E-Books

E-book challenges continued, perhaps even increased, in 2011. As libraries were dealing with rapidly changing devices available to consumers, and the "lease or own" question, HarperCollins announced it would set library per-copy use on new titles added to OverDrive and other vendors selling e-books to libraries. The cap was set at 26 circulations, at which time the library-purchased copy would "expire" and a new copy purchase would be required. It is unclear what research was done to determine the average number of circulations per title (the "turn rate") in order to arrive at this number, although Josh Marwell, president of sales for HarperCollins, indicated in a February 25, 2011, *Library Journal* article that the publisher determined this figure based on "the average lifespan of a print book, and wear and tear on circulating copies."[13] The question is what data were used, as they do not exist in any national public library data set. State-level total turn rate data are estimated, but do not distinguish format. At the time this report was prepared, no resolution had been achieved and the 26-circulation limit was still in place for HarperCollins titles included in OverDrive.

In a July 2011 household survey conducted by Harris Interactive,[14] 1 in 6 Americans (about 15 percent) reported using an e-reader (digital book reader)— nearly twice the percentage reported in 2010—and e-reader users were more likely to read books than those who did not yet own or have access to an e-reader (36 percent and 16 percent, respectively). Further, about 15 percent report they would likely purchase an e-reader in the next six months. The survey found that e-reader owners were more likely to purchase books than non-owners. The study details genre preferences by age and geographic region. Compare this with a September 2010 Harris Poll that found 8 percent of Americans used e-readers.[15] Although proportionally low, those with e-readers reported reading more than those reading only print. The poll found that "Overall, two in five Americans (40%) read 11 or more books a year with one in five reading 21 or more books in a year (19%). But among those who have an eReader, over one-third read 11–20 books a year (36%) and over one-quarter read 21 or more books in an average year (26%)." The 2010 poll also found that about 1 in 10 Americans planned to purchase an e-reader in the following six months. The 2011 results aligned closely with this projection, with about 15 percent more Americans reporting that they owned an e-reader in 2011 than in 2010.

A 2011 Pew Research Center study[16] found the greatest increase in e-reader ownership among adults, doubling between August 2010 and April 2011—the largest increase since Pew began collecting this information in 2006. In another article from this study, Kristen Purcell, associate director of research of the Pew Internet and American Life Project, provides demographic detail of 2010 and 2011 survey respondents.[17] Increased ownership was demonstrated in all but one demographic category (educational attainment, some high school). Ownership grew 8 percent among those self-reporting as Hispanic, 6 percent among those with some college, 5 percent among those completing college, and 8 percent among those earning $75,000 or more.

The first *Library Journal Patron Profiles* study, *Library Patrons and Ebook Usage*, provides extensive detail on public library patron behavior in library use and media consumption both inside and outside the library. The study describes "power patrons"—those who use the library more, borrow more when they visit (all formats), consider the library an excellent value, and "are more likely to read their books on multiple devices." The study found that e-book patrons resemble power patrons more than they resemble patrons overall, although there were some exceptions. Generally, patrons borrowing e-books tend to be male (49 percent, versus 45 percent of overall respondents), younger (age 41.5 versus age 47 overall), and more highly educated (pp. 20–21). Of particular interest was that about 84 percent of those with e-readers reported reading in multiple formats—print, audio, and digital print—compared with about 34 percent of the overall sample. Patron awareness of library e-book holdings is called out in the study (about 22 percent of all respondents versus about 40 percent of e-reader owners), but as e-reader adoption increases one would expect that gap to close (p. 23).

As e-reader adoption rates continue to climb, and as e-book circulation skyrockets in public libraries, one must ask what this trend means for libraries and their migration away from print collections to more digital content. A September 2011 *Publishers Weekly* article[18] highlights findings from the July 2011 Harris Poll and an industry study conducted by Aptara in which e-book publishing figures were outlined. Aptara reported that 76 percent of publishers currently produced e-books, and of these about 42 percent reported that between 76 percent and 100 percent of their books would be distributed as e-books in 2011. The profit margin for e-books is increasing, with about 20 percent of publishers reporting more than 10 percent of revenue from e-book sales. Publishers also anticipate continuing dual format distribution, with 87 percent reporting they would continue producing both print and digital content; only 10 percent indicated they would replace digital for print. Michael Kelley reported in an August 9, 2011, article for *Library Journal*,[19] with data from the BookStats study sponsored by the Association of American Publishers and the Book Industry Study Group, that e-book sales composed about 6.4 percent of the trade market in 2010 compared with only 0.6 percent in 2008, an increase of about 1,274 percent.

The results of Bowker's PubTrack Consumer survey for 2011, second quarter,[20] found that shifts in format sales from 2010 were growing. Specifically, print/paperback sales declined by 7.3 percent, print/hardback declined 4.7 percent, nonprint audio increased 0.4 percent, nonprint e-book increased 10.5 percent, and all remaining bindings sales increased 1.1 percent.

These trends do not predict the death of print books, but the data certainly demonstrate a growing strain on libraries' already stretched resources. If the *Library Journal Patron Profiles* report is any indication, libraries will need to maintain deep collections in multiple formats—expensive formats—as consumers adopt the various devices. Also, the lack of growth in format-agnostic devices will only exacerbate the challenges facing libraries. Following trends in e-content over the next year will continue to prove interesting, possibly in the Chinese sense of the word.

Awards and Grants that Support Excellent Research

The professional library associations offer many awards and grants to recognize and encourage research. The 2011 awards and grants here are listed under the name of the sponsoring association, and in the case of ALA by the awarding division, in alphabetical order. More-detailed information about the prizes and prizewinners can be found at the association Web sites. [For additional library awards, see "Library Scholarship and Award Recipients, 2011" in Part 3—*Ed.*]

American Library Association

Carroll Preston Baber Research Grant
Winner: Mary Wilkins Jordan, Simmons College, for "Public Library Stressors: Identification and Elimination."

Jesse H. Shera Award for Excellence in Published Research
Winner: M. Christina Patuelli for "Modeling Domain Ontology for Cultural Heritage," published in the *Journal of the American Society for Information Science and Technology* 62(2): 314–342, February 2011.

Jesse H. Shera Award for Support of Dissertation Research
Winner: Amy VanScoy for "Exploring the Meaning of Reference Work for Librarians in Academic Research Libraries."

American Society for Information Science and Technology

ASIS&T Best Information Science Book Award
Winner: Katy Börner for *Atlas of Science: Visualizing What We Know* (MIT).

History Fund Research Grant Award
Winners: Trudi Bellardo Hahn and Diane Barlow for "The Fortuitous Confluence of Helen Brownson, the National Science Foundation, and Information Science."

John Wiley Best JASIST Paper Award
Winners: Jim Jansen and Soo-Young Rieh for "The Seventeen Theoretical Constructs of Information Searching and Information Retrieval."

ProQuest Doctoral Dissertation Award
Winner: Shelagh K. Genuis for "Making Sense of Evolving Health Information: Navigating Uncertainty in Everyday Life."

Research in Information Science Award
Winner: Christine Borgman.

Thomson Reuters Doctoral Dissertation Proposal Scholarship
Winner: Amber Cushing for "Possession and Self Extension in Digital Environments: Implications for Maintaining Personal Information."

Association of College and Research Libraries

Coutts Nijhoff International West European Specialist Study Grant
Winner: Mara Degnan Rojeski, Dickinson College, for her project to construct a bibliography of the pamphlets of the Deutscher Fichte-Bund, a propaganda organization active in Hamburg, Germany, from 1914 to 1941.

Ilene F. Rockman Instruction Publication of the Year Award
Winner: Megan Jane Oakleaf for "Information Literacy Instruction Assessment Cycle: A Guide for Increasing Student Learning and Improving Librarian Instructional Skills."

Association for Library and Information Science Education

ALISE/Eugene Garfield Doctoral Dissertation Competition
Winners: Cassidy Sugimoto, Indiana University–Bloomington, for "Mentoring, Collaboration, and Interdisciplinary: An Evaluation of the Scholarly Development of Information and Library Science Doctoral Students"; Shari Ann Lee, St. John's University, for "Teen Space: Designed for Whom?"

ALISE Research Grant Competition
Winners: Gail Dickinson and Shana Pribesh, Old Dominion University, for "The Impact of National Board Certification of Library Media Specialists on Student Academic Achievement, a National Study (Impact NBC)."

Library and Information Technology Association/OCLC

Frederick G. Kilgour Award for Research in Library and Information Technology
Winner: Daniel J. Cohen, associate professor of history and art history at George Mason University and director of the Center for History and New Media.

Medical Library Association

Janet Doe Lectureship
Winner: Mark E. Funk, Samuel J. Wood Library, Weill Cornell Medical College.

Donald A. B. Lindberg Research Fellowship
Winner: Thane Chambers, Faculty of Nursing Library, University of Alberta–Edmonton.

MLA President's Award
Winner: Susan S. Starr (retired), Biomedical Library, University of California, San Diego.

Notes

1. American Library Association. *The State of America's Libraries 2011.* Digital Supplement to *American Libraries,* April 2011. Last accessed December 3, 2011. Available at http://www.ala.org/ala/newspresscenter/mediapresscenter/americaslibraries2011/state_of_ americas_libraries_report_2011.pdf.

2. Public Library Association. *Public Library Data Service 2011 Statistical Report.* Available at http://www.ala.org/pla/publications/plds. A summary article is available. Virgil E. Varvel, Jr., "The Public Library Data Service 2011 Statistical Report, Characteristics and Trends." *Public Libraries* 50(5):26-22. September/October 2011.

3. Harris Interactive. ALA January 2011 Harris Poll Quorum Results. Last accessed December 2, 2011. Available at http://www.ala.org/ala/research/librarystats/2011harrispoll.pdf.

4. Library Journal. *Library Journal Patron Profiles: Library Patrons and Ebook Usage. Patron Profiles* 1(1) October 2011. Available for purchase at http://www.patronprofiles.com.

5. ———. Figure 9 (p.12).

6. Hoffman, Judy, John Carlo Bertot, Denise M. Davis, and Larra Clark. *Libraries Connect Communities: Public Library Funding and Technology Access Study 2010–2011*. Digital supplement to *American Libraries* magazine, June 2011. Last accessed December 4, 2011. Available at http://viewer.zmags.com/publication/857ea9fd.

7. ———. Executive Summary. Last accessed December 4, 2011. Available at http://www.ala.org/ala/research/initiatives/plftas/2010_2011/plftas11-execsummary.pdf.

8. Matthews, Joseph R. "What's the Return on ROI? The Benefits and Challenges of Calculating Your Library's Return on Investment." *Library Leadership & Management* (25)1:1–14. February 1, 2011.

9. Phan, Tai, et al. *Academic Libraries: 2010*. U.S. Department of Education, National Center for Education Statistics. (NCES 2012-365, December 2011). Last accessed December18, 2011. Available at http://nces.ed.gov/pubsearch/pubsinfo.asp?pubid=2012365.

10. American Library Association. American Association of School Librarians. 2011 *School Libraries Count!* Last accessed December 5, 2011. Available at http://www.ala.org/aasl/slcsurvey.

11. ———. *Supplemental Report on Digital Citizenship*. Last accessed December 4, 2011. Available at http://www.ala.org/aasl/researchandstatistics/slcsurvey/2011/slc2011extra.

12. AASL. Urban Schools Task Force. *AASL Urban Schools Task Force Survey Report*. January 8, 2011. Last accessed December 5, 2011. Available at http://www.ala.org/aasl/sites/ala.org.aasl/files/content/researchandstatistics/AASL%20Urban%20Schools%20Taskforce%20Report_v2.pdf.

13. Hadro, Josh. "HarperCollins Puts 26 Loan Cap on Ebook Circulation." *Library Journal*. February 25, 2011. Last accessed November 26, 2011. Available at http://www.libraryjournal.com/lj/home/889452-264/harpercollins_puts_26_loan_cap.html.csp.

14. Harris Interactive. "One in Six Americans Now Use E-Reader with One in Six Likely to Purchase in Next Six Months." Last accessed December 18, 2011. Available at http://www.harrisinteractive.com/NewsRoom/HarrisPolls/tabid/447/mid/1508/articleId/864/ctl/ReadCustom%20Default/Default.aspx.

15. Harris Poll. Regina Corso, Director. *The Harris Poll* #108 (September 22, 2010). Survey question was "Do you use an electronic reader device, such as a Kindle, an iPad or a Nook, to read books?" Last accessed December 8, 2010. Available at http://www.harrisinteractive.com/NewsRoom/HarrisPolls/tabid/447/ctl/ReadCustom%20Default/mid/1508/ArticleId/568/Default.aspx.

16. "Gadget Ownership Over Time." Pew Research Center Internet and American Life Project, April 26–May 27, 2011 tracking survey. Trend Data. Last accessed December 1, 2011. Available at http://www.pewinternet.org/Static-Pages/Trend%20Data/Device-Ownership.aspx.

17. Purcell, Kristen. "E-reader Ownership Doubles in Six Months. Adoption Rate of E-readers Surges Ahead of Tablet Computers." June 27, 2011. "Who owns e-readers" P.5. Last accessed November 27, 2011. Available at http://pewinternet.org/Reports/2011/E-readers-and-tablets.aspx.

18. "More Readers, Sales of E-books: Two New Surveys Chart Rise of Digital Publishing." *Publishers Weekly* September 26, 2011:4. Information Science and Library Issues Collections. Web. November 5, 2011.

19. Kelley, Michael. "New Statistics Model for Book Industry Shows Trade Ebook Sales Grew Over 1000 Percent." *Library Journal*. August 9, 2011. Last accessed November 30, 2011. Available at http://www.libraryjournal.com/lj/home/891561-264/new_statistics_model_for_book.html.csp.

20. Milliot, Jim. "E-tailers, E-books Move Ahead: Both Grabbed More Market Share in Second Quarter." *Publishers Weekly* October 17, 2011:4. Information Science and Library Issues Collection. Web. November 5, 2011.

The Consortial Effect in Detail:
The SC LENDS Experience

Robert E. Molyneux

Rogan Hamby

Background

The "consortial effect" occurs when public libraries join in a resource-sharing consortium. The evidence so far indicates that as public libraries join a consortium, the ease of intra-consortial lending (ICL) results in a rapid increase in ICL traffic between the members of the consortium as users discover the larger pool of available library materials. The "consortial effect" is not to be confused with the related "Evergreen effect."[1]

The consortial effect was first posited in an April 2011 blog post[2] and examined further in the 2011 *Library and Book Trade Almanac*.[3] This report examines the question more closely following the development of a second, more granular set of data from one of the consortia discussed in the 2011 *Almanac*.

Why is it important to understand whether there is a consortial effect? In a time of declining budgets, creating a resource-sharing consortium appears to be a relatively inexpensive way to improve services. There is less pressure to purchase new materials, and existing materials are shared. Patron feedback has indicated that a deep collection of materials offsets the expectation of a large purchase of new materials. The result should be a virtual library of greater size to meet users' interests and the expected increase in circulations and in ICLs.

The evidence for the expected accompanying increase in circulations, however, is clouded by three data problems discussed in the previous *Almanac*. The most serious problem is that in those consortia examined, a change in integrated library systems (ILS) is followed by a drop in annual circulations—occasionally a dramatic one—in a few of the libraries joining the consortium. This drop is often large enough to affect the totals for the new consortium in the first few years. This behavior is consistent across all sets of consortia examined in the two studies and with migration to most ILS vendors' products. However, in almost all cases examined so far, ICLs—when compared with the historic interlibrary loans that were generated from the older systems—increase as soon as a trend can be established from reports from the new system. It appears it will take a few years of data after a library joins such a consortium for measured total annual circulations to begin to grow. In any case, the results presented here with a better dataset conform to expectations from this literature: circulations (mostly) down; intra-consortial lending up. Individual studies of this problem indicate that a significant factor is the lack of ILS standardization in how circulation is recorded and reported.

The two other data problems making analysis difficult are that it is often not certain from available documentation when the libraries actually migrated from

Robert E. Molyneux has worked on compiling, documenting, and analyzing library data for more than 25 years, taught in three library schools, and worked for two private firms supporting library software. Rogan Hamby is director of information technologies and innovation at the State Library of South Carolina.

Table 1 / Summary Data of SC LENDS Libraries, by Migration Wave

Go-Live Date	City		Population Served*	Total Circulations*	Book and Serial Volumes*	Total Circulations per capita*	Total Expenditures*	Total Operating Expenditures per capita*	Outlets*
Wave 1 2009-05-28	Beaufort	Beaufort County Library	142,045	799,383	248,230	5.6	4,430,899	31.19	5
2009-05-28	Union	Union County Library System	28,000	93,732	33,248	3.3	484,067	17.29	2
2009-05-28	Columbia	South Carolina State Library			304,282				1
Wave 2 2009-10-15	Chesterfield	Chesterfield County Library System	43,500	104,286	70,289	2.4	427,291	9.82	5
2009-10-15	Rock Hill	York County Library System	208,827	1,200,272	280,809	5.7	4,778,628	22.88	6
2009-10-15	St. George	Dorchester County Library System	96,413	671,590	147,568	7.0	2,409,180	24.99	3
2009-10-15	St. Matthews	Calhoun County Library System	14,777	42,628	28,416	2.9	299,172	20.25	2
Wave 3 2009-12-03	Anderson	Anderson County Library	193,277	679,811	340,340	3.5	4,249,492	21.99	10
2009-12-03	Florence	Florence County Library System	131,097	358,681	296,689	2.7	3,596,128	27.43	7
2009-12-03	Winnsboro	Fairfield County Library	24,435	79,768	82,511	3.3	527,773	21.60	3
Wave 4 2011-02-14	Allendale	Allendale Hampton Jasper Regional Library	58,325	75,639	70,937	1.3	569,809	9.77	6
2011-02-14	Camden	Kershaw County Library System	58,168	250,099	114,176	4.3	797,872	13.72	4
2011-02-14	Kingstree	Williamsburg County Library System	37,217	65,572	63,353	1.8	453,018	12.17	3
2011-02-14	Walterboro	Colleton County Library System	40,610	102,859	112,796	2.5	759,490	18.70	3
		Totals/averages	1,076,691	4,524,320	2,193,644	4.2	23,782,819	22.09	60

*Data for fiscal year 2009. The South Carolina fiscal year is from July to June. [Footnote 4]

one system to another, and, second, the data are annual and the migration may be mid-year. With annual summary data being all that is available in national-level data, for a deeper look we turn to detailed data available from reports from one such consortium.

Here we examine a new consortium, South Carolina's SC LENDS, which offers better data than available previously. The data used here come from the published annual public library data with the addition of data from reports generated from SC LENDS on monthly transaction summaries. This combination will give us a more granular view of the consortial effect than has been seen to date. This article replicates the results seen with the circulation experience reviewed above and shows dramatic increases in ICL traffic.

SC LENDS

SC LENDS is a public library resource-sharing consortium running Evergreen, the open-source ILS designed for geographically dispersed, resource-sharing networks (http://www.evergreen-ils.org). At the time this report was prepared, four "waves" of migrations had taken place with a fifth scheduled for April 2012. Table 1 introduces these libraries and the waves in which they migrated, with summary statistics[4] from fiscal year (FY) 2009. By Wave 4, SC LENDS[5] served a population of more than 1 million or a little under a fourth of South Carolina's population. Currently 14 of the state's 42 library systems are in SC LENDS. These 42 systems serve the entire state's population.

The public libraries in South Carolina are generally grouped into county systems with multiple libraries. The "outlet" (central libraries + branches + bookmobiles) count is included in this summary table to illustrate this aspect of these systems.

Two figures in Table 1 can be easily compared with other U.S. state figures: Total (annual) circulations per capita in these libraries are 4.2, while the U.S. average is 8.1. The average expenditures per capita are $22.09, while the U.S. average is $36.84. The state rankings for the South Carolina figures are 39th and 40th, respectively.[6]

In a story familiar to public librarians across the country, South Carolina is in the throes of a budget crisis, with declining funding for libraries. In the midst of this crisis, South Carolina took a bold course: under the leadership of the South Carolina State Library (SCSL), a set of public libraries has moved forward to form SC LENDS. SCSL was in the first wave, and has provided a great deal of support to the new consortium. It is the highest net lender to the consortium's other members.

The consortium member libraries hold 876,000 bibliographic items and 2.6 million physical items. After Wave 3, the number of bibliographic items was reduced by about 326,000 as a result of a deduplication project. This is a common project undertaken by resource-sharing consortia to make searching more efficient and the online catalog easier to use.[7]

What follows is a story told with data, but one that makes clear that SC LENDS has been a success from the perspective of its libraries' users.

Table 2 / Total Annual Circulations, SC LENDS Libraries, by Waves 1–3

		Fiscal Year Data Reported by IMLS/NCES						SC LENDS Reported Total Circulations, Annualized	
		FY 2005	FY 2006	FY 2007	FY 2008	FY 2009		FY 2010	FY 2011
Wave 1 (2009-05-28)	Beaufort County Library	516,992	519,267	747,079	602,588	799,383		866,137	794,062
	Union County Library System	52,752	69,924	80,926	88,978	93,732		77,488	67,797
Wave 2 (2009-10-15)	Calhoun County Library System	23,520	28,161	32,960	39,301	42,628			55,969
	Chesterfield County Library System	98,326	102,793	104,051	105,709	104,286			63,259
	Dorchester County Library System	531,257	560,193	576,402	600,067	671,590			632,549
	York County Library System	885,354	982,237	1,007,939	1,079,048	1,200,272			1,023,094
Wave 3 (2009-12-03)	Anderson County Library	585,364	570,767	590,135	635,656	679,811			635,730
	Fairfield County Library	81,975	74,050	72,606	73,187	79,768			60,253
	Florence County Library System	444,010	450,671	460,660	342,560	358,681			374,762

The South Carolina fiscal year is from July to June.

The Data Used

The analysis that follows uses annual summary data from historic sources, along with data from SC LENDS Evergreen reports. The latter data are summarized to make them compatible with the fiscal year (FY) data from these historic sources. Table 2 compares members' FY circulation data with monthly data from SC LENDS Evergreen reports summarized in comparable FY fashion. Table 3 is similar in that it compares historic FY Interlibrary Loan (ILL) figures with SC LENDS data summarized in comparable FY fashion. We then present four graphs—one for each wave—of the ICL data from SC LENDS summarized on a monthly basis.

The historic data are from the national Public Library Survey (PLS) recompiled in a longitudinal file.

Given the asynchronous aspect of these data—the latest annual public library data are for FY 2009 and the monthly Evergreen data are through December 2011—and with the varying go-live dates, there are gaps between the two series.

Analysis

Circulation Patterns

Table 2 presents the circulation data from three waves of SC LENDS libraries with historic annual data juxtaposed with data from the SC LENDS Evergreen system, reformatted to the base FY data. Data from these three waves are the only data from the Evergreen reports on circulation currently available that fit the format of the PLS survey. Given earlier results of post-migration circulation patterns discussed above, we should not be surprised that no clear trends emerge. Here we present data from FY 2005 (July 2004–June 2005) through FY 2009 (June 2008–July 2009) from the PLS data, compared with summarized annual data from Waves 1 through 3. From these fragmentary data, all but one member library (Florence County Library System in FY 2011) show declines in annual circulations between the two series. Let us await the vetting of the data that comes from the PLS series and come back in a few years. By then, we will also have data from other comparable libraries to compare circulation statistics with SC LENDS' libraries.

Intra-Consortial Lending

Fiscal Year Comparison

Table 3 presents data formatted in a manner similar to Table 2. By summarizing the FY PLS ILL data and SC LENDS ICL data we can present a comparable FY format. The reader will recall that the PLS data, being on a fiscal year basis, will not match the dates of the waves, but this table gives us a comparable review of the two series. Clearly, the change is dramatic after the libraries join the consortium.

ILLs and ICLs are not quite the same thing. ILL is the historic means used by libraries to share materials, usually by mail. ILL was usually not geographically bounded; that is, a library might well lend materials across state lines. ICLs however will be between members of the consortium and often transported by a courier system. For every item lent by one library in an ILL transaction, there is

Table 3 / Total Annual Interlibrary Loan (ILL) Compared with SC LENDS Inter-consortial Lending (ICL)

| | | ILL Fiscal Year data Reported by IMLS/NCES | | | | | | | | | | SC LENDS Reported ICLs | | | |
| | | FY 2005 | | FY 2006 | | FY 2007 | | FY 2008 | | FY 2009 | | FY 2010 | | FY 2011 | |
		Lent to	Borrowed from	Lent to	Borrowed from	Lent to	Borrowed from	Lent to	Borrowed from	Lent to	Borrowed from	Lent to	Borrowed from	Lent to	Borrowed from
Wave 1 (2009-05-28)	Beaufort County Library	444	2,790	456	1,655	372	1,584	405	1,759	409	2,258	20,611	16,180	30,759	20,783
	Union County Library System	0	63	0	112	0	250	0	413	3	481	3,336	1,486	2,733	1,966
	South Carolina State Library											5,683	535	6,468	635
Wave 2 (2009-10-15)	Calhoun County Library System	0	48	0	76	1	97	7	54	3	67			3,080	3,562
	Chesterfield County Library System	1	394	0	285	0	377	5	347	0	192			3,116	2,019
	Dorchester County Library System	0	137	0	239	0	203	0	163	0	181			18,617	19,908
	York County Library System	2	1,702	59	1,938	39	2,248	72	2,360	111	2,907			19,814	40,680
Wave 3 (2009-12-03)	Anderson County Library	2,269	1,319	2,475	1,256	3,016	1,448	3,057	1,623	2,322	1,759			21,517	26,473
	Fairfield County Library	3	148	2	168	0	229	0	153	0	62			5,564	1,863
	Florence County Library System	601	1,081	544	1,308	549	1,175	1,085	982	997	948			18,367	12,252
Wave 4 (2011-03-01)	Allendale Hampton Jasper Regional Library	1	34	2	15	10	25	15	30	16	40				
	Colleton County Library System	2	678	1	328	0	195	0	208	0	201				
	Kershaw County Library System	3	300	24	274	34	335	35	349	14	289				
	Williamsburg County Library System	2	129	1	141	5	127	7	84	10	55				

another count of the item as one that is borrowed. However, the ILL transaction may be between two libraries in different states or between two libraries of different types (say a public library and an academic library). A lot of labor is needed to locate and arrange lending of the materials, making the cost per item of lending very high. If the data were produced with sufficiently rigorous methods, we expect the number of items lent between all libraries of all types and all locations would equal those borrowed. The ILL data we have will not have this characteristic, and, typically, analysis of ILL data considers both items lent and items borrowed. However, for our purposes here, we are dealing with a closed system of counting transactions between members of SC LENDS, and the total number of items borrowed does equal the total number lent in the reported data, allowing for differences that reflect the dynamic aspect of a working consortium. Items are moving around, and those in transit will have been "sent" but not yet "received," for example. If we look at the consortium as a whole, we can use either number to represent that consortium—particularly given the level of the changes from the old series to the new one. However, net lending libraries will typically have relatively high "lent to" statistics and low "borrowed from" statistics. The high volume of materials shared as ICLs and casual means of handling them, in contrast to ILLs, make it more likely that routine errors occur in the process that have to be accounted for.

From the standpoint of a library user, the look of the online catalog after migration to the SC LENDS consortium will have changed. In addition, there is a new capability: consortial search is added. In practice, a user who learns to select a simple drop-down menu option can now search an entire consortium and place holds on those materials. The difference between placing a hold on local materials and across the consortium is completely transparent. The user searches the catalog locally and the system's display will give items owned and/or available; that is, items in this building, items in the local system, and items in the consortium at large. It does not take long (typically two mouse clicks) to see the larger catalog and, as we will see, the users take advantage of the longer tail of resources quickly. The SC LENDS courier system stops at locations with a frequency based on the volume of materials it transports. Many locations are serviced five days a week and all are visited a minimum of twice a week. Materials are picked up and distributed for transport on the same day. In a worst-case scenario, it may take 96 hours for an item to be transported between library systems, but many are delivered in less than 24 hours.

Wave 1 is a good place to start to understand this table. Two relatively large libraries (Beaufort County Library and the South Carolina State Library) and one relatively small library (Union County Library) were the founding members of SC LENDS. SCSL's data are not in the PLS survey, so the data that we have map uncertainly to the PLS data. Table 1 gives us raw physical item counts (FY 2009) for Beaufort County (248,000), SCSL (304,000), and Union County (33,000.) Returning to Table 3: note the jump between ILLs and ICLs for these libraries. Beaufort County lent 409 items through ILL in FY 2009 and in FY 2010 it lent more than 20,500. The next year, it lent almost 31,000. In FY 2009, it borrowed nearly 2,300 items while in FY 2010 it borrowed more than 16,000 items, followed by nearly 21,000 items in FY 2011. All three of these libraries are net lenders in these two years. The Wave 2 libraries that joined the consortium later in the year were net borrowers, but their figures are sufficient to include for the whole fiscal year. These missing data will be included in the charts that follow.

Similar dramatic changes occur between the ILL figures and the new ICL figures. With Waves 2 and 3, even though there is a year gap, the new summary figures are much higher than the ILL numbers. Wave 4 data were not yet available for a full fiscal year.

The comparison between the two series is not exact but quite close—each reports data on a method to supply materials from one library another library to another library's users. Traditional ILL was slow and cumbersome while ICLs are rapid. The libraries' users soon discovered the ICL system process and flocked to it.

These data suggest that library users' demand for materials was perhaps suppressed by the cumbersome process of ILL. In the case of SC LENDS, the ICL process is transparent and users do not require staff moderation to request the materials across systems.

Monthly Data

A look at monthly ICL data provides a more detailed picture of the transition that takes place as a library joins the consortium. Four graphs—one for the *lending* patterns of each of the waves—are presented.

In Wave 1, we see that ICL use is at a low level until September, when SC LENDS members discover the consortium's resources. Table 3 shows that Beaufort County is the biggest lender and borrower in the first fiscal year, and shows its lending pattern since joining. We see a characteristic dip in December and a characteristic summer peak in June 2010 with a higher peak in 2011. Union County's numbers do not appear as impressive, but graphing a small library with a larger one can mislead the eye. Consider that in the FY 2009 annual data in Table 3, Union County lent 3 items and borrowed 481. After joining, it regularly lent more than 300 items a month and in June 2011 lent 459 items.

Chart 2 shows us two relatively large libraries and two smaller ones. York County has the largest population served and the highest annual circulations of any of the libraries in SC LENDS. Not surprisingly, it shows very high usage, as does Dorchester County, a library smaller than York County but with the highest circulations per capita of these libraries at 7.

However, once again, the eyes can deceive. Calhoun County lent 3 items in FY 2009 and borrowed 67. Each month after joining, it has lent more than 200 items and in several months hit 400.

There are two large Wave 3 libraries and one smaller one. There are several aspects of the data charted here that are familiar now. There are peaks in the summer and dips in December. The large libraries lend and borrow more items, but the smallest of the three, Fairfield County, which lent no items in FY 2009, lent an impressive 5,600 in FY 2011.

Wave 4 began in 2011, so there are only a few months of experience, but this is perhaps the most interesting of the four. The libraries are about average size, but with relatively low circulations per capita. They joined the consortium late, but became active very quickly. And again, we have a library—Colleton County—that

(text continues on page 420)

SC LENDS Wave 1 / Intra-Consortial Lending

BCL = Beaufort County
SCSL = South Carolina State Library
UCCL = Union County

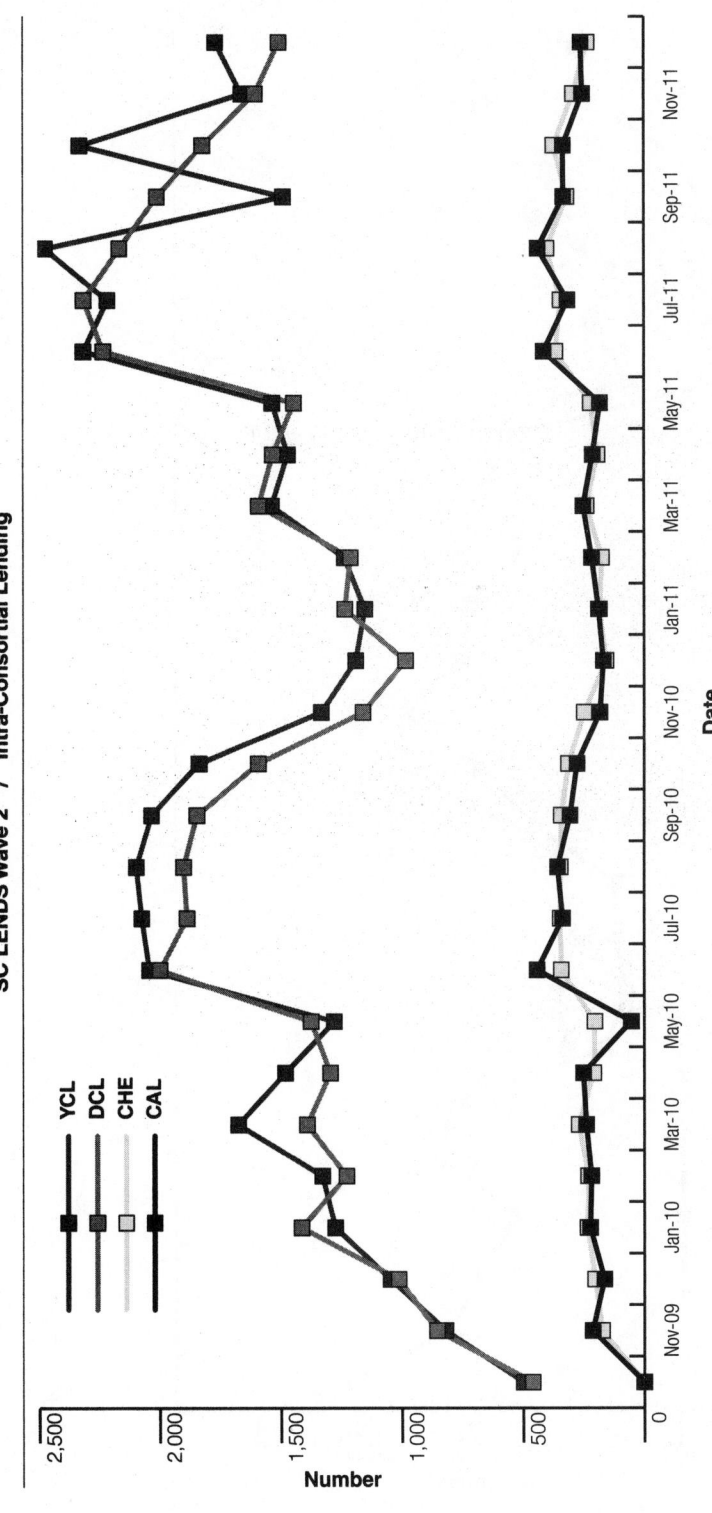

SC LENDS Wave 2 / Intra-Consortial Lending

Number

Date

CAL = Calhoun County
CHE = Chesterton County
DCL = Dorchester County
YCL = York County

SCLENDS Wave 3 / Intra-Consortial Lending

ACL = Anderson County
FCL = Fairfield County
FLO - Florence County

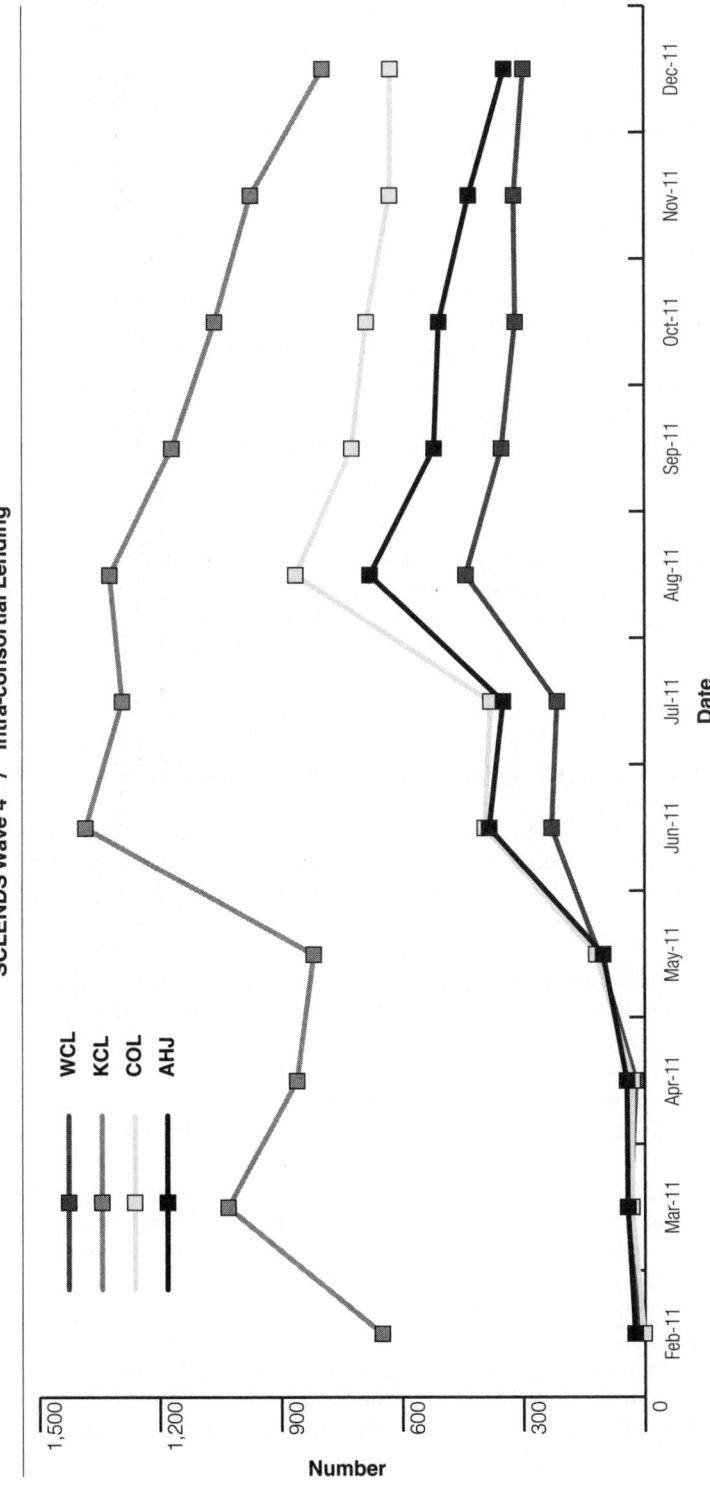

SCLENDS Wave 4 / Intra-consortial Lending

AHJ = Allendale Hampton Jasper Regional Library
COL = Colleton County
KCL = Kershaw County
WCL = Williamsburg County

(continued from page 415)
lent no items in FY 2009 but has lent many each month since joining. In August 2011 it lent 863 items. Kershaw County is the largest lender in this wave, reporting 1,385 items in June 2011. In FY 2009, it lent 14.

Conclusion

We present data here based on the experience of one new and expanding resource-sharing consortium. From these ICL data, we see the users at the various member libraries adapt quickly to the new system and its capabilities and change their patterns of lending and borrowing. As was pointed out above, although the large libraries and those with relatively high circulations per capita certainly have increases in ICLs that catch the eye, the smaller libraries have just as impressive experiences as the larger ones.

SC LENDS is a success based on what we see here. It appears from these data that the consortium is, indeed, greater than the sum of its parts.

There are other aspects of consortia that are relevant but not studied here and that may shed further light on other aspects of any consortial effects.

There are scale economies in running a consortium.[8] The savings incurred in joining many small libraries into a larger consortium come about for several reasons, including how vendors price integrated library systems. Typically, ten libraries with 10,000 bibliographic items will pay more for their ILSs than one system with 100,000 items. This pricing on the part of commercial vendors makes sense given that it is more difficult to manage the software for ten smaller libraries than for one bigger one.

Evergreen was designed for this kind of role, and its design architecture takes into account consortial requirements and uses modern software design practices to accomplish high scalability. As a result, the software and configuration aspects of SC LENDS arguably save money over the charges for the disparate ILS vendor products.

However, it also costs a great deal of money to move the items between libraries and the cost of the courier services subtracts from the considerable savings from running the Evergreen consortial library system used by SC LENDS. Net, the whole system still saves money over the former system and has happier users who have access to more materials than they had before—as evidenced by the rapid uptake of this new system. Net? The libraries cost less to run, use increases, and users are happier. That is not a bad argument to take to a funding source. We expect the circulation figures to show a similar increase in the years going forward. As this article was being written, the state legislature gave a vote of confidence to South Carolina libraries by recommending rare new recurring funds for SCSL, and SC LENDS has been part of the story of how they are optimizing South Carolina's investment in libraries.

In addition, there are anecdotal reports that might be investigated further.

It is a fact of most of these consortia that smaller and less affluent libraries are often the first to join. Representatives of the largest libraries are commonly of the opinion that they will be net lenders to these smaller libraries, thereby imposing costs without benefits. However, it has been said that experience does not support this belief because the flow both ways balances out: the smaller libraries lend the bigger libraries some of the older classics, while the newer titles move to the smaller libraries. This proposition should be tested. A surface examination of the data used here but not reported suggests that one should be skeptical of this idea except for the intriguing aspect of the small libraries discussed with the charts of ICL traffic. The smaller libraries clearly are contributing to the consortium. Other variables, including quality of collection, play a significant though difficult to measure role in lending and borrowing, as do borrowing traits of local communities. Small libraries may show more variability in borrowing habits than large libraries because smaller populations exhibit more variance. In any case, these large consortia find varying quality in the cataloging of their new members and typically embark on a program of improving the online catalogs. The deduplication project discussed above is one kind of common effort undertaken by consortia. While the SC LENDS catalog is not yet mature enough for this kind of test, there are other older consortia, and—if we can obtain the data—we can test this notion by investigating the character of the items borrowed and lent.

Another anecdotal report from SC LENDS members is that services such as technology classes and book clubs have been better attended since the libraries joined the consortium. These observations are not dissimilar to reports from the early days of the Georgia PINES consortium[9] that a spur to libraries' joining was the fact that any Georgia citizen could get a PINES card, and many library users consequently bypassed their local libraries to use PINES libraries. That belief would be more difficult to test because the data that would have to be examined might contain personal information that would have to be anonymized in some fashion.

Notes

1. Robert E. Molyneux, "Save the Time of the Reader" January 8, 2008, http://evergreen-ils. org/blog/?p=112. The "Evergreen effect" was posited based on the experience of the Georgia PINES resource-sharing network. In moving from its legacy integrated library system to Evergreen without any other changes, circulations and intra-consortial lending increased. It was speculated that given that Evergreen was designed for such a network and used more modern software development practices, library users found it easier to use. This notion awaits further testing.

2. Robert E. Molyneux, "The Consortial Effect," April 5, 2011, http://blog.esilibrary.com/2011/ 04/05/the-consortial-effect.

3. Robert E. Molyneux, "The Consortial Effect: Is a Consortium Greater than the Sum of Its Parts?" *Library and Book Trade Almanac,* vol. 56, 395–403 (2011).

4. Data are from three sources. Fiscal year 2009 data are the most current public library data from the Institute of Museum and Library Services' "Public Libraries Survey" (http://www. imls.gov/research/public_libraries_in_the_united_states_survey.aspx). This series of data is the premier public library data series. Historic data are from the PLDF3 dataset, a longitudinal recompilation of the annual data in the Public Libraries Survey and its predecessors (http://drdata.lrs.org/pldf3). Data on the SC LENDS intra-consorial lending and circulations after migration to SC LENDS were extracted from the Evergreen system by one of the authors of this study (Hamby).

5. An SC LENDS wiki is hosted by the South Carolina State Library. It has information on the background and workings of the consortium. The URL of the SC LENDS catalog is http://sclends.lib.sc.us/opac/en-US/skin/default/xml/index.xml.

6. These state ranks come from the "Rank Order Tables," a popular calculation published in the annual Public Libraries Survey. Data for fiscal year 2009 are from: Miller, K.; Swan, D.; Craig, T.; Dorinski, S.; Freeman, M.; Isaac, N.; O'Shea, P.; Schilling, P.; and Scotto, J.; *Public Libraries Survey: Fiscal Year 2009* (IMLS-2011–PLS-02) (2011). Institute of Museum and Library Services. Washington, D.C. Available at https://harvester.census.gov/imls/pubs/Publications/pls2009.pdf. See: Table A2, p. 173, for circulations per capita, and Table A10, p. 181, for total operating expenditures per capita.

7. Rogan Hamby and Shasta Brewer, "10% Wrong, 90% Done: A Practical Approach to Bibliographic De-duplication," 2011 Evergreen International Conference, April 27–30, Decatur, Georgia. http://pines.georgialibraries.org/evergreen2011/node/14#T. As a result of this deduplication effort, the bibliographic item count was reduced by 326,000 after Wave 3. We argue that from this evidence, the case of a "consortial effect" becomes stronger. The evidence is that resource-sharing consortia *do* improve service to a library's users as evidenced by the fact that users like the addition of more items to choose from.

8. Robert E. Molyneux and Mike Rylander, "Scale Economies," November 10, 2010, http://evergreen-ils.org/blog/?p=455.

9. The Georgia Public Library Service (the Georgia state library) initially developed Evergreen, and the Georgia PINES library network was the first network to migrate to Evergreen. The PINES Internet address is http://pines.georgialibraries.org.

Number of Libraries in the United States and Canada

Statistics are from *American Library Directory (ALD) 2011–2012* (Information Today, Inc., 2011). Data are exclusive of elementary and secondary school libraries.

Libraries in the United States

Public Libraries	16,922*
Public libraries, excluding branches	9,716†
Main public libraries that have branches	1,413
Public library branches	7,206
Academic Libraries	3,735*
Community college	1,156
Departmental	207
Law	1
Medical	10
Religious	11
University and college	2,579
Departmental	1,349
Law	183
Medical	241
Religious	240
Armed Forces Libraries	280*
Air Force	84
Medical	6
Army	129
Medical	26
Marine Corps	12
Navy	55
Law	1
Medical	12
Government Libraries	1,098*
Law	400
Medical	149
Special Libraries (excluding public, academic, armed forces, and government)	7,033*
Law	840
Medical	1,394
Religious	511
Total Special Libraries (including public, academic, armed forces, and government)	8,313
Total law	1,425
Total medical	1,838
Total religious	1,010
Total Libraries Counted(*)	29,068

Libraries in Regions Administered by the United States

Public Libraries	28*
Public libraries, excluding branches	11†
Main public libraries that have branches	3
Public library branches	17
Academic Libraries	37*
Community college	4
Departmental	3
Medical	0
University and college	33
Departmental	21
Law	3
Medical	2
Religious	1
Armed Forces Libraries	2*
Air Force	1
Army	1
Navy	0
Government Libraries	4*
Law	1
Medical	1
Special Libraries (excluding public, academic, armed forces, and government)	6*
Law	3
Medical	1
Religious	1
Total Special Libraries (including public, academic, armed forces, and government)	14
Total law	7
Total medical	4
Total religious	2
Total Libraries Counted(*)	77

Libraries in Canada

Public Libraries	2,047*
Public libraries, excluding branches	815†
Main public libraries that have branches	135
Public library branches	1,232
Academic Libraries	348*
Community college	85
Departmental	14
Medical	0
Religious	4
University and college	263

Departmental	176
Law	15
Medical	20
Religious	34
Government Libraries	283*
Law	37
Medical	7
Special Libraries (excluding public, academic, armed forces, and government)	8,949*
Law	103
Medical	173
Religious	26
Total Special Libraries (including public, academic, armed forces, and government)	1,011
Total law	155
Total medical	200
Total religious	90
Total Libraries Counted(*)	3,5724

Summary

Total U.S. Libraries	29,068
Total Libraries Administered by the United States	77
Total Canadian Libraries	3,572
Grand Total of Libraries Listed	32,717

Note: Numbers followed by an asterisk are added to find "Total libraries counted" for each of the three geographic areas (United States, U.S.-administered regions, and Canada). The sum of the three totals is the "Grand total of libraries listed" in *ALD*. For details on the count of libraries, see the preface to the 64th edition of *ALD—Ed.*

†Federal, state, and other statistical sources use this figure (libraries *excluding* branches) as the total for public libraries.

Highlights of IMLS and NCES Surveys

The Institute of Museum and Library Services (IMLS) and the National Center for Education Statistics (NCES) collect and disseminate statistical information about libraries in the United States and its outlying areas. Two major surveys are conducted by NCES, the Academic Libraries Survey and the School Library Media Centers Survey; two others, the Public Libraries Survey and the State Library Agencies Survey, were formerly conducted by NCES, but are now handled by IMLS. Both NCES and IMLS also conduct surveys on related topics.

This article presents highlights from two of the most recently conducted surveys. For more information on the surveys, see "National Center for Education Statistics Library Statistics Program" in Part 1 and "Institute of Museum and Library Services Library Programs" in Part 2 of this volume.

Public Libraries

The following are highlights from the publication *Public Libraries Survey: Fiscal Year 2009*, released in October 2011 by IMLS.

Number of Libraries

- There were 9,225 public libraries (administrative entities) in the 50 states and the District of Columbia in fiscal year (FY) 2009.
- Public libraries are widely distributed across the United States. Public library service areas encompassed 97.4 percent of the total population of the states and the District of Columbia in FY 2009, either in legally established service areas or in areas under contract.
- Out of all the public libraries surveyed, 1,089 (11.8 percent) served the majority of the population (73.0 percent) in legally served areas in the United States in FY 2009. Each of these libraries was in a more densely populated area (urban or suburban), and each had a legal service area population of 50,000 or more.
- Through openings and closings of public libraries, their number in FY 2009 had increased by a net of 151—an overall increase of 1.7 percent—since FY 2000. Most states (31 states, or 60.8 percent) saw an increase in their public libraries. However, this growth had been outpaced by changes in the national population, which had increased by 11.7 percent since FY 2000. Thus, the change in the number of public libraries per capita has decreased.

Library Services

Visits and Circulation

- In FY 2009 public libraries had 1.59 billion visits, an increase of 5.7 percent from 1.50 billion in the previous year. On average, individuals within a library service area visited the public library more than five times (5.3), an increase of 5.0 percent from FY 2008 and a ten-year increase of 24.3 percent since FY 2000.

- More than 169.7 million people were registered to borrow books at public libraries, comprising 57.1 percent of the population in the legal service area. This is a 4.8 percent increase from the number of registered borrowers in FY 2006, the first year in which this information was collected in the Public Libraries Survey.
- Overall, the nation's public libraries circulated 2.41 billion materials in FY 2009. Circulation per capita provides a measure of how many people within a public library service area checked out materials. Like visitation, circulation per capita also increased over the past ten years, with a per-person circulation of 8.1 in FY 2009. This was an increase of 5.2 percent from FY 2008 and a ten-year increase of 26.1 percent since FY 2000.
- Circulation of children's materials also increased. Per capita circulation of children's materials was 2.7 in FY 2009, a 3.1 percent increase from the previous year and a ten-year increase of 17.0 percent.
- Circulation per visits is an indication of how often someone who goes to a public library checks out materials during their visit, which allows examination of how patterns of library use may be changing. Circulation per 1,000 visits in FY 2009 was 1,517. Although there was an initial increase of 2.3 percent from FY 2000 to 2003, overall the metric has been stable across the observed period (FY 2000–2009), with a ten-year net increase of 1.5 percent, fluctuating from a low in FY 2000 (1,495) to a high in FY 2003 (1,530).
- Circulation of children's material per 1,000 visits was 513 in FY 2009, which was a decline of 1.8 percent since FY 2000. Circulation of children's material comprises 33.8 percent of total circulation, which was down 2.0 percent from FY 2008.

Reference Transactions

- Reference transactions decreased over the ten-year period from FY 2000 to FY 2009. Reference transactions per capita were 1.04 in FY 2009, down 4.8 percent since FY 2000. However, recent activity has evidenced a slight increasing trend of 4.1 percent since FY 2007.
- Reference transactions were lowest in towns and rural areas. Reference transactions per capita were 0.6 for towns and 0.7 for rural areas, levels that were below the national average by 40.4 percent and 29.0 percent, respectively. A similar pattern was seen in reference transactions per 1,000 visits. Per-visit reference transactions were 132.0 for towns and 153.1 for rural areas, which were 32.2 percent and 21.4 percent below the national average.

Computer Use and Availability

- The availability of computer terminals with Internet access in public libraries has doubled over the past ten years. There were 3.9 Internet PCs per 5,000 people in FY 2009, an increase of 109.3 percent since FY 2000.

This increase of Internet accessibility is even more profound in rural areas. Public libraries in rural areas have 5.9 PCs per 5,000 people in their legal service area, a number that is 52.7 percent above the national average.

Collections

- Despite some fluctuations, the number of print materials held by public libraries has shown an overall decline in the past decade, from 2,859 print materials (per 1,000 people) in FY 2000 to 2,745 in FY 2009, a decrease of 4.0 percent.
- While the per capita number of print materials has declined, the amount of all three types of non-print materials (audio and video materials and e-books) per 1,000 people has increased. In FY 2009 there were 178 audio materials per 1,000 people, up 5.9 percent from FY 2008 and up 48.2 percent over ten years. Similarly, there were 171 video materials per 1,000 people, an increase of 2.7 percent since FY 2008 and more than double (105.8 percent) over the prior ten years. And in the same period there were 51 e-books per 1,000 people, up 13.0 percent from FY 2008 and an increase of 224.3 percent since the addition of e-book volumes to the survey FY 2003.
- The decline in print materials is not an indication of shrinking collections. Total materials in public library collections in FY 2009 were more than 934.8 million, an increase of 14.8 percent since FY 2000.
- Although print materials are still the largest proportion of most public library collections, the ratio of print to nonprint materials has changed significantly over the past decade. In FY 2000 print materials comprised 93.4 percent of public library collections; in FY 2009 this had dropped to 87.3 percent. In contrast, audio and video materials combined made up only 6.6 percent of collections in FY 2000, but this proportion increased to 11.1 percent in FY 2009.
- Although still a small proportion of the total collections, e-books comprised 1.6 percent of the total public library collection in FY 2009, which is an increase of 89.2 percent since FY 2004.

Programs

- Public libraries offered 3.7 million programs to the public in FY 2009, more than 2.3 million of which were children's programs. This was an increase in the number of programs offered of 7.6 percent and 2.6 percent for total and child-focused programs from FY 2008.
- Children's programs comprised 64.1 percent of all public library programming in FY 2009, a decrease of 4.6 percent from the prior year.
- Public libraries offered 263,500 programs for young adult programs in FY 2009, making up 7.1 percent of all programs offered in U.S. public libraries. The number of programs per capita has increased since FY 2004, the first time this information was collected in the survey.
- Public libraries conducted 62.4 programs per 5,000 people in FY 2009, an increase of 36.1 percent since FY 2004. They also provided 40 children's

programs per 5,000 people, an increase of 20.9 percent since FY 2005. Finally, public libraries offered 4.4 programs per 5,000 people for young adults in FY 2009.

- Program attendance per capita is also on the rise, suggesting that public libraries are offering more programs to keep pace with the demand. Attendance for all programs in FY 2009 was 1,453.5 per 5,000 people, up 22.4 percent since 2004, and attendance at children's programs was 1036.5 per 5,000 people, up 11.9 percent since 2000. Programs at rural public libraries have the highest attendance rates for total programs and children's programs, at 11.6 percent and 13.8 percent higher than the national average.

Staffing

- In FY 2009 there were 48,015 librarians working at public libraries in the United States, 32,977 (68.7 percent) of whom had master's degrees in library science accredited by the American Library Association (ALA-MLS degrees). In addition to librarians, public libraries employed 96,246 paid staff.

- Staffing at public libraries has remained stable over the past ten years. The number of paid staff members per 25,000 people was 12.1 at public libraries in FY 2009. Of those paid staff per 25,000 people, 4.0 were librarians. For both paid staff and librarians, the ten-year change was less than 1.0 percent.

- The percentage of librarians with ALA-MLS degrees was 68.7 percent in FY 2009. Like staffing overall, this metric has also remained fairly flat since FY 2000, with an increase of 0.3 percent over ten years. In contrast, the number of library systems with at least one ALA-MLS degreed librarian on staff has increased over the study period. Of the 9,225 public libraries, 4,464 (48.4 percent) had an ALA-MLS librarian on staff, a gain of 8.9 percent since FY 2000.

Operating Revenues and Expenditures

- Total revenue for U.S. public libraries was $11.59 billion in FY 2009, a 1.8 percent increase over FY 2008 and a ten-year increase of 50.5 percent. Total expenditures were $10.95 billion in FY 2009, which was an increase of 2.1 percent from FY 2008 and a ten-year increase of 55.8 percent.

- Total revenue and expenses per capita also evidenced an increasing trend. In FY 2009 total revenue per capita was $39.01, a ten-year increase of 8.8 percent; total expenditures per capita were $36.84, a ten-year increase of 12.6 percent.

- Public libraries in suburban areas had the highest levels of per capita revenue and expenditures in FY 2009, at $44.50 and $42.10, respectively, both of which were 14 percent above the national average. Public libraries in towns and rural areas had the lowest levels of per capital revenue and expenditures.

Service Outlets, Legal Basis and Interlibrary Relationships

- Most public libraries (85.3 percent) are public agencies connected to some form of local government. In FY 2009, nearly 53 percent of public libraries were part of a municipal government, 14.7 percent were part of a separate government entity referred to as a library district, 9.8 percent were part of a county or parish, 3.4 percent had a multi-jurisdictional legal basis under an intergovernmental agreement, 2.0 percent were part of a school district, 1.0 percent were part of a city/county, and 1.5 percent reported a legal basis of "other." The remaining 14.8 percent of public libraries were operated by nonprofit associations or agencies.

- Although most public libraries report single jurisdictions, many belong to broader service networks. A majority of public libraries (76.7 percent) were members of a federation or cooperative service, and 1.2 percent of these served as the headquarters of a federation or cooperative service. The remaining public libraries (23.3 percent) were not a part of a federation or cooperative service.

Analysis by Locality

- Library services are delivered in many types of communities across the United States. Almost half (47.8 percent) of public library administrative entities are in a rural area, serving 12.3 percent of the population.

Academic Libraries

The following are highlights from the First Look publication *Academic Libraries, 2010,* released in December 2011 by NCES.

Services

- Academic libraries lent some 11.2 million documents to other libraries in fiscal year 2010 and borrowed approximately 10.2 million documents from other libraries and commercial services. Documents from commercial services accounted for about 176,000 of those documents borrowed.

- The majority of academic libraries, 2,362, were open between 60 and 99 hours during a typical week in fall 2010. Another 564 were open 100 or more hours per typical week.

- In FY 2010 academic libraries conducted approximately 34.6 million information services to individuals, including computer searches.

Collections

- At the end of FY 2010 there were 227 academic libraries that held at least 1 million or more books, serial backfiles, and other paper materials including government documents.

- Academic libraries held approximately 158.7 million e-books and about 1.8 million electronic reference sources and aggregation services at the end of FY 2010. During the fiscal year academic libraries added about 12.9 million audiovisual material units, making their total audiovisual material holdings more than 1.12 billion units.

Staff

- Academic libraries reported 88,943 full-time equivalent (FTE) staff working in academic libraries during fall 2010, and 26,706 FTE librarians working during the same period. Librarians accounted for about 30 percent of the total number of FTE staff in academic libraries.

Expenditures

- Just under half of academic libraries, 1,739, had total expenditures of $500,000 or more in FY 2010. Another 581 academic libraries had total expenditures under $100,000.
- During the fiscal year academic libraries spent about $3.4 billion on salaries and wages, representing approximately 50 percent of total library expenditures.
- Academic libraries spent approximately $152.4 million for electronic books, serial backfiles, and other materials in FY 2010. Expenditures for electronic current serial subscriptions totaled about $1.2 billion. During the fiscal year academic libraries spent approximately $142.7 million for computer hardware and software.

Electronic Services

- In fall 2010 about 41 percent of academic libraries reported providing documents digitized by staff.
- More than half (54 percent) reported providing technology to assist patrons with disabilities.

Virtual Reference

- During FY 2010 about 72 percent of academic libraries reported that they supported virtual reference services.
- About 32 percent reported that they utilized instant messaging applications.

Public Library State Rankings, 2009

State	Library Visits per Capita[1]	Reference Transactions per Capita	Circulation Transactions per Capita	Interlibrary Loans per 1,000 Population	Average Public-use Internet Computers per Outlet
Alabama	46	26	46	32	13
Alaska	30	37	37	30	48
Arizona	39	41	29	26	4
Arkansas	45	39	43	39	39
California	36	20	38	22	14
Colorado	12	12	5	19	9
Connecticut	5	9	16	14	18
Delaware	27	45	11	16	21
District of Columbia[2]	32	5	50	50	2
Florida	35	3	35	41	1
Georgia	41	21	45	24	8
Hawaii[3]	37	42	42	51	36
Idaho	10	24	13	25	41
Illinois	6	10	18	6	23
Indiana	2	16	3	38	7
Iowa	14	46	17	18	44
Kansas	13	15	7	12	40
Kentucky	38	36	34	42	6
Louisiana	49	6	48	36	28
Maine	24	49	25	7	50
Maryland	20	8	10	31	3
Massachusetts	15	28	20	4	33
Michigan	22	19	22	10	17
Minnesota	26	34	9	13	27
Mississippi	51	47	51	48	38
Missouri	23	14	14	27	29
Montana	33	51	33	15	42
Nebraska	8	30	12	34	45
Nevada	42	48	31	33	24
New Hampshire	25	43	21	17	49
New Jersey	21	18	27	11	19
New Mexico	31	27	36	45	31
New York	19	4	23	8	22
North Carolina	34	7	40	49	11
North Dakota	40	31	28	21	46
Ohio	1	2	1	5	15
Oklahoma	4	40	32	43	34
Oregon	9	33	2	3	30
Pennsylvania	44	35	41	9	32
Rhode Island	17	29	30	2	20
South Carolina	43	13	39	46	12
South Dakota	29	25	24	28	47
Tennessee	48	44	49	44	25
Texas	47	38	44	40	5

State	Library Visits per Capita[1]	Reference Transactions per Capita	Circulation Transactions per Capita	Interlibrary Loans per 1,000 Population	Average Public-use Internet Computers per Outlet
Utah	7	1	4	47	26
Vermont	16	32	26	23	51
Virginia	28	17	15	37	10
Washington	11	22	6	35	16
West Virginia	50	50	47	29	43
Wisconsin	18	23	8	1	35
Wyoming	3	11	19	20	37

State	Public-use Internet Computers per 5,000 Population	Print Materials per Capita	Audio Materials per 1,000 Population	Video Materials per 1,000 Population	Current Print Serial Subscriptions per 1,000 Population
Alabama	17	42	43	44	48
Alaska	22	17	27	5	8
Arizona	48	51	42	43	47
Arkansas	34	32	47	45	41
California	49	43	45	41	46
Colorado	26	35	17	17	26
Connecticut	9	9	11	6	14
Delaware	46	40	34	30	25
District of Columbia[2]	15	20	20	27	30
Florida	33	49	37	31	40
Georgia	42	50	51	50	50
Hawaii[3]	51	29	40	46	42
Idaho	23	23	26	26	34
Illinois	16	16	12	13	11
Indiana	6	8	6	2	4
Iowa	5	13	8	9	3
Kansas	4	10	19	3	16
Kentucky	28	41	36	37	36
Louisiana	18	30	44	34	29
Maine	8	1	22	12	10
Maryland	38	33	23	33	31
Massachusetts	30	2	7	11	12
Michigan	11	19	15	22	19
Minnesota	20	26	30	32	21
Mississippi	35	45	50	48	45
Missouri	24	22	25	28	15
Montana	13	24	28	29	27
Nebraska	2	5	13	14	5
Nevada	50	48	31	25	43
New Hampshire	19	4	18	10	2
New Jersey	29	18	24	21	20
New Mexico	21	25	32	38	23

State	Public-use Internet Computers per 5,000 Population	Print Materials per Capita	Audio Materials per 1,000 Population	Video Materials per 1,000 Population	Current Print Serial Subscriptions per 1,000 Population
New York	27	14	5	19	9
North Carolina	43	47	49	51	44
North Dakota	12	7	21	24	17
Ohio	14	15	3	1	1
Oklahoma	32	36	39	42	37
Oregon	41	28	4	15	28
Pennsylvania	47	37	14	35	32
Rhode Island	10	12	35	20	22
South Carolina	37	39	41	39	35
South Dakota	7	11	29	16	18
Tennessee	44	44	48	49	51
Texas	40	46	46	47	49
Utah	45	34	10	23	33
Vermont	1	3	9	7	6
Virginia	36	31	33	40	39
Washington	31	38	16	18	24
West Virginia	39	27	38	36	38
Wisconsin	25	21	1	4	13
Wyoming	3	6	2	8	7

State	Paid FTE Staff per 25,000 Population	Paid FTE Librarians per 25,000 Population	ALA-MLS Librarians per 25,000 Population	Other Paid FTE Staff per 25,000 Population	Total Operating Revenue per Capita
Alabama	42	34	44	43	47
Alaska	29	31	26	27	12
Arizona	50	48	38	46	37
Arkansas	39	44	50	31	44
California	48	47	27	44	29
Colorado	13	29	16	10	8
Connecticut	8	6	1	12	9
Delaware	35	30	37	33	24
District of Columbia[2]	6	24	4	2	1
Florida	43	43	24	36	32
Georgia	47	51	39	40	46
Hawaii[3]	36	36	11	29	42
Idaho	21	32	46	15	31
Illinois	5	8	6	6	3
Indiana	2	11	9	1	7
Iowa	17	4	29	37	28
Kansas	3	5	20	7	15
Kentucky	25	12	35	35	26
Louisiana	23	19	31	21	20
Maine	15	7	13	24	33

State	Paid FTE Staff per 25,000 Population	Paid FTE Librarians per 25,000 Population	ALA-MLS Librarians per 25,000 Population	Other Paid FTE Staff per 25,000 Population	Total Operating Revenue per Capita
Maryland	12	13	15	13	13
Massachusetts	18	10	7	28	18
Michigan	24	23	12	20	16
Minnesota	31	33	22	30	21
Mississippi	38	25	51	41	51
Missouri	14	37	33	8	17
Montana	41	20	45	50	41
Nebraska	11	9	34	14	27
Nevada	44	49	41	34	22
New Hampshire	10	1	10	25	19
New Jersey	7	22	3	5	4
New Mexico	30	28	28	39	38
New York	9	15	5	9	2
North Carolina	46	50	36	38	45
North Dakota	40	21	42	49	43
Ohio	4	14	8	3	6
Oklahoma	33	18	30	42	34
Oregon	28	35	19	18	11
Pennsylvania	34	38	23	26	39
Rhode Island	16	16	2	17	14
South Carolina	32	41	21	22	40
South Dakota	27	17	47	32	36
Tennessee	51	46	49	48	50
Texas	49	45	40	47	48
Utah	37	42	43	23	35
Vermont	19	3	32	45	30
Virginia	26	39	17	16	25
Washington	20	40	14	11	10
West Virginia	45	26	48	51	49
Wisconsin	22	27	18	19	23
Wyoming	1	2	25	4	5

State	State Operating Revenue per Capita	Local Operating Revenue per Capita	Other Operating Revenue per Capita	Total Operating Expenditures per Capita	Collection Expenditures per Capita
Alabama	30	45	33	47	49
Alaska	22	11	24	12	25
Arizona	43	33	49	39	37
Arkansas	14	41	45	44	41
California	35	24	28	24	42
Colorado	46	7	12	10	9
Connecticut	36	10	8	7	12
Delaware	4	34	18	23	5
District of Columbia[2]	50	1	51	1	2

State	State Operating Revenue per Capita	Local Operating Revenue per Capita	Other Operating Revenue per Capita	Total Operating Expenditures per Capita	Collection Expenditures per Capita
Florida	25	27	46	32	34
Georgia	8	47	48	46	47
Hawaii[3]	2	51	31	41	44
Idaho	34	31	22	34	39
Illinois	11	4	10	4	3
Indiana	9	8	14	9	4
Iowa	28	26	13	25	21
Kansas	16	13	9	14	13
Kentucky	19	23	26	37	33
Louisiana	20	16	36	26	32
Maine	40	37	3	29	40
Maryland	6	19	5	11	8
Massachusetts	18	17	15	16	14
Michigan	32	12	23	17	19
Minnesota	23	20	16	21	27
Mississippi	10	50	35	51	51
Missouri	29	14	17	19	7
Montana	37	39	34	42	43
Nebraska	38	21	25	28	20
Nevada	26	32	4	30	11
New Hampshire	47	15	20	18	24
New Jersey	33	2	27	6	10
New Mexico	24	35	44	36	38
New York	12	5	2	2	15
North Carolina	15	43	43	45	48
North Dakota	21	40	29	43	30
Ohio	1	42	6	3	1
Oklahoma	31	28	38	31	23
Oregon	42	9	21	13	18
Pennsylvania	5	46	11	38	36
Rhode Island	3	25	7	15	22
South Carolina	17	38	47	40	35
South Dakota	51	30	37	35	29
Tennessee	48	48	32	50	50
Texas	41	44	50	48	46
Utah	39	29	42	33	17
Vermont	49	36	1	27	31
Virginia	13	22	39	22	28
Washington	44	6	40	8	6
West Virginia	7	49	41	49	45
Wisconsin	27	18	30	20	26
Wyoming	45	3	19	5	16

State	Staff Expenditures per Capita	Salaries and Wages Expenditures per Capita	Registered Borrowers per Capita
Alabama	46	46	39
Alaska	12	17	19
Arizona	41	41	15
Arkansas	48	47	23
California	24	28	26
Colorado	13	12	27
Connecticut	4	3	32
Delaware	33	34	35
District of Columbia[2]	1	1	41
Florida	35	36	30
Georgia	44	45	49
Hawaii[3]	38	24	10
Idaho	32	31	24
Illinois	7	6	47
Indiana	11	10	7
Iowa	23	25	8
Kansas	16	14	2
Kentucky	40	40	21
Louisiana	31	32	31
Maine	25	23	12
Maryland	9	11	20
Massachusetts	14	9	34
Michigan	19	20	42
Minnesota	21	22	1
Mississippi	51	51	48
Missouri	22	21	22
Montana	42	42	44
Nebraska	26	27	4
Nevada	28	30	51
New Hampshire	17	15	29
New Jersey	6	7	36
New Mexico	36	37	3
New York	2	2	18
North Carolina	43	43	33
North Dakota	45	44	43
Ohio	5	5	5
Oklahoma	34	35	17
Oregon	15	16	38
Pennsylvania	37	38	46
Rhode Island	10	13	45
South Carolina	39	39	25
South Dakota	30	29	28
Tennessee	49	49	40

State	Staff Expenditures per Capita	Salaries and Wages Expenditures per Capita	Registered Borrowers per Capita
Texas	47	48	37
Utah	29	33	13
Vermont	27	26	14
Virginia	20	19	16
Washington	8	8	6
West Virginia	50	50	50
Wisconsin	18	18	11
Wyoming	3	4	9

FTE=full-time equivalent.

1. Per capita is based on the total unduplicated population of legal service areas.

2. The District of Columbia, while not a state, is included in the state rankings. Special care should be used in comparing its data to state data.

3. Caution should be used in making comparisons with the state of Hawaii, as Hawaii reports only one public library for the entire state.

Source: Compiled by Carol Collier from Survey of Public Libraries in the United States, Fiscal Year 2009, Institute of Museum and Library Services, 2010.

Library Acquisition Expenditures, 2010–2011: U.S. Public, Academic, Special, and Government Libraries

The information in these tables is taken from *American Library Directory* (*ALD*) *2011–2012* (Information Today, Inc., 2011). The tables report acquisition expenditures by public, academic, special, and government libraries.

The total number of libraries in the United States and in regions administered by the United States listed in this 64th edition of *ALD* is 29,145, including 16,950 public libraries, 3,772 academic libraries, 7,045 special libraries, and 1,102 government libraries.

Understanding the Tables

Number of libraries includes only those U.S. libraries in *ALD* that reported annual acquisition expenditures (1,826 public libraries, 775 academic libraries, 131 special libraries, and 44 government libraries). Libraries that reported annual income but not expenditures are not included in the count. Academic libraries include university, college, and junior college libraries. Special academic libraries, such as law and medical libraries, that reported acquisition expenditures separately from the institution's main library are counted as independent libraries.

The amount in the *total acquisition expenditures* column for a given state is generally greater than the sum of the categories of expenditures. This is because the total acquisition expenditures amount also includes the expenditures of libraries that did not itemize by category.

Figures in *categories of expenditure* columns represent only those libraries that itemized expenditures. Libraries that reported a total acquisition expenditure amount but did not itemize are only represented in the total acquisition expenditures column.

Table 1 / Public Library Acquisition Expenditures

State	Number of Libraries	Total Acquisition Expenditures	Books	Other Print Materials	Periodicals/ Serials	Manuscripts & Archives	AV Equipment	AV Materials	Microforms	Electronic Reference	Preservation
Alabama	26	18,071,933	1,304,778	9,100	43,038	2,000	297	201,933	1,963	16,711	400
Alaska	13	912,983	183,275	5,123	21,834	0	0	34,382	500	16,080	6,871
Arizona	21	13,035,919	3,064,616	4,727,824	179,869	0	0	2,367,928	50,656	2,043,038	8,876
Arkansas	17	4,163,551	2,567,385	22,064	172,035	0	23,105	454,518	1,640	314,435	8,270
California	74	87,333,489	33,625,465	1,939,761	3,907,294	6,500	8,430	10,050,725	173,241	7,496,631	9,990,836
Colorado	35	16,456,307	6,068,396	16,500	509,805	0	17,200	2,913,112	1,000	1,186,697	450
Connecticut	66	10,343,264	5,166,999	665,498	874,652	600	10,600	1,023,512	118,040	1,406,062	25,444
Delaware	5	632,708	130,294	0	0	0	0	26,263	0	1,500	0
District of Columbia	0	0	0	0	0	0	0	0	0	0	0
Florida	34	34,520,802	12,285,205	171,893	1,146,101	1,500	129,966	5,601,400	194,671	2,595,686	2,000
Georgia	13	9,643,657	3,114,935	1,068	143,850	0	2,026	589,730	740	424,470	583
Hawaii	1	2,930,469	0	0	170,259	0	0	0	67,819	1,487,608	0
Idaho	11	494,812	172,695	500	7,632	0	0	26,094	0	14,064	1,500
Illinois	93	39,180,132	8,274,976	81,696	662,985	10,000	86,253	2,755,821	45,346	2,747,337	19,429
Indiana	63	24,348,631	11,710,190	57,538	1,294,023	0	169,735	4,247,856	197,190	869,879	87,209
Iowa	60	7,056,124	1,935,948	90,161	221,474	0	13,768	587,565	2,530	216,488	0
Kansas	38	12,887,037	2,554,469	146,408	841,741	15	23,600	858,092	3,879	649,398	400
Kentucky	20	6,614,682	1,880,688	2,486	82,984	0	15,329	729,187	15,085	354,041	0
Louisiana	7	6,201,161	2,364,950	5,000	300,991	3,000	41,263	779,767	54,882	561,992	0
Maine	46	1,736,996	835,994	1,350	118,433	2,000	5,350	123,169	1,200	202,861	1,000
Maryland	3	10,293,959	1,771,917	0	88,452	0	0	942,122	0	197,079	0
Massachusetts	88	20,181,035	3,676,820	83,566	437,202	0	4,257	1,107,584	35,671	394,673	3,200
Michigan	82	25,240,830	8,867,540	18,763	625,445	0	34,000	2,113,452	21,468	1,346,387	12,475
Minnesota	37	16,969,129	4,073,240	7,447	104,300	0	4,500	961,474	6,039	464,790	668
Mississippi	9	2,560,287	457,474	0	33,331	0	0	153,542	400	114,559	2,162

Categories of Expenditures (in U.S. dollars)

Missouri	30	17,024,669	2,505,917	0	205,587	0	24,240	737,196	2,154	912,874	0
Montana	18	789,609	527,692	1,000	54,797	200	10,316	116,298	2,873	50,558	1,710
Nebraska	28	2,126,440	1,190,595	399,866	45,328	278	47	64,419	540	242,297	2,346
Nevada	5	1,157,070	128,500	1,193	10,558	0	0	19,634	0	20,000	0
New Hampshire	65	2,653,546	1,192,077	500	149,388	0	7,428	280,434	23,891	106,276	7,050
New Jersey	75	29,124,492	13,739,158	77,366	1,350,470	500	22,500	3,341,859	83,249	1,777,419	5,850
New Mexico	12	2,472,100	1,205,065	4,927	63,526	0	6,000	234,225	11,955	93,823	0
New York	132	41,694,902	21,559,340	367,583	1,730,525	5,000	145,183	3,911,312	108,967	2,361,584	23,873
North Carolina	28	13,212,900	7,539,792	1,344,458	261,369	0	31,840	952,062	15,540	512,475	0
North Dakota	16	1,726,020	741,349	4,085	86,568	0	35,000	135,462	3,500	121,887	1,000
Ohio	66	52,315,383	23,684,262	487,993	3,702,248	6,921	117,317	11,134,575	380,680	6,675,985	338,071
Oklahoma	10	11,780,850	5,299,655	11,498	860,493	0	0	1,582,848	2,945	921,466	0
Oregon	38	6,940,138	2,644,268	22,827	307,369	0	1,500	551,007	21,968	175,359	1,872,003
Pennsylvania	75	19,560,973	6,476,148	895,879	1,720,791	156,260	14,208	2,857,310	397,884	1,583,291	106,789
Rhode Island	9	9,931,828	548,865	71,214	63,771	0	0	95,864	70	761,361	1,000
South Carolina	17	11,553,069	6,824,187	22,222	423,116	5,000	90,907	1,851,105	23,809	1,456,764	12,235
South Dakota	18	1,917,118	962,969	1,000	96,933	0	395	302,516	50	119,547	0
Tennessee	24	5,746,936	1,447,585	0	185,617	0	11,600	331,822	1,200	463,767	1,315
Texas	95	57,115,793	10,483,513	530,811	1,081,891	200	287,296	1,981,221	67,524	1,683,410	18,424
Utah	10	3,806,788	958,665	1,203	58,063	245,000	0	219,375	30,367	108,754	70,000
Vermont	47	1,322,910	588,416	571	26,653	0	0	119,097	276	21,705	500
Virginia	29	11,071,389	3,986,745	3,148	476,764	56,278	0	958,769	79,578	836,025	1,904,800
Washington	25	24,389,966	2,909,461	531,228	140,284	0	54,230	767,015	3,211	549,602	400
West Virginia	16	4,051,488	1,506,927	4,086	97,400	9,000	24,000	246,527	13,810	855,055	2,900
Wisconsin	63	7,703,645	3,801,994	77,991	231,616	0	6,475	1,127,933	11,892	578,623	2,700
Wyoming	13	1,509,749	422,259	4,694	40,422	0	6,000	86,191	55	43,039	0
Puerto Rico	0	0	0	0	0	0	0	0	0	0	0
Total	1,826	714,509,668	238,963,653	12,921,089	25,459,277	510,252	1,486,161	72,655,304	2,281,948	48,155,412	14,544,739
Estimated % of Acquisition Expenditures		33.44	1.81		3.56	0.07	0.21	10.17	0.32	6.74	2.04

Table 2 / Academic Library Acquisition Expenditures

					Categories of Expenditures (in U.S. dollars)						
State	Number of Libraries	Total Acquisition Expenditures	Books	Other Print Materials	Periodicals/ Serials	Manuscripts & Archives	AV Equipment	AV Materials	Microforms	Electronic Reference	Preservation
Alabama	14	17,153,904	1,843,740	9,017	4,479,172	0	20,000	134,634	104,162	2,480,977	105,002
Alaska	5	6,687,613	532,433	10,000	2,446,408	0	300	74,887	17,307	888,392	18,827
Arizona	9	3,175,170	742,122	67,581	650,102	17,979	6,675	110,561	39,301	1,354,392	14,153
Arkansas	7	11,622,938	1,666,847	0	6,655,927	0	1,000	99,385	184,835	2,920,796	94,148
California	59	86,337,307	8,328,115	752,200	15,496,356	4,914	65,419	418,451	292,988	11,428,791	475,891
Colorado	12	25,658,341	3,332,850	902,987	9,901,588	0	0	144,413	70	7,946,268	62,126
Connecticut	11	9,115,689	1,602,056	340	3,760,480	0	80,478	145,090	122,636	1,680,093	94,852
Delaware	3	8,346,310	40,000	0	8,419	0	0	0	0	0	0
District of Columbia	3	11,667,126	1,973,224	0	6,269,488	0	0	8,100	99,300	1,012,392	94,154
Florida	30	26,216,683	5,100,878	705,997	11,034,496	0	26,000	531,180	185,418	6,773,183	202,663
Georgia	21	13,774,528	1,072,219	2,000	1,450,501	0	4,075	148,069	51,714	1,937,872	56,037
Hawaii	2	659,932	128,000	0	176,200	0	3,000	16,047	14,000	77,438	18,700
Idaho	4	9,452,279	832,363	0	3,584,197	2,470	0	28,897	0	879,501	56,780
Illinois	30	70,861,345	8,779,827	1,188	16,302,845	0	34,435	332,684	49,019	12,908,571	155,304
Indiana	17	22,271,905	3,790,801	24,211	13,222,044	0	44,452	175,948	33,331	2,040,908	86,883
Iowa	19	27,420,601	3,341,438	264,492	13,416,863	0	31,139	109,743	44,941	3,433,662	140,041
Kansas	17	9,113,988	1,608,412	24,000	6,229,888	0	8,718	37,678	23,753	724,296	62,577
Kentucky	13	19,659,850	2,641,435	11,300	8,556,521	28,000	2,747	161,244	194,218	5,485,729	205,935
Louisiana	8	5,389,739	535,560	36,361	3,390,304	3,427	3,720	6,387	68,382	1,193,211	42,718
Maine	3	7,905,379	1,509,525	0	5,842,437	0	0	44,812	62,500	251,231	74,374
Maryland	12	11,979,804	1,189,306	6,209	5,292,199	14,926	0	80,722	11,535	1,062,393	77,734
Massachusetts	27	181,994,832	4,214,684	36,256	13,485,943	0	107,000	244,004	47,480	5,780,165	169,820
Michigan	29	22,544,573	3,434,815	162,940	7,646,560	26,000	48,588	150,019	211,550	6,680,484	115,685
Minnesota	17	13,304,061	2,424,293	10,000	4,954,526	5,000	28,475	256,861	105,821	1,616,846	95,701
Mississippi	6	3,489,772	341,867	0	1,365,001	0	1,000	36,853	116,000	1,309,437	45,818

Missouri	17	12,778,268	738,036	19,916	2,478,514	2,326	11,254	116,815	135,273	784,858	52,344
Montana	5	374,497	164,301	0	154,767	0	10,000	9,069	3,000	20,000	0
Nebraska	9	10,619,597	570,597	123,250	2,235,302	15,000	0	144,276	51,129	784,278	17,930
Nevada	2	415,295	136,754	0	11,877	0	0	15,908	217	49,926	613
New Hampshire	6	9,351,484	1,195,724	0	4,180,222	0	0	700	21,116	1,351,794	76,271
New Jersey	9	6,688,942	814,873	69,154	1,365,700	0	0	33,684	22,586	745,053	5,620
New Mexico	5	5,124,302	44,000	0	8,800	0	0	11,000	4,300	24,400	2,200
New York	53	81,884,742	10,652,850	567,368	22,605,519	28,433	157,936	557,366	237,017	20,694,156	415,011
North Carolina	30	56,151,619	9,808,255	15,003	28,029,980	2,000	33,616	562,492	544,440	3,683,612	195,371
North Dakota	3	4,699,658	368,210	10,000	2,095,007	0	1,080	28,734	684	1,027,799	22,732
Ohio	31	28,893,218	5,709,650	78,695	8,959,901	2,461	27,829	259,764	144,094	6,532,447	281,498
Oklahoma	9	6,451,805	688,701	0	2,523,001	2,000	0	130,646	18,127	2,141,517	12,228
Oregon	16	29,464,004	1,438,337	4,488	3,509,981	0	43,675	116,010	0	1,734,265	102,981
Pennsylvania	31	20,179,884	4,165,519	18,108	9,505,064	35,314	71,203	294,221	269,315	2,915,835	200,011
Rhode Island	5	2,414,914	518,996	2,100	1,063,029	9,500	36,338	42,372	21,021	609,916	17,636
South Carolina	17	10,512,994	2,185,592	103,196	2,681,220	20,000	10,000	106,476	90,085	2,338,305	94,116
South Dakota	4	3,381,770	280,605	0	641,458	0	3,592	12,688	12,480	626,286	18,339
Tennessee	15	18,973,008	957,884	0	1,539,729	0	0	55,750	68,400	2,643,068	11,101
Texas	36	46,428,825	9,049,961	18,140	20,573,795	6,050	98,562	244,570	277,420	4,443,187	264,389
Utah	4	4,846,673	1,008,900	0	2,964,773	0	16,000	71,500	3,500	782,000	0
Vermont	6	1,788,682	484,963	0	812,980	3,500	5,000	41,550	1,770	365,719	9,000
Virginia	27	33,862,502	6,647,534	625,166	12,663,026	2,000	28,041	370,274	105,470	6,333,483	93,612
Washington	16	14,130,162	2,229,370	0	6,792,719	14,564	50,000	269,645	8,900	1,691,960	28,873
West Virginia	13	3,651,826	334,719	15,479	398,578	12,696	19,000	47,453	35,295	811,914	9,005
Wisconsin	18	21,693,523	2,683,558	7,573	6,037,582	2,000	23,109	159,960	96,412	984,466	65,227
Wyoming	3	7,480,309	3,458,937	0	2,201,321	0	0	13,200	0	863,481	0
Puerto Rico	7	6,235,838	804,121	1,000	4,649,922	5,000	34,527	49,638	0	674,235	10,000
Total	775	1,074,282,010	128,147,757	4,705,715	316,302,232	265,560	1,197,983	7,262,430	4,252,312	147,524,988	4,572,031
Estimated % of Acquisition Expenditures			11.93	0.44	29.44	0.02	0.11	0.68	0.40	13.73	0.43

Table 3 / Special Library Acquisition Expenditures

State	Number of Libraries	Total Acquisition Expenditures	Books	Other Print Materials	Periodicals/ Serials	Manuscripts & Archives	AV Equipment	AV Materials	Microforms	Electronic Reference	Preservation
Alabama	1	1,375	250	0	525	0	0	0	0	500	100
Alaska	0	0	0	0	0	0	0	0	0	0	0
Arizona	4	20,324	0	0	0	0	0	0	0	0	0
Arkansas	0	0	0	0	0	0	0	0	0	0	0
California	14	417,098	52,198	2,000	167,059	0	2,500	1,100	0	69,741	7,500
Colorado	1	10,000	7,000	0	1,000	0	0	2,000	0	0	0
Connecticut	0	0	0	0	0	0	0	0	0	0	0
Delaware	0	0	0	0	0	0	0	0	0	0	0
District of Columbia	3	877,714	124,027	0	57,110	0	0	261	25,000	13,000	504,877
Florida	5	97,760	46,650	1,000	31,230	0	0	0	0	6,630	11,400
Georgia	0	0	0	0	0	0	0	0	0	0	0
Hawaii	0	0	0	0	0	0	0	0	0	0	0
Idaho	0	0	0	0	0	0	0	0	0	0	0
Illinois	10	2,818,800	93,300	30,500	147,700	200	1,900	4,000	1,500	72,000	4,700
Indiana	2	43,625	37,725	0	120	500	0	0	3,780	0	1,500
Iowa	2	203,058	35,362	0	12,408	0	0	0	155,288	0	0
Kansas	2	12,581	4,400	4,000	4,081	0	0	0	0	0	100
Kentucky	0	0	0	0	0	0	0	0	0	0	0
Louisiana	0	0	0	0	0	0	0	0	0	0	0
Maine	1	200	0	0	0	0	0	0	0	0	0
Maryland	3	166,950	23,150	0	130,450	50	0	0	0	12,000	100
Massachusetts	3	81,891	0	0	0	0	0	0	0	0	0
Michigan	1	12,000	3,000	500	3,600	0	0	400	0	0	0
Minnesota	2	54,850	21,350	5,000	11,500	0	0	1,000	0	16,000	0
Mississippi	0	0	0	0	0	0	0	0	0	0	0

Categories of Expenditures (in U.S. dollars)

	Count										
Missouri	2	68,745	24,000	0	30,145	0	0	0	600	14,000	0
Montana	1	17,348	15,848	0	0	0	0	0	0	1,500	0
Nebraska	2	2,600	950	0	1,500	0	0	0	0	0	0
Nevada	1	1,000	0	0	0	0	0	0	0	0	0
New Hampshire	2	92,000	16,000	10,000	5,000	20,000	0	6,000	0	32,000	9,000
New Jersey	4	21,700	9,000	0	5,500	0	0	0	0	0	1,200
New Mexico	2	12,500	0	0	0	0	0	0	0	0	0
New York	21	470,956	118,545	50	53,450	20,000	3,452	11,662	1,000	8,475	19,320
North Carolina	0	0	0	0	0	0	0	0	0	0	0
North Dakota	2	11,598	2,660	0	5,475	2,000	0	0	0	0	1,463
Ohio	11	1,587,731	112,763	550	674,157	0	150	1,998	3,249	777,524	12,160
Oklahoma	3	101,050	15,000	1,250	36,800	12,000	20,000	1,000	3,000	12,000	0
Oregon	1	600	200	0	0	0	0	0	0	400	0
Pennsylvania	5	456,057	41,108	58,812	85,859	18,351	0	9,671	10,000	204,322	25,034
Rhode Island	1	75,313	44,726	0	5,000	15,387	0	0	0	0	10,200
South Carolina	1	29,600	14,000	0	5,000	0	0	6,000	3,000	0	0
South Dakota	0	0	0	0	0	0	0	0	0	0	0
Tennessee	2	26,000	12,500	0	6,000	0	500	3,000	0	4,000	0
Texas	7	1,319,360	37,556	43,992	2,393	500	670	765	0	29,000	2,056
Utah	1	75,000	5,000	5,000	10,000	5,000	5,000	0	0	50,000	0
Vermont	0	0	0	0	0	0	0	0	0	0	0
Virginia	5	383,110	102,159	12,600	51,030	40,373	48,265	5,380	4,200	27,975	91,128
Washington	1	1,500	0	0	0	0	0	0	0	0	0
West Virginia	0	0	0	0	0	0	0	0	0	0	0
Wisconsin	2	128,500	11,300	0	74,000	0	0	0	0	43,000	0
Wyoming	0	0	0	0	0	0	0	0	0	0	0
Puerto Rico	0	0	0	0	0	0	0	0	0	0	0
Total	131	9,700,494	1,031,727	175,254	1,618,092	129,361	82,437	54,237	210,617	1,394,067	701,838
Estimated % of Acquisition Expenditures			10.64	1.81	16.68	1.33	0.85	0.56	2.17	14.37	7.24

Table 4 / Government Library Acquisition Expenditures

State	Number of Libraries	Total Acquisition Expenditures	Books	Other Print Materials	Periodicals/ Serials	Manuscripts & Archives	AV Equipment	AV Materials	Microforms	Electronic Reference	Preservation
Alabama	2	626,295	243,777	0	575	0	0	0	0	381,472	471
Alaska	0	0	0	0	0	0	0	0	0	0	0
Arizona	0	0	0	0	0	0	0	0	0	0	0
Arkansas	0	0	0	0	0	0	0	0	0	0	0
California	10	2,553,176	781,727	174,358	537,590	0	7,472	6,245	17,804	399,163	4,432
Colorado	0	0	0	0	0	0	0	0	0	0	0
Connecticut	0	0	0	0	0	0	0	0	0	0	0
Delaware	1	50,000	7,000	1,000	9,000	0	0	0	0	33,000	0
District of Columbia	0	0	0	0	0	0	0	0	0	0	0
Florida	1	19,545	3,750	0	14,170	0	0	1,625	0	0	0
Georgia	0	0	0	0	0	0	0	0	0	0	0
Hawaii	0	0	0	0	0	0	0	0	0	0	0
Idaho	0	0	0	0	0	0	0	0	0	0	0
Illinois	0	0	0	0	0	0	0	0	0	0	0
Indiana	0	0	0	0	0	0	0	0	0	0	0
Iowa	0	0	0	0	0	0	0	0	0	0	0
Kansas	2	789,260	296,852	0	400,491	0	0	0	0	85,690	6,227
Kentucky	0	0	0	0	0	0	0	0	0	0	0
Louisiana	2	1,042,318	28,500	0	123,000	0	500	1,000	0	15,000	0
Maine	1	257,079	0	0	0	0	0	0	0	0	0
Maryland	3	589,000	358,000	11,800	196,000	0	0	7,700	0	0	3,500
Massachusetts	3	348,868	195,036	0	0	0	0	0	0	68,332	7,500
Michigan	1	35,000	0	0	0	0	0	0	0	0	0
Minnesota	2	134,500	18,000	0	61,500	0	0	0	0	55,000	0
Mississippi	0	0	0	0	0	0	0	0	0	0	0

Categories of Expenditures (in U.S. dollars)

State											
Missouri	0	0	0	0	0	0	0	0	0	0	0
Montana	1	425,961	328,391	0	0	0	0	0	0	97,570	0
Nebraska	0	0	0	0	0	0	0	0	3,151	186,357	5,802
Nevada	1	768,769	562,656	0	10,803	0	0	0	0	0	0
New Hampshire	1	70,000	0	0	0	0	0	0	0	0	0
New Jersey	0	0	0	0	0	0	0	0	0	0	0
New Mexico	0	0	0	0	0	0	0	0	0	0	5,300
New York	3	1,367,180	0	0	0	0	0	0	0	0	0
North Carolina	0	0	0	0	0	0	0	0	0	0	0
North Dakota	1	40,000	5,000	0	30,000	0	0	0	0	5,000	0
Ohio	0	0	0	0	0	0	0	0	0	0	0
Oklahoma	0	0	0	0	0	0	0	0	0	0	0
Oregon	0	0	0	0	0	0	0	0	0	0	0
Pennsylvania	4	575,000	71,500	0	500	0	0	0	0	10,000	0
Rhode Island	1	43,425	9,961	0	31,764	0	0	814	0	886	0
South Carolina	0	0	0	0	0	0	0	0	0	0	0
South Dakota	0	0	0	0	0	0	0	0	0	0	0
Tennessee	1	125,000	0	0	0	0	0	0	0	0	0
Texas	0	0	0	0	0	0	0	0	0	0	0
Utah	0	0	0	0	0	0	0	0	0	0	0
Vermont	0	0	0	0	0	0	0	0	0	0	0
Virginia	1	63,090	13,355	0	42,453	0	0	6,271	0	1,011	0
Washington	0	0	0	0	0	0	0	0	0	0	0
West Virginia	1	650,000	50,000	0	400,000	0	0	0	0	200,000	0
Wisconsin	1	81,000	45,000	0	0	0	0	0	0	36,000	0
Wyoming	0	0	0	0	0	0	0	0	0	0	0
Puerto Rico	0	0	0	0	0	0	0	0	0	0	0
Total	44	10,654,466	3,018,505	187,158	1,857,846	0	7,972	23,655	20,955	1,574,481	33,232
Estimated % of Acquisition Expenditures			28.33	1.76	17.44	0.00	0.07	0.22	0.20	14.78	0.31

Library Buildings 2011: Design of the Times

Bette-Lee Fox

Managing Editor, *Library Journal*

Whether sleek and modern, true to classic lines, or touched with whimsy, the projects that comprise the library construction landscape are greener than ever. U.S. Green Building Council silver, gold, and platinum shimmer from many of the 150 public projects and 26 academic library buildings completed between July 1, 2010, and June 30, 2011.

Leadership in Energy and Environmental Design (LEED) certification and practice is at the heart of much of today's library design, just as these new and updated buildings were designed to be at the heart of their communities.

What was cutting-edge in terms of sustainable features—solar roofs, recycled building materials, low-VOC paint, bicycle racks, high-efficiency windows, and under-floor heating, ventilating, and air-conditioning systems—is now more widespread and familiar in library planning. Yet, there are still a few new sustainable wheels rolling down the ecofriendly pike, such as a cupola at the North Kohala Public Library in Kapaau, Hawaii, for natural light and wind turbines for power; chilled beam technology to reduce energy and an innovative stormwater collection system at the Orange Branch Library in Delaware, Ohio; a collaboration between the Mission Branch of San Antonio Public Library and the San Antonio Water System for the installation and operation of a demonstration rainwater/air-conditioning condensate collection system for irrigation; and an anticipated electric vehicle charging station at the Fitchburg (Wisconsin) Public Library.

Creating Community

As well as being environmentally sound, these current projects focus on the needs of their constituents for a place to gather and to feel at home. The central atrium at the Vancouver (Washington) Community Library is considered the "city's living room," as it links the five levels of the new structure. For the kids, Vancouver offers a children's museum-like experience, which is also the thrust behind the remodel of New York's Queens Library Children's Library Discovery Center. San Diego's Fallbrook Library, winner of a People's Choice Orchid Award from the San Diego Architectural Foundation and also referred to as the community's living room, includes a Poet's Patio and an outdoor reading garden. Growing new readers is also on the agenda of Chicago's Greater Grand Crossing Branch, which features a family reading garden, while the walled story garden of the Fox Lake District Library in Illinois connects directly to the indoor children's space.

The Peoria (Illinois) Public Library North Branch encompasses a reading garden and vast prairie views, while the Caledonia Township (Michigan) Branch of Kent District Library has a children's garden that includes a giant checkerboard. A crowning achievement in imaginative children's spaces is the Robbie Waters Pocket-Greenhaven Branch of the Sacramento (California) Public Library, whose children's reading tower mimics a castle when seen from the outside.

Adapted from *Library Journal,* December 2011

Moving back inside, the project at Aspen Drive Library in Vernon Hills, Illinois, is a little fishy—it incorporates a children's aquarium. The remodel of the Phoenix Public Library's Juniper Branch has a designated "First Five Years" interactive literacy learning environment. And while information is key to library service, entertainment is right behind, as evidenced by the transformation of the multipurpose meeting room of Dallas's Pleasant Grove Public Library into a black-box theater and the addition of a 300-seat auditorium and art gallery at Las Vegas's Windmill Library and Service Center.

Restoring Community

Mother Nature offered challenges to many regions and their libraries over the last several years, but some are getting back on their feet. Mississippi's new Waveland Public Library replaces a Katrina-damaged facility with a structure that includes a welcoming front porch and a children's library called, fittingly, "Jean Lafitte's Pirate Cove." The Evelyn Meador Branch Library in Seabrook, Texas, supplants a building impacted by Hurricane Ike in 2008, while the Georgetown Neighborhood Library in Washington, D.C., has returned after a devastating 2007 fire.

Aside from physical disasters, economics has played havoc with our neighborhoods. Seeking to overturn some of the impact of the recent hard times, the Weaver Bolden Branch Library in Tuscaloosa is a joint venture with the Tuscaloosa Housing Authority to help revitalize the neighborhood, with the library next door to a community center. Denver's Fruita Branch is in a mixed-use facility with a recreation center, senior center, swimming pool, and gymnasium. The University Place Pierce County (Washington) Library combines with civic functions, police, city hall, and retail ventures. The Rita and Truett Smith Central Public Library in Wylie, Texas, takes its place in a municipal complex comprising city offices and a recreation center along a continuous 700-foot Texas limestone wall.

Preserving History

Updating historical buildings with fresh purpose means both green and community focus. The Scotts Valley Branch Library in California was once a roller rink; the Jackson Public Library in New Hampshire is made from an old barn dismantled by the local historical society; and the Twin Oaks Branch in Austin, Texas, is composed of salvaged bricks from the post office that formerly stood on the site. The Nesconset Branch, Smithtown (New York) Special Library District transformed a 25,000-square-foot 1961 National Guard armory building; the Dolley Madison Library in McLean, Virginia, maintains Jeffersonian detail with an oculus (oval window) at the entrance and geometric inlays in the millwork. Then there's Iowa's Mason City Public Library renovation of its 1939 building. Composer Meredith Willson, a Mason City native, based his iconic Marian the Librarian in *The Music Man* on a former Mason City library director.

Among the academic library constructions are the massive addition/renovation at the University of California, Santa Cruz; the project at the University of Missouri–Kansas City that includes a 12,800-square foot-addition standing 70 feet high; and the new Arlington Campus Library of George Mason University.

Where We Go from Here

The perseverance of library capital projects is heartening, considering fiscal situation nationwide. We all understand that libraries in these uncertain times are more valuable than ever. As they embrace sustainable features and save money on operations, they are a model to others. They also stand as a beacon to those whose lives have shifted with a collapsing economic framework. Libraries support us; we must continue to support them.

Table 1 / New Academic Library Buildings, 2011

Institution	Project Cost	Gross Area (Sq. Ft.)	Sq. Ft. Cost	Construction Cost	Furniture/ Equip. Cost	Book Capacity	Architect
Arlington Campus Library, George Mason University, Va.	$91,000,000	414,000	$212.32	$87,900,000	$700,000	150,000	SmithGroup
Georgia Gwinnett College Library, Lawrenceville	24,333,000	90,883	237.67	21,600,000	2,019,600	400,000	Leo A. Daly
Karen H. Huntsman Library, Snow College, Ephraim, Utah	20,000,000	72,000	208.33	15,000,000	3,000,000	65,000	CRSA
Marquette University Law Library,* Milwaukee	n.a.	34,545	292.37	10,100,000	n.a.	280,000	Shepley Bulfinch; Opus Group
Joe & Rika Mansueto Library, University of Chicago	n.a.	61,719	n.a.	n.a.	n.a.	3,500,000	Murphy/Jahn

*The new library is part of a larger law school construction project encompassing 200,000 square feet and costing upwards of $60 million.

n.a. = not available

Table 2 / Academic Library Buildings, Additions Only, 2011

Institution	Project Cost	Gross Area (Sq. Ft.)	Sq. Ft. Cost	Construction Cost	Furniture/ Equip. Cost	Book Capacity	Architect
John Grant Grabbe Library/Noel Studio for Academic Creativity, Eastern Kentucky University, Richmond	$2,851,569	17,000	$156.02	$2,652,303	n.a.	n.a.	Voelker Blackburn Niehoff
Library Learning Terrace, Drexel University, Philadelphia	950,000	3,000	295.00	885,000	$65,000	n.a.	Erdy McHenry

n.a. = not available

Table 3 / Academic Library Buildings, Renovations Only, 2011

Institution	Project Cost	Gross Area (Sq. Ft.)	Sq. Ft. Cost	Construction Cost	Furniture/ Equip. Cost	Book Capacity	Architect
Ingram Library, University of West Georgia, Carrollton	$6,875,698	59,600	n.a.	n.a.	n.a.	n.a.	Houser Walker; Parrish Construction Group
Jean & Alexander Heard Library, Vanderbilt University, Nashville	5,936,000	20,150	$179.65	$3,620,000	$715,000	n.a.	Gilbert | McLaughlin | Casella
Pannell Library, New Mexico Junior College, Hobbs	5,146,180	29,514	133.77	3,948,127	1,198,053	244,000	Dekker/Perich/Sabatini
Porter Henderson Library, Angelo State University, San Angelo, Tex.	4,380,000	83,290	122.78	2,455,689	510,000	55,000	SHW Group
Charles E. Young Research Library, University of California–Los Angeles	2,480,000	17,230	110.27	1,900,000	200,000	51,000	Perkins + Will
Pattee & Paterno Library, Penn State University, University Park	1,400,000	6,000	216.67	1,300,000	100,000	3,500	WTW Architects
North Carolina State University Libraries, Raleigh	910,380	8,930	42.57	380,216	530,164	0	RND Architects*
Gertrude Kistler Memorial Library, Rosemont College, Pa.	577,603	4,680	115.89	542,352	35,251	5,000	Kimmel Bogrette
Ryan Library, Iona College, New Rochelle, N.Y.	464,689	3,430	105.83	362,981	102,708	27,000	Dimitris Halaris
Charleston Division Library, West Virginia University	53,013	1,850	19.47	36,013	17,000	0	none**
Special Collections Research Center, Joseph Regenstein Library, University of Chicago	n.a.	15,160	n.a.	n.a.	n.a.	16,500	Booth Hansen

* This architect designed the terrace portion; other spaces designed by library staff.

**Work done by a variety of public contractors.

n.a. = not available

Table 4 / Academic Library Buildings, Additions and Renovations, 2011

Institution	Status	Project Cost	Gross Area (Sq. Ft.)	Sq. Ft. Cost	Construction Cost	Furniture/ Equip. Cost	Book Capacity	Architect
McHenry Library, University of California Santa Cruz	Total	$100,125,000	273,962	$321.10	$87,968,000	$1,911,000	824,349	Boora Architects
	New	46,333,000	112,264	351.23	39,431,000	1,588,000	710,520	
	Renovated	53,792,000	161,698	300.17	48,537,000	323,000	113,829	
Lemieux Library & McGoldrick Learning Commons, Seattle University	Total	55,000,000	125,700	246.62	31,000,000	4,768,000	380,000	Pfeiffer Partners
	New	n.a.	33,000	576.76	19,000,000	n.a.	n.a.	
	Renovated	n.a.	92,700	129.45	12,000,000	n.a.	n.a.	
Library & Academic Resources Center, Colorado State University, Pueblo	Total	24,802,638	123,686	142.77	17,658,913	1,636,941	n.a.	Bennett Wagner & Grody
	New	n.a.	22,600	255.51	5,774,554		326,432	
	Renovated	n.a.	101,086	116.34	11,760,673		n.a.	
Miller Nichols Library, University of Missouri, Kansas City	Total	15,400,000	76,769	137.10	10,525,000	4,875,000	1,004,500	PGAV Architects; Sasaki Associates
	New	13,000,000	27,552	308.51	8,500,000	4,500,000	1,000,000	
	Renovated	2,400,000	49,217	41.14	2,025,000	375,000	4,500	
Pierce College Library, Lakewood, Wash.	Total	8,580,000	61,000	108.20	6,600,000	1,980,000	90,000	McGranahan Architects
	New	n.a.	n.a.	n.a.	n.a.	n.a.	n.a.	
	Renovated	n.a.	n.a.	n.a.	n.a.	n.a.	n.a.	
John T. Hinckley Library, Northwest College, Powell, Wyo.	Total	2,563,000	7,553	286.91	2,167,000	200,000	n.a.	CTA Billings
	New	1,634,900	5,316	263.54	1,401,000	106,500	n.a.	
	Renovated	928,100	2,237	342.42	766,000	93,500	n.a.	
Berkeley Law Library, University of California, Berkeley	Total	n.a.	110,000	n.a.	n.a.	n.a.	900,000	Ratcliff
	New	n.a.	61,000	n.a.	n.a.	n.a.	800,000	
	Renovated	n.a.	49,000	n.a.	n.a.	n.a.	100,000	
Belk Library & Information Commons, Appalachian State University, Boone, N.C.	Total	11,925	310	27.74	8,600	3,325	500	NC State Dept. of Construction
	New	8,400	120	50.00	6,000	2,400	0	
	Renovated	3,525	190	13.68	2,600	925	500	

n.a. = not available

Table 5 / New Public Library Buildings, 2011

Community	Pop. ('000)	Code	Project Cost	Const. Cost	Gross Area (Sq. Ft.)	Sq. Ft. Cost	Equip. Cost	Site Cost	Other Costs	Volumes	Architect
Alabama											
Tuscaloosa	35	B	$2,622,848	$2,362,848	275	$8,592	$128,236	Leased	$131,764	40,000	Cohen, Carnaggio & Reynolds
Vestavia Hills	34	M	12,804,000	9,063,000	38,000	239	941,000	$850,000	1,950,000	112,000	Keith Design
Arizona											
Phoenix	62	B	22,374,152	16,821,504	53,500	314	3,308,698	Owned	2,243,950	83,394	richärd+bauer
Waddell	49	B	9,867,070	8,686,984	29,000	300	738,256	Owned	441,830	35,000	DWL Architects
Arkansas											
Little Rock	23	B	4,303,453	3,038,504	13,550	224	465,906	624,043	175,000	65,000	Allison Architects
Van Buren	23	MS	4,684,936	3,557,711	19,200	185	369,817	470,408	287,000	5,000	MAHG; MS&R Ltd.
California											
Acton	17	B	13,368,000	8,069,000	11,343	711	951,000	309,000	4,039,000	60,000	Tetra IBI Group
Fallbrook	49	B	10,567,334	9,703,814	19,151	507	863,520	Owned	0	5,064	Ferguson Pape Baldwin
Oakland	35	B	14,128,373	9,854,713	21,000	469	1,069,628	Leased	3,204,032	30,000	Group 4 Architecture
Ramona	36	B	13,947,663	11,700,000	21,500	544	847,663	1,400,000	0	5,250	Ferguson Pape Baldwin
Sacramento	57	B	13,751,831	8,812,377	15,387	573	907,000	1,820,185	2,212,269	67,000	WLC Architects
San José	47	BO	32,407,685	19,168,537	40,000	479	n.a.	7,700,000	5,539,148	121,730	Rob Wellington Quigley
San José	62	B	10,633,368	7,647,935	18,000	425	n.a.	Leased	2,985,433	113,225	Anderson Brulé
San José	58	BO	34,194,164	27,583,411	60,000	460	n.a.	Owned	6,610,753	121,290	Rob Wellington Quigley
Tulare	60	M	15,200,000	11,400,000	31,408	363	742,000	1,100,000	1,958,000	14,975	Paul Halajian
Uninc. Whittier	19	B	8,400,000	5,500,000	10,655	516	560,000	Owned	2,340,000	51,000	Carde Ten Architects
Colorado											
Denver	29	B	9,804,696	4,740,624	26,000	182	2,908,368	651,364	1,504,340	75,000	Humphries Poli
Fruita	14	B	1,281,000	1,024,000	7,000	146	160,000	Leased	97,000	1200	Humphries Poli
Peyton	23	B	2,586,575	1,347,755	6,008	224	321,345	770,140	147,335	14,550	Humphries Poli
District Of Columbia											
Washington	25	B	15,005,203	10,677,852	23,000	464	967,225	Owned	3,360,126	80,000	Aedas Architects
Washington	25	B	18,086,605	12,741,455	23,000	554	1,013,000	Owned	4,332,150	80,000	Freelon Group

Symbol Code: B=Branch Library; BS=Branch and System Headquarters; M=Main Library; MS=Main and System Headquarters; S=System Headquarters; O=combined use space; n.a.=not available

State / City		Code								Architect
Florida										
Dania Beach	30	B	3,516,338	2,819,232	10,000	282	354,819	Leased	342,287	40,000	Manuel Synalovski Associates
Georgia										
Covington	100	B	5,014,286	3,363,321	19,200	175	507,228	Owned	1,143,737	42,100	Craig Gaulden Davis
Hawaii										
Kapaau	6	M	8,463,823	7,800,000	6,000	1,300	183,823	n.a.	480,000	28,000	CDS International
Illinois										
Chicago	32	B	7,686,123	4,383,000	8,900	492	147,508	1,976,000	1,179,615	45,000	Lohan Anderson
Chicago	56	B	12,209,202	5,671,172	16,300	348	210,837	2,995,428	3,331,765	60,000	Lohan Anderson
Chicago	41	B	7,181,831	4,390,000	8,900	493	150,396	960,000	1,681,435	45,000	Jackson Harlan
Fox Lake	25	M	15,573,590	10,090,151	45,000	224	840,275	Owned	4,643,164	10,088	Dewberry
Glenview	45	M	30,600,303	21,235,378	87,000	244	1,706,063	Owned	7,658,862	366,000	Dewberry
Peoria	115	B	11,024,688	8,344,014	29,717	281	520,271	1,060,325	1,100,078	7,923	Farnsworth; Dewberry
Vernon Hills	60	M	7,359,762	5,612,693	20,251	277	295,459	1,008,500	443,110	94,992	Studio GC
Maryland										
Arbutus	20	B	4,448,314	2,845,841	25,000	114	604,589	Owned	997,884	103,937	Sanders Designs
Massachusetts										
Dudley	11	M	5,981,000	3,883,714	16,750	232	676,200	Owned	1,421,086	55,000	Johnson Roberts Associates
Westhampton	2	M	2,167,500	1,288,400	5,400	239	126,100	370,000	383,000	15,000	Tappé Associates
Michigan										
Caledonia	12	B	2,885,000	2,100,000	17,200	122	385,000	250,000	150,000	39,000	Fishbeck, Thompson, Carr…
Kentwood	48	B	7,943,775	5,140,680	47,000	109	1,123,770	969,982	709,343	125,000	Post Associates
Mississippi										
Waveland	5	B	2,270,834	1,474,149	10,065	146	576,000	Owned	220,685	15,000	Walter T. Bolton
Nevada										
Las Vegas	90	BS	45,700,000	33,900,000	142,149	238	1,700,000	Leased	10,100,000	130,000	JMA Architecture
New Hampshire										
Jackson	2	M	1,300,451	1,175,000	4,800	245	70,000	Owned	55,451	15,000	Dennis Mires
West Lebanon	13	M	5,723,854	4,061,055	15,400	264	235,542	525,000	902,257	47,225	Tappé Associates
New York										
Bronx	129	B	17,728,972	14,048,972	12,000	1,171	1,325,000	Owned	2,355,000	20,000	Prendergast Laurel

Symbol Code: B=Branch Library; BS=Branch and System Headquarters; M=Main Library; MS=Main and System Headquarters; S=System Headquarters; O=combined use space; n.a.=not available

455

Table 5 / New Public Library Buildings, 2011 (cont.)

Community	Pop. ('000)	Code	Project Cost	Const. Cost	Gross Area (Sq. Ft.)	Sq. Ft. Cost	Equip. Cost	Site Cost	Other Costs	Volumes	Architect
Ohio											
Delaware	143	B	8,935,871	5,889,000	33,000	178	1,140,150	750,000	1,156,721	104,000	Dewberry
Pennsylvania											
Lancaster*	36	M	7,700,000	5,500,000	33,500	164	933,000	Leased	1,267,000	80,000	Kimmel Bogrette
Rhode Island											
Johnston	29	M	3,240,000	2,590,000	11,400	227	300,000	Owned	350,000	60,000	Thomas Lonardo & Associates
Texas											
Austin	50	M	6,886,000	3,700,000	10,120	366	611,000	571,000	2,004,000	70,000	hatch + ulland owen
Dallas	82	B	4,626,229	3,781,229	20,800	182	325,000	Owned	520,000	1,086	Hidell & Associates
Dallas	60	B	6,842,420	4,050,000	18,000	225	356,155	907,634	1,548,631	63,695	DSGN Associates
Fort Worth	700	B	5,385,000	2,800,000	13,038	215	1,800,000	Owned	785,000	34,000	Komatsu Architecture
Irving	70	B	8,175,903	6,995,903	25,600	273	550,000	Owned	630,000	1,345	Hidell & Associates
San Antonio	54	B	9,384,200	4,985,000	17,000	293	400,000	3,049,200	950,000	5,292	Marmon Mok
San Antonio	128	B	7,157,000	5,300,000	16,450	322	400,000	570,000	887,000	4,320	Kell Muñoz
Seabrook	19	B	5,902,656	4,539,337	21,090	215	869,000	Owned	494,349	60,000	English Associates
Waco	35	B	5,906,990	2,013,766	32,196	63	459,091	2,885,370	548,763	145,000	RBDR, Inc.
Wylie	41	M	13,290,000	10,570,000	43,500	243	803,000	Owned	1,917,000	93,100	Holzman Moss Bottino

Symbol Code: B=Branch Library; BS=Branch and System Headquarters; M=Main Library; MS=Main and System Headquarters; S=System Headquarters; O=combined use space; n.a.=not available

Utah										
Herriman	M	5,902,412	4,015,454	20,000	201	894,803	Owned	992,155	120,000	EDA Architects
Magna	M	8,080,703	4,428,955	20,000	221	1,067,911	396,719	2,187,118	120,000	CRSA
Virginia										
Fredericksburg	B	10,531,218	9,641,218	30,775	313	n.a.	Owned	890,000	200,000	Lukmire Partnership
Washington										
Bellevue	B	2,779,000	1,604,000	10,000	160	630,000	Leased	545,000	55,700	ZGF Architects
Maple Falls**	B	408,570	195,544	3,120	63	6,839	163,903	42,284	8,450	KGA Architect
University Place***	O	2,939,146	1,697,449	10,000	170	289,486	Owned	952,211	80,000	Koppe-Wagoner Architects
Vancouver	MS	38,000,000	24,000,000	75,000	320	3,000,000	Owned	11,000,000	385,000	Miller Hull Partnership
Wisconsin										
Fitchburg	M	14,000,000	9,000,000	57,000	158	4,000,000	Owned	1,000,000	100,000	Engberg Anderson

* The building site is operated by a nonprofit, to which the municipality has a long-term lease for $1.

** Building owned by the Friends of the Library; land owned by the Whatcom County Library System.

*** Joint-use space with library, city hall, and retail establishments. Figures refer just to library expenditure.

Symbol Code: B=Branch Library; BS=Branch and System Headquarters; M=Main Library; MS=Main and System Headquarters; S=System Headquarters; O=combined use space; n.a.=not available

Table 6 / Public Library Buildings, Additions and Renovations, 2011

Community	Pop. ('000)	Code	Project Cost	Const. Cost	Gross Area (Sq. Ft.)	Sq. Ft. Cost	Equip. Cost	Site Cost	Other Costs	Volumes	Architect
Alaska											
Kenai	14	M	$6,203,376	$5,173,694	22,225	$233	$179,201	Owned	$850,481	7,284	ECI/HYER Architecture
Arizona											
Phoenix	128	MS	1,245,200	881,200	10,000	88	45,000	Owned	319,000	722,402	Will Bruder & Partners
Phoenix	122	B	446,400	332,900	9,000	37	38,000	Owned	75,500	74,380	Durkin + Durkin Architects
Phoenix	149	B	315,700	194,000	11,000	18	30,000	Owned	91,700	62,794	Wendell Burnette Architects
Tempe	170	M	8,000,000	5,725,000	100,000	57	1,285,000	Owned	990,000	350,000	Engberg Anderson
Arkansas											
Little Rock	20	B	744,382	671,284	8,500	79	35,000	Owned	38,098	30,000	Ruby Architects
California											
Alameda	6	B	978,290	627,828	2,700	233	129,432	Owned	221,030	19,267	Noll & Tam
Alameda	19	B	1,233,979	776,291	3,400	228	130,174	Owned	327,514	20,841	Noll & Tam
Castro Valley*	66	B	1,700,000	1,700,000	n.a.	n.a.	0	Owned	0	166,000	Noll & Tam
Fullerton	135	M	10,784,000	7,187,300	61,898	116	375,000	Owned	3,221,700	400,000	LPA, Inc.
Palo Alto	8	B	3,151,000	2,196,000	8,774	250	276,000	Owned	679,000	21,500	Group 4 Architecture
Palo Alto	7	BS	1,500,215	1,293,363	2,392	541	49,218	Owned	157,634	12,000	Dept. of Public Works
Sacramento	47	B	333,659	239,972	10,000	24	57,833	Owned	35,854	72,000	Rainforth Grau Architects
San Francisco	23	B	8,226,324	4,737,633	8,222	576	500,000	Owned	2,988,691	3,763	SF Dept. of Public Works
San Francisco	17	B	5,910,462	3,438,974	6,376	539	500,000	Owned	1,971,488	2,594	SF Dept. of Public Works
San Francisco	30	B	3,398,893	1,768,922	8,825	200	500,000	Owned	1,129,971	2,371	Field Paoli
San Francisco	21	B	5,199,217	3,189,198	6,890	463	500,000	Owned	1,510,019	2,582	THA & Karin Payson
San Francisco	16	B	4,681,646	2,498,767	10,205	245	500,000	Owned	1,682,879	2,519	Field Paoli
Scotts Valley	12	B	4,071,629	2,495,603	13,150	190	368,026	Leased	1,208,000	64,500	Group 4 Architecture

Symbol Code: B=Branch Library; BS=Branch and System Headquarters; M=Main Library; MS=Main and System Headquarters; S=System Headquarters; O=combined use space; n.a.=not available

Location										Architect
Colorado										
Commerce City	46	B	2,164,062	1,456,000	8,870	164	467,765	Owned	240,297	38,000	Humphries Poli
Denver	43	B	2,176,882	1,682,888	10,000	168	276,106	Owned	217,888	30,000	Humphries Poli
Sterling	14	M	2,544,202	2,042,009	17,000	120	265,131	Owned	237,062	68,000	Humphries Poli
Connecticut										
New Haven	129	MS	664,745	294,745	10,195	29	320,000	Owned	50,000	n.a.	New Haven Office City Engineer
District Of Columbia										
Washington	20	B	22,743,625	17,184,125	24,000	716	766,835	Owned	4,792,665	80,000	Martinez & Johnson
Washington	20	B	14,585,000	10,259,494	19,500	526	700,000	Leased	3,625,506	80,000	Franck & Lohsen Architects
Florida										
Miami	28	B	2,165,609	1,505,918	6,282	240	588,835	Owned	70,856	32,365	Richard George & Associates
Miami Springs	22	B	1,524,932	914,956	3,480	262,92	567,790	Owned	42,186	18,332	Office Elements
Palm Bch. Gardens.	85	B	11,444,337	8,714,953	40,000	218	1,481,943	Owned	1,247,441	11,800	PGAL
Georgia										
Blairsville	25	B	2,590,000	1,903,000	13,300	143	375,000	Owned	312,000	36,000	Bailey Associates
Canton	75	MS	1,402,191	956,625	31,100	31	297,907	Owned	147,659	88,000	Professional Design; Craig Caulden
Idaho										
Boise	25	B	250,000	205,000	16,877	12	40,000	Leased	5,000	35,000	habitec
Rexburg	36	M	3,920,000	2,550,000	26,000	98	860,000	$110,000	400,000	100,000	CRSA
Illinois										
Chicago	81	O	3,442,736	2,000,128	13,300	150	260,431	Owned	1,182,177	50,000	Interactive Design Eight
Libertyville	60	M	6,658,058	5,647,462	46,120	122	443,082	Leased	567,514	185,246	Studio GC
Peoria	115	M	10,323,562	8,459,656	94,080	90	841,568	Owned	1,022,338	16,344	Farnsworth; Dewberry
Indiana										
Kokomo	76	MS	4,230,263	3,420,910	45,000	76	237,090	Owned	572,263	200,000	krM Architecture+
Iowa										
Dubuque	60	M	6,346,305	4,837,130	46,904	103	432,000	Owned	1,077,175	12,627	OPN Architects
Mason City	27	M	9,372,851	6,960,447	44,419	157	558,805	Owned	1,853,599	120,000	Holabird & Root

Symbol Code: B=Branch Library; BS=Branch and System Headquarters; M=Main Library; MS=Main and System Headquarters; S=System Headquarters; O=combined use space; n.a.=not available

Table 6 / Public Library Buildings, Additions and Renovations, 2011 *(cont.)*

Community	Pop. ('000)	Code	Project Cost	Const. Cost	Gross Area (Sq. Ft.)	Sq. Ft. Cost	Equip. Cost	Site Cost	Other Costs	Volumes	Architect
Maine											
Biddeford	22	M	298,726	233,466	7,720	30	37,012	Owned	28,248	5,986	Oak Point Associates
Presque Isle	10	M	1,500,000	n.a.	17,500	n.a.	40,000	Owned	n.a.	n.a.	Northpeak Architecture
Maryland											
Cockeysville	64	B	1,994,016	1,213,978	25,500	48	422,972	Owned	357,066	159,838	Hord Coplan Macht
Massachusetts											
Boston	70	B	4,330,000	3,900,000	22,368	174	370,000	Owned	60,000	41,500	Johnson Roberts Associates
Springfield	29	B	1,512,428	241,865	17,141	14	344,403	850,000	76,160	26,000	Jablonski/Devriese
Michigan											
Monroe	145	M	2,700,000	2,170,000	31,000	70	300,000	Owned	230,000	140,000	Fanning/Riemenschneider
Minnesota											
Burnsville	60	B	2,684,000	2,111,000	26,775	79	404,000	Owned	169,000	11,829	Wold Architects
Minneapolis	28	B	4,411,963	2,850,079	16,900	169	356,050	Owned	1,205,834	50,653	Cuningham Group
Minneapolis	20	B	5,057,625	3,615,950	17,340	209	385,240	Owned	1,056,435	46,143	DLR Group
Mississippi											
Pearlington	4	B	818,223	668,223	7,218	93	90,000	Owned	60,000	10,000	Dean & Dean Architects
Missouri											
Kirkwood	26	M	5,111,250	4,615,014	24,152	191	238,325	Owned	257,911	87,000	Bond Wolfe Architects
Nebraska											
Omaha	15	O	972,972	853,682	7,412	115	30,790	Owned	88,500	36,925	RDG Planning & Design
Scottsbluff	15	M	3,885,000	2,900,000	22,000	132	435,000	Owned	550,000	100,748	Leo A. Daly
New Jersey											
Hackettstown	9	M	238,980	205,380	3,665	56	0	Owned	33,600	n.a.	Arcari & Iovino
Mahwah	26	M	1,691,626	1,407,446	7,000	201	113,192	Owned	170,988	210	Montoro Architectural
Maywood	9	M	222,966	188,366	585	322	0	Owned	34,600	n.a.	Arcari & Iovino

Symbol Code: B=Branch Library; BS=Branch and System Headquarters; M=Main Library; MS=Main and System Headquarters; S=System Headquarters; O=combined use space; n.a.=not available

Monmouth Junction	3	B	339,137	308,737	5,800	53	0	Owned	30,400	n.a.	Arcari & Iovino
Ramsey	15	M	4,248,120	2,823,378	14,000	202	758,253	Owned	666,489	90,000	Lothrop Associates
Swedesboro	3	B	1,327,084	1,102,505	6,500	169	112,000	Owned	112,579	1,129	Compass Architectural Design
New York											
Brooklyn	100	B	5,250,000	4,255,000	7,300	583	250,000	Owned	745,000	1,137	Vincent Benic Architect
Commack	24	B	4,018,470	3,478,367	13,074	266	250,000	Owned	290,103	5,700	BBS Architects
Jamaica	2,500	M	37,624,250	30,230,000	23,500	1,286	2,809,250	Owned	4,585,000	70,000	1100 Architect
Mamaroneck	18	M	19,546,000	12,646,000	33,000	383	800,000	Owned	6,100,000	120,000	BKSK Architects
Nesconset	17	BS	6,966,852	6,166,312	25,535	241	308,840	1	491,699	5,883	BBS Architects
New York	1,630	M	48,915,342	44,691,985	n.a.	n.a.	0	Owned	4,223,357	n.a.	Wiss, Janney, Elstner
Oakland Gardens	27	B	2,679,410	1,986,915	7,500	265	495,385	Owned	197,110	69,500	Belfiore Architects
Patchogue	51	M	1,082,115	714,510	10,000	71	169,259	Owned	198,346	85,000	H2M
Saugerties	20	M	7,254,213	4,886,389	13,162	371	586,972	400,000	1,380,852	4,608	Butler Rowland Mays
North Carolina											
Charlotte	920	B	3,296,060	2,650,000	18,550	143	321,060	Owned	325,000	4,519	Gantt Huberman
Sylva	40	O	8,844,549	6,755,431	26,000	260	1,500,000	Owned	589,118	5500	McMillan	Pazdan	Smith
Ohio											
Arlington	5	B	144,700	129,700	810	160	0	Owned	15,000	4,500	RCM Architects
Circleville	56	M	3,939,875	2,728,050	24,256	112	441,175	Owned	770,650	11,817	HBM Architects
Lorain	70	MS	683,458	442,707	5,000	89	190,751	Owned	50,000	321,661	Arkinetics Inc.
Shaker Heights	33	MS	823,240	659,596	5,813	113	57,008	Owned	106,636	n.a.	Van Dyke Architects
Pennsylvania											
Pittsburgh	45	B	8,690,000	5,200,000	40,000	130	690,000	1,000,000	1,800,000	84,808	EDGE Studio
Rhode Island											
Scituate	8	M	1,600,000	1,177,800	7,925	149	222,000	Owned	200,200	35,000	LLB Architects
Westerly	23	M	6,924,000	4,871,000	50,000	97	760,000	Owned	1,293,000	12,800	Tappé Associates

Symbol Code: B=Branch Library; BS=Branch and System Headquarters; M=Main Library; MS=Main and System Headquarters; S=System Headquarters; O=combined use space; n.a.=not available

Table 6 / Public Library Buildings, Additions and Renovations, 2011 *(cont.)*

Community	Pop. ('000)	Code	Project Cost	Const. Cost	Gross Area (Sq. Ft.)	Sq. Ft. Cost	Equip. Cost	Site Cost	Other Costs	Volumes	Architect
Texas											
Austin	45	B	146,261	132,561	8,320	16	13,700	Owned	0	70,000	Austin PL Library Facilities
Bedford	49	M	9,404,360	7,894,360	40,516	195	925,000	Owned	585,000	1,947	Hidell & Associates
Colleyville	24	M	755,788	561,482	10,800	52	130,306	Owned	64,000	1,544	Hidell & Associates
Houston	37	B	4,650,355	3,391,172	12,116	280	835,703	Owned	423,480	3777	James Ray Architects
Houston	55	B	983,968	721,355	8,391	86	138,000	Owned	124,613	3,564	Bailey Architects
Hurst	39	M	4,422,939	3,877,939	16,000	242	220,000	Owned	325,000	n.a.	Hidell & Associates
San Angelo	108	MS	19,187,301	12,472,079	82,500	151	1,492,589	3,400,000	1,822,633	8,400	Holzman Moss Bottino
Virginia											
Glade Spring	2	B	607,125	423,137	3,500	121	99,274	56,100	28,614	8,770	Beeson & Beeson
McLean	52	B	6,740,600	4,605,000	19,046	242	680,600	Owned	1,455,000	55,000	Bowie Gridley Architects
Richmond	23	B	773,652	370,733	6,000	62	253,459	Owned	149,460	30,000	Fanning Howey
Richmond	29	B	1,054,460	598,066	5,500	109	255,044	Owned	201,350	35,000	Fanning Howey; Rawlings Wilson
Washington											
Bellevue	20	B	3,493,000	2,439,000	8,690	281	612,000	Owned	442,000	56,500	Miller Hull Partnership
Milton	16	B	1,563,661	1,050,338	6,300	167	184,961	Leased	328,362	29,000	SHKS Architects
Wisconsin											
Fort Atkinson	19	M	5,500,000	3,620,000	33,000	110	665,000	117,030	1,097,970	154,000	Uihlein-Wilson Architects

* This LEED Gold project added 880 solar panels to the roof, providing 100 percent of the building's power.

Symbol Code: B=Branch Library; BS=Branch and System Headquarters; M=Main Library; MS=Main and System Headquarters; S=System Headquarters; O=combined use space; n.a.=not available

Expenditures for Resources in School Library Media Centers: 2010–2011

Lesley Farmer

Results of the *School Library Journal* (*SLJ*) spending survey for 2010–2011 show that the picture remains bleak. Librarians, especially in the West, are still struggling to get by on bare-bones budgets. Media specialists are still battling to keep pace with a slew of additional duties—everything from serving as student advisers to maintaining their buildings' online networks. And although most school libraries' doors remain open 35 to 40 hours a week, about 1 in 7 are open 20 hours per week or less.

On the other hand, book collections have grown slightly since the previous year's survey, media specialists' salaries in the survey sample have climbed 10 percent, and—perhaps best of all—there are signs that the worst of the budget cuts may be behind us.

School librarians who responded to the survey have used these tough times as a clarion call to action. It's time to "show your staff and students what you can do, don't just tell them," wrote a Texas elementary school librarian. "Don't wait for an invitation. Know the curriculum and how to use it!"

Other media specialists urged their colleagues to turn up the volume about the key role that school libraries play in boosting kids' academic achievement. "Speak at school board meetings and community forums," suggested a Pennsylvania high school librarian. "Get yourself on the schedule to speak to incoming students and their parents. Toot your own horn whenever possible (not something most librarians are comfortable doing, but you have to!). Get on state and local committees to review resources, or review for a journal and let administration know that you're donating those resources to the library." Such actions are essential to the profession's survival during these challenging times.

Budgets Still Dropping

School library media center (LMC) budgets have declined on average since *SLJ*'s 2009–2010 survey, and media specialists expect even more cuts this year. Those who work in elementary and middle schools reported a dip of 4.8 percent in their budgets. The situation was slightly better for high school librarians, who reported budget declines of 3.4 percent. Although budgets are expected to fall in 2012–2013, the cuts aren't likely to be as deep, with budgets for elementary schools expected to slump by an additional 2.9 percent, middle schools by 4.6 percent, and high schools by 2.4 percent. The picture is brightest in the Northeast, where school library budgets dropped by a comparatively low 2.9 percent, and dimmest in the West, where they plummeted 9.3 percent. Overall, those figures are consistent with trending seen in *SLJ*'s last couple of spending surveys.

Lesley Farmer coordinates the librarianship program at California State University, Long Beach.

Adapted from *School Library Journal*, March 2012

In some areas, private school libraries have outshone their public school counterparts. For example, although private schools' library budgets slipped 2.9 percent, public schools' dropped 6.1 percent. And while public schools spent $7.86
per student annually (down from $8.68 reported in last year's survey), private
schools spent nearly twice that amount, or $15.63 (compared with $20.96 the year
before).

Table 1 / Trends in Library Media Center Budgets

	Elem. school	Middle school	High school	Public school	Private school	Midwest	Northeast	South	West/ Mountain
Net change 2010–2011 to 2011–2012	-4.9%	-4.8%	-4.8%	-6.1%	2.9%	-2.4%	-2.9%	-5.7%	-9.3%
Projected change 2012–2013	-2.9%	-4.6%	-2.4%	-4.1%	4.2%	-2.1%	-1.8%	-1.2%	-9.9%

Source: *SLJ* School Library Spending Survey, 2012.

The bottom line? The median total school library budget was $7,000, ranging
from $4,485 in the West to $9,000 in the Northeast, and from $4,670 for elementa-
ry schools to $12,500 for high schools. That's a change from our previous survey,
when the median LMC budgets were $5,177 for elementary schools, $6,023 for
middle schools, and $12,485 for high schools. The mean figures in our most recent
report were sometimes as much as $4,000 higher, indicating that a few LMCs have
appreciably deeper pockets than the vast majority of their counterparts.

As mentioned earlier, most school libraries stay open between 35 and 40
hours a week. But parsing the data yields a less rosy picture: about 1 in 7 LMCs
were open roughly half that time or less—and that includes one-fifth of elementary
schools. One-tenth of LMCs in middle schools, high schools, and private schools
were open less than half the school day. Roughly 80 percent of LMCs reported no
change in hours.

Staffing and Salaries

Salary is one area in which public school librarians came out on top, with the median salary of head public school librarians at $55,000, compared with $43,000 for
those in private schools. In terms of dollars, media specialists in the Northeast led
the pack with a median salary of $68,000. And although overall salaries reported
in the survey were up 10 percent from the previous year, middle school and high
school librarians' earnings remained flat.

Almost 90 percent of respondents were full-time credentialed school librarians, although the number dips to 79 percent at the elementary school level and to
75 percent in private schools. Almost one-fourth of high schools had two or more
full-time school librarians. Part-time media specialists usually worked around 20
hours a week. Compared with the previous year, the professional staffing rate was
stable for 94 percent of LMCs.

A little more than half of public school respondents said they had a district-level library media coordinator or director, with three-fourths of them working full time. Districts in the Northeast and Midwest were least likely to have a coordinator or director (45 percent and 47 percent, respectively), while 54 percent of media centers in districts in the West and 70 percent of those in the South had one.

As for support staff, about one-third of LMCs had a full-time clerk (about 4 percent had two), with the positions mostly found in the Midwest (49 percent) or the South (44 percent). Media centers in the West (43 percent) and Northeast (38 percent) were more likely to employ a part-time clerk or aide, and private schools were the least likely to have one.

As a result of budget cuts, many school librarians have turned to adult volunteers for help. Overall, almost half (about 46 percent) of LMCs had adult volunteers, and two-thirds of elementary schools and three-fourths of private schools had an average of five and six volunteers, respectively. Only one-third of middle schools and a quarter of high schools had adult volunteers, since students' parents often aren't as involved in the upper grades. Three-fourths of school libraries saw no change in volunteer trends, but the remaining quarter experienced a net increase, particularly in the Midwest (23 percent) and middle schools (22 percent) where LMCs are finding alternative ways to staff the media center.

As student volunteers go, the usual patterns persisted: one-third of elementary schools, two-thirds of middle schools, and almost three-fourths of high schools used student helpers. Elementary schools averaged three volunteers, and middle and high schools twice that number. Only one-third of private schools had student volunteers (and averaged just two), probably because the responding schools serve mostly younger students.

In terms of regional representation, about two-thirds of western LMCs had student volunteers, compared with 56 percent in the Northeast and South, and 45 percent in the Midwest. But the average number of student volunteers per region reflected a different pattern, with a mean of three helpers in the Midwest, four in the West, and five in the Northeast and South.

Roles Broaden

Lean budgets and worries over possible layoffs have prompted many school librarians to volunteer—or administrators have asked them to "volunteer"—for additional duties. On the bright side, some new duties also stretch the potential impact of the person in the role. For instance, media specialists now routinely teach classes: about 89 percent say they offer instruction, although it's unclear if they're teaching traditional library classes or classroom courses. Elementary school librarians tend to teach the most (95 percent) and those in high schools the least (83 percent). About one-sixth of librarians also tutor students, with roughly 24 percent of private school librarians leading the way. When it comes to tutoring, there are also significant regional differences, with only 6 percent of Midwest media specialists offering that type of instruction, compared with 17 percent in the Northeast, 22 percent in the South, and 23 percent in the West.

Table 2 / Library Media Specialists' Top Tasks

	Total	Elementary school	Middle school	High school	Public school	Private school
Teaching classes	89%	95%	86%	83%	89%	88%
Tech troubleshooting	60	52	64	71	64	36
Faculty development	52	54	46	58	53	44
Yard, recess, bus, or lunch duty	33	52	30	10	33	28
Other tech duties	28	30	27	26	29	20
Tutoring	17	18	17	17	17	24
Textbooks	14	12	12	17	14	14
Network maintenance	4	3	5	3	4	2
Other duties	28	31	29	23	27	36

Source: *SLJ* School Library Spending Survey, 2012.

Overall, 60 percent of survey respondents also engaged in technology troubleshooting, including 52 percent of elementary school librarians, 64 percent of middle school media specialists, and 71 percent of those in high schools. Interestingly, only a third of private school media specialists handle that task, compared with two-thirds of their public school counterparts. About a quarter of school librarians also had other tech responsibilities, especially those in the South, where the figure was about a third. Again, private school librarians were least likely to have additional tech duties—approximately one-fifth.

Slightly more than half of all media specialists conduct professional development programs, although that percentage sinks to 44 percent in private schools.

As one might expect, elementary school librarians (52 percent) were at the top of the heap when it comes to covering playground duty or breaks—which makes us wonder how their media centers can possibly remain open during those times. Only 28 percent of private school librarians, who tend to work in K–8 schools, were responsible for supervising the playground and break times. About a quarter of school librarians also reported doing "other duties as assigned" (such as monitoring study halls, leading book fairs, and supervising morning announcements), particularly those in the South and in private schools (approximately one-third for each group). While it may appear that private school librarians are getting off a little easier—with more narrowly defined roles—than public school librarians, they're actually assuming many new duties that aren't traditionally associated with media specialists, such as serving as student advisers.

When asked for advice on how librarians can enhance their value as educators, many respondents mentioned the need to keep up to date with new developments, especially with the latest advances in technology. Several also encouraged librarians to learn about grants and how to write effective grant applications. Others brought up the importance of engaging in professional development opportunities (both at school and in professional associations) and staying current with the professional literature. Still other media specialists stressed the need to be proactive. "Find ways to become integrated into every course in the building," urged one school librarian. "Show your administrator what you are doing and how it reflects on student data. Make yourself the go-to person."

Another set of suggestions focused on sharing resources and forming partnerships, including networking with a variety of stakeholders, sponsoring book exchanges, and encouraging interlibrary loans. Respondents also urged libraries to host parent meetings, reading programs, and tutoring sessions. Some respondents reminded their peers to seek community sponsors for events and cultivate volunteers for the library. Several librarians also noted the need to volunteer for extra responsibilities, such as coordinating online learning and credit recovery programs.

Good old-fashioned competition also has a role to play, some noted. "Talk to other teacher-librarians in your state and find out how they got books, technology, etc. and formulate your own plan," recommended a Rhode Island librarian. "Don't be afraid to use a community's sense of healthy competition. For example, 'Town A has X and we don't. How do you feel about those children having a resource that our children don't? How can we work together to level the playing field?'"

Some Growth in Collections

Historically, the size of a school library's book collection has correlated positively with grade level and student enrollment. Elementary school LMCs have roughly 12,000 books on their shelves, middle schools around 13,000 titles, and high schools weigh in with 13,636 titles. Public school libraries edged out private, with an average of 12,500 volumes to 11,000, respectively. On the whole, book collections grew slightly, with a net increase of 200 titles each.

Table 3 / The State of Book Collections

	Elementary school		Middle school		High school	
	2009–2010	2010–2011	2009–2010	2010–2011	2009–2010	2010–2011
Total volumes (median)	12,111	12,000	12,000	13,000	13,966	13,636
Net number of books added to collection	200	152	100	243	196	150

Source: *SLJ* School Library Spending Surveys, 2012 and 2011.

The picture of LMCs' book expenditures is more varied. The median total book budget was $5,000, with elementary schools spending $4,500 and middle and high schools $6,000. Private school libraries spent a median of just $3,342, compared with $5,061 by public schools.

What was the average expenditure per pupil? The total for all school libraries was $11, which varied from $8 at the elementary level to $10 at the high school level, and ranged from $10 in the Midwest to $5 in the West. Private school libraries spent $16 per pupil, and public schools half that amount.

Reference collections have continued to shrink, possibly because some school librarians now put a greater emphasis on using subscription databases. Nevertheless, relative to the total collection, things were surprisingly stable. Although 1 percent to 2 percent of LMCs don't have a reference collection, elementary schools have a median of 100 volumes, middle schools 400, and high schools 1,000. LMCs

Table 4 / What School Libraries Spent Per Student

	Average Student enrollment		Total LMC budget (median)		Expenditure per student	
	2009–2010	2010–2011	2009–2010	2010–2011	2009–2010	2010–2011
Elementary school	540	558	$5,177	$4,670	9.58	8.36
Middle school	748	783	6,023	7,500	8.05	9.57
High school	1,269	1,258	12,485	12,500	9.83	9.93
Public school	806	890	7,000	7,000	8.68	7.86
Private school	477	422	10,000	6,600	20.96	15.63

Source: *SLJ* School Library Spending Surveys, 2012 and 2011.

in the Northeast had a median of 314 reference books, followed by those in the South with 280, the Midwest with 250, and the West with 200 volumes.

How many of those reference titles are digital? On average, about 6 percent. Surprisingly, the majority of LMCs don't have any digital reference works. Private schools boast an average of 9 percent digital reference books, compared with 6 percent for public schools. Elementary school collections average 5 percent, middle schools 7 percent, and high schools 8 percent. Among high schools there was a huge difference: 3.5 percent had reference collections in which the majority of titles were in digital format, but 50 percent of high schools didn't have a single digital reference title. The digital divide yawns (see Table 5).

Although digital books may be the rage, school libraries have been slow to join the party. About two-thirds of LMCs don't have any circulating e-books—ranging from four-fifths of elementary schools to about half of high schools. The difference between the mean (average) and median (the half-way point) was startling: an average 1,277 e-books, with 1,281 for elementary schools, 763 for middle schools, 1,741 for high schools, with a median of just 50 items. Nevertheless, overall spending for e-books rose an average of 8 percent over the previous year, with the greatest gains (around 14 percent) in high school libraries and in the Northwest and Midwest. E-book spending was pretty much flat in middle schools, the South, and the West.

Where are media specialists buying them? Fifty-seven percent of e-books come from Follett, with Gale/Cengage a distant second at 24 percent. About 11 percent of school libraries order directly from publishers, and other sources include NetLibrary and Barnes & Noble (8 percent each), Amazon (6 percent), OverDrive (4 percent), and public domain materials or other digital resources (28 percent).

How about e-readers? A full 84 percent of school libraries don't have any. For those LMCs fortunate enough to own some, the median number of digital devices is 12 (ranging from 10 in elementary schools to 20 in high schools). Not surprisingly, 84 percent of elementary school libraries that do have devices don't lend out their e-readers, while half of middle schools and two-thirds of high schools and private schools circulate theirs.

The overall budget for e-books remains small: an average of $275. Two-thirds of that money during the survey period came from local school board appropriations, another fifth came from federal funding, and the rest from local fund-raising efforts and gifts. Elementary schools and LMCs in the West fared the worst

Table 5 / The Latest On Digital Collections

	Elementary school	Middle school	High school
Percentage of LMCs with some digital reference	40%	45%	54%
Percentage of LMCs with circulating e-books	21%	39%	48%

E-book Spending on the RIse

	Elementary school	Middle school	High school
Net change in e-book spending since 2010–2011	+6.9%	-1.9%	+13.7%

E-readers Make Inroads

	Elementary school	Middle school	High school
Percentage of LMCs with e-readers	14%	12%	20%
Number of e-readers (median)	10	12	20
Percentage of e-readers that circulate	16%	56%	62%

Source: *SLJ* School Library Spending Survey, 2012.

(spending less than $70 on average for e-books), while private school LMCs did the best, with an average of $388.

As for the most popular e-readers, Nooks are the preferred choice in 50 percent of LMCs, with Kindles and iPads running neck and neck at about 40 percent, and Sony's e-Reader at 9 percent.

However, without the necessary infrastructure and hardware, e-book adoption remains purely a dream. One New York City elementary school librarian seemed to sigh as she wrote, "The reason I can't buy e-books is that the computers in my library are so old that the Web browsers don't load e-books. The Web browsers can't be updated until the operating systems on the computers are updated. That's why, even though I have $15,000 to spend from the Robin Hood Foundation, I spend $0 on e-books; no one will replace my computers. In such a high-poverty area, very few of my students have computer access at home either."

Digital Beyond Books

Sixty percent of LMCs spent money on Web-based information resources, averaging $1,509. Predictably, high school libraries racked up the biggest bill, averaging $3,259. Librarians in the Northeast and in private schools were also among the biggest spenders at $2,409 and $2,009, respectively. As expected, elementary school libraries were the most frugal in this category, spending just $373. More than 90 percent of the funding for online information resources came from local school boards.

Media specialists aren't spending much on audiovisual goods and services, such as CDs, DVDs, video players, digital cameras, camcorders, SMART boards, PDAs, and cable video streaming. The average amount they spent on these items was $510, with two-thirds spending a median of $100, and roughly 90 percent of those dollars came from local schools and districts. Curiously, librarians spend slightly more on the equipment needed to support audiovisual materials—an average of $668—than on the audiovisual products themselves.

About 56 percent of LMCs spent an average of $594 on computer software, although most libraries within that group laid out a miniscule amount, typically less than $200. Interestingly, the West fared best, spending an average of $974 on software (most likely on reading programs), and far outdistancing Midwest LMCs, which laid out an average of $358. Local school boards accounted for roughly 83 percent of the funding, with another 5 percent coming from federal funds and the balance from fund-raising activities.

School librarians are also reconsidering the desktop computer. On average, LMCs purchased just one desktop machine in 2010–2011, and 9 times out of 10 they used non-library funds to buy it. Media specialists plan to purchase the same number of desktops this year, which probably means they're just replacing existing machines. However, the other reason for the tiny number of desktop acquisitions is the rise of laptops and notebooks in LMCs: an average of 2.6 (2 in elementary schools, the South, and the West, compared with 6 in the Midwest). As with desktops, laptops are also bought with non-library funds more than 90 percent of the time, and LMCs anticipate buying only one or two laptops this year.

Tablets are also beginning to hit the scene, with LMCs likely to own one or two wireless devices. Most school libraries bought a tablet in 2010–2011, and they expected to buy another one this year, using non-library dollars.

Computer hardware was purchased by 56 percent of LMCs, averaging $1,182 per site. About two-thirds of the funds came from local school boards, with federal funding accounting for about 10 percent, and the rest coming from fund-raising activity.

If money talks, it's tough to tell if schools really value ethics and digital citizenship. Less than 5 percent of LMCs set aside funds for digital citizenship speakers or programs. Elementary school libraries (5 percent) were a little more likely than middle and high schools (3 percent each) to promote these programs. Private school LMCs (19 percent) were much more likely to allocate funding for ethics and digital citizenship than those in public schools.

Interestingly, almost 11 percent of school libraries used some kind of plagiarism software—about 7 percent of those in the Northeast and West and 3 percent in the Midwest and South. A strong positive correlation exists between plagiarism software and faculty workshops, which may imply that curative rather than preventative measures are being taken in regard to intellectual property issues.

Call to Advocate

Numbers, although important, tell only part of the story. When survey respondents were asked for a single piece of advice they'd like to share with their colleagues, the No. 1 suggestion was: Hang in there! The second most popular piece of advice: Advocate, advocate, advocate! Advocacy is an essential part of being a 21st century librarian—and not just for our own sakes, but for the sake of our students, our programs, and the teachers we work with. To that end, one media specialist encouraged her colleagues to take advantage of the American Association of

School Librarians (AASL), *SLJ,* and other sources of professional advocacy materials. Several respondents also urged peers to increase their visibility and tell the library story to stakeholders including other educators, administrators, parents, and school boards.

It was stressed that they must be ready to provide compelling evidence of how school libraries enhance student learning. It also never hurts, especially around budget or contract-renewal time, to have quantitative records of library usage (including records of circulation, individual and class visits, and space use), lessons taught, time spent on technology, staff requests, and student programs, links to library materials that support the school curriculum, evidence of the impact on student achievement, and a record of the increased cost of materials, items lost, extra duties performed, and tasks that can't be accomplished because of limited staffing or funds.

Remember, too, that it helps to keep things in perspective. "I've been a teacher-librarian for 28 years and budgets have been restrained for about 22 of those years," wrote a California middle school librarian. "We're always fighting for funding and recognition. Just remember that by working with students every day, we help educate them and assist them in becoming their best selves. No matter what the current fiscal crisis, we still foster in our students the love of reading, learning, and doing research. That makes all we do worthwhile."

About the Survey

This survey covers the 2010–2011 academic year. In November 2011 *SLJ* e-mailed its online survey to 6,500 school librarians. In total, 602 school libraries answered the survey; their representation by student enrollment or grade level doesn't differ significantly from a 2011 survey by the American Association of School Librarians (AASL): 41 percent elementary, 20 percent middle school, and 32 percent high school. The geographic spread is more evenly distributed than AASL's: 26 percent of the *SLJ* respondents were from the Northeast, 23 percent from the Midwest, 32 percent from the South, and 19 percent from the West and mountain states. The private sector proved to be an important source of information, with 65 respondents.

Book Trade Research and Statistics

2011: Another Year of Restructuring as Publishing and Bookselling Evolve

Jim Milliot
Co-Editorial Director, *Publishers Weekly*

The closing of Borders and the expansion of Amazon in 2011 reflected the two dominant trends: the acceleration of the growth in e-book sales and the decline in print book sales.

Once the nation's second-largest bookstore chain, Borders closed its final stores in September 2011 after an unsuccessful seven-month battle to try to reorganize under Chapter 11. The Borders bankruptcy went through several phases, starting with the closing of 220 stores, a search for a buyer for all or a portion of the remaining chain, and then liquidation. The decision to liquidate came at the end of July after one potential buyer for a portion of the chain failed to get the support of creditors for its plan.

Publishers were skeptical throughout the bankruptcy process that Borders could come up with a viable reorganization plan and preferred to see the chain close. Borders had hoped that publishers would return to selling to the chain on normal terms—something publishers refused to do, fearing the company would just go bankrupt again, costing them more money. In the end, publishers and landlords received about 10 cents on the dollar for money owed them by Borders.

Among the factors that led Borders to close was its lack of a meaningful e-bookstore and online bookstore to offset the decline in print book sales made through physical stores. In contrast, Amazon's e-book sales and print book sales continued to grow during the year, as did sales of digital reading devices. In the fall, Amazon introduced the Kindle Fire, a tablet meant to compete with Apple's iPad (at least in the digital reading space). Amazon also continued to lower the price of its e-ink Kindle devices with its lowest-priced model selling for $79.99. In addition, Amazon significantly increased its presence in the publishing field, forming Amazon Publishing and hiring former Time Warner Trade Books President Larry Kirshbaum to head the New York-based operation. At its Seattle headquarters, Amazon formed three new imprints: Montlake Romance, the mystery/thriller imprint Thomas & Mercer, and the science fiction/fantasy imprint 47North, which will release its first titles in 2012. In early December Amazon ramped up its presence in the children's book market with its purchase of Marshall Cavendish Children's Books, an acquisition that brought Amazon 450 titles.

Books-A-Million looked to take advantage of the closing of Borders by expanding its store footprint into eight new states through a combination of buying Borders stores and taking over closed Borders stores in 41 locations. The expansion, although it was accompanied by the closing of 21 outlets, put Books-A-Million stores in 31 states.

The demise of Borders left Barnes & Noble as the nation's lone national bookstore chain. But rather than look to expand its number of bricks-and-mortar outlets, B&N held its number of physical stores steady while putting more resources into its e-bookstore and family of Nook digital reading devices. B&N, which already had e-ink devices as well as Nook Color, introduced its own tablet, Nook Tablet, in the fall. B&N estimated that in its 2012 fiscal year digital content and hardware sales would be about $1.8 billion.

In other retailing developments, the multimedia chain Hastings Entertainment opened its own e-bookstores in the fall in an attempt to offset declining sales of print books.

Late in the year, Amazon launched the Kindle Owner Lending Library, a program that allows Amazon Prime customers to get one free e-book per month. None of the major trade houses put books in the program, and Amazon added books from smaller houses, sometimes without the permission or knowledge of the publishers. To entice smaller publishers and self-published authors into the program, Amazon created a $6 million fund that will make payments to authors based on the number of loans made. To participate in the program, publishers and authors need to give Amazon a 90-day exclusive on the e-books.

As publishing makes the transition from print to digital content, business models and rules are being rewritten, and, as is often the case, disruption led to litigation. In August the first of about a dozen class action lawsuits was filed against Apple and the largest trade publishers, charging that the companies had conspired to fix e-book prices through the adoption of the agency pricing model that allows publishers to set a price for a book and for which e-book retailers receive a 30 percent commission. The suits contend that such an arrangement inflates the price of e-books. The various lawsuits were consolidated in the U.S. District Court for the Southern District of New York with the law firm Hagens Berman named lead counsel. The European Commission also announced that it was investigating possible e-book price fixing, as did the U.S. Justice Department.

A long-running lawsuit brought by authors and publishers against Google's book-scanning program, thought to be settled at the end of 2010, was back in play after U.S. District Court Judge Denny Chin declined to ratify the revised settlement agreement in February. With the denial, publishers and authors began a new round of talks with Google to try to save the deal, but by the end of the year the Authors Guild had filed its own revised suit, while a hoped-for deal between publishers and Google had yet to materialize.

The Authors Guild filed a separate copyright infringement lawsuit against HathiTrust, a consortium of university libraries that has built a database of about 10 million digitized books scanned by Google. HathiTrust had planned to release 140 "orphan works" (copyrighted works for which a copyright holder cannot be identified or found) in digital form in October, but suspended that plan after it was discovered that several of the titles were ineligible because the copyright holders could easily be identified. HathiTrust said it would re-examine its book-identification procedures.

To fight digital piracy, John Wiley in November filed a copyright infringement suit against 27 "John Does" that it claimed were illegally copying ". . . For Dummies" titles through Bit Torrent file-sharing sites.

Library lending of e-books took a number of turns in the year. Kindle's lending program with OverDrive went live in September, offering e-book lending to 11,000 libraries. The major publishers, however, continued to be concerned about e-book library loans and only HarperCollins and Random House were allowing e-book loans of frontlist titles. Under Harper's terms however, libraries needed to buy new e-books after a particular title had been circulated 25 times.

The battle over collecting online sales tax heated up in 2011 as Amazon threatened not to build warehouses in states that passed sales tax legislation and/ or fired its affiliates in states where online sales tax bills were passed. The issue came to a head when California passed legislation to collect online sales tax, and other states followed suit. Amazon reached agreements with some states and said it would support federal online sales tax legislation, which Congress began to debate at the end of the year.

Digital Developments, Partnerships

Penguin, Hachette, and Simon & Schuster joined together in May to create Bookish, a Web site that will recommend and sell books, e-books, and audiobooks from all book publishers. Originally set to go live in September 2011, the launch of Bookish was delayed until spring 2012 following the appointment of a new CEO in the fall. Caroline Marks, formerly with Meredith, took over from Paulo Lemgruber, who resigned along with several of his top executives.

Other partnerships in the year involved the teaming up of technology and print companies. Kane Miller, the children's publishing division of Educational Development Corp. (EDC), teamed with the digital development company Demibooks to form the InkPad Press imprint that will let authors use its Composers platform to created digitally enhanced e-books in addition to print books. Earlier in the year EDC made an equity investment in Demibooks. The Random House Publishing Group and Blacklight Transmedia formed a partnership to create original transmedia intellectual properties as well as to coordinate the development of intellectual property material from other sources. Random also made a minority investment in Flat World Knowledge, publisher of digital and print-on-demand college textbooks. Perseus Books Group formed Argo Navis, a new unit to handle digital distribution and marketing for authors who want to self-publish their titles and who are represented by established literary agencies. Janklow & Nesbit and Curtis Brown were the first literary agencies to sign agreements with Argo Navis.

Hasbro and Ruckus Mobile Media signed a deal to jointly develop original mobile interactive storybook apps based on Hasbro brands. Ruckus also teamed with Scholastic to form the Scholastic Ruckus imprint, a joint venture that will publish a wide range of children's and YA content across a number of platforms and formats. Also in the children's area, Candlewick partnered with British independent publisher Nosy Crow to copublish its titles in print and digital format in the United States.

RossettaBooks teamed up with the Mayo Clinic to do a series of e-books based on Mayo content. The On Demand Company, parent company of the Espresso Book Machine, expanded into more outlets and struck deals with HarperCollins and Perseus Books Group to add thousands of backlist titles to the Espresso point-of-sale book printer.

Earlier in the year, Harper reached an agreement with R. R. Donnelley under which Donnelley will fulfill and ship orders for all new books while also serving as Harper's print-on-demand supplier in global markets. The Ingram Content Group launched Global Connect, a series of alliances to allow publishers to print books in overseas countries through Ingram's own facilities or through an affiliate partner. Books on Demand in Germany was its first partner. Ingram also struck various warehousing and inventory deals with several publishers. With O'Reilly Media, Ingram will use its print-on-demand facilities to replenish O'Reilly's backlist titles.

Most of the major trade houses accelerated the move from print catalogues to digital, with Random House announcing it would be using only digital catalogues by spring 2012.

People

Brian Napack resigned as president of Macmillan at the end of the year. He had joined the publisher in May 2006. Houghton Mifflin Harcourt ended a five-month search for a new CEO in September with the appointment of Linda Zecher, a vice president at Microsoft. Longtime Random House and Bertelsmann executive Richard Sarnoff, who also helped lead talks to reach a settlement in the Google book-scanning issue, left Bertelsmann to join the private-equity firm Kohlberg Kravis Roberts & Co. as a senior advisor. Mark Schoenwald, president and COO of Thomas Nelson, was promoted to CEO following the resignation of Michael Hyatt, who remained chairman of the publisher. At rival Zondervan, Scott Macdonald was named permanent CEO after serving as interim CEO. Robert Guth was named president and CEO of Reader's Digest. He had been a board member. Scott Lubeck resigned as executive director of the Book Industry Study Group (BISG) and joined the executive search firm Bert Davis. Len Vlahos, COO of the American Booksellers Association (ABA), was named to replace Lubeck at BISG. Michael Healy, who was director of the Book Rights Registry (BRR), joined the Copyright Clearance Center after the BRR failed to materialize following rejection of the Google Books settlement.

Niko Pfund was named president of Oxford University Press USA. Karen Rinaldi, after three years heading up Rodale's book group, left the company. Prior to her departure, Rodale vice president and publishing director Colin Dickerman left to go to Penguin Press, where he was named executive editor; following Rinaldi's exit, Pam Krauss, also an executive editor, returned to the Crown Publishing Group where she replaced Lauren Shakely in the top spot of Crown's Clarkson Potter group. Also within the Random House family, Betsy Mitchell, editor-in-chief of Del Rey for the past decade, took early retirement. Tricia Pasternak was promoted to editorial director of Del Rey Spectra. At "Little Random," Scott Shannon was named to the newly created position of senior vice president, publisher, digital content. The realignment of Random's Fodor's travel group led to the departure of longtime publisher Tim Jarrell. Crown Executive Editor John Glusman moved to Norton as editor-in-chief, succeeding Starling Lawrence, who was named editor at large.

Geoff Shandler was named vice president and editorial director at Little, Brown, stepping into a newly created position in which he will be tasked with expanding the Hachette imprint's nonfiction program. In a related promotion, Judy Clain was named editor in chief. Also at Hachette, Twelve publisher Susan Lehman stepped down after three months at the imprint, and was replaced by associate publisher Cary Goldberg. Joining Twelve as associate publisher was Brian McLendon, who moved over from Ballantine Bantam Dell. Aileen Boyle, former vice president and publisher at Simon & Schuster's flagship imprint, joined former boss David Rosenthal at his new Penguin imprint, Blue Rider Press, where she was named associate publisher. At Penguin's Penguin Press imprint, Scott Moyers was named publisher. Following the appointment of Larry Kirshbaum as head of its East Coast office, Amazon Publishing added editors in both New York and Seattle. Among those hired were Kelli Martin, who moved to Montlake Romance from Harlequin, and Ed Park, who was named general fiction editor in New York. Park had been an editor with the literary magazine *The Believer.*

Judy Hottensen resigned as publisher of Weinstein Books and returned to Grove/Atlantic as associate publisher. Jessica Tribble was promoted to publisher of Poisoned Pen Press. At Harper's imprint It Books, Carrie Kania stepped down to become an agent and Mauro DiPreta left to join Crown as editor-in-chief of its new Archetype imprint. Jill Lamar, head of Barnes & Noble's Discover Great New Writers program, was named editor-in-chief of Henry Holt in February, succeeding Marjorie Braman. Five months later, Lamar resigned and Gillian Blake was promoted to the position. Also at Holt, Barbara Jones was named executive editor.

National Book Network rehired Spencer Gale as national accounts manager, while promoting Jason Brockwell to director of sales. The moves followed the departures of Rich Freese as head of NBN and of sales director John Groton; Freese joined Recorded Books as president, while Groton moved to Innodata Isogen as account executive, e-book publishing. Nancy Miller was promoted to editor-in-chief of Bloomsbury USA from executive editor. Molly Barton, director of business development at Penguin, was promoted to vice president, digital publishing, business development, and strategy. Peter Miller was hired as director of publicity at Liveright & Company, W. W. Norton's dormant literary imprint that was being revived by executive editor Bob Weil. Miller was formerly with Bloomsbury and Walker & Company. Late in 2011 James Connolly was named publisher of Council Oak Books and began the process of moving the indie press from Tulsa to the San Francisco Bay area.

At Macmillan Children's Publishing Group, Angus Killick was named vice president and associate publisher. Ginee Seo was named children's publishing director at Chronicle Books. Josalyn Moran, who left her job as children's publishing director at Chronicle Books to become vice president of publishing at Albert Whitman in 2010, stepped down from that role at the end of the year.

In bookselling, Terry Finley was promoted to president of Books-A-Million, succeeding Clyde Anderson, who remained chairman. Joseph Lombardi resigned as CFO of Barnes & Noble. Former bookseller Shannon O'Connor was named manager of the ABC Children's Group at the American Booksellers Association.

Acquisitions

The biggest deal of the year—and the biggest in a number of years—was HarperCollins's surprise purchase of religion publisher Thomas Nelson for $200 million. Harper already owned Nelson's largest rival in the Christian publishing field, Zondervan. Nelson had been owned by a private equity firm that bought the company in 2006 for $473 million. A few weeks before it announced its purchase of Nelson, Harper made a much smaller deal, buying the independent publisher Newmarket Communications. Zondervan made its own smaller purchase in the summer, buying the Beginner's Bible line from Mission City Press.

Levy Home Entertainment, one of the largest distributors of books to mass merchandisers, changed hands in the year, acquired by Dennis Aboud, a one-time executive at Levy and managing partner in Treesdale Investments. Aboud was changing the name Levy to Readerlink Distribution Services to reflect his plan to add more digital distribution capabilities to the company.

Google acquired the restaurant guide publisher Zagat, explaining that Zagat would form the "cornerstone" of its local search offerings.

Random House divested two specialized publishers it had acquired when Peter Olsen ran the company. In July it sold illustrated publisher Monacelli Press back to founder Gianfranco Monacelli A month later Triumph Books was sold back to its president and founder Mitch Rogartz. Random House acquired the digital media agency Smashing Ideas, which has developed apps for Random's children's book group.

Bloomsbury Publishing acquired the academic and professional publisher Continuum for $32 million. With operations in both the United States and Britain, Continuum has annual sales of about $17 million. Fox Chapel Publishing made three acquisitions in 2011, adding about 300 titles in the do-it-yourself and hobby segments. The largest purchase was of Design Originals, publisher of 260 craft titles. Fox Chapel also bought the book publishing arm of Heliconia Press and Plain White Press. The Penguin Group acquired a 45 percent stake in Companhia das Letras, a 25-year-old publishing house founded by Luiz Schwarcz in São Paulo, Brazil. EBSCO Publishing acquired database and reference publisher H. W. Wilson. Greenleaf Books received a new round of funding from the private equity firm Noson Lawen Partners. F+W Media acquired Tyrus Books and hired its founder, Ben LeRoy, as publisher and community leader of a new vertical, F+W Crime. The imprint will publish a mix of e-books and print books.

A major technology deal in the book segment was the purchase of Kobo by the Japanese e-commerce company Rakuten Inc. for $315 million. Kobo, which manufactures digital reading devices as well as operating e-bookstores in a number of countries around the world, was launched by Canada's largest book retailer, Indigo Books & Music, but was looking for more financial resources to expand. Amazon acquired the British e-tailer The Book Depository. Launched in 2004, The Book Depository offers about 6 million titles for sale and ships to more than 100 countries. Nolo Inc., parent company of Nolo Press, was acquired by Internet Brands, a new online media company that operates online media, community, and e-commerce Web sites. The purchase price was $21 million. Worthy Publishing bought Freeman-Smith, a specialty publisher of gift books, devotionals, and custom projects. Cengage Learning bought the National Geographic Society's digital and print publishing educational unit. The Ingram Content Group expanded its digital textbook offerings with the acquisition of VPG Integrated Media, an interactive textbook producer based in Boston.

The private equity firm RLJ Equity Partners acquired Media Source Inc., parent company of *Library Journal, School Library Journal, Horn Book,* and the Junior Library Guild (formerly the Junior Literary Guild), a commercial book club devoted to juvenile literature. Abrams acquired SelfMadeHero, a British publisher of graphic novels. Baker & Taylor bought Bridgeall Libraries, a developer of software based in Glasgow, Scotland, that helps libraries manage their collections. The Japanese publishing giant Kodansha joined with Japanese printer Dai Nippon Printer to buy Vertical Inc., a publisher of Japanese prose fiction and nonfiction and classic manga in translation with offices in New York and Tokyo. Following the purchase, Kodansha closed Kodansha International.

Restructurings

The decline in both print book sales and number of physical bookstores prompted changes in the sales and marketing operations of most of the major houses. In addition to eliminating the sales rep who called on Borders, the publishers also shook up their overall sales divisions. Hachette Book Group was the first to make a move, cutting 11 sales positions and redrawing its sales territories. Simon & Schuster revamped its sales force during the year, eliminating ten positions and combining its field and national sales forces into a joint Retail Sales unit and creating a new Digital Sales operation. Simon & Schuster said it planned to hire several new marketing employees to increase its promotion of digital content as well as sales of print titles through online sales channels. Macmillan also revamped its sales operation, cutting six positions, but adding heads to the children's sales group and a position in merchandise sales. Penguin kept its sales force intact but gave its sales directors more responsibility for marketing, a change that was reflected in switching their titles from district sales managers to district sales and marketing managers.

The change at the retail level affected more than Borders. Nebraska Book Company, the nation's third-largest operator of college stores as well as a major distributor, filed for prepackaged bankruptcy at the end of June. Although the company expected a quick exit, it was still in Chapter 11 at the start of 2012. Leading independent Powell's Books of Portland, Oregon, laid off 7 percent of its unionized work force in January and made cuts in management late in the year. Joseph-Beth Booksellers filed for Chapter 7 and the regional Tennessee/Kentucky/Ohio chain's five stores were sold to two groups; prior to the auction, Joseph-Beth had closed three stores.

Two of the nation's largest educational publishing companies underwent extensive reorganizations in 2011. McGraw-Hill Education eliminated 550 jobs (10 percent of its work force) in December and cut 20 percent of its executives as part of its strategy to create a flatter, more agile company. The spin-off of McGraw-Hill Education from McGraw-Hill Companies was expected to be completed in

2012. McGraw-Hill Professional, like a number of its competitors, restructured its sales force to put more emphasis on selling digital content. Earlier in the fall, Houghton Mifflin Harcourt announced it was eliminating more than 200 positions and disbanding its education group. The HMH trade and reference group was not affected by the downsizing.

Reader's Digest completed another restructuring at the end of 2011, eliminating 150 positions across its worldwide operations. The cuts were in all business groups, including books, and were part of the company's strategy to refocus on its core "master brands," including *Reader's Digest, Taste of Home,* and *The Family Handyman.*

Marvel Comics laid off 11 employees, including three editors.

After selling off some of its titles to Berrett-Koehler Publishers and Paradigm, seven year-old PoliPoint Press closed in the summer. Canada's largest independent distributor, H. B. Fenn, went bankrupt and its imprint, Key Porter Books, suspended publication. Macmillan, a major Fenn distribution client, moved its Canadian business to Raincoast following the bankruptcy. Jordan Fenn, publisher of Key Porter, joined McClelland & Stewart as publisher of the new Fenn/McClelland & Stewart imprint.

Launches

An industrywide initiative took root in 2011 with the announcement of World Book Night U.S. (WBN US). Modeled after the original World Book Night held in Britain in 2011, WBN US aimed to give away 1 million copies of 30 selected books on April 23, 2012. The American publishing industry hopes the program will, in addition to providing positive press coverage of books and reading, boost sales of the selected titles—as occurred in the United Kingdom.

Responding to the dramatic decline in mass market paperback sales, Penguin announced a January 2012 launch for a new e-book imprint, InterMix. The imprint will focus on popular genres such as romance and mystery, publishing bestselling authors (Nora Roberts, for example) and new authors in $6.99 e-books. Harper's Avon Books imprint started Avon Impulse, a digital and print-on-demand publisher of novels and novellas. In another digital launch, Random House revived Bantam's Loveswept romance imprint as an e-books-only line that will feature reprints from the original Loveswept imprint as well as e-originals. Loveswept is a collaboration between Random U.S. and the Transworld unit of Random's British operation. Bloomsbury Publishing formed Bloomsbury Reader, a global digital publisher that publishes e-books and print-on-demand titles for authors who have regained publishing rights.

Random's Crown Publishing Group teamed with its British sister company Vintage Publishing to form Hogarth Books, an imprint that will publish 8 to 10 titles annually; Molly Stern will lead the imprint in the United States and Clara Farmer will head the British side. Abrams announced plans to launch a third children's imprint in spring 2012. Appleseed Books will be led by publishing director Cecily Kaiser and will produce 8 to 12 titles a year.

Algonquin Books launched a young adult line under the direction of Elise Howard, who had been at Harper Teen and Harper imprints. Prometheus Books' Pyr imprint also entered the young adult market with the launch of a new science fiction line published under the editorial direction of Lou Anders. At Atria Books, Emily Bestler, executive editorial director, was given her own imprint that launched in the spring. Penguin Press associate publisher Eamon Dolan returned to Houghton Mifflin Harcourt, where he was given his own imprint, Eamon Dolan Books.

William Morrow gave author Dennis Lehane his own imprint. Crown struck a similar deal with Deepak Chopra, who later in the year decided to publish a book with Amazon. At Harper, chef Anthony Bourdain was given his own line at Ecco—An Anthony Bourdain Book—that will do 3 to 5 titles a year. The Wharton School at the University of Pennsylvania launched Wharton Digital Press and signed with Perseus Books Group Constellation service to produce and distribute its titles; Wharton Digital plans to publish 25 to 30 titles annually.

The Hachette Book Group announced the creation of Jericho Books. Part of Hachette's Nashville division, Jericho will be led by Wendy Grisham, who has served as director of publishing for Hodder Faith, an imprint with Hodder & Stoughton, part of the Hachette UK federation. Regnery Publishing launched a history imprint under the direction of Alex Novak, Regnery associate publisher. Shambhala Publications created Roost Books, a lifestyle imprint. Simon & Schuster opened a new division in India, headed by S&S United Kingdom managing director Ian Chapman.

Amazon's Audible Inc. subsidiary launched ACX (ACX.com), an online audiobook rights marketplace, production platform, and online sales system. Officially known as the Audiobook Creation Exchange, ACX is aimed at increasing the number of audiobooks in the market by matching authors and other book-rights holders with actors, studios, and publishers. Tim Coates, former head of the British bookstore chain Waterstone's, announced plans for an early 2012 launch for Bilbary, a Web site that will sell e-books from publishers around the world. Harry Potter author J. K. Rowling announced plans to launch Pottermore, a Web site dedicated to her Potter franchise that will include the ability to buy e-books from the series for the first time. Originally set to launch in October, Pottermore's debut was delayed until 2012.

Bestsellers

Despite Stieg Larsson's Millennium Trilogy losing its grip on the *Publishers Weekly* bestsellers list in 2011, the year was still a good one for Larsson's American publisher, Random House. The country's largest trade publisher increased its share of *PW*'s bestsellers list in both the hardcover and paperback formats. (Bestsellers are based on print sales only).

Random House's performance was particularly impressive in the hardcover segment, where the company's market share rose by more than 10 percentage points to 31.4 percent. While the number of books that hit the hardcover list rose to 106 from 93 in 2010, the key to Random's 2011 gain was the number of weeks those titles spent on the list—in 2011 Random's bestsellers spent a combined 480 weeks on the hardcover list compared with 318 weeks in 2010. Random's strength in hardcover in 2011 is seen in the range of titles that stayed in the top 15 hardcover sellers: Larsson's *The Girl Who Kicked the Hornet's Nest* was on the list for 39 weeks, the longest of any title. *Hornet's Nest* was joined by *The Paris Wife* by Paula McLain and *A Dance with Dragons: A Song for Fire and Ice, Book 5* by George R. R. Martin, which had the second- and third-longest stays on the hardcover list. In nonfiction hardcover, Laura Hillenbrand's *Unbroken* was on the hardcover list for 50 weeks, while the second-longest run was 27 weeks for *The 17 Day Diet,* published by Free Press. Other Random titles that had extended stays were *The Dukantal Diet* (21 weeks), *In the Garden of Beasts* (22) and *The 4-Hour Body* (19).

Hachette Book Group took over second place in the hardcover rankings from Penguin even though its share fell from 18.3 percent to 16.2 percent; Penguin's share fell even more, dropping from 20.2 percent to 15.8 percent in 2011. And while the number of weeks Hachette's titles spent on the hardcover list fell, its number of bestsellers rose from 46 to 56. Its biggest bestseller was Tina Fey's *Bossypants.* Penguin's number of bestsellers also rose—by three to 86—but only *The Help* had an extended stay. Simon & Schuster and HarperCollins also lost market share to Random House, but stayed in fourth and fifth spots with S&S claiming an 11.1 percent share and HarperCollins an 8.2 percent share.

In paperback, Random House's share of the bestseller market rose to 29.5 percent from 24.2 percent. While its number of paperback bestsellers rose from 50 to 54, it was the length of time its books spent on the list that separated Random from its competitors. The company's paperbacks totaled 451 weeks on the paperback lists compared with 370 in 2010. Random's performance was helped by the paperback editions of Martin's Fire and Ice books with *A Game of Thrones, A Storm of Swords, A Clash of Kings,* and *A Feast for Crows* all spending at least 15 weeks on the mass market paperback list. (Martin's titles were aided in turn by the HBO series "Game of Thrones.") There was more variety on the trade paperback side with titles from a number of houses having extended bestseller stays. Thomas Nelson's *Heaven Is for Real* was on the list for 49 weeks and, along with Algonquin's *Water for Elephants,* was one of two titles from outside the "Big Six" publishers to place a bestseller on the paperback lists for a long run. Macmillan, the sixth-largest of the major houses, held even in paperback with a 7.0 percent share (and a 7.1 percent share in hardcover). Hachette managed to boost its paperback market share slightly for the year, from 12.7 percent to 12.9 percent, while Penguin, S&S, and Harper all saw their paperback shares decline.

Prices of U.S. and Foreign Published Materials

Narda Tafuri

Editor, ALA ALCTS Library Materials Price Index Editorial Board

The Library Materials Price Index (LMPI) Editorial Board of the American Library Association's Association for Library Collections and Technical Services' Publications Committee continues to monitor prices for a range of library materials from sources within North America and from other key publishing centers around the world.

The U.S. Consumer Price Index (CPI) increased 3.0 percent in 2011. This is the highest increase seen since 2007. Other indexes such as household energy, electricity, fuel oil, food, and apparel also experienced significant increases over 2010. During 2011 the average prices of serials, legal serials services, and British academic books saw the highest increases. Along with U.S. college books these categories all outperformed the CPI. In contrast, U.S. hardcover books, trade paperbacks, audiobooks, and e-books experienced dramatic declines in price. Mass market paperbacks did a little better but still underperformed the CPI. CPI data are obtained from the Bureau of Labor Statistics Web site at http://www.bls.gov.

The U.S. Periodicals Price Index (USPPI) (Table 1) has not been updated and is being repeated again from its initial publication in the 2010 article. It is hoped that this index will be re-established and made available in the future. Percent changes in average prices from previous years are noted in the chart below under the category "Periodicals."

The new Table 8 established last year by compiler Stephen Bosch has been continued in this year's article. The table, Average Price of Serials, is based on titles in select serials indexes and shows average price trends from 2008 through 2012. The table is based on titles indexed in ISI Arts and Humanities Citation Index, ISI Science Citation Index, ISI Social Sciences Citation Index, EBSCO Academic Search Complete, and EBSCO Masterfile Premier. It differs from the data that appear in the U.S. Periodicals Price Index (USPPI) by its inclusion of foreign serials prices as well as by using approximately three times the number of serials in its compilation. Changes in average prices from previous years are noted in the chart below under the category "Serials."

The Legal Serials Services Index (LSSI) established last year appears again this year as Table 2. The base year for this table is 2009. The British Academic Book index, also re-established last year, continues this year as Table 9.

A new index, U.S. E-Books, established by compiler Catherine Barr, is being introduced to track the general price trends of e-books. Data for this new index are being provided by Baker & Taylor. Changes in average prices for this index are noted in the chart below under the category "E-Books." Table 4A, "North American Academic E-Books" covers only those titles treated for academic library approval plan customers by Coutts Information Services and YBP Library Services. Changes in average prices for Table 4A are noted in the chart below under the category "Academic E-Books."

Readers should note that the data source for the North American Academic Books Index changed in 2009 and that this table is being indexed using combined

Table 1 / U.S Periodicals: Average Prices and Price Indexes, 2008–2010
Index Base: 1984 = 100

Subject Area	1984 Average Price	2008 Average Price	2008 Index	2009 Average Price	2009 Index	2010 Average Price	2010 Index
U.S. periodicals excluding Russian translations	$54.97	$436.90	794.8	$467.82	851.1	$497.63	905.3
U.S. periodicals including Russian translations	72.47	559.96	772.7	603.85	833.3	642.62	886.8
Agriculture	24.06	169.99	706.5	181.40	754.0	201.60	837.9
Business and economics	38.87	245.27	631.0	263.64	678.3	287.64	740.0
Chemistry and physics	228.90	2,333.37	1,019.4	2,482.16	1,084.4	2,622.14	1,145.5
Children's periodicals	12.21	29.98	245.5	33.43	273.8	35.87	293.8
Education	34.01	240.80	708.0	258.73	760.8	276.33	812.5
Engineering	78.70	688.98	875.5	734.14	932.8	786.72	999.6
Fine and applied arts	26.90	84.94	315.8	89.40	332.4	94.10	349.8
General interest periodicals	27.90	60.11	215.5	63.91	229.1	66.70	239.1
History	23.68	106.55	450.0	113.94	481.2	123.57	521.8
Home economics	37.15	225.51	549.5	246.26	600.1	260.64	635.1
Industrial arts	30.40	170.51	560.9	172.22	566.5	188.27	619.3
Journalism and communications	39.25	182.41	464.8	192.89	491.4	210.49	536.3
Labor and industrial relations	29.87	201.12	673.3	220.96	739.8	234.50	785.1
Law	31.31	141.02	450.4	149.04	476.0	157.88	504.2
Library and information sciences	38.85	161.15	414.8	172.63	444.4	179.80	462.8
Literature and language	23.02	96.35	418.5	102.92	447.1	109.32	474.9
Mathematics, botany, geology, general science	106.56	925.61	868.6	991.88	930.8	1,024.13	961.1
Medicine	125.57	1,224.41	975.1	1,317.81	1,049.5	1,427.56	1,136.9
Philosophy and religion	21.94	99.33	452.8	107.44	489.7	117.24	534.3
Physical education and recreation	20.54	81.79	398.2	87.73	427.1	91.48	445.4
Political science	32.43	241.37	744.3	261.05	805.0	273.80	844.3
Psychology	69.74	631.79	905.9	686.52	984.4	726.87	1,042.3
Russian translations	381.86	3,080.51	806.7	3,390.04	887.8	3,580.13	937.6
Sociology and anthropology	43.87	367.59	837.9	400.08	912.0	432.76	986.5
Zoology	78.35	911.89	1,163.9	980.66	1,251.6	1,047.35	1,336.8
Total number of periodicals							
Excluding Russian translations	3,731	3,728		3,728		3,728	
Including Russian translations	3,942	3,910		3,910		3,912	

Compiled by Brenda Dingley, University of Missouri, Kansas City, based on subscription information supplied by Swets Information Services.

data from Coutts Information Services and YBP Library Services. Prior years' data may not be applicable if compared with those presented with this year's table.

Index	Percent Change				
	2007	2008	2009	2010	2011
CPI	4.1	0.1	2.7	1.5	3.0
Periodicals	7.2	8.0	6.4	n.a.	n.a.
Legal serials services	n.a.	n.a.	n.a.	3.5	11.0
*Hardcover books	-39.00	2.81	0.34	5.54	1.07
+Academic books	1.1	3.9	-1.2	12.4	n.a.
+Academic e-books	n.a.	13.1	-18.4	13.7	n.a.
+Textbooks	n.a.	2.8	1.7	0.7	n.a.
College books	0.47	3.3	4.1	-2.3	4.6
*Mass market paperbacks	0.47	1.56	3.08	1.94	2.05
*Trade paperbacks	27.29	-9.75	-0.41	7.30	-12.08
*Audiobooks	8.44	11.39	9.88	-1.19	-4.25
E-books	n.a.	n.a.	-22.80	-6.07	-34.29
Serials	n.a.	7.7	8.3	3.8	9.2
British academic books	n.a.	n.a.	n.a.	-1.8	14.7

n.a. = not available
* = figures revised based on BISAC categories
+Beginning with 2009, new data source

U.S. Published Materials

Tables 1 through 7B indicate average prices and price indexes for library materials published primarily in the United States. These indexes are U.S. Periodicals (Table 1), Legal Serials Services (Table 2), U.S. Hardcover Books (Table 3), North American Academic Books (Table 4), North American Academic E-Books (Table 4A), North American Academic Textbooks (Table 4B), U.S. College Books (Table 5), U.S. Mass Market Paperback Books (Table 6), U.S. Paperbacks (Excluding Mass Market) (Table 7), U.S. Audiobooks (Table 7A), and U.S. E-Books (Table 7B).

Periodical and Serials Prices

The LMPI Committee and Swets Information Services jointly produced the U.S. Periodicals Price Index (Table 1). The subscription prices shown are publishers' list prices, excluding publisher discount or vendor service charges. This report includes 2008, 2009 and 2010 data indexed to the base year of 1984. Table 1 is compiled by Brenda Dingley using data provided by Swets Information Services. This index is being repeated from last year. It is hoped that an updated table will appear in next year's *Library and Book Trade Almanac.*

More extensive reports from the periodicals price index were published annually in the April 15 issue of *Library Journal* through 1992, in the May issue of *American Libraries* from 1993 to 2002, and in the October 2003 issue of *Library Resources and Technical Services.*

The Legal Serials Services Index (Table 2) was compiled by Ajaye Bloomstone using data collected from a number of different legal serials vendors. The base year for this index is 2009. This index presents price data covering the years

2009 through 2012. Vendors were asked to provide cost data on particular titles with the assumption that the title/set has been held by a large academic research law library, and the cost recorded in the index is that for upkeep of the title in question, *not* the cost incurred with purchasing a new set.

Table 2 / Legal Serials Services: Average Prices and Price Indexes, 2009–2012
Index Base: 2009 = 100

Year	Number of Titles	Average Price	Percent Change	Index
2009	217	$1,658.20	n.a.	100.0
2010	217	1,716.30	3.5	103.5
2011	217	1,905.20	11.0	114.9
2012	217	2,020.83	6.1	124.1

Finding serials publications available in print is challenging now and will undoubtedly become more challenging in the future as more of these publications migrate to an electronic-only status. Because the type of serial publication that is being tracked for this index is most commonly found in library collections—and not in private collections—vendors may be more likely to discontinue the print versions in favor of electronic versions. As the pool of available print titles becomes even smaller than it is now, there is concern that meaningful comparisons will become more difficult to make. Two titles used through 2011 have been discontinued, and one is no longer available in print. Titles in the same subject area have been substituted, trying to match the original titles' costs as closely as possible. The use of a new base year (2009) for this index shows smaller dollar amounts for the average costs than the previous base year used, in part because some of the more expensive materials may have already migrated to an electronic-only format. This lower dollar amount also reflects a smaller sample available.

As in the past, legal serials services titles were selected on the basis of their format: print, with the same continuing titles being tracked over time. In many cases, especially for U.S. state statutes and codes, there may be little or no consistency in the number of new volumes/revised volumes/updates/etc. that are published for any one title from any given year to the next, so the cost of those items may well bear no resemblance to the cost of the previous year(s).

Book Prices

Tables 3 (hardcover books), 6 (mass market paperbacks), 7 (other—trade—paperbacks), 7A (audiobooks), and new table 7B (e-books), prepared by Catherine Barr, are derived from data provided by book wholesaler Baker & Taylor. Figures for 2010 are revised to reflect late updates to the Baker & Taylor database (publishers were still adding 2010 titles in early 2011); the 2011 figures given here may be similarly revised in next year's tables and should be considered preliminary. These five tables use the Book Industry Study Group's BISAC categories; for more information on the BISAC categories, visit http://www.bisg.org.

Average book prices were again mixed in 2011. List prices for hardcovers (Table 3) rose only 1.07 percent after a climb of 5.54 percent in 2010. Mass market paperback prices (Table 6) continued their slow but steady increase, rising another 2.05 percent. In contrast, trade paperback prices (Table 7) lost ground in 2011, declining 12.08 percent after a surprising jump of 7.30 percent in 2010. Audiobook prices (Table 7A) saw drops of 1.19 percent in 2010 and 4.25 percent in 2011. And e-book prices (Table 7B) varied dramatically by category in 2011, with the children's and YA categories seeing large increases (up 43.49 percent and 75.33 percent, respectively), while other important categories such as fiction (down 24.79 percent) showed declines. There was an overall decrease of 34.29 percent in 2011.

The North American Academic Books Price Indexes (Tables 4, 4A, and 4B) are prepared by Stephen Bosch. The current version of North American Academic Books: Average Prices and Price Indexes 2008–2010 (Table 4) should not be compared with the versions published in 2009 or prior years. The North American Academic Books Price Index (NAABPI) now contains many more titles in the source data, which has impacted the index considerably. (In 2010 Blackwell Book Services was purchased by YBP Library Services. Blackwell and YBP had been the data sources for the index. Starting with 2009, the data sources will now be Coutts Information Services and YBP. The index was reconstructed back to 2007 using data from Coutts Information Services and YBP.) The year-to-year comparisons from 2007 onward are now based on this new data model, and the changes in price and number of titles are not as dramatic as when looking at comparable data in the indexes that were published prior to 2009.

There was a significant increase in the overall average price for books in the NAABPI for 2010 when compared with 2009. The average price of these books increased to $89.15 (2010) from $79.32 (2009), a 12 percent increase. The number of titles in the index remained relatively the same but the costs went up significantly. This index looks at all titles treated by approval book vendors including e-books, which have seen substantial price gains in 2010. This has affected the overall average price of North American Academic Books.

Since 2008 two additional indexes have been available, one for academic e-books only (Table 4A) and another for textbooks (Table 4B). Both of these indexes are of high interest to users and, based on that input, the indexes will continue to be published with the base index year set to 2007. In the academic market, it has always been assumed that e-books are more expensive than their print counterparts. Users might be surprised to find that the $9.95 versions of e-books, available to consumers through channels such as Amazon and the Apple Store are not available to libraries. The new index clearly points out the difference in price—the average price of an e-book in 2010 climbed to $116.25 while the average price for all books was $89.15. The average price for a print book dropped to $69.73. The price for e-books is not that surprising as most pricing models for academic e-books generally charge a large percentage of list print price for multiuser access to e-books. Responding to customer demands, vendors offer multiple platforms and pricing models for e-books; consequently there can be multiple prices for the same title. Only the first instance of a unique ISBN is included in the data, so if the same book was treated by a vendor from one e-book aggregator and then treated again from another aggregator, only the first instance of the e-book is in the index. Because electronic access is where the market is going, it is appropriate to have e-books as a separate index. It is also important to note that the e-book market is rapidly changing. This is reflected in the large swing in numbers of titles between

(text continues on page 492)

Table 3 / Hardcover Books: Average Prices and Price Indexes, 2008–2011
Index Base: 2005 = 100

BISAC Category	2005 Average Prices	2008 Final Volumes	2008 Final Average Prices	2008 Final Index	2009 Final Volumes	2009 Final Average Prices	2009 Final Index	2010 Final Volumes	2010 Final Average Prices	2010 Final Index	2011 Preliminary Volumes	2011 Preliminary Average Prices	2011 Preliminary Index
Antiques and collectibles	$71.07	195	$80.84	113.7	159	$46.98	66.1	179	$51.44	72.4	152	$53.64	75.5
Architecture	66.99	853	77.54	115.7	842	84.46	126.1	742	85.52	127.7	700	79.24	118.3
Art	62.33	1,681	84.79	136.0	1,688	75.13	120.5	1,687	71.53	114.8	1,678	75.03	120.4
Bibles	48.05	191	49.19	102.4	165	46.32	96.4	185	37.50	78.0	220	47.92	99.7
Biography and autobiography	46.20	1,714	57.55	124.6	1,652	50.08	108.4	1,658	53.41	115.6	1,588	50.66	109.7
Body, mind and spirit	26.76	233	26.12	97.6	194	27.60	103.1	177	36.91	137.9	136	30.38	113.5
Business and economics	120.56	3,581	134.29	111.4	3,913	123.46	102.4	3,977	134.61	111.7	4,127	132.21	109.7
Children	23.14	13,235	27.35	118.2	12,396	25.01	108.1	11,675	24.63	106.4	11,277	26.79	115.8
Comics and graphic novels	32.75	462	32.65	99.7	732	32.07	97.9	679	31.51	96.2	753	35.13	107.3
Computers	113.07	731	146.42	129.5	786	155.86	137.8	834	138.53	122.5	912	136.22	120.5
Cooking	28.68	1,015	29.99	104.6	814	29.54	103.0	1,016	30.91	107.8	956	29.65	103.4
Crafts and hobbies	28.82	267	27.57	95.7	237	29.94	103.9	217	33.28	115.5	216	30.70	106.5
Design	59.41	358	62.22	104.7	331	66.52	112.0	435	76.59	128.9	447	68.78	115.8
Drama	60.81	192	53.65	88.2	81	83.00	136.5	133	42.91	70.6	94	51.89	85.3
Education	95.10	1,330	111.90	117.7	1,392	105.56	111.0	1,345	117.59	123.6	1,397	118.46	124.6
Family and relationships	25.37	301	29.37	115.8	296	33.57	132.3	277	32.24	127.1	195	31.69	124.9
Fiction	28.37	4,976	29.03	102.3	4,556	28.78	101.4	4,464	32.20	113.5	4,169	29.61	104.4
Foreign language study	116.89	146	110.68	94.7	120	132.01	112.9	123	132.47	113.3	140	119.03	101.8
Games	32.07	145	39.16	122.1	167	37.48	116.9	163	52.07	162.4	96	36.63	114.2
Gardening	38.20	149	42.41	111.0	140	36.98	96.8	118	36.42	95.3	114	41.58	108.8
Health and fitness	54.05	449	61.08	113.0	356	50.78	94.0	309	48.51	89.8	326	61.99	114.7
History	88.17	4,795	87.46	99.2	4,687	84.41	95.7	4,927	82.65	93.7	4,618	83.49	94.7
House and home	31.51	117	40.85	129.6	113	40.44	128.3	90	44.61	141.6	93	38.00	120.6
Humor	19.00	241	20.42	107.5	229	20.24	106.5	221	21.94	115.5	195	19.66	103.5

Language arts and disciplines	120.71	1,300	133.45	110.6	1,485	131.36	108.8	1,613	117.67	97.5	1,541	116.38	96.4
Law	155.28	1,516	163.59	105.4	1,515	166.60	107.3	1,714	174.48	112.4	1,788	175.61	113.1
Literary collections	74.92	383	89.75	119.8	373	90.08	120.2	325	83.49	111.4	340	89.90	120.0
Literary criticism	123.84	1,707	106.08	85.7	1,903	108.05	87.2	1,955	117.63	95.0	2,053	119.86	96.8
Mathematics	144.88	916	127.81	88.2	895	117.08	80.8	1,028	133.23	92.0	1,079	128.77	88.9
Medical	156.54	3,076	154.91	99.0	2,924	165.92	106.0	3,153	171.13	109.3	3,096	163.77	104.6
Music	77.63	485	69.34	89.3	520	77.34	99.6	502	87.84	113.2	500	87.87	113.2
Nature	67.75	435	62.58	92.4	411	65.83	97.2	377	74.89	110.5	402	74.04	109.3
Performing arts	71.74	618	81.63	113.8	540	80.97	112.9	531	76.27	106.3	578	80.06	111.6
Pets	25.45	181	29.39	115.5	176	25.04	98.4	138	24.66	96.9	123	20.79	81.7
Philosophy	127.22	973	98.56	77.5	990	93.78	73.7	1,044	108.93	85.6	1,052	98.77	77.6
Photography	56.77	882	82.64	145.6	805	81.82	144.1	800	107.99	190.2	837	60.53	106.6
Poetry	36.58	339	42.50	116.2	293	45.48	124.3	294	40.76	111.4	241	39.62	108.3
Political science	103.39	2,492	97.13	93.9	2,698	108.10	104.6	2,671	110.32	106.7	2,687	106.94	103.4
Psychology	93.85	1,063	101.94	108.6	1,031	104.29	111.1	1,138	109.85	117.0	1,082	112.89	120.3
Reference	202.23	613	290.72	143.8	558	274.83	135.9	541	302.69	149.7	499	384.00	189.9
Religion	62.29	2,449	68.04	109.2	2,353	72.64	116.6	2,590	80.88	129.8	2,466	78.01	125.2
Science	203.44	3,171	204.74	100.6	3,161	190.41	93.6	3,557	192.20	94.5	3,590	189.92	93.4
Self-help	22.43	322	25.67	114.4	311	21.51	95.9	257	27.11	120.9	197	23.43	104.5
Social science	96.17	2,948	97.93	101.8	3,019	102.73	106.8	3,027	100.47	104.5	3,158	103.02	107.1
Sports and recreation	38.77	746	41.47	107.0	619	38.66	99.7	652	41.23	106.3	635	44.70	115.3
Study aids	105.28	17	78.49	74.6	24	114.64	108.9	17	101.54	96.4	19	100.59	95.5
Technology and engineering	187.80	2,145	158.80	84.6	2,439	160.83	85.6	2,455	164.66	87.7	2,770	164.03	87.3
Transportation	68.68	312	64.24	93.5	245	75.98	110.6	292	84.28	122.7	315	59.90	87.2
Travel	37.11	457	34.80	93.8	384	41.22	111.1	367	41.32	111.3	332	42.80	115.3
True crime	29.28	94	26.32	89.9	93	29.36	100.3	67	34.83	119.0	73	31.08	106.1
Young adult	50.17	2,256	49.41	98.5	2,466	37.38	74.5	2,653	35.99	71.7	2,561	37.07	73.9
Totals	$80.36	69,253	$84.55	105.2	68,277	$84.84	105.6	69,389	$89.54	111.4	68,613	$90.50	112.6

Compiled by Catherine Barr from data supplied by Baker & Taylor.

n.a. = not available.

Table 4 / North American Academic Books: Average Prices and Price Indexes 2008–2010
(Index Base: 1989 = 100)

Subject Area	LC Class	1989 No. of Titles	1989 Average Price	2008 No. of Titles	2008 Average Price	2009 No. of Titles	2009 Average Price	2010 No. of Titles	2010 Average Price	2010 % Change 2009–2010	2010 Index
Agriculture	S	897	$45.13	1,295	$96.70	1,253	$98.24	1,139	$107.44	9.4	238.1
Anthropology	GN	406	32.81	515	77.29	488	73.55	609	91.96	25.0	280.3
Botany	QK	251	69.02	272	172.18	286	118.52	260	125.84	6.2	182.3
Business and economics	H	5,979	41.67	9,852	92.69	10,070	89.33	10,916	97.31	8.9	233.5
Chemistry	QD	577	110.61	621	222.95	562	225.48	667	223.03	-1.1	201.6
Education	L	1,685	29.61	4,314	70.83	4,295	75.75	4,688	86.47	14.2	292.0
Engineering and technology	T	4,569	64.94	7,363	121.74	7,137	124.72	6,913	133.45	7.0	205.5
Fine and applied arts	M-N	3,040	40.72	6,767	54.17	6,647	54.07	5,535	57.17	5.7	140.4
General works	A	333	134.65	133	72.42	116	57.09	80	75.60	32.4	56.1
Geography	G	396	47.34	1,108	100.87	1,124	102.13	1,144	104.98	2.8	221.8
Geology	QE	303	63.49	318	123.68	278	125.35	276	114.34	-8.8	180.1
History	C-D-E-F	5,549	31.34	10,380	59.10	10,415	55.98	10,079	65.29	16.6	208.3
Home economics	TX	535	27.10	1,153	41.74	961	42.85	812	44.35	3.5	163.7
Industrial arts	TT	175	23.89	246	40.89	281	38.05	265	52.60	38.2	220.2
Law	K	1,252	51.10	4,119	103.47	4,522	113.24	4,596	125.35	10.7	245.3
Library and information science	Z	857	44.51	705	77.00	738	86.67	636	90.18	4.1	202.6
Literature and language	P	10,812	24.99	18,368	45.69	19,707	48.32	19,364	57.31	18.6	229.3
Mathematics and computer science	QA	2,707	44.68	4,204	101.69	3,902	103.90	3,965	103.85	-0.0	232.4
Medicine	R	5,028	58.38	9,089	109.35	8,603	101.97	8,679	112.66	10.5	193.0
Military and naval science	U-V	715	33.57	872	63.21	849	62.51	773	79.99	27.9	238.3
Philosophy and religion	B	3,518	29.06	7,522	65.79	7,574	67.91	7,386	81.75	20.4	281.3
Physical education and recreation	GV	814	20.38	1,728	49.51	1,807	49.75	1,788	56.03	12.6	274.9
Physics and astronomy	QB	1,219	64.59	1,522	134.91	1,551	138.92	1,627	128.36	-7.6	198.7
Political science	J	1,650	36.76	3,167	88.21	3,196	85.12	3,549	99.70	17.1	271.2
Psychology	BF	890	31.97	1,499	71.82	1,626	63.97	1,730	76.65	19.8	239.7
Science (general)	Q	433	56.10	515	106.31	552	122.02	631	108.40	-11.2	193.2
Sociology	HM	2,742	29.36	6,199	76.44	6,240	73.58	6,666	88.75	20.6	302.3
Zoology	QH,L,P,R	1,967	71.28	2,964	138.00	2,973	126.24	3,029	140.26	11.1	196.8
Average for all subjects		59,299	$41.69	106,810	$80.25	107,753	$79.32	107,802	$89.15	12.4	213.8

Compiled by Stephen Bosch, University of Arizona, from electronic data provided by Coutts Information Services, and YBP Library Services. The data represents all titles (includes hardcover, trade, and paperback books, as well as annuals) treated for all approval plan customers serviced by the vendors. This table covers titles published or distributed in the United States and Canada during the calendar years listed.

This index does include paperback editions. The inclusion of these items does impact pricing in the index.

Table 4A / North American Academic E-Books: Average Prices and Price Indexes 2007–2010
(Index Base: 2007 = 100)

Subject Area	LC Class	2007		2008		2009		2010			
		No. of Titles	Average Price	No. of Titles	Average Price	No. of Titles	Average Price	No. of Titles	Average Price	% Change 2009–2010	Index
Agriculture	S	894	$128.59	600	$158.42	1,416	$141.69	697	$168.73	19.1	131.2
Anthropology	GN	382	105.28	197	117.18	521	87.65	385	109.96	25.4	104.4
Botany	QK	287	168.18	191	244.50	347	167.31	190	175.23	4.7	104.2
Business and economics	H	9,807	97.25	5,892	105.84	12,542	87.02	8,481	102.87	18.2	105.8
Chemistry	QD	934	213.76	537	262.82	1,559	244.65	521	232.57	-4.9	108.8
Education	L	2,565	107.62	1,425	118.84	3,650	84.24	2,852	99.96	18.7	92.9
Engineering and technology	T	7,176	133.60	4,032	159.82	9,128	142.86	4,976	152.33	6.6	114.0
Fine and applied arts	M-N	1,141	84.30	924	86.89	2,174	70.91	1,493	83.35	17.5	98.9
General works	A	60	107.85	28	140.81	83	81.79	53	89.13	9.0	82.6
Geography	G	888	132.67	542	138.69	1,308	109.83	829	117.83	7.3	88.8
Geology	QE	201	136.49	187	172.39	358	135.90	178	146.85	8.1	107.6
History	C-D-E-F	4,452	93.55	3,220	90.04	8,519	73.99	5,189	89.42	20.9	95.6
Home economics	TX	255	104.31	149	113.72	468	80.49	211	78.08	-3.0	74.9
Industrial arts	TT	20	52.73	19	55.08	72	36.91	23	46.11	24.9	87.4
Law	K	1,743	99.61	1,415	120.39	3,711	113.49	2,433	147.66	30.1	148.2
Library and information science	Z	308	74.70	192	125.90	561	84.44	387	89.43	5.9	119.7
Literature and language	P	5,517	90.59	4,676	104.93	11,470	84.08	7,664	103.12	22.6	113.8
Mathematics and computer science	QA	4,285	102.93	2,559	129.34	4,387	109.20	3,000	112.65	3.2	109.4
Medicine	R	7,420	123.59	4,897	142.04	10,680	118.45	6,404	134.60	13.6	108.9
Military and naval science	U-V	684	82.89	399	92.37	736	86.28	487	105.07	21.8	126.8
Philosophy and religion	B	3,612	93.77	3,531	111.98	6,843	87.18	4,262	110.31	26.5	117.6
Physical education and recreation	GV	610	96.00	409	79.67	1,255	61.11	791	76.57	25.3	79.8
Physics and astronomy	QB	1,965	142.11	1,237	163.76	2,197	143.77	1,288	147.50	2.6	103.8
Political science	J	2,447	102.72	1,583	118.11	4,053	88.44	2,638	110.10	24.5	107.2
Psychology	BF	1,113	83.51	747	96.46	1,729	77.42	1,062	91.35	18.0	109.4
Science (general)	Q	468	117.19	340	135.07	640	107.75	462	122.51	13.7	104.5
Sociology	HM	4,139	98.02	2,953	105.59	7,141	82.60	4,520	103.73	25.6	105.8
Zoology	QH,L,P,R	3,394	154.01	2,124	189.08	4,066	145.77	2,336	164.82	13.1	107.0
Average for all subjects		66,767	$110.82	45,005	$125.33	101,614	$102.21	63,812	$116.25	13.7	104.9

Compiled by Stephen Bosch, University of Arizona, from electronic data provided by Coutts Information Services, and YBP Library Services. The data represents all e-book titles treated for all approval plan customers serviced by the vendors. This table covers titles published or distributed in the United States and Canada during the calendar years listed. It is important to note that e-books that were released in a given year may have been published in print much earlier.

(continued from page 487)

2007, 2008, 2009 and 2010. Vendors have reported large jumps in numbers of titles treated due to adding "catch up" titles to their database or adding titles from new publishers.

The cost of textbooks continues to be a hot topic on many college campuses. The index for textbooks documents price changes in this area. Indications are that textbooks tend to be much more expensive than other types of books with an average price of $107.94 in 2010. However, this was not a significant increase in price. The rate of price inflation seems to have plateaued.

The average price of North American Academic Books in 2010 (Table 4) increased by 12.4 percent as compared with the 2009 average price. This is mainly due to a large increase in the number of titles treated in the higher part of the price bands ($120 and up) as well as a large increase in the prices in the top price band. Nearly all price bands showed fewer titles between 2009 and 2010 except for the price bands above $90, which showed increases. This led to a large increase in the average price for all books. The increase in the upper price bands was primarily due to the increased cost of e-books. Remove e-books from this sample, and the upper price bands shrink considerably. See Figure 1.

Figure 1 / Comparison of Titles in Sample Grouped by Price

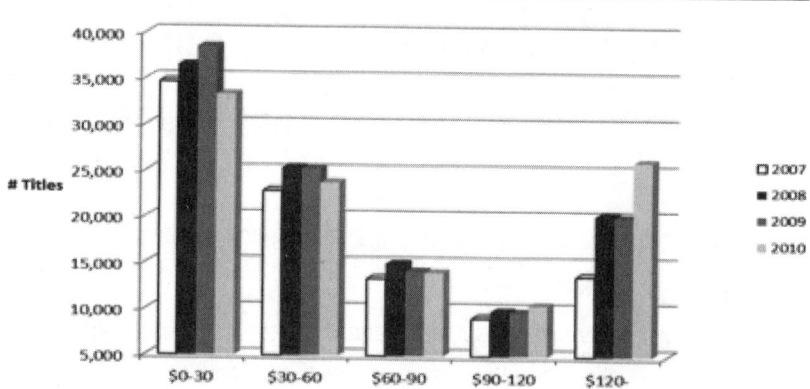

One thing that really stands out when looking at the data by price band is that the highest end of the price bands ($120 and up) has seen huge growth in the past three years, more than doubling in overall costs from $2.6 million (2007) to $5.8 million (2010). The impact on pricing from the titles in the $120 and up price band is confirmed if you look at the actual dollar values in groups (sum of all prices for titles in the group). It is clear that the increase in the top end of the index was the main component in the overall increase in the index for 2010. Although the $0–30 price area has the largest number of titles, dollar-wise it remains the smallest portion as far as total cost (sum of all prices) goes in the index. The increase in the prices in the upper end of the index was what added to the overall level of increase. See Figure 2.

Figure 2

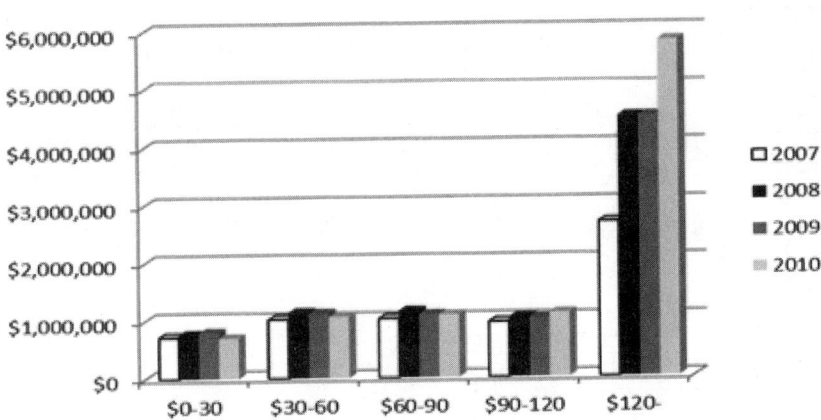

The data used for this index is derived from all titles treated by Coutts Information Services, and YBP Library Services in their approval plans during the calendar years listed. The index does include e-books as well as paperback editions as supplied by these vendors and this inclusion of paperbacks and e-books as distributed as part of the approval plans has clearly influenced the prices reflected in the index figures. The index is inclusive of the broadest categories of materials as that is the marketplace in which academic libraries operate, and the index attempts to chart price changes that impact that market.

E-books are also now being treated in a separate index (Table 4A), so the differences in the indexes will be interesting to observe. Currently the vast majority of titles are not published in both print and "e" version, so the number of titles in the e-book index should remain much smaller than the broader index. It is safe to say that in the future the number of titles in the broader index could decline and at the same time the number of e-books should rise, especially as we see more publishers move to publishing electronic versions of their books. Many e-book pricing models add extra charges of as much as 50 percent to 100 percent to the retail price for a multi-user license. This pricing model is reflected in the higher prices for e-books. The overall price for e-books did show a decline from 2008 to 2009, but in 2010 the prices shot up again. Since the number of titles treated has had a huge variation, it is not really possible to draw absolute conclusions about pricing trends in e-books at this time. The overall trend seems to indicate that prices are increasing. The index does clearly show that for the library market, e-books are much more expensive than print. Many publishers and e-book aggregators are still adding "e" versions of print books from backlists and these are showing up in the index; this is also the basis of the wide swings in numbers of titles in the index from year to year.

The price index for textbooks (Table 4B) shows a slight 0.7 percent increase for overall prices between 2009 and 2010. This increase is smaller than the increase seen for the broader print index, but the overall prices are higher. These are

(text continues on page 501)

Table 4B / North American Academic Textbooks: Average Prices and Price Indexes 2007–2010
(Index Base: 2007 = 100)

Subject Area	LC Class	2007 No. of Titles	2007 Average Price	2008 No. of Titles	2008 Average Price	2009 No. of Titles	2009 Average Price	2010 No. of Titles	2010 Average Price	% Change 2009–2010	Index
Agriculture	S	68	$134.75	67	$103.67	50	$102.37	49	$115.80	13.1	85.9
Anthropology	GN	40	89.15	31	90.75	27	82.21	35	90.65	10.3	101.7
Botany	QK	4	98.00	12	124.29	21	126.81	11	109.52	-13.6	111.8
Business and economics	H	666	110.18	740	115.69	674	115.47	694	121.36	5.1	110.1
Chemistry	QD	80	138.70	95	123.83	76	131.24	94	134.59	2.6	97.0
Education	L	235	79.58	269	84.55	220	84.49	271	87.75	3.9	110.3
Engineering and technology	T	668	106.13	835	110.98	790	113.64	744	116.38	2.4	109.7
Fine and applied arts	M-N	82	73.69	75	79.99	72	86.44	73	93.33	8.0	126.6
General works	A	1	48.00	2	53.48	1	90.00	0	0.00	0.0	0.0
Geography	G	59	100.42	72	105.24	82	104.79	78	105.21	0.4	104.8
Geology	QE	26	118.28	26	114.15	20	124.78	36	117.97	-5.5	99.7
History	C-D-E-F	72	78.41	102	73.85	72	87.34	81	81.49	-6.7	103.9
Home economics	TX	54	68.23	40	108.45	32	92.59	39	89.52	-3.3	131.2
Industrial arts	TT	13	73.90	16	86.76	13	91.87	14	84.72	-7.8	114.6
Law	K	163	87.67	271	90.51	241	100.38	242	102.09	1.7	116.5
Library and information science	Z	24	65.54	31	70.46	21	71.61	19	70.30	-1.8	107.3
Literature and language	P	269	71.35	263	73.50	284	73.56	309	77.71	5.6	108.9
Mathematics and computer science	QA	732	91.42	821	88.93	679	89.50	683	96.11	7.4	105.1
Medicine	R	1,210	126.37	1,375	133.27	1,375	131.12	1,512	126.75	-3.3	100.3
Military and naval science	U-V	10	104.58	10	109.19	8	138.90	3	122.65	-11.7	117.3
Philosophy and religion	B	85	55.51	107	56.83	98	57.11	101	72.13	26.3	129.9
Physical education and recreation	GV	47	72.14	59	74.89	45	84.99	51	79.39	-6.6	110.0
Physics and astronomy	QB	237	107.05	197	112.42	200	109.28	243	107.38	-1.7	100.3
Political science	J	104	74.21	116	80.58	100	86.36	110	80.09	-7.3	107.9
Psychology	BF	120	100.17	126	107.08	102	101.51	138	95.95	-5.5	95.8
Science (general)	Q	24	111.30	25	84.82	24	86.36	33	97.14	12.5	87.3
Sociology	HM	330	84.88	339	84.50	261	84.05	353	86.97	3.5	102.5
Zoology	QH,L,P,R	250	116.73	249	110.45	231	114.93	227	109.82	-4.4	94.1
Average for all subjects		5,673	$102.52	6,371	$105.34	5,819	$107.17	6,243	$107.94	0.7	105.3

Compiled by Stephen Bosch, University of Arizona, from electronic data provided by YBP Library Services. The data represents all Textbook titles treated for all approval plan customers serviced by the vendors. This table covers titles published or distributed in the United States and Canada during the calendar years listed.
This index does include paperback editions. The inclusion of these items does impact pricing in the index.

Table 5 / US College Books: Average Prices and Price Indexes 1989, 2009–2011
(Index Base for all years: 1989=100)

Subject	1989		2009				2010				2011				
	No. of Titles	Avg. Price per Title	No. of Titles	Avg. Price per Title	Indexed to 1989	Indexed to 2008	No. of Titles	Avg. Price per Title	Indexed to 1989	Indexed to 2009	No. of Titles	Avg. Price per Title	Indexed to 1989	Indexed to 2010	Percent Change 2010–2011
General*	19	$40.19	n.a.	n.a.	n.a.	n.a.	n.a.	n.a.	n.a.	n.a.	n.a.	n.a.	n.a.	n.a.	n.a.
Humanities	21	$32.33	80	$55.38	171.30	97.24	91	$58.99	182.46	106.52	87	$60.90	188.37	103.24	3.24
Art & Architecture	276	55.56	161	58.30	104.93	100.80	149	61.69	111.03	105.81	170	64.61	116.29	104.73	4.73
Fine Arts**	n.a.	n.a.	88	64.79	n.a.	94.21	92	67.13	n.a.	103.61	93	65.46	n.a.	97.51	-2.49
Architecture**	n.a.	n.a.	55	62.38	n.a.	80.89	48	61.53	n.a.	98.64	51	67.72	n.a.	110.06	10.06
Photography	24	44.11	30	54.44	123.42	116.72	28	53.02	120.20	97.39	25	51.87	117.59	97.83	-2.17
Communication	42	32.70	90	61.00	186.54	112.61	112	59.97	183.39	98.31	111	73.51	224.80	122.58	22.58
Language and Literature	110	35.17	73	60.76	172.76	93.81	94	68.66	195.22	113	124	70.09	199.29	102.08	2.08
Africa and Middle East**	n.a.	n.a.	30	48.68	n.a.	99.29	24	62.28	n.a.	127.94	30	63.93	n.a.	102.65	2.65
Asia and Oceania**	n.a.	n.a.	23	55.94	n.a.	89.83	24	71.99	n.a.	128.69	18	78.89	n.a.	109.58	9.58
Classical	75	43.07	29	74.51	173.00	91.27	24	78.76	182.87	105.70	34	92.32	214.35	117.22	17.22
English and American	547	30.27	382	62.74	207.27	106.65	394	61.96	204.69	98.76	376	68.92	227.68	111.23	11.23
Germanic	38	32.18	25	65.85	204.63	98.45	22	70.36	218.65	106.85	26	67.99	211.28	96.63	-3.37
Romance	97	30.30	70	63.77	210.46	118.22	70	59.00	194.72	92.52	70	68.69	226.70	116.42	16.42
Slavic	41	27.92	16	55.17	197.60	124.23	32	35.95	128.76	65.16	21	55.46	198.64	154.27	54.27
Other	63	25.09	n.a.	n.a.	n.a.	n.a.	n.a.	n.a.	n.a.	n.a.	n.a.	n.a.	n.a.	n.a.	n.a.
Performing Arts	20	29.41	34	55.77	189.63	102.48	30	61.97	210.71	111.12	26	46.03	156.51	74.28	-25.72
Film	82	33.00	163	66.89	202.70	115.09	130	64.13	194.33	95.87	138	64.97	196.88	101.31	1.31
Music	156	35.34	116	54.62	154.56	95.88	123	61.01	172.64	111.70	146	65.12	184.27	106.74	6.74

Table 5 / US College Books: Average Prices and Price Indexes 1989, 2009–2011 *(cont.)*
(Index Base for all years: 1989=100)

Subject	1989		2009				2010				2011				
	No. of Titles	Avg. Price per Title	No. of Titles	Avg. Price per Title	Indexed to 1989	Indexed to 2008	No. of Titles	Avg. Price per Title	Indexed to 1989	Indexed to 2009	No. of Titles	Avg. Price per Title	Indexed to 1989	Indexed to 2010	Percent Change 2010–2011
Theater and Dance	58	34.18	48	62.44	182.68	97.40	45	62.38	182.50	99.90	49	70.28	205.62	112.66	12.66
Philosophy	185	37.25	198	70.02	187.97	120.72	198	63.45	170.34	90.62	206	70.28	188.67	110.76	10.76
Religion	174	33.49	213	50.23	149.99	103.95	272	57.18	170.74	113.84	243	60.99	182.11	106.66	6.66
Total Humanities	2,009	$36.09	1,924	$60.85	168.61	104.25	2,002	$61.60	170.68	101.23	2,044	$66.89	185.34	108.59	8.59
Science and Technology	99	$46.90	89	$64.47	137.46	120.10	110	$58.09	123.86	90.10	93	$57.99	123.65	99.83	-0.17
History of Science and Technology	74	40.56	90	61.47	151.55	131.57	78	54.1	133.38	88.01	79	50.72	125.05	93.75	-6.25
Astronautics and Astronomy	22	50.56	82	54.41	107.61	107.44	63	55.58	109.93	102.15	69	55.96	110.68	100.68	0.68
Biology	97	51.01	140	72.10	141.34	101.11	151	72.74	142.60	100.89	153	73.42	143.93	100.93	0.93
Botany	29	63.91	82	86.09	134.71	110.87	85	85.09	133.14	98.84	75	70.92	110.97	83.35	-16.65
Zoology	53	49.21	107	64.28	130.62	95.05	121	64.33	130.73	100.08	114	61.00	123.96	94.82	-5.18
Chemistry	21	70.76	50	103.32	146.01	94.75	42	115.42	163.11	111.71	48	96.06	135.75	83.23	-16.77
Earth Science	34	79.44	111	77.25	97.24	104.76	102	63.33	79.72	81.98	113	64.02	80.59	101.09	1.09
Engineering	87	66.74	101	102.62	153.76	107.76	103	88.38	132.42	86.12	89	102.12	153.01	115.55	15.55
Health Sciences	94	34.91	191	52.90	151.53	93.98	146	56.14	160.81	106.12	154	57.98	166.08	103.28	3.28
Information and Computer Science	70	40.35	82	93.54	231.82	123.31	83	73.5	182.16	78.58	96	70.03	173.56	95.28	-4.72
Mathematics	60	48.53	117	67.75	139.60	98.22	108	61.97	127.69	91.47	104	69.89	144.01	112.78	12.78
Physics	22	43.94	47	64.30	146.34	101.37	50	54.74	124.58	85.13	64	65.59	149.27	119.82	19.82
Sports and Physical Education	18	27.46	56	51.82	188.71	133.83	67	54.06	196.87	104.32	52	63.91	232.74	118.22	18.22
Total Science	780	$49.54	1,345	$71.00	143.32	105.44	1,309	$67.13	135.51	94.55	1,303	$67.65	136.56	100.77	0.77

Social and Behavioral Sciences	92	$37.09	95	$64.92	175.03	107.64	129	$66.32	178.81	102.16	143	$68.64	185.06	103.50	3.50
Anthropology	96	39.94	125	68.14	170.61	120.79	139	63.6	159.24	93.34	134	68.46	171.41	107.64	7.64
Business Management and Labor	145	35.72	150	54.88	153.64	103.53	150	58	162.37	105.69	161	54.37	152.21	93.74	-6.26
Economics	332	40.75	292	63.56	155.98	101.92	270	61.16	150.09	96.22	281	59.01	144.81	96.48	-3.52
Education	71	34.50	170	58.33	169.07	110.66	158	62.56	181.33	107.25	153	69.54	201.57	111.16	11.16
History, Geography and Area Studies	59	42.10	102	53.59	127.29	104.4	154	58.16	138.15	108.53	109	71.73	170.38	123.33	23.33
Africa	44	34.85	24	63.61	182.53	102.56	38	69.05	198.13	108.55	46	65.28	187.32	94.54	-5.46
Ancient History**	n.a.	n.a.	44	63.06	n.a.	78.18	49	57.90	n.a.	91.82	62	74.41	n.a.	128.51	28.51
Asia and Oceania	76	34.75	82	71.83	206.71	131.24	72	60.88	175.19	84.76	61	61.86	178.01	101.61	1.61
Central and Eastern Europe**	n.a.	n.a.	60	68.85	n.a.	120.28	56	66.53	n.a.	96.63	61	64.22	n.a.	96.53	-3.47
Latin America and Caribbean	42	37.23	60	55.14	148.11	103.74	54	59.31	159.31	107.56	59	60.28	161.91	101.64	1.64
Middle East and North Africa	30	36.32	44	68.44	188.44	136.42	43	65.57	180.53	95.81	51	60.69	167.10	92.56	-7.44
North America	349	30.56	396	49.30	161.32	109.39	444	45.50	148.89	92.29	445	47.43	155.20	104.24	4.24
United Kingdom**	n.a.	n.a.	62	64.55	n.a.	110.12	80	69.56	n.a.	107.76	68	80.32	n.a.	115.47	15.47
Western Europe	287	42.08	144	69.55	165.28	106.95	138	59.14	140.54	85.03	141	69.66	165.54	117.79	17.79
Political Science	28	33.56	3	103.00	306.91	189.69	4	84.36	251.37	81.90	4	132.50	394.82	157.06	57.06
Comparative Politics	236	37.82	185	70.93	187.55	117.90	183	66.34	175.41	93.53	211	72.76	192.38	109.68	9.68
International Relations	207	35.74	171	66.19	185.20	111.32	213	65.64	183.66	99.17	167	72.47	202.77	110.41	10.41
Political Theory	59	37.76	89	61.13	161.89	97.92	73	56.74	150.26	92.82	91	59.06	156.41	104.09	4.09
U.S. Politics	212	29.37	218	50.30	171.26	102.34	253	53.03	180.56	105.43	213	55.86	190.19	105.34	5.34
Psychology	179	36.36	122	65.45	180.01	106.27	126	60.55	166.53	92.51	115	64.12	176.35	105.90	5.90
Sociology	178	36.36	258	59.86	164.63	97.99	226	60.71	166.97	101.42	241	64.48	177.34	106.21	6.21

Table 5 / US College Books: Average Prices and Price Indexes 1989, 2009–2011 (cont.)
(Index Base for all years: 1989=100)

Subject	1989		2009				2010				2011				
	No. of Titles	Avg. Price per Title	No. of Titles	Avg. Price per Title	Indexed to 1989	Indexed to 2008	No. of Titles	Avg. Price per Title	Indexed to 1989	Indexed to 2009	No. of Titles	Avg. Price per Title	Indexed to 1989	Indexed to 2010	Percent Change 2010–2011
Social and Behavioral Sciences	2,722	$36.43	2,896	$60.65	166.48	107.54	3,052	$59.09	162.20	97.43	3,017	$62.75	172.25	106.19	6.19
Total General, Humanities	5,511	$38.16	6,165	$62.97	165.02	106.10	6,363	$61.53	161.24	97.71	6,364	$65.08	170.55	105.77	5.77
Science, and Social Science Reference	636	$61.02	39	$93.36	153	129.02	29	$61.17	65.52	65.52	31	$91.40	149.79	149.42	49.42
Humanities**	n.a.	n.a.	115	112.72	n.a.	109.49	128	117.12	n.a.	103.9	109	126.39	n.a.	107.91	7.91
Science and Technology**	n.a.	n.a.	85	117.06	n.a.	80.21	76	133.19	n.a.	113.78	58	136.46	n.a.	102.46	2.46
Social and Behavioral Sciences**	n.a.	n.a.	185	150.72	n.a.	92.69	216	152.91	n.a.	101.45	216	144.23	n.a.	94.32	-5.68
Total Reference	636	$61.02	424	$128.60	210.75	94.38	449	$133.44	218.68	103.76	414	$134.49	220.40	100.79	0.79
Grand Total	6,147	$40.52	6,589	$67.18	165.79	104.12	6,812	$66.27	163.55	98.65	6,778	$69.32	171.08	104.60	4.60

Compiled by Frederick Lynden, Brown University. *General category no longer appears after 1999. **Began appearing as separate sections after 1989. n.a. = not available.

Table 6 / U.S. Mass Market Paperback Books: Average Prices and Price Indexes, 2008–2011

Index Base: 2005 = 100

BISAC Category	2005 Average Prices	2008 Final Volumes	2008 Final Average Prices	2008 Final Index	2009 Final Volumes	2009 Final Average Prices	2009 Final Index	2010 Final Volumes	2010 Final Average Prices	2010 Final Index	2011 Preliminary Volumes	2011 Preliminary Average Prices	2011 Preliminary Index
Antiques and collectibles	$7.69	10	$8.59	111.7	9	$8.66	112.6	9	8.77	114.0	5	8.79	114.3
Architecture	n.a.	n.a.	n.a.	n.a.	n.a.	n.a.	n.a.	n.a.	n.a.	n.a.	n.a.	n.a.	n.a.
Art	n.a.	n.a.	n.a.	n.a.	n.a.	n.a.	n.a.	n.a.	n.a.	n.a.	n.a.	n.a.	n.a.
Bibles	7.83	8	7.87	100.5	13	7.48	95.5	13	7.51	95.9	8	8.62	110.1
Biography and autobiography	7.11	14	7.13	100.3	13	7.99	112.4	17	7.99	112.4	17	7.93	111.5
Body, mind and spirit	12.47	1	7.99	64.1	1	9.99	80.1	3	9.32	74.7	2	7.99	64.1
Business and economics	5.29	239	5.94	112.3	238	6.12	115.7	257	6.22	117.6	244	6.47	122.3
Children	8.47	n.a.	n.a.	n.a.	n.a.	n.a.	n.a.	n.a.	n.a.	n.a.	n.a.	n.a.	n.a.
Comics and graphic novels	n.a.	n.a.	n.a.	n.a.	n.a.	n.a.	n.a.	n.a.	n.a.	n.a.	n.a.	n.a.	n.a.
Computers	n.a.	n.a.	n.a.	n.a.	n.a.	n.a.	n.a.	n.a.	n.a.	n.a.	n.a.	n.a.	n.a.
Cooking	7.50	n.a.	n.a.	n.a.	n.a.	n.a.	n.a.	n.a.	n.a.	n.a.	1	7.99	106.5
Crafts and hobbies	n.a.	n.a.	n.a.	n.a.	n.a.	n.a.	n.a.	n.a.	n.a.	n.a.	n.a.	n.a.	n.a.
Design	n.a.	n.a.	n.a.	n.a.	n.a.	n.a.	n.a.	n.a.	n.a.	n.a.	n.a.	n.a.	n.a.
Drama	6.32	2	5.99	94.8	3	5.98	94.6	3	6.30	99.7	1	8.95	141.6
Education	n.a.	n.a.	n.a.	n.a.	n.a.	n.a.	n.a.	n.a.	n.a.	n.a.	n.a.	n.a.	n.a.
Family and relationships	6.98	n.a.	n.a.	n.a.	1	4.99	71.5	1	7.99	114.5	1	8.99	128.8
Fiction	6.34	4,162	6.48	102.2	4,013	6.68	105.4	3,952	6.80	107.3	3,976	6.95	109.6
Foreign language study	n.a.	5	6.19	n.a.	4	6.99	n.a.	6	7.08	n.a.	n.a.	n.a.	n.a.
Games	7.14	13	5.45	76.3	5	4.99	69.9	n.a.	n.a.	n.a.	n.a.	n.a.	n.a.
Gardening	n.a.	n.a.	n.a.	n.a.	n.a.	n.a.	n.a.	n.a.	n.a.	n.a.	n.a.	n.a.	n.a.
Health and fitness	7.43	18	7.66	103.1	15	7.79	104.8	14	7.92	106.6	10	7.99	107.5
History	7.90	3	5.83	73.8	5	7.89	99.9	1	9.95	125.9	7	8.56	108.4
House and home	5.99	n.a.	n.a.	n.a.	n.a.	n.a.	n.a.	n.a.	n.a.	n.a.	n.a.	n.a.	n.a.
Humor	6.99	3	6.32	90.4	n.a.	n.a.	n.a.	n.a.	n.a.	n.a.	1	3.50	50.1
Language arts and disciplines	6.99	n.a.	n.a.	n.a.	n.a.	n.a.	n.a.	2	13.25	189.6	n.a.	n.a.	n.a.
Law	n.a.	1	4.99	n.a.	1	7.95	n.a.	1	5.95	n.a.	1	7.95	n.a.
Literary collections	n.a.	n.a.	n.a.	n.a.	n.a.	n.a.	n.a.	n.a.	n.a.	n.a.	n.a.	n.a.	n.a.
Literary criticism	7.95	1	7.95	100.0	1	7.99	100.5	1	7.99	100.5	1	9.99	125.7

Table 6 / U.S. Mass Market Paperback Books: Average Prices and Price Indexes, 2008–2011 *(cont.)*

Index Base: 2005 = 100

BISAC Category	2005 Average Prices	2008 Final Volumes	2008 Final Average Prices	2008 Final Index	2009 Final Volumes	2009 Final Average Prices	2009 Final Index	2010 Final Volumes	2010 Final Average Prices	2010 Final Index	2011 Preliminary Volumes	2011 Preliminary Average Prices	2011 Preliminary Index
Mathematics	n.a.	n.a.	n.a.	n.a.	n.a.	n.a.	n.a.	n.a.	n.a.	n.a.	n.a.	n.a.	n.a.
Medical	7.83	1	7.50	95.8	n.a.	n.a.	n.a.	1	8.99	114.8	n.a.	n.a.	n.a.
Music	7.95	n.a.	n.a.	n.a.	n.a.	n.a.	n.a.	n.a.	n.a.	n.a.	1	7.95	100.0
Nature	n.a.	n.a.	n.a.	n.a.	n.a.	n.a.	n.a.	n.a.	n.a.	n.a.	n.a.	n.a.	n.a.
Performing arts	8.23	1	9.99	121.4	1	9.99	121.4	1	9.99	121.4	2	8.99	109.2
Pets	n.a.	1	7.99	n.a.	n.a.	n.a.	n.a.	1	7.99	n.a.	1	7.99	n.a.
Philosophy	7.49	2	5.95	79.4	n.a.	n.a.	n.a.	2	6.47	86.4	n.a.	n.a.	n.a.
Photography	n.a.	n.a.	n.a.	n.a.	n.a.	n.a.	n.a.	n.a.	n.a.	n.a.	n.a.	n.a.	n.a.
Poetry	5.75	2	4.95	86.1	5	6.95	120.9	1	7.95	138.3	1	7.95	138.3
Political science	n.a.	2	7.99	n.a.	1	5.95	n.a.	2	7.97	n.a.	1	5.95	n.a.
Psychology	7.97	n.a.	n.a.	n.a.	n.a.	n.a.	n.a.	n.a.	n.a.	n.a.	1	7.99	100.3
Reference	6.85	3	7.16	104.5	3	7.66	111.8	1	7.99	116.6	2	7.99	116.6
Religion	9.96	4	7.74	77.7	3	6.98	70.1	2	7.99	80.2	2	7.49	75.2
Science	n.a.	1	6.95	n.a.	n.a.	n.a.	n.a.	n.a.	n.a.	n.a.	n.a.	n.a.	n.a.
Self-help	12.45	3	9.64	77.4	2	7.99	64.2	1	7.99	64.2	1	7.99	64.2
Social science	7.08	n.a.	n.a.	n.a.	n.a.	n.a.	n.a.	n.a.	n.a.	n.a.	n.a.	n.a.	n.a.
Sports and recreation	7.62	3	7.99	104.9	3	6.99	91.7	1	7.99	104.9	1	7.99	104.9
Study aids	n.a.	n.a.	n.a.	n.a.	n.a.	n.a.	n.a.	n.a.	n.a.	n.a.	n.a.	n.a.	n.a.
Technology and engineering	n.a.	n.a.	n.a.	n.a.	n.a.	n.a.	n.a.	n.a.	n.a.	n.a.	n.a.	n.a.	n.a.
Transportation	12.95	n.a.	n.a.	n.a.	1	14.00	108.1	n.a.	n.a.	n.a.	n.a.	n.a.	n.a.
Travel	n.a.	1	6.95	n.a.	1	4.95	n.a.	n.a.	n.a.	n.a.	n.a.	n.a.	n.a.
True crime	7.19	53	7.35	102.2	52	7.47	103.9	54	7.64	106.3	44	7.83	108.9
Young adult	6.46	142	7.10	109.9	96	7.63	118.1	83	8.13	125.9	49	8.44	130.7
Totals	$6.34	4,699	$6.50	102.5	4,490	$6.70	105.7	4,430	$6.83	107.7	4,381	$6.97	109.9

Compiled by Catherine Barr from data supplied by Baker & Taylor.

n.a. = not available.

(continued from page 493)

indicators that the angst experienced by students as they purchase their texts may well be justified; prices appear to be much higher than those of regular academic books. It may be that the public outcry about high textbook costs has had a dampening effect on price increases, but only time will tell if that trend continues. It will take a little more time and data before any real trends can be identified.

Price changes vary, as always, among subject areas. This year there were many double-digit increases in subject areas, and a few areas showed price decreases. The subjects with the highest price increases, as indicated by the 2010 data, were the social sciences and humanities. This may be due to increases in e-book publishing in these subject areas. STM publishers have tended to be early adopters and have been publishing e-books for a while. The large price increases in the social sciences and humanities reflect the increased availability of e-books in these areas.

It is good to remember that price indexes become less accurate at describing price changes the smaller the sample becomes. Industrial arts and general works are small samples that showed very large price changes, but to conclude that all books in those areas increased or decreased at like amounts is not correct. These areas have a small sample size (fewer than 500 titles) and the inclusion of just a few large, expensive items can have a major impact on prices for the category. In these areas there will be a lot of encyclopedias and other large reference works, so price volatility is expected.

The U.S. College Books Price Index (Table 5), prepared by Frederick C. Lynden, contains price and indexing information for the years 2009 through 2011 (index base year of 1989), and also the percentage change between 2010 and 2011. Data for the index were compiled from 6,778 reviews of books published in *Choice* during 2011; expensive titles ($500 or more) were omitted from the analysis, thus the total number of titles reported is smaller than the number reviewed. As with Table 4, this index includes some paperback prices; as a result, the average price of books is less than if only hardcover books were included. Table 5 reports the number of titles, dollar amounts, percentages, average price for books for the years 2009 through 2011 in each *Choice* subject category.

The average price for humanities titles in 2011 increased by 8.59 percent over the previous year. The average price for science and technology titles increased by only 0.77 percent, and the average price for social and behavioral sciences titles increased by 6.19 percent. Calculated separately, reference books for 2011 showed a 0.79 percent increase over the previous year. For all titles, there was a 4.60 percent average price increase for 2011, and a 71 percent average price increase since 1989.

For 2011 the overall average price for books in the humanities, sciences, and social and behavioral sciences (including reference books) was $69.32, an increase of 4.60 percent over the average 2010 book price of $66.27. Reference books calculated separately had an average price increase of 0.79 percent over the previous year, with a 2011 average of $134.49 compared with 2010's average price of $133.44. Excluding reference books, the 2011 average price was $65.08, a 5.77 percent increase compared with the average 2010 price of $61.53.

(text continues on page 508)

Table 7 / U.S. Paperback Books (Excluding Mass Market): Average Prices and Price Indexes, 2008–2011

Index Base: 2005 = 100

BISAC Category	2005 Average Prices	2008 Final Volumes	2008 Final Average Prices	2008 Final Index	2009 Final Volumes	2009 Final Average Prices	2009 Final Index	2010 Final Volumes	2010 Final Average Prices	2010 Final Index	2011 Preliminary Volumes	2011 Preliminary Average Prices	2011 Preliminary Index
Antiques and collectibles	$24.80	239	$27.08	109.2	191	$27.25	109.9	178	$25.53	102.9	137	$26.99	108.8
Architecture	38.90	694	41.89	107.7	692	44.89	115.4	752	45.31	116.5	697	42.69	109.7
Art	31.28	1,581	37.55	120.0	1,491	37.63	120.3	1,506	38.25	122.3	1,534	37.07	118.5
Bibles	36.87	363	49.29	133.7	307	40.67	110.3	430	38.66	104.9	746	40.97	111.1
Biography and autobiography	19.19	2,211	20.31	105.8	2,347	20.54	107.0	2,434	20.35	106.0	2,441	19.87	103.5
Body, mind and spirit	17.48	1,072	18.47	105.7	1,009	18.16	103.9	995	18.03	103.1	1,061	18.27	104.5
Business and economics	71.12	5,937	73.97	104.0	5,930	62.07	87.3	5,791	69.30	97.4	4,906	66.86	94.0
Children	11.11	9,099	10.79	97.1	9,716	10.91	98.2	8,612	10.42	93.8	8,562	10.04	90.4
Comics and graphic novels	12.75	2,407	14.15	111.0	2,173	15.42	120.9	1,863	16.11	126.4	1,890	16.26	127.5
Computers	57.01	3,279	87.12	152.8	3,795	97.47	171.0	3,460	70.42	123.5	3,171	66.75	117.1
Cooking	18.30	1,271	18.84	103.0	1,006	19.59	107.0	1,101	19.95	109.0	1,101	19.92	108.9
Crafts and hobbies	18.49	943	19.98	108.1	1,002	19.29	104.3	1,052	19.34	104.6	1,077	19.50	105.5
Design	32.87	381	34.18	104.0	397	37.00	112.6	440	63.98	194.6	397	41.78	127.1
Drama	16.40	521	18.66	113.8	581	21.70	132.3	739	18.95	115.5	413	19.40	118.3
Education	35.10	3,929	37.21	106.0	3,262	41.43	118.0	3,545	42.98	122.5	3,116	41.07	117.0
Family and relationships	17.10	951	17.78	104.0	884	19.63	114.8	782	18.72	109.5	641	18.86	110.3
Fiction	15.74	9,480	16.30	103.6	9,694	17.32	110.0	9,546	17.99	114.3	11,609	18.25	115.9
Foreign language study	41.90	1,405	30.19	72.1	977	32.31	77.1	1,280	31.33	74.8	1,179	32.53	77.6
Games	16.53	800	17.08	103.3	787	17.59	106.4	792	16.57	100.2	657	16.34	98.9
Gardening	20.59	368	18.93	91.9	256	20.96	101.8	241	23.45	113.9	239	23.33	113.3
Health and fitness	22.81	1,373	24.19	106.0	1,333	23.67	103.8	1,271	26.95	118.1	1,247	26.72	117.1
History	33.53	5,856	31.85	95.0	6,436	31.80	94.8	6,952	35.79	106.7	6,706	34.83	103.9
House and home	19.33	295	20.23	104.7	226	21.96	113.6	200	21.19	109.6	138	20.94	108.3
Humor	12.96	463	13.49	104.1	486	13.79	106.4	430	14.37	110.9	385	14.15	109.2

Category													
Language arts and disciplines	49.14	53.38	1,654	108.6	65.85	2,088	134.0	64.46	2,317	131.2	68.39	1,719	139.2
Law	60.92	115.14	3,781	189.0	75.41	2,711	123.8	72.07	3,179	118.3	69.47	3,090	114.0
Literary collections	28.07	35.23	540	125.5	35.01	581	124.7	36.42	672	129.7	29.91	477	106.6
Literary criticism	31.99	36.57	1,446	114.3	38.66	1,770	120.9	36.57	1,612	114.3	37.28	1,665	116.5
Mathematics	75.77	61.82	961	81.6	68.93	885	91.0	86.13	1,312	113.7	62.66	1,152	82.7
Medical	64.27	74.82	3,986	116.4	76.34	3,937	118.8	90.22	5,378	140.4	76.82	4,081	119.5
Music	22.66	21.67	2,921	95.6	23.22	2,975	102.5	22.83	3,020	100.8	23.85	2,533	105.3
Nature	26.90	25.42	604	94.5	27.02	613	100.4	37.28	565	138.6	32.20	502	119.7
Performing arts	27.85	31.01	991	111.3	33.65	934	120.8	33.53	1,030	120.4	32.65	910	117.2
Pets	18.86	18.70	292	99.2	19.01	299	100.8	17.34	249	91.9	19.87	196	105.4
Philosophy	31.40	30.93	1,271	98.5	34.33	1,465	109.3	52.66	1,391	167.7	42.32	1,324	134.8
Photography	27.74	32.87	535	118.5	31.13	539	112.2	31.30	546	112.8	32.33	539	116.5
Poetry	16.09	16.50	1,784	102.5	16.88	1,720	104.9	16.73	1,720	104.0	16.75	1,705	104.1
Political science	45.65	37.58	3,142	82.3	37.91	3,220	83.0	41.00	3,908	89.8	39.49	3,333	86.5
Psychology	45.74	41.37	1,377	90.4	43.08	1,256	94.2	47.98	1,578	104.9	45.99	1,334	100.5
Reference	52.54	68.97	1,353	131.3	90.69	1,307	172.6	84.85	1,057	161.5	99.79	1,065	189.9
Religion	20.54	20.12	5,796	98.0	21.31	6,052	103.7	22.08	6,955	107.5	21.38	6,400	104.1
Science	71.05	70.80	2,099	99.6	78.19	2,462	110.0	116.37	4,004	163.8	90.14	2,722	126.9
Self-help	16.36	17.17	1,148	105.0	17.84	1,047	109.0	17.84	1,121	109.0	18.21	1,008	111.3
Social science	36.83	40.16	4,037	109.0	42.51	3,998	115.4	45.05	4,270	122.3	41.59	3,761	112.9
Sports and recreation	21.82	23.77	1,331	108.9	23.39	1,259	107.2	22.30	1,315	102.2	24.49	1,140	112.2
Study aids	30.90	32.14	880	104.0	30.82	669	99.7	49.24	1,499	159.4	33.52	971	108.5
Technology and engineering	85.80	154.07	2,583	179.6	153.11	2,681	178.4	111.20	2,427	129.6	103.29	1,759	120.4
Transportation	40.19	39.28	430	97.7	36.61	459	91.1	36.26	507	90.2	36.79	437	91.5
Travel	19.18	20.33	3,077	106.0	20.51	2,852	106.9	20.93	2,585	109.1	19.71	2,384	102.8
True crime	17.71	18.17	144	102.6	19.00	156	107.3	20.94	195	118.2	19.15	169	108.1
Young adult	14.06	13.76	2,555	97.9	16.79	2,462	119.4	14.86	2,173	105.7	14.49	2,291	103.1
Totals	$33.90	$39.36	105,636	116.1	$39.20	105,375	115.6	$42.06	110,977	124.1	$36.98	102,717	109.1

Compiled by Catherine Barr from data supplied by Baker & Taylor.

Table 7A / U.S. Audiobooks: Average Prices and Price Indexes, 2008–2011

Index Base: 2005 = 100

BISAC Category	2005 Average Prices	2008 Final Volumes	2008 Final Average Prices	2008 Final Index	2009 Final Volumes	2009 Final Average Prices	2009 Final Index	2010 Final Volumes	2010 Final Average Prices	2010 Final Index	2011 Preliminary Volumes	2011 Preliminary Average Prices	2011 Preliminary Index
Antiques and collectibles	n.a.	n.a.	n.a.	n.a.	1	$74.95	n.a.	3	$36.66	n.a.	n.a.	n.a.	n.a.
Architecture	$68.95	2	$37.47	54.3	n.a.	n.a.	n.a.	4	41.24	59.8	3	39.97	58.0
Art	57.51	5	40.99	71.3	7	59.41	103.3	9	58.21	101.2	9	39.65	68.9
Bibles	47.08	20	41.83	88.8	9	75.53	160.4	7	43.28	91.9	10	44.49	94.5
Biography and autobiography	37.68	641	47.05	124.9	685	50.75	134.7	751	50.79	134.8	746	51.26	136.0
Body, mind and spirit	26.74	83	38.28	143.2	87	37.95	141.9	69	32.98	123.3	101	38.47	143.9
Business and economics	42.11	426	39.54	93.9	436	46.15	109.6	346	49.70	118.0	403	45.74	108.6
Children	26.57	733	31.09	117.0	832	36.22	136.3	899	37.80	142.3	968	34.53	130.0
Comics and graphic novels	n.a.	n.a.	n.a.	n.a.	n.a.	n.a.	n.a.	n.a.	n.a.	n.a.	n.a.	n.a.	n.a.
Computers	41.39	4	31.23	75.5	5	46.99	113.5	2	45.00	108.7	12	53.99	130.4
Cooking	14.45	4	14.71	101.8	14	44.70	309.3	2	44.97	311.2	12	47.40	328.0
Crafts and hobbies	n.a.	9	42.20	n.a.	4	38.72	n.a.	1	24.98	n.a.	n.a.	n.a.	n.a.
Design	n.a.	n.a.	n.a.	n.a.	n.a.	n.a.	n.a.	n.a.	n.a.	n.a.	n.a.	n.a.	n.a.
Drama	23.45	48	36.67	156.4	151	34.54	147.3	95	33.21	141.6	104	27.68	118.0
Education	27.46	17	29.78	108.4	22	45.34	165.1	20	45.71	166.5	34	43.99	160.2
Family and relationships	24.58	73	36.73	149.4	54	39.41	160.3	69	41.17	167.5	108	41.22	167.7
Fiction	41.47	4,379	48.43	116.8	6,278	52.62	126.9	7,649	50.38	121.5	7,138	48.24	116.3
Foreign language study	70.04	394	37.63	53.7	260	40.74	58.2	186	45.11	64.4	220	50.06	71.5
Games	32.68	1	14.95	45.7	6	14.12	43.2	n.a.	n.a.	n.a.	5	46.98	143.8
Gardening	n.a.	2	39.97	n.a.	n.a.	n.a.	n.a.	6	47.82	n.a.	n.a.	n.a.	n.a.
Health and fitness	26.61	83	33.32	125.2	82	46.09	173.2	85	43.09	161.9	110	47.46	178.4
History	41.61	577	54.71	131.5	450	57.69	138.6	563	58.07	139.6	444	59.36	142.7
House and home	25.00	n.a.	n.a.	n.a.	n.a.	n.a.	n.a.	n.a.	n.a.	n.a.	1	34.95	139.8
Humor	29.60	65	36.20	122.3	79	42.37	143.1	95	36.62	123.7	103	40.82	137.9

Language arts and disciplines	60.84	14	36.96	60.7	18	46.65	76.7	13	38.34	63.0	39	44.88	73.8
Law	55.32	18	54.21	98.0	9	49.75	89.9	10	64.49	116.6	7	70.14	126.8
Literary collections	24.71	16	38.91	157.5	20	32.34	130.9	11	52.07	210.7	34	51.45	208.2
Literary criticism	26.41	35	49.61	187.8	20	42.43	160.7	18	42.53	161.0	188	30.59	115.8
Mathematics	n.a.	n.a.	n.a.	n.a.	n.a.	n.a.	n.a.	n.a.	n.a.	n.a.	1	24.95	n.a.
Medical	153.72	25	96.61	62.8	13	60.66	39.5	28	40.13	26.1	24	45.58	29.7
Music	29.83	144	29.46	98.8	108	38.41	128.8	74	35.67	119.6	54	42.14	141.3
Nature	28.92	27	39.18	135.5	37	47.09	162.8	57	41.20	142.5	44	46.71	161.5
Performing arts	25.78	39	38.32	148.6	21	46.23	179.3	16	40.60	157.5	9	65.08	252.4
Pets	33.05	20	34.05	103.0	23	43.51	131.6	52	38.33	116.0	25	43.14	130.5
Philosophy	35.30	37	41.33	117.1	36	51.39	145.6	38	53.05	150.3	73	46.86	132.7
Photography	n.a.	n.a.	n.a.	n.a.	n.a.	n.a.	n.a.	n.a.	n.a.	n.a.	n.a.	n.a.	n.a.
Poetry	22.87	45	25.88	113.2	50	35.88	156.9	28	33.59	146.9	14	23.55	103.0
Political science	42.66	174	44.16	103.5	177	49.69	116.5	230	48.04	112.6	220	48.59	113.9
Psychology	35.70	31	37.38	104.7	54	52.13	146.0	46	45.42	127.2	91	48.66	136.3
Reference	21.20	15	32.78	154.6	7	40.55	191.3	2	59.99	283.0	19	42.62	201.0
Religion	26.52	313	30.20	113.9	418	33.50	126.3	425	33.94	128.0	460	31.52	118.9
Science	39.86	61	48.59	121.9	64	47.75	119.8	66	51.89	130.2	90	54.25	136.1
Self-help	23.58	207	29.98	127.1	289	38.30	162.4	192	39.43	167.2	199	41.37	175.4
Social science	35.73	55	40.17	112.4	79	50.36	140.9	90	48.07	134.5	100	48.86	136.7
Sports and recreation	28.46	57	39.75	139.7	41	45.78	160.9	58	48.48	170.3	38	46.57	163.6
Study aids	41.85	18	67.10	160.3	21	33.92	81.1	7	19.41	46.4	1	21.99	52.5
Technology and engineering	61.47	10	52.09	84.7	7	48.56	79.0	23	53.33	86.8	25	47.18	76.8
Transportation	28.00	n.a.	n.a.	n.a.	3	36.66	130.9	7	46.28	165.3	1	24.95	89.1
Travel	41.91	39	44.73	106.7	15	51.57	123.0	47	50.96	121.6	20	61.17	146.0
True crime	35.97	59	51.41	142.9	45	50.69	140.9	37	52.58	146.2	36	50.59	140.6
Young adult	35.68	269	45.52	127.6	527	44.85	125.7	888	44.81	125.6	960	41.69	116.8
Totals	$40.49	9,294	$44.21	109.2	11,564	$48.58	120.0	13,324	$48.00	118.5	13,303	$45.96	113.5

Compiled by Catherine Barr from data supplied by Baker & Taylor.
n.a. = not available.

Table 7B / U.S. E-Books: Average Prices and Price Indexes, 2008–2011
Index Base: 2008 = 100

BISAC Category	2008 Average Prices	2009 Final Volumes	2009 Final Average Prices	2009 Final Index	2010 Final Volumes	2010 Final Average Prices	2010 Final Index	2011 Preliminary Volumes	2011 Preliminary Average Prices	2011 Preliminary Index
Antiques and collectibles	$55.97	11	$89.97	160.7	62	$30.24	54.0	216	$22.13	39.5
Architecture	70.50	205	69.22	98.2	268	66.57	94.4	281	71.84	101.9
Art	45.41	166	27.92	61.5	199	41.56	91.5	645	16.20	35.7
Bibles	25.79	22	15.58	60.4	119	6.11	23.7	109	10.80	41.9
Biography and autobiography	14.58	1,464	14.25	97.7	1,828	15.47	106.1	2,794	12.08	82.9
Body, mind and spirit	12.41	362	11.71	94.4	628	13.95	112.4	1,104	12.34	99.4
Business and economics	57.52	4,707	48.46	84.2	5,603	44.82	77.9	5,365	45.10	78.4
Children	12.01	3,554	11.73	97.7	4,239	13.82	115.1	11,980	19.83	165.1
Comics and graphic novels	25.04	16	12.11	48.4	26	11.39	45.5	205	6.89	27.5
Computers	66.87	2,574	61.64	92.2	3,057	62.09	92.9	3,595	63.55	95.0
Cooking	20.20	508	16.04	79.4	715	16.79	83.1	1,147	16.66	82.5
Crafts and hobbies	14.35	211	12.91	90.0	340	17.63	122.9	622	17.32	120.7
Design	36.04	59	34.95	97.0	125	37.03	102.7	97	40.09	111.2
Drama	29.49	137	12.56	42.6	443	4.86	16.5	2,130	3.35	11.4
Education	51.98	1,397	55.18	106.2	1,537	45.95	88.4	1,310	48.22	92.8
Family and relationships	19.88	650	14.23	71.6	717	14.79	74.4	774	11.96	60.2
Fiction	8.71	13,364	8.21	94.3	18,043	7.06	81.1	39,886	5.31	61.0
Foreign language study	43.01	116	40.91	95.1	97	46.68	108.5	183	20.36	47.3
Games	17.73	84	16.60	93.6	120	12.85	72.5	218	13.07	73.7
Gardening	20.40	51	23.49	115.1	68	17.41	85.3	115	17.01	83.4
Health and fitness	18.54	755	18.23	98.3	920	18.78	101.3	1,283	16.06	86.6
History	57.53	1,929	46.95	81.6	2,641	48.20	83.8	3,171	36.64	63.7
House and home	22.89	103	23.70	103.5	121	21.57	94.2	147	17.21	75.2
Humor	11.27	232	12.39	109.9	322	11.15	98.9	410	8.51	75.5

Language arts and disciplines	93.27	566	88.14	94.5	582	75.61	81.1	784	65.64	70.4
Law	81.23	487	91.61	112.8	609	112.19	138.1	599	87.20	107.3
Literary collections	24.50	94	30.99	126.5	226	20.27	82.7	1,298	5.20	21.2
Literary criticism	86.62	447	81.55	94.1	608	87.17	100.6	822	54.73	63.2
Mathematics	106.16	530	101.96	96.0	801	112.32	105.8	987	100.36	94.5
Medical	135.21	1,676	123.67	91.5	1,575	135.71	100.4	2,065	117.03	86.6
Music	33.83	262	34.93	103.3	331	32.65	96.5	1,982	19.26	56.9
Nature	59.76	209	32.43	54.3	370	59.48	99.5	369	37.35	62.5
Performing arts	38.06	335	35.56	93.4	474	32.17	84.5	586	32.27	84.8
Pets	15.91	113	15.06	94.7	176	14.50	91.1	380	11.65	73.2
Philosophy	79.19	664	60.68	76.6	598	71.43	90.2	801	48.66	61.4
Photography	30.30	158	28.53	94.2	202	27.23	89.9	272	23.94	79.0
Poetry	13.66	257	13.70	100.3	332	9.54	69.8	1,165	6.25	45.8
Political science	59.03	1,451	62.19	105.4	1,427	59.74	101.2	1,546	50.55	85.6
Psychology	65.30	845	53.40	81.8	914	56.42	86.4	976	57.15	87.5
Reference	48.33	284	31.18	64.5	646	22.92	47.4	500	24.04	49.7
Religion	27.29	2,676	21.23	77.8	2,874	27.81	101.9	3,613	21.99	80.6
Science	210.57	2,770	194.27	92.3	2,915	155.80	74.0	2,750	142.18	67.5
Self-help	14.15	743	11.93	84.3	746	14.06	99.4	1,417	10.01	70.7
Social science	69.42	1,357	57.38	82.7	1,513	56.83	81.9	1,815	58.24	83.9
Sports and recreation	22.44	546	20.59	91.8	643	19.22	85.7	833	18.69	83.3
Study aids	21.95	147	15.96	72.7	305	13.94	63.5	445	15.32	69.8
Technology and engineering	153.73	1,633	143.51	93.4	2,618	158.44	103.1	2,240	137.15	89.2
Transportation	35.47	64	39.64	111.8	97	33.12	93.4	137	23.21	65.4
Travel	15.61	710	13.52	86.6	1,223	15.84	101.5	2,439	10.03	64.3
True crime	11.60	169	11.42	98.4	210	10.37	89.4	218	10.72	92.4
Young adult	8.83	1,861	9.61	108.8	1,892	11.96	135.4	2,324	20.97	237.5
Totals	$57.38	53,731	$44.30	77.2	67,145	$41.61	72.5	111,150	$27.34	47.6

(continued from page 501)
Questions regarding this index should be addressed to the author: Frederick Lynden, Retired Director, Scholarly Communication and Library Research, Brown University Library, Providence, RI 02912 (e-mail flynden@stanfordalumni.org).

Prices of Other Media

The Library Materials Price Index Editorial Board has continued its work on a price index for electronic journals. A preliminary pricing model and index may appear in next year's article.

Foreign Prices

The dollar posted only a slight decline from 2010 against the euro, the British pound sterling, and the Canadian dollar. The dollar continues to experience steep declines against the Japanese yen. Worldwide economic volatility was undiminished in 2011.

Dates	12/30/07*	12/31/08*	12/31/09*	12/31/10*	12/31/11*
Canada	0.9990	1.1910	1.0510	1.0200	1.0180
Euro	0.6800	0.7310	0.6950	0.7700	0.7650
U.K.	0.4860	0.6570	0.6160	0.6400	0.6370
Japan	110.8800	92.6500	92.3900	83.8300	8.0000

* Data from Financial Management Services. U.S. Treasury Department (http://fms.treas.gov/intn.html).

Serials Prices

Average Price of Serials (Table 8), compiled by Stephen Bosch, provides the average prices and percent increases for serials based on titles in select serials indexes. The serials included here are published in the United States as well as overseas and are indexed in ISI Arts and Humanities Citation Index, ISI Science Citation Index, ISI Social Sciences Citation Index, EBSCO Academic Search Complete, and EBSCO Masterfile Premier.

Table 8 covers prices for periodicals and serials for a five-year period, 2008 through 2012. The 2012 pricing is the renewal pricing for 2012. This table is derived from pricing data supplied by EBSCO Subscription Services and reflects broad pricing changes aggregated from titles that are indexed in the five major products mentioned above. The USPPI (Table 1) is based on price changes seen in a static set of approximately 3,700 serial titles, while Table 8 is based on a much broader set of titles, approximately 10,000. The titles are not static, so this pricing study does not rise to the level of a price index. This study is still useful, however, in showing price changes for periodicals. The indexes selected for this price survey were deemed to be fairly representative of serials that are frequently purchased in academic and public libraries. There are some foreign titles in the indexes, so the scope is broader and this may give a better picture of the overall price pressures experienced in libraries.

The most important trend seen in this data is that after a modest increase in prices for 2010 (3.8 percent), the overall price increase has risen to 9.2 percent in 2012. The respite in price increases seen in 2010 appears to be ending. Libraries were very vocal about not being able to sustain high rates of inflation, and in 2010 price increases moderated significantly. That moderation is now over. The price increase in 2012 is higher than those for 2008 (7.7 percent) and 2009 (8.3 percent) and is a large departure from the rate (3.8 percent) seen in 2010.

Another interesting trend is that the science areas do not dominate the list of subjects with the largest price increases. The subject areas that displayed large increases were quite varied and included history, health sciences, geography, sociology, technology, engineering, agriculture, recreation, and anthropology. Average prices of journals in the science and technology areas are higher by far than those in other areas, and that trend continues, with the average cost of chemistry and physics journals being $4,152 and $3,679, respectively. Although STM titles are not inflating at high rates, the impact of a 4.6 percent increase on a $4,000 title is much greater than a 9 percent increase on a $300 title.

In this price study, as in similar price surveys, the data become less accurate at describing price changes as the sample becomes smaller. For that reason, conclusions about price changes in subject areas with a limited number of titles will be less accurate than for large areas or the broader price survey. Price changes are far more volatile where smaller data sets are used. For example, anthropology (about 84 titles) showed price changes of 5.5 percent, 10.5 percent, 6.0 percent, 9.6 percent, and 37.5 percent between 2008 and 2012. Librarians are encouraged to look at an average price change over the period (anthropology averaged 13 percent) or the overall number for the price study (9.2 percent) to calculate inflation rates. Year-to-year price changes are too unstable to be used for this purpose.

Book Prices

British Academic Books (Table 9), compiled by Judy Jeng, indicates the average prices and price indexes for 2009 through 2011 with the percent of change from 2010 to 2011. This index has been re-established using data provided by Baker & Taylor. The previous index, compiled by Curt Holleman, was based on data supplied by Blackwell's Book Services, and may not be comparable.

The average price in pounds of a British academic book went from £51.97 in 2010 to £59.60 in 2011, a surprising increase of 14.7 percent. This index utilizes prices from cloth editions except when not available, and does not separate out more expensive reference titles. As previously mentioned, small numbers of titles that include higher-priced reference sets may not reliable indicators of price changes. This index does not include e-book prices.

British academic book production has seen a decline, from 18,490 titles in 2010 to 16,452 titles in 2011, a decrease of 11.02 percent.

(text continues on page 513)

Table 8 / Average Price of Serials, Based on Titles in Select Serials Indexes: 2008–2012

Subject	LC Class	2008			2009			2010			2011			2012		
		No. of Titles	Avg. Price	% of Price Increase	No. of Titles	Avg. Price	% of Price Increase	No. of Titles	Avg. Price	% of Price Increase	No. of Titles	Avg. Price	% of Price Increase	No. of Titles	Avg. Price	% of Price Increase
Agriculture	S	287	$760	8.1%	286	$819	7.8%	288	$869	6.1%	289	$958	10.2%	288	$1,156	20.6%
Anthropology	GN	84	286	5.5	80	316	10.5	81	335	6.0	84	367	9.6	81	504	37.5
Arts and architecture	N	168	272	11.0	165	294	8.1	169	324	10.2	171	343	5.9	169	298	-13.0
Astronomy	QB	46	1,722	7.1	47	1,852	7.5	47	1,968	6.3	50	2,067	5.0	47	2,211	7.0
Biology	QH	370	1,693	7.8	369	1,836	8.4	371	1,937	5.5	369	2,091	8.0	370	2,214	5.9
Botany	QK	91	1,416	7.5	92	1,537	8.5	92	1,631	6.1	94	1,725	5.8	93	1,772	2.7
Business and economics	HA-HJ	684	584	6.8	683	628	7.5	693	668	6.4	694	716	7.2	676	782	9.2
Chemistry	QD	308	3,334	6.8	313	3,548	6.4	315	3,702	4.3	320	3,969	7.2	318	4,152	4.6
Education	L	437	343	9.6	437	369	7.6	437	387	4.9	440	468	20.9	411	516	10.3
Engineering	T	536	1,488	7.2	539	1,604	7.8	540	1,690	5.4	543	1,796	6.3	713	2,124	18.2
Food science	TX	59	588	3.5	59	635	8.0	60	674	6.1	60	727	7.9	60	771	6.1
General science	Q	137	934	7.9	137	1,005	7.6	137	1,064	5.9	141	1,146	7.7	136	1,258	9.7
General works	A	238	132	6.5	235	135	2.3	238	142	5.2	236	149	4.9	232	136	-8.7
Geography	G-GF	147	773	10.1	153	818	5.8	153	886	8.3	151	949	7.1	152	1,099	15.8
Geology	QE	129	1,191	-5.8	131	1,438	20.7	132	1,511	5.1	126	1,621	7.3	125	1,731	6.8
Health sciences	R	2,435	1,137	8.6	2,440	1,241	9.1	2,444	1,233	-0.6	2,474	1,382	12.1	2,440	1,560	12.9
History	C,D,E,F	591	226	11.9	599	245	8.4	522	267	9.0	630	284	6.4	652	315	10.9
Language and literature	P	600	223	10.4	598	216	-3.1	626	260	20.4	660	271	4.2	663	288	6.3
Law	K	187	310	10.7	178	339	9.4	193	412	21.5	198	431	4.6	191	372	-13.8
Library science	Z	139	352	7.6	138	372	5.7	139	385	3.5	142	399	3.6	132	379	-5.1

Subject	LC Class	Titles	Price	%	Titles	Price	%	Titles	Price	%	Titles	Price	%	Titles	Price	%
Math and computer science	QA	371	1,317	7.1	371	1,411	7.1	372	1,466	3.9	384	1,550	5.7	373	1,660	7.1
Military and naval science	U,V	51	295	11.7	51	333	12.9	45	406	21.9	45	414	2.0	44	396	-4.4
Music	M	94	198	31.1	93	210	6.1	95	220	4.8	96	238	8.2	91	195	-18.0
Philosophy and religion	B-BD, BH-BX	343	262	9.2	341	289	10.3	386	322	11.4	396	344	6.8	397	329	-4.2
Physics	QC	353	3,077	5.3	356	3,256	5.8	360	3,386	4.0	360	3,531	4.3	347	3,679	4.2
Political science	J	158	463	7.9	158	508	9.7	163	527	3.7	166	577	9.5	165	601	4.2
Psychology	BF	176	581	9.0	177	638	9.8	181	679	6.4	182	722	6.3	260	771	6.8
Recreation	QV	72	193	11.6	70	212	9.8	71	218	2.8	73	230	5.5	74	282	22.5
Social sciences	H	101	456	9.1	100	501	9.9	101	525	4.8	103	547	4.2	102	555	1.4
Sociology	HM-HX	343	484	11.3	348	518	7.0	350	552	6.6	353	590	6.9	539	685	16.1
Technology	TA-TT	99	853	8.8	98	979	14.8	98	1,038	6.0	99	1,098	5.8	120	1,286	17.1
Zoology	QL	171	1,278	10.2	171	1,394	9.1	176	1,452	4.2	179	1,512	4.1	175	1,634	8.0
Totals		10,005	$950	7.7%	10,013	$1,029	8.3%	10,075	$1,068	3.8%	10,308	$1,144	7.1%	10,636	$1,250	9.2%

Compiled by Stephen Bosch, University of Arizona, from data on serial pricing supplied by EBSCO based on titles indexed in ISI Arts and Humanities Citation Index, ISI Science Citation Index, ISI Social Sciences Citation Index, EBSCO Academic Search Complete, and EBSCO Masterfile Premier.

Table 9 / British Academic Books: Average Prices and Price Indexes 2009–2011
(Index Base: 2009 = 100)

Subject	LC Class	2009 No. of Titles	2009 Average Price (£)	2010 No. of Titles	2010 Average Price (£)	2011 No. of Titles	2011 Average Price (£)	2011 % Change 2010–2011	2011 Index
Agriculture	S	140	53.96	154	63.97	177	58.83	-8.0%	109.0
Anthropology	GN	109	53.60	154	50.85	111	59.74	17.5	111.5
Botany	QK	22	145.94	45	66.08	39	85.29	29.1	58.4
Business and economics	H-HJ	2,439	59.12	2,874	61.09	1,690	63.89	4.6	108.1
Chemistry	QD	88	101.14	96	105.68	87	116.07	9.8	114.8
Education	L	386	49.70	558	52.21	456	52.98	1.5	106.6
Engineering and technology	T	716	65.60	655	65.73	639	81.66	24.2	124.5
Fine and applied arts	M, N	762	39.71	1,037	37.00	949	44.63	20.6	112.4
General works	A	15	76.73	30	60.03	24	69.50	15.8	90.6
Geography	G-GF, GR-GT	233	50.98	660	64.95	294	52.61	-19.0	103.2
Geology	QE	41	53.80	33	52.28	35	57.97	10.9	107.8
History	C,D,E,F	1,572	41.01	1,822	48.13	1,586	48.51	0.8	118.3
Home economics	TX	59	39.02	46	30.48	34	48.40	58.8	124.0
Industrial arts	TT	21	24.32	41	28.47	42	36.62	28.6	150.6
Law	K	1,117	76.13	1,153	83.10	1,159	78.79	-5.2	103.5
Library and information science	Z	98	60.32	100	53.58	104	61.51	14.8	102.0
Literature and language	P	2,928	34.77	3,987	31.58	3,526	32.71	3.6	94.1
Mathematics and computer science	QA	216	49.30	207	48.29	245	55.79	15.5	113.2
Medicine	R	1,110	48.50	1,182	55.12	1,177	55.02	-0.2	113.4
Military and naval sciences	U, V	112	83.99	184	38.00	133	45.16	18.8	53.8
Philosophy and religion	B	1,091	46.45	1,336	45.24	1,151	48.30	6.8	104.0
Physics and astronomy	QB, QC	196	54.54	214	59.69	215	62.78	5.2	115.1
Political Science	J	621	59.74	737	71.88	671	62.95	-12.4	105.4
Psychology	BF	195	44.46	265	39.69	264	46.77	17.8	105.2
Science (general)	Q	55	42.12	69	36.32	60	51.05	40.6	121.2
Sociology	HM-HX	153	74.17	208	70.13	1,069	62.67	-10.6	84.5
Sports & Recreation	GV	181	30.90	192	36.76	145	46.83	27.4	151.6
Zoology	QH, QL-QR	326	66.20	373	72.30	370	81.77	13.1	123.5
Total, All Books		15,432	52.91	18,490	51.97	16,452	59.60	14.7%	112.6

Compiled by Judy Jeng, University of Illinois at Urbana-Champaign, based on information provided by Baker & Taylor.

(continued from page 509)

Using the Price Indexes

Librarians are encouraged to monitor trends in the publishing industry and changes in economic conditions when preparing budget forecasts and projections. The ALA ALCTS Library Materials Price Index Editorial Board endeavors to make information on publishing trends readily available by sponsoring the annual compilation and publication of price data contained in Tables 1 to 9. The indexes cover newly published library materials and document prices and rates of percent changes at the national and international level. They are useful benchmarks against which local costs can be compared, but because they reflect retail prices in the aggregate, they are not a substitute for cost data that reflect the collecting patterns of individual libraries, and they are not a substitute for specific cost studies.

Differences between local prices and those found in national indexes arise partially because these indexes exclude discounts, service charges, shipping and handling fees, and other costs that a library might incur. Discrepancies may also relate to a library's subject coverage; mix of titles purchased, including both current and backfiles; and the proportion of the library's budget expended on domestic or foreign materials. These variables can affect the average price paid by an individual library, although the individual library's rate of increase may not differ greatly from the national indexes.

LMPI is interested in pursuing studies that would correlate a particular library's costs with the national prices. The group welcomes interested parties to its meetings at ALA Annual and Midwinter conferences.

The Library Materials Price Index Editorial Board consists of compilers Catherine Barr, Ajaye Bloomstone, Stephen Bosch, Brenda Dingley, Judy Jeng, Frederick C. Lynden, and editor Narda Tafuri.

Book Title Output and Average Prices: 2008–2011

Catherine Barr
Contributing Editor

Constance Harbison
Baker & Taylor

The print publishing industry is showing signs of recovering from the worst of the economic downturn even as the surge in popularity of e-books raises questions about the future of printed materials. From a high of 190,502 titles in 2007, overall American book title output fell to 178,841 in 2009 but climbed back to 186,344 in 2010; preliminary figures for 2011 showed a decline but are likely to be revised upward as late-arriving materials are added to the database (publishers were still submitting late 2011 titles in early 2012). The number of titles published dropped by 5.5 percent in 2008 and 0.66 percent in 2009, then rose by 4.2 percent in 2010 only to fall again by 4.95 percent in the preliminary figures for 2011.

The figures for this edition of the *Library and Book Trade Almanac* were provided by book wholesaler Baker & Taylor and are based on the Book Industry Study Group's BISAC categories. The BISAC juvenile category (fiction and non-fiction) has been divided into children's (Pre-K–6) and young adult (YA; grades 7–12). Figures for 2010 have been restated, reflecting late updates to the Baker & Taylor database.

For more information on the BISAC categories, visit http://www.bisg.org.

This year we have added a new table covering e-books, with historical data going back to 2008.

Output by Format and by Category

Output was generally lower in 2011, with the following formats showing varying degrees of decline: hardcover (down 1.12 percent following growth of 1.63 percent the previous year), hardcovers less than $81 (down 4.25 percent after a drop of 3.46 percent), mass market paperbacks (down 1.11 percent, slightly less than the previous 1.34 percent), trade paperbacks (down 7.44 percent, wiping out the 5.32 percent gain in 2010), and audiobooks (down 0.16 percent after rising 15.22 percent the previous year). Production of e-books, however, continued to soar, registering a gain of 65.54 percent and building on hikes of 24.97 percent in 2010 and 51.37 percent in 2009.

Fiction, a key category, rose 9.95 percent in 2011 after a disappointing performance in 2010 and registered overall output of 19,760. Hardcover fiction costing less than $81 (Table 3) has fallen steadily since 2008, declining 8.20 percent in 2009, 2.43 percent in 2010, and a further 6.31 percent in 2011. In the paperback sector, mass market fiction (Table 4) dropped 1.52 percent in 2010 but recovered slightly with a posting of 0.61 percent in 2011 while trade fiction (Table 5) fell 1.53 percent in 2010 but recovered by 21.61 percent in 2011. Audiobook fiction (Table 6), which had jumped an impressive 43.37 percent in 2009, registered a more modest increase of 21.84 percent in 2010 and fell 6.68 percent in 2011.

Table 1 / American Book Production, 2007–2011

BISAC Category	2007	2008	2009	2010	2011
Antiques and collectibles	485	445	359	366	296
Architecture	1,504	1,548	1,534	1,495	1,396
Art	3,347	3,261	3,181	3,213	3,233
Bibles	467	554	474	614	966
Biography and autobiography	4,116	3,935	4,012	4,105	4,038
Body, mind and spirit	1,276	1,319	1,216	1,189	1,213
Business and economics	14,593	9,593	10,006	10,024	9,278
Children	24,440	22,603	22,395	20,562	20,127
Comics and graphic novels	2,491	2,869	2,906	2,542	2,644
Computers	4,590	4,014	4,589	4,312	4,105
Cooking	1,957	2,294	1,835	2,131	2,061
Crafts and hobbies	1,247	1,212	1,240	1,271	1,294
Design	800	739	728	878	846
Drama	666	714	665	875	508
Education	5,428	5,277	4,673	4,955	4,573
Family and relationships	1,317	1,256	1,185	1,064	840
Fiction	18,471	18,638	18,272	17,971	19,760
Foreign language study	1,431	1,550	1,114	1,464	1,383
Games	1,022	958	959	955	754
Gardening	431	517	397	359	355
Health and fitness	1,962	1,847	1,710	1,601	1,607
History	11,526	10,658	11,157	11,975	11,409
House and home	481	412	340	290	231
Humor	710	708	715	651	580
Language arts and disciplines	3,436	2,967	3,590	3,985	3,386
Law	4,318	5,363	4,266	4,925	4,922
Literary collections	1,031	922	955	998	819
Literary criticism	3,401	3,158	3,679	3,580	3,720
Mathematics	2,025	1,888	1,829	2,549	2,380
Medical	7,331	7,092	6,891	8,574	7,206
Music	3,149	3,408	3,497	3,541	3,057
Nature	1,145	1,039	1,025	944	905
Performing arts	1,681	1,610	1,481	1,569	1,509
Pets	546	474	475	388	320
Philosophy	2,631	2,246	2,456	2,447	2,392
Photography	1,375	1,417	1,344	1,345	1,369
Poetry	2,215	2,126	2,018	2,015	1,947
Political science	5,988	5,655	5,927	6,703	6,057
Psychology	2,698	2,456	2,339	2,882	2,525
Reference	1,933	1,975	1,872	1,601	1,569
Religion	8,065	8,276	8,415	9,550	8,871
Science	5,596	5,324	5,740	7,782	6,475
Self-help	1,548	1,474	1,360	1,379	1,206
Social science	6,997	6,998	7,037	7,353	7,005
Sports and recreation	2,054	2,081	1,882	1,968	1,776
Study aids	704	898	694	1,519	990
Technology and engineering	4,642	4,739	5,134	4,907	4,561
Transportation	701	742	706	800	752
Travel	4,206	3,542	3,238	2,953	2,719
True crime	303	291	301	316	286
Young adult	6,025	4,950	5,028	4,909	4,905
Totals	190,502	180,032	178,841	186,344	177,126

E-books output (Table 7) may explain a lot of the declines in other fiction formats, with totals rising from 7,414 in 2008 to a whopping 39,886 in 2011 (with increases of 80.25 percent in 2009, 35.01 percent in 2010, and 121.06 percent in 2011).

Production of children's books (Pre-K–6) fell gradually from 2008 through 2011, with declines of 8.18 percent in 2010 and 2.12 percent in 2011. Hardcover children's books priced at less than $81 dropped from 12,796 titles in 2008 to 10,801 in 2011, a fall of 15.60 percent over the period. Mass market and trade paperbacks moved up and down over the four-year period, while audiobooks and e-books showed consistent growth, with audiobooks up 8.05 percent in 2010 and 7.68 percent in 2011; e-books registered gains of 84 percent in 2009, 19.27 percent in 2010, and an impressive 182.61 percent in 2011.

YA titles overall seemed more stable, registering output of 4,950 in 2008 and 4,905 in 2011, with fluctuations in the intervening years. Hardcover titles priced at less than $81 grew slightly over the period, with gains of 11.47 percent in 2009 and 8.87 percent in 2010, followed by a decline of 4.02 percent in 2011. Mass market paperbacks continued their steady decline, with a significant drop of 40.96 percent in 2011, while trade paperbacks fared slightly better with a hike of 5.43 percent in 2011 after two years of decline. YA audiobooks showed healthy growth in 2009 and 2010 (95.9 percent and 68.5 percent, respectively) before posting a more modest (8.11 percent) gain in 2011.

A review of overall output in nonfiction categories (Table 1) shows the usual variations. Of the 51 categories, 42 lost ground in 2011. The only categories that registered significant increases were Bibles (up 57.33 percent) and fiction (up 9.95 percent). Double-digit losses were common and covered the gamut from antiques and collectibles to study aids (down 34.83 percent).

Average Book Prices

Average book prices were mixed in 2011. List prices for hardcovers overall (Table 2) rose only 1.07 percent after a climb of 5.54 percent in 2010, and those for hard-covers under $81 increased just less than 1 percent.

Mass market paperback prices continued their slow but steady increase, rising another 2.05 percent. In contrast, trade paperback prices lost ground in 2011, declining 12.08 percent after a surprising jump of 7.30 percent in 2010. And audiobook prices (Table 6) saw drops of 1.19 percent in 2010 and 4.25 percent in 2011.

Average book prices for fiction were also mixed in 2011. Hardcover fiction titles priced at less than $81 edged up a mere 6 cents (0.21 percent) after rising 14 cents (0.50 percent) in 2010. Mass market fiction fared slightly better, rising 15 cents (2.21 percent), and trade fiction continued its steady climb, up 26 cents or 1.45 percent. Audiobook fiction prices, however, fell for the second year in a row, and e-book pricing was down a hefty 24.79 percent.

Average prices for hardcovers under $81 in the important children's category have been fairly stable over the last few years, falling 0.51 percent in 2010 and 1.23 percent in 2011. Children's mass market paperbacks, on the other hand, rose steadily, posting gains of 1.63 percent in 2010 and 4.02 percent in 2011; while the more important sector of trade paperbacks saw declines of 4.49 percent in 2010 and 3.65 percent in 2011. Children's audiobook prices fell 8.65 percent in 2011 after climbing 4.36 percent in 2010.

In the hardcovers under $81 sector, YA prices recovered 0.11 percent in 2011 after slipping fell by 2.01 percent in 2010, while trade paperback prices continued to slide (down 2.49 percent in 2011). YA audiobooks followed a similar trend, declining 6.96 percent in 2011.

Prices for e-books for Pre-K–12 readers have been climbing steadily, with children's prices rising from $12.01 in 2008 to $19.83 in 2011 and YA rising from $8.83 to $20.97 over the same period. The children's sector showed an average hike of 43.49 percent in 2011 and the YA sector was up a strong 75.33 percent.

Price declines exceeded increases in the hardcover sector (Table 2). Categories showing substantial price increases in 2011 included health and fitness (up 27.79 percent) and reference (up 26.86 percent). Double-digit declines were seen in categories with small numbers of titles.

There were some substantial swings in pricing for trade paperbacks, with many gains in 2010 being erased by losses in 2011.

The rise in audiobook prices generally stalled or declined in 2011, with popular categories such as biography and autobiography and history rising only 0.93 percent and 2.22 percent, respectively. (Audio fiction, children's, and YA sectors are discussed above.)

Despite the increases in prices for children's and YA e-books mentioned earlier, results for e-books are mixed, with 37 categories posting declines. Biography and autobiography, for example, showed a 21.91 percent drop; history was down 23.98 percent; medical lost 13.77 percent; and science was down 8.74. Gainers included business and economics, up 0.63 percent; computers, up 2.35 percent; and education, up 4.94 percent.

Table 2 / Hardcover Average Per-Volume Prices, 2008–2011

BISAC Category	2008			2009			2010			2011		
	Vols.	$ Total	Prices	Vols.	$ Total	Prices	Vols.	$ Total	Prices	Vols.	$ Total	Prices
Antiques and collectibles	195	$15,763.28	$80.84	159	$7,469.68	$46.98	179	$9,208.36	$5 1.44	152	$8,154.04	$53.64
Architecture	853	66,141.71	77.54	842	71,115.56	84.46	742	63,455.32	85.52	700	55,464.58	79.24
Art	1,681	142,524.38	84.79	1,688	126,824.23	75.13	1,687	120,672.85	71.53	1,678	125,904.09	75.03
Bibles	191	9,396.02	49.19	165	7,643.10	46.32	185	6,937.14	37.50	220	10,542.40	47.92
Biography and autobiography	1,714	98,643.35	57.55	1,652	82,734.86	50.08	1,658	88,546.37	53.41	1,588	80,451.97	50.66
Body, mind and spirit	233	6,085.82	26.12	194	5,355.04	27.60	177	6,532.28	36.91	136	4,131.10	30.38
Business and economics	3,581	480,896.85	134.29	3,913	483,112.81	123.46	3,977	535,329.39	134.61	4,127	545,644.60	132.21
Children	13,235	362,043.14	27.35	12,396	310,031.58	25.01	11,675	287,595.70	24.63	11,277	302,084.72	26.79
Comics and graphic novels	462	15,084.50	32.65	732	23,474.46	32.07	679	21,394.39	31.51	753	26,449.80	35.13
Computers	731	107,032.74	146.42	786	122,508.69	155.86	834	115,535.07	138.53	912	124,233.47	136.22
Cooking	1,015	30,443.41	29.99	814	24,041.89	29.54	1,016	31,405.09	30.91	956	28,348.83	29.65
Crafts and hobbies	267	7,361.24	27.57	237	7,094.80	29.94	217	7,222.08	33.28	216	6,630.57	30.70
Design	358	22,273.82	62.22	331	22,019.63	66.52	435	33,317.52	76.59	447	30,743.73	68.78
Drama	192	10,300.98	53.65	81	6,723.29	83.00	133	5,706.38	42.91	94	4,877.80	51.89
Education	1,330	148,820.74	111.90	1,392	146,944.34	105.56	1,345	158,158.85	117.59	1,397	165,488.30	118.46
Family and relationships	301	8,839.56	29.37	296	9,936.85	33.57	277	8,931.75	32.24	195	6,179.03	31.69
Fiction	4,976	144,477.84	29.03	4,556	131,127.58	28.78	4,464	143,724.29	32.20	4,169	123,464.65	29.61
Foreign language study	146	16,159.40	110.68	120	15,840.79	132.01	123	16,293.93	132.47	140	16,664.15	119.03
Games	145	5,678.75	39.16	167	6,258.91	37.48	163	8,486.77	52.07	96	3,516.03	36.63
Gardening	149	6,318.83	42.41	140	5,177.87	36.98	118	4,297.09	36.42	114	4,739.74	41.58
Health and fitness	449	27,425.63	61.08	356	18,078.72	50.78	309	14,990.57	48.51	326	20,209.78	61.99
History	4,795	419,378.14	87.46	4,687	395,609.19	84.41	4,927	407,233.60	82.65	4,618	385,577.20	83.49
House and home	117	4,779.14	40.85	113	4,569.88	40.44	90	4,014.78	44.61	93	3,534.20	38.00

Humor	241	4,921.32	20.42	229	4,635.89	20.24	221	4,849.44	21.94	195	3,834.67	19.66
Language arts and disciplines	1,300	173,479.85	133.45	1,485	195,067.50	131.36	1,613	189,802.42	117.67	1,541	179,347.77	116.38
Law	1,516	247,998.43	163.59	1,515	252,397.29	166.60	1,714	299,062.75	174.48	1,788	313,985.73	175.61
Literary collections	383	34,373.11	89.75	373	33,600.00	90.08	325	27,134.42	83.49	340	30,565.18	89.90
Literary criticism	1,707	181,073.91	106.08	1,903	205,616.68	108.05	1,955	229,962.69	117.63	2,053	246,065.52	119.86
Mathematics	916	117,073.40	127.81	895	104,786.72	117.08	1,028	136,962.32	133.23	1,079	138,941.25	128.77
Medical	3,076	476,516.50	154.91	2,924	485,153.60	165.92	3,153	539,557.59	171.13	3,096	507,020.45	163.77
Music	485	33,628.05	69.34	520	40,214.72	77.34	502	44,097.69	87.84	500	43,933.79	87.87
Nature	435	27,221.52	62.58	411	27,055.02	65.83	377	28,234.52	74.89	402	29,765.58	74.04
Performing arts	618	50,450.12	81.63	540	43,721.93	80.97	531	40,500.99	76.27	578	46,274.24	80.06
Pets	181	5,318.82	29.39	176	4,407.15	25.04	138	3,402.88	24.66	123	2,556.97	20.79
Philosophy	973	95,896.54	98.56	990	92,845.84	93.78	1,044	113,724.14	108.93	1,052	103,908.48	98.77
Photography	882	72,886.61	82.64	805	65,864.70	81.82	800	86,393.32	107.99	837	50,661.41	60.53
Poetry	339	14,406.45	42.50	293	13,324.37	45.48	294	11,982.30	40.76	241	9,548.62	39.62
Political science	2,492	242,055.07	97.13	2,698	291,658.10	108.10	2,671	294,673.30	110.32	2,687	287,352.40	106.94
Psychology	1,063	108,360.07	101.94	1,031	107,518.67	104.29	1,138	125,012.56	109.85	1,082	122,149.00	112.89
Reference	613	178,211.72	290.72	558	153,354.85	274.83	541	163,753.31	302.69	499	191,614.23	384.00
Religion	2,449	166,622.19	68.04	2,353	170,926.23	72.64	2,590	209,468.75	80.88	2,466	192,371.10	78.01
Science	3,171	649,242.37	204.74	3,161	601,882.90	190.41	3,557	683,655.73	192.20	3,590	681,807.55	189.92
Self-help	322	8,265.48	25.67	311	6,690.61	21.51	257	6,967.70	27.11	197	4,616.18	23.43
Social science	2,948	288,701.80	97.93	3,019	310,154.24	102.73	3,027	304,118.83	100.47	3,158	325,322.36	103.02
Sports and recreation	746	30,938.26	41.47	619	23,927.64	38.66	652	26,883.77	41.23	635	28,383.88	44.70
Study aids	17	1,334.40	78.49	24	2,751.35	114.64	17	1,726.24	101.54	19	1,911.30	100.59
Technology and engineering	2,145	340,632.86	158.80	2,439	392,271.18	160.83	2,455	404,250.43	164.66	2,770	454,356.24	164.03
Transportation	312	20,043.82	64.24	245	18,614.53	75.98	292	24,609.98	84.28	315	18,869.19	59.90
Travel	457	15,904.23	34.80	384	15,827.41	41.22	367	15,164.44	41.32	332	14,210.82	42.80
True crime	94	2,474.48	26.32	93	2,730.42	29.36	67	2,333.57	34.83	73	2,269.03	31.08
Young adult	2,256	111,464.02	49.41	2,466	92,170.46	37.38	2,653	95,478.35	35.99	2,561	94,934.08	37.07
Totals	69,253	$5,855,364.67	$84.55	68,277	$5,792,863.75	$84.84	69,389	$6,212,754.00	$89.54	68,613	$6,209,611.80	$90.50

Table 3 / Hardcover Average Per-Volume Prices, Less Than $81, 2008–2011

BISAC Category	2008			2009			2010			2011		
	Vols.	$ Total	Prices	Vols.	$ Total	Prices	Vols.	$ Total	Prices	Vols.	$ Total	Prices
Antiques and collectibles	158	$6,091.85	$38.56	140	$5,250.25	$37.50	147	$4,501.00	$30.62	125	$4,880.61	$39.04
Architecture	613	31,148.56	50.81	564	29,288.70	51.93	493	25,651.77	52.03	487	24,882.80	51.09
Art	1,333	62,046.12	46.55	1,364	63,705.85	46.71	1,335	62,565.70	46.87	1,316	61,578.27	46.79
Bibles	177	6,708.32	37.90	158	6,370.23	40.32	177	5,953.20	33.63	204	7,258.96	35.58
Biography and autobiography	1,510	47,377.50	31.38	1,482	45,428.56	30.65	1,466	46,136.67	31.47	1,402	43,543.62	31.06
Body, mind and spirit	222	4,861.07	21.90	183	4,031.74	22.03	166	4,356.88	26.25	129	3,403.21	26.38
Business and economics	1,615	66,649.41	41.27	1,814	72,002.39	39.69	1,617	64,601.18	39.95	1,668	70,067.62	42.01
Children	12,796	250,571.44	19.58	12,073	236,547.64	19.59	11,295	220,108.19	19.49	10,801	207,898.90	19.25
Comics and graphic novels	434	12,220.74	28.16	710	20,811.69	29.31	659	18,799.44	28.53	719	22,463.58	31.24
Computers	240	14,827.83	61.78	181	10,900.85	60.23	185	11,010.71	59.52	259	15,772.11	60.90
Cooking	987	26,659.53	27.01	805	23,192.54	28.81	977	25,089.56	25.68	934	24,675.83	26.42
Crafts and hobbies	266	7,276.24	27.35	232	6,590.35	28.41	209	6,158.08	29.46	209	5,970.67	28.57
Design	307	14,911.87	48.57	277	13,520.48	48.81	339	15,713.02	46.35	354	17,238.00	48.69
Drama	168	6,923.43	41.21	37	1,680.29	45.41	106	2,642.48	24.93	67	1,797.50	26.83
Education	625	35,825.96	57.32	649	36,057.56	55.56	471	24,227.11	51.44	494	26,183.98	53.00
Family and relationships	279	6,119.71	21.93	271	6,413.10	23.66	254	6,098.65	24.01	177	3,983.58	22.51
Fiction	4,935	136,931.49	27.75	4,530	127,152.18	28.07	4,420	124,701.19	28.21	4,141	117,085.40	28.27
Foreign language study	71	3,764.05	53.01	46	2,152.49	46.79	37	1,732.59	46.83	46	2,206.09	47.96
Games	139	4,415.85	31.77	161	5,377.91	33.40	157	4,176.77	26.60	91	2,842.03	31.23
Gardening	141	5,084.13	36.06	134	4,558.07	34.02	115	3,933.09	34.20	109	4,028.79	36.96
Health and fitness	342	10,366.78	30.31	303	10,085.59	33.29	260	8,412.02	32.35	258	7,829.69	30.35
History	3,210	139,908.95	43.59	3,066	136,103.66	44.39	3,076	140,793.51	45.77	2,762	121,380.75	43.95
House and home	110	3,874.20	35.22	107	3,928.93	36.72	85	3,060.93	36.01	91	3,064.20	33.67

Category												
Humor	238	4,483.44	18.84	226	4,301.94	19.04	218	4,491.49	20.60	193	3,589.67	18.60
Language arts and disciplines	517	28,871.62	55.84	551	32,192.66	58.43	669	38,841.54	58.06	579	34,166.04	59.01
Law	331	17,692.70	53.45	278	15,704.82	56.49	332	17,978.77	54.15	266	14,758.93	55.48
Literary collections	265	12,426.71	46.89	237	10,737.27	45.30	211	9,636.37	45.67	196	8,980.03	45.82
Literary criticism	841	47,022.07	55.91	872	47,594.62	54.58	783	44,251.02	56.51	823	48,219.39	58.59
Mathematics	255	16,019.92	62.82	264	16,163.72	61.23	227	14,162.41	62.39	220	13,962.85	63.47
Medical	572	32,413.01	56.67	450	25,644.77	56.99	448	24,869.75	55.51	416	24,042.18	57.79
Music	351	15,137.90	43.13	352	15,543.74	44.16	320	14,115.74	44.11	310	13,551.54	43.71
Nature	342	12,455.23	36.42	294	10,642.04	36.20	255	9,633.42	37.78	269	9,783.88	36.37
Performing arts	378	18,878.72	49.94	314	14,787.15	47.09	326	15,627.22	47.94	309	15,956.99	51.64
Pets	179	4,356.83	24.34	173	4,112.20	23.77	137	3,257.88	23.78	123	2,556.97	20.79
Philosophy	489	26,490.89	54.17	441	23,240.50	52.70	441	24,659.66	55.92	479	25,795.33	53.85
Photography	793	34,612.03	43.65	706	31,564.61	44.71	705	33,865.63	48.04	724	34,462.98	47.60
Poetry	303	9,594.30	31.66	255	7,652.03	30.01	263	7,886.00	29.98	222	6,716.22	30.25
Political science	1,258	61,728.66	49.07	1,175	57,443.46	48.89	1,030	49,757.20	48.31	944	45,419.44	48.11
Psychology	460	23,722.51	51.57	477	24,580.38	51.53	456	23,807.86	52.21	474	25,192.67	53.15
Reference	270	9,210.17	34.11	238	8,588.83	36.09	219	7,565.84	34.55	196	6,270.62	31.99
Religion	1,762	55,636.12	31.58	1,614	53,692.99	33.27	1,645	54,558.92	33.17	1,524	52,153.63	34.22
Science	645	32,356.74	50.17	683	33,617.88	49.22	655	33,131.00	50.58	650	32,389.12	49.83
Self-help	311	6,884.98	22.14	309	6,458.71	20.90	249	5,867.50	23.56	195	4,411.28	22.62
Social science	1,657	86,305.63	52.09	1,622	85,039.38	52.43	1,464	76,354.23	52.15	1,384	73,835.49	53.35
Sports and recreation	690	22,765.11	32.99	579	18,414.49	31.80	592	18,796.17	31.75	559	17,209.33	30.79
Study aids	12	558.50	46.54	15	661.50	44.10	12	514.59	42.88	13	562.60	43.28
Technology and engineering	305	16,902.02	55.42	269	15,258.54	56.72	248	13,114.69	52.88	294	16,998.76	57.82
Transportation	259	10,541.22	40.70	196	8,252.63	42.11	237	9,164.23	38.67	260	9,393.60	36.13
Travel	439	12,882.88	29.35	365	11,560.17	31.67	330	9,563.71	28.98	316	9,763.54	30.90
True crime	94	2,474.48	26.32	91	2,550.42	28.03	64	1,880.58	29.38	71	2,039.03	28.72
Young adult	2,093	56,380.12	26.94	2,333	67,217.00	28.81	2,540	71,701.20	28.23	2,438	68,890.45	28.26
Totals	46,787	$1,583,369.54	$33.84	44,666	$1,524,369.50	$34.13	43,122	$1,469,478.36	$34.08	41,290	$1,421,108.75	$34.42

Table 4 / Mass Market Paperbacks Average Per-Volume Prices, 2008–2011

BISAC Category	2008			2009			2010			2011		
	Vols.	$ Total	Prices	Vols.	$ Total	Prices	Vols.	$ Total	Prices	Vols.	$ Total	Prices
Antiques and collectibles	10	$85.90	$8.59	9	$77.91	$8.66	9	$78.91	$8.77	5	$43.95	$8.79
Architecture	n.a.	n.a.	n.a.	n.a.	n.a.	n.a.	n.a.	n.a.	n.a.	n.a.	n.a.	n.a.
Art	n.a.	n.a.	n.a.	n.a.	n.a.	n.a.	n.a.	n.a.	n.a.	n.a.	n.a.	n.a.
Bibles	n.a.	n.a.	n.a.	n.a.	n.a.	n.a.	n.a.	n.a.	n.a.	n.a.	n.a.	n.a.
Biography and autobiography	8	62.92	7.87	13	97.30	7.48	13	97.67	7.51	8	68.92	8.62
Body, mind and spirit	14	99.86	7.13	13	103.87	7.99	17	135.83	7.99	17	134.83	7.93
Business and economics	1	7.99	7.99	1	9.99	9.99	3	27.97	9.32	2	15.98	7.99
Children	239	1,420.29	5.94	238	1,456.16	6.12	257	1,597.94	6.22	244	1,579.56	6.47
Comics and graphic novels	n.a.	n.a.	n.a.	n.a.	n.a.	n.a.	n.a.	n.a.	n.a.	n.a.	n.a.	n.a.
Computers	n.a.	n.a.	n.a.	n.a.	n.a.	n.a.	n.a.	n.a.	n.a.	n.a.	n.a.	n.a.
Cooking	n.a.	n.a.	n.a.	n.a.	n.a.	n.a.	n.a.	n.a.	n.a.	1	7.99	7.99
Crafts and hobbies	n.a.	n.a.	n.a.	n.a.	n.a.	n.a.	n.a.	n.a.	n.a.	n.a.	n.a.	n.a.
Design	n.a.	n.a.	n.a.	n.a.	n.a.	n.a.	n.a.	n.a.	n.a.	n.a.	n.a.	n.a.
Drama	2	11.98	5.99	3	17.93	5.98	3	18.89	6.30	1	8.95	8.95
Education	n.a.	n.a.	n.a.	n.a.	n.a.	n.a.	n.a.	n.a.	n.a.	n.a.	n.a.	n.a.
Family and relationships	n.a.	n.a.	n.a.	1	4.99	4.99	1	7.99	7.99	1	8.99	8.99
Fiction	4,162	26,965.85	6.48	4,013	26,824.43	6.68	3,952	26,882.67	6.80	3,976	27,635.00	6.95
Foreign language study	5	30.95	6.19	4	27.96	6.99	6	42.45	7.08	n.a.	n.a.	n.a.
Games	13	70.87	5.45	5	24.95	4.99	n.a.	n.a.	n.a.	n.a.	n.a.	n.a.
Gardening	n.a.	n.a.	n.a.	n.a.	n.a.	n.a.	n.a.	n.a.	n.a.	n.a.	n.a.	n.a.
Health and fitness	18	137.82	7.66	15	116.85	7.79	14	110.86	7.92	10	79.90	7.99
History	3	17.48	5.83	5	39.46	7.89	1	9.95	9.95	7	59.89	8.56
House and home	n.a.	n.a.	n.a.	n.a.	n.a.	n.a.	n.a.	n.a.	n.a.	n.a.	n.a.	n.a.
Humor	3	18.97	6.32	n.a.	n.a.	n.a.	n.a.	n.a.	n.a.	1	3.50	3.50

Language arts and disciplines	n.a.	n.a.	n.a.	n.a.	n.a.	n.a.	n.a.	n.a.	n.a.	n.a.	n.a.	n.a.
Law	n.a.	n.a.	n.a.	n.a.	n.a.	n.a.	2	26.49	13.25	1	7.95	7.95
Literary collections	1	4.99	4.99	1	7.95	7.95	1	5.95	5.95	1	9.99	9.99
Literary criticism	1	7.95	7.95	1	7.99	7.99	1	7.99	7.99	n.a.	n.a.	n.a.
Mathematics	n.a.	n.a.	n.a.	n.a.	n.a.	n.a.	n.a.	n.a.	n.a.	1	7.95	7.95
Medical	1	7.50	7.50	n.a.	n.a.	n.a.	1	8.99	8.99	n.a.	n.a.	n.a.
Music	n.a.	n.a.	n.a.	n.a.	n.a.	n.a.	n.a.	n.a.	n.a.	2	17.98	8.99
Nature	n.a.	n.a.	n.a.	n.a.	n.a.	n.a.	n.a.	n.a.	n.a.	1	7.99	7.99
Performing arts	1	9.99	9.99	1	9.99	9.99	1	9.99	9.99	n.a.	n.a.	n.a.
Pets	1	7.99	7.99	n.a.	n.a.	n.a.	1	7.99	7.99	n.a.	n.a.	n.a.
Philosophy	2	11.90	5.95	n.a.	n.a.	n.a.	2	12.94	6.47	1	7.95	7.95
Photography	n.a.	n.a.	n.a.	n.a.	n.a.	n.a.	n.a.	n.a.	n.a.	1	5.95	5.95
Poetry	2	9.90	4.95	5	34.75	6.95	1	7.95	7.95	1	7.99	7.99
Political science	2	15.98	7.99	1	5.95	5.95	2	15.94	7.97	2	15.98	7.99
Psychology	n.a.	n.a.	n.a.	n.a.	n.a.	n.a.	n.a.	n.a.	n.a.	2	14.98	7.49
Reference	3	21.48	7.16	3	22.97	7.66	1	7.99	7.99	n.a.	n.a.	n.a.
Religion	4	30.96	7.74	3	20.93	6.98	2	15.98	7.99	1	7.99	7.99
Science	1	6.95	6.95	n.a.	n.a.	n.a.	n.a.	n.a.	n.a.	n.a.	n.a.	n.a.
Self-help	3	28.93	9.64	2	15.98	7.99	1	7.99	7.99	1	7.99	7.99
Social science	n.a.	n.a.	n.a.	n.a.	n.a.	n.a.	n.a.	n.a.	n.a.	n.a.	n.a.	n.a.
Sports and recreation	3	23.97	7.99	3	20.97	6.99	1	7.99	7.99	1	7.99	7.99
Study aids	n.a.	n.a.	n.a.	n.a.	n.a.	n.a.	n.a.	n.a.	n.a.	n.a.	n.a.	n.a.
Technology and engineering	n.a.	n.a.	n.a.	n.a.	n.a.	n.a.	n.a.	n.a.	n.a.	n.a.	n.a.	n.a.
Transportation	n.a.	n.a.	n.a.	n.a.	n.a.	n.a.	n.a.	n.a.	n.a.	n.a.	n.a.	n.a.
Travel	1	6.95	6.95	1	14.00	14.00	n.a.	n.a.	n.a.	n.a.	n.a.	n.a.
True crime	53	389.47	7.35	52	388.48	7.47	54	412.46	7.64	44	344.56	7.83
Young adult	142	1,007.71	7.10	96	732.61	7.63	83	674.68	8.13	49	413.51	8.44
Totals	4,699	$30,523.50	$6.50	4,490	$30,089.32	$6.70	4,430	$30,242.45	$6.83	4,381	$30,526.22	$6.97

n.a. = not available

Table 5 / Trade Paperbacks Average Per-Volume Prices, 2008–2011

BISAC Category	2008 Vols.	2008 $ Total	2008 Prices	2009 Vols.	2009 $ Total	2009 Prices	2010 Vols.	2010 $ Total	2010 Prices	2011 Vols.	2011 $ Total	2011 Prices
Antiques and collectibles	239	$6,471.72	$27.08	191	$5,204.12	$27.25	178	$4,544.12	$25.53	137	$3,697.02	$26.99
Architecture	694	29,074.36	41.89	692	31,060.73	44.89	752	34,075.86	45.31	697	29,752.66	42.69
Art	1,581	59,368.38	37.55	1,491	56,100.80	37.63	1,506	57,609.66	38.25	1,534	56,865.33	37.07
Bibles	363	17,891.83	49.29	307	12,484.70	40.67	430	16,622.32	38.66	746	30,565.86	40.97
Biography and autobiography	2,211	44,895.41	20.31	2,347	48,201.37	20.54	2,434	49,532.67	20.35	2,441	48,495.35	19.87
Body, mind and spirit	1,072	19,799.35	18.47	1,009	18,319.98	18.16	995	17,940.04	18.03	1,061	19,386.94	18.27
Business and economics	5,937	439,177.68	73.97	5,930	368,094.31	62.07	5,791	401,291.31	69.30	4,906	328,038.63	66.86
Children	9,099	98,172.30	10.79	9,716	105,976.59	10.91	8,612	89,751.55	10.42	8,562	85,934.76	10.04
Comics and graphic novels	2,407	34,048.57	14.15	2,173	33,503.48	15.42	1,863	30,016.52	16.11	1,890	30,733.25	16.26
Computers	3,279	285,682.16	87.12	3,795	369,895.63	97.47	3,460	243,654.22	70.42	3,171	211,658.62	66.75
Cooking	1,271	23,940.09	18.84	1,006	19,711.24	19.59	1,101	21,962.25	19.95	1,101	21,932.86	19.92
Crafts and hobbies	943	18,840.65	19.98	1,002	19,331.96	19.29	1,052	20,343.06	19.34	1,077	21,005.65	19.50
Design	381	13,021.49	34.18	397	14,690.39	37.00	440	28,152.04	63.98	397	16,584.93	41.78
Drama	521	9,719.82	18.66	581	12,607.20	21.70	739	14,006.42	18.95	413	8,012.57	19.40
Education	3,929	146,190.54	37.21	3,262	135,148.69	41.43	3,545	152,347.38	42.98	3,116	127,974.14	41.07
Family and relationships	951	16,908.59	17.78	884	17,351.78	19.63	782	14,642.51	18.72	641	12,089.94	18.86
Fiction	9,480	154,544.25	16.30	9,694	167,906.96	17.32	9,546	171,735.66	17.99	11,609	211,914.10	18.25
Foreign language study	1,405	42,411.50	30.19	977	31,564.73	32.31	1,280	40,097.96	31.33	1,179	38,356.48	32.53
Games	800	13,664.44	17.08	787	13,844.60	17.59	792	13,127.18	16.57	657	10,733.50	16.34
Gardening	368	6,967.28	18.93	256	5,364.93	20.96	241	5,651.33	23.45	239	5,575.53	23.33
Health and fitness	1,373	33,213.71	24.19	1,333	31,558.58	23.67	1,271	34,253.18	26.95	1,247	33,314.82	26.72
History	5,856	186,490.43	31.85	6,436	204,677.72	31.80	6,952	248,808.28	35.79	6,706	233,586.62	34.83

Category												
House and home	295	5,966.45	20.23	226	4,963.14	21.96	200	4,238.03	21.19	138	2,889.49	20.94
Humor	463	6,245.21	13.49	486	6,700.28	13.79	430	6,176.99	14.37	385	5,449.23	14.15
Language arts and disciplines	1,654	88,284.87	53.38	2,088	137,490.40	65.85	2,317	149,344.28	64.46	1,719	117,564.17	68.39
Law	3,781	435,331.41	115.14	2,711	204,427.95	75.41	3,179	229,116.93	72.07	3,090	214,672.49	69.47
Literary collections	540	19,026.29	35.23	581	20,338.04	35.01	672	24,471.28	36.42	477	14,267.65	29.91
Literary criticism	1,446	52,882.23	36.57	1,770	68,422.50	38.66	1,612	58,945.92	36.57	1,665	62,065.68	37.28
Mathematics	961	59,407.06	61.82	885	61,007.20	68.93	1,312	113,002.65	86.13	1,152	72,179.34	62.66
Medical	3,986	298,247.53	74.82	3,937	300,540.69	76.34	5,378	485,210.97	90.22	4,081	313,499.35	76.82
Music	2,921	63,289.38	21.67	2,975	69,079.36	23.22	3,020	68,935.86	22.83	2,533	60,409.30	23.85
Nature	604	15,354.00	25.42	613	16,565.41	27.02	565	21,064.03	37.28	502	16,164.40	32.20
Performing arts	991	30,729.49	31.01	934	31,428.80	33.65	1,030	34,531.78	33.53	910	29,711.77	32.65
Pets	292	5,460.59	18.70	299	5,683.91	19.01	249	4,317.85	17.34	196	3,895.15	19.87
Philosophy	1,271	39,313.80	30.93	1,465	50,292.43	34.33	1,391	73,256.72	52.66	1,324	56,030.41	42.32
Photography	535	17,583.24	32.87	539	16,778.30	31.13	546	17,087.12	31.30	539	17,426.36	32.33
Poetry	1,784	29,429.78	16.50	1,720	29,025.11	16.88	1,720	28,775.89	16.73	1,705	28,554.77	16.75
Political science	3,142	118,071.58	37.58	3,220	122,070.40	37.91	3,908	160,217.61	41.00	3,333	131,634.82	39.49
Psychology	1,377	56,963.01	41.37	1,256	54,111.63	43.08	1,578	75,710.56	47.98	1,334	61,354.87	45.99
Reference	1,353	93,313.81	68.97	1,307	118,538.30	90.69	1,057	89,691.16	84.85	1,065	106,271.48	99.79
Religion	5,796	116,639.69	20.12	6,052	128,974.55	21.31	6,955	153,538.88	22.08	6,400	136,848.44	21.38
Science	2,099	148,609.73	70.80	2,462	192,498.92	78.19	4,004	465,938.99	116.37	2,722	245,356.42	90.14
Self-help	1,148	19,714.93	17.17	1,047	18,675.96	17.84	1,121	20,002.38	17.84	1,008	18,359.19	18.21
Social science	4,037	162,110.83	40.16	3,998	169,968.27	42.51	4,270	192,361.40	45.05	3,761	156,425.91	41.59
Sports and recreation	1,331	31,637.86	23.77	1,259	29,445.35	23.39	1,315	29,326.75	22.30	1,140	27,914.53	24.49
Study aids	880	28,279.44	32.14	669	20,617.83	30.82	1,499	73,805.65	49.24	971	32,549.70	33.52
Technology and engineering	2,583	397,972.78	154.07	2,681	410,478.85	153.11	2,427	269,875.47	111.20	1,759	181,680.42	103.29
Transportation	430	16,891.62	39.28	459	16,804.27	36.61	507	18,385.24	36.26	437	16,078.70	36.79
Travel	3,077	62,556.02	20.33	2,852	58,486.95	20.51	2,585	54,099.71	20.93	2,384	46,985.58	19.71
True crime	144	2,616.49	18.17	156	2,964.75	19.00	195	4,083.57	20.94	169	3,236.95	19.15
Young adult	2,555	35,166.01	13.76	2,462	41,325.07	16.79	2,173	32,281.38	14.86	2,291	33,192.80	14.49
Totals	105,636	$4,157,589.68	$39.36	105,375	$4,130,305.11	$39.20	110,977	$4,667,960.57	$42.06	102,717	$3,798,878.93	$36.98

Table 6 / Audiobook Average Per-Volume Prices, 2008–2011

BISAC Category	2008			2009			2010			2011		
	Vols.	$ Total	Prices	Vols.	$ Total	Prices	Vols.	$ Total	Prices	Vols.	$ Total	Prices
Antiques and collectibles	n.a.	n.a.	n.a.	1	$74.95	$74.95	3	$109.97	$36.66	n.a.	n.a.	n.a.
Architecture	2	$74.94	$37.47	n.a.	n.a.	n.a.	4	164.97	41.24	3	$119.90	$39.97
Art	5	204.96	40.99	7	415.86	59.41	9	523.90	58.21	9	356.87	39.65
Bibles	20	836.66	41.83	9	679.75	75.53	7	302.93	43.28	10	444.86	44.49
Biography and autobiography	641	30,161.85	47.05	685	34,762.98	50.75	751	38,142.55	50.79	746	38,236.62	51.26
Body, mind and spirit	83	3,177.53	38.28	87	3,302.01	37.95	69	2,275.35	32.98	101	3,885.67	38.47
Business and economics	426	16,843.14	39.54	436	20,121.06	46.15	346	17,195.20	49.70	403	18,431.64	45.74
Children	733	22,787.18	31.09	832	30,132.89	36.22	899	33,981.63	37.80	968	33,421.34	34.53
Comics and graphic novels	n.a.	n.a.	n.a.	n.a.	n.a.	n.a.	n.a.	n.a.	n.a.	n.a.	n.a.	n.a.
Computers	4	124.91	31.23	5	234.95	46.99	2	89.99	45.00	12	647.86	53.99
Cooking	4	58.83	14.71	14	625.78	44.70	2	89.94	44.97	12	568.84	47.40
Crafts and hobbies	9	379.79	42.20	4	154.88	38.72	1	24.98	24.98	n.a.	n.a.	n.a.
Design	n.a.	n.a.	n.a.	n.a.	n.a.	n.a.	n.a.	n.a.	n.a.	n.a.	n.a.	n.a.
Drama	48	1,760.14	36.67	151	5,214.79	34.54	95	3,154.48	33.21	104	2,878.47	27.68
Education	17	506.32	29.78	22	997.47	45.34	20	914.22	45.71	34	1,495.73	43.99
Family and relationships	73	2,681.09	36.73	54	2,128.07	39.41	69	2,840.86	41.17	108	4,451.53	41.22
Fiction	4,379	212,093.98	48.43	6,278	330,348.73	52.62	7,649	385,381.14	50.38	7,138	344,325.43	48.24
Foreign language study	394	14,826.58	37.63	260	10,592.04	40.74	186	8,390.07	45.11	220	11,012.97	50.06
Games	1	14.95	14.95	6	84.74	14.12	n.a.	n.a.	n.a.	5	234.91	46.98
Gardening	2	79.94	39.97	n.a.	n.a.	n.a.	6	286.89	47.82	n.a.	n.a.	n.a.
Health and fitness	83	2,765.84	33.32	82	3,779.22	46.09	85	3,662.56	43.09	110	5,220.40	47.46
History	577	31,569.53	54.71	450	25,959.35	57.69	563	32,691.39	58.07	444	26,355.66	59.36
House and home	n.a.	n.a.	n.a.	n.a.	n.a.	n.a.	n.a.	n.a.	n.a.	1	34.95	34.95
Humor	65	2,353.30	36.20	79	3,347.29	42.37	95	3,479.34	36.62	103	4,204.81	40.82

Language arts and disciplines	14	517.38	36.96	18	839.65	46.65	13	498.43	38.34	39	1,750.18	44.88
Law	18	975.80	54.21	9	447.79	49.75	10	644.94	64.49	7	490.96	70.14
Literary collections	16	622.55	38.91	20	646.71	32.34	11	572.74	52.07	34	1,749.26	51.45
Literary criticism	35	1,736.31	49.61	20	848.60	42.43	18	765.61	42.53	188	5,750.66	30.59
Mathematics	n.a.	n.a.	n.a.	n.a.	n.a.	n.a.	n.a.	n.a.	n.a.	1	24.95	24.95
Medical	25	2,415.28	96.61	13	788.59	60.66	28	1,123.66	40.13	24	1,093.98	45.58
Music	144	4,241.96	29.46	108	4,148.22	38.41	74	2,639.78	35.67	54	2,275.61	42.14
Nature	27	1,057.98	39.18	37	1,742.43	47.09	57	2,348.20	41.20	44	2,055.28	46.71
Performing arts	39	1,494.32	38.32	21	970.78	46.23	16	649.63	40.60	9	585.74	65.08
Pets	20	681.06	34.05	23	1,000.67	43.51	52	1,993.21	38.33	25	1,078.57	43.14
Philosophy	37	1,529.12	41.33	36	1,850.21	51.39	38	2,015.98	53.05	73	3,420.46	46.86
Photography	n.a.	n.a.	n.a.	n.a.	n.a.	n.a.	n.a.	n.a.	n.a.	n.a.	n.a.	n.a.
Poetry	45	1,164.63	25.88	50	1,794.08	35.88	28	940.46	33.59	14	329.64	23.55
Political science	174	7,684.54	44.16	177	8,795.18	49.69	230	11,050.07	48.04	220	10,688.99	48.59
Psychology	31	1,158.63	37.38	54	2,815.00	52.13	46	2,089.19	45.42	91	4,428.36	48.66
Reference	15	491.73	32.78	7	283.85	40.55	2	119.98	59.99	19	809.77	42.62
Religion	313	9,452.23	30.20	418	14,002.55	33.50	425	14,426.23	33.94	460	14,501.02	31.52
Science	61	2,964.04	48.59	64	3,055.70	47.75	66	3,425.01	51.89	90	4,882.33	54.25
Self-help	207	6,205.85	29.98	289	11,067.31	38.30	192	7,571.23	39.43	199	8,232.65	41.37
Social science	55	2,209.62	40.17	79	3,978.46	50.36	90	4,326.20	48.07	100	4,886.44	48.86
Sports and recreation	57	2,265.59	39.75	41	1,877.15	45.78	58	2,811.69	48.48	38	1,769.47	46.57
Study aids	18	1,207.83	67.10	21	712.23	33.92	7	135.88	19.41	1	21.99	21.99
Technology and engineering	10	520.92	52.09	7	339.94	48.56	23	1,226.54	53.33	25	1,179.62	47.18
Transportation	n.a.	n.a.	n.a.	3	109.97	36.66	7	323.93	46.28	1	24.95	24.95
Travel	39	1,744.45	44.73	15	773.58	51.57	47	2,395.08	50.96	20	1,223.46	61.17
True crime	59	3,033.48	51.41	45	2,281.13	50.69	37	1,945.35	52.58	36	1,821.29	50.59
Young adult	269	12,244.65	45.52	527	23,638.46	44.85	888	39,789.54	44.81	960	40,022.94	41.69
Totals	9,294	$410,921.41	$44.21	11,564	$561,765.05	$48.58	13,324	$639,530.92	$48.00	13,303	$611,427.03	$45.96

n.a. = not available

Table 7 / E-Book Average Per-Volume Prices, 2008–2011

BISAC Category	2008			2009			2010			2011		
	Vols.	$ Total	Prices	Vols.	$ Total	Prices	Vols.	$ Total	Prices	Vols.	$ Total	Prices
Antiques and collectibles	6	$335.82	$55.97	11	$989.68	$89.97	62	$1,875.04	$30.24	216	$4,780.98	$22.13
Architecture	212	14,945.16	70.50	205	14,190.05	69.22	268	17,839.50	66.57	281	20,187.01	71.84
Art	86	3,905.66	45.41	166	4,635.21	27.92	199	8,270.92	41.56	645	10,447.08	16.20
Bibles	10	257.90	25.79	22	342.78	15.58	119	727.27	6.11	109	1,177.22	10.80
Biography and autobiography	874	12,740.60	14.58	1,464	20,866.88	14.25	1,828	28,271.22	15.47	2,794	33,751.42	12.08
Body, mind and spirit	238	2,953.97	12.41	362	4,238.07	11.71	628	8,759.51	13.95	1,104	13,618.73	12.34
Business and economics	3,129	179,984.95	57.52	4,707	228,107.43	48.46	5,603	251,141.29	44.82	5,365	241,939.32	45.10
Children	1,931	23,186.54	12.01	3,554	41,682.27	11.73	4,239	58,588.74	13.82	11,980	237,584.24	19.83
Comics and graphic novels	16	400.66	25.04	16	193.82	12.11	26	296.18	11.39	205	1,412.34	6.89
Computers	2,108	140,951.84	66.87	2,574	158,668.53	61.64	3,057	189,819.37	62.09	3,595	228,479.24	63.55
Cooking	237	4,787.07	20.20	508	8,147.74	16.04	715	12,007.93	16.79	1,147	19,106.07	16.66
Crafts and hobbies	72	1,033.03	14.35	211	2,724.58	12.91	340	5,995.40	17.63	622	10,772.95	17.32
Design	39	1,405.42	36.04	59	2,061.86	34.95	125	4,629.14	37.03	97	3,888.41	40.09
Drama	55	1,622.12	29.49	137	1,720.28	12.56	443	2,152.39	4.86	2,130	7,145.25	3.35
Education	1,111	57,748.68	51.98	1,397	77,081.31	55.18	1,537	70,625.15	45.95	1,310	63,172.65	48.22
Family and relationships	386	7,675.09	19.88	650	9,252.18	14.23	717	10,600.99	14.79	774	9,255.73	11.96
Fiction	7,414	64,608.97	8.71	13,364	109,681.11	8.21	18,043	127,403.62	7.06	39,886	211,633.05	5.31
Foreign language study	49	2,107.53	43.01	116	4,745.40	40.91	97	4,528.10	46.68	183	3,725.16	20.36
Games	56	993.03	17.73	84	1,394.05	16.60	120	1,542.19	12.85	218	2,848.51	13.07
Gardening	14	285.54	20.40	51	1,197.94	23.49	68	1,184.03	17.41	115	1,955.77	17.01
Health and fitness	488	9,047.11	18.54	755	13,762.20	18.23	920	17,276.85	18.78	1,283	20,604.39	16.06
History	1,270	73,062.00	57.53	1,929	90,563.42	46.95	2,641	127,292.83	48.20	3,171	116,197.74	36.64
House and home	55	1,258.72	22.89	103	2,441.51	23.70	121	2,610.21	21.57	147	2,530.13	17.21
Humor	157	1,770.14	11.27	232	2,875.31	12.39	322	3,589.47	11.15	410	3,490.90	8.51

Category											
Language arts and disciplines	437	40,758.37	93.27	566	49,885.85	88.14	582	44,003.09	75.61	784	51,461.90	65.64
Law	378	30,703.94	81.23	487	44,616.45	91.61	609	68,324.51	112.19	599	52,234.70	87.20
Literary collections	43	1,053.49	24.50	94	2,912.93	30.99	226	4,580.60	20.27	1,298	6,744.45	5.20
Literary criticism	462	40,019.59	86.62	447	36,454.50	81.55	608	53,002.07	87.17	822	44,986.46	54.73
Mathematics	571	60,619.24	106.16	530	54,040.15	101.96	801	89,965.18	112.32	987	99,053.79	100.36
Medical	1,645	222,417.52	135.21	1,676	207,275.36	123.67	1,575	213,740.04	135.71	2,065	241,666.72	117.03
Music	187	6,326.87	33.83	262	9,151.49	34.93	331	10,808.03	32.65	1,982	38,164.13	19.26
Nature	124	7,410.72	59.76	209	6,777.67	32.43	370	22,006.25	59.48	369	13,780.36	37.35
Performing arts	227	8,639.88	38.06	335	11,911.61	35.56	474	15,246.76	32.17	586	18,909.59	32.27
Pets	83	1,320.56	15.91	113	1,701.62	15.06	176	2,552.35	14.50	380	4,428.34	11.65
Philosophy	484	38,328.84	79.19	664	40,289.40	60.68	598	42,712.85	71.43	801	38,973.52	48.66
Photography	104	3,150.90	30.30	158	4,507.88	28.53	202	5,501.27	27.23	272	6,511.51	23.94
Poetry	138	1,885.05	13.66	257	3,521.91	13.70	332	3,167.52	9.54	1,165	7,278.82	6.25
Political science	1,243	73,375.04	59.03	1,451	90,231.19	62.19	1,427	85,245.96	59.74	1,546	78,152.71	50.55
Psychology	709	46,297.41	65.30	845	45,122.14	53.40	914	51,568.40	56.42	976	55,780.40	57.15
Reference	209	10,101.10	48.33	284	8,854.79	31.18	646	14,809.54	22.92	500	12,019.27	24.04
Religion	1,427	38,939.94	27.29	2,676	56,810.95	21.23	2,874	79,918.02	27.81	3,613	79,461.38	21.99
Science	2,111	444,503.24	210.57	2,770	538,120.20	194.27	2,915	454,162.54	155.80	2,750	390,983.56	142.18
Self-help	369	5,221.43	14.15	743	8,865.50	11.93	746	10,489.68	14.06	1,417	14,190.94	10.01
Social science	989	68,655.92	69.42	1,357	77,863.22	57.38	1,513	85,986.29	56.83	1,815	105,709.07	58.24
Sports and recreation	302	6,777.24	22.44	546	11,240.95	20.59	643	12,360.63	19.22	833	15,570.16	18.69
Study aids	46	1,009.89	21.95	147	2,346.28	15.96	305	4,250.35	13.94	445	6,817.44	15.32
Technology and engineering	1,653	254,111.08	153.73	1,633	234,354.76	143.51	2,618	414,799.35	158.44	2,240	307,214.60	137.15
Transportation	50	1,773.37	35.47	64	2,536.78	39.64	97	3,212.56	33.12	137	3,180.40	23.21
Travel	434	6,774.38	15.61	710	9,596.24	13.52	1,223	19,367.97	15.84	2,439	24,457.59	10.03
True crime	83	963.18	11.60	169	1,930.69	11.42	210	2,177.10	10.37	218	2,337.85	10.72
Young adult	975	8,604.91	8.83	1,861	17,889.85	9.61	1,892	22,635.77	11.96	2,324	48,744.27	20.97
Totals	35,496	$2,036,810.65	$57.38	53,731	$2,380,373.97	$44.30	67,145	$2,793,622.02	$41.61	111,150	$3,038,518.22	$27.34

How E-Books' 'Disruptive Technology' Affects U.S. Book Industry, Trade

Albert N. Greco

Professor of Marketing, Gabelli School of Business, Fordham University
E-mail agreco@fordham.edu

Clayton M. Christensen, in his pivotal book *The Innovator's Dilemma* (2000), outlined in detail how executives handle disruptive technologies. He wrote that "many executives would like to believe that they're in charge of their organizations, that they make the crucial decisions . . . In practice, it is a company's customers who effectively control what it can and cannot do . . ."[1] Michael E. Porter, creator of the strategic management school of thought, also stressed the importance of understanding how industries respond to challenges from customers and competitors, specifically addressing uncertainty, the rate and pattern of decline, and the remaining structure: "The process by which demand declines and the characteristics of the market segments that remain have a major influence on competition in the decline phase."[2] And many of these issues were discussed by Nassim Nicholas Taleb in his bestselling book *The Black Swan: The Impact of the Highly Improbable.*[3]

These authors did not specifically address the U.S. book industry, but their overarching narratives and theories do touch indirectly on the dramatic impact that e-books and e-readers—the disruptive technologies in this sector—have had on the entire book publishing industry, from publishers to retailers to libraries to institutions to consumers.

E-readers have been available for some time, but these devices gained little traction in the consumer market at first. The key turning points were the launches of the Kindle in November 2007, the Nook in November 2009, and the iPad in April 2010. All three of these e-readers gained significant market share in the middle of a debilitating recession, and all underwent a series of major technological changes that enriched the reading experiences of millions of consumers.

In about four and a half years, consumers adopted e-readers as a preferred platform for reading books and other print products. (Some of these devices were "tablets," offering other entertainment products such as movies and music.) The overall impact was dramatic.

In 2011 the Pew Research Center released a report outlining the pace of acceptance of e-readers.[4] Pew asked consumers whether they had an e-reader ("an electronic book device or e-book, such as a Kindle or Nook"). The results were unimpressive at first: 2 percent said yes in April 2009, 3 percent in September 2009, 4 percent in May 2010, 5 percent in September 2010, 6 percent in November 2010. Then there was a doubling to 12 percent in April 2011.

Note: The source of the exports and imports tables accompanying this article is the U.S. Department of Commerce, International Trade Administration (ITA). All numbers are rounded off to one or two decimal places and may not add to 100 percent. Only physical book exports and imports from ITA are analyzed in this research study; foreign rights and digital book data were not available. In addition, certain datasets were not available from ITA in a few book categories for 2010, including religion. The author estimated the total 2010 statistical data on book exports and imports. Because of changes in the classification of "U.S. traded products" and what constitutes products classified as "books," data prior to 1990 are not strictly comparable to data beginning in 1990. The Department of Commerce often updates previously released data incorporating changes in collection methodologies.

Pew also investigated tablet ownership ("a tablet computer like an iPad, Samsung Galaxy or Motorola Xoom") and came up with these figures: May 2010, 3 percent; September 2010, 4 percent; November 2010, 5 percent; January 2011, 7 percent; and April 2011, 8 percent.

By the third and fourth quarters of 2011, a sea change took place. Millions of e-readers and tablets were sold, transforming the book-publishing landscape. In January 2012 Pew Research Center reported significant changes[5] among consumers regarding e-readers and tablets: May 2011, e-book ownership 12 percent, tablet ownership (primarily the iPad) 8 percent; August 2011, e-book ownership 9 percent, tablet ownership 10 percent; December 2011, e-book ownership 10 percent, tablet ownership 10 percent; January 2012, e-book ownership 19 percent, tablet ownership 19 percent.

Pew also reported on the demographic characteristics of tablet (iPad) owners as of January 2012:

- Gender: males and females both at 19 percent
- Race/Ethnicity: 19 percent white, 21 percent for both African Americans and Hispanics
- Age: 18–29, 24 percent; 30–49, 27 percent; 50–64, 15 percent; 65+, 7 percent
- Education: some high school, 5 percent; high school graduate, 15 percent; some college, 18 percent; college graduate, 31 percent
- Annual household income: less than $30,000, 8 percent; $30,000–$49,999, 16 percent; $50,000–$74,000, 20 percent; $75,000+, 36 percent

The dataset for e-readers was equally intriguing.

- Gender: males 16 percent, females 21 percent
- Race/Ethnicity: 18 percent white; 20 percent African American, 19 percent Hispanic
- Age: 18–29, 18 percent; 30–49, 24 percent; 50–64, 19 percent; 65+, 12 percent
- Education: some high school, 6 percent; high school graduate, 14 percent; some college, 19 percent; college graduate, 30 percent
- Annual Household Income: less than $30,000, 8 percent; $30,000–$49,999, 19 percent; $50,000–$74,000, 19 percent; $75,000+, 31 percent

The Pearson Foundation reported dramatic increases in tablet ownership among high school seniors (2011, 4 percent; 2012, 17 percent) and college students (2011, 7 percent; 2012, 25 percent).[6]

The growth in the sale and usage of e-readers impacted in a substantive way the sale of e-books and printed books. In March 2012 *Publishers Weekly* released its anticipated unit sales data for 2011.[7] A detailed analysis of the top 20 bestseller datasets revealed conclusively a decline in the sale of printed books and sharp increases in the sale of e-books in a cluster of categories. These were the figures:

- Hardcover fiction 2011 unit sales: 10,852,819 (16.24 percent of total top 20 sales)

- Hardcover nonfiction 2011 unit sales: 9,936,615 (14.87 percent of total top 20 sales)
- Mass market paperback 2011 unit sales: 18,946,775 (28.36 percent of total top 20 sales)
- Adult trade paperback 2011 unit sales: 17,056,297 (25.53 percent of total top 20 sales)
- Adult E-Book unit 2011 sales: 10,016,936 (14.99 percent of total top 20 sales)
- Total (100 percent of total top 20 sales): 66,809,442

A more extensive analysis of trade e-book unit sales was equally impressive: top 30 sales, 12,495,066; top 40 sales, 14,465,802; and top 50 sales 16,004,965.

In the juvenile/young adult e-book category, the top 20 e-book unit sales topped 5,128,331.

This meant that total e-book unit sales among just the top 20 trade and juvenile/YA titles totaled 15,145,267. As more e-books and fewer printed books are sold to U.S. consumers, the impact on print publishing will be dramatic; hardcover fiction and nonfiction face a steady decline in the sales of printed books, and mass market paperbacks and adult trade paperbacks are likely to meet a similar fate. An examination of the *Publishers Weekly* e-book units for 2011 revealed that backlist classics (such as *The Sun Also Rises, Gone with the Wind,* and *The Great Gatsby*) experienced healthy sales as e-books. As the magazine remarked: "America is reading; but all signs point to rocketing e-book sales and continued declining of print."

Impact on International Trade

Newton was correct: For every action there is an equal and opposite reaction,[8] and the increase in e-book sales affected print sales. Newton's law of motion was evident in (a) a decline in the number of chain and independent bookstores in the United States; (b) a decline in comparative sales data at Barnes & Noble; (c) allocation of more floor space in bookstores for toys, games, and other products; (d) movement among some mass merchants, price clubs, terminals, supermarkets, convenience stores, and other outlets to reduce the number of books on sale or remove books from their inventory entirely; (e) changes for libraries in the availability and/or price of e-books; (f) declines in book exports and book imports as revealed in figures from the U.S. Department of Commerce's International Trade Administration (ITA); (g) Commerce's announcement in October 2011 that it would no longer publish the Statistical Abstract of the United States; and (h) the announcement in March 2012 that the *Encyclopaedia Britannica* would no longer be available in print, but as a digital product only.[9]

As fewer printed books are sold in the United States, a smaller number of printed books will be exported to or imported from abroad, including books printed (but not published and printed) in foreign nations.

During our analysis of the ITA statistics for exports and imports, certain methodological issues and problems emerged. Commerce did not have 2010 data for all book categories. This necessitated estimating certain book exports and imports. Data for 2011 were not available, because Commerce had not updated any totals since the first quarter of 2011. It is highly likely that when the 2011 data are released, declines—perhaps significant declines—will be evident in book imports and, possibly, in book exports because of the surge in e-book sales.

Drawing on Commerce's figures, the export and import revenues totals increased in 2010 over 2009. Table 1 has historical data back to 1970.

Table 1 / U.S. Trade in Books, 1970–2010
($ million)

Year	U.S. Book Exports	U.S. Book Imports	Ratio: U.S. Book Exports/Imports
1970	$174.9	$92.0	1.90
1975	269.3	147.6	1.82
1980	518.9	306.5	1.69
1985	591.2	564.2	1.05
1990	1,415.1	855.1	1.65
1995	1,779.5	1,184.5	1.50
1996	1,775.6	1,240.1	1.43
1997	1,896.6	1,297.5	1.46
1998	1,841.8	1,383.7	1.33
1999	1,871.1	1,441.4	1.30
2000	1,877.0	1,590.5	1.18
2001	1,712.3	1,627.8	1.05
2002	1,681.2	1,661.2	1.01
2003	1,693.6	1,755.9	0.96
2004	1,740.5	1,934.4	0.90
2005	1,894.3	2,026.3	0.93
2006	1,948.1	2,124.3	0.92
2007	2,135.2	2,281.3	0.94
2008	2,187.0	2,313.8	0.95
2009	1,987.3	1,746.1	1.13
2010 (est.)	2,010.8	1,847.0	1.08

Table 2 lists total U.S. book shipments (that is, net publishers' revenues) for the years 1970 to 2010 along with the ratio between shipments and exports. While both totals were up in 2010, the ratio has been falling precipitously since 2007. In fact, the high point was reached in 1990 when the ratio topped 9.4 percent.

Table 3 lists detailed data on specific book exports, although data were not available for three categories. Historically, the United States has been a major global source of printed books because of the ability of many publishers, primarily in the trade book sector, to acquire and publish major books from immensely popular authors. The data in Table 3 reflect this pattern. Hardcover books, an unusual amalgamation of many different fiction and nonfiction book categories and subcategories, generated an impressive 9.15 percent increase in export sales, although units declined 0.60 percent. This decrease may well be a harbinger of additional slippage over the next few years.

A book category that closely correlates to hardcover is the mass market paperback sector. Mass market paperback revenues increased 2.14 percent, and units declined 2.49 percent—another sign of weakness in the book export business.

Table 2 / U.S. Book Industry Shipments
Compared with U.S. Book Exports: 1970–2010
($ million)

Year	Total Shipments	U.S. Book Exports	Exports as a Percent of Total Shipments
1970	$2,434.2	$174.9	7.2%
1975	3,536.5	269.3	7.6
1980	6,114.4	518.9	8.5
1985	10,165.7	591.2	5.8
1990	14,982.6	1,415.1	9.4
1995	19,471.0	1,779.5	9.1
1996	20,285.7	1,775.6	8.8
1997	21,131.9	1,896.6	9.0
1998	22,480.0	1,841.8	8.2
1999	24,129.9	1,871.1	7.8
2000	25,235.0	1,877.0	7.4
2001	26,096.0	1,712.3	6.6
2002	27,203.0	1,681.2	6.2
2003	26,326.0	1,693.6	6.4
2004	27,903.0	1,740.5	6.2
2005	27,905.0	1,894.3	6.8
2006	28,236.0	1,948.1	6.9
2007	29,296.0	2,135.2	7.3
2008	31,812.4	2,187.0	6.9
2009	33,084.9	1,987.3	6.0
2010 (est.)	33,379.3	2,010.8	6.0

Technical, scientific, and professional books, another strong book category, posted exceptionally large export revenue and unit totals in 2010. Revenues topped the $453.38 million level (up 4.25 percent), and unit totals were exceptionally strong, up 6.15 percent.

In the "small" book category, art titles posted an interesting increases in revenues and units, indicating that certain books, including cookbooks (based on the *Publishers Weekly* unit datasets), remain popular printed products.

A series of analyses were undertaken to highlight trends in certain book categories in a selected list of countries. Table 4 addresses the volatile mass market paperback business. The United States continued to export these inexpensive books to a variety of nations. For decades, the best markets for these books have been Canada, the United Kingdom, and Australia. While Canada again generated a positive growth rate (up 12.61 percent), steep declines were recorded for both the United Kingdom (10.36 percent) and Australia (23.15 percent). In fact, six of the top ten export destinations bought fewer book in 2010. In terms of units, only two nations were up in 2010: Singapore and South Africa. The other eight nations showed declines, almost reaching the 2 percent mark.

Table 3 / U.S. Exports of Books: 2009–2010

Category	Value ($'000)		Percent Change	Units ('000)		Percent Change
	2009	2010	2009–2010	2009	2010	2009–2010
Dictionaries and thesauruses	n.a.	n.a.	n.a.	n.a.	n.a.	n.a.
Encyclopedias	n.a.	n.a.	n.a.	n.a.	n.a.	n.a.
Art books	$17,109	$18,388	7.48%	2,700	3,145	16.48%
Textbooks	476,625	453,482	-4.86	33,583	45,362	35.07
Religious books	n.a.	n.a.	n.a.	n.a.	n.a.	n.a.
Technical, scientific, and professional books	434,888	453,384	4.25	28,636	30,396	6.15
Hardcover books, n.e.s.	203,062	221,637	9.15	25,608	25,454	-0.60
Mass market paperbacks	307,358	313,937	2.14	89,846	87,610	-2.49

n.a. = not available
n.e.s. = not elsewhere specified

Table 4 / U.S. Exports of Mass Market Paperbacks (Rack Sized): Top Ten Markets 2009–2010

Country	Value ($'000) 2009	Value ($'000) 2010	Percent Change 2009–2010	Units ('000) 2009	Units ('000) 2010	Percent Change 2009–2010
Canada	$158,689	$178,581	12.61%	47,728	49,319	-5.10%
United Kingdom	43,064	38,602	-10.36	12,706	10,852	-14.59
Australia	20,574	15,811	-23.15	6,185	4,752	-23.14
Japan	11,680	10,357	-11.33	3,900	3,538	-9.28
Philippines	11,007	8,148	-25.97	3,461	2,806	-18.93
Singapore	10,875	13,513	24.26	2,287	2,950	28.99
South Africa	10,826	13,708	26.62	2,625	3,629	38.25
China	5,731	5,284	-7.80	1,614	1,564	-3.10
Brazil	4,100	2,357	-42.51	800	587	-26.63
Thailand	3,728	2,329	5.30	660	398	-39.70
Total	$280,174	$288,690	3.04	81,966	80,397	-1.91

The United States has a significant number of major scientific, technical, professional, and medical research facilities generating impressive research studies, and the U.S. book industry has been very active and successful in this category, releasing "must have" content. Many of the titles in this category have high suggested retail prices, often above $75. See Table 5 for an overview of this sector.

Between 2009 and 2010 revenues among the top ten nations increased 4.96 percent, paced by Japan (up 55.07 percent), Mexico (up 54.92 percent, and Brazil (up 52.36 percent). However, declines were recorded by Canada and the United Kingdom. In terms of units, the record was sterling, up 9.62 percent. However, our projections indicate that this category has moved aggressively into the e-book format. What can "save" print exports is the fact that digital e-reader and/or computer usage in certain parts of the world (especially India and parts of Latin America and Africa) remains uneven; because of that, many markets will continue to need printed books, at least for the next few years.

The higher education/college textbook category is also likely to experience a downward swing in export revenues and units as these books are moving inevitably toward digital e-books (Table 6 outlines these trends). In August 2007 the "big five" textbook publishers (Prentice Hall, Cengage, McGraw-Hill, Wiley, and Macmillan) created Coursesmart (http://www.coursesmart.com), a digital e-book (pdf) platform. By 2012 these publishers offered more than 13,000 e-book titles for rent at lower prices (often less than 50 percent of the price of a printed textbook). In addition, many of the publishers, through Inkling (http://www.inkling.com), offer "enriched" digital textbooks (with audio and video) for sale either as an entire book or by chapter. The National Association of College Stores alerted its more than 4,000 college bookstore members in March 2010 to be prepared for a massive digital e-book marketplace by 2015. Our projections for higher education textbook sales follow the inexorable adoption of digital e-textbooks in the United States. But once again, lagging e-reader and/or computer usage in certain parts of the world means that printed textbooks will remain a viable product for the next few years.

Table 5 / U.S. Exports of Technical, Scientific, and Professional Books: Top Ten Markets 2009–2010

Country	Value ($'000) 2009	Value ($'000) 2010	Percent Change 2009–2010	Units ('000) 2009	Units ('000) 2010	Percent Change 2009–2010
Canada	$129,830	$124,587	-4.04%	9,588	8,493	-11.42%
United Kingdom	92,344	83,546	-9.53	4,571	5,188	13.50
Japan	26,497	41,090	55.07	1,413	1,454	2.90
Mexico	23,134	35,840	54.92	2,257	5,852	159.28
Australia	21,753	26,718	22.82	1,581	1,986	25.62
Germany	16,385	17,448	6.49	812	703	-13.42
Hong Kong	15,676	12,142	-22.54	399	450	12.78
Singapore	14,755	9,651	-34.59	2,065	728	-64.75
India	10,159	12,199	20.08	606	609	0.50
Brazil	9,931	15,131	52.36	696	832	19.54
Total	$360,464	$378,452	4.96	23,988	26,295	9.62

Signs of this transformation toward digital e-books were evident in 2010 when revenues sagged by 5.16 percent. At the same time, unit totals surged 29.61 percent, indicating that unit sales generated smaller revenue streams. Additional revenue declines were likely in 2012 and beyond.

Table 6 / U.S. Exports of Textbooks: Top Ten Markets 2009-2010

Country	Value ($'000) 2009	Value ($'000) 2010	Percent Change 2009–2010	Units ('000) 2009	Units ('000) 2010	Percent Change 2009–2010
Canada	$108,956	$101,748	-6.62%	7,128	8,506	19.33%
United Kingdom	89,816	95,592	6.43	6,167	9,998	62.12
Australia	34,666	32,032	-7.60	2,588	3,456	33.54
South Korea	26,518	26,445	-0.28	1,811	1,535	-15.24
Singapore	25,368	24,574	-3.13	2,815	3,062	8.77
Japan	23,682	15,610	-34.08	1,320	1,094	-17.12
Germany	18,665	15,298	-18.04	1,208	665	-44.95
Mexico	14,850	15,298	3.02	1,270	3,613	184.49
United Arab Emirates	12,968	13,828	6.63	790	941	19.11
Taiwan	9,983	6,179	-38.10	520	331	-36.35
Total	$365,472	$346,604	-5.16	25,617	33,201	29.61

Hardcover books are in a vicious cycle of uncertainty and instability (Table 7). Increases in e-book sales will trigger declines in printed hardcover book sales, which will probably compel publishers to cut print runs, affecting the number of hardcover export sales. Revenue data for 2010 showed impressive growth of nearly 9 percent; but this could be the last year of strong growth rates. Unit sales declined 1.1 percent, a sign that this sector was affected by increases in suggested retail prices rather than any growth in the number of units shipped abroad.

Table 7 / U.S. Exports of Hardbound Books: Top Ten Markets 2009–2010

Country	Value ($'000) 2009	Value ($'000) 2010	Percent Change 2009–2010	Units ('000) 2009	Units ('000) 2010	Percent Change 2009–2010
Canada	$160,246	$176,225	9.97%	19,401	19,797	2.04%
United Kingdom	12,552	9,720	-22.56	2,031	1,230	-39.44
India	4,498	7,364	63.72	607	1,024	68.70
Australia	3,938	5,486	39.31	669	692	3.44
Singapore	1,941	998	-48.58	349	135	-61.32
Japan	1,909	2,530	32.53	212	248	16.98
Mexico	1,840	1,816	-1.30	307	228	-25.73
Philippines	1,089	1,590	46.01	111	206	85.59
South Korea	1071	791	-26.41	184	126	-31.52
New Zealand	817	440	-46.14	79	n.a.	n.a.
Total	$189,901	$206,960	8.98	23,950	23,686	-1.10

n.a. = not available

Art books remain a small bright spot for publishers active in this category. Revenues and units were both up in 2010, as shown in Table 8.

Table 8 / U.S. Exports of Art and Pictorial Books: Top Ten Markets 2009–2010

Country	Value ($'000) 2009	Value ($'000) 2010	Percent Change 2009–2010	Units ('000) 2009	Units ('000) 2010	Percent Change 2009–2010
United Kingdom	$7,295	$6,617	-9.29%	1,233	1,228	-0.41%
Canada	2,731	3,534	29.40	242	394	62.81
Mexico	1,106	721	-34.81	206	123	-40.29
Netherlands	797	539	-32.37	163	173	6.13
Singapore	610	733	20.16	106	121	14.15
Chile	525	n.a.	n.a.	89	n.a.	n.a.
Australia	391	658	68.29	62	119	91.94
United Arab Emirates	390	211	-45.90	64	26	-59.38
South Korea	349	1,324	279.37	52	227	336.54
Germany	236	593	151.27	46	105	128.26
Total	$14,430	$14,930	3.47	2,263	2,516	11.18

n.a. = not available

Some hardcover books are printed and published abroad and imported into the U.S. market (Table 9), but some are just printed abroad for U.S. publishers because the unit manufacturing costs for printing, paper, and binding (PPB), as well as for certain costs such as editorial, art, design, layout, and page make-up services are lower, especially in China and South Korea for PPB and in India, Singapore, and Hong Kong for plant operations.

The growth in e-books in the United States will have a considerable impact on many foreign PPB and plant operations, especially in Asia. Signs of this coming shift were evident in 2010. Imports from Singapore dropped 21.64 percent in value, from Hong Kong 36.66 percent, and from South Korea 55.11 percent in 2010, and the entire market for the top ten nations increased only 1.44 percent.

While units increased 6.54 percent, the results were not encouraging for Singapore (down 13.95 percent), the United Kingdom (down 39.11 percent), Hong Kong (down 37.62 percent), and South Korea (down 45.98).

Table 9 / U.S. Imports of Hardbound Books: Top Ten Markets 2009–2010

Country	Value ($'000)		Percent Change	Units ('000)		Percent Change
	2009	2010	2009–2010	2009	2010	2009–2010
China	$312,453	$346,284	10.83%	$134,108	$155,128	15.67%
Singapore	42,250	33,108	-21.64	16,988	14,619	-13.95
United Kingdom	36,712	38,462	4.77	4,505	2,743	-39.11
Hong Kong	23,405	14,824	-36.66	8,052	5,023	-37.62
Canada	21,647	19,004	-12.21	4,570	4,071	-10.92
Italy	19,971	20,769	4.00	1,914	2,258	17.97
Spain	10,628	9,352	-12.01	1,628	1,490	-8.49
Germany	9,131	7,713	-15.53	1,244	1,241	-0.24
France	7,294	4,524	-37.98	197	139	-29.44
South Korea	6,329	2,841	-55.11	4,137	2,235	-45.98
Total	$489,820	$496,881	1.44	177,343	188,947	6.54

The economics of publishing worked in favor of importing inexpensive mass market paperbacks (Table 10). Revenues and units increased in 2010, with a sharp surge in units. Yet the positive results of 2010 will probably be only a fond memory as fewer paperbacks are sold in the United States, which was evident in annual sales data released recently by the Association of American Publishers.

Table 10 / U.S. Imports of Mass Market Paperbacks (Rack Size): Top Ten Markets 2009–2010

Country	Value ($'000)		Percent Change	Units ('000)		Percent Change
	2009	2010	2009–2010	2009	2010	2009–2010
China	$24,503	$46,139	88.30%	16,348	27,744	69.71%
Canada	21,021	15,879	-24.46	10,832	5,690	-47.47
United Kingdom	18,716	7,854	-58.04	4,616	2,022	-56.20
Hong Kong	4,418	2,571	-41.81	2,783	1,324	-52.43
Italy	3,528	4,000	13.38	1,103	1,368	24.03
Singapore	3,498	4,218	20.58	2,650	3,245	22.45
Spain	2,178	2,195	0.78	1,207	1,267	4.97
Japan	1,146	548	-52.18	312	98	-68.59
Malaysia	684	783	14.47	234	867	270.51
Germany	636	447	-25.00	196	150	-23.47
Total	$80,328	$84,664	5.40	40,281	43,775	8.67

Imported art books (Table 11) grew in 2010 because of the appeal of sophisticated, lushly illustrated four-color lithographic or gravure books. While no category will be immune from the seductive appeal of e-books, the art category is well positioned to experience several more years of impressive growth figures.

Table 11 / U.S. Imports of Art and Pictorial Books: Top Ten Markets 2009–2010

Country	Value ($'000) 2009	Value ($'000) 2010	Percent Change 2009–2010	Units ('000) 2009	Units ('000) 2010	Percent Change 2009–2010
Germany	$5,927	$8,875	49.74%	421	584	38.72%
China	4,766	5,640	18.34	375	546	45.60
United Kingdom	4,567	6,217	36.13	225	382	69.78
Italy	3,768	12,980	244.48	227	257	13.22
Hong Kong	2,063	1,680	-18.57	210	177	-15.71
Singapore	925	1,801	94.70	95	129	35.79
Netherlands	552	896	62.32	25	37	48.00
France	535	1,475	175.70	18	55	205.56
Spain	496	621	25.20	25	27	8.00
Canada	479	384	-19.83	27	31	14.81
Total	$24,078	$40,569	68.49	1,648	2,225	35.01

The last two categories of imported books, higher education textbooks (Table 12) and technical, scientific, and professional books (Table 13), remained vibrant print categories as long as college students and scientists wanted printed products. But by 2011 individuals in both of these consumer groups started to adopt e-readers or tablets in large numbers. So the impressive 2010 totals for imported textbooks (up 6.16 percent in revenues and 11.57 percent in units) and technical titles (up 9.90 percent in revenues and 40.06 percent in units) are likely to dissipate because of the transformation of the marketplace from a print to a digital market.

Table 12 / U.S. Imports of Textbooks 2009-2010: Top Ten Markets

Country	Value ($'000) 2009	Value ($'000) 2010	Percent Change 2009–2010	Units ('000) 2009	Units ('000) 2010	Percent Change 2009–2010
Canada	$68,651	$53,666	-21.83%	11,799	10,649	-9.75%
United Kingdom	57,547	55,071	-4.30	3,510	4131	17.69
China	54,253	71,984	32.68	14,606	19,744	35.18
Hong Kong	16,823	27,657	64.40	2,551	1,943	-23.83
Singapore	10,309	10,377	0.66	2,988	3,224	7.90
United Arab Emirates	3,940	3,178	-19.34	289	242	-16.26
Mexico	3,678	2,854	-22.40	541	437	-19.22
India	2,920	3,808	30.41	170	201	18.24
Colombia	2,696	4,161	54.34	736	938	27.45
Germany	2,689	2,285	-15.02	134	132	-1.49
Total	$222,506	$235,041	6.16	37,324	41,641	11.57

Summation

It is regrettable that Commerce was unable to release 2011 statistical datasets by March 2012 (or to update the fragmentary 2009 religion totals). However, the

Table 13 / U.S. Imports of Technical, Scientific, and Professional Books
2009–2010: Top Ten Markets

Country	Value ($'000) 2009	Value ($'000) 2010	Percent Change 2009–2010	Units ('000) 2009	Units ('000) 2010	Percent Change 2009–2010
China	$33,721	$34,393	1.99%	11,922	15,448	29.58%
Japan	28,403	39,002	37.32	1,020	1,712	67.84
Germany	26,291	17,630	-32.94	1,104	805	-27.08
Canada	24,144	27,399	13.48	4,341	6,062	39.65
United Kingdom	22,653	30,414	34.26	3,171	2,309	-27.18
Hong Kong	7,805	2,495	-68.03	1,458	1,433	-1.71
India	5,898	7,935	34.54	1,456	1,149	-21.09
Singapore	5,710	6,109	6.99	1,551	1,141	-26.43
Mexico	4,357	9,918	127.63	3,208	11,062	244.83
France	3,566	3,353	-5.97	195	93	-52.31
Total	$162,548	$178,648	9.90	29,426	41,214	40.06

available data makes it obvious that publishers will generate fewer dollars in the next few years from the export of printed books.

Publishers have two possible strategies to replace these lost revenues. First, generate new revenues from the sales of e-books. Second, capitalize on the popularity of U.S. books by tapping into the burgeoning sub-rights and foreign rights markets.

If either of these strategies fails to compensate for the inevitable losses in export revenues, some publishing houses could face a severe cash flow problem, pushing a few into bankruptcy. On the other hand, the future looks very attractive for publishers able to exploit the digital book boom. But this means that many publishing companies will become de facto technology companies, a possibility that is somewhat unsettling to what has been, since the 17th century in the United States, a rather traditional enterprise.

References

1. Christensen, Clayton M. *The Innovator's Dilemma* (Harper Business, 2000), 117.

2. Porter, Michael E. *Competitive Strategy: Techniques for Analyzing Industries and Competitors* (Free Press, 1998), 256.

3. Taleb, Nassim Nicholas. *The Black Swan: The Impact of the Highly Improbable* (Random, 2007), 3–21.

4. Pew Research Center. "Spring Change Assessment Survey 2011." May 25, 2011. http://pewinternet.org/reports/2011/E-readers-and-tablets.aspx. Also see James L. McQuivey, "How E-Readers Will Fare in a Tablet PC World," Forrester Research, 2010; and Geoffrey A. Fowler and Marie C. Baca, "The ABCs of E-Reading," *Wall Street Journal,* August 24, 2010, http://online.wsj.com.

5. Pew Research Center. "Tablet and E-Book Reader Ownership Nearly Doubled Over the Holiday Gift-Giving Period." January 23, 2012, http://pewinternet.org/reports/2012/E-readers-and-tablets.aspx. Also see Christina Lewis Halpern, "Should Serious Readers Buy E-Books?" *Wall Street Journal,* March 13, 2012, http://online.wsj.com; Katherine Rosman, "Books Women Read When No One Can See the Cover." *Wall Street Journal,* March 14,

2012, http://online.wsj.com; Eric Savitz, "Amazon: Goldman Sees 19.2 Million 2012 Fire Units: Other Kindles Slide." *Forbes,* January 9, 2012, http://www.forbes.com.

6. Pearson Foundation. "New Survey from the Pearson Foundation Finds Dramatic Increase in Tablet Ownership Among College Students and High School Seniors." March 14, 2012, http:/www.pearsoned.com.

7. Maryles, Daisy. "E-books Boom: E-books: Facts and Figures 2012," *Publishers Weekly,* March 16, 2012, http://www/publishersweekly.com.

8. Newton, Sir Isaac. *Philosophiae Naturalis Principia Mathematica* (1687).

9. Ramachandran, Shalini, and Jeffrey A. Trachtenberg. "End of Era for Britannica." *Wall Street Journal,* March 14, 2012, B1, B9.

Number of Book Outlets
in the United States and Canada

The *American Book Trade Directory* (Information Today, Inc.) has been published since 1915. Revised annually, it features lists of booksellers, wholesalers, periodicals, reference tools, and other information about the U.S. and Canadian book markets. The data shown in Table 1, the most current available, are from the 2012–2013 edition of the directory.

The 17,205 stores of various types shown are located throughout the United States, Canada, and regions administered by the United States. "General" bookstores stock trade books and children's books in a general variety of subjects. "College" stores carry college-level textbooks. "Educational" outlets handle school textbooks up to and including the high school level. "Mail order" outlets sell general trade books by mail and are not book clubs; all others operating by mail are classified according to the kinds of books carried. "Antiquarian" dealers sell old and rare books. Stores handling secondhand books are classified as "used." "Paperback" stores have more than 80 percent of their stock in paperbound books. Stores with paperback departments are listed under the appropriate major classification ("general," "department store," "stationer," and so forth.). Bookstores with at least 50 percent of their stock on a particular subject are classified by subject.

Table 1 / Bookstores in the United States and Canada, 2011

Category	United States	Canada
Antiquarian General	681	65
Antiquarian Mail Order	269	9
Antiquarian Specialized	125	5
Art Supply Store	63	2
College General	3,041	146
College Specialized	115	5
Comics	207	26
Computer Software	2	0
Cooking	276	9
Department Store	1,536	9
Educational*	173	34
Federal Sites†	229	1
Foreign Language*	15	2
General	2,644	549
Gift Shop	127	7
Juvenile*	96	17
Mail Order General	81	8
Mail Order Specialized	322	15
Metaphysics, New Age, and Occult	136	19
Museum Store and Art Gallery	481	30
Nature and Natural History	38	6
Newsdealer	26	2
Office Supply	11	1
Other‡	2,428	446
Paperback§	82	3

Table 1 / Bookstores in the United States and Canada, 2011
(cont.)

Category	United States	Canada
Religious*	1,733	149
Self Help/Development	19	6
Stationer	3	3
Toy Store	36	18
Used*	538	80
Totals	15,533	1,672

* Includes Mail Order Shops for this topic, which are not counted elsewhere in this survey.

† National Historic Sites, National Monuments, and National Parks.

‡ Stores specializing in subjects or services other than those covered in this survey.

§ Includes Mail Order. Excludes used paperback bookstores, stationers, drugstores, or wholesalers handling paperbacks.

Review Media Statistics

Compiled by the staff of the *Library and Book Trade Almanac*

Number of Books and Other Media Reviewed by Major Reviewing Publications 2010–2011

	Adult		Juvenile		Young Adult		Total	
	2010	2011	2010	2011	2010	2011	2010	2011
Booklist[1]	4,876	4,479	3,581	3,499	—	—	8,457	7,978
Bookmarks	702	711	—	—	10	16	712	727
BookPage[2]	653	576	116	74	59	32	828	682
Bulletin of the Center for Children's Books[3]	—	—	726	n.a.	—	—	726	n.a.
Chicago Sun Times	n.a.	n.a.	n.a.	n.a.	—	—	n.a.	n.a.
Chicago Tribune Sunday Book Section[4]	250	260	250	240	—	—	500	500
Choice[5]	6,851	6,833	—	—	—	—	6,851	6,833
Horn Book Guide	—	—	3,046	3,155	921	1,111	3,967	4,266
Horn Book Magazine[6]	1	5	301	351	126	126	428	482
Kirkus Reviews[4]	2,279	3,231	2,245	2,966	—	—	4,524	6,197
Library Journal[7]	6,099	6,590	—	—	—	—	6,099	6,590
Los Angeles Times	n.a.	n.a.	—	—	—	—	n.a.	n.a.
Multicultural Review[8]	226	n.a.	121	n.a.	31	n.a.	378	n.a.
New York Journal of Books[9]	975	1,192	150	120	100	60	1,225	1,372
New York Review of Books[10]	394	n.a.	—	—	—	—	394	n.a.
New York Times Sunday Book Review	n.a.	n.a.	n.a.	n.a.	—	—	n.a.	n.a.
Publishers Weekly[11]	6,119	6,131	1,765	1,704	—	—	7,884	7,835
School Library Journal[4]	19	220	5,755	5,999	—	—	5,774	6,219
Washington Post Book World	839	1,100	45	36	—	—	884	1,136

n.a. = not available

1 All figures are for a 12-month period from September 1, 2010, to August 31, 2011 (vol. 107). YA books are included in the juvenile total. *Booklist* also reviewed 316 other media.

2 Of the total count, 184 were Web-only reviews. *BookPage* also published 37 audio reviews.

3 All figures are for a 12-month period beginning September and ending July/August. YA books are included in the juvenile total.

4 YA books are included in the juvenile total.

5 All materials reviewed in *Choice* are scholarly publications intended for undergraduate libraries. *Choice* also reviewed 427 Internet sites.

6 *Horn Book Magazine* also reviewed 14 audiobooks.

7 In addition, *Library Journal* reviewed 393 audiobooks; 458 DVDs/videos; 55 magazines and zines; 306 books, 160 DVDs, and 30 audiobooks in Collection Development; 96 online databases; and previewed 1,887 books in "Prepub Alert."

8 *MultiCultural Review* published three issues in 2010 rather than the usual four, and publication remained suspended in 2011.

9 *New York Journal of Books,* which began publication in 2010, is online only.

10 *New York Review of Books* in 2010 published 280 articles dealing directly with books or other media. These articles treated a cumulative 435 individual items, of which 10 were films, 2 operas, 2 television series, 3 plays, and 24 art exhibitions. The remainder (394) were adult books. Figures for 2011 were unavailable.

11 Of the total of 7,835 reviews, 1,255 were online only. *Publishers Weekly* also reviewed 232 audiobooks.

Part 5
Reference Information

Bibliographies

The Librarian's Bookshelf

Karen Muller

Librarian, American Library Association

Most of the books on this selective bibliography have been published since 2009; a few earlier titles are retained because of their continuing importance. Print publications are paperbound unless otherwise specified; many are also available as e-books.

General

American Library Directory, 2012–2013. 2v. Information Today, Inc., 2012. $349 (cloth). Also available online.

Annual Review of Information Science and Technology (ARIST). Ed. by Blaise Cronin. Information Today, Inc., 2011. $124.95.

The Atlas of New Librarianship. By R. David Lankes., MIT Press, 2011, $55 (cloth).

Books: A Living History. By Martyn Lyons. J. Paul Getty Museum, 2011. $34.95 (cloth).

Encyclopedia of Library and Information Science. 3rd ed. Ed. by Miriam A. Drake. CRC, 2009. $3,150 (cloth). Also available online.

The Library: An Illustrated History. By Stuart A. P. Murray. Skyhorse Publishing, 2009. $20 (cloth).

Library and Book Trade Almanac, 2012. Information Today, Inc., 2012. $249 (cloth).

Library, Information Science and Technology Abstracts (LISTA). EBSCO Publishing. Free to libraries (http://www.ebscohost.com).

Library, Information Science and Technology Abstracts with Full Text. EBSCO Publishing (http://www.ebscohost.com).

Library Literature and Information Science Full Text, 1984–. EBSCO Publishing (formerly H. W. Wilson) (http://www.ebscohost.com).

Library Literature and Information Science Retrospective: 1905–1983. EBSCO Publishing (formerly H. W. Wilson) (http://www.ebscohost.com).

Library World Records. 2nd ed. By Godfrey Oswald. McFarland, 2009. $39.95.

The Oxford Guide to Library Research. 3rd ed. By Thomas Mann. Oxford University Press, 2005. $19.99.

The Whole Library Handbook 5. Ed. by George Eberhart. American Library Association, 2012. $50.

Academic Libraries

Academic Librarianship. By Camila A. Alire and G. Edward Evans. Neal-Schuman, 2010. $70.

Building Bridges: Connecting Faculty, Students, and the College Library. By Monty L. McAdoo. American Library Association, 2010. $57.

Creating the Customer-Driven Academic Library. By Jeannette Woodward. American Library Association, 2008. $60.

Embedded Librarians: Moving Beyond One-Shot Instruction. Ed. by Cassandra Kvenild and Kaijsa Calkins. Association of College and Research Libraries, 2011. $48.

Envisioning Future Academic Library Services: Initiatives, Ideas and Challenges. Ed. by Sue Knight. Facet, 2010. $105.

The Expert Library: Staffing, Sustaining, and Advancing the Academic Library in the 21st Century. Ed. by Scott Walter and Karen Williams. Association of College and Research Libraries, 2010. $48.

A Field Guide to the Information Commons. By Charles Forrest and Martin Halbert. Scarecrow, 2009. $69.99.

Managing the Small College Library. By Rachel Applegate. Libraries Unlimited, 2010. $55.

Administration

The Complete Library Trustee Handbook. By Sally Gardner Reed and Jillian Kolonick. Neal-Schuman, 2010. $55.

Convergence of Project Management and Knowledge Management. Ed. by T. Kanti Srikantaiah, Michael E. D. Koenig, and Suliman Hawamdeh. Scarecrow, 2010. $65.

Developing a Compensation Plan for Your Library. 2nd ed. By Paula M. Singer and Laura L. Francisco. American Library Association, 2009. $57.

The Frugal Librarian: Thriving in Tough Economic Times. Ed. by Carol Smallwood. American Library Association, 2011. $42.

How to Thrive as a Solo Librarian. Ed. by Carol Smallwood and Melissa J. Clapp. Scarecrow, 2012. $45.

Implementing for Results: Your Strategic Plan in Action. By Sandra Nelson. American Library Association, 2009. $70.

Moving Materials: Physical Delivery in Libraries. Ed. by Valerie Horton and Bruce Smith. American Library Association, 2010. $85.

New Planning for Results: A Streamlined Approach. By Sandra Nelson. Public Library Association, 2001. $58.

Strategic Planning for Results. By Sandra Nelson. American Library Association, 2008. $72.

Streamlining Library Services: What We Do, How Much Time It Takes, What It Costs, and How We Can Do It Better. By Richard M. Dougherty. Scarecrow, 2008. $55.

The Successful Library Trustee Handbook. 2nd ed. By Mary Y. Moore. American Library Association, 2009. $47.

Advocacy and Funding

Advocacy, Outreach and the Nation's Academic Libraries: A Call for Action. Ed. by William C. Welburn, Janice Welburn, and Beth McNeil. Association of College and Research Libraries, 2010. $40.

ALA Book of Library Grant Money. 8th ed. American Library Association, 2012. $175.

A Book Sale How-to Guide: More Money, Less Stress. By Pat Ditzler and JoAnn Dumas. American Library Association. 2012. $40.

From Awareness to Funding: A Study of Library Support in America. OCLC, 2008. $10.

Inside, Outside, and Online: Building Your Library Community. By Chrystie Hill. American Library Association, 2009. $50.

Librarian's Handbook for Seeking, Writing, and Managing Grants. By Sylvia D. Hall-Ellis, Stacey L. Bowers, Christopher Hudson, Claire Williamson, and Joanne Patrick. Libraries Unlimited, 2011. $50.

Archives

Academic Archives: Managing the Next Generation of College and University Archives, Records, and Special Collections. By Aaron D. Purcell. Neal-Schuman, 2012. $95.

Archives: Principles and Practices. By Laura A. Millar. Neal-Schuman, 2010. $80.

Special Collections 2.0: New Technologies for Rare Books, Manuscripts, and Archival Collections. By Beth M. Whittaker and Lynne M. Thomas. Libraries Unlimited, 2009. $45.

Starting, Strengthening, and Managing Institutional Repositories: A How-to-Do-It Manual. By Jonathan A. Nabe. Neal-Schuman, 2010. $90.

Buildings and Space Planning

The Academic Library Building in the Digital Age: A Study of Construction, Planning, and

Design of New Library Space. By Christopher Stewart. Association of College and Research Libraries, 2010. $44.

Building Blocks for Planning Functional Library Space. 3rd ed. By Library Leadership and Management Association. Scarecrow, 2011. $45.

Building Science 101: A Primer for Librarians. By Lynn M. Piotrowicz and Scott Osgood. American Library Association, 2010. $40.

Countdown to a New Library: Managing the Building Project. 2nd ed. By Jeannette Woodward. American Library Association, 2010. $75.

Moving Your Library: Getting the Collection from Here to There. By Steven Carl Fortriede. American Library Association, 2010. $72.

Planning Academic and Research Library Buildings. 3rd ed. By Philip D. Leighton and David C. Weber. American Library Association, 1999. $165.

Teen Spaces: The Step-by-Step Library Makeover. 2nd ed. By Kimberly Bolan. American Library Association, 2009. $50.

Cataloging and Bibliographic Control

Cataloging Correctly for Kids: An Introduction to the Tools. 5th ed. By Sheila S. Intner and Joanna F. Fountain. American Library Association, 2011. $55.

Describing Electronic, Digital, and Other Media Using AACR2 and RDA. By Mary Beth Weber and Fay Austin. Neal-Schuman, 2010. $75.

FRBR: A Guide for the Perplexed. By Robert L. Maxwell. American Library Association, 2008. $65.

Introducing RDA: A Guide to the Basics. By Chris Oliver. American Library Association, 2010. $45.

Metadata. By Marcia Lei Zeng and Jian Qin. Neal-Schuman, 2008. $70.

Next-Gen Library Catalogs. By Marshall Breeding. Neal-Schuman, 2010. $55.

The Organization of Information. 3rd ed. By Arlene G. Taylor and Daniel N. Joudrey. Libraries Unlimited, 2009. $50.

RDA: Strategies for Implementation. By Magda El-Sherbini. American Library Association, 2012. $65.

Structures for Organizing Knowledge: Exploring Taxonomies, Ontologies, and Other Schemas. By June Abbas. Neal-Schuman, 2010. $90.

Children's and Young Adult Services and Materials

Children's Services: Partnerships for Success. Ed. by Betsy Diamant-Cohen. American Library Association, 2010. $50.

The Coretta Scott King Awards, 1970–2009. 4th ed. Ed. by Henrietta M. Smith, Ethnic and Multicultural Information Exchange Round Table, and Coretta Scott King Book Awards Committee. American Library Association, 2009. $50.

Crash Course in Library Services to Preschool Children. By Betsy Diamant-Cohen. Libraries Unlimited, 2010. $30.

In the Words of the Winners: The Newbery and Caldecott Medals, 2001–2010. By Association for Library Service to Children and Horn Book. American Library Association, 2011. $50.

Managing Children's Services in the Public Library. 3rd ed. By Adele M. Fasick and Leslie E. Holt. Libraries Unlimited, 2008. $45.

More Than MySpace: Teens, Librarians, and Social Networking. Ed. by Robyn M. Lupa. Libraries Unlimited, 2009. $40.

The Newbery and Caldecott Awards 2012: A Guide to the Medal and Honor Books. Association for Library Service to Children/ American Library Association, 2012. $30.

Risky Business: Taking and Managing Risks in Library Services for Teens. By Linda W. Braun, Hillias J. Martin, and Connie Urquhart. American Library Association, 2010. $55.

Serving Urban Teens. By Paula Brehm-Heeger. Libraries Unlimited, 2008. $40.

Teen-Centered Library Service: Putting Youth Participation into Practice. By Diane P. Tuccillo. Libraries Unlimited, 2009. $45.

Young Adults Deserve the Best: YALSA's Competencies in Action. By Sarah Flowers. American Library Association, 2010. $48.

Collection Development

Developing an Outstanding Core Collection. By Carol Alabaster. American Library Association, 2010. $60.

Fundamentals of Collection Development and Management. 2nd ed. By Peggy Johnson. American Library Association, 2009. $70.

The Kovacs Guide to Electronic Library Collection Development. 2nd ed. By Diane K. Kovacs. Neal-Schuman, 2009. $155.

Copyright

Copyright Law for Librarians and Educators: Creative Strategies and Practical Solutions. 3rd ed. By Kenneth D. Crews. American Library Association, 2012. $57.

Licensing Digital Content: A Practical Guide for Librarians. 2nd ed. By Lesley Ellen Harris. American Library Association, 2009. $57.

Smart Copyright Compliance for Schools: A How-to-Do-It Manual. By Rebecca P. Butler. Neal-Schuman, 2009. $80.

Digital Libraries

Digital Library Futures: User Perspectives and Institutional Strategies. Ed. by Ingeborg Verheul, Anna Maria Tammaro, and Steve Witt. De Gruyter Saur, 2009. $126.

Digitization in the Real World: Lessons Learned from Small and Medium-Sized Digitization Projects. Ed. by Kwong Bor Ng and Jason Kucsma. Metropolitan New York Library Council, 2010. $60.

Evaluating and Measuring the Value, Use and Impact of Digital Collections. By Lorna M. Hughes. Facet, 2012. $115.

No Shelf Required: E-Books in Libraries. By Sue Polanka. American Library Association, 2011. $65.

No Shelf Required 2: Use and Management of Electronic Books. By Sue Polanka. American Library Association, 2012. $65.

History

The Great Depression: Its Impact on Forty-Six Large American Public Libraries: An Inqui-ry Based on a Content Analysis of Published Writings of Their Directors. By Robert Scott Kramp. Library Juice, 2010. $18.

Librarianship in Gilded Age America: An Anthology of Writings, 1868–1901. Ed. by Leonard Schlup and Stephen H. Paschen. McFarland, 2009. $55.

Main Street Public Library. By Wayne Weigand. University of Iowa Press, 2011. $25.95.

The MLS Project: An Assessment After Sixty Years. By Boyd Keith Swigger. Scarecrow, 2010. $50.

Reading Places: Literacy, Democracy, and the Public Library in the Cold War. By Christine Pawley. University of Massachusetts Press, 2010. $28.95.

Right Here I See My Own Books: The Woman's Building Library at the World's Columbian Exposition. By Wayne A. Wiegand and Sarah Wadsworth. University of Massachusetts Press, 2012. $28.95.

Human Resources and Leadership

Being Indispensable: A School Librarian's Guide to Becoming an Invaluable Leader. Ruth Toor and Hilda K. Weisburg. American Library Association, 2011. $42.

Coaching in the Library: A Management Strategy for Achieving Excellence. 2nd ed. By Ruth F. Metz. American Library Association, 2011. $50.

Developing Library Leaders: A How-to-Do-It Manual for Coaching, Team Building, and Mentoring Library Staff. By Robert D. Stueart with Maureen Sullivan. Neal-Schuman, 2010. $80.

Fundamentals of Library Supervision. By Joan Giesecke and Beth McNeil. American Library Association, 2010. $55.

Hiring, Training, and Supervising Library Shelvers. By Patricia Tunstall. American Library Association, 2010. $56.

Interpersonal Skills, Theory, and Practice: The Librarian's Guide to Becoming a Leader. By Brooke E. Sheldon. Libraries Unlimited, 2010. $48.

"Leading from the Middle," and Other Contrarian Essays on Library Leadership. By John Lubans, Jr. Libraries Unlimited, 2010. $50.

Managing Library Volunteers. By Preston Driggers and Eileen Dumas. American Library Association, 2011. $55.

Personal Learning Networks: Professional Development for the Isolated School Librarian. By Mary Ann Harlan. Libraries Unlimited, 2009. $30.

Shaping the Future: Advancing the Understanding of Leadership. Ed. by Peter Hernon. Libraries Unlimited, 2010. $50.

Staff Development Strategies That Work! Stories and Strategies from New Librarians. Ed. by Georgie L. Donovan and Miguel A. Figueroa. Neal-Schuman, 2008. $80.

Succession Planning in the Library: Developing Leaders, Managing Change. By Paula M. Singer with Gail Griffith. American Library Association, 2010. $55.

Information Literacy

Going Beyond Google: The Invisible Web in Learning and Teaching. By Jane Devine and Francine Egger-Sider. Neal-Schuman, 2009. $70.

I Found It on the Internet: Coming of Age Online. By Frances Jacobson Harris. American Library Association, 2011. $45.

Information Literacy and Information Skills Instruction: Applying Research to Practice in the 21st Century School Library. 3rd ed. By Nancy Pickering Thomas, Sherry R. Crow, and Lori L. Franklin. Libraries Unlimited, 2011. $40.

Information Literacy Instruction: Theory and Practice. 2nd ed. By Esther S. Grassian and Joan R. Kaplowitz. Neal-Schuman, 2009. $80.

Instructional Design for Librarians and Information Professionals. By Lesley S. J. Farmer. Neal-Schuman, 2011. $80.

Reflective Teaching, Effective Learning: Instructional Literacy for Library Educators. By Char Booth. American Library Association, 2011. $60.

Teaching Generation M: A Handbook for Librarians and Educators. By Robert J. Lackie and Vibiana Bowman Cvetkovic. Neal-Schuman, 2009. $90.

Transforming Information Literacy Programs: Intersecting Frontiers of Self, Library Culture, and Campus Community. Ed. by Carroll Wilkinson and Courtney Bruch. Association of College and Research Libraries, 2011. $62.

Information Science

Foundations of Library and Information Science. 3rd ed. By Richard E. Rubin. Neal-Schuman, 2010. $80.

Information Technology in Librarianship: New Critical Approaches. Ed. by Gloria J. Leckie and John E. Buschman. Libraries Unlimited, 2009. $50.

Introduction to Information Science and Technology. Ed. by Charles H. Davis and Debora Shaw. Information Today, Inc., 2011. $59.50.

Knowledge Management: An Introduction. By Kevin C. Desouza and Scott Paquette. Neal-Schuman, 2011. $80.

Intellectual Freedom

Banned Books Resource Guide. American Library Association/Office of Intellectual Freedom, 2010. $39.

Intellectual Freedom Manual. 8th ed. American Library Association/Office of Intellectual Freedom, 2010. $65.

Library Ethics. By Jean L. Preer. Libraries Unlimited, 2008. $45.

Privacy and Confidentiality Issues: A Guide for Libraries and Their Lawyers. By Theresa Chmara. American Library Association, 2009. $50.

Protecting Intellectual Freedom in Your Academic Library. By Barbara M. Jones. American Library Association, 2009. $50.

Protecting Intellectual Freedom in Your Public Library. By June Pinnell-Stephens. American Library Association, 2009. $50.

Protecting Intellectual Freedom in Your School Library. By Pat R. Scales. American Library Association, 2009. $55.

Librarians and Librarianship

A Librarian's Guide to an Uncertain Job Market. By Jeannette Woodward. American Library Association, 2011. $45.

Libraries in the Information Age: An Introduction and Career Exploration. 2nd ed. By Denise K. Fourie and David R. Dowell. Libraries Unlimited, 2009. $45.

Library Camps and Unconferences. By Steve Lawson. Neal-Schuman, 2010. $55.

Mob Rule Learning: Camps, Unconferences, and Trashing the Talking Head. By Michelle Boule. CyberAge Books, 2011. $24.95.

A Strong Future for Public Library Use and Employment. By José-Marie Griffiths and Donald W. King. American Library Association, 2011. $70.

Outreach and Services

Academic Library Outreach: Beyond the Campus Walls. By Nancy Courtney. Libraries Unlimited, 2008. $45.

The Anywhere Library: A Primer for the Mobile Web. By Courtney Greene, Missy Roser, and Elizabeth Ruane. Association of College and Research Libraries, 2010. $30.

Assistive Technologies in the Library. By Barbara T. Mates; with contributions by William R. Reed IV. American Library Association, 2011. $55.

Easy Information Sources for ESL, Adult Learners, and New Readers. By Rosemarie Riechel. Neal-Schuman, 2008. $70.

50+ Services: Innovation in Action. By Diantha Dow Schull. American Library Association, 2012. $55.

Hola, Amigos! A Plan for Latino Outreach. By Susana G. Baumann. Libraries Unlimited, 2010.$40.

The Librarian's Guide to Micropublishing: Helping Patrons and Communities Use Free and Low-Cost Publishing Tools to Tell Their Stories. By Walt Crawford. Information Today, Inc., 2012. $49.50.

Librarians Serving Diverse Populations: Challenges and Opportunities. By Lori Mestre. Association of College and Research Libraries, 2010. $62.

Open Conversations: Public Learning in Libraries and Museums. By David Carr. Libraries Unlimited, 2011. $50.

The Prison Library Primer: A Program for the Twenty-First Century. By Brenda Vogel. Scarecrow, 2009. $64.99.

Public Library Services to the Poor: Doing All We Can. By Leslie Edmonds Holt and Glen E. Holt. American Library Association, 2010. $48.

Small Business and the Public Library: Strategies for a Successful Partnership. By Luise Weiss, Sophia Serlis-McPhillips, and Elizabeth Malafi. American Library Association, 2011. $55.

Successful Community Outreach: A How-to-Do-It Manual for Librarians. By Barbara Blake, Robert S. Martin, and Yunfei Du. Neal-Schuman, 2011. $64.95.

Technology Training in Libraries. By Sarah Houghton-Jan. Neal-Schuman, 2010. $55.

Without a Net: Librarians Bridging the Digital Divide. By Jessamyn C. West. Libraries Unlimited, 2011. $40.

Preservation, Disaster Response, and Security

Comprehensive Guide to Emergency Preparedness and Disaster Recovery. By Frances C. Wilkinson, Linda K. Lewis, and Nancy K. Dennis. Association of College and Research Libraries, 2010. $54.

Disaster Response and Planning for Libraries. By Miriam B. Kahn. American Library Association, 2012. $57.

Guide to Security Considerations and Practices for Rare Book, Manuscript, and Special Collection Libraries. Ed. by Everett C. Wilkie, Jr. Association of College and Research Libraries, 2011. $65.

The Library Security and Safety Guide to Prevention, Planning, and Response. By Miriam B. Kahn. American Library Association, 2008. $55.

Programming

El Día de los Niños/El Día de los Libros: Building a Culture of Literacy in Your Community Through Día. By Jeanette Larson. American Library Association, 2011. $45.

Everyone Plays at the Library: Creating Great Gaming Experiences for All Ages. By Scott Nicholson. Information Today, Inc., 2010. $39.50.

Game On! Gaming at the Library. By Beth Gallaway. Neal-Schuman, 2009. $60.

Gaming in Libraries. By Kelly N. Czarnecki. Neal-Schuman, 2010. $55.

Library Programs Online: Possibilities and Practicalities of Web Conferencing. By Thomas A. Peters. Libraries Unlimited, 2009. $40.

Library Videos and Webcasts. By Sean Robinson. Neal-Schuman, 2010. $55.

Multicultural Programs for Tweens and Teens. By Linda B. Alexander and Nahyun Kwon. American Library Association, 2010. $50.

Start-to-Finish YA Programs: Hip-hop Symposiums, Summer Reading Programs, Virtual Tours, Poetry Slams, Teen Advisory Boards, Term Paper Clinics, and More! By Ella W. Jones. Neal-Schuman, 2009. $80.

Technology and Literacy: 21st Century Library Programming for Children and Teens. By Jennifer Nelson and Keith Braafladt. American Library Association, 2012. $50.

Public Libraries

The American Public Library Handbook. By Guy A. Marco. Libraries Unlimited, 2012. $75.

IFLA Public Library Service Guidelines. Ed. by Christie Koontz and Barbara Gubbin. De Gruyter Saur, 2010. $126.

Opportunity for All: How Library Policies and Practices Impact Public Internet Access: The U.S. IMPACT Study: A Research Initiative Examining the Impact of Free Access to Computers and the Internet in Public Libraries. By Samantha Becker, et al. IMLS, 2011. Free: http://www.imls.gov/assets/1/AssetManager/OppForAll2.pdf.

Public Libraries and Internet Service Roles: Measuring and Maximizing Internet Services. By Charles R. McClure and Paul T. Jaeger. American Library Association, 2008. $45.

Public Libraries and the Internet: Roles, Perspectives, and Implications. By John Carlo Bertot and Paul T. Jaeger. Libraries Unlimited, 2010. $45.

Public Libraries Going Green. By Kathryn Miller. American Library Association, 2010. $45.

Public Libraries in the 21st Century. By Ann E. Prentice. Libraries Unlimited, 2011. $50.

The Public Library Policy Writer: A Guidebook with Model Policies on CD-ROM. By Jeanette C. Larson and Herman L. Totten. Neal-Schuman, 2008. Includes CD-ROM, $80.

Small Public Library Management. By Jane Pearlmutter and Paul Nelson. American Library Association, 2012. $50.

Public Relations/Marketing

Bite-Sized Marketing: Realistic Solutions for the Overworked Librarian. By Nancy Dowd, Mary Evangelista, and Jonathan Silberman. American Library Association, 2010. $48.

Building a Buzz: Libraries and Word-of-Mouth Marketing. By Peggy Barber and Linda Wallace. American Library Association, 2010. $45.

The Customer-Focused Library: Re-inventing the Library from the Outside-In. By Joseph R. Matthews. Libraries Unlimited, 2009. $50.

DIY Programming and Book Displays: How to Stretch Your Programming Without Stretching Your Budget and Staff. By Amanda Moss Struckmeyer and Svetha Hetzler. Libraries Unlimited, 2010. $36.

The Library PR Handbook: High-Impact Communications. Ed. by Mark R. Gould. American Library Association, 2009. $57.

Listening to the Customer. By Peter Hernon and Joseph R. Matthews. Libraries Unlimited, 2011. $50.

The Mobile Marketing Handbook: A Step-by-Step Guide to Creating Dynamic Mobile Marketing Campaigns. 2nd ed. By Kim Dushinski. Information Today, Inc., 2012. $29.95.

A Social Networking Primer for Librarians. By Cliff Landis. Neal-Schuman, 2010. $55.

Wikis for Libraries. By Lauren Pressley. Neal-Schuman, 2010. $55.

Readers' Advisory

A Few Good Books: Using Contemporary Reader's Advisory Strategies to Connect Readers with Books. By Stephanie L. Maatta. Neal-Schuman, 2009. $74.95.

Integrated Advisory Service: Breaking Through the Book Boundary to Better Serve Library Users. Ed. by Jessica E. Moyer. Libraries Unlimited, 2010. $58.

Outstanding Books for the College Bound: Titles and Programs for a New Generation. Ed. by Angela Carstensen. American Library Association, 2011. $50.

The Readers' Advisory Guide to Genre Fiction. 2nd ed. By Joyce G. Saricks. American Library Association, 2009. $65.

The Readers' Advisory Guide to Street Literature. By Vanessa Irvin Morris. American Library Association, 2012. $48.

The Reader's Advisory Handbook. Ed. by Jessica E. Moyer and Kaite Mediatore Stover. American Library Association, 2010. $55.

Readers' Advisory Service for Children and 'Tweens. By Penny Peck. Libraries Unlimited, 2010. $36.

Research-Based Readers' Advisory. By Jessica E. Moyer. American Library Association, 2008. $55.

Serving Boys Through Readers' Advisory. By Michael Sullivan. American Library Association, 2010. $48.

Reference Services

Conducting the Reference Interview: A How-to-Do-It Manual for Librarians. 2nd ed. By Catherine Sheldrick Ross, Kristi Nilsen, and Marie L. Radford. Neal-Schuman, 2009. $80.

Essential Reference Services for Today's School Media Specialists. 2nd ed. By Scott Lanning and John Bryner. Libraries Unlimited, 2010. $45.

Guide to Reference. American Library Association. Online database. http://www.guidetoreference.org.

Interlibrary Loan Practices Handbook. 3rd ed. Ed. by Cherié L. Weible and Karen L. Janke. American Library Association, 2011. $85.

The Librarian as Information Consultant: Transforming Reference for the Information Age. By Sarah Anne Murphy. American Library Association, 2011. $48.

Reference and Information Services: An Introduction. 4th ed. Ed. by Richard E. Bopp and Linda C. Smith. Libraries Unlimited, 2011. $50.

Reference and Information Services in the 21st Century: An Introduction. By Kay Ann Cassell and Uma Hiremath. Neal-Schuman, 2009. $69.95.

Reference Renaissance: Current and Future Trends. Ed. by Marie L. Radford and R. David Lankes. Neal-Schuman, 2010. $80.

Reference Sources and Services for Youth. By Meghan Harper. Neal-Schuman, 2011. $70.

Searching 2.0. By Michael P. Sauers. Neal-Schuman, 2009. $70.

Training Paraprofessionals for Reference Service. By Pamela J. Morgan. Neal-Schuman, 2008. $70.

Research and Statistics

Academic Library Trends and Statistics, 2010. Association of College and Research Libraries/American Library Association, 2012. 3 vols. $550.

The ALA-APA Salary Survey 2010: Librarian—Public and Academic: A Survey of Public and Academic Library Positions Requiring an ALA-Accredited Master's Degree. ALA-Allied Professional Association and the ALA Office for Research and Statistics. American Library Association, 2010. $90. Also available online.

ARL Annual Salary Survey, 2010–2011. Association of Research Libraries, 2011. Online, $170. http://www.arl.org.

ARL Statistics. Association of Research Libraries. Annual. $175 or online at http://www.arl.org/stats/annualsurveys/arlstats.

Assessing Information Needs: Managing Transformative Library Services. By Robert J. Grover, Roger C. Greer, and John Agada. Libraries Unlimited, 2010. $60.

Assessing Service Quality: Satisfying the Expectations of Library Customers. 2nd ed. By Peter Hernon and Ellen Altman. American Library Association, 2010. $65.

Basic Research Methods for Librarians. By Lynn Silipigni Connaway and Ronald R. Powell. 5th ed. Libraries Unlimited, 2010. $50.

Engaging in Evaluation and Assessment Research. By Peter Hernon, Robert E. Dugan, and Danuta A. Nitecki. Libraries Unlimited, 2011. $50.

Library Data: Empowering Practice and Persuasion. Ed. by Darby Orcutt. Libraries Unlimited, 2010. $50.

Public Library Data Service Statistical Report 2011 (PLDS). Public Library Association/ American Library Association, 2011. Spiral, $135.

School Libraries/Media Centers

Administering the School Library Media Center. 5th ed. By Betty J. Morris. Libraries Unlimited, 2010. $60.

Empowering Learners: Guidelines for School Library Programs. American Association of School Librarians, 2009. $39.

Essential Documents for School Libraries. 2nd ed. By Colleen MacDonell. Linworth, 2010. Paper and CD $50.

Fundamentals of School Library Media Management. By Barbara Stein Martin and Marco Zannier. Neal-Schuman, 2009. $64.95.

Guide for Developing and Evaluating School Library Programs. 7th ed. By Nebraska Educational Media Association. Libraries Unlimited, 2010. $45.

Independent School Libraries: Perspectives on Excellence. Ed. by Dorcas Hand. Libraries Unlimited, 2010. $45.

The School Library Media Manager. 4th ed. By Blanche Woolls. Libraries Unlimited, 2008. $45.

The School Library Media Specialist's Policy and Procedure Writer. By Elizabeth Downs. Neal-Schuman, 2010. With CD-ROM $80.

Simply Indispensable: An Action Guide for School Librarians. By Janice Gilmore-See. Libraries Unlimited, 2010. $35.

Standards for the 21st Century Learner. American Association of School Librarians, 2007. $14.95 for bundle of 12.

Standards for the 21st Century Learner in Action. American Association of School Librarians, 2009. $39.

Technology and the School Library: A Comprehensive Guide for Media Specialists and Other Educators. By Odin Jurkowski. Scarecrow, 2010. $50.

21st Century Learning in School Libraries: Putting the AASL Standards to Work. Ed. by Kristin Fontichiaro. Libraries Unlimited, 2009. $40.

Using Web 2.0 and Social Networking Tools in the K–12 Classroom. By Beverley E. Crane. Neal-Schuman, 2012. $65.

Technical Services

Acquisitions in the New Information Universe: Core Competencies and Ethical Practices. By Jesse Holden. Neal-Schuman, 2010. $80.

Electronics Resources Management in the Academic Library: A Professional Guide. By Karin Wikoff. Libraries Unlimited, 2012. $40.

Fundamentals of Technical Services Management. By Sheila S. Intner, with Peggy Johnson. American Library Association, 2008. $55.

Integrated Library Systems: Planning, Selecting, and Implementing. By Desiree Webber and Andrew Peters. Libraries Unlimited, 2010. $45.

Introduction to Technical Services. 8th ed. By C. Edward Evans, Sheila S. Intner, and Jean Weihs. Libraries Unlimited, 2011. $50.

Technology

Blogging and RSS: A Librarian's Guide. 2nd ed. By Michael P. Sauers. Information Today, Inc., 2010. $35.

Core Technology Competencies for Librarians and Library Staff: A LITA Guide. Ed. by Susan M. Thompson. Neal-Schuman, 2009. $70.

Library Mashups: Exploring New Ways to Deliver Library Data. Ed. by Nicole C. Engard. Information Today, Inc., 2009. $39.50

Mobile Technology and Libraries. By Jason Griffey. Neal-Schuman, 2010. $55.

Neal-Schuman Library Technology Companion: A Basic Guide for Library Staff. 3rd ed. By John J. Burke. Neal-Schuman, 2009. $70.

The Neal-Schuman Technology Management Handbook for School Library Media Cen-

ters. By Lesley S. J. Farmer and Marc E. McPhee. Neal-Schuman, 2010. $64.95.

Periodicals

This listing of key library publications includes ISSNs for print and online formats. All titles have been verified against the EBSCO database as active periodicals.

Against the Grain (1043-2094)

American Libraries (0002-9769)

American Libraries Direct (1559-369X)

Art Documentation (print, 0730-7187; online, 2161-9417)

Behavioral and Social Sciences Librarian (print, 0163-9269; online, 1544-4546)

Booklist (0006-7385)

Bottom Line: Managing Library Finances (0888-045X)

Cataloging and Classification Quarterly (print, 0163-9374; online, 1544-4554)

Catholic Library World (0008-820X)

Children and Libraries: The Journal of the Association for Library Service to Children (1542-9806)

CHOICE: Current Reviews for Academic Libraries (print, 0009-4978; online, 1523-8253)

Collection Building (0160-4953)

Collection Management (print, 0146-2679; online, 1545-2549)

College and Research Libraries (print, 0099-0086; online, 2150-6701)

College and Undergraduate Libraries (print, 1069-1316; online, 1545-2530)

Community and Junior College Libraries (print, 0264-0473; online, 1758-616X)

Computers in Libraries (1041-7915)

Congregational Libraries Today (1934-2292)

Documents to the People (DttP) (0091-2085)

Electronic Library (print, 0264-0473; online, 1758-616X)

Government Information Quarterly (0740-624X)

Horn Book Magazine (0018-5078)

IFLA Journal (print, 0340-0352; online, 1745-2651)

Indexer (print, 0019-4131; online, 1756-0632)

Information and Culture (2164-8034)

Information Outlook (print, 1091-0808; online, 1938-3819)

Information Standards Quarterly (1041-0031)

Information Technology and Libraries (2163-5226)

Interlending and Document Supply (print, 0264-1615; online, 1995–2006)

Internet @ Schools (2156-843X)

Internet Reference Services Quarterly (print, 1087-5301; online, 1540-4749)

Journal of Academic Librarianship (0099-1333)

Journal of Documentation (print, 0022-0418; online, 1758-7379)

Journal of Education for Library and Information Science (0748-5786)

Journal of Electronic Resources Librarianship (print, 1542-4065; online, 1532-3269)

Journal of Information Ethics (1061-9321)

Journal of Information Science (print, 0165-5515; online, 1061-9321)

Journal of Interlibrary Loan, Document Delivery, and Information Supply (print, 1072-303X; online, 1540-3572)

Journal of Librarianship and Information Science (print, 0961-0006; online 1741-6477)

Journal of Library Administration (print, 0193-0826; online, 1540-3564)

Journal of Library Metadata (print, 1938-6389; online, 1937-5034)

Journal of Research on Libraries and Young Adults (2157-3980)

Journal of the American Society for Information Science and Technology (1532-2882)

Journal of the Medical Library Association (1536-5050)

Journal of Web Librarianship (print, 1932-2909; online, 1932-2917)

Knowledge Quest (1094-9046)

Law Library Journal (0023-9283)

Legal Reference Services Quarterly (print, 0270-319X; online, 1540-949X)

Library and Archival Security (print, 0196-0075; online 1540-9511)

Library and Information Science Research (LIBRES) (0740-8188)

Library Hi-Tech Journal (0737-8831)

Library Issues: Briefings for Faculty and Academic Administrators (0734-3035)

Library Journal (0363-0277)

Library Leadership and Management (1945-886X)

Library Management (0143-5124)

Library Media Connection (1542-4715)

The Library Quarterly (print, 0024-2519; online, 1549-652X)

Library Resources and Technical Services (0024-2527)

Library Technology Reports (print, 0024-2586; online, 1945-4538)

Library Trends (print, 0024-2594; online, 1559-0682)

Library Worklife: HR e-news for Today's Leaders (1550-3534)

Librarysparks (1544-9092)

New Review of Children's Literature and Librarianship (print, 1361-4541; online, 1740-7885)

Newsletter on Intellectual Freedom (1945-4546)

Notes (Music Library Association) (print, 0027-4380; online, 1534-150X)

Online (0146-5422)

Portal: Libraries and the Academy (print, 1531-2542; online, 1530-7131)

Public Libraries (0163-5506)

Public Library Quarterly (print, 0161-6846; online, 1541-1540)

Publishing Research Quarterly (print, 1053-8801; online, 1936-4792)

RBM: A Journal of Rare Books, Manuscripts, and Cultural Heritage (1529-6407)

Reference and User Services Quarterly (1094-9054)

Reference Librarian (print, 0276-3877; online, 1541-1117)

Research Libraries Issues (1947-4911)

RSR: Reference Services Review (0090-7324)

Rural Library Services Newsletter (1520-8761)

School Library Journal (0362-8930)

School Library Research

Searcher: The Magazine for Database Professionals (1070-4795)

Serials Librarian (print, 0361-526X; online, 1541-1095)

Serials Review (0098-7913)

State of America's Libraries Report (annual, online only)

Technical Services Quarterly (print, 0731-7131; online, 1555-3337)

Technicalities (0272-0884)

Video Librarian (0887-6851)

Voice of Youth Advocates (*VOYA*) (0160-4201)

Blogs

(All sites checked March 12, 2012)

025.431: The Dewey Blog. Jonathan Furner, ed (http://ddc.typepad.com)

AASL Blog (http://www.aasl.ala.org/aaslblog)

ACRL Insider (http://www.acrl.ala.org/acrl insider)

ACRLog (http://acrlog.org)

AL Inside Scoop (http://americanlibraries magazine.org/insidescoop)

ALA Editions Blog (http://www.alaeditions. org/blog)

ALA Membership Blog (http://americanlibraries magazine.org/ala-members-blog)

ALA Student Member Blog (http://american librariesmagazine.org/student-member-blog)

ALSC Blog (http://www.alsc.ala.org/blog)

Annoyed Librarian (http://www.libraryjournal. com/annoyedlibrarian)

AOTUS: Collector in Chief. By David Ferriero (http://blogs.archives.gov/aotus)

Ask the ALA Librarian (http://www.american librariesmagazine.org/askthelibrarian)

Audiobooker. By Mary Burkey (http://audio booker.booklistonline.com)

Awful Library Books. By Holly Hibner and Mary Kelly (http://awfullibrarybooks.net)

Blue Skunk. By Doug Johnson (http://doug-johnson.squarespace.com)

Book Group Buzz (http://bookgroupbuzz. booklistonline.com)

Bookends. By Cindy Dobrez and Lynn Rutan (http://bookends.booklistonline.com)

Catalogablog. By David Bigwood (http://catalog ablog.blogspot.com)

Celeripedean. By Jennifer Eustis (http:// celeripedean.wordpress.com)

Censorship Watch (http://americanlibraries magazine.org/censorship-watch)

A Chair, a Fireplace, and a Tea Cozy. By Liz Burns (http://blog.schoollibraryjournal.com/ teacozy)

Copyfight: The Politics of IP. By Donna Wentworth, Ernest Miller, Elizabeth Rader, Jason Schultz, Wendy Seltzer, Aaron Schwartz, and Adam Wexelblat (http://copyfight. corante.com)

Copyright Matters: Digitization and Public Access (http://blogs.loc.gov/copyrightdigitization)

Copyrightlaws.com. By Lesley Ellen Harris (http://www.copyrightlaws.com)

COSWL Cause. By the ALA Committee on the Status of Women in Librarianship (http://www.discuss.ala.org/coswlcause)

Coyle's InFormation. By Karen Coyle (http://kcoyle.blogspot.com)

David Lee King. By David Lee King (http://www.davidleeking.com)

Designing Better Libraries: Exploring the Application of Design, Innovation, and New Media to Create Better Libraries and User Experiences (http://dbl.lishost.org/blog)

The Digital Shift (http://www.thedigitalshift.com)

Digitization 101. By Jill Hurst-Wahl (http://hurstassociates.blogspot.com)

District Dispatch. By the ALA Washington Office (http://www.districtdispatch.org)

Early Word. By Nora Rawlinson (http://www.earlyword.com)

E-Content (http://americanlibrariesmagazine.org/e-content)

Free Range Librarian. By Karen G. Schneider (http://freerangelibrarian.com)

A Fuse #8 Production. By Elizabeth Bird (http://blog.schoollibraryjournal.com/afuse8production)

GLBT-RT Reviews by the ALA Gay, Lesbian, Bisexual, and Transgendered Round Table (http://www.glbtrt.ala.org/reviews)

Global Reach (http://americanlibrariesmagazine.org/global-reach)

Go to Hellman. By Eric Hellman (http://go-to-hellman.blogspot.com)

Green Your Library (http://americanlibrariesmagazine.org/green-your-library)

Hack Library School (http://hacklibschool.wordpress.com)

Hangingtogether.org (http://hangingtogether.org)

Hey Jude. By Judy O'Connell (http://heyjude.wordpress.com)

The Hub: Your Connection to Teen Reads. By the Young Adult Library Services Association (http://www.yalsa.ala.org/thehub)

In the Library with the Lead Pipe (http://www.inthelibrarywiththeleadpipe.org)

INFOdocket. By Gary Price and Shirl Kennedy (http://infodocket.com)

Information Wants to Be Free. By Meredith Farkas (http://meredith.wolfwater.com/wordpress)

InfoViews: Insights About Libraries, Research and Learning. By Mike Diaz (http://mhdiaz.wordpress.com)

John Battelle's Searchblog (http://battellemedia.com)

Leads from LLAMA (http://www.llama.ala.org/llamaleads)

Librarian.net. By Jessamyn West (http://www.librarian.net)

LibrarianInBlack. By Sarah Houghton-Jan (http://librarianinblack.net/librarianinblack)

Library History Buff Blog. By Larry T. Nix (http://libraryhistorybuff.blogspot.com)

Library Juice. By Rory Litwin (http://libraryjuicepress.com/blog)

Library of Congress Blog (http://blogs.loc.gov/loc)

Library Renewal (http://libraryrenewal.org/)

Library Web Chic. By Karen A. Coombs (http://www.librarywebchic.net)

A Library Writer's Blog. By Corey Seeman (http://librarywriting.blogspot.com)

LibraryLaw Blog. By Mary Minow (http://blog.librarylaw.com)

Likely Stories. By Keir Graff (http://blog.booklistonline.com)

LIS News. By Blake Carver (http://lisnews.org)

LITA Blog (http://litablog.org)

Lorcan Dempsey's Weblog (http://orweblog.oclc.org)

The 'M' Word—Marketing in Libraries. By Kathy Dempsey (http://themwordblog.blogspot.com)

NeverEndingSearch. By Joyce Valenza (http://blog.schoollibraryjournal.com/neverendingsearch)

NMRT Notes (http://www.nmrt.ala.org/notes)

No Shelf Required. By Sue Polanka (http://www.libraries.wright.edu/noshelfrequired)

Office for Intellectual Freedom Blog (http://www.oif.ala.org/oif)

Pattern Recognition. By Jason Griffey (http://www.jasongriffey.net/wp)

Peer to Peer Review. By Barbara Fister (http://lj.libraryjournal.com/category/opinion/barbara-fister)

Perpetual Beta (http://americanlibrariesmagazine.org/perpetualbeta)

Phil Bradley's Weblog. By Phil Bradley (http://www.philbradley.typepad.com)

PLA Blog (http://plablog.org)

Planet Cataloging (http://planetcataloging.org)

Points of Reference (http://pointsofreference.booklistonline.com)

Programming Librarian Blog (http://www.programminglibrarian.org/blog.html)

RDA Toolkit Blog (http://www.rdatoolkit.org/blog)

RUSA Blog (http://rusa.ala.org/blog)

ShelfRenewal. By Karen Kleckner Keefe and Rebecca Vnuk (http://shelfrenewal.booklistonline.com)

The Signal: Digital Preservation (http://blogs.loc.gov/digitalpreservation)

SLA Blog (http://slablogger.typepad.com/sla_blog)

Solutions and Services (http://americanlibrariesmagazine.org/solutions-and-services)

Stephen's Lighthouse. By Stephen Abram (http://stephenslighthouse.com)

Swiss Army Librarian. By Brian Herzog (http://www.swissarmylibrarian.net)

Tame the Web: Libraries and Technology. By Michael Stephens (http://tametheweb.com)

TechSource Blog. By Jason Griffey, Tom Peters, Kate Sheehan, Michael Stephens, Cindi Trainor, Michelle Boule, and Richard Wallis (http://www.alatechsource.org/blog)

TeleRead: News and Views on E-Books, Libraries, Publishing and Related Topics (http://www.teleread.com)

The Travelin' Librarian. By Michael Sauers (http://www.travelinlibrarian.info)

Walking Paper. By Aaron Schmidt (http://www.walkingpaper.org/blog)

Walt at Random. By Walt Crawford (http://walt.lishost.org)

YALSA Blog (http://yalsa.ala.org/blog)

Ready Reference

How to Obtain an ISBN

Beat Barblan

United States ISBN/SAN Agency

The International Standard Book Numbering (ISBN) system was introduced into the United Kingdom by J. Whitaker & Sons Ltd. in 1967 and into the United States in 1968 by R. R. Bowker. The Technical Committee on Documentation of the International Organization for Standardization (ISO TC 46) is responsible for the international standard.

The purpose of this standard is to "establish the specifications for the International Standard Book Number (ISBN) as a unique international identification system for each product form or edition of a monographic publication published or produced by a specific publisher." The standard specifies the construction of an ISBN, the rules for assignment and use of an ISBN, and all metadata associated with the allocation of an ISBN.

Types of monographic publications to which an ISBN may be assigned include printed books and pamphlets (in various product formats); electronic publications (either on the Internet or on physical carriers such as CD-ROMs or diskettes); educational/instructional films, videos, and transparencies; educational/instructional software; audiobooks on cassette or CD or DVD; braille publications; and microform publications.

Serial publications, printed music, and musical sound recordings are excluded from the ISBN standard as they are covered by other identification systems.

The ISBN is used by publishers, distributors, wholesalers, bookstores, and libraries, among others, in 217 countries and territories as an ordering and inventory system. It expedites the collection of data on new and forthcoming editions of monographic publications for print and electronic directories used by the book trade. Its use also facilitates rights management and the monitoring of sales data for the publishing industry.

The "new" ISBN consists of 13 digits. As of January 1, 2007, a revision to the ISBN standard was implemented in an effort to substantially increase the numbering capacity. The 10-digit ISBN identifier (ISBN-10) is now replaced by the ISBN 13-digit identifier (ISBN-13). All facets of book publishing are now expected to use the ISBN-13, and the ISBN agencies throughout the world are now issuing only ISBN-13s to publishers. Publishers with existing ISBN-10s need to convert their ISBNs to ISBN-13s by the addition of the EAN prefix 978 and recalculation of the new check digit:

ISBN-10: 0-8352-8235-X
ISBN-13: 978-0-8352-8235-2

When the inventory of the ISBN-10s has been exhausted, the ISBN agencies will start assigning ISBN-13s with the "979" prefix instead of the "978." There is no 10-digit equivalent for 979 ISBNs.

Construction of an ISBN

An ISBN currently consists of 13 digits separated into the following parts:

1 A prefix of "978" for an ISBN-10 converted to an ISBN-13
2 Group or country identifier, which identifies a national or geographic grouping of publishers
3 Publisher identifier, which identifies a particular publisher within a group
4 Title identifier, which identifies a particular title or edition of a title
5 Check digit, the single digit at the end of the ISBN that validates the ISBN-13

For more information regarding ISBN-13 conversion services provided by the U.S. ISBN Agency at R. R. Bowker, LLC, visit the ISBN Agency Web site at http://www.isbn.org, or contact the U.S. ISBN Agency at isbn-san@bowker.com.

Publishers requiring their ISBNs to be converted from the ISBN-10 to ISBN-13 format can use the U.S. ISBN Agency's free ISBN-13 online converter at http://isbn.org/converterpub.asp. Large list conversions can be requested by e-mailing isbnconversion@bowker.com. Publishers can also subscribe to view their ISBN online log book by accessing their personal account at http://www.bowkerlink.com.

Displaying the ISBN on a Product or Publication

When an ISBN is written or printed, it should be preceded by the letters ISBN, and each part should be separated by a space or hyphen. In the United States, the hyphen is used for separation, as in the following example: ISBN 978-0-8352-8235-2. In this example, 978 is the prefix that precedes the ISBN-13, 0 is the group identifier, 8352 is the publisher identifier, 8235 is the title identifier, and 2 is the check digit. The group of English-speaking countries, which includes the United States, Australia, Canada, New Zealand, and the United Kingdom, uses the group identifiers 0 and 1.

The ISBN Organization

The administration of the ISBN system is carried out at three levels—through the International ISBN Agency in the United Kingdom, through the national agencies, and through the publishing houses themselves. The International ISBN

Agency, which is responsible for assigning country prefixes and for coordinating the worldwide implementation of the system, has an advisory panel that represents the International Organization for Standardization (ISO), publishers, and libraries. The International ISBN Agency publishes the *Publishers International ISBN Directory,* which is a listing of all national agencies' publishers with their assigned ISBN publisher prefixes. R. R. Bowker, as the publisher of *Books In Print* with its extensive and varied database of publishers' addresses, was the obvious place to initiate the ISBN system and to provide the service to the U.S. publishing industry. To date, the U.S. ISBN Agency has entered more than 180,000 publishers into the system.

ISBN Assignment Procedure

Assignment of ISBNs is a shared endeavor between the U.S. ISBN Agency and the publisher. Publishers can make online application through the ISBN Agency's Web site, or by phone or fax. After an application is received and processed by the agency, an ISBN Publisher Prefix is assigned, along with a computer-generated block of ISBNs that is mailed or e-mailed to the publisher. The publisher then has the responsibility to assign an ISBN to each title, keep an accurate record of each number assigned, and register each title in the *Books In Print* database at http://www.bowkerlink.com. It is the responsibility of the ISBN Agency to validate assigned ISBNs and keep a record of all ISBN publisher prefixes in circulation.

ISBN implementation is very much market-driven. Major distributors, wholesalers, retailers, and so forth recognize the necessity of the ISBN system and request that publishers register with the ISBN Agency. Also, the ISBN is a mandatory bibliographic element in the International Standard Bibliographical Description (ISBD). The Library of Congress Cataloging in Publication (CIP) Division directs publishers to the agency to obtain their ISBN prefixes.

Location and Display of the ISBN

On books, pamphlets, and other printed material, the ISBN shall be printed on the verso of the title leaf or, if this is not possible, at the foot of the title leaf itself. It should also appear on the outside back cover or on the back of the jacket if the book has one (the lower right-hand corner is recommended). The ISBN shall also appear on any accompanying promotional materials following the provisions for location according to the format of the material.

On other monographic publications, the ISBN shall appear on the title or credit frames and any labels permanently affixed to the publication. If the publication is issued in a container that is an integral part of the publication, the ISBN shall be displayed on the label. If it is not possible to place the ISBN on the item or its label, then the number should be displayed on the bottom or the back of the container, box, sleeve, or frame. It should also appear on any accompanying material, including each component of a multi-type publication.

Printing of ISBN in Machine-Readable Coding

All books should carry ISBNs in the EAN-13 bar code machine-readable format. All ISBN EAN-13 bar codes start with the EAN prefix 978 for books. As of January 1, 2007, all EAN bar codes should have the ISBN-13 appearing immediately above the bar code in eye-readable format, preceded by the acronym "ISBN." The recommended location of the EAN-13 bar code for books is in the lower right-hand corner of the back cover (see Figure 1).

Figure 1 / Printing the ISBN in Bookland/EAN Symbology

Five-Digit Add-On Code

In the United States, a five-digit add-on code is used for additional information. In the publishing industry, this code is used for price information. The lead digit of the five-digit add-on has been designated a currency identifier, when the add-on is used for price. Number 5 is the code for the U.S. dollar, 6 denotes the Canadian dollar, 1 the British pound, 3 the Australian dollar, and 4 the New Zealand dollar. Publishers that do not want to indicate price in the add-on should print the code 90000 (see Figure 2).

Figure 2 / Printing the ISBN Bookland/EAN Number in Bar Code with the Five-Digit Add-On Code

978 = ISBN Bookland/EAN prefix   90000 means no information
5 = Code for U.S. $ in the add-on code
2499 = $24.99

Reporting the Title and the ISBN

After the publisher reports a title to the ISBN Agency, the number is validated and the title is listed in the many R. R. Bowker hard-copy and electronic publications, including *Books in Print; Forthcoming Books; Paperbound Books in Print; Books in Print Supplement; Books Out of Print; Books in Print Online; Books in Print Plus-CD ROM; Children's Books in Print; Subject Guide to Children's Books in Print; Books Out Loud: Bowker's Guide to AudioBooks; Bowker's Complete Video Directory; Software Encyclopedia; Software for Schools; and other specialized publications.*

For an ISBN application and information, visit the ISBN Agency Web site at http://www.isbn.org, call the toll-free number 888-269-5372, fax 908-219-0188, or write to the United States ISBN Agency, 630 Central Ave., New Providence, NJ 07974.

The ISSN, and How to Obtain One

U.S. ISSN Center
Library of Congress

In the early 1970s the rapid increase in the production and dissemination of information and an intensified desire to exchange information about serials in computerized form among different systems and organizations made it increasingly clear that a means to identify serial publications at an international level was needed. The International Standard Serial Number (ISSN) was developed and became the internationally accepted code for identifying serial publications.

The ISSN is an international standard, ISO 3297: 2007, as well as a U.S. standard, ANSI/NISO Z39.9. The 2007 edition of ISO 3297 expands the scope of the ISSN to cover continuing resources (serials, as well as updating databases, looseleafs, and some Web sites).

The number itself has no significance other than as a brief, unique, and unambiguous identifier. The ISSN consists of eight digits in Arabic numerals 0 to 9, except for the last—or check—digit, which can be an X. The numbers appear as two groups of four digits separated by a hyphen and preceded by the letters ISSN—for example, ISSN 1234-5679.

The ISSN is not self-assigned by publishers. Administration of the ISSN is coordinated through the ISSN Network, an intergovernmental organization within the UNESCO/UNISIST program. The ISSN Network consists of national ISSN centers, coordinated by the ISSN International Centre, located in Paris. National ISSN Centers are responsible for registering serials published in their respective countries. Responsibility for the assignment of ISSN to titles from multinational publishers is allocated among the ISSN Centers in which the publisher has offices. A list of these publishers and the corresponding ISSN centers is located on the ISSN International Centre's Web site, http://www.issn.org.

The ISSN International Centre handles ISSN assignments for international organizations and for countries that do not have a national center. It also maintains and distributes the ISSN Register and makes it available in a variety of products, most commonly via the ISSN Portal, an online subscription database. The ISSN Register is also available via Z39.50 access, and as a data file. Selected ISSN data can also be obtained in customized files or database extracts that can be used, for example, to check the accuracy or completeness of a requestor's list of titles and ISSN. The ISSN Register contains bibliographic records corresponding to each ISSN assignment as reported by national ISSN centers. The database contains records for well over 1.5 million ISSNs.

The ISSN is used all over the world by serials publishers to identify their serials and to distinguish their titles from others that are the same or similar. It is used by subscription services and libraries to manage files for orders, claims, and back issues. It is used in automated check-in systems by libraries that wish to process receipts more quickly. Copyright centers use the ISSN as a means to collect and disseminate royalties. It is also used as an identification code by postal services and legal deposit services. The ISSN is included as a verification element in interlibrary lending activities and for union catalogs as a collocating device. In recent years, the ISSN has been incorporated into bar codes for optical recognition of serial publications and into the standards for the identification of issues and articles in serial publications. Other growing uses for the ISSN are in online systems where it can serve to connect catalog records or citations in abstracting and indexing databases with full-text journal content via OpenURL resolvers or reference linking services, and as an identifier and link in archives of electronic and print serials.

Because serials are generally known and cited by title, assignment of the ISSN is inseparably linked to the key title, a standardized form of the title derived from information in the serial issue. Only one ISSN can be assigned to a title in a particular medium. For titles issued in multiple media—e.g., print, online, CD-ROM—a separate ISSN is assigned to each medium version. If a major title change occurs or the medium changes, a new ISSN must be assigned. Centers responsible for assigning ISSNs also construct the key title and create an associated bibliographic record.

A significant new feature of the 2007 ISSN standard is the Linking ISSN (ISSN-L), a mechanism that enables collocation or linking among different media versions of a continuing resource. The Linking ISSN allows a unique designation (one of the existing ISSNs) to be applied to all media versions of a continuing resource while retaining the separate ISSN that pertains to each version. When an ISSN is functioning as a Linking ISSN, the eight digits of the base ISSN are prefixed with the designation "ISSN-L." The Linking ISSN facilitates search, retrieval, and delivery across all medium versions of a serial or other continuing resource for improved ISSN functionality in OpenURL linking, search engines, library catalogs, and knowledge bases. The 2007 standard also supports interoperability by specifying the use of ISSN and ISSN-L with other systems such as DOI, OpenURL, URN, and EAN bar codes. ISSN-L was implemented in the ISSN Register in 2008. To help ISSN users implement the ISSN-L in their databases, two free tables are available from the ISSN International Centre's home page: one lists each ISSN and its corresponding ISSN-L; the other lists each ISSN-L and its corresponding ISSNs.

In the United States, the U.S. ISSN Center at the Library of Congress is responsible for assigning and maintaining the ISSNs for all U.S. serial titles. Publishers wishing to have an ISSN assigned should download an application from the Center's Web site, and mail, e-mail, or fax the form to the U.S. ISSN Center. Assignment of the ISSN is free, and there is no charge for use of the ISSN.

To obtain an ISSN for a U.S. publication, or for further information about ISSN in the United States, libraries, publishers, and other ISSN users should visit the U.S. ISSN Center's Web site, http://www.loc.gov/issn, or contact the U.S. ISSN Center, U.S. and Publisher Liaison Division, Library of Congress, 101 Independence Ave. S.E., Washington, DC 20540-4284 (telephone 202-707-6452, fax 202-707-6333, e-mail issn@loc.gov).

For information about ISSN products and services, and for application procedures that non-U.S. parties should use to apply for an ISSN, visit the ISSN International Centre's Web site at http://www.issn.org or contact the International Centre at 45 rue de Turbigo, 75003 Paris, France (telephone 33-1-44-88-22-20, fax 33-1-40-26-32-43, e-mail issnic@issn.org).

How to Obtain an SAN

Beat Barblan

United States ISBN/SAN Agency

SAN stands for Standard Address Number. The SAN system, an American National Standards Institute (ANSI) standard, assigns a unique identification number that is used to positively identify specific addresses of organizations in order to facilitate buying and selling transactions within the industry. It is recognized as the identification code for electronic communication within the industry.

For purposes of this standard, the book industry includes book publishers, book wholesalers, book distributors, book retailers, college bookstores, libraries, library binders, and serial vendors. Schools, school systems, technical institutes, and colleges and universities are not members of this industry, but are served by it and therefore included in the SAN system.

The purpose of the SAN is to ease communications among these organizations, of which there are several hundreds of thousands that engage in a large volume of separate transactions with one another. These transactions include purchases of books by book dealers, wholesalers, schools, colleges, and libraries from publishers and wholesalers; payments for all such purchases; and other communications between participants. The objective of this standard is to establish an identification code system by assigning each address within the industry a unique code to be used for positive identification for all book and serial buying and selling transactions.

Many organizations have similar names and multiple addresses, making identification of the correct contact point difficult and subject to error. In many cases, the physical movement of materials takes place between addresses that differ from the addresses to be used for the financial transactions. In such instances, there is ample opportunity for confusion and errors. Without identification by SAN, a complex record-keeping system would have to be instituted to avoid introducing errors. In addition, problems with the current numbering system—such as errors in billing, shipping, payments, and returns—are significantly reduced by using the SAN system. The SAN also eliminates one step in the order fulfillment process: the "look-up procedure" used to assign account numbers. Previously a store or library dealing with 50 different publishers was assigned a different account number by each of the suppliers. The SAN solved this problem. If a publisher prints its SAN on its stationery and ordering documents, vendors to whom it sends transactions do not have to look up the account number, but can proceed immediately to process orders by SAN.

Libraries are involved in many of the same transactions as book dealers, such as ordering and paying for books and charging and paying for various services to other libraries. Keeping records of transactions—whether these involve buying, selling, lending, or donations—entails operations suited to SAN use. SAN stationery speeds up order fulfillment and eliminate errors in shipping, billing, and crediting; this, in turn, means savings in both time and money.

History

Development of the Standard Address Number began in 1968 when Russell Reynolds, general manager of the National Association of College Stores (NACS), approached R. R. Bowker and suggested that a "Standard Account Number" system be implemented in the book industry. The first draft of a standard was prepared by an American National Standards Institute (ANSI) Committee Z39 subcommittee, which was co-chaired by Russell Reynolds and Emery Koltay of Bowker. After Z39 members proposed changes, the current version of the standard was approved by NACS on December 17, 1979.

Format

The SAN consists of six digits plus a seventh *Modulus 11* check digit; a hyphen follows the third digit (XXX-XXXX) to facilitate transcription. The hyphen is to be used in print form, but need not be entered or retained in computer systems. Printed on documents, the Standard Address Number should be preceded by the identifier "SAN" to avoid confusion with other numerical codes (SAN XXXXXXX).

Check Digit Calculation

The check digit is based on *Modulus 11*, and can be derived as follows:

1. Write the digits of the basic number.   2 3 4 5 6 7
2. Write the constant weighting factors associated with
    each position by the basic number.   7 6 5 4 3 2
3. Multiply each digit by its associated weighting factor.   14 18 20 20 18 14
4. Add the products of the multiplications. $14 + 18 + 20 + 20 + 18 + 14 = 104$
5. Divide the sum by *Modulus 11* to find the remainder. $104 \div 11 = 9$ plus a remainder of 5
6. Subtract the remainder from the *Modulus 11* to generate the required check digit. If there is no remainder, generate a check digit of zero. If the check digit is 10, generate a check digit of X to represent 10, since the use of 10 would require an extra digit. $11 - 5 = 6$
7. Append the check digit to create the standard seven-digit Standard Address Number.   SAN 234-5676

SAN Assignment

R. R. Bowker accepted responsibility for being the central administrative agency for SAN, and in that capacity assigns SANs to identify uniquely the addresses of organizations. No SANs can be reassigned; in the event that an organization should cease to exist, for example, its SAN would cease to be in circulation entirely. If an organization using an SAN should move or change its name with no change in ownership, its SAN would remain the same, and only the name or address would be updated to reflect the change.

The SAN should be used in all transactions; it is recommended that the SAN be imprinted on stationery, letterheads, order and invoice forms, checks, and all other documents used in executing various book transactions. The SAN should always be printed on a separate line above the name and address of the organization, preferably in the upper left-hand corner of the stationery to avoid confusion with other numerical codes pertaining to the organization, such as telephone number, zip code, and the like.

SAN Functions

The SAN is strictly a Standard Address Number, becoming functional only in applications determined by the user; these may include activities such as purchasing, billing, shipping, receiving, paying, crediting, and refunding. It is the method used by Pubnet and PubEasy systems and is required in all electronic data interchange communications using the Book Industry Systems Advisory Committee (BISAC) EDI formats. Every department that has an independent function within an organization could have a SAN for its own identification.

For additional information or to make suggestions, write to ISBN/SAN Agency, R. R. Bowker, LLC, 630 Central Ave., New Providence, NJ 07974, call 888-269-5372, or fax 908-219-0188. The e-mail address is san@bowker.com. The SAN Web site for online applications is at http://www.isbn.org.

Distinguished Books

Notable Books of 2011

The Notable Books Council of the Reference and User Services Association, a division of the American Library Association, selected these titles for their significant contribution to the expansion of knowledge or for the pleasure they can provide to adult readers.

Fiction

Banks, Russell. *Lost Memory of Skin* (Ecco).

Barnes, Julian. *The Sense of an Ending* (Knopf).

deWitt, Patrick. *The Sisters Brothers* (Ecco).

Goldman, Francisco. *Say Her Name* (Grove).

Harbach, Chad. *The Art of Fielding* (Little, Brown).

MacLeod, Alexander. *Light Lifting* (Biblioasis).

Obreht, Téa. *The Tiger's Wife* (Random).

Ondaatje, Michael. *The Cat's Table* (Knopf).

Phillips, Arthur. *The Tragedy of Arthur* (Random).

Russell, Karen. *Swamplandia!* (Knopf).

Torres, Justin. *We the Animals* (Houghton Mifflin Harcourt).

Trevor, William. *Selected Stories* (Viking).

Nonfiction

Adams, Mark. *Right Turn at Machu Picchu: Rediscovering the Lost City One Step at a Time* (Dutton).

Bartók, Mira. *The Memory Palace* (Free Press).

Gleick, James. *The Information: A History, a Theory, a Flood* (Knopf).

Greenblatt, Stephen. *The Swerve: How the World Became Modern* (Norton).

Hillenbrand, Laura. *Unbroken: A World War II Story of Survival, Resilience, and Redemption* (Random).

Hitchens, Christopher. *Arguably: Essays* (Twelve).

Homans, Jennifer. *Apollo's Angels: A History of Ballet* (Random).

Kahneman, Daniel. *Thinking, Fast and Slow* (Farrar, Straus & Giroux).

Marable, Manning. *Malcolm X: A Life of Reinvention* (Viking).

Millard, Candace. *Destiny of the Republic: A Tale of Madness, Medicine, and the Murder of a President* (Doubleday).

Mukherjee, Siddhartha. *Emperor of All Maladies: A Biography of Cancer* (Scribner).

Reitman, Janet. *Inside Scientology: The Story of America's Most Secretive Religion* (Houghton Mifflin Harcourt).

Poetry

Rimbaud, Arthur. *Illuminations,* translated by John Ashbery (Norton).

Bartlett, Jennifer, Sheila Black, and Michael Northen. *Beauty is a Verb: The New Poetry of Disability* (Cinco Puntos).

Best Fiction for Young Adults

Each year a committee of the Young Adult Library Services Association (YALSA), a division of the American Library Association, compiles a list of the best fiction appropriate for young adults ages 12 to 18. Selected on the basis of each book's proven or potential appeal and value to young adults, the titles span a variety of subjects as well as a broad range of reading levels.

Fiction

Abel-Fattah, Randa. *Where the Streets Had a Name* (Scholastic).

Aguirre, Ann. *Enclave* (Feiwel & Friends).

Almond, David. *My Name is Mina* (Random).

Altebrando, Tara. *Dreamland Social Club* (Penguin).

Bauer, Joan. *Close to Famous* (Penguin).

Beam, Chris. *I am J.* (Little, Brown).

Billingsley, Franny. *Chime* (Penguin).

Black, Holly. *Red Glove* (Simon & Schuster).

Blake, Kendare. *Anna Dressed in Blood* (Tor).

Blundell, Judy. *Strings Attached* (Scholastic).

Bondoux, Anne-Laure. *A Time of Miracles* (Random).

Booth, Coe. *Bronxwood* (Scholastic).

Bray, Libba. *Beauty Queens* (Scholastic).

Brezenoff, Steve. *Brooklyn Burning* (Lerner).

Brooks, Martha. *Queen of Hearts* (Farrar, Straus & Giroux).

Brown, Jennifer. *Bitter End* (Little, Brown).

Bunce, Elizabeth C. *Liar's Moon* (Scholastic).

Caletti, Deb. *Stay* (Simon & Schuster).

Carson, Rae. *The Girl of Fire and Thorns* (HarperCollins).

Castle, Jennifer. *The Beginning of After* (HarperCollins).

Chayil, Eishes. *Hush* (Walker).

Chow, Cara. *Bitter Melon* (Egmont USA).

Clement-Moore, Rosemary. *Texas Gothic* (Random).

Cohen, Joshua C. *Leverage* (Penguin).

Cooper, Michelle. *The FitzOsbornes in Exile* (Random).

Cross, Gillian. *Where I Belong* (Holiday House).

De la Peña, Matt. *I Will Save You* (Random).

Dessen, Sarah. *What Happened to Goodbye* (Penguin).

DeStefano, Lauren. *Wither* (Simon & Schuster).

Deuker, Carl. *Payback Time* (Houghton Mifflin Harcourt).

Dixon, Heather. *Entwined* (HarperCollins).

Dowell, Frances O'Roark. *Ten Miles Past Normal* (Simon & Schuster).

Downham, Jenny. *You Against Me* (Random).

Edwardson, Debby Dahl. *My Name is Not Easy* (Marshall Cavendish).

Fisher, Catherine. *The Dark City* (Penguin).

Forman, Gayle. *Where She Went* (Penguin).

Freitas, Donna. *The Survival Kit* (Farrar, Straus & Giroux).

Friesner, Esther. *Threads and Flames* (Penguin).

Gantos, Jack. *Dead End in Norvelt* (Farrar, Straus & Giroux).

Gier, Kerstin. *Ruby Red* (Henry Holt).

Goldberg Sloan, Holly. *I'll Be There* (Little, Brown).

Goodman, Shawn. *Something Like Hope* (Random).

Handler, Daniel. *Why We Broke Up,* illustrated by Maira Kalman (Little, Brown).

Hautman, Pete. *The Big Crunch* (Scholastic).

Herback, Geoff. *Stupid Fast* (Sourcebooks).

Johnson, Maureen. *The Last Little Blue Envelope* (Harper).

Johnson, Maureen. *The Name of the Star* (Penguin).

King, A. S. *Everybody Sees the Ants* (Little, Brown).

Kirby, Matthew J. *Icefall* (Scholastic).

Kittredge, Caitlin. *The Iron Thorn* (Random).

Knowles, Jo. *Pearl* (Henry Holt).

Leavitt, Lindsey. *Sean Griswold's Head* (Bloomsbury).

Lo, Malinda. *Huntress* (Little, Brown).

Lu, Marie. *Legend* (Penguin).

Marchetta, Melina. *The Piper's Son* (Candlewick).

Marcus, Kimberly. *Exposed* (Random).

Martinez, Jessica. *Virtuosity* (Simon & Schuster).

McCall, Guadalupe Garcia. *Under the Mesquite* (Lee & Low).

McMann, Lisa. *Cryer's Cross* (Simon & Schuster).

Meloy, Maile. *The Apothecary* (Penguin).

Mullin, Mike. *Ashfall* (Tanglewood).

Myracle, Lauren. *Shine* (Abrams).

Nelson, Blake. *Recovery Road* (Scholastic).

Ness, Patrick. *A Monster Calls,* illustrated by Jim Kay (Candlewick).

Neumeier, Rachel. *The Floating Islands* (Random).

O'Brien, Caragh. *Prized* (Roaring Brook).

O'Neal, Eilis. *The False Princess* (Egmont).

Ockler, Sarah. *Fixing Delilah* (Little, Brown).

Okorafor, Nnedi. *Akata Witch* (Penguin).

Oliver, Lauren. *Delirium* (HarperCollins).

Oppel, Kenneth. *This Dark Endeavor: The Apprenticeship of Victor Frankenstein* (Simon & Schuster).

Ostlere, Cathy. *Karma, A Novel in Verse* (Penguin).

Perera, Anna. *Guantanamo Boy* (Albert Whitman).

Pérez, Ashley Hope. *What Can(t) Wait* (Lerner).

Perkins, Stephanie. *Anna and the French Kiss* (Penguin).

Perkins, Stephanie. *Lola and the Boy Next Door* (Penguin).

Porter, Tracey. *Lark* (HarperCollins).

Powers, J. L. *This Thing Called the Future* (Cinco Puntos).

Price, Charlie. *Desert Angel* (Farrar, Straus & Giroux).

Riggs, Ransom. *Miss Peregrine's Home for Peculiar Children* (Quirk).

Reedy, Trent. *Words in the Dust* (Scholastic).

Reeve, Philip. *A Web of Air* (Scholastic).

Resau, Laura, and Maria Virginia Farinango. *Queen of Water* (Random).

Riordan, Rick. *The Lost Hero* (Disney).

Roth, Veronica. *Divergent* (HarperCollins).

Sales, Leila. *Past Perfect* (Simon & Schuster).

Schmidt, Gary. *Okay for Now* (Houghton Mifflin Harcourt).

Sedgwick, Marcus. *White Crow* (Roaring Brook).

Selznick, Brian. *Wonderstruck* (Scholastic).

Sepetys, Ruta. *Between Shades of Gray* (Penguin).

Sharenow, Robert. *The Berlin Boxing Club* (Harper).

Silvey, Craig. *Jasper Jones* (Random).

Smith, Andrew. *Stick* (Feiwel & Friends).

Stiefvater, Maggie. *The Scorpio Races* (Scholastic).

Taylor, Laini. *Daughter of Smoke and Bone* (Little, Brown).

Thompson, Holly. *Orchards* (Random).

Valente, Catherynne M. *The Girl Who Circumnavigated Fairyland in a Ship of Her Own Making* (Feiwel & Friends).

Van Allsberg, Chris, editor. *The Chronicles of Harris Burdick: Fourteen Amazing Authors Tell the Tales* (Houghton Mifflin Harcourt).

Van Draanen, Wendelin. *The Running Dream* (Random).

Venkatraman, Padma. *Island's End* (Penguin).

Vernick, Shirley Reva. *The Blood Lie* (Cinco Puntos).

Wallace, Jason. *Out of Shadows* (Holiday House).

Warman, Jessica. *Between* (Walker).

Whaley, John Corey. *Where Things Come Back* (Simon & Schuster).

Williams, Carol Lynch. *Miles from Ordinary* (St. Martin's).

Williams, Michael. *Now Is the Time for Running* (Little, Brown).

Wolf, Allan. *The Watch That Ends the Night: Voices from the Titanic* (Candlewick).

Wynne-Jones, Tim. *Blink and Caution* (Candlewick).

Yee, Lisa. *Warp Speed* (Scholastic).

Young, Moira. *Blood Red Road* (Simon & Schuster).

Yovanoff, Brenna. *The Space Between* (Penguin).

Zarr, Sara. *How to Save a Life* (Little, Brown).

Quick Picks for Reluctant Young Adult Readers

The Young Adult Library Services Association, a division of the American Library Association, annually chooses a list of outstanding titles that will stimulate the interest of reluctant teen readers. This list is intended to attract teens who, for whatever reason, choose not to read.

The list includes fiction and nonfiction titles published from late 2010 through early 2012.

Fiction

Aguirre, Ann. *Enclave* (Feiwel & Friends).

Barnholdt, Lauren. *Sometimes it Happens* (Simon & Schuster).

Beam, Cris. *I am J* (Little, Brown).

Binns, B. A. *Pull* (WestSide).

Blake, Kendare. *Anna Dressed in Blood* (Tor).

Booth, Coe. *Bronxwood* (Scholastic).

Brooks, Kevin. *iBoy* (Scholastic).

Brosgol, Vera. *Anya's Ghost* (Macmillan).

Busch, Jeff. *Zombie High Yearbook '64* (Sterling).

Cerrito, Angela. *The End of the Line* (Holiday House).

Dean, Carolee. *Take Me There* (Simon & Schuster).

Elkeles, Simone. *Chain Reaction* (Walker).

50 Cent. *Playground,* illustrated by Lizzi Akana (Penguin).

Ford, Christopher. *Stickman Odyssey, Book 1: An Epic Doodle* (Penguin).

Gidwitz, Adam. *A Tale Dark and Grimm* (Penguin).

Greenman, Catherine. *Hooked* (Random).

Harrington, Kim. *Clarity* (Scholastic).

Harris, Carrie. *Bad Taste in Boys* (Random).

Hopkins, Ellen. *Perfect* (Simon & Schuster).

Hunter, Travis. *Two the Hard Way* (Kensington/Dafina).

Kessler, Jackie Morse. (Riders of the Apocalypse series) *Hunger; Rage* (Houghton Mifflin Harcourt).

Kowalski, William. *The Barrio Kings* (Orca).

Lancaster, Mike A. *Human.4* (Egmont).

Lewis, Stewart. *You Have Seven Messages* (Random).

Littman, Sarah Darer. *Want to Go Private?* (Scholastic).

Lore, Pittacus. *I Am Number Four* (Lorien Legacies No. 1) (HarperCollins).

Lost Zombies. *Dead Inside Do Not Enter: Notes from the Zombie Apocalypse* (Chronicle).

Marcus, Kimberly. *Exposed* (Random).

McClintock, Norah. *She Said/She Saw* (Orca).

McMann, Lisa. *Cryer's Cross* (Simon & Schuster).

Mlynowski, Sarah. *Ten Things We Did (And Probably Shouldn't Have)* (HarperCollins).

Nelson, Blake. *Recovery Road* (Scholastic).

Northrop, Michael. *Trapped* (Scholastic).

Patterson, James. *Middle School: The Worst Years of My Life,* illustrated by Lara Park and Chris Tebbets (Little, Brown).

Peirce, Lincoln. *Big Nate on a Roll* (HarperCollins).

Proimos, James. *12 Things to Do Before You Crash and Burn* (Roaring Book).

Reed, Amy. *Clean* (Simon & Schuster).

Restrepo, Bettina. *Illegal* (HarperCollins).

Roth, Veronica. *Divergent* (HarperCollins).

Rue, Ginger. *Jump* (Random).

Sanchez, Alex. *Boyfriends with Girlfriends* (Simon & Schuster).

Santat, Dan. *Sidekicks* (Scholastic).

Schraff, Anne. (Urban Underground series, Saddleback Educational) *To Catch a Dream; The Unforgiven; The Fairest; The Quality of Mercy; Wildflower; Dark Secrets; Deliverance; Leap of Faith; The Lost; No Fear; The Stranger; Time of Courage; The Water's Edge.*

Schroeder, Lisa. *The Day Before* (Simon & Schuster).

Schreiber, Joe. *Au Revoir, Crazy European Chick* (Houghton Mifflin Harcourt).

Shepard, Sara. *The Lying Game* (HarperCollins).

Smith, Alexander Gordon. *Death Sentence* (Escape From Furnace No. 3) (Farrar, Straus & Giroux).

Springer, Kristina. *My Fake Boyfriend is Better Than Yours* (Farrar, Straus & Giroux).

Strasnick, Lauren. *Her and Me and You* (Simon & Schuster).

Summers, Courtney. *Fall For Anything* (Macmillan).

TenNapel, Doug. *Ghostopolis* (Scholastic).

Van Cleave, Ryan G. *Unlocked* (Bloomsbury).

Vrettos, Adrienne Maria. *Burnout* (Simon & Schuster).

Wells, Robison. *Variant* (HarperCollins).

Wilkerson, Lili. *Pink.* (HarperCollins).

Multi-Author Series

Bluford Series

Folan, Karyn Langhorne. *Breaking Point* (Townsend).

Folan, Karyn Langhorne. *Pretty Ugly* (Townsend).

Kern, Peggy. *The Test* (Townsend).

Night Fall Series

Atwood, Megan. *Last Desserts* (Lerner).

Carr, Elias. *The Combination* (Lerner).

Jasper, Rick. *The Late Bus* (Lerner).

Harris, Ashley Rae. *The Prank* (Lerner).

Hoblin, Paul. *Foul* (Lerner).

Surviving South Side Series

Fontes, Justine. *Benito Runs* (Lerner).

Korman, Susan. *Bad Deal* (Lerner).

Simon, Charnan. *Plan B* (Lerner).

Simon, Charnan. *Shattered Star* (Lerner).

Weyn, Suzanne. *Beaten* (Lerner).

Weyn, Suzanne. *Recruited* (Lerner).

Nonfiction

Almerico, Kendall, and Tess Hottenroth. *Whoogles: Can a Dog Make a Woman Pregnant? And Hundreds of Other Searches That Make You Ask "Who Would Google That?"* (F+W Media).

Barton, Chris. *Can I See Your I.D.? True Stories of False Identities,* illustrated by Paul Hoppe (Penguin).

Beecroft, Simon. *Star Wars Character Encyclopedia* (DK).

Beever, Julian. *Pavement Chalk Artist: The Three-Dimensional Drawings of Julian Beever* (Firefly).

Benson, Richard. *F in Exams, The Very Best Totally Wrong Test Answers* (Chronicle).

Black, Jake. *The Ultimate Guide to WWE* (Penguin).

Bleiman, Andrew, and Chris Eastland *ZooBorns: The Newest, Cutest Animals from the World's Zoos and Aquariums* (Simon & Schuster).

BradyGames. *Guinness World Records, Gamers Edition 2011* (Jim Pattison Group/Guinness World Records Ltd.).

Bragg, Georgia. *How They Croaked: The Awful Ends of the Awfully Famous,* illustrated by Kevin O'Malley (Walker).

Buchholz, Rachel. *How to Survive Anything,* illustrated by Chris Philpot (National Geographic).

Claybourne, Anna. *100 Most Awesome Things on the Planet* (Scholastic).

Conrad, Lauren. *Lauren Conrad Style* (HarperCollins).

Cowsill, Alan. *Marvel Avengers: The Ultimate Character Guide* (DK/Marvel).

DK Publishing. *Big Questions* (DK).

Dugard, Jaycee. *A Stolen Life: A Memoir* (Simon & Schuster).

Guinness World Records. *Guinness World Records 2011* (Guinness).

Hammond, Paula. *The World's Strangest Animals* (Scholastic).

Haugen, Brenda. *The Zodiac Killer: Terror and Mystery* (Capstone).

Kaelin, Lauren, and Sophia Fraioli. *When Parents Text, So Much Said . . . So Little Understood.* (Workman).

Lee, J. H. *Boo: The Life of the World's Cutest Dog.* (Chronicle).

Levy, Joel. *Phobiapedia: All the Things We Fear the Most!* (Scholastic).

Murray, Peter, and Angela Sanchez. *Memorable Moments in NFL Football* (Murray).

Murray, Peter. *Basketball* (Murray).

Murray, Peter. *Memorable Moments in Baseball* (Murray).

Murray, Peter. *Soccer* (Murray).

Murrie, Steve, and Matthew Murrie. *Every Day on Earth,* illustrated by Tom Bloom (Scholastic).

Ripley's Believe It or Not! *Curioddities* (Scholastic).

Scholastic. *Ripley's Believe It or Not! Special Edition 2012*. (Scholastic).

Sherman, M. Zachary. *Fighting Phantoms* (Capstone).

Shoket, Ann. *Seventeen Ultimate Guide to Style: How to Find Your Perfect Look* (Running Press).

Shoreline Publishing. *Year in Sports 2012* (Scholastic).

Snider, Brandon T. *DC Comics: The Ultimate Character Guide* (DK).

Tebow, Tim. *Through My Eyes: A Quarterback's Journey* (HarperCollins).

Tibballs, Geoff, Judy Barratt, and Sally McFall (eds.). *Ripley's Believe it or Not! Strikingly True*. (Ripley Entertainment).

Willin, Melvyn. *Monsters Caught on Film* (David and Charles).

Amazing Audiobooks for Young Adults

Each year a committee of the Young Adult Library Services Association, a division of the American Library Association, compiles a list of the best audiobooks for young adults ages 12 to 18. The titles are selected for their teen appeal and recording quality, and because they enhance the audience's appreciation of any written work on which the recordings may be based. While the list as a whole addresses the interests and needs of young adults, individual titles need not appeal to this entire age range but rather to parts of it.

Nonfiction

How They Croaked by Georgia Bragg, read by L. J. Ganser. Recorded Books, 3 hours and 15 minutes, 3 discs or 3 cassettes.

Fiction

After Ever After by Jordan Sonnenblick, read by Nick Podehl. Brilliance Audio, 4 hours and 37 minutes, 4 discs.

Are These My Basoomas I See Before Me? by Louise Rennison, read by Stina Nielson. Recorded Books, 6 hours and 15 minutes, 5 discs.

The Ask and the Answer (Chaos Walking, Book 2) by Patrick Ness, read by Angela Dawe and Nick Podehl. Candlewick on Brilliance Audio, 13 hours, 11 discs.

Beauty Queens by Libba Bray, read by the author. Scholastic Audio, 14 hours and 30 minutes, 12 discs.

Behemoth by Scott Westerfeld, read by Alan Cumming. Simon & Schuster Audio, 9 hours and 30 minutes, 8 discs.

Books of Umber: Dragon Games by P. W. Catanese, read by Richard Poe. Recorded Books, 9 hours, 8 discs or 8 cassettes.

Bruiser by Neal Shusterman, read by Nick Podehl, Kate Rudd, Luke Daniels, and Laura Hamilton. Brilliance Audio, 7 hours, 6 discs.

Carter's Big Break by Brent Crawford, read by Nick Podehl. Brilliance Audio, 6 hours and 39 minutes, 6 discs.

Charlie Joe Jackson's Guide to Not Reading by Tommy Greenwald, read by MacLeod Andrews. Brilliance Audio, 3 hours and 29 minutes, 3 discs.

Chime by Franny Billingsley, read by Susan Duerden. Listening Library, 10 hours and 13 minutes, 8 discs.

Cosmic by Frank Cottrell Boyce, read by Kirby Heyborne. Listening Library, 7 hours and 42 minutes, 6 discs.

Curse of the Wendigo by Rick Yancey, read by Steven Boyer. Recorded Books, 12 hours and 15 minutes, 10 discs.

Fever Crumb by Philip Reeve, read by the author. Scholastic Audio, 7 hours, 6 discs.

Ghetto Cowboy by G. Neri, read by JD Jackson. Candlewick on Brilliance Audio, 4 hours, 4 discs.

Hero by Perry Moore, read by Michael Urie. Brilliance Audio, 11 hours and 21 minutes, 10 discs.

Marbury Lens by Andrew Smith, read by Mark Boyett. Brilliance Audio, 10 hours and 40 minutes, 10 discs.

Okay for Now by Gary Schmidt, read by Lincoln Hoppe. Listening Library, 9 hours and 18 minutes, 8 discs.

Operation Yes by Sara Lewis Holmes, read by Jessica Almasy. Brilliance Audio, 6 hours, 6 discs.

Paintings from the Cave by Gary Paulsen, read by Jim Bond, Kevin R Free, Sarah Grace, and Nick Podehl. Brilliance Audio, 3 hours and 23 minutes, 3 discs.

Pick-Up Game: A Full Day of Full Court, edited by Marc Aronson and Charles R. Smith Jr., read by Dion Graham and Quincy Tyler Berstine. Candlewick on Brilliance Audio, 4 hours, 3 discs.

Ring of Solomon by Jonathan Stroud, read by Simon Jones. Listening Library, 12 hours and 30 minutes, 10 discs.

Rotters by Daniel Kraus, read by Kirby Heyborne. Random House Audio, 16 hours and 13 minutes, 18 discs.

Sapphique by Catherine Fisher, read by Kim Mai Guest. Listening Library, 12 hours, 10 discs.

Scorch Trials by James Dashner, read by Mark Deakins. Listening Library, 10 hours and 30 minutes, 9 discs.

The Scorpio Races by Maggie Stiefvater, read by Steve West and Fiona Hardingham. Scholastic Audiobooks, 10 hours and 12 minutes, 7 discs.

The Sky is Everywhere by Jandy Nelson, read by Julia Whelan. Brilliance Audio, 7 hours and 15 minutes, 6 discs.

Some Girls Are by Courtney Summers, read by Katie Schorr. Brilliance Audio, 6 hours and 50 minutes, 6 discs.

Sophomore Switch by Abby McDonald, read by Katherine Kellgren. Candlewick on Brilliance Audio, 7 hours and 9 minutes, 6 discs.

Strange Case of Origami Yoda by Tom Angleberger, read by Mark Turetsky, Greg Steinbruner, Jonathan Todd Ross, Julia Gibson, and Charlotte Parry. Recorded Books, 2 hours and 25 minutes, 2 discs.

Wake of the Lorelei Lee: Being an Account of the Further Adventures of Jacky Faber, On Her Way to Botany Bay (Bloody Jack Adventures) by L. A. Meyer, read by Katherine Kellgren. Listen and Live Audio, 16 hours, 12 discs.

Water Seeker by Kimberly Willis Holt, read by Will Patton. Listening Library, 7 hours and 6 minutes, 6 discs.

Zombies v. Unicorns, edited by Holly Black and Justine Larbalestier, read by Ellen Grafton, Nick Podehl, Kate Rudd, Julia Whelan, and Phil Gigante. Brilliance Audio, 12 hours, 10 discs.

The Reading List

Established in 2007 by the Reference and User Services Association (RUSA), a division of the American Library Association, this list highlights outstanding genre fiction that merits special attention by general adult readers and the librarians who work with them.

RUSA's Reading List Council, which consists of 12 librarians who are experts in readers' advisory and collection development, selects books in eight categories: Adrenaline (suspense, thrillers, and action adventure), Fantasy, Historical Fiction, Horror, Mystery, Romance, Science Fiction, and Women's Fiction.

Adrenaline

Before I Go To Sleep by S. J. Watson (HarperCollins).

Fantasy

The Night Circus by Erin Morgenstern (Doubleday).

Historical Fiction

Doc by Mary Doria Russell (Random).

Horror

The Ridge by Michael Koryta (Little, Brown).

Mystery

The Devotion of Suspect X by Keigo Higashino (Minotaur).

Romance

Silk is for Seduction by Loretta Chase (Avon).

Science Fiction

Leviathan Wakes by James S. A. Corey (Orbit).

Women's Fiction

The Language of Flowers by Vanessa Diffenbaugh (Ballantine).

Notable Recordings for Children

This list of notable CD recordings for children was selected by the Association for Library Service to Children, a division of the American Library Association. Recommended titles are chosen by children's librarians and educators on the basis of their originality, creativity, and suitability.

Alcatraz Versus the Evil Librarians. Recorded Books, 7 hours. Ages 10–13. Ramón de Ocampo tells the story of how Alcatraz Smedry does battle with evil librarians who are trying to take over the world.

The Apothecary. Penguin, 8 hours. Ages 11–15. Cristin Milioti uses American, British, and Russian accents in her reading of this Cold War fantasy.

Beethoven's Wig: Sing Along Piano Classics. Beethoven's Wig, 46 minutes. Ages 4 and older. Richard Perlmutter and four other singers present a humorous introduction to some classics by noted composers.

Clementine and the Family Meeting. Recorded Books, 2 hours. Ages 7–10. Jessica Almasy tells the story of a third grader who is realizing that her family dynamics are about to change.

Countdown. Listening Library, 7 hours and 20 minutes. Ages 10–14. Emma Galvin's narration and historical audio clips tell the story of an 11-year-old girl during the Cuban missile crisis of the early 1960s.

Dead End in Norvelt. Macmillan, 7 hours. Ages 10–14. Jack Gantos tells this story of his boyhood summer escaping Hell's Angels and writing obituaries, all while he was grounded at home.

Dear America: Like the Willow Tree. Scholastic, 4 hours and 17 minutes. Ages 9–12. Sara Barnett relates the story of 11-year-old Lydia Amelia Pierce during the flu epidemic of 1918.

Don't Let the Pigeon Stay Up Late! Weston Woods, 5 minutes. Ages 3–7. Author-illustrator Mo Willems reads this adaptation of his popular book.

Ella Jenkins: A Life of Song. Smithsonian Folkways, 36 minutes. Ages 4 and up. Jenkins enlists children and others to help deliver a collection of stories and songs inspired by her early life.

Fletcher and the Springtime Blossoms. Weston Woods, 7 minutes. Ages 4–7. Katherine Kellgren portrays Fletcher, who warns his animal friends to return to their winter quarters when he mistakes blossoms for snow.

Ghetto Cowboy. Brilliance Audio, 4 hours. JD Jackson tells the story of a 12-year-old boy who grows from near-delinquent to responsible teen and passionate horseman.

The Incorrigible Children of Ashton Place, Book 2: The Hidden Gallery. Listening Library, 5 hours and 57 minutes. Ages 9–13. A gothic mystery read by Katherine Kellgren.

Ivy and Bean: What's the Big Idea? Recorded Books, 1 hour and 15 minutes. Ages 7–10. Cassandra Morris portrays Ivy and Bean as they search for the perfect science project.

Jefferson's Sons. Listening Library, 10 hours and 24 minutes. Ages 11–15. A young slave asks why he can't call his own father "papa." Adenrele Ojo tells the story.

Jessica. Live Oak Media, 7 minutes and 27 seconds. Ages 3–6. Ruthie's parents say her friend Jessica isn't real, but she is—to Ruthie. Read by Katherine Kellgren.

Jim Gill Presents Music Play for Folks of All Stripes. Jim Gill, 50 minutes. Ages 2–6. Gill's songs make use of catchy fingerplays and movements.

Looking Like Me. Live Oak Media, 8 minutes. Ages 7–12. Dion Graham and Quincy Tyler Bernstine perform rhyming couplets set against jazzy music and picture book collages.

Lucky for Good. Listening Library, 5 hours and 25 minutes. Ages 8–12. The final book in the Lucky series is narrated by Cassandra Campbell.

Mirror Mirror: A Book of Reversible Verse. Live Oak Media, 16 minutes and 18 seconds. Ages 8–12. Marilyn Singer and Joe Morton have fun with familiar fairy tales in 14 reverso poems.

Moon Over Manifest. Listening Library, 9 hours and 25 minutes. Ages 10–14. Jenna Lamia, Cassandra Campbell, and Kirby Heyborne tell the story of Abilene Tucker's adventures in Manifest during the summer of 1936.

Okay for Now. Listening Library, 9 hours and 18 minutes. Ages 11–15. Lincoln Hoppe voices Douglas Swieteck with all the attitude the young teen experiences in "stupid" Marysville, N.Y., in 1968.

Operation Yes. Brilliance Audio, 6 hours and 28 minutes. Ages 9–13. Jessica Almasy's performance reflects the ups and downs of sixth graders living on a military base while friends and relatives serve in Afghanistan.

The Other Half of My Heart. Listening Library, 7 hours and 50 minutes. Ages 10–13. Bahni Turpin's tells this moving story about biracial twin sisters.

Practically Ridiculous. Pluckypea, 40 minutes. Ages 5–12. The Jimmies bring a variety of musical styles to this celebration of childhood.

The Sisters Club: Cloudy with a Chance of Boys. Brilliance Audio, 3 hours and 6 minutes. Ages 9–12. With charm and humor, Jenna Lamia captures the perspectives of three sisters as boys begin to play a new role in their lives.

Songs from the Baobab: African Lullabies and Nursery Rhymes. Secret Mountain, 48 minutes. Ages 0–7. Lyrics in nearly a dozen African languages provide an experience of traditional lullabies and nursery rhymes.

Stone Soup. Weston Woods, 10 minutes and 12 seconds. Ages 5–8. B. D. Wong narrates a traditional folktale given a new twist.

Thunder over Kandahar. Listening Library, 6 hours and 36 minutes. Ages 12–16. Mozhan Marno reads a novel of friendship in the midst of the war in Afghanistan.

The Unforgotten Coat. Brilliance Audio, 1 hour and 40 minutes. Ages 10–13. Sarah Coomes's performance conveys Julie's feelings as she becomes the guide for two mysterious new students from Mongolia.

Young Fredle. Listening Library, 6 hours and 30 minutes. Wendy Carter voices young Fredle the mouse on Fredle's adventures inside and outside the house.

Notable Children's Books

A list of notable children's books is selected each year by the Notable Children's Books Committee of the Association for Library Service to Children, a division of the American Library Association. Recommended titles are selected by children's librarians and educators based on originality, creativity, and suitability for children. [See "Literary Prizes, 2011" later in Part 5 for Caldecott, Newbery, and other award winners—*Ed.*]

Books for Younger Readers

Bartoletti, Susan Campbell. *Naamah and the Ark at Night,* illustrated by Holly Meade (Candlewick).

Bently, Peter. *King Jack and the Dragon,* illustrated by Helen Oxenbury (Dial).

Burkert, Rand. *Mouse & Lion,* illustrated by Nancy Ekholm Burkert (Scholastic).

Cunnane, Kelly. *Chirchir Is Singing,* illustrated by Jude Daly (Schwartz & Wade).

Daly, Cathleen. *Prudence Wants a Pet,* illustrated by Stephen Michael King (Roaring Brook).

Harris, Robie H. *Who Has What? All About Girls' Bodies and Boys' Bodies,* illustrated by Nadine Bernard Westcott (Candlewick).

Henkes, Kevin. *Little White Rabbit,* illustrated by the author (Greenwillow).

Intriago, Patricia. *Dot,* illustrated by the author (Farrar, Straus & Giroux).

Klassen, Jon. *I Want My Hat Back,* illustrated by the author (Candlewick).

Lamb, Albert. *Tell Me the Day Backwards,* illustrated by David McPhail (Candlewick).

Lyon, George Ella. *All the Water in the World,* illustrated by Katherine Tillotson (Atheneum).

McDonnell, Patrick. *Me . . . Jane,* illustrated by the author (Little, Brown).

Martin, Bill Jr. *Ten Little Caterpillars,* illustrated by Lois Ehlert (Beach Lane).

Mason, Margaret H. *These Hands,* illustrated by Floyd Cooper (Houghton Mifflin Harcourt).

Medina, Meg. *Tia Isa Wants a Car,* illustrated by Claudio Muñoz (Candlewick).

Meisel, Paul. *See Me Run,* illustrated by the author (Holiday House).

Messner, Kate. *Over and Under the Snow,* illustrated by Christopher Silas Neal (Chronicle).

Ogburn, Jacqueline K. *Little Treasures: Endearments from Around the World,* illustrated by Chris Raschka (Houghton Mifflin Harcourt).

Raschka, Chris. *A Ball for Daisy,* illustrated by the author (Schwartz & Wade).

Ray, Mary Lyn. *Stars,* illustrated by Marla Frazee (Beach Lane).

Rinker, Sherri Duskey. *Goodnight, Goodnight, Construction Site,* illustrated by Tom Lichtenheld (Chronicle).

Rocco, John. *Blackout,* illustrated by the author (Disney/Hyperion).

Savage, Stephen. *Where's Walrus?* illustrated by the author (Scholastic).

Schneider, Josh. *Tales for Very Picky Eaters,* illustrated by the author (Clarion).

Shea, Susan A. *Do You Know Which Ones Will Grow?* illustrated by Tom Slaughter (Blue Apple).

Stockdale, Susan. *Bring on the Birds,* illustrated by the author (Peachtree).

Smith, Lane. *Grandpa Green,* illustrated by the author (Roaring Brook).

Vamos, Samantha R. *The Cazuela that the Farm Maiden Stirred,* illustrated by Rafael López (Charlesbridge).

Wild, Margaret. *Harry and Hopper,* illustrated by Freya Blackwood (Feiwel & Friends).

Willems, Mo. *I Broke My Trunk,* illustrated by the author (Hyperion).

Willems, Mo. *Should I Share My Ice Cream?* illustrated by the author (Hyperion).

Yu, Li-Qiong. *A New Year's Reunion: A Chinese Story,* illustrated by Zhu Cheng-Liang (Candlewick).

Middle Readers

Arnosky, Jim. *Thunder Birds: Nature's Flying Predators,* illustrated by the author (Sterling).

Aston, Dianna Hutts. *Dream Something Big: The Story of the Watts Towers,* illustrated by Susan L. Roth (Dial).

Boyce, Frank Cottrell. *The Unforgotten Coat,* illustrated by Carl Hunter and Clare Heney (Candlewick).

Brown, Don. *America is Under Attack: September 11, 2001: The Day the Towers Fell,* illustrated by the author (Roaring Brook).

Brown, Monica. *Marisol McDonald Doesn't Match/Marisol McDonald No Combina,* illustrated by Sara Palacios (Lee & Low).

Burleigh, Robert. *Night Flight: Amelia Earhart Crosses the Atlantic,* illustrated by Wendell Minor (Simon & Schuster).

Deedy, Carmen Agra, and Randall Wright. *The Cheshire Cheese Cat: A Dickens of a Tale,* illustrated by Barry Moser (Peachtree).

Duffy, Chris, editor. *Nursery Rhyme Comics: 50 Timeless Rhymes from 50 Celebrated Cartoonists* (First Second).

Ellis, Deborah. *No Ordinary Day* (Groundwood).

Evans, Shane. *Underground,* illustrated by the author (Roaring Brook).

Garza, Xavier. *Maximilian and the Mystery of the Guardian Angel: A Bilingual Lucha Libre Thriller* (Cinco Puntos).

George, Kristine O'Connell. *Emma Dilemma: Big Sister Poems,* illustrated by Nancy Carpenter (Clarion).

Greenfield, Eloise. *The Great Migration: Journey to the North,* illustrated by Jan Spivey Gilchrist (HarperCollins/Amistad).

Hatke, Ben. *Zita the Spacegirl,* illustrated by the author (First Second).

Henkes, Kevin. *Junonia* (Greenwillow).

Holm, Jennifer L. *The Trouble with May Amelia* (Atheneum).

Lai, Thanhha. *Inside Out and Back Again* (HarperCollins).

Lichtenheld, Tom. *E-mergency!* illustrated by Ezra Fields-Meyer (Chronicle).

Napoli, Donna Jo. *Treasury of Greek Mythology: Classic Stories of Gods, Goddesses, Heroes & Monsters,* illustrated by Christina Balit (National Geographic).

Park, Linda Sue. *The Third Gift,* illustrated by Bagram Ibatoulline (Clarion).

Raczka, Bob. *Lemonade, and Other Poems Squeezed from a Single Word,* illustrated by Nancy Doniger (Roaring Brook).

Roth, Susan L., and Cindy Trombore. *The Mangrove Tree: Planting Trees to Feed Families,* illustrated by Susan L. Roth (Lee & Low).

Selznick, Brian. *Wonderstruck,* illustrated by the author (Scholastic).

Sweet, Melissa. *Balloons over Broadway: The True Story of the Puppeteer of Macy's Parade,* illustrated by the author (Houghton Mifflin Harcourt).

Tak, Bibi Dumon. *Soldier Bear,* illustrated by Philip Hopman, translated by Laura Watkinson (Eerdmans).

Thor, Annika. *The Lily Pond,* translated by Linda Schenck (Delacorte).

Tonatiuh, Duncan. *Diego Rivera: His World and Ours,* illustrated by the author. (Abrams).

Trottier, Maxine. *Migrant,* illustrated by Isabelle Arsenault (Groundwood).

Voight, Cynthia. *Young Fredle,* illustrated by Louise Yates (Knopf).

Wardlaw, Lee. *Won-Ton: A Cat Tale Told in Haiku,* illustrated by Eugene Yelchin (Henry Holt).

Winter, Jeanette. *The Watcher: Jane Goodall's Life with the Chimps,* illustrated by the author (Schwartz & Wade).

Yelchin, Eugene. *Breaking Stalin's Nose,* illustrated by the author (Henry Holt).

Older Readers

Arni, Samhita. *Sita's Ramayana,* illustrated by Moyna Chitrakar. (Groundwood).

Blumenthal, Karen. *Bootleg: Murder, Moonshine, and the Lawless Years of Prohibition* (Roaring Brook).

Bradley, Kimberly Brubaker. *Jefferson's Sons: A Founding Father's Secret Children* (Dial).

Bragg, Georgia. *How They Croaked: The Awful Ends of the Awfully Famous,* illustrated by Kevin O'Malley (Walker).

Brimner, Larry Dane. *Black and White: The Confrontation between Reverend Fred L. Shuttlesworth and Eugene "Bull" Connor* (Calkins Creek).

Brooks, Martha. *Queen of Hearts* (Farrar, Straus & Giroux).

Brosgol, Vera. *Anya's Ghost* (First Second).

Christopher, Lucy. *Flyaway* (Chicken House).

Engle, Margarita. *Hurricane Dancers: The First Caribbean Pirate Shipwreck* (Henry Holt).

Fleming, Candace. *Amelia Lost: The Life and Disappearance of Amelia Earhart* (Schwartz & Wade).

Frost, Helen. *Hidden* (Farrar, Straus & Giroux).

Gantos, Jack. *Dead End in Norvelt* (Farrar, Straus & Giroux).

Gourlay, Candy. *Tall Story* (Random House).

Kent, Trilby. *Stones for My Father* (Tundra).

McCall, Guadalupe Garcia. *Under the Mesquite* (Lee & Low).

Ness, Patrick. *A Monster Calls* (Candlewick).

O'Connell, Caitlin, and Donna M. Jackson. *The Elephant Scientist*, illustrated by Caitlin O'Connell and Timothy Rodwell (Houghton Mifflin Harcourt).

Pringle, Laurence. *Billions of Years, Amazing Changes: The Story of Evolution*, illustrated by Steve Jenkins (Boyds Mills).

Ross, Stuart. *Into the Unknown: How Great Explorers Found Their Way by Land, Sea, and Air*, illustrated by Stephen Biesty (Candlewick).

Rubin, Susan Goldman. *Music Was It: Young Leonard Bernstein* (Charlesbridge).

Say, Allen. *Drawing from Memory*, illustrated by the author (Scholastic).

Schanzer, Rosalyn. *Witches! The Absolutely True Tale of Disaster in Salem*, illustrated by the author (National Geographic).

Schmatz, Pat. *Bluefish* (Candlewick).

Schmidt, Gary D. *Okay for Now* (Clarion).

Scott, Elaine. *Space, Stars, and the Beginning of Time: What the Hubble Telescope Saw* (Clarion).

Sepetys, Ruta. *Between Shades of Gray* (Philomel).

Stiefvater, Maggie. *The Scorpio Races* (Scholastic).

Tan, Shaun. *Lost & Found*, illustrated by the author (Arthur A. Levine).

Thomson, Ruth. *Terezin: Voices from the Holocaust* (Candlewick).

VanHecke, Susan. *Raggin', Jazzin', Rockin': A History of American Musical Instrument Makers* (Boyds Mills).

Walker, Sally M. *Blizzard of Glass: The Halifax Explosion of 1917* (Henry Holt).

Wolitzer, Meg. *The Fingertips of Duncan Dorfman* (Dutton).

Young, Ed, and Libby Koponen. *The House Baba Built: An Artist's Childhood in China*, illustrated by Ed Young (Little, Brown).

All Ages

Jenkins, Martin. *Can We Save the Tiger?* illustrated by Vicky White (Candlewick).

McGuirk, Leslie. *If Rocks Could Sing: A Discovered Alphabet*, illustrated by the author (Tricycle).

McKissack, Patricia. *Never Forgotten*, illustrated by Leo and Diane Dillon (Schwartz & Wade).

Nelson, Kadir. *Heart and Soul: The Story of America and African Americans*, illustrated by the author (Balzer + Bray).

Sidman, Joyce. *Swirl by Swirl: Spirals in Nature*, illustrated by Beth Krommes (Houghton Mifflin Harcourt).

Tullet, Hervé. *Press Here*, illustrated by the author, translated by Christopher Franceschelli (Chronicle).

Notable Children's Videos

These DVD titles are selected by a committee of the Association for Library Service to Children, a division of the American Library Association. Recommendations are based on originality, creativity, and suitability for children.

All the World. Weston Woods, 6 minutes. Ages 3–7.

A Child's Garden of Poetry. Warner Home Video, 27 minutes. Grades 2 and up.

Children Make Terrible Pets. Weston Woods, 6 minutes. Ages 4–8.

Choosing to Be a GFF (Good Friend Forever). Good Friend, 15 minutes. Ages 10–14.

Coming Out: What Every Teen (Gay and Straight) Needs to Know. Human Relations Media, 23 minutes. Ages 12–18.

The Day of the Dead. Weston Woods, 9 minutes. Ages 4–8.

Don't Let the Pigeon Stay Up Late! Weston Woods, 6 minutes. Ages 2–7.

Eric Carle, Picture Writer: The Art of the Picture Book. Eric Carle Studio, 32 minutes. All Ages.

Kitten's First Full Moon. Weston Woods, 9 minutes. Ages 2–7.

Party Day (The Laurie Berkner Band). Two Tomatoes/Razor & Tie, 49 minutes. Ages 3–8.

Private Eyes/Les Yeux Noirs. National Film Board of Canada, 15 minutes. Ages 4–8.

Robot Zot! Weston Woods, 8 minutes. Ages 3–7.

Safety Smart Science with Bill Nye the Science Guy: Germs and Your Health. Disney Educational, 26 minutes. Ages 9–13.

Scaredy Squirrel. Weston Woods, 7 minutes. Ages 4–8.

Stone Soup. Weston Woods, 12 minutes. Ages 4–8.

Too Many Toys. Weston Woods, 11 minutes. Ages 4–8.

Bestsellers of 2011

E-books Boom

Daisy Maryles
Contributing Editor, *Publishers Weekly*

Last year was the first time *Publishers Weekly* (*PW*) gathered annual sales on e-books. Criteria were at least 10,000 copies or more sold during 2010's 12 months and the publishers polled were the ones that also had print bestsellers. Not all publishers responded, and many submitted selected titles. Nevertheless, the annual list included about 275 titles, an impressive figure. With reports of e-book sales going through the roof last year, we wisely set 25,000 or more for this year's cutoff point. The 2011 total for 25,000+ is even more impressive—340 titles; only 100 books on the 2010 list hit that mark. Unit sales for the e-books bestsellers also exploded. In 2010 five e-books had sales of 200,000 or more units; in 2011, a whopping 35 titles had sales of more than 200,000. Once again, there were publishers who did not want to share their e-book data while others shared selected titles.

We were inundated with so many e-books bestsellers that a few new rules were put into play. First, e-book bestsellers would have to abide by the same rules as their print counterparts; specifically, only e-books published in 2010 and 2011 with sales of 25,000 or more in 2011 were to be considered. Exceptions were made for those e-book titles that are still on *PW*'s annual print charts. We did rule ineligible e-books that were priced at less than $5.

Not surprisingly, books that sold well in print also sold well as e-books. Top-sellers in print were also the leaders on the e-book charts. And except for cookbooks, all popular print categories were popular on the e-book list. Fiction was more popular than nonfiction; only 45 of the 340 e-book titles were nonfiction; still, half of the top ten were nonfiction. Admittedly, our instructions for e-books were not as clear as they were for print books, so many publishers gave us figures for backlist titles and classics. Perusing these lists indicates the strength of backlist for both classics and commercial fiction.

The Sun Also Rises, Gone with the Wind, and *The Great Gatsby* were among many classics with impressive e-book sales in 2011. Bestseller veterans such as James Patterson and Nora Roberts had an equal number of new books (e-books first released in 2010 and 2012) as well as backlist in the 25,000+ list: nine for Roberts and 11 for Patterson. Bestselling political thriller author Vince Flynn demonstrated the strength of backlist in e-books with his latest, *American Assassin,* enjoying more than 122,000 copies sold; 11 backlist titles over the 25,000 mark added up to more than 376,000 units in 2011. Many of Flynn's author colleagues enjoyed similar e-book experiences. Clearly, backlist thrives in the e-book world.

America is reading, but all signs point to rocketing e-book sales and continued dwindling of print.

(Note: Titles with an asterisk were submitted in confidence, for use only in placing the titles on the list. In a few cases, there are titles with asterisks and figures that were rounded down to indicate their relationship to other titles.)

Adapted from *Publishers Weekly,* March 19, 2012

E-book Sales, 2011

400,000+

The Help by Kathryn Stockett. Berkley (1,950,000)

Heaven Is for Real by Todd Burpo. Thomas Nelson (958,837)

Unbroken by Laura Hillenbrand. Random House (789,998)

Steve Jobs by Walter Isaacson. Simon & Schuster (624,595)

The Lincoln Lawyer by Michael Connelly. Little, Brown (481,985)

Explosive Eighteen by Janet Evanovich. Bantam (477,474)

Stolen Life by Jaycee Dugard. Simon & Schuster (457,724)

Bossypants by Tina Fey. Little, Brown/Reagan Arthur (431,117)

Now You See Her by James Patterson. Little, Brown (411,827)

250,000+

Something Borrowed by Emily Giffin, St. Martin's (351,993)

Smokin' Seventeen by Janet Evanovich. Bantam (335,669)

The Paris Wife by Paula McLain. Ballantine (332,169)

10th Anniversary by James Patterson. Little, Brown (325,678)

In the Garden of the Beasts by Erik Larson. Crown (323,775)

A Dance with the Dragons by George R. R. Martin. Bantam (321,439)

The Best of Me by Nicholas Sparks. Grand Central (309,724)

Kill Alex Cross by James Patterson. Little, Brown (298,578)

Room by Emma Donoghue. Little, Brown (289,564)

Tick Tock by James Patterson. Little, Brown (275,932)

Sarah's Key by Tatiana de Rosnay. St. Martin's (268,858).

11/22/63 by Stephen King. Scribner (266,417).

The Affair by Lee Child. Delacorte (264,328).

The Fifth Witness by Michael Connelly. Little, Brown (260,999).

The Sixth Man by David Baldacci. Grand Central (254,900).

Dead Reckoning by Charlaine Harris. Ace.

Killing Lincoln: The Shocking Assassination That Changed America Forever by Bill O'Reilly. Henry Holt.

The Immortal Life of Henrietta Lacks by Rebecca Skloot. Crown (250,507).

200,000+

Unfinished Business by Nora Roberts. Silhouette (234,800).

The Black Echo by Michael Connelly. Little, Brown (227,129).

Something Blue by Emily Giffin. St. Martin's (218,034).

Kill Me If You Can by James Patterson. Little, Brown (207,698).

The Drop by Michael Connelly. Little, Brown (206,184).

Zero Day by David Baldacci. Grand Central (204,289).

State of Wonder by Ann Patchett. Harper (203,109).

Decision Points by George W. Bush. Crown (202,005).

125,000+

Buried Prey by John Sandford. Putnam (195,000).

The Next Always by Nora Roberts. Berkley.

No Time Left (digital original) by David Baldacci. Grand Central (190,808).

Sing You Home by Jodi Picoult. Atria (185,508).

The 4-Hour Body by Timothy Ferriss. Crown (185,326).

Love You More by Lisa Gardner. Bantam (173,390).

A Discovery of Witches by Deborah Harkness. Penguin.

Crossfire by James Patterson. Little, Brown (168,129).

The Art of Racing in the Rain by Garth Stein. Harper (160,256).

Safe Haven by Nicholas Sparks. Grand Central (153,363).

The Christmas Wedding by James Patterson. Little, Brown (148,641).

The Black Ice by Michael Connelly. Little, Brown (145,192).

One Summer by David Baldacci. Grand Central (140,857).

The 17 Day Diet by Dr. Mike Moreno. Free Press (140,711).

I'll Walk Alone by Mary Higgins Clark. Simon & Schuster (140,494).

*V Is for Vengeance by Sue Grafton. Putnam/ Marion Wood.

*Red Mist by Patricia Cornwell. Putnam.

Before I Go to Sleep by S. J. Watson. Harper (136,720).

*Chasing Fire by Nora Roberts. Putnam.

*Dead or Alive by Tom Clancy. Putnam.

Lethal by Sandra Brown. Grand Central (131,582).

Suicide Run (digital original) by Michael Connelly. Little, Brown (130,902).

Portrait of a Spy by Daniel Silva. Harper (129,932).

Then Came You by Jennifer Weiner. Atria (128,954).

1225 Christmas Tree Lane by Debbie Macomber. Mira (128,600).

*Treachery in Death by J. D. Robb. Berkley.

Hell's Corner by David Baldacci. Grand Central (126,256).

100,000+

*Against All Enemies by Tom Clancy. Putnam.

*New York to Dallas by J. D. Robb. Putnam.

American Assassin by Vince Flynn. Atria (122,982).

The Reversal by Michael Connelly. Little, Brown (122,851).

Until Proven Guilty by J. A. Jance. Morrow (121,528).

Freedom by Jonathan Franzen. Farrar, Straus & Giroux (120,995).

Full Black by Brad Thor. Atria (120,745).

Shadowfever by Karen Marie Moning. Delacorte (120,612).

SEAL Team Six: Memoirs of an Elite Navy SEAL by Howard E. Wasdin and Stephen Templin. St. Martin's (120,505).

*Shockwave by John Sandford. Putnam.

Full Dark, No Stars by Stephen King. Scribner (119,464).

House Rules by Jodi Picoult. Atria (119,349).

*Stories I Only Tell My Friends: An Autobiography by Rob Lowe. Henry Holt.

Mystery by Jonathan Kellerman. Ballantine (118,942).

The Glass Castle by Jeannette Walls. Scribner (118,187).

The Jefferson Key by Steve Berry. Ballantine (116,025).

*Split Second by Catherine Coulter. Putnam.

The Silent Girl by Tess Gerritsen. Ballantine (113,416).

Night Road by Kristin Hannah. St. Martin's (108,654).

The Brass Verdict by Michael Connelly. Little, Brown (108,172).

Cleopatra by Stacy Schiff. Little, Brown (107,128).

A Turn in the Road by Debbie Macomber. Mira (104,600).

The Winter Sea by Susanne Kearsley. Sourcebooks Landmark (104,106).

*Live Wire by Harlan Coben. Dutton.

The 9th Judgment by James Patterson. Little, Brown (101,475).

Heart of the Matter by Emily Giffin. St. Martin's (101,083).

70,000+

*The Jungle by Clive Cussler. Putnam.

1105 Yakima Street by Debbie Macomber. Mira (98,400).

Dreams of Joy by Lisa See. Random House (98,305).

Happy Birthday by Danielle Steel. Delacorte (95,819).

Toys by James Patterson. Little, Brown (95,353).

Catherine the Great by Robert K. Massie. Random House (95,073).

Eve by Iris Johansen. St. Martin's (93,268).

*Fall of Giants by Ken Follett. Dutton.

44 Charles Street by Danielle Steel. Delacorte (92,454).

Lost in Shangri La by Mitchell Zuckoff. Harper (90,264).

Sizzling Sixteen by Janet Evanovich. St. Martin's (90,162).

Bonnie by Iris Johansen. St. Martin's (87,067).

The Tiger's Wife by Téa Obreht. Random House (84,496).

Half-Broke Horses by Jeannette Walls. Scribner (84,457).

Spontaneous by Brenda Jackson. Harlequin (84,100).

*Secrets to the Grave by Tami Hoag. Dutton.

The Search by Nora Roberts. Jove.

Quinn by Iris Johansen. St. Martin's (83,387).

Dead in the Family by Charlaine Harris. Ace.

Port Mortuary by Patricia Cornwell. Berkley.

Locked On by Tom Clancy. Putnam.

The Wise Man's Fear by Patrick Rothfuss. DAW.

The Dukan Diet by Pierre Dukan. Crown (80,308).

Strategic Moves by Stuart Woods. Signet.

The Fall of Shane Mackade by Nora Roberts. Silhouette (79,200).

Summer Rental by Mary Kay Andrews. St. Martin's (79,075).

The Marriage Plot by Jeffrey Eugenides. Farrar, Straus & Giroux (77,624).

Caleb's Crossing by Geraldine Brooks. Viking.

Hearts Aflame by Johanna Lindsey. Avon (76,825).

Chasing the Night by Iris Johansen. St. Martin's (75,604).

The Weird Sisters by Eleanor Brown. Putnam/ Amy Einhorn.

Battle Hymn of the Tiger Mother by Amy Chua. Penguin.

The Devil Colony by James Rollins. Morrow (72,204).

Bonhoeffer by Eric Meetaxas. Thomas Nelson (72,015).

World War Z by Max Brooks. Crown (71,828).

The Ideal Man by Julie Garwood. Dutton.

Rules of Civility by Amor Towles. Viking.

Go the F**k to Sleep by Adam Mansbach, illustrated by Ricardo Cortes. Akashic (70,000).

60,000+

Ghost Story by Jim Butcher. Roc.

A Dog's Purpose by W. Bruce Cameron. Forge (68,352).

The Heir by Grace Borrowes. Sourcebooks Casablanca (68,314).

Bring Me Home for Christmas by Robyn Carr. Mira (67,100).

Kitchen House by Kathleen Grissom. Touchstone (66,653).

What a Westmoreland Wants by Brenda Jackson. Harlequin (65,800).

The Sentry by Robert Crais. Berkley.

The Return of Rafe Mackade by Nora Roberts. Silhouette (65,300).

Are You There, Vodka? It's Me, Chelsea by Chelsea Handler. Gallery (64,772).

The Greater Journey by David McCullough. Simon & Schuster (62,910).

Heat Rises by Richard Castle. Hyperion (62,862).

River Marked by Patricia Briggs. Ace.

Flash and Bones by Kathy Reichs. Scribner (62,712).

Winter Garden by Kristin Hannah. St. Martin's (61,840).

Pale Demon by Kim Harrison. Harper Voyager (61,553).

Left Neglected by Lisa Genova. Pocket (61,046).

Emperor of All Maladies: A Biography of Cancer by Siddhartha Mukherjee. Scribner (60,365).

Just Like Heaven by Julia Quinn. Avon (60,137).

50,000+

77 Shadow Street by Dean Koontz. Bantam (59,802).

Moonwalking with Einstein by Joshua Foer. Penguin.

Marrying Daisy Bellamy by Susan Wiggs. Mira (58,700).

Baby Proof by Emily Giffin. St. Martin's (58,643).

The Kingdom by Clive Cussler. Putnam.

The Heart of Devin Mackade by Nora Roberts. Silhouette (58,500).

Worst Case by James Patterson. Little, Brown (56,457).

Bel-Air Dead by Stuart Woods. Signet.

Son of Stone by Stuart Woods. Putnam.

The Perfect Christmas by Debbie Macomber. Mira (55,600).

Sixhill by Robert Parker. Putnam.

An Engagement in Seattle by Debbie Macomber. Mira (55,400).

Hotel Vendome by Danielle Steel. Delacorte (55,236).

Carte Blanche by Jeffery Deaver. Simon & Schuster (54,831).

How to Win Friends and Influence People by Dale Carnegie. Simon & Schuster (54,148).

The Social Animal by David Brooks. Random House (53,708).

Fallen by Karin Slaughter. Delacorte (53,699).

Harvest Moon by Robyn Carr. Mira (53,600).

Towers of Midnight by Robert Jordan and Brandon Sanderson. Tor (53,400).

Save Me by Lisa Scottoline. St. Martin's (53,135).

*Happy Ever After by Nora Roberts. Berkley.

Yours to Keep by Stacey Shannon. Harlequin/ Carina Press (53,000).

Thunder Dog by Michael Hingson. Thomas Nelson (52,978).

Call Me Irresistible by Susan Elizabeth Phillips. Morrow (52,646).

Private by James Patterson. Little, Brown (52,103).

In My Time: A Personal and Political Memoir by Dick Cheney. Threshold (52,056).

Don't Blink by James Patterson. Little, Brown (51,840).

Dovekeepers by Alice Hoffman. Scribner (51,682).

Still Alice by Lisa Genova. Pocket (51,592).

Sisterhood Everlasting by Ann Brashares. Random House (50,600).

*Devil's Gate by Clive Cussler. Putnam.

Assholes Finish First by Tucker Max. Gallery (50,339).

40,000+

Radical by David Platt. Crown (48,338).

The Postcard Killers by James Patterson. Little, Brown (48,333).

*The Race by Clive Cussler. Putnam.

*Hit List by Laurell Hamilton. Berkley.

Athena Project by Brad Thor. Atria (47,844).

Crooked Letter Crooked Letter by Tom Franklin. Morrow (47,484).

*The Postmistress by Sarah Blake. Berkley.

The Language of Flowers by Vanessa Diffenbaugh. Ballantine (46,579).

Those Guys Have All the Fun by James Andrew Miller. Little, Brown (46,289).

*Damage by John Lescroart. Signet.

The 4-Hour Workweek, expanded edition, by Timothy Ferriss. Crown (45,983).

Naked Heat by Richard Castle. Hyperion (45,463).

Dreams of a Dark Warrior by Kresley Cole. Pocket (45,357).

This Side of the Grave by Jeaniene Frost. Avon (45,198).

The Happiness Project by Gretchen Rubin. Harper (44,790).

Tough Customer by Sandra Brown. Simon & Schuster (44,621).

Deeper than Midnight by Lara Adrian. Dell (44,337).

The Peach Keeper by Sarah Addison Allen. Bantam (43,782).

Sister by Rosamund Lupton. Crown (43,715).

Awaken the Highland Warrior by Anita Clenney. Sourcebooks Casablanca (43,411).

*What Alice Forgot by Liane Moriarty. Putnam/Amy Einhorn.

Micro by Michael Crichton. Harper (43,031).

The Informationist by Taylor Stevens. Crown (42,764).

Robert Ludlum's The Bourne Dominion by Robert Ludlum. Grand Central (42,603).

Empire of the Summer Moon by S. C. Gwynne. Scribner (42,578).

Betrayal of Trust by J. A. Jance. Morrow (42,457).

The Island by Erin Hilderbrand. Little, Brown/ Reagan Arthur (42,295).

Dead Zero by Stephen Hunter. Simon & Schuster (42,227).

*Crescent Dawn by Clive Cussler. Berkley.

*Reckless Endangerment by Gretchen Morgensen. Times.

That Used to Be Us: How America Fell Behind in the World It Invented and How We Can Come Back by Thomas L. Friedman and Michael Mandelbaum. Farrar, Straus & Giroux (41,445).

Retribution by Sherrilyn Kenyon. St. Martin's (41,234).

All That Is Bitter and Sweet by Ashley Judd. Ballantine (41,055).

High Five by Janet Evanovich. St. Martin's (41,035).

Hard Eight by Janet Evanovich. St. Martin's (40,389).

Shadow of Your Smile by Mary Higgins Clark. Simon & Schuster (40,265).

*Saving CeeCee Honeycutt by Beth Hoffman. Penguin.

30,000+

*Miracle Cure by Harlan Coben. Signet.

Hot Six by Janet Evanovich. St. Martin's (39,047).

Fly Away Home by Jennifer Weiner. Atria (38,990).

11/22/63 (enhanced e-book) by Stephen King. Scribner (38,847).

Reno's Chance by Lora Leigh. St. Martin's (38,545).

*Lover Mine by J. R. Ward. Signet.

Seven Up by Janet Evanovich. St. Martin's (38,212).

Blood, Bones & Butter by Gabrielle Hamilton. Random House (38,117).

Unbearable Lightness: A Story of Loss and Gain by Portia De Rossi. Atria (37,910).

The Host by Stephenie Meyer. Little, Brown (37,828).

Area 51 by Annie Jacobsen. Little, Brown (37,780).

Pride and Prejudice and Zombies by Seth Grahame-Smith. Quirk (37,535).

*Indulgence of Death by J. D. Robb. Berkley.

Fatal Error by J. A. Jance. Touchstone (37,367).

Is Everyone Hanging Out Without Me? (And Other Concerns) by Mindy Kaling. Crown (37,073).

No Rest for the Dead by Sandra Brown. Touchstone (36,910).

The Scottish Prisoner by Diana Gabaldon. Delacorte (36,838).

A Family Affair by Debbie Macomber. Morrow (36,551).

A Secret Kept by Tatiana de Rosnay. St. Martin's (36,545).

Wicked Appetite by Janet Evanovich. St. Martin's (36,524).

Folly Beach by Dorothea Benton Frank. Morrow (36,086).

Distant Hours by Kate Morton. Atria (36,043).

One Grave at a Time by Jeaniene Frost. Avon (35,806).

Ten Big Ones by Janet Evanovich. St. Martin's (35,193).

Extremely Loud and Incredibly Close by Jonathan Safran Foer. Houghton Mifflin Harcourt (35,081).

When Beauty Tamed the Beast by Eloisa James. Avon (34,964).

Rescue by Anita Shreve. Little, Brown (34,882).

*Victory and Honor by W. E. B. Griffin. Putnam.

Then Again by Diane Keaton. Random House (34,814).

Reamde by Neal Stephenson. Morrow (34,797).

*Envy by J. R. Ward. Signet.

Moonlight Mile by Dennis Lehane. Morrow (34,511).

Prey by Linda Howard. Ballantine (34,500).

*Storm Prey by John Sandford. Berkley.

*The Outlaws by W. E. B. Griffin. Jove.

Imperfect Justice by Jeff Ashton. Morrow (34,363).

Eat to Live, revised edition, by Joel Fuhrman. Little, Brown (34,294).

*The Secret Soldier by Alex Berenson. Putnam.

*Dark Predator by Christine Feehan. Berkley.

The Saturday Big Tent Wedding Party by Alexander McCall Smith. Pantheon (34,087).

Demonic by Ann Coulter. Crown (33,950).

In Bed with a Highlander by Maya Banks. Ballantine (33,911).

Eleven on Top by Janet Evanovich. St. Martin's (33,751).

Foreign Influence by Brad Thor. Atria (33,716).

True Colors by Kristin Hannah. St. Martin's (33,168).

The Soldier by Grace Burrowes. Sourcebooks Casablanca (33,099).

*The Psychopath Test by Jon Ronson. Riverhead.

A Heartbeat Away by Michael Palmer. St. Martin's (32,337).

A Place of Yes: 10 Rules for Getting Everything You Want Out of Life by Bethenny Frankel. Touchstone (32,004).

*Caught by Harlan Coben. Signet.

*Savor the Moment by Nora Roberts. Berkley.

*Time of Death by J. D. Robb. Berkley.

Trader of Secrets by Steve Martini. Morrow (31,293).

Once a Princess by Johanna Lindsey. Avon (31,143).

*Savage Nature by Christine Feehan. Jove.

*D. C. Dead by Stuart Woods. Putnam.

*The Judas Gate by Jack Higgins. Berkley.

Faith by Jennifer Haigh. Harper (31,054).

The Hypnotist by Lars Kepler. Farrar, Straus & Giroux/Sarah Crichton (30,835).

The Zombie Survival Guide by Max Brooks. Crown (30,829).

Only Time Will Tell by Jeffrey Archer. St. Martin's (30,750).

Eight Days to Live by Iris Johansen. St. Martin's (30,749).

Feast Day of Fools by James Lee Burke. Simon & Schuster (30,720).

The Red Queen by Philippa Gregory. Touchstone (30,555).

Jacqueline Kennedy—The Enhanced Edition: Historic Conversations on Life with John F. Kennedy by Caroline Kennedy and Michael Beschloss. Hyperion (30,451) (the plain edition sold 23,859).

Captured by the Highlander by Julianne Maclean. St. Martin's (30,319).

*The Magician King by Lev Grossman. Viking.

Halfway to the Grave by Jeaniene Frost. Avon (30,022).

25,000+

Live Wire by Lora Leigh. St. Martin's (29,907).

Crunch Time by Diane Mott Davidson. Morrow (29,858).

Eleven Scandals to Start a Duke's Heart by Sarah MacLean. Avon (29,619).

Ready Player One by Ernest Cline. Crown (29,468).

The Corrections by Jonathan Franzen. Farrar, Straus & Giroux (29,463).

From This Moment On by Shania Twain. Atria (29,461).

Nightwoods by Charles Frazier. Random House (29,241).

Never Love a Highlander by Maya Banks. Ballantine (29,148).

The King of Lies by John Hart. St. Martin's Minotaur (29,102).

Seduction of a Highlander by Maya Banks. Ballantine (29,048).

*Robert B. Parker's Killing the Blues by Michael Brandman. Putnam.

2030 by Albert Brooks. St. Martin's (28,963).

Viscount Breckenridge to the Rescue by Stephanie Laurens. Avon (28,707).

*Tinker, Tailor, Soldier, Spy by John le Carré. Penguin.

Goddess of Vengeance by Jackie Collins. St. Martin's (28,424).

Still Missing by Chevy Stevens. St. Martin's (28,399).

*Magic Slays by Ilona Andrews. Ace.

Trick of the Light by Louise Penny. Minotaur (28,283).

Vampire Mine by Kerrelyn Sparks. Avon (28,029).

Spider Bones by Kathy Reichs. Scribner (27,831).

*Quicksilver by Amanda Quick. Putnam.

*In Too Deep by Jayne Ann Krentz. Putnam.

Enigma by Lora Leigh. St. Martin's (27,519).

*Faithful Place by Tana French. Penguin.

The Final Storm by Jeff Shaara. Ballantine (27,277).

The Red Garden by Alice Hoffman. Crown (26,657).

Thinking, Fast and Slow by Daniel Kahneman. Farrar, Straus & Giroux (26,598).

Breaking the Rules by Suzanne Brockman. Ballantine (26,552).

The God Delusion by Richard Dawkins. Houghton Mifflin Harcourt (26,483).

Angel Fire by Lisa Unger. Crown (26,442).

In Pursuit of Eliza Cynster by Stephanie Laurens. Avon (26,418).

*The Secret by Julie Garwood. Dutton.

*The Rembrandt Affair by Daniel Silva. Signet.

Switch by Chip Heath and Dan Heath. Crown (26,280).

Those Who Save Us by Jenna Blum. Houghton Mifflin Harcourt (26,201).

*Bad Blood by John Sandford. Putnam.

*Spirit Bound by Christine Feehan. Jove.

The Confidence Man by Ron Suskind. Harper (25,962).

*The Bride by Julie Garwood. Dutton.

Prey by Michael Crichton. Harper (25,845).

*Whiplash by Catherine Coulter. Jove.

New Atkins for a New You by Dr. Eric C. Westman. Touchstone (25,725).

Island of Lost Girls by Jennifer McMahon. Harper (25,682).

*Navarro's Promise by Lora Leigh. Berkley.

How to Woo a Reluctant Lady by Sabrina Jeffries. Pocket (25,303).

*Getting Things Done by David Allen. Penguin.

The Reluctant Vampire by Lynsay Sands. Avon (25,280).

The Scent of Jasmine by Jude Deveraux. Pocket (25,219).

Hardcover: Lower Unit Sales, Fewer Titles

Daisy Maryles

For both fiction and nonfiction hardcover titles, name-brand recognition is the key to bestseller success. While that is not new, the 2011 annual chart had fewer than usual new players. In fiction, there were two novelists debuting in the top 30. George R. R. Martin's A Song of Ice and Fire series, with five titles, was perhaps the most successful franchise last year.

Martin's *A Dance with Dragons* is No. 5, with sales of about 750,000. Random House reports that last year his books sold about 8.4 million copies across all formats, including print, digital, and audio. The other newcomer to the top 30 is Paula McLain (*The Paris Wife*); she also had the second-longest-running fiction bestseller last year, with 23 appearances on *Publishers Weekly*'s weekly top 15 list. Four other novelists made a first appearance on this end-of-year chart. All were first fiction; they are *The Night Circus, Dollhouse, The Art of Fielding,* and *The Tiger's Wife.*

All other authors are veteran chart occupiers, and many regularly have multiple titles in the top slots. James Patterson had seven top-sellers, with combined sales of about 2.4 million, making him the leader in the competitive hardcover fiction race. Janet Evanovich had two winners in the top 10, *Smokin' Seventeen* and *Explosive Eighteen*; their combined sales of more than 1.4 million makes her the female winner for hardcover fiction. Nora Roberts, Danielle Steel, and Clive Cussler each had three books topping 100,000 and more. Check the lists for many more authors with two books on the chart.

In nonfiction, the operative words are celebrity and renown, with books by or about familiar faces in the news, including politicians, talk show hosts, thespians—and the revolutionary tech guru who died in fall 2011. Walter Isaacson's bio of Steve Jobs, with sales of more than 2,246,000 copies, was the most popular hardcover by a margin of more than 2:1. The other familiar faces in hardcover nonfiction included Tina Fey, Ellen DeGeneres, Diane Keaton, Jane Fonda, Mindy Kaling, Lady Gaga, Gwyneth Paltrow, Rob Lowe, the Kardashians, and the irrepressible Betty White, not to mention Katie Couric, Bill Maher, Bill O'Reilly, Glenn Beck, and Suze Orman. Religion leaders such as Joel Osteen, Billy Graham, and Joyce Meyer land their books in the top 30. There were two books about Navy SEALs (one just missed the top 30) and four featuring a Kennedy. Politicos such as Dick Cheney, Condoleezza Rice, Bill Clinton, and Herman Cain were bestseller winners.

A popular category on these year-end charts is cookbooks and also some advice for healthier lifestyles. Three on the latter subject, *The 17 Day Diet, The Dukan Diet,* and *The 4-Hour Body,* are in the top 30. *Paula Deen's Southern Cooking Bible* was the most popular food book, with sales of more than 372,000. *Guy Fieri Food,* Pat Neely's *Celebration Cookbook,* and Buddy Valastro's *Baking with the Cake Boss* were also tasty bestsellers. And Gwyneth Paltrow's *My Father's Daughter* featured recipes for family togetherness.

One nonfiction book was the benefactor of a new happening—going viral. Akashic Books, a first-timer on our annual charts, has a book at No. 7, *Go the F**k to Sleep* by Adam Mansbach. When word on the book hit the Internet, Akashic had to get the book out faster than planned and it became the gift book of 2011.

One unfortunate trend that continues is that fewer books make these end-of-year charts. In 2011, 113 fiction titles and 83 nonfiction books achieved the 100,000+ level. In 2010, the fiction number was 126; in 2009, 130 and in 2008, 156. The nonfiction drop was a bit steeper. In 2010 there were 108 titles, more than the 91 in 2009 but fewer than the 132 in 2008. Bestseller pundits would bet on even lower figures for this year. They might also guess that the e-book explosion could be the culprit.

The Usual Disclaimer

As in previous years, all the calculations on the following pages are based on shipped-and-billed figures supplied by publishers for new books with sales of 100,000+; all reflect only 2011 domestic retail sales for print books. We asked publishers to take into account returns through mid-February; it would be safe to assume that not all did. Sales figures on all these pages should not be considered final. For many books, especially those published in the final third of the year, returns were still being calculated. Perhaps the beauty of the e-book figures is that they are direct to consumer and not returnable. Please note that e-books priced at less than $5 were deemed ineligible.

Fiction Top 15

1. *The Litigators* by John Grisham. Doubleday (10/25). 1,100,000.
2. *11/23/1963* by Stephen King. Scribner (11/08). 919,524.
3. *The Best of Me* by Nicholas Sparks. Grand Central (10/11). 850,653.
4. *Smokin' Seventeen* by Janet Evanovich. Bantam (6/21). 751, 899.
5. *A Dance with Dragons* by George R. R. Martin. Bantam (7/12). 750,000.
6. *Explosive Eighteen* by Janet Evanovich. Bantam (11/22). 744,029.
7. *Kill Alex Cross* by James Patterson. Little, Brown (11/11). 619,406.
8. *Micro* by Michael Crichton. Harper (11/22). 537,835.
9. **Dead Reckoning* by Charlaine Harris. Ace (5/3). 500,000.
10. **Locked On* by Tom Clancy with Mark Greaney. Putnam (12/8). 450,000.
11. *The Land of Painted Caves* by Jean M. Auel. Crown (3/29). 447,626.
12. *The Girl Who Kicked the Hornet's Nest* by Stieg Larsson. Knopf (5/25). 422,000.
13. **V Is for Vengeance* by Sue Grafton. Putnam/Marian Woods Books (11/14).
14. **Red Mist* by Patricia Cornwell. Putnam (12/6).
15. *10th Anniversary* by James Patterson and Maxine Paetro. Little, Brown (5/11). 419,105.

Nonfiction Top 15

1. *Steve Jobs* by Walter Isaacson. Simon & Schuster (10/11). 2,246,569.
2. *Unbroken: A World War II Story of Survival, Resilience, and Redemption* by Laura Hillenbrand. Random House (11/10), 1,100,000.
3. *Killing Lincoln: The Shocking Assassination that Changed America Forever* by Bill O'Reilly and Martin Dugard. Henry Holt (9/11). 997,731.
4. *The 17 Day Diet: A Doctor's Plan Designed for Rapid Results* by Dr. Mike Moreno. Free Press (3/11). 833,847.
5. *Stolen Life: A Memoir* by Jaycee Dugard. Simon & Schuster (7/11). 782,452.
6. *Bossypants* by Tina Fey. Little, Brown/Reagan Arthur (4/11). 671,106.
7. *Go the F**k to Sleep* by Adam Mansbach, illustrated by Ricardo Cortes. Akashic Books (6/11). 550,000.
8. *Every Day a Friday: How to Be Happier 7 Days a Week* by Joel Osteen. FaithWords (9/11), 513,681.
9. *Gabby: A Story of Courage and Hope* by Gabrielle Gifford, Mark Kelly, and Jeffrey Zaslow. Scribner (11/11). 479,618.
10. *In the Garden of Beasts: Love, Terror, and an American Family in Hitler's Berlin* by Erik Larson. Crown (5/11). 476,121.
11. *Through My Eyes* by Tim Tebow and Nathan Whitaker. Harper (5/11). 448,190.
12. *The Money Class: Learn to Create Your New American Dream* by Suze Orman. Spiegel & Grau (3/11). 419,893.
13. *Being George Washington: The Indispensable Man as You've Never Seen Him* by Glenn Beck. Threshold (11/11). 384,265.
14. *Paula Deen's Southern Cooking Bible* by Paula Deen. Simon & Schuster (10/11). 372,676.
15. *Nearing Home—Life, Faith, and Finishing Well* by Billy Graham. Thomas Nelson (10/11). 358,300.

Hardcover Fiction Runners-Up

16. *Tick Tock* by James Patterson and Michael Ledwidge. Little, Brown (417,115).
17. *Snow Angel* by Glenn Beck. Threshold (408,832).
18. *Now You See Her* by James Patterson and Michael Ledwidge. Little, Brown (399,210).
19. *The Affair* by Lee Child. Delacorte (386,385).
20. *The Christmas Wedding* by James Patterson and Richard DiLallo. Little, Brown (385,200).
21. *Zero Day* by David Baldacci. Grand Central (376,501).
22. *Happy Birthday* by Danielle Steel. Delacorte (344,352).
23. *44 Charles Street* by Danielle Steel. Delacorte (344,110).
24. *Hotel Vendome* by Danielle Steel. Delacorte (318,783).

25. *Sing You Home* by Jodi Picoult. Atria (344,264).
26. *The Drop* by Michael Connelly. Little, Brown (311,135).
27. *The Paris Wife* by Paula McClain. Ballantine (301,883).
28. *Kill Me if You Can* by James Patterson and Marshall Karp. Little, Brown (297,089).
29. **Against All Enemies* by Tom Clancy with Peter Telep. Putnam.
30. *The Sixth Man* by David Baldacci. Grand Central (286,378).

200,000+

Toys by James Patterson and Neil McMahon. Little, Brown (280,776).

77 Shadow Street by Dean Koontz. Random House (275,000).

The Fifth Witness by Michael Connelly. Little, Brown (234,679).

I'll Walk Alone by Mary Higgins Clark. Simon & Schuster (232,363).

*Chasing Fire by Nora Roberts. Putnam.

The Night Circus by Erin Morgenstern. Doubleday (218,000).

Lost December by Richard Paul Evans. Simon & Schuster (215,823).

State of Wonder by Ann Patchett. Harper (214,664).

*Devil's Gate by Clive Cussler and Graham Brown. Putnam.

Lethal by Sandra Brown. Grand Central (207,787).

Night Road by Kristin Hannah. St. Martin's (207,592).

One Summer by David Baldacci. Grand Central (205,226).

Death Comes to Pemberley by P. D. James. Knopf (200,000).

175,000+

1Q84 by Haruki Murakami. Knopf (197,000).

*Buried Prey by John Sandford. Putnam.

*New York to Dallas by J. D. Robb. Putnam.

Ghost Story by Jim Butcher. Roc (190,420).

*The Jungle by Clive Cussler with Jack Du Brul. Putnam.

*A Discovery of Witches by Deborah Harkness. Viking.

*Treachery in Death by J. D. Robb. Putnam.

Sisterhood Everlasting by Ann Brashares. Random House (182,238).

150,000+

*Lover Un-leashed by J. R. Ward. NAL.

1225 Christmas Tree Lane by Debbie Macomber. Mira (173,987).

The Marriage Plot by Jeffrey Eugenides. Farrar, Straus & Giroux (171,718).

*Shock Wave by John Sandford. Putnam.

Dreams of Joy by Lisa See. Random House (162,621).

Then Came You by Jennifer Weiner. Atria (161,575).

Portrait of a Spy by Daniel Silva. Harper (160,174).

Minding Frankie by Maeve Binchy. Knopf (158,000).

Twilight: The Graphic Novel, Vol. 2 by Stephenie Meyer and Young Kim. Hachette/Yen (155,202).

*Live Wire by Harlan Coben. Dutton.

Mystery by Jonathan Kellerman. Ballantine (150,183).

125,000+

*Split Second by Catherine Coulter. Putnam.

Love You More by Lisa Gardner. Bantam (148,180).

*The Race by Clive Cussler and Justin Scott. Putnam.

Eve by Iris Johansen. St. Martin's (144,472).

The Wise Man's Fear by Patrick Rothfuss. DAW (144,122).

The Jefferson Key by Steve Berry. Bantam (143,939).

The Devil Colony by James Rollins. Morrow (143,072).

*The Kingdom by Clive Cussler with Grant Blackwood. Putnam.

The Silent Girl by. Tess Gerritsen. Ballantine (142,717).

Save Me by Lisa Scottoline. St. Martin's (142,477).

Shadow Fever by Karen Marie Moning. Delacorte (141,101).

Out of Oz by Gregory Maguire. Morrow (140,149).

Nightwoods by Charles Frazier. Random House (139,496).

Retribution by Sherrilyn Kenyon. St. Martin's (137,542).

Full Black by Brad Thor. Atria (136,547).

Hit List by Laurell K. Hamilton. Berkley.

Goddess of Vengeance by Jackie Collins. St. Martin's (133,309).

Quinn by Iris Johansen. St. Martin's (130,093).

Blake by Iris Johansen. St. Martin's (129,123).

The Scottish Prisoner by Diana Gabaldon. Delacorte (128,553).

The Inner Circle by Brad Meltzer. Grand Central (127,810).

100,000+

Folly Beach by Dorothea Benton Frank. Morrow (124,813).

Dollhouse by Kourtney Kardashian, Kim Kardashian, and Khloe Kardashian. Morrow (124,523).

Down the Darkest Road by Tami Hoag. Dutton.

The Art of Fielding by Chad Harbach. Little, Brown (117,954).

The Tiger's Wife by Téa Obreht. Random House (116,777).

Pale Demon by Kim Harrison. Morrow (115,252).

D.C. Dead by Stuart Woods. Putnam.

Dark Predator by Christine Feehan. Berkley.

Son of Stone by Stuart Woods. Putnam.

Dovekeepers by Alice Hoffman. Scribner (110,046).

Saturday Big Tent Wedding Party by Alexander McCall Smith. Pantheon (110,000).

Cold Vengeance by Douglas Preston and Lincoln Child. Grand Central (109,549).

Only Time Will Tell by Jeffrey Archer. St. Martin's (109,362).

A Turn in the Road by Debbie Macomber. Mira (109,342).

The Omen Machine by Terry Goodkind. Tor (108,809).

Maine by J. Courtney Sullivan. Knopf (107,000).

The Snowman by Jo Nesbø. Knopf (107,000).

Covert Warriors by W. E. B. Griffin and William E. Butterworth IV. Putnam.

Summer Rental by Mary Kay Andrews. St. Martin's (106,385).

Abuse of Power by Michael Savage. St. Martin's (106,133).

Flash and Bones by Kathy Reichs. Scribner (105,981).

The Sense of an Ending by Julian Barnes. Knopf (104,000).

Lady of the Rivers by Philippa Gregory. Touchstone (103,742).

Carte Blanche by Jeffery Deaver. Simon & Schuster (102,399).

Caleb's Crossing by Geraldine Brooks. Viking.

The Christmas Note by Donna Van Liere. St. Martin's (102,014).

Iron House by John Hart. St. Martin's (101,516).

Heat Rises by Richard Castle. Hyperion (101,260).

Reamde by Neal Stephenson. Morrow (100,047).

Hardcover Nonfiction Runners-Up

16. *The Dukan Diet: 2 Steps to Lose the Weight, 2 Steps to Keep It Off Forever* by Dr. Pierre Dukan. Crown Archetype (345,762).

17. *One Thousand Gifts: A Dare to Live Fully Right Where You Are* by Ann Voskamp. Zondervan (11/11) 345,000.

18. *Seriously . . . I'm Kidding* by Ellen DeGeneres. Grand Central (335,563).

19. *In My Time: A Personal and Political Memoir* by Dick Cheney. Threshold (334,670).

20. *Lies That Chelsea Handler Told Me* by Chelsea Handler, et al. Grand Central (313,032).
21. *The Greater Journey* by David McCullough. Simon & Schuster (306,108).
22. **Boomerang: Travels in the New Third World* by Michael Lewis. Norton.
23. *Jacqueline Kennedy: Historic Conversations on Life with John F. Kennedy* by Caroline Kennedy and Michael Beschloss. Hyperion (302,321).
24. *SEAL Six: Memoirs of an Elite Navy Seal* by Howard E. Wasdin and Stephen Templin. St. Martin's (287,676).
25. *Living Beyond Your Feelings: Controlling Emotions so They Don't Control You* by Joyce Meyer. FaithWords (269,677).
26. *Back to Work* by Bill Clinton. Knopf (254,000).
27. *The Time of Our Lives* by Tom Brokaw. Random House (236,607).
28. *Guy Fieri Food* by Guy Fieri. Morrow (232,154).
29. *The 4-Hour Body: An Uncommon Guide to Rapid Fat-Loss, Incredible Sex, and Becoming Superhuman* by Timothy Ferriss. Crown Archetype (229,421).
30. *Jack Kennedy* by Chris Matthews. Simon & Schuster (226,635).

150,000+

Pioneer Woman Cooks by Ree Drummond. Morrow (216,230).

Love Wins: A Book About Heaven, Hell, and the Fate of Every Person Who Ever Lived by Rob Bell. HarperOne (213,469).

SEAL Target Geronimo: The Inside Story of the Mission to Kill Osama bin Laden by Chuck Pfarrer. St. Martin's (210,319).

From This Moment On by Shania Twain. Atria (209,540).

Then Again by Diane Keaton. Random House (203,090).

Catherine the Great by Robert K. Massie. Random House (199,177).

Great by Choice: Uncertainty, Chaos, and Luck—Why Some Thrive Despite Them All by Jim Collins. Harper Business (187,076).

The Social Animal by David Brooks. Random House (181,263).

Imperfect Justice: Prosecuting Casey Anthony by Jeff Ashton. Morrow (177,815).

That Used to Be Us: How America Fell Behind in the World It Invented and How We Can Come Back by Thomas L. Friedman and Michael Mandelbaum. Farrar, Straus & Giroux (173,221).

Thinking Fast and Slow by Daniel Kahneman. Farrar, Straus & Giroux (172,253).

No Higher Honor: A Memoir of My Years in Washington by Condoleezza Rice. Crown (171,382).

Pioneer Woman by Ree Drummond. Morrow (153,696).

Prime Time by Jane Fonda. Random House (150,588).

*Stories I Only Tell My Friends: An Autobiography by Rob Lowe. Henry Holt (150,000).

125,000+

Is Everyone Hanging Out Without Me? (And Other Concerns) by Mindy Kaling. Crown Archetype (149,536).

Lady Gaga X Terry Richardson by Lady Gaga and Terry Richardson. Grand Central (148,674).

I'd Never Thought I'd See the Day: Culture at the Crossroads by David Jeremiah. FaithWords (148,483).

The Confident Woman Devotional by Joyce Meyer. Faith Words (144,005).

*If You Ask Me (And of Course You Won't) by Betty White. Putnam.

Demonic: How the Liberal Mob Is Endangering America by Ann Coulter. Crown Forum (142,444).

Heaven Is for Real deluxe edition by Todd Burpo. Thomas Nelson (140,409).

Blue Nights by Joan Didion. Knopf (139,000).

20 Years Younger: Look Younger, Feel Younger, Be Younger! by Bob Greene et al. Little, Brown (137,068).

Throw Them All Out by Peter Schweizer. Houghton Mifflin Harcourt (134,907).

William and Catherine by Andrew Morton. St. Martin's (132,326).

Neelys' Celebration Cookbook by Pat Neely. Knopf (132,000).

The Best Advice I Ever Got: Lessons from Extraordinary Lives by Katie Couric. Random House (129,344).

My Father's Daughter: Delicious, Easy Recipes Celebrating Family and Togetherness by Gwyneth Paltrow. Grand Central (127,888).

Moonwalking with Einstein by Joshua Foer. Penguin.

100,000+

The Investment Answer: Learn to Manage Your Money and Protect Your Financial Future by Gordon Murray and Daniel C. Goldie. Grand Central (124,235).

The Christian Atheist: Believing in God but Living As If He Doesn't Exist by Craig Groeschel. Zondervan (120,000).

Battle Hymn of the Tiger Mother by Amy Chua. Penguin.

Rin Tin Tin by Susan Orlean. Simon & Schuster (117,723).

Baking with the Cake Boss by Buddy Valastro. Free Press (117,273).

Switch by Chip Heath and Dan Heath. Crown Business (116,769).

The New New Rules: A Funny Look at How Everybody But Me Has Their Head Up Their Asses by Bill Maher. Blue Rider Press (115,590).

This Is Herman Cain! My Journey to the White House by Herman Cain. Threshold (111,437).

The 4-Hour Workweek, Expanded Edition by Timothy Ferriss. Crown Archetype (110,473).

Spontaneous Happiness by Andrew Weil, M.D. Little, Brown (109,759).

1493 by Charles C. Mann. Knopf (109,000).

A Place of Yes: 10 Rules for Getting Everything You Want Out of Life by Bethenny Frankel. Touchstone (108,206).

The Swerve by Stephen Greenblatt. Norton.

The Hidden Reality by Brian Greene. Knopf (106,000).

The Black Banners: The Inside Story of 9/11 by Ali H. Soufan. Norton.

She Walks in Beauty: A Woman's Journey Through Poems by Caroline Kennedy. Voice (105,339).

Cook Like a Rock Star by Anne Burrell. Clarkson Potter (102,765).

Those Guys Have All the Fun: Inside the World of ESPN by James Andrew Miller and Tom Shales. Little, Brown (101,968).

A History of the World in 100 Objects by Neil MacGregor. Viking.

I Beat the Odds: From Homelessness, to the Blind Side, and Beyond by Michael Oher. Avery (101,571).

This Is Gonna Hurt by Nikki Sixx. Morrow (101,253).

Unlimited: How to Build an Exceptional Life by Jillian Michaels. Crown Archetype (101,032).

Kardashian Konfidential by Kim Kardashian, Khloe Kardashian, and Kourtney Kardashian. St. Martin's (100,632).

Paperbacks: Less Is Just Less

Daisy Maryles

Back in *Publishers Weekly*'s bestsellers report of 2002, there were an astounding number of mass market bestsellers with sales over the million-copy mark. A total of eight books boasted sales of 2 million and more; an additional 39 claimed more than 1 million. That's a dramatic contrast to the total of 6 million+ players noted in our 2012 report. Two current million-copy authors, John Grisham and Nora Roberts, were among the 2 million+ group in 2002, and Roberts had three on that list. The newcomer to the 2011 million-copy club is George R. R. Martin, with four books totaling more than 5.5 million copies.

There were 48 mass market bestsellers with units of more than 500,000+ on this year's list—the lowest figure we've recorded. In 2010, the previous low record, 58 bestsellers reached 500,000+. And in the 2002 report, for which we collected sales only on 750,000+, there were 72 mass markets that hit that number.

What did not change among the 2011 top sellers were the authors. They include the usual winners who have multiple hits—James Patterson with five, and Janet Evanovich, Danielle Steel, Dean Koontz, Debbie Macomber, and Iris Johansen, with three each. For most of these authors, unit sales dropped from previous years. In 2010 Evanovich went over the 1 million mark with *Finger Lickin' Fifteen* and Koontz's highest was 948,000 for *Restless*; Patterson got to about 927,000 with *Cross Fire,* and Macomber reached more than 900,000 with *One Night.* The two perennial high rollers that did go higher from 2010 to 2011 were Grisham and Roberts.

Fewer Trade Titles

For trade paperbacks, we again asked publishers to report on titles that sold 100,000 or more during the 2011 calendar year. The figure for last year was 106, a record low. In 2010 we had 134 books reporting sales of 100,000+, and the record high was in 2005 with 226. Also waning were unit sales. In 2011 there were eight books with sales of 500,000+ compared with 12 in 2010 and 22 in 2009. Two of the high rollers, *The Help* and *Water for Elephants,* appeared twice—the second time for their movie tie-in editions. Both racked up very impressive sales when combining the two editions. *The Help* went over the 5 million mark (all the Academy Award Oscar buzz certainly helped), and *Water* rose to about 1,263,000. Topping the charts for the first time is publisher Thomas Nelson, for *Heaven Is for Real,* the story of a young child whose trip to heaven during surgery made a book that sold more than 4.6 million in paper.

Eclectic is always the best adjective for trade paper, where commercial and literary fiction reign and how-to and serious nonfiction hold court. There was also a stronger-than-usual showing of titles by religion publishers—while Nelson topped the list, Zondervan had eight 100,000-copy top-sellers. Since Harper now owns both publishers, it will be interesting to see what happens next year. And that goes for all publishers.

(Note: All the figures that follow on the two paperback lists were provided by publishers. An asterisk denotes a title for which sales figures were provided in confidence, to be used for ranking purposes only. In a few cases, we rounded down numbers to indicate their relationship to figures for other titles.)

Mass Market Fiction

1,000,000+

A Feast for Crows by George R. R. Martin. Bantam (1,632,878).

The Confession by John Grisham. Dell (1,576,834).

A Game of Thrones by George R. R. Martin. Bantam (1,539,783).

A Clash of Kings by George R. R. Martin. Bantam (1,204,723).

A Storm of Swords by George R. R. Martin. Bantam (1,136,075).

The Search by Nora Roberts. Jove (1,039,005).

700,000+

Sizzling Sixteen by Janet Evanovich. St. Martin's (900,000).

Worth Dying For by Lee Child. Dell (862,852).

Big Girl by Danielle Steel. Dell (848,608).

Smokin' Seventeen by Janet Evanovich. Bantam (833,763).

What the Night Knows by Dean Koontz. Bantam (775,584).

The Girl with the Dragon Tattoo (movie tie-in) by Stieg Larsson. Vintage (752,000).

Family Ties by Danielle Steel. Dell (750,053).

Wicked Appetite by Janet Evanovich. St. Martin's (750,000).

Legacy by Danielle Steel. Dell (749,623).

Frankenstein: The Dead Town by Dean Koontz. Bantam (739,456).

Deception by Jonathan Kellerman. Ballantine (734,607).

*Caught by Harlan Coben. Signet.

Toys by James Patterson and Neil McMahon. Vision (708,618).

Frankenstein: Lost Souls by Dean Koontz. Bantam (703,694).

Cross Fire by James Patterson. Vision (703,594).

550,000+

*Port Mortuary by Patricia Cornwell. Berkley.

*Whiplash by Catherine Coulter. Jove.

Chasing the Night by Iris Johansen. St. Martin's (650,000).

*Storm Prey by John Sandford. Berkley.

Water for Elephants (movie tie-in) by Sara Gruen. Algonquin (610,515).

Deliver Us from Evil by David Baldacci. Vision (578,240).

Something Borrowed (movie tie-in) by Emily Giffin. St. Martin's Griffin (575,000).

*The Silent Sea by Clive Cussler. Berkley.

Worst Case by James Patterson and Michael Ledwidge. Vision (561,674).

Touched by Angels by Debbie Macomber. Avon (556,719).

Sizzle by Julie Garwood. Ballantine (554,058).

A Season for Angels by Debbie Macomber. Avon (553,906).

Quinn by Iris Johansen. St. Martin's (550,000).

Eve by Iris Johansen. St. Martin's (550,000).

500,000+

The Shadow of Your Smile by Mary Higgins Clark. Pocket (544,747).

Broken by Karin Slaughter. Dell (537,546).

Just Like Heaven by Julia Quinn. Avon (535,299).

1105 Yakima Street by Debbie Macomber. Mira (528,717).

Swimsuit by James Patterson and Maxine Paetro. Grand Central (520,007).

In Pursuit of Eliza Cynster by Stephanie Laurens. Avon (519,525).

*Miracle Cure by Harlan Coben. Signet.

The Jefferson Key by Steve Berry. Ballantine (515,924).

*Bad Blood by John Sandford, Berkley.

Private by James Patterson and Maxine Paetro. Grand Central (507,105).

The Girl Who Played with Fire by Stieg Larsson. Vintage (502,200).

*Indulgence in Death by J. D. Robb. Berkley.

*Secrets to the Grave by Tami Hoag. Signet.

Trade Paperbacks

4,000,000+

Heaven Is for Real by Todd Burpo. Thomas Nelson (4,679,793).

2,000,000+

*The Help by Kathryn Stockett. Berkley.
*The Help (movie tie-in) by Kathryn Stockett. Berkley.

1,000,000+

The Girl with Dragon Tattoo (movie tie-in) by Stieg Larsson. Vintage (1,100,000).

550,000+

Water for Elephants by Sara Gruen. Algonquin (723,249).
*The Next Always by Nora Roberts. Berkley.
Sarah's Key by Tatiana de Rosnay. St. Martin's Griffin (600,000).
Water for Elephants (movie tie-in). Sara Gruen. Algonquin (540,000).
Cutting for Stone by Abraham Verghese. Vintage (496,000).
One Day by David Nicholls. Vintage (496,000).
Safe Haven by Nicholas Sparks. Grand Central (438,133).
Inside of a Dog: What Dogs See, Smell, and Know by Alexandra Horowitz. Scribner (421,123).
Room by Emma Donoghue. Little, Brown/Back Bay (411,742).
Heart of the Matter by Emily Giffin. St. Martin's Griffin (400,000).

300,000+

Outliers: The Story of Success by Malcolm Gladwell. Little, Brown/Back Bay (391,884).
The Art of Racing in the Rain by Garth Stein. Harper Perennial (370,686).
The Happiness Project by Gretchen Rubin. Harper Perennial (367,686).
The Girl Who Played with Fire by Stieg Larsson. Vintage (366,000).

A Visit from the Goon Squad by Jennifer Egan. Anchor (329,000).
Hungry Girl: 300 Under 300 by Lisa Lillien. St. Martin's Griffin (325,000).
A Game of Thrones by George R. R. Martin. Bantam (322,029).
Unlikely Friendships: 47 Remarkable Stories from the Animal Kingdom by Jennifer S. Holland. Workman (314,778).
The Glass Castle: A Memoir by Jeannette Walls. Scribner (314,121).
*The Postmistress by Sarah Blake. Berkley.
Born to Run by Christopher McDougall. Vintage (307,000).

250,000+

The Alchemist by Paulo Coelho. HarperOne (295,405).
*Dead or Alive by Tom Clancy. Berkley.
The Imperfectionists by Tom Rachman. Dial (278,965).
The 9th Judgment by James Patterson. Grand Central (278,735).
The Tiger's Wife by Téa Obreht. Random House (271,866).
Longing by Karen Kingsbury. Zondervan (260,000).
Empire of the Summer Moon by S. C. Gwynne. Scribner (257,079).
Something Borrowed (movie tie-in) by Emily Giffin. St. Martin's Griffin (255,500).
Night Road by Kristin Hannah. St. Martin's Griffin (255,000).
Little Bee by Chris Cleave. Simon & Schuster (254,197)
*Fall of Giants by Ken Follett. NAL.
Made to Crave: Satisfying Your Deepest Desire with God, Not Food by Lysa TerKeurst. Zondervan (250,000).

225,000+

*The Big Short: Inside the Doomsday Machine by Michael Lewis. Norton.
Original Argument: The Federalist Case for the Constitution, Adapted for the 21st Century by Glenn Beck. Threshold (249,618).
*Moneyball (movie tie-in) by Michael Lewis. Norton.

Leaving by Karen Kingsbury. Zondervan (245,000).

A Dog's Purpose by W. Bruce Cameron. Forge (243,433).

Not a Fan: Becoming a Completely Committed Follower of Jesus by Kyle Idleman. Zondervan (240,000).

The Island by Elin Hilderbrand. Little, Brown/ Back Bay (237,086).

Private by James Patterson and Maxine Paetro. Grand Central (233,820).

The Postcard Killers by James Patterson and Liza Marklund. Grand Central (232,867).

The Passage by Justin Cronin. Ballantine (231,505).

Unlocked: A Love Story by Karen Kingsbury. Zondervan (230,000).

200,000+

Take Three by Karen Kingsbury. Zondervan (220,000).

Take Four by Karen Kingsbury. Zondervan (220,000).

Think Twice by Lisa Scottoline. St. Martin's Griffin (220,000).

Tick Tock by James Patterson and Michael Ledwidge. Grand Central (219,497).

Life by Keith Richards with James Fox. Little, Brown/Back Bay (218,620).

Secret Daughter by Shilpi Somaya Gowda. Morrow (214,241).

The Sixth Man by David Baldacci. Grand Central (208,382).

The Devil in the White City by Erik Larson, Vintage (207,000).

One for the Money (movie tie-in) by Janet Evanovich. St. Martin's Griffin (200,000).

Secret Kept by Tatiana de Rosnay. St. Martin's Griffin (200,000).

Sarah's Key (movie tie-in) by Tatiana de Rosnay. St. Martin's Griffin (200,000).

Learning by Karen Kingsbury. Zondervan (200,000).

170,000+

Now Eat This! Diet: Lose Up to 10 Pounds in Just 2 Weeks Eating 6 Meals a Day! by Rocco DiSpirito. Grand Central (195,253).

Mini Shopaholic by Sophie Kinsella. Random House (192,201).

Don't Blink by James Patterson and Howard Roughan. Grand Central (190,586).

Are You There, Vodka? It's Me, Chelsea by Chelsea Handler. Gallery (185,483).

Extremely Loud and Incredibly Close (movie tie-in) by Jonathan Safran Foer. Houghton Mifflin Harcourt (181,337).

Soul Surfer by Bethany Hamilton. Gallery (181,167).

The Other Wes Moore: One Name, Two Fates by Wes Moore. Random/Spiegel & Grau (177,571).

Major Pettigrew's Last Stand by Helen Simonson. Random House (176,701).

Something Borrowed by Emily Giffin. St. Martin's Griffin (175,000).

Left Neglected by Lisa Genova. Gallery (173,685).

Distant Shores by Kristin Hannah. Ballantine (171,94).

Winter Garden by Kristin Hannah. St. Martin's Griffin (170,000).

150,000+

Cleopatra: A Life by Stacy Schiff. Little, Brown/Back Bay (169,126).

Eat to Live, revised edition, by Dr. Joel Fuhrman. Little, Brown/Back Bay (167,439).

The Red Queen by Philippa Gregory. Touchstone (162,728).

A Clash of Kings by George R. R. Martin. Bantam (162,561).

*A Discovery of Witches by Deborah Harkness. Penguin.

The Descendants (movie tie-in) by Kaui Hart Hemmings. Random House (158,463).

Extremely Loud and Incredibly Close by Jonathan Safran Foer. Houghton Mifflin Harcourt (156,734).

Have a Little Faith by Mitch Albom. Hyperion (154,902).

The Fifth Witness by Michael Connelly. Grand Central (153,078).

*The Kite Runner by Khaled Hosseini. Riverhead.

125,000+

Silver Girl by Elin Hilderbrand. Little, Brown/ Back Bay (147,597).

Full Dark, No Stars by Stephen King. Gallery (146,804).

*Committed: A Love Story by Elizabeth Gilbert. Penguin.

New Atkins for a New You by Dr. Eric C. Westman. Fireside (145,036).

Chelsea Chelsea Bang Bang by Chelsea Handler. Grand Central (143,114).

I Still Dream About You by Fannie Flagg. Random House (138,138).

Every Last One by Anna Quindlen. Random House (136,686).

Shanghai Girls by Lisa See. Random House (132,230).

How to Win Friends and Influence People by Dale Carnegie. Gallery (132,178).

These Things Hidden by Heather Gudenkauf. Mira (129,398).

What's New, Cupcake? Ingeniously Simple Designs for Every Occasion by Karen Tack and Alan Richardson. Houghton Mifflin Harcourt (129,282).

The Invisible Bridge by Julie Orringer. Vintage (126,000).

100,000+

1,000 Places to See Before You Die, 2nd edition, by Patricia Schultz. Workman (121,749).

*Drive: The Surprising Truth About What Motivates Us by Daniel Pink. Riverhead.

Perks of Being a Wallflower by Stephen Chbosky. Gallery (117,395).

Innocent by Scott Turow. Grand Central (116,597).

Clark Howard's Living Large in Lean Times by Clark Howard. Avery (116,044).

Still Missing by Chevy Stevens. St. Martin's Griffin (115,000).

Squirrel Seeks Chipmunk: A Modern Bestiary by David Sedaris. Little, Brown (114,812).

Thank You Notes by Jimmy Fallon and the Writers of Late Night. Grand Central (114,189).

The Land of Painted Caves by Jean M. Auel. Bantam Books (113,472).

Abraham Lincoln: Vampire Hunter by Seth Grahame-Smith. Grand Central (112,314).

One Good Dog by Susan Wilson. St. Martin's Griffin (110,000).

Assholes Finish First by Max Tucker. Gallery (109,783).

Still Alice by Lisa Genova. Gallery (109,071).

Crooked Letter, Crooked Letter by Tom Franklin. Morrow (108,549).

Food Network Magazine Great Easy Meals by Food Network Magazine. Hyperion (106,923).

Between Friends by Debbie Macomber. Mira (106,803).

A Feast for Crows by George R. R. Martin. Bantam (102,122).

The Calhouns: Catherine, Amanda and Lilah by Nora Roberts. Silhouette (102,114).

We Need to Talk About Kevin by Lionel Shriver. Harper Perennial (101,754).

Prevent and Reverse Heart Disease: The Revolutionary, Scientifically Proven, Nutrition-Based Cure by Dr. Caldwell B. Esselstyn Jr. Avery (100,058).

Superfreakonomics by Steven D. Levitt and Stephen J. Dubner. Morrow (100,029).

Super Sad True Love Story by Gary Shteyngart. Random House (105,000).

One Thousand White Women by Jim Fergus. St. Martin's Griffin (100,000). (Published in 1999, it was a Target Book Club Pick in July 2011.)

Look Again by Lisa Scottoline. St. Martin's Griffin (100,000).

Children's Bestsellers: 'Hunger Games' Rule, E-Books Ascend

Diane Roback
Senior Editor, Children's Books, *Publishers Weekly*

With the movie version of The Hunger Games out this month, Panem fever is everywhere. But the enthusiasm for this trilogy has been building for a some time. Last year, fans bought a total of 9.2 million Hunger Games books (6.4 million print copies, 2.8 million e-books), up from 4.3 million total in 2010. E-book sales were just 430,000 in 2010, making for a 550 percent gain in just one year.

In other bestselling series news, books about that Wimpy Kid sold 6 million copies, down from 11 million in 2010; the sixth title in the series, which came out in November, sold 3.3 million copies. The widely anticipated final volume in Christopher Paolini's Inheritance Cycle sold 1.8 million print copies, but just 616,000 copies were sold from the series's backlist. Rick Riordan's various myth-based series sold slightly under 5 million copies, down from 10 million the previous year, but his e-book sales increased from just over half a million to just under 1 million. Harry Potter was still going strong, thanks to the July 2011 release of the final movie in that series: 2.5 million copies sold in the wizard's swan song year. That other big movie franchise, Twilight, sold 1.6 million print copies, down from 8.5 million in 2010; e-book sales jumped to 778,000, from 560,000 in the previous year.

Plenty more to peruse here; happy reading!

(Note: the figures that follow were provided by the publishers, reflecting book sales in the calendar year 2011. In the e-books section, Penguin and Random House supplied titles for ranking purposes only; Open Road Media declined to participate.)

Hardcover Frontlist

1,000,000+

1. *Cabin Fever* (Diary of a Wimpy Kid No. 6) by Jeff Kinney. Abrams/Amulet (3,321,388).
2. *Inheritance* (Inheritance Cycle No. 4) by Christopher Paolini. Knopf (1,811,022).
3. *The Son of Neptune* (Heroes of Olympus No. 2) by Rick Riordan. Disney-Hyperion (1,781,189).
4. *The Throne of Fire* (Kane Chronicles No. 2) by Rick Riordan. Disney-Hyperion (1,187,604).

600,000+

5. *Destined* (House of Night No. 9) by P. C. and Kristin Cast. St. Martin's Griffin (625,000).

500,000+

6. *Middle School, the Worst Years of My Life* by James Patterson and Chris Tebbetts, illustrated by Laura Park. Little, Brown (543,254).
7. *Every Thing on It* by Shel Silverstein. HarperCollins (511,389).
8. *If You Give a Dog a Donut* by Laura Numeroff, illustrated by Felicia Bond. HarperCollins/Balzer + Bray (508,884).

400,000+

9. *City of Fallen Angels* (Mortal Instruments No. 4) by Cassandra Clare. Simon & Schuster/McElderry (495,766).
10. *Tales from a Not-So-Talented Pop Star* (Dork Diaries No. 3) by Rachel Renée Russell. Simon & Schuster/Aladdin (492,832).
11. *Silverlicious* by Victoria Kann. HarperCollins (481,227).
12. *LEGO Star Wars Character Encyclopedia* by Hannah Dolan. DK (425,306).
13. *The LEGO Ideas Book* by Daniel Lipkowitz. DK (413,348).
14. *The Twilight Saga: The Official Illustrated Guide* by Stephenie Meyer. Little, Brown/Tingley (413,204).

300,000+

15. *The Wimpy Kid Movie Diary (Revised and Expanded)* by Jeff Kinney. Abrams/Amulet (398,588).
16. *Angel* (Maximum Ride No. 7) by James Patterson. Little, Brown (382,683).
17. *Heaven Is for Real for Kids* by Todd and Sonja Burpo, illustrated by Wilson Ong. Thomas Nelson (380,061).
18. *The Fire* (Witch & Wizard No. 3) by James Patterson and Jill Dembowski. Little, Brown (357,277).
19. *Big Nate on a Roll* by Lincoln Peirce. HarperCollins (302,164).
20. *Passion* (Fallen No. 3) by Lauren Kate. Delacorte (301,474).

200,000+

21. *Cars 2 Little Golden Book* (Disney/Pixar Cars 2). Golden/Disney (287,702).
22. *How to Dork Your Diary* (Dork Diaries 31/2) by Rachel Renée Russell. Simon & Schuster/Aladdin (282,627).
23. *The Power of Six* (Lorien Legacies) by Pittacus Lore. HarperCollins (282,054).
24. *Cars Storybook Collection.* Disney Press (278,103).
25. *Miss Peregrine's Home for Peculiar Children* by Ransom Riggs. Quirk (275,820).

26. *Theodore Boone: The Abduction* by John Grisham. Dutton (266,860).

27. *Big Nate Boredom Buster* by Lincoln Peirce. HarperCollins (253,401).

28. *Clockwork Prince* (Infernal Devices No. 2) by Cassandra Clare. Simon & Schuster/McElderry (252,169).

29. *Dragon's Oath* (House of Night No. 10) by P. C. and Kristin Cast. St. Martin's Griffin (250,000).

30. *Tales from a Not-So-Popular Party Girl* (Dork Diaries No. 2) by Rachel Renée Russell. Simon & Schuster/Aladdin (249,671).

31. *Everlasting* (Immortals No. 6) by Alyson Noël. St. Martin's Griffin (225,000).

32. *The Bippolo Seed and Other Lost Stories* by Dr. Seuss. Random House (224,101).

33. *Wonderstruck* by Brian Selznick. Scholastic (218,547).

34. *The Invasion of the Potty Snatchers* (Super Diaper Baby No. 2) by Dav Pilkey. Scholastic (202,746).

35. *Vespers Rising* (The 39 Clues No. 11) by Rick Riordan. Scholastic (202,460).

36. *Invincible* (Chronicles of Nick No. 2) by Sherrilyn Kenyon. St. Martin's Griffin (200,000).

100,000+

37. *What Happened to Goodbye* by Sarah Dessen. Viking (198,872).

38. *Forever* by Maggie Stiefvater. Scholastic (198,382).

39. *Darth Paper Strikes Back: An Origami Yoda Book* by Tom Angleberger. Abrams/Amulet (194,257).

40. *The Vampire Diaries: The Return: Midnight* by L. J. Smith. HarperTeen (187,388).

41. *The Night Before Christmas* (Little Golden Book) by Clement C. Moore, illustrated by Corinne Malvern. Random House/Golden (184,101).

42. *The Wizard of Oz: A Scanimation Book* by Rufus Butler Seder. Workman (181,031).

43. *Bloodlines* by Richelle Mead. Penguin/Razorbill (179,827).

44. *Twisted* (Pretty Little Liars No. 9) by Sara Shepard. HarperTeen (177,145).

45. *A Bad Kitty Christmas* by Nick Bruel. Roaring Brook/Porter (173,056).

46. *Michael Vey: The Prisoner of Cell 25* by Richard Paul Evans. Simon & Schuster/Mercury (172,984).

47. *Crossed* by Ally Condie. Dutton (167,850).

48. *The Medusa Plot* (The 39 Clues, Cahills vs. Vespers No. 1). Gordon Korman. Scholastic (166,381).

49. *Delirium* by Lauren Oliver. HarperCollins (164,554).

50. *Silence* (Hush, Hush No. 3) by Becca Fitzpatrick. Simon & Schuster (163,068).

51. *The Warlock* (Secrets of the Immortal Nicholas Flamel) by Michael Scott. Delacorte (161,267).

52. *World Without Heroes* (Beyonders No. 1) by Brandon Mull. Simon & Schuster/Aladdin (160,848).

53. *Awakened* (House of Night No. 8) by P. C. and Kristin Cast. St. Martin's Griffin (160,000).

54. *Divergent* by Veronica Roth. HarperCollins/Tegen (159,020).

55. *The Death Cure* (Maze Runner No. 3) by James Dashner. Delacorte (155,552).

56. *You Are My Sunshine* (board book) by Jimmie Davis, illustrated by Caroline Jayne Church. Scholastic/Cartwheel (155,037).

57. *The Emperor of Nihon-Ja* (Ranger's Apprentice No. 10) by John Flanagan. Philomel (152,463).

58. *Splish, Splash, Splat!* by Rob Scotton. HarperCollins (151,053).

59. *Perfect* by Ellen Hopkins. Simon & Schuster/McElderry (148,328).

60. *The Future of Us* by Jay Asher and Carolyn Mackler. Penguin/Razorbill (148,074).

61. *Ruthless* (Pretty Little Liars No. 10) by Sara Shepard. HarperTeen (143,641).

62. *Summer and the City* (Carrie Diaries) by Candace Bushnell. HarperCollins/Balzer + Bray (138,382).

63. *A Crazy Day with Cobras* (Magic Tree House No. 45) by Mary Pope Osborne, illustrated by Sal Murdocca. Random House (137,852).

64. *The Artist Who Painted a Blue Horse* by Eric Carle. Philomel (136,610).

65. *A King's Ransom* (The 39 Clues, Cahills vs. Vespers No. 2) by Jude Watson. Scholastic (133,068).

66. *Dogs in the Dead of Night* (MTH No. 46) by Mary Pope Osborne, illustrated by Sal Murdocca. Random House (131,797).

67. *Fancy Nancy: Aspiring Artist* by Jane O'Connor, illustrated by Robin Preiss Glasser. HarperCollins (128,363).

68. *Scorpia Rising* (Alex Rider) by Anthony Horowitz. Philomel (127,387).

69. *Never Have I Ever* (Lying Game No. 2) by Sara Shepard. HarperTeen (124,464).

70. *Happy Hippo, Angry Duck* (board book) by Sandra Boynton. Little Simon (122,512).

71. *The Vampire Diaries: The Hunters: Phantom* by L. J. Smith. HarperTeen (120,696).

72. *The Lost Stories* (Ranger's Apprentice) by John Flanagan. Philomel (118,759).

73. *Princess Charm School* by Mary Tillworth. Random House/Golden (118,441).

74. *5-Minute Princess Stories.* Disney (118,259).

75. *The Outcasts* (Brotherband Chronicles No. 1) by John Flanagan. Philomel (118,037).

76. *The Ghoul Next Door* (Monster High No. 2) by Lisi Harrison. Little, Brown/Poppy (118,016).

77. *Dora and the Unicorn King* (Dora the Explorer Little Golden Book) by Molly Reisner, illustrated by David Aikins. Random House/Golden (116,992).

78. *Fancy Nancy: Stellar Stargazer!* by Jane O'Connor, illustrated by Robin Preiss Glasser. HarperCollins (116,241).

79. *Phineas and Ferb's Guide to Life.* Disney (113,701).

80. *Bumble-Ardy* by Maurice Sendak. HarperCollins (113,397).

81. *Pete the Cat: Rocking in My School Shoes* by Eric Litwin, illustrated by James Dean. HarperCollins (112,592).

82. *Bloodrose* (Nightshade No. 3) by Andrea Cremer. Philomel (111,400).

83. *Home for Christmas* by Jan Brett. Putnam (110,258).

84. *Abe Lincoln at Last!* (MTH No. 47) by Mary Pope Osborne, illustrated by Sal Murdocca. Random House (107,249).

85. *Tractor Trouble* (Disney/Pixar Cars Little Golden Book) by Frank J. Berrios. Golden/Disney (106,036).

86. *Llama Llama Home with Mama* by Anna Dewdney. Viking (105,593).

87. *The Big Book of Berenstain Bears Beginner Books* by Stan and Jan Berenstain. Random House (104,679).

88. *Beautiful Chaos* (Beautiful Creatures No. 3) by Kami Garcia and Margaret Stohl. Little, Brown (104,257).

89. *Bad Kitty Meets the Baby* by Nick Bruel. Roaring Brook/Porter (103,742).

90. *Sign of the Moon* (Warriors: Omen of the Stars No. 4) by Erin Hunter. HarperCollins (101,438).

91. *The Emerald Atlas* by John Stephens. Knopf (101,187).

92. *The Scorpio Races* by Maggie Stiefvater. Scholastic (100,963).

93. *Tiger's Curse* by Colleen Houck. Sterling/Splinter (100,000).

Hardcover Backlist

1,000,000+

1. *Catching Fire* (Hunger Games No. 2) by Suzanne Collins. Scholastic, 2009 (1,671,902).

2. *Mockingjay* (Hunger Games No. 3) by Suzanne Collins. Scholastic, 2010 (1,450,207).

500,000+

3. *Rodrick Rules* (Diary of a Wimpy Kid No. 2) by Jeff Kinney. Abrams/Amulet, 2008 (741,944).

4. *The Ugly Truth* (Diary of a Wimpy Kid No. 5) by Jeff Kinney. Abrams/Amulet, 2010 (696,518).

5. *The Last Straw* (Diary of a Wimpy Kid No. 3) by Jeff Kinney. Abrams/Amulet, 2009 (632,534).

6. *Diary of a Wimpy Kid* by Jeff Kinney. Abrams/Amulet, 2007 (622,871).

7. *The Hunger Games* by Suzanne Collins. Scholastic, 2008 (594,562).

8. *Dog Days* (Diary of a Wimpy Kid No. 4) by Jeff Kinney. Abrams/Amulet, 2009 (582,729).

9. *Green Eggs and Ham* by Dr. Seuss. Random House, 1960 (569,371).

10. *Goodnight Moon* (board book) by Margaret Wise Brown, illustrated by Clement Hurd. HarperFestival, 1991 (557,602).

250,000+

11. *Guess How Much I Love You* (all editions) by Sam McBratney, illustrated by Anita Jeram. Candlewick, 1995 (488,245).

12. *One Fish Two Fish Red Fish Blue Fish* by Dr. Seuss. Random House, 1960 (464,016).

13. *Clifford the Big Red Dog* by Norman Bridwell. Scholastic/Cartwheel, 2005 (463,876).

14. *Brown Bear, Brown Bear, What Do You See?* (board book) by Bill Martin, Jr., illustrated by Eric Carle. Holt, 1996 (437,518).

15. *The Cat in the Hat* by Dr. Seuss. Random House, 1957 (393,893).

16. *Dr. Seuss's ABC* (board book) by Dr. Seuss. Random House, 1996 (355,657).

17. *The Very Hungry Caterpillar* (board book) by Eric Carle. Philomel, 2004 (348,079).

18. *Oh, the Places You'll Go!* by Dr. Seuss. Random House, 1990 (328,486).

19. *Tales from a Not-So-Fabulous Life* (Dork Diaries No. 1) by Rachel Renée Russell. Simon & Schuster/Aladdin, 2009 (318,944).

20. *Princess Bedtime Stories.* Disney, 2010 (299,222).

21. *Going-to-Bed Book* (board book) by Sandra Boynton. Little Simon, 1982 (272,638).

22. *Justin Bieber: First Step 2 Forever* by Justin Bieber. HarperCollins, 2010 (257,213).

23. *First 100 Words* by Roger Priddy. Priddy Books, 2005 (253,634).

24. *Big Nate: In a Class by Himself* by Lincoln Peirce. HarperCollins, 2010 (251,024).

25. *Mr. Brown Can Moo! Can You?* (board book) by Dr. Seuss. Random House, 1996 (250,997).

200,000+

26. *I Am Number Four* by Pittacus Lore. HarperCollins, 2010 (244,217).

27. *On the Night You Were Born* (board book) by Nancy Tillman. Feiwel & Friends, 2010 (241,672).

28. *Moo, Baa, La La La!* (board book) by Sandra Boynton. Little Simon, 1982 (238,840).

29. *Disney Bedtime Favorites.* Disney, 2007 (235,808).

30. *Go, Dog. Go!* by P. D. Eastman. Random House, 1961 (234,427).

31. *Clifford the Firehouse Dog* by Norman Bridwell. Scholastic/Cartwheel, 2010 (233,670).

32. *Big Nate Strikes Again* by Lincoln Peirce. HarperCollins, 2010 (233,652).

33. *Clifford's First Day of School* by Norman Bridwell. Scholastic/Cartwheel, 1999 (231,390).

34. *Clifford's Birthday Party* by Norman Bridwell. Scholastic/Cartwheel, 1997 (230,640).

35. *The Lost Hero* (Heroes of Olympus No. 1) by Rick Riordan. Disney-Hyperion, 2010 (224,955).

36. *I Love You Through and Through* (board book) by Bernadette Rossetti Shustak, illustrated by Caroline Jayne Church. Scholastic/Cartwheel, 2005 (219,935).

37. *The Big Blue Book of Beginner Books.* Random House, 2008 (216,843).

38. *The Giving Tree* by Shel Silverstein. HarperCollins, 2003 (213,182).

39. *Where Is Baby's Belly Button?* (board book) by Karen Katz. Little, Simon, 2000 (211,046).

40. *A Sick Day for Amos McGee* by Philip Stead, illustrated by Erin E. Stead. Roaring Brook/Porter, 2010 (203,426).

41. *Fox in Socks* by Dr. Seuss. Random House, 1965 (202,580).

42. *Where the Sidewalk Ends* (30th anniversary edition) by Shel Silverstein. HarperCollins, 2003 (200,595).

43. *Baby Einstein: First Words.* Disney, 2008 (200,038).

100,000+

44. *The Big Green Book of Beginner Books.* Random House, 2009 (197,712).

45. *Hop on Pop* by Dr. Seuss. Random House, 2004 (195,761).

46. *Disney Princess Collection.* Disney, 2009 (192,109).

47. *Are You My Mother?* by P. D. Eastman. Random House, 1960 (187,997).

48. *A Treasury of Curious George* by H. A. Rey. Houghton Mifflin, 2004 (177,357).

49. *Are You My Mother?* (board book) by P. D. Eastman. Random House, 1998 (169,816).

50. *Barnyard Dance!* by Sandra Boynton. Workman, 1993 (165,554).

51. *Dr. Seuss's ABC* by Dr. Seuss. Random House, 1960 (162,243).

52. *Brown, Bear, Brown Bear, What Do You See?* (Slide and Find) by Bill Martin, Jr., illustrated by Eric Carle. Priddy Books, 2010 (159,722).

53. *Slide and Find—Trucks* by Roger Priddy. Priddy Books, 2007 (155,037).

54. *The Strange Case of Origami Yoda* by Tom Angleberger. Abrams/Amulet, 2010 (152,887).

55. *Wherever You Are: My Love Will Find You* by Nancy Tillman. Feiwel & Friends, 2010 (152,622).

56. *Snuggle Puppy* by Sandra Boynton. Workman, 2003 (150,394).

57. *The Invention of Hugo Cabret* by Brian Selznick. Scholastic, 2007 (150,324).

58. *Pat the Bunny* by Dorothy Kunhardt. Random House/Golden, 1940 (145,500).

59. *Hand, Hand, Fingers, Thumb* by Al Perkins, illustrated by Eric Gurney. Random House, 1998 (144,957).

60. *The Polar Express* by Chris Van Allsburg. Houghton Mifflin, 1985 (144,175).

61. *Little Blue Truck* (board book) by Alice Schertle, illustrated by Jill McElmurry. Harcourt, 2004 (140,679).

62. *The Foot Book* by Dr. Seuss. Random House, 1996 (137,533).

63. *The Big Red Book of Beginner Books.* Random House, 2010 (136,643).

64. *Hop on Pop* (board book) by Dr. Seuss. Random House, 2004 (135,256).

65. *There's No Place Like Space* by Tish Rabe, illustrated by Aristides Ruiz. Random House, 1999 (133,618).

66. *Five Little Monkeys Jumping on the Bed* (board book) by Eileen Christelow. Clarion, 1989 (133,581).

67. *My First Read and Learn Bible* by American Bible Society. Scholastic/Little Shepherd, 2006 (132,459).

68. *How the Grinch Stole Christmas!* by Dr. Seuss. Random House, 1957 (127,485).

69. *Fancy Nancy: Splendiferous Christmas* by Jane O'Connor, illustrated by Robin Preiss Glasser. HarperCollins, 2009 (126,933).

70. *On the Night You Were Born* by Nancy Tillman. Feiwel & Friends, 2006 (126,474).

71. *The Poky Little Puppy* by Janette Sebring Lowery, illustrated by Gustaf Tenggren. Random House/Golden, 1942 (124,417).

72. *The Lion King* by Justine Korman, illustrated by Don Williams and H. R. Russell. Golden/Disney, 2003 (124,376).

73. *Rudolph the Red-Nosed Reindeer.* Random House/Golden, 2000 (123,000).

74. *I Love You, Stinky Face* (board book) by Lisa McCourt, illustrated by Cyd Moore. Scholastic/Cartwheel, 2004 (122,718).

75. *The Lorax* by Dr. Seuss. Random House, 1971 (122,074).

76. *Pinkalicious* by Victoria Kann. HarperCollins, 2006 (121,501).

77. *Moon over Manifest* by Clare Vanderpool. Delacorte, 2010 (121,064).

78. *I'm a Big Sister* by Joanna Cole, illustrated by Rosalinda Kightley. Harper-Festival, 2009 (120,967).

79. *Disney Christmas Storybook Collection.* Disney, 2009 (120,761).

80. *The Red Pyramid* (Kane Chronicles No. 1) by Rick Riordan. Disney-Hyperion, 2010 (120,519).

81. *Nursery Rhymes* by Roger Priddy. Priddy Books, 2006 (116,226).

82. *Belly Button Book* by Sandra Boynton. Workman, 2005 (113,251).

83. *The Maze of Bones* (The 39 Clues No. 1) by Rick Riordan. Scholastic, 2008 (112,821).

84. *The Christmas Story* (Little Golden Book) by Jane Werner Watson. Random House/Golden, 2000 (110,301).

85. *The Monster at the End of This Book* by Jon Stone, illustrated by Michael Smollin. Random House/Golden, 1999 (109,273).

86. *Go, Dog. Go!* (board book) by P. D. Eastman. Random House, 1997 (107,764).

87. *I Can Read with My Eyes Shut!* by Dr. Seuss. Random House, 1978 (107,456).

88. *The Runaway Bunny* (board book) by Margaret Wise Brown, illustrated by Clement Hurd. HarperFestival, 1991 (104,972).

89. *Pajama Time!* by Sandra Boynton. Workman, 2000 (104,300).

90. *Happy Birthday to You!* by Dr. Seuss. Random House, 1959 (103,361).

91. *Interrupting Chicken* by David Ezra Stein. Candlewick, 2010 (102,552).

92. *The Nose Book* (board book) by Al Perkins, illustrated by Joe Mathieu. Random House, 2003 (102,320).

93. *Cars Puzzle Book.* Random House/Disney, 2003 (102,065).

94. *Harry Potter: The Tales of Beedle the Bard* by J. K. Rowling. Scholastic/Levine, 2008 (101,893).

95. *Baby Einstein: Mirror Me!* Disney, 2002 (101,810).

96. *If You Give a Mouse a Cookie* by Laura Numeroff, illustrated by Felicia Bond. HarperCollins, 1985 (100,819).

97. *Tangled* (Little Golden Book) by Ben Smiley, illustrated by Victoria Ying. Golden/Disney, 2010 (100,691).

98. *Harry Potter and the Sorcerer's Stone* by J. K. Rowling. Scholastic/Levine, 1998 (100,499).

99. *Another Monster at the End of This Book* by Jon Stone, illustrated by Michael Smollin. Random House/Golden, 1999 (100,355).

100. *Night-Night, Little Pookie* by Sandra Boynton. Random House/Corey, 2009 (100,307).

101. *There's a Wocket in My Pocket!* (board book) by Dr. Seuss. Random House, 1996 (100,180).

102. *Oh, Say, Can You Say Di-no-saur?* by Bonnie Worth. Random House, 1999 (100,166).

103. *Ten Apples Up on Top!* by Dr. Seuss (writing as Theo. LeSieg). Random House, 1961 (100,126).

104. *The Cat in the Hat Comes Back* by Dr. Seuss. Random House, 1958 (100,008).

Paperback Frontlist

500,000+

1. *Breaking Dawn* (Twilight Saga No. 4) (trade and mass market media tie-in editions) by Stephenie Meyer. Little, Brown/Tingley (753,888).
2. *Witch & Wizard* (mass market). James Patterson and Gabrielle Charbonnet. Little, Brown (656,665).
3. *Phineas and Ferb: Across the 2nd Dimension.* Disney (516,007).

400,000+

4. *Pinkalicious: Pinkie Promise* by Victoria Kann. HarperCollins (457,416).
5. *The Last Olympian* (Percy Jackson and the Olympians No. 5) by Rick Riordan. Disney-Hyperion (448,672).
6. *Phineas and Ferb: Agent P's Top-Secret Joke Book.* Disney (403,950).

300,000+

7. *Race Around the World* (Disney/Pixar Cars 2). Random House/Disney (356,822).
8. *Fang* (Maximum Ride No. 6) (mass market edition) by James Patterson. Little, Brown (330,806).

200,000+

9. *African Cats: A Lion's Pride.* Disney (296,077).
10. *Beastly* (movie tie-in edition) by Alex Flinn. HarperTeen (276,033).
11. *Judy Moody and the NOT Bummer Summer* (movie tie-in) by Megan McDonald, illustrated by Peter H. Reynolds. Candlewick (270,040).
12. *The Red Pyramid* (Kane Chronicles No. 1) by Rick Riordan. Disney-Hyperion (252,495).
13. *Super Spies* (Disney/Pixar Cars 2). Random House/Disney (251,343).
14. *Tempted* (House of Night No. 6) by P. C. and Kristin Cast. St. Martin's Griffin (250,000).
15. *Thirteen Reasons Why* by Jay Asher. Penguin/Razorbill (242,097).
16. *Racing Rivals* (Disney/Pixar Cars 2). Random House/Disney (236,088).
17. *Red Riding Hood* (media tie-in edition) by Catherine Hardwicke, Sarah Blakeley-Cartwright, and David Leslie Johnson. Little, Brown/Poppy (229,728).
18. *Theodore Boone: Kid Lawyer* by John Grisham. Dutton (227,356).
19. *Splat the Cat: Good Night, Sleep Tight* by Rob Scotton. HarperCollins (224,111).
20. *A Horse and a Hero* (Disney Tangled) by Daisy Alberto. Random House/Disney (215,263).
21. *Burned* (House of Night No. 7) by P. C. and Kristin Cast. St. Martin's Griffin (200,000).

100,000+

22. *War Horse* (trade and movie tie-in editions) by Michael Morpurgo. Scholastic (187,731).

23. *Torment* (Fallen No. 2) by Lauren Kate. Delacorte (186,113).

24. *Pinkalicious: The Pinkerrific Playdate* by Victoria Kann. HarperCollins (165,944).

25. *Barbie: A Fairy Secret* (Step into Reading) by Christy Webster. Random House (164,919).

26. *Barbie: Princess Charm School* (Step into Reading) by Ruth Homberg. Random House (164,553).

27. *Fancy Nancy and the Too-Loose Tooth* by Jane O'Connor, illustrated by Robin Preiss Glasser. HarperFestival (163,236).

28. *Alvin and the Chipmunks: Chipwrecked: Too Cool for Rules* by J. E. Bright. HarperCollins (156,893).

29. *The Twilight Saga: Breaking Dawn, Part 1: The Official Illustrated Movie Companion* by Stephenie Meyer. Little, Brown (154,335).

30. *Racing in the Rain* by Garth Stein. HarperCollins (148,307).

31. *Along for the Ride* by Sarah Dessen. Penguin/Speak (148,273).

32. *I Am Number Four* by Pittacus Lore. HarperCollins (146,383).

33. *Barbie: A Fairy Secret* (Pictureback) by Mary Man-Kong. Random House (142,991).

34. *Clockwork Angel* (Infernal Devices No. 1) by Cassandra Clare. Simon & Schuster/McElderry (142,046).

35. *Fancy Nancy and the Mean Girl* by Jane O'Connor, illustrated by Robin Preiss Glasser. HarperFestival (142,020).

36. *The Gift* (Witch & Wizard No. 2) by James Patterson and Ned Rust. Little, Brown (138,862).

37. *Summer of the Sea Serpent* (Magic Tree House No. 43) by Mary Pope Osborne, illustrated by Sal Murdocca. Random House (138,092).

38. *Go, Go, Go* (Disney/Pixar Cars) by Melissa Lagonegro, illustrated by Ron Cohee. Random House/Disney (134,851).

39. *Marley: Messy Dog* by John Grogan, illustrated by Richard Cowdrey. HarperCollins (133,086).

40. *Nightshade* by Andrea Cremer. Penguin/Speak (129,905).

41. *Transformers: Dark of the Moon: The Junior Novel* by Michael Kelly. Little, Brown (124,817).

42. *The Vampire Diaries: The Return: Shadow Souls* by L. J. Smith. HarperTeen, (124,329).

43. *Nine Lives of Chloe King* by Liz Braswell. Simon Pulse (123,438).

44. *Olivia the Princess* by Natalie Shaw, illustrated by Shane L. Johnson. Simon Spotlight (123,310).

45. *Dora and the Unicorn King* by Ellie Seiss, illustrated by Victoria Miller. Simon & Schuster/Nickelodeon (122,585).

46. *Wanted* (Pretty Little Liars No. 8) by Sara Shepard. HarperTeen (121,993).
47. *Meet Smurfette* by Peyo. Simon Spotlight (121,478).
48. *Matched* by Ally Condie. Penguin/Speak (121,243).
49. *Spooky Buddies Junior Novel* (Disney Buddies). Disney (120,484).
50. *The Vampire Diaries: Stefan's Diaries No. 3* by L. J. Smith. HarperTeen (119,893).
51. *Thor Junior Novel.* Marvel (119,074).
52. *Thirst No. 4* by Christopher Pike. Simon Pulse (118,865).
53. *Where the Mountain Meets the Moon* by Grace Lin. Little, Brown (114,161).
54. *A Tale of Two Pretties* (Clique No. 14) by Lisi Harrison. Little Brown/Poppy (110,080).
55. *Winter of the Ice Wizard* (MTH No. 32) by Mary Pope Osborne, illustrated by Sal Murdocca. Random House (108,651).
56. *Barbie: Princess Charm School* (Pictureback) by Mary Man-Kong. Random House (107,565).
57. *Pirates of the Caribbean: On Stranger Tides* (junior novel). Disney (107,498).
58. *A Smurfin' Big Adventure!* by Fern Alexander, illustrated by Mel Milton. Simon Spotlight (106,332).
59. *Hop: The Chapter Book,* adapted by Annie Auerbach. Little, Brown (106,329).
60. *Fancy Nancy: Hair Dos and Hair Don'ts* by Jane O'Connor, illustrated by Robin Preiss Glasser. HarperCollins (106,005).
61. *Infinity* (Chronicles of Nick No. 1) by Sherrilyn Kenyon. St. Martin's Griffin (105,000).
62. *Barbie: A Perfect Christmas* (Step into Reading) by Christy Webster. Random House (102,125).
63. *The Magician's Elephant* by Kate DiCamillo, illustrated by Yoko Tanaka. Candlewick (101,452).
64. *Judy Moody and the Poop Picnic* (movie tie-in) by Jamie Michalak. Candlewick (100,874).
65. *Five Fast Tales* (Disney/Pixar Cars). Random House/Disney (100,068).
66. *Forever Summer* by Alyson Noël. St. Martin's Griffin (100,000).

Paperback Backlist

2,000,000+

1. *The Hunger Games* by Suzanne Collins. Scholastic, 2010 (2,696,707).

400,000+

2. *Harry Potter and the Sorcerer's Stone* by J. K. Rowling, illustrated by Mary GrandPré. Scholastic, 1999 (452,076).

3. *The Giver* by Lois Lowry. Bantam, 1999 (435,710).

300,000+

4. *Love You Forever* by Robert Munsch, illustrated by Sheila McGraw. Firefly, 1986 (381,347).
5. *Harry Potter and the Deathly Hallows* by J. K. Rowling, illustrated by Mary GrandPré. Scholastic, 2009 (371,873).
6. *The Lightning Thief* (Percy Jackson and the Olympians No. 1) by Rick Riordan. Disney-Hyperion, 2006 (358,706).
7. *Dinosaurs Before Dark* (MTH No. 1). Mary Pope Osborne, illustrated by Sal Murdocca. Random House, 1992 (345,220).
8. *Harry Potter and the Chamber of Secrets* by J. K. Rowling, illustrated by Mary GrandPré. Scholastic, 2000 (343,735).
9. *Harry Potter and the Prisoner of Azkaban* by J. K. Rowling, illustrated by Mary GrandPré. Scholastic, 2001 (309,458).

200,000+

10. *Harry Potter and the Order of the Phoenix* by J. K. Rowling, illustrated by Mary GrandPré. Scholastic, 2004 (296,849).
11. *Harry Potter and the Goblet of Fire* by J. K. Rowling, illustrated by Mary GrandPré. Scholastic, 2002 (296,582).
12. *Harry Potter and the Half-Blood Prince* by J. K. Rowling, illustrated by Mary GrandPré. Scholastic, 2006 (290,351).
13. *The Book Thief* by Markus Zusak. Knopf, 2007 (281,846).
14. *Mr. Popper's Penguins* (trade paperback and media tie-in editions) by Richard Atwater and Florence Atwater. Little Brown/Tingley, 1992 (275,054).
15. *The Sea of Monsters* (Percy Jackson and the Olympians No. 2) by Rick Riordan. Disney-Hyperion, 2007 (270,953).
16. *The Knight at Dawn* (MTH No. 2) by Mary Pope Osborne, illustrated by Sal Murdocca. Random House, 1993 (256,065).
17. *The Care and Keeping of You: The Body Book for Girls* by Valorie Schaefer, illustrated by Norm Bendel. American Girl, 1998 (248,051).
18. *Mummies in the Morning* (MTH No. 3) by Mary Pope Osborne, illustrated by Sal Murdocca. Random House, 1993 (240,511).
19. *Holes* by Louis Sachar. Random House/Yearling, 2000 (239,708).
20. *Pinkalicious: Pink Around the Rink* by Victoria Kann. HarperCollins (231,293).
21. *Eragon* (Inheritance Cycle No. 1) by Christopher Paolini. Knopf, 2005 (230,876).
22. *The Outsiders* by S. E. Hinton. Penguin/Speak, 1997, and Puffin, 2006 (230,565).
23. *The Titan's Curse* (Percy Jackson and the Olympians No. 3) by Rick Riordan. Disney-Hyperion, 2008 (224,991).

24. *Where the Wild Things Are* by Maurice Sendak. HarperCollins, 1988 (224,608).
25. *Pirates Past Noon* (MTH No. 4) by Mary Pope Osborne, illustrated by Sal Murdocca. Random House, 1994 (221,714).
26. *Pretty Little Liars* by Sara Shepard. HarperTeen, 2007 (219,296).
27. *Breaking Dawn* (Twilight Saga No. 4) by Stephenie Meyer. Little Brown/ Tingley, 2010 (217,375).
28. *Charlotte's Web* by E. B. White, illustrated by Garth Williams. HarperCollins, 1974 (216,565).
29. *The Absolutely True Diary of a Part-Time Indian* by Sherman Alexie. Little, Brown, 2009 (214,344).
30. *The Battle of the Labyrinth* (Percy Jackson and the Olympians No. 4) by Rick Riordan. Disney-Hyperion, 2009 (211,200).
31. *Disney Tangled: Kingdom of Color* (Step into Reading) by Melissa Lagonegro, illustrated by Jean-Paul Orpinas. Random House/Disney (208,958).
32. *Pinkalicious: School Rules!* by Victoria Kann. HarperCollins, 2010 (207,465).
33. *A Wrinkle in Time* by Madeleine L'Engle. Macmillan/Square Fish, 2007 (207,442).
34. *Fallen* by Lauren Kate. Random House/Ember (202,278).
35. *Brisingr* (Inheritance Cycle No. 3) by Christopher Paolini. Knopf, 2009 (201,057).

100,000+

36. *Twilight* by Stephenie Meyer. Little Brown/Tingley, 2006 (196,146).
37. *Ramona Quimby, Age 8* by Beverly Cleary, illustrated by Tracy Dockray. HarperCollins, 1992 (193,420).
38. *Fancy Nancy and the Delectable Cupcakes* by Jane O'Connor, illustrated by Robin Preiss Glasser. HarperCollins, 2010 (189,826).
39. *Eldest* (Inheritance Cycle No. 2) by Christopher Paolini. Knopf (184,881).
40. *Judy Moody* by Megan McDonald, illustrated by Peter H. Reynolds. Candlewick, 2002 (180,340).
41. *Night of the Ninjas* (MTH No. 5) by Mary Pope Osborne, illustrated by Sal Murdocca. Random House, 1995 (176,174).
42. *The Boy in the Striped Pajamas* by John Boyne. Random House/Ember, 2007 (172,618).
43. *The Maze Runner* by James Dashner. Random House/Ember, 2010 (171,782).
44. *Fancy Nancy Sees Stars* by Jane O'Connor, illustrated by Robin Preiss Glasser. HarperCollins, 2008 (170,668).
45. *Hatchet* by Gary Paulsen. Simon & Schuster, 2006 (164,808).
46. *The Lion, the Witch and the Wardrobe* by C. S. Lewis, illustrated by Pauline Baynes. HarperCollins, 1994 (161,502).

47. *Disney Princess: What Is a Princess?* by Jennifer Liberts Weinberg, illustrated by Atelier Philippe Harchy. Random House/Disney, 2004 (161,004).

48. *Because of Winn-Dixie* (trade paper and movie tie-in editions) by Kate DiCamillo. Candlewick, 2001 (156,677).

49. *Ramona the Pest* by Beverly Cleary, illustrated by Tracy Dockray. HarperCollins, 1992 (155,852).

50. *Junie B. Jones and the Stupid Smelly Bus* (JBJ No. 1) by Barbara Park, illustrated by Denise Brunkus. Random House, 1992 (155,465).

51. *Goodnight Moon* by Margaret Wise Brown, illustrated by Clement Hurd. HarperCollins, 1977 (154,113).

52. *Danny and the Dinosaur* by Syd Hoff. HarperCollins, 1978 (153,784).

53. *The Cricket in Times Square* by George Selden, illustrated by Garth Williams. Macmillan/Square Fish, 2008 (152,822).

54. *Number the Stars* by Lois Lowry. Random House/Yearling, 1990 (152,287).

55. *Flawless* (Pretty Little Liars No. 2) by Sara Shepard. HarperTeen, 2008 (153,252).

56. *Perfect* (Pretty Little Liars No. 3) by Sara Shepard. HarperTeen, 2008 (150,258).

57. *Splat the Cat: Splat the Cat Sings Flat* by Rob Scotton. HarperCollins, 2010 (147,571).

58. *Biscuit Goes to School* by Alyssa Satin Capucilli, illustrated by Pat Schories. HarperCollins, 2003 (146,179).

59. *Ramona the Brave* by Beverly Cleary, illustrated by Tracy Dockray. HarperCollins, 1995 (145,374).

60. *City of Bones* by Cassandra Clare. Simon & Schuster/McElderry, 2008 (145,334).

61. *Afternoon on the Amazon* (MTH No. 6) by Mary Pope Osborne, illustrated by Sal Murdocca. Random House, 1995 (145,279).

62. *Frog and Toad Are Friends* by Arnold Lobel. HarperCollins, 1979 (142,123).

63. *Unbelievable* (Pretty Little Liars No. 4) by Sara Shepard. HarperTeen, 2008 (140,748).

64. *Midnight on the Moon* (MTH No. 8) by Mary Pope Osborne, illustrated by Sal Murdocca. Random House, 1996 (140,216).

65. *The Mysterious Benedict Society* by Trenton Lee Stewart, illustrated by Carson Ellis. Little, Brown/Tingley, 2008 (139,397).

66. *The Mouse and the Motorcycle* by Beverly Cleary, illustrated by Tracy Dockray. HarperCollins, 1990 (138,490).

67. *Dolphins at Daybreak* (MTH No. 9) by Mary Pope Osborne, illustrated by Sal Murdocca. Random House, 1997 (137,956).

68. *Beezus and Ramona* by Beverly Cleary, illustrated by Tracy Dockray. HarperCollins, 1990 (137,436).

69. *DC Super Friends: Super Friends Flying High.* Random House, 2008 (137,247).

70. *Where the Red Fern Grows* by Wilson Rawls. Random House/Yearling, 1996 (136,804).

71. *Amelia Bedelia* by Peggy Parish, illustrated by Fritz Siebel. HarperTrophy, 1992 (134,440).

72. *Judy Moody Gets Famous* by Megan McDonald, illustrated by Peter H. Reynolds. Candlewick, 2003 (132,605).

73. *Eclipse* (Twilight Saga No. 3) by Stephenie Meyer. Little Brown/Tingley, 2009 (131,517).

74. *The Voyage of the Dawn Treader* by C. S. Lewis, illustrated by Pauline Baynes. HarperCollins, 1994 (131,111).

75. *Fancy Nancy: Pajama Day* by Jane O'Connor, illustrated by Robin Preiss Glasser. HarperCollins, 2009 (130,803).

76. *New Moon* (Twilight Saga No. 2) by Stephenie Meyer. Little Brown/Tingley, 2008 (130,596).

77. *Flat Stanley* by Jeff Brown, illustrated by Macky Pamintuan. HarperCollins, 2003 (130,048).

78. *Marked* (House of Night No. 1) by P. C. and Kristin Cast. St. Martin's Griffin, 2007 (130,000).

79. *Little Critter: Going to the Sea Park* by Mercer Mayer. HarperCollins, 2009 (127,816).

80. *Sleepover Party Mad Libs* by Roger Price and Leonard Stern. Price Stern Sloan, 2008 (127,665).

81. *Biscuit* by Alyssa Satin Capucilli, illustrated by Pat Schories. HarperCollins, 1997 (127,417).

82. *Junie B. Jones and a Little Monkey Business* (JBJ No.2) by Barbara Park, illustrated by Denise Brunkus. Random House (125,699).

83. *Maniac Magee* by Jerry Spinelli. Little, Brown, 1999 (124,471).

84. *Island of the Blue Dolphins* by Scott O'Dell. Houghton Mifflin, 2010 (124,216).

85. *Fancy Nancy: The Dazzling Book Report* by Jane O'Connor, illustrated by Robin Preiss Glasser. HarperCollins, 2009 (122,848).

86. *Tales of a Fourth Grade Nothing* by Judy Blume. Puffin, 2007 (122,353).

87. *The Name of This Book Is Secret* by Pseudonymous Bosch. Little, Brown, 2008 (120,595).

88. *Barbie: I Can Be a Pet Vet* (Step into Reading) by Mary Man-Kong, illustrated by Jiyoung An. Random House, 2010 (120,239).

89. *Polar Bears Past Bedtime* (MTH No. 12) by Mary Pope Osborne, illustrated by Sal Murdocca. Random House, 1998 (119,113).

90. *The Phantom Tollbooth* by Norton Juster, illustrated by Jules Feiffer. Random House/Yearling, 1988 (118,699).

91. *Ramona and Her Father* by Beverly Cleary, illustrated by Tracy Dockray. HarperCollins, 1990 (118,565).

92. *The Watsons Go to Birmingham—1963* by Christopher Paul Curtis. Random House/Yearling, 1997 (116,521).

93. *Little Critter: Just Go to Bed* by Mercer Mayer. Random House, 2001 (114,600).

94. *Junie B. Jones and Her Big Fat Mouth* (JBJ No.3) by Barbara Park, illustrated by Denise Brunkus. Random House, 1993 (113,870).

95. *Bad Kitty Gets a Bath* by Nick Bruel. Macmillan/Square Fish, 2009 (113,686).

96. *Miss Daisy Is Crazy!* (My Weird School No. 1) by Dan Gutman, illustrated by Jim Paillot. HarperCollins, 2004 (112,953).

97. *Ghost Town at Sundown* (MTH No. 10) by Mary Pope Osborne, illustrated by Sal Murdocca. Random House, 1997 (112,630).

98. *The Night Before Kindergarten* by Natasha Wing, illustrated by Julie Durrell. Grosset & Dunlap, 2001 (112,258).

99. *Star Wars Mad Libs* by Roger Price and Leonard Stern. Price Stern Sloan, 2008 (112,217).

100. *The Original Mad Libs 1* by Roger Price and Leonard Stern. Price Stern Sloan, 2008 (111,728).

101. *Frog and Toad Together* by Arnold Lobel. HarperCollins, 1979 (111,365).

102. *The Berenstain Bears and Too Much Junk Food* by Stan and Jan Berenstain. Random House, 1985 (110,595).

103. *Fancy Nancy: Splendid Speller* by Jane O'Connor, illustrated by Robin Preiss Glasser. HarperCollins, 2010 (110,199).

104. *Fancy Nancy: At the Museum* by Jane O'Connor, illustrated by Robin Preiss Glasser. HarperCollins, 2008 (109,516).

105. *Sunset of the Sabertooth* (MTH No. 7) by Mary Pope Osborne, illustrated by Sal Murdocca. Random House, 1996 (108,773).

106. *Bridge to Terabithia* by Katherine Paterson, illustrated by Donna Diamond. HarperCollins, 1987 (108,171).

107. *Junie B. Jones and Some Sneaky Peeky Spying* (JBJ No. 4) by Barbara Park, illustrated by Denise Brunkus. Random House, 1994 (107,079).

108. *Wicked* (Pretty Little Liars No. 5) by Sara Shepard. HarperTeen, 2009 (106,596).

109. *Frindle* by Andrew Clements. Simon & Schuster/Atheneum, 1998 (106,552).

110. *Tuck Everlasting* by Natalie Babbitt. Macmillan/Square Fish, 2007 (106,205).

111. *Touching Spirit Bear* by Ben Mikaelsen. HarperCollins, 2002 (106,145).

112. *Judy Moody Saves the World!* by Megan McDonald, illustrated by Peter H. Reynolds. Candlewick, 2004 (105,408).

113. *Where's Waldo?* by Martin Handford. Candlewick, 2007 (104,880).

114. *Harold and the Purple Crayon* by Crockett Johnson. HarperCollins, 1981 (104,819).

115. *Into the Wild* (Warriors No. 1) by Erin Hunter. HarperCollins, 2003 (104,683).

116. *Hoot* by Carl Hiaasen. Random House/Yearling, 2004 (104,430).

117. *Frog and Toad All Year* by Arnold Lobel. HarperCollins, 1984 (104,370).

118. *Stink: The Incredible Shrinking Kid* by Megan McDonald, illustrated by Peter H. Reynolds. Candlewick, 2006 (104,323).

119. *Killer* (Pretty Little Liars No. 6) by Sara Shepard. HarperTeen, 2009 (103,659).

120. *When You Reach Me* by Rebecca Stead. Random House/Yearling, 2010 (103,145).

121. *Esperanza Rising* by Pam Muñoz Ryan. Scholastic, 2002 (103,002).

122. *If I Stay* by Gayle Forman. Penguin/Speak (102,997).

123. *Fancy Nancy: Poison Ivy Expert* by Jane O'Connor, illustrated by Robin Preiss Glasser. HarperCollins, 2008 (102,685).

124. *The Tale of Despereaux: Being the Story of a Mouse, a Princess, Some Soup, and a Spool of Thread* by Kate DiCamillo, illustrated by Timothy Basil Ering. Candlewick, 2006 (102,421).

125. *Spider-Man: Spider-Man versus Electro* by Susan Hill. HarperCollins, 2009 (102,045).

126. *Disney/Pixar Cars: Race Team.* Random House, 2008 (101,508).

127. *Disney/Pixar Cars: Old, New, Red, Blue!* Random House/Disney, 2006 (101,446).

128. Junie B., First Grader: Toothless Wonder (JBJ No. 20) by Barbara Park, illustrated by Denise Brunkus. Random House, 2003 (101,272).

129. *The Adventures of Captain Underpants* by Dav Pilkey. Scholastic, 1997 (100,907).

130. *Ramona and Her Mother* by Beverly Cleary, illustrated by Tracy Dockray. HarperCollins, 1990 (100,268).

131. *Fancy Nancy and the Boy from Paris* by Jane O'Connor, illustrated by Robin Preiss Glasser. HarperCollins, 2008 (100,085).

132. *The City of Ember* by Jeanne DuPrau. Random House/Yearling, 2004 (100,456).

133. *Lions at Lunchtime* (MTH No. 11) by Mary Pope Osborne, illustrated by Sal Murdocca. Random House, 1998 (100,215).

134. *Betrayed* (House of Night No. 2) by P. C. and Kristin Cast. St. Martin's Griffin, 2007 (100,000).

E-Books

1,000,000+

1. *The Hunger Games* by Suzanne Collins. Scholastic (1,093,091).

500,000+

2. *Catching Fire* (Hunger Games No. 2) by Suzanne Collins. Scholastic (849,957).

3. *Mockingjay* (Hunger Games No. 3) by Suzanne Collins. Scholastic (782,445).

200,000+

4. *Breaking Dawn* (Twilight Saga No. 4) by Stephenie Meyer. Little, Brown (296,366).

5. *Inheritance* (Inheritance Cycle No. 4) by Christopher Paolini. Knopf.

6. *The Son of Neptune* (Heroes of Olympus No. 2) by Rick Riordan. Disney-Hyperion (204,500).

100,000+

7. *Twilight* by Stephenie Meyer. Little, Brown (174,672).

8. *I Am Number Four* by Pittacus Lore. HarperCollins (158,552).

9. *The Throne of Fire* (Kane Chronicles No. 2) by Rick Riordan. Disney-Hyperion. (137,917).

10. *Eclipse* (Twilight Saga No. 3) by Stephenie Meyer. Little, Brown (137,164).

11. *New Moon* (Twilight Saga No. 2) by Stephenie Meyer. Little, Brown (134,903).

12. *Miss Peregrine's Home for Peculiar Children* by Ransom Riggs. Quirk (134,348).

13. *The Lost Hero* (Heroes of Olympus No. 1) by Rick Riordan. Disney-Hyperion. (132,814).

14. *Awakened* (House of Night No. 8) by P. C. and Kristin Cast. St. Martin's (130,000).

15. *The Hunger Games Trilogy* by Suzanne Collins. Scholastic (121,518).

50,000+

16. *The Lightning Thief* (Percy Jackson and the Olympians No. 1) by Rick Riordan. Disney-Hyperion (93,311).

17. *The Power of Six* by Pittacus Lore. HarperCollins (89,176).

18. *City of Fallen Angels* (Mortal Instruments No. 4) by Cassandra Clare. Simon & Schuster/McElderry (88,365).

19. *The Red Pyramid* (Kane Chronicles No. 1) by Rick Riordan. Disney-Hyperion (85,732).

20. *The Book Thief* by Markus Zusak. Knopf.

21. *The Giver* by Lois Lowry. Houghton Mifflin (78,999).

22. *The Sea of Monsters* (Percy Jackson and the Olympians No. 2) by Rick Riordan. Disney-Hyperion (75,605).

23. *Destined* (House of Night No. 9) by P. C. and Kristin Cast. St. Martin's (75,000).

24. *The Last Olympian* (Percy Jackson and the Olympians No. 5) by Rick Riordan. Disney-Hyperion (72,792).

25. *The Gift* (Witch & Wizard No. 2) by James Patterson and Ned Rust. Little, Brown (71,423).

26. *Witch & Wizard* by James Patterson and Gabrielle Charbonnet. Little, Brown (70,020).

27. *Pretty Little Liars* by Sara Shepard. HarperCollins (69,643).

28. *The Titan's Curse* (Percy Jackson and the Olympians No. 3) by Rick Riordan. Disney-Hyperion (67,346).

29. *The Battle of the Labyrinth* (Percy Jackson and the Olympians No. 4) by Rick Riordan. Disney-Hyperion (65,326).

30. *Marked* (House of Night No. 1) by P. C. and Kristin Cast. St. Martin's (65,000).

31. *Angel* (Maximum Ride No. 7) by James Patterson. Little, Brown (63,342).

32. *Evermore* (Immortals No. 1) by Alyson Noël. St. Martin's (60,000).

33. *Beastly* by Alex Flinn. HarperTeen (59,122).

34. *Matched* by Ally Condie. Dutton.

35. *Passion* (Fallen No. 3) by Lauren Kate. Delacorte.

36. *Thirteen Reasons Why* by Jay Asher. Penguin/Razorbill.

37. *Flawless* (Pretty Little Liars No. 2) by Sara Shepard. HarperCollins (50,449).

25,000+

38. *Divergent* by Veronica Roth. HarperCollins/Tegen (49,904).

39. *Wicked Lovely* (with bonus material) by Melissa Marr. HarperCollins (47,901).

40. *Burned* (House of Night No. 7) by P. C. and Kristin Cast. St. Martin's (45,000).

41. *I Am Number Four: The Lost Files: Six's Legacy* by Pittacus Lore. HarperCollins (44,112).

42. *Twisted* (Pretty Little Liars No. 9) by Sara Shepard. HarperCollins (43,398).

43. *Perfect* (Pretty Little Liars No. 3) by Sara Shepard. HarperCollins (42,577).

44. *The Angel Experiment* (Maximum Ride No. 2) by James Patterson. Little, Brown (42,559).

45. *Fallen* by Lauren Kate. Delacorte.

46. *Betrayed* (House of Night No. 2) by P. C. and Kristin Cast. St. Martin's (40,000).

47. *The Lying Game* by Sara Shepard. HarperCollins (39,865).

48. *The Maze Runner* by James Dashner. Delacorte.

49. *Torment* (Fallen No. 2) by Lauren Kate. Delacorte.

50. *Unbelievable* (Pretty Little Liars No. 4) by Sara Shepard. HarperCollins (38,647).

51. *Last Sacrifice* (Vampire Academy No. 6) by Richelle Mead. Penguin/Razorbill.

52. *School's Out—Forever* (Maximum Ride No. 2) by James Patterson. Little, Brown (37,728).

53. *Wicked* (Pretty Little Liars No. 5). Sara Shepard. HarperCollins (37,268).

54. *Clockwork Angel* (Infernal Devices No. 1) by Cassandra Clare. Simon & Schuster/McElderry (37,628).

55. *The Fire* (Witch & Wizard No. 3) by James Patterson and Jill Dembowski. Little, Brown (37,113).

56. *Judy Moody* by Megan McDonald, illustrated by Peter H. Reynolds. Candlewick (36,609).

57. *Saving the World and Other Extreme Sports* (Maximum Ride No. 3) by James Patterson. Little, Brown (36,352).

58. *Eragon* (Inheritance Cycle No. 1). Christopher Paolini. Knopf.

59. *The Warlock* (Secrets of the Immortal Nicholas Flamel No. 5) by Michael Scott. Delacorte.

60. *The Vampire Diaries: The Awakening* by L. J. Smith. HarperTeen (36,295).

61. *Crossed* (Matched No. 2) by Ally Condie. Dutton.

62. *Chosen* (House of Night No. 3) by P. C. and Kristin Cast. St. Martin's (35,000).

63. *Hunted* (House of Night No. 5) by P. C. and Kristin Cast. St. Martin's (35,000).

64. *Tempted* (House of Night No. 6) by P. C. and Kristin Cast. St. Martin's (35,000).

65. *Untamed* (House of Night No. 4) by P. C. and Kristin Cast. St. Martin's (35,000).

66. *MAX* (Maximum Ride No. 6) by James Patterson. Little, Brown (34,987).

67. *The Name of This Book Is Secret* by Pseudonymous Bosch. Little, Brown (34,854).

68. *Wanted* (Pretty Little Liars No. 8) by Sara Shepard. HarperCollins (34,519).

69. *City of Bones* (Mortal Instruments No. 1) by Cassandra Clare. Simon & Schuster/McElderry (34,481).

70. *Killer* (Pretty Little Liars No. 6) by Sara Shepard. HarperCollins (33,859).

71. *Brisingr* (Inheritance Cycle No. 3) by Christopher Paolini. Knopf.

72. *What Happened to Goodbye* by Sarah Dessen. Viking.

73. *The Scorch Trials* (Maze Runner No. 2) by James Dashner. Delacorte.

74. *Gregor the Overlander* (Underland Chronicles No. 1) by Suzanne Collins. Scholastic (33,075).

75. *The Death Cure* (Maze Runner No. 3) by James Dashner. Delacorte.

76. *Bloodlines* by Richelle Mead. Penguin/Razorbill.

77. *Heartless* (Pretty Little Liars No.7) by Sara Shepard. HarperCollins (32,542).
78. *Summer and the City* (Carrie Diaries) by Candace Bushnell. HarperCollins/ Balzer + Bray (32,042).
79. *Shelter* by Harlan Coben. Putnam.
80. *City of Glass* (Mortal Instruments No. 3) by Cassandra Clare. Simon & Schuster/McElderry (30,442).
81. *Everlasting* (Immortals No. 6) by Alyson Noël. St. Martin's (30,000).
82. *Nightstar* (Immortals No. 5) by Alyson Noël. St. Martin's (30,000).
83. *Eldest* (Inheritance Cycle No. 2) by Christopher Paolini. Knopf.
84. *The Emperor of Nihon-Ja* (Ranger's Apprentice No. 10) by John Flanagan. Philomel.
85. *Crescendo* (Hush, Hush No. 2) by Becca Fitzpatrick. Simon & Schuster (29,618).
86. *Tales from a Not-So-Talented Pop Star* (Dork Diaries No. 3) by Rachel Renée Russell. Simon & Schuster/Aladdin (29,317).
87. *City of Ashes* (Mortal Instruments No. 2) by Cassandra Clare. Simon & Schuster/McElderry (29,307).
88. *Forever* (Wolves of Mercy Falls No. 3) by Maggie Stiefvater. Scholastic (29,030).
89. *The Lion, the Witch and the Wardrobe* by C. S. Lewis, illustrated by Pauline Baynes. HarperCollins (28,470).
90. *Shiver* (Wolves of Mercy Falls No. 1) by Maggie Stiefvater. Scholastic (27,827).
91. *The Miraculous Journey of Edward Tulane* by Kate DeCamillo, illustrated by Bagram Ibatoulline. Candlewick (27,523).
92. *Fang* (Maximum Ride No. 6) by James Patterson. Little, Brown (26,843).
93. *Tales from a Not-So-Fabulous Life* (Dork Diaries No. 1) by Rachel Renée Russell. Simon & Schuster/Aladdin (26,597).
94. *Never Have I Ever* (Lying Game No. 2) by Sara Shepard. HarperTeen (26,199).
95. *Graceling* by Kristin Cashore. Harcourt (26,180).
96. *Inheritance Cycle Omnibus: Eragon, Eldest, and Brisingr* by Christopher Paolini. Knopf.
97. *Delirium: The Special Edition* by Lauren Oliver. HarperCollins (25,758).
98. *Vampire Academy* by Richelle Mead. Penguin/Razorbill.
99. *Silence* (Hush, Hush No. 3) by Becca Fitzpatrick. Simon & Schuster (25,419).
100. *Spirit Bound* (Vampire Academy No. 5) by Richelle Mead. Penguin/Razorbill.
101. *Ruthless* (Pretty Little Liars No. 10) by Sara Shepard. HarperTeen (25,202).
102. *A Wrinkle in Time* by Madeleine L'Engle. Macmillan (25,062).
103. *Blue Moon* (Immortals No. 2). Alyson Noël, St. Martin's (25,000).
104. *Dark Flame* (Immortals No. 4) by Alyson Noël, St. Martin's (25,000).

105. *Invincible* (Chronicles of Nick No. 2) by Sherrilyn Kenyon. St. Martin's (25,000).

106. *Shadowland* (Immortals No. 3) by Alyson Noël, St. Martin's (25,000).

10,000+

107. *Tales from a Not-So-Popular Party Girl* (Dork Diaries No. 2) by Rachel Renée Russell. Simon & Schuster/Aladdin (24,855).

108. *Hatchet* by Gary Paulsen. Simon & Schuster (24,719).

109. *The Final Warning* (Maximum Ride No. 5) by James Patterson. Little, Brown (24,663).

110. *We'll Always Have Summer* by Jenny Han. Simon & Schuster (24,417).

111. *Linger* (Wolves of Mercy Falls No. 2) by Maggie Stiefvater. Scholastic (24,328).

112. *Dinosaurs Before Dark* (MTH No. 1) by Mary Pope Osborne, illustrated by Sal Murdocca. Random House.

113. *Hush, Hush* by Becca Fitzpatrick. Simon & Schuster (23,934).

114. *The Poky Little Puppy* by Janette Sebring Lowrey. Random House/Golden.

115. *Where the Red Fern Grows* by Wilson Rawls. Random House/Laurel Leaf.

116. *The Tale of Despereaux: Being the Story of a Mouse, a Princess, Some Soup, and a Spool of Thread* by Kate DiCamillo, illustrated by Timothy Basil Ering. Candlewick (23,533).

117. *The Vampire Diaries: The Struggle* by L. J. Smith. HarperTeen (23,573).

118. *The Boy in the Striped Pajamas* by John Boyne. Random House/Fickling.

119. *Beautiful Creatures* (Caster Chronicles No. 1) by Kami Garcia and Margaret Stohl. Little, Brown (23,218).

120. *Michael Vey: The Prisoner of Cell 25* by Richard Paul Evans. Simon & Schuster/Mercury (23,191).

121. *The Short Second Life of Bree Tanner: An Eclipse Novella* by Stephenie Meyer. Little, Brown (22,734).

122. *The Lemonade War* by Jacqueline Davies. Houghton Mifflin (22,503).

123. *Judy Moody and the NOT Bummer Summer* (movie tie-in) by Megan McDonald, illustrated by Peter H. Reynolds. Candlewick (22,210).

124. *Blood Promise* (Vampire Academy No. 4) by Richelle Mead. Penguin/Razorbill.

125. *Before I Fall* by Lauren Oliver. HarperCollins (22,162).

126. *War Horse* by Michael Morpurgo. Scholastic (22,090).

127. *Frostbite* (Vampire Academy No. 2) by Richelle Mead. Penguin/Razorbill.

128. *The Ruins of Gorlan* (Ranger's Apprentice No. 1) by John Flanagan. Puffin.

129. *The Vampire Diaries: The Return: Midnight* by L. J. Smith. HarperTeen (22,001).

130. *Curious George Goes to an Ice Cream Shop* by H. A. Rey, illustrated by Allen Shalleck. Houghton Mifflin (21,980).

131. *Shadow Kiss* (Vampire Academy No. 3) by Richelle Mead. Penguin/Razorbill.

132. *If I Stay* by Gayle Forman. Penguin/Speak.

133. *The Vampire Diaries: The Fury* by L. J. Smith. HarperTeen (21,301).

134. *Go, Dog. Go!* by P. D. Eastman. Random House.

135. *The Death of Joan of Arc* (Secrets of the Immortal Nicholas Flamel) by Michael Scott. Delacorte.

136. *Scorpia Rising* by Anthony Horowitz. Philomel.

137. *The Magician's Nephew* by C. S. Lewis, illustrated by Pauline Baynes. HarperCollins (20,532).

138. *The Summer I Turned Pretty* by Jenny Han. Simon & Schuster (20,163).

139. *Junie B., First Grader: Jingle Bells, Batman Smells! (P.S. So Does May)* (JBJ No. 25) by Barbara Park, illustrated by Denise Brunkus. Random House.

140. *Dragon's Oath* (House of Night No. 10) by P. C. and Kristin Cast. St. Martin's (20,000).

141. *The Alchemyst* (Secrets of the Immortal Nicholas Flamel No. 1) by Michael Scott. Delacorte.

142. *Because of Winn-Dixie* by Kate DiCamillo. Candlewick (19,768).

143. *Uglies* by Scott Westerfield. Simon Pulse (19,129).

144. *Artemis Fowl* by Eoin Colfer. Disney-Hyperion (18,712).

145. *It's Not Summer Without You* by Jenny Han. Simon & Schuster (18,587).

146. *The Magician's Elephant* by Kate DiCamillo, illustrated by Yoko Tanaka. Candlewick (18,460).

147. *Percy Jackson: The Demigod Files* by Rick Riordan. Disney-Hyperion (18,421).

148. *Halt's Peril* (Ranger's Apprentice No. 9) by John Flanagan. Philomel.

149. *The Last Little Blue Envelope* by Maureen Johnson. HarperTeen (18,237).

150. *The Burning Bridge* (Ranger's Apprentice No. 2) by John Flanagan. Puffin.

151. *Sign of the Moon* (Warriors: Omen of the Stars No. 4) by Erin Hunter. HarperCollins (18,173).

152. *Sugar and Spice: An L.A. Candy Novel* by Lauren Conrad. HarperCollins (18,135).

153. *Gregor and the Prophecy of Bane* (Underland Chronicles No. 2) by Suzanne Collins. Scholastic (18,105).

154. *The Boxcar Children* by Gertrude Chandler Warner. Albert Whitman/Open Road (17,697).

155. *Gone* by Michael Grant. HarperCollins/Tegen (17,329).

156. *Bloody Valentine: A Blue Bloods Novel* by Melissa de la Cruz. Disney-Hyperion (17,270).

157. *Middle School, the Worst Years of My Life* by James Patterson and Chris Tebbetts. Little, Brown (17,246).

158. *The Necromancer* (Secrets of the Immortal Nicholas Flamel No. 4) by Michael Scott. Delacorte.

159. *Red Riding Hood* by Catherine Hardwicke, Sarah Blakeley-Cartwright, and David Leslie Johnson. Little, Brown/Poppy (17,108).

160. *Kings of Clonmel* (Ranger's Apprentice No. 8) by John Flanagan. Puffin.

161. *The City of Ember* by Jeanne DuPrau. Random House.

162. *Island of the Blue Dolphins* by Scott O'Dell. Houghton Mifflin (16,812).

163. *The Icebound Land* (Ranger's Apprentice No. 3) by John Flanagan. Puffin.

164. *The Battle for Skandia* (Ranger's Apprentice No. 4) by John Flanagan. Puffin.

165. *Misguided Angel: A Blue Bloods Novel* by Melissa de la Cruz. Disney-Hyperion (16,425).

166. *Erak's Ransom* (Ranger's Apprentice No. 7) by John Flanagan. Puffin.

167. *Plague: A Gone Novel* by Michael Grant. HarperCollins/Tegen (16,261).

168. *Daughter of Smoke and Bone* by Laini Taylor. Little, Brown (16,095).

169. *Gregor and the Curse of the Warmbloods* (Underland Chronicles No. 3) by Suzanne Collins. Scholastic (15,990).

170. *The Graveyard Book* by Neil Gaiman, illustrated by Dave McKean. HarperCollins (15,829).

171. *The Magician* (Secrets of the Immortal Nicholas Flamel No. 2) by Michael Scott. Delacorte.

172. *The Little Mermaid: A Special Song*. Disney (15,783).

173. *Into the Wild* (Warriors No. 1) by Erin Hunter. HarperCollins (15,778).

174. *The Sorcerer of the North* (Ranger's Apprentice No. 5) by John Flanagan. Puffin.

175. *Tangled*. Disney (15,591).

176. *Unwind* by Neal Shusterman. Simon & Schuster (15,569).

177. *Rapunzel's Tale*. Disney (15,441).

178. *The Sorceress* (Secrets of the Immortal Nicholas Flamel No. 3) by Michael Scott. Delacorte.

179. *Pretties* by Scott Westerfield. Simon Pulse (15,381).

180. *Lost in Time: A Blue Bloods Novel* by Melissa de la Cruz. Disney-Hyperion (15,322).

181. *The Vampire Diaries: Stefan's Diaries No. 1: Origin* by L. J. Smith. HarperTeen (15,251).

182. *The Siege of Macindaw* (Ranger's Apprentice No. 6) by John Flanagan. Puffin.

183. *Where She Went* by Gayle Forman. Dutton.

184. *Gregor and the Marks of Secret* (Underland Chronicles No. 4) by Suzanne Collins. Scholastic (15,164).

185. *Gregor and the Code of Claw* (Underland Chronicles No. 5) by Suzanne Collins. Scholastic (15,110).

186. *Tamar* by Mal Peet. Candlewick (15,073).

187. *Fallout* by Ellen Hopkins. Simon & Schuster/McElderry (15,068).

188. *Infinity* (Chronicles of Nick No. 1) by Sherrilyn Kenyon. St. Martin's (15,000).

189. *Number the Stars* by Lois Lowry. Houghton Mifflin (14,936).

190. *Bridge to Terabithia* by Katherine Paterson, illustrated by Donna Diamond. HarperCollins (14,821).

191. *L.A. Candy* by Lauren Conrad. HarperCollins (14,744).

192. *The Vampire Diaries: Stefan's Diaries No. 2: Bloodlust* by L. J. Smith. HarperTeen (14,605).

193. *Illusions* by Aprilynne Pike. HarperTeen (14,547).

194. *The Carrie Diaries* by Candace Bushnell. HarperCollins/Balzer + Bray (14,313).

195. *Beautiful Darkness* (Caster Chronicles No. 2) by Kami Garcia and Margaret Stohl. Little, Brown (14,206).

196. *Clockwork Prince* (Infernal Devices No. 2) by Cassandra Clare. Simon & Schuster/McElderry (14,195).

197. *Twenty Boy Summer* by Sarah Ockler. Little, Brown (14,180).

198. *Darke* (Septimus Heap No. 6) by Angie Sage, illustrated by Mark Zug. HarperCollins/Tegen (14,158).

199. *The Forgotten Warrior* (Warriors: Omen of the Stars No. 5) by Erin Hunter. HarperCollins (14,143).

200. *Darkest Mercy* by Melissa Marr. HarperCollins (14,039).

201. *Blue Bloods* by Melissa de la Cruz. Disney-Hyperion (13,992).

202. *The Bad Beginning* (A Series of Unfortunate Events No. 1) by Lemony Snicket, illustrated by Brett Helquist. HarperCollins (13,967).

203. *Looking for Alaska* by John Green. Penguin/Speak.

204. *Pathfinder* by Orson Scott Card. Simon Pulse (13,736).

205. *The Gathering* by Kelley Armstrong. HarperCollins (13,612).

206. *Entwined* by Heather Dixon. Greenwillow (13,519).

207. *The Golden Compass* (His Dark Materials No. 1) by Philip Pullman. Knopf.

208. *Eve of the Emperor Penguin* (MTH No. 40) by Mary Pope Osborne, illustrated by Sal Murdocca. Random House.

209. *The Phantom Tollbooth* by Norton Juster, illustrated by Jules Feiffer. Knopf.

210. *The Lost Stories* by John Flanagan. Philomel.

211. *Night Whispers* (Warriors: Omen of the Stars No. 3) by Erin Hunter. HarperCollins (13,071).

212. *Fire and Ice* (Warriors: No. 2) by Erin Hunter. HarperCollins (12,952).

213. *Ten Things We Did (and Probably Shouldn't Have)* by Sarah Mlynowski. HarperTeen (12,712).

214. *Nine Lives of Chloe King* by Liz Braswell. Simon Pulse (12,638).

215. *Demonglass: A Hex Hall Novel* by Rachel Hawkins. Disney-Hyperion (12,636).

216. *Along for the Ride* by Sarah Dessen. Penguin/Speak.
217. *Ramona Quimby, Age 8* by Beverly Cleary, illustrated by Tracy Dockray. HarperCollins (12,447).
218. *The Atlantis Complex* (Artemis Fowl No. 7) by Eoin Colfer. Disney-Hyperion (12,387).
219. *Specials* by Scott Westerfield. Simon Pulse (12,345).
220. *Flyte* (Septimus Heap No. 2) by Angie Sage. HarperCollins/Tegen (12,339).
221. *Spells* by Aprilynne Pike. HarperCollins (12,329).
222. *Hunger: A Gone Novel* by Michael Grant. HarperCollins/Tegen (12,254).
223. *The People of Sparks* (Books of Ember No. 2) by Jeanne DuPrau. Random House.
224. *Justin Bieber: First Step 2 Forever* by Justin Bieber. HarperCollins (12,179).
225. *Frindle* by Andrew Clements. Atheneum (12,053).
226. *Born at Midnight* (A Shadow Falls No. 1) by C. C. Hunter. St. Martin's (12,000).
227. *Life as We Knew It* by Susan Beth Pfeffer. Harcourt. (11,991).
228. *The Twilight Saga: The Official Illustrated Guide* by Stephenie Meyer. Little, Brown (11,961).
229. *When You Reach Me* by Rebecca Stead. Random House/Lamb.
230. *Lies: A Gone Novel* by Michael Grant. HarperCollins/Tegen (11,744).
231. *Beautiful Chaos* (Caster Chronicles No. 3) by Kami Garcia and Margaret Stohl. Little, Brown (11,713).
232. *Are You My Mother?* by P. D. Eastman. Random House.
233. *Sweet Little Lies: An L.A. Candy Novel* by Lauren Conrad. HarperCollins (11,663).
234. *Two-Way Street* by Lauren Barnholdt. Simon Pulse (11,647).
235. *Cars: Friday Night Fun.* Disney (11,600).
236. *The Voyage of the Dawn Treader* by C. S. Lewis, illustrated by Pauline Baynes. HarperCollins (11,600).
237. *Big Egg* by Molly Coxe. Random House.
238. *Ink Exchange* by Melissa Marr. HarperCollins (11,526).
239. *World Without Heroes* (Beyonders No. 1) by Brandon Mull. Simon & Schuster/Aladdin (11,471).
240. *The Van Alen Legacy: A Blue Bloods Novel* by Melissa de la Cruz. Disney-Hyperion (11,452).
241. *The Vampire Diaries: The Return: Nightfall* by L. J. Smith. HarperTeen (11,447).
242. *Someone Like You* by Sarah Dessen. Penguin/Speak.
243. *Never Glue Your Friends to Chairs* (Roscoe Riley Rules No. 1) by Katherine Applegate, illustrated by Brian Biggs. HarperCollins (11,427).
244. *Crookedstar's Promise* (Warriors Super Edition) by Erin Hunter. HarperCollins (11,376).
245. *Crank* by Ellen Hopkins. Simon & Schuster/McElderry (11,247).

246. *Dreamland* by Sarah Dessen. Penguin/Speak.
247. *Stormbreaker* (Alex Rider No. 1) by Anthony Horowitz. Puffin.
248. *Wolfsbane* (Nightshade No. 2) by Andrea Cremer. Philomel.
249. *The Gray Wolf Throne: A Seven Realms Novel* by Cinda Williams Chima. Disney-Hyperion (11,002).
250. *Racing in the Rain* by Garth Stein. HarperCollins (10,955).
251. *Tuck Everlasting* by Natalie Babbitt. Macmillan (10,876).
252. *Nightshade* by Andrea Cremer. Penguin/Speak.
253. *The Body Finder* by Kimberly Derting. HarperCollins (10,667).
254. *Found* (The Missing No. 1) by Margaret Peterson Haddix. Simon & Schuster (10,635).
255. *Among the Hidden* (Shadow Children No. 1) by Margaret Peterson Haddix. Simon & Schuster (10,519).
256. *A Tale of Two Pretties* (Clique No. 14) by Lisi Harrison. Little, Brown/Poppy (10,489).
257. *Unearthly* by Cynthia Hand. HarperTeen (10,448).
258. *The Westing Game* by Ellen Raskin. Puffin.
259. *Forest of Secrets* (Warriors No. 3) by Erin Hunter. HarperCollins (10,419).
260. *Mastiff* (Beka Cooper No. 3) by Tamora Pierce. Random House.
261. *Judy Moody Gets Famous* by Megan McDonald, illustrated by Peter H. Reynolds. Candlewick (10,362).
262. *Virals* by Kathy Reichs. Penguin/Razorbill.
263. *The Truth About Forever* by Sarah Dessen. Penguin/Speak.
264. *Go Ask Alice* by Anonymous. Simon Pulse (10,257).
265. *Splat the Cat and the Duck with No Quack* by Rob Scotton. HarperCollins (10,236).
266. *The Knight at Dawn* (MTH No. 2) by Mary Pope Osborne, illustrated by Sal Murdocca. Random House.
267. *Hoot* by Carl Hiaasen. Knopf.
268. *This Lullaby* by Sarah Dessen. Penguin/Speak.
269. *Prince Caspian* by C. S. Lewis, illustrated by Pauline Baynes. HarperCollins (10,192).
270. *Holes* by Louis Sachar. Random House/Yearling.
271. *The Subtle Knife* (His Dark Materials No. 2) by Philip Pullman. Knopf.
272. *Hex Hall* by Rachel Hawkins. Disney-Hyperion (10,163).
273. *The Amber Spyglass* (His Dark Materials No. 3) by Philip Pullman. Knopf.
274. *Beezus and Ramona* by Beverly Cleary, illustrated by Tracy Dockray. HarperCollins (10,129).
275. *Tonight on the Titanic* (MTH No. 17) by Mary Pope Osborne, illustrated by Sal Murdocca. Random House.
276. *Masquerade: A Blue Bloods Novel* by Melissa de la Cruz. Disney-Hyperion (10,095).

277. *Dolphins at Daybreak* (MTH No. 9) by Mary Pope Osborne, illustrated by Sal Murdocca. Random House.
278. *Gathering Blue* by Lois Lowry. Houghton Mifflin (10,084).
279. *Speak* by Laurie Halse Anderson. Macmillan (10,072).
280. *Uncommon Criminals: A Heist Society Novel* by Ally Carter. Disney-Hyperion (10,063).
281. *Stink: The Incredible Shrinking Kid* by Megan McDonald, illustrated by Peter H. Reynolds. Candlewick (10,055).
282. *Kingdom Keepers: Disney After Dark* by Ridley Pearson. Disney-Hyperion (10,052).
283. *Monster High* by Lisi Harrison. Little, Brown/Poppy (10,050).
284. *The Warrior Heir* by Cinda Williams Chima. Disney-Hyperion (10,029).
285. *Flush* by Carl Hiaasen. Knopf.
286. *Shadowspell* (Faeriewalker No. 2) by Jenna Black. St. Martin's (10,000).

Literary Prizes, 2011

Compiled by the staff of the *Library and Book Trade Almanac*

Jane Addams Children's Book Awards. For children's books that effectively promote the cause of peace, social justice, world community, and equality. *Offered by:* Women's International League for Peace and Freedom and the Jane Addams Peace Association. *Winners:* (younger children) Linda Glaser and Claire A. Nivola, illustrator, for *Emma's Poem: The Voice of the Statue of Liberty* (Houghton Mifflin); (older children) Linda Sue Park for *A Long Walk to Water* (Clarion).

Aesop Prize. For outstanding work in children's folklore, both fiction and nonfiction. *Offered by:* American Folklore Society. *Winner:* Matt Dembicki, editor, for *Trickster: Native American Tales, A Graphic Collection* (Fulcrum).

Agatha Awards. For mystery novels written in the method exemplified by author Agatha Christie. *Offered by:* Malice Domestic Ltd. *Winners:* (novel) Louise Penny for *Bury Your Dead* (Minotaur); (best first novel) Avery Aames for *The Long Quiche Goodbye* (Berkley); (nonfiction) John Curran for *Agatha Christie's Secret Notebooks: 50 Years of Mysteries in the Making* (HarperCollins); (short story) Mary Jane Maffini for "So Much in Common" in *Ellery Queen Mystery Magazine*; (children's/young adult) Sarah Smith for *The Other Side of Dark* (Atheneum).

Alex Awards. To the authors of ten books published for adults that have high potential appeal to teenagers. *Sponsor:* Margaret Alexander Edwards Trust and *Booklist.* Winners: DC Pierson for *The Boy Who Couldn't Sleep and Never Had To* (Vintage); Liz Murray for *Breaking Night: A Memoir of Forgiveness, Survival, and My Journey from Homeless to Harvard* (Hyperion); Jean Kwok for *Girl in Translation* (Riverhead); Peter Bognanni for *The House of Tomorrow* (Putnam); Steve Hamilton for *The Lock Artist* (St. Martin's); Aimee Bender for *The Particular Sadness of Lemon Cake* (Doubleday); Matt Haig for *The Radleys* (Simon & Schuster); Alden Bell for *The Reapers Are the Angels* (Holt);

Emma Donoghue for *Room* (Little, Brown); Helen Grant for *The Vanishing of Katharina Linden* (Delacorte).

Ambassador Book Awards: To honor an exceptional contribution to the interpretation of life and culture in the United States. *Offered by:* English-Speaking Union of the United States. *Winners:* Rebecca Skloot for *The Immortal Life of Henrietta Lacks* (Crown); Alan Brinkley for *The Publisher: Henry Luce and His American Century* (Knopf); Christian Wiman for *Every Riven Thing* (Farrar, Straus & Giroux); Deborah Eisenberg for *Collected Stories of Deborah Eisenberg* (Picador); (special distinction) Tony Judt (posthumously) for *The Memory Chalet* (Penguin); (lifetime achievement) Janet Malcolm.

American Academy of Arts and Letters Award of Merit ($10,000). To an American author of novels, poetry, short stories, or drama. *Offered by:* American Academy of Arts and Letters. *Winner:* playwright John Patrick Shanley.

American Academy of Arts and Letters Awards in Literature ($7,500). To honor writers of fiction and nonfiction, poets, dramatists, and translators of exceptional accomplishment. *Offered by:* American Academy of Arts and Letters. *Winners:* Mark Doty, Alice Fulton, John Koethe, Colum McCann, Suzan-Lori Parks, Alex Ross, Leslie Marmon Silko, Joseph Stroud.

American Academy of Arts and Letters Award of Merit Medal for Drama ($10,000) To an outstanding playwright. *Winner:* John Patrick Shanley.

American Academy of Arts and Letters Rome Fellowships. For a one-year residency at the American Academy in Rome for young writers of promise. *Offered by:* American Academy of Arts and Letters. *Winners:* Matt Donovan, Suzanne Rivecca.

American Book Awards. For literary achievement by people of various ethnic backgrounds. *Offered by:* Before Columbus Foundation. *Winners:* Keith Gilyard for *John Oliver Killens: A Life of Black Liter-*

ary Activism (University of Georgia Press); Akbar Ahmed for *Journey Into America* (Brookings Institution); Camille Dungy for *Suck on the Marrow* (Red Hen); Karen Tei Yamashita for *I Hotel* (Coffee House); William W. Cook and James Tatum for *African American Writers and Classical Tradition* (University of Chicago Press); Gerald Vizenor for *Shrouds of White Earth* (SUNY Press); Eric Gansworth for *Extra Indians* (Milkweed); Ivan Arguelles for *The Death of Stalin* (Beatitude); Geoffrey Alan Argent for *The Complete Plays of Jean Racine: The Fratricides* (Penn State University Press); Neela Vaswani for *You Have Given Me a Country* (Sarabande); Sasha Pimentel Chacon for *Insides She Swallowed* (West End); Miriam Jimenez Roman and Juan Flores for *The Afro-Latin@ Reader: History of Culture in the United States* (Duke University Press); Carmen Gimenez Smith for *Bring Down the Little Birds* (University of Arizona Press); (lifetime achievement) John A. Williams, Luis Valdez.

American Indian Youth Literature Awards. Offered biennially to recognize excellence in books by and about American Indians. *Offered by:* American Indian Library Association. *Winners:* To be awarded next in 2012.

American Poetry Review/Honickman First Book Prize in Poetry ($3,000). To encourage excellence in poetry and to provide a wide readership for a deserving first book of poems. *Winner:* Nathaniel Perry for *Nine Acres* (American Poetry Review).

Américas Book Award for Children's and Young Adult Literature. To recognize U.S. works of fiction, poetry, folklore, or selected nonfiction that authentically and engagingly portray Latin America, the Caribbean, or Latinos in the United States. *Sponsored by:* Consortium of Latin American Studies Programs (CLASP). *Winners:* Willie Perdomo and Bryan Collier, illustrator, for *Clemente!* (Holt); Pam Muñoz Ryan and Peter Sís, illustrator, for *The Dreamer* (Scholastic).

Rudolfo and Patricia Anaya Premio Aztlan Literary Prize ($1,000 and a lectureship). To honor a Chicano or Chicana fiction writer who has published no more than two books. *Offered by:* University of New Mexico. *Winner:* Denise Chávez.

Hans Christian Andersen Awards. Awarded biennially to an author and an illustrator whose body of work has made an important and lasting contribution to children's literature. *Offered by:* International Board on Books for Young People (IBBY). *Sponsor:* Nami Island, Inc. *Winners:* To be awarded next in 2012.

Hans Christian Andersen Literature Award (500,000 Danish kroner, about $90,000). To a writer whose work can be compared with that of Andersen. *Offered by:* Hans Christian Andersen Literary Committee. *Winner:* Isabel Allende.

Anthony Awards. For superior mystery writing. *Offered by:* Boucheron World Mystery Convention. *Winners:* (novel) Louise Penny for *Bury Your Dead* (Minotaur); (first novel) Hilary Davidson for *The Damage Done* (Forge); (paperback original) Duane Swierczynski for *Expiration Date* (Minotaur); (short story) Dana Cameron for "Swing Shift" in *Crimes By Moonlight: Mysteries from the Dark Side* (Berkley); (graphic novel) Jason Starr for *The Chill* (Vertigo); (critical nonfiction) John Curran for *Agatha Christie's Secret Notebooks: 50 Years of Mysteries in the Making* (HarperCollins).

Asian American Literary Awards. To Asian American writers for excellence in poetry, fiction, and creative nonfiction. *Sponsor:* Asian American Writers' Workshop. *Winners:* (fiction) Yiyun Li for *Gold Boy, Emerald Girl* (Random); (nonfiction) Amitava Kurman for *A Foreigner Carrying in the Crook of His Arm, a Bomb* (Duke University Press); (poetry) Kimiko Hahn for *Toxic Flora* (Norton).

Asian/Pacific American Awards for Literature. For books that promote Asian/Pacific American culture and heritage. *Sponsor:* Asian/Pacific American Librarians Association (APALA). *Winners:* (2010–2011) (picture book) Ann Malaspina and Doug Chayka, illustrator, for *Yasmin's Hammer* (Lee and Low); (children's literature) Margi Preus for *Heart of a Samurai* (Abrams); (young adult) N. H. Senzai for *Shooting Kabul* (Simon & Schuster); (adult fiction) Karen Tei Yamashita for *I Hotel* (Coffee House); (adult nonfiction) Erika Lee and Judy Yung for *Angel Island: Immigration Gateway to America* (Oxford University Press).

Audio Publishers Association awards (Audies). To recognize excellence in audiobooks. *Winners:* (audiobook of the year and biography/memoir) *Life* by Keith Richards, read by Richards, Johnny Depp, and Joe Hurley (Hachette Audio); (drama) George Bernard Shaw's *Saint Joan: A Chronicle Play in Six Scenes and an Epilogue,* read by Amy Irving, Edward Herrmann, Stefan Rudnicki, and others (Blackstone); (audiobook adaptation) *No Country for Old Men* by Cormac McCarthy, read by Sean Barrett (Naxos); (business/educational) *The Intelligent Entrepreneur* by Bill Murphy, Jr., read by L. J. Ganser and Fred Berman (Audible); (children's, up to age 8) *This Jazz Man* by Karen Ehrhardt, read by James "D Train" Williams (Live Oak); (children's, ages 8–12) *The Evolution of Calpurnia Tate* by Jacqueline Kelly, read by Natalie Ross (Brilliance); (classics) *The Woman in White* by Wilkie Collins, read by Roger Rees, Rosalyn Landor, John Lee, and Judy Geeson (Blackstone); (distinguished achievement in production) *Here in Harlem: Poems in Many Voices* by Walter Dean Myers, read by Muhammad Cunningham, Michael Early, Patricia R. Floyd, Kevin R. Free, Arthur French, Dion Graham, Nathan Hinton, Ezra Knight, Robin Miles, Lizan Mitchell, Gail Nelson, Monica Patton, and Charles Turner (Live Oak); (fiction) *Winter's Bone* by Daniel Woodrell, read by Emma Galvin (Hachette); (history) *Empire of Liberty: A History of the Early Republic* by Gordon S. Wood, read by Robert Fass (Audible); (humor) *Old Jews Telling Jokes: 5,000 Years of Funny Bits and Not-So-Kosher Laughs* by Sam Hoffman and Eric Spiegelman, read by Sam Hoffman, Eric Spiegelman, and others (HighBridge); (inspirational/faith-based fiction) *Fireflies in December* by Jennifer Erin Valent, read by Kate Forbes (Recorded Books); (inspirational/faith-based nonfiction) *In a Heartbeat* by Leigh Anne Tuohy and Sean Tuohy, with Sally Jenkins, read by Leigh Anne Tuohy, Sean Tuohy, and others (Macmillan); (judges' award—paranormal) *Beautiful Creatures* by Kami Garcia and Margaret Stohl, read by Kevin T. Collins (Hachette); (literary fiction) *Snakewoman of Little Eqypt* by Robert Hellenga, read by Coleen Marlo (Tantor); (multi-voiced performance) *Jit-* *ters: A Quirky Little Audio Book* by Adele Park, read by a full cast (Straight to Audio); (mystery and suspense) *The Reversal* by Michael Connelly, read by Peter Giles (Hachette); (narration by the author) *Nanny McPhee Returns* by Emma Thompson (Macmillan); (nonfiction) *The Immortal Life of Henrietta Lacks* by Rebecca Skloot, read by Cassandra Campbell and Bahni Turpin (Random); (original work) *The New Adventures of Mickey Spillane's Mike Hammer, Vol. 2: The Little Death* by Mickey Spillane and Max Allan Collins, read by Stacy Keach and others (Blackstone); (science fiction/fantasy) *The Stainless Steel Rat* by Harry Harrison, read by Phil Gigante (Brilliance); (short stories/collections) *Stories* by Neil Gaiman and Al Sarrantonio, editors, and Joe Hill, Lawrence Block, Carolyn Parkhurst, Joanne Harris, and others, read by Anne Bobby, Jonathan Davis, Peter Francis James, Katherine Kellgren, and Euan Morton (Harper); (solo narration—female) *Glorious* by Bernice L. McFadden, read by Alfre Woodard (Audible); (solo narration—male) *Zorgamazoo* by Robert Paul Weston, read by Alan Cumming (Penguin); (teens) *The Rock and the River* by Kekla Magoon, read by Dion Graham (Brilliance); (thriller/suspense) *The Girl Who Kicked the Hornet's Nest* by Stieg Larsson, read by Simon Vance (Random); (package design) *The Very Best of Bob and Ray: Legends of Comedy* (HighBridge).

Bad Sex in Fiction Award (United Kingdom). *Sponsor: Literary Review. Winner:* David Guterson for *Ed King,* a modern version of the fable of Oedipus (Knopf).

Bakeless Literary Publication Prizes (publication by Graywolf and fellowships to attend the 2012 Bread Loaf Writers' Conference). For promising new writers. *Offered by:* Bread Loaf Writers' Conference of Middlebury College. *Winners:* (fiction) Ted Sanders for *No Animals We Could Name*; (creative nonfiction) Carmen Bugan for *Burying the Typewriter*; (poetry) Jo Sarzotti for *Mother Desert.*

Bancroft Prizes ($10,000). For books of exceptional merit and distinction in American history, American diplomacy, and the international relations of the United States. *Offered by:* Columbia University. *Winners:* Sara Dubow for *Ourselves Unborn: A Histo-*

ry of the Fetus in Modern America (Oxford University Press); Eric Foner for *The Fiery Trial: Abraham Lincoln and American Slavery* (Norton); Christopher Tomlins for *Freedom Bound: Law, Labor, and Civic Identity in Colonizing English America* (Cambridge University Press).

Barnes & Noble Discover Great New Writers Awards. To honor a first novel and a first work of nonfiction by American authors. *Offered by:* Barnes & Noble. *Winners:* (fiction) Kim Echlin for *The Disappeared* (Hamish Hamilton Canada); (nonfiction) David R. Dow for *The Autobiography of an Execution* (Twelve).

Mildred L. Batchelder Award. For an American publisher of a children's book originally published in a language other than English and subsequently published in English in the United States. *Offered by:* American Library Association, Association for Library Service to Children. *Winner:* Delacorte for *A Time of Miracles* by Anne-Laure Bondoux, translated by Y. Maudet.

BBC National Short Story Award (£15,000). *Winner:* D. W. Wilson for "The Dead Roads."

Beacon of Freedom Award. For the best title introducing American history, from colonial times through the Civil War, to young readers. *Offered by:* Williamsburg (Virginia) Regional Library and the Colonial Williamsburg Foundation. *Winner:* Ken Stark for *Marching to Appomattox* (Putnam).

Pura Belpré Awards. To a Latino/Latina writer and illustrator whose work portrays, affirms, and celebrates the Latino cultural experience in an outstanding work of literature for children and youth. *Offered by:* American Library Association, Association for Library Service to Children. *Winners:* Pam Muñoz Ryan for *The Dreamer,* illustrated by Peter Sís (Scholastic); (illustrator) Eric Velasquez for *Grandma's Gift* (Walker).

Curtis Benjamin Award. To an outstanding individual within the U.S. publishing industry who has shown exceptional innovation and creativity in the field of publishing. *Offered by:* Association of American Publishers. *Winner:* Not awarded in 2011.

Helen B. Bernstein Award ($15,000). To a journalist who has written at book length about an issue of contemporary concern. *Offered by:* New York Public Library. *Winner:* Shane Harris for *The Watchers: The Rise of America's Surveillance State* (Penguin).

Black Caucus of the American Library Association (BCALA) Literary Awards. *Winners:* (fiction) Bernice L. McFadden for *Glorious* (Akashic); (nonfiction) Wes Moore for *The Other Wes Moore: One Name, Two Fates* (Random); (first novelist award) Dolen Perkins-Valdez for *Wench* (HarperCollins); (outstanding contribution to publishing citation) Harold Battiste, Jr. and Karen Celestan for *Unfinished Blues: Memories of a New Orleans Music Man* (Historic New Orleans Collection).

Irma Simonton Black and James H. Black Award for Excellence in Children's Literature. To a book for young children in which the text and illustrations work together to create an outstanding whole. *Offered by:* Bank Street College of Education. *Winner:* Tad Hills for *How Rocket Learned to Read* (Random).

James Tait Black Memorial Prize (United Kingdom) (£10,000). To recognize literary excellence in biography and fiction. *Offered by:* University of Edinburgh. *Winners:* (fiction) Tatjani Soli for *The Lotus Eaters* (St. Martin's); (biography) Hilary Spurling for *Burying the Bones: Pearl Buck in China* (Profile).

Blue Peter Book of the Year (United Kingdom). To recognize excellence in children's books. *Winner:* Lauren St John for *Dead Man's Cove* (Orion).

Rebekah Johnson Bobbitt National Prize for Poetry ($10,000). *Offered biennially by:* Library of Congress. *Winner:* To be awarded next in 2012.

Bookseller/Diagram Prize for Oddest Title of the Year *Sponsor: The Bookseller* magazine. *Winner: Managing a Dental Practice the Genghis Khan Way* by Michael R. Young (Radcliffe).

BookSense Book of the Year Awards. See Indies Choice Book Awards.

Booktrust Teenage Prize (United Kingdom) (£2,500). *Offered by:* Booktrust. *Winner:* Not awarded in 2011.

Boston Globe/Horn Book Awards. For excellence in children's literature. *Winners:* (fiction) Tim Wynne-Jones for *Blink and Caution* (Candlewick); (nonfiction) Steve

Sheinkin for *The Notorious Benedict Arnold: A True Story of Adventure, Heroism, and Treachery* (Roaring Brook); (picture book) Salley Mayor for *Pocketful of Posies: A Treasury of Nursery Rhymes* (Houghton).

W. Y. Boyd Literary Award ($5,000). For a military novel that honors the service of American veterans during a time of war. *Offered by:* American Library Association. *Donor:* W. Y. Boyd II. *Winner:* Karl Marlantes for *Matterhorn, a Novel of the Vietnam War* (Atlantic Monthly).

Branford Boase Award (United Kingdom). To the author and editor of an outstanding novel for young readers by a first-time writer. *Winners:* Jason Wallace and Charlie Sheppard, editor, for *Out of Shadows* (Andersen).

Michael Braude Award for Light Verse ($5,000). *Offered biennially by:* American Academy of Arts and Letters. *Winner:* To be awarded next in 2012.

Bridport International Creative Writing Prizes (United Kingdom). For poetry and short stories. *Offered by:* Bridport Arts Centre. *Winners:* (short story, first place, £5,000) Kitty Aldridge for "Arrivederci Les"; (poetry, first place, £5,000) Terry Jones for "Endowments"; (flash fiction—250 word maximum—first place, £1,000) Becky Tipper for "Meeting the Lobster."

British Fantasy Awards (United Kingdom). *Offered by:* British Fantasy Society. *Winners:* (novel—August Derleth Fantasy Award) Sam Stone for *Demon Dance* (House of Murky Depths); (novella) Simon Clark for *Humpty's Bones* (Telos); (short story) Sam Stone for "Fool's Gold" in *The Bitten Word* (NewCon); (collection) Stephen King for *Full Dark, No Stars* (Hodder & Stoughton); (anthology) Johnny Mains, editor, for *Back From The Dead: The Legacy of the Pan Book of Horror Stories* (Noose & Gibbet); (nonfiction) Vincent Chong for *The Art of Vincent Chong* (Telos); (graphic novel) I. N. J. Culbard for *At the Mountains of Madness* (SelfMadeHero).

Sophie Brody Medal. For the U.S. author of the most distinguished contribution to Jewish literature for adults published in the preceding year. *Donors:* Arthur Brody and the Brodart Foundation. *Offered by:* Reference and User Services Association, American Library Association. *Winner:* Judith Shulev-

itz for *The Sabbath World: Glimpses of a Different Order of Time* (Random).

Caine Prize for African Writing (£10,000). For a short story by an African writer, published in English. *Winner:* NoViolet Bulawayo for her short story "Hitting Budapest" published in the *Boston Review,* vol. 35, no. 6.

Randolph Caldecott Medal. For the artist of the most distinguished picture book. *Offered by:* American Library Association, Association for Library Service to Children. *Winner:* Erin E. Stead for *A Sick Day for Amos McGee,* written by Philip C. Stead (Roaring Brook).

California Book Awards. To California residents to honor books of fiction, nonfiction, and poetry published in the previous year. *Offered by:* Commonwealth Club of California. *Winners:* (poetry) Alexandra Teague for *Mortal Geography* (Persea); (nonfiction) Yunte Huang for *Charlie Chan* (Norton); (first fiction) Zachary Mason for *The Lost Books of the Odyssey* (Picador); (fiction) Karen Tei Yamashita for *I Hotel* (Coffee House); (juvenile) Cecil Castellucci for *Grandma's Gloves,* illustrated by Julia Denos (Candlewick); (young adult) Dana Reinhardt for *The Things a Brother Knows* (Wendy Lamb); (contribution to publishing) University of California Press Berkeley and Los Angeles for *Autobiography of Mark Twain, Volume 1*; (Californiana) Laura Cunningham for *A State of Change: Forgotten Landscapes of California* (Heyday).

John W. Campbell Award. For the best new science fiction or fantasy writer whose first work of science fiction or fantasy was published in a professional publication in the previous two years. *Offered by:* Dell Magazines. *Winner:* Lev Grossman.

John W. Campbell Memorial Award. For science fiction writing. *Offered by:* Center for the Study of Science Fiction. *Winner:* Ian McDonald for *The Dervish House* (Pyr).

Canadian Library Association Book of the Year for Children. *Sponsor:* Library Services Centre. *Winner:* Kenneth Oppel for *Half Brother* (HarperCollins).

Canadian Library Association Amelia Frances Howard-Gibbon Illustrator's Award. *Sponsor:* Library Services Centre. *Winner:* Marie-Louise Gay, writer and illustrator, for

Roslyn Rutabaga and the Biggest Hole on Earth! (Groundwood).

Canadian Library Association Young Adult Book Award. *Winner:* Kenneth Oppel for *Half Brother* (HarperCollins).

Center for Fiction Flaherty-Dunnan First Novel Prize ($10,000). *Offered by:* Center for Fiction, Mercantile Library of New York. *Winner:* Bonnie Nadzam for *Lamb* (Other).

Chicago Tribune Heartland Prize for Fiction ($7,500). *Offered by: Chicago Tribune. Winner:* Jonathan Franzen for *Freedom* (Farrar, Straus & Giroux).

Chicago Tribune Heartland Prize for Nonfiction ($7,500). *Offered by: Chicago Tribune. Winner:* Isabel Wilkerson for *The Warmth of Other Suns: The Epic of America's Great Migration* (Random).

Chicago Tribune Literary Prize. For a lifetime of literary achievement by an author whose body of work has had great impact on American society. *Offered by: Chicago Tribune. Winner:* Stephen Sondheim.

Chicago Tribune Nelson Algren Short Story Award ($5,000). For unpublished short fiction. *Offered by: Chicago Tribune. Winner:* Billy Lombardo for "Clover."

Chicago Tribune Young Adult Literary Prize. To recognize a distinguished literary career. *Winner:* Joan Bauer.

Children's Africana Book Awards. To recognize and encourage excellent children's books about Africa. *Offered by:* Outreach Council of the African Studies Association. *Winners:* Jen Cullerton Johnson and Sonia Lynn Sadler, illustrator, for *Seeds of Change: Planting a Path to Peace* (Lee & Low).

Children's Book Council of Australia Children's Book of the Year Awards. *Winners:* (older readers) Sonja Hartnett for *The Midnight Zoo* (Penguin); (younger readers) Isobelle Carmody for *The Red Wind* (Penguin); (early childhood) Jan Ormerod and Freya Blackwood, illustrator, for *Maudie and Bear* (Little Hare); (picture book—tie) Jeannie Baker for *Mirror* (Walker), Nicki Greenberg for *Hamlet* (Allen & Unwin); (Eve Pownall Award for Information Books) Ursula Dubosarsky and Tohby Riddle, illustrator, for *The Return of the Word Spy* (Penguin).

Children's Poet Laureate ($25,000). For lifetime achievement in poetry for children. Honoree holds the title for two years. *Offered by:* The Poetry Foundation. *Winner:* J. Patrick Lewis.

Cholmondeley Awards for Poets (United Kingdom) (£2,500). For a poet's body of work and contribution to poetry. *Winners:* Imtiaz Dharker, Michael Haslam, Lachlan Mackinnon.

CILIP Carnegie Medal (United Kingdom). For the outstanding children's book of the year. *Offered by:* CILIP: The Chartered Institute of Library and Information Professionals (formerly the Library Association). *Winner:* Patrick Ness for *Monsters of Men* (Walker).

CILIP Kate Greenaway Medal and Colin Mears Award (United Kingdom) (£5,000 plus £500 worth of books donated to a library of the winner's choice) For children's book illustration. *Offered by:* CILIP: The Chartered Institute of Library and Information Professionals. *Winner:* Grahame Baker-Smith for *FArTHER* (Templar).

Arthur C. Clarke Award (United Kingdom). For the best science fiction novel published in the United Kingdom. *Offered by:* British Science Fiction Association. *Winner:* Lauren Beukes for *Zoo City* (Angry Robot).

David Cohen Prize for Literature (United Kingdom) (£40,000). Awarded biennially to a living British writer, novelist, poet, essayist, or dramatist in recognition of an entire body of work written in the English language. *Offered by:* David Cohen Family Charitable Trust. *Winner:* Julian Barnes.

Matt Cohen Award: In Celebration of a Writing Life (Canada) (C$20,000). To a Canadian author whose life has been dedicated to writing as a primary pursuit, for a body of work. *Offered by:* Writers' Trust of Canada. *Sponsors:* Marla and David Lehberg. *Winner:* David Adams Richards.

Commonwealth Writers' Prize (United Kingdom). To reward and encourage new Commonwealth fiction and ensure that works of merit reach a wider audience outside their country of origin. *Offered by:* Commonwealth Institute. *Winners:* (best book) Aminatta Forna for *The Memory of Love* (Grove); (best first book) Craig Cliff for *A Man Melting* (Random); (short story) Philip Nash for "Rejoinder."

Olive Cook Prize. See Tom-Gallon Trust Award and Olive Cook Prize.

Cork City–Frank O'Connor Short Story Award (€35,000). An international award for a collection of short stories. *Offered by:* Munster Literature Centre, Cork, Ireland. *Sponsor:* Cork City Council. *Winner:* Edna O'Brien for *Saints and Sinners* (Faber).

Costa Book Awards (United Kingdom) (formerly Whitbread Book Awards). For literature of merit that is readable on a wide scale. *Offered by:* Booksellers Association of Great Britain and Costa Coffee (£5,000 plus an additional £25,000 for Book of the Year). *Winners:* (novel and Book of the Year) Andrew Miller for *Pure* (Sceptre); (first novel) Christie Watson for *Tiny Sunbirds Far Away* (Quercus); (biography) Matthew Hollis for *Now All Roads Lead to France: The Last Years of Edward Thomas* (Faber); (poetry) Carol Ann Duffy for *The Bees* (Picador); (children's) Moira Young for *Blood Red Road* (Marion Lloyd).

Crab Orchard Review Series in Poetry Open Competition. For poetry collections. *Winners:* (editor's selection) Amy Fleury for "Sympathetic Magic"; (first book award) Tyler Mills for "Tongue"; (open competition award) Jacob Shores-Arguello for "In the Absence of Clocks," Wally Swist for "Huang Po and the Dimensions of Love."

Crime Writers' Association (CWA) Dagger Awards (United Kingdom). *Winners:* (Gold Dagger, for outstanding achievement in the field of crime writing) Tom Franklin for *Crooked Letter, Crooked Letter* (Macmillan); (Ian Fleming Steel Dagger, £2,000) Steve Hamilton for *The Lock Artist* (Orion); (John Creasey New Blood Dagger, for a first book by a previously unpublished writer) S. J. Watson for *Before I Go to Sleep* (Doubleday); (International Dagger) Anders Roslund and Börge Hellström for *Three Seconds,* translated by Kari Dickson (Quercus); (Nonfiction Dagger) Douglas Starr for *The Killer of Little Shepherds: A True Crime Story and the Birth of Forensic Science* (Vintage); (Dagger in the Library, to the author of crime fiction whose work is currently giving the greatest enjoyment to library users) Mo Hayder; (Short Story Dagger) Phil Lovesey for "Homework"; (Debut Dagger, for an author who has not yet had a novel published commercially) Michele Rowe for "What Hidden Lies"; (Ellis Peters Historical

Award) Andrew Martin for *The Somme Stations* (Faber).

Roald Dahl Funny Prize (United Kingdom) (£2,500). *Offered by:* Booktrust. *Winners:* (ages 0–6) Peter Bently and Jim Field, illustrator, for *Cats Ahoy!* (Pan Macmillan Children's); (ages 7–14) Liz Pichon for *The Brilliant World of Tom Gates* (Scholastic).

Benjamin H. Danks Award ($20,000). To a promising young writer, playwright, or composer, in alternate years. *Offered by:* American Academy of Arts and Letters. *Winner:* (writer) Karen Russell.

Dartmouth Medal. For creating current reference works of outstanding quality and significance. *Donor:* Dartmouth College. *Winner: Encyclopedia of World Dress and Fashion* (Oxford University Press) and its companion online database, the Berg Fashion Library.

Derringer Awards. To recognize excellence in short crime and mystery fiction. *Sponsor:* Short Mystery Fiction Society. *Winners:* (flash story, up to 1,000 words—tie) Kathy Chencharik for "The Book Signing" in *Thin Ice: Crime Stories by New England Writers* (Level Best), Jane Hammons for "The Unknown Substance" in the online *A Twist of Noir*; (short story, 1,001–4,000 words) Michael J. Solender for "Pewter Badge" in *Yellow Mama* magazine; (long story, 4,001–8,000 words—tie) Sean Doolittle for "Care of the Circumcised Penis" in *Thuglit Presents: Blood, Guts & Whiskey* (Kensington) and B. K. Stevens for "Interpretation of Murder" in *Alfred Hitchcock Mystery Magazine*; (best novelette, 8,001–17,500 words) Art Taylor for "Rearview Mirror" in *Ellery Queen Mystery Magazine*.

Philip K. Dick Award. For a distinguished science fiction paperback published in the United States. *Sponsor:* Philadelphia Science Fiction Society and the Philip K. Dick Trust. *Winner:* Mark Hodder for *The Strange Affair of Spring Heeled Jack* (Pyr).

Dundee International Book Prize (Scotland) (£10,000). For an unpublished novel on any theme, in any genre. *Winner:* Simon Ashe-Browne for the thriller "Nothing Human Left," to be published by Cargo.

Dundee Picture Book Award (Scotland) (£1,000). To recognize excellence in storytelling for children. The winner is chosen by the schoolchildren of Dundee. *Winner:* Alex T. Smith for *Bella and Monty: A Hairy, Scary Night* (Hodder Children's).

Educational Writers' Award (United Kingdom) (£2,000). For noteworthy educational non-fiction for children. *Offered by:* Authors' Licensing and Collecting Society and Society of Authors. *Winner:* Stewart Ross for *Moon: Apollo 11 and Beyond—The Ultimate Guide to Our Nearest Neighbour* (Oxford University Press).

Margaret A. Edwards Award ($2,000). To an author whose book or books have provided young adults with a window through which they can view their world and which will help them to grow and to understand themselves and their role in society. *Donor: School Library Journal. Winner:* Sir Terry Pratchett, whose books include *The Amazing Maurice and His Educated Rodents* and *Small Gods* (both HarperCollins).

Encore Award (United Kingdom) (£10,000). Awarded for the best second novel of the previous two years. *Offered by:* Society of Authors. *Winner:* Adam Foulds for *The Quickening Maze* (Cape).

European Union Prize for Literature (€5,000). To recognize outstanding European writing. *Sponsors:* European Commission, European Booksellers Federation, European Writers' Council, Federation of European Publishers. The 2011 round of the competition involved writers from Bulgaria, the Czech Republic, Greece, Iceland, Latvia, Liechtenstein, Malta, Montenegro, Serbia, the Netherlands, Turkey and the United Kingdom. *Winners:* (Bulgaria) Kalin Terziyski for the short story "Is There Anybody to Love You?"; (Czech Republic) Tomáš Zmeškal for *A Love Letter in Cuneiform Script*; (Greece) Kostas Hatziantoniou for *Agrigento*; (Iceland) Ófeigur Sigurðsson for *Jon*; (Latvia) Inga Zolude for the collection of stories *A Solace for Adam's Tree*; (Liechtenstein) Iren Nigg for *Wording the Places Oneself*; (Malta) Immanuel Mifsud for *In the Name of the Father (and of the Son)*; (Montenegro) Andrej Nikolaidis for *The Son*; (the Netherlands) Rodaan Al Galidi for *The Autist and the Carrier-Pigeon*; (Serbia) Jelena Lengold for *Fairground Magician*; (Turkey) Ciler Ilhan for *Exile*; (United Kingdom) Adam Foulds for *The Quickening Maze* (Cape).

Fairfax Prize ($10,000). For a body of work that has "made significant contributions to American and international culture." *Sponsors:* Fairfax County (Virginia) Public Library Foundation and George Mason University. *Winner:* Amy Tan.

FIELD Poetry Prize ($1,000). For a book-length poetry collection. *Offered by: FIELD: Contemporary Poetry and Poetics. Winner:* Mark Neely for *Beasts of the Hill* (Oberlin College Press).

FIL Literary Award in Romance Languages (formerly the Juan Rulfo International Latin American and Caribbean Prize (Mexico) ($150,000). For lifetime achievement in any literary genre. *Offered by:* Juan Rulfo International Latin American and Caribbean Prize Committee. *Winner:* Fernando Vallejo.

Financial Times/Goldman Sachs Business Book of the Year Award (£30,000). To recognize books that provide compelling and enjoyable insight into modern business issues. *Winner:* Abhijit Banerjee and Esther Duflo for *Poor Economics* (PublicAffairs).

ForeWord Magazine Book of the Year Awards ($1,500). For independently published books. *Offered by: ForeWord* magazine. *Winners:* (fiction) Brian Doyle for *Mink River* (Oregon State University Press); (nonfiction) Veronica Kavass and Thomas Sanders, photographer, for *The Last Good War* (Welcome).

E. M. Forster Award ($20,000). To a young writer from England, Ireland, Scotland, or Wales, for a stay in the United States. *Offered by:* American Academy of Arts and Letters. *Winner:* Rachel Seiffert.

Forward Prizes (United Kingdom). For poetry. *Offered by: The Forward. Winners:* (best collection, £10,000), John Burnside for *Black Cat Bone* (Jonathan Cape); (Felix Dennis Prize for best first collection, £5,000) Rachel Boast for *Sidereal* (Picador); (best single poem, £1,000) R. F. Langley for "To a Nightingale" in *London Review of Books*, vol. 32, no. 22.

H. E. Francis Short Story Competition ($1,000). For an unpublished short story no more than 5,000 words in length. *Sponsors:* Ruth Hindman Foundation and English Department, University of Alabama, Huntsville. *Winner:*

Joanna Frieda Mulder for "This Will Be Our Year."

Josette Frank Award (formerly the Children's Book Award). For a work of fiction in which children or young people deal in a positive and realistic way with difficulties in their world and grow emotionally and morally. *Offered by:* Bank Street College of Education and the Florence M. Miller Memorial Fund. *Winner:* Sharon Draper for *Out of My Mind* (Athenaeum).

George Freedley Memorial Award. For the best English-language work about live theater published in the United States. *Offered by:* Theatre Library Association. *Winners:* James Shapiro for *Contested Will: Who Wrote Shakespeare?* (Simon & Schuster); (special jury prize) Stephen Sondheim for *Finishing the Hat: Collected Lyrics (1954– 1981) with Attendant Comments, Principles, Heresies, Grudges, Whines and Anecdotes.* (Knopf).

French-American Foundation Translation Prizes. For a translation or translations from French into English of works of fiction and nonfiction. *Offered by:* French-American Foundation. *Winners:* Mitzi Angel for *03* by Jean-Christophe Valtat (Farrar, Straus & Giroux); Lydia Davis for *Madame Bovary* by Gustave Flaubert (Viking/Penguin); Frederick Brown for *Letters from America* by Alexis de Tocqueville (Yale University Press); Jane MarieTodd for *Reading and Writing in Babylon* by Dominique Charpin (Harvard University Press).

Frost Medal. To recognize achievement in poetry over a lifetime. *Offered by:* Poetry Society of America. *Winner:* Charles Simic.

Lewis Galantière Award. A biennial award for a literary translation into English from any language other than German. *Offered by:* American Translators Association. *Winner:* To be awarded next in 2012.

Galaxy National Book Awards (United Kingdom). *Winners:* (Galaxy book of the year and More4 popular nonfiction book of the year) Caitlin Moran for *How to Be a Woman* (Harper Perennial); (Waterstone's UK author of the year) Alan Hollinghurst for *The Stranger's Child* (Picador); (Specsavers popular fiction book of the year) Dawn French for *A Tiny Bit Marvellous* (Penguin); (crime and thriller of the year) S. J. Watson for *Before I Go to Sleep* (Doubleday); (*Daily Telegraph* biography of the year) Claire Tomalin for *Charles Dickens* (Viking); (international author of the year) Jennifer Egan for *A Visit From the Goon Squad* (Corsair); (food and drink book of the year) Simon Hopkinson for *The Good Cook* (BBC Books); (WHSmith paperback of the year) Emma Donoghue for *Room* (Picador); (National Book Tokens Children's Book of the Year) Patrick Ness for *A Monster Calls* (Walker) (Audible.Co.UK audiobook of the year) *My Dear, I Wanted to Tell You* by Louisa Young, read by Dan Stevens (HarperAudio); (Galaxy new writer of the year) Sarah Winman for *When God was a Rabbit* (Bloomsbury USA); (outstanding achievement award) Jackie Collins.

Theodor Seuss Geisel Medal. For the best book for beginning readers. *Offered by:* American Library Association, Association for Library Service to Children. *Winners:* Kate DiCamillo, Alison McGhee, and Tony Fucile, illustrator, for *Bink and Gollie* (Candlewick).

David Gemmell Legend Award for Fantasy. For the best full-length fantasy novel published for the first time in English during the year of nomination. *Winners:* (Legend Award for best novel) Brandon Sanderson for *The Way of Kings* (Tor); (Morningstar Award for best newcomer) Darius Hinks for *Warrior Priest* (Black Library); (Ravenheart Award for best cover artist) Olof Erla Einarsdottir for *Power and Majesty* by Tansy Rayner Roberts (HarperCollins Australia).

Giller Prize (Canada). See Scotiabank Giller Prize.

Gival Press Novel Award ($3,000 and publication by Gival Press). *Winner:* Perry Glasser for *Riverton Noir.*

Giverny Award. For an outstanding children's science picture book. *Offered by:* 15 Degree Laboratory. *Winner:* Mary Ann Rodman and Tatjama Mai-Wyss, illustrator, for *A Tree for Emmy* (Peachtree).

Alexander Gode Medal. To an individual or institution for outstanding service to the translation and interpreting professions. *Offered by:* American Translators Association. *Winner:* Holly Mikkelson.

Goldberg Prize for Jewish Fiction by Emerging Writers ($2,500). To highlight new works by contemporary writers exploring Jewish themes. *Offered by:* Foundation for Jewish Culture. *Donor:* Samuel Goldberg and Sons Foundation. *Winner:* Sharon Pomerantz for *Rich Boy* (Twelve).

Golden Duck Awards for Excellence in Children's Science Fiction Literature. *Sponsored by:* Super-Con-Duck-Tivity. *Winners:* (picture book) Mac Bannett and Dan Santat, illustrator, for *Oh No, or How My Science Project Destroyed the World* (Hyperion); (Eleanor Cameron middle grades award) Pamela F. Service and Mike Gorman, illustrator, for *Alien Encounter* (Carolrhoda); (Hal Clement young adult award) Robert Sawyer for *www.Watch* (Ace).

Golden Kite Awards ($2,500). For children's books. *Offered by:* Society of Children's Book Writers and Illustrators. *Winners:* (fiction) Jennifer Holm for *Turtle in Paradise* (Random); (nonfiction) Tanya Lee Stone for *The Good, the Bad, and the Barbie* (Viking); (picture book text) Rukhsana Khan for *Big Red Lollipop* (Viking); (picture book illustration) Salley Mavor for *A Pocket Full of Posies* (Houghton Mifflin).

Governor General's Literary Awards (Canada) (C$25,000, plus C$3,000 to the publisher). For works, in English and in French, of fiction, nonfiction, poetry, drama, and children's literature, and for translation. *Offered by:* Canada Council for the Arts. *Winners:* (fiction, English) Patrick deWitt for *The Sisters Brothers* (Ecco); (fiction, French) Perrine Leblanc for *L'Homme-Blanc* (Gallimard); (nonfiction, English) Charles Foran for *Mordecai: The Life and Times* (Knopf Canada); (nonfiction, French) Georges Leroux for *Wanderer: Essai sur le Voyage d'Hiver de Franz Schubert* (Nota Bene); (children's text, English) Christopher Moore for *From Then to Now: A Short History of the World* (Tundra); (children's text, French) Martin Fournier for *Les Aventures de Radisson— L'Enfer Ne Brûle Pas* (Septentrion); (children's illustration, English) Cybèle Young for *Ten Birds* (Kids Can); (children's illustration, French) Caroline Merola for *Lili et les Poilus* (Héritage); (drama, English) Erin Shields for *If We Were Birds* (Playwrights Canada); (drama, French) Normand Chaurette for *Ce Qui Meurt en Dernier* (Leméac); (poetry, English) Phil Hall for *Killdeer* (Book Thug); (poetry, French) Louise Dupre

for *Plus Haut que les Flammes* (Noroît);. (translation, English) Donald Winkler for *Partita for Glenn Gould* (McGill-Queen's University Press); (translation, French) Maryse Warda for *Toxique: Ou l'Incident dans l'Autobus* (Dramaturges Éditeurs).

Dolly Gray Children's Literature Awards. Presented biennially for fiction or biographical children's books with positive portrayals of individuals with developmental disabilities. *Offered by:* Council for Exceptional Children, Division on Autism and Developmental Disabilities. *Winners:* (intermediate/young adult award) Kathryn Erskine for *Mocking Bird* (Penguin), Beverley Brenna for *Waiting for No One* (Red Deer); (picture book) Rebecca Elliott, author and illustrator, for *Just Because* (Lion Children's), Holly Robinson Peete and Ryan Elizabeth Peete (authors) and Shane W. Evans (illustrator) for *My Brother Charlie* (Scholastic).

Eric Gregory Awards (United Kingdom) (£4,200). For a published or unpublished collection by poets under the age of 30. *Winners:* Niall Campbell, Tom Chivers, Holly Hopkins, Martin Jackson, Kim Moore.

Griffin Poetry Prizes (Canada) (C$200,000 total). To a living Canadian poet or translator and a living poet or translator from any country, which may include Canada. *Offered by:* Griffin Trust. *Winners:* (international) Gjertrud Schnackenberg for *Heavenly Questions* (Farrar, Straus & Giroux); (Canadian) Dionne Brand for *Ossuaries* (McClelland and Stewart).

Gryphon Award ($1,000). To recognize a noteworthy work of fiction or nonfiction for younger children. *Offered by:* The Center for Children's Books. *Winner:* Mo Willems for *We Are in a Book!* (Hyperion).

Guardian Children's Fiction Prize (United Kingdom) (£1,500). For an outstanding children's or young adult novel. *Offered by:* The *Guardian*. *Winner:* Andy Mulligan for *Return to Ribblestrop* (Simon & Schuster).

Guardian First Book Award (United Kingdom) (£10,000). To recognize a first book. *Offered by:* The *Guardian*. *Winner:* Siddhartha Mukherjee for *The Emperor of All Maladies: A Biography of Cancer* (Scribner).

Dashiell Hammett Prize. For a work of literary excellence in the field of crime writing. *Offered by:* North American Branch, International Association of Crime Writers. *Winner:* Olen Steinhauer for *The Nearest Exit* (St. Martin's).

O. B. Hardison, Jr. Poetry Prize ($10,000). To a U.S. poet who has published at least one book in the past five years, and has made important contributions as a teacher, and is committed to furthering the understanding of poetry. *Offered by:* Folger Shakespeare Library. *Winner:* Award discontinued in 2009.

Harvey Awards. To recognize outstanding work in comics and sequential art. *Winners:* (syndicated strip or panel) Garry Trudeau for "Doonesbury" (Universal Press Syndicate); (online comics) Kate Beaton for "Hark! A Vagrant"; (writer) Roger Langridge for "Thor: The Mighty Avenger" (Marvel); (cover artist) Mike Mignola for "Hellboy" (Dark Horse).

R. R. Hawkins Award. For the outstanding professional/scholarly work of the year. *Offered by:* Association of American Publishers. *Winner:* McGraw-Hill Professional for *The Diffusion Handbook: Applied Solutions for Engineers.*

Anthony Hecht Poetry Prize ($3,000 and publication by Waywiser Press). For an unpublished first or second book-length poetry collection. *Winner:* Mark Kraushaar for *The Uncertainty Principle.*

Drue Heinz Literature Prize ($15,000 and publication by University of Pittsburgh Press). For short fiction. *Winner:* Shannon Cain for *The Necessity of Certain Behaviors.*

O. Henry Awards. See PEN/O. Henry Prize.

William Dean Howells Medal. In recognition of the most distinguished novel published in the preceding five years. *Offered by:* American Academy of Arts and Letters. *Winner:* To be awarded next in 2015.

Hugo Awards. For outstanding science fiction writing. *Offered by:* World Science Fiction Convention. *Winners:* (novel) Connie Willis for *Blackout* and *All Clear* (Random); (novella) Ted Chiang for *The Lifecycle of Software Objects* (Subterranean); (novelette) Allen M. Steele for *The Emperor of Mars* in *Asimov's,* June 2010; (short story) Mary Robinette Kowal for "For Want of a Nail" in *Asimov's,* September 2010; (best related work) Lynne M. Thomas and Tara O'Shea, editors, for *Chicks Dig Time Lords: A Celebration of Doctor Who by the Women Who Love It* (Mad Norwegian); (graphic story) Phil and Kaja Foglio and Cheyenne Wright for *Girl Genius, Volume 10: Agatha Heterodyne and the Guardian Muse* (Airship Entertainment); (John W. Campbell Award for best new writer) Lev Grossman.

Hurston/Wright Legacy Awards. To writers of African American descent for a book of fiction, a book of nonfiction, and a book of poetry. *Offered by:* Hurston/Wright Foundation. *Sponsor:* Busboys and Poets. *Winners:* (fiction) Danielle Evans for *Before You Suffocate Your Own Fool Self* (Riverhead); (nonfiction) Isabel Wilkerson for *The Warmth of Other Suns: The Epic Story of America's Great Migration* (Vintage); (poetry) Elizabeth Alexander for *Crave Radiance: New and Selected Poems 1990–2010* (Graywolf).

IMPAC Dublin Literary Award (Ireland) (€100,000). For a book of high literary merit, written in English or translated into English. *Offered by:* IMPAC Corp. and the City of Dublin. *Winner:* Colum McCann for *Let the Great World Spin* (Random).

Independent Foreign Fiction Prize (United Kingdom) (£5,000 each for author and translator). For a work of fiction by a living author that has been translated into English from any other language and published in the United Kingdom. *Winners:* Santiago Roncagliolo and Edith Grossman, translator from Spanish, for *Red April* (Atlantic).

Indies Choice Book Awards (formerly BookSense Book of the Year Awards). Chosen by owners and staff of American Booksellers Association member bookstores. *Winners:* (adult fiction) Emma Donoghue for *Room* (Little, Brown); (adult nonfiction) Laura Hillenbrand for *Unbroken* (Random); (adult debut) Karl Marlantes for *Matterhorn* (Atlantic Monthly and El León Literary Arts); (young adult) Jennifer Donnelly for *Revolution* (Delacorte); (most engaging author) Laurie Halse Anderson.

International Prize for Arabic Fiction. To reward excellence in contemporary Arabic creative writing. *Sponsors:* Booker Prize Foundation, Emirates Foundation for Philanthropy. *Winners:* Mohammed Achaari for *The Arch and the Butterfly*; Raja Alem for *The Dove's Necklace.*

Iowa Poetry Prize. For book-length poetry collections by new or established poets. *Sponsor:* University of Iowa Press. *Winners:* Joseph Campana for *Natural Selections*; Kerri Webster for *Grand and Arsenal* (both to be published by University of Iowa Press).

IPPY Peacemaker Award. To honor the best book promoting world peace and human tolerance. *Offered by:* Jenkins Group and *Independent Publisher* online. *Winner:* Paul K. Chappell for *The End of War: How Waging Peace Can Save Humanity, Our Planet and Our Future* (Easton Studio).

IRA Children's and Young Adult Book Awards. For first or second books in any language published for children or young adults. *Offered by:* International Reading Association. *Winners:* (primary fiction) Fiona Roberton for *Wanted: The Perfect Pet* (Penguin); (primary nonfiction) Michael Hall for *My Heart Is Like a Zoo* (HarperCollins); (intermediate fiction) Kathryn Erskine for *Mockingbird* (Penguin); (young adult fiction) Swati Avasthi for *Split* (Knopf).

Rona Jaffe Foundation Writers' Awards ($25,000). To identify and support women writers of exceptional talent in the early stages of their careers. *Offered by:* Rona Jaffe Foundation. *Winners:* Melanie Drane, Apricot Irving, Fowzia Karimi, Namwali Serpell, Merritt Tierce, JoAnn Wypijewski.

Jerusalem Prize (Israel). Awarded biennially to a writer whose works best express the theme of freedom of the individual in society. *Offered by:* Jerusalem International Book Fair. *Winner:* Ian McEwan.

Jewish Book of the Year (Everett Family Foundation Award). For outstanding writing. *Offered by:* Jewish Book Council. *Winner:* Simon Sebag Montefiore for *Jerusalem: The Biography* (Knopf).

Samuel Johnson Prize for Nonfiction (United Kingdom) (£20,000). For an outstanding work of nonfiction. *Offered by:* British Broadcasting Corporation. *Winner:* Frank Dikötter for *Mao's Great Famine* (Bloomsbury).

Sue Kaufman Prize for First Fiction ($5,000). For a first novel or collection of short stories. *Offered by:* American Academy of Arts and Letters. *Winner:* Brando Skyhorse for *The Madonnas of Echo Park* (Free Press).

Ezra Jack Keats Awards. For children's picture books. *Offered by:* New York Public Library and the Ezra Jack Keats Foundation. *Winners:* (new writer award) Laurel Croza for *I Know Here,* illustrated by Matt James (Groundwood); (new illustrator award) Tao Nyeu for *Bunny Days* (Dial).

Kerlan Award. To recognize singular attainments in the creation of children's literature and in appreciation for generous donation of unique resources to the Kerlan Collection for the study of children's literature. *Offered by:* Kerlan Children's Literature Research Collections, University of Minnesota. *Winner:* Jane Kurtz.

Coretta Scott King Book Awards ($1,000). To an African American author and illustrator of outstanding books for children and young adults. *Offered by:* American Library Association, Social Responsibilities Roundtable. *Winners:* (author) Rita Williams-Garcia for *One Crazy Summer* (HarperCollins); (illustrator) Bryan Collier for *Dave the Potter: Artist, Poet, Slave,* written by Laban Carrick Hill (Little, Brown).

Coretta Scott King/John Steptoe Award for New Talent. To offer visibility to a writer or illustrator at the beginning of a career. *Sponsor:* Coretta Scott King Book Award Committee. *Winners:* Victoria Bond and T. R. Simon for *Zora and Me* (Candlewick).

Coretta Scott King/Virginia Hamilton Award for Lifetime Achievement. Given in even-numbered years to an African American author, illustrator, or author/illustrator for a body of books for children or young adults. In odd-numbered years, the award honors substantial contributions through active engagement with youth, using award-winning African American literature for children or young adults. *Winner:* Henrietta Mays Smith.

Kiriyama Pacific Rim Book Prize ($30,000). For a book of fiction or a book of nonfiction that best contributes to a fuller understanding among the nations and peoples of the Pacific Rim. *Offered by:* Pacific Rim Voices. *Winner:* Not awarded in 2011.

Robert Kirsch Award for Lifetime Achievement ($1,000). To a living author whose residence or focus is the American West, and whose contributions to American letters clearly merit body-of-work recognition. *Offered by: Los Angeles Times. Winner:* Beverly Cleary. Lambda Literary Awards. To honor outstanding lesbian, gay, bisexual, and transgendered (LGBT) literature. *Offered by:* Lambda Literary Foundation. *Winners:* (bisexual fiction) Myrlin A. Hermes for *The Lunatic, the Lover, and the Poet* (Harper Perennial); (bisexual nonfiction) Maria Pallotta-Chiarolli for *Border Sexualities, Border Families in Schools* (Rowman & Littlefield); (transgender fiction) Zoe Whittall for *Holding Still for As Long As Possible* (House of Anansi); (transgender nonfiction) Noach Dzmura, editor, for *Balancing on the Mechitza: Transgender in Jewish Community* (North Atlantic); (LGBT anthology) Kate Bornstein and S. Bear Bergman, editors, for *Gender Outlaws: The Next Generation* (Seal); (LGBT children's/young adult) Jane Eagland for *Wildthorn* (Houghton Mifflin Harcourt); (LGBT drama) Maureen Angelos, Dominique Dibbell, Peg Healey, and Lisa Kron for *Oedipus at Palm Springs: A Five Lesbian Brothers Play* (Samuel French); (LGBT nonfiction) Virginie Despentes for *King Kong Theory* (Feminist Press); (SF/fantasy/horror) Sandra McDonald for *Diana Comet and Other Improbable Stories* (Lethe); (LGBT studies—tie) Scott Herring for *Another Country: Queer Anti-Urbanism* (New York University Press); Gayle Salamon for *Assuming a Body: Transgender and Rhetorics of Materiality* (Columbia University Press); (lesbian debut fiction) Amber Dawn for *Sub Rosa* (Arsenal Pulp); (lesbian erotica) Tristan Taormino, editor, for *Sometimes She Lets Me: Best Butch/Femme Erotica* (Cleis); (lesbian fiction) Eileen Myles for *Inferno: A Poet's Novel* (OR); (lesbian memoir/biography—tie) Barbara Hammer for *Hammer! Making Movies Out of Sex and Life* (Feminist Press), Julie Marie Wade for *Wishbone: A Memoir in Fractures* (Colgate University Press); (lesbian mystery) Val McDermid for *Fever of the Bone* (HarperCollins); (lesbian poetry) Anna Swanson for *The Nights Also* (Tightrope); (lesbian romance) Cate Culpepper for *River Walker* (Bold Strokes); (gay debut fiction) David Pratt for *Bob the Book* (Chelsea Station); (gay erotica) Jon Macy for *Teleny and Camille* (Northwest);

(gay fiction) Adam Haslett for *Union Atlantic* (Doubleday); (gay memoir/biography) Justin Spring for *Secret Historian: The Life and Times of Samuel Steward, Professor, Tattoo Artist and Sexual Renegade* (Farrar, Straus & Giroux); (gay mystery) David Lennon for *Echoes* (Blue Spike); (gay poetry) Brian Teare for *Pleasure* (Ahsahta); (gay romance) Erik Orrantia for *Normal Miguel* (Cheyenne).

Harold Morton Landon Translation Award ($1,000). For a book of verse translated into English by a single translator. *Offered by:* Academy of American Poets. *Winner:* Jeffrey Angles for his translation from Japanese of Tada Chimako's *Forest of Eyes* (University of California Press).

David J. Langum, Sr. Prize in American Historical Fiction ($1,000). To honor a book of historical fiction published in the previous year. *Winner:* Ann Weisgarber for *The Personal History of Rachel DuPree* (Viking).

Lannan Foundation Literary Fellowships. To recognize young and mid-career writers of distinctive literary merit who demonstrate potential for continued outstanding work. *Offered by:* Lannan Foundation. *Winners:* Sherwin Bitsui, Atsuro Riley.

James Laughlin Award ($5,000). To commend and support a second book of poetry. *Offered by:* Academy of American Poets. *Winner:* Anna Moschovakis for *You and Three Others Are Approaching a Lake* (Coffee House).

Claudia Lewis Award. For the year's best poetry book or books for young readers. *Offered by:* Bank Street College of Education and the Florence M. Miller Memorial Fund. *Winners:* Bob Raczka and Peter H. Reynolds, illustrator, for *Guyku: A Year of Haiku for Boys* (Houghton Mifflin).

Library of Congress Lifetime Achievement Award for the Writing of Fiction. For a distinguished body of work. *Offered by:* Library of Congress. *Winner:* Not awarded in 2011.

Ruth Lilly Fellowships ($15,000). To emerging poets to support their continued study and writing of poetry. *Offered by:* the Poetry Foundation. *Winners:* Olivia Clare, T. Zachary Cotler, Farnoosh Fathi, Alison Seay, Marcus Wicker.

Ruth Lilly Poetry Prize ($100,000). To a U.S. poet in recognition of lifetime achievement. *Offered by:* the Poetry Foundation. *Winner:* David Ferry.

Astrid Lindgren Memorial Award (Sweden) (5 million kroner, approximately $725,000). In memory of children's author Astrid Lindgren, to honor outstanding children's literature and efforts to promote it. *Offered by:* Government of Sweden and the Swedish Arts Council. *Winner:* author and illustrator Shaun Tan.

Locus Awards. For science fiction writing. *Offered by:* Locus Publications. *Winners:* (novel) Connie Willis for *Blackout* and *All Clear* (Random); (fantasy novel) China Miéville for *Kraken* (Del Rey); (first novel) N. K. Jemisin for *The Hundred Thousand Kingdoms* (Orbit); (young adult book) Paolo Bacigalupi for *Ship Breaker* (Little, Brown); (novella) Ted Chiang for *The Lifecycle of Software Objects* (Subterranean); (novelette) Neil Gaiman for *The Truth Is a Cave in the Black Mountains* in *Stories* (Morrow); (short story) Neil Gaiman for "The Thing About Cassandra" in *Songs of Love and Death: All Original Tales of Star Crossed Love* (Gallery); (anthology) George R. R. Martin and Gardner Dozois, editors, for *Warriors* (Tor); (collection) Jonathan Strahan and Charles N. Brown, editors, for *Fritz Leiber: Selected Stories* (Night Shade); (nonfiction) William H. Patterson, Jr. for *Robert A. Heinlein: In Dialogue with His Century: Volume 1 (1907–1948): Learning Curve* (Tor); (art book) Cathy and Arnie Fenner, editors, for *Spectrum 17* (Underwood).

London Book Festival Awards. To honor books worthy of further attention from the international publishing community. *Winner:* (grand prize) Rick Robinson for *Writ of Mandamus* (Headline).

Elizabeth Longford Prize for Historical Biography (United Kingdom) (£5,000). *Sponsors:* Flora Fraser and Peter Soros. *Winner:* Philip Ziegler for *Edward Heath: The Authorised Biography* (HarperPress).

Los Angeles Times Book Prizes. To honor literary excellence. *Offered by: Los Angeles Times. Winners:* (biography) Laura Hillenbrand for *Unbroken: A World War II Story of Survival, Resilience and Redemption* (Random); (current interest) Michael Lewis

for *The Big Short: Inside the Doomsday Machine* (Norton); (Art Seidenbaum Award for First Fiction) Peter Bognanni for *The House of Tomorrow* (Putnam); (fiction) Jennifer Egan for *A Visit From the Goon Squad* (Knopf); (graphic novel) Adam Hines for *Duncan the Wonder Dog: Show One* (Adhouse); (history) Thomas Powers for *The Killing of Crazy Horse* (Knopf); (mystery/thriller) Tom Franklin for *Crooked Letter, Crooked Letter* (Morrow); (poetry) Maxine Kumin for *Where I Live: New and Selected Poems 1990–2010 (Norton); (science and technology)* Oren Harman for The Price of Altruism: George Price and the Search for the Origins of Kindness (Norton); (young adult literature) Megan Whalen Turner for *A Conspiracy of Kings* (HarperCollins); (Robert Kirsch Award) Beverly Cleary; (Innovator's Award) Powell's Books.

Amy Lowell Poetry Traveling Scholarship. For one or two U.S. poets to spend one year outside North America in a country the recipients feel will most advance their work. *Offered by:* Amy Lowell Poetry Traveling Scholarship. *Winners:* Paisley Rekdal, Mark Spencer Reece.

J. Anthony Lukas Awards. For nonfiction writing that demonstrates literary grace, serious research, and concern for an important aspect of American social or political life. *Offered by:* Columbia University Graduate School of Journalism and the Nieman Foundation for Journalism at Harvard. *Winners:* (Lukas Book Prize) ($10,000) Eliza Griswold for *The Tenth Parallel: Dispatches from the Fault Line Between Christianity and Islam* (Farrar, Straus & Giroux); (Mark Lynton History Prize) ($10,000) Isabel Wilkerson for *The Warmth of Other Suns: The Epic Story of America's Great Migration* (Random); (Lukas Work-in-Progress Award) ($30,000) Alex Tizon for *Big Little Man: The Asian Male at the Dawn of the Asian Century* (to be published by Houghton Mifflin Harcourt).

Macavity Awards. For excellence in mystery writing. *Offered by:* Mystery Readers International. *Winners:* (novel) Louise Penny for *Bury Your Dead* (Minotaur); (first novel) Bruce DeSilva for *Rogue Island* (Forge); (mystery-related nonfiction) John Curran for *Agatha Christie's Secret Notebooks:*

Fifty Years of Mysteries in the Making (HarperCollins); (short story) Dana Cameron for "Swing Shift" in *Crimes by Moonlight: Mysteries from the Dark Side* (Berkley); (Sue Feder Memorial Historical Mystery Award) Kelli Stanley for *City of Dragons* (Minotaur).

McKitterick Prize (United Kingdom) (£4,000). To an author over the age of 40 for a first novel, published or unpublished. *Winner:* Emma Henderson for *Grace Williams Says It Loud* (Sceptre).

Man Booker International Prize (United Kingdom) (£60,000). Awarded biennially to a living author for a significant contribution to world literature. *Offered by:* Man Group. *Winner:* Philip Roth.

Man Booker Prize for Fiction (United Kingdom) (£50,000). For the best novel written in English by a Commonwealth author. *Offered by:* Booktrust and the Man Group. *Winner:* Julian Barnes for *The Sense of an Ending* (Jonathan Cape).

Lenore Marshall Poetry Prize ($25,000). For an outstanding book of poems published in the United States. *Offered by:* Academy of American Poets. *Winner:* C. D. Wright for *One With Others* (Copper Canyon).

Mason Award ($10,000). To honor an author whose body of work has made extraordinary contributions to bringing literature to a wide reading public. *Sponsors:* George Mason University and Fall for the Book. *Winner:* Stephen King.

Somerset Maugham Awards (£3,500) (United Kingdom). For works in any genre except drama by a writer under the age of 35, to enable young writers to enrich their work by gaining experience of foreign countries. *Winners:* Miriam Gamble for *The Squirrels Are Dead* (Bloodaxe), Alexandra Harris for *Romantic Moderns* (Thames and Hudson), Adam O'Riordan for *In the Flesh* (Chatto).

Addison M. Metcalf Award in Literature ($10,000). Awarded biennially to a young writer of great promise. *Offered by:* American Academy of Arts and Letters. *Winner:* Matthea Harvey.

Vicky Metcalf Award for Children's Literature (Canada) (C$20,000). To a Canadian writer of children's literature for a body of work. *Offered by:* Metcalf Foundation. *Winner:* Iain Lawrence.

Midwest Booksellers Choice Awards. *Offered by:* Midwest Booksellers Association. *Winners:* (fiction) Nina Revoyr for *Wingshooters* (Akashic); (nonfiction) Wendy McClure for *The Wilder Life: My Adventures in the Lost World of Little House on the Prairie* (Riverhead); (children's literature) Clare Vanderpool for *Moon Over Manifest* (Random); (children's picture book) Jane Yolen and David Small, illustrator, for *Elsie's Bird* (Penguin); (poetry) William Kloefkorn for *Swallowing the Soap* (University of Nebraska Press).

William C. Morris YA Debut Award. To honor a debut book published by a first-time author writing for teens and celebrating impressive new voices in young adult literature. *Offered by:* American Library Association, Young Adult Library Services Association. *Donor:* William C. Morris Endowment. *Winner:* Blythe Woolston for *The Freak Observer* (Carolrhoda).

Gustavus Myers Awards. For outstanding books that extend understanding of the root causes of bigotry. *Offered by:* Gustavus Myers Center for the Study of Bigotry and Human Rights in North America. *Winners:* Awarded suspended in 2009.

Mythopoeic Fantasy Awards. To recognize fantasy or mythic literature for children and adults that best exemplifies the spirit of the Inklings, a group of fantasy writers that includes J. R. R. Tolkien, C. S. Lewis, and Charles Williams. *Offered by:* Mythopoeic Society. *Winners:* (children's) Megan Whalen Turner for The Queen's Thief Series, *The Thief, The Queen of Attolia, The King of Attolia,* and *A Conspiracy of Kings* (Greenwillow); (adult) Karen Lord for *Redemption in Indigo* (Small Beer).

National Book Awards. For the best books of the year published in the United States. *Offered by:* National Book Foundation. *Winners:* (fiction) Jesmyn Ward for *Salvage the Bones* (Bloomsbury USA); (nonfiction) Stephen Greenblatt for *The Swerve: How the World Became Modern* (Norton); (poetry) Nikky Finney for *Head Off and Split* (Northwestern University Press); (young people's literature) Thanhha Lai for *Inside Out and Back Again* (HarperCollins).

National Book Critics Circle Awards. For literary excellence. *Offered by:* National Book

Critics Circle. *Winners:* (fiction) Jennifer Egan for *A Visit from the Goon Squad* (Knopf); (nonfiction) Isabel Wilkerson for *The Warmth of Other Suns: The Epic Story of America's Great Migration* (Random); (biography) Sarah Bakewell for *How To Live: Or, A Life of Montaigne in One Question and Twenty Attempts at an Answer* (Other); (autobiography) Darin Strauss for *Half a Life* (McSweeney's); (poetry) C. D. Wright for *One with Others* (Copper Canyon); (criticism) Clare Cavanagh for *Lyric Poetry and Modern Politics: Russia, Poland, and the West* (Yale University Press); (Nona Balakian Citation for Excellence in Reviewing) Parul Sehgal; (Ivan Sandrof Lifetime Achievement Award) Dalkey Archive Press.

National Book Festival Award for Creative Achievement. *Offered by:* Center for the Book, Library of Congress. *Winner:* Toni Morrison.

National Book Foundation Literarian Award for Outstanding Service to the American Literary Community. *Offered by:* National Book Foundation. *Winner:* Mitchell Kaplan.

National Book Foundation Medal for Distinguished Contribution to American Letters ($10,000). To a person who has enriched the nation's literary heritage over a life of service or corpus of work. *Offered by:* National Book Foundation. *Winner:* John Ashbery.

National Endowment for the Arts Literature Fellowships for Creative Writing (prose) ($25,000). *Winners:* Paul Bergstraesser, Sean Bernard, Eula Biss, Belle Boggs, Veronica Chambers, Jennifer Clement, Katherine Leonard Czepiel, Carolina De Robertis, Amber Dermont, Karen Fisher, Jennifer Haigh, Jean Harper, Alan Heathcock, Paul Hendrickson, Richard Holeton, Abeer Hoque, Nalini Jones, Tayari Jones, Nadia Kalman, Porochista Khakpour, Paul La Farge, Victoria Lancelotta, William Lychack, Peter Manseau, Suzanne Matson, Susan McCallum-Smith, Sabina Murray, Joseph O'Neill, Benjamin Percy, Jennifer Percy, Pedro Ponce, Shann Ray, Ted Sanders, Elisabeth Sheffield, Stephanie Soileau, Gregory Spatz, Sarah A.Strickley, Jonathan Tel, René Georg Vasicek, Mitch Wieland.

National Translation Awards ($5,000). To honor translators whose work has made a valuable contribution to literary translation into English. *Offered by:* American Literary Translators Association. *Winners:* (National Translation Award) Lisa Rose Bradford for *Between Words: Juan Gelman's Public Letter* (Coimbra); (Lucien Stryk Asian Translation Prize) Charles Egan for *Clouds Thick, Whereabouts Unknown: Poems by Zen Monks of China* (Columbia University Press).

Nebula Awards. For science fiction writing. *Offered by:* Science Fiction and Fantasy Writers of America (SFWA). *Winners:* The 2011 winners were to be announced in mid-May, 2012. See http://www.sfwa.org/nebula-awards for more information.

Nestlé Children's Book Prizes (formerly Smarties Book Prizes) (United Kingdom). To encourage high standards and to stimulate interest in books for children. *Offered by:* Nestlé UK Ltd. *Winners:* Award discontinued.

John Newbery Medal. For the most distinguished contribution to literature for children. *Offered by:* American Library Association, Association for Library Service to Children. *Winner:* Clare Vanderpool for *Moon over Manifest* (Random).

Nimrod Literary Awards ($2,000 plus publication). *Offered by:* Nimrod International Journal of Prose and Poetry. *Winners:* (Pablo Neruda Prize in Poetry) Hayden Saunier for "Sideways Glances in the Rear-View Mirror"; (Katherine Anne Porter Prize in Fiction) Sultana Banulescu for "Beggars and Thieves."

Nobel Prize in Literature (Sweden). For the total literary output of a distinguished career. *Offered by:* Swedish Academy. *Winner:* Tomas Tranströmer.

Eli M. Oboler Memorial Award. Given biennially to an author of a published work in English or in English translation dealing with issues, events, questions, or controversies in the area of intellectual freedom. *Offered by:* Intellectual Freedom Round Table, American Library Association. *Winner:* To be awarded next in 2012.

Flannery O'Connor Awards for Short Fiction. For collections of short fiction. *Offered by:* University of Georgia Press. *Winners:* Melinda Moustakis for *Bear Down, Bear North: Alaska Stories* (University of Georgia Press); Amina Gautier for *At-Risk* (University of Georgia Press).

Frank O'Connor Short Story Award. See Cork City–Frank O'Connor Short Story Award.

Oddest Book Title of the Year Award. See Bookseller/Diagram Prize for Oddest Title of the Year.

Scott O'Dell Award for Historical Fiction ($5,000). *Offered by: Bulletin of the Center for Children's Books,* University of Chicago. *Winner:* Rita Williams-Garcia for *One Crazy Summer* (Amistad).

Odyssey Award. To the producer of the best audiobook for children and/or young adults available in English in the United States. *Sponsors:* American Library Association, ALSC/Booklist/YALSA. *Winner:* Listening Library for *The True Meaning of Smekday* by Adam Rex, narrated by Bahni Turpin.

Sean O'Faoláin Short Story Competition (€1,500 and publication in the literary journal *Southword. Offered by:* Munster Literature Centre, Cork, Ireland. *Winner:* P. G. O'Connor for "The Haggard."

Dayne Ogilvie Grant for an Emerging Gay Writer (C$4,000). *Offered by:* Writers' Trust of Canada. *Sponsor:* Robin Pacific. *Winner:* Farzana Doctor.

Orange Award for New Writers (United Kingdom) (£10,000). For a first novel or short story collection written by a woman and published in the United Kingdom. *Offered by:* Orange plc and Arts Council London. *Winner:* Not awarded in 2011.

Orange Prize for Fiction (United Kingdom) (£30,000). For the best novel written by a woman and published in the United Kingdom. *Offered by:* Orange plc. *Winner:* Téa Obreht for *The Tiger's Wife* (Random).

Orbis Pictus Award. For outstanding nonfiction for children. *Offered by:* National Council of Teachers of English. *Winners:* Jan Greenberg and Sandra Jordan, and Brian Floca, illustrator, for *Ballet for Martha: Making Appalachian Spring* (Roaring Brook).

Orion Book Award ($3,000). To recognize books that deepen connection to the natural world, present new ideas about mankind's relationship with nature, and achieve excellence in writing. *Sponsors: Orion Magazine* and the Geraldine R. Dodge Foundation. *Winner:* Hugh Raffles for *Insectopedia* (Pantheon).

PEN Award for Poetry in Translation ($3,000). For a book-length translation of poetry from any language into English and published in the United States. *Offered by:* PEN American Center. *Winner:* Khaled Mattawa for *Adonis: Selected Poems* (Yale University Press).

PEN/Saul Bellow Award for Achievement in American Fiction ($25,000). Awarded biennially to a distinguished living American author of fiction. *Offered by:* PEN American Center. *Winner:* Not awarded in 2011.

PEN Beyond Margins Awards. See PEN Open Book Awards.

PEN/Robert Bingham Fellowship ($25,000). To a writer whose first novel or short story collection represents distinguished literary achievement and suggests great promise. *Offered by:* PEN American Center. *Winners:* Susanna Daniel for *Stiltsville* (Harper Perennial), Danielle Evans for *Before You Suffocate Your Own Fool Self* (Riverhead).

PEN/Diamonstein-Spielvogel Award for the Art of the Essay ($5,000). For a book of essays by a single author that best exemplifies the dignity and esteem of the essay form. *Winner:* Mark Slouka for *Essays from the Nick of Time: Reflections and Refutations* (Graywolf).

PEN Emerging Writers Awards ($1,660). *Winner:* Smith Henderson.

PEN/ESPN Lifetime Achievement Award for Literary Sports Writing ($5,000). For a writer whose body of work represents an exceptional contribution to the field. *Winner:* Roger Angell.

PEN/ESPN Award for Literary Sports Writing ($5,000). To a living writer for exceptional contributions to the field of literary sports writing. *Winner:* George Dohrmann for *Play Their Hearts Out* (Ballantine).

PEN/Faulkner Award for Fiction ($15,000). To honor the best work of fiction published by an American. *Winner:* Not awarded in 2011.

PEN/John Kenneth Galbraith Award ($10,000). Given biennially for a distinguished book of general nonfiction. *Offered by:* PEN American Center. *Winner:* Robert Perkinson for *Texas Tough: The Rise of America's Prison Empire* (Metropolitan).

PEN/Ernest Hemingway Foundation Award. For a distinguished work of first fiction by an American. *Offered by:* PEN New England. *Winner:* Brando Skyhorse for *The Madonnas of Echo Park* (Free Press).

PEN/Nora Magid Award ($5,000) To honor a magazine editor who has contributed significantly to the excellence of the publication he or she edits. *Winner:* Brigid Hughes, founding editor of *A Public Space.*

PEN/Ralph Manheim Medal for Translation. Given every three years to a translator whose career has demonstrated a commitment to excellence. *Winner:* To be awarded next in 2012.

PEN/Nabokov Award ($20,000). To celebrate the accomplishments of a living author whose body of work, either written in or translated into English, represents achievement in a variety of literary genres. *Winner:* Not awarded in 2011.

PEN/Phyllis Naylor Working Writer Fellowship ($5,000). *Offered by:* PEN American Center. *Winner:* Lucy Frank for *Two Girls Staring at the Ceiling,* a novel in verse.

PEN/O. Henry Prize. To strengthen the art of the short story. *Winners:* Jim Shepard for "Your Fate Hurtles Down at You" in *Electric Literature*; Helen Simpson for "Diary of an Interesting Year" in the *New Yorker*; Judy Doenges for "Melinda" in the *Kenyon Review*; Kenneth Calhoun for "Nightblooming" in the *Paris Review*; Tamas Dobozy for "The Restoration of the Villa Where Tíbor Kálmán Once Lived" in *One Story*; Lily Tuck for "Ice" in the *American Scholar*; Jennine Capó Crucet for "How to Leave Hialeah" in *Epoch*; David Means for "The Junction" in *Ecotone*; Susan Minot for "Pole, Pole" in the *Kenyon Review*; Brad Watson for "Alamo Plaza" in *Ecotone*; Chris Adrian for "The Black Square" in *McSweeney's*; Jane Delury for "Nothing of Consequence" in *Narrative*; Adam Foulds for "The Rules Are the Rules" in *Granta*; Leslie Parry for "The Vanishing American" in *Virginia Quarterly Review*; Mark Slouka for "Crossing" in the *Paris Review*; Lori Ostlund for "Bed Death" in the *Kenyon Review*; Brian Evenson for "Windeye" in *PEN America*; Lynn Freed for "Sunshine" in *Narrative*; Elizabeth Tallent for "Never Come Back" in the *Threepenny Review*; Matthew Neill Null for "Something You Can't Live Without" in *Oxford American.*

PEN Open Book Award (formerly PEN Beyond Margins Award) ($1,000). For book-length writings by authors of color, published in the United States during the current calendar year. *Offered by:* PEN American Center. *Winner:* Manu Joseph for *Serious Men* (Norton).

PEN/Joyce Osterweil Award for Poetry ($5,000). A biennial award to recognize a new and emerging American poet. *Offered by:* PEN American Center. *Winner:* Ishion Hutchinson for *Far District* (Peepal Tree).

PEN/Laura Pels Foundation Awards for Drama. To recognize a master American dramatist and an American playwright in mid-career. *Offered by:* PEN American Center. *Winners:* (master dramatist) David Henry Hwang; (mid-career) Marcus Gardley.

PEN Prison Writing Awards. To provide support and encouragement to prison inmates whose writing shows merit or promise. *Offered by:* PEN American Center. *Winners:* (poetry) Gene Walker for "Longevity"; (essay) Thomas Bartlett Whitaker for "Hell's Kitchen"; (drama) Robert Weaver for "The Secret of Sky, Act 3"; (memoir) D Ka Lani Raposa for "A Fine, Fine Day"; (fiction) Robert Weaver for "The Blessing of Jebidiah Goodytake."

PEN/W. G. Sebald Award ($10,000). For a fiction writer in mid-career who has published at least three significant works of literary fiction. *Winner:* Aleksandar Hemon.

PEN Translation Fund Grants. To support the translation of book-length works of fiction, creative nonfiction, poetry, or drama that have not previously appeared in English or have appeared only in an egregiously flawed translation. *Winners:* Amiri Ayanna, Neil Blackadder, Clarissa Botsford, Steve Bradbury, Annmarie S. Drury, Diane Nemec Ignashev, Chenxin Jiang, Hilary B. Kaplan, Catherine Schelbert, Joel Streicker, Sarah L. Thomas.

PEN Translation Prize ($3,000). To promote the publication and reception of translated world literature in English. *Winner:* Ibrahim Muhawi for *Journal of an Ordinary Grief* by Mahmoud Darwish (Archipelago).

PEN/Voelcker Award for Poetry. Given in even-numbered years to an American poet at the height of his or her powers. *Offered by:* PEN

American Center. *Winner:* Not awarded in 2011.

PEN/Jacqueline Bograd Weld Award for Biography ($5,000). To the author of a distinguished biography published in the United States during the previous calendar year. *Offered by:* PEN American Center. *Winner:* Stacy Schiff for *Cleopatra: A Life* (Little, Brown).

PEN/E. O. Wilson Literary Science Writing Award ($10,000). For a book of literary nonfiction on the subject of the physical and biological sciences. *Winner:* Siddhartha Mukherjee for *The Emperor of All Maladies: A Biography of Cancer* (Scribner).

Maxwell E. Perkins Award. To honor an editor, publisher, or agent who has discovered, nurtured, and championed writers of fiction in the United States. *Offered by:* Center for Fiction, Mercantile Library of New York. *Winner:* Nan Graham, senior vice president and editor-in-chief, Scribner.

Phoenix Award. To the author of an English-language children's book that failed to win a major award at the time of its publication 20 years earlier. *Winner:* Virginia Euwer Wolff for *The Mozart Season* (Holtzbrinck, 1991).

Edgar Allan Poe Awards. For outstanding mystery, suspense, and crime writing. *Offered by:* Mystery Writers of America. *Winners:* (novel) Steve Hamilton for *The Lock Artist* (Minotaur); (first novel by an American author) Bruce DeSilva for *Rogue Island* (Forge); (paperback original) Robert Goddard for *Long Time Coming* (Random); (fact crime) Ken Armstrong and Nick Perry for *Scoreboard, Baby: A Story of College Football, Crime and Complicity* (University of Nebraska Press); (critical/biographical) Yunte Huang for *Charlie Chan: The Untold Story of the Honorable Detective and his Rendez-vouz with American History* (Norton); (short story) Doug Allyn for "The Scent of Lilacs" in *Ellery Queen Mystery Magazine* (Dell); (juvenile) Dori Hillestad Butler for *The Buddy Files: The Case of the Lost Boy* (Albert Whitman); (young adult) Charlie Price for *Interrogation of Gabriel James* (Farrar, Straus & Giroux); (play) Sam Bobrick for "The Psychic" (Falcon Theatre, Burbank, California); (television episode teleplay) Neil Cross for episode 1 of "Luther" (BBC America); (Robert L. Fish Memorial Award)

Evan Lewis for "Skyler Hobbs and the Rabbit Man" in *Ellery Queen Mystery Magazine* (Dell); (grand master) Sara Paretsky; (Simon & Schuster/Mary Higgins Clark Award) Elly Griffiths for *The Crossing Places* (Houghton Mifflin Harcourt).

Poets Out Loud Prize ($1,000 and publication by Fordham University Press). For a book-length poetry collection. *Sponsor:* Fordham University at Lincoln Center. *Winners:* Julie Choffel for "The Hello Delay"; (editor's prize) Michelle Naka Pierce for "Continuous Frieze Bordering [Red]."

Katherine Anne Porter Award ($20,000). Awarded biennially to a prose writer of demonstrated achievement. *Offered by:* American Academy of Arts and Letters. *Winner:* Not awarded in 2011.

Michael L. Printz Award. For excellence in literature for young adults. *Offered by:* American Library Association, Young Adult Library Services Association. *Winner:* Paolo Bacigalupi for *Ship Breaker* (Little, Brown).

V. S. Pritchett Memorial Prize (United Kingdom) (£1,000). For a previously unpublished short story. *Offered by:* Royal Society of Literature. *Winner:* Carys Davies for "The Redemption of Galen Pike."

Pritzker Military Library Literature Award ($100,000). To recognize a living author for a body of work that has profoundly enriched the public understanding of American military history. *Sponsor:* Tawani Foundation. *Winner:* Carlo D'Este.

Prix Aurora Awards (Canada). For science fiction writing. *Winners:* (novel) Robert J. Sawyer for *WWW: Watch* by Robert J. Sawyer (Penguin Canada); (short form, English): Hayden Trenholm for "The Burden of Fire" in *Neo-Opsis* No. 19; (best poem/song) Carolyn Clink for "The ABCs of the End of the World" in *A Verdant Green*; (graphic novel, English) Tarol Hunt for *Goblins* (goblinscomic.com); (related work, English) Derwin Mak and Eric Choi, editors, for *The Dragon and the Stars* (DAW); (artist) Erik Mohr.

Prix Goncourt (France). For "the best imaginary prose work of the year." *Offered by:* Société des Gens des Lettres. *Winner:* Alexis Jenni for *L'Art Francais De La Guerre* (*The French Art of War*) (Gallimard).

Pulitzer Prizes in Letters ($10,000). To honor distinguished work dealing preferably with American themes. *Offered by:* Columbia University Graduate School of Journalism. *Winners:* (fiction) Jennifer Egan for *A Visit from the Goon Squad* (Knopf); (drama) Bruce Norris for "Clybourne Park"; (history) Eric Foner for *The Fiery Trial: Abraham Lincoln and American Slavery* (Norton); (biography) Ron Chernow for *Washington: A Life* (Penguin); (poetry) Kay Ryan for *The Best of It: New and Selected Poems* (Grove Press); (general nonfiction) Siddhartha Mukherjee for *The Emperor of All Maladies: A Biography of Cancer* (Scribner); (music) Zhou Long for "Madame White Snake."

Raiziss/De Palchi Translation Award ($5,000 prize and a $25,000 fellowship, awarded in alternate years). For a translation into English of a significant work of modern Italian poetry by a living translator. *Offered by:* Academy of American Poets. *Winner:* (fellowship, $25,000) Dominic Siracusa for *Oramai* by Emilio Villa.

Raven Awards. For outstanding achievement in the mystery field outside the realm of creative writing. *Offered by:* Mystery Writers of America. *Winners:* Centuries & Sleuths bookshop, Forest Park, Illinois (Augie Aleksy, owner); Once Upon a Crime bookshop, Minneapolis (Pat Frovarp and Gary Shulze, owners).

RBC Bronwen Wallace Award for Emerging Writers (Canada) ($5,000). For a writer under the age of 35 who has not yet been published in book form. *Sponsor:* RBC Foundation. *Winner:* Garth Martens for "Inheritance and Other Poems."

Arthur Rense Poetry Prize ($20,000). Awarded triennially to an exceptional poet. *Offered by:* American Academy of Arts and Letters. *Winner:* David Wagoner.

John Llewellyn Rhys Prize (United Kingdom) (£5,000). For a work of literature by a British or Commonwealth author 35 or younger and published in the United Kingdom. *Offered by:* Booktrust. Winner: Not awarded in 2011.

Harold U. Ribalow Prize. For Jewish fiction published in English. *Sponsor:* Hadassah magazine. *Winner:* Howard Jacobson for *The Finkler Question* (Bloomsbury USA).

Rita Awards. *Offered by:* Romance Writers of America. *Winners:* (historical romance) Sherry Thomas for *His at Night* (Random); (regency historical romance) Lauren Willig for *The Mischief of the Mistletoe* (Penguin); (inspirational romance) Irene Hannon for *In Harm's Way* (Baker); (young adult romance) Julie Kagawa for *The Iron King* (Harlequin); (contemporary series romance) Karen Templeton for *Welcome Home, Cowboy* (Silhouette); (contemporary series romance: suspense/adventure) Helen Brenna for *The Moon That Night* (Harlequin); (novel with strong romantic elements) Jodi Thomas for *Welcome to Harmony* (Penguin); (romance novella) Virginia Kantra for *Shifting Sea* in *Burning Up* (Penguin); (romantic suspense) Karen Rose for *Silent Scream* (Grand Central); (paranormal romance) Sharon Ashwood for *Unchained: The Dark Forgotten* (Penguin); (best first book) Kaki Warner for *Pieces of Sky* (Penguin); (contemporary single title romance) Jill Shalvis for *Simply Irresistible* (Grand Central); (Nora Roberts Lifetime Achievement Award) Sharon Sala.

Rita Golden Heart Awards. For worthy unpublished romance manuscripts. *Winners:* (regency historical romance) Anne Barton for "The Proper Miss's Guide to Bad Behavior"; (historical romance) Maire Shelley for "The Dark Lady"; (inspirational romance) Ruth Kaufman for "At His Command"; (young adult romance) Suzanne Kaufman Kalb for "Irresistible"; (contemporary series romance) Jo Anne Banker for "Lost and Found"; (contemporary series romance: suspense/adventure) Robin Lynn Perini for "Stolen Lullaby"; (novel with strong romantic elements) Anne Charles for "Nearly Departed in Deadwood"; (romantic suspense) Diana Van Dyke for "Spy in the Mirror"; (paranormal romance) Trisza Ray for "The Blood Sworn King"; (contemporary single title romance) Lisa Connelly for "The Sinners."

Rodda Book Award. To recognize a book that exhibits excellence in writing and has contributed significantly to congregational libraries through promotion of spiritual growth. The award is given to books for adults, young adults, and children on a three-year-rotational basis. *Offered by:* Church and Synagogue Library Association. *Win-*

ners: Maya Ajmera, Magda Nakassis, and Cynthia Pon for *Faith* (Charlesbridge).

Rogers Writers' Trust Fiction Prize (Canada) (C$25,000). To a Canadian author of a novel or short story collection. *Offered by:* Rogers Communications. *Winner:* Patrick deWitt for *The Sisters Brothers* (House of Anansi).

Sami Rohr Prize for Jewish Literature ($100,000 first place, $25,000 first runner-up). For emerging writers of Jewish literature. *Offered by:* Family of Sami Rohr. *Winners:* (first place) Austin Ratner for *The Jump Artist* (Bellevue Literary); (first runner-up) Joseph Skibell for *A Curable Romantic* (Algonquin).

Rosenthal Foundation Award ($5,000). To a young novelist of considerable literary talent. *Offered by:* American Academy of Arts and Letters. *Winner:* Monique Truong for *Bitter in the Mouth* (Random).

Royal Society of Literature Benson Medal (Great Britain). To recognize meritorious works in poetry, fiction, history and belles letters, honoring an entire career. The recipient may be someone who is not a writer but has done conspicuous service to literature. *Winners:* Diana Athill, Francis King,

Royal Society of Literature Jerwood Awards for Nonfiction (United Kingdom). For authors engaged on their first major commissioned works of nonfiction. *Offered by:* Royal Society of Literature. *Winners:* (£10,000) Alexander Monro for *The Paper Trail* (Penguin); (£5,000) Roger Beam for *Englandspiel* (Haynes); (£5,000) Jonathan Beckman for *Cardinal Sins—Marie Antoinette and the Affair of the Necklace* (to be published by Fourth Estate).

Royal Society of Literature Ondaatje Prize (£10,000). For a distinguished work of fiction, nonfiction or poetry evoking the spirit of a place. *Offered by:* Royal Society of Literature. *Winner:* Edmund de Waal for *The Hare with Amber Eyes* (Chatto).

Juan Rulfo International Latin American and Caribbean Prize (Mexico). See FIL Literary Award in Romance Languages.

Carl Sandburg Literary Awards. To honor a significant body of work that has enhanced public awareness of the written word. *Sponsor:* Chicago Public Library Foundation. *Winners:* (Sandburg Award) Roger Ebert; (21st Century Award, recognizing a Chica-

go-area writer for recent noteworthy accomplishments) Rebecca Skloot.

Schneider Family Book Awards ($5,000). To honor authors and illustrators for books that embody artistic expressions of the disability experience of children and adolescents. *Offered by:* American Library Association. *Donor:* Katherine Schneider. *Winners:* (young readers) George Ella Lyon and Lynne Avril, illustrator, for *The Pirate of Kindergarten* (Athenium); (middle school readers) Jordan Sonnenblick for *After Ever After* (Scholastic); (teen readers) Antony John for *Five Flavors of Dumb* (Penguin).

Scotiabank Giller Prize (Canada) (C$50,000). For the best Canadian novel or short story collection written in English. *Offered by:* Giller Prize Foundation and Scotiabank. *Winner:* Esi Edugyan for *Half-Blood Blues* (Thomas Allen).

Scottish Book of the Year Awards. *Sponsor:* Scottish Arts Council. *Donor:* Scottish Mortgage Investment Trust. *Winners:* (book of the year, £30,000) Jackie Kay for *Red Dust Road* (Picador); (category winners, £5,000) (fiction) Leila Aboulelas for *Lyrics Alley* (Weidenfeld & Nicolson); (nonfiction) Jackie Kay for *Red Dust Road* (Picador); (poetry) Stewart Conn for *The Breakfast Room* (Bloodaxe); (first book) Sue Peebles for *The Death of Lomond Friel* (Vintage).

Shamus Awards. To honor mysteries featuring independent private investigators. *Offered by:* Private Eye Writers of America. *Winners:* (hardcover novel) Lori Armstrong for *No Mercy* (Touchstone); (first novel) Michael Ayoob for *In Search of Mercy* (Minotaur); (paperback original) Christopher G. Moore for *Asia Hand* (Grove/Atlantic); (short story Gar Anthony Haywood for "The Lamb Was Sure to Go" in *Alfred Hitchcock Mystery Magazine,* November 2010); (Hammer Award for best series character) Sara Paretsky for V. I. Warshawski; (the EYE lifetime achievement award) Ed Gorman.

Shelley Memorial Award ($6,000 to $9,000). To a poet or poets living in the United States, chosen on the basis of genius and need. *Offered by:* Poetry Society of America. *Winners:* Rigoberto Gonzales, Joan Larkin.

Robert F. Sibert Medal. For the most distinguished informational book for children. *Offered by:* American Library Association,

Association for Library Service to Children. *Winners:* Sy Montgomery and Nic Bishop, photographer, for *Kakapo Rescue: Saving the World's Strangest Parrot* (Houghton Mifflin Harcourt).

Society of Authors Travelling Scholarships (£2,000) (Great Britain). *Winners:* Mark Cocker, Rose George, Ben Markovits.

Spur Awards. *Offered by:* Western Writers of America. *Winners:* (long novel) Lucia St. Clair Robson for *Last Train from Cuernavaca* (Tom Doherty Associates); (short novel) Richard S. Wheeler for *Snowbound* (Tom Doherty Associates); (original mass market paperback) Max McCoy for *Damnation Road* (Kensington); (first novel) Nick Pizolatto for *Galveston* (Simon & Schuster); (nonfiction biography) James Haley for *Wolf: The Lives of Jack London* (Basic); (nonfiction contemporary) Lawrence Culver for *The Frontier of Leisure: Southern California and the Shaping of Modern America* (Oxford University Press); (short fiction) K. L. Cook for "Bonnie and Clyde in the Backyard" in *Glimmer Train Stories*; (short nonfiction) Lee Niedringhaus for "The N Bar N Ranch: A Legend of the Open-Range Cattle Industry, 1885–99" in *Montana: The Magazine of Western History*; (juvenile nonfiction) Ronald A. Reis for *Buffalo Bill Cody* (Chelsea House); (storyteller award) Aaron Frisch and Chris Sheban, illustrator, for *A Night on the Range* (Creative Editions); (western drama—tie) Christopher Monger and William Merritt Jonson for *Temple Grandin* (HBO Films), Joel and Ethan Coen for *True Grit* (Paramount); (western documentary) Rob Rapley for *American Experience: Wyatt Earp* (PBS); (poem) Red Shuttleworth for "Roadside Attractions" in *The Basement*; (audiobook) Kirby Jonas for *Secret of Two Hawks* (Books in Motion).

Wallace Stevens Award ($100,000). To recognize outstanding and proven mastery in the art of poetry. *Offered by:* Academy of American Poets. *Winner:* Yusef Komunyakaa.

Bram Stoker Awards. For superior horror writing. *Offered by:* Horror Writers Association. *Winners:* (novel) Peter Straub for *A Dark Matter* (Doubleday); (first novel—tie) Benjamin Kane Ethridge for *Black and Orange* (Bad Moon), Lisa Morton for *The Castle of Los Angeles* (Gray Friar; (long fiction) Norman Prentiss for *Invisible Fences* (Cemetery Dance); (short fiction) Joe R. Lansdale for "The Folding Man" in *Haunted Legends* (Tor); (anthology) Ellen Datlow and Nick Mamatas, editors, for *Haunted Legends* (Tor); (fiction collection) Stephen King for *Full Dark, No Stars* (Simon & Schuster); (nonfiction) Gary Braunbeck for *To Each Their Darkness* (Apex); (poetry collection) Bruce Boston for *Dark Matters* (Bad Moon); (lifetime achievement) Ellen Datlow, Al Feldstein; (Silver Hammer Award) Angel Leigh McCoy; (Richard Laymon President's Award) Michael Colangelo.

Stonewall Book Awards. *Offered by:* Gay, Lesbian, Bisexual, and Transgendered Round Table, American Library Association. *Winners:* (children's and young adult literature) Brian Katcher for *Almost Perfect* (Delacourte); (Barbara Gittings Literature Award) Barb Johnson for *More of This World or Maybe Another* (Harper); (Israel Fishman Nonfiction Award) Emma Donoghue for *Inseparable: Desire between Women in Literature* (Knopf).

Story Prize. For a collection of short fiction. *Offered by:* Story magazine. *Winner:* Anthony Doerr for *Memory Wall* (Scribner).

Flora Stieglitz Straus Award. For nonfiction books that serve as an inspiration to young readers. *Offered by:* Bank Street College of Education and the Florence M. Miller Memorial Fund. *Winners:* Andrea Davis Pinkney and Brian Pinkney, illustrator, for *Sit-In: How Four Friends Stood Up by Sitting Down* (Little, Brown).

Mildred and Harold Strauss Livings ($50,000 a year for five years). To two writers of English prose literature to enable them to devote their time exclusively to writing. *Winners:* To be awarded next in 2013.

Theodore Sturgeon Memorial Award for the best short science fiction of the year. *Offered by:* Center for the Study of Science Fiction. *Winner:* Geoffrey A. Landis for "The Sultan of the Clouds."

Sunburst Awards for Canadian Literature of the Fantastic (C$1,000). *Winners:* (adult) Guy Gavriel Kay for *Under Heaven* (Penguin); (young adult) Paul Glennon for *Bookweirder* (Doubleday).

Charles Taylor Prize for Literary Nonfiction (Canada) (C$25,000). To honor a book of creative nonfiction widely available in Canada and written by a Canadian citizen or landed immigrant. *Offered by:* Charles Taylor Foundation. *Winner:* Charles Foran for *Mordecai: The Life and Times,* a biography of Mordecai Richler (Knopf Canada).

Sydney Taylor Children's Book Awards. For a distinguished contribution to Jewish children's literature. *Offered by:* Association of Jewish Libraries. *Winners:* (younger readers) Howard Schwartz and Kristina Swarner (illustrator), for *Gathering Sparks* (Roaring Brook); (older readers) Barry Deutsch for *Hereville: How Mirka Got Her Sword* (Abrams); (teen readers) Dana Reinhardt for *The Things a Brother Knows* (Random).

Sydney Taylor Manuscript Competition ($1,000). For the best fiction manuscript appropriate for readers ages 8–11, both Jewish and non-Jewish, revealing positive aspects of Jewish life, and written by an unpublished author. *Winner:* Susan Ross for "In Search of Lottie."

Theatre Library Association Award. See Richard Wall Memorial Award.

Dylan Thomas Prize (£30,000). For a published or produced literary work in the English language, written by an author under 30. *Offered by:* University of Wales. *Winner:* Lucy Caldwell for *The Meeting Point* (Faber).

Thriller Awards. *Offered by:* International Thriller Writers. *Winners:* (hardcover novel) John Sandford for *Bad Blood* (Putnam); (paperback original) J. T. Ellison for *The Cold Room* (Mira); (first novel) Chevy Stevens for *Still Missing* (St. Martin's); (short story) Richard Helms for "The Gods for Vengeance Cry" (*Dell Magazine*).

Thurber Prize for American Humor ($5,000). For a humorous book of fiction or nonfiction. *Offered by:* Thurber House. *Winner:* David Rakoff for *Half Empty* (Doubleday).

Tom-Gallon Trust Award and Olive Cook Prize (£1,000). For a short story. Each is awarded biennially in alternate years. *Winner:* (Tom-Gallon Trust Award) Emma Timpany for "The Pledge."

Betty Trask Prize and Award (United Kingdom). To Commonwealth writers under the age of 35 for "romantic or traditional" first novels. *Offered by:* Society of Authors. *Winners:* (Betty Trask Prize, £10,000) Anjali Joseph for *Saraswati Park* (Fourth Estate); (Betty Trask Award, £6,000) Laura Barton for *Twenty-One Locks* (Quercus); (£2,500) Simon Lelic for *Rupture* (Picador); (£2,500) Robert Williams for *Luke and Jon* (Faber).

Kate Tufts Discovery Award ($10,000). For a first or very early book of poetry by an emerging poet. *Offered by:* Claremont Graduate School. *Winner:* Atsuro Riley for *Romey's Order* (University of Chicago Press).

Kingsley Tufts Poetry Award ($100,000). For a book of poetry by a mid-career poet. *Offered by:* Claremont Graduate School. *Winner:* Chase Twichell for *Horses Where the Answers Should Have Been* (Copper Canyon).

21st Century Award. To honor recent achievement in writing by an author with ties to Chicago. See Carl Sandburg Literary Awards.

UKLA Children's Book Awards (United Kingdom). *Sponsor:* United Kingdom Literacy Association. *Winners:* (younger readers) Ellie Sandall for *Birdsong* (Egmont); (older readers) Jason Wallace for *Out of Shadows* (Andersen).

Ungar German Translation Award. Awarded biennially for a distinguished literary translation from German into English that has been published in the United States. *Offered by:* American Translators Association. *Winner:* Robert E. Norton for his translation of Ernst Bertram's *Nietzsche: Attempt at a Mythology* (University of Illinois Press).

John Updike Award ($20,000). Given biennially to a writer in mid-career who has demonstrated consistent excellence. *Offered by:* American Academy of Arts and Letters. *Winner:* Tom Sleigh.

VCU/Cabell First Novelist Award ($5,000). For a first novel published in the previous year. *Offered by:* Virginia Commonwealth University. *Winner:* David Gordon for *The Serialist* (Simon & Schuster).

Harold D. Vursell Memorial Award ($10,000). To a writer whose work merits recognition for the quality of its prose style. *Offered by* American Academy of Arts and Letters. *Winner:* Thomas Mallon.

Amelia Elizabeth Walden Award ($5,000). To honor a book relevant to adolescents that has enjoyed a wide teenage audience. *Sponsor:* Assembly on Literature for Adolescents, National Council of Teachers of English. *Winner:* Francisco X. Stork for *The Last Summer of the Death Warriors* (Scholastic).

Richard Wall Memorial Award (formerly the Theatre Library Association Award). To honor an English-language book of exceptional scholarship in the field of recorded performance, including motion pictures, television, and radio. *Offered by:* Theatre Library Association. *Winners:* Scott Eyman for *Empire of Dreams: The Epic Life of Cecil B. DeMille* (Simon & Schuster); (special jury prize) Yunte Huang for *Charlie Chan: The Untold Story of the Honorable Detective and His Rendezvous with American History* (Norton).

Kim Scott Walwyn Prize (United Kingdom) (£1,000). To recognize the professional achievements of women in publishing. *Offered by:* Booktrust. *Winner:* Kay Peddle.

George Washington Book Prize ($50,000). To recognize an important new book about America's founding era. *Offered by:* Washington College and the Gilder Lehrman Institute of American History. *Winner:* Pauline Maier for *Ratification: The People Debate the Constitution, 1787–1788* (Norton).

Carole Weinstein Poetry Prize ($10,000). To poets with strong connections to central Virginia who have made a "significant recent contribution to the art of poetry." *Winner:* Lisa Russ Spaar.

Witter Bynner Poetry Fellowships. To encourage poets and poetry. *Sponsor:* Witter Byner Foundation. *Winners:* Robert Bringhurst, Forrest Gander.

Hilary Weston Writers' Trust of Canada Prize for Nonfiction (C$60,000). *Winner:* Charles Foran for *Mordecai: The Life and Times,* a biography of Mordecai Richler (Knopf).

Whitbread Book Awards. See Costa Book Awards.

E. B. White Read-Aloud Awards. For children's books with particular appeal as read-aloud books. *Offered by:* American Booksellers Association/Association of Booksellers for Children. *Winners:* (picture book) Peter Brown for *Children Make Terrible Pets* (Little, Brown); (middle readers) Tom Angleberger for *The Strange Case of Origami Yoda* (Amulet).

Whiting Writers' Awards ($50,000). For emerging writers of exceptional talent and promise. *Offered by:* Mrs. Giles Whiting Foundation. *Winners:* (fiction) Scott Blackwood, Ryan Call, Daniel Orozco, Teddy Wayne; (nonfiction) Paul Clemens; (poetry) Don Mee Choi, Eduardo Corral, Shane McCrae, Kerri Webster; (plays) Amy Herzog.

Walt Whitman Award ($5,000). To a U.S. poet who has not published a book of poems in a standard edition. *Offered by:* Academy of American Poets. *Winner:* Elana Bell for *Eyes, Stones* (LSU Press).

Richard Wilbur Award ($1,000 and publication by University of Evansville Press). For a book-length poetry collection. *Winner:* Robert W. Crawford for *The Empty Chair.*

Laura Ingalls Wilder Award. Awarded biennially to an author or illustrator whose books have made a substantial and lasting contribution to children's literature. *Offered by:* American Library Association, Association for Library Service to Children. *Winner:* Tomie dePaola.

Thornton Wilder Prize for Translation ($20,000). To a practitioner, scholar, or patron who has made a significant contribution to the art of literary translation. *Offered by:* American Academy of Arts and Letters. *Winner:* Not awarded in 2011.

Robert H. Winner Memorial Award ($2,500). To a mid-career poet over 40 who has published no more than one book of poetry. *Offered by:* Poetry Society of America. *Winner:* Kathy Nilsson.

George Wittenborn Memorial Book Awards. To North American art publications that represent the highest standards of content, documentation, layout, and format. *Offered by:* Art Libraries Society of North America (ARLIS/NA). *Winners:* Ruth Barnes and Mary Hunt Kahlenberg for *Five Centuries of Indonesian Textiles: The Mary Hunt Kahlenberg Collection* (Prestel USA).

Thomas Wolfe Award and Lecture. To honor writers with distinguished bodies of work. *Offered by:* Thomas Wolfe Society and University of North Carolina at Chapel Hill. *Winner:* Al Young.

Thomas Wolfe Fiction Prize ($1,000). For a short story that honors Thomas Wolfe. *Offered by:* North Carolina Writers Network. *Winner:* Kristin Fitzpatrick for "Queen City Playhouse."

Helen and Kurt Wolff Translator's Prize ($10,000). For an outstanding translation from German into English, published in the United States. *Offered by:* Goethe Institut

Inter Nationes, Chicago. *Winner:* Jean M. Snook for her translation of Gert Jonke's *The Distant Sound* (Dalkey Archive).

World Fantasy Convention Awards. For outstanding fantasy writing. *Offered by:* World Fantasy Convention. *Winners:* (novel) Nnedi Okorafor for *Who Fears Death* (DAW); (novella) Elizabeth Hand for *The Maiden Flight of McCauley's Bellerophon* in *Stories: All-New Tales* (Morrow); (short story) Joyce Carol Oates for "Fossil-Figures" in *Stories: All-New Tales* (Morrow); (anthology) Kate Bernheimer, editor, for *My Mother She Killed Me, My Father He Ate Me* (Penguin); (collection) Karen Joy Fowler for *What I Didn't See and Other Stories* (Small Beer); (artist) Kinuko Y. Craft; (lifetime achievement) Peter S. Beagle, Angélica Gorodischer.

Writers' Trust Distinguished Contribution Award (Canada). To an individual or an organization in recognition of their long-standing involvement with the Writers' Trust of Canada. *Winner:* Alma Lee.

Writers' Trust Shaughnessy Cohen Prize for Political Writing (Canada) (C$25,000). For a nonfiction book that captures a subject of political interest. *Sponsor:* CTV. *Winner:* Anna Porter for *The Ghosts of Europe: Journeys Through Central Europe's Troubled Past and Uncertain Future* (Douglas & McIntyre).

Writers' Trust Engel/Findley Award (C$25,000). To a Canadian writer predominantly of fiction, for a body of work. *Winner:* Wayne Johnston.

Writers' Trust/McClelland & Stewart Journey Prize (Canada) (C$10,000). To a new, developing Canadian author for a short story or an excerpt from a novel in progress. *Offered by:* McClelland & Stewart. *Winner:* Miranda Hill for "Petitions to Saint Chronic" in the *Dalhousie Review.*

Writers' Trust Hilary Weston Prize for Nonfiction (Canada). See Hilary Weston Writers' Trust of Canada Prize for Nonfiction.

YALSA Award for Excellence in Nonfiction. For a work of nonfiction published for young adults (ages 12–18). *Offered by:* American Library Association, Young Adult Library Services Association. *Winner:* Ann Angel for *Janis Joplin: Rise Up Singing* (Amulet).

Young Lions Fiction Award ($10,000). For a novel or collection of short stories by an American under the age of 35. *Offered by:* Young Lions of the New York Public Library. *Winner:* Adam Levin for *The Instructions* (McSweeney's).

Morton Dauwen Zabel Award ($10,000). Awarded biennially to a progressive and experimental writer. *Offered by:* American Academy of Arts and Letters. *Winner:* To be awarded next in 2012.

Zoetrope Short Fiction Prizes. *Offered by:* Zoetrope: All-Story. *Winners:* (first, $1,000) Aimee LaBrie for "A Good Thing"; (second, $500) Amina Gautier for "Now We Will Be Happy"; (third, $250) B. G. Firmani for "How I Married Philip Glass."

Charlotte Zolotow Award. For outstanding writing in a picture book published in the United States in the previous year. *Offered by:* Cooperative Children's Book Center, University of Wisconsin–Madison. *Winner:* Rukhsana Khan for *Big Red Lollipop,* illustrated by Sophie Blackall (Viking).

Part 6
Directory of Organizations

Directory of Library and Related Organizations

Networks, Consortia, and Other Cooperative Library Organizations

United States

Alabama

Alabama Health Libraries Assn., Inc. (AL-HeLa), Lister Hill Lib., Univ. of Alabama, Birmingham 35294-0013. SAN 372-8218. Tel. 205-975-8313, fax 205-934-2230. *Pres.* Lee Vacovich.

Library Management Network, Inc. (LMN), 2132 6th Ave S.E., Suite 106, Decatur 35601. SAN 322-3906. Tel. 256-308-2529, fax 256-308-2533. *Systems Coord.* Charlotte Moncrief.

Marine Environmental Sciences Consortium, Dauphin Island Sea Laboratory, Dauphin Island 36528. SAN 322-0001. Tel. 251-861-2141, fax 251-861-4646, e-mail disl@disl.org. *Coord.* John Dindo.

Network of Alabama Academic Libraries, c/o Alabama Commission on Higher Education, Montgomery 36104. SAN 322-4570. Tel. 334-242-2211, fax 334-242-0270. *Dir.* Ron P. Leonard.

Alaska

Alaska Library Network (ALN), P.O. Box 100585, Anchorage 99501-0585. SAN 371-0688. Tel. 907-269-6567. *Exec. Dir.* Nina Malyshev.

Arizona

Maricopa County Community College District/Library Technology Services, 2411 W. 14 St., Tempe 85281-6942. SAN 322-0060. Tel. 480-731-8774, fax 480-731-8787. *Dir. of Technical Services* Thomas Saudargas.

Arkansas

Arkansas Area Health Education Center Consortium (AHEC), Sparks Regional Medical Center, Fort Smith 72917-7006. SAN 329-3734. Tel. 479-441-5337, fax 479-441-5339. *Dir.* Grace Anderson.

Arkansas Independent Colleges and Universities, Firstar Bldg., 1 Riverfront Place, Suite 610, North Little Rock 72114. SAN 322-0079. Tel. 501-378-0843, fax 501-374-1523. *Pres.* Kearney E. Dietz.

Mid-America Law Library Consortium (MALLCO), UALR Bowen School of Law Lib., 1203 McMath Ave., Little Rock 72202. Tel. 501-324-9980, fax 501-324-9447, e-mail sdgoldner@ualr.edu. *Exec. Dir.* Susan Goldner.

Northeast Arkansas Hospital Library Consortium, 223 E. Jackson, Jonesboro 72401. SAN 329-529X. Tel. 870-972-1290, fax 870-931-0839. *Dir.* Karen Crosser.

South Arkansas Film Coop., c/o Malvern-Hot Spring County Lib., Malvern 72104. SAN 321-5938. Tel. 501-332-5441, fax 501-332-6679, e-mail hotspringcountylibrary@yahoo.com. *Dir.* Tammy Carter.

California

49-99 Cooperative Library System, c/o Southern California Lib. Cooperative, Monrovia 91016. SAN 301-6218. Tel. 626-359-6111, fax 626-359-0001. *Dir.* Rosario Garza.

Bay Area Library and Information Network (BayNet), c/o San Francisco Public Lib., San Francisco 94702. SAN 371-0610. Tel. 415-355-2826, e-mail infobay@baynetlibs. org. *Pres.* Linda Suzukie.

Berkeley Information Network (BIN), Berkeley Public Lib., Berkeley 94704. Tel. 510-981-6166; 510-981-6150, fax 510-981-6246. *Mgr.* Jane Scantlebury.

Califa, 32 W. 25 Ave., Suite 201, San Mateo 94403. Tel. 650-572-2746, fax 650-349-5089, e-mail califa@califa.org. *Exec. Dir.* Linda Crowe.

Claremont University Consortium (CUC), 150 E. 8 St., Claremont 91711. Tel. 909-621-8026; 909-621-8150, fax 909-621-8681. *CEO* Robert Walton.

Consortium for Open Learning, 333 Sunrise Ave., No. 229, Roseville 95661-3480. SAN 329-4412. Tel. 916-788-0660, fax 916-788-0696. *Operations Mgr.* Sandra Scott-Smith.

Consumer Health Information Program and Services (CHIPS), 12350 Imperial Hwy., Norwalk 90650. SAN 372-8110. Tel. 562-868-4003, fax 562-868-4065, e-mail reference services@gw.colapl.org. *Libn.* Amy Beteilho.

Gold Coast Library Network, 3437 Empresa Drive, Suite C, San Luis Obispo 93401-7355. Tel. 805-543-6082, fax 805-543-9487. *Admin. Dir.* Maureen Theobald.

Kaiser Permanente Library System–Southern California Region (KPLS), Health Sciences Lib., Riverside 92505. SAN 372-8153. Tel. 951-353-3659, fax 951-353-3262. *Dir.* William Paringer.

Monterey Bay Area Cooperative Library System (MOBAC), 2471 Flores St., San Mateo 94403. SAN 301-2921. Tel. 650-349-5538, fax 650-349-5089. *Exec. Dir.* Linda Crowe.

Mountain Valley Library System (MVLS), 55 E St., Santa Rosa 95404. Tel. 707-544-0142, fax 707-544-8411 ext. 101. *Exec. Dir.* Annette Milliron.

National Network of Libraries of Medicine–Pacific Southwest Region (NN/LM-PSR), Louise M. Darling Biomedical Lib., Los Angeles 90095-1798. SAN 372-8234. Tel. 310-825-1200, fax 310-825-5389, e-mail psr-nnlm@library.ucla.edu. *Dir.* Judy Consales.

Nevada Medical Library Group (NMLG), Barton Memorial Hospital Lib., South Lake Tahoe 96150. SAN 370-0445. Tel. 530-543-5844, fax 530-541-4697. *Senior Exec. Coord.* Laurie Anton.

Northern California Assn. of Law Libraries (NOCALL), 268 Bush St., No. 4006, San Francisco 94104. SAN 323-5777. E-mail admin@nocall.org. *Pres.* Coral Henning.

Northern California Consortium of Psychology Libraries (NCCPL), Argosy Univ., San Francisco Bay Area Campus, Alameda 94133. SAN 371-9006. Tel. 510-837-3715. *Pres.* Julie Griffith.

Peninsula Libraries Automated Network (PLAN), 2471 Flores St., San Mateo 94403-4000. SAN 371-5035. Tel. 650-349-5538, fax 650-349-5089. *Dir., Information Technology.* Monica Schultz.

San Bernardino, Inyo, Riverside Counties United Library Services (SIRCULS), 3581 Mission Inn Ave., Riverside 92501-3377. SAN 322-0222. Tel. 951-369-7995, fax 951-784-1158, e-mail sirculs@inlandlib.org. *Exec. Dir.* Kathleen F. Aaron.

San Francisco Biomedical Library Network (SFBLN), San Francisco General Hospital UCSF/Barnett-Briggs Medical Lib., San Francisco 94110. SAN 371-2125. Tel. 415-206-6639, e-mail fishbon@ucsfmedctr.org.

Santa Clarita Interlibrary Network (SCILNET), Powell Lib., Santa Clarita 91321. SAN 371-8964. Tel. 661-259-3540 ext. 3420, fax 661-222-9159. *Libn.* John Stone.

Serra Cooperative Library System, c/o San Diego Public Library, San Diego 92101. SAN 301-3510. Tel. 619-232-1225, fax 619-696-8649, e-mail mad@serralib.org. *Head, ILL* Ralph DeLauro.

Southern California Library Cooperative (SCLC), 248 E. Foothill Blvd., Suite 101, Monrovia 91016-5522. SAN 371-3865. Tel.

626-359-6111, fax 626-359-0001, e-mail sclchq@socallibraries.org. *Dir.* Rosario Garza.

Substance Abuse Librarians and Information Specialists (SALIS), P.O. Box 9513, Berkeley 94709-0513. SAN 372-4042. Tel. 510-769-1831, fax 510-865-2467, e-mail salis@salis.org. *Exec. Dir.* Andrea L. Mitchell.

Colorado

Automation System Colorado Consortium (ASCC), c/o Delta Public Lib., Delta 81416. Tel. 970-872-4317. *Technology Consultant* Connie Wolfrom.

BCR (Bibliographical Center for Research), 14394 E. Evans Ave., Aurora 80014-1408. SAN 322-0338. Tel. 303-751-6277, fax 303-751-9787, e-mail info@bcr.org. *Pres. and CEO* Brenda Bailey-Hainer.

Colorado Alliance of Research Libraries, 3801 E. Florida Ave., Suite 515, Denver 80210. SAN 322-3760. Tel. 303-759-3399, fax 303-759-3363. *Exec. Dir.* Alan Charnes.

Colorado Assn. of Law Libraries, P.O. Box 13363, Denver 80201. SAN 322-4325. Tel. 303-492-7535, fax 303-492-2707. *Pres.* Tracy Leming.

Colorado Council of Medical Librarians (CCML), P.O. Box 101058, Denver 80210-1058. SAN 370-0755. Tel. 303-724-2124, fax 303-724-2154. *Pres.* Gene Gardner.

Colorado Library Consortium (CLiC), 7400 E. Arapahoe Rd., Suite 75, Centennial 80112. SAN 371-3970. Tel. 303-422-1150, fax 303-431-9752. *Dir.* Valerie Horton.

Connecticut

Bibliomation, 32 Crest Rd., Middlebury 06762. Tel. 203-577-4070, fax 203-577-4077. *CEO* Mike Simonds.

Capital Area Health Consortium, 270 Farmington Ave., Suite 352, Farmington 06032-1994. SAN 322-0370. Tel. 860-676-1110, fax 860-676-1303. *Pres.* Karen Goodman.

Connecticut Library Consortium, 234 Court St., Middletown 06457-3304. SAN 322-0389. Tel. 860-344-8777, fax 860-344-9199, e-mail clc@ctlibrarians.org. *Exec. Dir.* Christine Bradley.

Council of State Library Agencies in the Northeast (COSLINE), Connecticut State Lib., Hartford 06106. SAN 322-0451. Tel. 860-757-6510, fax 860-757-6503.

CTW Library Consortium, Olin Memorial Lib., Middletown 06459-6065. SAN 329-4587. Tel. 860-685-3889, fax 860-685-2661. *Systems Libn.* Steve Bischof.

Hartford Consortium for Higher Education, 950 Main St., Suite 314, Hartford 06103. SAN 322-0443. Tel. 860-906-5016, fax 860-906-5118. *Exec. Dir.* Rosanne Druckman.

LEAP, 110 Washington Ave., North Haven 06473. SAN 322-4082. Tel. 203-239-1411, fax 203-239-9458. *Exec. Dir.* Diana Sellers.

Libraries Online, Inc. (LION), 100 Riverview Center, Suite 252, Middletown 06457. SAN 322-3922. Tel. 860-347-1704, fax 860-346-3707. *Exec. Dir.* Alan Hagyard.

Library Connection, Inc., 599 Matianuck Ave., Windsor 06095-3567. Tel. 860-298-5322, fax 860-298-5328. *Exec. Dir.* George Christian.

Delaware

Central Delaware Library Consortium, Dover Public Lib., Dover 19901. SAN 329-3696. Tel. 302-736-7030, fax 302-736-5087. *Dir.* Margery Kirby Cyr.

Delaware Library Consortium (DLC), Delaware Academy of Medicine, Newark 19713. SAN 329-3718. Tel. 302-733-1122, fax 302-733-3885, e-mail library@delamed.org. *Dir.* P. J. Grier.

District of Columbia

Computer Sciences Corporation/ERIC Project, 655 15th St. N.W., Suite 500, Washington 20005. SAN 322-161X. Tel. 202-741-4200, fax 202-628-3205. *Dir.* Lawrence Henry.

Council for Christian Colleges and Universities, 321 8th St. N.E., Washington 20002. SAN 322-0524. Tel. 202-546-8713, fax 202-546-8913, e-mail council@cccu.org. *Pres.* Paul R. Corts.

District of Columbia Area Health Science Libraries (DCAHSL), American College of Obstetrics and Gynecology Resource Center, Washington 20024. SAN 323-9918. Tel. 202-863-2518, fax 202-484-1595, e-mail resources@acog.org. *Pres.* Rudine Anderson.

FEDLINK/Federal Library and Information Network, c/o Federal Lib. and Info. Center Committee, Washington 20540-4935. SAN 322-0761. Tel. 202-707-4800, fax 202-707-4818, e-mail flicc@loc.gov. *Exec. Dir.* Roberta I. Shaffer.

Interlibrary Users Assn. (IUA), c/o Urban Institute Lib., Washington 20037. SAN 322-1628. Tel. 202-261-5534, fax 202-223-3043. *Pres.* Nancy L. Minter.

OCLC Eastern,11 Dupont Circle N.E., Suite 550, Washington 20036-3430. SAN 321-5954. Tel. 202-331-5771, fax 202-331-5788, e-mail eastern@oclc.org. *Exec. Dir.* Irene M. Hoffman.

Transportation Research Board, 500 5th St. N.W., Washington 20001. SAN 370-582X. Tel. 202-334-2990, fax 202-334-2527. *Mgr., Info. Services* Barbara Post.

Veterans Affairs Library Network (VALNET), Lib. Programs Office 19E, Washington 20420. SAN 322-0834. *Dir. of Lib. Programs* Ginny DuPont.

Washington Theological Consortium, 487 Michigan Ave. N.E., Washington 20017-1585. SAN 322-0842. Tel. 202-832-2675, fax 202-526-0818, e-mail wtc@washtheocon.org. *Exec. Dir.* Larry Golemon.

Florida

Central Florida Library Cooperative (CFLC), 431 E. Horatio Ave., Suite 230, Maitland 32751. SAN 371-9014. Tel. 407-644-9050, fax 407-644-7023, e-mail contactus@cflc.net. *Exec. Dir.* Marta Westall.

College Center for Library Automation (CCLA), 1753 W. Paul Dirac Drive, Tallahassee 32310. Tel. 850-922-6044, fax 850-922-4869, e-mail servicedesk@cclaflorida.org. *Exec. Dir.* Richard Madaus.

Consortium of Southeastern Law Libraries (COSELL), Lawton Chiles Legal Information Center, Gainesville 32611. SAN 372-8277. Tel. 352-273-0710, fax 352-392-5093. *Chair* Gordon Russell.

Florida Center for Library Automation (FCLA), 5830 N.W. 39 Ave., Gainesville 32606. Tel. 352-392-9020, fax 352-392-9185, e-mail fclmin@ufl.edu. *Dir.* James Corey.

Florida Library Information Network, R. A. Gray Bldg., Tallahassee 32399-0250. SAN 322-0869. Tel. 850-245-6600, fax 850-245-6744, e-mail library@dos.myflorida.com. *Lending Services Libn.* Linda Pulliam.

Miami Health Sciences Library Consortium (MHSLC), Miami VA Healthcare System, Miami 33125-1624. SAN 371-0734. Tel. 305-575-3187, fax 305-575-3118, e-mail vhamialibrary@va.gov. *Pres.* Devica Samsundar.

Northeast Florida Library Information Network (NEFLIN), 2233 Park Ave., Suite 402, Orange Park 32073. Tel. 904-278-5620, fax 904-278-5625, e-mail office@neflin.org. *Exec. Dir.* Brad Ward.

Panhandle Library Access Network (PLAN), Five Miracle Strip Loop, Suite 8, Panama City Beach 32407-3850. SAN 370-047X. Tel. 850-233-9051, fax 850-235-2286. *Exec. Dir.* William P. Conniff.

SEFLIN/Southeast Florida Library Information Network, Inc, Wimberly Lib., Office 452, Boca Raton 33431. SAN 370-0666. Tel. 561-208-0984, fax 561-208-0995. *Interim Dir.* Jeannette Smithee.

Southwest Florida Library Network (SWFLN), Bldg. III, Unit 7, Fort Myers 33913. Tel. 239-225-4225, fax 239-225-4229, e-mail swfln@fgcu.edu. *Exec. Dir.* Sondra Taylor-Furbee.

Tampa Bay Library Consortium, Inc., 1202 Tech Blvd., Suite 202, Tampa 33619. SAN 322-371X. Tel. 813-740-3963; 813-622-8252, fax 813-628-4425. *Exec. Dir.* Charlie Parker.

Tampa Bay Medical Library Network (TA-BAMLN), Florida Hospital College of Health Sciences, Orlando 32803-1226. SAN 322-0885. Tel. 407-303-9798, fax 407-303-9408. *Pres.* Deanna Stevens.

Georgia

Assn. of Southeastern Research Libraries (ASERL), c/o LYRASIS, Atlanta 30309-2955. SAN 322-1555. Tel. 404-892-0943, fax 404-892-7879. *Exec. Dir.* John Burger.

Atlanta Health Science Libraries Consortium, Fran Golding Medical Lib. at Scottish Rite, Atlanta 30342-1600. Tel. 404-785-2157, fax 404-785-2155. *Pres.* Kate Daniels.

Atlanta Regional Council for Higher Education (ARCHE), 50 Hurt Plaza, Suite 735, Atlanta 30303-2923. SAN 322-0990. Tel. 404-651-

2668, fax 404-880-9816, e-mail arche@atlantahighered.org. *Pres.* Michael Gerber.

Georgia Interactive Network for Medical Information (GAIN), c/o Mercer Univ. School of Medicine, Macon 31207. SAN 370-0577. Tel. 478-301-2515, fax 478-301-2051, e-mail gain.info@gain.mercer.edu. *Dir.* Jan H. LaBeause.

Georgia Online Database (GOLD), c/o Public Lib. Services, Atlanta 30345-4304. SAN 322-094X. Tel. 404-235-7200, fax 404-235-7201. *Dir., Resource Sharing and Interlibrary Cooperation* Toni Zimmerman.

LYRASIS, 1438 W. Peachtree St. N.W., Suite 200, Atlanta 30309-2955. SAN 322-0974. Tel. 404-892-0943, fax 404-892-7879. *Exec. Dir.* Kate Nevins.

Metro Atlanta Library Assn. (MALA), P.O. Box 14948, Atlanta 30324. SAN 378-2549. Tel. 678-915-7207, fax 678-915-7471, e-mail mala-a@comcast.net. *Pres.* Steven Vincent.

Hawaii

Hawaii Library Consortium (HLC), c/o Hawaii Business Research Lib., Kihei 96753. Tel. 808-875-2408. *Pres.* Sonia I. King.

Hawaii-Pacific Chapter, Medical Library Assn. (HPC-MLA), Health Sciences Lib., Honolulu 96813. SAN 371-3946. Tel. 808-692-0810, fax 808-692-1244. *Chair* A. Lee Adams.

Idaho

Canyon Owyhee Library Group, Ltd. (COLG), 203 E. Owyhee Ave., Homedale 83628. Tel. 208-337-4613, fax 208-337-4933. *Pres.* Bonnie Speas.

Cooperative Information Network (CIN), 8385 N. Government Way, Hayden 83835-9280. SAN 323-7656. Tel. 208-772-5612, fax 208-772-2498, e-mail hay@cin.kcl.org. *Fiscal Agent* John W. Hartung.

Idaho Health Information Assn. (IHIA), c/o Eastern Idaho Regional Medical Center, Idaho Falls 83403. SAN 371-5078. Tel. 208-529-6077, fax 208-529-7014. *Dir.* Kathy Fatkin.

Library Consortium of Eastern Idaho (LCEI), 149 South Main, Soda Springs 83276. SAN

323-7699. Tel. 208-547-2606. *Pres.* Cindy Erickson.

LYNX Consortium, c/o Boise Public Lib., Boise 83702-7195. SAN 375-0086. Tel. 208-384-4238, fax 208-384-4025.

Western Council of State Libraries, Inc., c/o Idaho Commission for Libraries, Boise 83702-6055. Tel. 208-334-2150, fax 208-334-4016. *Pres.* Ann Joslin.

Illinois

American Theological Library Assn. (ATLA), 300 S. Wacker Drive, Suite 2100, Chicago 60606-5889. SAN 371-9022. Tel. 312-454-5100, fax 312-454-5505, e-mail atla@atla.com. *Exec. Dir.* Dennis A. Norlin.

Areawide Hospital Library Consortium of Southwestern Illinois (AHLC), c/o St. Elizabeth Hospital Health Sciences Lib., Belleville 62222. SAN 322-1016. Tel. 618-234-2120 ext. 2011, fax 618-222-4614.

Assn. of Chicago Theological Schools (ACTS), Univ. of St. Mary of the Lake, Mundelein 60060-1174. SAN 370-0658. Tel. 847-566-6401. *Chair* Thomas Baima.

Capital Area Consortium, 701 N. 1 St., Springfield 62781. *Coord.* Lynne Ferrell.

Center for Research Libraries, 6050 S. Kenwood, Chicago 60637-2804. SAN 322-1032. Tel. 773-955-4545, fax 773-955-4339. *Pres.* Bernard F. Reilly.

Chicago and South Consortium, Jackson Park Hospital and Medical Center, Chicago 60649-3993. SAN 322-1067. Tel. 773-947-7653. *Coord.* Andrew Paradise.

Chicago Area Museum Libraries (CAML), c/o Lib., Field Museum, Chicago 60605-2496. SAN 371-392X. Tel. 312-665-7970, fax 312-665-7893. *Museum Libn.* Christine Giannoni.

Committee on Institutional Cooperation, 1819 S. Neil St., Suite D, Champaign 61820-7271. Tel. 217-333-8475, fax 217-244-7127, e-mail cic@staff.cic.net. *Dir.* Barbara Mcfadden Allen.

Council of Directors of State University Libraries in Illinois (CODSULI), Southern Illinois Univ. School of Medicine Lib., Springfield 62702-4910. SAN 322-1083. Tel. 217-545-0994, fax 217-545-0988.

East Central Illinois Consortium, Booth Lib., Eastern Illinois Univ., Charleston 61920.

SAN 322-1040. Tel. 217-581-7549, fax 217-581-7534. *Mgr.* Stacey Knight-Davis.

Fox Valley Health Science Library Consortium, c/o Delnor-Community Hospital, Geneva 60134. SAN 329-3831. Tel. 630-208-4299.

Heart of Illinois Library Consortium, 511 N.E. Greenleaf, Peoria 61603. SAN 322-1113. *Chair* Leslie Menz.

Illinois Library and Information Network (IL-LINET), c/o Illinois State Lib., Springfield 62701-1796. SAN 322-1148. Tel. 217-782-2994, fax 217-785-4326. *Dir.* Anne Craig.

Illinois Office of Educational Services, 2450 Foundation Drive, Suite 100, Springfield 62703-5464. SAN 371-5108. Tel. 217-786-3010, fax 217-786-3020, e-mail info@ioes. org. *Dir.* Rebecca Woodhull.

LIBRAS, Inc., North Park Univ., Chicago 60625-4895. SAN 322-1172. Tel. 773-244-5584, fax 773-244-4891. *Pres.* Mark Vargas.

Metropolitan Consortium of Chicago, Chicago School of Professional Psychology, Chicago 60610. SAN 322-1180. Tel. 312-329-6633, fax 312-644-6075. *Coord.* Margaret White.

National Network of Libraries of Medicine–Greater Midwest Region (NN/LM-GMR), c/o Lib. of Health Sciences, Univ. of Illinois at Chicago, Chicago 60612-4330. SAN 322-1202. Tel. 312-996-2464, fax 312-996-2226. *Dir.* Kathryn Carpenter.

Network of Illinois Learning Resources in Community Colleges (NILRC), PO Box 120, Blanchardville 53516-0120. Tel. 608-523-4094, fax 608-523-4072. *Business Mgr.* Lisa Sikora.

Quad Cities Libraries in Cooperation (Quad-LINC), 220 W. 23 Ave., Coal Valley 61240. SAN 373-093X. Tel. 309-799-3155 ext. 3254, fax 309-799-7916.

System Wide Automated Network (SWAN), c/o Metropolitan Lib. System, Burr Ridge 60527-5783. Tel. 630-734-5000, fax 630-734-5050. *Dir.* Aaron Skog.

Indiana

Central Indiana Health Science Libraries Consortium, Indiana Univ. School of Medicine Lib., Indianapolis 46202. SAN 322-1245. Tel. 317-274-8358, fax 317-274-4056. *Officer* Elaine Skopelja.

Collegiate Consortium Western Indiana, c/o Cunningham Memorial Lib., Terre Haute 47809. SAN 329-4439. Tel. 812-237-3700, fax 812-237-3376. *Interim Dean* Alberta Comer.

Consortium of College and University Media Centers (CCUMC), Indiana Univ., Bloomington 47405-1223. SAN 322-1091. Tel. 812-855-6049, fax 812-855-2103, e-mail ccumc @ccumc.org. *Exec. Dir.* Aileen Scales.

Consortium of Foundation Libraries, IUPUI Univ. Lib., Indianapolis 46202. SAN 322-2462. Tel. 317-278-2329. *Chair* Brenda Burk.

Evansville Area Library Consortium, 3700 Washington Ave., Evansville 47750. SAN 322-1261. Tel. 812-485-4151, fax 812-485-7564. *Coord.* Jane Saltzman.

Indiana State Data Center, Indiana State Lib., Indianapolis 46202. SAN 322-1318. Tel. 317-232-3733, fax 317-232-3728. *Coord.* Katie Springer.

Northeast Indiana Health Science Libraries Consortium (NEIHSL), Univ. of Saint Francis Vann Lib., Fort Wayne 46808. SAN 373-1383. Tel. 260-399-7700 ext. 6065, fax 260-399-8166. *Coord.* Lauralee Aven.

Northwest Indiana Health Science Library Consortium (NIHSLC), c/o N.W. Center for Medical Education, Gary 46408-1197. SAN 322-1350. Tel. 219-980-6852; 219-980-6709, fax 219-980-6524; 219-980-6566. *Coord. Lib. Services* Corona Wiley.

Iowa

Consortium of User Libraries (CUL), Lib. for the Blind and Physically Handicapped, Des Moines 50309-2364. Tel. 515-281-1333, fax 515-281-1378; 515-281-1263. *Pres.* Karen Keninger.

Dubuque (Iowa) Area Library Information Consortium, c/o Burton Payne Lib., N.E. Iowa Community College, Peosta 52068. Tel. 563-556-5110 ext. 269, fax 563-557-0340. *Coord.* Deb Seiffert.

Iowa Private Academic Library Consortium (IPAL), c/o Buena Vista Univ. Lib., Storm Lake 50588. SAN 329-5311. Tel. 712-749-2127, 712-749-2203, fax 712-749-2059, e-mail library@bvu.edu. *Pres.* Rodney N. Henshaw.

Linn County Library Consortium, Russell D. Cole Lib., Mount Vernon 52314-1012. SAN 322-4597. Tel. 319-895-4259. *Pres.* Jason Bengtson.

Polk County Biomedical Consortium, c/o Broadlawns Medical Center Lib., Des Moines 50314. SAN 322-1431. Tel. 515-282-2394, fax 515-282-5634. *Treas.* Elaine Hughes.

Quad City Area Biomedical Consortium, Great River Medical Center Lib., West Burlington 52655. SAN 322-435X. Tel. 319-768-4075, fax 319-768-4080. *Coord.* Judy Hawk.

Sioux City Library Cooperative (SCLC), c/o Sioux City Public Lib., Sioux City 51101-1203. SAN 329-4722. Tel. 712-255-2933 ext. 255, fax 712-279-6432. *Chair* Betsy Thompson.

State of Iowa Libraries Online (SILO), State Lib. of Iowa, Des Moines 50319. SAN 322-1415. Tel. 515-281-4105, fax 515-281-6191. *State Libn.* Mary Wegner.

Kansas

Associated Colleges of Central Kansas (ACCK), 210 S. Main St., McPherson 67460. SAN 322-1474. Tel. 620-241-5150, fax 620-241-5153.

Dodge City Library Consortium, c/o Comanche Intermediate Center, Dodge City 67801. SAN 322-4368. Tel. 620-227-1609, fax 620-227-4862.

Kansas Regents Library Database Consortium (RLDC), c/o Emporia State Univ., Emporia 66801. Tel. 620-341-5480, e-mail rldc@ku.edu. *Chair* Cynthia Akers.

State Library of Kansas/Statewide Resource Sharing Div., 300 S.W. 10 Ave., Room 343 N., Topeka 66612-1593. SAN 329-5621. Tel. 785-296-3875, fax 785-368-7291. *Dir.* Patti Butcher.

Kentucky

Assn. of Independent Kentucky Colleges and Universities (AIKCU), 484 Chenault Rd., Frankfort 40601. SAN 322-1490. Tel. 502-695-5007, fax 502-695-5057. *Pres.* Gary S. Cox.

Eastern Kentucky Health Science Information Network (EKHSIN), c/o Camden-Carroll Lib., Morehead 40351. SAN 370-0631. Tel.

606-783-6860, fax 606-784-2178. *Lib. Dir.* Tammy Jenkins.

Kentuckiana Metroversity, Inc., 109 E. Broadway, Louisville 40202. SAN 322-1504. Tel. 502-897-3374, fax 502-895-1647.

Kentucky Medical Library Assn., VA Medical Center, Lib. Serices 142D, Louisville 40206-1499. SAN 370-0623. Tel. 502-287-6240, fax 502-287-6134. *Head Libn.* Gene M. Haynes.

Kentucky Virtual Library (KVL), 1024 Capital Center Drive, Suite 320, Frankfort 40601. Tel. 502-573-1555, fax 502-573-0222, e-mail kyvl@ky.gov. *Dir.* Enid Wohlstein.

Southeastern Chapter of the American Assn. of Law Libraries (SEAALL), c/o Univ. of Kentucky Law Lib., Lexington 40506-0048. Tel. 859-257-8347, fax 859-323-4906. *Pres.* Amy Osborne.

Theological Education Assn. of Mid America (TEAM-A), Southern Baptist Theological Seminary, Louisville 40280. SAN 377-5038. Tel. 502-897-4807, fax 502-897-4600. *Dir., Info. Resources* Ken Boyd.

Louisiana

Central Louisiana Medical Center Library Consortium (CLMLC), 2495 Shreveport Hwy., 142D, Alexandria 71306. Tel. 318-619-9102, fax 318-619-9144, e-mail clmlc8784@yahoo.com. *Coord.* Miriam J. Brown.

Health Sciences Library Assn. of Louisiana (HSLAL), LSUHSC Lib., Shreveport 71103. SAN 375-0035. *Pres.* Jessica Delgado

Loan SHARK, State Lib. of Louisiana, Baton Rouge 70802. SAN 371-6880. Tel. 225-342-4920, 342-4918, fax 225-219-4725. *Head, Access Services* Kytara A. Gaudin.

LOUIS/Louisiana Library Network, Info. Technology Services, Baton Rouge 70803. *Exec. Dir.* Ralph Boe.

New Orleans Educational Telecommunications Consortium, 6400 Press Dr., New Orleans 70126. SAN 329-5214. Tel. 504-524-0350, e-mail noetc@noetc.org. *Exec. Dir.* Susan M. Simkowski.

Maine

Health Science Library Information Consortium (HSLIC), 211 Marginal Way, No 245, Portland 04101. SAN 322-1601. Tel. 207-

795-2561, fax 207-795-2569. *Chair* Kathy Brunjes.

Maryland

Maryland Assn. of Health Science Librarians (MAHSL), VA Medical HealthCare System Medical Lib., Baltimore 21201. SAN 377-5070. Tel. 401-605-7093. *Co-Pres.* Brittany Rice.

Maryland Interlibrary Loan Organization (MILO), c/o Enoch Pratt Free Lib., Baltimore 21201-4484. SAN 343-8600. Tel. 410-396-5498, fax 410-396-5837, e-mail milo@prattlibrary.org. *Mgr.* Emma E. Beaven.

National Network of Libraries of Medicine (NN/LM), National Lib. of Medicine, Bethesda 20894. SAN 373-0905. Tel. 301-496-4777, fax 301-480-1467. *Dir.* Angela Ruffin.

National Network of Libraries of Medicine–Southeastern Atlantic Region (NN/LM-SEA), Univ. of Maryland Health Sciences and Human Services Lib., Baltimore 21201-1512. SAN 322-1644. Tel. 410-706-2855, fax 410-706-0099, e-mail hshsl-nlmsea@hshsl.umaryland.edu. *Dir.* Mary J. Tooey.

Regional Alcohol and Drug Abuse Resource Network (RADAR), National Clearinghouse on Alcohol and Drug Info., Rockville 20852. SAN 377-5569. Tel. 301-468-2600, fax 301-468-6433.

U.S. National Library of Medicine (NLM), 8600 Rockville Pike, Bethesda 20894. SAN 322-1652. Tel. 301-594-5983, fax 301-402-1384, e-mail custserv@nlm.nih.gov. *Coord.* Martha Fishel.

Washington Research Library Consortium (WRLC), 901 Commerce Drive, Upper Marlboro 20774. SAN 373-0883. Tel. 301-390-2031, fax 301-390-2020. *Dir. of Lib. Services* Bruce Hulse.

Massachusetts

Boston Biomedical Library Consortium (BBLC), c/o Dana Farber Cancer Trust, Boston 02115. SAN 322-1725. *Pres.* Christine Fleuriel.

Boston Library Consortium, Inc., McKim Bldg., Boston 02117. SAN 322-1733. Tel. 617-262-6244, fax 617-262-0163, e-mail

mtrevvett@blc.org. *Exec. Dir.* Melissa Trevvett.

Cape Libraries Automated Materials Sharing Network (CLAMS), 270 Communication Way, Unit 4E, Hyannis 02601. SAN 370-579X. Tel. 508-790-4399, fax 508-771-4533. *Exec. Dir.* Gayle Simundza.

Central and Western Massachusetts Automated Resource Sharing (C/W MARS), 67 Millbrook St., Suite 201, Worcester 01606. SAN 322-3973. Tel. 508-755-3323 ext. 30, fax 508-755-3721. *Exec. Dir.* Joan Kuklinski.

Cooperating Libraries of Greater Springfield (CLGS), Springfield Technical Community College, Springfield 01102. SAN 322-1768. Tel. 413-755-4565, fax 413-755-6315, e-mail lcoakley@stcc.edu. *Coord.* Lynn Coakley.

Fenway Libraries Online, Inc. (FLO), c/o Wentworth Institute of Technology, Boston 02115. SAN 373-9112. Tel. 617-442-2384, fax 617-442-1519. *Exec. Dir.* Walter Stine.

Massachusetts Health Sciences Libraries Network (MAHSLIN), Brigham and Women's Hospital Medical Lib., Boston 02115. SAN 372-8293. Tel. 617-632-2489. *Chair* Christine Fleuriel.

Massachusetts Library System (MLS), 225 Cedar Hill St., Suite 229, Marlborough 01752. Tel. 508-357-2121. *Pres.* Dianna Magnoni.

Merrimack Valley Library Consortium, 1600 Osgood St., North Andover 01845. SAN 322-4384. Tel. 978-557-1050, fax 978-557-8101, e-mail netmail@mvlc.org. *Exec. Dir.* Lawrence Rungren.

Minuteman Library Network, 10 Strathmore Rd., Natick 01760-2419. SAN 322-4252. Tel. 508-655-8008, fax 508-655-1507. *Exec. Dir.* Susan McAlister.

National Network of Libraries of Medicine–New England Region (NN/LM-NER), Univ. of Massachusetts Medical School, Shrewsbury 01545-2732. SAN 372-5448. Tel. 508-856-5979, fax 508-856-5977. *Dir.* Elaine Martin.

North of Boston Library Exchange, Inc. (NOBLE), 26 Cherry Hill Drive, Danvers 01923. SAN 322-4023. Tel. 978-777-8844, fax 978-750-8472. *Exec. Dir.* Ronald A. Gagnon.

Northeast Consortium of Colleges and Universities in Massachusetts (NECCUM), Merrimack College, North Andover 01845. SAN

371-0602. Tel. 978-556-3400, fax 978-556-3738. *Pres.* Richard Santagati.

Northeastern Consortium for Health Information (NECHI), Lowell General Hospital Health Science Lib., Lowell 01854. SAN 322-1857. Tel. 978-937-6247, fax 978-937-6855. *Libn.* Donna Beales.

SAILS, Inc., 547 W. Groves St., Suite 4, Middleboro 02346. SAN 378-0058. Tel. 508-946-8600, fax 508-946-8605. *Pres.* Robin Glasser.

Southeastern Massachusetts Consortium of Health Science Libraries (SEMCO), Youngdahl Lib., Norwood Hospital, Norwood 02062. SAN 322-1873. Tel. 781-278-6243, fax 781-769-9622. *Chair* Denise Corless.

Western Massachusetts Health Information Consortium, Baystate Medical Center Health Sciences Lib., Springfield 01199. SAN 329-4579. Tel. 413-794-1865, fax 413-794-1974. *Pres.* Susan La Forter.

Michigan

Detroit Area Consortium of Catholic Colleges, c/o Sacred Heart Seminary, Detroit 48206. SAN 329-482X. Tel. 313-883-8500, fax 313-883-8594. *Acting Dir.* Chris Spilker.

Detroit Area Library Network (DALNET), 6th Floor SEL, 5048 Gullen Mall, Detroit 48202. Tel. 313-577-6789, fax 313-577-1231. *Exec. Dir.* Steven K. Bowers.

Kalamazoo Consortium for Higher Education (KCHE), Kalamazoo College, Kalamazoo 49006. SAN 329-4994. Tel. 269-337-7220, fax 269-337-7219. *Pres.* Eileen B. Wilson-Oyelaran.

Lakeland Library Cooperative, 4138 Three Mile Rd. N.W., Grand Rapids 49534-1134. SAN 308-132X. Tel. 616-559-5253, fax 616-559-4329. *Dir.* Sandra Wilson.

The Library Network (TLN), 13331 Reeck Rd., Southgate 48195-3054. SAN 370-596X. Tel. 734-281-3830, fax 734-281-1905. *Dir.* James Pletz.

Michigan Health Sciences Libraries Assn. (MHSLA), 1407 Rensen St., Suite 4, Lansing 48910. SAN 323-987X. Tel. 517-394-2774, fax 517-394-2675. *Pres.* Sheila Bryant.

Mideastern Michigan Library Cooperative, 503 S. Saginaw St., Suite 839, Flint 48502. SAN

346-5187. Tel. 810-232-7119, fax 810-232-6639. *Dir.* Roger Mendel.

Mid-Michigan Library League, 210 1/2 N Mitchell, Cadillac 49601-1835. SAN 307-9325. Tel. 231-775-3037, fax 231-775-1749. *Dir.* James Lawrence.

Midwest Collaborative for Library Services, 1407 Rensen St., Suite 1, Lansing 48910-3657. Tel. 800-530-9019, fax 517-394-2096. *Exec. Dir.* Randy Dykhuis.

PALnet, 1040 W Bristol Rd., Flint 48507. Tel. 810-766-4070. *Dir.* Stephanie C. John.

Southeastern Michigan League of Libraries (SEMLOL), Lawrence Technological Univ., Southfield 48075. SAN 322-4481. Tel. 248-204-3000, fax 248-204-3005. *Treas.* Gary Cocozzoli.

Southwest Michigan Library Cooperative, Willard Public Library, Battle Creek, 49017. SAN 308-2156. Tel. 269-968-8166, email rhulsey@willard.lib.mi.us. *Dir.* Rick Hulsey.

Suburban Library Cooperative (SLC), 44750 Delco Blvd., Sterling Heights 48313. SAN 373-9082. Tel. 586-685-5750, fax 586-685-3010. *Interim Dir.* Arthur M. Woodford.

Upper Peninsula of Michigan Health Science Library Consortium, c/o Marquette Health System Hospital, Marquette 49855. SAN 329-4803. Tel. 906-225-3429, fax 906-225-3524. *Lib. Mgr.* Janis Lubenow.

Upper Peninsula Region of Library Cooperation, Inc., 1615 Presque Isle Ave., Marquette 49855. SAN 329-5540. Tel. 906-228-7697, fax 906-228-5627. *Treas.* Suzanne Dees.

Valley Library Consortium, 3210 Davenport Ave., Saginaw 48602-3495. Tel. 989-497-0925, fax 989-497-0918. *Exec. Dir.* Karl R. Steiner.

Minnesota

Capital Area Library Consortium (CALCO), c/o Minnesota Dept. of Transportation, Lib. MS155, Saint Paul 55155. SAN 374-6127. Tel. 651-296-5272, fax 651-297-2354. *Libn.* Shirley Sherkow.

Central Minnesota Libraries Exchange (CMLE), Miller Center, Room 130-D, Saint Cloud 56301-4498. SAN 322-3779. Tel. 320-308-2950, fax 320-654-5131, e-mail cmle@stcloudstate.edu. *Dir.* Patricia A. Post.

Cooperating Libraries in Consortium (CLIC), 1619 Dayton Ave., Suite 204, Saint Paul 55104. SAN 322-1970. Tel. 651-644-3878, fax 651-644-6258. *System Admin.* Deb Bergeron.

Metronet, 1619 Dayton Ave., Suite 314, Saint Paul 55104. SAN 322-1989. Tel. 651-646-0475, fax 651-649-3169, e-mail information @metrolibraries.net. *Exec. Dir.* Ann Walker Smalley.

Metropolitan Library Service Agency (MEL-SA), 1619 Dayton Ave., No. 314, Saint Paul 55104-6206. SAN 371-5124. Tel. 651-645-5731, fax 651-649-3169, e-mail melsa@melsa.org. *Exec. Dir.* Chris D. Olson.

MINITEX Library Information Network, 15 Andersen Lib., Univ. of Minnesota–Twin Cities, Minneapolis 55455-0439. SAN 322-1997. Tel. 612-624-4002, fax 612-624-4508. *Dir.* William DeJohn.

Minnesota Library Information Network (MnLINK), Univ. of Minnesota–Twin Cities, Minneapolis 55455-0439. Tel. 612-624-8096, fax 612-624-4508. *Info. Specialist* Nick Banitt.

Minnesota Theological Library Assn. (MTLA), Luther Seminary Lib., Saint Paul 55108. SAN 322-1962. Tel. 651-641-3447. *Chair* David Stewart.

North Country Library Cooperative, 5528 Emerald Ave., Mountain Iron 55768-2069. SAN 322-3795. Tel. 218-741-1907, fax 218-741-1908. *Dir.* Linda J. Wadman.

Northern Lights Library Network, 103 Graystone Plaza, Detroit Lakes 56501-3041. SAN 322-2004. Tel. 218-847-2825, fax 218-847-1461, e-mail nloffice@nlln.org. *Exec. Dir.* Kathy B. Enger.

SMILE (Southcentral Minnesota Inter-Library Exchange), 1400 Madison Ave., No. 622, Mankato 56001. SAN 321-3358. Tel. 507-625-7555, fax 507-625-4049, e-mail smile@tds.lib.mn.us. *Dir.* Nancy Katharine Steele.

Southeastern Libraries Cooperating (SELCO), 2600 19th St. N.W., Rochester 55901-0767. SAN 308-7417. Tel. 507-288-5513, fax 507-288-8697. *Exec. Dir.* Ann Hutton.

Southwest Area Multicounty Multitype Interlibrary Exchange (SAMMIE), 109 S. 5 St., Suite 30, Marshall 56258-1240. SAN 322-2039. Tel. 507-532-9013, fax 507-532-2039, e-mail info@sammie.org. *Dir.* Robin Chaney.

Twin Cities Biomedical Consortium (TCBC), c/o Fairview Univ. Medical Center, Minneapolis 55455. SAN 322-2055. Tel. 612-273-6595, fax 612-273-2675. *Mgr.* Colleen Olsen.

Mississippi

Central Mississippi Library Council (CMLC), c/o Millsaps College Lib., Jackson 39210. SAN 372-8250. Tel. 601-974-1070, fax 601-974-1082. *Admin./Treas.* Tom Henderson.

Mississippi Electronic Libraries Online (MELO), Mississippi State Board for Community and Junior Colleges, Jackson 39211. Tel. 601-432-6518, fax 601-432-6363, e-mail melo@colin.edu. *Dir.* Audra Kimball.

Missouri

Greater Western Library Alliance (GWLA), 5109 Cherry St., Kansas City 64110. Tel. 816-926-8765, fax 816-926-8790. *Exec. Dir.* Joni Blake.

Health Sciences Library Network of Kansas City (HSLNKC), Univ. of Missouri–Kansas City Health Sciences Lib., Kansas City 64108-2792. SAN 322-2098. Tel. 816-235-1880, fax 816-235-6570. *Dir.* Peggy Mullaly-Quijas.

Kansas City Library Service Program (KC-LSP), 14 W. 10 St., Kansas City 64105.Tel. 816-701-3520, fax 816-701-3401, e-mail kclcsupport@kclibrary.org. *Dir. of Business and Library Systems* Steven Knapp.

Kansas City Metropolitan Library and Information Network, 15624 E. 24 Hwy., Independence 64050. SAN 322-2101. Tel. 816-521-7257, fax 816-461-0966. *Exec. Dir.* Susan Burton.

Missouri Library Network Corp. (MLNC), 8045 Big Bend Blvd., Suite 202, Saint Louis 63119-2714. SAN 322-466X. Tel. 314-918-7222, fax 314-918-7727, e-mail support@mlnc.org. *Exec. Dir.* Tracy Byerly.

Saint Louis Regional Library Network, 341 Sappington Rd., Saint Louis 63122. SAN 322-2209. Tel. 314-395-1305.

Nebraska

ICON Library Consortium, McGoogan Lib. of Medicine, Univ. of Nebraska, Omaha

68198-6705. Tel. 402-559-7099, fax 402-559-5498.

Southeast Nebraska Library System, 5730 R St., Suite C-1, Lincoln 68505. SAN 322-4732. Tel. 402-467-6188, fax 402-467-6196. *Pres.* Glenda Willnerd.

Nevada

Desert States Law Library Consortium, Wiener-Rogers Law Lib., William S. Boyd School of Law, Las Vegas 89154-1080. Tel. 702-895-2400, fax 702-895-2416. *Collection Development Libn.* Matthew Wright.

Information Nevada, Interlibrary Loan Dept., Nevada State Lib. and Archives, Carson City 89701-4285. SAN 322-2276. Tel. 775-684-3328, fax 775-684-3330. *Asst. Admin., Lib. and Development Services* Karen Starr.

New Hampshire

Carroll County Library Cooperative, c/o Conway Public Lib., P.O. Box 2100, Conway 03818. Tel. 603-447-5552, fax 603-447-6921, e-mail tthomas@conway.lib.nh.us. *Dir.* Tara Thomas.

GMILCS, Inc., 1701B Hooksett Rd., Hooksett 03106. Tel. 603-485-4286, fax 603-485-4246, e-mail helpdesk@gmilcs.org. *Chair* Dianne Hathaway.

Health Sciences Libraries of New Hampshire and Vermont, Breene Memorial Lib., New Hampshire Hospital, Concord 03246. SAN 371-6864. Tel. 603-527-2837, fax 603-527-7197. *Admin. Coord.* Marion Allen.

Librarians of the Upper Valley Coop. (LUV Coop), c/o Hanover Town Lib., Etna 03750. SAN 371-6856. Tel. 603-643-3116. *Coord.* Barbara Prince.

Merri-Hill-Rock Library Cooperative, c/o Manchester City Lib., 405 Pine St., Manchester 03104. Tel. 603-624-6550, fax 603-624-6559, e-mail aletourn@manchesternh. gov. *Chair* Arlene Letourneau.

New England Law Library Consortium, Inc. (NELLCO), 9 Drummer Rd., Keene 03431. SAN 322-4244. Tel. 603-357-3385, fax 603-357-2075. *Exec. Dir.* Tracy L. Thompson.

New Hampshire College and University Council, Three Barrell Court, Suite 100, Concord 03301-8543. SAN 322-2322. Tel. 603-225-

4199, fax 603-225-8108. *Pres.* Thomas R. Horgan.

Nubanusit Library Cooperative, c/o Peterborough Town Lib., Peterborough 03458. SAN 322-4600. Tel. 603-924-8040, fax 603-924-8041.

Scrooge and Marley Cooperative, 695 Main St., Laconia 03246. SAN 329-515X. Tel. 603-524-4775. *In Charge* Randy Brough.

New Jersey

Basic Health Sciences Library Network (BHSL), Overlook Hospital Health Science Lib., Summit 07902. SAN 371-4888. Tel. 908-522-2886, fax 908-522-2274. *Coord.* Pat Regenberg.

Bergen Passaic Health Sciences Library Consortium, c/o Health Sciences Lib., Englewood Hospital and Medical Center, Englewood 07631. SAN 371-0904. Tel. 201-894-3069, fax 201-894-9049. *Coord.* Lia Sabbagh.

Burlington Libraries Information Consortium (BLINC), 5 Pioneer Blvd., Westampton 08060. Tel. 609-267-9660, fax 609-267-4091, e-mail hq@bcls.lib.nj.us. *Coord.* Gale Sweet.

Central New Jersey Health Science Libraries Consortium (CNJHSLA), Saint Francis Medical Center Medical Lib., Trenton 08629. SAN 370-0712. Tel. 609-599-5068, fax 609-599-5773. *Libn.* Donna Barlow.

Cosmopolitan Biomedical Library Consortium (CBLC), Overlook Hospital Medical Lib., Summit 07902. SAN 322-4414. Tel. 908-522-2886, fax 908-522-2274. *Coord.* Pat Regenberg.

Health Sciences Library Assn. of New Jersey (HSLANJ), Saint Michaels Medical Center, Newark 07102. SAN 370-0488. Tel. 973-877-5471, fax 973-877-5378. *Dir.* Peter Cole.

Integrated Information Solutions, 600 Mountain Ave., Room 1B 202, Murray Hill 07974. SAN 329-5400. Tel. 908-582-4840, fax 908-582-3146. *Mgr.* M. E. Brennan.

Libraries of Middlesex Automation Consortium (LMxAC), 1030 Saint Georges Ave., Suite 203, Avenel 07001. SAN 329-448X. Tel. 732-750-2525, fax 732-750-9392. *Exec. Dir.* Eileen Palmer.

LibraryLinkNJ, New Jersey Library Cooperative, 44 Stelton Rd., Suite 330, Piscataway 08854. SAN 371-5116. Tel. 732-752-7720, fax 732-752-7785. *Exec. Dir.* Cheryl O'Connor.

Monmouth-Ocean Biomedical Information Consortium (MOBIC), Community Medical Center, Toms River 08755. SAN 329-5389. Tel. 732-557-8117, fax 732-557-8354. *Libn.* Reina Reisler.

Morris Automated Information Network (MAIN), c/o Morris County Lib., 30 East Hanover Ave., Whippany 07981. SAN 322-4058. Tel. 973-631-5353, fax 973-631-5366. *Dir.* Jeremy Jenynak.

Morris-Union Federation, 214 Main St., Chatham 07928. SAN 310-2629. Tel. 973-635-0603, fax 973-635-7827.

New Jersey Health Sciences Library Network (NJHSN), Overlook Hospital Lib., Summit 07902. SAN 371-4829. Tel. 908-522-2886, fax 908-522-2274. *Lib. Mgr.* Patricia Regenberg.

New Jersey Library Network, Lib. Development Bureau, Trenton 08608. SAN 372-8161. Tel. 609-278-2640 ext. 152, fax 609-278-2650. *Assoc. State Libn. for Lib. Development* Kathleen Moeller-Peiffer.

Virtual Academic Library Environment (VALE), William Paterson Univ. Lib., Wayne 07470-2103. Tel. 973-720-3179, fax 973-720-3171. *Coord.* Judy Avrin.

New Mexico

Alliance for Innovation in Science and Technology Information (AISTI), 369 Montezuma Ave., No. 237, Santa Fe 87501. *Exec. Dir.* Corinne Lebrunn.

Estacado Library Information Network (ELIN), 509 N. Shipp, Hobby 88240. Tel. 505-397-9328, fax 505-397-1508. *System Admin.* Cristine Adams.

New Mexico Consortium of Academic Libraries, Dean's Office, Albuquerque 87131-0001. SAN 371-6872. *Pres.* Ruben Aragon.

New Mexico Consortium of Biomedical and Hospital Libraries, c/o St. Vincent Hospital, Santa Fe 87505. SAN 322-449X. Tel. 505-820-5218, fax 505-989-6478. *Chair* Albert Robinson.

New York

Academic Libraries of Brooklyn, Long Island Univ. Lib. LLC 517, Brooklyn 11201. SAN 322-2411. Tel. 718-488-1081, fax 718-780-4057.

Associated Colleges of the Saint Lawrence Valley, SUNY Potsdam, Potsdam 13676-2299. SAN 322-242X. Tel. 315-267-3331, fax 315-267-2389. *Exec. Dir.* Anneke J. Larrance.

Capital District Library Council (CDLC), 28 Essex St., Albany 12206. SAN 322-2446. Tel. 518-438-2500, fax 518-438-2872. *Exec. Dir.* Jean K. Sheviak.

Central New York Library Resources Council (CLRC), 6493 Ridings Rd., Syracuse 13206-1195. SAN 322-2454. Tel. 315-446-5446, fax 315-446-5590. *Exec. Dir.* Penelope J. Klein.

Connect NY, Rochester Institute of Technology, Rochester 14623. Tel. 585-475-2050. *Dir. of Technology* Chris Lerch.

Council of Archives and Research Libraries in Jewish Studies (CARLJS), 330 7th Ave., 21st flr., New York 10001. SAN 371-053X. Tel. 212-629-0500, fax 212-629-0508, e-mail fjc@jewishculture.org. *Operations Dir.* Michelle Moskowitz Brown.

Library Assn. of Rockland County (LARC), P.O. Box 917, New City 10956-0917. Tel. 845-359-3877. *Pres.* Sara Nugent.

Library Consortium of Health Institutions in Buffalo (LCHIB), Abbott Hall, SUNY at Buffalo, Buffalo 14214. SAN 329-367X. Tel. 716-829-3900 ext. 143, fax 716-829-2211, e-mail hubnet@buffalo.edu; ulb-lchib@buffalo.edu. *Exec. Dir.* Martin E. Mutka.

Long Island Library Resources Council (LILRC), 627 N. Sunrise Service Rd., Bellport 11713. SAN 322-2489. Tel. 631-675-1570. *Dir.* Herbert Biblo.

Medical and Scientific Libraries of Long Island (MEDLI), c/o Palmer School of Lib. and Info. Science, Brookville 11548. SAN 322-4309. Tel. 516-299-2866, fax 516-299-4168. *Chair* Mary Westermann-Cicio.

Metropolitan New York Library Council (METRO), 57 E. 11 St., 4th flr., New York 10003-4605. SAN 322-2500. Tel. 212-228-2320, fax 212-228-2598. *Exec. Dir.* Dottie Hiebing.

National Network of Libraries of Medicine–Middle Atlantic Region (NN/LM-MAR), NYU Medical Center, New York 10010. E-mail rml@library.med.nyu.edu. *Assoc. Dir.* Kathel Dunn.

New York State Higher Education Initiative (NYSHEI), 22 Corporate Woods Blvd., Albany 12211-2350. Fax 518-432-4346, e-mail nyshei@nyshei.org. *Exec. Dir.* Jason Kramer.

Northeast Foreign Law Libraries Cooperative Group, Columbia Univ. Lib., New York 10027. SAN 375-0000. Tel. 212-854-1411, fax 212-854-3295. *Coord.* Silke Sahl.

Northern New York Library Network, 6721 U.S. Hwy. 11, Potsdam 13676. SAN 322-2527. Tel. 315-265-1119, fax 315-265-1881, e-mail info@nnyln.org. *Exec. Dir.* John J. Hammond.

Nylink, 22 Corporate Woods, 3rd flr., Albany 12211. SAN 322-256X. Tel. 518-443-5444, fax 518-432-4346, e-mail nylink@nylink. org. *Exec. Dir.* David Penniman.

Research Library Assn. of South Manhattan, Bobst Lib., New York Univ., New York 10012. SAN 372-8080. Tel. 212-998-2477, fax 212-995-4366. *Dean of Lib.* Carol Mandel.

Rochester Regional Library Council, 390 Packetts Landing, Fairport 14450. SAN 322-2535. Tel. 585-223-7570, fax 585-223-7712, e-mail rrlc@rrlc.org. *Exec. Dir.* Kathleen M. Miller.

South Central Regional Library Council, Clinton Hall, Ithaca 14850. SAN 322-2543. Tel. 607-273-9106, fax 607-272-0740, e-mail scrlc@scrlc.org. *Exec. Dir.* Mary-Carol Lindbloom.

Southeastern New York Library Resources Council (SENYLRC), 21 S. Elting Corners Rd., Highland 12528-2805. SAN 322-2551. Tel. 845-883-9065, fax 845-883-9483. *Exec. Dir.* John L. Shaloiko.

SUNYConnect, Office of Lib. and Info. Services, Albany 12246. Tel. 518-443-5577, fax 518-443-5358. *Asst. Provost for Lib. and Info. Services* Carey Hatch.

United Nations System Electronic Information Acquisitions Consortium (UNSEIAC), c/o United Nations Lib., New York 10017. SAN 377-855X. Tel. 212-963-2026, fax 212-963-2608, e-mail unseiac@un.org. *Coord.* Noriko Gines.

Western New York Library Resources Council, 4455 Genesee St., Buffalo 14225. SAN 322-2578. Tel. 716-633-0705, fax 716-633-1736. *Exec. Dir.* Sheryl Knab.

North Carolina

Cape Fear Health Sciences Information Consortium, 1601 Owen Drive, Fayetteville 28301. SAN 322-3930. Tel. 910-671-5046, fax 910-671-5337. *Dir.* Katherine Mcginniss.

North Carolina Area Health Education Centers, Univ. of North Carolina Health Sciences Lib., CB 7585, Chapel Hill 27599-7585. SAN 323-9950. Tel. 919-962-0700. *Dir.* Diana McDuffee.

North Carolina Community College System, 200 W. Jones St., Raleigh 27603-1379. SAN 322-2594. Tel. 919-807-7100, fax 919-807-7175; 919-807-7164. *Assoc. V.P. for Learning Technology Systems* Bill Randall.

North Carolina Library and Information Network, State Lib. of North Carolina, Raleigh 27601-2807. SAN 329-3092. Tel. 919-807-7400, fax 919-733-8748. *State Libn.* Mary L. Boone.

Northwest AHEC Library at Hickory, Catawba Medical Center, Hickory 28602. SAN 322-4708. Tel. 828-326-3662, fax 828-326-3484. *Dir.* Karen Lee Martinez.

Northwest AHEC Library at Salisbury, c/o Rowan Regional Medical Center, Salisbury 28144. SAN 322-4589. Tel. 704-210-5069, fax 704-636-5050.

Northwest AHEC Library Information Network, Wake Forest Univ. School of Medicine, Winston-Salem 27157-1060. SAN 322-4716. Tel. 336-713-7700, fax 336-713-7701. *Dir.* Mike Lischke.

Triangle Research Libraries Network, Wilson Lib., Chapel Hill 27514-8890. SAN 329-5362. Tel. 919-962-8022, fax 919-962-4452. *Dir.* Mona C. Couts.

Western North Carolina Library Network (WNCLN), c/o Appalachian State Univ., Boone 28608. SAN 376-7205. Tel. 828-262-2774, fax 828-262-3001. *Libn.* Catherine Wilkinson.

North Dakota

Central Dakota Library Network, Morton Mandan Public Lib., Mandan 58554-3149. SAN 373-1391. Tel. 701-667-5365, e-mail mortonmandanlibrary@cdln.info. *Dir.* Kelly Steckler.

Tri-College University Libraries Consortium, NDSU Downtown Campus, Fargo 58102. SAN 322-2047. Tel. 701-231-8170, fax 701-231-7205. *In Charge* Sonia Hohnadel.

Ohio

Assn. of Christian Librarians (ACL), P.O. Box 4, Cedarville 45314. Tel. 937-766-2255, fax 937-766-5499, e-mail info@acl.org. *Pres.* Linda Poston.

Central Ohio Hospital Library Consortium, 127 S. Davis Ave., Columbus 43222. SAN 371-084X. Tel. 614-234-5214, fax 614-234-1257, e-mail library@mchs.com. *Dir.* Stevo Roksandic.

Christian Library Consortium (CLC), c/o ACL, Cedarville 45314. Tel. 937-766-2255, fax 937-766-5499, e-mail info@acl.org. *Coord.* Beth Purtee.

Columbus Area Library and Information Council of Ohio (CALICO), c/o Westerville Public Lib., Westerville 43081. SAN 371-683X. Tel. 614-882-7277, fax 614-882-5369.

Consortium of Popular Culture Collections in the Midwest (CPCCM), c/o Popular Culture Lib., Bowling Green 43403-0600. SAN 370-5811. Tel. 419-372-2450, fax 419-372-7996. *Head Libn.* Nancy Down.

Five Colleges of Ohio, 102 Allen House, Gambier 43022. Tel. 740-427-5377, fax 740-427-5390, e-mail ohiofive@gmail.com. *Exec. Dir.* Susan Palmer.

Northeast Ohio Regional Library System (NEO-RLS), 4445 Mahoning Ave. N.W., Warren 44483. SAN 322-2713. Tel. 330-847-7744, fax 330-847-7704. *Exec. Dir.* William Martino.

Northwest Regional Library System (NOR-WELD), 181½ S. Main St., Bowling Green 43402. SAN 322-273X. Tel. 419-352-2903, fax 419-353-8310. *Dir.* Allan Gray.

OCLC Online Computer Library Center, Inc., 6565 Kilgour Place, Dublin 43017-3395. SAN 322-2748. Tel. 614-764-6000, fax 614-718-1017, e-mail oclc@oclc.org. *Pres./CEO* Jay Jordan.

Ohio Health Sciences Library Assn. (OHSLA), Medical Lib., South Pointe Hospital, Warrensville Heights 44122. Tel. 216-491-7454, fax 216-491-7650. *Pres.* Michelle Kraft.

Ohio Library and Information Network (Ohio-LINK), 2455 N. Star Rd., Suite 300, Columbus 43221. SAN 374-8014. Tel. 614-728-3600, fax 614-728-3610, e-mail info@ohiolink.edu.

Ohio Network of American History Research Centers, Ohio Historical Society Archives-Lib., Columbus 43211-2497. SAN 323-9624. Tel. 614-297-2510, fax 614-297-2546, e-mail reference@ohiohistory.org.

Ohio Public Library Information Network (OPLIN), 2323 W. 5 Ave., Suite 130, Columbus 43204. Tel. 614-728-5252, fax 614-728-5256, e-mail support@oplin.org. *Exec. Dir.* Stephen Hedges.

OHIONET, 1500 W. Lane Ave., Columbus 43221-3975. SAN 322-2764. Tel. 614-486-2966, fax 614-486-1527. *Exec. Officer* Michael P. Butler.

Rural Ohio Valley Health Sciences Library Network (ROVHSLN), Southern State Community College–South, Sardinia 45171. Tel. 937-695-0307 ext. 3681, fax 937-695-1440. *Mgr.* Mary Ayres.

Southeast Regional Library System (SERLS), 252 W. 13 St., Wellston 45692. SAN 322-2756. Tel. 740-384-2103, fax 740-384-2106, e-mail dirserls@oplin.org. *Exec. Dir.* Mary Leffler.

SouthWest Ohio and Neighboring Libraries (SWON), 10815 Indeco Drive, Suite 200, Cincinnati 45241-2926. SAN 322-2675. Tel. 513-751-4422, fax 513-751-0463, e-mail info@swonlibraries.org. *Exec. Dir.* Anne K. Abate.

Southwestern Ohio Council for Higher Education (SOCHE), Miami Valley Research Park, Dayton 45420-4015. SAN 322-2659. Tel. 937-258-8890, fax 937-258-8899, e-mail soche@soche.org.

State Assisted Academic Library Council of Kentucky (SAALCK), c/o SWON Libs., Cincinnati 45241. SAN 371-2222. Tel. 513-751-4422, fax 513-751-0463, e-mail saalck@saalck.org. *Exec. Dir.* Anne Abate.

Theological Consortium of Greater Columbus (TCGC), Trinity Lutheran Seminary, Columbus 43209-2334. Tel. 614-384-4646, fax 614-238-0263. *Lib. Systems Mgr.* Ray Olson.

Oklahoma

Greater Oklahoma Area Health Sciences Library Consortium (GOAL), Resource Center, Mercy Memorial Health Center, Ardmore 73401. SAN 329-3858. Tel. 580-220-6625, fax 580-220-6599. *Pres.* Catherine Ice.

Oklahoma Health Sciences Library Assn. (OHSLA), HSC Bird Health Science Lib., Univ. of Oklahoma, Oklahoma City 73190. SAN 375-0051. Tel. 405-271-2285 ext. 48755, fax 405-271-3297. *Dir.* Clinton M. Thompson.

Oregon

Chemeketa Cooperative Regional Library Service, c/o Chemeketa Community College, Salem 97305-1453. SAN 322-2837. Tel. 503-399-5105, fax 503-399-7316, e-mail cocl@chemeketa.edu. *Coord.* Linda Cochrane.

Coastal Resource Sharing Network (CRSN), c/o Tillamook County Lib., Tillamook 97141. Tel. 503-842-4792, fax 503-815-8194. *Pres.* Jill Tierce.

Coos County Library Service District, Tioga, 3rd flr., 1988 Newmark, Coos Bay 97420. SAN 322-4279. Tel. 541-888-1529, fax 541-888-1529. *Dir.* Mary Jane Fisher.

Gorge LINK Library Consortium, c/o Hood River County Lib., Hood River 97031. Tel. 541-386-2535, fax 541-386-3835, e-mail gorgelinklibrary@gorge.net. *System Admin.* Jayne Guidinger.

Library Information Network of Clackamas County (LINCC), 16239 S.E. McLoughlin Blvd., Suite 208, Oak Grove 97267-4654. SAN 322-2845. Tel. 503-723-4888, fax 503-794-8238. *Lib. System Analyst* George Yobst.

Orbis Cascade Alliance, 1501 Kincaid, No. 4, Eugene 97401-4540. SAN 377-8096. Tel. 541-346-1832, fax 541-346-1968. *Chair* Lee Lyttle.

Oregon Health Sciences Libraries Assn. (OHSLA), Oregon Health and Science Univ. Lib., Portland 97239-3098. SAN 371-2176. Tel. 503-494-3462, fax 503-494-3322, e-mail library@ohsu.edu.

Portland Area Library System (PORTALS), Port Community College, SYLIB202, Portland 97219. Tel. 503-977-4571, fax 503-977-4977. *Coord.* Roberta Richards.

Southern Oregon Library Federation, c/o Klamath County Lib., Klamath Falls 97601. SAN 322-2861. Tel. 541-882-8894, fax 541-882-6166. *Dir.* Andy Swanson.

Southern Oregon Library Information System (SOLIS), 724 S. Central Ave., Suite 112, Medford 97501. Tel. 541-772-2141, fax 541-772-2144, e-mail solis_97501@yahoo. com. *System Admin.* Marian Stoner.

Washington County Cooperative Library Services, 111 N.E. Lincoln St., MS No. 58, Hillsboro 97124-3036. SAN 322-287X. Tel. 503-846-3222, fax 503-846-3220. *Mgr.* Eva Calcagno.

Pennsylvania

Associated College Libraries of Central Pennsylvania, P.O. Box 39, Grantham 17027. E-mail aclcp@aclcp.org. *Pres.* Gregory Crawford.

Berks County Library Assn. (BCLA), Reading Public Lib., Reading 19602. SAN 371-0866. Tel. 610-478-9035; 610-655-6350. *Pres.* Jennifer Balas.

Central Pennsylvania Consortium (CPC), Dickinson College, Carlisle 17013. SAN 322-2896. Tel. 717-245-1984, fax 717-245-1807, e-mail cpc@dickinson.edu. *Pres.* Katherine Haley Will.

Central Pennsylvania Health Sciences Library Assn. (CPHSLA), Office for Research Protections, Pennsylvania State Univ., University Park 16802. SAN 375-5290. Fax 814-865-1775. *Pres.* Tracie Kahler.

Cooperating Hospital Libraries of the Lehigh Valley Area, Estes Lib., Saint Luke's Hospital, Bethlehem 18015. SAN 371-0858. Tel. 610-954-3407, fax 610-954-4651. *Chair* Sharon Hrabina.

Delaware Valley Information Consortium (DEVIC), St. Mary Medical Center Medical Lib., Langhorne 19047. Tel. 215-710-2012, fax 215-710-4638. *Dir.* Jacqueline Luizzi.

Eastern Mennonite Associated Libraries and Archives (EMALA), 2215 Millstream Rd., Lancaster 17602. SAN 372-8226. Tel. 717-393-9745, fax 717-393-8751. *Chair* Edsel Burdge.

Erie Area Health Information Library Cooperative (EAHILC), Nash Lib., Gannon Univ., Erie 16541. SAN 371-0564. Tel. 814-871-7667, fax 814-871-5566. *Chair* Deborah West.

Greater Philadelphia Law Library Assn. (GPLLA), Wolf, Block, Schorr and Solis-Cohen LLP Lib., 25th flr., Philadelphia 19103. SAN 373-1375. *Pres.* Monica Almendarez.

HSLC/Access PA (Health Science Libraries Consortium), 3600 Market St., Suite 550, Philadelphia 19104-2646. SAN 323-9780. Tel. 215-222-1532, fax 215-222-0416, e-mail support@hslc.org. *Exec. Dir.* Joseph C. Scorza.

Interlibrary Delivery Service of Pennsylvania (IDS), c/o Bucks County IU, No. 22, Doylestown 18901. SAN 322-2942. Tel. 215-348-2940 ext. 1620, fax 215-348-8315, e-mail ids@bucksiu.org. *Admin. Dir.* Beverly J. Carey.

Keystone Library Network, Dixon Univ. Center, Harrisburg 17110-1201. Tel. 717-720-4088, fax 717-720-4453. *Coord.* Mary Lou Sowden.

Laurel Highlands Health Science Library Consortium, 361 Sunrise Rd., Dayton 16222. SAN 322-2950. Tel. 814-341-0242, fax 814-266-8230. *Dir.* Rhonda Yeager.

Lehigh Valley Assn. of Independent Colleges, 130 W. Greenwich St., Bethlehem 18018. SAN 322-2969. Tel. 610-625-7888, fax 610-625-7891. *Exec. Dir.* Bonnie Lynch.

Montgomery County Library and Information Network Consortium (MCLINC), 301 Lafayette St., 2nd flr., Conshohocken 19428. Tel. 610-238-0580, fax 610-238-0581, e-mail webmaster@mclinc.org. *Pres.* Carrie L. Turner.

Northeastern Pennsylvania Library Network, c/o Marywood Univ. Lib., Scranton 18509-1598. SAN 322-2993. Tel. 570-348-6260, fax 570-961-4769. *Exec. Dir.* Catherine H. Schappert.

Northwest Interlibrary Cooperative of Pennsylvania (NICOP), Mercyhurst College Lib., Erie 16546. SAN 370-5862. Tel. 814-824-2190, fax 814-824-2219. *Archivist* Earleen Glaser.

Pennsylvania Library Assn., 220 Cumberland Pkwy, Suite 10, Mechanicsburg 17055. Tel. 717-766-7663, fax 717-766-5440. *Exec. Dir.* Glenn R. Miller.

Philadelphia Area Consortium of Special Collections Libraries (PACSCL), P.O. Box 22642, Philadelphia 19110-2642. Tel. 215-985-1445, fax 215-985-1446, email lblanchard@pacscl.org. *Exec. Dir.* Laura Blanchard.

Southeastern Pennsylvania Theological Library Assn. (SEPTLA), c/o Biblical Seminary, Hatfield 19440. SAN 371-0793. Tel. 215-368-5000 ext. 234. *Chair* Daniel LaValla.

State System of Higher Education Library Cooperative (SSHELCO), c/o Bailey Lib., Slippery Rock 16057. Tel. 724-738-2630, fax 724-738-2661. *Dir.* Philip Tramdack.

Susquehanna Library Cooperative (SLC), Stevenson Lib., Lock Haven Univ., Lock Haven 17745. SAN 322-3051. Tel. 570-484-2310, fax 570-484-2506. *Dean of Lib. and Info. Services.* Tara Lynn Fulton.

Tri-State College Library Cooperative (TCLC), c/o Rosemont College Lib., Rosemont 19010-1699. SAN 322-3078. Tel. 610-525-0796, fax 610-525-1939, e-mail office@tclclibs.org. *Coord.* Ellen Gasiewski.

Rhode Island

Library of Rhode Island Network (LORI), c/o Office of Lib. and Info. Services, Providence 02908-5870. SAN 371-6821. Tel. 401-574-9300, fax 401-574-9320. *Lib. Services Dir.* Howard Boksenbaum.

Ocean State Libraries (OSL), 300 Centerville Rd., Suite 103S, Warwick 02886-0226. SAN 329-4560. Tel. 401-738-2200, fax 401-736-8949, e-mail support@oslri.net. *Exec. Dir.* Joan Gillespie.

South Carolina

Charleston Academic Libraries Consortium (CALC), P.O. Box 118067, Charleston 29423-8067. SAN 371-0769. Tel. 843-574-6088, fax 843-574-6484. *Chair* Drucie Gullion.

Columbia Area Medical Librarians' Assn. (CAMLA), School of Medicine Lib., Univ. of South Carolina, Columbia 29209. SAN 372-9400. Tel. 803-733-3361, fax 803-733-1509. *Pres.* Roz Anderson.

Partnership Among South Carolina Academic Libraries (PASCAL), 1333 Main St., Suite

305, Columbia 29201. Tel. 803-734-0900, fax 803-734-0901. *Exec. Dir.* Rick Moul.

South Carolina AHEC, c/o Medical Univ. of South Carolina, Charleston 29425. SAN 329-3998. Tel. 843-792-4431, fax 843-792-4430. *Exec. Dir.* David Garr.

South Carolina State Library/South Carolina Library Network, 1430 and 1500 Senate St., Columbia 29201. SAN 322-4198. Tel. 803-734-8666,fax803-734-8676,e-mail reference @statelibrary.sc.gov. *Dir. of Lib. and Info. Services.* Mary Morgan.

South Dakota

South Dakota Library Network (SDLN), 1200 University, Unit 9672, Spearfish 57799-9672. SAN 371-2117. Tel. 605-642-6835, fax 605-642-6472, e-mail help@sdln.net. *Dir.* Warren Wilson.

Tennessee

Consortium of Southern Biomedical Libraries (CONBLS), Meharry Medical College, Nashville 37208. SAN 370-7717. Tel. 615-327-6728, fax 615-327-6448. *Chair* Barbara Shearer.

Knoxville Area Health Sciences Library Consortium (KAHSLC), Univ. of Tennessee Preston Medical Lib., Knoxville 37920. SAN 371-0556. Tel. 865-305-9525, fax 865-305-9527. *Pres.* Cynthia Vaughn.

Mid-Tennessee Health Science Librarians Assn., VA Medical Center, Nashville 37212. SAN 329-5028. Tel. 615-327-4751 ext. 5523, fax 615-321-6336.

Tennessee Health Science Library Assn. (THeSLA), Holston Valley Medical Center Health Sciences Lib., Kingsport 37660. SAN 371-0726. Tel. 423-224-6870, fax 423-224-6014. *Coord., Lib. Services* Sharon M. Brown.

Tri-Cities Area Health Sciences Libraries Consortium (TCAHSLC), James H. Quillen College of Medicine, East Tennessee State Univ., Johnson City 37614. SAN 329-4099. Tel. 423-439-6252, fax 423-439-7025. *Dir.* Biddanda Ponnappa.

Wolf River Library Consortium, c/o Germantown Community Lib., Germantown 38138-2815. Tel. 901-757-7323, fax 901-756-9940. *Dir.* Melody Pittman.

Texas

Abilene Library Consortium, 3305 N. 3 St., Suite 301, Abilene 79603. SAN 322-4694. Tel. 325-672-7081, fax 325-672-7082. *Coord.* Edward J. Smith.

Amigos Library Services, Inc., 14400 Midway Rd., Dallas 75244-3509. SAN 322-3191. Tel. 972-851-8000, fax 972-991-6061, e-mail amigos@amigos.org. *Exec. Dir.* Bonnie Juergens.

Council of Research and Academic Libraries (CORAL), P.O. Box 290236, San Antonio 78280-1636. SAN 322-3213. Tel. 210-458-4885. *Coord.* Rosemary Vasquez.

Del Norte Biosciences Library Consortium, El Paso Community College, El Paso 79998. SAN 322-3302. Tel. 915-831-4149, fax 915-831-4639. *Coord.* Becky Perales.

Harrington Library Consortium, 413 E. 4 Ave., Amarillo 79101. SAN 329-546X. Tel. 806-378-6037, fax 806-378-6038. *Dir.* Donna Littlejohn.

Health Libraries Information Network (Health LINE), Univ. of Texas Southwestern Medical Center Lib., Dallas 75390-9049. SAN 322-3299. Tel. 214-648-2626, fax 214-648-2826.

Houston Area Library Automation Network (HALAN), Houston Public Lib., Houston 77002. Tel. 832-393-1411, fax 832-393-1427, e-mail website@hpl.lib.tx.us. *Chief* Judith Hiott.

Houston Area Research Library Consortium (HARLiC), c/o Univ. of Houston Libs., Houston 77204-2000. SAN 322-3329. Tel. 713-743-9807, fax 713-743-9811. *Pres.* Dana Rooks.

National Network of Libraries of Medicine–South Central Region (NN/LM-SCR), c/o HAM-TMC Library, Houston 77030-2809. SAN 322-3353. Tel. 713-799-7880, fax 713-790-7030, e-mail nnlm-scr@exch.library. tmc.edu. *Dir.* L. Maximillian Buja.

Northeast Texas Library System (NETLS), 4845 Broadway Blvd., Garland 75043-7016. SAN 370-5943. Tel. 972-205-2566, fax 972-205-2767. *Major Resource Center Dir.* Claire Bausch.

South Central Academic Medical Libraries Consortium (SCAMeL), c/o Lewis Lib.-UNTHSC, Fort Worth 76107. SAN 372-8269. Tel. 817-735-2380, fax 817-735-5158.

Assoc. V.P. for Info. Resources/Treas. Bobby Carter.

Texas Council of Academic Libraries (TCAL), VC/UHV Lib., Victoria 77901. SAN 322-337X. Tel. 361-570-4150, fax 361-570-4155. *Chair* Joe Dahlstrom.

Texnet, P.O. Box 12927, Austin 78711. SAN 322-3396. Tel. 512-463-5406, fax 512-936-2306, e-mail ill@tsl.state.tx.us.

Western Council of State Libraries, Inc., c/o Texas State Library & Archives Commission, P.O. Box 12927, Austin 78711-2927. Tel. 512-463-5460, fax 512-463-5436, e-mail peggy.rudd@tsl.state.tx.us. *Pres.* Ann Joslin.

Utah

National Network of Libraries of Medicine–MidContinental Region (NN/LM-MCR), Spencer S. Eccles Health Sciences Lib., Univ. of Utah, Salt Lake City 84112-5890. SAN 322-225X. Tel. 801-587-3412, fax 801-581-3632. *Dir.* Wayne J. Peay.

Utah Academic Library Consortium (UALC), Univ. of Utah, Salt Lake City 84112. -0860. SAN 322-3418. Tel. 801-581-7701, 801-581-3852, fax 801-585-7185, e-mail UALCmail@library.utah.edu. *Fiscal Agent* Carol Jost.

Utah Health Sciences Library Consortium, c/o Spencer S. Eccles Health Sciences Lib., Univ. of Utah, Salt Lake City 84112-5890. SAN 376-2246. Tel. 801-585-5743, fax 801-581-3632. *Chair* John Bramble.

Vermont

North Atlantic Health Sciences Libraries, Inc. (NAHSL), Dana Medical Lib., Univ. of Vermont Medical School, Burlington 05405. SAN 371-0599. Tel. 508-656-3483, fax 508-656-0762. *Chair* Katherine Stemmer Frumento.

Vermont Resource Sharing Network, c/o Vermont Dept. of Libs., Montpelier 05609-0601. SAN 322-3426. Tel. 802-828-3261, fax 802-828-1481. *Libn.* Gerrie Denison.

Virgin Islands

Vilinet/Virgin Islands Library and Information Network, c/o Div. of Libs., Archives, and Museums, Saint Thomas 00802. SAN 322-3639. Tel. 340-773-5715, fax 340-773-3257, e-mail info@vilinet.net. *Territorial Dir. of Libs., Archives, and Museums* Ingrid Bough.

Virginia

American Indian Higher Education Consortium (AIHEC), 121 Oronoco St., Alexandria 22314. SAN 329-4056. Tel. 703-838-0400, fax 703-838-0388, e-mail info@aihec.org.

Lynchburg Area Library Cooperative, c/o Sweet Briar College Lib., Sweet Briar 24595. SAN 322-3450. Tel. 434-381-6315, fax 434-381-6173.

Lynchburg Information Online Network (LION), 2315 Memorial Ave., Lynchburg 24503. SAN 374-6097. Tel. 434-381-6311, fax 434-381-6173. *Dir.* John G. Jaffee.

NASA Libraries Information System–NASA Galaxie, NASA Langley Research Center, MS 185-Technical Lib., Hampton 23681-2199. SAN 322-0788. Tel. 757-864-2356, fax 757-864-2375, e-mail tech-library@larc.nasa.gov. *Coord.* Manjula Ambur.

Richmond Academic Library Consortium (RALC), James Branch Cabell Lib., Virginia Commonwealth Univ., Richmond 23284. SAN 322-3469. Tel. 804-828-1110, fax 804-828-1105.

Southside Virginia Library Network (SVLN), Longwood Univ., Farmville 23909-1897. SAN 372-8242. Tel. 434-395-2431; 434-395-2433, fax 434-395-2453. *Dir.* Suzy Szasz.

Southwestern Virginia Health Information Librarians (SWVAHILI), Carilion Health Sciences Lib., Roanoke 24033. SAN 323-9527. Tel. 540-433-4166, fax 540-433-3106. *Chair* George Curran.

United States Army Training and Doctrine Command (TRADOC)/Lib. Program Office, U.S. Army Hq TRADOC, Fort Monroe 23651. SAN 322-418X. Tel. 757-788-2155, fax 757-788-5544. *Dir.* Amy Loughran.

Virginia Independent College and University Library Assn., c/o Mary Helen Cochran Lib., Sweet Briar 24595. SAN 374-6089. Tel. 434-381-6139, fax 434-381-6173. *Dir.* John Jaffee.

Virginia Tidewater Consortium for Higher Education (VTC), 4900 Powhatan Ave., Norfolk 23529. SAN 329-5486. Tel. 757-683-3183, fax 757-683-4515, e-mail lgdotolo@aol. com. *Pres.* Lawrence G. Dotolo.

Virtual Library of Virginia (VIVA), George Mason Univ., Fairfax 22030. Tel. 703-993-4652, fax 703-993-4662. *Dir.* Katherine Perry.

Washington

Cooperating Libraries in Olympia (CLIO), Evergreen State College Library, L2300, Olympia 98505. SAN 329-4528. Tel. 360-867-6260, fax 360-867-6790. *Dean, Lib. Services* Lee Lyttle.

Inland NorthWest Health Sciences Libraries (INWHSL), P.O. Box 10283, Spokane 99209-0283. SAN 370-5099. Tel. 509-368-6973, fax 509-358-7928. *Treas.* Robert Pringle.

National Network of Libraries of Medicine–Pacific Northwest Region (NN/LM-PNR), T-344 Health Sciences Bldg., Univ. of Washington, Seattle 98195. SAN 322-3485. Tel. 206-543-8262, fax 206-543-2469, e-mail nnlm@u.washington.edu. *Assoc. Dir.* Catherine Burroughs.

Palouse Area Library Information Services (PALIS), c/o Neill Public Lib., Pullman 99163. SAN 375-0132. Tel. 509-334-3595, fax 509-334-6051. *Dir.* Andriette Pieron.

Washington Idaho Network (WIN), Foley Center Lib., Gonzaga Univ., Spokane 99258. Tel. 509-323-6545, fax 509-324-5904, e-mail winsupport@gonzaga.edu. *Pres.* Eileen Bell-Garrison.

West Virginia

Mid-Atlantic Law Library Cooperative (MALLCO), College of Law Lib., Morgantown 26506-6135. SAN 371-0645. Tel. 304-293-7641, fax 304-293-6020. *Lib. Dir.* Camille M. Riley.

Wisconsin

Arrowhead Health Sciences Library Network, Wisconsin Indianhead Technical College, Shell Lake 54817. SAN 322-1954. Tel. 715-468-2815 ext. 2298, fax 715-468-2819. *Coord.* Judy Lyons.

Fox River Valley Area Library Consortium (FRVALC), c/o Polk Lib., Univ. of Wisconsin–Oshkosh, Oshkosh 54901. SAN 322-

3531. Tel. 920-424-3348, 920-424-4333, fax 920-424-2175.

Fox Valley Library Council, c/o OWLS, Appleton 54911. SAN 323-9640. Tel. 920-832-6190, fax 920-832-6422. *Pres.* Joy Schwarz.

Library Council of Southeastern Wisconsin, Inc., 814 W. Wisconsin Ave., Milwaukee 53233-2309. SAN 322-354X. Tel. 414-271-8470, fax 414-286-2798. *Exec. Dir.* Susie M. Just.

North East Wisconsin Intertype Libraries, Inc. (NEWIL), 515 Pine St., Green Bay 54301. SAN 322-3574. Tel. 920-448-4412, fax 920-448-4420. *Dir.* Mark Merrifield.

Northwestern Wisconsin Health Science Library Consortium, c/o Gundersen Lutheran Medical Center, Lacrosse 54601. Tel. 608-775-5410, fax 608-775-6343. *Treas.* Eileen Severson.

South Central Wisconsin Health Science Library Consortium, c/o Fort Healthcare Medical Lib., Fort Atkinson 53538. SAN 322-4686. Tel. 920-568-5194, fax 920-568-5195. *Coord.* Carrie Garity.

Southeastern Wisconsin Health Science Library Consortium, Veterans Admin. Center Medical Lib., Milwaukee 53295. SAN 322-3582. Tel. 414-384-2000 ext. 42342, fax 414-382-5334. *Coord.* Janice Curnes.

Southeastern Wisconsin Information Technology Exchange, Inc. (SWITCH), 6801 N. Yates Rd., Milwaukee 53217-3985. SAN 371-3962. Tel. 414-351-2423, fax 414-228-4146. *Coord.* William A. Topritzhofer.

University of Wisconsin System School Library Education Consortium (UWSSLEC), Graduate and Continuing Educ., Univ. of Wisconsin–Whitewater, Whitewater 53190. Tel. 262-472-1463, fax 262-472-5210, e-mail lenchoc@uww.edu. *Co-Dir.* E. Anne Zarinnia.

Wisconsin Library Services (WILS), 728 State St., Room 464, Madison 53706-1494. SAN 322-3612. Tel. 608-265-0580, 608-263-4981, 608-265-4167, fax 608-262-6067, 608-263-3684. *Dir.* Kathryn Schneider Michaelis.

Wisconsin Public Library Consortium (WPLC), c/o South Central Lib. System, Madison 53718. *Dir.* Phyllis Davis.

Wisconsin Valley Library Service (WVLS), 300 N. 1 St., Wausau 54403. SAN 371-3911.

Tel. 715-261-7250, fax 715-261-7259. *Dir.* Marla Rae Sepnafski.

WISPALS Library Consortium, c/o Gateway Technical College, Kenosha 53144-1690. Tel. 262-564-2602, fax 262-564-2787.

Wyoming

WYLD Network, c/o Wyoming State Lib., Cheyenne 82002-0060. SAN 371-0661. Tel. 307-777-6339, fax 307-777-6289, e-mail wyldstaff@will.state.wy.us. *State Libn.* Lesley Boughton.

Canada

Alberta

The Alberta Library (TAL), 6-14, 7 Sir Winston Churchill Sq., Edmonton T5J 2V5. Tel. 780-414-0805, fax 780-414-0806, e-mail admin@thealbertalibrary.ab.ca. *CEO* Maureen Woods.

NEOS Library Consortium, Cameron Lib., 5th flr., Edmonton T6G 2J8. Tel. 780-492-0075, fax 780-492-8302. *Mgr.* Margaret Law.

British Columbia

British Columbia Academic Health Council (BCAHC), 402-1770 W. 7 Ave., Vancouver V6J 4Y6. Tel. 604-739-3910 ext. 228, fax 604-739-3931, e-mail info@bcahc.ca. *CEO* George Eisler.

British Columbia College and Institute Library Services, Langara College Lib., Vancouver V5Y 2Z6. SAN 329-6970. Tel. 604-323-5639, fax 604-323-5544, e-mail cils@langara.bc.ca. *Dir.* Mary Anne Epp.

British Columbia Electronic Library Network (BCELN), WAC Bennett Lib., 7th flr., Simon Fraser Univ., Burnaby V5A 1S6. Tel. 778-782-7003, fax 778-782-3023, e-mail office@eln.bc.ca. *Exec. Dir.* Anita Cocchia.

Council of Prairie and Pacific University Libraries (COPPUL), 2005 Sooke Rd., Victoria V9B 5Y2. Tel. 250-391-2554, fax 250-391-2556, e-mail coppul@royalroads.ca. *Exec. Dir.* Alexander Slade.

Electronic Health Library of British Columbia (e-HLbc), c/o Bennett Lib., Burnaby V5A 1S6. Tel. 778-782-5440, fax 778-782-3023,

e-mail info@ehlbc.ca. *Coord.* JoAnne Newyear-Ramirez.

Public Library InterLINK, c/o Burnaby Public Lib.–Kingsway Branch, Burnaby V5E 1G3. SAN 318-8272. Tel. 604-517-8441, fax 604-517-8410, e-mail info@interlinklibraries.ca. *Operations Mgr.* Rita Avigdor.

Manitoba

Manitoba Government Libraries Council (MGLC), c/o Instructional Resources Unit, Winnipeg R3G 0T3. SAN 371-6848. Tel. 204-945-7833, fax 204-945-8756. *Chair* John Tooth.

Manitoba Library Consortium, Inc. (MLCI), c/o Lib. Admin., Univ. of Winnipeg, Winnipeg R3B 2E9. SAN 372-820X. Tel. 204-786-9801, fax 204-783-8910. *Chair* Patricia Burt.

Nova Scotia

Maritimes Health Libraries Assn. (MHLA-AB-SM), W. K. Kellogg Health Sciences Lib., Halifax B3H 1X5. SAN 370-0836. Tel. 902-494-2483, fax 902-494-3750. *Libn.* Shelley McKibbon.

NOVANET, 84 Chain Lake Drive, Suite 402, Halifax B3S 1A2. SAN 372-4050. Tel. 902-453-2461, fax 902-453-2369, e-mail office@novanet.ns.ca. *Mgr.* Bill Slauenwhite.

Ontario

Canadian Assn. of Research Libraries (Association des Bibliothèques de Recherche du Canada), Morisset Hall, Room 238, Ottawa K1N 9A5. SAN 323-9721. Tel. 613-562-5385, fax 613-562-5297, e-mail carladm@uottawa.ca. *Exec. Dir.* Brent Roe.

Canadian Health Libraries Assn. (CHLA-AB-SC), 39 River St., Toronto M5A 3P1. SAN 370-0720. Tel. 416-646-1600, fax 416-646-9460, e-mail info@chla-absc.ca. *Pres.* Miriam Ticoll.

Canadian Research Knowledge Network (CRKN), Preston Sq., Tower 2, Ottawa K1S IN4. Tel. 613-907-7040, fax 866-903-9094. *Exec. Dir.* Deb deBruijn.

Consortium of Ontario Libraries (COOL), 111 Peter St., Suite 902, Toronto M5V 2H1. Tel.

416-961-1669, fax 416-961-5122. *Dir.* Barbara Franchetto.

Hamilton and District Health Library Network, c/o St Josephs Healthcare Hamilton, Sherman Lib., Room T2305, Hamilton L8N 4A6. SAN 370-5846. Tel. 905-522-1155 ext. 3410, fax 905-540-6504. *Coord.* Jean Maragno.

Health Science Information Consortium of Toronto, c/o Gerstein Science Info. Center, Univ. of Toronto, Toronto M5S 1A5. SAN 370-5080. Tel. 416-978-6359, fax 416-971-2637. *Exec. Dir.* Miriam Ticoll.

Ontario Council of University Libraries (OCUL), 130 Saint George St., Toronto M5S 1A5. Tel. 416-946-0578, fax 416-978-6755. *Exec. Dir.* Kathy Scardellato.

Ontario Health Libraries Assn. (OHLA), c/o Salt Area Hospital Lib., Sault Ste. Marie P6A 2C4. SAN 370-0739. Tel. 705-759-3434, fax 705-759-3640. *Pres.* Kimberley Aslett.

Ontario Library Consortium (OLC), Owen Sound and North Grey Union Public Lib., Owen Sound N4K 4K4. *Pres.* Judy Armstrong.

Parry Sound and Area Access Network, c/o Parry Sound Public Lib., Parry Sound P2A 1E3. Tel. 705-746-9601, fax 705-746-9601, e-mail pspl@vianet.ca. *Chair* Laurine Tremaine.

Perth County Information Network (PCIN), c/o Stratford Public Lib., Stratford N5A 1A2. Tel. 519-271-0220, fax 519-271-3843, e-mail webmaster@pcin.on.ca.

Shared Library Services (SLS), South Huron Hospital, Exeter N0M 1S2. SAN 323-9500. Tel. 519-235-5168, fax 519-235-4476, e-mail shha.sls@shha.on.ca. *Libn.* Linda Wilcox.

Southwestern Ontario Health Libraries and Information Network (SOHLIN), St. Joseph's Health Care London–Regional Mental Health Staff Libs., St. Thomas N5P 3V9. Tel. 519-631-8510 ext. 49685. *Pres.* Elizabeth Russell.

Toronto Health Libraries Assn. (THLA), 3409 Yonge St., Toronto M4N 2L0. SAN 323-9853. Tel. 416-485-0377, fax 416-485-6877, e-mail medinfoserv@rogers.com. *Pres.* Graziela Alexandria.

Quebec

Assn. des Bibliothèques de la Santé Affiliées a l'Université de Montréal (ABSAUM), c/o Health Lib., Univ. of Montreal, Montreal H3C 3J7. SAN 370-5838. Tel. 514-343-6826, fax 514-343-2350. *Dir.* Monique St-Jean.

Canadian Heritage Information Network (CHIN), 15 Eddy St., 4th flr., Gatineau K1A 0M5. SAN 329-3076. Tel. 819-994-1200, fax 819-994-9555, e-mail service@chin.gc.ca. *CEO* Gabrielle Blais.

National Library and Information-Industry Associations, United States and Canada

American Association of Law Libraries

Executive Director, Kate Hagan
105 W. Adams St., Suite 3300, Chicago, IL 60603
312-939-4764, fax 312-431-1097, e-mail khagan@aall.org
World Wide Web http://www.aallnet.org

Object

The American Association of Law Libraries (AALL) is established for educational and scientific purposes. It shall be conducted as a nonprofit corporation to promote and enhance the value of law libraries to the public, the legal community, and the world; to foster the profession of law librarianship; to provide leadership in the field of legal information; and to foster a spirit of cooperation among the members of the profession. Established 1906.

Membership

Memb. 5,000+. Persons officially connected with a law library or with a law section of a state or general library, separately maintained. Associate membership available for others. Dues (Indiv.) $222; (Associate) $222; (Retired) $56; (Student) $56. Year. July 1–June 30.

Officers

Pres. Darcy Kirk, Univ. of Connecticut School of Law Lib., 39 Elizabeth St., Hartford, CT 06105-2287. Tel. 860-570-5109, fax 860-570-5104, e-mail darcy.kirk@law.uconn.edu; *V.P.* Jean M. Wenger, 6963 N. Bell Ave., Unit 101, Chicago, IL 60645-4880. Tel. 312-603-5131, fax 312-603-4716, e-mail jean.wenger@cook countyil.gov; *Secy.* Deborah L. Rusin. E-mail deborah.rusin@kattenlaw.com; *Treas.* Susan J. Lewis. E-mail slewis@wcl.american.edu; *Past Pres.* Joyce Manna Janto, Univ. of Richmond School of Law Lib., 28 Westhampton Way, Richmond, VA 23173-0002. Tel. 804-289-8223, fax 804-289-8683, e-mail jjanto@richmond.edu.

Executive Board

Kathleen Brown, Lucy Curci-Gonzalez, Gregory R. Lambert, Diane Rodriguez, Ronald E. Wheeler, Jr., Donna S. Williams.

American Library Association

Executive Director, Keith Michael Fiels
50 E. Huron St., Chicago, IL 60611
800-545-2433, 312-280-1392, fax 312-440-9374
World Wide Web http://www.ala.org

Object

The mission of the American Library Association (ALA) is to provide leadership for the development, promotion, and improvement of library and information services and the profession of librarianship in order to enhance learning and ensure access to information for all. Founded 1876.

Membership

Memb. (Indiv.) 56,839; (Inst.) 2,765; (Corporate) 220; (Total) 59,824 (as of December 2011). Any person, library, or other organization interested in library service and librarians. Dues (Indiv.) 1st year, $65; 2nd year, $98; 3rd year and later, $130; (Trustee and Assoc. Memb.) $59; (Lib. Support Staff) $46; (Student) $33; (Foreign Indiv.) $78; (Other) $46; (Inst.) $110 and up, depending on operating expenses of institution.

Officers (2011–2012)

Pres. Molly Raphael, Multnomah County (Oregon) Lib. E-mail mraphael@rapgroup.com; *Pres.-Elect* Maureen Sullivan, Organization Development Consultant. E-mail msull317@aol.com; *Past Pres.* Roberta Stevens, Lib. of Congress. E-mail rlste@loc.gov.com; *Treas.* James Neal, Columbia Univ. E-mail jneal@columbia.edu.

Executive Board

Dora Ho (2014), Patricia M. Hogan (2012), Stephen L. Matthews (2012), Sylvia Norton (2014), Michael Porter (2014), Kevin Reynolds (2013), J. Linda Williams (2013), Courtney L. Young (2012).

Endowment Trustees

Daniel J. Bradbury (chair), John Vitali, Robert A. Walton; *Exec. Board Liaison* James Neal; *Staff Liaison* Gregory L. Calloway.

Divisions

See the separate entries that follow: American Assn. of School Libns.; Assn. for Lib. Collections and Technical Services; Assn. for Lib. Service to Children; Assn. of College and Research Libs.; Assn. of Lib. Trustees, Advocates, Friends, and Foundations; Assn. of Specialized and Cooperative Lib. Agencies; Lib. Leadership and Management Assn.; Lib. and Info. Technology Assn.; Public Lib. Assn.; Reference and User Services Assn.; Young Adult Lib. Services Assn.

Publications

ALA Handbook of Organization (online).
American Libraries (10 a year; memb.; organizations $70; foreign $80; single copy $7.50).
Booklist (22 a year; U.S. and Canada $147.50; foreign $170; single copy $9).

Round Table Chairs

(ALA staff liaison in parentheses)
Continuing Library Education Network and Exchange. To be announced (Darlena Davis).
Ethnic and Multicultural Information Exchange. Homa Naficy (Miguel A. Figueroa).
Exhibits. Gene Shimshock (Amy McGuigan).
Federal and Armed Forces Libraries. Vicky Crone (Rosalind Reynolds).
Games and Gaming. To be announced.
Gay, Lesbian, Bisexual, Transgendered. Anne Moore (Elliot Mandel).

Government Documents. Kirsten Clark (Rosalind Reynolds).

Intellectual Freedom. Pat Scales (Nanette Perez).

International Relations. Eve Nyren (Delin Guerra).

Learning. Sharon Morris (Kimberly Redd).

Library History. Tom Glynn (Norman Rose).

Library Instruction. Linda Goff (Beatrice Calvin).

Library Research. John Budd (Norman Rose).

Library Support Staff Interests. Jason Rendleton (Darlena Davis).

Map and Geography. Hallie Pritchett (Danielle M. Alderson).

New Members. Linda Crook (Kimberly Sanders).

Retired Members. To be announced (Danielle M. Alderson).

Social Responsibilities. Mike Marlin (Elliot Mandel).

Staff Organizations. Leon S. Bey (Kimberly Redd).

Video. Tom Ipri (Danielle M. Alderson).

Committee Chairs

(ALA staff liaison in parentheses)

Accreditation (Standing). Ken Haycock (Karen L. O'Brien).

American Libraries Advisory (Standing). Andrew K. Pace (George Eberhart).

Appointments (Standing). Maureen Sullivan (Delores Yates).

Awards (Standing). Andrea R. Lapsley (Cheryl Malden).

Budget Analysis and Review (Standing). Clara Nalli Bohrer (Gregory L. Calloway).

Chapter Relations (Standing). Cynthia Czesak (Don Wood).

Committee on Committees (Elected Council Committee). Maureen Sullivan (Delores Yates).

Conference Committee (Standing). Stephen Matthews (Carrie Mehrhoff).

Conference Program Coordinating Team. (Amy McGuigan).

Constitution and Bylaws (Standing). Steven Bowers (JoAnne M. Kempf).

Council Orientation (Standing). Barbara Genco (Lois Ann Gregory-Wood).

Diversity (Standing). Alexandra Rivera (Gwendolyn Prellwitz).

Education (Standing). Ismail Abdullahi (Lorelle R. Swader).

Election (Standing). Karen Danczak-Lyons (Eileen Mahoney).

Human Resource Development and Recruitment (Standing). Pat Hawthorne (Lorelle R. Swader).

Information Technology Policy Advisory (Standing). Bonnie Tijerina (Alan Inouye).

Intellectual Freedom (Standing). Pat Scales (Nanette Perez).

International Relations (Standing). Sha Li Zhang (Michael P. Dowling).

Legislation (Standing). Eva Poole (Lynne E. Bradley).

Literacy (Standing). Juliet I. Machie (Dale Lipschultz).

Literacy and Outreach Services Advisory (Standing). John Sandstrom (Dale Lipschultz).

Membership (Standing). Kay Cassell (Cathleen Bourdon).

Membership Meetings. Loida Garci-Febo (Lois Ann Gregory-Wood).

Nominating. To be announced (Joanne Kempf).

Organization (Standing). James R. Rettig (Delores Yates).

Orientation, Training, and Leadership Development. Catharine Freeman (Lorelle Swader).

Policy Monitoring (Standing). John Allyn Moorman (Lois Ann Gregory-Wood).

Professional Ethics (Standing). (Angela Maycock).

Public and Cultural Programs Advisory (Standing). Terrilyn Chun (Deborah Anne Robertson).

Public Awareness (Standing). Sonia Alcantara-Antoine (Megan McFarlane).

Publishing (Standing). Gail A. Schlachter (Donald E. Chatham).

Research and Statistics (Standing). Wanda V. Dole (Norman Rose).

Resolutions. Larry Romans (Lois Ann Gregory-Wood).

Rural, Native, and Tribal Libraries of All Kinds. Jennifer Lee Peterson (Miguel A. Figueroa).

Scholarships and Study Grants. Toni Carter (Lorelle R. Swader).

Status of Women in Librarianship (Standing). To be announced (Lorelle R. Swader).

Web Site Advisory. Aaron W. Dobbs (Sherri L. Vanyek).

American Library Association
American Association of School Librarians

Executive Director, Julie A. Walker
50 E. Huron St., Chicago, IL 60611
312-280-4382, 800-545-2433 ext. 4382, fax 312-280-5276, e-mail aasl@ala.org
World Wide Web http://www.aasl.org.

Object

The mission of the American Association of School Librarians (AASL) is to advocate excellence, facilitate change, and develop leaders in the school library field. AASL works to ensure that all members of the field collaborate to provide leadership in the total education program; participate as active partners in the teaching/learning process; connect learners with ideas and information; and prepare students for lifelong learning, informed decision making, a love of reading, and the use of information technologies.

Established in 1951 as a separate division of the American Library Association.

Membership

Memb. 8,000+. Open to all libraries, school librarians, interested individuals, and business firms, with requisite membership in ALA.

Officers (2011–2012)

Pres. Carl A. Harvey II; *Pres.-Elect* Susan D. Ballard; *Treas.* Karen R. Lemmons; *Past Pres.* Nancy Everhart.

Board of Directors

Jay Bansbach, Deborah Jean Christensen, Audrey P. Church, Sally A. Daniels, Valerie Diggs, Valerie A. Edwards, Karen L. Egger, Louis Matthew Greco, Jr., Susi Parks Grissom, Dorcas Hand, Sara Kelly Johns, Bonnie S. Kel-ley, Linda Anne Roberts, David A. Sonnen, Deborah Svec.

Publications

AASL Hotlinks (mo.; electronic, memb.).
Knowledge Quest (5 a year; $50, $60 outside USA). *Ed.* Markisan Naso. E-mail mnaso@ala.org.
School Library Media Research (electronic, free, at http://www.ala.org/aasl.slmr). *Eds.* Jean Donham. E-mail jean.donham@uni.edu; Carol L. Tilley. E-mail ctilley@uiuc.edu.

Section Leadership

AASL/ESLS Executive Committee. Audrey P. Church, Jody K. Howard, Michelle Kowalsky, Barbara J. Ray.
AASL/ISS Executive Committee. Carla Bosco, Dorcas Hand, Judith L. Hill, Barbara L. Spivey, Alicia S. Q. Yao.
AASL/SPVS Executive Committee. John P. Brock, Judith Dzikowski, Eva Efron, Bonnie S. Kelley.

Committee Chairs

AASL/ACRL Joint Information Literacy Committee. Lesley S. J. Farmer, Scott B. Mandernack.
AASL/ALSC/YALSA Interdivisional Committee on School/Public Library Cooperation. Randall Enos.
Advocacy. Judi Repman.
Affiliate Assembly. Geraldine J. Fegan.

Alliance for Association Excellence. Karen R. Lemmons.

American University Press Book Selection. Linda J. Underwood.

Annual Conference. Melissa P. Johnston, Terrence E. Young, Jr.

Appointments. Robbie Leah Nickel.

Awards. Nancy Dickinson.

Best Web Sites for Teaching and Learning. Heather Michele Moorefield-Lang.

Blog Editorial Board. Carolyn J. Starkey, Wendy Steadman Stephens.

Bylaws and Organization. Dolores D. Gwaltney.

Intellectual Freedom. Helen Ruth Adams.

Knowledge Quest Editorial Board. Ann M. Martin.

Legislation. Connie Hamner Williams.

National Institute 2012. Barbara A. Jansen.

NCATE Coordinating Committee. Rebecca J. Pasco.

Nominating. Barbara J. Ray.

Research/Statistics. Gail K. Dickinson.

School Library Month Committee. Cassandra G. Barnett.

SLMR Editorial Board. Jean Donham, Carol L. Tilley.

Essential Links Editorial Board. Vicki C. Builta.

Task Force Chairs

Educator Pre-Service. Shonda Layne Brisco.

Leadership Development. Ann M. Martin.

Planned Giving Initiative. Frances R. Roscello.

Retirees. Irene Kwidzinski.

Standards and Guidelines Implementation. Karen W. Gavigan.

Urban Schools. To be appointed.

Awards Committees and Chairs

AASL Research Grant. Ann Marie Pipkin.

ABC-CLIO Leadership Grant. Mary O. Keeling.

Collaborative School Library Award. Leslie M. Forsman.

Distinguished School Administrator Award. Douglas Allan Johnson.

Distinguished Service Award. Diane R. Chen.

Frances Henne Award. Janice C. Ostrom.

Information Technology Pathfinder Award. Kelly S. Brannock.

Innovative Reading Grant. Ernie J. Cox.

Intellectual Freedom Award. Joanne M. Proctor.

National School Library Program of the Year Award. Bonnie J. Grimble.

American Library Association
Association for Library Collections and Technical Services

Executive Director, Charles Wilt
50 E. Huron St., Chicago, IL 60611
800-545-2433 ext. 5030, fax 312-280-5033, e-mail cwilt@ala.org
World Wide Web http://www.ala.org/alcts

Object

The Association for Library Collections and Technical Services (ALCTS) envisions an environment in which traditional library roles are evolving. New technologies are making information more fluid and raising expectations. The public needs quality information anytime, anyplace. ALCTS provides frameworks to meet these information needs.

ALCTS provides leadership to the library and information communities in developing principles, standards, and best practices for creating, collecting, organizing, delivering, and preserving information resources in all forms. It provides this leadership through its members by fostering educational, research, and professional service opportunities. ALCTS is committed to quality information, universal access, collaboration, and lifelong learning.

Standards—Develop, evaluate, revise, and promote standards for creating, collecting, organizing, delivering, and preserving information resources in all forms.

Best practices—Research, develop, evaluate, and implement best practices for creating, collecting, organizing, delivering, and preserving information resources in all forms.

Education—Assess the need for, sponsor, develop, administer, and promote educational programs and resources for lifelong learning.

Professional development—Provide opportunities for professional development through research, scholarship, publication, and professional service.

Interaction and information exchange—Create opportunities to interact and exchange information with others in the library and information communities.

Association operations—Ensure efficient use of association resources and effective delivery of member services.

Established 1957; renamed 1988.

Membership

Memb. 4,200. Any member of the American Library Association may elect membership in this division according to the provisions of the bylaws.

Officers (2011–2012)

Pres. Betsy Simpson, Smathers Lib., Univ. of Florida, P.O. Box 117004, Gainesville, FL 32611. Tel. 352-273-2730, fax 352-392-7365, e-mail betsys@uflib.ufl.edu; *Pres.-Elect* Carolynne Myall, Kennedy Lib., Eastern Washington Univ., 816 F St., Cheney, WA 99004. Tel. 509-359-6967, fax 509-359-2476, e-mail cmyall@ewu.edu; *Past Pres.* Cynthia Whitacre, OCLC, 6565 Kilgour Place, Dublin, OH 43017. Tel. 614-764-6183, fax 614-718-7397, e-mail whitacrc@oclc.org; *Councilor* Brian E. C. Schottlaender, Lib., Univ. of California, San Diego, 9500 Gilman Dr., No. 0175G, La Jolla, CA 92093. Tel. 858-534-3060, fax 858-534-6193, e-mail becs@ucsd.edu.

Address correspondence to the executive director.

Board of Directors

Elizabeth Appleton, Stephen Bosch, Susan A. Davis, Marlene Harris, Harriet Lightman, Janet Lute, Mary Mastraccio, Norm Medeiros, Margaret Mering, Arthur Miller, Carolynne Myall, Mary Page, Alice Platt, Brian E. C. Schottlaender, Betsy Simpson, Timothy Strawn, Cynthia Whitacre, Ann Marie Willer, Charles Wilt.

Publications

ALCTS Newsletter Online (q.; free; posted at http://www.ala.org/alcts). *Ed.* Alice Platt, Boston Athenaeum, 101/2 Beacon St., Boston, MA 02108. Tel. 617-720-7609 ext. 241, e-mail platt@bostonathenaeum.org.

Library Resources and Technical Services (q.; nonmemb. $95; international $110). *Ed.* Peggy Johnson, Univ. of Minnesota Libs., 499 Wilson Lib., 309 19th Ave. S., Minneapolis, MN 55455. Tel. 612-624-2312, fax 612-626-9353, e-mail m-john@tc.umn.edu.

Section Chairpersons

Acquisitions. Stephen Bosch.
Cataloging and Metadata Management. Mary Mastraccio.
Collection Management. Harriet Lightman.
Continuing Resources. Margaret Mering.
Preservation and Reformatting. Ann Marie Willer.

Committee Chairpersons

ALCTS Outstanding Publications Award Jury. Mary Beth Weber.
Hugh C. Atkinson Memorial Award (ALCTS/ACRL/LAMA/LITA). Lisa Thomas.
Ross Atkinson Lifetime Achievement Award Jury. Bruce Chr. Johnson.
Budget and Finance. Janet Lute.
Continuing Education. Pamela Bluh.
Fundraising. Genevieve Owens.
International Relations. David Miller.
Leadership Development. Miranda Bennett.
LRTS Editorial Board. Peggy Johnson.
Membership. Deborah Ryszka.

Nominating. Mary Case.

Organization and Bylaws. Arthur Miller.

Outstanding Collaboration Citation Jury. Elaine Yontz.

Esther J. Piercy Award Jury. Steven Kelley.

Planning. Norm Medeiros.

Program. Susan Wynne, Angie Ohler.

Publications. Dina Giambi.

Edward Swanson Memorial Best of *LRTS* Award Jury. Alex Thurman.

Interest Groups

Authority Control (ALCTS/LITA). Melanie McGurr.

Automated Acquisitions/In-Process Control Systems. Sharon Marshall.

Creative Ideas in Technical Services. Libbie Crawford.

Electronic Resources. Elizabeth Babbit.

FRBR. Karen Anderson.

Linked Library Data (ALCTS/LITA). Karen Coyle, Corey Harper.

MARC Formats (ALCTS/LITA). Chiat Naun Chew.

New Members. Amy Jackson.

Newspapers. Brian Geiger.

Public Libraries Technical Services. Donna Cranmer.

Role of the Professional in Academic Research Technical Service Departments. Erica Olivier, Shoko Tokoro.

Scholarly Communications. Sarah Shreeves.

Technical Services Directors of Large Research Libraries. Joseph Kiegel.

Technical Services Managers in Academic Libraries. Judy Garrison.

Technical Services Workflow Efficiency. Eric Brownell, Megan Dazey.

American Library Association
Association for Library Service to Children

Executive Director, Aimee Strittmatter
50 E. Huron St., Chicago, IL 60611
312-280-2163, 800-545-2433 ext. 2163, fax 312-280-5271, e-mail alsc@ala.org
World Wide Web http://www.ala.org/alsc

Object

The core purpose of the Association for Library Service to Children (ALSC) is to create a better future for children through libraries. Its primary goal is to lead the way in forging excellent library services for all children. ALSC offers creative programming, information about best practices, continuing education, a prestigious award and media evaluation program, and professional connections. Founded 1901.

Membership

Memb. 4,000. Open to anyone interested in library services to children. For information on dues, see ALA entry.

Address correspondence to the executive director.

Officers

Pres. Mary Fellows; *V.P./Pres.-Elect* Carolyn S. Brodie; *Past Pres.* Julie Corsaro; *Fiscal Officer* Tali Balas; *Division Councilor* Rhonda Puntney.

Directors

Ernie Cox, Nina Lindsay, Cecelia McGowan, Leslie Molnar, Elizabeth Orsburn, Jennifer Ralston, Ellen Riordan, Michael Santangelo, Lisa Von Drasek, Jan Watkins.

Publications

Children and Libraries: The Journal of the Association for Library Service to Children (q.; memb.; nonmemb. $40; foreign $50).

ALSConnect (q., electronic; memb. Not available by subscription.)

Committee Chairs

AASL/ALSC/YALSA Interdivisional Committee on School/Public Library Cooperation. Randy Enos.

ALSC/*Booklist*/YALSA Odyssey Award Selection 2012. Lizette Hannegan.

Arbuthnot Honor Lecture 2012. Shawn Brommer.

Arbuthnot Honor Lecture 2013. Susan Pine.

Arbuthnot Honor Lecture 2014. Susan Moore.

Mildred L. Batchelder Award 2012. Susan Stan.

Mildred L. Batchelder Award 2013. Jean Hatfield.

Pura Belpré Award 2012. Jamie Campbell Naidoo.

Pura Belpré Award 2013. Charmette Kuhn-Kendrick.

Budget. Alison Ernst.

Randolph Caldecott Award 2012. Steven Herb.

Randolph Caldecott Award 2013. Sandra Imdieke.

Andrew Carnegie Medal/Notable Children's Videos. Maeve Visser-Knoth.

Children and Libraries Advisory Committee. Christina Desai.

Children and Technology. Gretchen Caserotti.

Distinguished Service Award 2012. Jennifer Brown.

Distinguished Service Award 2013. Carol Doll.

Early Childhood Programs and Services. Kathy Jarombek.

Education. Linda Ward-Callaghan.

Theodor Seuss Geisel Award 2012. Carole Fiore.

Theodor Seuss Geisel Award 2013. Carla Morris.

Grant Administration Committee. Nancy Baumann.

Great Web Sites. Kimberly Grad, Denise Vallandingham.

Intellectual Freedom. Erlene Bishop.

Legislation. Penny Markey.

Liaison with National Organizations. Nancee Dahms-Stinson, Stephanie Bange.

Library Service to Special Population Children and Their Caregivers. Paula Holmes.

Local Arrangements (Anaheim). Madeline Kerr.

Managing Children's Services. Anitra Steele.

Membership. A. Charlene McKenzie.

John Newbery Award 2012. Viki Ash.

John Newbery Award 2013. Steven Engelfried.

Nominating 2012. Pat Scales.

Nominating 2013. Thom Barthelmess.

Notable Children's Books. Wendy Woodfill.

Notable Children's Recordings. Lynda Poling.

Oral History. Kathleen T. Horning.

Organization and Bylaws. Susan Polos, Melissa McBride.

Program Coordinating. Angela Nolet.

Public Awareness. Barbara Scotto.

Quicklists Consulting. Natasha J. Forrester, Laura Jenkins.

Charlemae Rollins President's Program 2012. Tessa Michaelson.

Scholarships. Janis Cooker.

School Age Programs and Service. Tami L. Chumbley Finley.

Robert F. Sibert Award 2012. Andrew Medlar.

Robert F. Sibert Award 2013. Kathie Meizner.

Special Collections and Bechtel Fellowship. Ellen Ruffin.

Laura Ingalls Wilder Award 2013. Martha Parravano.

American Library Association
Association of Library Trustees, Advocates, Friends, and Foundations

Executive Director, Sally Gardner Reed
109 S. 13 St., Suite 117B, Philadelphia, PA 19107
Tel. 312-280-2161, fax 215-545-3821, e-mail sreed@ala.org
World Wide Web http://www.ala.org/altaff

Object

The Association for Library Trustees, Advocates, Friends, and Foundations (ALTAFF) was founded in 1890 as the American Library Trustee Association (ALTA). It was the only division of the American Library Association dedicated to promoting and ensuring outstanding library service through educational programs that develop excellence in trusteeship and promote citizen involvement in the support of libraries. In 2008 the members of ALTA voted to expand the division to more aggressively address the needs of friends of libraries and library foundations, and through a merger with Friends of Libraries USA (FOLUSA) became ALTAFF. ALTA had become an ALA division in 1961.

Membership

Memb. 5,200. Open to all interested persons and organizations. For dues and membership year, see ALA entry.

Officers (2011–2012)

Pres. Donna McDonald; *V.P./Pres.-Elect* Gail Guidry Griffin; *Councilor* Susan Schmidt; *Past. Pres.* Rod Gauvin.

Publications

The Voice for America's Libraries (q.; memb.).
101+ Great Ideas for Libraries and Friends.
Even More Great Ideas for Libraries and Friends.
The Complete Trustee Handbook.

Committee Chairs

ALTAFF Leaders Orientation. Peggy Danhof.
Annual Conference Program. Robin Hoklotubbe.
Library Issues. Shirley Bruursema.
Newsletter and Web Site Advisory. Diane Sarantakos.
Nominating. Rose Mosley.
PLA Conference Program. Margaret Schuster, Gail Griffin.

American Library Association
Association of College and Research Libraries

Executive Director, Mary Ellen K. Davis
50 E. Huron St., Chicago, IL 60611-2795
312-280-2523, 800-545-2433 ext. 2523, fax 312-280-2520, e-mail acrl@ala.org
World Wide Web http://www.ala.org/acrl

Object

The Association of College and Research Libraries (ACRL) leads academic and research librarians and libraries in advancing learning and scholarship. Founded 1940.

Membership

Memb. 12,500. For information on dues, see ALA entry.

Officers

Pres. Joyce L. Ogburn, 327 J. Willard Marriott Lib., Univ. of Utah, Salt Lake City, UT 84103-3322. Tel. 801-585-9775, fax 801-585-7185, e-mail joyce.ogburn@utah.edu; *Pres.-Elect* Steven J. Bell, Paley Lib., Temple Univ., Philadelphia, PA 19122-6086. Tel. 215-204-5023, fax 215-204-5201, e-mail bells@temple.edu; *Past Pres.* Lisa Janicke Hinchliffe, Univ. of Illinois, Urbana, IL 61801-3607. Tel. 217-333-1323, fax 217-244-4358, e-mail ljanicke@illinois.edu; *Budget and Finance Chair* Cynthia K. Steinhoff, Anne Arundel Community College, 101 College Pkwy., Arnold, MD 21012-1895. Tel. 410-777-2483, fax 410-777-4483, e-mail cksteinhoff@aacc.edu; *ACRL Councilor* Maggie Ferrell, Univ. of Wyoming, 1000 E. University Ave., Laramie, WY 82071-2000. Tel. 307-766-3279, fax 307-766-2510, e-mail-farrell@uwyo.edu.

Board of Directors

Officers; Lisabeth A. Chabot, Mark Emmons, Irene M. H. Herold, Linda A. Kopecky, John A. Lehner, Loretta R. Parham, Ann Campion Riley, Mary Ann Sheble.

Publications

Choice (12 a year; $370; Canada and Mexico $420; other international $490). *Ed.* Irving Rockwood.

Choice Reviews-on-Cards (available only to subscribers of *Choice* and/or *Choice Reviews Online*); $460; Canada and Mexico $510; other international $590).

ChoiceReviews Online 2.0 ($510).

College & Research Libraries (*C&RL*) (6 a year; memb.; nonmemb. $75; Canada and other PUAS countries $80; other international $85). *Ed.* Joseph J. Branin.

College & Research Libraries News (*C&RL News*) (11 a year; memb.; nonmemb. $50; Canada and other PUAS countries $55; other international $60). *Ed.* David Free.

Publications in Librarianship (formerly ACRL Monograph Series) (occasional). *Ed.* Craig Gibson.

RBM: A Journal of Rare Books, Manuscripts, and Cultural Heritage (s. ann.; $45; Canada and other PUAS countries $50; other international $60). *Ed.* Beth M. Whittaker.

Committee and Task Force Chairs

AASL/ACRL Information Literacy (interdivisional). Lesley S. J. Farmer, Scott B. Mandernack.

Academic/Research Librarian of the Year Award. John M. Budd.

ACRL Academic Library Trends and Statistics Survey. Charles C. Stuart.

ACRL/LLAMA Interdivisional Committee on Building Resources. Kathleen Gallagher, Ann H. Hamilton.

Advocacy. Eric L. Frierson.

Annual Conference Programs. Sarah E. Sheehan.

Appointments. John H. Pollitz.

Assessment. Jennifer Anne Rutner.

Hugh C. Atkinson Memorial Award. Larry P. Alford.

Budget and Finance. Cynthia K. Steinhoff.

Choice Editorial Board. Dalia Lapatinskas Corkrum.

Colleagues. Marianne I. Gaunt, Lorraine J. Haricombe.

College & Research Libraries Editorial Board. Joseph Branin.

College & Research Libraries News Editorial Board. Joan F. Cheverie.

Copyright. Tim Gritten.

Doctoral Dissertation Fellowship. Dana M. Sally.

Ethics. Rebecca Blakiston.

Excellence in Academic Libraries Award. Lori Goetsch.

Friends Fund. Frances J. Maloy.

Friends Fund Disbursement. Ethan A. Henderson.

Government Relations. Jeffrey Scott Bullington.

Immersion Program. Mark Szarko.

Information Literacy Coordinating. Sarah E. McDaniel.

Information Literacy Standards. Christy R. Stevens.

Information Literacy Web Site. Kathy L. Magarrell.

Intellectual Freedom. Steven L. Irving.

International Relations. Binh P. Le.

E. J. Josey Spectrum Scholar Mentor. Nancy H. Allen.

Leadership Recruitment and Nomination. Theresa S. Byrd.

Liaison Assembly. Susan Barnes Whyte.

Liaison Coordinating. Debbie L. Malone.

Liaison Grants. Marilyn Nabua Ochoa.

Liaisons Training and Development. Susan Barnes Whyte.

Marketing Academic and Research Libraries. Douglas K. Lehman.

Membership Coordinating. Allie Flanary.

Membership Promotion. Alex Hodges.

Membership Recruitment. Amanda Dinscore.

Membership Retention. Miriam Rigby.

Midwinter Preconferences and Annual Workshops. Jennifer R. Kolmes.

National Conference Coordinating Committee (Philadelphia). Erika C. Linke.

New Publications Advisory. Joan K. Lippincott.

President's Program Planning Committee, 2012. Richard W. Clement.

President's Program Planning Committee, 2013. To be appointed.

Professional Development Coordinating. Marla E. Peppers.

Publications Coordinating. Christopher Millson-Martula.

Publications in Librarianship Editorial Board. Craig Gibson.

Racial and Ethnic Diversity. Charlene Maxey-Harris.

RBM Editorial Board. Beth M. Whittaker.

Research Coordinating. Marie L. Radford.

Research Planning and Review. Lynn Silipigni Connaway.

Research Program. Sheril Hook.

Resources for College Libraries Editorial Board. Nancy P. O'Brien.

Scholarly Communications. C. Jeffrey Belliston.

Scholarships. Gladys Smiley Bell.

Section Membership. Kimberley Bugg.

Standards and Accreditation. Jeanne R. Davidson.

Status of Academic Librarians. Connie M. Strittmatter.

Virtual Institutes. Courtney R. Greene.

Discussion Group Chairs

Balancing Baby and Book. Cynthia M. Dudenhoffer.

Continuing Education/Professional Development. To be appointed.

Copyright. Tomas A. Lipinski.

Digital Humanities. Kate Mary Brooks.

Heads of Public Services. Jan H. Kemp.

Information Commons. Rudy Leon, Michael Whitchurch.

Leadership. Rudy Leon.

Librarianship in For-Profit Educational Institutions. Tabitha Dillon.

Libraries and Information Science Collections. Rebecca Vargha.

Media Resources. Catherine Helen Michael.

MLA International Bibliography. Sarah G. Wenzel.

New Members. Bohyun Kim, Elizabeth Psyck, Lindsay C. Sarin.
Personnel Administrators and Staff Development Officers. Emily Backe.
Philosophical, Religious, and Theological Studies. Joshua Barton.
Popular Cultures. Kimberley Bugg.
Regional Campus Libraries. To be appointed.
Scholarly Communications. Lisa A. Macklin.
Undergraduate Libraries. Carrie J. Kruse.

Interest Group Conveners

Academic Library Services to International Students. Victor Dominguez Baeza.
Digital Curation. Marisa Ramirez.
Health Sciences. Shannon Fay Johnson.
Image Resources. Shilpa Rele.
Numeric and Geospatial Data Services in Academic Libraries. Scott R. McEathron.
Residency Programs. Hannah Kyung Lee.
Universal Accessibility. Sherry E. Gelbwasser.
Virtual Worlds. Marcia Meister.

Section Chairs

African American Studies Librarians. Rebecca Hankins.
Anthropology and Sociology. Terrence W. Epperson.
Arts. Claudia Trevathan Covert.
Asian, African, and Middle Eastern. Binh P. Le.
College Libraries. Douglas K. Lehman.
Community and Junior College Libraries. Nan Schichtel.
Distance Learning. Samantha Hines.
Education and Behavioral Sciences. Sally R. Neal.
Instruction. Stephanie A. Michel.
Law and Political Science. Chad Kahl.
Literatures in English. Faye Christenberry.
Rare Books and Manuscripts. Mike Kelly.
Science and Technology. Mary Beth Slebodnik.
Slavic and East European. Liladhar Ramchandra Pendse.
University Libraries. Karl F. Bridges.
Western European Studies. Gail P. Hueting.
Women and Gender Studies. Pamela Mann.

American Library Association
Association of Specialized and Cooperative Library Agencies

Executive Director, Susan Hornung
50 E. Huron St., Chicago, IL 60611-2795
312-280-4395, 800-545-2433 ext. 4395, fax 312-280-5273
E-mail shornung@ala.org
World Wide Web http://www.ala.org/ascla

Object

The Association of Specialized and Cooperative Library Agencies (ASCLA) represents specialized library agencies, state library agencies, library cooperatives, and independent librarians.

Library agencies provide library materials and service to populations with special needs, such as those with sensory, physical, health, or behavioral conditions or those who are incarcerated or detained. The ASCLA LSSP (Library Services to Special Populations) Interest Group represents members with interests in this area.

State library agencies are those organizations created or authorized by the state government to promote library services in the state through the organization and coordination of a variety of library services. The ASCLA SLA (State Library Agencies) Interest Group represents members with interests in this area.

Library cooperatives are combinations, mergers, or contractual associations of one or more types of libraries (academic, public, special, or school) crossing jurisdictional, institutional, or political boundaries, working together to achieve maximum effective use of funds to provide library and information services to all citizens above and beyond those that can be provided through one institution. Such cooperative organizations or agencies may be designated to serve a community, a metropolitan area, a region within a region, or may serve a statewide or multi-state area. The ASCLA ICAN (InterLibrary Cooperation and Networking) Interest Group represents members with interests in this area.

The ASCLA ILEX (Independent Librarians' Exchange) Interest Group represents independent librarians who work outside traditional library settings.

Within the interests of these types of library organizations, ASCLA has specific responsibility for:

1. Development and evaluation of goals and plans for state library agencies and library cooperatives to facilitate the implementation, improvement, and extension of library activities designed to foster improved user services, coordinating such activities with other appropriate ALA units

2. Representation and interpretation of the role, function, and services of state library agencies, specialized library agencies, and library cooperatives within and outside the profession, including contact with national organizations and government agencies

3. Development of policies, studies, and activities in matters affecting state library agencies and library cooperatives relating to: (a) state and local library legislation, (b) state grants-in-aid and appropriations, and (c) relationships among state, federal, regional, and local governments, coordinating such activities with other appropriate ALA units

4. Establishment, evaluation, and promotion of standards and services guidelines relating to the concerns of the association

5. Identifying the library interests and needs of all persons, encouraging the creation

of services to meet these needs within the areas of concern of the association, and promoting the use of these services provided by state library agencies, specialized library agencies, and library cooperatives

6. Stimulating the professional growth and promoting the specialized training and continuing education of library personnel at all levels in the areas of concern of this association and encouraging membership participation in appropriate type-of-activity divisions within ALA

7. Assisting in the coordination of activities of other units within ALA that have a bearing on the concerns of this association

8. Granting recognition for outstanding library service within the areas of concern of this association

9. Acting as a clearinghouse for the exchange of information and encouraging the development of materials, publications, and research within the areas of concern of this association

Membership

Memb. 800+. For information on dues, see ALA entry.

Officers (2011–2012)

Pres. Norma E. Blake; *V.P.* Stacey Aldrich; *Past Pres.* Diana Reese; *Div. Councilor* Kendall French Wiggin.

Interest Groups

ASCLA ICAN (InterLibrary Cooperation and Networking) Consortium Management Discussion Interest Group; ASCLA ICAN Collaborative Digitization Interest Group; ASCLA ICAN Interlibrary Cooperation Interest Group; ASCLA ICAN Physical Delivery Interest Group; ASCLA Library Consultants Interest Group; ASCLA Library Services for Incarcerated Youth (LSSP); ASCLA LSSP Bridging Deaf Cultures @your library Interest Group; ASCLA LSSP (Libraries Serving Special Populations) Library Services to People with Visual or Physical Disabilities that Prevent Them from Reading Standard Print Interest Group; ASCLA LSSP Library Services to the Incarcerated and Detained; ASCLA LSSP Universal Access Interest Group; ASCLA SLA State Library Agencies/Library Development Interest Group; ASCLA SLA/LSTA Coordinators Interest Group; ASCLA SLA Youth Services Consultants Interest Group.

Publication

Interface (q.; memb.). *Ed.* Anne Abate. E-mail anne@librarydiscountnetwork.com.

Committees

Accessibility Assembly; Awards; Finance and Planning; Guidelines for Library and Information Services for the American Deaf Community; Legislation; Membership; Nominating; Online Continuing Education; Publications; Standards Review; Web Presence.

American Library Association
Library Leadership and Management Association

Executive Director, Kerry Ward
50 E. Huron St., Chicago, IL 60611
312-280-5032, 800-545-2433 ext. 5032, fax 312-280-5033
e-mail kward@ala.org
World Wide Web http://www.ala.org/llama

Object

The Library Leadership and Management Association (LLAMA) Strategic Plan sets out the following:

Mission: The Library Leadership and Management Association encourages and nurtures current and future leaders, and develops and promotes outstanding leadership and management practices.

Vision: LLAMA will be the foremost organization developing present and future leaders in library and information services.

Image: LLAMA is a welcoming community where aspiring and experienced leaders from all types of libraries, as well as those who support libraries, come together to gain skills in a quest for excellence in library management, administration, and leadership.

In addition

- LLAMA will be an organization in which value to its members drives decisions.

- LLAMA will expand and strengthen leadership and management expertise at all levels for all libraries.

- LLAMA will facilitate professional development opportunities to enhance leadership and management.

- LLAMA will be the preeminent professional organization that develops and supports library leaders and managers.

Established 1957.

Membership

Memb. 4,800. For information on dues, see ALA entry.

Officers (July 2011–June 2012)

Pres. Janine Golden; *V.P.* Pat Hawthorne; *Past Pres.* Gail A. Kennedy.

Address correspondence to the executive director.

Publications

Library Leadership and Management (open access: http://journals.tdl.org/index.php/llm). *Eds.* Wendi Arant Kaspar, Pixey Mosley.

Committee Chairs

Financial Advancement. Katharina J. Blackstead.

Leadership Development. Alison Armstrong.

LL&M Advisory. Wendi Arant Kaspar, Pixey Mosley.

Marketing Communications. Elisabeth Leonard.

Membership. Krisellen Maloney.

Mentoring. Kay L. Bauman.

Nominating. Gina J. Millsap.

Program. Lee Anne Hooley.

American Library Association
Library and Information Technology Association

Executive Director, Mary C. Taylor
50 E. Huron St., Chicago, IL 60611
312-280-4267, 800-545-2433, e-mail mtaylor@ala.org
World Wide Web http://www.lita.org

Object

As a center of expertise about information technology, the Library and Information Technology Association (LITA) leads in exploring and enabling new technologies to empower libraries. LITA members use the promise of technology to deliver dynamic library collections and services.

LITA educates, serves, and reaches out to its members, other ALA members and divisions, and the entire library and information community through its publications, programs, and other activities designed to promote, develop, and aid in the implementation of library and information technology.

Membership

Memb. 3,352. For information on dues, see ALA entry.

Officers (2011–2012)

Pres. Colleen Cuddy; *V.P./Pres.-Elect* Elizabeth A. Stewart-Marshall; *Past Pres.* Karen Starr.

Directors

John F. Blyberg, Aaron W. Dobbs, Jason Griffey, David Lee King, Lauren Pressley, Cindi Trainor, Maurice York; *Exec. Dir.* Mary C. Taylor.

Publication

Information Technology and Libraries (*ITAL*) (q.; memb.; nonmemb. $65; single copy $30). *Ed.* Marc Truitt. For information or to send manuscripts, contact the editor.

American Library Association
Public Library Association

Executive Director, Barbara A. Macikas
50 E. Huron St., Chicago, IL 60611
312-280-5752, 800-545-2433 ext. 5752, fax 312-280-5029, e-mail pla@ala.org
World Wide Web http://www.pla.org

The Public Library Association (PLA) has specific responsibility for

1. Conducting and sponsoring research about how the public library can respond to changing social needs and technical developments

2. Developing and disseminating materials useful to public libraries in interpreting public library services and needs

3. Conducting continuing education for public librarians by programming at national and regional conferences, by publications such as the newsletter, and by other delivery means

4. Establishing, evaluating, and promoting goals, guidelines, and standards for public libraries

5. Maintaining liaison with relevant national agencies and organizations engaged in public administration and human services, such as the National Association of Counties, the Municipal League, and the Commission on Postsecondary Education

6. Maintaining liaison with other divisions and units of ALA and other library organizations, such as the Association for Library and Information Science Education and the Urban Libraries Council

7. Defining the role of the public library in service to a wide range of user and potential user groups

8. Promoting and interpreting the public library to a changing society through legislative programs and other appropriate means

9. Identifying legislation to improve and to equalize support of public libraries

PLA enhances the development and effectiveness of public librarians and public library services. This mission positions PLA to

• Focus its efforts on serving the needs of its members

• Address issues that affect public libraries

• Commit to quality public library services that benefit the general public

The goals of PLA are

• Advocacy and Awareness: PLA is an essential partner in public library advocacy.

• Leadership and Transformation: PLA is the leading source for learning opportunities to advance transformation of public libraries.

• Literate Nation: PLA will be a leader and valued partner of public libraries' initiatives to create a literate nation.

• Organizational Excellence: PLA is positioned to sustain and grow its resources to advance the work of the association.

Membership

Memb. 10,000+. Open to all ALA members interested in the improvement and expansion of public library services to all ages in various types of communities.

Officers (2011–2012)

Pres. Marcia A. Warner, Grand Rapids (Michigan) Public Library. E-mail pla@ala.org; *Pres.-Elect* Eva D. Poole, Denton (Texas) Public Library. E-mail eva.poole@cityofdenton.com; *Past Pres.* Audra L. Caplan. E-mail caplan@hcplonline.info.

Publication

Public Libraries (bi-mo.; memb.; nonmemb. $65; foreign $75; single copy $10). *Ed.* Kathleen Hughes, PLA, 50 E. Huron St., Chicago, IL 60611. E-mail khughes@ala.org.

Committee Chairs

Annual Conference Program Subcommittee. Cathy E. Sanford.

Baker & Taylor Entertainment Audio Music/ Video Product Award. Roxy L. Ekstrom.

Budget and Finance. Audra L. Caplan.

Gordon M. Conable Award Jury. Valerie Rowe-Jackson.

Continuing Education Advisory Group. Larry P. Neal.

DEMCO New Leaders Travel Grant Jury. Daisy Porter.

EBSCO Excellence in Small and/or Rural Public Library Service Award. Carol R. Bara.

Highsmith Library Innovation Award Jury. Irmgarde B. Brown.

Intellectual Freedom. Kenton L. Oliver.

Leadership Development Task Force. Carolyn A. Anthony.

Legislation and Advocacy. Victoria L. Yarbrough.

Allie Beth Martin Award Jury. Judy Sasges.

Membership Advisory Group. Jennifer L. Giltrop.

Nominating 2012. Sari Feldman.

Nominating 2013. Audra L. Caplan.

PLA/ALSC Every Child Ready to Read Oversight Committee. Judy T. Nelson.

PLA National Conference 2012. Karen Danczak-Lyons.

PLA National Conference 2012 Program Subcommittee. Sara Dallas.

PLA 2012 Local Arrangements. Siobhan A. Reardon.

PLDS Statistical Report Advisory. Ingrid M. Norris.

Polaris Innovation in Technology John Iliff Award. Sharon R. Castleberry.

Public Libraries Advisory. Anne L. Coriston.

Charlie Robinson Award Jury. Toni A. Garvey.

Romance Writers of America Library Grant Jury. Jill Garcia.

Technology Committee. Amy Frances Terlaga.

American Library Association
Reference and User Services Association

Executive Director, Susan Hornung
50 E. Huron St., Chicago, IL 60611
Tel. 800-545-2433 ext. 4395, 312-280-4395, fax 312-280-5273
E-mail shornung@ala.org
World Wide Web http://www.ala.org/rusa

Object

The Reference and User Services Association (RUSA) is responsible for stimulating and supporting excellence in the delivery of general library services and materials, and the provision of reference and information services, collection development, readers' advisory, and resource sharing for all ages, in every type of library.

The specific responsibilities of RUSA are:

1. Conduct of activities and projects within the association's areas of responsibility

2. Encouragement of the development of librarians engaged in these activities, and

stimulation of participation by members of appropriate type-of-library divisions

3. Synthesis of the activities of all units within the American Library Association that have a bearing on the type of activities represented by the association

4. Representation and interpretation of the association's activities in contacts outside the profession

5. Planning and development of programs of study and research in these areas for the total profession

6. Continuous study and review of the association's activities

Membership

Memb. 4,200+

Officers (2011–2012)

Pres. Gary W. White; *Pres.-Elect* Mary Pagliero Popp; *Secy.* Carolyn Larson; *Past Pres.* Barry Trott; *Div. Councilor* M. Kathleen Kern.

Publication

Reference and User Services Quarterly online only, rusa.metapress.com. (q.; memb.). *Ed.* Diane M. Zabel, Schreyer Business Lib., 309 Paterno Lib., Pennsylvania State Univ., University Park, PA 16802. E-mail dxz2@psu.edu.

Sections

Business Reference and Services (BRASS); Collection Development and Evaluation (CODES); History (HS); Emerging Technologies in Reference (MARS); Reference Services (RSS); Sharing and Transforming Access to Resources (STARS).

Committees

Access to Information; AFL/CIO Joint Committee on Library Services to Labor Groups; Awards; Budget and Finance; Conference Program; Membership; Nominating; Organization and Planning; Professional Development; Publications and Communications; Standards and Guidelines.

American Library Association
Young Adult Library Services Association

Executive Director, Beth Yoke
50 E. Huron St., Chicago, IL 60611
312-280-4390, 800-545-2433 ext. 4390, fax 312-280-5276, e-mail yalsa@ala.org
World Wide Web http://www.ala.org/yalsa
Blog http://yalsa.ala.org/blog, Wiki http://wikis.ala.org/yalsa, Twitter http://twitter.com/yalsa,
Facebook http://www.facebook.com/YALSA.

Object

In every library in the nation, high-quality library service to young adults is provided by a staff that understands and respects the unique informational, educational, and recreational needs of teenagers. Equal access to information, services, and materials is recognized as a right, not a privilege. Young adults are actively involved in the library decision making process. The library staff collaborates and co-operates with other youth-serving agencies to provide a holistic, community-wide network of activities and services that support healthy youth development. To ensure that this vision becomes a reality, the Young Adult Library Services Association (YALSA)

1. Advocates extensive and developmentally appropriate library and information services for young adults ages 12 to 18

2. Promotes reading and supports the literacy movement

3. Advocates the use of information and communications technologies to provide effective library service

4. Supports equality of access to the full range of library materials and services, including existing and emerging information and communications technologies, for young adults

5. Provides education and professional development to enable its members to serve as effective advocates for young people

6. Fosters collaboration and partnerships among its individual members with the library community and other groups involved in providing library and information services to young adults

7. Influences public policy by demonstrating the importance of providing library and information services that meet the unique needs and interests of young adults

8. Encourages research and is in the vanguard of new thinking concerning the provision of library and information services for youth

Membership

Memb. 5,400. Open to anyone interested in library services, literature, and technology for young adults. For information on dues, see ALA entry.

Officers

Pres. Sarah Flowers. E-mail sarahflowers@charter.net; *V.P./Pres.-Elect* Jack Martin. E-mail jackmartin@nypl.org; *Division Councilor* Nick Buron. E-mail nickburon.ala@gmail.com; *Fiscal Officer* Penny Johnson. E-mail pj librarylady@gmail.com; *Secy.* Sarajo Wentling. E-mail sjwentling@gmail.com; *Past Pres.* Kim Patton. E-mail kimpatton@kclibrary.org.

Directors

Priscille Dando, Sandra Hughes-Hassell, Monique leConge, Shannon Peterson, Sara Ryan, Chris Shoemaker, Stephanie Squicciarini, Gail Tobin, Christian Zabriskie.

Publications

Journal of Research on Libraries and Young Adults (q.) (online, open source, peer-reviewed).

Young Adult Library Services (q.) (memb.; nonmemb. $70; foreign $80). Ed. Megan Honig.

YALSA E-News (memb.) *Ed.* Stephanie Kuenn.

AIIM—The Enterprise Content Management Association

President, John F. Mancini
1100 Wayne Ave., Suite 1100, Silver Spring, MD 20910
800-477-2446, 301-587-8202, e-mail aiim@aiim.org
World Wide Web http://www.aiim.org
European Office: 8 Canalside, Lowesmoor Wharf, Worcester WR1 2RR, England. Tel. 44-1905-727613, fax 44-1905-727609, e-mail info@aiim.org.uk

Object

AIIM is an international authority on enterprise content management, the tools and technologies that capture, manage, store, preserve, and deliver content in support of business processes. Founded in 1943 as the Association for Information and Image Management.

Officers

Chair John Chickering, Fidelity Investments; *V. Chair* John Opdyke, Hyland Software; *Treas.* Timothy Elmore, Bank-Fund Staff Federal Credit Union; *Past Chair* Lynn Fraas, Crown Partners.

Publications

Infonomics magazine (bi-mo.; memb., print and online); *Infonomics Weekly eNewsletter.*

American Indian Library Association

President, Sandy Littletree
World Wide Web http://www.ailanet.org

Objective

To improve library and information services for American Indians. Founded in 1979; affiliated with American Library Association 1985.

Large David Hurley. E-mail david.hurley@gmail.com; David Ongley. E-mail david.ongley@tuzzy.org; Melanie Toledo. E-mail mtoledo@ak-chin.nsn.us; *Executive Director* Kelly Webster. E-mail kellypster@gmail.com.

Membership

Any person, library, or other organization interested in working to improve library and information services for American Indians may become a member. Dues (Inst.) $40; (Indiv.) $20; (Student) $10.

Officers (July 2011–June 2012)

Pres. Sandy Littletree. E-mail sandy505@email.arizona.edu; *V.P./Pres.-Elect* Janice Kowemy. E-mail jkowemy@lagunatribe.org; *Secy.* Heather Devine. E-mail hhdevine@gmail.com; *Treas.* Carlene Engstrom. E-mail carleneengstrom@yahoo.com; *Past. Pres.* Jody Gray. E-mail grayjl@umn.edu; *Members at*

Publication

AILA Newsletter (q.).

Committee Chairs

Development and Fund Raising. To be announced.
Distinguished Service Award. David Ongley.
Membership and Publications. To be announced.
Nominating. Jody Gray.
Programming. Jody Gray.
Scholarship Review Board. Holly Tomren.
Talk Story Grant. Liana Juliano.
Web Site. Heather Devine.
Youth Literature Award. Lisa Mitten.

American Merchant Marine Library Association

Executive Director, Roger T. Korner
635 Fourth Ave., Brooklyn, NY 11232
Tel. 718-369-3818, e-mail ussammla@ix.netcom.com
World Wide Web http://unitedseamensservice.org

Object

Known as "the public library of the high seas," the association provides ship and shore library

service for American-flag merchant vessels, and for the Military Sealift Command, the U.S. Coast Guard, and other waterborne operations of the U.S. government. Established 1921.

Executive Committee

John M. Bowers; John L. DeGurse, Jr.; Capt. Fred Finger; Capt. Robert E. Hart; David Hei-ndel; James Henry; Donald E. Kadlac; Roger T. Korner; Edward R. Morgan; George E. Murphy; F. Anthony Naccarato; William D. Potts; Kenneth R. Wykle.

American Society for Information Science and Technology

Executive Director, Richard B. Hill
1320 Fenwick Lane, Suite 510, Silver Spring, MD 20910
301-495-0900, fax 301-495-0810, e-mail f@asis.org
World Wide Web http://www.asis.org

Object

The American Society for Information Science and Technology (ASIS&T) provides a forum for the discussion, publication, and critical analysis of work dealing with the design, management, and use of information, information systems, and information technology.

Membership

Memb. (Indiv.) 3,000; (Student) 800; (Inst.) 250. Dues (Indiv.) $140; (Student) $40; (Inst.) $650 and $800.

Officers

Pres. Diane Sonnenwald, Univ. College Dublin (Ireland); *Pres.-Elect* Andrew Dillon, Univ. of Texas at Austin; *Treas.* Vicki Gregory, Univ. of South Florida; *Past Pres.* Linda C. Smith, Univ. of Illinois at Urbana-Champaign.

Address correspondence to the executive director.

Board of Directors

Dirs.-at-Large Katriina Byström, Prudence Dalrymple, Jens-Erik Mai, Diane Neal, Cassidy Sugimoto, Elaine Toms, Shelly Warwick, Marcia Lei Zeng.

Publications

ASIS&T Thesaurus of Information Science, Technology, and Librarianship, 3rd edition, ed. by Alice Redmond-Neal and Marjorie M. K. Hlava.

Computerization Movements and Technology Diffusion: From Mainframes to Ubiquitous Computing, ed. by Margaret S. Elliott and Kenneth L. Kraemer.

Covert and Overt: Recollecting and Connecting Intelligence Service and Information Science, ed. by Robert V. Williams and Ben-Ami Lipetz.

Editorial Peer Review: Its Strengths and Weaknesses, by Ann C. Weller.

Electronic Publishing: Applications and Implications, ed. by Elisabeth Logan and Myke Gluck.

Evaluating Networked Information Services: Techniques, Policy and Issues, by Charles R. McClure and John Carlo Bertot.

From Print to Electronic: The Transformation of Scientific Communication, by Susan Y. Crawford, Julie M. Hurd, and Ann C. Weller.

Historical Information Science: An Emerging Unidiscipline, by Lawrence J. McCrank.

Historical Studies in Information Science, ed. by Trudi Bellardo Hahn and Michael Buckland.

The History and Heritage of Scientific and Technological Information Systems, ed. by W. Boyd Rayward and Mary Ellen Bowden.

Information and Emotion: The Emergent Affective Paradigm in Information Behavior Research and Theory, ed. by Dania Bilal and Diane Nahl.

Information Management for the Intelligent Organization: The Art of Environmental Scanning, 3rd edition, by Chun Wei Choo.

Information Representation and Retrieval in the Digital Age, by Heting Chu.

Intelligent Technologies in Library and Information Service Applications, by F. W. Lancaster and Amy Warner.
Introduction to Information Science and Technology, ed. by Charles H. Davis and Debora Shaw.
Introductory Concepts in Information Science, by Melanie J. Norton.
Knowledge Management for the Information Professional, ed. by T. Kanti Srikantaiah and Michael E. D. Koenig.
Knowledge Management in Practice: Connections and Context, ed. by T. Kanti Srikantaiah and Michael E. D. Koenig.
Knowledge Management Lessons Learned: What Works and What Doesn't, ed. by T. Kanti Srikantaiah and Michael E. D. Koenig.
Knowledge Management: The Bibliography, compiled by Paul Burden.
Proceedings of ASIS&T Annual Meetings.
Statistical Methods for the Information Professional, by Liwen Vaughan.
Theories of Information Behavior, ed. by Karen E. Fisher, Sanda Erdelez, and Lynne E. F. McKechnie.
The Web of Knowledge: A Festschrift in Honor of Eugene Garfield, ed. by Blaise Cronin and Helen Barsky Atkins.
The above publications are available from Information Today, Inc., 143 Old Marlton Pike, Medford, NJ 08055.

American Theological Library Association

Executive Director, Brenda Bailey-Hainer
300 S. Wacker Drive, Suite 2100, Chicago, IL 60606-6701
Tel. 888-665-2852, 312-454-5100, fax 312-454-5505, e-mail atla@atla.com
World Wide Web http://www.atla.com

Mission

The mission of the American Theological Library Association (ATLA) is to foster the study of theology and religion by enhancing the development of theological and religious libraries and librarianship.

Membership

(Inst.) 258; (International Inst.) 14; (Indiv.) 444; (Student) 98; (Lifetime) 87; (Affiliates) 65.

Officers

Pres. John Weaver, Abilene Christian Univ., 221 Brown Lib., ACU Box 29208, Abilene, TX 79699-9208. Tel. 325-674-2476, fax 325-674-2202, e-mail jbw11a@acu.edu; *V.P.* Andrew Keck, Duke Univ. Divinity School Lib., Box 90972, Durham, NC 27708-0972. Tel. 919-660-3549, fax 919-681-7594, e-mail andy. keck@duke.edu; *Secy.* Carrie M. Hackney, Howard Univ. School of Divinity Lib., 1400 Shepherd St. N.E., Washington, DC 20017.

Tel. 202-806-0760, fax 202-806-0711, e-mail chackney@howard.edu.

Directors

H. D. Sandy Ayer, Carisse Mickey Berryhill, Beth Bidlack, Kelly Campbell, Douglas L. Gragg, Saundra Lipton, André Paris, Eileen K. Saner, Laura C. Wood.

Publications

ATLA Indexes in MARC Format (q.).
ATLA Religion Database, 1949– (q., on EBSCO, OCLC, Ovid).
ATLASerials, 1949– (q., full-text, on EBSCO, OCLC, Ovid).
ATLA Catholic Periodical and Literature Index (q., on EBSCO).
Old Testament Abstracts (ann. on EBSCO).
New Testament Abstracts (ann. on EBSCO).
Proceedings (ann.; memb.; nonmemb. $60).
Ed. Sara Corkery.
Research in Ministry: An Index to Doctor of Ministry Project Reports (ann., online).

Archivists and Librarians in the History of the Health Sciences

President, Stephen J. Greenberg
E-mail patzere4@gmail.com
World Wide Web http://www.alhhs.org

Object

The association was established exclusively for educational purposes, to serve the professional interests of librarians, archivists, and other specialists actively engaged in the librarianship of the history of the health sciences by promoting the exchange of information and by improving the standards of service.

Membership

Memb. 170. Dues $15 (Americas), $21 (other countries).

Officers

Pres. Stephen J. Greenberg. E-mail patzere4@ gmail.com; *Pres.-Elect* Christopher Lyons. E-mail christopher.lyons@mcgill.ca; *Secy.* Crystal Smith. E-mail crys_smith@verizon. net; *Treas.* Arlene Shaner. E-mail ashaner@ nyam.org; *Membs.-at-Large* Megan Curran, John Hellebrand, Jennifer Kane Nieves, Martha Stone; *Past Pres.* Lisa A. Mix. E-mail lisa. mix@library.ucsf.edu.

Publication

Watermark (q.; memb.). *Ed.* Stephen E. Novak, Archives and Special Collections, Columbia Univ. Medical Center. E-mail sen13@ columbia.edu.

ARMA International

Executive Director, Marilyn Bier
11880 College Blvd., Suite 450, Overland Park, KS 66210
Tel. 800-422-2762, 913-341-3808, fax 913-341-3742
World Wide Web http://www.arma.org

Object

To advance the practice of records and information management as a discipline and a profession; to organize and promote programs of research, education, training, and networking within that profession; to support the enhancement of professionalism of the membership; and to promote cooperative endeavors with related professional groups.

Membership

Memb. 11,000. Annual dues $175 for international affiliation (student/retired $25). Chapter dues vary.

Pres. Galina Datskovsky, Autonomy, 21-00 Rte. 208 S., Fair Lawn, NJ 07410; *Pres.-Elect* Komal Gulich, FirstEnergy Service Co., 76 S. Main St., Akron, OH 44308; *Treas.* Fred Pulzello, 26 Holt Court, Glen Rock, NJ 07452; *Past Pres./Chair* Nicholas De Laurentis, State Farm, 3 State Farm Plaza S., L3, Bloomington, IL 61791-0001.

Directors

Beverly Bishop, Julie J. Colgan, Ilona Koti, Peter Kurilecz, William LeFevre, Samantha Lofton, Mike Marsh, Brian A. Moriki, Paula Sutton, Sean Tanner, Alice Young.

Publication

Information Management (IM) (bi-mo.).

Art Libraries Society of North America

President, Jon Evans
Executive Management, Scott Sherer
Tel. 414-768-8000 ext. 104, fax 414-768-8001, e-mail sherer@techenterprises.net

Object

The object of the Art Libraries Society of North America (ARLIS/NA) is to foster excellence in art librarianship and visual resources curatorship for the advancement of the visual arts. Established 1972.

Membership

Memb. 1,000+. Dues (Inst./Business Affiliate) $145; (Introductory) $90 (one-year limit); (Indiv.) $120; (Student) $50 (three-year limit); (Retired/Unemployed) $60. Year. Jan. 1–Dec. 31. Membership is open to all those interested in visual librarianship, whether they be professional librarians, students, library assistants, art book publishers, art book dealers, art historians, archivists, architects, slide and photograph curators, or retired associates in these fields.

Officers

Pres. Jon Evans, Hirsch Lib., Museum of Fine Arts—Houston, P.O. Box 6826, Houston, TX 77265-6826. Tel. 713-639-7393, e-mail jevans@mfah.org; *V.P./Pres.-Elect* Deborah Kempe, Frick Art Reference Lib., 10 E. 71 St., New York, NY 10021. Tel. 212-547-0658, e-mail kempe@frick.org; *Secy.* Alan Michelson, Built Environments Lib., Univ. of Washington Libs., Gould Hall, Box 355730, Seattle, WA 98195. Tel. 206-543-7091, e-mail alanmich@u. washington.edu; *Treas.* Tom Riedel, Dayton Memorial Lib., Regis Univ., 3333 Regis Blvd., D-20, Denver, CO 80221. Tel. 303-458-4261,

e-mail triedel@regis.edu; *Past Pres.* Marilyn Russell, Haskell Indian Nations Univ., 155 Indian Ave., Lawrence, KS 66046. Tel. 785-832-6661, e-mail mrussell@haskell.edu.

Address correspondence to Scott Sherer, Technical Enterprises, Inc., 7044 S. 13 St., Oak Creek, WI 53154.

Publications

ARLIS/NA Update (bi-mo.; memb.).
Art Documentation (2 a year; memb., subscription).
Handbook and List of Members (ann.; memb.).
Occasional papers (price varies).

Miscellaneous others (request current list from headquarters).

Committee Chairs

Awards. Jennifer Parker.
Cataloging Advisory. Sherman Clarke.
Communications and Publications. Jonathan Franklin.
Development. Sonja Staum.
Diversity. Meredith Kahn.
Finance. Ted Goodman.
International Relations. Katie Keller.
Membership. Jamie Lausch Vander Broek.
Nominating. Daniel Starr.
Professional Development. Stacy Brinkman.
Public Policy. Roger Lawson, Carmen Orth-Alfie.
Strategic Planning. Patricia Barnett.

Asian/Pacific American Librarians Association

Executive Director, Buenaventura "Ven" Basco
P.O. Box 1669, Goleta, CA 93116-1669
E-mail buenaventura.basco@ucf.edu
World Wide Web http://www.apalaweb.org

Object

To provide a forum for discussing problems and concerns of Asian/Pacific American librarians; to provide a forum for the exchange of ideas by Asian/Pacific American librarians and other librarians; to support and encourage library services to Asian/Pacific American communities; to recruit and support Asian/Pacific American librarians in the library/information science professions; to seek funding for scholarships in library/information science programs for Asian/Pacific Americans; and to provide a vehicle whereby Asian/Pacific American librarians can cooperate with other associations and organizations having similar or allied interests. Founded in 1980; incorporated 1981; affiliated with American Library Association 1982.

Membership

Open to all librarians and information specialists of Asian/Pacific descent working in U.S. libraries and information centers and other related organizations, and to others who support the goals and purposes of the association. Asian/Pacific Americans are defined as people residing in North America who self-identify as Asian/Pacific American.

Officers (July 2011–June 2012)

Pres. Sandy Wee, San Mateo County Lib., 1 Library Ave., Millbrae, CA 94030. Tel. 650-697-7607, e-mail wee@smcl.org *V.P./Pres.-Elect* A. Jade Alburo, UCLA. E-mail jalburo@library.ucla.edu; *Secy.* Lessa K. Pelayo-Lozada, Palos Verdes Lib. Dist. E-mail lessalozada@gmail.com; *Treas.* Shoko Tokoro, Univ. of North Carolina at Charlotte. E-mail stokoro@uncc.edu; *Past Pres.* Florante Peter Ibanez, William M. Rains Lib., Loyola Law School, Los Angeles. E-mail florante.ibanez@lls.edu.

Publication

APALA Newsletter (q.).

Committee Chairs

Constitution and Bylaws. Ben Wakashige.
Finance and Fund Raising. Eileen Bosch.
Literature Awards. Dora Ho.
Membership. Rebecca Kennedy.
Newsletter and Publications. Gary Colmenar.
Nominating. Florante Ibanez.
Program Planning. A. Jade Alburo.
Publicity. Heawon Paick.
Scholarships and Awards. Safi Safiullah, Gayatri Singh.
Web. Angela Boyd.

Association for Library and Information Science Education

Executive Director, Kathleen Combs
ALISE Headquarters, 65 E. Wacker Place, Suite 1900, Chicago, IL 60601-7246
312-795-0996, fax 312-419-8950, e-mail contact@alise.org
World Wide Web http://www.alise.org

The Association for Library and Information Science Education (ALISE) is an independent nonprofit professional association whose mission is to promote excellence in research, teaching, and service for library and information science education through leadership, collaboration, advocacy, and dissemination of research. Its enduring purpose is to promote research that informs the scholarship of teaching and learning for library and information science, enabling members to integrate research into teaching and learning. The association provides a forum in which to share ideas, discuss issues, address challenges, and shape the future of education for library and information science. Founded in 1915 as the Association of American Library Schools, it has had its present name since 1983.

Membership

700+ in four categories: Personal, Institutional, International Affiliate Institutional, and Associate Institutional. Personal membership is open to anyone with an interest in the association's objectives.

Officers (2011–2012)

Pres. Lynne Howarth, Univ. of Toronto. E-mail lynn.howarth@utoronto.ca; *V.P./Pres.-Elect* Melissa Gross, Florida State University; *Past Pres.* Lorna Peterson, Univ. at Buffalo; *Secy.-Treas.* Jean Preer, Indiana Univ., Indianapolis; *Dirs.* Susan Roman, Dominican Univ.; Anne Weeks, Univ. of Maryland; Andrew Wertheimer, Univ. of Hawaii; Louise Spiteri, Dalhousie University.

Publications

Journal of Education for Library and Information Science (JELIS) (q.). *Co-Eds.* Michelle Kazmer, Kathleen Burnett. E-mail jeliseditors@gmail.com; *ALISE News* (q.)

Association for Rural and Small Libraries

201 E. Main St., Suite 1405, Lexington, KY 40507
Tel. 859-514-9178, e-mail szach@amrms.com
World Wide Web http://www.arsl.info

Object

The Association for Rural and Small Libraries (ARSL) was established in 1978 as the Center for Study of Rural Librarianship in the Department of Library Science at Clarion University of Pennsylvania.

ARSL is a network of persons throughout the United States dedicated to the positive growth and development of libraries. ARSL believes in the value of rural and small libraries, and strives to create resources and services that address national, state, and local priorities for libraries situated in rural communities.

Its objectives are

- To organize a network of members concerned about the growth and development of useful library services in rural and small libraries

- To provide opportunities for the continuing education of members

- To provide mechanisms for members to exchange ideas and to meet on a regular basis
- To cultivate the practice of librarianship and to foster a spirit of cooperation among members of the profession, enabling them to act together for mutual goals
- To serve as a source of current information about trends, issues, and strategies
- To partner with other library and nonlibrary groups and organizations serving rural and small library communities
- To collect and disseminate information and resources that are critical to this network
- To advocate for rural and small libraries at the local, state, and national levels

Officers

Pres. Becky Heil, Iowa Lib. Services/State Lib., 1401 Fifth St., Coralville, IA 52241. Tel. 563-542-0519, e-mail becky.heil@ lib.state.ia.us; *V.P./Pres.-Elect* Andrea Berstler, Wicomico Public Lib., 122 S. Division St., Salisbury, MD 21801. Tel. 717-669-9960, e-mail andrea.berstler@gmail.com; *Past Pres.* Sonja Plummer-Morgan, Turner Memorial Lib., 39 Second St., Presque Isle, ME 04769. Tel. 207-764-2571, e-mail sonjaplummer@presqueisle.lib.me.us.

Association of Academic Health Sciences Libraries

Executive Director, Louise S. Miller
2150 N. 107 St., Suite 205, Seattle, WA 98133
206-367-8704, fax 206-367-8777, e-mail aahsl@sbims.com
World Wide Web http://www.aahsl.org

Object

The Association of Academic Health Sciences Libraries (AAHSL) comprises the libraries serving the accredited U.S. and Canadian medical schools belonging to or affiliated with the Association of American Medical Colleges. Its goals are to promote excellence in academic health science libraries and to ensure that the next generation of health practitioners is trained in information-seeking skills that enhance the quality of health care delivery, education, and research. Founded in 1977.

Membership

Memb. 150+. Regular membership is available to nonprofit educational institutions operating a school of health sciences that has full or provisional accreditation by the Association of American Medical Colleges. Full members are represented by the chief administrative officer of the member institution's health sciences library. Associate membership (and nonvoting representation) is available to organizations having an interest in the purposes and activities of the association.

Officers (2011–2012)

Pres. Gary Freiburger, Arizona Health Sciences Lib., Univ. of Arizona; *Pres.-Elect* M. J. Tooey, Health Sciences and Human Services Lib., Univ. of Maryland, Baltimore; *Secy./Treas.* Jett McCann, Dahlgren Memorial Lib., Georgetown Univ. Medical Center; *Past Pres.* Pat Thibodeau, Medical Center Lib., Duke Univ.

Directors

Karen Butter, Lib. and Center for Knowledge Management, Univ. of California, San Francisco; Sandra Franklin, Woodruff Health Sciences Center Lib., Emory Univ.; Neil Rambo, NYU Health Sciences Lib., NYU Langone Medical Center.

Association of Independent Information Professionals

8550 United Plaza Blvd., Suite 1001, Baton Rouge, LA 70809
225-408-4400, fax 225-408-4422, e-mail office@aiip.org
World Wide Web http://www.aiip.org

Object

Members of the Association of Independent Information Professionals (AIIP) are owners of firms providing such information-related services as online and manual research, document delivery, database design, library support, consulting, writing, and publishing. The objectives of the association are

- To advance the knowledge and understanding of the information profession
- To promote and maintain high professional and ethical standards among its members
- To encourage independent information professionals to assemble to discuss common issues
- To promote the interchange of information among independent information professionals and various organizations
- To keep the public informed of the profession and of the responsibilities of the information professional

Membership

Memb. 50+.

Officers (2011–2012)

Pres. Cynthia Hetherington, Hetherington Group. E-mail president@aiip.org; *Pres.-Elect* Scott Brown, Social Information Group; *Secy.* Vada Repta, Precision Research Link; *Treas.* Lark Birdsong, Birdsong Information Services; *Past Pres.* Margaret King, InfoRich Group.

Publications

AIIP Connections (q.).
Membership Directory (ann.).
Professional papers series.

Association of Jewish Libraries

P.O. Box 1118, Teaneck, NJ 07666
World Wide Web http://www.jewishlibraries.org

Object

The Association of Jewish Libraries (AJL) promotes Jewish literacy through enhancement of libraries and library resources and through leadership for the profession and practitioners of Judaica librarianship. The association fosters access to information, learning, teaching, and research relating to Jews, Judaism, the Jewish experience, and Israel.

AJL membership is open to individuals and libraries, library workers, and library support-ers. There are two divisions within AJL: RAS (Research Libraries, Archives, and Special Collections) and SSC (Schools, Synagogues, and Centers). The diverse membership includes libraries in synagogues, JCCs, day schools, yeshivot, universities, Holocaust museums, and the Library of Congress. Membership is drawn from North America and beyond, including from China, the Czech Republic, the Netherlands, Israel, Italy, South Africa, Switzerland, and the United Kingdom.

Goals

- Maintain high professional standards for Judaica librarians and recruit qualified individuals into the profession
- Facilitate communication and exchange of information on a global scale
- Encourage quality publication in the field in all formats and media
- Stimulate publication of high-quality children's literature
- Facilitate and encourage establishment of Judaica library collections
- Enhance information access for all through application of advanced technologies
- Publicize the organization and its activities in all relevant venues
- Stimulate awareness of Judaica library services among the public at large
- Promote recognition of Judaica librarianship within the wider library profession
- Encourage recognition of Judaica library services by other organizations and related professions
- Ensure continuity of the association through sound management, financial security, effective governance, and a dedicated and active membership

AJL conducts an annual convention in the United States or Canada in late June.

Membership

Memb. 1,000+. Dues $70; (First Year Student) free; (Second and Third Year Student/Retired) $35; (Large institutions) $100; (Small Institutions) $75; (Trial Membership—one month) $10. Year. July 1–June 30.

Officers (July 2010–June 2012)

Pres. James P. Rosenbloom. E-mail rosenbloom @brandeis.edu; *V.P./Pres.-Elect* Heidi Estrin. E-mail heidi@cbiboca.org; *V.P. Memb.* Laurie Haas; *V.P. Publications* Deborah Stern; *Recording Secy.* Elana Gensler; *Corresponding Secy.* Rachel Glasser; *Treas.* Sheryl Stahl; *Past Pres.* Susan Dubin.

Address correspondence to the association.

Publications

AJL News & Reviews (q., digital); *Judaica Librarianship* (annual).

Division Presidents

Research Libraries, Archives, and Special Libraries. Rachel Leket-Mor.

Synagogue, School, and Center Libraries. Joyce Levine.

Association of Research Libraries

Executive Director, Charles B. Lowry
21 Dupont Circle N.W., Suite 800, Washington, DC 20036
202-296-2296, fax 202-872-0884, e-mail arlhq@arl.org
World Wide Web http://www.arl.org

Object

The Association of Research Libraries (ARL) is a nonprofit organization of 126 research libraries in North America. Its mission is to influence the changing environment of scholarly communication and the public policies that affect research libraries and the diverse communities they serve. ARL pursues this mission by advancing the goals of its member research libraries, providing leadership in public and information policy to the scholarly and higher education communities, fostering the exchange of ideas and expertise, facilitating the emergence of new roles for research libraries, and shaping a future environment that leverages its interests with those of allied organizations.

Membership

Memb. 126. Membership is institutional. Dues: $24,954 for 2012.

Officers

Pres. Winston Tabb, Johns Hopkins Univ.; *V.P./Pres.-Elect* Wendy Pradt Lougee, Univ. of Minnesota; *Past Pres.* Carol A. Mandel, New York Univ.

Board of Directors

Deborah Carver, Univ. of Oregon; Carol Pitts Diedrichs, Ohio State Univ.; Joan Giesecke, Univ. of Nebraska–Lincoln; Ernie Ingels, Univ. of Alberta; Deborah Jakubs, Duke Univ.; Anne R. Kenney, Cornell Univ.; Wendy Pradt Lougee, Univ. of Minnesota; Charles B. Lowry (ex officio), ARL; Carol A. Mandel, New York Univ.; Carton Rogers (ex officio), Univ. of Pennsylvania; Judith C. Russell, Univ. of Florida; Jay Schafer, Univ. of Massachusetts Amherst; Winston Tabb, Johns Hopkins Univ.; James F. Williams II (ex officio), Univ. of Colorado at Boulder; Ann J. Wolpert (ex officio), Massachusetts Institute of Technology.

Publications

Research Library Issues: A Bimonthly Report from ARL, CNI, and SPARC (bi-mo.).
ARL Academic Health Sciences Library Statistics (ann.).
ARL Academic Law Library Statistics (ann.).
ARL Annual Salary Survey (ann.).
ARL Statistics (ann.).
SPEC Kit series (6 a year).

Committee and Working Group Chairs

Diversity and Leadership. Nancy Baker, Univ. of Iowa.
E-Science Working Group. James Mullins, Purdue Univ.
Fair Use and Related Exemptions Working Group. Betsy Wilson, Univ. of Washington.
Membership. Paula Kaufman, Univ. of Illinois at Urbana-Champaign.
Influencing Public Policies. James F. Williams II, Univ. of Colorado at Boulder.
Regional Federal Depository Libraries Working Group. Judith C. Russell, Univ. of Florida.
Transforming Research Libraries. Carton Rogers, Univ. of Pennsylvania.
Reshaping Scholarly Communication. Ann J. Wolpert, Massachusetts Institute of Technology.
Transforming Special Collections in the Digital Age Working Group, Anne Kenney, Cornell Univ.
Statistics and Assessment. William Potter, Univ. of Georgia.

ARL Membership

Non-university Libraries

Boston Public Lib., Canada Inst. for Scientific and Technical Info., Center for Research Libs., Lib. and Archives Canada, Lib. of Congress, National Agricultural Lib., National Archives, National Lib. of Medicine, New York Public Lib., New York State Lib., Smithsonian Institution Libs.

University Libraries

Alabama; Albany (SUNY); Alberta; Arizona; Arizona State; Auburn; Boston College; Boston Univ.; Brigham Young; British Columbia; Brown; Buffalo (SUNY); Calgary; California, Berkeley; California, Davis; California, Irvine; California, Los Angeles; California, Riverside; California, San Diego; California, Santa Barbara; Case Western Reserve; Chicago; Cincinnati; Colorado; Colorado State; Columbia; Connecticut; Cornell; Dartmouth; Delaware; Duke; Emory; Florida; Florida State; George Washington; Georgetown; Georgia; Georgia Inst. of Technology; Guelph; Harvard; Hawaii; Houston; Howard; Illinois, Chicago; Illinois, Urbana-Champaign; Indiana; Iowa; Iowa State; Johns Hopkins; Kansas; Kent State; Kentucky; Laval; Louisiana State; Louisville; McGill; McMaster; Manitoba; Maryland; Massachusetts; Massachusetts Inst. of Technology; Miami (Florida); Michigan; Michigan State; Minnesota; Missouri; Montreal; Nebraska, Lincoln; New Mexico; New York; North Carolina; North Carolina State; Northwestern; Notre Dame; Ohio; Ohio State; Oklahoma; Oklahoma State; Oregon; Ottawa; Pennsylvania; Pennsylvania State; Pittsburgh; Princeton; Purdue; Queen's (Kingston, Ontario); Rice; Rochester; Rutgers; Saskatchewan; South Carolina; Southern California; Southern Illinois; Stony Brook (SUNY); Syracuse; Temple; Tennessee; Texas; Texas A&M; Texas Tech; Toronto; Tulane; Utah; Vanderbilt; Virginia; Virginia Tech; Washington; Washington (Saint Louis): Washington State; Waterloo; Wayne State; Western Ontario; Wisconsin; Yale; York.

Association of Vision Science Librarians

Chair, 2010–2012, Gale A. Oren, Kellogg Eye Center, Univ. of Michigan, 1000 Wall St., Ann Arbor, MI 48105
Tel. 734-763-9468, fax 734-936-9050, e-mail goren@umich.edu
World Wide Web http://www.avsl.org

Object

To foster collective and individual acquisition and dissemination of vision science information, to improve services for all persons seeking such information, and to develop standards for libraries to which members are attached. Founded in 1968.

Membership

Memb. (U.S.) 62; (International) 60.

Publications

Core List of Audio-Visual Related Serials.
Guidelines for Vision Science Libraries.
Opening Day Book, Journal and AV Collection—Visual Science.
Publication Considerations in the Age of Electronic Opportunities.
Standards for Vision Science Libraries.
Union List of Vision-Related Serials (irreg.).

Meetings

Annual meeting held in the fall, mid-year mini-meeting with the Medical Library Association.

Beta Phi Mu
(International Library and Information Studies Honor Society)

Executive Director, Christie Koontz
College of Communication and Information
Florida State University, Tallahassee, FL 32306-2100
850-644-3907, fax 850-644-9763, e-mail ckoontz@cci.fsu.edu
World Wide Web http://www.beta-phi-mu.org

Object

To recognize distinguished achievement in and scholarly contributions to librarianship, information studies, or library education, and to sponsor and support appropriate professional and scholarly projects relating to these fields. Founded at the University of Illinois in 1948.

Membership

Memb. 36,000. Open to graduates of library school programs accredited by the American Library Association who fulfill the following requirements: complete the course requirements leading to a fifth year or other advanced degree in librarianship with a scholastic average of 3.75 where A equals 4 points (this provision shall also apply to planned programs of advanced study beyond the fifth year that do not culminate in a degree but that require full-time study for one or more academic years) and rank in the top 25 percent of their class; and receive a letter of recommendation from the faculty of their respective library schools attesting to their professional promise.

Officers

Pres. Marie L. Radford, Rutgers Univ., 4 Huntington St., New Brunswick, NJ 08901; *V.P./Pres.-Elect* Beth Paskoff, Louisiana State Univ., Baton Rouge, LA 70803; *Treas.* Bob Branciforte, College of Communication and Info., Florida State Univ., Tallahassee, FL 32306-2100; *Exec. Dir.* Christie Koontz, College of Communication and Info., Florida State Univ., Tallahassee, FL 32306-2100. Tel. 850-644-3907, fax 850-644-9763, e-mail betaphimuinfo@admin.fsu.edu.

Directors

Eileen G. Abels, Susan W. Alman, John M. Budd, Elizabeth Figa, Carrie Hurst, Charles McElroy, Amanda Ros, Shannon Tennant, Elaine Yontz.

Publications

Beta Phi Mu Monograph Series. Book-length scholarly works based on original research in subjects of interest to library and information professionals. Available from ABC-CLIO, 130 Cremona Drive, Santa Barbara, CA 93117. *Ed.* Lorraine J. Haricombe; *Assoc. Ed.* Keith Russell.
The Pipeline (electronic only). *Ed.* John Paul Walters.

Chapters

Alpha. Univ. of Illinois, Grad. School of Lib. and Info. Science; *Gamma.* Florida State Univ., College of Communication and Info.; *Epsilon.* Univ. of North Carolina, School of Info. and Lib. Science; *Theta.* Pratt Inst., Grad. School of Lib. and Info. Science; *Iota.* Catholic Univ. of America, School of Lib. and Info. Science; Univ. of Maryland, College of Info. Studies; *Lambda.* Univ. of Oklahoma, School of Lib. and Info. Studies; *Mu.* Univ. of Michigan, School of Info; *Xi.* Univ. of Hawaii, Grad. School of Lib. and Info. Studies; *Omicron.* Rutgers Univ., Grad. School of Communication, Info. and Lib. Studies; *Pi.* Univ. of Pittsburgh, School of Info. Sciences; *Rho.* Kent State Univ., School of Lib. and Info. Science; *Sigma.* Drexel Univ., College of Info. Science and Technology; *Upsilon.* Univ. of Kentucky, School of Lib. and Info. Science; *Phi.* Univ. of Denver, Grad. School of Lib. and Info. Science; *Chi.* Indiana Univ., School of Lib. and Info. Science; *Psi.* Univ. of Missouri at Columbia, School of Lib. and Info. Science; *Omega.* San Jose State Univ., School of Lib. and Info. Science; *Beta Alpha.* Queens College, City College of New York, Grad. School of Lib. and Info. Studies; *Beta Beta.* Simmons College, Grad. School of Lib. and Info. Science; *Beta Delta.* State Univ. of New York at Buffalo, Dept. of Lib. and Info. Studies; *Beta Epsilon.* Emporia State Univ., School of Lib. and Info. Management; *Beta Zeta.* Louisiana State Univ., Grad. School of Lib. and Info. Science; *Beta Eta.* Univ. of Texas at Austin, Grad. School of Lib. and Info. Science; *Beta Iota.* Univ. of Rhode Island, Grad. School of Lib. and Info. Studies; *Beta Kappa.* Univ. of Alabama, Grad. School of Lib. and Info. Studies; *Beta Lambda.* Texas Woman's Univ., School of Lib. and Info. Sciences; *Beta Mu.* Long Island Univ., Palmer Grad. School of Lib. and Info. Science; *Beta Nu.* Saint John's Univ., Div. of Lib. and Info. Science; *Beta Xi.* North Carolina Central Univ., School of Lib. and Info. Sciences; *Beta Omicron.* Univ. of Tennessee at Knoxville, Grad. School of Info. Sciences; *Beta Pi.* Univ. of Arizona, Grad. School of Info. Resources and Lib. Science; *Beta Rho.* Univ. of Wisconsin at Milwaukee, School of Info.; *Beta Sigma.* Clarion Univ. of Pennsylvania, Dept. of Lib. Science; *Beta Tau.* Wayne State Univ., Lib. and Info. Science Program; *Beta Phi.* Univ. of South Florida, Grad. School of Lib. and Info. Science; *Beta Psi.* Univ. of Southern Mississippi, School of Lib. and Info. Science; *Beta Omega.* Univ. of South Carolina, College of Lib. and Info. Science; *Beta Beta Gamma.* Dominican Univ., Grad. School of Lib. and Info. Science; *Beta Beta Epsilon.* Univ. of Wisconsin at Madison, School of Lib. and Info. Studies; *Beta Beta Zeta.* Univ. of North Carolina at Greensboro, Dept. of Lib. and Info. Studies; *Beta Beta Theta.* Univ. of Iowa, School of Lib. and Info. Science; *Beta Beta Iota.* State Univ. of New York, Univ. at Albany, School of Info. Science and Policy; *Beta Beta Kappa.* Univ. of Puerto Rico, Grad. School of Info. Sciences and Technologies; *Pi Lambda Sigma.* Syracuse Univ., School of Info. Studies; *Beta Beta Mu.* Valdosta State Univ., School of Lib. and Info. Science; *Beta Beta Nu.* Univ. of North Texas, College of Info.

Bibliographical Society of America

Executive Secretary, Michèle E. Randall
P.O. Box 1537, Lenox Hill Sta., New York, NY 10021
212-452-2710 (tel./fax), e-mail bsa@bibsocamer.org
World Wide Web http://www.bibsocamer.org

Object

To promote bibliographical research and to issue bibliographical publications. Organized 1904.

Membership

Memb. Dues (Indiv.) $65; (Sustaining) $250; (Contributing) $100; (Student) $20; (Inst.) $100; (Lifetime) $1,250. Year. Jan.–Dec.

Officers

Pres. Claudia Funke. E-mail claudiafunke@mac.com; *V.P.* John Crichton. E-mail jcrichton@brickrow.com; *Secy.* Caroline Duroselle-Melish. E-mail cmelish@fas.harvard.edu; *Treas.* G. Scott Clemons. E-mail scott.clemons@bbh.com; *Past Pres.* John Neal Hoover. E-mail jhoover@umsl.edu.

Council

(2012) David L. Gants, Barbara Shailor, Daniel

Slive, David Supino; (2013) Gerald Cloud, Eugene S. Flamm, David Alan Richards, Carolyn L. Smith; (2014) Douglas F. Bauer, John Crichton, Joan Friedman, Gregory A. Pass.

Publication

Papers of the Bibliographical Society of America (q.; memb.). *Ed.* Gregory A. Pass; *Managing Ed.* Travis Gordon. E-mail travisgordon@mindspring.com.

Committee Chairs

Audit. R. Dyke Benjamin.
Fellowship. David L. Gants.
Finance. David J. Supino.
Program. Marcia Reed.
Publications. Gregory A. Pass.

Bibliographical Society of Canada
(La Société Bibliographique du Canada)

President, Janet Friskney
P.O. Box 575, Postal Station P, Toronto, ON M5S 2T1
World Wide Web http://www.bsc-sbc.ca/index.html

Object

The Bibliographical Society of Canada is a bilingual (English/French) organization that has as its goal the scholarly study of the history, description, and transmission of texts in all media and formats, with a primary emphasis on Canada, and the fulfillment of this goal through the following objectives:

- To promote the study and practice of bibliography: enumerative, historical, descriptive, analytical, and textual
- To further the study, research, and publication of book history and print culture
- To publish bibliographies and studies of book history and print culture
- To encourage the publication of bibliographies, critical editions, and studies of book history and print culture
- To promote the appropriate preservation and conservation of manuscript, archival, and published materials in various formats
- To encourage the utilization and analysis of relevant manuscript and archival sources as a foundation of bibliographical scholarship and book history
- To promote the interdisciplinary nature of bibliography, and to foster relationships with other relevant organizations nationally and internationally
- To conduct the society without purpose of financial gain for its members, and to ensure that any profits or other accretions to the society shall be used in promoting its goal and objectives

Membership

The society welcomes as members all those who share its aims and wish to support and participate in bibliographical research and publication.

Officers

Pres. Janet Friskney. E-mail president@bsc-sbc.ca; *Senior V.P.* Linda Quirk; *2nd V.P.* Don McLeod; *Secy.* Greta Golick. E-mail secretary@bsc-sbc.ca; *Treas.* Tom Vincent.

Publications

Papers of the Bibliographical Society of Canada/Cahiers de la Société Bibliographique du Canada (s. ann).
The Bulletin/Le Bulletin (s. ann).

For a full list of the society's publications, see http://www.library.utoronto.ca/bsc/publicationseng.html.

Committee Chairs

Awards. Julie Frédette.
Publications. Geoffrey Little.
Scholarships. Jillian Tomm.

Black Caucus of the American Library Association

President, Jos N. Holman, Tippecanoe County Public Library, 627 South St., Lafayette, IN 47901. Tel. 765-429-0118, fax 765-429-0150, e-mail jholman@tcpl.lib.in.us
World Wide Web http://www.bcala.org

Mission

The Black Caucus of the American Library Association (BCALA) serves as an advocate for the development, promotion, and improvement of library services and resources for the nation's African American community and provides leadership for the recruitment and professional development of African American librarians. Founded in 1970.

Membership

Membership is open to any person, institution, or business interested in promoting the development of library and information services for African Americans and other people of African descent and willing to maintain good financial standing with the organization. The membership is currently composed of librarians and other information professionals, library support staff, libraries, publishers, authors, vendors, and other library-related organizations in the United States and abroad. Dues (Corporate) $200; (Institutional) $60; (Regular) $45; (Student) $10.

Officers

Pres. Jos N. Holman. Tel. 765-429-0118, e-mail jholman@ tcpl.lib.in.us; *V.P./Pres.-Elect* Jerome Offord, Jr.; *Secy.* Jannie R. Cobb; *Treas.* Stanton F. Biddle; *Past Pres.* Karolyn S. Thompson.

Executive Board

Jason K. Alston, Gladys Smiley Bell, Vivian Bordeaux, Diane Covington, Anna Marie Ford, D. L. Grant, Emily Guss, Dorothy Guthrie, Sylvia Sprinkle Hamlin, Allene Hayes, Andrew Jackson (Sekou Molefi Baako), Leroy Robinson, Eboni Stokes, Kelvin Watson, Roberta Webb.

Publication

BCALA Newsletter (bi-mo; memb.). *Contact* Makiba J. Foster. E-mail makibaj27@yahoo.com.

Committee Chairs

Affiliated Chapters. Sylvia Sprinkle-Hamlin, Lainey Westbrooks.
Affirmative Action. Howard F. McGinn, Darren Sweeper.
ALA Relations. Allene Hayes.
Awards. Richard Bradberry, ayo dayo.
Budget/Audit. Bobby Player.
Constitution and Bylaws. D. L. Grant, Gerald Holmes.
Fund Raising. Makiba J. Foster, Kelvin Watson.
History. Sibyl E. Moses.
International Relations. Vivian Bordeaux, Eboni M. Stokes.
E. J. Josey Scholarship. Billy Beal, Joyce E. Jelks.

Literary Awards. Virginia Toliver, Joel White.
Membership. Rudolph Clay, Allison M. Sutton.
Newsletter. Makiba J. Foster.
Nominations/Elections. Wanda K. Brown.
Programs. Jos N. Holman.
Public Relations. Barbara E. Martin.

Recruitment and Professional Development. Andrew P. Jackson (Sekou Molefi Baako).
Services to Children of Families of African Descent. Karen Lemmons.
Smiley Fund. Gladys Smiley Bell.
Technology Advisory. H. Jamane Yeager.
Dr. John C. Tyson Award. Alys Jordan, Esmeralda M. Kale.

Canadian Association for Information Science
(L'Association Canadienne des Sciences de l'Information)

President, Nadia Caidi
Faculty of Information, University of Toronto, 45 Willcocks St., No. 335, Toronto, ON M5S 1C7
World Wide Web http://www.cais-acsi.ca

Object

To promote the advancement of information science in Canada and encourage and facilitate the exchange of information relating to the use, access, retrieval, organization, management, and dissemination of information.

Membership

Institutions and individuals interested in information science and involved in the gathering, organization, and dissemination of information (such as information scientists, archivists, librarians, computer scientists, documentalists, economists, educators, journalists, and psychologists) and who support CAIS's objectives can become association members. Dues (Inst.) $109; (Personal) $75; (Student) $49.

Directors

Pres. Siobhan Stevenson, Univ. of Toronto. E-mail siobhan.stevenson@utoronto.ca; *V.P.* Heather O'Brien, Univ. of British Columbia. E-mail h.obrien@ubc.ca; *Secy.* Jen Pecoskie, Wayne State Univ.; *Treas.* Anatoliy Gruzd, Dalhousie Univ.; *Dir., Communications* Cameron Hoffman, Univ. of Western Ontario; *Dir., Membership* Heather Hill, Univ. of Western Ontario; *Past Pres.* Nadia Caidi, Univ. of Toronto.

Publication

Canadian Journal of Information and Library Science. Ed. Clément Arsenault, Univ. de Montréal.

Canadian Association of Research Libraries
(Association des Bibliothèques de Recherche du Canada)

Brent Roe, Executive Director
600-350 Albert St., Ottawa, ON K1R 1B1
Tel. 613-482-9344, e-mail brent.roe@carl-abrc.ca
World Wide Web http://www.carl-abrc.ca

Membership

The Canadian Association of Research Libraries (CARL), established in 1976, is the leadership organization for the Canadian research library community. The association's members are the 29 major academic research libraries across Canada together with Library and Archives Canada, the Canada Institute for Scientific and Technical Information (CISTI), and the Library of Parliament. Membership is institutional, open primarily to libraries of Canadian universities that have doctoral graduates in both the arts and the sciences. CARL is an associate member of the Association of Universities and Colleges of Canada (AUCC) and is incorporated as a not-for-profit organization under the Canada Corporations Act.

CARL strives to enhance the capacity of Canada's research libraries to partner in research and higher education, seeking effective and sustainable scholarly communication and public policy encouraging research and broad access to scholarly information. CARL's strategic directions for 2010–2012 focus on the continuing transformation of scholarly communication, advocacy for a favorable federal public policy environment, and the strengthening and promotion of Canada's research libraries.

Officers

Pres. (2011–2013) Thomas Hickerson, MacKimmie Lib. Tower, Univ. of Calgary, 2500 University Drive N.W., Calgary, AB T2N 1N4.

E-mail tom.hickerson@ucalgary.ca; *V.P./Pres.-Elect (2011–2013)* Gerald Beasley, Concordia Univ., Montréal; *Secy.* Richard Dumont, Univ. de Montréal; *Treas.* John Teskey, Univ. of New Brunswick; *Dirs. (2010–2012)* Karen Adams, Univ. of Manitoba Libs., Winnipeg, MB R3T 2N2; Mark Haslett, Univ. of Waterloo Lib., 200 University Ave. West, Waterloo, ON N2L 3G1; *Past Pres.* Ernie Ingles, 5-07 Cameron Lib., Univ. of Alberta, Edmonton, AB T6G 2J8.

Member Institutions

Univ. of Alberta, Univ. of British Columbia, Brock Univ., Univ. of Calgary, Carleton Univ., CISTI (Canada Institute for Scientific and Technical Information), Concordia Univ., Dalhousie Univ., Univ. of Guelph, Université Laval, Univ. of Manitoba, Lib. and Archives Canada, Lib. of Parliament, McGill Univ., McMaster Univ., Memorial Univ. of Newfoundland, Université de Montréal, Univ. of New Brunswick, Univ. of Ottawa, Université du Québec à Montréal, Queen's Univ., Univ. of Regina, Ryerson Univ., Univ. of Saskatchewan, Université de Sherbrooke, Simon Fraser Univ., Univ. of Toronto, Univ. of Victoria, Univ. of Waterloo, Univ. of Western Ontario, Univ. of Windsor, York Univ.

Publications

For a full list of publications, see http://www.carl-abrc.ca/publications/publications-e.html.

Canadian Library Association
(Association Canadienne des Bibliothèques)

Executive Director, Kelly Moore
1150 Morrison Drive, Suite 400, Ottawa, ON K2H 8S9
613-232-9625 ext. 306, fax 613-563-9895, e-mail kmoore@cla.ca
World Wide Web http://www.cla.ca

Object

The Canadian Library Association (CLA) is the national public voice for Canada's libraries. CLA champions library values and the value of libraries, influences public policy impacting libraries, inspires and supports learning, and collaborates to strengthen the library community. The association represents Canadian librarianship to the federal government and media, carries on international liaison with other library associations and cultural agencies, offers professional development programs, and supports such core library values as intellectual freedom and access to information, particularly for disadvantaged populations. Founded in 1946, CLA is a not-for-profit voluntary organization governed by an elected executive council.

Membership

Memb. (Indiv.) 3,750; (Inst.) 450. Open to individuals, institutions, library boards, and groups interested in librarianship and in library and information services.

Officers

Pres. Karen Adams, Univ. of Manitoba Libraries; *V.P./Pres.-Elect* Pilar Martinez, Edmonton Public Lib.; *Treas.* Mary-Jo Romaniuk, Univ. of Alberta.

Publications

Feliciter: Linking Canada's Information Professionals (6 a year; magazine/journal).
CLA Digest (bi-weekly; electronic newsletter).

Catholic Library Association

Acting Executive Director, Malachy R. McCarthy
205 W. Monroe St., Suite 314, Chicago, IL 60606
312-739-1776, fax 312-739-1778, e-mail cla@cathla.org
World Wide Web http://www.cathla.org

Object

The promotion and encouragement of Catholic literature and library work through cooperation, publications, education, and information. Founded in 1921.

Membership

Memb. 1,000. Dues $55–$500. Year. July–June.

Officers (2011–2013)

Pres. Malachy R. McCarthy, Claretian Missionaries Archives, 205 W. Monroe St., Chicago, IL 60606; *V.P./Pres.-Elect* Sara B. Baron, Regent Univ. Lib., 1000 Regent University Drive, Virginia Beach, VA 23464; *Past Pres.* Nancy K. Schmidtmann, 174 Theodore Drive, Coram, NY 11727.

Address correspondence to the executive director.

Executive Board

Officers; Jean Elvekrog, 401 Doral Court, Waunakee, WI 53597; Susan B. Finney, St. Mary's Dominican H.S., 7701 Walmsley Ave., New Orleans, LA 70125; Cait C. Kokolus, St. Charles Borromeo Seminary, 100 E. Wynnewood Rd., Wynnewood, PA 19096; Frances O'Dell, OSF, Barry Univ. Lib., 11300 N.E. 2 Ave., Miami Shores, FL 33161.

Publications

Catholic Library World (q.; memb.; nonmemb. $125). *General Ed.* Sigrid Kelsey.

Chief Officers of State Library Agencies

Association Director, Laura Singler-Adams
201 E. Main St., Suite 1405, Lexington, KY 40507
859-514-9151, fax 859-514-9166, e-mail lsingler-adams@amrms.com
World Wide Web http://www.cosla.org

Object

Chief Officers of State Library Agencies (COSLA) is an independent organization of the chief officers of state and territorial agencies designated as the state library administrative agency and responsible for statewide library development. Its purpose is to identify and address issues of common concern and national interest; to further state library agency relationships with federal government and national organizations; and to initiate cooperative action for the improvement of library services to the people of the United States.

COSLA's membership consists solely of these top library officers, variously designated as state librarian, director, commissioner, or executive secretary. The organization provides a continuing mechanism for dealing with the problems and challenges faced by these officers. Its work is carried on through its members, a board of directors, and committees.

Officers (2010–2012)

Pres. Lamar Veatch, State Libn., Georgia Public Lib. Service, 1800 Century Place, Suite 150, Atlanta, GA 30345-4304. Tel. 404-235-7200, e-mail lveatch@georgialibraries.org; *V.P./Pres.-Elect* Ann Joslin, State Libn., Idaho Commission for Libs., 325 W. State St., Boise, ID 83702. Tel. 208-334-2150, e-mail ann.joslin@libraries.idaho.gov; *Secy.* Margaret Conroy, State Libn., Missouri State Lib., P.O. Box 387, Jefferson City, MO 65102. Tel. 573-526-4783, e-mail margaret.conroy@sos.mo.gov; *Treas.* David Goble, Dir. and State Libn., South Carolina State Lib., P.O. Box 11469, Columbia, SC 29211. Tel. 803-734-8656, e-mail dgoble@statelibrary.sc.gov; *Past Pres.* Susan McVey, State Libn., Oklahoma Dept. of Libs., 200 N.E. 18 St., Oklahoma City, OK 73105-3298. Tel. 405-521-2502, e-mail smcvey@oltn.odl.state.ok.us; *Dirs.* Jo Budler, State Libn., State Lib. of Kansas, Capitol Bldg., Room 343-N, 300 S.W. 10 Ave., Topeka, KS 66612. Tel. 785-296-5466, e-mail jobudler@kslib.info; Michael York, State Libn., New Hampshire State Lib., 20 Park St., Concord, NH 03301. Tel. 603-271-2397, e-mail michael.york@dcr.nh.gov.

Chinese American Librarians Association

Executive Director, Haipeng Li
E-mail haipeng4cala@gmail.com
World Wide Web http://www.cala-web.org

Object

To enhance communications among Chinese American librarians as well as between Chinese American librarians and other librarians; to serve as a forum for discussion of mutual problems and professional concerns among Chinese American librarians; to promote Sino-American librarianship and library services; and to provide a vehicle whereby Chinese American librarians can cooperate with other associations and organizations having similar or allied interests.

Membership

Memb. 1,400+. Open to anyone who is interested in the association's goals and activities. Dues (Regular) $30; (International/Student/Nonsalaried) $15; (Inst.) $100; (Affiliated) $100; (Life) $300.

Officers

Pres. Min Chou. E-mail minchou.njcu@gmail.com; *V.P./Pres.-Elect* Esther Lee. E-mail eyw888lee@gmail.com; *Incoming V.P./Pres.-Elect* Lisa Zhao. E-mail zhls50@yahoo.com; *Treas.* Songqian Lu. E-mail songqian4cala@gmail.com; *Past Pres.* Zhijia Shen. E-mail zhijia@u.washington.edu; *Exec. Dir. (2010–2013)* Haipeng Li. E-mail haipeng4cala@gmail.com.

Publications

Journal of Library and Information Science (*JLIS*) (2 a year). *Editorial Board Chair (2011-2014)* Nancy Hershoff, Florida International Univ. Libs. E-mail sunn@fiu.edu.
Membership Directory (memb.).
Newsletter (2 a year; memb.; online). *Eds.* Priscilla Yu. E-mail pcyu@illinois.edu; Sai Deng. E-mail sai.deng@wichita.edu.
Occasional Paper Series (OPS) (online). *Ed. (2009–2012)* Xue-Ming Bao. E-mail baoxuemi@shu.edu.

Committee Chairs

Alire Initiative Task Force. Nancy Hershoff, Dora Ho.
Annual Conference, Program Planning (2011–2012). Esther Lee.
Awards. Maria Fung, Liana Zhou.
Best Book Award. Min Tong, Chengzhi Wang.
Constitution and Bylaws. Kuei Chiu, Manuel Urrizola.
Elections. Haipeng Li.
Finance. Clement Lau.
International Relations. Michael Bailou Huang.
Membership. Weiling Liu, Lian Ruan.
Mentorship Program. Ying Zhong, Hong Miao.
Nominating. Zhijia Shen.
Public Relations/Fund Raising. Yi Liang, Jia Mi.
Publications. Jia Mi, Dajin Sun.
Sally C. Tseng's Professional Development Grant Committee. Ying Xu.
Scholarship Committee. Vincci Kwong, Jian Anna Xiong.

Church and Synagogue Library Association

10157 SW Barbur Blvd., No.102C, Portland, OR 97219
503-244-6919, 800-542-2752, fax 503-977-3734, e-mail CSLA@worldaccessnet.com
World Wide Web http://www.cslainfo.org

Object

The Church and Synagogue Library Association (CSLA) provides educational guidance in the establishment and maintenance of congregational libraries.

Its purpose is to act as a unifying core for congregational libraries; to provide the opportunity for a mutual sharing of practices and problems; to inspire and encourage a sense of purpose and mission among congregational librarians; to study and guide the development of congregational librarianship toward recognition as a formal branch of the library profession. Founded in 1967.

Membership

Memb. 1,300. Dues (Inst.) $200; (Affiliated) $100; (Church or Synagogue) $70 ($75 foreign); (Indiv.) $50 ($55 foreign).

Officers (July 2011–July 2012)

Pres. Evelyn Pockrass; *1st V.P./Pres.-Elect* To be announced; *2nd V.P.* David Reid; *Treas.* Dick Burgduff; *Past Pres.* Marjorie Smink; *Ed., Congregational Libraries Today* Jeri Zulli; *Admin.* Judith Janzen.

Executive Board

Officers; committee chairs.

Publications

Bibliographies (4; price varies).
Congregational Libraries Today (q.; memb.; nonmemb. $50; Canada $60).
CSLA Guides (price varies).

Committee Chairs

Awards. Mary Lou Henneman.
Conference. Marianne Stowers.
Finance. Pat Shufeldt.
Nominations and Elections. Marjorie Smink.
Publications. Dotty Lewis.

Coalition for Networked Information

Executive Director, Clifford A. Lynch
21 Dupont Circle, Suite 800, Washington, DC 20036
202-296-5098, fax 202-872-0884, e-mail http://www.cni.org/contact
World Wide Web http://www.cni.org

Mission

The Coalition for Networked Information (CNI) is an organization to advance the transformative promise of networked information technology for the advancement of scholarly communication and the enrichment of intellectual productivity.

Membership

Memb. 210. Membership is institutional. Dues $6,900. Year. July–June.

Steering Committee

Daniel Cohen, George Mason Univ.; Jeffrey Horrell, Dartmouth College; Charles B. Lowry, Assn. of Research Libs.; Clifford A. Lynch, CNI; Kathryn Joan Monday, Univ. of Richmond; Diana G. Oblinger, EDUCAUSE; Patti Orr, Baylor Univ.; Carrie E. Regenstein, Carnegie Mellon Univ.; Sherrie Schmidt, Arizona State Univ.; Tyler O. Walters, Virginia Polytechnic Institute and State Univ.; Donald J. Waters, Andrew W. Mellon Foundation.

Publication

CNI-Announce (subscribe by e-mail to cni-announce-subscribe@cni.org).

Council on Library and Information Resources

1752 N St. N.W., Suite 800, Washington, DC 20036
202-939-4750, fax 202-939-4765
World Wide Web http://www.clir.org

Object

In 1997 the Council on Library Resources (CLR) and the Commission on Preservation and Access (CPA) merged and became the Council on Library and Information Resources (CLIR). CLIR is an independent, nonprofit organization that forges strategies to enhance research, teaching, and learning environments in collaboration with libraries, cultural institutions, and communities of higher learning.

CLIR promotes forward-looking collaborative solutions that transcend disciplinary, institutional, professional, and geographic boundaries in support of the public good. CLIR identifies and defines the key emerging issues relating to the welfare of libraries and the constituencies they serve, convenes the leaders who can influence change, and promotes collaboration among the institutions and organizations that can achieve change. The council's interests embrace the entire range of information resources and services from traditional library and archival materials to emerging digital formats. It assumes a particular interest in helping institutions cope with the accelerating pace of change associated with the transition into the digital environment.

While maintaining appropriate collaboration and liaison with other institutions and organizations, CLIR operates independently of any particular institutional or vested interests. Through the composition of its board, it brings the broadest possible perspective to bear upon defining and establishing the priority of the issues with which it is concerned.

Board

CLIR's Board of Directors currently has 15 members.

Officers

Chair Stephen Nichols; *Pres.* Charles Henry. E-mail chenry@clir.org; *V. Chair* Wendy Lou-gee; *Secy.* Stephen Rhind-Tutt; *Treas.* Joseph King.

Address correspondence to headquarters.

Publications

Annual Report.
CLIR Issues (bi-mo.).
Technical reports.

Council on Library/Media Technicians

Executive Director, Margaret Barron
PMB 168, 28262 Chardon Rd., Willoughby Hills, OH 44092
216-261-0776, e-mail margaretrbarron@aol.com
World Wide Web http://colt.ucr.edu

The Council on Library/Media Technicians (COLT), an affiliate of the American Library Association, is an international organization that works to address the issues and concerns of library and media support staff personnel.

Since 1967 COLT has addressed issues covering such areas as technical education, continuing education, certification, job description uniformity, and the more elusive goals of gaining recognition and respect for the professional work that its members do.

Objectives

COLT's objectives are

* To function as a clearinghouse for information relating to library support staff personnel
* To advance the status, employment, and certification of library staff
* To promote effective communication and cooperation with other organizations whose purposes and objectives are similar to those of COLT

COLT's Web site provides information on library technician programs, a speaker exchange listing for help in organizing workshops and conferences, bibliographies on needed resources, and jobline resource links.

COLT holds an annual conference, generally immediately preceding the American Library Association Annual Conference.

Membership

Membership is open to all library employees. Dues (Inst.) $70 ($95 foreign); (Indiv.) $45 ($70 foreign); (Student) $35. Year. Jan.–Dec.

Officers

Pres. Jackie Hite. Tel. 202-231-3836, fax 202-231-3838, e-mail jmhite0@dia.mil; *V.P./ Pres.-Elect.* Chris Egan. E-mail egan@rand.org; *Secy.* Robin Martindill. E-mail rmartind@sdccd.edu; *Treas.* Stan Cieplinski. E-mail stan.cieplinski@domail.maricopa.edu; *Past Pres.* Jackie Lakatos. E-mail jlakatos@lemontlibrary.org.

Federal Library and Information Center Committee

Executive Director, Blane K. Dessy
Library of Congress, Washington, DC 20540-4935
202-707-4800
World Wide Web http://www.loc.gov/flicc

Object

The Federal Library and Information Center Committee (FLICC) makes recommendations on federal library and information policies, programs, and procedures to federal agencies and to others concerned with libraries and information centers. The committee coordinates cooperative activities and services among federal libraries and information centers and serves as a forum to consider issues and policies that affect federal libraries and information centers, needs and priorities in providing information services to the government and to the nation at large, and efficient and cost-effective use of federal library and information resources and services. Furthermore, the committee promotes improved access to information, continued development and use of the Federal Library and Information Network (FEDLINK), research and development in the application of new technologies to federal libraries and information centers, improvements in the management of federal libraries and information centers, and relevant education opportunities. Founded in 1965.

Membership

Libn. of Congress, Dir. of the National Agricultural Lib., Dir. of the National Lib. of Medicine, Dir. of the National Lib. of Educ., repre-

sentatives of each of the cabinet-level executive departments, and representatives of each of the following agencies: National Aeronautics and Space Admin., National Science Foundation, Smithsonian Institution, U.S. Supreme Court, National Archives and Records Admin., Admin. Offices of the U.S. Courts, Defense Technical Info. Center, Government Printing Office, National Technical Info. Service (Dept. of Commerce), Office of Scientific and Technical Info. (Dept. of Energy), Exec. Office of the President, Dept. of the Army, Dept. of the Navy, Dept. of the Air Force, and chair of the FEDLINK Advisory Council. Fifteen additional voting member agencies are selected on a rotating basis by the voting members of FEDLINK. These rotating members serve three-year terms. One representative of each of the following agencies is invited as an observer to committee meetings: Government Accountability Office, General Services Admin., Joint Committee on Printing, Office of Mgt. and Budget, Office of Personnel Mgt., and U.S. Copyright Office.

Officers

Chair Deanna Marcum, Assoc. Libn. for Lib. Services, Lib. of Congress; *Co-Chair* Kathryn Mendenhall; *Exec. Dir.* Blane K. Dessy.

Address correspondence to the executive director.

Medical Library Association

Executive Director, Carla Funk
65 E. Wacker Place, Suite 1900, Chicago, IL 60601-7298
312-419-9094, fax 312-419-8950, e-mail info@mlahq.org
World Wide Web http://www.mlanet.org

Object

The Medical Library Association (MLA) is a nonprofit professional education organization with more than 4,000 health sciences information professional members and partners worldwide. MLA provides lifelong educational opportunities, supports a knowledgebase of health information research, and works with a global network of partners to promote the importance of high-quality information for improved health to the health care community and the public.

Membership

Memb. (Inst.) 600+; (Indiv.) 3,400+, in 56 countries. Institutional members are medical and allied scientific libraries. Individual members are people who are (or were at the time membership was established) engaged in professional library or bibliographic work in medical and allied scientific libraries or people who are interested in medical or allied scientific libraries. Members can be affiliated with one or more of MLA's more than 20 special-interest sections and its regional chapters.

Officers

Pres. Gerald Perry. E-mail jerry.perry@ucdenver.edu; *Pres-Elect* Jane Blumenthal. E-mail janeblum@umich.edu; *Past Pres.* Ruth Holst. E-mail rholst@uic.edu.

Directors

Ysabel Bertolucci (2014), Marianne Comegys (2013), Cynthia Henderson (2012), Michelle Kraft (2014), Ann McKibbon (2012), Rikke Ogawa (2013), Gabriel Rios (2014), Julia Shaw-Kokot (2013), Joy Summers-Ables (2014).

Publications

Journal of the Medical Library Association (q.; $190).
MLA News (10 a year; $120).

Miscellaneous (request current list from association headquarters).

Music Library Association

8551 Research Way, Suite 180, Middleton, WI 53562
608-836-5825, e-mail mla@areditions.com
World Wide Web http://www.musiclibraryassoc.org

Object

The Music Library Association provides a professional forum for librarians, archivists, and others who support and preserve the world's musical heritage. To achieve this mission, it

- Provides leadership for the collection and preservation of music and information about music in libraries and archives

- Develops and delivers programs that promote continuing education and professional development in music librarianship

- Ensures and enhances intellectual access to music for all by contributing to the development and revision of national and international codes, formats, and other standards for the bibliographic control of music

- Ensures and enhances access to music for all by facilitating best practices for housing, preserving, and providing access to music

- Promotes legislation that strengthens music library services and universal access to music

- Fosters information literacy and lifelong learning by promoting music reference services, library instruction programs, and publications

- Collaborates with other groups in the music and technology industries, government, and librarianship, to promote its mission and values

Membership

Memb. 1,200+. Dues (Inst.) $135; (Indiv.) $100; (Retired or Assoc.) $70; (Paraprofessional) $55; (Student) $45. (Foreign, add $10.) Year. July 1–June 30.

Officers

Pres. Ruthann B. McTyre, 2000 Voxman Music Bldg., Univ. of Iowa, Iowa City, IA 52242-1795. Tel. 319-335-3088, fax 319-335-2637, e-mail ruthann-mctyre@uiowa.edu; *V.P./Pres.-elect* Jerry L. McBride. E-mail jerry.mcbride@stanford.edu; *Rec. Secy.* Pamela Bristah. E-mail pbristah@wellesley.edu; *Treas./Exec. Secy.* Michael Rogan. E-mail michael.rogan@tufts.edu; *Past Pres.* Philip R. Vandermeer, Music Lib., Wilson Lib. CB3906, Univ. of North Carolina at Chapel Hill, Chapel Hill, NC 27514. Tel. 919-966-1113, fax 919-843-0418, e-mail vanderme@email.unc.edu.

Members-at-Large

Members-at-Large (2010–2012) Susannah Cleveland, Cheryl Taranto, Liza Vick.

Publications

MLA Index and Bibliography Series (irreg.; price varies).
MLA Newsletter (q.; memb.).
MLA Technical Reports (irreg.; price varies).
Music Cataloging Bulletin (mo.; online subscription only, $35).
Notes (q.; indiv. $85; inst. $100).

National Association of Government Archives and Records Administrators

1450 Western Ave., Suite 101, Albany, NY 12203
518-694-8472, e-mail nagara@caphill.com
World Wide Web http://www.nagara.org

Object

Founded in 1984, NAGARA is a growing nationwide association of local, state, and federal archivists and records administrators, and others interested in improved care and management of government records. NAGARA promotes public awareness of government records and archives management programs, encourages interchange of information among government archives and records management agencies, develops and implements professional standards of government records and archival administration, and encourages study and research into records management problems and issues.

Membership

Most NAGARA members are federal, state, and local archival and records management agencies.

Officers

Pres. Paul R. Bergeron, City of Nashua, 229 Main St., Nashua, NH 03060. Tel. 603-589-3010, fax 603-589-3029, e-mail bergeronp@nashuanh.gov; *V.P.* Daphne DeLeon, Nevada State Lib. and Archives, 100 N. Stewart St., Carson City, NV 89701-4285. Tel. 775-684-3315, fax 775-684-3311, e-mail ddeleon@nevadaculture.org; *Secy.* Caryn Wojcik, Records Management Services, Michigan Dept. of Technology, Management, and Budget, 3400

N. Grand River Ave., P.O. Box 30026, Lansing, MI 48909. Tel. 517-335-8222, fax 517-321-3408, e-mail wojcikc@michigan.gov; *Treas.* Nancy Fortna, National Archives and Records Administration, Seventh and Pennsylvania Ave. N.W., Room G-13 NWCC, Washington, DC 20408-0001. Tel. 202-357-5288, e-mail nancy.fortna@nara.gov; *Past Pres.* Tracey Berezansky, Alabama Dept. of Archives and History, P.O. Box 300100, Montgomery, AL 36130-0100. Tel. 334-353-4604, fax 334-353-4321, e-mail tracey.berezansky@archiveds.alabama.gov.

Directors

Jim Corridan, Indiana Commission on Public Records; Bonnie Curtin, Federal Trade Commission; John Paul Deley, Office of Info. Technology; Sandy Hart, McKinney, Texas; Sandra Jaramillo, New Mexico State Records Center and Archives; Douglas K. King, Sedgwick County (Kansas) Government; Val Wood, Records and Licensing Services, King County, Washington.

Publications

Clearinghouse (q.; memb.).
Crossroads (q.; memb.).
Government Records Issues (series).
Preservation Needs in State Archives.
Program Reporting Guidelines for Government Records Programs.

National Church Library Association

Executive Director, Susan Benish
275 S. 3 St., Suite 204, Stillwater, MN 55082
651-430-0770, e-mail info@churchlibraries.org
World Wide Web http://www.churchlibraries.org

Object

The National Church Library Association (NCLA), formerly the Lutheran Church Library Association, is a nonprofit organization that serves the unique needs of congregational libraries and those who manage them. NCLA provides inspiration, solutions, and support to church librarians in the form of printed manuals and guidelines, booklists, the quarterly journal *Libraries ALIVE,* national conferences, a mentoring program, online support, and personal advice. Regional chapters operate throughout the United States.

Membership

Memb. $55. Year. Jan.–Jan.

Officers

Pres. Kathleen Bowman; *Treas.* Moe Conley *Past Pres.* Charles Mann.

Directors

Gordon Duffy, Bev Etzelmueller, Sandra Neal, Sally Onstad, Sandy Sharps, Kay Smith.

Address correspondence to the executive director.

Publication

Libraries ALIVE (q.; memb.).

National Federation of Advanced Information Services

Executive Director, Bonnie Lawlor
1518 Walnut St., Suite 1004, Philadelphia, PA 19102
215-893-1561, fax 215-893-1564,e-mail nfais@nfais.org
World Wide Web http://www.nfais.org

Object

The National Federation of Advanced Information Services (NFAIS) is an international nonprofit membership organization composed of leading information providers. Its membership includes government agencies, nonprofit scholarly societies, and private sector businesses. NFAIS is committed to promoting the value of authoritative content. It serves all groups that create, aggregate, organize, or facilitate access to such information. In order to improve members' capabilities and to contribute to their ongoing success, NFAIS provides opportunities for education, advocacy, and a forum in which to address common interests. Founded in 1958.

Membership

Memb. 60. Full members are organizations whose main focus is any of the following activities: information creation, organization, aggregation, dissemination, access, or retrieval. Organizations are eligible for associate member status if they do not meet the qualifications for full membership.

Officers (2010–2011)

Pres. Judith Russell, Univ. of Florida; *Pres.-Elect* Keith MacGregor, Thomson Reuters; *Secy.* Barbara Dobbs Mackenzie, *RILM Abstracts of Music Literature*; *Treas.* Suzanne Be-Dell, Dialog; *Past Pres.* Terence Ford, J. Paul Getty Trust.

Staff

Exec. Dir. Bonnie Lawlor. E-mail blawlor@nfais.org; *Dir., Planning and Communications* Jill O'Neill. E-mail jilloneill@nfais.org; *Customer Service* Margaret Manson. E-mail mmanson@nfais.org.

Directors

David Brown, Mark Gauthier, David Gillikin, Ellen Herbst, Chris McCue, Judy Salk, Lynn Willis.

Publications

For a detailed list of NFAIS publications, see the NFAIS Web site, http://www.nfais.org.

National Information Standards Organization

Managing Director, Todd Carpenter
1 N. Charles Ave., Suite 1905, Baltimore, MD 21201
301-654-2512, fax 410-685-5278, e-mail nisohq@niso.org
World Wide Web http://www.niso.org

Object

NISO, the National Information Standards Organization, a nonprofit association accredited by the American National Standards Institute (ANSI), identifies, develops, maintains, and publishes technical standards to manage information in our changing and ever-more-digital environment. NISO standards apply both traditional and new technologies to the full range of information-related needs, including discovery, retrieval, repurposing, storage, metadata, business information, and preservation.

Experts from the information industry, libraries, systems vendors, and publishing participate in the development of NISO standards. The standards are approved by the consensus body of NISO's voting membership, which consists of more than 80 voting members representing libraries, publishers, vendors, government, associations, and private businesses and organizations. In addition, approximately 30 libraries are NISO Library Standards Alliance members. NISO is supported by its membership and corporate grants. NISO is a nonprofit educational organization. It is accredited by ANSI and serves as the U.S. Technical Advisory Group to ISO/TC 46 Information and Docu-

mentation as well as the secretariat for ISO/TC 46/SC 9, Identification and Description.

Membership

Memb. 80+. Open to any organization, association, government agency, or company willing to participate in and having substantial concern for the development of NISO standards. Libraries may support NISO as members of the Library Standards Alliance.

Officers

Chair Janice Fleming, American Psychological Assn., 750 First St. N.E., Washington, DC 20002-4242. Tel. 202-336-5500, e-mail jfleming@apa.org; *V. Chair/Chair-Elect* Bruce Heterick, Ithaka, 149 Fifth Ave., New York, NY 10010. Tel. 212-358-6400, fax 212-358-6499, e-mail bruce.heterick@ithaka.org; *Past Chair* Chuck Koscher, CrossRef, 40 Salem St., Lynnfield, MA 01940. Tel. 781-295-0072 ext. 26, fax 781-295-0077, e-mail ckoscher@crossref.org; *Treas.* Barbara Preece, California State Univ., San Marco, 333 S. Twin Oaks Valley

Rd., San Marcos, CA 92096. Tel. 760-750-4350, e-mail bpreece@csusm.edu.

Directors

Nancy Barnes, Nancy Davenport, John Harwood, Charles Lowry, Oliver Pesch, Heather Reid, Bruce Rosenblum, Winston Tabb, Mike Teets.

Publications

Information Standards Quarterly ($130/year, foreign $165, back issues $40).

NISO Newsline (free monthly e-letter released on the first Wednesday of each month. See the NISO Web site for details on subscribing and archived issues).

For other NISO publications, see the article "National Information Standards Organization (NISO) Standards" later in Part 6.

NISO published standards, recommended practices, and technical reports are available free of charge as downloadable pdf files from the NISO Web site (http://www.niso.org). Standards in hard copy are available for sale on the Web site.

Patent and Trademark Depository Library Association

World Wide Web http://www.ptdla.org

Object

The Patent and Trademark Depository Library Association (PTDLA) provides a support structure for the more than 80 patent and trademark depository libraries (PTDLs) affiliated with the U.S. Patent and Trademark Office (USPTO). The association's mission is to discover the interests, needs, opinions, and goals of the PTDLs and to advise USPTO in these matters for the benefit of PTDLs and their users, and to assist USPTO in planning and implementing appropriate services. Founded in 1983 as the Patent Depository Library Advisory Council; name changed to Patent and Trademark Depository Library Association in 1988; became an American Library Association affiliate in 1996.

Membership

Open to any person employed in a patent and trademark depository library whose responsibilities include the patent collection. Affiliate membership is also available. Dues $25.

Officers (2011–2012)

Pres. Marian Armour Gemmen. E-mail marmour@wvu.edu; *V.P./Pres-Elect* Walt Johnson. E-mail wjohnson@hclib.org; *Secy.* Martin Wallace. E-mail martin.wallace@umit.maine.edu; *Treas.* Jim Miller. E-mail jmiller2@umd.edu; *Past Pres.* Robert Klein. E-mail patents@mdpls.org.

Divisional Representatives

(Academic) John Meier. E-mail meier@psu.edu; Suzanne Reinman. E-mail suzanne.reinman@okstate.edu; (Public) Michael Strickland. E-mail michaels@library.arkansas.gov; Spruce Fraser. E-mail sfraser@slpl.org.

Publications

PTDLA Newsletter. Ed. Suzanne Reinman. E-mail suzanne.reinman@okstate.edu.

Intellectual Property (IP). Electronic at http://www.ptdla.org/ipjournal.html. *Ed.* Michael White.

REFORMA (National Association to Promote Library and Information Services to Latinos and the Spanish-Speaking)

President, Lucía González
National Office Manager, Sandra Rios Balderrama
P.O. Box 4386, Fresno, CA 93744
Tel. 480-734-4460, e-mail reformaoffice@riosbalderrama.com
World Wide Web http://www.reforma.org

Object

Promoting library services to the Spanish-speaking for nearly 40 years, REFORMA, an affiliate of the American Library Association, works in a number of areas to promote the development of library collections to include Spanish-language and Latino-oriented materials; the recruitment of more bilingual and bicultural professionals and support staff; the development of library services and programs that meet the needs of the Latino community; the establishment of a national network among individuals who share its goals; the education of the U.S. Latino population in regard to the availability and types of library services; and lobbying efforts to preserve existing library resource centers serving the interest of Latinos.

Membership

Memb. 800+. Any person who is supportive of the goals and objectives of REFORMA.

Officers

Pres. Lucía M. González, 16410 Miami Drive, Apt. 404, North Miami Beach, FL 33162. Tel. 305-335-8215, e-mail inotherwordsllc@gmail.com; *Pres.-Elect* Maria Kramer. E-mail mkramer@redwoodcity.org; *Secy./Recorder* Tiffany Herbon. E-mail therbon@slcpl.org; *Treas.* Robin Imperial. E-mail robin.imperial@gmail.com; *Memb.-at-Large* Roberto C. Delga-

dillo. E-mail rdelgadillo@lib.ucdavis.edu; *Past Pres.* Loida García Febo. E-mail loidagarcia febo@gmail.com.

Committees

Pura Belpré Award. Jamie Campbell Naidoo.
Children's and Young Adult Services. Alma Ramos-McDermott, Jamie Campbell Naidoo.
Education. Siobhan Champ-Blackwell.
Finance. Loida García Febo.
Fund Raising. Sylvia D. Hall-Ellis.
Information Technology. Juan Carlos Rodríguez.
International Relations. Miguel Garcia Colon.
Legislative. Carol Brey-Casiano.
Membership. Daniel Berdaner.
Nominations. Oscar Baeza.
Organizational Development. Yolanda Valentín.
Public Relations. Jessica Hernandez.
Recruitment and Mentoring. To be announced.
Scholarship. Ramona Grijalva.
Translations. Armando Trejo.

Publication

REFORMA Newsletter (s. ann; memb.).

Meetings

General membership and board meetings take place at the American Library Association Midwinter Meeting and Annual Conference.

Society for Scholarly Publishing

Executive Director, Ann Mehan Crosse
10200 W. 44 Ave., Suite 304, Wheat Ridge, CO 80033
303-422-3914, fax 303-422-8894, e-mail info@sspnet.org or amehan@resourcecenter.org
World Wide Web http://www.sspnet.org

Object

To draw together individuals involved in the process of scholarly publishing. This process requires successful interaction of the many functions performed within the scholarly community. The Society for Scholarly Publishing (SSP) provides the leadership for such interaction by creating opportunities for the exchange of information and opinions among scholars, editors, publishers, librarians, printers, booksellers, and all others engaged in scholarly publishing.

Membership

Memb. 1,000. Open to all with an interest in the scholarly publishing process and dissemination of information. Dues (New Member) $140; (Indiv. Renewal) $155; (Libn.) $75; (Student) $30; (Supporting) $1,390; (Sustaining) $3,375. Year. Jan. 1–Dec. 31.

Executive Committee

Pres. Theresa Van Schaik, American Society of Clinical Oncology. E-mail: terry.vanschaik@asco.org; *Pres.-Elect* Carol Anne Meyer, CrossRef. E-mail cmeyer@crossref.org; *Secy./Treas.* Todd Carpenter, National Info. Standards Organization. E-mail tcarpenter@niso.org; *Past Pres.* Lois Smith, Human Factors and Ergonomics Society. E-mail lois@hfes.org.

Directors

Michael T. Clarke, Alice Meadows, Eileen Kiley Novak, Anne Orens, Kristen Fisher Ratan, Howard Ratner, Adrian Stanley, William M. Wakeling, Charles Watkinson.

Meetings

An annual meeting is held in late May/early June. SSP also conducts a Fall Seminar Series (November), Librarian Focus Group (February), and the IN Conference (September).

Society of American Archivists

Executive Director, Nancy Perkin Beaumont
17 N. State St., Suite 1425, Chicago, IL 60602
866-722-7858, 312-606-0722, fax 312-606-0728, nbeaumont@archivists.org
http://www.archivists.org

Object

Founded in 1936, the Society of American Archivists (SAA) is North America's oldest and largest national archival professional association. SAA's mission is to serve the educational and informational needs of more than 6,000 individual and institutional members and to provide leadership to ensure the identification, preservation, and use of records of historical value.

Membership

Memb. 6,000. Dues (Indiv.) $47 to $225, graduated according to salary; (Assoc.) $80, domestic; (Student or Bridge) $47; (Inst.) $265; (Sustaining Inst.) $500.

Officers (2011–2012)

Pres. Gregor Trinkaus-Randall, Massachusetts Board of Lib. Commissioners. Tel. 617-725-1860 ext. 236, e-mail gregor.trinkaus-randall@ state.ma.us; *V.P.* Jackie M. Dooley, OCLC Research, San Clemente, CA 92673. Tel. 949-492-5060, e-mail dooleyj@oclc.org.

Staff

Exec. Dir. Nancy Perkin Beaumont. E-mail nbeaumont@archivists.org; *Dir., Publishing* Teresa Brinati. E-mail tbrinati@archivists.org;

Dir., Educ. Solveig De Sutter. E-mail sdesutter@archivists.org; *Dir., Member and Technical Services* Brian Doyle. E-mail bdoyle@ archivists.org; *Dir., Finance and Admin.* Tom Jurczak. E-mail tjurczak@archivists.org; *Educ. Program Coord.* Amanda Look. E-mail alook@ archivists.org.

Publications

American Archivist (2 a year) individual print or online edition, $139; print and online, $169; institutional, $169 print or online, $199 print and online). *Ed.* Gregory Hunter; *Reviews Ed.* Amy Cooper Cary.

Archival Outlook (bi-mo.; memb.). *Ed.* Teresa Brinati.

Software and Information Industry Association

1090 Vermont Ave. N.W., Washington, DC 20005
Tel. 202-289-7442, fax 202-289-7097
World Wide Web http://www.siia.net

Membership

Memb. 520 companies. The Software and Information Industry Association (SIIA) was formed January 1, 1999, through the merger of the Software Publishers Association (SPA) and the Information Industry Association (IIA). Open to companies involved in the creation, distribution, and use of software, information products, services, and technologies. For details on membership and dues, see the SIIA Web site.

Staff

Pres. Kenneth Wasch. E-mail kwasch@siia. net; *V.P. Educ. Div.* Karen Billings; *V.P. Software Div.* Rhianna Collier.

Board of Directors

Suresh Balasubramanian, Adobe Systems, Inc.; Cynthia Braddon, McGraw-Hill; Daniel Burton, Salesforce.com; Alan Davidson, Google, Inc.; Joseph T. FitzGerald, Symantec; Kenneth J. Glueck, Oracle; Kathy Hurley, Pearson School and Pearson Foundation; Steve Manzo, Reed Elsevier; Randy Marcinko, Marcinko Enterprises; Bernard McKay, Intuit; Calvin A. Mitchell, Thomson Reuters; Jim Panos, Houghton Mifflin Harcourt; Tom B. Rabon, Jr., Red Hat; Scott Schulman, Dow Jones; Timothy Sheehy (chair), IBM; Ken Wasch, SIIA.

SPARC

Executive Director, Heather Joseph
21 Dupont Circle, Suite 800, Washington, DC 20036
202-296-2296, fax 202-872-0884
E-mail sparc@arl.org
World Wide Web http://www.arl.org/sparc

SPARC, the Scholarly Publishing and Academic Resources Coalition, is a global organization that promotes expanded sharing of scholarship in the networked digital environment. Developed by the Association of Research Libraries, SPARC has become a catalyst for change. Its pragmatic focus is to stimulate the emergence of new scholarly communication models that expand the dissemination of scholarly research and reduce financial pressures on libraries. Action by SPARC in collaboration with stakeholders—including authors, publishers, and libraries—builds on the unprecedented opportunities created by the networked digital environment to advance the conduct of scholarship.

SPARC's role in stimulating change focuses on

- Educating stakeholders about the problems facing scholarly communication and the opportunities for them to play a role in achieving positive change
- Advocating policy changes that advance scholarly communication and that explicitly recognize that dissemination of scholarship is an essential, inseparable component of the research process
- Incubating demonstrations of new publishing and sustainability models that benefit scholarship and academe

SPARC is a visible advocate for changes in scholarly communication that benefit more than the academic community alone. Founded in 1997, SPARC has expanded to represent more than 800 academic and research libraries in North America, the United Kingdom, Europe, and Japan.

Membership

SPARC membership is open to international academic and research institutions, organizations, and consortia that share an interest in creating a more open and diverse marketplace for scholarly communication. Dues are scaled by membership type and budget. For more information, visit SPARC's Web site at http://www.arl.org/sparc, SPARC Europe at http://www.sparceurope.org, or SPARC Japan at http://www.nii.ac.jp/sparc.

Publications

Open-Access Journal Publishing Resource Index (2011) by Raym Crow.

Library Publishing Services: Strategies for Success (2011) by Raym Crow, October Ivins, Allyson Mower, Daureen Nesdill, Mark Newton, Julie Speer, and Charles Watkinson.

Library Publishing Services: Strategies for Success Report Version 1.0 (2011) by Raym Crow, October Ivins, Allyson Mower, Daureen Nesdill, Mark Newton, Julie Speer, and Charles Watkinson.

Campus-Based Publishing Partnerships: A Gguide to Critical Issues (2009) by Raym Crow.

Income Models for Open Access: An Overview of Current Practice (2009) by Raym Crow.

The Right to Research: The Student Guide to Opening Access to Scholarship (2008), part of a campaign to engage students on the issue of research access.

Greater Reach for Research: Expanding Readership Through Digital Repositories (2008), the initiative to educate faculty on the benefits of open repositories and emerging research access policies.

Author Rights (2006), an educational initiative and introduction to the SPARC Author Addendum, a legal form that enables authors of journal articles to modify publishers' copyright transfer agreements and allow authors to keep key rights to their articles.

"Open Access News Blog," daily updates on the worldwide movement for open access to science and scholarship written by Peter Suber and cosponsored by SPARC.

SPARC Open Access Newsletter, a monthly roundup of developments relating to open access publishing, written by Peter Suber.

SPARC e-news, SPARC's monthly newsletter featuring SPARC activities, an industry roundup, upcoming workshops and events, and articles relating to developments in scholarly communication.

Publishing Cooperatives: An Alternative for Society Publishers (2006) by Raym Crow.

Sponsorships for Nonprofit Scholarly and Scientific Journals: A Guide to Defining and Negotiating Successful Sponsorships (2005) by Raym Crow.

A more complete list of SPARC publications, including brochures, articles, and guides, is available at http://www.arl.org/sparc.

Special Libraries Association (SLA)

Chief Executive Officer, Janice R. Lachance
331 S. Patrick St., Alexandria, VA 22314
703-647-4900, fax 703-647-4901, e-mail resources@sla.org
World Wide Web http://www.sla.org

Mission

The Special Libraries Association promotes and strengthens its members through learning, advocacy, and networking initiatives.

Strategic Vision

SLA is a global association of professionals who are employed in every sector of the information and knowledge economy. Its members thrive where data, information, and knowledge intersect, and its strategic partners support SLA because they believe in the association's mission and the future of its members. SLA's goal is to support information professionals as they contribute, in their varied and evolving roles, to the opportunities and achievements of organizations, communities, and society.

Membership

Memb. 9,200. Dues (Organizational) $750; (Indiv.) $114–$200; (Student/Retired/Salary less than $18,000 a year) $40.

Officers

Pres. Brent Mai, Concordia Univ. E-mail bmai@cu-portland.edu; *Pres.-Elect* Deb Hunt, Information Edge. E-mail dhunt@information-edge.com; *Treas.* Dan Trefethen, Boeing. E-mail daniel.b.trefethen@boeing.com; *Chapter Cabinet Chair* Ulla de Stricker, de Stricker Associates. E-mail ulla@destricker.com; *Chapter Cabinet Chair-Elect* Debbie Schachter, Douglas College. E-mail schachterd@douglas.bc.ca; *Div. Cabinet Chair* Richard Huffine, U.S. Geological Survey. E-mail richardhuffine@yahoo.com; *Div. Cabinet Chair-Elect* Ann Koopman, Thomas Jefferson University. E-mail ann.koopman@jefferson.edu

Directors

Officers; Jill Hurst-Wahl, Sara Tompson, Marilyn Bromley, Hal Kirkwood.

Publication

Information Outlook (memb., nonmemb. $125/yr.)

Theatre Library Association

c/o The New York Public Library for the Performing Arts
40 Lincoln Center Plaza, New York, NY 10023
E-mail info@tla-online.org, World Wide Web http://www.tla-online.org

Object

To further the interests of collecting, preserving, and using theater, cinema, and performing arts materials in libraries, museums, and private collections. Founded in 1937.

Membership

Memb. 327. Dues (Indiv.) $20–$40, (Inst.) $40–$50. Year. Jan. 1–Dec. 31.

Officers

Pres. Kenneth Schlesinger, Lehman College, City Univ. of New York; *V.P.* Nancy Friedland, Columbia Univ.; *Exec. Secy.* David Nochimson, New York Public Lib.; *Treas.* Colleen Reilly, Slippery Rock Univ.

Executive Board

Susan Brady, John Calhoun, Charlotte Cubbage, Phyllis Dircks, Beth Kattelman, Diana King, Stephen Kuehler, Francesca Marini, Karen Nickeson, Tiffany Nixon, Doug Reside, Cynthia Tobar, Angela Weaver, Sarah Zimmerman; *Honorary* Louis A. Rachow, Marian Seldes; *Legal Counsel* Georgia Harper; *Past Pres.* Martha S. LoMonaco.

Publications

Broadside (3 a year; memb.). *Ed.* Angela Weaver. *Performing Arts Resources* (occasional; memb.). *Membership Directory* (annual; memb.). *Ed.* David Nochimson.

Committee Chairs

Book Awards. Flordalisa Lopez, Cynthia Tobar.
Conference Planning. Nancy Friedland.
Finance and Fund Raising. Colleen Reilly.
Membership. Beth Kerr.
Nominating. Martha S. LoMonaco.
Professional Award. Phyllis Dircks.
Publications. Leakhim Gannett.
Strategic Planning. Nancy Friedland.
Web Site. David Nochimson.

Urban Libraries Council

125 S. Wacker Drive, Suite 1050, Chicago, IL 60606
312-676-0999, fax 312-676-0950, e-mail info@urbanlibraries.org
World Wide Web http://www.urbanlibraries.org

Object

Since 1971 the Urban Libraries Council (ULC) has worked to strengthen public libraries as an essential part of urban life. A member organization of North America's leading public library systems, ULC serves as a forum for research widely recognized and used by public and private sector leaders. Its members are thought leaders dedicated to leadership, innovation, and the continuous transformation of libraries to meet community needs.

ULC's work focuses on helping public libraries to identify and utilize skills and strategies that match the challenges of the 21st century.

Membership

Membership is open to public libraries and to corporate partners specializing in library-related materials and services. The organization also offers associate memberships.

Officers (2011–2012)

Chair Keith B. Simmons; *V. Chair/Chair-Elect* Joan Prince; *Secy./Treas.* John F. Szabo; *Past Chair* Melinda Cervantes; *Member-at-Large* Melanie Huggins.

Officers serve one-year terms, members of the executive board two-year terms. New officers are elected and take office at the summer annual meeting of the council.

Executive Board

Susan Adams, Ruth Anna, Karen E. "Kari" Glover, Jan Harder, Patrick Losinski, Robert S. Martin, Dennis B. Martinez, Matthew K. Poland, Gloria Rubio-Cortés, Rivkah Sass, Rashad Young.

Key Staff

CEO and Pres. Susan Benton; *Media and Marketing* Mary Colleen Bragiel; *Finance and Admin.* Angela Goodrich; *Communications and Member Services* Jodi Lazar; *Writer* Sheila Murphy; *Senior Communications* Alison Saffold; *Exec. Assistant to the Pres.* Erika Slaughter.

State, Provincial, and Regional Library Associations

The associations in this section are organized under three headings: United States, Canada, and Regional. Both the United States and Canada are represented under Regional associations.

United States

Alabama

Memb. 1,200. Term of Office. Apr. 2011–Apr. 2012. Publication. *The Alabama Librarian* (q.).

Pres. Steven Yates, Mountain Brook H.S., 3650 Bethune Drive, Birmingham 35223. Tel. 205-826-3303, e-mail yatess@mtnbrook.k12. al.us; *Pres.-Elect* Emily Tish, Trussville Public Lib., 201 Parkway Drive, Trussville 35173. Tel. 205-559-4639, e-mail etish@bham.lib.al.us; *Secy.* Alyssa Martin, Rosa Parks Lib., Troy Univ.–Montgomery, 252 Montgomery St., Montgomery 36104. Tel. 334-241-8601, e-mail almartin@troy.edu; *Treas.* Tim Bailey, Auburn Univ. at Montgomery, P.O. Box 244023, Montgomery 36124-4023. Tel. 334-398-0825, e-mail tbailey1@aum.edu; *Past Pres.* Jodi Poe, Houston Cole Lib., Jacksonville State Univ., 700 Pelham Rd. N., Jacksonville 36265. Tel. 256-782-8103, e-mail jpoe@jsu.edu.

Address correspondence to the association, 9154 Eastchase Pkwy., Suite 418, Montgomery 36117. Tel. 334-414-0113, e-mail admin@allanet.org.

World Wide Web http://allanet.org.

Alaska

Memb. 450+. Publication. *Newspoke* (q.).

Pres. Michael Robinson. E-mail afmcr@uaa. alaska.edu; *Pres.-Elect* Linda Wynne. E-mail lindaleewynne@gmail.com; *Secy.* Julie Niederhauser. E-mail julie.niederhauser@alaska. gov; *Treas.* Patricia Linville. E-mail plinville @cityofseward.net; *Conference Coord.* Diane Ruess. E-mail deruess@alaska.edu; *Past Pres.* David Ongley. E-mail david.ongley@ tuzzy.org; *Exec. Officer* Mary Jennings. E-mail maryj@gci.net.

Address correspondence to the secretary, Alaska Lib. Assn., P.O. Box 81084, Fairbanks 99708. Fax 877-863-1401, e-mail akla@akla.org.

World Wide Web http://www.akla.org.

Arizona

Memb. 1,000. Term of Office. Nov. 2011–Nov. 2012. Publication. *AzLA Newsletter* (mo.).

Pres. Nancy Deegan, South Mountain Community College, 7050 S. 24 St., Phoenix 85042-5806. Tel. 602-305-5877, e-mail president@ azla.org or nancy.deegan@smcmail.maricopa. edu; *Pres.-Elect* Tom Wilding, SIRLS, Univ. of Arizona, 1515 E. 1 St., Tucson 85719. E-mail presidentelect@azla.org or wilding@email. arizona.edu; *Secy.* Ann M. Boles, Yavapai County Free Lib. Dist., 172 E. Merritt, Suite E, Prescott 86301. Tel. 928-442-5387, fax 928-771-3113, e-mail ann.boles@co.yavapai.az.us; *Treas.* Claudia Leon, Glendale Public Lib. Tel. 623-930-3570, e-mail cleon@glendaleaz. com; *Past Pres.* Nancy Ledeboer, Pima County Public Lib., 101 N. Stone Ave., Tucson 85701-1501. Tel. 520-594-5601, fax 520-594-5621, e-mail nancy.ledeboer@pima.gov; *Exec. Secy.* Debbie J. Hanson, Arizona Lib. Assn., 1030 E. Baseline Rd., No. 105-1025, Tempe 85283. Tel. 480-609-3999, fax 480-609-3939, e-mail admin@azla.org.

Address correspondence to the executive secretary.

World Wide Web http://www.azla.org.

Arkansas

Memb. 600. Term of Office. Jan.–Dec. 2012. Publication. *Arkansas Libraries* (bi-mo.).

Pres. Jim Robb, North Arkansas College, 1515 Pioneer Drive, Harrison 72601. Tel. 870-391-3359, e-mail jrobb@northark.edu; *V.P./ Pres.-Elect* Trish Miller, Remington College, 19 Remington Rd., Little Rock 72204. Tel. 501-312-0007, e-mail trish.miller@remington-college.edu; *Secy./Treas.* Michael Strickland, Arkansas State Lib., 900 W. Capitol, Suite 100, Little Rock 72201. Tel. 501-682-2053, e-mail michaels@library.Arkansas.gov; *Past Pres.* Shawn Pierce, Lonoke/Prairie County Regional Lib., 2504 S. Tyler St., Little Rock 72204. Tel.

501-676-6608, e-mail spierce@lpregional.lib.
ar.us; *Exec. Admin.* Lynda Hampel, Arkansas
Lib. Assn., P.O. Box 958, Benton 72018-0958.
Tel. 501-860-7585, fax 501-778-4014, e-mail
arlib2@sbcglobal.net.

Address correspondence to the executive
administrator.

World Wide Web http://www.arlib.org.

California

Memb. 2,500. Publication. *Clarion* (s. ann.).
Pres. Wayne Disher, Hemet Public Lib. Tel.
951-765-2441, e-mail wdisher@cityofhemet.
org; *V.P./Pres.-Elect* Derek Wolfgram, Santa
Clara County Lib. E-mail dwolfgram@sccl.
org; *Treas.* Jan Sanders, Pasadena Public Lib.
E-mail jsanders@cityofpasadena.net; *Past
Pres.* Paymaneh Maghsoudi, Whittier Public
Lib. Tel. 562-464-3452, e-mail pmaghsoudi@
whittierpl.org; *Exec. Dir.* Carol Simmons. Tel.
650-376-0886, e-mail csimmons@cla-net.org.

Address correspondence to the executive director, California Lib. Assn., 2471 Flores St.,
San Mateo 94403. Tel. 650-376-0886, fax 650-
539-2341.

World Wide Web http://www.cla-net.org.

Colorado

Pres. Linda Conway. E-mail linda.conway@
rocketmail.com; *V.P./Pres.-Elect* Stephen
Sweeney. E-mail Stephen.Sweeney@archden.
org; *Secy.* Denise Muniz. E-mail dmuniz@
broomfield.org; *Treas.* Chris Brogan. E-mail
cgbrogan@msn.com; *Past Pres.* Teri Switzer.
E-mail switzer@uccs.edu.

Address correspondence to the president,
Colorado Assn. of Libs., 3030 W. 81 Ave.,
Westminster 80031. Tel. 303-463-6400, fax
303-458-0002.

World Wide Web http://www.cal-webs.org.

Connecticut

Memb. 1,000+. Term of Office. July 2011–June
2012. Publication. *CLA Today* (online). *Ed.*
Lisa Carlucci Thomas. E-mail editor@ctlibrar-
ians.org.

Pres. Elizabeth Anne Reiter, Groton Public
Lib. Tel. 860-441-6750, fax 860-448-0363,
e-mail breiter@town.groton.ct.us; *V.P./Pres.-
Elect* Carl R. DeMilia, New Milford Public

Lib., 24 Main St., New Milford 6776. Tel. 860
355-1191 ext. 210, fax 860-350-9579, e-mail
cdemilia@biblio.org; *Treas.* Alison Wang,
Naugatuck Valley Community College, Water-
bury. Tel. 203-575-8250, e-mail awang@nvcc.
commnet.edu; *Recording Secy.* Beth Crowley,
Scranton Lib., 801 Boston Post Rd., Madison
06443. Tel. 203-245-7365, e-mail crowleyb@
madisonct.org; *Past Pres.* Debbie Herman,
Central Connecticut State Univ. Tel. 860-832-
2084, fax 860-832-2118, e-mail hermand@
ccsu.edu.

Address correspondence to Connecticut Lib.
Assn., 234 Court St., Middletown 06457. Tel.
860-346-2444, fax 860-344-9199, e-mail cla@
ctlibrarians.org.

World Wide Web http://www.ctlibraryasso-
ciation.org.

Delaware

Memb. 200+. Term of Office. Apr. 2011–Apr.
2012. Publication. *DLA Bulletin* (online only).

Pres. Patty Langley, Delaware Div. of Libs.,
121 Duke of York St., Dover 19901. Tel. 800-
282-8696 (302-739-4748 in Kent County), fax
302-739-6787, e-mail patty.langley@state.
de.us; *V.P.* Terri Jones, Hockessin Lib., 1023
Valley Rd., Hockessin 19707. Tel. 302-239-
5160, e-mail terrijones18@gmail.com; *Secy.*
Maureen S. Miller, Lewes Public Lib., 111
Adams Ave., Lewes 19958. Tel. 302-645-4633,
e-mail maureen.miller@lib.de.us; *Treas.* Pauly
Iheanacho, Univ. of Delaware Lib., 181 S. College Ave., Newark 19717-5267. Tel. 302-831-
6946, fax 302-831-1631, e-mail pinacho@
udel.edu; *Past Pres.* Margery Cyr, Dover Public Lib. Tel. 302-736-7032, fax 302-736-5087,
e-mail margery.cyr@lib.de.us.

Address correspondence to the association,
Box 816, Dover 19903-0816. E-mail dla@dla.
lib.de.us.

World Wide Web http://www2.lib.udel.edu/
dla.

District of Columbia

Memb. 300+. Term of Office. July 2011–June
2012. Publication. *Capital Librarian* (s. ann.).

Pres. Megan Sheils; *V.P./Pres.-Elect* Jacqueline Protka; *Secy.* Jessica McGilvray; *Treas.*
Roman Santillan; *Past Pres.* Richard Huffine.

Address correspondence to the association, Box 14177, Benjamin Franklin Sta., Washington 20044.

World Wide Web http://www.dcla.org.

Florida

Memb. (Indiv.) 1,000+. Term of Office. May 2011–Apr. 2012. Publication. *Florida Libraries* (s. ann.). *Ed.* Maria Gebhardt. Tel. 954-357-7570, e-mail mariagfla@gmail.com.

Pres. Gloria Colvin, 2505 Blarney Drive, Tallahassee 32309. Tel. 850-645-1680, e-mail gpcolvin@yahoo.com; *V.P./Pres.-Elect* Barbara Stites, Florida Gulf Coast Univ., 10501 FGCU Blvd. S., Fort Myers 33965-6501. Tel. 239-590-7602, e-mail bstites@fgcu.edu; *Secy.* Ruth O'Donnell, 3509 Trillium Court, Tallahassee 32312. Tel. 850-668-6911, e-mail ruth.odonnell@comcast.net; *Treas.* Susan D. Dillinger, New Port Richey Public Lib., 5939 Main St., New Port Richey 34652. Tel. 727-853-1262, e-mail sddillinger@gmail.com; *Past Pres.* John J. Callahan III, Palm Beach County Lib. System, 3650 Summit Blvd., West Palm Beach 33406-4198. Tel. 561-233-2600, e-mail callahanj@pgclibrary.org; *Exec. Dir.* Faye Roberts, P.O. Box 1571, Lake City 32056-1571. Tel. 386-438-5795, e-mail faye.roberts@comcast.net.

Address correspondence to the executive director.

World Wide Web http://www.flalib.org.

Georgia

Memb. 800+. Publication. *Georgia Library Quarterly. Interim Ed.* Jeff Heck, Reese Lib., Augusta State Univ., 2500 Walton Way, Augusta 30904-2200. E-mail jheck@aug.edu.

Pres. Carolyn Fuller, Henry County Public Lib. Tel. 770-954-2806, e-mail cfuller@mail.henry.public.lib.ga.us; *1st V.P./Pres.-Elect* Elizabeth Bagley, McCain Lib., Agnes Scott College, 141 E. College Ave., Decatur 30030. Tel. 404-471-5277, e-mail ebagley@agnesscott.edu; *2nd V.P.* Kim Eccles, Monroe F. Swilley, Jr. Lib., Mercer Univ. Atlanta Campus, 3001 Mercer University Drive, Atlanta 30341. Tel. 678-547-6271, e-mail eccles.kl@mercer.edu; *Secy.* Debbie Holmes, Gould Memorial Lib., College of Coastal Georgia, 3700 Altama Ave., Brunswick 31520. Tel. 912-279-5787, e-mail deholmes@ccga.edu; *Treas.* Cathy Jeffrey,

Clayton State Univ. Lib., 2000 Clayton State University Blvd., Morrow 30260. Tel. 678-466-4336, e-mail cathyjeffrey@clayton.edu; *Past Pres.* Carol Stanley, Athens Technical College, 1317 Athens Hwy., Elberton 30635. Tel. 706-213-2116, e-mail cstanley@athenstech.edu.

Address correspondence to the president, Georgia Lib. Assn., P.O. Box 793, Rex 30273-0793.

World Wide Web http://gla.georgialibraries.org.

Hawaii

Memb. 250. Publication. HLA Blog, "Hawaii Library Association" (http://hawaiilibraryassociation.blogspot.com).

Pres. Christine Pawliuk, Hawaii Business Research Center and Lib. E-mail christine.pawliuk@hisbdc.org; *V.P./Pres-Elect* Christina Abelardo, Sgt. Yano Lib. E-mail christinathelibrarian@gmail.com; *Treas.* Naomi Chow, Univ. of Hawaii. E-mail nchow@hawaii.edu; *Past Pres.* Stewart Chun, Hawaii State Lib. Tel. 808-586-3477, e-mail stewart.chun@imail.librarieshawaii.org; *Secy.* Kimball Boone, Brigham Young Univ.–Hawaii. E-mail kimball.boone@byuh.edu; *Treas.* Naomi Chow, Univ. of Hawaii at Manoa.

Address correspondence to the association at hawaii.library.association@gmail.com.

World Wide Web http://hla.chaminade.edu.

Idaho

Memb. 420. Term of Office. Oct. 2011–Oct. 2012.

Pres. Gena Marker, Centennial H.S., 12400 W. McMillan Rd., Boise 83713. Tel. 208-855-4261, e-mail marker.gena@meridianschools.org; *V.P./Pres.-Elect* Karen Yother, Community Lib. Network, 8385 N. Government Way, Hayden 83835. Tel. 208-772-5612 ext. 121, e-mail kareny@communitylibrary.net; *Secy.* Megan Egbert, Meridian Lib. Dist., 1326 W. Cherry Lane, Meridian 83642. Tel. 208-888-4451, e-mail megan@mld.org; *Treas.* Steve Poppino, College of Southern Idaho, 315 Falls Ave., Twin Falls 83383-1238. Tel. 208-732-6504, fax 208-732-3087, e-mail spoppino@csi.edu; *Past Pres.* Ben Hunter, Univ. of Idaho Lib., P.O. Box 442350, Moscow 83844-2350. Tel. 208-885-5858, e-mail bhunter@uidaho.edu.

Address correspondence to the association, P.O. Box 8533, Moscow 83844.

World Wide Web http://www.idaholibraries.org.

Illinois

Memb. 3,500. Term of Office. July–July. Publication. *ILA Reporter* (bi-mo.).

Pres. Lynn Elam, Algonquin Area Public Lib. Dist., 2600 Harnish Drive, Algonquin 60102. Tel. 847-458-6069, fax 847-458-9370, e-mail lelam@aapld.org; *V.P./Pres.-Elect* Pamela Van Kirk, 708 N. I St., Monmouth 61462. Tel. 309-734-3922, e-mail pamela.vankirk@gmail.com; *Treas.* Cynthia L. Fuerst, Vernon Area Public Lib. Dist., 300 Olde Half Day Rd., Lincolnshire 60069. Tel. 847-634-3650, fax 847-634-8449, e-mail cynthialfuerst@gmail.com; *Past Pres.* Gail Bush, National Louis Univ. Center for Teaching Through Children's Books, 5202 Old Orchard Rd., Suite 300, Skokie 60077. Tel./fax 224-233-2522, e-mail gail.bush@nl.edu; *Exec. Dir.* Robert P. Doyle, Illinois Lib. Assn., 33 W. Grand Ave., Suite 401, Chicago 60654-6799. Tel. 312-644-1896, fax 312-644-1899, e-mail doyle@ila.org.

Address correspondence to the executive director.

World Wide Web http://www.ila.org.

Indiana

Memb. 2,000+. Publications. *Indiana Libraries* (s. ann.). *Ed.* Kristi Palmer, IUPUI Univ. Lib., 755 W. Michigan, Indianapolis 46202. Tel. 317-274-8230, e-mail klpalmer@iupui.edu; *Focus on Indiana Libraries* (11 a year, memb.). *Ed.* Diane J. Bever, Kokomo Lib., Indiana Univ., 2300 S. Washington St., P.O. Box 9003, Kokomo 46904-9003. Tel. 765-455-9345, fax 765-455-9276, e-mail dbever@iuk.edu.

Pres. Dennis LeLoup, Avon Intermediate School East, Avon 46123. E-mail djleloup@avon-schools.org; *Pres.-Elect* Robin Crumrin, IUPUI Univ. Lib., Indianapolis. E-mail rcrumrin@iupui.edu; *Secy.* Kelly Ehinger, Adams Public Lib. System, 128 S. 3 St., Decatur 46733. E-mail ehinger@apls.lib.in.us; *Treas.* Jason Hatton, Bartholomew County Public Lib., 536 Fifth St., Columbus 47201. Tel. 812-379-1255, e-mail jhatton@barth.lib.in.us; *Past Pres.* John Borneman, Tipton County Public

Lib., 10373 W. 650 N., Sharpsville 46068. E-mail johnborneman@gmail.com; *Exec. Dir.* Susan Akers. Tel. 317-257-2040 ext. 101, e-mail sakers@ilfonline.org.

Address correspondence to Indiana Lib. Federation, 941 E. 86 St., Suite 260, Indianapolis 46240. Tel. 317-257-2040, fax 317-257-1389.

World Wide Web http://www.ilfonline.org.

Iowa

Memb. 1,500. Publication. *The Catalyst* (bi-mo.).

Pres. Lorraine Borowski, Decorah Public Lib., 202 Winnebago St., Decorah 52101. Tel. 563-382-3717, e-mail lborowski@decorah.lib.ia.us; *Exec. Board* Louise Alcorn, Mary Cameron, Maeve Clark, Tena Hanson, Mary Heinzman, John Lerdal, Marilyn Murphy, Ellen Nauhaus, Kathy A. Parsons, Duncan Stewart; *Past Pres.* Dale Vande Haar, Des Moines Public Schools, 1800 Grand Ave., Mezzanine 253, Des Moines 50309. Tel. 515-242-7569, fax 515-242-7359, e-mail dale.vandehaar@dmps.k12.ia.us.

Address correspondence to the association, 525 S.W. 5 St., Suite A, Des Moines 50309. Tel. 515-273-5322, fax 515-309-4576.

World Wide Web http://www.iowalibraryassociation.org.

Kansas

Memb. 1,500. Term of Office. July 2011–June 2012. Publication. *KLA Connects* (q.).

Pres. Royce Kitts, Tonganoxie Public Lib., 303 S. Bury, Tonganoxie 66086. Tel. 913-845-3281, fax 913-845-2962, director@tonganoxielibrary.org; *V.P.* Mickey Coalwell, Northeast Kansas Lib. System, 4317 W. 6, Lawrence 66049. Tel. 785-838-4090, e-mail mcoalwell@nekls.org; *2nd V.P.* Cathy Reeves, Dodge City Public Lib., 1001 N. 2 Ave., Dodge City 67801. E-mail cathyr@dcpl.info; *Secy.* Cindi Hickey, State Lib. of Kansas, 343-N, 300 S.W. 10 Ave., Topeka 66612-1593. Tel. 785-296-3296, e-mail chickey@kslib.info; *Treas.* Candi Hemel, Cimarron City Library, 120 N. Main, P.O. Box 645, Cimarron 67835. Tel. 620-855-3808, e-mail cimarroncitylibrary@gmail.com; *Past Pres.* Emily Sitz, Southwest Kansas Lib. System, 100 Military Ave., Suite 210, Dodge

City 67801. Tel. 620-225-1231, e-mail esitz@ swkls.org.

Address correspondence to the president, Kansas Lib. Assn., 1020 S.W. Washburn, Topeka 66604. Tel. 785-580-4518, fax 785-580-4595, e-mail kansaslibraryassociation@yahoo.com.

World Wide Web http://www.kslibassoc.org.

Kentucky

Memb. 1,800. Term of Office. Oct. 2011–Oct. 2012. Publication. *Kentucky Libraries* (q.).

Pres. Terry Buckner, Learning Resource Center, Bluegrass Community and Technical College, 222B Oswald Bldg., 460 Cooper Drive, Lexington 40506. Tel. 859-246-6397, e-mail terry.buckner@kctcs.edu; *Pres.-Elect* Lisa Rice, Warren County Public Lib., 1225 State St., Bowling Green 42101. Tel. 270-781-4882 ext. 202, e-mail lisar@warrenpl.org; *Secy.* Brenda Metzger, Lone Oak H.S., 225 John E. Robinson Ave., Paducah 42003. Tel. 270-554-2920 e-mail brenda.metzger@mccracken.kyschools.us; *Past Pres.* Leoma Dunn, Thomas More College, 333 Thomas More Pkwy., Crestview Hills 41017. Tel. 859-344-3524, e-mail leoma.dunn@thomasmore.edu; *Exec. Dir.* Tom Underwood, 1501 Twilight Trail, Frankfort 40601. Tel. 502-223-5322, fax 502-223-4937, e-mail info@kylibasn.org.

Address correspondence to the executive director.

World Wide Web http://www.klaonline.org

Louisiana

Memb. 1,000+. Term of Office. July 2011–June 2012. Publication. *Louisiana Libraries* (q.). *Ed.* Vivian Solar. Tel. 225-647-8924, e-mail vsolar@state.lib.la.us.

Pres. Carla Clark. Tel. 801-223-5734, e-mail carla.clark@sirsidynix.com; *1st V.P.* Charlene Picheloup. Tel. 337-229-4701, e-mail crpeachy@yahoo.com; *2nd V.P.* Helen Curol. Tel. 337-217-4250 ext. 3101, e-mail helen.curol@cpsb.org; *Secy.* Laura-Ellen Ayres. Tel. 318-442-1858 ext. 225, e-mail lea@rpl.org; *Past Pres.* Randy Allen DeSoto. Tel. 985-651-6733, e-mail radesoto@stjohn.lib.la.us; *Exec. Dir.* Bland O'Connor. E-mail execdirector@llaonline.org.

Address correspondence to Louisiana Lib. Assn., 8550 United Plaza Blvd., Suite 1001, Baton Rouge 70809. Tel. 225-922-4642, 877-550-7890, fax 225-408-4422, e-mail office@llaonline.org.

World Wide Web http://www.llaonline.org.

Maine

Memb. 950. Publication. *MLA-to-Z* (q., online).

Pres. Andi Jackson-Darling, Falmouth Memorial Lib., 5 Lunt Rd., Falmouth 04105. Tel. 207-781-2351, e-mail mlatoznewsletter@gmail.com; *V.P./Pres.-Elect* Nissa Flanagan, Merrill Memorial Lib., 215 Main St., Yarmouth 04096. Tel. 207-846-4763; *Secy.* Leigh Hallett, Newport Public Lib., 154 Main St., Newport 04953. Tel. 207-368-2193; *Treas.* Mamie Ney, South Berwick Public Lib., P.O. Box 35, South Berwick 03908-0035. Tel. 207-384-3308; *Past Pres.* Sonja Plummer-Morgan, Mark and Emily Turner Memorial Lib., 39 Second St., Presque Isle 04769. Tel. 207-764-2571, e-mail sonjapmorgan@presqueislelibrary.org.

Address correspondence to the association, P.O. Box 634, Augusta 04332-0634. Tel. 207-441-1410.

World Wide Web http://mainelibraries.org.

Maryland

Memb. 1,100. Term of Office. July 2011–July 2012. Publication. *The Crab* (q., online). *Ed.* Annette Haldeman. E-mail annette.haldeman@mlis.state.md.us.

Pres. Lucy Holman, Univ. of Baltimore. Tel. 410-837-4333, e-mail lholman@ubalt.edu; *1st V.P./Pres.-Elect* Lynn Wheeler; *Secy.* Donna Sebly; *Treas.* Daria Parry; *Past Pres.* Glennor Shirley, Dept. of Labor, Licensing, and Regulation. Tel. 410-767-9761, e-mail gshirley@dllr.state.md.us; *Exec. Dir.* Margaret Carty. E-mail mcarty@carr.org.

Address correspondence to the association, 1401 Hollins St., Baltimore 21223. Tel. 410-947-5090, fax 410-947-5089, e-mail mla@mdlib.org.

World Wide Web http://www.mdlib.org.

Massachusetts

Memb. (Indiv.) 1,000; (Inst.) 100. Publication. *Bay State Libraries* (q.).

Pres. Ruth Urell, Reading Public Lib., 64 Middlesex Ave., Reading 01867. Tel. 781-942-6725, e-mail urell@noblenet.org; *V.P.* Dinah O'Brien, Plymouth Public Lib., 132 South St., Plymouth 02360. Tel. 508-830-4250, e-mail do'brien@townhall.plymouth.ma.us; *Secy.* Nancy Siegel Dellapenna, West Springfield Public Lib., 200 Park St., West Springfield 01089-3314. Tel. 413-736-4561, e-mail ndellape@cwmars.org; *Treas.* Bernadette D. Rivard, Bellingham Public Lib., 100 Blackstone St., Bellingham 02019. Tel. 508-966-1660, e-mail brivard@bellinghamma.org; *Past Pres.* Jacqueline Rafferty, Paul Pratt Memorial Lib., 35 Ripley Rd., Cohasset 02025. Tel. 781-383-1348, e-mail jrafferty@ocln.org; *Exec. Mgr.* Elizabeth Hacala, Massachusetts Lib. Assn., P.O. Box 535, Bedford 01730. Tel. 781-275-7729, fax 781-998-0393, e-mail mlaoffice@masslib.org.

Address correspondence to the executive manager.

World Wide Web http://www.masslib.org.

Michigan

Memb. (Indiv.) 2,000+. Publications. *Michigan Librarian Newsletter* (6 a year), *Michigan Library Association Forum* (s. ann., online).

Pres. Richard Cochran, Central Michigan Univ.; *Pres.-Elect* Lance Werner, Kent Lib. Dist.; *Treas.* Ed Repik, Howell Carnegie Dist. Lib.; *Past Pres.* Christine Berro, Portage Dist. Lib.

Address correspondence to Gretchen Couraud, Exec. Dir., Michigan Lib. Assn., 1407 Rensen St., Suite 2, Lansing 48910. Tel. 517-394-2774 ext. 224, e-mail couraudg@mlcnet.org.

World Wide Web http://www.mla.lib.mi.us.

Minnesota

Memb. 1,100. Term of Office. (Pres., Pres.-Elect) Jan.–Dec. 2012.

Pres. Carla Urban. E-mail dewey002@umn.edu; *Pres.-Elect* Kristen Mastel. E-mail meye0539@umn.edu; *Secy.* Jenny Trushenski. E-mail jjepse@tds.lib.mn.us; *Treas.* Anna Hulseberg. E-mail ahulsebe@gac.edu; *Past Pres.* Robin Ewing. E-mail rlewing@stcloudstate.edu.

Address correspondence to the association, 1821 University Ave. W., Suite S256, Saint Paul 55104. Tel. 651-999-5343, fax 651-917-1835, e-mail office@mnlibraryassociation.org.

World Wide Web http://www.mnlibrary association.org.

Mississippi

Memb. 650. Term of Office. Jan.–Dec. 2012. Publication. *Mississippi Libraries* (q.).

Pres. Stephen Cunetto, MSU-Mitchell Memorial Lib. Tel. 662-325-8542, e-mail scunetto @library.msstate.edu; *V.P./Pres.-Elect* Lynn F. Shurden, Bolivar County Lib. System. Tel. 662-843-2774 ext. 102, e-mail lshurden@bolivar.lib.ms.us; *Secy.* Patricia Matthes, MSU. Tel. 662-325-7662, e-mail pmatthes@library.msstate.edu; *Treas.* Kathy Buntin, Mississippi Lib. Commission. Tel. 601-432-4111, e-mail kbuntin@mlc.lib.ms.us; *Past Pres.* Jennifer A. Smith, Warren County–Vicksburg Public Lib. Tel. 601-636-6411, e-mail jensmith@warren.lib.ms.us; *Exec. Secy.* Mary Julia Anderson, P.O. Box 13687, Jackson 39236-3687. Tel. 601-981-4586, fax 601-981-4501, e-mail info@misslib.org or marjulia@misslib.org.

Address correspondence to the executive secretary.

World Wide Web http://www.misslib.org.

Missouri

Memb. 800+. Term of Office. Jan.–Dec. 2012. Publication. *MO INFO* (bi-mo.).

Pres. Glenda Hunt, Adair County Public Lib., 1 Library Lane, Kirksville 63501. Tel. 660-665-6038, e-mail ghunt@adairco.org; *Pres.-Elect* Carol Smith, James C. Kirkpatrick Lib., JCKL 2464, Univ. of Central Missouri, Warrensburg 64093. Tel. 660-543-8639, e-mail csmith@libserv.ucmo.edu; *Secy.* To be announced; *Treas.* Neosha Mackey, Duane G. Meyer Lib., Missouri State Univ., Springfield 65897. Tel. 417-836-4525, e-mail neoshamackey@missouristate.edu; *Past Pres.* Karen Hicklin, Trails Regional Lib., 432 N. Holden St., Warrensburg 64093. Tel. 660-747-1699, e-mail hicklink@trailslibrary.org.

Address correspondence to the president.

World Wide Web http://www.molib.org.

Montana

Memb. 600. Term of Office. July 2011–June 2012. Publication. *Focus* (bi-mo.).

Pres. Kim Crowley, Flathead County Lib. System, 247 1st Ave. E., Kalispell 59901. Tel. 406-758-5820, fax 406-758-5868, e-mail kcrowley@flathead.mt.gov; *V.P.* Anne Kish, Carson Lib., Univ. of Montana–Western, Dillon 59725. Tel. 406-683-7495, fax 406-683-7493, e-mail a_kish@umwestern.edu; *Secy./Treas.* Sarah Daviau, Lincoln County Public Libs., 220 W. 6 St., Libby 59923. Tel. 406-293-2778, fax 406-293-4235, e-mail sdaviau@lincolncountylibraries.com; *Past Pres.* Samantha Pierson, Lincoln County Public Libs., 220 W. 6 St., Libby 59427. Tel. 406-293-2778, fax 406-293-4235, e-mail spierson@lincolncountylibraries.com; *Admin. Dir.* Debra Kramer, P.O. Box 1352, Three Forks 59752. Tel. 406-285-3090, fax 406-285-3091, e-mail debkmla@hotmail.com.

Address correspondence to the administrative director.

World Wide Web http://www.mtlib.org.

Nebraska

Term of Office. Jan.–Dec. 2012.

Pres. Jan Boyer, UNO. E-mail jboyer@mail.unomaha.edu; *V.P./Pres.-Elect* Gordon Wynant, Bellevue Public Lib. E-mail gordon.wyant@bellevue.net; *Secy.* Joanne Ferguson Cavanaugh, Omaha Public Lib. E-mail jferguson@omahapubliclibrary.org; *Treas.* Barbara Hegr, Nebraska City Lib. E-mail barbarahegr@neb.rr.com; *Past Pres.* Christine Walsh, Kearney Public Lib. E-mail cwalsh@kearneygov.org; *Exec. Dir.* Michael Straatmann. E-mail nla executivedirector@gmail.com.

Address correspondence to the executive director.

World Wide Web http://www.nebraskalibraries.org.

Nevada

Memb. 450. Term of Office. Jan.–Dec. 2012. Publication. *Nevada Libraries* (q.).

Pres. Robbie DeBuff, Las Vegas-Clark County Lib. Dist. E-mail rjdebuff@hotmail.com; *V.P./Pres.-Elect* John Crockett, Washoe County Lib. System. E-mail jcrockett@washoecounty.us; *Treas.* Larry Johnson, Las Vegas-Clark County Lib. Dist. E-mail johnsonl@lvccld.org; *Past Pres.* Barbara Mathews, Churchill County Lib. E-mail blmathew@clan.lib.nv.us;

Exec. Secy. Lauren Campbell, Las Vegas-Clark County Lib. Dist. E-mail ltcampbell10@gmail.com.

Address correspondence to the executive secretary.

World Wide Web http://www.nevadalibraries.org.

New Hampshire

Memb. 700. Publication. *NHLA News* (q.).

Pres. Lori Fisher, Baker Free Lib., 509 South St., Bow 03304. Tel. 603-224-7113, e-mail bfl director@comcast.net; *V.P./Pres.-Elect* Diane Lynch, Laconia Public Lib., 695 Main St., Laconia 03246. Tel. 603-524-4775 ext. 12, e-mail dlynchlpl@metrocast.net; *Secy.* Carl Heidenblad, Nesmith Lib., 8 Fellows Rd., Windham 03087. Tel. 603-432-7154, e-mail cheidenblad@nesmithlibrary.org; *Treas.* Sean Fleming, Lebanon Public Lib., 9 E. Park St., Lebanon 03766. Tel. 603-448-2459, e-mail sean.fleming@lebcity.com; *Past Pres.* Mary White, Howe Lib., 13 South St., Hanover 03755. Tel. 603-643-4120, e-mail mary.h.white@thehowe.org.

Address correspondence to the association, c/o LGC, P.O. Box 617, Concord 03302-0617.

World Wide Web http://nhlibrarians.org.

New Jersey

Memb. 1,800. Term of Office. July 2011–June 2012. Publication. *New Jersey Libraries Newsletter* (q.).

Pres. Susan O'Neal, Middletown Twp. Public Lib., 55 New Monmouth Rd., Middletown 07748. Tel. 732-671-3703, fax 732-671-5839, e-mail soneal@mtpl.org; *V.P.* Karen Klapperstuck, Monroe Twp. Pubic Lib., 4 Municipal Plaza, Monroe Twp. 08831. Tel. 732-521-5000, fax 732-521-4766, e-mail librarykar@gmail.com; *2nd V.P.* Jayne Beline, Parsippany-Troy Hills Lib., 449 Halsey Rd., Parsippany 07054. Tel. 973-887-8907 ext. 219, fax 973-887-0062, e-mail jayne.beline@parsippanylibrary.org; *Secy.* Anne M. Wodnick, Gloucester County Lib. System, 389 Wolfert Station Rd., Mullica Hill 08062. Tel. 856-223-6010, fax 856-223-6039, e-mail awodnick@gcls.org; *Treas.* Brett Bonfield, Collingswood Public Lib., 771 Haddon Ave., Collingswood 08108. Tel. 856-858-0649, fax 856-858-5016, e-mail bonfield@collingswoodlib.org; *Past Pres.* Mary Romance,

West Orange Public Lib., 46 Mount Pleasant Ave., West Orange 07052. Tel. 973-736-0191, fax 973-324-9817, e-mail mromance@west orangelibrary.org; *Exec. Dir.* Patricia Tumulty, NJLA, P.O. Box 1534, Trenton 08607. Tel. 609-394-8032, fax 609-394-8164, e-mail ptumulty @njla.org.

Address correspondence to the executive director.

World Wide Web http://www.njla.org.

New Mexico

Memb. 550. Term of Office. Apr. 2011–Apr. 2012. Publication. *New Mexico Library Association Newsletter* (6 a year).

Pres. Mary Alice Tsosie. E-mail mtsosie@ unm.edu; *V.P.* Tina Glatz. E-mail tglatz@lcps. k12.nm.us; *Secy.* Lynette Schurdevin. E-mail lschurdevin@las-cruces.org; *Treas.* Norice Lee. E-mail nlee@nmsu.edu; *Past Pres.* Barbara Lovato. E-mail drbarbaralovato@gmail. com; *Admin.* Lorie Christian. E-mail admin@ nmla.org.

Address correspondence to the association, Box 26074, Albuquerque 87125. Tel. 505-400-7309, fax 505-891-5171, e-mail admin@nmla. org.

New York

Memb. 4,000. Term of Office. Oct. 2011–Oct. 2012. Publication. *NYLA Bulletin* (q.). *Ed.* To be announced.

Pres. Matthew Bollerman. Tel. 631-979-1600, e-mail mbollerm@suffolk.lib.ny.us; *Pres.-Elect* Carol Anne Germain. Tel. 518-442-3590, e-mail cgermain@albany.edu; *Treas.* Christine McDonald. Tel. 518-792-6508 ext. 300, e-mail mcdonald@crandalllibrary.org; *Past Pres.* Marcia Eggleston. Tel. 315-250-0352, e-mail megglest@nncsk12.org; *Interim Exec. Dir.* Jeremy Johannesen.

Address correspondence to the executive director, New York Lib. Assn., 6021 State Farm Rd., Guilderland 12084. Tel. 518-432-6952, fax 518-427-1697, e-mail director@nyla.org.

World Wide Web http://www.nyla.org.

North Carolina

Memb. 1,100. Term of Office. Oct. 2011–Oct. 2013. Publications. *North Carolina Library Association E-news* (bi-mo.). *Ed.* Marilyn Schus-

ter, Local Documents/Special Collections, Univ. of North Carolina–Charlotte. E-mail mbschust@email.uncc.edu; *North Carolina Libraries Online* (2 a year). *Ed.* Ralph Scott, Joyner Lib., East Carolina Univ., Greenville 27858. Tel. 252-328-0265, e-mail scottr@ecu. edu.

Pres. Wanda Brown, Z. Smith Reynolds Lib., Wake Forest Univ., Box 7777 Reynolda Sta., Winston-Salem 27109. Tel. 336-758-5094, e-mail brownw@wfu.edu; *V.P./Pres.-Elect* Dale Cousins, Wake County Public Libs., 1930 Clark Ave., Raleigh 27605. Tel. 919-856-6726, dale.cousins@wakegov.com; *Secy.* Eleanor Cook, Joyner Lib., East Carolina Univ., E. Fifth St., Greenville 27858. Tel. 252-328-2598, e-mail cooke@ecu.edu; *Treas.* Mary Sizemore, High Point Public Lib., 301 N. Main St., High Point 27262. Tel. 336-883-3694, e-mail mary sizemore@highpointnc.org; *Past Pres.* Sherwin Rice, Bladen Community College, P.O. Box 266, Dublin 28332. Tel. 910-879-5641, e-mail srice@bladencc.edu; *Admin. Asst.* Kim Parrott, North Carolina Lib. Assn., 1811 Capital Blvd., Raleigh 27604. Tel. 919-839-6252, fax 919-839-6253, e-mail nclaonline@gmail.com.

Address correspondence to the administrative assistant.

World Wide Web http://www.nclaonline. org.

North Dakota

Memb. (Indiv.) 317; (Inst.) 9. Term of Office. Sept. 2011–Sept. 2012. Publication. *The Good Stuff* (q.). *Ed.* Marlene Anderson, Bismarck State College Lib., Box 5587, Bismarck 58506-5587. Tel. 701-224-5578.

Pres. Aubrey Madler, Univ. of North Dakota Center for Rural Health, School of Medicine and Health Sciences, Room 4520, 501 N. Columbia Rd., Stop 9037, Grand Forks 58202-9037. Tel. 701-777-6025, e-mail aubrey.madler@med. und.edu; *Pres.-Elect* Alfred L. Peterson, North Dakota State Lib. Tel. 701-328-3495, fax 701-328-2040, e-mail alpeterson@nd.gov; *Secy.* Brianne Schmidt, Fargo Public Lib. Tel. 701-476-5978, e-mail bschmidt@cityoffargo.com; *Treas.* Michael Safratowich, Harley French Lib. of the Health Sciences, Univ. of North Dakota, Box 9002, Grand Forks 58202-9002. Tel. 701-777-2602, fax 701-777-4790, e-mail michael.safratowich@med.und.edu; *Past Pres.*

Rita Ennen, Stoxen Lib., Dickinson State Univ., 291 Campus Drive, Dickinson 58601. Tel. 701-483-2883, fax 701-483-2006, e-mail rita.ennen@dickinsonstate.edu. Address correspondence to the president. World Wide Web http://www.ndla.info.

Ohio

Memb. 2,700+. Term of Office. Jan.–Dec. 2012. Publication. *Access* (memb., weekly, online only).

Pres. Virginia Sharp March, Perry Public Lib., 3753 Main St., Perry 44081-8501. Tel. 440-259-3300, e-mail marchvi@oplin.org; *V.P./Pres.-Elect* Christine Taylor, Columbus Metropolitan Lib., 96 S. Grant Ave., Columbus 43215. Tel. 614-894-1265, e-mail ctaylor @columbuslibrary.org; *Secy./Treas.* Steve Gregory, Shawnee State Univ., 940 Second St., Portsmouth 45662. Tel. 740-351-3259, e-mail sgregory@shawnee.edu; *Past Pres.* Molly Carver, Bellevue Public Lib., 224 E. Main St., Bellevue 44811-1409. Tel. 419-483-4769 ext. 14, e-mail mcarver@bellevue.lib.oh.us; *Exec. Dir.* Douglas S. Evans. E-mail devans@olc. org.

Address correspondence to the executive director, OLC, 1105 Schrock Rd., Suite 440, Columbus 43229-1174. Tel. 614-410-8092, fax 614-410-8098, e-mail olc@olc.org.

World Wide Web http://www.olc.org.

Oklahoma

Memb. (Indiv.) 1,000; (Inst.) 60. Term of Office. July 2011–June 2012. Publication. *Oklahoma Librarian* (bi-mo.).

Pres. Cheryl Suttles; *V.P./Pres.-Elect* Sarah Robbins; *Secy.* Jane Long; *Treas.* Tim Miller; *Past Pres.* Leslie Langley; *Exec. Dir.* Kay Boies, 300 Hardy Drive, Edmond 73013. Tel. 405-525-5100, fax 405-525-5103, e-mail kboies@ sbcglobal.net.

Address correspondence to the executive director.

World Wide Web http://www.oklibs.org.

Oregon

Memb. (Indiv.) 1,000+. Publications. *OLA Hotline* (bi-w.), *OLA Quarterly.*

Pres. Abigail Elder, Tualatin Public Lib. E-mail aelder@ci.tualatin.or.us; *V.P./Pres.-Elect*

To be announced; *Secy.* Arlene Weible, Oregon State Lib. E-mail arlene.weible@state.or.us; *Treas.* Liisa Sjoblom, Deschutes Public Lib. E-mail liisas@deschuteslibrary.org; *Past Pres.* Robert Everett, Springfield Public Lib. E-mail reverett@ci.springfield.or.us.

Address correspondence to Oregon Lib. Assn., P.O. Box 3067, La Grande 97850. Tel. 541-962-5824, e-mail olaweb@olaweb.org.

World Wide Web http://www.olaweb.org.

Pennsylvania

Memb. 1,900+. Term of Office. Jan.–Dec. 2012. Publication. *PaLA Bulletin* (10 a year).

Pres. Debbie Malone, DeSales Univ. Tel. 610-282-1100 ext. 253, e-mail debbie.malone@desales.edu; *1st V.P.* Paula Gilbert, Martin Lib. Tel. 717-846-5300, e-mail pgilbert@ yorklibraries.org; *2nd V.P./Conference Chair* Karla Trout, Palmyra Public Lib. Tel. 717-838-1347, e-mail ktrout@lclibs.org; *3rd V.P./Membership Chair* Jeff Swope, Dauphin County Lib. System. Tel. 717-234-4961, e-mail jswope @dcls.org; *Treas.* David Schappert, Moravian College. Tel. 610-861-1540; *Past Pres.* Robin Lesher, Adams County Lib. System. Tel. 717-334-5716, e-mail robinl@adamslibrary.org; *Exec. Dir.* Glenn R. Miller, Pennsylvania Lib. Assn., 220 Cumberland Pkwy., Suite 10, Mechanicsburg 17055. Tel. 717-766-7663, fax 717-766-5440, e-mail glenn@palibraries.org.

Address correspondence to the executive director.

World Wide Web http://www.palibraries. org.

Rhode Island

Memb. (Indiv.) 350+; (Inst.) 50+. Term of Office. June 2011–June 2013. Publication. *RILA Bulletin.*

Pres. Eileen Dyer, Cranston Public Lib., 140 Sockanossett Cross Rd., Cranston 02920. Tel. 401-943-9080 ext. 119, e-mail president@ rilibraryassoc.org; *V.P./Pres.-Elect* Jenifer Bond, Douglas and Judith Krupp Lib., Bryant Univ., Smithfield 02917. Tel. 401-232-6299, e-mail vicepresident@rilibraryassoc.org; *Secy.* Adrienne Gallo. Tel. 401-942-1787, e-mail secretary@rilibraryassoc.org; *Treas.* Patricia Schultz. Tel. 401-232-6296, e-mail treasurer@ rilibraryassoc.org; *Past Pres.* Laura Marlane,

Providence Community Lib., South Providence Lib., 441 Prairie Ave., Providence 02905. Tel. 401-467-2700 ext. 1610, e-mail pastpresident@rilibraries.org.

Address correspondence to Rhode Island Library Assn., P.O. Box 6765, Providence 02940.

World Wide Web http://www.rilibraries.org.

South Carolina

Memb. 350+. Term of Office. Jan.–Dec. 2012. Publication. *News and Views.*

Pres. Yvonne Davis, Rogers Lib., Francis Marion Univ., P.O. Box 100547, Florence 29502. Tel. 843-661-1303, e-mail ydavis@fmarion.edu; *1st V.P./Pres.-Elect* Jonathan Newton, Sarah Dobey Jones Branch, Greenville Public Lib., 11 N. Hwy. 25 Bypass, Greenville 29617. Tel. 864-246-1695, fax 864-246-1765, e-mail jnewton@greenvillelibrary.org; *2nd V.P.* Edward Rock, Clemson Univ. Libs., Box 343001, Clemson 29643. Tel. 864-656-1879, fax 864-656-7608, e-mail erock@clemson.edu; *Secy.* Todd Rix, Charles W. and Joan S. Coker Lib., 300 E. College Ave., Hartsville 29550. Tel. 843-383-8270, fax 843-383-8129, e-mail trix@coker.edu; *Treas.* Crystal L. Johnson. Richland County Public Lib., 1431 Assembly St., Columbia 29201-3101. Tel. 803-929-3400, fax 803-929-3476, e-mail cjohnson@myRCPL. com; *Past Pres.* Adam Haigh, Jackson Lib., Lander Univ., 320 Stanley Ave., Greenwood 29649. Tel. 864-388-8029, fax 864-388-8816, e-mail ahaigh@lander.edu; *Exec. Secy.* Donald Wood, SCLA, P.O. Box 1763, Columbia 29202. Tel. 803-252-1087, fax 803-252-0589. E-mail scla@capconsc.com.

Address correspondence to the executive secretary.

World Wide Web http://www.scla.org.

South Dakota

Memb. (Indiv.) 462; (Inst.) 67. Term of Office. Oct. 2011–Oct. 2012. Publication. *Book Marks* (q.).

Pres. Annie Brunskill, Haakon County Public Lib., Phillip. E-mail library@gwtc.net; *V.P./ Pres.-Elect* Jan Brue Enright, Augustana College Lib., Sioux Falls. E-mail jenright@augie. edu; *Recording Secy.* Kathy Jacobs, Yankton Community Lib. E-mail kjacobs@sdln.net;

Past Pres. Kay Christensen, Augustana College Lib., Sioux Falls. E-mail kay.christensen@augie.edu; *Exec. Secy./Treas.* Laura G. Olson. E-mail sdlaest@gmail.com.

Address correspondence to the executive secretary, SDLA, 28363 472nd Ave., Worthing 57077-5722. Tel. 605-372-0235, e-mail sdlaest @gmail.com.

World Wide Web http://www.sdlibraryasso-ciation.org.

Tennessee

Memb. 600+. Term of Office. July 2011–June 2012. Publications. *Tennessee Libraries* (q.), *TLA Newsletter* (bi-mo.). Both online only at http://www.tnla.org.

Pres. Wendy Cornelisen. E-mail wendy. cornelisen@gmail.com; *V.P./Pres.-Elect* Dinah Harris. E-mail library@bellsouth.net; *Recording Secy.* Christi Underdown-DuBois. E-mail cunderdown@gmail.com; *Past Pres.* Susan Earl. E-mail earls@brentwood-tn.org; *Exec. Dir.* Annelle R. Huggins, Tennessee Lib. Assn., Box 241074, Memphis 38124. Tel. 901-485-6952, e-mail arhuggins1@comcast.net.

Address correspondence to the executive director.

World Wide Web http://tnla.org.

Texas

Memb. 7,600+. Term of Office. Apr.–Apr. Publications. *Texas Library Journal* (q.), *TLACast* (9 a year).

Pres. Jerilynn A. Williams, Montgomery County Lib. System. E-mail jeri.williams@countylibrary.org; *Pres.-Elect* Sherilyn Bird, Texas Woman's Univ.; *Treas.* Jesús Campos, South Texas College; *Past Pres.* Maribel Castro, Lubbock ISD; *Exec. Dir.* Patricia H. Smith, TXLA, 3355 Bee Cave Rd., Suite 401, Austin 78746-6763. Tel. 512-328-1518, fax 512-328-8852, e-mail pats@txla.org or tla@txla.org.

Address correspondence to the executive director.

World Wide Web http://www.txla.org.

Utah

Memb. 650. Publication. *Utah Libraries News* (bi-mo.) (online at http://www.ula.org/newsletter).

Pres. Linda Tillson, Park City Lib., P.O. Box 668, Park City 84060. Tel. 435-615-5605, e-mail ltillson@parkcity.org; *V.P./Pres.-Elect* Adriane Juarez, Salt Lake City Public Lib., Sprague Branch Lib., 2131 South 1100 East, Salt Lake City 84106. Tel. 801-594-8643, fax 801-322-8183, e-mail ajuarez@slcpl.org; *Recording Secy.* Trish Hull, Magna Branch, Salt Lake County Lib. Services, 8339 West 3500 South, Magna 84044. Tel. 801-944-7626, fax 801-250-6927, e-mail phull@slcolibrary.org; *Treas. (acting)* Javaid Lal. E-mail jlal@slcolibrary.org; *Past Pres.* Andy Spackman, Harold B. Lee Lib., Brigham Young Univ., 1212 HBLL, Provo 84602. Tel. 801-422-3924, e-mail andy_spackman@byu.edu; *Exec. Dir.* Anna Neatrour, No. 101, 845 E. 100 S., Salt Lake City 84102. Tel. 801-200-3129, e-mail anna.neatrour@gmail.com.

Address correspondence to the executive director.

World Wide Web http://www.ula.org.

Vermont

Memb. 400. Publication. *VLA News* (6 a year). *Pres.* Joseph Farara, Willey Lib., Johnson State College, 337 College Hill, Johnson 05656. Tel. 802-635-1272, e-mail joseph.farara@jsc.edu; *V.P./Pres.-Elect* Deborah Gadwah-Lambert, Alice M. Ward Memorial Lib., P.O. Box 134, Canaan 05903. Tel. 802-266-7135, e-mail deborahlle@yahoo.com; *Secy.* Heidi Steiner, Kreitzberg Lib., Norwich Univ., 158 Harmon Drive, Northfield 05663. Tel. 802-485-2171, e-mail hsteiner@norwich.edu; *Treas.* Wynne Browne, Downs Rachlin Martin, St. Johnsbury 05819-0099. Tel. 802-473-4216, e-mail wbrowne@drm.com; *Past Pres.* Marti Fiske, Dorothy Alling Memorial Lib., 21 Library Lane, Williston 05495. Tel. 802-878-4918, e-mail marti@williston.lib.vt.us.

Address correspondence to VLA, Box 803, Burlington 05402.

World Wide Web http://www.vermontlibraries.org.

Virginia

Memb. 900+. Term of Office. Oct. 2011–Oct. 2012. Publication. *Virginia Libraries* (q.). *Pres.* Connie Gilman, Chinn Park Regional Lib., 13065 Chinn Park Drive, Prince William 22192. Tel. 703-792-6199, e-mail cgilman@pwcgov.org; *V.P./Pres.-Elect* Lisa Lee Brough-

man, Randolph College, 2500 Rivermont Ave., Lynchburg 24503. Tel. 434-947-8481, e-mail llee@randolphcollege.edu; *2nd V.P.* Mark Lenker, Longwood Univ., 201 High St., Farmville 23909. Tel. 434-395-257, e-mail lenkermn@longwood.edu; *Secy.* Diane Adkins, Pittsylvania County Public Lib., 24 Military Drive, Chatham 24531. Tel. 434-432-3271; *Treas.* Maryke Barber, Hollins Univ. Lib., P.O. Box 9000, Roanoke 24020. Tel. 540-362-6328, e-mail mbarber@hollins.edu; *Past Pres.* Matthew Todd, NOVA, 3001 N. Beauregard St., Alexandria 22331. Tel. 703-845-6033, e-mail mtodd@nvcc.edu; *Exec. Dir.* Lisa Varga, P.O. Box 56312, Virginia Beach 23456. Tel. 757-689-0594, fax 757-447-3478, e-mail vla.lisav@cox.net.

Address correspondence to the executive director.

World Wide Web http://www.vla.org.

Washington

Memb. 750+. Term of Office. Apr. 2011–Apr. 2013. Publication. *Alki: The Washington Library Association Journal* (3 a year). *Ed.* Bo Kinney, Seattle Public Lib., 1000 Fourth Ave., Seattle 98104. E-mail alkieditor@wla.org.

Pres. Brian Soneda, Mount Vernon City Lib., 315 Snoqualmie St., Mount Vernon 98273. Tel. 360-336-6209, e-mail brians@ci.mount-vernon.wa.us; *V.P./Pres.-Elect* Jennifer Wiseman, King County Lib. System, P.O. Box 199, Snoqualmie 98068. Tel. 425-369-3221, e-mail jlwiseman@kcls.org; *Secy/Treas.* Phil Heikkinen, Orcas Island Public Lib., 500 Rose St., Eastsound 98245. Tel. 360-376-2308, e-mail pheikkinen@orcaslibrary.org; *Exec. Dir.* Dana Murphy-Love, WLA, 23607 Hwy. 99, Suite 2-C, Edmonds 98026. Tel. 425-967-0739, fax 425-771-9588, e-mail dana@wla.org.

Address correspondence to the executive director.

World Wide Web http://www.wla.org.

West Virginia

Memb. 650+. Publication. *West Virginia Libraries* (6 a year). *Ed.* Pam Coyle, Martinsburg Public Lib., 101 W. King St., Martinsburg 25401. Tel. 304-267-8933, fax 304-267-9720, e-mail pcoyle@martin.lib.wv.us.

Pres. Crystal Hamrick, Bridgeport Public Lib., 1200 Johnson Ave., Bridgeport 26330. Tel. 304-842-8248, e-mail chamrick@bridgeport wv.com; *1st V.P./Pres.-Elect* Myra Ziegler, Summers County Public Lib., 201 Temple St., Hinton 25951. Tel. 304-466-4490, e-mail zieglm@mail.mln.lib.wv.us; *2nd V.P.* Christine P. Lewis, Marshall Univ. Libs., 1 John Marshall Drive, Huntington 25755. Tel. 304-696-4356, fax 304-696-5228, e-mail lewis47@marshall. edu; *Secy.* Angela Strait, Cabell County Public Lib., 455 9th St., Huntington 25701. Tel. 304-528-5700, fax 304-528-5701, e-mail angela. strait@cabell.lib.wv.us; *Treas.* Brian E. Raitz, Parkersburg and Wood County Public Lib., 3100 Emerson Ave., Parkersburg 26104-2414. Tel. 304-420-4587 ext. 11, fax 304-420-4589, e-mail raitzb@park.lib.wv.us.

Address correspondence to the president. World Wide Web http://www.wvla.org.

Wisconsin

Memb. 1,900. Term of Office. Jan.–Dec. Publication. *WLA Newsletter* (q.).

Pres. Ron McCabe, McMillan Memorial Lib., 490 E. Grand Ave., Wisconsin Rapids 54494-4898. E-mail rmccabe@wctc.net; *Pres.-Elect* Paula Ganyard, Cofrin Lib., Univ. of Wisconsin–Green Bay. E-mail ganyardp@uwgb. edu; *Secy.* Tasha Saecker, Elisha D. Smith Public Lib., 440 First St., Menasha 54952-3191. E-mail saecker@menashalibrary.org; *Treas.* Jan Berg, DeForest Public Lib., 203 Library St., DeForest 53532. E-mail bergjd@scls.lib. wi.us; *Past Pres.* Rhonda K. Puntney, Lakeshores Lib. System, 725 Cornerstone Crossing, Suite C, Waterford 53185. E-mail rpuntney@ lakeshores.lib.wi.us; *Exec. Dir.* Lisa K. Strand, Wisconsin Lib. Assn., 4610 S. Biltmore Lane, Suite 100, Madison 53718-2153. Tel. 608-245-3640, fax 608-245-3646, e-mail strand@scls. lib.wi.us.

Address correspondence to the association. World Wide Web http://www.wla.lib.wi.us.

Wyoming

Memb. 450+. Term of Office. Oct. 2011–Oct. 2012.

Pres. Sukey Hohl, Sublette County Lib. Tel. 307-367-4114, fax 307-367-6722, e-mail shohl@sublettecountylibrary.org; *V.P.* Debbie McCarthy, Coe Lib., Univ. of Wyoming. Tel. 307-766-4228, e-mail mccarthy@uwyo.edu; *Past Pres.* Sue Knesel, Campbell County Public Lib. System. Tel. 307-687-9229, fax 307-686-4009, e-mail sknesel@will.state.wy.us; *Exec. Secy.* Laura Grott, Box 1387, Cheyenne 82003. Tel. 307-632-7622, fax 307-638-3469, e-mail grottski@aol.com.

Address correspondence to the executive secretary. World Wide Web http://www.wyla.org.

Canada

Alberta

Memb. 500. Term of Office. May 2011–Apr. 2012. Publication. *Letter of the LAA* (q.).

Pres. Pat Sandercock, Univ. of Calgary. E-mail president@laa.ca or psandercock@shaw. ca; *1st V.P.* Diane Clark, 5-02A Cameron Lib., Univ. of Alberta Libs., Edmonton T6G 2J8. E-mail 1stvicepresident@laa.ca; *2nd V.P.* Linda Williams, Edmonton Public Lib. E-mail lwilliams@epl.ca; *Treas.* Julia Reinhart, Alberta Lib. E-mail jreinhart@thealbertalibrary. ab.ca; *Past Pres.* Mary Jane Bilsland, Edmonton Public Lib. E-mail mjbilsland@epl.ca; *Exec. Dir.* Christine Sheppard, 80 Baker Crescent N.W., Calgary T2L 1R4. Tel. 403-284-5818, fax 403-282-6646, e-mail info@laa.ca.

Address correspondence to the executive director. World Wide Web http://www.laa.ca.

British Columbia

Memb. 750+. Term of Office. April 2011–April 2012. Publication. *BCLA Browser* (online at http://bclabrowser.ca). *Ed.* Leanna Jantzi.

Pres. Christopher Kevlahan, Vancouver Public Lib., 7110 Kerr St., Vancouver, BC V5S 4W2. Tel. 604-665-3955, e-mail christopher. kevlahan@vpl.ca; *V.P./Pres.-Elect* June Stockdale, Nelson Municipal Lib. E-mail jstockdale @nelson.ca; *2nd V.P.* Heather Morrison, Simon Fraser Univ. E-mail heatherm@eln.bc.ca; *Treas.* Debbie Schachter, Douglas College. E-mail schachterd@douglascollege.ca; *Past Pres.* Marjorie Mitchell, Univ. of British Columbia, Okanagan, 3333 University Way, Kelowna V1V 1V7. Tel. 250-807-9147, fax 250-807-

8057, e-mail marjorie.mitchell@ubc.ca; *Exec. Dir.* Annette DeFaveri. E-mail execdir@bcla.bc.ca.

Address correspondence to the association, 900 Howe St., Suite 150, Vancouver V6Z 2M4. Tel. 604-683-5354, e-mail office@bcla.bc.ca. World Wide Web http://www.bcla.bc.ca.

Manitoba

Memb. 500+. Term of Office. May 2011–May 2012. Publication. *Newsline* (mo.).

Pres. Emma Hill Kepron, Elizabeth Dafoe Lib., Winnipeg. Tel. 204-474-6710, e-mail emma_kepron@umanitoba.ca; *V.P.* Alex Homanchuk, Univ. of Winnipeg Lib., 515 Portage Ave., Winnipeg R3B 2E9. Tel. 204-786-9940, e-mail a.homanchuk@uwinnipeg.ca; *Secy.* Katherine Penner, Elizabeth Dafoe Lib., Univ. of Manitoba, Winnipeg R3T 2N2. Tel. 204-474-6846, e-mail katherine_penner@umanitoba.ca; *Treas.* Kathy Rusnak, Univ. of Manitoba Libs., Winnipeg R3T 2N2. Tel. 204-474-8858, fax 204-474-7581, e-mail kathy_rusnak@umanitoba.ca; *Past Pres.* Sherri Vokey, Neil John Maclean Health Sciences Lib., 770 Bannatyne Ave., Winnipeg R3B 0W3. Tel. 204-789-3344, e-mail sherri_vokey@umanitoba.ca.

Address correspondence to the association, 606-100 Arthur St., Winnipeg R3B 1H3. Tel. 204-943-4567, e-mail manitobalibrary@gmail.com.

World Wide Web http://www.mla.mb.ca.

Ontario

Memb. 5,200+. Publications. *Access* (q.); *Teaching Librarian* (3 a year).

Pres. Karen McGrath, Niagara College Libs. E-mail kmcgrathniagara@gmail.com; *V.P./Pres.-Elect* Susanna Hubbard Krimmer, London Public Lib. E-mail susanna.krimmer@lpl.london.on.ca; *Treas.* Paul Takala, Hamilton Public Lib. E-mail ptakala@hpl.ca; *Past Pres.* Tanis Fink, Seneca College Libs. E-mail tanis.fink@senecac.on.ca; *Exec. Dir.* Shelagh Paterson. E-mail spaterson@accessola.com.

Address correspondence to the association, 50 Wellington St. E., Suite 201, Toronto M5E 1C8. Tel. 416-363-3388, fax 416-941-9581, e-mail info@accessola.com.

World Wide Web http://www.accessola.com.

Quebec

Memb. (Indiv.) 100+. Term of Office. May 2011–April 2012. Publication. *ABQLA Bulletin* (3 a year).

Pres. Julie-Anne Cardella; *V.P.* Luigina Vileno; *Secy.* Margaret Goldik; *Exec. Secy./Treas.* Janet Ilavsky, P.O. Box 1095, Pointe-Claire H9S 4H9. Tel. 514-697-0146, e-mail abqla@abqla.qc.ca; *Past Pres.* Anne Wade.

Address correspondence to the executive secretary.

World Wide Web http://www.abqla.qc.ca.

Saskatchewan

Memb. 200+. Publication. *Forum* (q.).

Pres. Amber Christensen, Prince of Wales Branch, Regina Public Lib., P.O. Box 2311, Regina S4P 3Z5. Tel. 306-777-6140, e-mail msamberdawn@gmail.com; *V.P.* Robert G. Thomas, Dr. John Archer Lib., Univ. of Regina, 3737 Wascana Pkwy., Regina S4S 0A2. Tel. 306-585-4398, e-mail robert.thomas@uregina.ca; *Treas.* Elgin Bunston, Provincial Lib. and Literacy Office, Ministry of Educ., 409A Park St., Regina S4N 5B2. Tel. 306-787-2355, fax 306-787-2029, e-mail elgin.bunston@gov.sk.ca; *Exec. Dir.* Loraine Thompson, Saskatchewan Lib. Assn., 2010 Seventh Ave., No. 15, Regina S4R 1C2. Tel. 306-780-9413, fax 306-780-9447, e-mail slaexdir@sasktel.net.

Address correspondence to the executive director.

World Wide Web http://www.saskla.ca.

Regional

Atlantic Provinces: N.B., N.L., N.S., P.E.I.

Memb. (Indiv.) 300+; (Inst.) 26. Publications. *APLA Bulletin* (5 a year).

Pres. Jocelyne Thompson, Univ. of New Brunswick Libs. Tel. 506-458-7053, e-mail jlt@unb.ca; *V.P./Pres.-Elect* Lou Duggan, Patrick Power Lib., Saint Mary's Univ. Tel. 902-420-5534, e-mail lou.duggan@smu.ca; *V.P., Membership* Ann Smith, Vaughan Memorial Lib., Acadia Univ., Wolfville, NS B4P 2R6. Tel. 902-585-1723, fax 902-585-1748, e-mail apla_executive@yahoo.ca; *Secy.* Debbie Costelo, Nova Scotia Community College.

Tel. 902-491-1031, fax 902-491-1292, e-mail debbie.costelo@nscc.ca; *Treas.* Bill Slauenwhite, Novanet, 1550 Bedford Hwy., Suite 501, Bedford, NS B4A 1E6. Tel. 902-453-2461, fax 902-453-2369, e-mail bill.slauenwhite@novanet.ns.ca; *Past Pres.* Sarah Gladwell, Saint John Free Public Lib. Tel. 506-643-7224, e-mail sarah.gladwell@gnb.ca.

Address correspondence to Atlantic Provinces Lib. Assn., c/o School of Info. Mgt., Faculty of Mgt., Kenneth C. Rowe Mgt. Bldg., 6100 University Ave., Halifax, NS B3H 3J5. World Wide Web http://www.apla.ca.

Mountain Plains: Ariz., Colo., Kan., Mont., Neb., Nev., N.Dak., N.M., Okla., S.Dak., Utah, Wyo.

Memb. 820. Term of Office. May 2011–May 2012. Publications. *MPLA Newsletter* (bi-mo.). *Ed./Advertising Mgr.* Judy Zelenski, 14293 W. Center Drive, Lakewood, CO 80228. Tel. 303-985-7795, e-mail editor@mpla.us.

Pres. Dana Braccia, Scottsdale Public Lib. System, 3839 N. Drinkwater Blvd., Scottsdale, AZ 85258. Tel. 480-312-7949, fax 480-312-7993, e-mail dbraccia@scottsdaleaz.gov or president@mpla.us; *Pres.-Elect* JaNae Kinikin, Stewart Lib., Weber State Univ., 2901 University Circle, Ogden, UT 84408-2901. Tel. 801-626-6093, fax 801-626-8521, e-mail vice president@mpla.us; *Recording Secy.* Royce Kitts, Washburn Univ. Lib., 1700 S.W. College Ave., Topeka, KS 66621. Tel. 785-670-1010, e-mail secretary@mpla.us; *Past Pres.* Elvita Landau, Brookings Public Lib., 515 Third St., Brookings, SD 57006. Tel. 605-692-9407, fax 605-692-9386, e-mail elandau@sdln.net; *Exec. Secy.* Judy Zelenski, 14293 W. Center Drive, Lakewood, CO 80228. Tel. 303-985-7795, e-mail execsecretary@mpla.us.

Address correspondence to the executive secretary.

World Wide Web http://www.mpla.us.

New England: Conn., Maine, Mass., N.H., R.I., Vt.

Memb. (Indiv.) 700. Term of Office. Nov. 2011–Oct. 2012. Publication. *NELA News* (online, mo.).

Pres. Mary Ann List, Portsmouth Public Lib., 175 Parrott Ave., Portsmouth, NH 03801.

Tel 603-766-1719, e-mail president@nela1.org; *V.P.* Deborah Kelsey, Medfield Public Lib, 468 Main St., Medfield, MA 02052. Tel. 508-359-4544, e-mail vicepresident@nela1.org; *Secy.* Kirsten Corbett, Lane Memorial Lib., 2 Academy Ave., Hampton, NH 03842. Tel. 603-926-3368, fax 603-926-1348, e-mail secretary@nela1.org; *Treas.* Karen Patterson, 83 Elizabeth St., South Windsor, CT 08074. E-mail treasurer@nela1.org; *Past Pres.* Jen Alvino Leo, Walker Memorial Lib., 800 Main St., Westbrook, ME 04092. Tel. 207-854-0630, e-mail pastpresident@nela1.org; *Exec. Mgr.* Mary Ann Rupert, 31 Connor Lane, Wilton, NH 03086. Tel. 603-654-3533, fax 603-654-3526, e-mail executivemanager@nela1.org.

Address correspondence to the executive manager.

World Wide Web http://www.nelib.org.

Pacific Northwest: Alaska, Idaho, Mont., Ore., Wash., Alberta, B.C.

Memb. (Active) 170+. Term of Office. Aug.–Aug. Publication. *PNLA Quarterly. Ed.* Mary Bolin, 322B Love Lib., Univ. of Nebraska, P.O. Box 881140, Lincoln, NE 68588-4100. Tel. 402-472-4281, e-mail mbolin2@unlnotes.unl.edu.

Pres. Michael Burris, Public Lib. Inter-LINK, 7252 Kingsway, Burnaby, BC V5E 1G3. Tel. 604-517-8441, fax 604-517-8410, e-mail michael.burris@interlinklibraries.ca; *1st V.P./Pres.-Elect* Heidi Chittim, Eastern Washington Univ. Libs., 100 LIB, 816 F St., Cheney, WA 99004-2453. Tel. 509-359-2303, fax 509-359-2476, e-mail hchittim@ewu.edu; *2nd V.P.* Jason Openo, Edmonton Public Lib., 145 Whitemud Crossing Shopping Centre, 4211 106th St., Edmonton, AB T6J 6L7. Tel. 780-496-8348, e-mail jopeno@epl.ca; *Secy.* Darlene Hert, Montana State Univ.–Billings. E-mail dhert@msubillings.edu; *Treas.* Katie Cargill, Eastern Washington Univ. Libs., 816 F St., Cheney, WA 99004. Tel. 509-359-2385, fax 509-359-2476, e-mail kcargill@mail.ewu.edu; *Past Pres.* Samantha Hines, Univ. of Montana Mansfield Lib., Missoula, MT 59812. Tel. 406-243-4558, e-mail samantha.hines@umontana.edu.

Address correspondence to the president, Pacific Northwest Lib. Assn.

World Wide Web http://www.pnla.org.

Southeastern: Ala., Ark., Fla., Ga., Ky., La., Miss., N.C., S.C., Tenn., Va., W.Va.

Memb. 500. Publication. *The Southeastern Librarian (SELn)* (q.). *Ed.* Perry Bratcher, *SELn* Editor, 503A Steely Lib., Northern Kentucky Univ., Highland Heights, KY 41099. Tel. 859-572-6309, fax 859-572-6181, e-mail bratcher@nku.edu.

Pres. Michael Seigler, Smyrna Public Lib., 100 Village Green Circle, Smyrna, GA 30080. Tel. 770-431-2860, fax 770-431-2862, e-mail m.seigler@ci.smyrna.ga.us; *V.P.* Gordon N. Baker. E-mail gordonbaker@mail.clayton.edu; *Secy.* Camille McCutcheon. E-mail cmccutcheon@uscupstate.edu; *Treas.* Beverly James. E-mail bjames@greenvillelibrary.org; *Past Pres.* Kathleen R. T. Imhoff, 3617 Gloucester Drive, Lexington, KY 40510. Tel. 859-225-9310, e-mail kathleenrtimhoff@gmail.com.

Address correspondence to Southeastern Lib. Assn., Admin. Services, P.O. Box 950, Rex, GA 30273-0950. Tel. 770-961-3520, fax 770-961-3712.

World Wide Web http://sela.jsu.edu.

State and Provincial Library Agencies

The state library administrative agency in each of the U.S. states will have the latest information on its state plan for the use of federal funds under the Library Services and Technology Act (LSTA). The directors and addresses of these state agencies are listed below.

Alabama

Rebecca Mitchell, Dir., Alabama Public Lib. Service, 6030 Monticello Drive, Montgomery 36130-6000. Tel. 334-213-3901, fax 334-213-3993, e-mail rmitchell@apls.state.al.us. World Wide Web http://statelibrary.alabama.gov/Content/Index.aspx.

Alaska

Linda S. Thibodeau, State Libn. and Dir., Alaska Dept. of Educ., Div. of Libs., Archives, and Museums, P.O. Box 110571, Juneau 99811. Tel. 907-465-2911, fax 907-465-2151, e-mail linda.thibodeau@alaska.gov. World Wide Web http://library.state.ak.us.

Arizona

Janet Fisher, Acting State Libn., Arizona State Lib., Archives, and Public Records, Rm. 200, 1700 W. Washington, Phoenix 85007. Tel. 602-926-4035, fax 602-256-7983, e-mail jfisher@lib.az.us. World Wide Web http://www.lib.az.us.

Arkansas

Carolyn Ashcraft, State Libn., Arkansas State Lib., 900 W. Capitol, Suite 100, Little Rock 72201-3108. Tel. 501-682-1526, fax 501-682-1899, e-mail carolyn@library.arkansas.gov. World Wide Web http://www.asl.lib.ar.us.

California

Stacey Aldrich, State Libn., California State Lib., P.O. Box 942837, Sacramento 94237. Tel. 916-654-0174, fax 916-654-0064, e-mail saldrich@library.ca.gov. World Wide Web http://www.library.ca.gov.

Colorado

Eugene Hainer, Dir. and State Libn., Colorado State Lib., Rm. 309, 201 E. Colfax Ave., Denver 80203-1799. Tel. 303-866-6733, fax 303-866-6940, e-mail hainer_g@cde.state.co.us. World Wide Web http://www.cde.state.co.us/cdelib.

Connecticut

Kendall F. Wiggin, State Libn., Connecticut State Lib., 231 Capitol Ave., Hartford 06106. Tel. 860-757-6510, fax 860-757-6503, e-mail kwiggin@cslib.org. World Wide Web http://www.cslib.org.

Delaware

Annie Norman, State Libn. and Dir., Delaware Div. of Libs., 121 Duke of York St., Dover 19901. Tel. 302-739-4748 ext. 5126, fax 302-739-8436, e-mail annie.norman@state.de.us. World Wide Web http://www.state.lib.de.us.

District of Columbia

Ginnie Cooper, Chief Libn., District of Columbia Public Lib., 901 G St. N.W., Suite 400, Washington 20001-4599. Tel. 202-727-1101, fax 202-727-1129, e-mail ginnie.cooper@dc.gov. World Wide Web http://www.dclibrary.org.

Florida

Judith A. Ring, State Libn., Div. of Lib. and Info. Services, R. A. Gray Bldg., 500 S. Bronough St., Tallahassee 32399-0250. Tel. 850-245-6600, fax 850-245-6282, e-mail judith.ring@dos.myflorida.com. World Wide Web http://dlis.dos.state.fl.us/stlib.

Georgia

Lamar Veatch, State Libn., Georgia Public Lib. Services, 1800 Century Place N.E., Suite 150, Atlanta 30345-4304. Tel. 404-235-7200, fax 404-235-7201, e-mail lveatch@georgialibraries.org. World Wide Web http://www.georgialibraries.org.

Hawaii

Richard Burns, State Libn., Hawaii State Public Lib. System, 44 Merchant St., Honolulu 96813. Tel. 808-586-3704, fax 808-586-3715, e-mail richard.burns@librarieshawaii.org. World Wide Web http://www.librarieshawaii.org.

Idaho

Ann Joslin, State Libn., Idaho Commission for Libs., 325 W. State St., Boise 83713-6072. Tel. 208-334-2150 ext. 134, fax 208-334-4016, e-mail ann.joslin@libraries.idaho.gov. World Wide Web http://libraries.idaho.gov.

Illinois

Anne Craig, Dir., Illinois State Lib., 300 S. 2 St., Springfield 62701-1703. Tel. 217-782-2994, fax 217-785-4326, e-mail acraig@ilsos.net. World Wide Web http://www.cyber driveillinois.com/departments/library/home. html.

Indiana

Roberta L. Brooker, Dir. and State Libn., Indiana State Lib., 140 N. Senate Ave., Indianapolis 46204. Tel. 317-232-3693, fax 317-232-3713, e-mail rbrooker@library.in.gov. World Wide Web http://www.in.gov/library.

Iowa

Mary Wegner, State Libn., State Lib. of Iowa, 1112 E. Grand Ave., Des Moines 50319. Tel. 515-281-4105, fax 515-281-6191, e-mail mary. wegner@lib.state.ia.us. World Wide Web http:// www.statelibraryofiowa.org.

Kansas

Jo Budler, State Libn., Capitol Bldg., Rm. 343N, 300 S.W. 10 Ave., Topeka 66612-1593. Tel. 785-506-4563, fax 785-368-7291, e-mail jo.budler@library.ks.gov. World Wide Web http://skyways.org/KSL.

Kentucky

Wayne Onkst, State Libn. and Commissioner, Kentucky Dept. for Libs. and Archives, P.O. Box 537, Frankfort 40602-0537. Tel. 502-564-8300 ext. 312, fax 502-564-5773, e-mail wayne.onkst@ky.gov. World Wide Web http:// www.kdla.ky.gov.

Louisiana

Rebecca Hamilton, State Libn., State Lib. of Louisiana, P.O. Box 131, Baton Rouge 70821-0131. Tel. 225-342-4923, fax 225-219-4804, e-mail rhamilton@crt.la.gov. World Wide Web http://www.state.lib.la.us.

Maine

Linda Lord, State Libn., Maine State Lib., 64 State House Sta., Augusta 04333-0064. Tel. 207-287-5600, fax 207-287-5624, e-mail linda. lord@maine.gov. World Wide Web http://www. maine.gov/msl.

Maryland

Irene Padilla, Asst. State Superintendent for Libs., State Dept. of Educ., Div. of Lib. Development and Services, 200 W. Baltimore St., Baltimore 21201. Tel. 410-767-0435, fax 410-333-2507, e-mail ipadilla@msde.state.md.us. World Wide Web http://www.marylandpublic schools.org/MSDE/divisions/library.

Massachusetts

Robert Maier, Dir., Massachusetts Board of Lib. Commissioners, 98 N. Washington St., Suite 401, Boston 02114-1933. Tel. 617-725-1860, fax 617-725-0140, e-mail robert.maier@ state.ma.us. World Wide Web http://mblc.state. ma.us.

Michigan

Nancy R. Robertson, State Libn., Lib. of Michigan, 702 W. Kalamazoo St., P.O. Box 30007, Lansing 48909-7507. Tel. 517-373-5511, fax 517-373-4480, e-mail robertsonn@michigan. gov. World Wide Web http://www.michigan. gov/libraryofmichigan.

Minnesota

Nancy K. Walton, State Libn. and Dir., Minnesota State Lib. Agency, Div. of State Lib. Services, Dept. of Educ., 1500 Hwy. 36 W., Roseville 55113-4266. Tel. 651-582-8881, fax 651-582-8752, e-mail nancy.walton@state.mn.us. World Wide Web http://education.state.mn.us/

MDE/learning_support/library_services/
index.html.

Mississippi

Sharman Bridges Smith, Exec. Dir., Mississippi Lib. Commission, 3881 Eastwood Drive, Jackson 39211. Tel. 601-432-4039, fax 601-432-4480, e-mail sharman@mlc.lib.ms.us. World Wide Web http://www.mlc.lib.ms.us.

Missouri

Margaret Conroy, State Libn., Missouri State Lib., P.O. Box 387, Jefferson City 65102-0387. Tel. 573-526-4783, fax 573-751-3612, e-mail margaret.conroy@sos.mo.gov. World Wide Web http://www.sos.mo.gov/library.

Montana

Jennie Stapp, State Libn., Montana State Lib., 1515 E. 6 Ave., P.O. Box 201800, Helena 59620-1800. Tel. 406-444-4799, fax 406-444-0266, e-mail jstapp2@mt.gov. World Wide Web http://msl.mt.gov.

Nebraska

Rodney G. Wagner, Dir., Nebraska Lib. Commission, Suite 120, The Atrium, 1200 N St., Lincoln 68508-2023. Tel. 402-471-4001, fax 402-471-2083, e-mail rod.wagner@nebraska.gov. World Wide Web http://www.nlc.state.ne.us.

Nevada

Daphne DeLeon, State Lib. and Archives Admin., Nevada State Lib. and Archives, 100 N. Stewart St., Carson City 89701-4285. Tel. 775-684-3315, fax 775-684-3311, e-mail ddeleon@admin.nv.gov. World Wide Web http://www.nevadaculture.org/docs/nsla.

New Hampshire

Michael York, State Libn., New Hampshire State Lib., 20 Park St., Concord 03301-6314. Tel. 603-271-2397, fax 603-271-6826, e-mail michael.york@dcr.nh.gov. World Wide Web http://www.nh.gov/nhsl.

New Jersey

Norma E. Blake, State Libn., New Jersey State Lib., P.O. Box 520, 185 W. State St., Trenton 08625-0520. Tel. 609-278-2640, fax 609-278-2652, e-mail nblake@njstatelib.org. World Wide Web http://www.njstatelib.org.

New Mexico

Devon Skeele, State Libn., New Mexico State Lib., 1209 Camino Carlos Rey, Santa Fe 87507. Tel. 505-476-9762, fax 505-476-9761, e-mail devon.skeele@state.nm.us. World Wide Web http://www.nmstatelibrary.org.

New York

Bernard Margolis, State Libn. and Assistant Commissioner for Libs., New York State Lib., Room 10C34, Cultural Educ. Center, Empire State Plaza, Albany 12230. Tel. 518-474-5930, fax 518-486-6880, e-mail bmargolis@mail.nysed.gov. World Wide Web http://www.nysl.nysed.gov.

North Carolina

Caroline "Cal" Shepard, State Libn., State Lib. of North Carolina, 4640 Mail Service Center, Raleigh 27699-4640. Tel. 919-807-7410, fax 919-733-8748, e-mail cal.shepard@ncdcr.gov. World Wide Web http://statelibrary.ncdcr.gov.

North Dakota

Hulen Bivins, State Libn., North Dakota State Lib., 604 E. Boulevard Ave., Bismarck 58505-0800. Tel. 701-328-4654, fax 701-328-2040, e-mail hbivins@nd.gov. World Wide Web http://www.library.nd.gov.

Ohio

Beverly Cain, State Libn., State Lib. of Ohio, Suite 100, 274 E. 1 Ave., Columbus 43201. Tel. 614-644-6843, fax 614-466-3584, e-mail bcain@library.ohio.gov. World Wide Web http://www.library.ohio.gov.

Oklahoma

Susan C. McVey, Dir., Oklahoma Dept. of Libs., 200 N.E. 18 St., Oklahoma City 73105-

3298. Tel. 405-522-3173, fax 405-521-1077, e-mail smcvey@oltn.odl.state.ok.us. World Wide Web http://www.odl.state.ok.us.

Oregon

MaryKay Dahlgreen, State Libn., Oregon State Lib., 250 Winter St. N.E., Salem 97301. Tel. 503-378-5012, fax 503-585-8059, e-mail marykay.dahlgreen@state.or.us. World Wide Web http://oregon.gov/OSL.

Pennsylvania

Alice Lubrecht, Interim Deputy Secy. of Educ., Office of Commonwealth Libs., 607 South Drive, Harrisburg 17120-0600. Tel. 717-783-5968, fax 717-772-8268, e-mail alubrecht@pa.gov. World Wide Web http://www.education.state.pa.us/portal/server.pt/community/commonwealth_libraries/7225.

Rhode Island

Howard Boksenbaum, Chief Lib. Officer, Rhode Island Office of Lib. and Info. Services, 1 Capitol Hill, 4th flr., Providence 02908-5803. Tel. 401-574-9301, fax 401-574-9320, e-mail howard.boksenbaum@olis.ri.gov. World Wide Web http://www.olis.ri.gov.

South Carolina

David S. Goble, Agency Dir. and State Libn., South Carolina State Lib., 1430 Senate St., P.O. Box 11469, Columbia 29211. Tel. 803-734-8656, fax 803-734-8676, e-mail dgoble@statelibrary.sc.gov. World Wide Web http://www.statelibrary.sc.gov.

South Dakota

Dan J. Siebersma, State Libn., South Dakota State Lib., 800 Governors Drive, Pierre 57501-2294. Tel. 605-773-3131, fax 605-773-6962, e-mail dan.siebersma@state.sd.us. World Wide Web http://sdstatelibrary.com.

Tennessee

Charles Sherrill, State Libn. and Archivist, Tennessee State Lib. and Archives, 403 Seventh Ave. N., Nashville 37243-0312. Tel. 615-741-7996, fax 615-532-9293, e-mail chuck.sherrill@tn.gov. World Wide Web http://www.tennessee.gov/tsla.

Texas

Peggy D. Rudd, Dir. and Libn., Texas State Lib. and Archives Commission, P.O. Box 12927, Austin 78711-2927. Tel. 512-463-5460, fax 512-463-5436, e-mail prudd@tsl.state.tx.us. World Wide Web http://www.tsl.state.tx.us.

Utah

Donna Jones Morris, Dir. and State Libn., Utah State Lib. Div., Suite A, 250 N. 1950 W., Salt Lake City 84116. Tel. 801-715-6770, fax 801-715-6767, e-mail dmorris@utah.gov. World Wide Web http://library.utah.gov.

Vermont

Martha Reid, State Libn., Vermont Dept. of Libs., 109 State St., Montpelier 05609. Tel. 802-828-3265, fax 802-828-2199, e-mail martha.reid@state.vt.us. World Wide Web http://libraries.vermont.gov.

Virginia

Sandra Treadway, Libn. of Virginia, Lib. of Virginia, 800 E. Broad St., Richmond 23219-8000. Tel. 804-692-3535, fax 804-692-3594, e-mail sandra.treadway@lva.virginia.gov. World Wide Web http://www.lva.virginia.gov.

Washington

Rand Simmons, Acting State Libn., Washington State Lib., P.O. Box 42460, Tumwater 98504. Tel. 360-570-5585, fax 360-586-7575, e-mail rand.simmons@sos.wa.gov. World Wide Web http://www.sos.wa.gov/library.

West Virginia

Karen Goff, Dir./State Libn., West Virginia Lib. Commission, Cultural Center, 1900 Kanawha Blvd. E., Charleston 25305. Tel. 304-558-2041, fax 304-558-2044, e-mail karen.e.goff@wv.gov. World Wide Web http://librarycommission.lib.wv.us.

Wisconsin

Kurt Kiefer, State Libn., Div. for Libs., Technology, and Community Learning, Dept. of Public Instruction, P.O. Box 7841, Madison 53707. Tel. 608-266-2205, fax 608-266-8770, e-mail kurt.kiefer@dpi.wi.gov. World Wide Web http://dpi.wi.gov/dltcl/index.html.

Wyoming

Lesley Boughton, State Libn., Wyoming State Lib., 2800 Central Ave., Cheyenne 82002. Tel. 307-777-5911, fax 307-777-5920, e-mail lesley.boughton@wyo.gov. World Wide Web http://www.will.state.wy.us.

American Samoa

Cheryl Polataivao, Territorial Libn., Feleti Barstow Public Lib., P.O. Box 997687, Pago Pago, AS 96799. Tel./fax 684-633-5816, e-mail feletibarstow@yahoo.com. World Wide Web http://fbpl.org.

Federated States of Micronesia

Rufino Mauricio, Secy., National Archives, Culture, and Historic Preservation, P.O. Box PS 175, Palikir, Pohnpei, FM 96941. Tel. 691-320-2643, fax 691-320-5634, e-mail hpo@mail.fm. World Wide Web http://www.fsmgov.org.

Guam

Sandra Stanley, Admin. Officer, Guam Public Lib. System, 254 Martyr St., Hagatna 96910-5141. Tel. 671-475-4765, fax 671-477-0888, e-mail sandra.stanley@gpls.guam.gov. World Wide Web http://gpls.guam.gov.

Northern Mariana Islands

John Oliver Gonzales, Exec. Dir., CNMI Joeten-Kiyu Public Lib., P.O. Box 501092, Saipan, MP 96950-1092. Tel. 670-235-7322, fax 670-235-7550, e-mail jcpl.admin@gmail.com. World Wide Web http://www.cnmilibrary.com.

Palau

Sinton Soalablai, Minister of Educ., Republic of Palau, P.O. Box 7080, Koror, PW 96940. Tel. 680-488-2570, fax 680-488-2830, e-mail ssoalablai@palaumoe.net. World Wide Web http://www.palaugov.net/palaugov/executive/ministries/MOE/MOE.htm.

Puerto Rico

Sandra Castro, Dir., Lib. and Info. Services Program, Puerto Rico Dept. of Educ., P.O. Box 190759, San Juan 00919-0759. Tel. 787-773-3564, fax 787-753-6945, e-mail castroas @de.gobierno.pr. World Wide Web http://de.gobierno.pr/deportal/escuelas/bibliotecas/bibliotecarios.aspx.

Republic of the Marshall Islands

Newton Lajuan, Dir., Alele Museum and Public Lib., P.O. Box 629, Majuro, MH 96960. Tel. 692-625-3372, fax 692-625-3226, e-mail alele_inc@ntamar.net. World Wide Web http://rmigovernment.org/index.jsp.

Virgin Islands

Ingrid A. Bough, Territorial Dir. of Libs., Archives, and Museums, 1122 Kings St., Christiansted, St. Croix 00820. Tel. 340-773-5715, fax 340-773-5327, e-mail ingrid.bough@dpnr.gov.vi. World Wide Web http://www.virginislandspubliclibraries.org/usvi.

Canada

Alberta

Diana Davidson, Dir., Public Lib. Services Branch, Alberta Municipal Affairs, 803 Standard Life Centre, 10405 Jasper Ave., Edmonton T5J 4R7. Tel. 780-427-4871, fax 780-415-8594, e-mail diana.davidson@gov.ab.ca or libraries@gov.ab.cam. World Wide Web http://www.municipalaffairs.alberta.ca/mc_libraries.cfm.

British Columbia

Jacqueline van Dyk, Dir., Public Lib. Services Branch, Ministry of Educ., 605 Robson St., Suite 850, Vancouver V6B 5J3. Tel. 250-356-1791, fax 250-953-3225, e-mail jacqueline.vandyk@gov.bc.ca. World Wide Web http://www.bced.gov.bc.ca/pls.

Manitoba

Trevor Surgenor, Dir., Public Lib. Services, Manitoba Dept. of Culture, Heritage, and Tourism, 300-1011 Rosser Ave., Brandon R7A OL5. Tel. 204-726-6590, e-mail pls@gov.mb.ca. World Wide Web http://www.gov.mb.ca/chc/pls/index.html.

New Brunswick

Sylvie Nadeau, Exec. Dir., New Brunswick Public Lib. Service, Place 2000, 250 King St., P.O. Box 6000, Fredericton E3B 5H1. Tel. 506-453-7141, fax 506-444-4064, e-mail sylvie.nadeau@gnb.ca. World Wide Web http://www.gnb.ca/0003/index-e.asp.

Newfoundland and Labrador

Shawn Tetford, Exec. Dir., Provincial Info. and Lib. Resources Board, 48 St. George's Ave., Stephenville A2N 1K9. Tel. 709-643-0902, fax 709-643-0925, e-mail stetford@nlpl.ca. World Wide Web http://www.nlpl.ca.

Northwest Territories

Alison Hopkins, Territorial Libn., NWT Lib. Services, 75 Woodland Drive, Hay River X0E 1G1. Tel. 867-874-6531, fax 867-874-3321, e-mail alison_hopkins@gov.nt.ca. World Wide Web http://www.nwtpls.gov.nt.ca.

Nova Scotia

Jennifer Evans, Dir., Nova Scotia Provincial Lib., 2021 Brunswick St., P.O. Box 578, Halifax B3J 2S9. Tel. 902-424-2457, fax 902-424-0633, e-mail evansjl@gov.ns.ca. World Wide Web http://www.library.ns.ca.

Nunavut

Ron Knowling, Mgr., Nunavut Public Lib. Services, Box 270, Baker Lake X0C 0A0. Tel. 867-793-3353, fax 867-793-3360, e-mail rknowling@gov.nu.ca. World Wide Web http://www.publiclibraries.nu.ca.

Ontario

Michael Chan, Minister, Ontario Government Ministry of Tourism, Culture, and Sport, Hearst Block, 900 Bay St., Toronto M7A 2E1. Tel. 416-326-9326. World Wide Web http://www.ontario.ca/en/your_government/009887.html.

Ontario Lib. Service–North, 334 Regent St., Sudbury P3C 4E2. Tel. 705-675-6467. World Wide Web http://www.olsn.ca. Joyce Cunningham, Chair.

Southern Ontario Lib. Service, 111 Peter St., Suite 902, Toronto M5V 2H1. Tel. 416-961-1669 ext. 5118. World Wide Web http://www.sols.org. Brenda Carrigan, Chair.

Prince Edward Island

Public Lib. Service of Prince Edward Island, P.O. Box 7500, Morell C0A 1S0. Tel. 902-961-7320, fax 902-961-7322, e-mail plshq@gov.pe.ca. World Wide Web http://www.library.pe.ca/index.php3?lang=E.

Quebec

Guy Berthiaume, Chair and CEO, Bibliothèque et Archives Nationales du Québec (BAnQ), 2275 rue Holt, Montreal H2G 3H1. Tel. 800-363-9028 or 514-873-1100, fax 514-873-9312, info@banq.qc.ca. World Wide Web http://www.banq.qc.ca/portal/dt/accueil.jsp.

Saskatchewan

Brett Waytuck, Provincial Libn., Provincial Lib. and Literacy Office, Ministry of Educ., 409A Park St., Regina S4N 5B2. Tel. 306-787-2972, fax 306-787-2029, e-mail brett.waytuck@gov.sk.ca. World Wide Web http://www.education.gov.sk.ca/provincial-library.

Yukon Territory

Julie Ourom, Dir., Public Libs., Community Development Div., Dept. of Community Services, Box 2703, Whitehorse Y1A 2C6. Tel. 867-667-5447, fax 867-393-6333, e-mail julie.ourom@gov.yk.ca. World Wide Web http://www.ypl.gov.yk.ca.

State School Library Media Associations

Alabama

Children's and School Libns. Div., Alabama Lib. Assn. Memb. 650. Publication. *The Alabama Librarian* (q.).

Chair Jana Fine, Tuscaloosa Public Lib., 1801 Jack Warner Pkwy., Tuscaloosa 35401. Tel. 205-391-9025, e-mail jfine@tuscaloosalibrary.org; *V. Chair/Chair-Elect* Carolyn Jo Starkey, Buckhorn H.S., 25 Warren Rd., Albertville 35950. Tel. 256-302-1009, e-mail admin @jojo-starkey.com.

Address correspondence to the association administrator, Alabama Lib. Assn., 9154 Eastchase Pkwy., Suite 418, Montgomery 36117. Tel. 334-414-0113, e-mail admin@allanet.org. World Wide Web http://allanet.org.

Alaska

Alaska Assn. of School Libns. Memb. 130. Publication. *The Puffin* (3 a year), online at http://puffin.akasl.org. *Ed.* Piper Coulter, Ocean View Elementary. E-mail pcoulter@ acsalaska.net.

Pres. Robin Turk, Palmer. E-mail rturk@ matsuk12.us; *Pres.-Elect* Nicole Roohi, Anchorage. E-mail roohi_nicole@asdk12.org; *Secy.* Kari Sagel, Sitka. E-mail sagelk@mail. ssd.k12.ak.us; *Treas.* Kerri Geppert, Anchorage. E-mail geppert_kerri@asdk12.org; *Past Pres.* Ann Morgester, Anchorage. E-mail morgester_ ann@asdk12.org.

World Wide Web http://www.akasl.org.

Arizona

Teacher-Libn. Div., Arizona Lib. Assn. Memb. 1,000. Publication. *AZLA Newsletter.*

Chair Tanya Molina, Centerra Mirage Elementary School. E-mail tmolina@avondale. k12.az.us; *Past Co-Chairs* Jean Kilker, Maryvale H.S., Kerrlita Westrick, Verrado Middle School.

Address correspondence to the chairperson. World Wide Web http://www.azla.affiniscape. com.

Arkansas

Arkansas Assn. of School Libns., Div. of Arkansas Lib. Assn.

Chair Cathy Toney, Sally Cone Elementary, 1629 South Blvd., Conway 72034. Tel. 501-450-4835, e-mail toneyc@conwayschools.net; *V. Chair* Tracy McAllister, Bob Courtway Middle School, 1200 Bob Courtway Drive, Conway 72032. Tel. 501-450-4832, e-mail mcallistert@ conwayschools.net; *Past Chair* Devona Pendergrass, Mountain Home H.S., 149 Brushy Knob Trail, Mountain Home 72653. Tel. 870-425-2541, e-mail dpendergrass@mtnhome. k12.ar.us.

Address correspondence to the president. World Wide Web http://www.arlib.org/ organization/aasl/index.php.

California

California School Lib. Assn. Memb. 1,200+. Publications. *CSLA Journal* (2 a year). *Ed.* Marilyn Robertson. E-mail mnroberts@earthlink.net; *CSLA Newsletter* (10 a year).

Pres. Pam Oehlman, Polytechnic H.S., 1600 Atlantic Ave., Long Beach 90813. Tel. 562-400-6422, pjoehlman@aol.com; *Pres.-Elect* Jane Lofton, Mira Costa H.S., 1401 Artesia Blvd., Manhattan Beach 90266. E-mail jane@ lofton.com; *Secy.* Nina Jackson, Franklin Classical Middle School, 540 Cerritos Ave., Long Beach 90802. E-mail njcatsandbooks@gmail. com; *Treas.* Sandra Patton, Lakewood H.S., 3461 Lilly Ave., Long Beach 90808-3214. Tel. 562-997-8000 ext. 3129, e-mail sgpatton@ lbschools.net; *Past Pres.* Diane Alexander, 540 Discovery Bay Blvd., Discovery Bay 94505. Tel. 925-634-5456, e-mail dapa@comcast.net.

Address correspondence to the association at 950 Glenn Drive, Suite 150, Folsom 95630. Tel. 916-447-2684, fax 916-447-2695, e-mail info@csla.net.

World Wide Web http://www.csla.net.

Colorado

Colorado Assn. of School Libns. Memb. 260+.

Becky Johnson, Mesa County Valley School District 51. E-mail caslprez@gmail.com; *Pres.-Elect* Christine Schein, Academy 20 Dist., Colorado Springs. E-mail christine.schein@asd20. org; *Secy.* Molly Gibney, Mount View Elementary. E-mail mgibney@comcast.net; *Past Pres.* Yvonne Miller, Douglas County Schools. E-mail yvonne.miller@dcsdk12.org; *Business Admin.* Catherine Spatz, Colorado Assn. of School Libns., 3030 W. 81 Ave., Westminster 80031. Tel. 303-433-4446, fax 303-458-0002, e-mail cal@cal-webs.org.

World Wide Web http://cal-webs.org/CASL_.html.

Connecticut

Connecticut Assn. of School Libns. (formerly Connecticut Educ. Media Assn.). Memb. 500+. Term of Office. July 2011–June 2012.

Pres. Jacqueline Galante. E-mail jgalante@fairfield.k12.ct.us; *V.P.* Sara Kelley-Mudie. E-mail sara.kelley-mudie@formanschool.org; *Recording Secy.* Christopher Barlow. E-mail christophbarlow@sbcglobal.net; *Treas.* Martha Djang. E-mail mdjang@hamdenhall.org; *Admin. Secy.* Anne Weimann, 25 Elmwood Ave., Trumbull 06611. Tel. 203-372-2260, e-mail anneweimann@gmail.com.

Address correspondence to the administrative secretary.

World Wide Web http://www.ctcasl.com.

Delaware

Delaware School Lib. Assn., div. of Delaware Lib. Assn. Memb. 100+. Publications. *DSLA Newsletter* (online; irreg.); column in *DLA Bulletin* (3 a year).

Pres. Ed Hockersmith, Delcastle Technical H.S., 1417 Newport Rd., Wilmington 19804. Tel. 302-995-8100, e-mail charles.hockersmith@nccvt.k12.de.us.

Address correspondence to the president.

World Wide Web https://sites.google.com/site/delawaresla.

District of Columbia

District of Columbia Assn. of School Libns. Memb. 8. Publication. *Newsletter* (4 a year).

Pres. André Maria Taylor. E-mail divalibrarian2@aol.com; *V.P.* To be announced.

Address correspondence to André Maria Taylor, 330 10th St. N.E., Washington, DC 20002. Tel. 301-502-4203.

Florida

Florida Assn. for Media in Educ. Memb. 1,400+. Term of Office. Nov. 2011–Oct. 2012. Publication. *Florida Media Quarterly. Ed.* Rhoda Cribbs. E-mail rcribbs@pasco.k12.fl.us.

Pres. Lou Greco. E-mail grecol@stjohns.k12.fl.us; *Pres.-Elect* Cora Dunkley. E-mail cdunkley@usf.edu; *Secy.* Deborah McNeil. E-mail Debora.mcneil@ocps.net; *Treas.* Lorri Cosgrove. E-mail cosgrol@stjohns.k12.fl.us; *Past Pres.* Pat Dedicos. E-mail dedicosp@duvalschools.org; *Exec. Dir.* Larry E. Bodkin, Jr. Tel. 850-531-8351, fax 850-531-8344, e-mail lbodkin@floridamedia.org.

Address correspondence to FAME, 1876-B Eider Court, Tallahassee 32308. Tel. 850-531-8351, fax 850-531-8344, e-mail info@floridamedia.org.

World Wide Web http://www.floridamedia.org.

Georgia

School Lib. Media Div., Georgia Lib. Assn.

Chair Stephanie Jones, Georgia Southern Univ. College of Education, P.O. Box 8131, Statesboro 30460-8131. Tel. 912-478-5250, e-mail sjones@georgiasouthern.edu; *Chair-Elect* To be announced; *Past Chair* Tim Wojcik, Our Lady of Mercy Catholic H.S. Tel. 770-461-2202, e-mail wojcikt@bellsouth.net.

Address correspondence to School Lib. Media Div., Georgia Lib. Assn., P.O. Box 793, Rex, GA 30273.

World Wide Web http://gla.georgialibraries.org/div_media.htm.

Georgia Lib. Media Assn. Memb. 700+.

Pres. Valerie Ayer. E-mail valerie_ayer@dekalb.k12.ga.us; *Pres.-Elect* Betsy Razza. E-mail betsy_razza@dekalb.k12.ga.us; *Secy.* Ann Schaub. E-mail schaub@fulton.k12.ga.us; *Treas.* Nan Brown. E-mail brownnt@fulton.k12.ga.us; *Past Pres.* Susan Grigsby. E-mail susan.grigsby@gmail.com; *Exec. Dir.* Lasa Joiner.

Address correspondence to GLMA Executive Office, 2711 Irvin Way, Suite 111, Decatur 30030. Tel. 404-299-7700, e-mail glma@jlhconsulting.com.

World Wide Web http://www.glma-inc.org.

Hawaii

Hawaii Assn. of School Libns. Memb. 145. Term of Office. June 2011–May 2012. Publication. *HASL Newsletter* (3 a year).

Co-Pres. Lynette Kam, Diane Mokuau; *V.P., Programming* Michelle Colte; *V.P., Membership* Denise Sumida; *Corresponding Secy.* Donna Takara; *Recording Secy.* Ruby Redona; *Treas.* Jo-An Ishida; *Past Pres.* Debbie Lum.

Address correspondence to the association, P.O. Box 235284, Honolulu 96823.

World Wide Web http://hasl.ws.

Idaho

Educational Media Div., Idaho Lib. Assn. Memb. 44.

Chair Dennis Hahs, Rocky Mountain H.S., 5450 N. Linder Rd., Meridian 83646. Tel. 208-350-4340 ext. 1530, e-mail hahs.dennis@meridianschools.org; *Past Chair* Glynda Pflieger, Melba School Dist., 6870 Stokes Lane, P.O. Box 185, Melba 83641. Tel. 208-495-2221, e-mail gpflieger@melbaschools.org.

Address correspondence to the chairperson.

World Wide Web http://www.idaholibraries.org/node/94.

Illinois

Illinois School Lib. Media Assn. Memb. 1,050. Term of Office. July 2011–June 2012. Publications. *ISLMA News* (4 a year); *Linking for Learning: The Illinois School Library Media Program Guidelines* (3rd ed., 2010); *Powerful Libraries Make Powerful Learners: The Illinois Study.*

Pres. Sarah Hill, Paris Cooperative H.S., 309 S. Main St., Paris 61944. Tel. 217-466-1175, fax 217-466-1903, e-mail president@islma.org; *Pres.-Elect* Christine Graves, Jefferson Middle School, 1151 Plum St., Aurora 60506. Tel. 630-301-5320, fax 630-844-5711, e-mail cgraves@sevarg.net; *Secy.* Jennifer Bromann-Bender, Lincoln-Way West H.S. E-mail bromannj@hotmail.com; *Past Pres.* Jeremy Dunn, Chicago Public Schools Dept. of Libs. E-mail jldunn2@gmail.com; *Exec. Secy.* Kay Maynard, ISLMA, P.O. Box 598, Canton 61520. Tel. 390-649-0911, fax 309-649-0916, e-mail islma@islma.org.

World Wide Web http://www.islma.org.

Indiana

Assn. of Indiana School Library Educators (AISLE). Publications. *Focus on Indiana Libraries* (mo.); *Indiana Libraries* (q.).

Pres. Denise Keogh, Tipton Middle School, 817 S. Main St., Tipton 46072. Tel. 765-675-7521 ext. 225, e-mail dkeogh@tcsc.k12.in.us; *Pres.-Elect* Leslie Sutherlin, South Dearborn Middle School/H.S., 5850 Squire Place, Aurora 47001. Tel. 812-926-6298, e-mail leslie.sutherlin@sdcsc.k12.in.us; *Secy.* Susie Highley, Creston Middle School, 10925 E. Prospect, Indianapolis 46239. Tel. 812-532-6806, fax 812-532-6891, e-mail shighley@warren.k12.in.us; *Treas.* Kris Borrelli, Yost Elementary, 100 W. Beam St., Chesterton 46304. Tel. 219-983-3640, e-mail kristen.borrelli@duneland.k12.in.us; *Past Pres.* Lael Dubois, Plainfield H.S., 709 Stafford Rd., Plainfield 46168. Tel. 317-839-7711 ext. 1212, fax 317-838-3682, e-mail ldubois@plainfield.k12.in.us.

Address correspondence to the association, c/o Indiana Lib. Federation, 941 E. 86 St., Suite 260, Indianapolis 46240. Tel. 317-257-2040, fax 317-257-1389, e-mail ilf@indy.net.

World Wide Web http://www.ilfonline.org/units/aisle.

Iowa

Iowa Assn. of School Libns., Subdivision of the Iowa Lib. Assn. Memb. 180+. Term of Office. Jan.–Jan. Publication. *IASL Journal* (online, 4 a year). *Eds.* Karla Krueger. E-mail karla.krueger@uni.edu; Becky Johnson. E-mail bcjohnson@cr.k12.ia.us.

Pres. Becky Johnson, Jefferson H.S., Cedar Rapids. E-mail bcjohnson@cr.k12.ia.us; *V.P./Pres.-Elect* Susan Feuerbach, Commanche CSD. E-mail susan.feuerbach@comanche.k12.ia.us; *Secy./Treas.* To be announced; *Past Pres.* Erin Feingold, Marshalltown CSD. E-mail efeingold@marshalltown.k12.ia.us.

Address correspondence to the president.

World Wide Web http://www.iasl-ia.org.

Kansas

Kansas Assn. of School Libns. Memb. 600. Publication. *KASL News* (online; q.).

Pres. Juanita Jameson. Tel. 620-805-8412, e-mail juanitajameson@cox.net; *Pres.-Elect* Gwen Lehman. Tel. 620-285-8430, e-mail gwen.lehman@usd495.net; *Secy.* Jane Maresch. Tel. 785-309-4544, e-mail jane.maresch@usd305.com; Diane Leupold. Tel. 785-295-3941, e-mail dleupold@topeka.k12.ks.us; *Past Pres.* Debbi Maddy. Tel. 913-422-5121, e-mail maddyd@usd204.net; *Exec. Secy.* Barb Bahm. Tel. 913-845-2627, e-mail bbahm@tong464.org.

Address correspondence to the executive secretary.

World Wide Web http://kasl.typepad.com/kasl.

Kentucky

Kentucky School Media Assn., Section of the Kentucky Lib. Assn. Memb. 600+. Publication. *KSMA Newsletter* (q.).

Pres. Tara Griffith, W. R. McNeill Elementary School, 1800 Creason Drive, Bowling Green 42101. E-mail tara.griffith@bgreen.ky schools.us; *Pres.-Elect* Adele Koch, St. Patrick School, 1000 N. Beckley Station Rd., Louisville 40245. E-mail akoch@stpatrick-lou.org; *Secy.* Fred Tilsley, Sandgap Elementary. E-mail fred.tilsley@jackson.kyschools.us; *Past Pres.* Brenda Metzger, Lone Oak H.S., 225 John E. Robinson Ave., Paducah 42003. E-mail brenda.metzger@mccracken.kyschools.us.

Address correspondence to the president.

World Wide Web http://www.kysma.org.

Louisiana

Louisiana Assn. of School Libns. Memb. 230. Term of Office. July 2011–June 2012.

Pres. Paula Clemmons. E-mail pclemmons @episcopaldayschool.org; *1st V.P.* Cathy Smith. E-mail csmith@caddo.k12.la.us; *2nd V.P.* Amanda Graves. E-mail agraves@catholichigh. org; *Secy.* Janet Lathrop. E-mail lathropj@wfpsb.org.

Address correspondence to the association, c/o Louisiana Lib. Assn., 8550 United Plaza Blvd., Suite 1001, Baton Rouge 70809. Tel.

225-922-4642, fax 225-408-4422, e-mail office @llaonline.org.

World Wide Web http://www.llaonline.org/sig/lasl, wiki http://lasl2.wikispaces.com.

Maine

Maine School Lib. Assn. Memb. 230+.

Pres. Eileen Broderick. E-mail ebroderick@rus10.org; *V.P.* Joyce Lucas; *Secy.* Tina Taggart. E-mail tina.taggart@staff.foxcroft academy.org; *Treas.* Dorothy Hall-Riddle. E-mail hall-riddled@rsu5.org; *Past Pres.* Peg Becksvoort, Falmouth Middle School. E-mail pbecksvoort@falmouthschools.org; *Business Mgr.* Edna Comstock. E-mail empoweredna@gwi.net.

Address correspondence to the president.

World Wide Web http://www.maslibraries. org.

Maryland

Maryland Assn. of School Libns. (formerly Maryland Educ. Media Organization).

Pres. Michele Forney, High Bridge Elementary, Prince Georges County Public Schools. E-mail michele.forney@pgcps.org; *Pres.-Elect* To be announced; *Secy.* Lori M. Carter, Howard County Public Schools. E-mail lori_carter @hcpss.org; *Treas.* Jennifer Harner, Rising Sun Elementary, Cecil County Public Schools. E-mail jharner@ccps.org; *Past Pres.* Elizabeth Napier, North Carroll H.S. E-mail eanapie@k12.carr.org.

Address correspondence to the association, Box 21127, Baltimore 21228.

World Wide Web http://maslmd.org.

Massachusetts

Massachusetts School Lib. Assn. Memb. 800. Publication. *MSLA Forum* (3 a year, 1 in print, 2 online).

Pres. Valerie Diggs, Chelmsford H.S. Tel. 978-251-5111; *Past Pres.* Gerri Fegan, High Plain Elementary School, Andover. Tel. 978-623-8914, e-mail feganpkt@comcast.net; *Secy.* Judi Paradis, Plympton Elementary School, Waltham. Tel. 781-314-5767, e-mail judiparadis @gmail.com; *Treas.* Linda Friel. E-mail lafriel @comcast.net; *Exec. Dir.* Kathy Lowe, Massachusetts School Lib. Assn., P.O. Box 658,

Lunenburg 01462. Tel. 978-582-6967, e-mail klowe@maschoollibraries.org.

Address correspondence to the executive director.

World Wide Web http://www.maschoollibraries.org.

Michigan

Michigan Assn. for Media in Educ. Memb. 1,200. Publications. *Media Spectrum* (2 a year); *MAME Newsletter* (6 a year).

Pres. Sue Lay, Birmingham School Dist., 1300 Derby Rd., Birmingham 48009. Tel. 248-203-5068, e-mail bookwoman0122@ sbcglobal.net; *Pres.-Elect* Thomas Stream, Grand Haven Area Public Schools, 1050 Pennoyer Ave., Grand Haven 49417. Tel. 616-850-5322, fax 616-850-5310, e-mail tom.stream@ gmail.com; *Secy.* Jeanna Walker, Portage Public Schools, 1000 Idaho St., Portage 49024. Tel. 269-926-3525, e-mail jwalker@portageps.org; *Treas.* Bruce Popejoy, East Jackson Community Schools, 4340 Walz Rd., Jackson 49201. Tel. 517-764-6010, e-mail mameexhibits@aol. com; *Past Pres.* Rachel Markel, Bangor Public Schools, 309 S. Walnut St., Bangor 49013. Tel. 269-427-6800, e-mail rmarkel@bangor vikings.org; *Exec. Dir.* Tim Staal, MAME, 1407 Rensen, Suite 3, Lansing 48910. Tel. 517-394-2808, fax 517-394-2096, e-mail tstaal@ gmail.com.

Address correspondence to the executive director.

World Wide Web http://www.mame.gen. mi.us.

Minnesota

Minnesota Educ. Media Organization. Memb. 832. Term of Office. July 2011–July 2012. Publication. *MEMOrandom.*

Pres. Sally Mays, Robbinsdale Spanish Immersion School, 8808 Medicine Lake Rd., New Hope 55427. Tel. 763-504-4408, e-mail sally_ mays@rdale.org; *Pres.-Elect* Dhaivyd Hilgendorf, Park Center Senior H.S., 7300 Brooklyn Blvd., Brooklyn Park 55443. Tel. 763-569-7629, e-mail memodhaivyd@gmail.com; *Secy.* Mary Mehsikomer, TIES, 1667 Snelling Ave. N., St. Paul 55108. Tel. 651-999-6510, e-mail mary. mehsikomer@ties.k12.mn.us; *Treas.* Laura Gudmundson, Kingsland Public School, 705

North Section Ave., Spring Valley 55975. E-mail lauragud79@gmail.com; *Past Pres.* Tori Jensen, LEAP H.S. Tel. 651-483-1064, e-mail sunbear.t@gmail.com; *Admin. Asst.* Deanna Sylte, P.O. Box 130555, Roseville 55113. Tel. 651-771-8672, e-mail admin@memoweb.org.

World Wide Web http://memoweb.org.

Mississippi

School Section, Mississippi Lib. Assn. Memb. 1,300.

Co-Chairs Susan Sparkman, Rowan Middle School. Tel. 601-960-5349, e-mail ssparkman @jackson.k12.ms.us; Venetia Oglesby, New Hope Elementary. Tel. 662-244-4769, e-mail venetia.oglesby@lowndes.k12.ms.us; *Exec. Secy.* Mary Julia Anderson.

Address correspondence to School Section, Mississippi Lib. Assn., P.O. Box 13687, Jackson 39236-3687. Tel. 601-981-4586, fax 601-981-4501, e-mail info@misslib.org.

World Wide Web http://www.misslib.org.

Missouri

Missouri Assn. of School Libns. Memb. 1,000. Term of Office. June 2011–June 2012. Publication. *Connections* (q.).

Pres. Curtis Clark, Harrisonville Middle School. E-mail msmediacenter@harrisonville. k12.mo.us; *1st V.P./Pres.-Elect* Vickie Howard, Cape Girardeau Public Schools. E-mail howard vickie53@yahoo.com; *2nd V.P.* Ellen Wickham, Raytown South H.S. E-mail wickhame@ raytownschools.org; *Secy.* Toni Howe, Sikeston Fifth and Sixth Grade Center. E-mail thowe@ sikeston.k12.mo.us; *Treas.* Jenny Robins, UCMO. E-mail jrobins@ucmo.edu; *Past Pres.* Patricia Antrim. E-mail antrim@ucmo.edu.

Address correspondence to the association, P.O. Box 2107, Jefferson City 65102. Tel. 573-893-4155, fax 573-635-2858, e-mail info@ maslonline.org.

World Wide Web http://www.maslonline. org.

Montana

Montana School Lib. Media Div., Montana Lib. Assn. Memb. 200+. Publication. *FOCUS* (published by Montana Lib. Assn.) (q.).

Chair Kari Eliason, Manhattan Community School Lib., 308 Al Drive, Belgrade 59714. Tel.

406-388-2575, e-mail keliason@manhattan.
k12.mt.us; *Past Chair* Nancy Pensa, Russell
Elementary, Kalispell 59901. Tel. 406-751-
3915; *Exec. Asst., Montana Lib. Assn.* Debra
Kramer, P.O. Box 1352, Three Forks 59752.
Tel. 406-285-3090, fax 406-285-3091, e-mail
debkmla@hotmail.com.
World Wide Web http://www.mtlib.org.

Nebraska

Nebraska Educ. Media Assn. Memb. 370. Term
of Office. July 2011–June 2012. Publication.
NEMA News (q.).
Pres. Karen Buckley; *Pres.-Elect* Stacy
Lickteig; *Secy.* Beth Kabes; *Treas.* Tammi
Mans; *Past Pres.* Betty Meyer; *Exec. Secy.* Kim
Gangwish. E-mail nemacontact@gmail.com.
Address correspondence to the executive
secretary.
World Wide Web http://www.schoollibraries
rock.org.

Nevada

Nevada School and Children's Libs. Section,
Nevada Lib. Assn. Memb. 120.
Chair Leona Vittum-Jones, Henderson Libs.
E-mail lvittum-jones@hdpl.org; *Past Chair*
Jennifer Jost, Las Vegas-Clark County Lib.
Dist. E-mail jostj@lvccld.org; *Exec. Secy.* Lau-
ren Campbell, Las Vegas-Clark County Lib.
Dist. E-mail ltcampbell10@gmail.com.
Address correspondence to the executive
secretary.
World Wide Web http://www.nevadalibrar-
ies.org/handbook/nscls.html.

New Hampshire

New Hampshire School Lib. Media Assn.
(NHSLMA), Box 418, Concord 03302-0418.
Memb. 271. Term of Office. June 2011–June
2012. Publication. *Online News* (winter,
spring; online and print).
Pres. Helen Burnham, Lincoln Street
School, 25 Lincoln St., Exeter 03833. Tel. 603-
775-8851, e-mail hburnham@sau16.org; *V.P.*
To be announced; *Recording Secy.* Jill Canillas
Daley, Plainfield Elementary School. E-mail
jdaley@plainfieldschool.org; *Treas.* Jeff Kent,
43 E. Ridge Rd., Merrimack 03054. E-mail
jkent@comcast.net; *Past Pres.* Kathy Lane, G.

H. Hood Middle School, Derry 03038. E-mail
klane@derry.k12.nh.us.
Address correspondence to the president.
World Wide Web World Wide Web http://
nhslma.org.

New Jersey

New Jersey Association of School Librarians
(NJASL). Memb. 1,100. Term of Office. Aug.
2011–July 2012.
Pres. Fran King, Lincoln Middle School,
291 Lafayette Ave., Passaic 07055. E-mail
president@njasl.org; *V.P.* Pam Gunter. E-mail
vicepresident@njasl.org; *Pres.-Elect* April Bunn.
E-mail presidentelect@njasl.org; *Recording
Secy.* Patty Huizing. E-mail recordingsecretary
@njasl.org; *Corresponding Secy.* Amy Romi-
niecki. E-mail correspondingsecretary@njasl.
org; *Treas.* Michelle Marhefka. E-mail treasurer
@njasl.org; *Past Pres.* Pat Massey. E-mail
immediatepastpresident@njasl.org.
Address correspondence to Elizabeth McArthur, Assn. Mgr., NJASL, Box 610, Trenton
08607. E-mail associationmanager@njasl.org.
World Wide Web http://www.njasl.org.

New York

New York Lib. Assn./Section of School Libns,
252 Hudson St., Albany 12210. Tel. 518-432-
6952. Memb. 820. Term of Office. Nov. 2011–
Oct. 2012. Publications. *SLMSGram* (q.); participates in *NYLA Bulletin* (mo. except July and
Aug.).
Pres. Pauline Herr. E-mail pherr@acsdny.
org; *V.P. Conferences* Livia Sabourin. E-mail
krnsprrzz@gmail.com; *V.P. Communications*
Ellen Rubin. E-mail erubin@frontiernet.net;
Pres.-Elect Sue Kowalski. E-mail kowalski
423@yahoo.com; *Secy.* Michelle Miller. E-
mail mmiller@mwcsd.org; *Treas.* Patty Mar-
tire. E-mail pmartire@mtmorriscsd.org; *Past
Pres.* Fran Roscello. E-mail fran@roscello
associates.com.
World Wide Web http://www.nyla.org/display
common.cfm?an=1&subarticlenbr=403.

North Carolina

North Carolina School Lib. Media Assn. Memb.
1,000+. Term of Office. Nov. 2011–Oct. 2012.
Pres. Sarah Justice, Transylvania County
Schools, 749 Pickens Hwy., Rosman 28772.

Tel. 828-862-4284, fax 828-885-5572, e-mail sjustice@tcsnc.org; *Pres.-Elect* April Dawkins, Union County Public Schools, 2839 Ridge Rd., Indian Trail 28079. Tel. 704-292-7662, fax 704-296-9733, e-mail april.dawkins@ucps.k12.nc.us; *Treas.* Laura Bowers, Westwood Elementary School, 4083 U.S. Hwy 221 S., West Jefferson 28694. Tel. 336-877-2921, e-mail laura.bowers@ashe.k12.nc.us; *Past Pres.* Deanna Harris, Wake County Public Schools, 1111 S.E. Maynard Rd., Cary 27511. Tel. 919-466-4377, fax 919-466-4388, e-mail ncslma.deanna@gmail.com.

Address correspondence to the president.

World Wide Web http://www.ncslma.org.

North Dakota

School Lib. and Youth Services Section, North Dakota Lib. Assn. Memb. 100. Publication. *The Good Stuff* (q.).

Chair Lesley Gunderson, Sunrise Elementary, Bismarck Public Schools. Tel. 701-323-4300, e-mail lesley_gunderson@bismarckschools.org.

World Wide Web http://ndlaonline.org.

Ohio

Ohio Educ. Lib. Media Assn. Memb. 1,000. Publications. *OELMA News* (3 a year); *Ohio Media Spectrum* (q.).

Pres. Sue Subel. E-mail sue.subel@kenstonlocal.org; *V.P.* Susan Yutzey. E-mail syutzey@uaschools.org; *Secy.* Sheila Campbell. E-mail librarian@columbuszoo.com; *Treas.* Brenda Gehm. E-mail bgehm@monroelocalschools.com; *Past Pres.* Krista Taracuk. E-mail ktaracuk@columbus.rr.com; *Dir. of Services* Kate Brunswick, 17 S. High St., Suite 200, Columbus 43215. Tel. 614-221-1900, fax 614-221-1989, e-mail kate@assnoffices.com.

Address correspondence to the director of services.

World Wide Web http://www.oelma.org.

Oklahoma

Oklahoma School Libs. Div., Oklahoma Lib. Assn. Memb. 300+. Publication. *Oklahoma Librarian.*

Chair John Allen; *Chair-Elect* Earon Cunningham; *Secy.* Stephanie Brucks; *Treas.* Michelle Robertson; *Past Chair* Patty Zody.

Address correspondence to the chairperson, School Libs. Div., Oklahoma Lib. Assn., 300 Hardy Drive, Edmond 73013. Tel. 405-348-0506.

World Wide Web http://www.ola.oklibs.org/organization/Divisions/oksl.htm.

Oregon

Oregon Assn. of School Libs. Memb. 600. Publication. *Interchange* (3 a year).

Pres. Susan Stone. E-mail sstone@pps.net; *Pres.-Elect* Nancy Sullivan. E-mail nsulliva@pps.net; *Secy.* Jenny Takeda. E-mail jenny_takeda@beavton.k12.or.us; *Treas.* Stuart Levy. E-mail oasltreasurer@gmail.com; *Past Pres.* Ruth Murray. E-mail murrayr@pdx.edu.

Address correspondence to the association at OASL, 860 S. Clematis Rd., West Linn 97068.

World Wide Web http://oasl.memberclicks.net.

Pennsylvania

Pennsylvania School Libns. Assn. Memb. 1,400+. Publication. *Learning and Media* (q.).

Pres. Doug Francis. E-mail dfrancisd@psla.org; *V.P./Pres.-Elect* Eileen Kern. E-mail ekern@psla.org; *Secy.* Lindsey Long. E-mail llong@psla.org; *Treas.* Natalie Hawley. E-mail nhawley@psla.org; *Past Pres.* Nancy Smith Latanision. E-mail nlatanision@psla.org.

Address correspondence to the president.

World Wide Web http://www.psla.org.

Rhode Island

School Libns. of Rhode Island (formerly Rhode Island Educ. Media Assn.). Memb. 350+.

Pres. Darshell Silva. E-mail ucaplibrarian@verizon.net; *V.P.* To be announced; *Secy.* Jane Perry; *Treas.* Jen Simoneau. E-mail jsimoneau4@cox.net; *Past Pres.* Jamie Greene. E-mail greenej@bw.k12.ri.us.

Address correspondence to the president.

World Wide Web http://www.slri.info.

South Carolina

South Carolina Assn. of School Libns. Memb. 1,100. Term of Office. June 2011–May 2012.

Pres. Kathy Sutusky. E-mail ksutusky@sc.rr.com; *V.P./Pres.-Elect* Heather Loy. E-mail holy@mac.com; *Secy.* Kelly Knight. E-mail klknight@greenville.k12.sc.us; *Treas.* Steve Reed. E-mail screed3103@aol.com; *Past Pres.* Joe Myers. E-mail joemyers1961@yahoo.com; *Exec. Secy.* Diane Ervin. E-mail ervinscasl@gmail.com.

Address correspondence to the association at SCASL, P.O. Box 2442, Columbia 29202. Tel./fax 803-492-3025.

World Wide Web http://www.scasl.net.

South Dakota

South Dakota School Lib. Media Section, South Dakota Lib. Assn., 28363 472nd Ave., Worthing 57077. Tel. 605-372-0235. Memb. 140+. Term of Office. Oct. 2011–Oct. 2012.

Chair Jeanne Conner, Roosevelt H.S., Sioux Falls. E-mail jeanne.connerie@k12.sd.us.

Tennessee

Tennessee Assn. of School Libns. Memb. 450. Term of Office. Jan.–Dec. 2012. Publication. *TASL Talks.*

Pres. Hannah Little, Webb School, P.O. Box 488, Bell Buckle 37020. E-mail hlittle@webbschool.com; *V.P./Pres.-Elect* Beth Frerking, Northwest H.S., 800 Lafayette Rd., Clarksville 37042. E-mail frerking.tasl@gmail.com; *Secy.* Sarah Searles, West H.S., 5423 Oak Harbor Lane, Knoxville 37921. E-mail sarah. searles@knoxschools.org; *Treas.* Nancy Dickinson, Hillsboro Elementary, 23 Belmar Rd., Manchester 37355; *Past Pres.* Pam Renfrow, St. Agnes Academy-St. Dominic School, 4830 Walnut Grove Rd., Memphis 38117. E-mail prenfrow@ssa-sds.org.

Address correspondence to the president.

World Wide Web http http://www.tasltn.org.

Texas

Texas Assn. of School Libns., Div. of Texas Lib. Assn. Memb. 4,000+. Term of Office. Apr. 2011–Apr. 2012.

Chair Naomi M. Bates, Northwest H.S. Tel. 817-215-0203, e-mail nbates@nisdtx.org; *Chair-Elect* Mary Woodard. E-mail mwoodard@mesquiteisd.org; *Secy.* Faye L. Hagerty, Northside ISD. Tel. 210-397-8199, e-mail faye.hagerty@nisd.net; *Past Chair* Susan Y. Geye, Everman ISD. Tel. 817-568-3560, e-mail sgeye@eisd.org.

Address correspondence to Texas Lib. Assn., 3355 Bee Cave Rd., Suite 401, Austin 78746. Tel. 512-328-1518, fax 512-328-8852, e-mail tla@txla.org.

World Wide Web http://www.txla.org/groups/tasl.

Utah

Utah Educ. Lib. Media Assn. Memb. 500+. Publication. *UELMA Newsletter* (q.).

Pres. Andrea Woodring, Bonneville H.S., 251 E. Laker Way, Ogden 84405. Tel. 801-452-4050, e-mail anwoodring@weber.k12.ut.us; *Pres.-Elect* Shelly Ripplinger, Polk Elementary, 2615 Polk Ave., Ogden 84401. Tel. 801-737-8308, e-mail ripplingers@ogdensd.org; *Secy.* Celia Powell, Granite School Dist., Instructional Technology, Room D-229, 2500 S. State St., Salt Lake City 84115. Tel. 385-646-4110, e-mail cpowell@graniteschools.org; *Past Pres.* Brent Jones, Fremont H.S., 1900 N. 4700 W., Plain City 84404. Tel. 801-453-4034, e-mail bjones@wsd.net; *Exec. Dir.* John L. Smith, High Ridge Media, 714 W. 1900 N., Clinton 84015. Tel. 801-776-6829, fax 801-773-8708, e-mail jlsutah@comcast.net.

Address correspondence to the executive director.

World Wide Web http://www.uelma.org.

Vermont

Vermont School Lib. Assn. (formerly Vermont Educ. Media Assn.). Memb. 220+. Term of Office. May 2011–May 2012. Publication. *VSLA Newsletter Online* (q.).

Pres. Anna Bolognani, Twin Valley H.S., 1 School St., Wilmington 05363. Tel. 802-464-5255 ext. 119, e-mail rebolibrary@hotmail.com; *Pres.-Elect* To be announced; *Secy.* Lindy Sargent, Newport Elementary, 166 Sias Ave., Newport 05855. Tel. 802-334-2455, e-mail lsargent@northcountryschools.org; *Treas.* Donna Smyth, Proctor Elementary, 14 School St., Proctor 05765. Tel. 802-459-2225 ext. 2005, e-mail smythd@rcsu.org; *Past Pres.* Claire Buckley, South Burlington H.S., 550 Dorset St., South Burlington 05403. Tel. 802-652-7085, e-mail cbuckley@sbschools.net.

Address correspondence to the president.

World Wide Web https://sites.google.com/site/vermontschoolibraries/home.

Virginia

Virginia Educ. Media Assn. Memb. 1,073. Term of Office. (Pres., Pres.-Elect) Nov. 2011–Nov. 2012 (other officers two years in alternating years). Publication. *Mediagram* (q.).

Pres. Julie Tate, Hanover Public Schools, Hanover. E-mail president@vaasl.org; *Pres.-Elect* Frances Reeve. E-mail presidentelect@vaasl.org; *Secy.* Earlene Lester. E-mail secretary @vaasl.org; *Treas.* Lori Donovan, Thomas Dale H.S., Chester. E-mail treasurer@vaasl.org; *Past Pres.* Mary Keeling, Newport News Public Schools, Newport News. E-mail past president@vaasl.org; *Exec. Dir.* Margaret Baker. Tel. 540-416-6109, e-mail executive@vaasl.org.

Address correspondence to the association, P.O. Box 2015, Staunton 24402-2015.

World Wide Web http://www.vemaonline.org.

Washington

Washington Lib. Media Assn. Memb. 1,450+. Term of Office. Oct.–Oct. Publication. *The Medium* (3 a year).

Pres. Craig Seasholes. E-mail president@wlma.org; *Pres.-Elect* Leigh Lohrasbi. E-mail leigh.lohrasbi@gmail.com; *V.P.* Sharyn Merrigan. E-mail smerrigan28@gmail.com; *Secy.* Jeanne Staley. E-mail staleyj54@gmail.com; *Treas.* Kate Pankiewicz. E-mail kate.pankiewicz @shorelineschools.org; *Past Pres.* Stephen Coker. E-mail stephenjcoker@gmail.com.

Address correspondence to the association, 10924 Mukilteo Speedway, PMB 142, Mukilteo 98275. E-mail wlma@wlma.org.

World Wide Web http://www.wlma.org.

West Virginia

School Lib. Div., West Virginia Lib. Assn. Memb. 50. Term of Office. Nov.–Nov. Publication. *WVLA School Library News* (5 a year).

Chair Cathy Davis, East Fairmont Junior H.S., 1 Orion Lane, Fairmont 26554. Tel. 304-367-2123, e-mail ctdavis@access.k12.wv.us.

Address correspondence to the chairperson.

World Wide Web http://www.wvla.org.

Wisconsin

Wisconsin Educ. Media and Technology Assn. Memb. 1,100+. Publication. *WEMTA Dispatch* (q.).

Pres. Annette Smith. E-mail arsmith14@gmail.com; *Pres.-Elect* Jo Ann Carr. E-mail carr@education.wisc.edu; *Secy.* Vicki Santacroce. E-mail vsantacroce@ashwaubenon.k12.wi.us; *Treas.* Sandy Heiden. E-mail sheiden@seymour.k12.wi.us; *Assn. Mgr.* Courtney Rounds. Tel. 608-375-6020, e-mail wemamanager@hughes.net.

Address correspondence to WEMA, P.O. Box 206, Boscobel 53805.

World Wide Web http://www.wemaonline.org.

Wyoming

Teacher-Librarian Interest Group, Wyoming Lib. Assn. Memb. 100+.

Co-Chairs Ron Chesmore. E-mail rpchesmore@yahoo.com; Mary Wegher. E-mail mwegher@ccsd.k12.wy.us.

Address correspondence to the co-chairpersons.

World Wide Web https://sites.google.com/site/wlateacherlibrarians.

International Library Associations

International Association of Agricultural Information Specialists

Edith Hesse, President
IAALD, P.O. Box 63, Lexington, KY 40588-0063
Fax 859-257-8379, e-mail info@iaald.org
World Wide Web http://www.iaald.org

Object

The International Association of Agricultural Information Specialists (IAALD) facilitates professional development of and communication among members of the agricultural information community worldwide. Its goal is to enhance access to and use of agriculture-related information resources. To further this mission, IAALD will promote the agricultural information profession, support professional development activities, foster collaboration, and provide a platform for information exchange. Founded 1955.

Membership

Memb. 400+ in 80 countries. Dues (Inst.) US$110; (Indiv.) US$50.

Officers

Pres. Edith Hesse (Colombia). E-mail e.hesse @cgiar.org; *Pres.-Elect* Federico Sancho Guevara (Costa Rica); *Secy.-Treas.* Toni Greider (USA). P.O. Box 63, Lexington, KY 40588-0063. Tel. 859-254-0752, fax 859-257-8379, e-mail toni.greider@iaald.org; *Past Pres.* Barbara Hutchinson (USA). E-mail barbara.hutchinson@iaald.org.

Publication

Agricultural Information Worldwide (q.) (memb.).

International Association of Law Libraries

Petal Kinder, President
High Court of Australia, Canberra, ACT 2600
61-2-6270-6922, fax 61-2-6273-2110, e-mail pkinder@hcourt.gov.au
World Wide Web http://www.iall.org

Object

The International Association of Law Libraries (IALL) is a worldwide organization of librarians, libraries, and other persons or institutions concerned with the acquisition and use of legal information emanating from sources other than their jurisdictions and from multinational and international organizations.

IALL's purpose is to facilitate the work of librarians who acquire, process, organize, and provide access to foreign legal materials. IALL has no local chapters but maintains liaison with national law library associations in many countries and regions of the world.

Membership

More than 800 members in more than 50 countries on five continents.

Officers

Pres. Petal Kinder, High Court of Australia, Parkes Place, Parkes, Canberra, ACT 2600. Tel. 61-2-6270-6922, fax 61-2-6273-2110, e-mail pkinder@hcourt.gov.au; *1st V.P.* Jeroen Vervliet, Peace Palace Lib., Carnegieplein 2, 2517 KJ The Hague, Netherlands. Tel. 31-70-302-4242, e-mail j.vervliet@ppl.nl; *2nd V.P.* Jennefer Aston, 47 St. Kevin's Park, Dublin 6, Ireland. Tel. 353-1-497-4385, e-mail jennefera@gmail.com; *Secy.* Barbara Garavaglia, Univ. of Michigan Law Lib., Ann Arbor, MI 48109-1210. Tel. 734-764-9338, fax 734-764-5863, e-mail bvaccaro@umich.edu; *Treas.* Xinh Luu, Univ. of Virginia Law Lib., 580 Massie Rd., Charlottesville, VA 22903. E-mail xtl5d@virginia.edu; *Past Pres.* Jules Winterton, Institute of Advanced Legal Studies, Univ. of London, 17 Russell Sq., London WCIB 5DR, England. Tel. 44-20-7862-5884, fax 44-20-7862-5850, e-mail julesw@sas.ac.uk.

Board Members

Ruth Bird, Bodleian Law Lib., Oxford Univ., England; Ligita Gjortlere, Riga Graduate School of Law Lib., Riga, Latvia; Mari Hoffman (ex officio), Univ. of California, Berkeley, School of Law Lib.; Mark D. Engsberg (ex officio), MacMillan Law Lib., Emory Univ. School of Law, Atlanta; Janice L. Johnston, Albert E. Jenner, Jr. Memorial Law Lib., Univ. of Illinois; Uma Narayan, Bombay High Court, Mumbai, India; Pedro Padilla-Rosa, Univ. of Puerto Rico Law Lib., San Juan; Anita Soboleva, JURIX (Jurists for Constitutional Rights and Freedoms), Moscow, Russia; Ivo Vogel, Sondersammelgebiet und Virtuellen Fachbibliothek Recht, Berlin, Germany; Bård Tuseth, Dept. of Public and International Law Lib., Oslo, Norway.

Publication

International Journal of Legal Information (3 a year; US$60 indiv.; US$95 institutions).

International Association of Music Libraries, Archives and Documentation Centres

Pia Shekhter, Secretary-General
Gothenburg University Library, P.O. Box 222, SE 405 30 Gothenburg, Sweden
Tel. 46-31-786-4057, cell 46-703-22-62, fax 46-31-786-40-59, e-mail secretary@iaml.info
World Wide Web http://www.iaml.info

Object

The object of the International Association of Music Libraries, Archives, and Documentation Centres (IAML) is to promote the activities of music libraries, archives, and documentation centers and to strengthen the cooperation among them; to promote the availability of all publications and documents relating to music and further their bibliographical control; to encourage the development of standards in all areas that concern the association; and to support the protection and preservation of musical documents of the past and the present.

Membership

Memb. 2,000.

Board Members

Pres. Roger Flury, National Lib. of New Zealand, P.O. Box 1467, Wellington, NZ. Tel. 64-4-474-3039, fax 64-4-474-3035; *Secy.-Gen.* Pia Shekhter, Academy of Music and Drama, Univ. of Gothenburg Lib., Box 210, SE-405 30 Gothenburg, Sweden. Tel. 46-31-786-40-57, fax 46-31-786-40-59; *V.P.s* Stanislaw Hrabia, Biblioteka i Fonoteka, Instytut Muzykologii,

Uniwersytet Jagiellonski, ul. Westerplatte 10, 31-033 Kraków, Poland. Tel. 48-12-663-1673, fax 48-12-663-1671; Antony Gordon, British Lib. Sound Archive, 96 Euston Rd., London NW1 2DB. Tel. 44-20-7412-7412, fax 44-20-7412-7441; Johan Eeckeloo, Koninklijk Conservatorium Brussel, Regentschapsstraat 30, B-1000 Brussels. Tel. 32-2-213-41-30; Jutta Lambrecht, WDR D&A / Recherche, Leitung Musik und Notenarchiv, Appellhofplatz 1, D-50667 Köln, Germany. Tel. 49-221-220-3376, fax 49-221-220-9217; *Treas.* Kathryn Adamson, Libn., Royal Academy of Music, Marylebone Rd., London NW1 5HT, England. Tel. 44-20-7873-7321; *Past Pres.* Martie Severt, Netherlands Radio Music Lib., Postbus 125, NL-1200 AC Hilversum, Netherlands. Tel. 31-35-6714181, fax 31-35-6714189.

Publication

Fontes Artis Musicae (4 a year; memb.). *Ed.* Maureen Buja, Hong Kong Gold Coast Block 22, Flat 1-A, 1 Castle Peak Rd., Tuen Mun, NT, Hong Kong. Tel. 852-2146-8047, e-mail mbuja@earthlink.net.

Professional Branches

Archives and Documentation Centres. Marguerite Sablonnière, Bibliothèque Nationale de France, Département de la Musique, 58 rue de Richelieu, 75002 Paris, France.
Broadcasting and Orchestra Libraries. Angela Escott, Royal College of Music, Prince Consort Rd., London SW7 2BS, England.
Libraries in Music Teaching Institutions. Pia Shekhter, Gothenburg Univ. Lib., P.O. Box 222, SE 405 30 Gothenburg, Sweden.
Public Libraries. Hanneke Kuiper, Public Lib., Oosterdoksstraat 143, 1011 DK Amsterdam, Netherlands.
Research Libraries. Stanislaw Hrabia, Uniwersytet Jagiellonski Instytut Muzykologii Biblioteka, ul. Westerplatte 10 31-033 Kraków, Poland.

International Association of School Librarianship

Carla Funk, Executive Secretary
65 E. Wacker Place, Suite 1900, Chicago, IL 60601
e-mail iasl@mlahq.org
World Wide Web http://www.iasl-online.org

Object

The mission of the International Association of School Librarianship (IASL) is to provide an international forum for those interested in promoting effective school library programs as viable instruments in the educational process. The association provides guidance and advice for the development of school library programs and the school library profession. IASL works in cooperation with other professional associations and agencies.

The objectives of IASL are to advocate the development of school libraries throughout all countries; to encourage the integration of school library programs into the instructional and curriculum development of the school; to promote the professional preparation and con-

tinuing education of school library personnel; to foster a sense of community among school librarians in all parts of the world; to foster and extend relationships between school librarians and other professionals connected with children and youth; to foster research in the field of school librarianship and the integration of its conclusions with pertinent knowledge from related fields; to promote the publication and dissemination of information about successful advocacy and program initiatives in school librarianship; to share information about programs and materials for children and youth throughout the international community; and to initiate and coordinate activities, conferences, and other projects in the field of school librarianship and information services. Founded 1971.

Membership

Approximately 600.

Officers and Executive Board

Pres. Diljit Singh, Malaysia; *V.P.s* Katharina B. L. Berg, Latin America/Caribbean; Madhu Bhargava, Asia; Barbara Combes, Australia; Lourense Das, Europe; Lesley Farmer, USA; *Treas.* Katy Manck, USA; *Dirs.* Pat Carmichael, Oceania; Busi Dlamini, Africa–Sub Sahara; Betty Chu Wah Hing, East Asia; Luisa Marquardt, Europe; Dianne Oberg, Canada; Ingrid Skirrow, International Schools; Blanche Woolls, USA; Ayse Yuksel-Durukan, North Africa/Middle East.

Publications

Selected papers from proceedings of annual conferences (all prices are exclusive of postage):

34th Annual Conference, 2005, Hong Kong. *Information Leadership in a Culture of Change.* US$20.

35th Annual Conference, 2006, Lisbon, Portugal. *The Multiple Faces of Literacy: Reading. Knowing. Doing.* US$20.

36th Annual Conference, 2007, Taipei, Taiwan. *Cyberspace, D-world, E-learning: Giving Libraries and Schools the Cutting Edge.* US$20.

37th Annual Conference, 2008, Berkeley, California. *World Class Learning and Literacy Through School Libraries.* US$20.

38th Annual Conference 2009, Abano Terme, Italy. *Preparing Pupils and Students for the Future: School Libraries in the Picture.* US$20.

39th Annual Conference 2010, Brisbane, Australia. *Diversity Challenge Resilience: School Libraries in Action.* US$20.

40th Annual Conference 2011, Kingston, Jamaica. *School Libraries: Empowering the 21st Century Learner.* US$20.

International Association of Scientific and Technological University Libraries

President, Ainslie Dewe
World Wide Web http://www.iatul.org

Object

The main object of the International Association of Scientific and Technological University Libraries (IATUL) is to provide a forum where library directors and senior managers can meet to exchange views on matters of current significance and to provide an opportunity for them to develop a collaborative approach to solving problems. IATUL also welcomes into membership organizations that supply services to university libraries, if they wish to be identified with the association's activities.

Membership

239 (in 42 countries).

Officers

Pres. Ainslie Dewe, Univ. Libn., La Trobe Univ. Lib., Australia; *Secy.* Elisha R. T. Chiware, Dir., Libs., Cape Peninsula Univ. of Technology, South Africa; *Treas.* Irma Pasanen, Assoc. Lib. Dir. for Info. Services, Aalto Univ. Lib., Finland.

Publication

IATUL Conference Proceedings (on IATUL Web site, http://www.iatul.org). (ann.).

International Council on Archives

David A. Leitch, Secretary-General
60 rue des Francs-Bourgeois, 75003 Paris, France
Tel. 33-1-40-27-63-06, fax 33-1-42-72-20-65, e-mail ica@ica.org
World Wide Web http://www.ica.org

Object

The mission of the International Council on Archives (ICA) is to establish, maintain, and strengthen relations among archivists of all lands, and among all professional and other agencies or institutions concerned with the custody, organization, or administration of archives, public or private, wherever located. Established 1948.

Membership

Memb. Approximately 1,500 (representing about 195 countries and territories).

Officers

Pres. Martin Berendse, Netherlands; *V.P.s* Lewis J. Bellardo, USA; David Fricker, Australia; Andreas Kellerhals, Switzerland; Vu Thi Minh Huong, Vietnam; Henri Zuber, France.

Board

Paola Caroli, Italy; Daniel J. Caron, Canada; Kim Eberhard, Australia; William J. Maher, USA; Angelika Menne-Haritz, Germany; Marietta Minotos, Greece; Amela Silipa, Western Samoa; Kenth Sjöblom, Finland; David Sutton, United Kingdom; João Vieira, Portugal; Geir Magnus Walderhaug, Norway; Sureerat Wongsangiem, Thailand.

Publications

Comma (memb.) (CD-ROM only.)
Flash (3 a year; memb.).
Guide to the Sources of the History of Nations (Latin American Series, 11 vols. pub.; Africa South of the Sahara Series, 20 vols. pub.; North Africa, Asia, and Oceania Series, 15 vols. pub.).
Guide to the Sources of Asian History (English-language series [India, Indonesia, Korea, Nepal, Pakistan, Singapore], 14 vols. pub.; national language series [Indonesia, Korea, Malaysia, Nepal, Thailand], 6 vols. pub.; other guides, 3 vols. pub.).

International Federation of Film Archives
(Fédération Internationale des Archives du Film)

Secretariat, 1 rue Defacqz, B-1000 Brussels, Belgium
Tel. 32-2-538-3065, fax 32-2-534-4774, e-mail info@fiafnet.org
World Wide Web http://www.fiafnet.org

Object

Founded in 1938, the International Federation of Film Archives (FIAF) brings together not-for-profit institutions dedicated to rescuing films and any other moving-image elements considered both as cultural heritage and as historical documents.

FIAF is a collaborative association of the world's leading film archives whose purpose has always been to ensure the proper preservation and showing of motion pictures. A total of 153 archives in more than 75 countries collect, restore, and exhibit films and cinema documentation spanning the entire history of film.

FIAF seeks to promote film culture and facilitate historical research, to help create new archives around the world, to foster training and expertise in film preservation, to encourage the collection and preservation of documents and other cinema-related materials, to develop cooperation between archives, and to ensure the international availability of films and cinema documents.

Officers

Pres. Eric Le Roy; *Secy.-Gen.* Meg Labrum; *Treas.* Patrick Loughney; *Membs.* Francisco Gaytan Fernandez, Anne Fiaccarini, Sylvia Frank, Olga Futemma, Mimi Gjorgoska-Ilievska, Lise Gustavson, Dennis Maake, Hisashi Okajima, Vladimir Opela, Esteve Riambau.

Address correspondence to Christophe Dupin, Senior Administrator, c/o FIAF Secretariat. E-mail c.dupin@fiafnet.org.

Publications

Journal of Film Preservation.
International Index to Film Periodicals.
FIAF International Filmarchive database (OVID).
FIAF International Index to Film Periodicals (ProQuest).
For additional FIAF publications, see http://www.fiafnet.org.

International Federation of Library Associations and Institutions

Jennefer Nicholson, Secretary-General
P.O. Box 95312, 2509 CH The Hague, Netherlands
Tel. 31-70-314-0884, fax 31-70-383-4827
E-mail ifla@ifla.org, World Wide Web http://www.ifla.org

Object

The object of the International Federation of Library Associations and Institutions (IFLA) is to promote international understanding, cooperation, discussion, research, and development in all fields of library activity, including bibliography, information services, and the education of library personnel, and to provide a body through which librarianship can be represented in matters of international interest. IFLA is the leading international body representing the interests of library and information services and their users. It is the global voice of the library and information profession. Founded 1927.

Officers and Governing Board

Pres. Ingrid Parent, Univ. of British Columbia; *Pres.-Elect* Sinikka Sipilä, Finnish Lib. Assn.; *Treas.* Donna Scheeder, Lib. of Congress.

Governing Board

Kent Skov Andreasen, Odense Central Public Lib.; Frédéric Blin, Bibliothèque Nationale et Universitaire de Strasbourg; Ingrid Bon, Biblioservice Gelderland; Genevieve Clavel-Merrin, Swiss National Lib.; Barbara Lison, Bremen Public Libs.; Inga Lundén, Stockholm Public Lib.; Christine Mackenzie, Yarra Plenty Regional Lib.; Buhle Mbambo-Thata, UNISA; Paul Whitney, Vancouver Public Lib.; Ann Okerson, Yale Univ.; Lynne M. Rudasill, Univ. of Illinois at Urbana-Champaign; Tone Eli Moseid, ABM-Utvikling; Anna Maria Tammaro, Univ. of Parma; Filiberto Felipe Martínez-Arellano, National Autonomous Univ. of Mexico; Gerald Leitner, Austrian Lib. Assn.; Secy.-Gen. Jennefer Nicholson.

Publications

IFLA Annual Report.
IFLA Journal (4 a year).

IFLA Professional Reports.
IFLA Publications Series.
IFLA Series on Bibliographic Control.
International Preservation News.

American Membership

Associations

American Lib. Assn., Assn. for Lib. and Info. Science Educ., Assn. of Research Libs., Chief Officers of State Lib. Agencies, Medical Lib. Assn., Special Libs. Assn., Urban Libs. Council, Chinese American Libns. Assn.

Institutional Members

There are 130 libraries and related institutions that are institutional members or consultative bodies and sponsors of IFLA in the United States (out of a total of 1,130 members globally), and 125 individual affiliates (out of a total of 357 members globally).

International Organization for Standardization

Robert Steele, Secretary-General
ISO Central Secretariat, 1 ch. de la Voie-Creuse, Case postale 56,
CH-1211 Geneva 20, Switzerland
41-22-749-01-11, fax 41-22-733-34-30, e-mail central@iso.org
World Wide Web http://www.iso.org

Object

The International Organization for Standardization (ISO) is a worldwide federation of national standards bodies, founded in 1947, at present comprising 162 members, one in each country. The object of ISO is to promote the development of standardization and related activities in the world with a view to facilitating international exchange of goods and services, and to developing cooperation in the spheres of intellectual, scientific, technological, and economic activity. The scope of ISO covers international standardization in all fields except electrical and electronic engineering standardization, which is the responsibility of the International Electrotechnical Commission

(IEC). The results of ISO technical work are published as international standards.

Officers

Pres. Boris Aleshin, Russian Federation; *V.P. (Policy)* Sadao Takeda, Japan; *V.P. (Technical Management)* Elisabeth Stampfl-Blaha, Austria; *Treas.* Julien Pitton, Switzerland.

Technical Work

The technical work of ISO is carried out by more than 200 technical committees. These include:

ISO/TC 46–Information and documentation (Secretariat, Association Française de Normal-ization, 11 ave. Francis de Pressensé, 93571 Saint-Denis La Plaine, Cedex, France). Scope: Standardization of practices relating to librar-ies, documentation and information centers, indexing and abstracting services, archives, information science, and publishing.

ISO/TC 37–Terminology and language and content resources (Secretariat, INFOTERM, Aichholzgasse 6/12, 1120 Vienna, Austria, on behalf of Österreichisches Normungsinstitut). Scope: Standardization of principles, methods, and applications relating to terminology and other language and content resources in the contexts of multilingual communication and cultural diversity.

ISO/IEC JTC 1–Information technology (Secretariat, American National Standards In-stitute, 25 W. 43 St., 4th fl., New York, NY 10036). Scope: Standardization in the field of information technology.

Publications

ISO Annual Report.

ISO Catalogue on CD-ROM (combined catalog of published standards and technical work program) (ann.).

ISO Focus+ (10 a year).

ISO International Standards.

ISO Memento (ann.).

ISO Online information service on World Wide Web (http://www.iso.org).

Foreign Library Associations

The following is a list of regional and national library associations around the world. A more complete list can be found in *International Literary Market Place* (Information Today, Inc.).

Regional

Africa

Standing Conference of Eastern, Central, and Southern African Lib. and Info. Assns. (SCECSAL), c/o Constantine M. Nyamboga, Chair, Kenya Assn. of Lib. and Info. Professionals, P.O. Box 46031, Nairobi 00100, Kenya. E-mail constantinebu@yahoo.com or constantinenyamboga@gmail.com.

The Americas

Asociación de Bibliotecas Universitarias, de Investigación e Institucionales del Caribe (ACURIL) (Assn. of Caribbean Univ., Research, and Institutional Libs.), Box 23317, UPR Sta., San Juan, PR 00931-3317. Tel./fax 787-790-8054, e-mail acurilsec@yahoo.com or acuril@gmail.com, World Wide Web http://acuril.uprrp.edu. *Pres.* Ardis R Hanson. E-mail hanson@fmhi.usf.edu; *Exec. Secy.* Luisa Vigo-Cepeda.

Seminar on the Acquisition of Latin American Lib. Materials (SALALM), c/o *Exec. Secy.* Hortensia Calvo, SALALM Secretariat, Latin American Lib., 422 Howard Tilton Memorial Lib., 7001 Freret St., New Orleans, LA 70118-5549. Tel. 504-247-1366, fax 504-247-1367, e-mail salalm@tulane.edu, World Wide Web http://www.salalm.org. *Pres.* Fernando Acosta-Rodriguez. E-mail facosta@princeton.edu.

Asia

Congress of Southeast Asian Libns. (CONSAL), c/o Jl Salemba Raya 28A, Jakarta10430, Indonesia. Tel. 21-310-3554, World Wide Web http://www.consal.org. *Secy.-Gen.* Aristaianto Hakim.

The Commonwealth

Commonwealth Lib. Assn. (COMLA), Learning Resources Center, Univ. of the West Indies, Bridgetown Campus, P.O. Box 144, Mona, Kingston 7, Jamaica. Tel. 876-927-0083, fax 876-927-1926, e-mail nkpodo@uwimonal.edu.jm. *Pres.* Anthony Evans; *Exec. Secy.* Norma Y. Amenu-Kpodo.

Standing Conference on Lib. Materials on Africa (SCOLMA), Social Science Collections and Research, British Library St. Pancras, 96 Euston Rd., London NW1 2DB, England. Tel. 20-7412-7567, fax 20-7747-6168, fax 20-7747-6168, e-mail scolma@hotmail.com, World Wide Web http://www2.lse.ac.uk/library/scolma.

National and State Libs. Australasia, c/o State Lib. of Victoria, 328 Swanston St., Melbourne, Vic. 3000, Australia. Tel. 3-8664-7512, fax 3-9639-4737, e-mail nsla@slv.vic.gov.au, World Wide Web http://www.nsla.org.au. *Chair* Alan Smith.

Europe

Ligue des Bibliothèques Européennes de Recherche (LIBER) (Assn. of European Research Libs.), Postbus 90407, 2509 LK The Hague, Netherlands. Tel. 070-314-07-67, fax 070-314-01-97, e-mail liber@kb.nl, World Wide Web http://www.libereurope.eu. *Pres.* Hans Geleijnse. E-mail hans.geleijnse@uvt.nl; *Exec. Dir.* Wouter Schallier. E-mail wouter.schallier@kb.nl.

National

Argentina

Asociación de Bibliotecarios Graduados de la República Argentina (ABGRA) (Assn. of Graduate Libns. of Argentina), Parana 918, 2do Piso, C1017AAT Buenos Aires. Tel. 11-4811-0043, fax 11-4816-2234, e-mail info@abgra.org.ar, World Wide Web http://www.abgra.org.ar. *Pres.* Rosa Emma Monfasani.

Australia

Australian Lib. and Info. Assn., Box 6335, Kingston, ACT 2604. Tel. 2-6215-8222, fax 2-6282-2249, e-mail enquiry@alia.org.au, World Wide Web http://www.alia.org.au. *Pres.* Jan Richards. E-mail jan.richards@alia.org.au; *Exec. Dir.* Sue Hutley. E-mail sue.hutley@alia.org.au.

Australian Society of Archivists, GPO Box 1293, Brisbane, Qld. 4001. Tel. 800-622-251, e-mail office@archivists.org.au, World Wide Web http://www.archivists.org.au. *Pres.* Patricia Jackson; *V.P.* Louise Trott; *Secy.-Treas.* Clive Smith.

Austria

Österreichische Gesellschaft für Dokumentation und Information (Austrian Society for Documentation and Info.), c/o OGDI, Wollzeile 1-3, P.O. Box 46, 1010 Vienna. E-mail office@oegdi.at, World Wide Web http://www.oegdi.at. *Chair* Hermann Huemer.

Vereinigung Österreichischer Bibliothekarinnen und Bibliothekare (Assn. of Austrian Libns.), Voralberg State Lib., Fluherstr. 4, 6900 Bregenz. E-mail voeb@ub.tuwein.ac.at, World Wide Web http://www.univie.ac.at/voeb/php. *Pres.* Harald Weigel.

Bangladesh

Lib. Assn. of Bangladesh, Dhaka Univ. Lib., Shahbagh, Dhaka 1000. Tel. 2-966-190-79, World Wide Web http://www.lab-bd.org; *Pres.* Nasir Uddin Munshi; *Gen. Secy.* Syed Ali Akbor.

Barbados

Lib. Assn. of Barbados, P.O. Box 827E, Bridgetown, Barbados. E-mail milton@uwich.ill.edu.bb. *Pres.* Junior Browne.

Belgium

Archief- en Bibliotheekwezen in België (Belgian Assn. of Archivists and Libns.), Blvd. de l'Empereur 4, 1000 Brussels. Tel. 2-519-53-93, fax 2-519-56-10. *Pres.* Frank Daelemans. E-mail frank.daelemans@kbr.be.

Association Belge de Documentation/Belgische Vereniging voor Documentatie (Belgian Assn. for Documentation), chaussée de Wavre 1683, B-1160 Brussels. Tel. 2-675-58-62, fax 2-672-74-46, e-mail abdbvd@abd-bvd.be, World Wide Web http://www.abd-bvd.be. *Pres.* Vincent Maes; *Secy. Gen.* Christopher Boon.

Association Professionnelle des Bibliothécaires et Documentalistes (Assn. of Libns. and Documentation Specialists), Place de la Wallonie 15, 6140 Fontaine-l'Eveque. Tel. 71-52-31-93, fax 71-52-23-07, e-mail biblio.hainaut@skynet.be, World Wide Web http://www.apbd.be. *Pres.* Laurence Baker; *Secy.* Fabienne Gerard.

Vlaamse Vereniging voor Bibliotheek-, Archief-, en Documentatiewezen (Flemish Assn. of Libns., Archivists, and Documentalists), Statiestraat 179, B-2600 Berchem, Antwerp. Tel. 3-281-44-57, e-mail vvbad@vvbad.be, World Wide Web http://www.vvbad.be. *Exec. Dir.* Marc Storms.

Belize

Belize National Lib. Service and Info. System (BNLSIS), P.O. Box 287, Belize City. Tel. 223-4248, 223-4249, fax 223-4246, e-mail nls@btl.net, World Wide Web http://www.nlsbze.bz. *Chief Libn.* Joy Ysaguirre.

Bolivia

Centro Nacional de Documentacion Cientifica y Tecnologica (National Scientific and Technological Documentation Center), Av. Mariscal Santa Cruz 1175, Esquina c Ayacucho, La Paz. Tel. 02-359-583, fax 02-359-586, e-mail iiicndct@huayna.umsa.edu.bo, World Wide Web http://www.bolivian.com/industrial/cndct. *Contact* Ruben Valle Vera.

Bosnia and Herzegovina

Drustvo Bibliotekara Bosne i Hercegovine (Libns. Society of Bosnia and Herzegovina), Zmaja od Bosne 8B, 71000 Sarajevo. Tel. 33-275-5325, fax 33-212-435, e-mail nubbih @nub.ba, World Wide Web http://www. nub.ba. *Pres.* Nevenka Hajdarovic. E-mail nevenka@nub.ba; *Secy.* Dijana Bilos. E-mail dijana@nub.ba.

Botswana

Botswana Lib. Assn., Box 1310, Gaborone. Tel. 371-750, fax 371-748. *Chair* Bobana Badisang.

Brazil

Associação dos Arquivistas Brasileiros (Assn. of Brazilian Archivists), Av. Presidente Vargas 1733, Sala 903, 20210-030 Rio de Janiero RJ. Tel. 21-2507-2239, fax 21-3852-2541, e-mail aab@aab.org.br, World Wide Web http://www.aab.org.br. *Pres.* Lucia Maria Velloso de Oliveira.

Brunei Darussalam

Persatuan Perpustakaan Kebangsaan Negara Brunei (National Lib. Assn. of Brunei), Perpustakaan Universiti Brunei Darussalam, Jl. Tungku Link, Gadong BE 1410. Tel. 2-249-001, fax 2-249-504, e-mail chieflib@lib.ubd. edu.bn, World Wide Web http://www.ppkn-bd.org.bn. *Pres.* Nellie Dato Haji Sunny.

Cameroon

Association des Bibliothécaires, Archivistes, Documentalistes et Muséographes du Cameroun (Assn. of Libns., Archivists, Documentalists, and Museum Curators of Cameroon), BP 14077, Yaoundé. Tel. 222-6362, fax 222-4785, e-mail abadcam@yahoo.fr. *Pres.* Jerome Ndjock.

Chile

Colegio de Bibliotecarios de Chile (Chilean Lib. Assn.), Avda. Diagonal Paraguay 383, Torre 11, of. 122, 6510017 Santiago. Tel. 2-222-5652, fax 2-635-5023, e-mail cbc@ bibliotecarios.cl, World Wide Web http://www.bibliotecarios.cl. *Pres.* Paola Roncatti Galdames; *Secy.-Gen.* Carlos Pena Mardones.

China

Lib. Society of China, 33 Zhongguancun S, Beijing 100081. Tel. 10-8854-5563, fax 10-6841-7815, e-mail ztxhmsc@nlc.gov. cn, World Wide Web http://www.nlc.gov. cn. *Secy.-Gen.* Gensheng Tang; *Pres.* Zhan Furui.

Colombia

Asociación Colombiana de Bibliotecólogos y Documentalistas (Colombian Assn. of Libns. and Documentalists), Calle 21, No. 6-58, Of. 404, Bogotá. Tel. 1-282-3620, fax 1-282-5487, World Wide Web http://www. ascolbi.org. *Pres.* Edgar Allan Degado.

Congo (Republic of)

Association des Bibliothécaires, Archivistes, Documentalistes et Muséologues du Congo (ABADOM) (Assn. of Librarians, Archivists, Documentalists, and Museologists of Congo), BP 3148, Kinshasa-Gombe. *Pres.* Desire Didier Tengeneza. E-mail didier teng@yahoo.fr.

Costa Rica

Asociación Costarricense de Bibliotecarios (Costa Rican Assn. of Libns.), Apdo. 3308, San José. Tel. 234-9989, e-mail info@ cesdepu.com.

Côte d'Ivoire

Direction des Archives Nationales et de la Documentation, BP V 126, Abidjan, Tel. 20-21-74-20, fax 20-21-75-78. *Dir.* Venance Bahi Gouro.

Croatia

Hrvatsko Knjiznicarsko Drustvo (Croatian Lib. Assn.), c/o National and Univ. Lib., Hrvatske bratske zajednice 4, 10 000 Zagreb. Tel./fax 385-1-615-93-20, e-mail hkd@nsk.hr, World Wide Web http://www.hkdrustvo.hr. *Pres.* Zdenka Sviben. E-mail z.sviben@kqz. hr.

Cuba

Asociación Cubana de Bibliotecarios (AS-CUBI) (Lib. Assn. of Cuba), Biblioteca Nacional Jose Marti, Ave. Independencia 20 de Mayo, Plaza de la Revolucion, Havana. Tel. 7-555-442, fax 7-816-224, e-mail publiweb @bnjm.cu, World Wide Web http://www. bnjm.cu/ascubi. *Pres.* Margarita Bellas Vilarino.

Cyprus

Kypriakos Synthesmos Vivliothicarion (Lib. Assn. of Cyprus), c/o Pedagogical Academy, P.O. Box 1039, Nicosia.

Czech Republic

Svaz Knihovniku a Informacnich Pracovniku Ceske Republiky (SKIP) (Assn. of Lib. and Info. Professionals of the Czech Republic), National Lib., Klementinum 190, 110 00 Prague 1. Tel. 221-663-379, fax 221-663-175, e-mail vit.richter@nkp.cz, World Wide Web http://skip.nkp.cz. *Pres.* Vit Richter.

Denmark

Arkivforeningen (Archives Society), c/o Rigsarkivet, Rigsdagsgarden 9, 1218 Copenhagen. Tel. 3392-3310, fax 3315-3239, World Wide Web http://www.arkivarforeningen. no. *Pres.* Christian Larsen. E-mail cla@ ra.sa.dk.

Danmarks Biblioteksforening (Danish Lib. Assn.), Farvergade 27D, 1463 Copenhagen K. Tel. 3325-0935, fax 3325-7900, e-mail dbf@dbf.dk, World Wide Web http://www. dbf.dk. *Dir.* Vagn Ytte Larsen. E-mail vyl@ odsherred.dk.

Danmarks Forskningsbiblioteksforening (Danish Research Lib. Assn.), c/o Statsbiblioteket, Tangen 2, 8200, Arhus N. Tel. 89-46-22-07, e-mail df@statsbiblioteket.dk, World Wide Web http://www.dfdf.dk. *Pres.* Michael Cotta-Schonberg. E-mail mcs@ kb.dk; *Secy.* Hanne Dahl.

Dansk Musikbiblioteks Forening (Assn. of Danish Music Libs.), c/o Erling Dujardin, Aspegarden 38, 2670 Count. E-mail sekretariat @iaml.dk, World Wide Web http://www. dmbf.nu. *Pres.* Ole Bisbjerg.

Kommunernes Skolebiblioteksforening (Assn. of Danish School Libs.), Åboulevard 5, 2 th, DK-1635 Copenhagen V. Tel. 33-11-13-91, fax 33-11-13-90, e-mail ksbf@ksbf.dk, World Wide Web http://www.ksbf.dk. *Admin.* Gitte Frausing.

Dominican Republic

Asociación Dominicana de Bibliotecarios (Dominican Assn. of Libns.), c/o Biblioteca Nacional, Cesar Nicolás Penson 91, Plaza de la Cultura, Pichincha, Santo Domingo. Tel. 809-688-4086, fax 809-688-5841.

Ecuador

Asociación Ecuatoriana de Bibliotecarios (Ecuadoran Lib. Assn.), c/o Casa de la Cultura Ecuatoriana, Casilla 87, Quito. Tel. 9832-258-7666, fax 9832-258-8516, e-mail asoebfp @hotmail.com. *Pres.* Amparo Nuñez.

El Salvador

Asociación de Bibliotecarios de El Salvador (ABES) (Assn. of Salvadorian Libns.), Jardines de la Hacienda Block D pje, 19 No. 158, Ciudad Merliot, Antiguo Cuscatlan, La Libertad, El Salvador. Tel. 503-2241-4464, fax 523-2228-2956, World Wide Web http://www.abes.org.sv. *Pres.* Yensi Vides Ramirez.

Ethiopia

Ye Ethiopia Betemetshaft Serategnoch Mahber (Ethiopian Lib. and Info. Assn.), P.O. Box 30530, Addis Ababa. Tel. 1-511-344 ext. 223.

Finland

Suomen Kirjastoseura (Finnish Lib. Assn.), Runeberginkatu 15 A 23, 00100 Helsinki.

Tel. 9-6221-340, fax 9-6221-466, e-mail fla@fla.fi, World Wide Web http://www.fla. fi. *Exec. Dir.* Sinikka Sipila.

France

Association des Archivistes Français (Assn. of French Archivists), 8 rue Jean-Marie Jego, 75013 Paris. Tel. 1-46-06-39-44, fax 1-46-06-39-52, e-mail secretariat@archivistes. org, World Wide Web http://www.archivistes. org. *Pres.* Xavier de la Selle; *Secy.* Marie-Edith Enderle-Naud.

Association des Bibliothécaires Français (Assn. of French Libns.), 31 rue de Chabrol, F-75010 Paris. Tel. 1-55-33-10-30, fax 1-55-30-10-31, e-mail abf@abf.asso.fr, World Wide Web http://www.abf.asso.fr. *Pres.* Pascal Wagner; *Gen. Secy.* Maité Vanmarque.

Association des Professionnels de l'Information et de la Documentation (Assn. of Info. and Documentation Professionals), 25 rue Claude Tillier, F-75012 Paris. Tel. 1-43-72-25-25, fax 1-43-72-30-41, e-mail adbs@ adbs.fr, World Wide Web http://www.adbs. fr. *Commissioner Gen.* Flora Lagneau.

Germany

Arbeitsgemeinschaft der Spezialbibliotheken (Assn. of Special Libs.), c/o Herder-Institute eV, Bibliothek, Gisonenweg 5-7, 35037 Marburg. Tel. 6421-184-151, fax 6421-184-139, e-mail geschaeftsstelle@aspb.de, World Wide Web http://www.aspb.de. *Chair* Juergen Warmbrunn. E-mail warmbrunn@ herder-institut.de.

Berufsverband Information Bibliothek (Assn. of Info. and Lib. Professionals), Gartenstr. 18, 72764 Reutlingen. Tel. 7121-3491-0, fax 7121-3004-33, e-mail mail@bib-info. de, World Wide Web http://www.bib-info. de. *Pres.* Susanne Riedel. E-mail susanne. riedel@uni-bielefeld.de.

Deutsche Gesellschaft für Informationswissenschaft und Informationspraxis eV (German Society for Info. Science and Practice), Hanauer Landstr. 151-153, 60314 Frankfurt-am-Main 1. Tel. 69-43-03-13, fax 69-490-90-96, e-mail mail@dgi-info.de, World Wide Web http://www.dgd.de. *Pres.* Stefan Gradmann.

Deutscher Bibliotheksverband eV (German Lib. Assn.), Str. des 17 Juni 114, 10623 Berlin. Tel. 30-644-98-99-10, fax 30-64-49-89-92-9, e-mail dbv@bibliotheksverband. de, World Wide Web http://www.bibliotheks verband.de. *Chair* Gabriele Beger. E-mail beger@dgi-info.de.

VdA—Verband Deutscher Archivarinnen und Archivare (Assn. of German Archivists), Woerthstr. 3, 36037 Fulda. Tel. 661-29-109-72, fax 661-29-109-74, e-mail info@vda.ar chiv.net, World Wide Web http://www.vda. archiv.net. *Chair* Michael Diefenbacher.

Verein Deutscher Bibliothekare eV (Society of German Libns.), Universitaetsbibliothek Augsburg, Universitaetsstr. 22, 86159 Augsburg. Tel. 821-598-5300, fax 821-598-5354, e-mail sekr@bibliothek.uni-augsburg.de, World Wide Web http://www.vdb-online. org. *Chair* Ulrich Hohoff.

Ghana

Ghana Lib. Assn., c/o INSTI, P.O. Box GP 4105, Accra. Tel. 244-17-4930, e-mail info@librarygla.org, World Wide Web http://gla-net.org. *Pres.* Valentina J. A. Bannerman. E-mail valnin@yahoo.com.

Greece

Enosis Hellinon Bibliothekarion (Greek Lib. Assn.), Skoufa 52, P.O. Box 10672, Athens. Tel./fax 210-330-2128, World Wide Web http://www.eebep.gr. *Pres.* Christina Kyriakopoulou.

Guyana

Guyana Lib. Assn., c/o National Lib., P.O. Box 10240, Georgetown. Tel. 222-486, fax 223-596, e-mail londonh@uog.ed.gy, World Wide Web http://www.natlib.gov.gy. *Pres.* Wendy R. Stephenson, *Secy.* Althea John.

Honduras

Asociación de Bibliotecarios y Archiveros de Honduras (Assn. of Libns. and Archivists of Honduras), 11a Calle, 1a y 2a Avdas., No. 105, Comayagüela DC, Tegucigalpa. *Secy.-Gen.* Juan Angel R. Ayes.

Hong Kong

Hong Kong Lib. Assn., GPO Box 10095, Hong Kong. E-mail hkla@hkla.org, World Wide Web http://www.hkla.org. *Pres.* Peter Sidroko. E-mail peters@hkucc.hku.hk.

Hungary

Magyar Könyvtárosok Egyesülete (Assn. of Hungarian Libns.), Budavari Palota F, epulet 439 szoba, Budapest. Tel./fax 1-311-8634, e-mail mke@oszk.hu, World Wide Web http://www.mke.oszk.hu. *Pres.* Klara Bakos; *Secy. Gen.* Nagy Aniko.

Iceland

Upplysing—Felag bokasafns-og upplysinga-fraeoa (Information—The Icelandic Lib. and Info. Science Assn.), Lyngasi 18, 210 Garda-baer. Tel. 864-6220, e-mail upplysing@upplysing.is, World Wide Web http://www.upplysing.is. *Chair* Hrafnhildur Hreinsdottir. E-mail hrafnhildur@velvakandi.is; *Secy.* Ingibjorg Osp Ottarsdottir.

India

Indian Assn. of Special Libs. and Info. Centres, P-291, CIT Scheme 6M, Kankurgachi, Kolkata 700054. Tel. 33-2362-9651, e-mail iaslic@vsnl.net. *Pres.* J. N. Satpathi. E-mail satpathijn@rediffmail.com.

Indian Lib. Assn., A/40-41, Flat 201, Ansal Bldg., Mukerjee Nagar, New Delhi 110009. Tel./fax 11-2765-1743, e-mail dvs-srcc@rediffmail.com, World Wide Web http://www.ilaindia.net. *Gen. Secy.* R. Chandra.

Indonesia

Ikatan Pustakawan Indonesia (Indonesian Lib. Assn.), Jl. Merdeka Selatan No. 11, 10110 Jakarta, Pusat. Tel./fax 21-385-5729, World Wide Web http://ipri.pnri.go.id. *Pres.* S. Kartosdono.

Ireland

Cumann Leabharlann Na h-Eireann (Lib. Assn. of Ireland), 53 Upper Mount St., Dublin 2. Tel. 1-6120-2193, fax 1-6121-3090, e-mail president@libraryassociation.ie, World Wide Web http://www.libraryassociation.ie. *Pres.* Siobhan Fitzpatrick.

Israel

Israel Libns. and Info. Specialists Assn., 9 Beit Hadfus St., Givaat Shaul, Jerusalem. Tel. 2-658-9515, fax 2-625-1628, e-mail icl@icl.org.il. *Pres.* Benjamin Schachter.

Israeli Center for Libs., P.O. Box 801, 51108 Bnei Brak. Tel. 03-618-0151, fax 3-579-8048, e-mail icl@icl.org.il, World Wide Web http://www.icl.org.il.

Israeli Society for Libs. and Info. Centers (ASMI), Blum 8, 44253 Kfar Saba. Tel. 77-215-1800, fax 77-434-509, e-mail agudatasmi@gmail.com, World Wide Web http://www.asmi.org.il. *Chair* Hagafni Shahaf.

Italy

Associazione Italiana Biblioteche (Italian Lib. Assn.), C.P. 2461, 00185 Rome AD. Tel. 6-446-3532, fax 6-444-1139, e-mail aib@aib.it, World Wide Web http://www.aib.it. *Pres.* Mauro Guerrini.

Jamaica

Lib. and Info. Assn. of Jamaica., P.O. Box 125, Kingston 5. Tel./fax 876-927-1614, e-mail liajapresident@yahoo.com, World Wide Web http://www.liaja.org.jm. *Pres.* Paulette Stewart.

Japan

Joho Kagaku Gijutsu Kyokai (Info. Science and Technology Assn.), Sasaki Bldg., 2-5-7 Koisikawa, Bunkyo-ku, Tokyo 112-0002. Tel. 3-3813-3791, fax 3-3813-3793, e-mail infosta@infosta.or.jp, World Wide Web http://www.infosta.or.jp. *Pres.* Onodera Natsuo.

Nihon Toshokan Kyokai (Japan Lib. Assn.), 1-11-14 Shinkawa, Chuo-ku, Tokyo 104 0033. Tel. 3-3523-0811, fax 3-3523-0841, e-mail info@jla.or.jp, World Wide Web http://www.jla.or.jp. *Pres.* Shiomi Noboru.

Senmon Toshokan Kyogikai (Japan Special Libs. Assn.), c/o Japan Lib. Assn., Bldg. F6, 1-11-14 Shinkawa Chuo-ku, Tokyo 104-0033. Tel. 3-3537-8335, fax 3-3537-8336, e-mail jsla@jsla.or.jp, World Wide Web http://www.jsla.or.jp. *Pres.* Kousaku Inaba; *Exec. Dir.* Fumihisa Nakagawa.

Jordan

Arab Archives Institute, P.O. Box 815454, Amman. Tel. 6-465-6694, fax 6-465-6693, e-mail aainstitute@gmail.com, World Wide Web http://www.alarcheef.com. *Dir.* Sa'eda Kilani.
Jordan Lib. Assn., P.O. Box 6289, Amman 11118. Tel./fax 6-462-9412, e-mail info@jorla.org, World Wide Web http://www.jorla.org. *Pres.* Anwar Akroush.

Kenya

Kenya Assn. of Lib. and Info. Professionals (formerly Kenya Lib. Assn.), P.O. Box 46031, 00100 Nairobi. Tel. 20-733-732-799, fax 20-811-455, e-mail talktochairman@gmail.com, World Wide Web http://www.klas.or.ke. *Chair* Rosemary Gitachu. E-mail gitachur@yahoo.com.

Korea (Democratic People's Republic of)

Lib. Assn. of the Democratic People's Republic of Korea, c/o Grand People's Study House, P.O. Box 200, Pyongyang. E-mail nsj@co.chesin.com.

Korea (Republic of)

Korean Lib. Assn., San 60-1, Banpo-dong, Seocho-gu, Seoul 137-702. Tel. 2-535-4868, fax 2-535-5616, e-mail license@kla.kr, World Wide Web http://www.kla.kr. *Pres.* Ki Nam Shin; *Exec. Dir.* Won Ho Jo.

Laos

Association des Bibliothécaires Laotiens (Lao Lib. Assn.), c/o Direction de la Bibliothèque Nationale, Ministry of Info. and Culture, BP 704, Vientiane. Tel. 21-21-2452, fax 21-21-2408, e-mail bailane@laotel.com.

Latvia

Latvian Libns. Assn., Terbatas iela 75, Riga LV-1001. Tel./fax 6731-2792, e-mail lbb@lbi.lnb.lv, World Wide Web http://www.lnb.lv.

Lebanon

Lebanese Lib. Assn., P.O. Box 13-5053, Beirut 1102 2801. Tel. 1-786-456, e-mail kjaroudy@lau.edu.lb; World Wide Web http://www.llaweb.org/index.php. *Pres.* Fawz Abdalleh.

Lesotho

Lesotho Lib. Assn., Private Bag A26, Maseru 100. Tel./fax 213-420, e-mail s.mohai@nul.ls. *Chair* Celina K. M. Qobo; *Secy.* Makemang Ntsasa.

Lithuania

Lietuvos Bibliotekininku Draugija (Lithuanian Libns. Assn.), Sv Ignoto 6-108, LT-1120 Vilnius. Tel./fax 5-262-55-70, e-mail lbd_sekretore@amb.lt, World Wide Web http://www.lbd.lt. *Pres.* Petras Zurlys.

Luxembourg

Association Luxembourgeoise des Bibliothécaires, Archivistes, et Documentalistes (ALBAD) (Luxembourg Assn. of Libns., Archivists, and Documentalists), c/o National Lib. of Luxembourg, BP 295, L-2012 Luxembourg. Tel. 352-22-97-55-1, fax 352-47-56-72, World Wide Web http://www.albad.lu. *Pres.* Jean-Marie Reding. E-mail jean-marie.reding@bnl.etat.lu; *Secy.-Gen.* Michel Donven. E-mail michel.donven@bnl.etat.lu.

Macedonia

Bibliotekarsko Drustvo na Makedonija (Union of Libns.' Assns. of Macedonia), Blvd. Gotse Delcev 6, 1000 Skopje. E-mail bdm@bdm.org.mk, World Wide Web http://www.bdm.org.mk. *Pres.* Kiril Angelov; *Secy.* Elena Tevcheva.

Malawi

Malawi Lib. Assn., c/o Univ. Libn., P.O. Box 429, Zomba. *Pres.* Diston Chiweza. E-mail librarian@medcol.mw.

Malaysia

Persatuan Perpustakaan Malaysia (Lib. Assn. of Malaysia), P.O. Box 12545, 50782 Kuala Lumpur. Tel./fax 3-2694-7390, e-mail ppm55@po.jaring.my. *Pres.* Raslin Abu Bakar. E-mail raslin@pnm.my.

Mali

Association Malienne des Bibliothécaires, Archivistes et Documentalistes (Mali Assn. of Libns., Archivists, and Documentalists), BP E4473, Bamako. Tel. 20-29-94-23, fax 20-29-93-76, e-mail dnbd@afribone.net.ml. *Pres.* Mamadou Konoba Keita.

Malta

Malta Lib. and Info. Assn. (MaLIA), c/o Univ. of Malta Lib., Msida MSD 2080. E-mail info@malia-malta.org, World Wide Web http://www.malia-malta.org. *Chair* Laurence Zerafa.

Mauritania

Association Mauritanienne des Bibliothécaires, Archivistes et Documentalistes (Mauritanian Assn. of Libns., Archivists, and Documentalists), c/o Bibliothèque Nationale, BP 20, Nouakchott. Tel. 525-18-62, fax 525-18-68, e-mail bibliothequenationale@yahoo.fr.

Mauritius

Mauritius Lib. Assn., Ministry of Educ. Public Lib., Moka Rd., Rose Hill. Tel. 403-0200, fax 454-9553. *Pres.* Abdool Fareed Soogali.

Mexico

Asociación Mexicana de Bibliotecarios (Mexican Assn. of Libns.), Apdo. 12-800, Admon Postal Obreto Mundial, 03001 México DF 06760. Tel. 155-5575-3396, fax 155-5575-1136, e-mail correo@ambac.org.mx, World Wide Web http://www.ambac.org.mx. *Pres.* Oscar Saavedra; *Secy.* Maria Asuncion Mendoza.

Myanmar

Myanmar Lib. Assn., c/o National Lib., 85 Thirimingalar Ave., Yankin, Yangon. Tel. 1-28-3332.

Nepal

Nepal Lib. Assn., GPO 2773, Kathmandu. Tel. 977-1-441-1318, e-mail info@nla.org.np, World Wide Web http://www.nla.org.np. *Contact* Rudra Prasad Dulal.

The Netherlands

Nederlandse Vereniging voor Beroepsbeoefenaren in de Bibliotheek-Informatie-en Kennissector (Netherlands Assn. of Libns., Documentalists, and Info. Specialists), Mariaplaats 3, 3511 LH Utrecht. Tel. 30-233-00-50, fax 30-238-00-30, e-mail info@nvbonline.nl, World Wide Web http://www.nvbonline.nl. *Managing Dir.* Jan van der Burg. E-mail burg@nvbonline.nl.

New Zealand

New Zealand Lib. Assn. (LIANZA), P.O. Box 12-212, Thorndon, Wellington 6144. Tel. 4-801-5542, fax 4-801-5543, e-mail admin @lianza.org.nz, World Wide Web http://www.lianza.org.nz. *Exec. Dir.* Alli Smith. E-mail alli@lianza.org.nz.

Nicaragua

Asociación Nicaraguense de Bibliotecarios y Profesionales Afines (ANIBIPA) (Nicaraguan Assn. of Libns.), Bello Horizonte, Tope Sur de la Rotonda 1/2 cuadra abajo, Casa J-11-57, Managua. Tel. 277-4159 ext. 335, e-mail anibipa@hotmail.com. *Pres.* Yadira Roque. E-mail r-yardira@hotmail.com.

Nigeria

Nigerian Lib. Assn., c/o National Lib. of Nigeria, Sanusi Dantata House, Central Business District, PMB 1, Abuja GPO 900001. Tel. 803-334-8817, fax 9-234-6773, e-mail info@nla-ng.org, World Wide Web http://www.nla-ng.org. *Pres.* Victoria Okojie; *Secy.* D. D. Bwayili.

Norway

Arkivforeningen (Assn. of Archivists), Postboks 4013, Ulleval Stadion, 0806 Oslo. Tel. 22-02-26-03, fax 22-23-74-89, e-mail linhol@

arkivverket.no, World Wide Web http://www. arkivarforeningen.no. *Chair* Linda Holmans. Norsk Bibliotekforening (Norwegian Lib. Assn.), Postboks 6540, 0606 Etterstad. Tel. 23-24-34-30, fax 22-67-23-68, e-mail nbf@ norskbibliotekforening.no, World Wide Web http://www.norskbibliotekforening.no. *Gen. Secy.* Tore Andersen.

Pakistan

Library Promotion Bureau, Karachi Univ. Campus, P.O. Box 8421, Karachi 75270. Tel. 21-3632-1959, fax 21-857-6301, e-mail lpb_pakistan_bb@yahoo.com.

Panama

Asociación Panameña de Bibliotecarios (Panama Lib. Assn.), c/o Biblioteca Interamericana Simón Bolivar, Estafeta Universitaria, Panama City. E-mail biblis2@arcon.up.ac. pa.

Paraguay

Asociación de Bibliotecarios Graduados del Paraguay (Assn. of Paraguayan Graduate Libns.), Facultad Politecnica, Universidad Nacional de Asunción, 2160 San Lorenzo. Tel. 21-585-588, e-mail abigrap@pol.una. py, World Wide Web http://www.pol.una.py/ abigrap. *Pres.* Emilce Noemi Sena Correa.

Peru

Asociación de Archiveros del Perú (Peruvian Assn. of Archivists), Av. Manco Capacc No. 1180, Dpto 201, La Victoria, Lima. Tel. 1-472-8729, fax 1-472-7408, e-mail contactos@adapperu.com. *Pres.* Juan Manuel Serrano Valencia.
Asociación Peruana de Bibliotecarios (Peruvian Assn. of Libns.), Bellavista 561 Miraflores, Apdo. 995, Lima 18. Tel. 1-474-869. *Pres.* Martha Fernandez de Lopez.

Philippines

Assn. of Special Libs. of the Philippines, Rm. 301, National Lib. Bldg., T. M. Kalaw St., 1000 Ermita, Manila. Tel. 2-740-9625, e-mail aslpboard@yahoo.com.ph, World Wide

Web http://aslpboard.multiply.com. *Pres.* Wilhelmina Lopez.
Philippine Libns. Assn., P.O. Box 2926, 1000 Ermita, Manila. Tel./fax 2-525-9401, World Wide Web http://web.nlp.gov.ph/nlp. *Pres.* Lilia F Echiverri. E-mail lily.echiverri@ gmail.com.

Poland

Stowarzyszenie Bibliotekarzy Polskich (Polish Libns. Assn.), al Niepodleglosci 213, 02-086 Warsaw. Tel. 22-825-83-74, fax 22-825-53-49, e-mail biurozgsbp@sbp.pl, World Wide Web http://www.sbp.pl. *Pres.* Elzbieta Stefanczyk; *Secy.-Gen.* Marzena Przybysz.

Portugal

Associação Portuguesa de Bibliotecários, Arquivistas e Documentalistas (Portuguese Assn. of Libns., Archivists, and Documentalists), Rua Morais Soares, 43C, 1 Dto, 1900-341 Lisbon. Tel. 21-816-19-80, fax 21-815-45-08, e-mail apbad@apbad. pt, World Wide Web http://www.apbad.pt/ edicoes/edicoes_cadernos.htm. *Pres.* Maria Paula Santos.

Puerto Rico

Sociedad de Bibliotecarios de Puerto Rico (Society of Libns. of Puerto Rico), Apdo 22898, San Juan 00931-2898. Tel./fax 787-764-0000, World Wide Web http://www.sociedadbibliotecarios.org. *Pres.* Ivan Calimano. E-mail kalimano@gmail.com.

Russia

Rossiiskaya Bibliotechnaya Assotsiatsiya (Russian Lib. Assn.), 18 Sadovaya St., St. Petersburg 191069. Tel. 812-118-85-36, fax 812-710-58-61, e-mail rba@nlr.ru, World Wide Web http://www.rba.ru. *Pres.* Vladimir Zaitsev; *Exec. Secy.* Elena Tikhonova.

Senegal

Association Sénégalaise des Bibliothécaires, Archivistes et Documentalistes (Senegalese Assn. of Libns., Archivists, and Documentalists), BP 2006, Dakar. Tel. 77-651-00-33, fax

33-824-23-79, e-mail asbad200@hotmail.
com, World Wide Web http://www.asbad.
org. *Pres.* Adama Aly Pam; *Secy.-Gen.*
Alassane Ndiath.

Serbia and Montenegro

Jugoslovenski Bibliografsko Informacijski In-
stitut, Terazije 26, 11000 Belgrade. Tel. 11-
2687-836, fax 11-2687-760. *Dir.* Radomir
Glavicki.

Sierra Leone

Sierra Leone Assn. of Archivists, Libns., and
Info. Scientists, c/o Sierra Leone Lib. Board,
Rokel St., Freetown. Tel. 22-22-0758. *Pres.*
Oliver Harding.

Singapore

Lib. Assn. of Singapore, National Lib. Board,
100 Victoria St., No. 14-01, Singapore
188064. Tel. 6332-3255, fax 6332-3248,
e-mail lassec@las.org.sg, World Wide Web
http://www.las.org.sg. *Pres.* Puspa Yeow.

Slovenia

Zveza Bibliotekarskih Društev Slovenije
(Union of Assns. of Slovene Libns.),
Turjaška 1, 1000 Ljubljana. Tel. 01-20-01-
207, fax 01-42-57-293, e-mail zbds2010@
gmail.com, World Wide Web http://www.
zbds-zveza.si. *Pres.* Melita Ambrozic.

South Africa

Lib. and Info. Assn. of South Africa, Dept. of
Info. Science, Univ. of South Africa, P.O.
Box 392, Pretoria 0003. Tel. 12-328-2010,
fax 12-323-1033, e-mail liasa@liasa.org.
za, World Wide Web http://www.liasa.org.
za. *Pres.* Rachel More; *National Secy.* Judy
Henning.

Spain

Federación Española de Archiveros, Bibliotecarios, Museólogos y Documentalistas
(ANABAD) (Spanish Assn. of Archivists,
Libns., Curators, and Documentalists), de
las Huertas, 37, 28014 Madrid. Tel. 34-
91-575-1727, fax 34-91-578-1615, e-mail

anabad@anabad-clm.org, World Wide Web
http://www.anabad.org. *Pres.* Gacho Miguel
Ángel Santamaría.

Sri Lanka

Sri Lanka Lib. Assn., 275/75 OPA Centre,
Stanley Wijesundara Mawatha, Colombo 7.
Tel./fax 11-258-9103, e-mail slla@slltnet.
lk, World Wide Web http://www.slla.org.lk.
Pres. Upali Amarasiri; *Gen. Secy.* Pushpa-
mala Perera.

Swaziland

Swaziland Lib. Assn., P.O. Box 2309, Mbabane
H100. Tel. 404-2633, fax 404-3863, e-mail
fmkhonta@uniswacc.uniswa.sz, World Wide
Web http://www.swala.sz. *Chair* Faith Mk-
honta.

Sweden

Svensk Biblioteksförening Kansli (Swedish
Lib. Assn.), Box 70380, 107 24 S-Stock-
holm. Tel. 8-545-132-30, fax 8-545-132-
31, e-mail info@biblioteksforeningen.org,
World Wide Web http://www.biblioteks
foreningen.org. *Secy.-Gen.* Niclas Lindberg.
Svensk Förening för Informationsspecialis-
ter (Swedish Assn. for Info. Specialists),
Osquars backe 25, SE-100 44 Stockholm.
Tel. 8-678-23-20, e-mail kansliet@sfis.nu,
World Wide Web http://www.sfis.nu. *Pres.*
Peter Almerud. E-mail peter.almerud@
gmail.com.
Svenska Arkivsamfundet (Swedish Assn. of
Archivists), c/o Swedish Stockholms stad-
sarkiv, Box 22063, 104 22 Stockholm.
Tel. 46-19-70-00, fax 46-19-70-70, e-mail
info@arkivsamfundet.se, World Wide Web
http://www.arkivsamfundet.se. *Pres.* Sara
Naeslund.

Switzerland

Association des Bibliothèques et Bibliothé-
caires Suisses/Vereinigung Schweizerischer
Bibliothekare/Associazione dei Bibliotecari
Svizzeri (Assn. of Swiss Libs. and Libns.),
Hallestr. 58, CH-3012 Bern. Tel. 31-382-42-
40, fax 31-382-46-48, e-mail info@bis.info.
Schweizerische Vereinigung für Dokumenta-
tion/Association Suisse de Documentation

(Swiss Assn. of Documentation), Hallestr. 58, CH-3012 Bern. Tel. 31-382-42-40, fax 31-382-46-48, e-mail info@bis.info, World Wide Web http://www.svd-asd.org. *Gen. Secy.* Barbara Kraeuchi. E-mail b.kraeuchi@bbs.ch.

Verein Schweizer Archivarinnen und Archivare (Assn. of Swiss Archivists), Schweizerisches Bundesarchiv, Office Pontri GmbH, Solohurnstr. 13, CH-3322, Urtenen Schönbühl. Tel. 31-312-26-66, fax 31-312-26-68, e-mail info@vsa-aas.org, World Wide Web http://www.vsa-aas.org. *Pres.* Anna Pia Maissen, Zurich City Archives. E-mail annapia.maissen@zuerich.ch.

Taiwan

Lib. Assn. of the Republic of China (LAROC), 20 Zhongshan South Rd., Taipei 100. Tel. 2-2331-9132, fax 2-2370-0899, e-mail lac@msg.ncl.edu.tw. *Secy.-Gen.* Teresa Wang Chang.

Tanzania

Tanzania Lib. Assn., P.O. Box 33433, Dar es Salaam. Tel./fax 744- 296-134, e-mail tla_tanzania@yahoo.com, World Wide Web http://www.tla.or.tz. *Chair* Alli Mcharazo. E-mail amcharazo@hotmail.com.

Thailand

Thai Lib. Assn., 1346 Akarnsongkrau Rd. 5, Klongchan, Bangkapi, 10240 Bangkok. Tel. 02-734-9022, fax 02-734-9021, e-mail tla2497@yahoo.com, World Wide Web http://tla.or.th. *Pres.* Chutima Sacchanand; *Exec. Secy.* Suwadee Vichetpan.

Trinidad and Tobago

Lib. Assn. of Trinidad and Tobago, P.O. Box 1275, Port of Spain. Tel. 868-313-6321, e-mail info@latt.org.tt, World Wide Web http://www.latt.org.tt.

Tunisia

Association Tunisienne des Documentalistes, Bibliothécaires et Archivistes (Tunisian Assn. of Documentalists, Libns., and Archivists), Centre de Documentation Nationale, 8004 rue Kheredinne Pacha, 1002 Tunis. Tel. 7165-1924.

Turkey

Türk Kütüphaneciler Dernegi (Turkish Libns. Assn.), Necatibey Cad Elgun Sok 8/8, 06440 Kizilay, Ankara. Tel. 312-230-13-25, fax 312-232-04-53, e-mail tkd.dernek@gmail.com, World Wide Web http://www.kutuphaneci.org.tr. *Pres.* Ali Fuat Kartal; *Secy.* Hakan Anameric.

Uganda

Uganda Lib. and Info. Assn., P.O. Box 8147, Kampala. Tel. 141-256-77-467698. *Pres.* Innocent Rugambwa; *Gen. Secy.* Sarah Kaddu.

Ukraine

Ukrainian Lib. Assn., Vasylkovska 12, office 5, code 5, 01004, Kyiv. Tel. 380-44-239-74-87, fax 380-44-35-45-47, e-mail u_b_a@ukr.net, World Wide Web http://www.uba.org.ua. *Exec. Dir.* Soshynska Yaroslav.

United Kingdom

ASLIB, the Assn. for Info. Management, 207 Howard House, Wagon Lane, Bingley BD16 1WA, England. Tel. 01274-777-700, fax 01274-785-201, e-mail support@aslib.com, World Wide Web http://www.aslib.com.

Bibliographical Society, Institute of English Studies, Rm. 306, Senate House, Malet St., London WC1E 7HU, England. Tel. 20-7611-7244, fax 20-7611-8703, World Wide Web http://www.bibsoc.org.uk/bibsoc.htm. *Pres.* David Pearson.

Chartered Institute of Lib. and Info. Professionals (CILIP) (formerly the Lib. Assn.), 7 Ridgmount St., London WC1E 7AE, England. Tel. 20-7255-0500, fax 20-7255-0501, e-mail info@cilip.org.uk, World Wide Web http://www.cilip.org.uk. *Chief Exec.* Bob McKee.

School Lib. Assn., Unit 2, Lotmead Business Village, Wanborough, Swindon SN4 0UY, England. Tel. 1793-791-787, fax 1793-791-786, e-mail info@sla.org.uk, World Wide Web http://www.sla.org.uk. *Pres.* Miranda McKearney.

Scottish Lib. and Info. Council, 1st fl., Bldg. C, Brandon Gate, Leechlee Rd., Hamilton ML3 6AU, Scotland. Tel. 1698-458-888, fax 1698-283-170, e-mail slic@slainte.org.uk, World Wide Web http://www.slainte.org.uk/slic/slicindex.htm. *Dir.* Elaine Fulton.

Society of Archivists, Prioryfield House, 20 Canon St., Taunton TA1 1SW, England. Tel. 1823-327-030, fax 1823-271-719, e-mail societyofarchivists@archives.org.uk, World Wide Web http://www.archives.org.uk. *Chair* Peter Emmerson; *Exec. Dir.* John Chambers.

Society of College, National, and Univ. Libs (SCONUL) (formerly Standing Conference of National and Univ. Libs.), 102 Euston St., London NW1 2HA, England. Tel. 20-7387-0317, fax 20-7383-3197, e-mail info@sconul.ac.uk, World Wide Web http://www.sconul.ac.uk. *Chair* Jane Core.

Uruguay

Agrupación Bibliotecológica del Uruguay (Uruguayan Lib. and Archive Science Assn.), Cerro Largo 1666, 11200 Montevideo. Tel. 2-400-57-40, e-mail lama@adinet.com.uy. *Pres.* Luis Alberto Musso.

Asociación de Bibliotecólogos del Uruguay, Eduardo V. Haedo 2255, 11200 Montevideo.

Tel./fax 2-4099-989, e-mail abu@adinet.com.uy, World Wide Web http://www.abu.net.uy. *Pres.* Alicia Ocaso Ferreira.

Venezuela

Colegio de Bibliotecólogos y Archivólogos de Venezuela (Venezuelan Lib. and Archives Assn.), Apdo. 6283, Caracas. Tel. 212-572-1858.

Vietnam

Hôi Thu-Vien Viet Nam (Vietnamese Lib. Assn.), National Lib. of Vietnam, 31 Trang Thi, 10000 Hanoi. Tel. 4-8254-938, fax 4-8-253-357, e-mail info@nlv.gov.vn, World Wide Web http://www.nlv.gov.vn.

Zambia

Zambia Lib. Assn., P.O. Box 32379, Lusaka. *Chair* Benson Njobvu. E-mail bensonnjobvu@gmail.com.

Zimbabwe

Zimbabwe Lib. Assn., P.O. Box 3133, Harare. Tel. 4-692-741, e-mail zimlanec@gmail.com, World Wide Web http://zimbabwereads.org/zimla. *Chair* T. G. Bohwa.

Directory of Book Trade and Related Organizations

Book Trade Associations, United States and Canada

For more extensive information on the associations listed in this section, see the annual edition of *Literary Market Place* (Information Today, Inc.).

AIGA—The Professional Assn. for Design (formerly the American Institute of Graphic Arts), 164 Fifth Ave., New York, NY 10010. Tel. 212-807-1990, fax 212-807-1799, e-mail aiga@aiga.org, World Wide Web http://www.aiga.org. *Pres.* Doug Powell, Schwartz Powell, 330 Elmwood Place W., Minneapolis, MN 55419. Tel. 612-875-6702, e-mail doug@schwartzpowell.com; *Exec. Dir.* Richard Grefe. E-mail grefe@aiga.org.

American Book Producers Assn. (ABPA), 151 W. 19 St., Third fl., New York, NY 10011. Tel. 917-741-1919, fax 212-675-1364, e-mail office@ABPAonline.org, World Wide Web http://www.abpaonline.org. *Pres.* Richard Rothschild; *V.P.* Nancy Hall; *Admin.* Kirsten Hall.

American Booksellers Assn., 200 White Plains Rd., Tarrytown, NY 10591. Tel. 800-637-0037, 914-591-2665, fax 914-591-2720, World Wide Web http://www.bookweb.org. *Pres.* Becky Anderson, Anderson's Bookshops, 123 W. Jefferson Ave., Naperville, IL 60540 . Tel. 630-355-2665, fax 630-355-3470, e-mail becky@andersonsbookshop. com; *V.P./Secy.* Steve Bercu, BookPeople, 603 N. Lamar, Austin, TX 78703. Tel. 512-472-5050, e-mail steve@bookpeople.com; *CEO* Oren Teicher. E-mail oren@bookweb. org.

American Literary Translators Assn. (ALTA), Univ. of Texas at Dallas, 800 W. Campbell Rd., Mail Sta. JO51, Richardson, TX 75080. Tel. 972-883-2092, fax 972-883-6303, World Wide Web http://www.utdallas.edu/ alta. *Pres.* Gary Racz; *V.P.* Elizabeth Lowe; *Secy./Treas.* Russell Valentino.

American Medical Publishers Committee (AMPC), c/o Sara Pinto, dir., Professional/ Scholarly Publishing Div., Assn. of American Publishers, 71 Fifth Ave., New York, NY 10003-3004. Tel. 212-255-0200 ext. 257, fax 212-255-7007, e-mail spinto@publishers. org, World Wide Web http://www.psp central.org/rtcommittees/ampc/ampc_001. cfm.

American Printing History Assn., Box 4519, Grand Central Sta., New York, NY 10163-4519. World Wide Web http://www.printinghistory.org. *Pres.* Robert McCamant; *Exec. Secy.* Lyndsi Barnes. E-mail secretary@ printinghistory.org.

American Society for Indexing, 10200 W. 44 Ave., Suite 304, Wheat Ridge, CO 80033. Tel. 303-463-2887, fax 303-422-8894, e-mail info@asindexing.org, World Wide Web http://www.asindexing.org. *Pres.* Richard Shrout. E-mail president@asindexing.org; *V.P./Pres.-Elect* Pilar Wyman. E-mail pilarw @wymanindexing.com; *Exec. Dir.* Annette Rogers. E-mail arogers@asindexing.org.

American Society of Journalists and Authors, 1501 Broadway, Suite 403, New York, NY 10036. Tel. 212-997-0947, fax 212-937-3215, e-mail director@asja.org, World Wide Web http://www.asja.org. *Pres.* Salley Shannon. E-mail president@asja.org; *Exec. Dir.* Alexandra Owens.

American Society of Media Photographers, 150 N. 2 St., Philadelphia, PA 19106. Tel.

215-451-2767, fax 215-451-0880, e-mail mopsik@asmp.org, World Wide Web http://www.asmp.org. *Pres.* Jim Cavanaugh; *Exec. Dir.* Eugene Mopsik.

American Society of Picture Professionals, 217 Palos Verdes Blvd., No. 700, Redondo Beach, CA 90277. Tel. 424-247-9944, fax 424-247-9844, e-mail director@aspp.com, World Wide Web http://www.aspp.com. *Pres.* Michael Masterson; *Exec. Dir.* Jain Lemos.

American Translators Assn., 225 Reinekers Lane, Suite 590, Alexandria, VA 22314. Tel. 703-683-6100, fax 703-683-6122, e-mail ata@atanet.org, World Wide Web http://www.atanet.org. *Pres.* Dorothee Racette; *Pres.-Elect* Caitilin Walsh; *Secy.* Boris Silversteyn; *Treas.* Gabe Bokor; *Exec. Dir.* Walter W. Bacak, Jr. E-mail walter@atanet.org.

Antiquarian Booksellers Assn. of America, 20 W. 44 St., No. 507, New York, NY 10036-6604. Tel. 212-944-8291, fax 212-944-8293, e-mail inquiries@abaa.org, World Wide Web http://www.abaa.org. *Pres.* Sarah Baldwin; *V.P./Secy.* John Thomson; *Treas.* Thomas Goldwasser; *Exec. Dir.* Susan Benne. E-mail sbenne@abaa.org.

Assn. Media and Publishing (formerly Society of National Assn. Publications, or SNAP), 1760 Old Meadow Rd., Suite 500, McLean, VA 22102. Tel. 703-506-3285, fax 703-506-3266, e-mail info@associationmediaand publishing.org, World Wide Web http://www.associationmediaandpublishing.org. *Pres.* Greg Fine; *V.P.* Gary Rubin; *Exec. Dir.* Amy Lestition. Tel. 703-506-3285, e-mail a lestition@associationmediaandpublishing.org.

Assn. of American Publishers, 71 Fifth Ave., New York, NY 10003. Tel. 212-255-0200, fax 212-255-7007. *Washington Office* 455 Massachusetts Ave. N.W., Suite 700, Washington, DC 20001. Tel. 202-347-3375, fax 202-347-3690. *Pres./CEO* Tom Allen; *V.P.s* Allan R. Adler, Tina Jordan, Andi Sporkin, John Tagler; *Dir., Free Expression Advocacy* Judith Platt; *Exec. Dir., School Div.* Jay Diskey; *Exec. Dir., Higher Education* J. Bruce Hildebrand; *Exec. Dir., International Copyright Enforcement and Trade Policy* M. Lui Simpson; *Exec. Dir., Digital, Environmen-*

tal, and Accessibility Affairs Ed McCoyd; *Dir., Membership Marketing* Gail Kump.

Assn. of American University Presses, 28 W. 36 St., Suite 602, New York, NY 10018. Tel. 212-989-1010, fax 212-989-0275, e-mail info@aaupnet.org, World Wide Web http://aaupnet.org. *Pres.* MaryKatherine Callaway, Louisiana State; *Pres.-Elect* Richard Dougherty, Princeton; *Past Pres.* Richard Brown, Georgetown; *Exec. Dir.* Peter J. Givler. E-mail pgivler@aaupnet.org.

Assn. of Canadian Publishers, 174 Spadina Ave., Suite 306, Toronto, ON M5T 2C2. Tel. 416-487-6116, fax 416-487-8815, World Wide Web http://www.publishers.ca. *Pres.* Margie Wolfe, Second Story Press, 20 Maud St., Suite 401, Toronto, ON M5V 2M5. Tel. 416-537-7850, fax 416-537-0588, e-mail margie@secondstorypress.ca; *V.P.* Bill Harnum, Dept. of Publications, Pontifical Institute of Mediaeval Studies, 59 Queen's Park Crescent E., Toronto, ON M5S 2C4. Tel. 416-926-7144, fax 416-926-7258, e-mail bill.harnum@gmail.com; *Exec. Dir.* Carolyn Wood. Tel. 416-487-6116 ext. 222, e-mail carolyn_wood@canbook.org.

Assn. of Educational Publishers (AEP), 300 Martin Luther King Blvd., Suite 200, Wilmington, DE 19801. Tel. 302-295-8350, fax 302-778-1110, e-mail mail@aepweb.org, World Wide Web http://www.aepweb.org. *Pres.* Neal Goff; *Pres.-Elect* Lee Wilson; *V.P.* Greg Worrell; *Treas.* Randy Wilhelm; *Past Pres.* Dan Caton; *CEO* Charlene F. Gaynor. E-mail cgaynor@aepweb.org.

Authors Guild, 31 E. 32 St., Seventh fl., New York, NY 10016. Tel. 212-563-5904, fax 212-564-5363, e-mail staff@authorsguild.org, World Wide Web http://www.authors guild.org. *Pres.* Scott Turow.

Book Industry Study Group, 370 Lexington Ave., Suite 900, New York, NY 10017. Tel. 646-336-7141, fax 646-336-6214, e-mail info@bisg.org, World Wide Web http://www.bisg.org. *Co-Chairs* Dominique Raccah, Sourcebooks; Kenneth Michaels, Hachette; *Exec. Dir.* Len Vlahos. E-mail len@bisg.org; *Deputy Exec. Dir.* Angela Bole. E-mail angela@bisg.org.

Book Manufacturers' Institute, 2 Armand Beach Drive, Suite 1B, Palm Coast, FL 32137. Tel. 386-986-4552, fax 386-986-4553, e-mail info@bmibook.com, World

Wide Web http://www.bmibook.org. *Pres.* Mike Collinge; *V.P./Pres.-Elect* Jac B. Garner; *Exec. V.P./Secy.* Daniel N. Bach. Address correspondence to the executive vice president.

Bookbuilders of Boston, 44 Vinal Rd., Scituate, MA 02066. Tel. 781-378-1361, fax 419-821-2171, e-mail office@bbboston.org, World Wide Web http://www.bbboston.org. *Pres.* Tom Plain. E-mail tomp@hpcbook.com; *1st V.P.* Michael Mozina. E-mail mmozina@brillusa.com; *Treas.* Scott Payne. E-mail scott_payne@malloy.com; *Clerk* Anny DiCiccio. E-mail anny.diciccio@yahoo.com.

Canadian Booksellers Assn., 1255 Bay St., Suite 902, Toronto, ON M5R 2A9. Tel. 866-788-0790, e-mail enquiries@cbabook.org, World Wide Web http://www.cbabook.org. *Pres.* Mark Lefebvre, Titles Bookstore, McMaster Univ., Hamilton, Ontario. E-mail lefebvr@mcmaster.ca; *V.P.* Christopher Smith, Collected Works, Ottawa. E-mail christopher@collected-works.com; *Treas.* Ellen Pickle, Tidewater Books, Sackville. E-mail tidebook@nb.sympatico.ca; *Senior Mgr.* Jodi White. Tel. 416-467-7883 ext. 227, e-mail jwhite@cbabook.org.

Canadian International Standard Numbers (ISN) Agency, c/o Published Heritage, Library and Archives Canada, 395 Wellington St., Ottawa, ON K1A 0N4. Tel. 866-578-7777 (toll-free) or 613-996-5115, World Wide Web http://www.collectionscanada.ca/isn/index-e.html.

Canadian Printing Industries Assn., 151 Slater St., Suite 1110, Ottawa, ON K1P 5H3. Tel. 613-236-7208, fax 613-232-1334, e-mail belliott@cpia-aci.ca, World Wide Web http://www.cpia-aci.ca. *Pres.* Bob Elliott; *Chair* Sandy Stephens. E-mail sstephens@informco.com.

Chicago Book Clinic, 310 W. Lake St., Suite 111, Elmhurst, IL 60126. Tel. 630-833-4220, fax 630-563-9181, e-mail klabounty@apexmanage.com, World Wide Web http://www.chicagobookclinic.org. *Pres.* Eric Platou. E-mail eric_platou@malloy.com; *V.P.* Jason Berg. E-mail jberg@precisiongraphics.com; *Contact* Kimberly LaBounty, Apex Management and Special Events. E-mail klabounty@apexmanage.com or cbc@apexmanage.com.

Children's Book Council, 54 W. 39 St., 14th fl., New York, NY 10018. Tel. 212-966-1990, fax 212-966-2073, e-mail cbc.info@cbcbooks.org, World Wide Web http://www.cbcbooks.org. *Chair* Nancy Feresten; *V. Chair* Betsy Groban; *Secy.* Susan Van Metre; *Treas.* Simon Tasker; *Exec. Dir.* Robin Adelson. E-mail robin.adelson@cbcbooks.org.

Copyright Society of the USA, 352 Seventh Ave., Suite 739, New York, NY 10001. World Wide Web http://www.csusa.org. *Pres.* Corey Field; *V.P./Pres.-Elect* Joseph Salvo; *Secy.* Nancy Wolff; *Treas.* Eric Scwartz; *Operations Dir.* Amy Nickerson. E-mail amy@csusa.org.

Council of Literary Magazines and Presses, 154 Christopher St., Suite 3C, New York, NY 10014. Tel. 212-741-9110, fax 212-741-9112, e-mail info@clmp.org, World Wide Web http://www.clmp.org. *Co-chairs* Gerald Howard, Nicole Dewey; *Exec. Dir.* Jeffrey Lependorf. E-mail jlependorf@clmp.org.

Educational Book and Media Assn. (formerly Educational Paperback Assn.), P.O. Box 3363, Warrenton, VA 20188. Tel. 540-318-7770, e-mail bgorg@edupaperback.org, World Wide Web http://www.edupaperback.org. *Pres.* Gene Bahlman; *V.P.* Jennifer Allen; *Treas.* Michael Raymond; *Exec. Secy.* Brian Gorg.

Evangelical Christian Publishers Assn., 9633 S. 48 St., Suite 140, Phoenix, AZ 85044. Tel. 480-966-3998, fax 480-966-1944, e-mail info@ecpa.org, World Wide Web http://www.ecpa.org. *Pres./CEO* Mark W. Kuyper; *Chair* Cris Doornbos.

Graphic Artists Guild, 32 Broadway, Suite 1114, New York, NY 10004. Tel. 212-791-3400, fax 212-792-0333, e-mail admin@gag.org, World Wide Web http://www.graphicartistsguild.org. *Pres.* Haydn S. Adams. E-mail president@gag.org; *V.P.* Chuck Schultz; *Exec. Dir.* Patricia McKiernan. E-mail admin@gag.org.

Great Lakes Independent Booksellers Assn., c/o *Exec. Dir.* Deb Leonard, 2113 Roosevelt, Ypsilanti, MI. Tel. 888-736-3096, fax 734-879-11291, e-mail deb@gliba.org, World Wide Web http://www.gliba.org. *Pres.* Terry Whittaker. E-mail viewpointbooks@tls.net; *V.P.* Robin Allen. E-mail foreverbooks@qtm.net; *Past Pres.* Cynthia Compton. E-mail kidsbooks4@msn.com.

Guild of Book Workers, 521 Fifth Ave., New York, NY 10175. Tel. 212-292-4444, e-mail communications@guildofbookworkers.org, World Wide Web http://www.guildofbook workers.org. *Pres.* Andrew Huot. E-mail president@guildofbookworkers.org; *V.P.* Anna Embree. E-mail vicepresident@guildofbook workers.org.

Horror Writers Assn., 244 Fifth Ave., Suite 2767, New York, NY 10001. E-mail hwa@horror. org, World Wide Web http://www.horror. org. *Pres.* Rocky Wood. E-mail president@ horror.org; *V.P.* Lisa Morton. E-mail vp@ horror.org; *Secy.* Vince Liaguno. E-mail secretary@horror.org; *Treas.* Les Klinger. E-mail treasurer@horror.org.

IAPHC—The Graphic Professionals Resource Network (formerly the International Assn. of Printing House Craftsmen), P.O. Box 2549, Maple Grove, MN 55311-7549. Tel. 800-466-4274 (toll-free) or 763-560-1620, fax 763-560-1350, e-mail headquarters@iaphc. org, World Wide Web http://www.iaphc. org. *Pres./CEO* Kevin P. Keane. E-mail headquarters@iaphc.com.

Independent Book Publishers Assn. (formerly PMA), 1020 Manhattan Beach Blvd., Suite 204, Manhattan Beach, CA 90266. Tel. 310-546-1818, fax 310-546-3939, e-mail info@ ibpa-online.org, World Wide Web http:// www.ibpa-online.org. *Chair* Steve Mettee, The Write Thought, 1254 Commerce Ave., Sanger, CA 93657. Tel. 559-876-2170, fax 559-876-2180, e-mail mettee@thewrite thought.com; *Exec. Dir.* Terry Nathan. E-mail terry@ibpa-online.org.

International Standard Book Numbering U.S. Agency, 630 Central Ave., New Providence, NJ 07974. Tel. 888-269-5372, fax 908-219-0188, e-mail isbn-san@bowker.com, World Wide Web http://www.isbn.org. *Dir., Identifier Services* Beat Barblan.

Jewish Book Council, 520 Eighth Ave., Fourth fl., New York, NY 10018. Tel. 212-201-2920, fax 212-532-4952, e-mail jbc@jewish books.org, World Wide Web http://www. jewishbookcouncil.org. *Pres.* Lawrence J. Krule; *V.P.s* Harry L. Freund, Judith Lieberman; *Secy.* Mimi S. Frank; *Dir.* Carolyn Starman Hessel.

Library Binding Institute/Hardcover Binders International, 4400 PGA Blvd., Suite 600, Palm Beach Gardens, FL 33410. Tel. 561-745-6821, fax 561-775-0089, e-mail info@ lbibinders.org, World Wide Web http://www. lbibinders.org. *Pres.* Jack Tolbert, National Lib. Bindery Co. of Georgia. E-mail nlbga@ mindspring.com; *V.P.* Duncan Campbell, Campbell-Logan Bindery. E-mail duncan@ campbell-logan.com; *Exec. Dir.* Debra Nolan. E-mail dnolan@lbibinders.org.

Midwest Independent Booksellers Assn., 2355 Louisiana Ave. N., Suite A, Golden Valley, MN 55427. Tel. 800-784-7522 (toll-free) or 763-544-2993, fax 763-544-2266, e-mail info@idwestbooksellers.org. *Exec. Dir.* Carrie Obry. E-mail carrie@midwestbooksellers. org.

Midwest Independent Publishers Assn., P.O. Box 65686, St. Paul, MN 55165. Tel. 651-917-0021 or 651-797-3801, World Wide Web http://www.mipa.org. *Pres.* Seal Dwyer, North Star Press, P.O. Box 451, St. Cloud, MN 56302. Tel. 320-558-9062, e-mail info@northstarpress.com; *V.P.* Dorothy Molstad, Molstad Marketing. Tel. 651-342-0447, e-mail dendoor@aol.com; *Secy.* Sheyna Galyan, Yaldah Publishing. Tel. 651-470-3853, e-mail publisher@yaldapublishing. com; *Treas.* Dorie McClelland, Spring Book Design. Tel. 651-457-0258, e-mail dorie@ springbookdesign.com.

Miniature Book Society. *Pres.* Mark Palkovic. E-mail mark.palkovic@uc.edu; *V.P.* Stephen Byrne. E-mail sb@finalscore.demon.co.uk; *Secy.* Edward Hoyenski. E-mail ehoyensk@ library.unt.edu; *Treas.* Karen Nyman. E-mail karennyman@cox.net; *Past Pres.* Julian I. Edison. E-mail jiestl@mac.com. World Wide Web http://www.mbs.org.

Minnesota Book Publishers Roundtable. E-mail information@publishersroundtable. org, World Wide Web http://www.publishers roundtable.org. *Pres.* Steven M. Pomije, Llewellyn Worldwide, Ltd. E-mail stevenp @llewellyn.com.

Mountains and Plains Independent Booksellers Assn., 8020 Springshire Drive, Park City, UT 84098. Tel. 800-752-0249 (toll-free) or 435-649-6079, fax 435-649-6105, e-mail laura@mountainsplains.org, World Wide Web http://www.mountainsplains.org. *Pres.* Meghan Goel, BookPeople Bookstore, 603 N. Lamar Blvd., Austin, TX 78703. Tel. 512-472-5050, fax 512-482-8495, e-mail kids_buyer@bookpeople.com; *V.P./Secy.*

Nicole Magistro, Bookworm of Edwards, 295 Main St., Unit C101, Edwards, CO 81632. Tel. 970-926-7323, fax 970-926-7324, e-mail nicole@bookwormofedwards. com; *Exec. Dir.* Laura Ayrey.

MPA—The Assn. of Magazine Media (formerly Magazine Publishers of America), 810 Seventh Ave., 24th fl., New York, NY 10019. Tel. 212-872-3700, e-mail mpa@magazine.org, World Wide Web http://www.magazine.org. *Pres./CEO* Nina Link. Tel. 212-872-3710, e-mail president@magazine.org; *Chair* Michael A. Clinton, Hearst Magazines; *V. Chair* Efrem Zimbalist III, Active Interest Media.

NAPL (formerly National Assn. for Printing Leadership), 1 Meadowlands Plaza, Suite 1511, East Rutherford, NJ 07073. Tel. 800-642-6275, 201-634-9600, fax 201-634-0324, e-mail info@napl.org, World Wide Web http://www.napl.org. *Pres./CEO* Joseph P. Truncale. E-mail jtruncale@napl.org.

National Assn. of College Stores, 500 E. Lorain St., Oberlin, OH 44074-1294. Tel. 800-622-7498, 440-775-7777, fax 440-775-4769, e-mail info@nacs.org, World Wide Web http://www.nacs.org. *Pres.* Mary Ellen Martin; *Pres.-Elect* George Masforroll; *CEO* Brian Cartier. E-mail bcartier@nacs.org.

National Coalition Against Censorship (NCAC), 19 Fulton St., Suite 407, New York, NY 10038. Tel. 212-807-6222, fax 212-807-6245, e-mail ncac@ncac.org, World Wide Web http://www.ncac.org. *Exec. Dir.* Joan E. Bertin; *Dirs.* Michael Bamberger, Chris Csikszentmihalyi, Judy Blume, Susan Clare, Chris Finan, Eric M. Freedman, Robie Harris, Michael Jacobs, Chris Peterson, Larry Siems, Emily Whitfield.

New Atlantic Independent Booksellers Assn. (NAIBA), 2667 Hyacinth St., Westbury, NY 11590. Tel. 516-333-0681, fax 516-333-0689, e-mail info@naiba.com, World Wide Web http://www.newatlanticbooks.com. *Pres.* Lucy Kogler, Talking Leaves, 951 Elmwood Ave., Buffalo, NY 14222. Tel. 716-884-9524, fax 716-332-3625, e-mail lucyk@tleavesbooks.com; *V.P.* Margot Sage-El, Watchung Booksellers, Watchung Plaza, 54 Fairfield St., Montclair, NJ 07042. Tel. 973-744-7177, fax 973-783-5899, e-mail margot@watchungbooksellers.com; *Exec. Dir.* Eileen Dengler.

New England Independent Booksellers Assn., 297 Broadway, Arlington, MA 02474. Tel. 781-316-8894, fax 781-316-2605, e-mail steve@neba.org, World Wide Web http://www.newenglandbooks.org. *Pres.* Annie Philbrick, Bank Square Books, Mystic, Connecticut. E-mail banksquarebks@msn.com; *V.P.* Lisa Sullivan, Bartleby's Books, Wilmington, Vermont. E-mail lisa@bookcellarvt.com; *Treas.* Michael Hermann, Gibson's Bookstore, Concord, New Hampshire. E-mail gibsons@totalnetnh.net; *Exec. Dir.* Steve Fischer.

New York Center for Independent Publishing (formerly the Small Press Center), c/o General Society Lib., 20 W. 44 St., New York, NY 10036. Tel. 212-921-1767, fax 212-840-2046, e-mail library@generalsociety.org, World Wide Web http://nycip.wordpress.com.

North American Bookdealers Exchange (NABE), Box 606, Cottage Grove, OR 97424. Tel./fax 541-942-7455, e-mail nabe@bookmarketingprofits.com, World Wide Web http://bookmarketingprofits.com. *Dir.* Al Galasso.

Northern California Independent Booksellers Assn., Presidio National Park, 1007 General Kennedy Ave., P.O. Box 29169, San Francisco, CA 94129. Tel. 415-561-7686, fax 415-561-7685, e-mail office@nciba.com, World Wide Web http://www.nciba.com. *Pres.* Michael Barnard; *V.P.* Calvin Crosby; Exec. Dir. Hut Landon.

Pacific Northwest Booksellers Assn., 338 W. 11 Ave., Eugene, OR 97401-3062. Tel. 541-683-4363, fax 541-683-3910, e-mail info@pnba.org, World Wide Web http://www.pnba.org, blog Northwest Book Lovers (http://www.nwbooklovers.org). *Pres.* Jamil Zaidi, Elliott Bay Book Co. E-mail jzaidi@elliottbaybook.com; *Exec. Dir.* Thom Chambliss.

PEN American Center, Div. of International PEN, 588 Broadway, Suite 303, New York, NY 10012. Tel. 212-334-1660, fax 212-334-2181, e-mail pen@pen.org, World Wide Web http://www.pen.org. *Pres.* Kwame Anthony Appiah; *Exec. V.P.* Laurence J. Kirshbaum; *V.P.s* Jessica Hagedorn, Victoria Redel; *Secy.* Roxana Robinson; *Exec. Dir.* Steven L. Isenberg. E-mail sisenberg@pen.org.

Periodical and Book Assn. of America, 481 Eighth Ave., Suite 526, New York, NY

10001. Tel. 212-563-6502, fax 212-563-4098, World Wide Web http://www.pbaa.net. *Exec. Dir.* Lisa W. Scott. E-mail lisaw scott@hotmail.com; *Assoc. Dir.* Jose Cancio. E-mail jcancio@@pbaa.net; *Chair* Will Michalopoulos. E-mail wmichalopoulos@hearst.com.

Romance Writers of America, 14615 Benfer Rd., Houston, TX 77069. Tel. 832-717-5200, fax 832-717-5201, e-mail info@rwa.org, World Wide Web http://www.rwa.org. *Pres.* Linda Winstead Jones; *Pres.-Elect* Sylvia Day; *Exec. Dir.* Allison Kelley. E-mail allison.kelley@rwa.org.

Publishing Professionals Network (formerly Bookbuilders West), 9328 Elk Grove Blvd., Suite 105, Elk Grove, CA 95624. Tel. 415-670-9564, e-mail operations@bookbuilders.org, World Wide Web http://www.bookbuilders.org. *Pres.* David Zielonka, McGraw-Hill Professional. E-mail david_zielonka@mcgraw-hill.com; *V.P.* Andrea Helmbolt, McGraw-Hill Higher Educ. E-mail andrea_helmbolt@mcgraw-hill.com.

Science Fiction and Fantasy Writers of America, P.O. Box 3238, Enfield, CT 06083-3238. World Wide Web http://www.sfwa.org. *Pres.* John Scalzi. E-mail president@sfwa.org; *V.P.* Mary Robinette Kowal. E-mail vp@sfwa.org; *Secy.* Robert J. Howe. E-mail secretary@sfwa.org; *Treas.* Bud Sparhawk. E-mail treasurer@sfwa.org.

Small Publishers Assn. of North America (SPAN), P.O. Box 9725, Colorado Springs, CO 80932. Tel. 719-924-5534, fax 719-213-2602, e-mail brad@spannet.org, World Wide Web http://www.spannet.org.

Society of Children's Book Writers and Illustrators (SCBWI), 8271 Beverly Blvd., Los Angeles, CA 90048. Tel. 323-782-1010, fax 323-782-1892, e-mail scbwi@scbwi.org, World Wide Web http://www.scbwi.org. *Pres.* Stephen Mooser. E-mail stephenmooser @scbwi.org; *Exec. Dir.* Lin Oliver.

Society of Illustrators (SI), 128 E. 63 St., New York, NY 10065. Tel. 212-838-2560, fax 212-838-2561, e-mail info@societyillustrators.org, World Wide Web http://www.society illustrators.org. *Pres.* Dennis Dittrich; *Exec. V.P.* Tim O'Brien; *V.P.* Victor Juhasz; *Secy.* Joan Chiverton; *Exec. Dir.* Anelle Miller. E-mail anelle@societyillustrators.org.

Southern Independent Booksellers Alliance (SIBA), 3806 Yale Ave., Columbia, SC 29205. Tel. 803-994-9530, fax 309-410-0211, e-mail info@sibaweb.com, World Wide Web http://www.sibaweb.com. *Exec. Dir.* Wanda Jewell.

Technical Assn. of the Pulp and Paper Industry, 15 Technology Pkwy. S., Norcross, GA 30092 (P.O. Box 105113, Atlanta, GA 30348). Tel. 770-446-1400, fax 770-446-6947, World Wide Web http://www.tappi.org. *Pres./CEO* Larry N. Montague. E-mail lmontague@tappi.org; *Chair* Norman Marsolan; *V. Chair* Tom Garland.

Western Writers of America, c/o Candy Moulton, exec. dir., 271 CR 219, Encampment, WY 82325 Tel. 307-329-8942, e-mail wwa. moulton@gmail.com, World Wide Web http://www.westernwriters.org. *Pres.* Robert J. Conley; *V.P.* Dusty Richards; *Exec. Dir./Secy.-Treas.* Candy Moulton.

Women's National Book Assn., c/o Susannah Greenberg Public Relations, P.O. Box 237, FDR Sta., New York, NY 10150. Tel./fax 212-208-4629, e-mail publicity@bookbuzz.com, World Wide Web http://www.wnba-books.org. *Pres.* Mary Grey James; *V.P./Pres.-Elect* Valerie Tomaselli; *Secy.* Ruth Light; *Treas.* Margaret E. Auer.

International and Foreign Book Trade Associations

For Canadian book trade associations, see the preceding section, "Book Trade Associations, United States and Canada." For a more extensive list of book trade organizations outside the United States and Canada, with more detailed information, consult *International Literary Market Place* (Information Today, Inc.), which also provides extensive lists of major bookstores and publishers in each country.

International

African Publishers' Network, BP 3429, Abidjan 01, Côte d'Ivoire. Tel. 2021-1801, fax 2021-1803, e-mail apnet@zol.co.zw, World Wide Web http://www.african-publishers. net. *Chair* Mamadou Aliou Sow; *Exec. Secy.* Akin Fasemore.

Afro-Asian Book Council, 4835/24 Ansari Rd., New Delhi 110002, India. Tel. 11-2325-8865, fax 11-2326-7437, e-mail afro@aab council.org, World Wide Web http://www. aabcouncil.org. *Secy.-Gen.* Sukumar Das; *Dir.* Saumya Gupta.

Centro Régional para el Fomento del Libro en América Latina y el Caribe (CERLALC) (Regional Center for Book Promotion in Latin America and the Caribbean), Calle 70, No. 9-52, Bogotá DC, Colombia. Tel. 1-540-2071, fax 1-541-6398, e-mail libro@cerlalc. com, World Wide Web http://www.cerlalc. org. *Dir.* Fernando Zapata Lopez.

Federation of European Publishers, rue Montoyer 31, Boîte 8, 1000 Brussels, Belgium. Tel. 2-770-11-10, fax 2-771-20-71, e-mail info@fep-fee.eu, World Wide Web http:// www.fep-fee.be. *Pres.* Frederico Motto; *Dir.-Gen.* Anne Bergman-Tahon.

International Assn. of Scientific, Technical, and Medical Publishers (STM), Prama House, 267 Banbury Rd., Oxford OX2 7HT, England. Tel. 44-1865-339-321, fax 44-1865-339-325, e-mail info@stm-assoc.org, World Wide Web http://www.stm-assoc.org. *Chair* Jerry Cowhig; *CEO* Michael Mabe.

International Board on Books for Young People (IBBY), Nonnenweg 12, 4003 Basel, Switzerland. Tel. 61-272-29-17, fax 61-272-27-57, e-mail ibby@ibby.org, World Wide Web http://www.ibby.org. *Exec. Dir.* Elizabeth Page.

International League of Antiquarian Booksellers (ILAB), c/o 112 Glebe Point Rd., Sydney, NSW 2037, Australia. Tel. 2-9660-4889, fax 2-9552 2670, World Wide Web http://www. ilab.org. *Pres.* Adrian Harrington; *Gen. Secy.* Paul Feain.

International Publishers Assn. (Union Internationale des Editeurs), ave. de Miremont 3, CH-1206 Geneva, Switzerland. Tel. 22-704-1820, fax 22-704-1821, e-mail secretariat@ internationalpublishers.org, World Wide Web http://www.internationalpublishers.org. *Pres.* Y. S. Chi; *Secy.-Gen.* Jens Bammel.

National

Argentina

Cámara Argentina del Libro (Argentine Book Assn.), Av. Belgrano 1580, 4 piso, C1093AAQ Buenos Aires. Tel. 11-4381-8383, fax 11-4381-9253, e-mail cal@editores. org.ar, World Wide Web http://www.editores. org.ar. *Dir.* Norberto J. Pou.

Fundación El Libro (Book Foundation), Hipolito Yrigoyen 1628, 5 piso, C1089AAF Buenos Aires. Tel. 11-4370-0600, fax 11-4370-0607, e-mail fundacion@el-libro.com. ar, World Wide Web http://www.el-libro. com.ar. *Pres.* Horacio Garcia; *Dir.* Marta V. Diaz.

Australia

Australian and New Zealand Assn. of Antiquarian Booksellers, P.O. Box 1610, Carindale, Qld. 4152. Tel./fax 07-3843-0556, e-mail admin@anzaab.com, World Wide Web http://www.anzaab.com. *Pres.* Sally Burdon.

Australian Booksellers Assn., 828 High St., Unit 9, Kew East, Vic. 3102. Tel. 3-9859-7322, fax 3-9859-7344, e-mail mail@aba. org.au, World Wide Web http://www.aba.

org.au. *Pres.* Fiona Stager; *CEO* Joel Becker.

Australian Publishers Assn., 60/89 Jones St., Ultimo, NSW 2007. Tel. 2-9281-9788, fax 2-9281-1073, e-mail apa@publishers.asn. au, World Wide Web http://www.publishers. asn.au. *CEO* Maree McCaskill.

Austria

Hauptverband des Österreichischen Buchhandels (Austrian Publishers and Booksellers Assn.), Grünangergasse 4, A-1010 Vienna. Tel. 1-512-15-35, fax 1-512-84-82, e-mail sekretariat@hvb.at, World Wide Web http://www.buecher.at. *Mgr.* Inge Kralupper.

Verband der Antiquare Österreichs (Austrian Antiquarian Booksellers Assn.), Grünangergasse 4, A-1010 Vienna. Tel. 1-512-15-35, fax 1-512-84-82, e-mail sekretariat@hvb.at, World Wide Web http://www.antiquare.at. *Pres.* Norbert Donhofer.

Belarus

National Book Chamber of Belarus, 31a V Khoruzhei Str., Rm. 707, 220002 Minsk. Tel. 17-289-33-96, fax 17-334-78-47, World Wide Web http://www.natbook.org.by. *Dir.* Elena V. Ivanova. E-mail elvit@natbook. org.by.

Belgium

Vlaamse Boekverkopersbond (Flemish Booksellers Assn.), Te Buelaerlei 37, 2140 Borgerhout. Tel. 03-230-89-23, fax 3-281-22-40, World Wide Web http://www.boek.be. *Contact* Patricia De Laet. E-mail patricia. delaet@boek.be.

Vlaamse Uitgevers Vereniging (Flemish Publishers Assn.), Huis van het Boek, Te Boelaerlei 37, 2140 Borgerhout. Tel. 03-287-66-91, fax 03-281-22-40, e-mail vuv@boek.be, World Wide Web http://boekenvak.boek.be. *Contact* Geert Van den Bossche.

Bolivia

Cámara Boliviana del Libro (Bolivian Booksellers Assn.), Calle Capitan Ravelo No. 2116, 682 La Paz. Tel. 2-211-3264, e-mail cabolib @entelnet.bo, World Wide Web http://www.

cabolib.org.bo. *Gen. Mgr.* Ana Patricia Navarro.

Brazil

Cámara Brasileira do Livro (Brazilian Book Assn.), Rua Cristiano Viana 91, Pinheiros 05411-000 Sao Paulo-SP. Tel./fax 11-3069-1300, e-mail cbl@cbl.org.br, World Wide Web http://www.cbl.org.br. *Pres.* Rosely Boschini.

Sindicato Nacional dos Editores de Livros (Brazilian Publishers Assn.), Rue da Ajuda 35-18 andar, 20040-000 Rio de Janeiro-RJ. Tel. 21-2533-0399, fax 21-2533-0422, e-mail snel@snel.org.br, World Wide Web http://www.snel.org.br. *Pres.* Sonia Machado Jardim.

Chile

Cámara Chilena del Libro AG (Chilean Assn. of Publishers, Distributors, and Booksellers), Av. Libertador Bernardo O'Higgins 1370, Oficina 501, Santiago. Tel. 2-672-0348, fax 2-687-4271, e-mail prolibro@tie. cl, World Wide Web http://www.camlibro.cl. *Pres.* Eduardo Castillo Garcia.

Colombia

Cámara Colombiana del Libro (Colombian Book Assn.), Calle 35, No. 5A 05, Bogotá. Tel. 1-323-01-11, fax 1-285-10-82, e-mail camlibro@camlibro.com.co, World Wide Web http://www.camlibro.com.co. *Pres.* Enrique Gonzalez Villa.

Czech Republic

Svaz českých knihkupců a nakladatelů (Czech Publishers and Booksellers Assn.), P.O. Box 177, 110 01 Prague. Tel. 224-219-944, fax 224-219-942, e-mail sckn@sckn.cz, World Wide Web http://www.sckn.cz. *Pres.* Vladimir Pistorius.

Denmark

Danske Boghandlerforening (Danish Booksellers Assn.), Langebrogade 6 opgang J, 1 sal, 1411 Copenhagen K. Tel. 3254-2255, fax 3254-0041, e-mail ddb@bogpost.dk, World Wide Web http://www.bogguide.dk.

Danske Forlæggerforening (Danish Publishers Assn.), Borsen 1217, Copenhagen K. Tel. 3315-6688, e-mail danishpublishers@danish publishers.dk, World Wide Web http://www. danskeforlag.dk. *Dir.* Anette Wad.

Ecuador

Cámara Ecuatoriana del Libro, Avda. Eloy Alfaro, N29-61 e Inglaterra, Edf. Eloy Alfaro, 9 no. piso, Quito. Tel. 2-2577-531, fax 2-222-150, e-mail celnp@uio.satnet.net, World Wide Web http://celibro.org.ec. *Pres.* Fabian Luzuriaga.

Egypt

General Egyptian Book Organization, P.O. Box 235, Cornich El-Nil, Ramlat Boulaq, Cairo 11511. Tel. 2-257-7531, fax 2-2575-4213, e-mail info@egyptianbook.org.eg, World Wide Web http://www.egyptianbook.org.eg. *Chair* Nasser Al-Ansary.

Estonia

Estonian Publishers Assn., Roosikrantsi 6-207,10119 Tallinn, Tel. 372-644-9866, fax 372-617-7550, e-mail kirjastusteliit@eki.ee, World Wide Web http://www.estbook.com. *CEO* Kaidi Chauncey.

Finland

Kirjakauppaliitto Ry (Booksellers Assn. of Finland), Urho Kekkosen Katu 8 C 34b, 00100 Helsinki. Tel. 9-6859-9110, fax 9-6859-9119, e-mail toimisto@kirjakauppaliitto.fi, World Wide Web http://www.kirjakauppaliitto. fi. *Pres.* Tuula Korte; *Managing Dir.* Jarmo Oksaharju.

Suomen Kustannusyhdistys (Finnish Book Publishers Assn.), P.O. Box 177, Lönnrotinkatu 11 A, FIN-00121, Helsinki. Tel. 358-9-228-77-250, fax 358-9-612-1226, World Wide Web http://www.publishers.fi/ en. *Dir.* Sakari Laiho.

France

Bureau International de l'Edition Française (BIEF) (International Bureau of French Publishing), 115 blvd. Saint-Germain, F-75006 Paris. Tel. 01-44-41-13-13, fax 01-46-34-63-

83, e-mail info@bief.org, World Wide Web http://www.bief.org. *Dir.* Jean-Guy Boin. New York Branch French Publishers Agency, 853 Broadway, Suite 1509, New York, NY 10003-4703. Tel./fax 212-254-4540, World Wide Web http://frenchpubagency. com.

Cercle de la Librairie (Circle of Professionals of the Book Trade), 35 rue Grégoire-de-Tours, F-75006 Paris. Tel. 01-44-41-28-05, fax 01-44-41-28-19, World Wide Web http:// www.electre.com.

Syndicat de la Librairie Française, Hotel de Massa, 38 rue du Faubourg Saint-Jacques, F-75014 Paris. Tel. 01-53-62-23-10, fax 01-53-62-10-45, e-mail contact@union-librairie. fr, World Wide Web http://www.syndicat-librairie.fr. *Pres.* Benoit Bougerol.

Syndicat National de la Librairie Ancienne et Moderne (SLAM) (National Assn. of Antiquarian and Modern Booksellers), 4 rue Gît-le-Coeur, F-75006 Paris. Tel. 01-43-29-46-38, fax 01-43-25-41-63, e-mail slam-livre@ wanadoo.fr, World Wide Web http://www. slam-livre.fr. *Pres.* Frederic Castaing.

Syndicat National de l'Edition (SNE) (National Union of Publishers), 115 blvd. Saint-Germain, F-75006 Paris. Tel. 01-44-41-40-50, fax 01-44-41-40-77, World Wide Web http:// www.sne.fr. *Pres.* Antoine Gallimard.

Germany

Börsenverein des Deutschen Buchhandels e.V. (Stock Exchange of German Booksellers), Grosser Hirschgraben 17-21, 60311 Frankfurt-am-Main. Tel. 69-13-06-0, fax 069-13-06-201, e-mail info@boev.de, World Wide Web http://www.boersenverein.de. *Pres.* Gottfried Honnefelder.

Verband Deutscher Antiquare e.V. (German Antiquarian Booksellers Assn.), Geschäftsstelle, Seeblick 1, 56459 Elbingen. Tel. 6435-90-91-47, fax 6435-90-91-48, e-mail buch@antiquare.de, World Wide Web http:// www.antiquare.de. *Pres.* Eberhard Koestler.

Greece

Hellenic Federation of Publishers and Booksellers, 73 Themistocleous St., 106 83 Athens. Tel. 2103-300-924, fax 2133-301-617, e-mail secretary@poev.gr, World Wide Web http://www.poev.gr. *Pres.* Annie Ragia.

Hungary

Magyar Könyvkiadók és Könyvterjesztök Egyesülése (Assn. of Hungarian Publishers and Booksellers), Postfach 130, 1367 Budapest. Tel. 1-343-2540, fax 1-343-2541, e-mail mkke@mkke.hu, World Wide Web http://www.mkke.hu. *Dir.* Istvan Bart.

Iceland

Félag Islenskra Bókaútgefenda (Icelandic Publishers Assn.), Baronsstig 5, 101 Reykjavik. Tel. 511-8020, fax 511-5020, e-mail baekur@simnet.is, World Wide Web http://www.bokautgafa.is.

India

Federation of Indian Publishers, Federation House, 18/1C Institutional Area, Aruna Asaf Ali Marg, New Delhi 110067. Tel. 11-2696-4847, fax 11-2686-4054, e-mail fip1@satyam.net.in, World Wide Web http://www.fipindia.org. *Pres.* Anand Bhushan.

Indonesia

Ikatan Penerbit Indonesia (Assn. of Indonesian Book Publishers), Jl. Kalipasir 32, Jakarta 10330. Tel. 21-314-1907, fax 21-314-6050, e-mail ikapi@cbn.net.id, World Wide Web http://www.ikapi.org. *Pres.* Dharma Madjid; *Secy.-Gen.* Wanti Syaifullah.

Ireland

Publishing Ireland/Foilsiu Eireann (formerly CLÉ: The Irish Book Publishers' Assn.), Guinness Enterprise Centre, Taylor's Lane, Dublin 8. Tel. 1-415-1210, e-mail info@publishingireland.com, World Wide Web http://www.publishingireland.com. *Pres.* Jean Harrington. E-mail president@publishingireland.com.

Israel

Book Publishers' Assn. of Israel, P.O. Box 20123, 61201 Tel Aviv. Tel. 3-561-4121, fax 3-561-1996, e-mail hamol@tbpai.co.il, World Wide Web http://www.tbpai.co.il. *Managing Dir.* Amnon Ben-Shmuel; *Chair* Yaron Sadan.

Italy

Associazione Italiana Editori (Italian Publishers Assn.), Corso di Porta Romana 108, 20122 Milan. Tel. 2-89-28-0800, fax 2-89-28-0860, e-mail aie@aie.it, World Wide Web http://www.aie.it. *Dir.* Ivan Cecchini.

Associazione Librai Antiquari d'Italia (Antiquarian Booksellers Assn. of Italy), Via Cassia 1020, Rome. Tel. 39-347-64-6-9147, fax 39-06-2332-8979, e-mail alai@alai.it, presidente@alai.it, World Wide Web http://www.alai.it. *Pres.* Umberto Pregliasco.

Japan

Antiquarian Booksellers Assn. of Japan, 27 Sakamachi, Shinjuku-ku, Tokyo, 160-0002. Tel. 81-03-3357-1417, fax 81-03-3356-8730, e-mail abaj@abaj.gr.jp, World Wide Web http://www.abaj.gr.jp. *Pres.* Takao Nakao.

Japan Assn. of International Publications (formerly Japan Book Importers Assn.), c/o UPS, 1-32-5 Higashi-shinagawa, Shinagawa-ku, Toyko 140-0002. Tel. 3-5479-7269, fax 3-5479-7307, e-mail office@jaip.jp, World Wide Web http://www.jaip.jp. *Exec. Dir.* Takashi Yamakawa; *Dir.* Mark Gresham.

Japan Book Publishers Assn., 6 Fukuro-machi, Shinjuku-ku, Tokyo 162-0828. Tel. 3-3268-1302, fax 3-3268-1196, e-mail research@jbpa.or.jp, World Wide Web http://www.jbpa.or.jp. *Pres.* Masahiro Oga.

Kenya

Kenya Publishers Assn., P.O. Box 42767, Nairobi 00100. Tel. 20-375-2344, fax 20-375-4076, e-mail info@kenyapublishers.org, World Wide Web http://www.kenyapublishers.org. *Chair* Lawrence Njagi; *Exec. Officer* James Odhiambo.

Korea (Republic of)

Korean Publishers Assn., 105-2 Sagan-dong, Jongro-gu, Seoul 110-190. Tel. 70-7126-4720, fax 2-738-5414, e-mail webmaster@

kpa21.or.kr, World Wide Web http://www. kpa21.or.kr. *Pres.* Sok-Ghee Baek; *Secy.- Gen.* Jon Jin Jung.

Latvia

Latvian Publishers' Assn., Baznicas 37, LV-1010 Riga. Tel./fax 67-217-730, e-mail lga@gramatizdeveji.lv, World Wide Web http://www.gramatizdeveji.lv. *Pres.* Janis Leja; *Exec. Dir.* Dace Pugaca.

Lithuania

Lithuanian Publishers Assn., A Jaksto 9-231, LT-01105 Vilnius. Tel./fax 5-261-77-40, e-mail lla@centras.lt, World Wide Web http://www.lla.lt. *Pres.* Lolita Varanaviciene; *Exec. Dir.* Aida Dobkeviciute-Dzioveniene.

Malaysia

Malaysian Book Publishers' Assn., D/a Sasbabi Sdn Bhd No 12, Jl. Teknologi 3/4, Taman Sains, Selangor 1, Kota Damansara, 47810 Petaling Jaya, Selangor. Tel. 3-5637-9044, fax 3-5637-9043, e-mail inquiry@cerdik.com.my; World Wide Web http://www.mabopa.com.my. *Pres.* Law King Hui.

Mexico

Cámara Nacional de la Industria Editorial Mexicana (Mexican Publishers' Assn.), Holanda No 13, Col San Diego Churubusco, Deleg Coyoacan, 04120 Mexico DF. Tel. 155-5605-8784, fax 155-56-04-31-47, e-mail contacto@caniem.com, World Wide Web http://www.caniem.com. *Pres.* Victorico Albores Santiago.

The Netherlands

KVB—Koninklijke Vereeniging van het Boekenvak (formerly Koninklijke Vereeniging ter Bevordering van de Belangen des Boekhandels) (Royal Dutch Book Trade Assn.). Herengracht 166, 1016 BP Amsterdam. Tel. 20-624-02-12, fax 20-620-88-71, e-mail info@kvb.nl, World Wide Web http://www.kvb.nl. *Dir.* Marty Langeler.

Nederlands Uitgeversverbond (Royal Dutch Publishers Assn.), Postbus 12040, 1100 AA Amsterdam. Tel. 20-43-09-150, fax 20-43-09-199, e-mail info@nuv.nl, World Wide Web http://www.nuv.nl. *Pres.* Henk J. L. Vonhoff.

Nederlandsche Vereeniging van Antiquaren (Netherlands Assn. of Antiquarian Booksellers), Prinsengracht 15, 2512 EW The Hague. Tel. 70-364-98-40, fax 70-364-33-40, e-mail kok@xs4all.nl, World Wide Web http://www.nvva.nl. *Pres.* Ton Kok.

Nederlandse Boekverkopersbond (Dutch Booksellers Assn.), Postbus 32, 3720 AA Bilhoven. Tel. 30-22-87-956, fax 030-22-84-566, e-mail nbb@boekbond.nl, World Wide Web http://www.boekbond.nl. *Dir.* Ari Doeser.

New Zealand

Booksellers New Zealand, P.O. Box 25-033, Wellington 6146. Tel. 4-472-1908, fax 4-472-1912, e-mail info@booksellers.co.nz, World Wide Web http://www.booksellers.co.nz. *CEO* Lincoln Gould.

Nigeria

Nigerian Publishers Assn., GPO Box 2541, Ibadan. Tel. 2-751-5352, e-mail info@nigerianpublishers.org, World Wide Web http://www.nigerianpublishers.org. *Pres.* Samuel Kolawole.

Norway

Norske Bokhandlerforening (Norwegian Booksellers Assn.), Øvre Vollgate 15, 0158 Oslo. Tel. 22-40-45-40, fax 22-41-12-89, e-mail post@bokogsamfunn.no, World Wide Web http://www.bokogsamfunn.no. *Editor* Dag H. Nestegard.

Norske Forleggerforening (Norwegian Publishers Assn.), Øvre Vollgate 15, 0158 Oslo. Tel. 22-00-75-80, fax 22-33-38-30, e-mail dnf@forleggerforeningen.no, World Wide Web http://www.forleggerforeningen.no. *Managing Dir.* Christian Opsahl.

Peru

Cámara Peruana del Libro (Peruvian Publishers Assn.), Av. Cuba 427, Jesús María, Apdo. 10253, Lima 11. Tel. 1-472-9516, fax 1-265-0735, e-mail cp-libro@cpl.org.

pe, World Wide Web http://www.cpl.org.pe. *Pres.* Gladys Diaz Carrera.

Philippines

Philippine Educational Publishers Assn., c/o St. Mary's Publishing Corp., 1308 P Guevarra St., Santa Cruz, 1308 Manila. Tel. 2-734-7790, fax 2-735-0955, e-mail dbuhain @cnl.net, World Wide Web http://nbdb.gov. ph/publindust.htm. *Pres.* Dominador D. Buhain.

Poland

Polskie Towarzystwo Wydawców Książek (Polish Society of Book Editors), ul. Swietokrzyska 30, lok 156, 00-116 Warsaw. Tel. 22-407-77-30, fax 22-850-34-76, e-mail ptwk @wp.pl, World Wide Web http://www. wydawca.com.pl. *Dir.* Maria Kuisz.

Stowarzyszenia Księgarzy Polskich (Assn. of Polish Booksellers), ul. Mazowiecka def. 414, 00-048 Warsaw. Tel./fax 0-22-827-93-81, e-mail skp@ksiegarze.org.pl, World Wide Web http://www.ksiegarze.org.pl. *Chair* Waldemar Janaszkiewicz.

Portugal

Associação Portuguesa de Editores e Livreiros (Portuguese Assn. of Publishers and Booksellers), Av. dos Estados Unidas da America 97, 6 Esq., 1700-167 Lisbon. Tel. 21-843-51-80, fax 21-848-93-77, e-mail geral@ apel.pt, World Wide Web http://www.apel. pt. *Pres.* Graca Didier.

Russia

Assn. of Book Publishers of Russia, ul. B. Nikitskaya 44, 121069 Moscow. Tel. 495-202-1174, fax 495-202-3989, e-mail aski@ rol.ru, World Wide Web http://www.aski.ru. *Pres.* Konstantin V. Chechenev.

Rossiiskaya Knizhnaya Palata (Russian Book Chamber), Kremlin Embankment, 1/9, 119019 Moscow. Tel. 495-688-96-89, fax 495-688-99-91, e-mail bookch@postman.ru, World Wide Web http://www.bookchamber. ru. *Dir. Gen.* Elena Nogina.

Serbia and Montenegro

Assn. of Yugoslav Publishers and Booksellers, Kneza Milosa 25/I, 11000 Belgrade. Tel. 11-642-533, fax 11-686-539, e-mail ognjenl@ eunet.yu.

Singapore

Singapore Book Publishers Assn., 86 Marine Parade Central No. 03-213, Singapore 440086. Tel. 6344-7801, fax 6344-0897, e-mail twcsbpa@singnet.com.sg, World Wide Web http://www.publishers-sbpa.org.sg. *Pres.* Triena Ong.

Slovenia

Zdruzenie Zaloznikov in Knjigotrzcev Slovenije Gospodarska Zbornica Slovenije (Assn. of Publishers and Booksellers of Slovenia), Dimiceva 13, SI 1000 Ljubljana. Tel. 1-5898-000, fax 1-5898-100, e-mail info@ gzs.si, World Wide Web http://www.gzs.si/ sloi. *Pres.* Milan Matos.

South Africa

Publishers Assn. of South Africa (PASA), P.O. Box 106, Green Point 8051. Tel. 21-425-2721, fax 21-421-3270, e-mail pasa@ publishsa.co.za, World Wide Web http:// www.publishsa.co.za. *Exec. Dir.* Brian Wafawarowa.

South African Booksellers Assn. (formerly Associated Booksellers of Southern Africa), P.O. Box 870, Bellville 7535. Tel. 21-945-1572, fax 21-945-2169, e-mail saba@ sabooksellers.com, World Wide Web http:// sabooksellers.com. *Chair and Pres.* Guru Redhi.

Spain

Federación de Gremios de Editores de España (Federation of Spanish Publishers Assns.), Cea Bermúdez 44-2 Dcha, 2003 Madrid. Tel. 91-534-51-95, fax 91-535-26-25, e-mail fgee@fge.es, World Wide Web http:// www.federacioneditores.org. *Pres.* Pedro de Andres; *Exec. Dir.* Antonio María Avila.

Sri Lanka

Sri Lanka Book Publishers Assn., 61 Ven Hik-kaduwe Sri Sumangala Nahimi Mawatha, Maradana, Colombo 10. Tel. 74-304-546, fax 1-821-454, e-mail bookpub@sltnet.lk, World Wide Web http://www.bookpublishers. lk. *Gen. Secy.* Upali Wanigasooriya.

Sudan

Sudanese Publishers' Assn., c/o Institute of African and Asian Studies, Khartoum Univ., P.O. Box 321, Khartoum 11115. Tel. 11-77-0022. *Dir.* Al-Amin Abu Manga Mohamed.

Sweden

Svenska Förläggareföreningen (Swedish Publishers Assn.), Drottninggatan 97, S-11360 Stockholm. Tel. 8-736-19-40, fax 8-736-19-44, e-mail info@forlaggare.se, World Wide Web http://www.forlaggare.se. *Dir.* Kristina Ahlinder.

Switzerland

Association Suisse des Éditeurs de Langue Française (ASELF) (Swiss Assn. of French-Language Publishers), 2 ave. Agassiz, 1001 Lausanne. Tel. 21-319-71-11, fax 21-319-79-10, e-mail aself@centrezational.cl, World Wide Web http://www.culturactif.ch/ editions/asef1.htm. *Pres.* Francine Bouchet.

Schweizerischer Buchhandler- und Verleger-Verband (Swiss German-Language Book-sellers and Publishers Assn.), Alderstr. 40, Postfach, 8034 Zurich. Tel. 044-421-36-00, fax 044-421-36-18, e-mail sbvv@sbvv.ch, World Wide Web http://www.swissbooks. ch. *CEO* Dani Landolf.

Thailand

Publishers and Booksellers Assn. of Thailand, 83/156 Soi Chinnakhet 2, Ngam Wong Wan Rd., Thung Song Hong, Lak Si, Bangkok 10210. Tel. 662-954-9560-4, fax 662-954-9565-6, e-mail info@pubat.or.th, World Wide Web http://www.pubat.or.th.

Uganda

Uganda Publishers Assn., P.O. Box 7732, Kampala. Tel. 41-428-6093, fax 41-428-6397, e-mail mbd@infocom.co.ug. *Chair* David Kibuuka; *Gen. Secy.* Martin Okia.

United Kingdom

Antiquarian Booksellers Assn., Sackville House, 40 Piccadilly, London W1J 0DR, England. Tel. 20-7439-3118, fax 20-7439-3119, e-mail admin@aba.org.uk, World Wide Web http://www.aba.org.uk. *Admin.* Clare Pedder; *Secy.* John Critchley.

Assn. of Learned and Professional Society Publishers, 1-3 Ship St., Shoreham-by-Sea, West Sussex BN43 5DH, England. Tel. 1275-858-837, World Wide Web http://www.alpsp.org. *Chief Exec.* Ian Russell.

Booktrust, Book House, 45 East Hill, Wandsworth, London SW18 2QZ, England. Tel. 20-8516-2977, fax 20-8516-2978, e-mail query@ booktrust.org.uk, World Wide Web http:// www.booktrust.org.uk. *CEO* Viv Bird.

Educational Publishers Council, 29B Montague St., London WC1B 5BW, England. Tel. 20-7691-9191, fax 20-7691-9199, e-mail mail@publishers.org.uk, World Wide Web http://www.publishers.org.uk/en/educational. *Chair* Rob Ince; *Dir.* Graham Taylor.

Publishers Assn., 29B Montague St., London WC1B 5BW, England. Tel. 20-7691-9191, fax 20-7691-9199, e-mail mail@publishers. org.uk, World Wide Web http://www. publishers.org.uk. *Pres.* Rod Bristow; *Chief Exec.* Richard Mollet.

Scottish Book Trust, Sandeman House, Trunk's Close, 55 High St., Edinburgh EH1 1SR, Scotland. Tel. 131-524-0160, fax 131-524-0161, e-mail info@scottishbooktrust.com, World Wide Web http://www.scottishbook trust.com. *CEO* Marc Lambert.

Welsh Books Council (Cyngor Llyfrau Cymru), Castell Brychan, Aberystwyth, Ceredigion SY23 2JB, Wales. Tel. 1970-624-151, fax 1970-625-385, e-mail castellbrychan@ wbc.org.uk, World Wide Web http://www. cllc.org.uk. *Dir.* Elwyn Jones.

Uruguay

Cámara Uruguaya del Libro (Uruguayan Publishers Assn.), Colon 1476, Apdo. 102, 11 200 Montevideo. Tel. 2-916-93-74, fax 2-916-76-28, e-mail gerencia@camaradellibro.com.uy, World Wide Web http://www.camara dellibro.com.uy. *Pres.* Alvaro Juan Risso Castellanos.

Venezuela

Cámara Venezolana del Libro (Venezuelan Publishers Assn.), Av. Andrés Bello, Centro Andrés Bello, Torre Oeste 11, piso 11, of. 112-0, Caracas 1050. Tel. 212-793-1347, fax 212-793-1368, e-mail unegi@cavelibro. org, World Wide Web http://www.cavelibro. org. *Pres.* Leonardo Ramos.

Zambia

Booksellers Assn. of Zambia, P.O. Box 51109, 10101 Lusaka. Tel./fax 211-255-166, e-mail bpaz@zamtel.zm. *Contact* Enock Mwale.

Zimbabwe

Zimbabwe Book Publishers Assn., P.O. Box 3794, Harare. Tel./fax 4-754-256, e-mail engelbert@collegepress.co.zw.

National Information Standards Organization (NISO) Standards

Information Retrieval

Z39.2-1994 (R2009)   Information Interchange Format
Z39.19-2005 (R2010) Guidelines for the Construction, Format, and
                     Management of Monolingual Controlled Vocabularies
Z39.47-1993 (R2003) Extended Latin Alphabet Coded Character Set for
                     Bibliographic Use (ANSEL)
Z39.50-2003 (R2009) Information Retrieval (Z39.50) Application Service
                     Definition and Protocol Specification
Z39.56-1996 (R2002) Serial Item and Contribution Identifier (SICI)
Z39.64-1989 (R2002) East Asian Character Code for Bibliographic Use
Z39.76-1996 (R2002) Data Elements for Binding Library Materials
Z39.84-2005 (R2010) Syntax for the Digital Object Identifier
Z39.85-2007   Dublin Core Metadata Element Set
Z39.88-2004 (R2010) The OpenURL Framework for Context-Sensitive Services
Z39.89-2003 (R2009) The U.S. National Z39.50 Profile for Library Applications
Z39.93-2007   The Standardized Usage Statistics Harvesting Initiative
                     (SUSHI) Protocol

Library Management

Z39.7-2004   Information Services and Use: Metrics and statistics for
                     libraries and information providers—Data Dictionary
Z39.71-2006   Holdings Statements for Bibliographic Items
Z39.73-1994 (R2001) Single-Tier Steel Bracket Library Shelving
Z39.76-1996 (R2002) Data Elements for Binding Library Materials
Z39.83-1-2008   NISO Circulation Interchange Part 1: Protocol (NCIP)
Z39.83-2-2008   NISO Circulation Interchange Protocol (NCIP) Part 2:
                     Implementation Profile 1
Z39.93-2007   The Standardized Usage Statistics Harvesting Initiative
                     (SUSHI) Protocol

Preservation and Storage

Z39.32-1996 (R2002) Information on Microfiche Headers
Z39.48-1992 (R2009) Permanence of Paper for Publications and Documents in
                     Libraries and Archives

Z39.74-1996 (R2002) Guides to Accompany Microform Sets
Z39.78-2000 (R2006) Library Binding
Z39.79-2001   Environmental Conditions for Exhibiting Library and
                     Archival Materials
Z39.87-2006 (R2011) Data Dictionary–Technical Metadata for Digital Still
                     Images

Publishing and Information Management

Z39.9-1992 (R2001)   International Standard Serial Numbering (ISSN)
Z39.14-1997 (R2009) Guidelines for Abstracts
Z39.18-2005 (R2010) Scientific and Technical Reports—Preparation,
                     Presentation, and Preservation
Z39.19-2005 (R2010) Guidelines for the Construction, Format, and
                     Management of Monolingual Controlled Vocabularies
Z39.23-1997 (R2009) Standard Technical Report Number Format and Creation
Z39.26-1997 (R2002) Micropublishing Product Information
Z39.29-2005 (R2010) Bibliographic References
Z39.41-1997 (R2009) Printed Information on Spines
Z39.43-1993 (R2011) Standard Address Number (SAN) for the Publishing
                     Industry
Z39.56-1996 (R2002) Serial Item and Contribution Identifier (SICI)
Z39.82-2001   Title Pages for Conference Publications
Z39.85-2007   Dublin Core Metadata Element Set
Z39.86-2005   Specifications for the Digital Talking Book
ANSI/NISO/ISO
12083-1995 (R2009)   Electronic Manuscript Preparation and Markup

In Development/NISO Initiatives

NISO develops new standards, reports, and best practices on a continuing basis
to support its ongoing standards development program. NISO working groups are
currently developing or exploring the following:

- Authoring and Interchange Framework for Adaptive XML Publishing
  Specification (NISO Z39.98-201x)
- Digital Bookmarking and Annotation Sharing (NISO Z39.97-201x)
- E-book Accessibility, Discovery Tools and Linking, Distribution, and
  Metadata
- Improving OpenURLs Through Analytics (IOTA)
- Institutional Identifiers (I^2)
- Knowledge Base and Related Tools (KBART) Phase II
- NISO SUSHI Protocol: COUNTER-SUSHI Implementation Profile (NISO
  RP-14-201x)
- Online Supplemental Journal Article Materials (NISO RP-15-201x)
- Open Discovery Initiative

- Presentation and Identification of E-Journals (PIE-J)
- Providing a Test Mode for SUSHI Servers (NISO RP-13-201x)
- RFID in U.S. Libraries, revision (NISO-RP-6-201x)
- Shared Electronic Resource Understanding (SERU), revision (NISO RP-7-201x)
- Standardized Markup for Journal Articles (NISO Z39.96-201x)
- Web Resource Synchronization (NISO Z39.99-201x)

NISO Technical Reports and Recommended Practices

Best Practices for Designing Web Services in the Library Context (NISO RP-2006-01)

Cost of Resource Exchange (CORE) Protocol (NISO RP-10-2010)

Environmental Guidelines for the Storage of Paper Records (NISO TR01-1995), by William K. Wilson

ESPReSSO: Establishing Suggested Practices Regarding Single Sign-On (NISO RP-11-2011)

A Framework of Guidance for Building Good Digital Collections, 3rd ed., 2007

Guidelines for Indexes and Related Information Retrieval Devices (NISO TR02-1997), by James D. Anderson

Guidelines for Alphabetical Arrangement of Letters and Sorting of Numerals and Other Symbols (NISO TR03-1999), by Hans H. Wellisch

Journal Article Versions (JAV) (NISO RP-8-2008)

KBART: Knowledge Bases and Related Tools (NISO RP-9-2010)

Networked Reference Services: Question/Answer Transaction Protocol (NISO TR04-2006)

NISO Metasearch XML Gateway Implementers Guide (NISO RP-2006-02)

Physical Delivery of Library Resources (NISO RP-12-2012)

Ranking of Authentication and Access Methods Available to the Metasearch Environment (NISO RP-2005-01)

RFID in U.S. Libraries (NISO RP-6-2008)

Search and Retrieval Citation Level Data Elements (NISO RP-2005-03)

Search and Retrieval Results Set Metadata (NISO RP-2005-02)

SERU: A Shared Electronic Resource Understanding (NISO RP-7-2008)

Other NISO Publications

The Case for New Economic Models to Support Standardization, by Clifford Lynch

The Exchange of Serials Subscription Information, by Ed Jones

ISQ: Information Standards Quarterly NISO quarterly open access magazine)

Internet, Interoperability and Standards—Filling the Gaps, by Janifer Gatenby

Issues in Crosswalking Content Metadata Standards, by Margaret St. Pierre and William P. LaPlant

Making Good on the Promise of ERM: A Standards and Best Practices Discussion Paper, by the ERM Data Standards and Best Practices Review Steering Committee

Metadata Demystified: A Guide for Publishers, by Amy Brand, Frank Daly, and Barbara Meyers

The Myth of Free Standards: Giving Away the Farm, by Andrew N. Bank

NISO Newsline (free monthly e-newsletter)

NISO Working Group Connection (free quarterly supplement to *Newsline*)

Patents and Open Standards, by Priscilla Caplan

The RFP Writer's Guide to Standards for Library Systems, by Cynthia Hodgson

Streamlining Book Metadata Workflow, by Judy Luther

Understanding Metadata

Up and Running: Implementing Z39.50—Proceedings of a Symposium Sponsored by the State Library of Iowa, edited by Sara L. Randall

Z39.50: A Primer on the Protocol

Z39.50 Implementation Experiences

NISO standards are available online at http://www.niso.org/standards. Recommended Practices, Technical Reports, White Papers, and other publications are available on the NISO Web site at http://www.niso.org/publications.

For more information, contact NISO, 1 North Charles St., Suite 1905, Baltimore, MD 21201. Tel. 301-654-2512, fax 410-685-5278, e-mail nisohq@niso.org, World Wide Web http://www.niso.org.

Calendar, 2012–2021

The list below contains information on association meetings or promotional events that are, for the most part, national or international in scope. State and regional library association meetings are also included. To confirm the starting or ending date of a meeting, which may change after the *Library and Book Trade Almanac* has gone to press, contact the association directly. Addresses of library and book trade associations are listed in Part 6 of this volume. For information on additional book trade and promotional events, see *Literary Market Place* and *International Literary Market Place,* published by Information Today, Inc., and other library and book trade publications such as *Library Journal, School Library Journal,* and *Publishers Weekly. American Libraries,* published by the American Library Association (ALA), maintains an online calendar at http://www.ala.org/ala/alonline/calendar/calendar.cfm, and ALA keeps a separate calendar at http://www.ala.org/ala/conferencesevents/afficalendar/index.cfm. An Information Today events calendar can be found at http://www.infotoday.com/calendar.shtml.

2012

June

4–7	International Assn. of Scientific and Technological University Libraries (IATUL)	Singapore
4–8	International Assn. for Social Science and Information Technology	Washington, DC
4–8	Standing Conference of Eastern, Central, and South Africa Library and Information Assns.	Nairobi, Kenya
5–6	Digital Book 2012	New York
5–6	New Jersey Library Assn.	Atlantic City
5–7	BookExpo America (BEA)	New York
6–8	Adventures in Copyright: Navigating Your Way Through Intellectual Property	Baltimore
7–9	Assn. of Canadian Archivists	Whitehorse, YK
7–10	North American Serials Interest Group	Nashville
11–14	Assn. of Christian Librarians	Palm Beach
11–14	Polar Libraries Colloquy	Boulder, CO

June 2012 *(cont.)*

14–15	International Conference on Electronic Publishing	Guimarães, Portugal
14–16	Assn. of Canadian Publishers	Saskatoon, SK
15–16	Milwaukee Conference on the Ethics of Information	Milwaukee
15–17	Cape Town Book Fair	Cape Town, South Africa
15–18	Special Libraries Assn.	Chicago
17–20	Assn. of Jewish Libraries	Pasadena
18–20	Assn. of American University Presses	Chicago
20–24	Seoul International Book Fair	Seoul, Korea
21–26	American Library Assn. Annual Conference	Anaheim
24–28	Media and Information Literacy for Knowledge Societies	Moscow, Russia
25–28	International Conference on Information Society (i-Society 2012)	London, England
27–30	American Theological Library Assn.	Scottsdale, AZ
27–30	Assn. of European Research Libraries	Tartu, Estonia
30–7/1	International Conference on the Book	Barcelona, Spain

July

2–4	International Conference on Libraries (ICOL 2012)	Kota Bharu, Malaysia
4–6	European Assn. for Health Information and Libraries (EAHIL 2012)	Brussels, Belgium
5–8	Tokyo International Book Fair	Tokyo, Japan
9–10	Library Management Institute	Philadelphia
9–13	International Conference on Open Repositories	Edinburgh, Scotland
10–13	Australian Library and Information Assn.	Sydney, Australia
10–13	International Conference on Trends in Knowledge and Information Dynamics	Bangalore, India
12–14	Wikimania International Wikimedia Conference	Washington, DC
13–15	Pacific Asia Conference on Information Systems (PACIS)	Ho Chi Minh City, Vietnam
13–15	University of Virginia Scholarly Communication Institute	Charlottesville
17–19	Shanghai International Library Forum	Shanghai, China
18–21	National Assn. of Government Archives and Records Administrators (NAGARA)	Santa Fe, NM

18–24	Hong Kong Book Fair	Hong Kong
21–24	American Assn. of Law Libraries	Boston
22–27	International Assn. of Music Libraries, Archives, and Documentation Centres	Montreal, QC
29–31	Church and Synagogue Library Assn.	Springfield, IL

August

2–3	Pacific Northwest Library Assn.	Anchorage
3	Indiana University Libraries Information Literacy Colloquium	New Albany
7–12	Society of American Archivists	San Diego
9–19	International Book Biennial of São Paulo	São Paulo, Brazil
11–17	IFLA General Conference and Assembly	Helsinki, Finland
23–26	International Board on Books for Young People	London, England
29–9/2	Beijing International Book Fair	Beijing, China

September

5–10	Moscow International Book Fair	Moscow, Russia
6–7	European Conference on Knowledge Management (ECKM-2012)	Cartagena, Spain
7	Ohio Library Council Expo	Columbus
11–13	Assn. of Learned and Professional Society Publishers	Sutton Coldfield, England
13–14	European Conference on Information Management and Evaluation (ECIME-2012)	Cork, Ireland
13–14	Northwest Interlibrary Loan and Resource Sharing Conference	Portland
13–14	WebSearch University 2012	Washington, DC
19–21	International Symposium on Information Management in a Changing World	Ankara, Turkey
19–22	North Dakota Library Assn.	Fargo
19–23	National Joint Conference of Librarians of Color	Kansas City
20–22	Assn. for Library Service to Children National Institute	Indianapolis
20–22	Kentucky Library Assn.	Louisville
21–22	Georgia International Conference on Information Literacy	Savannah
23–25	ARMA International Annual Conference and Expo	Chicago
26–29	Wyoming Library Assn.	Casper

September 2012 *(cont.)*

26–30	Nairobi International Book Fair	Nairobi, Kenya
27–30	Göteborg Book Fair	Göteborg, Sweden
28–10/1	Kentucky Library Assn.	Louisville
30–10/3	Pennsylvania Library Assn.	Gettysburg
30–10/6	Banned Books Week	

October

3–5	LIBER International Book Fair	Barcelona, Spain
3–5	Minnesota Library Assn.	St. Paul
3–5	Missouri Library Assn.	Springfield
3–5	South Dakota Library Assn.	Huron
4–6	Nevada Library Assn.	Las Vegas
4–7	Library and Information Technology Assn. National Forum	Columbus, OH
9–11	Illinois Library Assn.	Peoria
10–12	Iowa Library Assn.	Dubuque
10–14	Frankfurt Book Fair	Frankfurt, Germany
12–13	American Assn. of School Librarians Fall Forum	Greenville, SC
16–17	Streaming Media Europe 2012	London, England
17–19	KMWorld 2012	Washington, DC
17–19	Nebraska Library Assn./Mountain Plains Library Assn./Nebraska Educational Media Assn.	La Vista
18–20	Colorado Assn. of Libraries	Keystone
21–27	National Friends of Libraries Week	
22–24	Internet Librarian 2012	Monterey, CA
23–26	Wisconsin Library Assn.	La Crosse
23–30	International Belgrade Book Fair	Belgrade, Serbia
25–28	Helsinki Book Fair	Helsinki, Finland
26–31	American Society for Information Science & Technology (ASIS&T)	Baltimore
30–31	Internet Librarian International	London, England

November

2–4	YALSA Young Adult Literature Symposium	St. Louis
7–9	Michigan Library Assn.	Dearborn
7–10	New York Library Assn.	Saratoga Springs
8–10	Arizona Library Assn.	Phoenix

9–11	Basel Book Fair	Basel, Switzerland
12–14	Indiana Library Federation	Indianapolis
14–19	Montreal Book Fair	Montreal, QC
16–18	Dublin Book Festival	Dublin, Ireland
17–25	Istanbul International Book Fair	Istanbul, Turkey
24–12/2	Guadalajara International Book Fair	Guadalajara, Mexico

2013

January

| 25–29 | American Library Assn. Midwinter Meeting | Seattle |

April

| 8–12 | Texas Library Assn. | San Antonio |
| 10–13 | Assn. of College and Research Libraries | Indianapolis |

June

| 27–7/2 | American Library Assn. Annual Conference | Chicago |

September

| 25–27 | Mountain Plains Library Assn./North Dakota Library Assn./South Dakota Library Assn. | Sioux Falls, SD |

October

| 16–18 | Iowa Library Assn. | Coralville |

2014

January

| 24–28 | American Library Assn. Midwinter Meeting | Philadelphia |

March

| 11–15 | Public Library Assn. | Indianapolis |

April

| 8–11 | Texas Library Assn. | Dallas |

June

| 26–7/1 | American Library Assn. Annual Conference | Las Vegas |

October 2014

1–3	South Dakota Library Assn.	Pierre
15–17	Iowa Library Assn.	Cedar Rapids

2015

January

23–27	American Library Assn. Midwinter Meeting	Chicago

April

10–17	Texas Library Assn.	Austin

June

25–30	American Library Assn. Annual Conference	San Francisco

October

14–16	Iowa Library Assn.	Council Bluffs

2016

January

22–26	American Library Assn. Midwinter Meeting	Boston

April

5–9	Public Library Assn.	Denver

June

23–28	American Library Assn. Annual Conference	Orlando

October

12–14	Iowa Library Assn.	Dubuque

2017

January

20–24	American Library Assn. Midwinter Meeting	Atlanta

June

22–27	American Library Assn. Annual Conference	Chicago

2018

January

19–23   American Library Assn. Midwinter Meeting   Los Angeles

March

20–24   Public Library Assn.   Philadelphia

June

21–26   American Library Assn. Annual Conference   New Orleans

2019

January

25–29   American Library Assn. Midwinter Meeting   Seattle

June

27–7/2   American Library Assn. Annual Conference   New York

2020

January

24–27   American Library Assn. Midwinter Meeting   Philadelphia

June

27–7/2   American Library Assn. Annual Conference   To be announced

2021

January

22–26   American Library Assn. Midwinter Meeting   Indianapolis

June

24–29   American Library Assn. Annual Conference   San Francisco

Acronyms

A

AALL. American Association of Law Libraries

AASL. American Association of School Librarians

ABA. American Booksellers Association

ACRL. Association of College and Research Libraries

AFSIC. National Agricultural Library, Alternative Farming Systems Information Center

AIIP. Association of Independent Information Professionals

AILA. American Indian Library Association

AJL. Association of Jewish Libraries

ALA. American Library Association

ALAC. Council on Library and Information Resources, Academic Library Advisory Committee

AL21C. American Library Association, AL21C (Program on America's Libraries for the 21st Century)

ALCTS. Association for Library Collections and Technical Services

ALIC. National Archives and Records Administration, Archives Library Information Center

ALISE. Association for Library and Information Science Education

ALS. National Center for Education Statistics, Academic Library Survey

ALSC. Association for Library Service to Children

ALTAFF. Association of Library Trustees, Advocates, Friends, and Foundations

AMMLA. American Merchant Marine Library Association

APA. Allied Professional Association

APALA. Asian/Pacific American Librarians Association

ARL. Association of Research Libraries

ARLIS/NA. Art Libraries Society of North America

ARSL. Association for Rural and Small Libraries

ASCLA. Association of Specialized and Cooperative Library Agencies

ASIS&T. American Society for Information Science and Technology

ATLA. American Theological Library Association

AWIC. National Agricultural Library, Animal Welfare Information Center

B

BBW. Banned Books Week

BCALA. Black Caucus of the American Library Association

BEA. BookExpo America

BSA. Bibliographical Society of America

C

CACUL. Canadian Association of College and University Libraries

CAIS. Canadian Association for Information Science

CALA. Chinese-American Librarians Association

CAPL. Canadian Association of Public Libraries

CARL. Canadian Association of Research Libraries

CASLIS. Canadian Association of Special Libraries and Information Services

CCL. American Library Association, Center for Civic Life

CDNL. Conference of Directors of National Libraries

CDRP. Government Printing Office, Cataloging Record Distribution Project

CHEMM. National Library of Medicine, Chemical Emergency Medical Management

CLA. Canadian Library Association

CLIR. Council on Library and Information Resources

CLTA. Canadian Library Trustees Association

CNI. Coalition for Networked Information

COAPI. Coalition of Open Access Policy Institutions

COLT. Council on Library/Media Technicians

COSLA. Chief Officers of State Library Agencies

CPSIA. Consumer Product Safety Improvement Act

CSLA. Church and Synagogue Library Association

CWA. Crime Writers' Association

D

DPLA. Digital Public Library of America

DRM. Digital rights management

DTIC. Defense Technical Information Center

E

EAR. National Technical Information Service, Export Administration Regulations

EBM. Espresso Book Machine

EDB. National Technical Information Service, Energy Science and Technology Database

EDC. Educational Development Corp.

EMIERT. American Library Association, Ethnic and Multicultural Information and Exchange Round Table

EQUACC. Equitable Access to Electronic Content, Presidential Task Force on

ERA. National Archives and Records Administration, Electronic Records Archives

ESEA. Elementary and Secondary Education Act

F

FAFLRT. American Library Association, Federal and Armed Forces Librarians Round Table

FAIFE. International Federation of Library Associations and Institutions, Freedom of Access to Information and Freedom of Expression

FDLP. Government Printing Office, Federal Depository Library Program

FDsys. FDsys (Federal Digital System)

FEDRIP. National Technical Information Service, FEDRIP (Federal Research in Progress Database)

FIAF. International Federation of Film Archives

FLICC. Federal Library and Information Center Committee

FNIC. National Agricultural Library, Food and Nutrition Information Center

FSRS. National Technical Information Service, Federal Science Repository Service

G

GLBT. American Library Association, Gay, Lesbian, Bisexual, and Transgendered Round Table

GLIN. Global Legal Information Network

GODORT. American Library Association, Government Documents Round Table

GPO. Government Printing Office

I

IAALD. International Association of Agricultural Information Specialists

IACs. Defense Technical Information Center, Information Analysis Centers

IALL. International Association of Law Libraries

IAML. International Association of Music Libraries, Archives and Documentation Centres

IASL. International Association of School Librarians

ICA. International Council on Archives

ICBS. International Committee of the Blue Shield

IFLA. International Federation of Library
Associations and Institutions

ILS. Government Printing Office, Integrated
Library System

IMLS. Institute of Museum and Library
Services

ISBN. International Standard Book Number

ISO. International Organization for
Standardization

ISOO. National Archives and Records
Administration, Information Security
Oversight Office

ISSN. International Standard Serial Number

ISTE. International Society for Technology
in Education

L

LC. Library of Congress

LCA. Library Copyright Alliance

LCDP. Association of Research Libraries,
Leadership and Career Development
Program

LHRT. American Library Association,
Library History Round Table

LIS. Library/information science

LITA. Library and Information Technology
Association

LJ. Library Journal

LRRT. American Library Association,
Library Research Round Table

LSCM. Government Printing Office, Library
Services and Content Management

LSP. National Center for Education
Statistics, Library Statistics Program

LSTA. Library Services and Technology Act

M

MLA. Medical Library Association; Music
Library Association

N

NAGARA.

NAL. National Agricultural Library

NARA. National Archives and Records
Administration

NCBI. National Center for Biotechnology
Information

NCES. National Center for Education
Statistics

NCLA. National Church Library Association

NCSS. National Council for the Social
Studies

NDC. National Archives and Records
Administration, National
Declassification Center

NDIIPP. National Digital Information
Infrastructure and Preservation
Program

NDNP. Newspapers, National Digital
Newspaper Program

NEH. National Endowment for the
Humanities

NFAIS. National Federation of Advanced
Information Services

NIH. National Institutes of Health

NISO. National Information Standards
Organization

NLE. National Library of Education

NLM. National Library of Medicine

NMRT. American Library Association, New
Members Round Table

NTIS. National Technical Information
Service

NTRL. National Technical Information
Service, National Technical Reports
Library

O

OGIS. Government Information Services,
Office of

OITP. American Library Association,
Information Technology Policy,
Office for

OPAL. Association of Research Libraries,
Organizational Performance
Assessment for Libraries

ORCID. ORCID (Open Researcher and
Contributor ID)

OWLL. One World Law Library

P

PACER. Public Access to Court Electronic
Records

PIPS. Partners in Public Service

PLA. Public Library Association

PMC. PubMedCentral

PPO. American Library Association, Public Programs Office

PTDLA. Patent and Trademark Depository Library Association

PW. Publishers Weekly

R

RDA. Library of Congress, Resource Description and Access

REMM. National Library of Medicine, Radiation Emergency Medical Management

RL/RC. National Library of Education, Research Library/Reference Center

RUSA. Reference and User Services Association

S

SAA. Society of American Archivists

SAN. Standard Address Number

SASS. National Center for Education Statistics, Schools and Staffing Survey

SIIA. Software and Information Industry Association

SLA. Special Libraries Association

SPARC. SPARC (Scholarly Publishing and Academic Resources Coalition)

SRIM. National Technical Information Service, Selected Research in Microfiche

SRRT. American Library Association, Social Responsibilities Round Table

SSP. Society for Scholarly Publishing

STEM. Education, STEM (science, technology, engineering, and mathematics)

StLA. State libraries and library agencies, IMLS State Library Agencies

T

TLA. Theatre Library Association

TPS. Library of Congress, Teaching with Primary Sources

U

ULC. Urban Libraries Council

V

VHP. History, Veterans History Project

W

WDL. World Digital Library

WNC. World News Connection

WPLC. Wisconsin Public Library Consortium

Y

YALSA. Young Adult Library Services Association

Index of Organizations

Please note that many cross-references refer to entries in the Subject Index.

A

AGRICOLA (Agricultural OnLine Access), 127, 128, 157

AGRIS (Agricultural Science and Technology database), 157

AIIM (The Enterprise Content Management Association), 702–703

Akashic Books, 595

Allied Professional Association (APA), 374

Amazon.com, 20, 23, 473, 478, 487
  Audible Inc., 481
  e-book sales, 17, 23, 473
  Kindle, 17, 23–24, 473, 475, 530
  Kindle Fire, 473
  Kindle Owner Lending Library, 474, 475

American Association of Law Libraries (AALL), 684
  scholarships, 367, 371

American Association of School Librarians (AASL), 687–688
  awards/scholarships/grants, 200, 374
  DigitalLiteracy.gov, partner in, 34–35
  interactive planning tool for library development, 202–203
  placement assistance, 338
  School Libraries Count!, 402
  Standards for the 21st-Century Learner, 38–39
  Urban Schools Task Force Survey Report, 402–403

American Booksellers Association (ABA), 214–220
  advocacy, 219–220
  conferences, 216, 218
  education for booksellers, 218
  Espresso Book Machine, 219
  governance activity, 215
  IndieCommerce, 218–219
  membership growth, 214–215
  staffing changes, 217

American Folklife Center, 113

American Indian Library Association (AILA), 703

American Library Association (ALA), 197–213, 685–702
  action areas, 27
  ALA Editions, 209
  ALA Graphics, 210
  AL21C (Program on America's Libraries for the 21st Century), 3–5, 11, 290
  American Libraries, 210–211
  awards, 213
  Banned Books Week (BBW), 200
  Booklist Publications, 211
  bookmobiles, 207
  campaign partnerships, 204
  Center for Civic Life (CCL), 87
  Checking Out the Future, 5
  conferences, 199, 203, 206–209
  Confronting the Future, 5, 11
  Digital Content in Libraries Working Group, 27
  Digital Libraries and Libraries Initiative, 13
  digital revolution and, 3, 5, 12–13
  DigitalLiteracy.gov, partner in, 34–35
  "Digitizing Hidden Collections in Public Libraries", 290
  Diversity, Office for, 198–199, 207, 381
  e-books, activities related to, 12–13
  Ethnic and Multicultural Information and Exchange Round Table (EMIERT) awards, 378
  Exhibits Round Table awards, 378
  Federal and Armed Forces Librarians Round Table (FAFLRT) awards, 378–379
  future, focus of, 12–13
  Gay, Lesbian, Bisexual, and Transgendered Round Table (GLBT), 379

Subject Index

Please note that many cross-references refer to entries in the Index of Organizations.

A

Academic books
  export revenues, 536
  prices and price indexes
    British books, 509, 512(table), 513
    North American, 483–484, 487, 490(table), 492
    U.S. college books, 493, 494(table), 495–498(table), 501
  See also Society for Scholarly Publishing; SPARC; Textbooks
Academic libraries, *see* College and research libraries; National Center for Education Statistics, Academic Libraries Survey
Acquisitions
  expenditures, 439–447
    academic libraries, 442–443(table)
    government libraries, 446–447(table)
    public libraries, 440–441(table)
    school library media centers, (table)
    special libraries, 444–445(table)
  LC, 104–105
  See also specific types of libraries, e.g., Public libraries
Adults, services for
  best books, 573
  RUSA's Reading List, 580
  See also Literacy programs; Reference and User Services Association
Agencies, library, *see* Library associations and agencies
Agricultural libraries, *see* International Association of Agricultural Information Specialists; National Agricultural Library
Alabama
  humanities councils, 297

library associations, 741
networks and cooperative library organizations, 663
school library media associations, 762
Alaska
  humanities councils, 297
  library associations, 741
  networks and cooperative library organizations, 663
  school library media associations, 762
Alcott, Louisa May, 213
Alexandria Declaration, 33
American Assassin (Flynn), 587
American Libraries, 210–211
American Samoa; humanities council, 301
Angleberger, Tom, 217
Animal welfare, NAL Web site, 130–131
Archives
  acquisition expenditures
    academic libraries, 442–443(table)
    government libraries, 446–447(table)
    public libraries, 440–441(table)
    special libraries, 444–445(table)
  bibliography for librarians, 550
  CLIR program, 249
  digital, 8–9, 19
  placement and salaries, 346
  Web archiving, 115
  See also International Council on Archives; International Federation of Film Archives; Internet Archive; National Archives and Records Administration; Presidential papers
Arizona
  humanities councils, 297
  library associations, 741
  networks and cooperative library organizations, 683
  school library media associations, 762

B